THIS CANCELS ALL PREVIOUS LISTS.

# *British Red Cross*

— AND —

# *Order of St. John.*

# ENQUIRY LIST

**No. 14, 1917.**

**Wounded and Missing**

***Containing all Enquiries up to and including July 20th, 1917.***

***August 1st, 1917.***


**18, CARLTON HOUSE TERRACE,**
**LONDON, S.W. 1**

**Telephone: REGENT 6151. (*EXTENSION* 26).**

## THE FOLLOWING REGIMENTS HAVE ALTERNATIVE NAMES:

| | |
|---|---|
| **Black Watch** ... ... ... ... | Royal Highlanders. |
| **Dragoons** ... ... ... ... ... | 1st Royal.<br>2nd Royal Scots Greys.<br>6th Inniskilling. |
| **Dragoon Guards** ... ... ... ... | 1st King's (K.D.G's.)<br>2nd Queen's Bays.<br>3rd Prince of Wales's.<br>4th Royal Irish.<br>5th Princess Charlotte of Wales's.<br>6th Carabiniers.<br>7th Princess Royal's. |
| **Hussars** ... ... ... ... ... | 3rd King's Own.<br>4th and 7th Queen's Own.<br>8th King's Royal Irish.<br>10th Prince of Wales's Own Regiment.<br>18th Queen Mary's Own.<br>19th Queen Alexandra's Own Royal. |
| **East Kent** ... ... ... ... ... | The Buffs. |
| **Lancers** ... ... ... ... ... | 5th Royal Irish.<br>9th Queen's Royal.<br>12th Prince of Wales's R.<br>16th The Queen's.<br>17th Duke of Cambridge's Own.<br>21st Empress of India's. |
| **Royal Fusiliers** ... ... ... ... | (1) The Royal Fusiliers (*Regulars*) are also known as the City of London Regiment. (2) In the London Regiment (*Territorials*) the first four battalions are called Royal Fusiliers. Where therefore a man is in the "Royal Fusiliers," it is necessary to ascertain whether it is the Regulars or Territorials. |
| **Royal Scots** ... ... ... ... | Lothian Regiment. |
| **Scottish Rifles** ... ... ... ... | The Cameronians. |
| **Sherwood Foresters** ... ... ... | Notts and Derby. |
| **R. W. Surrey** ... ... ... ... | The Queens. |
| **West Riding** ... ... ... ... | Duke of Wellington's Regiment. |

## CERTAIN BATTALIONS IN THE FOLLOWING REGIMENTS ARE KNOWN BY NAMES AS WELL AS NUMERALS.

| | |
|---|---|
| **Highland Light Infantry** ... ... | 9th Glasgow Highlanders. |
| **Liverpool Regiment** ... ... ... | 10th Liverpool Scottish.<br>11th Isle of Man. |
| **London Regiment** ... ... ... | 1st-4th Royal Fusiliers (T.F.).<br>5th London Rifle Brigade.<br>8th Post Office Rifles.<br>9th Queen Victoria's Rifles.<br>10th Hackney.<br>11th Finsbury Rifles.<br>12th The Rangers.<br>13th Princess Louise's Kensington.<br>14th London Scottish.<br>16th Queen's Westminster Rifles.<br>17th Poplar and Stepney Rifles.<br>18th London Irish Rifles.<br>19th St. Pancras.<br>21st First Surrey Rifles.<br>22nd and 24th The Queen's.<br>25th Cyclist Battalion.<br>28th Artists Rifles. |

**The first column of figures prefixed to the names indicates the Battalion; the second column of figures or letters indicates the Company; the third (Roman numerals) the Platoon.**

---

**THE FOLLOWING ABBREVIATIONS ARE USED:—**

| | | | |
|---|---|---|---|
| C.Q.M.S. | Company-Quarter-Master-Sergeant. | L.G.S. ... | Lewis Gun Section. |
| C.S.M.... | Company-Sergeant-Major. | M.G.S.... | Machine Gun Section. |
| Det. D/B. | Details Death and Burial asked. | Pl. ... | Platoon. |
| D/Dis. ... | Died of Disease. | R/Enq.... | Renewed Enquiry. |
| D/W ... | Died of Wounds. | R.S.M.... | Regimental Serjeant-Major. |
| Gren. ... | Grenade. | S. ... | Section. |
| H.Q. ... | Headquarters. | S/B ... | Stretcher-bearer. |
| I.T.M. ... | Infantry Trench Mortar. | W.O.L.... | War Office List. |

**N.B.**—In Regiments where the Men's numbers have been changed, the old number is placed in brackets.

---

## OFFICERS' CASUALTIES.

**The letters W.O.L. which in some cases precede the date of an Officer's casualty, refer to the date of the Communique and not to the actual date of the casualty, which is always previous.**

---

## NOTICE.

**Trench Mortar Batteries will now be found after Royal Sussex Regiment.**

---

## AUGUST 1st, 1917.

---

**For English searchers both single and double asterisks denote new enquiries.**

**The names with double asterisks are new for foreign searchers.**

---

### SOUTH AFRICAN INFANTRY.

*B.E.F.*

| | | |
|---|---|---|
| 1 B. VIII | Pearce, G. 3160. | M. Oct. 18/16. |
| 1 C. IX | Symons, C. S. 4084. | M. Oct. 18/16. |
| ‡1 D. | Carstairs, Arthur Kenneth. 10411. | K. April 12/17. Det.D./B. |
| 1 ? | Arnold, A. W. A. 6857. | M. Oct. 18/16. |
| 1 ? | Conchar, Sydney. 3907. | M. April 9/17. |
| 1 ? | Edmunds, John Percival. 4210. | M. April 12/17. |
| ‡1 ? | Matthews, Percy. 8663. | M. Oct. 18/16. |
| 1 ? | Milne, C. S. 9366. | M. Jan. 10/17. |
| 1 ? | Van Hooven, Andrew Ebenezer. 2631. | M. April 12/17. |
| 2 | Beddy, 2nd Lieut. N. | W. and M. about May 20/17. |
| 2 | Forth, 2nd Lieut. D. W. | M. April 12/17. |
| 2 | Ross, 2nd Lieut. J. M. | K. April 12/17. Det.D./B. R/Enq. |

**African Infantry, South—contd.**

## *B.E.F.*

| | | |
|---|---|---|
| 2 | **Tooke, 2nd Lieut. W. M. B.** | M. April 12/17. |
| 2 A. | Bruce, Patrick Tyrell Frank. 7532. | K. April 12/17. Det.D./B. |
| 2 B. | Charlton, George Wm. 9038. | M. Oct. 12/16. |
| 2 B. | Docker, Rupert Eley. 7258. | K. April 12/17. Det.D./B. |
| 2 B. | McLachlin, James. 5401. | M. Oct. 12/16. |
| 2 B. | Massey, Thos. Haisman. 9210. | M. Oct. 12/16. R/Enq. |
| 2 B. | Spence, Wm. John Hicks. 8632. | M. Oct. 12/16. |
| 2 B. | Upton, Edward Arthur. 8051. | K. April 12/17. Det.D./B. R/Enq. |
| 2 C. IX | Crampton, Sig. C. Owen. 4705. | K. April 12/17. Det.D./B. |
| *2 C. | Creighton, Vernon R. 8685. | M. Oct. 12/16. R/Enq. |
| ‡2 C. | Reynolds, George. 10013. | K. April 12/17. Det.D./B. R/Enq. |
| 2 D. | Batham, Charles A. F. 8639. | M. Oct. 12/16. R/Enq. |
| 2 D. | Carnegie, R. G. G. 8022. | M. Oct. 12/16. |
| 2 D. | Harvard, J. Mawson. 7450. | M. Oct. 12/16. |
| 2 D. | Manning, Fredk. Mark. 7952. | M. Oct. 12/16. R/Enq. |
| *2 ? | Blair, L.-Cpl. Andrew Edward. 8929. | K. April 12/17. Det.D./B. R/Enq. |
| ‡2 ? | Calett, Vincent Frank. 182. | K. Feb. 22/17. Det.D./B. |
| 2 ? | Clark, Bertie. 7059. | M. April 12/17. |
| 2 ? | Feinberg, M. 7502. | M. Oct. 12/16. |
| 2 ? | Ferguson, Duncan Victor McNair. 7254. | M. April 12/17. |
| 2 ? | Gray, Cpl. Raymond Barrett. 7064. | K. Oct. 12/16. Det.D./B. |
| 2 ? | Harris, E. G. 8211. | M. Oct. 12/16. |
| 2 ? | Ledger, Sergt. S. H. 6004. | W. and M. April 12/17. |
| 2 ? | Masson, Bruce. 7992. | M. Oct. 12/16. |
| 2 ? | Nicholls, Harry Edward. 10115. | M. April 12/17. |
| 2 ? | Rudd, C. 9147. | W. and M. April 12/17. |
| 2 ? | Shewan, William. 9883. | M. April 12/17. |
| 2 ? | Speed, Cpl. Fredk. Chas. 851. | M. April 12/17. |
| 2 ? | Upton, Arthur Edward. 8051. | M. April 12/17. R/Enq. |
| 2 ? | Woodrow, Edwin Chris. Angelo. 9053. | M. April 12/17. |
| 3 ? | McLachlan, Alexander. 9725. | M. April 12/17. |
| 4 | **Brown, Lieut. A. H.** | K. July 20/16. Det.D./B. |
| 4 A. | Burrough, Percy C. V. 9023. | K. April 9/17. Det.D./B. |
| 4 B. L.G.S. | Arbuckle, Robert Irvin. 9373. | W. Unoff. M. April 12/17. |
| 4 D. | Leddra, Geo. Hosking. 5352. | M. July 15-16/17. |
| 4 ? | Campbell, Hugh. 5438. | M. April 12/17. |
| 4 ? | Donald, William. 9178. | M. April 12/17. |
| 4 ? | *Fairweather, Herbert Wm. 9212. | M. April 12/17. |
| 4 ? | Grimsley, Francis Richd. 5292. | M. April 12/17. |
| *4 ? | Kegg, Henry. 33. | W. and M. April 12/17. |
| 4 ? | Oostermeyer, John James. 5874. | M. April 9/17. |
| *4 ? | Rodda, Thomas Edward. X/238. | W. and M. April 12/17. |
| 4 ? | Tod, L.-Cpl. James. 8103. | W. and M. April 9/17. |
| 4 ? I.T.M. | Wrigley, Chas. Kemble. 7148. (26 Bgde.) | W. and M. April 9/17. |

## ARMY CYCLIST CORPS.

### *B.E.F.*

6 Co. Butler, Joseph Arthur. 10860. M. April 10/17.
‡13 Topham, L. 5206. W. and M. June 7/17.
‡15 Clayton, H. 536. M. May 20/17.

### *BALKANS.*

‡16 Co. Hogg, H. 2621. M. June 16/17.
‡16 Jones, C. 3317. M. June 17/17.

### *E.E.F.*

52 Div. 155 Bgde. Wileman, Maurice. 20325. M. April 19/17.
52 ? Campbell, L.-Cpl. John. 16947. W. and M. April 19/17.
*? Gallacher, P. 19636. W. and M. April 19/17.
? Graham, C. L. 19826. M. April 19/17.
*? O'Rawe, B. 19796. W. and M. April 19/17.
*? Robertson, S. 19799. W. and M. April 19/17.

## ARMY SERVICE CORPS.

### *B.E.F.*

46 Res. Park Cooper, 2nd Lieut. G. F. K. Feb. 24/17. Det.D./B.
‡207 Co. Barnaham, Thos. T3/029312. M. May 25/17.

### *BALKANS.*

708 M.T. Coy. Evans, Henry. 166179. M. Dec. 18/16.

### *E.E.F.*

*120 Co. Hill, Dvr. Sam. T.3/031110. M., bel. drowned June 2/17. "Cameronian."

‡120 Co. Hunt, Arthur Victor. T4/243234. (3rd Horse Base Depot.) M., bel. drowned June 2/17, "Cameronian"

*478 Wheel Co. Smith, Cpl. F. J. T.4/212749. M., bel. drowned June 2/17. "Cameronian."

*485 Co. Hartley, Shoeing Smith Jesse. T.4/174446. M., bel. drowned June 2/17. "Cameronian."

855 Co. 27 Div. Train. Taylor, Lt. Wm. E. M., bel. drowned June 2/17, "Cameronian"

895 M.T. Co. Pibel, 2nd Lieut. Leo. Maxse. M., bel. drowned April 4/17.
895 Halford, W. H. D.M./2/221302. M., bel. drowned, April 15/17.
*? Ince, W. A. 156427. M., bel. drowned April 15/17. "Arcadian."

*Fld. Amb. Page, Wm. 045038. M., bel. drowned June 2/17. "Cameronian."

*Transport S. Walker, Robt. S. T.4/186925. M., bel. drowned June 2/17. "Cameronian."

? Axford, C. D.M./2/223762. M., bel. drowned, April 15/17.
? Burton, Dvr. G. H. T. 4/071029. M., bel. drowned Mar. 6-9/17.
? ? Tudgay, A. 110349. M., bel. drowned June 2/17, "Cameronian"

‡? Wynn, W. W. D. T4/212865. (3rd Horse Base Depot.) M., bel. drowned June 2/17, "Cameronian"

11 Armoured Motor Batty. Blamire, O. M. 2/156091. M. March 27/17.

Army Service Corps—contd.

*PERSIAN GULF.*

Scott, J. A. D.M. 2/169642. M. Nov. 26/16.

## ARMY VETERINARY CORPS.

*E.E.F.*

Reid, William. 17876. M. Jan. 1/17, from S.S. "Ivernia." Details.

## ARTILLERY.

### ROYAL FIELD ARTILLERY.

*B.E.F.*

| Bgde. | Batty. |  |  |
|---|---|---|---|
| 13 Bgde. | 8 Batty. | Price, Albert. 74359. | M. April 14/17. |
| 17 | 13 | Thonemann, 2nd Lieut. E. H. | M. May 3/17. |
| 17 | 13 | Brown, John. 38105. (Fr. H.Q.) | W. and M. April 28/17. |
| 29 | 127 | Parkes, Dvr. Cecil. 84052 | M. May 2/17. |
| 34 | C. | McCann, Sgt. A. 92962. | M. April 22/17. |
| 35 | 12 | Dixon, C. T. 3107. | M. May 4/17. |
| ‡39 | 54 | Townsend, 2nd Lt. H. | M. July 10/17. |
| 42 | 45 | Smith, W. T. 134692. | K. April 6/17. Det.D./B. |
| ‡59 | B. | Clough, B. 136424. | M. April 15/17. |
| 63 | D. | Perry, Hugh Luscombe. 87328. | M. April 13/17. |
| *86 | C. | Allan, D. 650278. | W. Unoff. M. May 27/17. |
| 86 | C. | Smith, Charles A. 650296 | M. May 14/17. |
| 93 | A. | Drayson, Capt. J. D. | K. April 10/17. Det.D./B. |
| 93 | A. or C. | Lock, Samuel Fredk. 57381. | W. and M. April 9/17. |
| 106 | C. | Hemsted, 2nd Lieut. J. | M. April 16/17. |
| †106 | C. | Mutton, Sh.-Smith J. 106389. | M. June 3/17. |
| ‡106 | D. | Curran, J. 168837. | M. June 6/17. |
| *112 | A. | Campbell, M.C., Major D. D. H. | K. June 7/17. Det.D./B. |
| 148 | M. | Brookes, Frank. 17537. | Unoff. M. 2nd week April/17. |
| 156 | | Barlow, 2nd Lieut. C. G. | D/W. May 17/17. Det.D./B. |
| 156 | M. | Grant, 2nd Lieut. N. | K. May 25/17. Det.D./B. |
| 171 | B. | Lovett-Thomas, 2nd Lt. R. S. | D/W. Mar. 11/17. Det.D./B. |
| ‡231 | ? | Singleton, Bdr. A. E. 810431. | W. and M., bel. K. May 6/17. |

**Artillery, Royal Field—contd.**

## *B.E.F.*

| | | | |
|---|---|---|---|
| *232 | C. | Cooper, Sgt. Noel Conrad. 1246. | K. April 27/17. Det.D./B. |
| 235 | C. | Bretton, Cpl. Horace Gordon. 902. | W. and M. Sept. 19/16. R/Enq. |
| ‡242 | D. | Pollard, E. A. 112995. | K. April 28/17. Det.D./B. |
| 250 | A. | Carver, William. 751633. | M. May 3/17. |
| ‡252 | D. | Monk, W. 136773. | W. and M. May 3/17. |
| *255 | D. | McNeill, Robt. 631590. (3 Howitzers.) | W. and M. May 4/17. |
| *283 | 109 | Bakewell, Dvr. A. 14085 | Unoff. W. and M. May 9/17. |
| *311 | D. | Fenton. 976357. (11052.) | K. April 5/17. Det.D./B. |
| ‡315 | ? | Walker, P. 645731. (Army F.A.) | M. June 2/17. |
| ? | ? | **Pearce, 2nd Lieut. J. B. H.** (Traffic Officer). | D/W. April 27/17. Det.D./B. |

**Divisional Ammunition Column.**

| | | |
|---|---|---|
| 4 | **Belas, Capt. G. H.** | K. about June 3/17. Det.D./B. |
| 4 | Ripton, Gnr. William. 31803. | K. April 6/17. Det.D./B. |
| ‡5 | Erwin, J. 101037. | M. April 23/17. |
| ‡23 | Cove, W. 49898. | W. Unoff M. June 8/17. |
| ‡29 | Tamplin, Cpl. F. 62475. | M., bel. K. April 22/17. |
| 33 | Stewart, J. L. 96978. (Late 192835, R.E.) | W. and M. Dec. 9/16. |
| 57 | Meldon, Joseph. 695717. | K. May 2/17. Det.D./B. |

## *BALKANS.*

| | | | |
|---|---|---|---|
| 19 Bgde. | 131 Batty. | Weddell, Bombdr. Andrew. 54516. | M. April 20-24/17. |
| ? | ? | **Humphreys, M.C., 2nd Lieut. S. N.** | M., bel. K. Feb. 10/17. |

## *E.E.F.*

| | | | |
|---|---|---|---|
| 20 | D. | **Clarke, Lieut. Roland Harwood.** | M., bel. drowned Feb. 20-24/17. |
| 20 | D. | Dale, Sgt. Arthur. 2840. | M., bel. drowned Feb. 22-24/17. |
| 20 | D. | Dale, R. 2839. | M., bel. drowned Feb. 22-24/17. |
| ‡28 | 31 | Charie, Wm. 66292. | M. June 6/17. |
| 266 | ? | Smith, A/Bombdr. D. G. 740469. | M. Mar. 27/17. |
| 267 | ? | James, H. 730139. | M., bel. K. April 20/17. |
| ? | 131 | Keenan, Thos. 32064. | M., bel. drowned Feb. 20-24/17. |
| ? | ? | Hall, Henry. 154644. | M., bel. drowned, "Cameronia," April 15/17. |
| ? | ? | Minney, Arthur. 174331. | M., bel. drowned April 15/17, "Arcadian" |
| ? | ? | Purcell, Jos. John. 71303. | M., bel. drowned, "Arcadian," April 15/17. |

## *PERSIAN GULF.*

| | | | |
|---|---|---|---|
| *14 Bgde. | 44 Batty. | Wallace, Dvr. H. 61802. | M. April 30/17. |
| ‡55 | ? | McKenzie, K. 64948. | M. Mar. 29/17. |
| 69 | A. | Wyatt, Thos. 68018. | M. Nov. 4/16. |
| ‡169 | C. | Workman, Edw. John. 103566. | W. and M. April 30/17. |
| ? | 44 | Lambert, Dvr. H. 1161. | D./Dis. Jan. 10/17. Det.D./B. |
| ? | ? | Crompton, Dvr. John. 37914. | D. April 23/17. Basra. Det.D./B. |

**Artillery, Royal Field—contd.**

## *PERSIAN GULF.*

**Divisional Ammunition Column.**

Sweeney, John. 49549. M. July/16.

## ROYAL GARRISON ARTILLERY.

### *B.E.F.*

| | | |
|---|---|---|
| 151 Heavy Batty. | Gibson, F. 116289. | M., bel. K. May 4/17. |
| ‡1 Siege Batty. | Briggs, Amos. 141950. | M. May 27/17. |
| ‡1 | Murray, John Edwin. 74255. | M. May 27/17. |
| 4 | Cowan, Wm. 10448. | M. Mar. 29/17. |
| ‡13 | Collins, Major P. R. M. | K. June 25/17. Det.D./B. |
| ‡113 | Bannister, S. 67988. | M. April 9/17. |
| *116 | Hickman, A. L. 145308. | K. May 27/17. Det.D./B. |
| ‡249 | Harris, J. W. 110824. | M. June 7/17. |
| ‡287 | Evans, Jas. 97527. | K. June 28/17. Det.D./B. |
| 9 Corps. N. Riding Batty. | Jones, David. 380. | M. Mar. 13/17. |
| '? | Remington, 2nd Lieut. F. G. | M. May 11-12/17 |
| ‡2nd A. Sub. S. London Hy Batty. | Wilson, Chas. Shafto. 31827. (855.) | M. June 7/17. |

### *E.E.F.*

| | | |
|---|---|---|
| 188 Heavy Batty. | Boulton, John. 108797. | M., bel. drowned May 5/17. |

## ROYAL HORSE ARTILLERY.

### *B.E.F.*

| | | |
|---|---|---|
| *Z. Batty. | Jarvis, Bombr. W. H. 40003. | D/W. Nov. 8/16. Det.D./B. |

## HONOURABLE ARTILLERY COMPANY.

### *B.E.F.*

| | | |
|---|---|---|
| ‡1 A. I | Barnes, George E. 7280. | K. April 23/17. Det.D./B. |
| 1 A. I | Hull, Arthur Wm. 4754. | M. Nov. 13-15/16. R/Enq. |
| ‡1 A. | Shears, E. G. 10060. | M. May 22/17. |
| 1 B. | Bush, C. M. 9373. | M. April 29/17. |
| 1 B. VI | Fergusson, L.-Cpl. Albert. 4547. | M. April 28/17. |
| 1 B. | Goldstein, S. W. 3556. | W. and M. Feb. 7/17. |
| 1 B. VI | Langridge, Bomber John Edwd. 3494. | M. April 17/17. |
| ‡1 B. VIII | Stephens, S/B. J. H. 7276. | K. April 21/17. Det.D./B. |
| 1 D. | Carpenter, Cecil Henry. 4740. | M., bel. K. Nov. 14/16. R/Enq. |

**Artillery Company, Honourable—contd.**

## *B.E.F.*

| | | |
|---|---|---|
| 2/1 | **Beck, 2nd Lieut. A. A. M.** | M. May 15/17. |
| 2/1 | **Bockett, 2nd Lieut. H. A. P.** | K. May 3/17. Det.D./B. |
| 2/1 | **Gander-Dower, 2nd Lieut. L. F.** | M., bel. K. May 3/17. |
| 2 | **Fedden, 2nd Lieut. R. H.** | K. May 3/17. Det.D./B. |
| 2 A. IV | L.G.S. Ayling, T. L. 7684. | M. May 3/17. |
| 2 A. III | Barney, Joseph Gilbert. 7330. | M. April 1/17. |
| 2 A. III | Bex, P. F. 9848. | M. May 3/17. |
| 2 A. | Brewster, Cpl. John. 6821. | M. May 3/17. |
| 2 A. III | Couling, Frank Herbert. 9715. | M. May 3/17. |
| 2 A. | Court, E. 9358. | M. May 3/17. |
| 2 A. II | Gentry, Frank Graham. 7360. | M. May 3/17. |
| ‡2 A. | Johnston, W. A. 9429. | M. May 3/17. |
| 2 A. III | Lockerbie, Andrew T. 9618. | M. May 3/17. |
| 2 A. | Moysey, L. J. S. 6755. | M. May 3/17. |
| 2 A. III | Parry, P. F. 9724. | M. May 3/17. |
| 2 A. IV | Porter, Arthur Wilmot. 9878. | M. May 3/17. |
| ‡2 A. | Rogers, F. G. 9905. | M. May 3/17. |
| 2 A. III | Seamark, Henry Reginald. 9728. | M. May 3/17. |
| *2 A. II | Seymour, W. Percy. 9170. | M. May 3/17. |
| 2 A. | Simpkin, T. 9866. | M. May 3/17. |
| ‡2 A. | Sinclair, G. S. 9942. | M. May 3/17. |
| 2 A. IV | Taylor, Arthur George. 5115. | K. Mar. 31/17. Det.D./B. |
| 2 A. | Waters-Bailey, L. 9846. | M. May 3/17. |
| 2 A. I | Watkins, C. F. 5554. | M. May 3/17. |
| 2 A. III | Watson, Thos. Tosh. 9856. | M. May 3/17. |
| 2 A. I | Wiles, S. 9832. | M. May 3/17. |
| 2 B. VII | Buckeridge, E. G. 9945. | M. May 3-4/17. |
| 2 B. | Crawford, A. L. 9889. | M. May 3/17. |
| 2 B. VI | Dowden, Jack D. 9786. | M. May 3/17. |
| 2 B. V | Dunn, Arthur Mare. 6961. | M. May 3/17. |
| 2 B. | Edwards, Arthur Edward. 7367. | M. May 3/17. |
| 2 B. | Gatward, L.-Cpl. W. J. 7549. | M. May 3/17. |
| 2 B. VI | Grimwood, Edward Wm. 7026. | M. May 3/17. |
| 2 B. VI | Grocott, Fredk. 9200. | M. May 3/17. |
| 2 B. VII | Haime, L. H. 7553. | M. May 3/17. |
| 2 B. V | Hedgecock, Ernest. 9921. | M. May 3/17. |
| 2 B. | Heggie, L.-Cpl. Fredk. W. 4456. | M., bel. K. May 3/17. |
| 2 B. | Mahr, Augustin Harry. 9932. | M. May 3/17. |
| 2 B. V | Morris, Ernest Walter. 9303. | M. May 3/17. |
| 2 B. VIII | Nixon, Ernest Harry. 9900. | M. May 3-5/17. |
| 2 B. | Proverbs, Stuart Elwyn. 7499. | M. May 3/17. |
| 2 B. | Robertson, Corpl. Noel S. 7303. | M. May 3/17. |
| 2 B. VIII | Selby, L.-Cpl. D. F. G. 3632. | M. May 3/17. |
| 2 B. | Sheppard, Duncan G. E. 9254. | M. May 3/17. |
| 2 B. VI | Simpson, V. L. 7362. | M. May 3/17. |
| 2 B. V | Whear, R. M. 9897. | M. May 3/17. |
| ‡2 B. VII | White, C. W. H. 7293. | M. May 3/17. R/Enq. |
| ‡2 B. | Wood, C. E. 7651. | M. May 3/17. |
| *2 B. | Woodger, Sergt. Noel Edwd. 3644. | K. May 15/17. Det.D./B. |
| *2 C. or D. | Bishop, H. R. G. 9733. | M. May 15/17. |
| 2 C. IX | Brown, R. T. 9785. | M. May 15/17. |
| 2 C. | Criswick, J. V. 5058. | M. May 3/17. |
| 2 C. X | Crompton, C. S. 9708. | M. May 14/17. |
| *2 C. X | Cutting, Chas. Henry. 4943. | M. May 15/17. |
| 2 C. X | Davis, F. G. 7141. | M. May 15/17. |
| 2 C. X | Dering, Cyril. 6837. | M. May 15/17. |
| ‡2 C. XI | Dix, S. H. 9005 | M. May 15/17. |
| ‡2 C. | Double, H. 9627. | M. May 15/17. |

**Artillery Company, Honourable—contd.**

*B.E.F.*

| | | |
|---|---|---|
| 2 C. | Elphick, C. D. 7379. | M. May 15/17. |
| 2 C. | Farrow, P. R. 5227. | M. May 15/17. |
| 2 C. | Forrest, L.-Cpl. E. J. 6855. | M. May 15/17. |
| ‡2 C. | Garrad, H. E. 6744. | M. May 15/17. |
| ‡2 C. | Hart, B. E. 9231. | M. May 15/17. |
| 2 C. IX | Hunt, H. C. 9644. | M. May 14/17. |
| 2 C. | Jenkins, George. 9247. | Unoff. M. May 15/17. |
| 2 C. IX | Laming, W. 9789. | M. May 14/17. |
| ‡2 C. | Lupkin, C. A. H. 9248. | M. May 15/17. |
| *2 C. | Mann, Sergt. James E. H. 9054. | M. May 15/17. |
| 2 C. IX | Meech, E. G. 9801. | M. May 15/17. |
| ‡2 C. | Monroe, Arthur S. 9225. | M. May 15/17. |
| 2 C. X | Peel, Edw. 4968. | M. May 14/17. |
| 2 C. | Prockter, F. C. 9546. | M. May 15/17. |
| *2 C. IX | Spears, Eric. 9819. | M. about May 15/17. |
| ‡2 C. | Springfield, R. W. 9820. | M. May 15/17. |
| 2 C. Bomb. S. | Summers, Robert Rendel. 4922. | M. May 3/17. |
| 2 C. | Walby, L.-Cpl. Arthur Gordon. 5303. | M. May 15/17. |
| ‡2 C. | Whiting, E. A. 9466. | M. May 15/17. |
| 2 C. X | Wright, Benjamin Joseph. 9795. | M. May 3/17. |
| 2 D. | Abbott, P. M. E. 7457. | M. May 3/17. |
| 2 D. | Arnold, A. E. 6503. | M. May 3/17. |
| 2 D. | Brayfield, Sgt. Arthur James. 3544. | M. May 3/17. |
| 2 D. | Calder, M. W. 9041. | M. May 3/17. |
| 2 D. | Clemmetsen, S. 7140. | M. May 3/17. |
| 2 D. | Cornish, Jas. Edward. 7657. | M. May 15/17. |
| 2 D. XIII | Crawford, Regd. Hugh. 5761. | M. May 3/17. |
| 2 D. XVI | Davies, Gilbert Lawrence. 7190. | M. May 3/17. |
| 2 D. | Dickson, M. J. B. 6959. | M. May 3/17. |
| 2 D. | Dodds, Douglas Geo. 7080. | M. May 3/17. |
| 2 D. | Greig, Roderick M. John. 9071. | M. May 3/17. |
| 2 D. | Hanford, Arthur T. 5103. | M. May 3/17. |
| 2 D. | Hardingham, F. F. 9055. | M. May 3/17. |
| 2 D. XIV | Heryet, L.-Cpl. Cyril. 6648. | M. May 3/17. |
| 2 D. XIV | Hill, Wm. Oswyn. 7559. | M. May 3/17. |
| 2 D. XIII | Jeaffreson, Ronald P. 5019. | M. May 3/17. |
| 2 D. XIV | Johnson, R. 9496. | M. May 3/17. |
| 2 D. XIV | Lee, Thomas George. 7054. | K. May 3/17. Det.D./B. |
| 2 D. | Oldreive, Reg. Richd. 9194. | M. May 3/17. |
| ‡2 D. | Walker, L. A. 7097. | M. May 3/17. |
| ‡2 D. | Wilson, A. G. 4272. | M. May 3/17. |

**ARGYLL AND SUTHERLAND HIGHLANDERS.**

*B.E.F.*

| | | |
|---|---|---|
| 2 A. | Charlton, John R. 11326. | K. April 24/17. Det.D./B. |
| 2 A. | Fraser, W. 11186. | M. April 23/17. |
| 2 A. | Grant, J. S. 16634. | M. April 24/17. |
| 2 A. | Hill, Hugh. 17309. (Fr. 3rd.) | M. April 24/17. |

**Argyll and Sutherland Highlanders.—contd.**

## *B.E.F.*

| | | |
|---|---|---|
| 2 A. | Leitch, A. 9460. (Fr. 4th.) | M. **April 23/17.** |
| 2 A. | Lynn, S. 15153. | M. **April 24/17.** |
| 2 A. II | McKechnie, Angus. S/43058. (320118.) | W. and M. **April 24/17.** |
| 2 A. | Martin, N. 6439. | M. **April 24/17.** |
| 2 A. | Miller, L.-Cpl. J. A. 16434. | M. **April 24/17.** |
| 2 A. | Moffat, A. 10486. | W. and M. **April 24/17.** |
| 2 A. | Munro, J. 9271. | W. and M. **April 24/17.** |
| 2 A. IV | Stewart, Thos. C. 43060. (Fr. 4th.) | W. and M. **April 24/17.** |
| 2 A. | Wilson, J. 8819. | M. **April 24/17.** |
| 2 B. | Caskie, L.-Cpl. John B. S/14966. | W. and M. **April 24/17.** |
| 2 B. | Clelland, Chas. 14117. | M. **April 24/17.** |
| 2 B. | Innes, J. 6867. | M. **April 24/17.** |
| 2 B. | McGarvey, John. 12158. | K. **April 24/17.** Det.D./B. |
| 2 B. | Marriott, Sgt. A. 9729. | M. **April 24/17.** |
| 2 B. | Miller, J. 11978. | W. and M. **April 24/17.** |
| 2 B. | Smith, A. 17500. | W. and M. **April 24/17.** |
| 2 D. | Campbell, Gershom. 16257. | K. **April 23/17.** Det.D./B. |
| 2 D. | Hughes, Sergt. R. C. S/12730. | M. **April 23/17.** |
| 2 D. | Stevenson, Robt. 4/6663. | W. and M. **April 23/17.** |
| *6 A. | Chalmers, Thomas. 5864. | M. **Sept. 26/16.** R/Enq. |
| 7 | **Milligan, 2nd Lieut. A.** | D/W. **April 23/17.** Det./Cas. |
| 7 | **Wilson, 2nd Lieut. T. D.** | Unoff. M., bel. W. **April 23/17.** |
| 7 A. | Campbell, D. 278640. | M. **April 23/17.** |
| 7 A. I | Hogg, Michael L. 278462. | M. **April 23/17.** |
| 7 A. III | Mackintosh, H. G. 276016. (3483.) | M. **April 23/17.** |
| 7 B. VIII | Bryce, John Henry. 278920. | W. and M. **April 23/17.** |
| 7 B. | McDonald, H. 278469. | M. **April 23/17.** |
| ‡7 B. | McKinlay, J. Mc. 325944. | M., bel. drowned **May 22-23/17.** |
| 7 C. XII | Boyle, Patrick. 276773. | W. and M. **April 23/17.** |
| 7 C. | Greenaway, J. 278613. | W. and M. **April 23/17.** |
| 7 C. IX | McAllister, Andrew. 278995. | K. **April 23/17.** Det.D./B. |
| ‡7 C. | Macdougall, R. 27851. (7294.) | K. **April 23/17.** Det.D./B. |
| 7 C. | Maismith, W. 278559. | M. **April 23/17.** |
| 7 C. X | Thomson, H. 278965. | W. and M. **April 23/17.** |
| ‡7 C. | Tyfe, J. B. 276586. | M. **May 5/17.** |
| 7 D. XVI | Currie, Joseph. 278661. | M **April 23/17.** |
| 7 D. XVI | Jenkins, L.-Cpl. T. Y. 278452. | M. **April 23/17.** |
| 7 D. XIV | McIntyre, Patrick. 278891. (7670.) | W. and M. **April 23/17.** |
| 7 D. XIV | McKechnie, Wm. 275991. (3437.) | W. and M. **April 23/17.** |
| 7 D. | Shields, W. K. 278976. | M. **April 23/17.** |
| 7 D. XIV | White, Jas. 278973. | M. **April 23/17.** |
| 8 | **Brown, 2nd Lt. C. T.** (Fr. 5th.) | W. and M. **March 17/17.** |
| 8 | **Munro, Capt. W. D.** | M. **May 15/17.** |
| 8 | **Watson, 2nd Lieut. P. S.** (Fr. 5th.) | M., bel. K. **April 9/17.** |
| ‡8 A. | Anderson, W. 10409. | M. **May 16/17.** |
| ‡8 A. | Bremner, H. 303097. | M. **May 16/17.** |
| *8 A. IV | Brown, Robt. 14239. | M. **May 16/17.** |
| 8 A. I | Brown, Samuel C. 500544. | M. **May 16/17.** |
| 8 A. IV | Cameron, D. 302838. (Late 5617.) | M. **March 17/17.** |
| 8 A. I | Cliff, C. H. 300469. (1995.) | M. **May 16/17.** |
| ‡8 A. | Duncan, L.-Cpl. M. 302989. | M. **May 16/17.** |
| ‡8 A. | Forster, Cpl. J. 301149. | M. **May 16/17.** |
| *8 A. IV | Hughes, Andrew. 303015. | M. **May 16/17.** |
| ‡8 A. | Miller, A. 303240. | M. **May 16/17.** |
| 8 A. or D. L.G.S. | Nicholson, Donald Alexander. 302982. | M. **April 9/17.** |
| 8 A | Smith, Cpl. J. 301284. | M. **Mar. 17/17.** |
| ‡8 A. | Wilson, Cpl. T. 301101. | M. **May 16/17.** |

**Argyll and Sutherland Highlanders—contd.**

***B.E.F.***

| | | |
|---|---|---|
| *8 B. VII | Blair, John. 303400. (6394.) | M. May 16/17. |
| ‡8 B. | Dowling, J. 302380. | M. May 16/17. |
| *8 B. VI | Duncan, David. 276641. (Fr. 7th.) | M. May 16/17. |
| 8 B. VII | Flockhart, William. 303378. | M. April 23/17. |
| *8 B. VI | Goldie, W. 12859. | M. May 16/17. |
| ‡8 B. | Granf, Geo. 325174. | M. May 16/17. |
| 8 B. | Gray, W. 303120. | M. Mar. 17/17. |
| 8 B. | Hay, A. 302979. | M. Mar. 17/17. |
| 8 B. | Howarth, J. 301336. | M. Mar. 17/17. |
| 8 B. VI | Jackson, Thos. 300897. (2747.) | M. April 23/17. |
| 8 B. VII | McCall, Wm. 8982. (Fr. 4th.) | M. May 16/17. |
| ‡8 B. | McCormack, P. 3/7400. | M. May 16/17. |
| 8 B. VI | McEwan, David. 303163. (Late 5963.) | M. March 17/17. |
| ‡8 B. | McGill, P. 301548. | M. May 16/17. |
| 8 B. | MacGregor, Sergt. H. 300101. | W. and M. April 9/17. |
| ‡8 B. | McLean, Sergt. J. 300053. | M. May 16/17. |
| ‡8 B. | Morgan, L.-Cpl. D. 7624. | M. May 16/17. |
| ‡8 B. | Wilson, L.-Cpl. H. 303079. | M. May 16/17. |
| ‡8 C. | Armstrong, A. 16163. | M. May 16/17. |
| ‡8 C. | Cuthbertson, D. 303055. | M. May 16/17. |
| 8 C. XI | Dillon, Robt. 303006. | M. April 9/17. |
| *8 C. X | Glynn, Wm. 301180. (3252.) | M. May 16/17. |
| 8 C. IX | Grey, E. 302104. (Late 4590.) (Fr. 5 Middlx., 29494.) | M. March 17/17. |
| 8 C. | Johnstone, J. 303192. | M. Mar. 17/17. |
| 8 C. | Kennedy, R. 303219. | M. April 23/17. |
| ‡8 C. | McBride, J. 302887. | M. May 16/17. |
| *8 C. IX | Mather, Cpl. J. S/3234. | M. May 16/17. |
| ‡8 C. | Muir, J. 300575. | M. May 16/17. |
| *8 C. X | Sloan, Thomas. 15928. | K. May 16/17. Det.D./B. |
| 8 D. | Farrar, F. 301421. | M. Mar. 17/17. |
| 8 D. XV | Landels, W. A. 301603. (Late 3906.) | M. Mar. 17/17. |
| 8 D. XVI | Thomson, Geo. 301772. (Late 4134.) | M. March 17/17. |
| 8 D. | Wilson, John. 303385. | M. Mar. 17/17. |
| *8 ? L.G.S. | McGregor, James. 300944. | M. May 16/17. |
| ‡9 B. | Jennings, B. 325586. | M. May 16/17. |
| 10 | **Duncan, 2nd Lieut. R. G. C.** | M. May 3/17. |
| 10 | **Law, Lieut. A. D.** | W. and M. May 3/17. |
| ‡10 A. | Fraser, W. 8272. | M. May 13/17. |
| 10 A. | Johnstone, A. 7918. | M. April 9/17. |
| 10 A. | McGregor, W. 14473. | M. April 15/17. |
| 10 A. III | Wilson, Wm. 16156. | M. Oct. 20/16. R/Enq. |
| 10 B. | Waterfield, V. H. 789. | M. April 30/17. |

**Argyll and Sutherland Highlanders—contd.**

## *B.E.F.*

| | | |
|---|---|---|
| 10 C. XII | Bartell, Albert Frederick. 13765. | M. **May 5/17.** |
| ‡10 C. | Birt, L.-Sergt. R. 11002. | M. **May 5/17.** |
| *10 C. XII | Flynn, L.-Cpl. T. 7588. | W. and M. **May 5/17.** |
| 10 C. X | Hamilton, Tom. 277207. | W. and M. **May 5/17.** |
| *10 C. M.G.S. | Hardie, Graham G. 13483. | M. **May 5/17.** |
| 10 C. | McGregor, J. D. 10308. | M. **April 15/17.** |
| 10 C. XI | McLachlan, Cpl. Duncan McNerchy. 10270. | M. **April 15/17.** |
| 10 C. IX | Morton, David. 11742. | M. **May 5/17.** |
| 10 C. X | Robinson, Harry. 48683. | W. and M. **May 5/17.** |
| 10 C. XII | Struthers, Robt. Murray. 14415. | W. and M. **April 5/17.** |
| ‡10 C. | Taylor, J. 40700. | M. **May 5/17.** |
| 10 D. IV | Anderson, Cpl. J. 12679. | M. **May 3/17.** |
| ‡10 D. XVI | Carey, Chas. 40018. | M. **May 3/17.** |
| *10 D. XVI | Currie, John. 17685. | M. **May 3/17.** |
| ‡10 D. | Haxton, L.-Sergt. G. 10663. | M. **May 3/17.** |
| 10 D. **Bomb.** S. | Hendry, Cpl. John. 2577. | M. **May 3/17.** |
| ‡10 D | Kennedy, R. 8092. | M. **May 3/17.** |
| ‡10 D. XVI | Lamont, Hugh. 16864. | M. **May 3/17.** |
| ‡10 D. | Lawson, A. 13748. | M. **May 3/17.** |
| ‡10 D. | Love, J. 3202. | M. **May 3/17.** |
| ‡10 D. XIV | Diarmid, J. John. 40078. | M. **May 3/17.** |
| ‡10 D. | McKillop, J. 13794. | M. **May 3/17.** |
| ‡10 D. | MacKinnon, J. 9235. | M. **May 3/17.** |
| 10 D. XVI | McClymont, John. 40076. (2389.) (Fr. 2/9 and 9 Entrench. Batt.) | M. **April 15/17.** |
| 10 D. XIV | Milne, William. 15580. | W. and M. **May 3/17.** |
| ‡10 D. | Mitchell, R. 15159. | M. **May 3/17.** |
| *10 D. | Rigg, Cpl. Ernest. S/9473. | M. **May 3/17.** |
| 11 A. M.G.S. | Ferguson, L.-Cpl. D. 7683. | M. **April 23/17.** |
| 11 A. or D. | Grieve, J. C. 9285. | M. **April 23/17.** |
| 11 A. | McArthur. L. 40191. | M. **April 23/17.** |
| ‡11 A. | Robertson, J. 11243. | M. **April 23/17.** |
| ‡11 A. | Galbraith, A. 17017. | W. and M. **April 23/17.** |
| ‡11 A. | Lafferty, L.-Cpl. O. 4823. | W. and M. **April 23/17.** |
| 11 A. | Simpson, J. 17605. | M. **April 23/17.** |
| 11 A. | Taylor, W. 40175. | M. **April 23/17.** |
| 11 A. or B. | Wilson, John. 7736. | M. **April 23/17.** |
| 11 A. or D. | Young, William. 18759. | M. **April 23/17.** |
| 11 B. VIII | Clancy, James B. 43145. | K. **April 23/17.** Det.D./B. |
| 11 D. XIII | Craik, L.-Cpl. John Kendrick. 40163. | M. **April 23/17.** |
| 11 D. | Graham, Jas. 278862. (Fr. 7th.) | M. **April 23/17.** |
| *11 D. | McColloch, Robt. S/40214. | W. and M. **April 23/17.** |
| 11 D. | Wilson, Thos. 7090. | M. **April 9/17.** |
| 14 D. | Henderson, L.-Cpl. R. H. 13650. | M. **April 24/17.** |

## *BALKANS.*

| | | |
|---|---|---|
| 1 ? | McAuslan, P. 7565 | W. and M. **Oct. 1/16.** |
| 12 | **Andrew, Lieut. R.** | M., bel. K. **May 8-9/17.** |
| 12 B. | **Andrews, 2nd Lieut. R. H. C.** | M., bel. K. **May 8-9/17.** |
| 12 A. | McConnell, Cpl. A. 5347. | M. **May 8-9/17.** |
| 12 A. | Mackenzie, Roderick James Balfour. 16482. | M. **May 8-9/17.** |
| 12 B. | Goldie, Wm. 5216. | M. **May 8-9/17.** |
| 12 B. | Harvey, Cpl. W. J. 4639. | W. and M. **May 8-9/17.** |
| 12 B. | Maclaren, Cpl. John M. S/5798. | M. Unoff. W. **May 8-9/17.** |

**Argyll and Sutherland Highlanders—contd.**

## *BALKANS.*

| | | |
|---|---|---|
| 12 B. | Mann, Cpl. Robert. S/5626. | M. May 8-9/17. |
| 12 B. | Norrie, Sergt. Geo. Lennox. 4454. | M. May 8-9/17. |
| 12 B. | Smith, Ernest. 4930. | M. May 8-9/17. |
| 12 B. | Wardrop, Geo. 14065. | M. May 8-9/17. |
| 12 C. | Bradley, L.-Cpl. E. 5271. | M. May 8-9/17. |
| 12 C. | Burge, Cpl. C. 5364. | M. May 8-9/17. |
| 12 C. | Condie, Thos. 5380. | M. May 8-9/17. |
| 12 C. | Dawson, F. 5426. | M. May 8-9/17. |
| 12 C. IX | Galbraith, Donald. 18151. | M. May 8-9/17. |
| 12 C. | Howie, Robt. M. 5212. | M. May 8-9/17. |
| 12 C. | King, David. 5469. | M. May 8-9/17. |
| 12 C. | Lumsden, Gordon. 5414. | M. May 8-9/17. |
| 12 C. | Michie, Wm. 5453. (Fr. 77 Bgde. M.G.C.) | M. April 24/17. |
| 12 C. | Rae, L.-Sergt, James. 1641. | M. May 8-9/17. |
| ‡12 C. XII | Scott, Cpl. G. M. 11048. | M. May 8-9/17. |
| 12 C. | *Sherman, John. 18137. | M. May 8-9/17. |
| 12 C. | Waddell, John Henderson. 18176. | M. May 8-9/17. |
| 12 D. | Brown, Sergt. John. S/5726. | M. May 8-9/17. |
| 12 D. | Dawson, John. 5913. | M. May 8-9/17. |
| 12 D. | Finlay, William. S/5713. | M. May 8-9/17. |
| 12 D. XIII. | James, A. J. 18384. | M. May 8-9/17. |
| 12 D. | Lindsay, John. 7024. | M. May 8-9/17. |
| 12 ? | Adam, A. 5522. | M. May 8-9/17. |
| *12 ? | Aitchison, J. 1334. | M. May 8-9/17. |
| 12 ? | Barclay, M. 8861. | M. May 8-9/17. |
| 12 ? | Boyle, T. 4955. | M. May 8-9/17. |
| 12 ? | Buchanan, A. 5878. | M. May 8-9/17. |
| 12 ? | Cameron, D. 4618. | M. May 8-9/17. |
| 12 ? | Campbell, Cpl. P. 5730. | M. May 8-9/17. |
| *12 ? | Craig, T. 4934. | M. May 8-9/17. |
| 12 ? | Currie, Sergt. G. 5645. | M. May 8-9/17. |
| 12 ? | Laidlaw, J. 2100. | M. May 8-9/17. |
| 12 ? | Leishman, Wm. Parker. 18166. | M. May 8-9/17. |
| 12 ? | Leitch, A.-Cpl. A. 5873. | M. May 8-9/17. |
| 12 ? | McIntyre, J. 5442. | M. May 8-9/17. |
| 12 ? | McKenzie, W. 17733. | M. May 8-9/17. |
| 12 ? | McLean, L.-Cpl. L. 4729. | M. May 8-9/17. |
| 12 ? | Miller, D. 5619. | M. May 8-9/17. |
| 12 ? | Owens, J. 5531. | M. May 8-9/17. |
| *12 ? | Paterson, A. 5357. | M. May 8-9/17. |
| 12 ? | Ponten, D. 7065. | M. May 8-9/17. |
| 12 ? | Rennie, J. 7163. | M. May 8-9/17. |
| ‡12 ? | Ritchie, D. 16558. | M. May 8-9/17. |
| ‡12 ? | Robertson, Chas. 18152. (Fr. 1st.) | M. May 8-9/17. |
| 12 ? | Robertson, Cpl. J. 5660. | M. May 8-9/17. |
| 12 ? | Shaw, A. 7424. | M. May 8-9/17. |
| 12 ? | Spence, J. 5682. | M. May 8-9/17. |
| 12 ? | Stirling, J. 6564. | M. May 8-9/17. |
| 12 ? | Thomson, A. 4908. | M. May 8-9/17. |
| 12 ? | Wilson, W. 7508. | M. May 8-9/17. |
| *12 ? | Wood, J. 18413. | M. May 8-9/17. |

**AUSTRALIAN IMPERIAL FORCE.**
**Vide end of List.**

## BEDFORDSHIRE REGIMENT.

### B.E.F.

| | | |
|---|---|---|
| 1 A. | Ayles, H. R. 32930. | W. and M. April 23/17. |
| 1 A. | Baker, H. E. 12210. | M. April 23/17. |
| 1 A. | Ball, Cpl. H. E. 32950. | M. April 23/17. |
| 1 A. IV | Barnes, Sidney. 32939. | M. April 23/17. |
| 1 A. | Beauchamp, H. 15891. | M. April 23/17. |
| 1 A. IV | Frost, L.-Cpl. Walter Samuel. 28970. | M. April 23/17. |
| 1 A. | Gore, T. 27645. | M. April 23/17. |
| 1 A. | Linsdell, W. J. 12677. | M. April 23/17. |
| 1 A. | Runham, Cpl. C. 10352. | M. April 23/17. |
| 1 A. | Sage, F. 25625. | M. April 23/17. |
| 1 B. | Andrews, H. 27863. | M. April 23/17. |
| 1 B. | Betts, G. W. 33601. | M. April 23/17. |
| 1 B. VII | Borlase, E. A. 32945. | M. April 23/17. |
| 1 B. | Bovingdon, W. E. 32954. | M. April 23/17. |
| 1 B. | Bracey, A. W. 18316. | M. April 23/17. |
| 1 B. | Brown, F. 33594. | M. April 23/17. |
| 1 B. | Cleaver, F. J. 43118. | M. April 23/17. |
| 1 B. V | Crawley, Sidney Geo. 33617. | M. April 23/17. |
| 1 B. L.G.S. | Darnell, Geo. 27837. | W. and M. April 23/17. |
| 1 B. | Deller, R. 43052. | M. April 23/17. |
| 1 B. | Emmington, W. 19535. | M. April 23/17. |
| 1 B. | Fountain, H. 20099. | W. and M. April 23/17. |
| 1 B. | Gaffer, J. 26874. | M. April 23/17. |
| 1 B. | Gaunt, C. P. 43426. | M. April 23/17. |
| 1 B. V | Harris, L.-Cpl. Ernest. 15732. | M. April 23/17. |
| 1 B. V | Harris, H. 18204. | M. April 23/17. |
| 1 B. | Hill, G. 10969. | M. April 23/17. |
| 1 B. | Hobbs, A. G. 10209. | M. April 23/17. |
| 1 B. VII | Holyoak, C. 27817. | M. April 23/17. |
| 1 B. L.G.S. | Izzard, L.-Cpl. A. 7118. (Fr. 4th.) | M. April 23/17. |
| 1 B. VI | Jones, J. J. 21250. | M. April 23/17. |
| 1 B. | Keep, Cpl. Alfred. 23286. | W. and M. April 23/17. |
| 1 B. VI | Lake, Harold Alfred. 31484. | M. April 23/17. |
| 1 B. VII | Lawson, C. H. 33347. | M. April 23/17. |
| 1 B. VI | Mardell, James. 30958. | W. and M. April 23/17. |
| 1 B. | Murphy, F. 33357. | M. April 23/17. |
| 1 B. | Page, A. 10408. | M. April 23/17. |
| 1 B. | Shepherd, Cpl. G. 16532. | M. April 23/17. |
| 1 B. VII | Slack, C. V. 43445. | M. April 23/17. |
| 1 B. | Smart, J. G. 31709. | M. April 23/17. |
| 1 B. | Smith, F. 5571. | M. April 23/17. |
| *1 B. V | Tear, Cpl. A. G. 12289. | M. April 23/17. |
| 1 B. | Torrance, V. G. H. 33351. | M. April 23/17. |
| 1 B. | Whittering, A. C. 31497. | M. April 23/17. |
| 1 B. | Williams, G. H. 13291. | M. April 23/17. |
| 1 B. | Wood, C. 33370. | M. April 23/17. |
| 1 C. | Anderson, J. W. 40036. | M. April 23/17. |
| 1 C. | Burr, A. W. 18122. | M. April 23/17. |
| 1 C. | Butler, H. 43107. | M. April 23/17. |
| 1 C. | Clarke, G. 32976. | M. April 23/17. |

**Bedfordshire Regiment**—contd.

## *B.E.F.*

| | | |
|---|---|---|
| 1 C. | Cole, L.-Cpl. Geo. 33373. | M. April 23/17. |
| 1 C. XI | Darnell, H. A. 32980. | W. and M. April 23/17. |
| 1 C. | Fensome, G. E. 12089. | M. April 23/17. |
| 1 C. | Hitchcock, A. E. 43409. | W. and M. April 23/17. |
| 1 C. or D. | Shadbolt, Alfred. 18592. | W. and M. April 23/17. |
| 1 C. IX | Smith, Albert Chas. 3/6620. | M. May 14/17. |
| 1 C. IX | Smith, Fred. 43064. | M. April 23/17. |
| 1 C. | Smith, L.-Cpl. M. 33350. | M. April 23/17. |
| 1 D. | Adams, F. 33587. | M. April 23/17. |
| 1 D. XV | Allen, A. G. 33588. | M. April 23/17. |
| 1 D. | Carpenter, Walter. 13926. | M. April 23/17. |
| 1 D. XIV | Clark, S. C. 43008. | M. April 23/17. |
| 1 D. VIII | Cuffe, J. 43102. | M. April 23/17. |
| 1 D. XVI | Davis, Harry. 14295. | M. April 23/17. |
| 1 D. XVI | Dighton, J. H. 40315. | M. April 23/17. |
| 1 D. | Dilley, Cpl. G. 22019. | M. April 23/17. |
| 1 D. XIII | Dray, Arthur. 32986. | M. April 23/17. |
| 1 D. XVI | Gilbert, G. W. 33010. | W. and M. April 23/17. |
| 1 D. XV | Gilder, Fredk. Harry. 33009. | W. and M. April 23/17. |
| 1 D. | Hitchcock, G. 40028. | M. April 23/17. |
| 1 D. | Kefford, F. 19499. | K. Oct. 31/16. Det.D./B. |
| 1 D. | Matthews, Sergt. G. E. 30471. | M. April 23/17. |
| 1 D. | Munns, G. 12804. | M. April 23/17. |
| 1 D. | Norris, A.-Cpl. T. W. 40007. | M. April 23/17. |
| 1 D. XVI | Parker, Bert. 33082. | M. April 23/17. |
| 1 D. | Peters, Sergt. G. E. 18641. | M. April 23/17. |
| 1 D. | Reynolds, H. 33383. | M. April 23/17. |
| 1 D. XIII | Robinson, Cpl. W. 43439. | M. Sept. 3/16. R/Enq. |
| 1 D. XIII | Saunders, A. G. 16973. | M. April 23/17. |
| 1 D. | Turner, Cpl. S. 6639. | M. April 23/17. |
| 1 D. | Walker, Stanley Geo. 40057. (Fr. H.Q.) | W. and M. April 23/17. |
| 1 D. | Wicks, F. C. 40043. | M. April 23/17. |
| 2 A. | Church, A.-Sergt. P. 9663. | M. April 8/17. |
| 2 B. | Minett, Ainger Harry. 26651. (Fr. 9th.) | M. Oct. 12/16. R/Enq. |
| 4 A. | **Muir, 2nd Lieut. H. W.** | M., bel. K. April 24/17. |
| *4 B. | **Mulligan, 2nd Lieut. S. G.** | K. April 23/17. Det.D./B. |
| 4 A. L.G.S. | Allen, W. S. 15225. | M. April 23/17. |
| ‡4 A. | Barker, L. A. 27713. | W. and M. April 29/17. |
| ‡4 A. | Bellamy, Sergt. C. C. 15169. | K. April 23/17. Det.D./B. |
| 4 A. | Bird, A.-Cpl. C. 19347. | M. April 29/17. |
| ‡4 A. | Boulton, J. 3/7205. | M. April 29/17. |
| 4 A. | Bradford, Reuben. 26710. | W. and M. April 3/17. |
| 4 A. I | Brittain, Fredk. Stanley. 16059. | M. April 23/17. |
| 4 A. | Cherry, Harry. 40581. | W. and M. April 23/17. |
| ‡4 A. IV | Dickerson, Ralph George. 28133. | M. April 23/17. |
| 4 A. | Eames, A. 18439. | M. April 29/17. |
| 4 A. | Goward, H. 30458. | M. April 29/17. |
| ‡4 A. | Islip, H. 23415. | W. and M. April 23/17. |
| 4 A. I | Jackson, John Albert. 35997. | M. April 23/17. |
| 4 A. | Mart, Fredk. Chas. 7873. | W. and M. April 29/17. |
| 4 A. | Mitchell, B. 26205. | M. April 23/17. |
| 4 A. I | Peacock, Fredk. J. 25572. | W. and M. April 29/17. |
| 4 A. | Rogers, J. W. 29048. | M. April 23/17. |
| 4 A. | Roper, A.-Cpl. H. J. 33707. | M. April 23/17. |
| 4 A. | Thorpe, Robt. Geo. Smith. 40606. | M. April 23/17. |
| 4 B. or C. | Barnes, Maurice. 14041. | M. April 23/17. |
| ‡4 B. | Burrell, W. 8836. | M. April 29/17. |

**Bedfordshire Regiment—contd.**

## *B.E.F.*

| | | |
|---|---|---|
| **4 B. VIII** | Caron, Corpl. William. 17011. | M. **April 23/17.** |
| **4 B.** | Coleman, W. H. 17151. | M. **April 29/17.** |
| **4 B. or C.** | Day, F. C. 40572. | M. **April 23/17.** |
| **4 B. M.G.S.** | Edwards, L.-Cpl. J. 23660. | W. and M. **April 29/17.** |
| **4 B. VIII** | Folkes, L.-Cpl. Thomas. 40112. | M. **April 23/17.** |
| **4 B. VIII** | Fountain, F. 27828. | M. **April 23/17.** |
| **4 B. VI** | Gilby, L.-Cpl. J. W. 40180. | K. **Nov. 13/16.** Det.D./B. |
| **4 B.** | Kingston, J. W. 23617. | M. **Nov. 13/16.** R./Enq. |
| **4 B.** | Lawrence, W. 23274. | M. **April 29/17.** |
| **4 B. L.G.S.** | Layton, Fred. 23304. | W. and M. **April 23/17.** |
| **4 B. V** | Peddar, W. 22970. | W. Unoff. M. **April 29/17.** |
| **4 B. VI** | Rawlings, O. G. 23219. | M. **April 23/17.** |
| **4 B.** | Reid, Cpl. Oscar Harold. 33476. | M. **April 23/17.** |
| **4 B.** | Scrivener, Sergt. Albert Edwin. 7319. | M. **April 23/17.** |
| **4 B.** | Stocker, T. 23473. | W. and M. **April 23/17.** |
| **4 B. VIII** | Winteringham, Sergt. C. 29745. | W. and M. **April 29/17.** |
| **4 C. IX** | Bird, A. 30815. | M. **Feb. 11/17.** |
| **4 C. IX** | Butterwick, Alfred. 25449. | W. and M. **Feb. 11/17.** |
| **4 C. IX** | Clark, Stanley. 29696. | M. **Feb. 11/17.** |
| **4 C. IX** | Coughtrey, L.-Cpl. F. 23540. | M. **Feb. 11/17.** |
| **4 C. IX** | Curston, Harry. 29071. | M. **April 29/17.** |
| **4 C.** | Dines, Sergt. C. W. 23125. | M. **April 23/17.** |
| **4 C. IX** | Durham, T. H. 23285. | W. and M. **April 29/17.** |
| **4 C. M.G.S.** | George, Albert. 23272. | W. and M. **Nov. 13/16.** |
| **4 C. X** | Hearne, Herbert W. 23801. | M. **April 29/17.** |
| **4 C. XI** | Manning, F. G. 22956. | M. **April 30/17.** |
| **4 C.** | Mills, Alfred Wm. 30026. | M. **April 29/17.** |
| **4 C.** | Odell, H. 23466. | M. **April 23/17.** |
| **4 C. X** | Stock, L.-Cpl. Frank. 22815. | M. **April 29/17.** |
| **4 C.** | Triplow, A. 20864. | M. **April 23/17.** |
| **4 C.** | Winch, Cpl. M. 13043. | M. **April 23/17.** |
| **4 C. IX** | Worker, Sgt. Thos. 22677. | W. and M. **April 23/17.** |
| **4 C.** | Wright, W. E. 40201. | M. **Nov. 13/16.** |
| **4 D.** | Booth, R. A. 7167. | W. and M. **April 29/17.** |
| **4 D. XVI** | Burrows, Samuel Foster. 18551. | M. **Feb. 11/17.** |
| **4 D.** | Calver, Isaac. 12351. | M. **Feb. 11/17.** |
| **4 D. M.G.S.** | Clack, C. T. 20433. | M. **Nov. 13/16.** R/Enq. |
| **‡4 D.** | Drage, G. 23044. | W. and M. **April 23/17.** |
| **4 D.** | Evans, Cpl. W. P. 23328. | M. **Feb. 10/17.** |
| **4 D.** | Froy, Bertram. 30592. | M. **Feb. 11/17.** |
| **4 D. XVI** | Kemp, G. A. 25655. | M. **Feb. 11/17.** |
| **4 D. XIV** | Moore, J. G. 30078. | W. and M. **April 23/17.** |
| **4 D. XIV** | Oliver, Fredk. Geo. 20112. | M. **Feb. 11/17.** |
| **4 D.** | Reynolds, F. J. 25135. | M. **April 29/17.** |
| **‡4 D.** | Sanford, W. 43058. | W. and M. **April 23/17.** |
| **4 D. XVI** | Smith, Ernest Jesse. 18904. | M. **April 23/17.** |
| **4 D. XVI** | Stoughton, E. 14429. | W. and M. **April 23/17.** |
| **4 D. XIV** | Sycamore, A. E. 30163. | M. **Feb. 11/17.** |
| **‡4 D.** | Weever, W. H. 12392. | M. **May 31/17.** |
| **‡4 H.Q.** | Cox, Sergt. N. F. 22757. | K. **April 29/17** Det.D./B. |
| **6** | **Smith, 2nd Lt. C. R. B.** (Fr. 3rd.) | M. **April 28/17.** |
| **‡6 A.** | Bettles, B. 32204. | W. and M. **April 23-29/17.** |
| **6 A.** | Cavill, L.-Cpl. C. 12214. | M. **April 23-29/17.** |
| **6 A.** | Drake, A. 10603. | W. and M. **April 23-29/17.** |
| **‡6 A.** | Gurney, G. F. 31982. | M. **April 23-29/17.** |
| **6 A. II** | King, L.-Cpl. Robt. Wm. 19322. | M. **April 23-29/17.** |
| **6 A. III** | Priest, W. F. 31980. | M. **April 23-29/17.** |

**Bedfordshire Regiment—contd.**

## *B.E.F.*

| | | |
|---|---|---|
| 6 A. | Reynolds, John. 52252. | M. April 23-29/17. |
| 6 A. | Taylor, H. 31918. | M. April 23-29/17. |
| 6 A. | Wightman, F. H. 14761. | M. April 23-29/17. |
| ‡6 A. | Willis, F. C. 31783. | M. April 23-29/17. |
| 6 A. | Wilson, Sergt. A. 43256. | M. April 23-29/17. |
| 6 B. | Andrews, H. 32009. | M. April 23-29/17. |
| 6 B. | Bishop, G. 31893. | M. April 23-29/17. |
| 6 B. | Coleman, L. J. 32029. | M. April 28/17. |
| *6 B. V | Fisher, Samuel. 10761. | M. April 9-12/17. |
| 6 B. | Green, J. 14457. | M. April 23-29/17. |
| 6 B. VIII | Herbert, Thos. 12347. | M. April 23-29/17. |
| 6 B. | King, L.-Cpl. Geo. Sam. 20135. | M. April 23-29/17. |
| 6 B. | Knell, Edw. 12420. | M. April 27/17. |
| 6 B. | Scroggs, G. E. 33080. | M. April 23-29/17. |
| 6 B. VIII | Spreckley, J. R. 32161. | M. April 23-29/17. |
| 6 B. VIII | Titmuss, A. G. 32174. | M. April 23/17. |
| 6 B. | Weeden, Horace. 20768. | M. April 23-29/17. |
| 6 C. XII | Baldwin, E. 12057. | M. April 23-29/17. |
| 6 C. | Brind, Sergt. Edward. 10535. | M. April 23-29/17. |
| 6 C. IX | Bundy, F. C. 22580. | W. and M. Nov. 16/16. R/Enq. |
| 6 C. | Day, A. 32114. | M. April 28/17. |
| 6 C. | Durrant, Cpl. Joseph. 14735. | M. April 23-29/17. |
| 6 C. | Hulles, Cpl. Monty. 12502. | M. April 23-29/17. |
| 6 C. | Humphrey, F. 18946. | M. April 23-29/17. |
| 6 C. | Long, A. 4/7185. | M. April 23-29/17. |
| 6 C. XI | Neal, W. J. 18626. | M. April 23-29/17. |
| 6 C. IX | Nye, John Henry. 33064. | M. April 23-29/17. |
| 6 C. X | Odell, Sergt. Walter. 32106. | M. April 23-29/17. |
| ‡6 C. | Ruddick, L.-Cpl. J. R. 43215. | M. May 26/17. |
| 6 C. | Rusdale, J. 32154. | M. April 23-29/17. |
| 6 C. | Rutt, L.-Cpl. J. 32257. | M. April 23-29/17. |
| 6 C. X | Sewell, Wm. 35962. | M. April 23-29/17. |
| 6 C. | Simpson, T. 32170. | M. April 23-29/17. |
| 6 C. IX | Smith, Alfred Henry. 43146. | W. and M. April 9-12/17. |
| 6 C. | Smith, Leonard. 35961. | M. April 23-29/17. |
| 6 C. | Thurley, G. L. 33736. | M. April 23-29/17. |
| 6 C. XI | Timson, G. A. 32171. | M. April 23-29/17. |
| 6 D. XV | Ambrose, A. 32202. | K. April 9/17. Det.D./B. |
| 6 D. | Beaver, J. J. 32105. | M. April 28/17. |
| 6 D. | Chapman, C. 32053. | M. April 28/17. |
| 6 D. XV | Costin, Fred. 31786. | M. April 28/17. |
| 6 D. | Currington, Ernest. 1939. | M. April 28/17. |
| 6 D. XIV | Rawlings, E. 30427. | W. and M. April 28/17. |
| ‡6 D. | Thomas, S. M. 37879. | M. May 23/17. |
| 6 D. | Wilder, G. 14733. | M. Nov. 16/16. R/Enq. |
| *7 C. | **Luscombe, 2nd Lieut. C. J.** | K. May 3/17. Conf. and Det.D./B. |
| 7 A. I | Barker, Sergt. T. E. 33559. | W. and M. May 3/17. |
| *7 A. | Bass, Cpl. Wm. Geo. 15339. | M. May 3/17. |
| ‡7 A. | Courtnell, F. 15018. | M. May 3/17. |
| ‡7 A. L.G.S. | Day, G. 19873. | M. May 3/17. |
| ‡7 A. | Dunn, L.-Cpl. Anthony. 19764. (Fr. 9th.) | M. May 3/17. |
| 7 A. II | George, Sergt. Stanley O. 33540. (Fr. Northants.) | M. May 3/17. |
| *7 A. IV. | Goldfinch, A. J. 40536. | M. May 3/17. |
| ‡7 A. | Racher, W. 20832. | M. May 3/17. |
| ‡7 A. | Smith, Cpl. E. T. 14519. | M., bel. K. May 3/17. |
| *7 A. or D. L.G.S. | Smith, F. J. 22714. | W. and M. May 3/17. |

**Bedfordshire Regiment**—contd.

## *B.E.F.*

‡7 A. Smith, L.-Cpl. G. A. 10750. M. May 3/17.
7 A. IV Summerlin, George. 30601. M. May 3/17.
7 A. IV Tokens, C. 30619. M. May 3/17.
7 A. I Tompkins, W. G. 31254. M. May 3/17.
‡7 A. Tye, L. A. 12957. M. May 3/17.
‡7 B. Blott, G. H. 30861. M. May 3/17.
‡7 B. Bourne, J. 40518. M. May 3/17.
7 B. Clapham, Albert J. 14149. M. May 3/17.
7 B. XV Heger, John. 7002. (Fr. 4th.) M. Sept. 28/16.
7 B. Langdon, L. A. 18565. W. and M. July 1/16. R/Enq.
7 B. I.T.M. Leach, L.-Cpl. E. C. 19968. (54 Bgde.) M. Feb. 17/17.
7 B. Osborn, Albert. 26375. M. May 3/17.
‡7 B. VIII Packham, W. A. 10116. M. May 3/17.
•7 B. Pearce, Wm. Jas. 7178. (Fr. 4th.) M. Sept. 28/16.
7 B. Reeve, L. T. 31176. M. May 3/17.
7 B. VI Saddington, C. W. 30618. M., bel. K. May 3/17.
7 B. Stone, Sgt. H. J. 14850. W. Unoff. M. May 3/17.
‡7 B. Taylor, L.-Cpl. C. 15341. W. and M. May 3/17.
7 B. or C. Tebbutt, W. 43363. M. May 3/17.
7 B. Wood, J. T. 40512. M. May 3/17.
7 C. Barcock, F. 25147. W. and M., bel. K. Mar. 15/17.
7 C. Cochrane, L.-Cpl. J. 15754. M. Sept. 28/16. R/Enq.
7 C. IX Higby, R. 29474. M. May 3/17.
7 C. Short, L.-Cpl. Edw. 13328. W. and M. May 3/17.
‡7 C. Whittle, D. 25167. M. May 3/17.
‡7 D. Anstee, E. 30849. W. and M. May 3/17.
‡7 D. Armer, C. F. 31166. M. May 3/17.
‡7 D. Brunt, W. J. 201555. M. May 3/17.
7 D. Calver, Claude Hilton. 30928. M. May 3/17.
‡7 D. Harding, H. 19203. M. May 3/17.
7 D. XV Harris, Horace. 15817. M. Sept. 27/16.
‡7 D. Hawes, E. 29849. M. May 3/17.
‡7 D. King, A. 20601. M. May 3/17.
7 D. Kingham, Ernest Frank. 15047. W. and M. May 3/17.
7 D. Lowe, A. G. 23583. M. May 3/17.
‡7 D. Mansfield, John. 14577. M. May 3/17.
7 D. XIV Mead, A. 3/7947. M. May 3/17.
7 D. XIII Mutch, Geo. 43322. M. May 3/17.
‡7 D. Odell, H. 43270. M. May 3/17.
‡7 D. Sammons, J. E. 23288. M. May 3/17.
•7 D. Trott, L.-Cpl. G. 7607. M. May 3/17.
‡7 D. Trundell, Maurice. 25959. W. and M. May 3/17.
7 D. Waite, C. 19164. M. May 3/17.
•7 D. XIII Welch, Charles. 18707. W. and M. May 3/17.
‡7 D. XV Willby, R. N. 29301. M. May 3/17.
7 ? Mortimer, E. 40523. W. and M. May 3/17.
8 A. I Bullimore, W. 29243. M. Sept. 18/16. R/Enq.
8 A. II Hall, Bertie S. 40265. W. and M. April 19/17.
8 A. III Knight, W. 33518. M. April 16/17.
‡8 B. Camp, A. J. 39555. M. June 22/17.
8 C. Allen, Ernest. 40075. M. Sept. 25/16. R/Enq.
8 C. Boneham, Cyril Seymour. 40091. M Sept. 25/16. R/Enq.
8 C. M.G.S. Edgeley, G. H. 16110. M. Sept. 15/16. R/Enq.
8 C. XI Fripp, William. 33484. K. April 19/17. Det.D./B.
8 C. Hall, Julian. 33802. M. April 19/17.
8 C. Hawken, Horace. 15675. M. Sept. 25/16. R/Enq.
•8 C. X Hemming, L.-Cpl. Stanley. 33494. K. April 19/17. Det.D./B.

**Bedfordshire Regiment**—contd.

## *B.E.F.*

| | | |
|---|---|---|
| †8 C. | Hughes, J. 32228. | W. and M. **April 19/17.** |
| *8 C. | Lambert, L. 20276. | W. and M. **April 19/17.** |
| 8 C. X | Mitchell, E. J. 19502. | W. and M. **Sept. 15/16.** R/Enq. |
| †8 C. | Stevens, W. 22435. | M. **Sept. 15/16.** R/Enq. |
| 8 D. | Abbott, W. J. 22851. | M. **April 19/17.** |
| 8 D. | Church, Edward. 33327. | M. **April 18-19/17.** |
| 8 D. | Shemmings, E. 33309. | M. **April 20/17.** |
| 8 D. XV | Webb, G. 15580. | K. **Sept. 15/16.** Det.D./B. R/Enq. |

## *E.E.F.*

| | | |
|---|---|---|
| 5 D. | Topham, C.-Q.-M.-S. A. 200337. (3778.) | W. and M. **April 19/17.** |
| 5 ? | White, F. 203213. | M., bel. K. **April 19/17.** |

## ROYAL BERKSHIRE REGIMENT.

## *B.E.F.*

| | | |
|---|---|---|
| 1 | **Dowson, Capt. O. J.** | M. **May 3/17.** |
| 1 | **Gibbs, 2nd Lieut. H. A.** | M. **April 29/17.** |
| 1 | **Merrick, Lieut. H. F. R.** | M. **May 3/17.** |
| 1 A. | Ayres, Henry. 26000. | M. **April 29/17.** |
| 1 A. | Bell, T. F. 10084. | M. **April 29/17.** |
| 1 A. IV | Bishop, T. O. 8869. | M. **May 3/17.** |
| 1 A. II | Donovan, Timothy. 17607. | M. **May 3/17.** |
| 1 A. II | Freeth, Cpl. Thos. A. 10177. | M. **May 3/17.** |
| 1 A. L.G.S. | Genler, L.-Cpl. H. 15850. | M. **May 3/17.** |
| 1 A. | Godwin, W. 19250. | M. **May 3/17.** |
| 1 A. II | Hambleton, B. 21585. | M. **April 29/17.** |
| 1 A. L.G.S. | Harris, Chas. 17609. | M. **May 3/17.** |
| 1 A. | Hessey, G. 19383. | M. **May 3/17.** |
| *1 A. L.G.S. | Hicks, F. 26083. | W. and M. **April 29/17.** |
| 1 A. | Hillier, Sgt. Geo. 10461. | W. and M. **April 29/17.** |
| 1 A. | Hiscock, E. C. 33287. | M. **May 3/17.** |
| 1 A. | Jones, L.-Cpl. S. 8557. | M. **May 3/17.** |
| 1 A. | Kemp, J. W. 27039. | W. and M. **April 29/17.** |
| 1 A. | Matthews, E. 25931. | M. **April 29/17.** |
| 1 A. | Pennell, F. 28750. | M. **April 29/17.** |
| 1 A. or D. | Sear, Arthur Henry. 16879. | W. and M. **Mar. 10/17.** |
| 1 A. | Sullivan, Geo. 12181. | M. **May 3/17.** |
| 1 A. | Watkinson, H. 7983. | M. **April 29/17.** |
| 1 A. L.G.S. | Woodham, J. 25578. | M. **Feb. 17/17.** |
| 1 B. | Anness, Tom Leslie. 21526. | M. **April 29/17.** |
| 1 B. L.G.S. | Bagley, W. W. 20177. | M. **May 3/17.** |
| *1 B. | Baldwin, Thos. Staines. 11143. | W. and M. **April 29/17.** |
| 1 B. | Barlow, Cpl. F. J. 9178. | M. **May 3/17.** |
| 1 B. | Brown, P. F. 10454. | M. **May 3/17.** |
| 1 B. V | Carter, V. T. 17774. | M. **April 29/17.** |
| *1 B. or D. | Clark, L.-Cpl. Leonard. 8259. | W. and M. **April 29/17.** |
| 1 B. | Clements, B. 39288. | M. **May 3/17.** |
| 1 B. VIII | Cobb, Victor Percival. 33294. | M. **April 29/17.** |

**Berkshire Regiment, Royal—contd.**

## *B.E.F.*

1 B. Collins, W. 13019. M. April 29/17.
1 B. Farrell, L.-Cpl. Fred. 11940. M. Feb. 5/17.
*1 B. Gomm, Wm. 33024. M. April 29/17.
1 B. or D. XIII Harris, L.-Sergt. Chas. 33039. M. May 3/17.
1 B. or C. Heath, C. 15765. W. and M. May 3/17.
*1 B. VII Kerr, John. 10906. W. and M. April 29/17.
1 B. V Mitchell, Arthur Richard. 28818. M. May 3/17.
1 B. Morton, T. G. 30133. M. May 3/17.
1 B. Oliver. 12121. M. April 29/17.
1 B. VIII Ostridge, E. 30132. M. April 29/17.
1 B. V Read, Walter Jessie. 30434. M. May 3/17.
1 B. Rossi, F. 33289. M. May 3/17.
1 B. Watts, P. E. 39259. M. May 3/17.
1 C. Alcock, Y. 18380. M. May 3/17.
*1 C. X Almeroth, C. W. 11930. M. April 29/17.
1 C. Belsham, George. 18889. M. May 3/17.
1 C. IX Carlton, W. H. 39299. M. April 29/17.
1 C. XI Donnelly, A. 17004. W. and M. May 3/17.
1 C. L.G.S. Dring, L.-Cpl. S. S. 27007. M. April 29/17.
1 C. Fathers, A. 37070. M. April 29/17.
1 C. Fentan, L.-Sergt. R. 10480. M. May 3/17.
1 C. Giles, J. 37570. M. May 3/17.
1 C. XI Gladwell, L.-Cpl. F. 21661. M. April 29/17.
1 C. X Gomm, Cpl. A., 20173. W. and M. April 29/17.
1 C. Haines, G. 25237. M. May 3/17.
1 C. IX Meller, Charles E. 6730. W. and M. July 27/16. R/Enq
1 C. Pilcher, T. 37565. M. May 3/17.
1 C. Sap. S. Powell, L. C. 37582. W. and M. April 29/17.
1 C. IX Purchell, A. J. 10254. M. May 3/17.
1 C. M.G.S. Robertson, L.-Cpl. Herbert. 11842. W. and M. April 29/17.
1 C. Roddes, A. W. 11841. W. and M. Mar. 6/17.
1 C. IX Skinner, S. 19441. M. May 3/17.
1 C. Slade, L.-Cpl. W. 37575. M. May 3/17.
1 C. Watmore, E. 37672. M. May 3/17.
‡1 C. Wells, G. H. 37574. W. and M. April 29/17.
1 C. Winfield, Sgt. A. H. 14855. M. April 29/17.
1 C. XI Wingfield, A. 17631. W. and M. July 27/16. R/Enq.
1 D. Barnett, Wm. E. 17328. ((Fr. H.Q. Sig. S.) M. April 29/17.
1 D. Blackall, Cpl. Alb. Wm. 12835. M. May 3/17.
1 D. L.G.S. Blazeby, Stanley Geo. 17131. M. May 3/17.
1 D. Bushnel, L.-Cpl. 11752. M. May 3/17.
1 D. XIV Collins, Ernest. 33045. M. May 3/17.
1 D. XIII Cox, Percy. 37680. M. April 29/17.
1 D. Crowe, W. 39303. M. May 3/17.
1 D. Hancock, G. 10206. M. May 3/17.
1 D. Hayles, B. 39422. M. May 3/17.
1 D. XVI Hopkins, E. W. 21782. M. May 3/17.
1 D. XIII Huggins, F. 22626. M. May 3/17.
1 D. L.G.S. Jackson, R. 20040. W. and M. April 28/17.
1 D. XV Newell, Fredk. Geo. 33285. M. April 29/17.
1 D. XIV Pallett, L.-Cpl. W. J. 33042. M. April 29/17.
1 D. Palmer, Sgt. E. 8725. M. April 29/17.
1 D. Parkes, H. 37539. M. May 3/17.
1 D. Smith, H. 21315. M. May 3/17.
1 D. Strong, Cpl. J. 11776. M. May 3/17.
1 D. XV Warren, A. E. 33305. M. April 29/17.
1 D. Webb, A. 18179. M. May 3/17.

**Berkshire Regiment, Royal—contd.**

*B.E.F.*

| | | |
|---|---|---|
| 1 D. | Wright, W. 39418. | M. May 3/17. |
| 1 D. | Young, E. 33057. | M. May 3/17. |
| 1 ? | Finlan, Sergt. R. 10480. | M. May 3/17. |
| 2 A. II | Harris, L.-Cpl. S. 23762. | M. March 4/17. |
| 2 B. | Bulkeley, T. J. 11442. | W. and M. Mar. 4/17. |
| 2 B. | Butcher, Albert. 27113. | W. and M. Mar. 4/17. |
| 2 B. VIII | Cox, Tom. 17800. | W. and M. Mar. 4/17. |
| 2 B. VIII | Gutteridge, Wm. 37658. | W. and M. March 4/17. |
| 2 B. | Harrington, L.-Cpl. A. W. 37215. (Fr. 4th.) | M. Mar. 4/17. |
| 2 B. | Lester, J. L. 19819. | M. Mar. 4/17. |
| 2 B. XI | Parsons, H. J. 37295. | M. Mar. 4/17. |
| 2 B. | Piercy, A. 17151. | M. Mar. 4/17. |
| 2 B. VII | Yates, Thomas. 37485. | K. April 4/17. Det.D./B. |
| 2 C. | Brant, E. 8402. | Unoff. M. Dec. 3/16. |
| 2 C. | Day, L. A. 20218. | M. Mar. 5/17. |
| 2 C. | Derrick, H. 37597. | M. Mar. 5/17. |
| 2 C. | Heredge, F. 16656. | W. and M. Mar. 4/17. |
| 2 C. M.G.S. | Maccabee, L.-Cpl. H. 7841. | W. and M. March 4/17. |
| 2 C. | Townley, C. 33344. | W. and M. Mar. 4/17. |
| 2 C. IX | Wallen, James. 22549. | M. Mar. 5/17. |
| 2 D. XIV | Davis, E. S. 37297. | D/W. April 4/17. Det.D./B. |
| 2 D. | Downes, H. A. 27296. | W. and M. April 4/17. |
| 2 D. XVI | Holland, J. H. 37243. | K. Oct. 23-28/16. Det.D./B. |
| 2 D. | Warwick, S. 7247. | W. and M. March 5/17. |
| 2 H.Q. | Gillingham, Roland Cuthbert. 15648. | K. April 4/17. Det.D./B. |
| ‡2 ? | Barnard, Cpl. Hubert Wm. 7511. | K. Mar. 4/17. Det.D./B. |
| 4 D. XV | Belcher, H. 200157. (Late 1801.) | M. April 5/17. |
| *2/4 D. XV | Pusey, F. 202755. | K. June 3/17. Det.D./B. |
| 5 | **Hughes, 2nd Lt. G. MacG. (Fr. 9th.)** | W. and M. Aug. 8/16. R/Enq. |
| ‡5 A. | Edwards, A. 37710. | M. May 1/17. |
| 5 A. IV | Gray, L.-Cpl. Norman Arthur. 9596. | M. April 9/17. |
| *5 A. | Hull, J. 202798. | M. April 29/17. |
| 5 A. | Johnson, Cpl. Chris. J. 10911. | W. and M., bel. K. March 17/17. |
| *5 A. I | Kimber, Tom Hellard. 19418. | M. April 29/17. |
| 5 A. | Pavey, A. 22473. | M. April 9/17. |
| 5 A. | Read, G. 10635. | M. May 1/17. |
| 5 B. | Ashford, Ernest Harry. 223002. (Fr. Ox. & Bucks.) | W. and M. April 9/17. |
| 5 B. | Holt, John Oakley. 202721. | M. April 29/17. |
| ‡5 B. | Palmer, G. 34997. | W. and M. April 28/17. |
| 5 B. L.G.S. | Spear, James. 9570. (Fr. 3rd.) | M. April 9/17. |
| ‡5 C. | Brewer, Henry. 35018. | M. April 28/17. |
| ‡5 C. | Didcock, G. 31107. | M. April 28/17. |
| 5 C. XII | Drury, C. V. 37737. (Late 6 Ox. & Bucks, 27521.) | M. May 5/17. |
| ‡5 C. | Henderson, A. 33675. | M. April 28/17. |
| 5 C. X | Hoddinott, H. H. 24205. | M. April 28/17. |
| 5 C. XII | Holmes, A. 23712. | M. April 28/17. |
| 5 C. | Langsbury, Chas. Alfred Geo. 201433. (Fr. 4th.) | M. April 28/17. |
| *5 C. X | Lewis, Albert Victor. 39348. | M. April 28/17. |
| ‡5 C. | Lind, W. 33679. | M. April 28/17. |
| 5 C. XII | Marshall, Sig. W. H. 33320. | M. March 17/17. |
| 5 C. | Silverthorne, Chas. Arthur. 23630. | M. April 28/17. |
| ‡5 C. | Withers, J. 22434. | M. April 28/17. |
| 5 D. | Askey, Cpl. A. J. 13565. | M. April 26/17. |
| 5 D. | Bowers, Cpl. Francis Fredk. 12050. | W. and M. April 28/17. |
| ‡5 D. | Cutler, S. 34993. | M. April 28/17. |

**Berkshire Regiment, Royal—contd.**

## *B.E.F.*

| | | | |
|---|---|---|---|
| *5 D. | | Emberry, Thomas H. 28798. | M. April 28/17. |
| 5 D. | XVI | Langman, A. W. 35019. | W. and M. April 9/17. |
| 5 D. | | Lawrence, D. 5804. | M. April 27/17. |
| ‡5 D. | | Lefevre, J. 36917. | M. April 27/17. |
| 5 D. | XIII | Pearson, A. J. 37368. | M. April 28/17. |
| 6 A. | | Adams, F. W. 36523. | W. and M. Sept. 29/16. |
| 6 A. | IV | Burnham, T. S. 36530. | W. and M. Feb. 17/17. |
| 6 A. | | Matthews, T. 36593. | W. and M. Sept. 29/16. |
| 6 A. | | Perrin, O. 36607. | W. and M. Sept. 29/16. |
| 6 A. | | Scott, H. A. 24744. | M. Mar. 12/17. |
| 6 A. | | Wilson, G. H. 39400. | W. and M. Sept. 29/16. |
| 6 B. | | Cowell, Walter. 36285. | M. Feb. 17/17. |
| 6 B. | | Grange, L.-Cpl. Jas. Edward. 36905. (Fr. 8 Lincolns, 12105.) | M. Feb. 17/17. |
| ‡6 B. | | Gutteridge, A. 36321. | M. May 9/17. |
| *6 B. | V | Lawrence, J. 7950. | M. May 9/17. |
| 6 B. | | Shaw, A. 12151. | M. May 9/17. |
| ‡6 B. | | Tate, J. 202629. | M. May 9/17. |
| 6 B. | V | Terry, A. E. 33700. | K. Feb. 17/17. Det.D./B. |
| 6 B. | VIII | Webb, T. 33694. | Unoff. W. and M. Feb. 17/17. |
| 6 C. | | Phipps, John. 12266. | W. Unoff. M. Feb. 17/17. |
| 6 C. | | Quelch, Sergt. Ernest. 13202. | W. and M. Feb. 17/17. |
| 6 C. | | Stanley, A. S. 31345. | M. Feb. 17/17. |
| 6 D. | XVI | Abbott, Edgar. 26356. | M. Feb. 17/17. |
| 6 D. | XVI | Edgington, J. 33720. | M. Feb. 17/17. |
| 6 D. | XIII | Pateman, L. M. 36423. | M. Feb. 17/17. |
| 6 D. | | Payne, L.-Cpl. F. E. 23419. | M. Feb. 17/17. |
| 6 D. | | Ridge, Chas. Edward. 33722. | M. Feb. 17/17. |
| 6 D. | | Sims, L.-Cpl. A. H. 36466. | M. Feb. 17/17. |
| 6 D. | L.G.S. | Sinfield, Wm. 11465. | M. Feb. 17/17. |
| 6 D. | | Smith, Alfred. 36478. | M. Feb. 17/17. |
| 6 D. | | Winkworth, Cpl. Herbert. 10876. | M. Feb. 17/17. |
| 6 D. | | Woodger, Lawrence. 19321. | M. Feb. 17/17. |
| 6 ? | | Glover, Geo. Coulson. 36325. | K. Feb. 17/17. Det.D./B. |
| ‡8 A. | III | Beckett, J. H. 21582. | M. Sept. 3/16. R/Enq. |
| 8 A. | | Hosier, H. J. 17980. | M. Sept. 3/16. R/Enq. |
| *8 C. | | Holmes, C. L. 19989. | K. Sept. 3/16. Det.D./B. R/Enq. |
| 8 C. | XII | Morcombe, G. J. 17287. | M. Sept. 3/16. |
| 9 A. | | Packham, G. F. S/28380. | M. May 3/17. |

## *BALKANS.*

| | | | |
|---|---|---|---|
| 7 C. | | **Day, 2nd Lieut. G. H.** | M., bel. K. April 24/17. |
| 7 | | **Gillespie, Major W. R. B.** | M., bel. K. May 8-9/17. |
| 7 | | **Thompson, 2nd Lieut. H. B.** | M. April 24/17. |
| 7 A. | IV | Matteri, L.-Cpl. H. 13397. | W. and M. Oct. 1/16. |
| 7 B. | | Brown, P. G. 23446. | M. May 9/17. |
| *7 B. | VII | Durbin, Edward. 22111. | M. May 9/17. |
| ‡7 B. | | Flood, C.-S.-M. Robert. 27224. | K. May 9/17. Conf. and Det. asked. |
| *7 B. | | Heath, A. T. 15568. | W. and M. May 9/17. |
| 7 B. | V | Tovey, Leslie H. 23415. | M. May 9/17. |
| 7 C. | | Allwright, W. J. 19975. | M. May 9/17. |
| 7 C. | XI | Boundy, H. H. 25581. | M. April 24/17. |
| 7 C. | | Branson, Sergt. Robert. 10276. | M. April 24/17. |
| 7 C. | XI | Clayson, J. W. 26072. | M. April 24/17. |
| ‡7 C. | | Fitzgerald, L.-Cpl. G. L. 10698. | W. and M. April 26/17. |
| 7 C. | XI | Hook, Geo. Walter. 25568. | M. April 24-25/17. |
| *7 C. | X | Kew, W. D. 23478. | M. May 9/17. |
| ‡7 C. | | Marriner, Cpl. Wm. 5585. | W. and M. April 24/17. |

**Berkshire Regiment, Royal—contd.**

## *BALKANS.*

7 C. XI Morris, Wilfred Hry. 23496. M. April 24/17.
7 C. Norris, C. J. 32890. M. April 24/17.
7 C. XII Parker, Henry. 15954. M. April 24/17.
7 C. XI Randell, L.-Cpl. W. N. 23507. M. April 24/17.
7 C. XII Showler, Joseph. 13526. M. May 9/17.
7 C. Woodage, H. G. 19066. M. April 24-25/17.
*7 D. XVI Anthony, D. 14265. W. and M. April 24/17.
‡7 D. M.G.S. Arnold, D. 13713. W. and M. April 26/17.
7 D. XIV Beckingham, George E. 23953. M. April 24/17.
*7 D. XVI Bircher, W. E. 14259. W. and M. April 24/17.
*7 D. Brett, J. 14366. W. and M. April 24/17.
7 D. Davies, Herbert S. 13316. M. May 11/17.
*7 D. Fogg, Sgt. W. J. 11443. W. and M. April 24/17.
7 D. XIII Holmes, Edward Robert. 10361. M. April 24/17.
7 D. XIII Norris, Herbert Jas. Alfred. 23874. M. April 24-25/17.
7 D. Pike, Sergt. Ernest Hy. 13759. M. April 24/17.
*7 D. XIV Seaman, B. 24692. W. and M. April 24/17.
7 D. Somerville, C.-S.-M. E. T. 14495. M. April 24/17.
‡7 ? Booth, A. 36954. M. April 24/17.
7 ? Bradshaw, H. 14778. W. and M. May 9/17.
‡7 ? Church, A. 14405. M. June 20/17.
*7 ? Dursley, Jas. Henry. 25582. M. April 24/17.
7 ? Garnett, Cpl. S. 13344. M. April 24/17.
7 ? Harris, L.-Cpl. A. R. 27412. M. April 24/17.
7 ? Kew, W. 23478. W. and M. May 9/17.
7 ? Mander, W. 23360. M. April 24/17.
7 ? Mitchell, E. T. 23702. M. April 24/17.
7 ? Nicholls, S. 20016. M. Dec. 23/16.
7 ? Reeve, Sergt. H. 8757. M. April 24/17.
‡7 ? Rixon, F. 19413. M. June 20/17.
7 ? Sadler, G. W. 14531. M. April 24/17.
‡7 ? Waring, C. S. 9729. M. April 24/17.
‡7 ? Watson, F. P. A. 25510. M. April 24/17.
7 ? York, E. 14743. M. April 24/17.
7 ? Young, F. A. 17209. M. April 24/17.

**BERKSHIRE YEOMANRY.**

## *E.E.F.*

? Squad. Eldridge, W. 70661. M. April 19/17.

**BLACK WATCH.**

## *B.E.F.*

1 A. Findleton, R. 40153. M. Sept. 22/16.
1 A. McDonald, Hugh. 200164. (1894.) (Fr. 4th.) M. Sept. 3/16. R/Enq.
1 A. IV Middleton, Jas. Johnston. 3185. M. Sept. 3/16. R/Enq.
1 B. VI Talkington, Harry. 5884. M. Sept. 4/16. R./Enq.

**Black Watch—contd.**

## B.E.F.

| | | |
|---|---|---|
| 1 C. | Aitken, Wm. 548. | M. Sept. 25/16. R/Enq. |
| 1 C. X | Ellis, A. E. 11848. | M. Sept. 3/16. R/Enq. |
| 1 C. | Simpson, Andrew. 3086. (Fr. 4th.) | M. Sept. 3/16. R/Enq. |
| 4 A. IV | McLeod, Alex. 2616. | M. Sept. 3/16. R./Enq. |
| 4 B. | Alcorn, L.-Cpl. Wm. J. 2697. | M. Oct. 14/16. R/Enq. |
| *4 B. | Campbell, Jas. 202330. (6438.) (Fr. 6th.) | W. and M. April 23/17. |
| *4 B. VI | Gray, Geo. 4310. | M. Oct. 14/16. R/Enq. |
| ‡4 B. VIII | Philp, John. 4640. | M. Oct. 14/16. R/Enq. |
| *4 C. IX | Downton, Percy. 201370. (4897.) | M. Oct. 25/16. R/Enq. |
| 4 C. | McBain, William. 4482. | W. and M. Sept. 3/16. R./Enq. |
| 4 D. XVI | Croll, W. L. 6347. | M. Nov. 13/16. R/Enq. |
| *4 D. XV | Gordon, John. 202079. (6163.) | M. Nov. 14/16. R/Enq. |
| 5 D. XV | Brand, David. 1482. | W. and M. Oct. 14/16. R/Enq. |
| 5 D. XIII | Couper, Frank H. 3386. | W. and M. Oct. 14/16. R/Enq. |
| 6 A. III | Hindle, Cpl. P. U. 267936. | M. April 23/17. |
| 6 A. | Hulme, C. N. 268399. (6634.) | M. Mar. 31/17. |
| 6 A. or B. | McLaren, John. 265997. | M. April 23/17. |
| 6 A. | Stewart, A. K. 267702. | M. April 23/17. |
| 6 B. | Nicholson, Cpl. H. 266276. | M. April 23/17. |
| ‡6 B. VIII | Shearer, Adam. 268262. | M. April 23/17. |
| 6 B. VII | Thomson, Robt. 268388. | W. and M. April 23/17. |
| 6 C. | Black, J. 265785. | M. Mar. 31/17. |
| 6 C. | McBride, T. 266829. | M. Mar. 31/17. |
| 6 C. | Macdonald, L.-Cpl. Tom. 265142. | M. April 23/17. |
| 6 C. | McPherson, Duncan. 266653. | M. April 23/17. |
| 6 D. XVI | Scott, Ralph. 266919. | W. and M. April 23/17. |
| ‡6 D. | Stewart, Duncan. 266102. | M. April 23/17. |
| 7 A. II | Doig, Wm. 6268. | M. April 23-25/17. |
| 7 A. | O'Shea, Robert. 292683. | M. April 23/17. |
| 7 B. VIII | Douglas, Geo. 291924. | M. April 23-25/17. |
| ‡7 C. | Bell, W. 292733. | W. and M. April 23/17. |
| 7 C. IX | Ferguson, James H. R. 292482. | M. April 23/17. |
| 7 C. IX | Hollebon, Wm. John. 292468. | M. April 23/17. |
| 7 C. XII | Laurie, Sig. Wm. 290311. | M. April 23/17. |
| 7 C. | McDonald, Jas. 292538. (6382.) | M. April 23/17. |
| 7 C. XII | Parkin, Charles. 292547. | M. April 23-25/17. |
| 7 C. | Watson, P. 293172. | M. April 23-25/17. |
| 8 | **Bell, 2nd Lieut. W.** (Fr. 5th.) | M. May 3/17. |
| 8 | **Fraser, 2nd Lieut. P. G.** (Fr. 3rd Gordons.) | W. and M. May 3/17. |
| 8 | **Harrison, 2nd Lieut. D. R.** | W. and M. May 3/17. |
| 8 | **Taylor, Capt. N. R.** (Fr. 5th.) | W. and M. May 3/17. |
| 8 A. | Baxter, A. 2957. | M. May 3/17. |
| 8 A. | Bowman, Cpl. A. 7698. | M. May 3/17. |
| 8 A. | Brash, J. 268709. | M. May 3/17. |
| ‡8 A. | Gillies, H. 40559. | W. and M. May 3/17. |
| 8 A. | Lawson, Patrick D. 268713. | M. May 3/17. |
| 8 A. | Lunn, G. 19925. | M. May 3/17. |
| 8 A. IV | Malpas, H. S/40567. | M. May 3/17. |
| 8 A. II | Okell, J. E. S/12133. | W. and M. Oct. 19/16. R/Enq. |
| 8 A. | Robertson, J. 16317. | M. May 3/17. |
| 8 A. | Ross, A. 40588. | M. May 3/17. |
| 8 A. II | Starr, Alfred. 10243. | W. and M. May 3/17. |
| 8 B. V | Constable, Albert. S/12987. | M. May 3/17. |
| ‡8 B. | Cooke, H. M. 8762. | M. May 3/17. |
| 8 B. VI | Dowie, Robt. 13696. | M. May 3/17. |
| 8 B. | Fisher, C. 19910. | M. May 3/17. |
| *8 B. VI | Grieve, Jas. 3/13338. | W. and M. April 9/17. |

**Black Watch—contd.**

## *B.E.F.*

| | | | |
|---|---|---|---|
| 8 B. VI | Hastie, Alexr. 4435. | M. May 3/17. |
| 8 B. | Moulter, E. 19930. | M. May 3/17. |
| 8 B. | Plumley, G. 19934. | M. May 3/17. |
| 8 B. | Reid, W. 3477. | M. May 3/17. |
| 8 C. X | Dalrymple, Jas. 16202. | M. May 3/17. |
| 8 C. IX | Felgate, W. 16899. | M. May 3/17. |
| 8 C. | McLeod, Joseph. 475. | M. May 3/17. |
| 8 C. | Rennie, Cpl. W. 9244. | M. May 3/17. |
| ‡8 C. | Robertson, R. 9315. | W. and M. May 3/17. |
| 8 C. | Rogers, John Thos. 19936. | M. May 3/17. |
| 8 C. | Smith, J. 19974. | M. May 3/17. |
| 8 C. | Threlfell, A. 9897. | M. May 3/17. |
| 8 C. | Tompkins, L. 17615. | M. May 3/17. |
| 8 C. | Walker, A. 16605. | M. May 3/17. |
| 8 C. | Wilson, T. 43319. | M. May 3/17. |
| 8 C. X | Woolnough, L.-Cpl. F. J. 17536. | M. May 3/17. |
| *8 D. | Bruce, Thos. Walter. 43194 | W. and M. May 3/17. |
| 8 D. | Collins, Sergt. George. 678. | M. May 3/17. |
| *8 D. XIII | Diamond, Patrick. 18025. | W. Unoff. M. May 3/17. |
| 8 D. XV | Ferguson, L.-Cpl. J. 10399. | M. May 3/17. |
| 8 D. | Hamilton, Cpl. A. 9286. | M. May 3/17. |
| 8 D. | Hannah, J. 3/4283. | M. May 3/17. |
| 8 D. XVI | Hodge, John. 19917. | M. May 3/17. |
| 8 D. | Kinnear, W. 11893. | M. May 3/17. |
| 8 D. | Langlands, A. 40516. | M. May 3/17. |
| 8 D. XIII | Littlejohn, Sergt. D. 3445. | M. May 3/17. |
| 8 D. | McDonald, R. 16612. | M. May 3/17. |
| 8 D. | Smart, A.-Sergt. A. 43010. | M. May 3/17. |
| 8 D. XVI | Smith, S. P. 19941. | M. May 3/17. |
| *8 D. XVI | Vass, T. 40757. | M. May 3/17. |
| 9 | **Burton, 2nd Lt. J. L.** (Fr. 1 H.L.I.) | M. April 27/17. |
| 9 A. III | Gayton, W. L. S/11169. | W. and M. April 23/17. |
| 9 A. II | McAinsh, James. 40230. | M. April 24/17. |
| 9 B. | Ferguson, John. 11271. | M. Sept. 8/16. |
| 9 B. VIII | Smedley, John. S/12228. | W. and M. April 7/17. |
| 9 C. IX | Barnett, Sigr. Mark. 291850. (Fr. 7.) | M. April 26/17. |
| ‡9 C. | Clunie, A. 18570. | M. April 26/17. |
| 9 C. | Cormack, George. 202758. | M. April 26/17. |
| 9 C. XI | Duncan, Andrew. 5/18558. | M. April 26/17. |
| 9 C. XI | Lister, Andrew. 14606. | M. April 26/17. |
| ‡9 C. | Martin, J. 16782. | M. April 26/17. |
| ‡9 C. | Maxwell, J. 9226. | W. and M. April 26/17. |
| 9 C. | Nellies, H. 15795. | M. April 9/17. |
| 9 C. | Potter, Cpl. Alex. S/9400. | M. April 9/17. |
| 9 D. XIII | Pert, Williams. 240496. | M. April 23/17. |
| ‡9 D. | Russell, C. 7756. | M. April 26/17. |

## *BALKANS.*

| | | |
|---|---|---|
| 10 A. | **Alexander, Lieut. T. L.** | M. May 8-9/17. |
| 10 B. | **Don, Lieut. R. N.** | M. May 8-9/17. |
| 10 B. | **Hebden, 2nd Lt. Alan.** (Fr. 6th.) | M. May 8-9/17. |
| 10 A. | **Nicol, Capt. Chas. A.** | M. May 8-9/17. |
| 10 A. II | Cuff, L.-Cpl. W. Y. 4238. | M. May 8-9/17. |
| 10 A. II | Grant, John. 17896. | M. May 8-9/17. |
| 10 A. | Gunn, L.-Cpl. Robert. 6104. | M. May 8-9/17. |
| 10 A. | Henshilwood, C.-S.-M. Thos. L. 5619 | M. May 8-9/17. |
| 10 A. | King, Juden. 6036. | M. May 8-9/17. |

Black Watch—contd.

## BALKANS.

10 A. II Macnab, L.-Cpl. David. 13380. M. May 8-9/17.
10 A. Nelson, W. 5598. M. May 8-9/17.
10 A. IV Spence, J. F. 17924. M. May 8-9/17.
‡10 B. Cooper, A. S/17438. W. and M. May 8-9/17
10 B. Hind, Joseph. 17460. M. May 8-9/17.
10 B. Miller, R. 17187. M. May 8-9/17.
10 B. Skinner, Wm. 5259. M. May 8-9/17
10 B. Wightman, T. 14098. M. May 8-9/17.
10 C. XII Bremner, L.-Cpl. Donald. 5960. M. May 8-9/17.
10 C. McGregor, Cpl. J. 7350. M. May 8-9/17.
10 C. XI Sloan, E. 14541. M. May 8-9/17.
10 D. Ferguson, David. S/16327. M. May 8-9/17.
10 ? Anderson, Act.-Q.-M.-S. J. 5422. M. May 8-9/17.
10 ? Brunton, G. 4967. M. May 8-9/17.
10 ? Culshaw, J. 6058. M. May 8-9/17.
10 ? Dewar, A. 4973. M. May 8-9/17.
10 ? Duthie, A. 14542. M. May 8-9/17.
10 ? Edwards, P. 2579. M. May 8-9/17.
10 ? Fraser, R. 14185. M. April 24-25/17.
10 ? Garth, D. 4985. M. May 8-9/17.
10 ? Howard, W. 12776. M. May 8-9/17.
10 ? Johnston, J. 15099. M. May 8-9/17.
10 ? Kennedy, D. 13417. M. May 8-9/17.
10 ? Laing, A. 7988. M. May 8-9/17.
‡10 ? McCabe, B. 10968. M. No date.
10 ? McGill, R. 5439. M. May 8-9/17.
10 ? McGregor, J. 12868. M. May 8-9/17.
10 ? McIntyre, H. 17909. M. May 8-9/17.
10 ? McKenzie, A. 5082. M. May 8-9/17.
10 ? McKenzie, A. 5521. M. May 8-9/17.
10 ? Millar, Sgt. W. 3863. M. May 8-9/17.
10 ? Murphy, R. 6894. M. May 8-9/17.
10 ? Paterson, W. 15908. M. May 8-9/17.
10 ? Patterson, R. 16086. M. May 8-9/17.
10 ? Rennie, E. 17994. M. May 8-9/17.
10 ? Robertson, D. 5575. M. May 8-9/17.
10 ? Simpson, A. 9232. M. May 8-9/17
10 ? Stein, D. 11419. M. May 8-9/17.
10 ? Stevenson, Sgt. W. 5554. M. May 8-9/17.
10 ? Stewart, C. 5574. M. May 8-9/17.
10 ? Stewart, D. 6112. W. and M. April 24-25/17.
10 ? Stewart, R. 17981. M. May 8-9/17.
10 ? Strachan, W. 557. M. May 8-9/17.
10 ? Turner, T. 17332. M. May 8-9/17.
10 ? Turner, W. 5608. M. May 8-9/17.
10 ? Walker, A. 5610. M. May 8-9/17.
10 ? Wright, W. 5547. M. May 8-9/17.
10 ? Younger, J. 13342. M. May 8-9/17.
*13 ? Stephenson, W. 316534. M. May 8-9/17.

## E.E.F.

‡? ? Williams, Alfred. 18697. (Fr. 3rd.) M., bel. drowned April 15/17, "Arcadian"

## PERSIAN GULF.

2 1 Barbour, Wm. Pattison. S/10576. M. April 22/16. R/Enq.
2 1 IV Haig, L.-Cpl. Wm. G. 10496. W. and M. Jan. 7/16. R./Enq.

**Black Watch—contd.**

## *PERSIAN GULF.*

*2 1 L.G.S. Hutcheson, L.-Cpl. John. S/11307. W. and M. Mar. 14/17.
2 1 III Jennings, R. S/15888. W. Unoff. M. Mar. 14/17.
*2 2 Gillillan, T. S/17494. M. April 24/17.
*2 2 Gregory, R. 13995. W. and M. Mar. 14/17.
2 2 Morrison, Stewart. 8166. M. April 22/16. R/Enq.
2 3 Kerwin, J. 1891. M. Jan. 13/16.
2 3 IX Mackay, Wm. S/15866. K. Mar. 14/17. Det.D./B.
‡2 3 Urquhart, David. S/7399. D/W. April 20/16. Det.D./B.
2 4 Burnett, W. A. S/11835. M. April 21/17.
*2 4 Campbell, John. 3569. M. April 21/17.
2 4 XIV Graham, Archie. 10477. K. before April 21/17. Conf. and Det.D./B.
‡2 4 XIV McDonald, Wallace. 3551. W. and M. Mar. 14/17.
*2 ? Batchelor, C. 13905. M. April 21/17.
2 ? Carlyle, E. 15657. M. Mar. 14/17.
*2 ? Cook, J. 15613. W. and M. Mar. 14/17.
‡2 ? Harris, A. 10222. W. and M. Mar. 14/17.
‡2 ? Hewitt, John Gordon. S/11776. W. and M. Mar. 14/17.
2 ? Irving, R. 10029 M. Jan. 28/16.
2 ? Robertson, Norman. 659. M. Jan. 21/16.
2 ? Smith, Andrew. 11557. M. April 22/16. R/Enq.
‡2 ? Watt, J. 15080. W. and M. Mar. 14/17.

### BORDER REGIMENT.

## *B.E.F.*

*1 Armstrong, 2nd Lieut. L. W. M., bel. K. May 19/17.
1 Jackson, 2nd Lieut. L. M. July 1/16. R/Enq.
1 Layard, 2nd Lieut. F. S. W. and M. May 19/17.
1 New, Lieut. P. M. May 19/17.
1 Pooley, 2nd Lt. R. (Fr. 8 Scot Fus.) K. April 23/17. Det.D./B.
‡1 A. Bewley, J. 32293. M. May 19/17.
‡1 A. I Bond, J. T. 25542. M. May 19/17.
‡1 A. IV Bottomley, S. 33859. M. May 19/17.
‡1 A. III Calvert, H. B. 202112. M. May 19/17.
1 A. Collins, C. 23030. M. Jan. 27/17.
‡1 A. Coyne, Sergt. T. 18189. M. May 19/17.
1 A. or D. Drake, Richard Henry. 16930. M. Jan. 27/17.
‡1 A. Harvey, F. 33729. M. May 19/17.
‡1 A. Hogarth, R. 23734. M. May 19/17.
‡1 A. Karaselchik, M. 33891. M. May 19/17.
‡1 A. Kinge, A. 33740. M. May 19/17.
1 A. Johnston, R. 24212. M. Unoff. W. Jan. 27/17.
1 A. Kew, Arthur. 33637. (Late R.F.A., 178352.) M. Jan. 27/17.
1 A. M.G.S. Lincoln, W. 22854. W. and M. Jan. 27/17.
1 A. I.T.M. Morley, L.-Cpl. Wm. 23646. (87 Bgde.) M. April 23/17.
*1 A. I Nugent, J. 241335. (3587.) W. and M. Unoff. K. May 19/17.
‡1 A. Sunderland, F. 26376. M. May 19/17.
‡1 A. Taylor, T. D. 20498. M. May 19/17.
1 A. IV Tucker, Fredk. John. 33707. M. Jan. 27/17.
1 A. I Walker, F. C. 33799. M. Jan. 28/17.

**Border Regiment—contd.**

## *B.E.F.*

| | | |
|---|---|---|
| 1 A. II | Wallin, H. Laurence. 33800. | M. **May 19/17.** |
| ‡1 B. | Arrowsmith, J. 202391. | M. **May 19/17.** |
| ‡1 B. | Atkinson, W. 240919. | M. **May 19/17.** |
| 1 B. V | Claridge, G. E. 32507. | Unoff. W. and M. **April 16/17.** |
| 1 B. VI | Crumpton, L.-Cpl. G. 241997. | M. **May 19/17.** |
| 1 B. VI | Dando, C. E. 33619. | W. and M. **Feb. 3/17.** |
| *1 B. | Elliff, Ernest F. 23024. | M. **May 19/17.** |
| *1 B. | Gibbs, L.-Cpl. C. 22838. | M. **May 19/17.** |
| 1 B. V | Greenhalgh, Cpl. Fred. 19055. | M. **May 19/17.** |
| ‡1 B. | Hamer, E. 202294. | M. **May 19/17.** |
| 1 B. | King, John Rich. 22954. | M. **Jan. 27/17.** |
| ‡1 B. | Little, T. 25669. | M. **May 19/17.** |
| *1 B. VIII | Linney, L.-Cpl. Thos. Henry. 13313. | M. **May 19/17.** |
| ‡1 B. | McCluskey, J. 241481. | M. **May 19/17.** |
| 1 B. VII | Manley, J. T. 33643. | W. and M. **Feb. 3/17.** |
| *1 B. VI | Murgatroyd, Richard. 26345. | M. **May 19/17.** |
| ‡1 B. | Pickering, F. 241870. | M. **May 19/17.** |
| ‡1 B. | Ritson, Cpl. J. 201482. | M. **May 19/17.** |
| 1 B. V | Walton, Thos. 24652. | M. **May 19/17.** |
| 1 C. XI | Andrews, W. 33443. | M. **April 23/17.** |
| 1 C. | Clayton, Horace Arthur. 33705. | M. **Jan. 27/17.** |
| *1 C. XI | Christmas, Walter H. 33703. | M. **May 19/17.** |
| *1 C. IX | Crilley, L.-Cpl. Peter. 17552. | M. **May 19/17.** |
| 1 C. X | Davis, Percy Wm. 33714. | M. **Jan. 27/17.** |
| 1 C. | Dewhurst, R. 21714. | M. **April 23/17.** |
| 1 C. | Earnshaw, J. H. 33865. | M. **April 23/17.** |
| 1 C. | Graham, John. 24887. | M. **May 19/17.** |
| ‡1 C. IX | Gregory, H. 33727. | M. **May 19/17.** |
| ‡1 C. | Lowery, J. 16618. | M. **May 19/17.** |
| 1 C. | Sheard, C. 33877. | M. **April 23/17.** |
| *1 C. or D. | Smith, L.-Cpl. Ernest. 25580. | M. **May 19/17.** |
| 1 C. XI | Turner, L.-Cpl. W. W. 21300. | M. **April 23/17.** |
| ‡1 D. | Alderson, J. 25783. | M. **May 19/17.** |
| ‡1 D. | Applin, L.-Cpl. W. 9813. | M. **May 19/17.** |
| 1 D. XVI | Atkinson, Harry H. 26455. | M. **Jan. 27/17.** |
| 1 D. XIV | Bowness, T. D. 23484. | M. **April 23/17.** |
| 1 D. XIII | Carter, Edward Henry. 33012. | M. **Jan. 27/17.** |
| 1 D. XVI | Clarke, Arthur. 33614. | M. **Feb. 3/17.** |
| ‡1 D. | Gibson, J. 23075. | M. **May 19/17.** |
| 1 D. | Gill, Bomber Thos. 20844. | W. and M. **Jan. 27/17.** |
| 1 D. XV | Grainger, R. W. 26094. | M. **May 19/17.** |
| ‡1 D. | Haney, H. 32497. | M. **May 19/17.** |
| ‡1 D. | Johnston, J. 14012. | M. **April 28/17.** |
| ‡1 D. | Latham, W. 17696. | M. **May 19/17.** |
| 1 D. XIV | McConnell, L.-Cpl. J. 20733. | M. **April 23/17.** |
| 1 D. XVI | Molyneux, L.-Cpl. Thos. 11820. | M. **April 23/17.** |
| 1 D. XV | Morris, Francis. 33649. | M. **Feb. 3/17.** |
| ‡1 D. | Nutter, T. 202164. | M. **May 19/17.** |
| 1 D. XIV | Oxbrow, E. J. 33810. | M. **Jan. 27/17.** |
| *1 D. XIII | Rouson, C. 30042. | M. **May 19/17.** |
| ‡1 D. | Skurr, R. 211000. | M. **May 19/17.** |
| 1 D. XIV | Taylor, John Henry. 33793. | M. **Jan. 27/17.** |
| 1 D. | Woof, J. 21833. | M. **April 23/17.** |
| ‡1 ? | Smith, J. 26506. | M. **May 19/17.** |
| 1 ? | Whichelo, Sniper Fredk. John. 22508. | M. **May 19/17.** |
| 2 A. | Tillotson, H. 30047. | M. **Mar. 30/17.** |
| 2 B. | Doran, L.-Cpl. William. 4316. | M. **Mar. 30/17.** |

**Border Regiment—contd.**

## *B.E.F.*

| | | |
|---|---|---|
| 2 C. XII | Partington, Wm. 18992. | M. Feb. 27/17. |
| 2 ? | Potter, Fredk. 32544. | K. May 10/17. Det.D./B. |
| ‡5 A. | Davis, W. 240952. | W. and M. April 23/17. |
| 5 A. | Graham, William. 240840. | M. April 23/17. |
| 5 B. | Beaty, Isaac Albert. 241485. | M. April 23/17. |
| 5 C. | Wilkin, Herbert. 241946. | W. and M. April 23/17. |
| ‡5 D. | Arnold, L. H. J. 241974. | W. and M. April 23/17. |
| 5 D. XVI | Fox, Charles. 242112. (4570.) | W. and M. April 24/17. |
| 5 D. | Graham, Cpl. Thos. 240019. | W. and M. April 23/17. |
| 5 D. XVI | Payne, Ernest Wm. 241983. (5542.) | M. April 23/17. |
| *5 D. | Wilkinson, D. 242067. (3524.) | W. and M. April 23/17. |
| 7 | **Audrew, 2nd Lieut. F.** | M., bel. K. April 23/17. |
| 7 | **Birch, Capt. L.** | M., bel. K. April 23/17. |
| 7 | **Brett, 2nd Lieut. E. E.** | M., bel. K. April 23/17. |
| 7 | **Campbell, 2nd Lieut. W. C.** | M. April 23/17. |
| 7 | **Clarke, 2nd Lieut. E. G.** | M., bel. K. April 23/17. |
| 7 | **Heath, 2nd Lieut. S. S.** | M. April 23/17. |
| 7 | **Kennedy, 2nd Lieut. J.** (Fr. 3 Scot. Rifles.) | M., bel. K. April 24/17. |
| 7 | **Nasmith, D.S.O., Capt. A. P.** | M., bel. K. April 23/17. |
| 7 | **Turner, 2nd Lieut. C.** (Fr. 4th.) | M. April 23/17. |
| 7 | **Welsh, Capt. R. M. B.** | M., bel. K. April 23/17. |
| 7 A. | Atkinson, J. J. 5465. | M. April 23/17. |
| 7 A. IV | Basson, L.-Cpl. John. 16522. | M. April 23/17. |
| 7 A. | Bellis, J. 19826. | M. April 23/17. |
| 7 A. III | Bennett, Harry. 14814. | M. April 23/17. |
| 7 A. | Bird, C. F. 23727. | M. April 23/17. |
| 7 A. I | Bradberry, T. 25229. | M. April 23/17. |
| 7 A. M.G.S. | Casson, James. 12764. | M. April 23/17. |
| 7 A. | Clelland, Arthur. 23850. | M. April 23/17. |
| 7 A. III | Constantine, L.-Cpl. Wm. Vernon. 27511. | M. April 23/17. |
| 7 A. IV | Cork, Jas. Auckland. 28338. (Late E. Surrey.) | M. April 23/17. |
| 7 A. | Cox, H. 28357. | M. April 23/17. |
| 7 A. | Cunningham, A. 20369. | M. April 23/17. |
| 7 A. II | Dunleary, John. 12067. | M. April 23/17. |
| 7 A. IV | Elliott, Oswald W. 20013. | M. April 23/17. |
| 7 A. | English, A.-Sergt. L. 14601. | M. April 23/17. |
| 7 A. | Evans, F. 28337. | M. April 23/17. |
| 7 A. | Faulder, John. 27928. | M. April 23/17. |
| 7 A. | Gamman, T. 28334. | M. April 23/17. |
| 7 A. or C. | Goodwin, Harold. 32350. | M. April 23/17. |
| 7 A. III | Hardman, Richard. 21442. | M. April 23/17. |
| 7 A. | Hogg, Sergt. J. 12639. | M. April 23/17. |
| 7 A. | Holmes, J. 18461. | M. April 23/17. |
| 7 A. IV | Howarth, Fred. 6968. | M. April 23/17. |
| 7 A. | Irving, G. 12797. | M. April 23/17. |
| 7 A. | Lippman, Simon. 9321. | M. April 23/17. |
| 7 A. | Lowman, L.-Cpl. J. N. 19564. | M. April 23/17. |
| 7 A. III | Marsh, Wilfred. 28100. | M. April 23/17. |
| 7 A. I | Nattrass, Thos. Wm. 25820. | M. April 23/17. |
| 7 A. III | Nethersell, John. 28340. | M. April 23/17. |
| 7 A. II | Rickers, George Henry. 25040. | M. April 23/17. |
| 7 A. | Rigg, D. T. 23414. | M. April 23/17. |
| 7 A. II | Robinson, Thos. 28106. | M. April 23/17. |
| 7 A. | Simmonds, L.-Cpl. H. 17753. | M. April 23/17. |
| 7 A. IV | Smith, Tom. 25041. | M. April 23/17. |
| 7 A. | Thompson, C. W. 20947. | M. April 23/17. |

**Border Regiment**—contd.

## *B.E.F.*

7 A. Towers, T. 27450. **M. April 23/17.**
7 A. Turner, F. 28356. **M. April 23/17.**
7 A. III Ward, T. G. 21405. **M. April 23/17.**
7 A. Watson, Frank. 19963. **M. April 23/17.**
7 A. or B. VIII Watson, Frank. 14631. **M. April 23/17.**
7 A. Wilson, R. 27452. **M. April 23/17.**
7 A. I Wright, Maurice. 25839. **M. April 23/17.**
7 B. Agnew, S. 23771. **M. April 23/17.**
7 B. Ainscough, L.-Cpl. Richard. 19998. **M. April 23/17.**
7 B. Auburn, L.-Cpl. E. 27478. **M. April 23/17.**
7 B. Bell, R. 14583. **M. April 23/17.**
7 B. VIII Bell, Robert James. 32015. **M. April 23/17.**
7 B. VIII Boxall, W. H. 28367. **M. April 23/17.**
7 B. Bradley, R. 18462. **M. April 23/17.**
7 B. X Bramwell, John. 18397. **M. April 23/17.**
7 B. V Browne, Bernard M. 32314. **M. April 23/17.**
7 B. Burgess, W. 25032. **M. April 23/17.**
7 B. VI Coles, Harry. 23553. **M. April 23/17.**
7 B. VII Davenport, Wm. Henry. 26468. **M. April 23/17.**
7 B. Egan, F. W. 28359. **M. April 23/17.**
7 B. Evans, D. W. 28368. **M. April 23/17.**
7 B. VII Everett, Walter Hubert. 27540. **M. April 23/17.**
7 B. Galling, Sergt. Daniel. 18357. **M. April 23/17.**
7 B. Gibbs, Robert. 28122. **M. April 23/17.**
7 B. Henninger, A. 22829. **M. April 23/17.**
7 B. or H.Q. Hewitt, Wm. Alfred. 16199. (Snip. Sec.) **M. April 23/17.**
7 B. Heywood, S. 18420. **M. April 23/17.**
7 B. Hogan, J. 26340. **M. April 23/17.**
7 B. Huggins, Cpl. E. A. 23055. **M. April 23/17.**
7 B. Leach, G. J. 23200. **M. April 23/17.**
7 B. VIII Loomes, Wm. 27599. **M. April 23/17.**
7 B. VI Mays, G. C. 23139. **M. April 23/17.**
7 B. Miller, J. 20867. **M. April 23/17.**
7 B. VI Mobbs, Ennett James. 23096. **M. April 23/17.**
7 B. Murray, P. 24841. **M. April 23/17.**
7 B. Phillips, Edw. 33763. **M. April 23/17.**
7 B. Price, J. 18370. **M. April 23/17.**
7 B. Roberts, W. 25375. **M. April 23/17.**
7 B. Rowntree, C. 10137. **M. April 23/17.**
7 B. Sanderson, S/B. J. W. 24842 M. Unoff. K. **April 23/17.**
7 B. Scott, Albert. 20102. **M. April 23/17.**
7 B. VIII Shannon, Ben. 22259. **M. April 23/17.**
7 B. Smith, J. 26083. **M. April 23/17.**
7 B. Stanton, J. W. 23746. **M. April 23/17.**
7 B. Tandy, W. J. 23498. **M. April 23/17.**
*7 B. VI Tempkin, Arthur. 28363. (Fr. E. Surrey.) **M. April 23/17.**
7 B. Tomkins, A. 28363. **M. April 23/17.**
7 B. VII Wheelan, E. 26608. **M. April 23/17.**
7 B. Wimhurst, Chas. 10632. (Fr. H.Q.) **M. April 23/17.**
7 C. Allonby, Sig. Robt. Stan. 23802. (Fr. H.Q.) **M. April 23/17.**
7 C. Bartlett, H. J. 27489. (Fr. H.Q.) **M. April 23/17.**
7 C. XII Bragg, A. W. 27494. **M. April 23/17.**
7 C. IX Bridgewater, L.-Cpl. Frank. 12608. **M. April 23/17.**
7 C. Button, H. J. 27492. **M. April 23/17.**
7 C. XII Carloss, E. L. 28329. **M. April 23/17.**
7 C. XII Cottam, Joseph. 28394. **M. April 23/17.**

**Border Regiment—contd.**

## *B.E.F.*

| | | | |
|---|---|---|---|
| 7 C. | | Coultrup, S. H. 28325. | M. April 23/17. |
| 7 C. | | Craven, W. 21445. | M. April 23/17. |
| 7 C. | | Dawson, E. W. 27536. | M. April 23/17. |
| 7 C. | | Delty, A.-Sergt. W. 14927. | M. April 23/17. |
| 7 C. | X | Finn, Charles. 20125. | M. April 23/17. |
| 7 C. | | Fitzpatrick, J. 11781. | M. April 23/17. |
| 7 C. | | Geoghegan, M. 16992. | M. April 23/17. |
| 7 C. | IX | Garwood, Alfred Joseph. 25725. | M. April 23/17. |
| 7 C. | X | Griffiths, Cpl. J. 22030. | M. April 23/17. |
| 7 C. | | Hinde, H. 23520. | M. April 23/17. |
| 7 C. | | Hindmoor, F. 23507. | M. April 23/17. |
| 7 C. | IX | Hodgson, Robert. 28391. | M. April 23/17. |
| 7 C. | | Hopplestone, R. 28398. | M. April 23/17. |
| 7 C. | XII | Howarth, Thos. 20246. | M. April 23/17. |
| 7 C. | X | Hulme, Wm. T. 28093. | M. April 23/17. |
| 7 C. | | Jobson, A. T. 27590. | M. April 23/17. |
| 7 C. | X | Jones, Thos. 28403. (Late N. Lancs., 32612.) | M. April 23/17. |
| 7 C. | | McDonald, John. 14840. (Known as Shoemaker.) | M. April 23/17. |
| 7 C. | | Moore, Dickinson. 22391. | M. April 23/17. |
| 7 C. | | Moseley, Michael Samuel Cecil. 27605 | M. April 23/17. |
| 7 C. | XII | Mullen, Thomas. 28099. | M. April 23/17. |
| 7 C. | | Nixon, F. 28331. | M. April 23/17. |
| 7 C. | XII | Oliphant, James. 33483. | M. April 23/17. |
| 7 C. | | Pressey, L. H. 28321. | M. April 23/17. |
| 7 C. | | Ralston, A. 4233. | M. April 23/17. |
| 7 C. | XI | Robinson, Albert. 28399. | M. April 23/17. |
| 7 C. | | Saville, A. E/28333. | M. April 23/17. |
| 7 C. | | Shore, E. W. 28111. | M. April 23/17. |
| 7 C. | | Smiles, A.-C.-S.-M. T. H. 12659. | M. April 23/17. |
| 7 C. | | Spilsbury, J. 20836. | M. April 23/17. |
| 7 C. | | Stagg, Chas. Arthur. 33785. | M. April 23/17. |
| 7 C. | M.G.S. | Thistlethwaite, L.-Cpl. Frank. 12430. | M. April 23/17. |
| 7 C. | X | Thompson, Alfred. 21638. | M. April 23/17. |
| 7 C. | XII | Whalley, Thos. 11798. | M. April 23/17. |
| 7 D. | M.G.S. | Barnes, G. 27497. | M. April 23/17. |
| 7 D. | XV | Blamire, Sergt. G. N. 4542. | M. April 23/17. |
| 7 D. | | Bostock, L.-Cpl. W. L. 13086. | M. April 23/17. |
| 7 D. | | Boustead, L. 23505. | M. April 23/17. |
| 7 D. | | Boustead, T. 23504. | M. April 23/17. |
| 7 D. | | Burr, W. 27496. | M. April 23/17. |
| 7 D. | | Catterall, A.-Cpl. W. 14387. | M. April 23/17. |
| 7 D. | | Clarke, F. 27525. | M. April 23/17. |
| 7 D. | | Collyer, T. 28414. | M. April 23/17. |
| 7 D. | | Curry, J. 6507. | M. April 23/17. |
| 7 D. | | Deakin, J. G. 22745. | M. April 23/17. |
| 7 D. | XIII | Dean, J. 22322. | M. April 23/17. |
| 7 D. | | Dixon, Frank. 28415. (Fr. 3 L.N. Lancs., 32662.) | M. April 23/17. |
| 7 D. | Sig. S. | Elliott, Robt. 23697. | M. April 23/17. |
| 7 D. | | English, A.-Sgt. A. 14599. | M. April 23/17. |
| 7 D. | | Gray, G. A. 13174. | M. April 23/17. |
| 7 D. | | Hampson, C. 28419. | M. April 23/17. |
| 7 D. | XV | Hayes, Albert. 28420. | M. April 23/17. |
| 7 D. | XIII | Heap, Basil Whitehead. 28421. | M. April 28/17. |
| 7 D. | | Irving, L.-Cpl. D. 16222. | M. April 23/17. |
| 7 D. | XV | Ithell, John. 28423. (Late L.N.L.) | M. April 23/17. |

**Border Regiment—contd.**

## *B.E.F.*

| | | |
|---|---|---|
| 7 D. | Lomas, Leonard Beaman. 28428. | M. April 23/17. |
| 7 D. XIII | Lovegrove, W. 27594. | K. April 25/17. Det.D./B. |
| 7 D. | Makepeace, J. 28430. | M. April 23/17. |
| 7 D. XIV | Matthews, Edward James. 28352. | M. April 23/17. |
| 7 D. XIV | Middleton, A. H. 28429. | M. April 23/17. |
| 7 D. | Morgan, B. 20926. | M. April 23/17. |
| 7 D. M.G.S. | Mould, Robert. 16554. | M. April 23/17. |
| 7 D. | Padgham, J. 27629. | M. April 23/17. |
| 7 D. | Phanp, W. 28435. | M. April 23/17. |
| 7 D. | Ramsay, W. 27637. | M. April 23/17. |
| 7 D. XVI | Richards, T. M. 18471. | M. April 23/17. |
| 7 D. XV | Riches, Tom. 28347. | M. April 23/17. |
| 7 D. XV | Riley, Helliwell. 28107. | M. April 23/17. |
| 7 D. XIV | Sharwin, Harold. 28437. | M. April 23/17. |
| 7 D. | Swindle, P. 28109. | M. April 23/17. |
| 7 D. | Welsh, H. 19834. | M. April 23/17. |
| 7 D. | Wilkin, A.-Sgt. W. 19937. | M. April 23/17. |
| 7 D. | Williams, Cpl. J. 33252. | M. April 23/17. |
| 7 D. | Williamson, A. 21259. | M. April 23/17. |
| 7 D. XV | Willimott, Wm. 21127. | M. April 23/17. |
| 7 D. | Willmer, L.-Cpl. Leonard Ernest. 28332. | M. April 23/17. |
| 7 D. | Yorke, L.-Sergt. E. 14952. | M. April 23/17. |
| 7 D. | Young, Bowman. 23806. (Fr. H.Q. Sig.) | M. April 23/17. |
| 7 D. | Youngs, T. W. 21366. | M. April 23/17. |
| 8 A. IV | Crone, Thomas. 12539. | M. Oct. 21/16. R/Enq |
| ‡8 B. VII | Brindle, William. 27398. | M. Oct. 21/16. R/Enq. |
| ‡8 B. VI | Nuttall, John. 30213. | M. Oct. 21/16. R/Enq. |
| *11 A. | Barnes, J. H. 17372. | M. Nov. 18/16. R/Enq. |
| 11 A. | Derrick, L.-Cpl. J. 33349. | M. Feb. 11/17. |
| 11 A. | Edgar, D. 24748. | M. Nov. 18/16. R/Enq. |
| ‡11 A. | Hughes, A. J. 27681 | M. Nov. 18/16. R/Enq. |
| 11 A. | Metcalf, Richard. 33561. | W. and M. Feb. 10/17. |
| ‡11 A. | Robson, John. 17415. | M. Nov. 18/16. R/Enq. |
| 11 A. | Stokes, A. E. 27692. | M. Jan. 12/17. Unoff. K. Det.D./B. |
| 11 B. VII | East, L. J. 27737. | M. Nov. 18/16. R/Enq. |
| 11 B. VI | Haycroft, Thomas. 16362. | M. Nov. 18/16. R/Enq. |
| 11 B. VII | Hicks, Albert Edward. 27758. | M. Nov. 18/16. R/Enq. |
| 11 B. | Isles, Sergt. J. M. 13654. | M. Nov. 18/16. |
| 11 B. | Lakin, S. 15316. | W. and M. Feb. 10/17. |
| 11 B. VII | Mounsey, Bugler Tom Fallowfield. 17665. | M. Nov. 18/16. R/Enq. |
| 11 B. | Stockdale, A. 26066. | M. April 15/17. |
| 11 C. | Nash, R. 27789. | M. Nov. 18/16. |
| ‡11 C. | Phillips, Wm. Henry. 27802. | M. Nov. 18/16. R/Enq. |
| ‡11 C. | Prickett, L.-Sergt. J. H. 13420. | M. Nov. 18/16. R/Enq. |
| 11 C. M.G.S. | Swift, H. 33137. | K. April 1/17. Det.D./B. |
| ‡11 D. | Jefferson, John. 23364. | M. Nov. 18/16. R/Enq. |
| ‡11 D. XIII | Johnson, James. 24686. | W. and M. Nov. 18/16. R/Enq. |
| 11 D. | McGann, Owen. 19345. | M. Feb. 11/17. |

## BUCKINGHAMSHIRE YEOMANRY.

### *E.E.F.*

| | | |
|---|---|---|
| A. Squad. | Roper, Frank. 2503. | M. April 19/17. |
| ? | Badcock, P. H. 204634. | M. April 19/17. |
| ? | Paxton, A. T. 205471. | M. April 19/17. |

## IMPERIAL CAMEL CORPS.

### *E.E.F.*

| | | |
|---|---|---|
| ? Squad. | Wilson, W. 2682. (Fr. 1 Hereford.) | M. Jan. 9/17. |

## CAMBRIDGESHIRE REGIMENT.

### *B.E.F.*

| | | |
|---|---|---|
| 1 A. I | Thaxter, C. 4614. | W. and M. Oct. 14/16. R/Enq. |
| *1 C. | Johnson, P. E. 4173. | M. Oct. 14/16. R/Enq. |
| 1 D. | Hitch, George William. 2883. | M. Oct. 14/16. R./Enq. |

## CAMERON HIGHLANDERS.

### *B.E.F.*

| | | |
|---|---|---|
| 1 A. | Cruickshank, J. 22656. | M. Sept. 3/16. R./Enq. |
| ‡1 A. | Liston, R. 13153. | M. Sept. 3/16. R/Enq. |
| 1 A. III | MacDonald, Donald. 20293. | M. Sept. 3/16. R/Enq. |
| *1 A. IV | Marshall, Thos. Wm. 4692. (Fr. 4.) | M. Sept. 3/16. R/Enq. |
| ‡1 A. IV | Smith, Jas. B. 1523. | W. and M. July 23/17. |
| 4 B. | Ward, Walter H. 3694. | M. Sept. 3/16. R/Enq. |
| 4 C. | Cawthra, Herbert. 3723. | M. Sept. 3/16. R/Enq. |
| 4 C. | McEachen, Jn. C. 200180. (Fr. 11th Entrenching Bn.) | M. April 23-28/17. |
| 5 | **Cameron, Capt. A.** (Fr. 3rd.) | M. May 3/17. |
| 5 | **Drummond, 2nd Lieut. D. T.** | M., bel. W. May 3/17. |
| 5 | **Lee, 2nd Lieut. H. M.** | W. and M. (W.O.L. March 28/17) |
| 5 | **Lorimer, Capt. J. B.** | M. May 3/17. |
| 5 A. II | Bardley, Hugh. 27492 | M. May 3/17. |
| *5 A. IV | Benson, John. 22105. | M. May 3/17. |
| ‡5 A. | Currie, Cpl. C. 26778. | M. May 3/17. |
| ‡5 A. | Fraser, L.-Cpl. J. 22369. | M. May 3/17. |
| ‡5 A. | Hewitt, A.-Cpl. L. 25315. | M. May 3/17. |
| *5 A. I | Johnstone, George. 40773. | M. May 3-4/17. |
| 5 A. I | McLellan, Joe. 14269. | M. May 3/17. |
| ‡5 A. | McMillan, L.-Cpl. J. 14476. | M. May 3/17. |
| *5 A. or C. | Millar, William. 23295. | M. May 3/17. |

**Cameron Highlanders—contd.**

*B.E.F.*

| | | | |
|---|---|---|---|
| 5 | A. | Spence, Cpl. Hugh. 5769. | M. May 3/17. |
| *5 | A. IV | Tomlinson, W. 23963. | M. May 3/17. |
| 5 | A. L.G.S. | Wood, L.-Cpl. Thomson. 12689. | M. May 3/17. |
| 5 | B. L.G.S. | Anderson, John. 10693. | W. and M. Oct. 18/16. R/Enq. |
| 5 | B. or D. | Bolton, L.-Cpl. J. 22604. | M. May 3/17. |
| 5 | B. V | Brooks, John. 18260. | M. May 3/17. |
| ‡5 | B. VIII | Cantley, A. 24958. | M. May 3/17. |
| ‡5 | B. | Clements, W. 9835. | M. May 3/17. |
| ‡5 | B. | Cullen, F. 26785. | M. May 3/17. |
| *5 | B. VI | Dunlop, Alex. C. S/22329. | W. and M. Oct. 18/16. R/Enq. |
| 5 | B. VI | Gardiner, Geo. A. V. 23750. | M. May 3/17. |
| 5 | B. VIII | Grant, L.-Cpl. James. 22491. | W. and M. Oct. 18/16. R/Enq. |
| 5 | B. VI | Hewat, L.-Cpl. W. B. 22661. | M. May 3/17. |
| ‡5 | B. | Hope, J. 18531. | M. May 3/17. |
| ‡5 | B. VIII | Laing, Alex. 27498. | M. May 3/17. |
| ‡5 | B. | McCartney, J. 9127. | M. May 3/17. |
| ‡5 | B. | McInnes, D. 23169. | M. May 3/17. |
| *5 | B. VIII | Matheson, L.-Cpl. John. 23877. | M. May 3/17. |
| ‡5 | B. | Robertson, James A. S/27507. | M. May 3/17. |
| ‡5 | B. | Ross, J. 40804. | M. May 3/17. |
| 5 | B. VII | Stewart, Murdo. 10652. | M. May 3/17. |
| ‡5 | B. | Wright, Sergt. A. 12688. | M. May 3/17. |
| ‡5 | C. | Cameron, A. 11577. | M. May 3/17. |
| ‡5 | C. | Cochrane, A. 8244. | M. May 3/17. |
| 5 | C. XII | Gibb, John H. 40885. | M. May 3/17. |
| ‡5 | C. | Good, J. 40883. | M. May 3/17. |
| 5 | C. | Hendry, Thos. 18977. | M. May 3/17. |
| 5 | C. V | Hunter, C. S. S/12432. | M. May 3/17. |
| 5 | C. X | Jardine, Joseph. 40890. | M. May 3/17. |
| 5 | C. X | Johnstone, James. 22288. | M. Oct. 18/16. R/Enq. |
| ‡5 | C. | McLennan, D. 27481. | M. May 3/17. |
| 5 | C. XII | McLennan, Cpl. John. 25384. | M. May 3/17. |
| ‡5 | C. | McRorie, J. 11591. | M. May 3/17. |
| 5 | C. X | Nicoll, Alex. 20505. | M. Oct. 18/16. R/Enq. |
| ‡5 | C. | Ogilvie, L.-Cpl. J. 9965. | M. May 3/17. |
| 5 | C. IX | Turnbull, Alex. 40828. | M. May 3/17. |
| 5 | C. X | Turnbull, James. 5918. | M. May 3/17. |
| ‡5 | C. IX | Walker, L.-Cpl. H. 22467. | M. May 3/17. |
| *5 | C. X | Yeats, Harry. 15881. | M. May 3/17. |
| 5 | D. XIV | Armstrong, John Taylor. S/40851. | M. May 3/17. |
| ‡5 | D. | Bain, J. 40859. | M. May 3/17. |
| 5 | D. | Boyd, Robt. 5647. | M. May 3/17. |
| ‡5 | D. | Chenie, L.-Cpl. A. 9259 | M. May 3/17. |
| ‡5 | D. | Chisholm, R. 40872. | M. May 3/17. |
| 5 | D. XIII | Fuller, Leonard Walter. 27548. | M. May 3/17. |
| ‡5 | D. | Grant, J. 40764. | M. May 3/17. |
| 5 | D. XIV | Jamieson, L.-Cpl. John. R/5162. (Fr. 1st.) | W. and M. Oct. 18/16. R/Enq. |
| 5 | D. XVI | Keiguin, F. 27551. | M. May 3/17. |
| 5 | D. | Larkins, Robert. 40895. | M. May 3/17. |
| *5 | D. XIII | McKay, John. 9356. | M. May 3/17. |
| *5 | D. XIII | McKenzie, Alick. S/27537. | M. May 3/17. |
| 5 | D. XVI | McKenzie, James. S/22841. | M. May 3/17. |
| *5 | D. XV | McQueen, John. 27529. | M. May 3/17. |
| 5 | D. | Martin, Thomas. 22407. | M. May 3/17. |
| *5 | D. M.G.S. | Miles, C. 40468. | M. May 3/17. |
| ‡5 | D. | Smart, D. 18105. | M. May 3/17. |
| 6 | | **Paterson, Lt. C. C.** (Fr. 19 R. Scots.) | W. and M. April 11/17. |
| 6 | A. IV | Baillie, Hugh. 40518. | M. April 11/17. |

**Cameron Highlanders—contd.**

*B.E.F.*

6 A. IV Brand, James. 40512. M. April 26/17.
6 A. Burns, Robt. Wm. 25092. M. April 26/17.
6 A. I Campbell, Sgt. Wm. Warrington. 27405. W. and M. April 26/17.
6 A. M.G.S. Cook, L.-Cpl. Matthew. 16543. M. April 26/17.
6 A. II Currie, Colin. 24380. M. April 26/17.
6 A. Dunbar, Robt. 43253. M. April 11/17.
6 A. Graham, Wm. 12092. M. April 26/17.
6 A. Greaves, W. 26370. M. April 26/17.
6 A. I Hewitt, David. 26315. M. April 26/17.
6 A. Hodge, George. 13641. W. and M. April 11/17.
6 A. Irvine, M. 24969. M. April 26/17.
6 A. I Laing, L.-Cpl. John. 40702. W. and M. April 11/17.
6 A. III McCallum, Duncan. F/40676. M. April 26/17.
6 A. IV McDonald, Murdo. 18892. M. April 11/17.
6 A. I MacDougall, A.-Cpl. S/40560. M. April 26/17.
6 A. McGill, A.-Cpl. T. 8250. W. and M. April 11/17.
6 A. MacKenzie, D. McD. 43262. W. and M. April 11/17.
6 A. I McKeown, George. 40680. M. April 26/17.
6 A. McKnight, J. 21868. M. April 11/17.
6 A. McWatt, W. 22140. W. and M. April 11/17.
6 A. Mitchell, Cpl. A. 25347. W. and M. April 11/17.
*6 A. IV Morris, L. B. 27422. Unoff. M., bel. K. April 23/17.
6 A. Muir, And. 21768. M. April 11/17.
6 A. Murchison, J. 40688. M. April 26/17.
6 A. II Ramsay, James. 26478. M. April 11/17.
6 A. Richardson, H. 20360. M. April 26/17.
6 A. III Ross, James. 22635. M. April 27/17.
6 A. Urwin, R. 21092. M. April 26/17.
6 A. Young, A. 12579. M. April 26/17.
6 B. VIII Cardie, Sergt. Wm. 12560. M. April 11/17.
6 B. VIII Davidson, G. B. 22976. Unoff. W. and M. April 11/17.
6 B. VII Edgar, Thomas. S/27001. M. April 11/17.
6 B. M.G.S. Ferguson, Alexander. 23241. W. and M. April 11/17.
6 B. Finlayson, R. 5506. M. April 11/17.
6 B. Haggan, A.-Cpl. W. 7781. W. and M. April 24/17.
6 B. Horne, P. 43282. M. April 24/17.
6 B. V MacDiarmid, L.-Sgt. Alex. S/16245. W. and M. April 24/17.
*6 B. VI McGhee, Hans. S/40677. K. April 21/17. Det.D./B.
6 B. McGregor, J. 40657. M. April 11/17.
6 B. V Macintyre, Hugh. S/27109. M. April 11/17.
6 B. VI Mackenzie, John M. S/26148. W. and M. April 11/17.
6 B. VIII McKinnon, Angus. 6219. M. April 11/17.
6 B. V MacLeod, Alex. 40720. M. April 11/17.
6 B. Maxwell, W. 17046. M. April 11/17.
6 B. VIII Reidpath, W. 40424. M. April 11/17.
6 B. Spence, Sergt. J. C. 8875. M. April 11/17.
6 B. Stewart, A.-Cpl. J. 8643. M. April 24/17.
6 B. VIII Young, James. 14271. M. April 24/17.
6 C. IX Briggs, Andrew. 40523. M. April 11/17.
6 C. Campbell, L.-Cpl. Alex. 8240. M. April 11/17.
6 C. XII Clark, Duncan A. 40130. W. and M. April 11/17.
6 C. Fillingham, Alfred. 12427. W. and M. April 11/17.
6 C. Fraser, Cpl. Donald. 27403. W and M. April 11/17.
6 C. Halliday, R. 26209. M. April 11/17.
6 C. XII Henderson, L.-Cpl. Tom. 21511. M. April 11/17.
6 C. McEwan, J. 10035. W. and M. April 11/17.

**Cameron Highlanders—contd.**

## *B.E.F.*

6 C. XI McNeilly, Thomas. 40660. M. April 11/17.
6 C. Mason, P. 43303. M. April 11/17.
6 C. Oliver, John. 40982. M. April 11/17.
6 C. Ravey, H. 20583. M. April 11/17.
6 C. XI Young, L.-Cpl. Andrew. 13915. M. April 11/17.
6 D. XIV Bell, James R. 24972. M. April 11/17.
6 D. XIII MacDonald, Peter. 23244. M. April 11/17.
6 D. McGregor, Sergt. John Alex. 13876. M. April 11/17.
6 D. XVI Reid, L.-Cpl. Jas. 7674. M. April 23/17.
6 D. XI Stephen, Hry. Burness. 27418. M. April 11/17.
6 D. XV Sutherland, A. F. 26069. W. and M. April 11/17.
7 **MacGillivray, 2nd Lieut. A.** W. Unoff. M. May 3/17.
*7 A. II McKechan, Walter. 21844. K. April 23/17. Det.D./B.
7 A. MacKenzie, G. 12857. M. April 23-28/17.
7 A. McLeod, G. 9555. M. April 23-28/17.
7 A. McNeill, A.-Cpl. D. 29385. M. April 23-28/17.
7 A. II Mitchell, R. R. S/22928. M. April 23-28/17.
7 B. M.G.S. Busby, Alex. 20225. M. April 23-28/17.
7 B. Downie, John C. 9552. M. April 23-28/17.
7 B. V Fletcher, Donald. 26398. M. April 23-28/17.
7 B. VI Glen, L.-Cpl. Thomas. S/22368. M. April 23-28/17.
7 B. VIII Kennedy, John. S/23280. W. and M. Jan. 28/17.
7 B. VII Lockhead, John. 27176. M. April 23-28/17.
7 B. McDonald, A. 21705. M. April 23-28/17.
7 B. McLeod, C. 13747. M. April 23-28/17.
7 B. VIII Rowley, S. S/23954. M. April 23-28/17.
7 C. XII Andrews, Fred H. 12949. M. April 23-28/17.
7 C. Edgar, L.-Cpl. R. 13600. W. and M. April 9-12/17.
7 C. Leigh, C. 17925. M. April 9-12/17.
7 C. Standish, H. 22332. M. April 23-28/17.
*7 D. Davidson, Robert. 22798. K. April 23-28/17. Det.D./B.
7 D. XIV Hardie, Andrew. 10999. (Fr. 1st, late 6th.) W. and M. April 23-28/17.
7 D. M.G.S. Jolly, Wm. 20787. M. April 23-28/17.
7 D. McKenzie, Donald. 14034. M. April 23-28/17.

## *BALKANS.*

*2 B. VIII Thomson, David. 20433. K. May 19/17. Det.D./B.
2 C. XI Latto, Geo. 10504. M. Mar. 16/17.
2 ? Logan, J. 18133. M. Mar. 16/17.
2 ? O'Brien, John. 8481. K. March 16/17. Det.D./B.
10 A. I McDonald, John. 2392. (Fr. Lovat's Scouts.) M. Dec. 15/16.

**CANADIAN IMPERIAL FORCES.**

**Vide end of List.**

## CHESHIRE REGIMENT.

### B.E.F.

|  |  |  |
|---|---|---|
| 1 A. | Dodd, C. 45943. | M. April 14/17. |
| 1 A. III | Mullins, Alfred. 50560. | K. April 14/17. Det.D./B. |
| 1 A. or B. | Parrott, Edward. 12227. | M. Sept. 5/16. R/Enq. |
| 1 A. or D. | Rimmer, Cpl. G. H. 50543. | M. April 14/17. |
| 1 A. | Walton, S. 49373. | M. April 13/17. |
| 1 C. | Davies, R. 28393. | M. April 13/17. |
| 1 D. | Berry, Fred. 12331. | W. and M. Sept. 5/16. R/Enq. |
| 1 D. XIV | Davies, Edward. 17569. | M. Sept. 5/16. R/Enq. |
| ‡5 B. | Ashley, E. 10/13569. | M. May 8/17. |
| ‡5 B. | Carter, A. W. H. 3/52118. | M. May 8/17. |
| ‡5 B. | Peers, L.-Sergt. F. 240518. | M. May 8/17. |
| ‡5 B. | Poole, W. M. 240321. | M. May 13/17. |
| ‡5 D. | Hoey, Edward. 20850. | K. May 3/17. Det.D./B. |
| ‡6 | **Crew, Lieut. D. M.** | M., bel. K. July 5/17. |
| 6 B. | Street, John. 3989. | M. Nov. 13/16. R/Enq. |
| 6 D. XIII | Howarth, Travis. 4515. | K. Nov. 13/16. Det.D./B. |
| 6 ? | Rose, Sam. 49637. (Fr. 13th.) | K. Oct. 21/16. Det.D./B. |
| 10 A. or C. | Barlow, H. 49431. | M Feb. 17/17. |
| 10 A. | Booth, F. 49446. | M. Feb. 17/17. |
| 10 A. | Cliffe, C. 434. | M. Feb. 17/17. |
| 10 A. | Hodkinson, C. 49406. (Late 5th, 2558.) | W. and M. Oct. 9/16. |
| 10 A. | Holland, Joe. 11137 | M. Feb. 17/17. |
| 10 A. | Leadbeater, J. 316. | M. Feb. 17/17. |
| 10 A. IV | Lloyd, Stephen. 13238. | W. and M. Feb. 17/17. |
| 10 A. | Spilsbury, J. 35282. | M. Feb. 17/17. |
| ‡10 B. M.G.S. | Blackhurst, Frank. 18003. | M. June 7/17. |
| 10 B. VI | Carlisle, F. J. 49459. | M. Oct. 9/16. R/Enq. |
| 10 B. | Dagger, T. H. 24817. | W. and M., bel. K. Feb. 17/17. |
| 10 C. | Barlow, H. 11049. | M. Feb. 17/17. |
| 10 C. | Burke, E. 10746. | M. Feb. 17/17. |
| 10 C. | Dodd, J. G. 10055. | M. April 15/17. |
| 10 C. XI | Freeman, J. E. 34520. | M. Feb. 17/17. |
| 10 C. | Hall, L. 44253. | M. Feb. 17/17. |
| 10 C. | Harris, Fred. 52400. (Fr. Shropshire Yeomanry.) | W. and M. Oct. 10/16. R/Enq. |
| 10 C. | Helsby, Harry. 35698. | M. Feb. 17/17. |
| 10 C. | Hickson, L.-Cpl. T. 13115. | M. Feb. 17/17. |
| 10 C. | Hughes, Thos. 35717. | M. Feb. 17/17. |
| 10 C. | Jones, G. 36169. | M. Feb. 17/17. |
| 10 C. | Little, Jack. 35848. | W. and M. Feb. 17/17. |
| 10 C. | Loughlin, J. 15518. | M. Feb. 17/17. |
| 10 C. | Lowcock, Harold Fielding. 35435. | M. Feb. 17/17. |
| 10 C. | Norman, A. E. 27173. | M. April 15/17. |
| 10 C. | Smith, J. 10801. | M. Feb. 17/17. |
| 10 C. IX | Tilsley, J. 44158. | M. Feb. 17/17. |
| 10 C. | Wainwright, Sergt. P. 18468. | M. Feb. 17/17. |
| 10 D. XVI | Houghton, Percy. 39996. | M. Feb. 17/17. |
| ‡10 D. XIV | Mongon, Owen. 33088. | M. June 7/17. |
| ‡10 D. XIV | Stanley, Dan. 28780. | M. June 6/17. |
| ‡11 A. III | Beresford, Sergt. William. 8869. | M. Oct. 21/16. R/Enq. |
| ‡11 A. | Peakman, T. E. 13838. | W. Unoff. M. June 7/17. |
| ‡11 A. III | Radcliffe, Arthur. 35375. | M. Oct. 21/16. |
| 11 C. | Morris, J. 49535. | M. Oct. 17/16. |
| ‡11 C. | Palmer, W. E. 50789. | Unoff. K. June 16/17. |
| ‡13 | **Walsh, 2nd Lieut. G. C. L.** | M. June 22/17. |
| ‡13 I II | Bellis, William. 45750. | M. May 24/17. |
| *13 I II | Cartwright, A. 6923. | W. and M. May 16/17. R/Enq. |

**Cheshire Regiment—contd.**

## *B.E.F.*

| | | |
|---|---|---|
| 13 1 III | Clegg, A. 52914. | M. Oct. 21/16. |
| ‡13 1 | Findlater, A. 36763. | M. May 24/17. |
| ‡13 1 | Fletcher, H. 26893. | M. May 24/17. |
| 13 1 | Hardy, H. W. 57618. (Late Dragoon Guards) (21580.) | W. and M. May 23/17. |
| *13 1 | Heywood, John. 16915. | K. June 7/17. Det.D./B. |
| ‡13 1 | Smalley, H. 20250. | M. May 24/17. |
| ‡13 1 | Storey, Sergt. R. J. 3/9777. | M. May 16/17. |
| 13 2 | Burgess, J. S. 16118. | M. Oct. 21/16. R/Enq. |
| 13 2 VII | Clifton, A.-Cpl. Arthur Percy. 52910. (Fr. 18 Welsh Fus., 35404.) | K. Oct. 21/16. Det.D./B. |
| ‡13 2 | Foxley, F. H. 33000. | M. May 24/17. |
| 13 2 VII | Price, G. 52885. | W. and M. Oct. 21/16. R/Enq. |
| 13 3 XI | Hoole, Cpl. H. 4/32659. | M. Oct. 21/16. R./Enq. |
| 13 3 XIII | Taylor, J. 10391. | W. and M., bel. P/W. May 16/17. |
| ‡13 4 | Turnock, D. 24082. | M. Oct. 21/16. R/Enq. |
| ‡13 4 | Woods, B. R. 1122. | M. Unoff. W. June 7/17. |
| ‡15 2 XVI | King, N. 45754. | M. April 30/17. |
| ‡16 W. | Bunting, R. 202048. | M. May 19/17. |
| ‡16 W. | Collier, W. H. 58223. | M. May 19/17. |
| 16 X. | Harvey, G. 57854. | M. April 28-29/17. |
| ‡16 Y. | Kelly, R. C. E. 61977. | W. and M. April 28-29/17. |
| 16 Y. XII | Rhodes, Geo. 50438. | M. April 28-29/17. |
| 16 ? | Adshead, Cpl. R. 50293. | W. and M. April 28-29/17. |

## *E.E.F.*

| | | |
|---|---|---|
| 4 A. I | Garlick, Arthur. 266756. (4542.) | W. and M. Mar. 26/17. |
| 4 D. XVI | Halsall, J. 241877. | W. and M. Mar. 26/17. |
| 4 ? | Hartley, A. 201740. | W. and M. Mar. 26/17. |
| 7 | **Gregg, 2nd Lt. Geo. Philip.** | W. and M., bel. K. March 26/17. |
| 7 A. II | Hall, Fred. 291460. | W. and M. Mar. 26/17. |
| 7 B. | Gallimore, J. 290804. (2861.) | W. and M. Mar. 26/17. |
| 7 B. | Postles, Luther. 290821. (2893.) | W. and M. Mar. 26/17. |
| 7 D. | Swindells, J. 290174. (Late 1606.) | W. and M. Mar. 26/17. |
| 7 D. | Wyatt, Charlie. 291537. (Late 4344.) | W. and M. Mar. 26/17. |
| 7 ? | Davies, A. V. 290885. | W. and M. Mar. 26/17. |
| 7 ? | Davies, J. C. 291176. | W. and M. Mar. 26/17. |
| 7 ? | Mottershead, J. 291044. | W. and M. Mar. 26/17. |
| 7 ? | O'Conner, J. 291025. | M. Mar. 26/17. |
| 7 ? | Ormes, A. 291217. | W. and M. Mar. 26/17. |
| 7 ? | Pomfret, L.-Cpl. J. E. 291040. | W. and M. Mar. 26/17. |
| 7 ? | Tickle, T. 291035. | W. and M. Mar. 26/17. |
| 7 ? | Turner, R. 291081. | W. and M. Mar. 26/17. |
| 7 ? | Warburton, James. 291520. | W. and M. Mar. 26/17. |
| 7 ? | Williamson, H. 291014. | W. and M. Mar. 26/17. |

## *PERSIAN GULF.*

| | | |
|---|---|---|
| 8 | **Jones, 2nd Lt. A. B.** (Fr. Liverpools) | M. April 30/17. |
| ‡8 A. | Boothby, A. 24261. | M. April 30/17. |
| ‡8 A. | Fraser, Sergt. W. P. 10654. | M. April 30/17. |
| 8 A. | Spann, Chas. Hry. 10873. | M. Jan. 9/17. |
| *8 B. | Beswick, Kenneth. 27058. | M. April 30/17. |
| 8 B. | Camble, L.-Cpl. Jas. E. 17917. | D/W. Feb. 17/17. Det.D./B. |
| 8 B. | Harper, W. 11576. | W. and M. April 11/17. |
| 8 B. | Pollard, John. 33367. | M. April 30/17. |
| 8 B. | Voss, Sgt. H. H. 28304. | M. April 30/17. |
| ‡8 B. | Williams, Frank. 12384. | M. April 30/17. |
| ‡8 B. | Wilson, Jas. Wm. 35458. | M. April 30/17. |

**Cheshire Regiment—contd.**

## *PERSIAN GULF.*

8 B. Woodfine, Geo. 24306. M., bel. K. Feb. 12/17.
8 C. XII Buckley, S. 34537. M. April 30/17.
8 C. Ferguson, L.-Cpl. R. 11099. K. April 30/17. Det.D./B.
‡8 C. XII Massey, John Henry. 10917. M. April 30/17.
8 C. Perrin, S. 11223. W. and M. April 9/16
‡8 C. XII Ward, William. 33428. M. April 30/17.
8 D. Broderick, James. 12463. M. April 9/16. R/Enq.
‡8 D. Ennett, Edward. 33736. M. April 30/17.
8 D. Horne, F. 12024. M. April 30/17.
*8 D. McArthur, J. 33265. M. April 30/17.
8 D. Norman, John. 28333. M. Feb. 1/17.
8 D. North, Daniel. 32840. M. April 30/17.
8 D. Wilson, F. 18214. M. Feb. 1/17.
‡8 ? Bell, D. M. 11717. M. April 30/17.
‡8 ? Brambley, F. 58990. M. April 30/17.
‡8 ? Brereton, J. 32800. M. April 30/17.
8 ? Brown, Sergt. H. 10149. W. and M. April 9/16.
‡8 ? Buckley, F. 35242. M. April 30/17.
‡8 ? Casey, G. 1102. M. April 30/17.
‡8 ? Castledine, Cpl. Ernest. 11882. M. April 30/17.
8 ? Currie, J. C. 10600. W. and M. April 5/16.
‡8 ? Dale, Cpl. T. 58993. W. and M. April 30/17.
‡8 ? Elgey, R. N. 58996. M. April 30/17.
‡8 ? Fletcher, E. 10806. W. and M. April 30/17.
‡8 ? Foster, J. 32891. M. April 30/17.
‡8 ? Hallworth, W. 27270. M. April 30/17.
‡8 ? Hampson, J. 34871. M. April 30/17.
‡8 ? Hatton, W. 30627. M. April 30/17.
‡8 ? Hilton, L.-Sergt. J. T. 59001. M. April 30/17.
8 ? Hunt, D. 10612. W. and M. April 21/16.
*8 ? Johnson, G. 26993. W. and M. April 11/17.
8 ? Kiddis, F. 27348. W. and M. Feb. 1/17.
‡8 ? Larby, L.-Cpl. A. G. 59003. M. April 30/17.
8 ? Ledsham, R. J. J. 34890. M. Feb. 15/17.
‡8 ? Lee, C. 26796. M. April 30/17.
‡8 ? Lewis, F. 18400. W. and M. April 30/17.
‡8 ? Lloyd, T. 33422. M. April 30/17.
‡8 ? McKivragen, H. 11311. M. April 30/17.
‡8 ? Mayman, P. 34749. W. and M. April 30/17.
‡8 ? Meakin, T. 24056. W. and M. April 30/17.
‡8 ? Moore, J. 32789. M. April 30/17.
8 ? Morton, G. 27806. M. Feb. 1/17.
‡8 ? Newby, J. W. 17473. M. April 30/17.
‡8 ? Ollier, W. 33490. M. April 30/17.
‡8 ? Orton, Sergt. J. 59011. M. April 30/17.
‡8 ? Parry, A. 26380. W. and M. April 30/17.
‡8 ? Pounall, E. 35350. W. and M. April 30/17.
‡8 ? Riley, G. 18772. M. April 30/17.
‡8 ? Rothery, N. B. J. 45266. M. April 30/17.
‡8 ? Sadler, J. 11140. M. April 30/17.
‡8 ? Saunders, W. 11476. M. April 30/17.
‡8 ? Sherwood, L.-Cpl. F. 32973. M. April 30/17.
‡8 ? Shirley, C. 26284. M. April 30/17.
‡8 ? Smith, J. 33442. M. April 30/17.
‡8 ? Stokes, P. 35020. M. April 30/17.
‡8 ? Sweeney, Sergt. T. 11465. M. April 30/17.
‡8 ? Wadsworth, W. 10631. M. April 30/17.
8 ? Walker, F. 25423. M. Feb. 1/17.

**Cheshire Regiment—contd.**

## *PERSIAN GULF.*

| | | |
|---|---|---|
| 18 ? | Ward, L. 59018. | M. April 30/17. |
| 18 ? | Whalley, F. 35767. | M. April 30/17. |
| 18 ? | Wood, G. 33190. | M. April 30/17. |
| 18 ? | Yarwood, J. W. 25922. | M. April 30/17. |

# CONNAUGHT RANGERS.

## *B.E.F.*

| | | |
|---|---|---|
| 6 A. | Doherty, T. 5904. | W. and M. Sept. 3/16. |
| 6 B. | Mulligan, T. 5720. | M. Sept. 3/16. |
| 6 C. XIII | MacLaughlan, John. 1635. | M. Sept. 3/16. R./Enq. |
| 6 C. | O'Donnell, B. 7303 | W. and M. Sept. 8/16. |
| 6 D. | Carragher, J. 4385. | W. and M. Sept. 9/16. |
| 6 D. | Fenoughty, M. 11029. | W. and M. Sept 3/16. |
| 6 D. | McDermott, D. 6184. | W. and M. Sept. 3/16. |
| 6 D. | Reilly, M. 6298. | M. Sept. 10/16. R/Enq. |
| 6 D. | Warren, F. M. 3106. | W. and M. Sept. 3/16. |
| 6 ? | Murphy, J. P. 6787. (Fr. 3rd.) | M. Sept. 3/16. |

## *PERSIAN GULF.*

| | | |
|---|---|---|
| *1 A. | Tolan, Thomas. 5939. • | D/W. April 8/17. Det.D./B. |
| 1 ? | Baker, Bernard. 6905. (Fr. 2 W. Kents.) | K. April/16. Det.D./B. |
| 1 ? | Carey, Thomas. 9670. | W. and M. April 17/16. R/Enq. |
| 1 ? | McNeill, Wm. Edward. 5672. (Fr. 3.) | W. and M. April 17/16. R/Enq. |
| 1 ? | Mulrooney, P. 9657. | W. and M. Jan. 21/17. |
| *1 ? | Welsh, J. 3/6859. | M., bel. K. Feb. 20/17. |
| 1 ? | Welsh, Peter. 6533. | W. and M. April 17/16. |

# DERBYSHIRE YEOMANRY.

## *BALKANS.*

| | | |
|---|---|---|
| 11 C. Squad. | Thornby, J. A. 75976. | W. and M., bel. P/W. June 25/17. |
| 11 ? | Labane, W. 75653. | M. June 23/17. |

## DEVONSHIRE REGIMENT.

### *B.E.F.*

| | | |
|---|---|---|
| 1 | **Bush, 2nd Lieut. F. W.** | W. and M. **May 9/17.** |
| 1 | **Grigson, 2nd Lt. L. H. S.** (Fr. 3rd.) | M. **May 9/17.** |
| 1 | **Hamilton, 2nd Lieut. R. E.** | W. and M. **April 23/17.** |
| *1 | **Hardwick, 2nd Lieut. O. W.** | K. **May 9/17.** Det.D./B. |
| 1 | **Malone, Lieut. B. W. L'E.** | W. and M. **April 23/17.** |
| 1 | **Wonnacott, 2nd Lieut. T. H.** | W. and M. **May 9/17.** |
| 1 1 or 3 | Boundy, A. L. 30282. | W. and M. **April 23/17.** |
| 1 1 L.G.S. | Carter, Edward J. 24047. | W. and M. **May 9/17.** |
| ‡1 1 | Collier, H. J. 38036. | M. **May 9/17.** |
| ‡1 1 | Downing, W. H. 21845. | M. **May 9/17.** |
| 1 1 III | Chiswell, P. J. 25729. | M. **May 9/17.** |
| 1 1 L.G.S. | Dunn, John Henry 16470. | K. **Sept. 25/16.** Det.D./B. R/Enq. |
| ‡1 1 I | Fancey, E. 49013. | M. **April 23/17.** |
| 1 1 III | Garnish, Walter J. 30304. (Fr. R.N. Devon Hussars.) | M. **May 9/17.** |
| ‡1 1 I | Grant, P. H. 23201. | M. **April 24/17.** |
| ‡1 II | Knight, P. J. 30297. | W. and M. **May 9/17.** |
| ‡1 1 | Lakeman, J. 26685. | M. **May 9/17.** |
| 1 2 V | Anning, L.-Cpl. F. 16631. | W. and M. **April 23/17.** |
| 1 2 V | Ball, J. H. 27611. | M. **April 23/17.** |
| 1 2 VI | Batten, F. P. 30413. | M. **April 23/17.** |
| 1 2 | Bearne, E. J. 20493. | M. **April 23/17.** |
| 1 2 | Berry, F. G. 26756. | M. **April 23/17.** |
| 1 2 | Dayies, A. E. 16157. | W. and M. **April 23/17.** |
| *1 2 VII | Dawe, C. 30297. (3057.) (Fr. N. Devon Hussars.) | W. and M. **May 9/17.** |
| 1 2 | Doidge, F. 30656. | M. **April 23/17.** |
| 1 2 | French, J. P. 15289. | M. **April 23/17.** |
| 1 2 | Hastie, A.-C.-S.-M. F. 28441. | M. **April 24/17.** |
| 1 2 | Hole, V. G. R. 14625. | M. **April 23/17.** |
| 1 2 | Hooking, W. J. 12960. | M. **April 23/17.** |
| 1 2 | James, A. C. B. 11138. | M. **April 23/17.** |
| 1 2 | Shambrook, N. 30349. | M. **April 23/17.** |
| 1 2 VII | Snow, Thos. John. 3288. (Fr. 1st Devon Yeo.) | K. **Sept. 3/16.** Det.D./B. |
| 1 2 VIII | Withy, S. A. 11484. | W. and M. **April 23/17.** |
| 1 3 L.G.S. | Bellchambers, Percy Frank. 20973. | M. **May 9/17.** |
| 1 3 | Branch, L.-Cpl. Wilfred. 9644. | M. **April 23/17.** |
| 1 3 IX | Bromell, Edm. Westaway. 25933. | M. **April 23/17.** |
| ‡1 3 IX | Cattanack, J. 225071. | W. and M. **May 9/17.** |
| *1 3 XI | Coles, James. 15913. | W. and M. **April 23/17.** |
| 1 3 | Friend, Ernest W. 30386. | W. and M. **April 23/17.** |
| ‡1 3 | Greeman, A. 27688. | M. **May 9/17.** |
| 1 3 XI | Higgins, Cpl. S. 20914. | M. **April 23/17.** |
| 1 3 | Hill, F. 20717. | W. and M. **April 23/17.** |
| *1 3 IX | Hill, T. 20771. | Unoff. W. and M. abt. **April 25/17.** |
| ‡1 3 XI | Maidstone, R. A. 38521. | W. and M. **April 23/17.** |
| 1 3 | Oakshott, Percy. 10925. | W. and M. **April 23/17.** |
| 1 3 | Parsons, Cpl. S. 8328. | M. **April 23/17.** |
| 1 3 | Partridge, A. C. 14824. | W. and M. **April 23/17.** |
| *1 3 | Petchey, J. W. 15444. | W. and M. **April 23/17.** |
| 1 3 | Polkinghorne, Sergt. Leo. B. 11260. | M. **April 23/17.** |
| 1 3 | Polland, G. 45637. | W. and M. **April 23/17.** |
| ‡1 3 | Slee, Sergt. G. 7633. | M. **May 9/17.** |
| 1 3 L.G.S. | Smith, L.-Cpl. Robert. 15906. | W. and M. **April 23/17.** |
| 1 3 X | Smith, L.-Cpl. W. 25611. | M. **April 23/17.** |
| 1 3 | Stone, W. E. 26978. | W. and M. **April 23/17.** |

Devonshire Regiment—contd.

*B.E.F.*

| | | |
|---|---|---|
| 1 4 | Bastow, W. 20800. | M. April 23/17. |
| ‡1 4 | Bennett, A. H. 26681. | W. and M. May 9/17. |
| 1 4 | Brookling, H. 23474. | W. and M. April 23/17. |
| ‡1 4 | Coombes, F. 24718. | M. May 9/17. |
| 1 4 | Endicroft, L.-Cpl. A. T. 25818. | M. April 23/17. |
| ‡1 4 | Fishleigh, P. 15674. | M. May 9/17. |
| 1 4 XVI | Jones, L.-Cpl. Wm. Henry. 23760. | M. April 24/17. |
| ‡1 4 | Marsden, W. E. 15283. | M. May 9/17. |
| ‡1 4 | Olliver, W. 45539. | M. May 9/17. |
| 1 4 XVI | Prentice, W. G. 30019. | M. April 23/17. |
| 1 4 XV | Richards, Cpl. Albert. 18659. | M. May 9/17. |
| ‡1 4 | Shears, L.-Cpl. George F. 11498. | W. and M. May 9/17. |
| 1 4 XV | Sherwin L.-Cpl. Peter Jas. 20659. | M. April 23/17. |
| 1 4 | Taylor, F. 36803. | M. April 23/17. |
| 1 4 | Tucker, C. 26698. | M. April 23/17. |
| ‡1 4 | Wakeley, F. H. 30370. | M. May 9/17. |
| 1 4 XIV | Williams, R. 30377. | W. and M. May 9/17. |
| 1 H.Q. | Winsor, G. 8559. (Fr. 1st.) | W. and M. May 9/17. |
| 2 B. VI | Pears, Cpl. Alf. Richd. 16512. | M. May 6/17. |
| ‡2 B. | Wilcocks, H. 26117. | M. May 6/17. |
| 8 A. or B. | Clark, Thos. Jarvis. 33492. | M. April 2/17. |
| 8 A. | Norman, R. 12130. (Fr. 11th.) | M. Aug. 17/16. |
| 8 A. III | Ray, Frank Percy. 58052. | K. May 7/17. Det.D./B. |
| 8 B. VI | Balson, Cpl. Fredk. 9086. | M. May 9/17. |
| 8 B. VII | Braddon, F. 28489. | W. and M., bel. K. May 9/17. |
| ‡8 B. | Counter, W. 38057. | W. and M. May 9/17. |
| ‡8 B. | Crabb, W. G. 45610. | M. May 9/17. |
| ‡8 B. | Discombe, W. S. 24897. | W. and M., bel. K. May 9/17. |
| 8 B. VIII | McBrion, L.-Cpl. Wilfred. 19893. | M. April 2/17. |
| ‡8 B. | Patey, A. 14989. | W. and M., bel. K. May 9/17. |
| 8 B. | Schofield, Thos. 16020. | W. and M., bel. K. May 9/17. |
| ‡8 C. | Andrews, R. 26499. | M. May 9/17. |
| 8 C. | Beesley, Howard Reginald. 49007. | K. May 9/17. Det.D./B. |
| 8 C. | Davis, Cpl. Wm. Jas. 16140. | M. May 9/17. |
| *8 C. IX | Dyer, Albert Chas. 45673. | W. and M. May 9/17. |
| ‡8 C. | George, W. 45678. | W. and M., bel. K. May 9/17. |
| *8 C. X | Parkin, W. J. 30673. | W. and M., bel. K. May 9/17. |
| 8 C. | Stone L.-Cpl. P. J. C. 3469. | M. Mar. 27/17. |
| ‡8 C. | Wigley, R. V. 30697. | W. and M., bel. K. May 9/17. |
| 8 C. XII | Wood, W. 28512. | W. and M. May 6/17. |
| ‡8 D. | Brimblecombe, E. J. 16943. | M. May 7/17. |
| ‡8 D. | Cann, A. 15405. | M. May 9/17. |
| *8 D. | Fernley, Thos. 17042. | W. and M., bel. K. May 9/17. |
| ‡8 D. | Glover, S. G. 42666. | M. May 9/17. |
| 9 A. I | Austin, W. A. 30125. | K. April 2/17. Det.D./B. |
| 9 B. | Clarke, Edw. 17591. (Fr. 8th.) | W. and M. April 2/17. |
| ‡9 B. | Hemmingway, L. 15537. | M. May 7/17. |
| ‡9 C. or D. | Davey, Horace G. 18441. | W. and M. Oct. 4-6/16. R/Enq. |
| *9 C. | Jones, John. 12908. | M. Sept. 4-6/16. R/Enq. |
| ‡9 C. | Mears, T. 30191. | W. and M. May 7-10/17. |
| 9 C. IX | Parker, Wm. 21198. (Fr. 6 Som. L.I.) | M. Sept. 4/16. R/Enq. |
| 9 C. | Smith, J. H. 14928. | M. Sept. 4-6/16. R./Enq. |
| 9 C. L.G.S. | Stallabrass, A.-L.-Cpl. Harry. 9994 | M. May 7/17. |
| 9 C. X | Williams, Arthur Thos. 3/20396. | W. and M. May 7-10/17. |
| 9 C. | Wilmott, C. 4113. (Fr. 6th Glos.) | M. Sept. 6/16. R/Enq. |

**Devonshire Regiment—contd.**

## B.E.F.

*9 D. XIV Britton, F. G. 50323. — M. May 8/17.
9 D. Eastment, W. 17493. — W. and M. April 2/17.
9 D. XV Manning, G. 50330. — M. May 8/17.
9 D. Troke, W. 14343. — M. April 2/17.
*9 D. Warren, Fredk. S. H. 17076. — K. Sept. 4-6/16. Det.D./B.
9 ? Bennett, John. 21477. (Fr. 6 Som. L.I.) — M. Sept. 4/16. R/Enq.

## BALKANS.

10 **Hancock, Lieut. W. R.** — M. April 24/17.
10 **Harris, 2nd Lieut. W. L.** — W. and M. Feb. 10/17.
10 **Lovett, Capt. O.** — M. Mar. 25/17.
10 **Miller, Lieut. W. R. F.** — M., bel. K. April 24/17.
10 **Partridge, Lieut. W. J.** — M. April 24-25/17.
10 **Prynne, 2nd Lieut. N. F.** — M. April 24-25/17.
10 D. **Thorne, 2nd Lieut. S. C.** — M. April 24-25/17.
10 **Wilson, 2nd Lieut. W. J.** — M., bel. K. April 24-25/17.
10 A. Damerell, Francis Geo. Lawrence. 12006 — M. April 24-25/17.
10 A. M.G.S. Gregory, Sergt. Chas. 7673. — M. April 24/17.
10 A. Merriman, James. 11739. — M. Feb. 10/17.
10 A. I Parish, A. J. 16785. — M. April 24-25/17.
10 A. Shute, S. J. 15194. — M. April 24-25/17.
10 A. Street, L.-Cpl. A. E. 11604. — W. and M. Feb. 10/17.
10 A. Ward, Cpl. Arthur John. 12837. — M. April 24-25/17.
10 B. Brett, J. K. 43418. — D/W. April 27/17. Det.D./B.
10 B. VIII James, L.-Cpl. Ernest. 13937. — W. and M. Mar. 14/17.
10 B. Kilby, Allan S. 17786. — K. Feb. 10/17. Conf. and det.
10 B. McLaren, W. Neil. 55786. — M. April 24-25/17.
10 B. Pennington, Leonard George. 17858. — W. and M. Feb. 10/17.
10 B. Troacke, A. J. 26071. — M. April 24-25/17.
10 C. Andrews, A. W. 13945. — M. Feb. 10/17.
10 C. Burnett, Fred. 13434. — M. Feb. 10/17.
10 C. IX Collinge, Arthur G. 16253. — M. Feb. 10/17.
10 C. Cudlip, Archibald. 20819. — M. Feb. 10/17.
10 C. Higgins. W. J. 13879. — M. Feb. 10/17.
10 C. X Milford, J. 14616. — M. Feb. 10/17.
10 C. Robinson, J. 13744. — W. and M. Feb. 10/17.
10 D. XV King, Wm. 21523. — W. and M. April 24-25/17.
10 D. XIV Morrish, J. 15668. — M. April 24/17.
10 D. Simmons, Frank. 12072. — M. April 24-25/17.
10 D. Smith, C. 11705. — M. April 24-25/17.
10 D. XVI Woolway, C. W. 25862. — M. April 24-25/17.
10 D. XVI Youles, C. 43366. — M. April 24-25/17.
10 ? Bagwell, Cpl. C. 13958. — M. April 24-25/17.
10 ? Bird, Cpl. W. E. 11809. — K. April 24/17. Det.D./B.
10 ? Bullen, A. 12860. — M. Feb. 10/17.
10 ? Chaplin, J. 11911. — M. April 24-25/17.
10 ? Chapman, J. W. 15065. — M. April 24-25/17.
10 ? Clifford, T. 15187. — M. April 24-25/17.
10 ? Cook, W. H. 20970. — M. Feb. 10/17.
10 ? Dening, Cpl. W. 13561. — M. April 24-25/17.
10 ? Edwards, A. H. 13594. — M. April 24-25/17.
10 ? Ellis, J. S. 15189. — M. April 24-25/17.
10 ? Evans, A. A. 8169. — M. Feb. 10/17.
10 ? Farrant, A. J. 11563. — M. April 24-25/17.
10 ? Geen, W. H. 13983. — M. Feb. 10/17.
10 ? Glenister, Cpl. J. 13210. — M. April 24-25/17.

**Devonshire Regiment—contd.**

## *BALKANS.*

10 ? Goodman, C. 13448. M. April 24-25/17.
10 ? Greenwood, F. 13306. M. April 24-25/17.
10 ? Gregory, B. H. 55783. M. April 24-25/17.
10 ? Hampson, T. 20893. M. April 24-25/17.
10 ? Hayes, E. 11743. M. April 24-25/17.
'10 ? Haynes, A. R. 14988. M. April 24-25/17.
10 ? Holman, G. J. 12029. M. April 24-25/17.
10 ? Jennings, Frank. 17783. D/W. April 26/17. Det.D./B.
10 ? Johnson, E. 16727. M. April 24-25/17.
10 ? Johnstone, D. L. 20788. M. April 24-25/17.
10 ? Kable, A. 13466. M. April 24-25/17.
10 ? King, J. H. 17803. M. April 24-25/17.
10 ? Lang, T. H. 11902. M. April 24-25/17.
10 ? Matthews, W. A. 13788. M. April 24-25/17.
10 ? Monk, W. J. 18557. M. April 24-25/17.
10 ? Mutters, F. 26059. M. April 24-25/17.
10 ? Partridge, F. F. 55789. M. April 24-25/17.
10 ? Rowcliffe, J. 17829. M. Feb. 10/17.
10 ? Ruckley, W. 13742. M. Feb. 10/17.
10 ? Sargant, L.-Sergt. F. A. 13657. M. April 24/17.
10 ? Stapleton, W. 25912. M. April 24-25/17.
10 ? Tomlin, G. J. H. 13159. M. April 24-25/17.
10 ? Turner, R. 13768. M. Feb. 10/17.
10 ? Weekes, J. T. 15230. M. April 24-25/17.
10 ? Wilcox, F. 13546. M. April 24-25/17.
10 ? Williams, G. 14904. M. April 24-25/17.

## *E.E.F.*

1 Garr. ? Hill, Geo. Wm. 59186. M., bel. drowned April 15/17.

## *PERSIAN GULF.*

4 **Woollcombe, Major John North.** K. Feb. 3/17. Det.D./B.
4 B. Gollop, Cpl. J. 2379. M. Feb. 3/17.
4 B. Rowland, W. 2165. W. and M. Feb. 3/17.
4 ? Sellars, W. G. 5690. W. and M. Feb. 3/17.
6 B. Brown, H. H. 1423. (Fr. 4th.) W. and M. Mar. 8/16. R/Enq.
6 ? Shaddick, Wm. W. 3356. W. and M. Mar. 8/16. R/Enq.

# DORSETSHIRE REGIMENT.

## *B.E.F.*

1 A. Symes, T. H. 17585. M. April 5/17.
1 C. IX Adlam, Frank Hart. 22253. M. April 15/17.
‡1 C. Cook, A. C. 22189. W. and M. April 14/17.
*1 C. XI Haycox, Bert. 8168. W. and M. April 15/17.
*1 C. IX Stevens, A. 17345. W. and M. April 14/17.
1 C. XI Trevett, S. F. 17341. M. April 14/17.
1 D. XVI Judd, Ernest Fredk. 22208. M. April 15/17.
1 D. Pearce, F. G. 17333. M. April 14/17.
*5 A. Featherstone, Cpl. Ernest Victor. 13876. M. Sept. 26/16. R/Enq.

**Dorsetshire Regiment—contd.**

## *B.E.F.*

| | | |
|---|---|---|
| 5 A. | Lidiard, W. G. 19450. | K. Jan. 11/17. Det.D./B. |
| *5 B. | Fosh, J. W. 14606. | M. Sept. 26/16. R/Enq. |
| 5 B. or D. | Furness, L.-Cpl. C. E. 9751. | M. Jan. 11/17. |
| 5 B. | Stanley, Samuel. 18085. | M. Jan. 11/17. |
| 5 C. | Burnett, L.-Cpl. George A. 13121. | M. Jan. 11/17. |
| 5 D. XIII | Griffin, Charles. 19254. | M. Jan. 11/17. |
| 5 D. | Masters, William. 19260. | M. Jan. 11/17. |
| 5 D. | Newcombe, E. 19280. | M. Jan. 11/17. |
| 5 D. | Rayson, W. A. 3/7715. | K. Sept. 26/16. Det.D./B. R/Enq. |
| 6 | **Goodman, 2nd Lieut. E. G.** | M., bel. K. (W.O.L. April 23/17). |
| ‡6 A. M.G.S. | Blinkhorn, L.-Cpl. J. 8906. | M. May 16/17. |
| 6 A. | Cash, H. 18453. | M. May 16/17. |
| 6 A. | Collis, J. L. 27183. | M. May 16/17. |
| ‡6 A. | Foxwell, F. B. 18414. | W. and M. May 11/17. |
| 6 A. or D. L.G.S. | Jones, A. 13236. | M. May 16/17. |
| ‡6 X. | Joyce, M. 15895. | W. and M. April 23/17. |
| *6 A. | Kennard, C. G. 10219. | M. May 16/17. |
| ‡6 A. | Kingdon, G. H. 13229. | M. May 16/17. |
| ‡6 A. | Roper, W. H. 27111. | M. May 16/17. |
| ‡6 A. | Sergent, W. H. 17179. | M. May 16/17. |
| ‡6 A. | Smith, G. 18925. | M. May 16/17. |
| ‡6 A. | Tucker, Thos. 19579. | M. May 16/17. |
| 6 B. VII | Brimblecombe, John. 22143. | W. and M. April 23/17. |
| ‡6 B. | Evans, W. J. 22168. | W. and M. April 25/17. |
| 6 B. | Lee, T. 14553. | M. April 23/17. |
| 6 B. | Mills, J. E. 22172. | M. April 23/17. |
| ‡6 B. | Ridout, R. H. 19555. | W. and M. May 15/17. |
| 6 C. | Briers, Sergt. J. 5833. | M. April 12/17. |
| 6 C. XII | Goldring, L.-Cpl. Fredk. Wm. 17421. | W. and M. April 22/17. |
| 6 D. XV | Conquest, J. W. 10529. | M. May 15/17. |
| ‡6 D. | Cribb, W. M. 10914. | M. May 16/17. |
| ‡6 D. | Dore, W. T. 10696. | M. May 16/17. |
| ‡6 D. | Watkins, Sergt. J. 10203. | W. and M. May 15/17. |
| 6 D. | White, G. 18869. | W. and M. April 12/17. |
| 6 ? | Foster, H. 9214. | M. Dec. 26/16. |
| *6 ? | Mathews, S/B. W. S. 11778. | W. and M. May 15/17. |

## *PERSIAN GULF.*

| | | |
|---|---|---|
| 2 | **Griffith, Lieut. Alex. J. W.** | W. and M. March 25/17. |
| 2 | **Thomson, M.C., Capt. W. B.** | M. March 25/17. |
| 2 | **Weldon, Major A. S. (Fr. N. Staffs.)** | K. March 25/17. Det.D./B. |
| 2 E. II | Mills, Ernest Hry. 16412. | W. and M. March 25/17. |
| 2 E. | Plummer, L.-Cpl. E. 16038. | M. Mar. 25/17. |
| 2 E. | Ryall, L.-Cpl. E. 16548. | M. Mar. 25/17. |
| 2 E. | Wrench, Cpl. Rupert Sydney. 24184. | W. and M. Mar. 25/17. |
| 2 F. | Baker, L.-Cpl. Reginald Wm. 17587. | W. and M. Mar. 25/17. |
| 2 F. | Edmonds, A. G. 8779. | W. and M. Mar. 25/17. |
| 2 F. | Gale, A. J. B. 17665. | W. and M. Mar. 25/17. |
| 2 F. | Lane, J. C. 16262. | M. Mar. 25/17. |
| 2 F. V | Lawrence, J. 15156. | W. and M. Mar. 25/17. |
| *2 F. | Livermore, Fredk. I. 12669. | W. and M. Mar. 25/17. |
| 2 F. | Luscombe, T. 14195. | M. Mar. 25/17. |
| 2 F. | Mayo, Harold. 18807. | W. and M. Mar. 25/17. |
| 2 F. | Read, Wm. 16731. | M. Mar. 25/17. |
| 2 F. | Tucker, Fredk. Geo. 17568. | M. Mar. 25/17. |
| 2 G. M.G.S. | Biss, L.-Cpl. Jesse. 15507. | W. and M. March 25/17. |
| 2 G. | Foxwell, Harry. 15992. | W. and M. Mar. 25/17. |

**Dorsetshire Regiment—contd.**

## *PERSIAN GULF.*

2 G. Harrison, Richard M. 24282. W. and M. Mar. 25/17.
2 G. Jackson, Fredk. Geo. 15374. M. Mar. 25/17.
2 G. Jackson, Geo. 14940. W. and M. Mar. 25/17.
2 G. Johnson, H. 8873. M. March 25/17.
2 G. Stanley, C.S.-M. 15922. M. March 25/17.
2 G. Tizzard, A. T. 16384. M. Mar. 25/17.
2 G. Trowbridge, W. G. 16673. M. Mar. 25/17.
2 G. Wilson, R. L. 9058. W. and M. Mar. 25/17.
2 H. Dawe, P. G. 9296. M. Mar. 25/17.
2 H. Frampton, B. 16313. M. Mar. 25/17.
2 H. Hall, Walter Henry. 8739. M. Mar. 25/17.
2 H. XV Hannaford, L.-Cpl. J. S. 14193. W. and M. Mar. 25/17.
2 H. Loader, T. F. 17758. M. Mar. 25/17.
2 H. Miller, G. J. 16293. M. Mar. 25/17.
2 H. New, T. 17738. W. and M. Mar. 25/17.
2 H. Snell, Cpl. Jack. 14214. M. Mar. 25/17.
2 H. Stamp, W. 24197. M. March 25/17.
2 H. Walker, R. W. 24294. M. Mar. 25/17.
2 ? Adams, T. 16409. W. and M. Mar. 25/17.
2 ? Arthurs, J. O. 16941. M. Mar. 25/17.
2 ? Bennett, S. 24270. W. and M. Mar. 25/17.
2 ? Beale, S. 15239. M. Mar. 25/17.
2 ? Biddlecombe, A. W. W. 16250. M. Mar. 25/17.
2 ? Blank, H. M. 24185. W. and M. Mar. 25/17.
2 ? Chainey, J. 16907. M. Mar. 25/17.
2 ? Crabb, W. V. 9001. W. and M. Mar. 25/17.
2 ? Credland, G. 14905. M. Mar. 25/17.
2 ? Donaldson, J. A. 16493. W. and M. Mar. 25/17.
2 ? Drake, C. H. 15381. M. Mar. 25/17.
2 ? Elliott, J. W. 14102. M. Mar. 25/17.
2 ? Endacott, L.-Cpl. R. H. F. 14188. W. and M. Mar. 25/17.
2 ? Farmer, J. 15950. W. and M. Mar. 25/17.
2 ? Fidler, H. 16484. W. and M. Mar. 25/17.
2 ? Follett, B. 16549. W. and M. Mar. 25/17.
2 ? Fosell, H. 15992. W. and M. Mar. 25/17.
2 ? Fowles, A. 7359. M. Mar. 23/17.
2 ? Gifford, W. R. 17848. M. Mar. 25/17.
2 ? Gooding, T. 16014. M. Mar. 25/17.
2 ? Hallett, C. G. J. 15158. M. Mar. 25/17.
2 ? Hartley, E. 16496. W. and M. Mar. 25/17.
2 ? Hayward, W. F. 10755. M. Mar. 25/17.
2 ? Holloway, E. 18815. W. and M. Mar. 25/17.
2 ? Hooten, H. 24326. M. Mar. 25/17.
2 ? Impey, C. 14263. W. and M. Mar. 25/17.
2 ? Jeffrey, C. P. 14988. W. and M. Mar. 25/17.
2 ? Kirby, A. 9230. W. and M. Mar. 25/17.
2 ? Langworthy, J. 24193. M. Mar. 25/17.
2 ? Lazarus, L.-Cpl. F. 15914. M. Mar. 25/17.
2 ? Leggett, W. 8610. W. and M. Mar. 25/17.
2 ? M.G.S. Livings, S. C. 14316. M. March 25/17.
2 ? Long, Sergt. W. H. 14861. M. Mar. 25/17.
2 ? Luscombe, T. 14195. M. Mar. 25/17.
2 ? Peaty, R. 8581. M. Mar. 25/17.
2 ? Richard, W. 17530. W. and M. Mar. 25/17.
2 ? Rodgers, R. J. 24249. W. and M. Mar. 25/17.
2 ? Sartin, T. J. R. E. 9208. M. Mar. 25/17.
2 ? Sawford, F. C. 9012. M. Mar. 25/17.
2 ? Sawyer, W. T. 14162. M. Mar. 25/17.
2 ? Tucker, O. E. 13357. (Fr. R.G.A.) D/Dis. April 26/16. Det.D./B.

**Dorsetshire Regiment—contd.**

## *PERSIAN GULF.*

| | | |
|---|---|---|
| 2 ? | Wareham. 17618. | W. and M. **Mar. 25/17.** |
| 2 ? | Wayborne, J. 8959. | W. and M. **Mar. 25/17.** |
| 2 ? | Webb, W. S. 14111. | M. **Mar. 25/17.** |
| 2 ? | White, A. 16317. | M. **Mar. 25/17.** |
| 2 ? | Whitehead, W. 24291. | W. and M. **Mar. 25/17.** |
| 2 ? | Whittle, W. 16765. | W. and M. **Mar. 25/17.** |
| 2 ? | Wilde, L.-Cpl. S. T. 17361. | M. **March 25/17.** |
| 4 Sig. S. | King, Wm. Henry. 3066. | M. **Feb. 2/17.** |

## DORSETSHIRE YEOMANRY.

## *BALKANS.*

| | | |
|---|---|---|
| 3 Squad. | Herity, P. 1793. | M. **Oct. 1/16.** |

## DRAGOON GUARDS.

## *B.E.F.*

| | | |
|---|---|---|
| 3 | **Dulson, 2nd Lieut. H. M.** | W. and M. **April 11/17.** |
| 3 ? | Burnett, H. D. 1949. | M. **April 12/17.** |
| ‡3 ? | Talby, Arthur. 2647. | Unoff. M. **July 1/16.** R/Enq. |
| ‡6 ? | Bailey, J. 5256. | M. **May 18/17.** |
| ‡6 ? | Killer, L.-Cpl. E. 5405. | M. **May 18/17.** |
| ‡6 ? | Sanderson, D. 4623. | M. **May 18/17.** |

## ROYAL DUBLIN FUSILIERS.

## *B.E.F.*

| | | |
|---|---|---|
| 1 W. | Anderson, Thomas. 20134. | W. and M. **April 24/17.** |
| 1 W. | Campbell, F. 9741. | M. **Feb. 28—Mar. 1/17.** |
| 1 W. | McCabe, Cpl. Jas. Patrick. 11342. | M. **Feb. 28—March 1/17.** |
| 1 W. | McKenna, T. 23148. | W. and M. **Feb. 28—Mar. 1/17.** |
| 1 W. II | McMahon, Michael. 40124. | Unoff. W. and M. **March 31/17.** |
| 1 W. or X. | Mullen, Joseph. 24601. | M. **Feb. 28—Mar. 1/17.** |
| 1 W. | O'Keefe, A.-Sgt. W. 26955. | M. **April 16/17.** |
| 1 X. VI | Byrne, Christopher. 28109. | M. **April 24/17.** |
| *1 X. VII | Jarvis, E. 40413. | W. and M. **April 24/17.** |
| 1 X. | Kenny, J. 43122. | W. and M. **Feb. 28—Mar. 1/17.** |
| 1 X. V | Sharry, T. 40092. | M. **Feb. 28/17.** |
| 1 X. | Upton, Wm. Thos. 40383. (40218.) | M. **April 24/17.** |
| 1 Y. | Burke, Wm. 40061. | W. and M. **Feb. 28—Mar. 1/17.** |
| 1 Y. | Cooper, Walter John. 40400. | M. **April 24/17.** |

**Dublin Fusiliers, Royal—contd.**

## *B.E.F.*

| | | |
|---|---|---|
| 1 Y. | Finnegan, T. 13488. | W. and M. Feb. 28—Mar. 1/17. |
| 1 Y. XI | Harris, Sidney Raymond. 40412. | M. April 24/17. |
| 1 Y. XI | Humphreys, Wm. 40083. | M. April 24/17. |
| 1 Y. | Janes, S/B. Wm. Henry. 14331. | W. and M. Feb. 28—March 1/17. |
| 1 Y. XI | Lambert, F. O. 40414. | M. April 24/17. |
| ‡1 Y. | McBride, J. 27685. | W. and M. April 24/17. |
| 1 Y. I.T.M. | Murphy, Owen. 20189. (86 Bgde.) | W. and M. Feb. 28—March 1/17. |
| 1 Z. | Callon, F. 40361. | M. April 24/17. |
| 1 Z. XIV | Cantwell, Wm. 40074. | M. Feb. 28—Mar. 1/17. |
| 1 Z. | Edwards, Ralph Alex. 40372. (Late 2 Suffolks, 36208.) | M. April 24/17. |
| ‡1 Z. | Flanagan, T. 21651. | M. April 24/17. |
| 1 Z. | Kearney, P. 8851. | M. April 24/17. |
| ‡1 Z. | Larkin, T. 27770. | W. and M. April 24/17. |
| 1 Z. | O'Keefe, J. 40305. | M. April 24/17. |
| *2 A. or C. | Coleman, Mark. 25062. | M. Oct. 23/16. R/Enq. |
| 2 A. | Sproule, Cpl. W. 43055. (Fr. 2 Irish Regt., 9684.) | M. Oct. 23/16. R./Enq. |
| ‡2 A. | White, W. 43206. | M. May 27/17. |
| ‡2 B. V | Cox, L.-Cpl. Edw. 27509. | M. May 27/17. |
| ‡2 B. | Donoghue, L.-Cpl. M. 40036. | M. May 3/17. |
| 2 C. or D. | Foley, Daniel. 21420. | W. and M. Oct. 23/16. R/Enq. |
| ‡2 C. | Jenkins, T. 14996. | M. May 27/17. |
| 2 C. | Molloy, J. B. 20590. | K. Oct. 23/16. Det.D./B. R/Enq. |
| ‡2 C. | Murphy, P. 27521. | M. May 27/17. |
| ‡2 C. | Punter, H. 25823. | M. May 27/17. |
| ‡2 D. | McGlynn, John D. 20009. | M. May 3/17. |
| ‡8 A. | Fleming, L.-Cpl. Thos. 19944. | K. Sept. 6/16. Det.D./B. |
| *8 C. | Davis, J. 21369. | W. and M. Sept. 9/16. R/Enq. |
| 8 C. | Markey, J. 21373. | M. Sept. 9/16. R/Enq. |
| 8 C. | O'Rourke, John J. 23289. | M. Sept. 9/16. R/Enq. |
| 8 D. XIII | Hartford, J. 24749. | M. Sept. 9/16. R/Enq. |
| 9 A. | Davies, Thomas. 14255. | M. Sept. 7/16. R/Enq. |
| 9 C. | Byrne, L.-Cpl. Jas. 23331. | K. Sept. 9/16. Det.D./B. R/Enq. |
| 10 A. | Murphy, P. J. 26832. | M. Feb. 26/17. |
| 10 A. I | Fennell, Henry. 43436. (Trans. S.) | M. April 22/17. |
| 10 B. | Flanagan, John. 26907. | M. April 15/17. |
| ‡10 B. | McDonnel, M. 25604. | W. and M. April 23/17. |
| 10 C. | Byrne, J. 27534. | M. April 15/17. |
| 10 C. | Holman, E. R. 6208. (Fr. 13 Lond.) | M. Feb. 2/17. |
| 10 C. L.G.S. | Shekleton, Cpl. H. A. 26166. | K. April 15/17. Det.D./B. |
| 10 D. | Bartrup, A. 43456. | M. April 28/17. |
| 10 D. | Carter, J. J. 40325. | M. April 28/17. |
| 10 D. XV | Gallagher, Sgt. Geo. M. 17393. | M. April 28/17. |
| 10 D. | Leath, J. 26607. | M. April 28/17. |
| 10 D. XIII | Nicholson, J. J. 43345. | M. April 28/17. |
| 10 D. | Nixon, F. 40336. | M. April 28/17. |
| 10 D. | Solomons, A. 43440. | M. April 28/17. |
| 10 ? | Franklin, Sergt. Thos. Jas. 9313. | W. and M. April 15/17. |

## *BALKANS.*

| | | |
|---|---|---|
| 6 B. V | Hanley, Michael. 23124. | K. Feb. 27/17. Det.D./B. |
| 6 ? | Brady, M. 17186. | W. and M. Oct. 3/16. |
| 6 ? | Keaveney, F. 22038. | W. and M. April 24-25/17. |
| 6 ? | Minton, T. 10035. (Fr. 1st.) | M. Oct. 3/16. |
| *7 D. | Harris, James. 28483. | M. June 1/17. |
| 7 ? | Hemsley. 6272. (Fr. 2 W. Kents.) | W. and M. Sept. 23/16. |

## DUKE OF CORNWALL'S LIGHT INFANTRY.

### B.E.F.

| | | | |
|---|---|---|---|
| 1 | | **Tremellan, 2nd Lieut. D. H.** | W. and M. April 23/17. |
| ‡1 | A. | Bugler, G. E. 27814. | M. April 23/17. |
| ‡1 | A. | Jones, W. 12004. | W. and M. April 23/17. |
| 1 | A. | King, H. W. 10655. | M. April 23/17. |
| 1 | B. | Blaby, J. 26607. | M. April 23/17. |
| *1 | B. VI | Brown, F. J. 34698. | K. May 8/17. Det.D./B. |
| 1 | B. | Butcher, Cpl. A. 12033. | M. April 23/17. |
| 1 | B. | Chapman, John. 24474. | M. April 23/17. |
| 1 | B. VI | Coleman, Herbert Richd. 29168. | M. April 23/17. |
| ‡1 | B. | Dryden, R. 11498. | M. April 23/17. |
| 1 | B. | Forsey, A. H. 31698. | M. April 23/17. |
| 1 | B. VI | Hankins, H. G. 27681. | M. April 23/17. |
| 1 | B. VII | Kelly, Edw. 22166. | M. April 23/17. |
| 1 | B. | Nicholas, L.-Cpl. C. H. 16166. | M. April 23/17. |
| 1 | B. | Parsons, C. 31773. | M. April 23/17. |
| 1 | B. | Pettitt, A.-Cpl. C. 7013. | M. April 23/17. |
| 1 | B. | Waters, Sgt. Fred. 9081. | M. April 23/17. |
| 1 | B. | Woodrow, F. 31832. | M. April 23/17. |
| 1 | C. XII | Beard, L.-Cpl. David. 26329. | M. April 23/17. |
| 1 | C. | Burden, R. J. 31656. | M. April 23/17. |
| 1 | C. | Buxton, C. 27762. | M. April 23/17. |
| 1 | C. | Chenoweth, S. J. 33951. | M. April 23/17. |
| 1 | C. | Colenso, C. H. 24435. | M. April 23/17. |
| 1 | C. X | Collins, E. J. 16896. | M. April 23/17. |
| 1 | C. | Crook, John. 27272. (Co. H.Q.) | M. April 23/17. |
| 1 | C. | Eales, W. F. 34031. | M. April 23/17. |
| 1 | C. | Hambly, W. H. 28513. | M. April 23/17. |
| 1 | C. | Hocking, A. A. 16574. | M. April 23/17. |
| 1 | C. | Jolley, S. P. 33822. | M. April 23/17. |
| 1 | C. | Kempton, Arthur. 28441. | M. April 23/17. |
| 1 | C. | Locke, Cpl. H. C. 10121. | M. April 23/17. |
| 1 | C. X | Mennear, Thos. H. 29172. | M. April 23/17. |
| 1 | C. | Morgan, L.-Cpl. Herbert. 24156. | K. April 23/17. Det.D./B. |
| 1 | C. X | Powell, William. 28444. | M. April 23/17. |
| 1 | C. IX | Treverrow. 12895. | M. April 23/17. |
| 1 | C. XIII | Wenborn, Alfred Wm. 17235. | M. April 23/17. |
| 1 | C. XI | Wilkes, J. M. 6029. | M. April 23/17. |
| ‡1 | D. | Bullock, J. 31651. | M. May 8/17. |
| ‡1 | D. | Creech, W. J. R. 27845. | M. May 8/17. |
| *1 | D. XV | Gates, G. W. 27136. | M. Unoff. K. May 8/17. |
| 1 | D. XIV | Lamb, Geo. 5860. | M. April 23/17. |
| 1 | H.Q. | Herbert, A. 5332. | M. Sept. 5/16. R/Enq. |
| 6 | C. IX | Merson, L.-Cpl. Clifford. 27740. | K. Sept. 16/16. Det.D./B. |
| ‡6 | C. | Prior, T. H. 28698. | W. and M. Sept. 16/16. R/Enq. |
| ‡6 | C. | Sanders, H. J. 19853. | M. Sept. 16/16. |
| 6 | C. | Sly, Philip Henry. 27512. | M. Sept. 16/16. |
| 7 | A. | Buscombe, P. 16169. | W. and M. Oct. 7/16. |
| 7 | D. | Kelly, Maurice. 23586. | M. Feb. 18/17. |
| 10 | | **Lockyer, 2nd Lieut. F. C. (Fr. 8th Devon.)** | M. Feb. 12/17. |

**Duke of Cornwall's Light Infantry—contd.**

## *BALKANS.*

| | | |
|---|---|---|
| 2 A. | Boyden, W. A. 17668. | W. and M. **Nov. 17/16.** |
| 2 B. | Daniels, C. H. 5368. | W. and M. **Nov. 17/16.** |
| 2 D. | Edmunds, Percy F. 20487. | W. and M. **Nov. 17/16.** |
| 2 D. | Legg, A.-Sergt. Chas. Russell. 20407. | W. and M. **Nov. 17/16.** |
| 2 ? | Cooper, J. W. 9632. | W. and M. **Nov. 17/16.** |
| 2 ? | Cottell, W. J. 24497. | W. and M. **Nov. 17/16.** |
| 2 ? | Tregunna, F. 17616. | W. and M. **Nov. 17/16.** |
| *8 A. | Magor, Harry. 16069. | W. and M. **April 25/17.** |
| 8 A. M.G.S. | Williams, W. H. 16242. | M. **April 25/17.** |
| *8 B. VIII | Cottom, Wm. Henry. 22514. | M. **June 7/17.** |
| 8 C. | Rayment, George. 15152. | M. **April 25/17.** |
| 8 C. X | Sloan, J. Wm. N. 34590. | M. **April 25/17.** |
| 8 C. | Tyler, L.-Cpl. Richard Geo. 35609. (Fr. R. Irish Fus.) | M. **April 24-25/17.** |
| 8 C. M.G.S. | Williams, Albert L. 15937. | M. **April 25/17.** |
| 8 ? | Eagles, L.-Cpl. S. 22095. | M. **April 25/17.** |
| 8 ? | Fox, H. 18180. | M. **April 25/17.** |
| ‡8 ? | Goldsworthy, M. 16897. | W. and M. **April 25/17.** |
| ‡8 ? | Knight, J. T. 16235. | W. and M. **June 7/17.** |
| 8 ? | Munt, E. 23719. | M. **April 25/17.** |
| ‡8 ? | Short, C. 16318. | M. **June 7/17.** |
| 8 ? | Sly, P. H. 27512. | M. **April 25/17.** |
| ‡8 ? | Wheatley, J. 16413. | W. and M. **June 7/17.** |

## DURHAM LIGHT INFANTRY.

## *B.E.F.*

| | | |
|---|---|---|
| 2 | **Wilson, Capt. F. G.** | K. **May 1/17.** Det.D./B. |
| 2 B. | Bryden, W. 43112. | M. **April 4/17.** |
| *2 B. VIII | Dennison, H. 27997. | M. **Oct. 15/16.** R/Enq. |
| 2 B. | Faulkner, W. 26778. | M. **April 9/17.** |
| 2 B. | Parkes, J. 9023. | M. **April 9/17.** |
| 2 B. | Shrimpton, L.-Sergt. George. 10978. | W. and M. **Oct. 15/16.** R./Enq. |
| ‡2 C. | Hodgson, A. H. 38425. | M. **May 16/17.** |
| 2 C. | Raine, Arthur. 43137. | M. **April 9/17.** |
| 2 C. XI | Taylor, L.-Cpl. Robt. 32995. | M., bel. K. **April 9/17.** |
| 2 C. | Walker, C. 32760. | M. **April 9/17.** |
| ‡2 D. | Reid, A. 31751. | M. **May 16/17.** |
| 2 D. | Tait, John G. 38899. | W. and M. **May 17/17.** |
| 2 D. XIV | Watson, John. 36733. | W. and M. **April 9/17.** |
| 5 A. | Birch, W. J. 200838. | M. **April 23/17.** |
| 5 A. | Eadington, T. 200556. | M. **April 23/17.** |
| 5 A. | Elliott, Thos. H. 295045. | M. **April 23/17.** |
| 5 A. | Gillespie, M. 295046. | M. **April 23/17.** |
| 5 A. | Griffin, T. 200614. | M. **April 23/17.** |
| 5 A. | Hewgill, H. B. 260873. | M. **April 23/17.** |
| 5 A. | Hutchinson, T. 201079. | M. **April 23/17.** |
| 5 A. III | Jago, George. 200665. (5494.) | W. and M. **April 24/17.** |
| 5 A. IV | Linton, John. 295049. | M. **April 23/17.** |
| 5 A. IV | McAdam, John. 270132. | M. **April 23/17.** |
| 5 A. | McKenzie, A. W. 201086. | M. **April 23/17.** |
| 5 A. | Porter, R. W. 200954. | M. **April 23/17.** |
| 5 A. | Potter, J. 201003. | M. **April 23/17.** |

**Durham Light Infantry—contd.**

## *B.E.F.*

| | | |
|---|---|---|
| 5 A. | Robinson, R. 200133. | M. April 23/17. |
| 5 A. | Robson, Cpl. J. G. 200238. | M. April 23/17. |
| 5 A. II | Sharp, Thos. 200892. (8799.) | M. April 23/17. |
| 5 A. | Simpson, A. 200733. | M. April 23/17. |
| 5 A. | Swan, Cpl. J. 204484. (4026.) | M. April 23/17. |
| 5 A. | Williams, J. B. 200402. | M. April 23/17. |
| 5 A. | Wood, S. 204485. (8739.) | M. April 23/17. |
| 5 B. or D. | Bowman, Rybt. 200862. (8527.) | W. and M. April 23/17. |
| 5 B. | Gray, W. 200466. | M. April 23/17. |
| 5 B. VI | Inkersole, Joseph Wm. 200962. | W. and M. April 23/17. |
| 5 B. | Sterling, William. 200848. (8361.) | M. April 23/17. |
| 5 C. | Glancy, Cpl. O. 200305. | M. April 23/17. |
| 5 C. | Wood, C. 200480. | M. April 23/17. |
| 5 D. | Boynton, F. W. 200694. | M. April 23/17. |
| 5 D. | Bryan, W. 248015. | M. April 23/17. |
| 5 D. | Cahn, H. 201146. | M. April 23/17. |
| 5 D. | Clarke, R. 200768. | M. April 23/17. |
| 5 D. | Dendy, J. H. 201149. | M. April 23/17. |
| 5 D. XIII | Ferguson, Walter Stokell. 4409. | W. and M. Sept. 15/16. R./Enq. |
| 5 D. | Hall, J. 273030. | M. April 23/17. |
| 5 D. | Horswill, R. 200766. | M. April 23/17. |
| 5 D. XIII | Langston, Joseph. 200167. | M. April 23/17. |
| 5 D. | Moore, F. T. 248034. | M. April 23/17. |
| 5 D. XIII | Mould, Cpl. Fairless. 200175. | M. April 23/17. |
| 5 D. XIII | Overfield, Thos. 200479. (3609.) | M. April 23/17. |
| ‡5 D. | Peacock, W. 200528. | W. and M. April 23/17. |
| 5 D. XIV | Pickering, Alf. Jas. 270150. | M. April 23/17. |
| 5 D. | Reed, R. H. 200958. | M. April 23/17. |
| 5 D. | Reynolds, H. E. 251093. | M. April 23/17. |
| 5 D. | Rowe, B. 200957. | M. April 23/17. |
| *5 D. XIV | Smith, Arthur. 200756. | Unoff. M. April 23/17. |
| 5 D. | Smith, J. F. 200079. | M. April 23/17. |
| 5 D. | Uphill, S. 201144. | M. April 23/17. |
| 5 D. | Wilkinson, T. H. 200410. | M. April 23/17. |
| 5 D. XIV | Wilson, Edw. 201131. (6151.) | M. April 23/17. |
| *5 ? | Vart, Harold. 6229. (Fr. 5th D.L.I., 32169.) | K. Nov. 7/16. Det.D./B. |
| 6 | **Greener, Lieut. H.** | K. April 14/17. Det.D./B. |
| 6 W. II | Broadbelt, Wm. 5832. | M. Jan. 12/17. |
| 6 W. III | Curtis, Albert Edward. 250649. | M. April 14/17. |
| 6 W. L.G.S. | Jackson, Robt. 250274. (2818.) | M. April 14/17. |
| 6 W. II | Little, Albert. 251034. (6167.) | M. April 14/17. |
| 6 W. II | Little, A. J. 4280. | M. April 14/17. |
| 6 W. | McPartlin, Peter. 251025. (6158.) | M. April 14/17. |
| 6 W. | Sleight, G. 273092. | W. and M. April 14/17. |
| 6 W. | Thorogood, G. 7196. | M. Oct. 1/16. |
| 6 X. or Y. | Barker, Norman. 2077. | W. and M. Nov. 5/16. R/Enq. |
| 6 X. VII | Copeman, Frederick. 251635. (5636.) | W. and M., Unoff. K. April 14/17. Conf. and Det.D./B. |
| 6 X. | Cotton, Alfred Geo. 273085. | M. April 14/17. |
| 6 X. | Owen, A. 251539. | W. and M. April 14/17. |
| 6 X. | Reveley, T. W. 5695. | M. Nov. 5/16. R/Enq. |
| 6 Y. XI | Ainsley, Sig. R. R. 6125. | M. Nov. 5/16. R/Enq. |
| 6 Y. | Butterworth, W. H. 251102. | W. and M. April 14/17. |
| 6 Y. | Campion, George. 5546. (Late 5th, No. 1386.) | M. Nov. 5/16. R./Enq. |

**Durham Light Infantry—contd.**

## *B.E.F.*

‡6 Y. IX Edmed, L.-Cpl. Walter S. 204476. (8500.) W. and M. **April 14/17.**
‡6 Y. Gringham, O. 250895. M. **Oct. 1/16.**
6 Y. Henderson, E. J. 251006. M. **April 14/17.**
6 Y. Muir, J. 250564. M. **April 14/17.**
6 Y. Mulholland, J. 251079. M. **April 14/17.**
6 Y. Simpson, C. 250297. M. **April 14/17.**
6 Y. Webster, W. 251005. M. **April 14/17.**
‡6 Y. Wilkinson, Thos. 4759. M. **Nov. 5/16.** R/Enq.
6 Z. L.G.S. Chapman, T. 250585. (5535.) M. **April 14/17.**
6 Z. Corker, S. 273087. M. **April 14/17.**
6 Z. Edgar, R. 250982. (5973.) W. and M. **April 14/17.**
‡6 Z. Howarth, R. 250465. W. and M. **Oct. 1/16.**
6 Z. XVI Moore, John Geo. 3295. W. and M. **Oct. 1/16.** R/Enq.
*6 Z. XIV Smith, T. L. 5521. W. and M. **Nov. 5/16.** R/Enq.
6 Z. L.G.S. Wallace, R. W. 3974. K. **Oct. 1/16.** Det.D./B.
8 A. Atkinson, L. 6123. M. **Nov. 5/16.**
8 A. I Chaplin, F. 6533. M. **Nov. 5/16.** R/Enq.
*8 A. Illingworth, Charles Wilton. 6098. M. **Nov. 5/16.** R/Enq.
8 A. III Mitton, Harry Collingwood. 312139. (Late 6614.) W. and M. **Sept. 29/16.**
8 A. Pearson, Thomas. 2239 M. **Nov. 5/16.**
‡8 B. Kaye, Harold. 6138. K. **Nov. 5/16.** Det.D./B. R/Enq.
8 C. Forrest, S. 301902. M. **April 17/17.**
8 C. XII Gorrill, H. 301877. (6256.) M. **April 25/17.**
8 C. McPherson, L.-Cpl. J. 301064. M. **April 24/17.**
8 C. XII Sawyer, John. 6187. M. Unoff. K. **Nov. 5/16.** Conf. and Det. R/Enq.
8 D. XIII Benzie, H. E. 6194. M. **Nov. 5/16.** R/Enq.
8 D. Clarke, H. W. 6202. M. **Nov. 5/16.** R/Enq.
*8 D. Harrison, John. 300908. (3694.) M. **Nov. 5/16.** R/Enq.
‡8 D. Palmer, Thos. Chas. 6211. M. **Nov. 5/16.** R/Enq.
8 ? Robson, R. W. 6656. (Fr. 9, 5749.) M. **Sept. 29/16.** R/Enq.
9 A. Carlton, Geo. 7090. M. **Nov. 5/16.** R/Enq.
‡9 A. I Garbutt, Wm. 7259. (Late 28642, Yorks Regt.) M. **Nov. 5/16.** R/Enq.
‡9 B. VIII Lynn, Thos. 204473. (7139.) (Fr. 5.) M. **April 23/17.**
9 B. Platts, W. M. 201324. M. **April 23/17.**
9 B. VIII Stephens, Alex. 325951. M. **April 23/17.**
9 B. Taylor, A. 4087. (Fr. 5th.) M. Unoff. K. **Nov. 5/16.** R/Enq.
9 C. X Loch, Geo. 7013. K. **Nov. 5/16.** Det.D./B.
*9 C. X MacKinnon, Angus. 325838. (7486.) W. and M. **April 23/17.**
9 C. XI Mallett, Arthur Albert. 7055. M. **Nov. 5/16.**
‡9 C. Scott, Cpl. R. 325249. W. and M. **April 23/17.**
9 C. L.G.S. Tench, R. 5055. M. **Nov. 5/16.** R/Enq.
9 D. XV Thompson, Fredk. Walker. 7173. M. **Nov. 5/16.**
*9 D. Wilson, Stanley. 2493. M. **Sept. 15/16.** R/Enq.
‡10 A. Hutchison, Robt. 42723. M. **Sept. 16/16.** R/Enq.
10 A. O'Brien, Michael. 14538. M. **Sept. 16/16.** R/Enq.
10 B. VII Fenton, Geo. 11913. W. and M. **Sept. 16/16.** R/Enq.
10 B. Hodgson, G. W. 27691. W. and M. **Sept. 16/16.** R/Enq.
10 B. or D. Earl, Charles. 11892. W. and M. **Sept. 16/16.** R/Enq.
10 B. M.G.S. Linwood, A. 43351. M. **April 9/17.**
10 B. McPherson, Joseph. 20586. W. and M. **Sept. 16/16.** R/Enq.
*10 B. Simpson, Joseph. 31743. W. and M. **Sept. 16/16.** R/Enq.
10 D. Anthony, J. 24106. M. **Sept. 16/16.** R/Enq.
10 D. XIII Copeland, Robt. A. 37392. M. **April 9/17.**
10 D. XIII Elliott, Arthur. 31767. W. and M. **Sept. 16/16.** R/Enq.
10 D. Jewett, J. J. 26221. M. **April 9/17.**

**Durham Light Infantry—contd.**

## *B.E.F.*

‡12 A. IV Hunt, A. 42866. M. June 7/17.
‡12 A. II Marshall, John Wesley. 33075. W. and M. June 7/17.
‡12 A. II Morris, Jas. 270054. M. June 7/17.
‡12 A. I Thompson, L.-Cpl. Thos. Hy. 16470 M. June 7/17.
‡12 A. West, L.-Cpl. Wm. Arthur. 52684. M. June 7/17.
*12 B. VIII Bates, James A. 31710. M. May 17/17.
‡12 B. Bull, A. 54265. W. and M. June 7/17.
‡12 B. Herries, L.-Sergt. Chas. 18263. W. and M. June 7/17.
*12 B. Hooks, George. 36921. W. and M., bel. K. June 7/17.
*13 B. Dixon, David. 62. (Fr. 20 North. Fus.) M. Oct. 7/16. R/Enq.
13 B. V Lawson, Arthur. 21750. W. and M. Sept. 19/16. R/Enq.
‡12 B. VI Parry, Richard. 52659. W. and M. June 7/17.
‡12 B. V Reed, Albert Edw. 21460. M. June 7/17.
‡12 B. VII Stone, C. 43852. W. and M. June 7/17.
‡12 C. XI Batey, Daniel. 31794. M. June 7/17.
‡12 D. XIII Dukes, S. H. 54222. M. June 7/17.
‡13 A. Porritt, J. 43408. M. May 13/17.
‡13 B. VIII Loveridge, Elias Walter. 54273. M. June 11/17.
‡13 B. Watson, L.-Sergt. John Edw. 13632. Unoff. M. or K. June 10/17.
‡13 B. VIII Wright, Albert. 52923. M. June 11/17.
‡13 C. XI Jones, F. H. 52892. W. and M. June 9/17.
13 C. Wilson, William. 23291. W. and M. Oct. 7/16.
‡13 D. XIII Johnson, Robt. Wilson. 33264. M. June 12/17.
14 Macdonald, 2nd Lieut. R. H. C. K. Dec. 10/16. Det.D./B. R/Enq.
14 A. I Anderson, Peter. 53733. M. April 20-22/17.
14 A. Gill, W. 53412. W. and M. April 20-22/17.
14 A. I Hood, George Alfred. 39272. W. and M. April 20-22/17.
14 A. L.G.S. Jobes, Robt. W. 38900. M. April 20-22/17.
‡14 A. Longstaff, Thos. 39293. M. April 22/17.
14 A. I Piggin, L.-Cpl. R. A. 43081. M. April 20-22/17.
14 A. Rose, H. 39136. M. April 20-22/17.
14 A. Watson, F. 53746. M. April 20-22/17.
14 B. Bentley, R. 43667. M., bel. K. April 21/17.
14 B. Blenkinsopp, A. 30259. M. Oct. 12/16.
*14 B. VI Cable, Cpl. S. 4/6121. W. and M. April 20-22/17.
‡14 B. VI Dixon, Willie. 1584. (Fr. 18th.) W. and M. Sept. 18/16. R/Enq.
14 B. VI Oddy, Charles. 43200. W. and M. April 21/17.
‡14 B. Williams, J. 4/12410. W. and M. April 20-22/17.
14 C. Conner, William. 14751. M. Sept. 18/16. R/Enq.
‡14 C. McGregor, L.-Cpl. J. 53750. W. and M. April 20-22/17.
‡14 D. XIV Clark, Robert H. G. 26759. M. April 22/17.
14 D. Hall, D. 4/39098. M. April 20-22/17.
14 D. XIV Happs, Arthur James. 27900. M. April 20-22/17.
‡14 D. Jackson, Jos. 19659. M. Sept. 18/16. R/Enq.
14 D. Kelly, M. 4/39176. M. April 20-22/17.
14 D. Shannon, John. 45867. M. April 20-22/17.
*15 A. II Bridge, Stanley Geo. 63042. K. April 9-10/17. Det.D./B.
15 A. II Goodman, L.-Sergt. H. J. 53179. M. April 9-10/17.
*15 A. Whitehead, Cpl. J. A. 22165. M. May 3/17.
15 A. or C. XII Richardson, Edward. 201259. M. May 3/17.
‡15 B. VI Ashbridge, Thos. 45664. M. Sept. 18/16. R/Enq.
15 B. Burnett, A. E. 53436. K. April 10/17. Det.D./B.
15 B. H.Q. Scouts S. Martin, L.-Cpl. 53108. K. April 9/17. Det.D./B.
‡15 B. VIII Etherington, L.-Cpl. T. 1854. K. April 9-10/17. Det.D./B.
*15 C. IX Atkinson, Fred. 45674. M. Sept. 16/16. R/Enq.
*15 C. Coleman, Ernest. 28158. K. Sept. 16/16. Det.D./B.
15 C. XII Greener, Wm. 13696. M. Sept. 16/16. R/Enq.
15 C. Lumley, W. 39522. M. April 9-10/17.

**Durham Light Infantry**—contd.

## *B.E.F.*

| | | |
|---|---|---|
| 15 C. X | Nattrass, T. J. 201296. | W. and M. **May 3/17.** |
| *15 C. X | Richardson, John Thos. 45665. (Late 6th Bn., 3769.) | M. Unoff. W. **Sept. 16/17.** R/Enq. |
| 15 C. | Taylor, V. 53491. | M. **April 9/17.** |
| 15 D. XIII | Perryman, Thos. 28647. | M. **May 3/17.** |
| 15 D. | Phillips, F. 42469. | M. **Sept. 16/16.** R./Enq. |
| ‡15 D. XIII | Rothwell, Thos. Edw. 201372. | W. and M. **May 3/17.** |
| ‡15 D. | Summers, J. W. 53487. | M. **May 3/17.** |
| 15 D. | Wilton, L.-Cpl. J. 53502. | W. and M. **April 9-10/17.** |
| ‡18 A. | Dobson, R. 30299. | M. **May 18/17.** |
| ‡18 A. | Forster, J. E. 43452. | M. **May 18/17.** |
| ‡18 A. | Renney, W. 751. | M. **May 18/17.** |
| ‡18 A. | Robinson, A.-Sergt. W. 141. | M. **May 18/17.** |
| ‡18 A. | Short, E. 70119. | M. **May 18/17.** |
| ‡18 A. | Whaley, G. 25563. | M. **May 18/17.** |
| *18 B. VI | Bradley, G. 36819. | M. **May 18/17.** |
| ‡18 B. | Marshall, L.-Cpl. W. E. 324. | M. **May 3/17.** |
| ‡18 C. | Cameron, R. A. 38620. | M. **May 3/17.** |
| ‡18 C. | Douglas, W. 36480. | W. and M. **May 3/17.** |
| 18 C. X | Harrison, Peter Mec. 36213. | M. **May 3/17.** |
| 18 C. XII | Middleton, A. 35860. | M. **May 18/17.** |
| 18 C. IX | Nicholson, J. 38469. | M. **May 3/17.** |
| ‡18 C. | Taylor, W. 625. | W. and M. **May 3/17.** |
| ‡18 ? | Bennett, W. 35817. | W. and M. **May 18/17.** |
| ‡18 ? | Marshall, S. 31655. | W. and M. **May 18/17.** |
| *18 ? | Morris, Chas. 554. | M. **May 18/17.** |
| ‡18 ? | Rodin, K. 38447. | W. and M. **May 18/17.** |
| 19 | **Blenkinsop, 2nd Lt. F.** (Fr. 5th.) | M., bel. K. **May 6/17.** |
| 19 W. | Brady, P. 38511. | M. **April 12/17.** |
| 19 W. | Robinson, W. 43585. | M. **April 12/17.** |
| ‡19 Y. | Gillan, Sgt. T. 320007. | M. **May 5-6/17.** |
| 19 Y. XII | Marshall, Thos. Edmund. 43787. (9540.) | M. **May 5-6/17.** |
| ‡19 Y. | Wilson, T. 43647. | M. **May 5-6/17.** |
| ‡19 Z. | Hobroyde, C.-S.-M. G. 9129. | M. **May 5-6/17.** |
| 19 Z. XVI | Lister, Arthur Edw. 23/487. | M. **May 5-6/17.** |
| ‡19 Z. | Smith, W. 512. | M. **May 5-6/17.** |
| ‡20 B. | Skimmings, Jos. 19/963. | M. **Sept. 16/16.** R/Enq. |

## *BALKANS.*

| | | |
|---|---|---|
| 2/5 | **Riddle, Lieut. A. B.** | M. **June 7/17.** |
| 2/5 ? | Sanders, Geo. Oscar. 6756. (Fr. 2/9 B.) | M. Unoff. P/W. **June 7/17.** |

**ROYAL ENGINEERS.**

## *B.E.F.*

| | | |
|---|---|---|
| 7 Field Co. | **Chaplin, Lieut. R. E. E.** | K. **April 21/17.** Det.D./B. |
| 11 | Morris, Henry. 159633. | W. and M. **May 20/17.** |
| 64 | Hobday, L.-Cpl. Albert Thos. 89614. | M. **Oct. 12/16.** R/Enq. |
| 73 | Dunn, A/2nd Cpl. C. J. 19685. | M., bel. K. **April 23/17.** |
| 73 | Ellis, W. C. 164760. | M., bel. K. **April 23/17.** |

**Engineers, Royal—contd.**

*B.E.F.*

| | | |
|---|---|---|
| 73 | Fletcher, Norman. 166445. | M. April 23/17. |
| 73 | Mew, John. 99644. | M., bel. K. April 23/17. |
| 73 | Mogridge, H. 140389. | W. and M. April 23/17. |
| 84 | Cowell, H. W. 56832. | M. Oct. 1-2/16. R/Enq. |
| *91 | McCrae, Alexander. 52210. (Fr. 9th Cheshire.) | K. June 7/17. Det.D./B. |
| 106 | Manley, Arthur. 62333. | M. Feb. 17/17. |
| 106 1 S. | Miller, Matthew K. 58065. | M. Feb. 17/17. |
| 106 | Phillips, Jas. 58904. | M. Feb. 17/17. |
| 124 | Davies, C. G. 34869. (Fr. 13 Welsh Fus.) | M. Mar. 22-24/17. |
| 177 | Dodd, William. 2387. | M. Oct. 12/16. R/Enq. |
| ‡184 | Roberts, E. 86672. | M. May 16/17. |
| ‡184 | Willmetts, Cpl. T. H. 147657. | M. May 16/17. |
| 185 | Howells, N. J. 79104. | W. and M. April 9/17. |
| 222 | Bessent, A.-Cpl. A. J. 96111. | M, April 23/17. |
| 222 1 S. | Cleverly, H. 96173. | M. April 23/17. |
| 222 | Harris, Edw. W. 96050. | M. April 23/17. |
| 222 | Nelson, W. G. 96230. | M. April 23/17. |
| 222 | Robinson, L.-Cpl. G. W. 96255. | M. April 23/17. |
| 222 | Sanderson, W. J. 96136. | M. April 23/17. |
| 222 | Shippam, Pnr. Arthur C. 96089. | M. April 23/17. |
| 222 | Webber, H. 166381. | M. April 28/17. |
| 222 | Wilson, W. 166913. | M. April 23/17. |
| 248 | **Saint, 2nd Lieut. J. H.** | K. June 3/17. Det.D./B. |
| 248 | **Shaw, Lieut. H.** | Fatally W. April 25/17. Det. cas. |
| 251 3 S. | Martin, Neil. 6439. | M. April 24/17. |
| *255 | Ward, G. 20565. (Fr. 8th E. Lancs.) | M. Nov. 16/16. R/Enq. |
| 279 | **Hodson, 2nd Lieut. R. C.** | D/W. May 8/17. Det.D./B. |
| ‡421 | Harris, H. 426810. (West Lancs.) | K. May 7/17. Det.D./B. |
| 438 | Pennington, H. 446724. | M. Mar. 22/17. |
| ‡438 | Slight, Oliver. 25639. (Fr. 8th E. Yorks.) | W. and M. May 3/17. |
| ‡455 | Jeffries, F. 476032. | W. and M. April 23/17. |
| *466 | Smith, William. 235028. | Unoff. M., bel. D/W. April 22/17. |
| ‡504 | Abbott, Alonzo Thos. 183535. | M. June 14-15/17. |
| 509 | Horsley, C. W. 548833. | M. April 22/17. |
| 517 | Brown, Alfred. 550068. | M., bel. K. April 7/17. |
| 517 4 S. | Olley, A.-L.-Cpl. W. G. 550093. (845.) | M. April 7/17. |
| ‡529 | Fletcher, G. W. 474642. (E. Riding.) | W. and M. June 14/17. |
| *178 Tunn. Co. | McGrath, John. 24661. (Fr. 1st Irish Fus.) | K. April 15/17. Det.D./B. |
| ‡184 | Gray, John. 325760. (3549.) | M. May 16/17. |
| ‡184 | Lucas, Sergt. T. 11410. (Fr. 6th K.O.Y.L.I.) | M. May 16/17. |
| 250 | McFarlane, D. 132414. | W. and M. Feb. 24/17. |
| 252 | Strachan, Andrew. 11318. (Fr. 1st Scots Guards.) | W. and M. Sept. 15/16. |
| 254 | Sansom, Cpl. Fredk. A. C/4227. (Fr. 17 K.R.R.C.) | M. Sept. 3/17. |
| 33 Lght. Op. Rly. Co. | Williams, E. S. SS/3786. (Fr. A.S.C.) | K. May 29/17. Det.D./B. |

**Special Brigade.**

| | | |
|---|---|---|
| 2 A. S. | Watson, F. 146638. | Unoff. W. and M. about end Mar./17. |
| *4 ? | Scammell, W. H. 197119. | K. June 3/17. Det.D./B. |
| ‡"O" S. 70 | Neville, L.-Cpl. J. O. 146503. | K. June 4/17. Det.D./B. |
| *"P" ? | Pike, 2/Cpl. Rolfe Wilson. 167286. | K. May 6/17. Det.D./B. |

**Engineers, Royal**—contd.

## *BALKANS.*

| | | |
|---|---|---|
| **108 Field Co.** | Elgar, H. 65925. | M. **May 8/17.** |
| ? | Charnley, Cpl. C. 50391. | M. **May 8/17.** |
| ? | Harthill, L.-Cpl. W. 95825 | M. **May 9/17.** |
| '? | Heaton, E. 53316. | M. **May 8/17.** |
| ? | Lundie, A.-L.-Cpl. R. 65869. | W. and M. **April 25/17.** |
| ? | Weight, W. 97130. | M., bel. K. **April 25/17.** |
| ? | Wiles, J. 65422. | M. **May 8/17.** |

## *E.E.F.*

| | | |
|---|---|---|
| **486 Field Co.** | Andrews, Horace G. 3337. | W. and M. **Mar. 27/17.** |
| ,**Motor Cyclist W. Corps (Sig. Co., 3 Sec.)** | Riley, Cpl. H. 77881. | W. and M. **Mar. 27/17.** |
| ? | **Curtis, 2nd Lt. H. E.** | M., bel. drowned (W.O.L. **May 9/16.)** |
| ? | Hodgkinson, E. S. 183708. | M., bel. drowned **April 15/17.** |
| ? | Wilson, F. 131895. | M. **Mar. 27/17.** |
| ? | Young, R. 414273. | M. **April 16/17.** |

## *PERSIAN GULF.*

| | | |
|---|---|---|
| **‡71 Fld. Co. 13 Div.** | Gosling, S. 37193. | M., bel. K. **May 8/17.** |
| **9 Bgde. 3 Div. Sig. S.** | Edwards, L.-Cpl. H. 27053. | W. and M. **Mar. 25/17.** |
| **14 Co. Div. Sig. S.** | Cockerton, W. J. 200476. (Fr. 2/4 Wilts, 2002. ) | M. **Feb. 2/17.** |
| **14** | Johns, Sgt. W. 200519. (Fr. 4th D.C.L.I.) | W. **April 27/17.** |
| **14** | King, W. H. 201276. (Fr. 2/4 Dorsets, No. 3066.) | M. **Feb. 2/17.** |
| **‡Inland Water Transport** | **Davies, 2nd Lt. T. L.** | M. **June 17/17.** |

## ROYAL ENGINEERS TERRITORIAL FORCE.

## *B.E.F.*

| | | |
|---|---|---|
| **2/1 W. Lancs. Field Co.** | Beardword, Joseph. 426416. (Late 8644.) | M. **Jan. 10/17.** |
| **2/2** | Fearnley, Charles. 6528. | M. **Aug. 8/16. R/Enq.** |

## *E.E.F.*

| | | |
|---|---|---|
| **2/1 E. Ang. Fld. Co.** | Bennett, C. E. 522326. | W. and M. **Mar. 27/17.** |
| **2/1** | Croot, G. V. 522308. | M. **Mar. 27/17.** |
| **E. Ang. Div. Sig. Co.** | Sore, H. 528081. | W. and M. **April 19/17.** |

## ENTRENCHING BATTALION.

### B.E.F.

| | | |
|---|---|---|
| 2 | **Hewlett, 2nd Lt. H. C. (Fr. 7th Suffolks.)** | K. about May 3/17. Det.D./B. |

## ESSEX REGIMENT.

### B.E.F.

| | | |
|---|---|---|
| 1 | **Brown, M.C., Lieut. C. R.** | M. April 14/17. |
| 1 | **Coombs, 2nd Lieut. P. D.** | M. April 16/17. |
| 1 | **Eyre, 2nd Lieut. S. H. R.** | M. April 14/17. |
| 1 | **Flinn, 2nd Lieut. C. H.** | W. and M. April 14/17. |
| 1 | **Foster, Capt. H. J. B. (Fr. Bedfords.)** | W. and M. April 14/17. |
| 1 | **Newth, Lieut. H. R.** | M. April 14/17. |
| 1 | **Portway, 2nd Lieut. L. F.** | M. April 14/17. |
| 1 A. | Ali, Cpl. A. E. 41650. | M. April 14/17. |
| 1 A. | Amos, Sergt. Albert. 9222. | M. April 14/17. |
| 1 A. | Andrews, L.-Cpl. R. 30610. | M. April 14/17. |
| 1 A. | Antingham, G. 41513. | M. April 14/17. |
| 1 A. II | Bacon, A. H. 27836. | M. April 14/17. |
| 1 A. | Badcock, Tom. 41515. | M. April 14/17. |
| 1 A. | Balls, F. A. 41517. | M. April 14/17. |
| 1 A. III | Barber, A. 2920. | M. April 14/17. |
| 1 A. | Barker, G. C. 41654. | M. April 14/17. |
| 1 A. IV | Bartholomew, Shirley Jas. 34175. (Fr. Essex Yeo.) | M. April 14/17. |
| 1 A. II | Baxter, W. 33038. | M. April 14/17. |
| 1 A. I | Beckett, Chas. Edwin. 32860. | M. April 14/17. |
| 1 A. | Bird, Arthur W. 20758. | M. April 14/17. |
| 1 A. III | Bishop, W. W. 32822. | M. April 14/17. |
| 1 A. | Bradley, L.-Cpl. R. 19235. | M. April 14/17. |
| 1 A. | Bray, J. 41653. | M. April 14/17. |
| 1 A. IV | Brazier, Wm. 32976. | M. April 14/17. |
| 1 A. or C. | Bullimore, C. 41527. | M. April 14/17. |
| 1 A. II | Bund, Cpl. H. 17110. | M. April 14/17. |
| 1 A. III | Bunfield, Charles. 41655. | M. April 14/17. |
| 1 A. | Chalk, J. 7857. | M. April 14/17. |
| 1 A. I | Cole, Stanley. 41534. (Fr. 5 Norfolks) | M. April 14/17. |
| 1 A. III | Copestake, Frank. 32082. | M. April 14/17. |
| 1 A. I | Cox, Cpl. E. 10428. | M. April 14/17. |
| 1 A. | Crick, Ernest. 32155. | M. April 14/17. |
| 1 A. | Dent, J. 13164. | M. April 14/17. |
| 1 A. | Edwards, E. 28890. | M. April 14/17. |
| 1 A. | Edwards, William. 41657. | M. April 14/17. |
| 1 A. | Eves, Robert Wm. 20953. | W. Oct. 12/16. R/Enq. |
| 1 A. | Fellers, P. 14944. | M. Oct. 12/16. R./Enq. |
| 1 A. | Fenn, W. G. 32136. | M. April 14/17. |
| 1 A. | Flack, John Edmond. 14805. | M. April 14/17. |
| 1 A. | Franklin, C. T. 19633. | M. April 14/17. |
| 1 A. | Fussell, F. 40710. | M. April 14/17. |
| 1 A. IV | Garnham, J. 41662. (150947.) | M. April 14/17. |
| 1 A. III | Gidney, F. J. 41543. | M. April 14/17. |
| 1 A. | Goodson, T. 41545. | M. April 14/17. |
| 1 A. II | Green, Alfred Jas. 32132. | M. April 14/17. |
| 1 A. | Green, J. 32982. | M. April 14/17. |

**Essex Regiment**—contd.

## *B.E.F.*

| | | |
|---|---|---|
| 1 A. | Gulston, R. 33044. | M. April 14/17. |
| 1 A. | Hancock, J. G. 20249. | M. April 14/17. |
| 1 A. | Hardy, D. 30587. | M. April 14/17. |
| 1 A. III | Harrington, A. 34192. | M. April 14/17. |
| 1 A. | Hatherill, L.-Cpl. J. 20278. | M. April 14/17. |
| 1 A. I | Holland, Arthur. 20866. | M. April 14/17. |
| 1 A. | Hooke, A. W. 41556. | M. April 14/17. |
| 1 A. IV | Ireson, L.-Cpl. J. E. 41678. | M. April 14/17. |
| 1 A. II | Jackson, G. 41619. | M. April 14/17. |
| 1 A. | Jones, W. 15416. | M. April 14/17. |
| 1 A. | Lambert, G. 41560. | M. April 14/17. |
| 1 A. II | Lilley, E. 32986. | M. April 14/17. |
| 1 A. | Lister, C. 32862. | M. April 14/17. |
| 1 A. | Lythgoe, L.-Cpl. T. 20155. | M. April 14/17. |
| 1 A. L.G.S. | Milne, L.-Cpl. A. 20188. | M. April 14/17. |
| 1 A. | Morrist, H. 20041. | M. April 14/17. |
| 1 A. I | Newman, Cpl. W. J. 11067. | M. April 14/17. |
| 1 A. | Norman, I. 12857. | M. April 14/17. |
| ‡1 A. | Oakley, C. A. 26246. | M. April 14/17. |
| 1 A. III | Paris, L.-Cpl. Charles Henry. 20258. | M. April 14/17. |
| 1 A. IV | Parkins, L.-Cpl. Wm. Geo. 33045. | M. April 14/17. |
| 1 A. | Parsons, H. 41669. | M. April 14/17. |
| 1 A. | Pendle, J. 41571. | M. April 14/17. |
| 1 A. III | Petchell, Ralph. 41572. | M. April 14/17. |
| 1 A. III | Pilgrim, E. W. 34173. | M. April 14/17. |
| 1 A. | Powter, G. W. 19301. | M. April 14/17. |
| 1 A. IV | Raggett, Walter Edgar. 40705. | M. April 14/17. |
| ‡1 A. II | Reed, George. 27826. | M. April 14/17. |
| 1 A. IV | Reeve, F. A. 32991. | M. April 14/17. |
| ‡1 A. | Richards, B. 23188. | M. April 13/17. |
| 1 A. III | Richardson, L.-Cpl. Jack. 30346. | M. April 14/17. |
| 1 A. III | Runnacles, P. A. 34183. | M. April 14/17. |
| ‡1 A. IV | Russell, F. 4070. | M. April 14/17. |
| 1 A. I | Sach, Fredk. 30640. | M. April 14/17. |
| 1 A. II | Samwell, F. 28977. | M. April 14/17. |
| 1 A. IV | Sandell, L.-Cpl. A. 41576. | M. April 14/17. |
| 1 A. II | Simpson, Arnold Augustus. 32993. | M. April 14/17. |
| 1 A. | Smith, C. W. 19560. | M. April 14/17. |
| 1 A. I | Smith, Fred. Jas. Langtry. 34143. | M. April 14/17. |
| 1 A. L.G.S. | Smith, L.-Cpl. J. 10338. | M. April 14/17. |
| 1 A. I | Smith, John. 20934. | M. April 14/17. |
| 1 A. | Smith, S. 40715. | M. April 14/17. |
| 1 A. III | Spratt, Edwin Victor. 41577. | M. April 14/17. |
| 1 A. | Stacey, A. 40713. | M. April 14/17. |
| 1 A. | Staff, Cpl. Walter. 9941. | M. April 14/17. |
| 1 A. or C. | Stewart, Arthur Edward. 32955. | M. April 14/17. |
| 1 A. II | Stock, Geo. Albert. 32996. | M. April 14/17. |
| 1 A. | Surridge, A. 9982. | M. April 14/17. |
| ‡1 A. I | Tack, Fred. 30640. | M. April 14/17. |
| 1 A. III | Thompson, A. 41642. | M. April 14/17. |
| 1 A. | Thompson, Leonard. 3/2178. | M. April 14/17. |
| 1 A. | Thompson, W. 41590. | M. April 14/17. |
| 1 A. | Thorn, A. 41645. | M. April 14/17. |
| 1 A. II | Turner, L.-Cpl. Albert. 32997. | M. April 14/17. |
| 1 A. | Turner, C. 41592. | M. April 14/17. |
| 1 A. II | Walder, George. 31577. | W. and M. April 13/17. |
| 1 A. | Watson, J. 43672. | M. April 14/17. |
| 1 A. | West, W. 43665. | M. April 14/17. |

**Essex Regiment—contd.**

## *B.E.F.*

| | | | |
|---|---|---|---|
| 1 A. IV | Whitehand, W. H. 41674. | M. April 14/17. | |
| 1 A. | Wingar, Fredk. Wm. 19431. | M. April 14/17. | |
| 1 A. I | Worship, G. C. 41600. | M. April 14/17. | |
| 1 A. I | Wright, E. B. 41595. | M. April 14/17. | |
| 1 A. | Young, V. C. 9068. | M. April 14/17. | R/Enq. |
| 1 B. | Alderton, W. 41639. | M. April 14/17. | |
| 1 B. | Andrews, Foster. 17085. | M. April 14/17. | |
| 1 B. V | Baines, Wm. 16346. | M. April 14/17. | |
| ‡1 B. VIII | Baker, H. 30510. | W. and M. Oct. 12/16. | R/Enq. |
| 1 B. | Banham, G. 41518. | M. April 14/17. | |
| 1 B. | Barker, S. 32149. | M. April 14/17. | |
| 1 B. | Barr, A. W. 18214. | M. April 14/17. | |
| 1 B. | Blake, Sergt. Oswald Merton. 41649. (Fr. 59 Div. Works Bn.) | M April 14/17. | |
| 1 B. V | Bradley, L.-Cpl. H. 20030. | M. April 13/17. | |
| 1 B. | Brister, G. E. 41523. | M. April 14/17. | |
| 1 B. | Broyde, S. 19477. | M. Oct. 12/16. | |
| 1 B. VII | Carr, Albert Edw. 41533. | M. April 14/17. | |
| 1 B. L.G.S. | Carr, S. 19628. | W. and M. Oct. 28/16. | |
| 1 B. V | Carter, Clarence Wm. 34212. | M. April 14/17. | |
| 1 B. | Cook, C. 2342. | M. April 14/17. | |
| 1 B. | Cooper, C. 28830. | M. April 14/17. | |
| 1 B. | Cooper, G. W. E. 32179. | M. April 14/17. | |
| 1 B. VI | Cross, L. C. 30601. | M. April 14/17. | |
| 1 B. V | Curson, Francis Albert. 41612. | M. April 14/17. | |
| 1 B. | Dicks, A. 32961. | M. April 14/17. | |
| 1 B. | Duncombe, W. E. 32158. | M. April 14/17. | |
| 1 B. | Elliott, R. C. 32074. | M. April 14/17. | |
| 1 B. | Forsdyke, L.-Cpl. W. 1813. (Fr. 3rd) | M. April 14/17. | |
| '1 B. VII | Frary, R. T. 41540. | M. April 14/17. | |
| 1 B. VII | Gibbons, R. A. 34188. | M. April 14/17. | |
| 1 B. | Gunn, W. 18908. | M. April 14/17. | |
| 1 B. VII | Hobbs, L.-Cpl. Reginald V. 32941. | M. April 14/17. | |
| 1 B. | Holmes, C. 41663. | M. April 14/17. | |
| 1 B. VI | Holsey, E. 41555. | M. April 14/17. | |
| 1 B. VII | Howe, Cpl. Albert Ed. 8397. | M. April 14/17. | |
| 1 B. | Howlett, V. 31262. | M. April 14/17. | |
| 1 B. | Ironside, J. 13142. | M. April 14/17. | |
| 1 B. V | King, Andrew J. 41643. | M. April 14/17. | |
| 1 B. VII | King, Sergt. O. G. 29323. | M. April 14/17. | |
| 1 B. | Leach, C. 34147. | M. April 14/17. | |
| 1 B. VII | Lee, B. H. 32119. | M. April 14/17. | |
| 1 B. VII | Loveday, B. J. (41563.) | M. April 14/17. | |
| 1 B. VII | Marshall, Harry E. 30521. | M. Oct. 12/16. | R/Enq. |
| 1 B. | Mayes, C. 41564. | M. April 14/17. | |
| 1 B. | Meek, H. 41365. | M. April 14/17. | |
| 1 B. | Mera, H. C. 26671. | M. April 14/17. | |
| 1 B. VIII | Miles, John Henry. 32110. | M. April 14/17. | |
| 1 B. V | Monument, L.-Cpl. A. R. 41622. | M. April 14/17. | |
| 1 B. VI | Munford, J. 41636. | M. April 14/17. | |
| 1 B. VII | Mynard, L. 34162. | M. April 14/17. | |
| 1 B. V | Newman, L.-Cpl. D. G. 34178. | Unoff. M. April 14/17. | |
| 1 B. VII | Nichols, Henry. 15752. | M. April 14/17. | |
| 1 B. VI | Norton, W. G. 43481. | M. April 14/17. | |
| '1 B. | Outram, L.-Cpl. Wm. 20085. | M. Oct. 12/16. | R/Enq. |
| 1 B. VIII | Parnell, L.-Cpl. A. E. R. J. 32388. | M. April 14/17. | |
| 1 B. VII | Richardson, Stanley. 43489. | M. April 14/17. | |
| 1 B. | Ridgway, Ernest John. 41574. | M. April 14/17. | |

Essex Regiment—contd.

## *B.E.F.*

1 B. Ringer, A. W. 41634. M. April 14/17.
1 B. Sargeant, S. 32949. M. April 14/17.
1 B. Shelley, Wm. 28818. M. April 14/17.
1 B. Shinn, Robt. Ridley. 41580. M. April 14/17.
1 B. V Simpson, Cpl. David. 9047. M. April 14/17.
1 B. Smart, Henry Edward. 3/1865. M. Oct. 12/16. R/Enq.
1 B. VIII Smith, Charles. 32952. M. April 14/17.
1 B. Smith, Sergt. C. J. 31194. M. April 14/17.
1 B. VIII Smith, Frank. 40717. M. April 14/17.
1 B. Spalding, S. 32159. M. April 14/17.
1 B. Thake, W. 40721. M. April 14/17.
1 B. Todd, J. 41389. M. April 14/17.
1 B. Tomalin, C. L. 41472. M. April 28/17.
1 B. or D. Tubb, Charles Wm. 29554. M. April 14/17.
*1 B. VI Wanford, J. 41636. M. April 14/17.
1 B. Ward, L.-Cpl. A. 20753. M. April 14/17.
1 B. VIII Wedd, Fred Leonard. 32960. M. April 14/17.
1 B. L.G.S. Whitehouse, Chas. Lyle. 19748. M. April 14/17.
1 B. VI Wilson, Bertie Alfred. 41601. M. April 14/17.
1 B. V Wire, Tom. 34161. M. April 14/17.
1 B. Woodley, W. 40732. M. April 14/17.
1 B. Wreford, A.-Cpl. J. S. 10097. M. April 14/17.
1 B. or D. XV Wright, R. 18413. M. April 14/17.
*1 C. X Adams, A. T. 28080. M. April 14/17.
1 C. L.G.S. Alford, H. 20229. M. April 14/17.
1 C. X Baily, W. C. 29530. M. April 14/17.
1 C. Baker, L.-Cpl. P. W. 12247. M. April 14/17.
1 C. XII Barrett, C. 15441. M. April 15/17.
1 C. Bartley, Arthur Thos. 13018. M. April 14/17.
1 C. XII Bassett, C. W. 29533. M April 14/17.
1 C. X Baxter, Wm. 29534. M. April 14/17.
1 C. L.G.S. Bennett, Ernest Chas. 41607. M. April 14/17.
1 C. XI Blyth, R. S. 29340. M. April 14/17.
1 C. Burton, J. A. 18922. M. April 14/17.
1 C. Bush, E. 24912. M. April 14/17.
1 C. Challis, L.-Cpl. C. S. 26705. M. April 14/17.
1 C. XI Clements, Arthur Fredk. 29358. M. April 14/17.
‡1 C. XII Clements, Fred. 29539. M. April 14/17. R./Enq.
1 C. Connelly, Samuel Edw. 13154. M. April 14/17.
1 C. Cooper, Cpl. T. D. 9363. M. April 14/17.
1 C. Cresswell, Frank. 3433. (Fr. 3rd.) M. April 14/17.
1 C. XII Crosby, G. 21654. M. April 14/17.
1 C. IX Denny, W. 28915. M. April 14/17.
1 C. Dorling, F. 3/2600. M. April 13/17.
1 C. Drake, W. J. 41613. M. April 14/17.
1 C. Durrant, C. 41323. M. April 14/17.
1 C. Fisher, H. 31143. M. April 14/17.
1 C. Franklin, W. C. 32980. M. April 14/17.
1 C. Frost, Robert. 20855. M. April 14/17.
1 C. Fust, P. 19571. M. April 14/17.
1 C. Germany, Ernest. 20860. M. April 14/17.
*1 C. IX Gilks, John Fredk. 30502. (Fr. 3rd.) M. Oct. 12/16. R/Enq.
1 C. Goddard, J. 20957. M. April 14/17.
1 C. Goodhew, L.-Cpl. H. 10437. M. April 14/17.
‡1 C. IX Greenway, H. W. 10387. M. April 14/17.
1 C. XII Gregory, F. S. 30875. M. April 14/17.
1 C. Hall, W. C. 20221. M. April 14/17.
1 C. Hardy, Sgt. Augustus H. (Jim). 29322. M. April 14/17.

**Essex Regiment—contd.**

## *B.E.F.*

1 C. XII Harris, Sydney. 30592. M. April 14/17.
1 C. XII Harrison, L.-Cpl. Thomas. 20146. M. April 14/17.
1 C. Hartwell, H. F. 20326. M. April 14/17.
1 C. IX Hawkes, Cpl. Wm. 20327. M. April 14/17.
1 C. Hayes, L. A. 28546. M. April 14/17.
1 C. L.G.S. Herbert A. R. 31254. M. April 14/17.
1 C. Hicks, Cpl. A. G. 32940. M. April 14/17.
1 C. Hilling, H. G. 28671. M. April 14/17.
1 C. XII Howlett, L.-Cpl. Arthur. 20869. M. April 14/17.
1 C. X Hutley, E. 40072. M. April 14/17.
1 C. Jenkins, L.-Cpl. J. 15445. M. April 14/17.
1 C. Jenkinson, L. 9203. M. April 14/17.
1 C. X Johnson, Ernest Wm. 18427. M. April 14/17.
1 C. IX Jones, Henry. 20158. M. April 14/17.
1 C. XI King, Arthur Mason. 12278. M. April 14/17.
1 C. XII Lefevre, F. S. 2229. (Fr. 3rd.) M. April 14/17.
1 C. Lincoln, J. W. 19841. M. April 14/17.
1 C. Litt, Edward. 20199. M. April 14/17.
1 C. McGorrock, J. 24792. M. April 14/17.
1 C. Marchant, F. J. 24798. M. April 14/17.
1 C. IX Matthams, B. 34186. M. April 14/17.
1 C. Merry, Sergt. Tom. 8610. M. April 14/17.
1 C. Mogford, Sergt. Jas. 9057. M. April 14/17.
1 C. Money, Fred W. 29546. M. April 14/17.
1 C. Ogden, C. 32957. M. April 14/17.
1 C. Ong, L.-Cpl. W. 10321. M. April 14/17.
1 C. Overton, L.-Cpl. B. E. 20883. M. April 14/17.
1 C. Raven, F. W. 26695. M. April 14/17.
1 C. Robinson, W. 19238. M. April 14/17.
1 C. IX Roebuck, George. 14102. M. April 14/17.
1 C. XII Rowe, Walter John. 20367. M. April 14/17.
1 C. Rust, Philip. 19571. M. April 14/17.
1 C. XII Samuel, W. 29314. M. April 14/17.
1 C. Saunders, W. 17071. M. April 14/17.
1 C. Snow, F. N. 29487. M. April 14/17.
1 C. Swann, W. 5499. M. April 14/17.
1 C. X Tampkins, James. 30583. M. April 14/17.
1 C. XII Thomas, L.-Cpl. Wm. Edmead. 32948 M. April 14/17.
1 C. X Upton, A. 20774. M. April 14/17.
1 C. Warner, E. 31487. M. April 14/17.
1 C. Webb, R. E. 32969. M. April 14/17.
1 C. Wilson, A. E. 20923. M. April 14/17.
1 D. XV Ainge, L.-Cpl. A. G. 29074. M. April 14/17.
1 D. Andrews, L. 19290. M. April 14/17.
1 D. XIII Auger, G. 33021. M. April 14/17.
1 D. Bagdatopulos, John Graham. 29529. M. April 14/17.
1 D. XVI Bareham, L.-Cpl. H. E. 29332. M. April 14/17.
1 D. XVI Bartram, Aruth. 29081. M. April 14/17.
1 D. Bodman, Edward Benj. 9107. M. April 14/17.
1 D. Britten, G. 29535. M. April 14/17.
1 D. Brooker, E. J. 29339. M. April 14/17.
1 D. L.G.S. Butter, L.-Cpl. R. S. 26713. M. April 14/17.
1 D. XIV Card, L.-Cpl. Wm. John. 23969. (Sig.) M. April 14/17.
1 D. XVI Clark, Gilbert. 30315. M. April 14/17.

**Essex Regiment—contd.**

*B.E.F.*

| | | | |
|---|---|---|---|
| 1 D. | | Cornell, E. 29305. | M. April 14/17. |
| 1 D. | XIII | Dann, Sergt. H. K. 35530. | M. April 14/17. |
| 1 D. | | Davis, L.-Cpl. G. 9353. | M. April 14/17. |
| 1 D. | | Denney, C. F. 34145. | M. April 14/17. |
| 1 D. | | Dixon, Arthur Wm. 28635. | M. April 14/17. |
| 1 D. | | Downing, S. G. 28848. | M. April 14/17. |
| 1 D. | XIV | Eaton, Stephen. 40494. | M. April 14/17. |
| 1 D. | | Edden, S. 29442. | M. April 14/17. |
| 1 D. | | Egner, L. 29326. | M. April 14/17. |
| 1 D. | XVI | Everett, L.-Cpl. Ernest. 29334. | M. April 14/17. |
| 1 D. | | Hazell, Cpl. Samuel. 19303. | M. April 14/17. |
| 1 D. | | Hersom, L.-Cpl. Leonard. 10250. | M. April 14/17. |
| 1 D. | | Hollingshead, J. R. 23535. | M. April 14/17. |
| 1 D. | | Humphries, Cpl. H. G. 10943. | M. April 14/17. |
| 1 D. | | Hurrell, L.-Cpl. Geo. 28805. | M. April 14/17. |
| 1 D. | XIII | Ingram, J. 24560. | M. April 14/17. |
| 1 D. | | Ireland, A. E. 28487. | M. April 14/17. |
| 1 D. | XIV | Jackson, Fredk. Geo. 29308. | M. April 14/17. |
| 1 D. | XIII | Johnson, Christopher Geo. 12738. | M. April 14/17. |
| 1 D. | XIII | King, Alb. Hy. 29453. | M. April 14/17. |
| 1 D. | XVI | Leigh, Frank Shire. 32827. | M. April 14/17. |
| 1 D. | XIV | London, John. 29309. | M. April 14/17. |
| 1 D. | XIII | Marshall, L.-Cpl. P. D. 28772. | M. April 14/17. |
| 1 D. | | Metford, Ed. Floyd. 24046. | M. April 14/17. |
| 1 D. | XIII | Narvige, John. 10722. | M. April 14/17. |
| 1 D. | | Neave, C. 31514. | M. April 14/17. |
| 1 D. | XIII | Nightingale, L.-Cpl. A. 43480. | M. April 14/17. |
| 1 D. | XIII | Palmer, A. 29461. | M. April 14/17. |
| 1 D. | | Palmer, F. C. H. 29480. | M. April 14/17. |
| 1 D. | | Palmer, Cpl. R. 41629. | M. April 14/17. |
| 1 D. | | Peck, Chas. Rowland. 29069. | M. April 14/17. |
| 1 D. | | Perry, F. 29073. | M. April 14/17. |
| 1 D. | | Petrie, C. H. 6373. | M. April 14/17. |
| ‡1 D. | | Pocknell, H. 29482. | M. April 14/17. |
| 1 D. | | Radley, C.-S.-M. Sidney. 7790. | W. and M. April 14/17. |
| 1 D. | | Rawlinson, H. 30400. | M. April 14/17. |
| 1 D. | | Reeves, John. 19439. | M. April 14/17. |
| 1 D. | | Richer, Sergt. J. 25. (Fr. 3rd.) | M. April 14/17. |
| 1 D. | | Roat, C. 14642. | M. April 14/17. |
| 1 D. | | Rogers, L.-Cpl. W. G. 19053. | M. April 14/17. |
| 1 D. | | Secker, Wilfred. 20052. | M. April 14/17. |
| 1 D. | | Sewell, E. 20537. | M. April 14/17. |
| 1 D. | XIII | Smith, L.-Cpl. Herbert. 34200. | M. April 14/17. |
| 1 D. | XIII | Smith, H. E. 5935. | M. April 14/17. |
| ‡1 D. | | Spray, Ernest. 24988. | K. April 24/17. Det.D./B. |
| 1 D. | | Steed, F. 29036. | M. April 14/17. |
| 1 D. | | Stracy, Cpl. Victor Alfred. 29456. | W. and M. April 14/17. |
| 1 D. | | Taylor, L.-Cpl. C. 34171. | M. April 14/17. |
| 1 D. | | Thompson, E. 20814. | M. April 14/17. |
| 1 D. | | Thomson, Cpl. Wm. 10911. | M. April 14/17. |
| 1 D. | | Thorogood, L.-Cpl. Cecil. 12442. | M. April 14/17. |
| 1 D. | | Thorogood, L.-Cpl. J. D. 26779. | M. April 14/17. |
| 1 D. | | Tiffen, L.-Cpl. C. W. 19040. | M. April 14/17. |
| 1 D. | | Tuckwell, F. J. 30792. | M. April 14/17. |
| 1 D. | | Turner, A. W. 13685. | M. April 14/17. |

**Essex Regiment—contd.**

## *B.E.F.*

| | | |
|---|---|---|
| 1 D. | Waller, Fred. 10829. | M. April 14/17. |
| 1 D. XVI | Wells, L.-Cpl. Walter Robt. 31105. | M. April 14/17. |
| 1 D. | Western, G. H. 20032. | M. April 14/17. |
| 1 D. | Witney, Cpl. A. W. 9058. | M. April 14/17. |
| 1 D. | Wright, Arthur Geo. Leslie. 9281. | M. April 14/17. |
| 2 | **Croager, 2nd Lieut. L. W.** | M. May 3/17. |
| 2 | **Evans, 2nd Lieut. P. H.** | M. May 3/17. |
| 2 C. | **McNeill, Lieut. J. C.** | M. May 3/17. |
| 2 A. III | Bailey, A. E. 33885. | W. and M. May 3/17. |
| 2 A. | Batterbury, Cpl. J. 34451. | M. May 3/17. |
| ‡2 A. | Benton, A. 41015. | M. May 3/17. |
| ‡2 A. | Biddle, G. 10800. | M. May 3/17. |
| *2 A. III | Breadmore, H. J. 35388. | M. May 3/17. |
| 2 A. IV | Burnham, Maurice George. 35384. | M. May 3/17. |
| ‡2 A. | Bush, Geo. 40150. | M. Oct. 23/16. R/Enq. |
| 2 A. | Choat, Porter. 16880. | M. Oct. 23/16. R/Enq. |
| 2 A. III | Constable, Geo. 35409. | M. May 3/17. |
| ‡2 A. | Cooch, W. 1993. | M. Oct. 23/16. R/Enq. |
| ‡2 A. | Croome, L. 35398. | M. May 3/17. |
| ‡2 A. | Ellis, J. R. 40462. | M. May 3/17. |
| ‡2 A. | Farrow, A. 28860. | M. Dec. 12/16. R/Enq. |
| ‡2 A. | Garrett, W. J. D. 30776. | M. May 3/17. |
| 2 A. III | Hicks, A.-L.-Cpl. A. J. 35373. | M. May 3/17. |
| 2 A. II | Holloway, H. F. 41159. | M. May 3/17. |
| 2 A. I | Laver, Cpl. W. 13209. | M. Oct. 23/16. R/Enq. |
| ‡2 A. | Page, R. 35368. | M. May 3/17. |
| ‡2 A. I | Reepe, E. 41180. | M. May 3/17. |
| ‡2 A. | Reeve, E. 41077. | M. May 3/17. |
| 2 A. | Reeve, Fred. 17444. | M. Oct. 23/16. R./Enq. |
| 2 A. | Rose, L.-Cpl. H. A. 32217. | M. May 3/17. |
| ‡2 A. IV | Rowcroft, L.-Cpl. J. J. 35358. | M., bel. K. June 5/17. Conf. and Details. |
| ‡2 A. | Saunders, B. 41061. | M. May 3/17. |
| 2 A. II | Shadbolt, Laurence. 33049. | W. and M. May 3/17. |
| ‡2 A. I | Turner, S. 34590. | M. May 3/17. |
| 2 A. III | Wright, Alfred S. T. 35351. | M. May 3/17. |
| 2 B. | Band, Arthur A. 34444. | M. May 3/17. |
| ‡2 B. | Bareford, Sgt. A. 7953. | M. May 3/17. |
| 2 B. VII | Barnes, Chas. 40145. | M. May 1/17. |
| 2 B. V | Barnsley, Jas. Foster. 34448. | M. May 1/17. |
| 2 B. VIII | Brown, A. 15976. | W. and M. May 3/17. |
| 2 B. | Bullock, Arthur. 23933. | M. Oct. 23/16. R/Enq. |
| 2 B. VI | Coles, David. 41005. | M. May 3/17. |
| 2 B. | Grant, Jack H. 40185. | M. May 3/17. |
| ‡2 B. | Harley, W. 27742. | M. May 3/17. |
| ‡2 B. | Kelly, L.-Cpl. G. W. 3/2220 | M. May 3/17. |
| 2 B. VI | MacDermott, T. 35459. | M. May 3/17. |
| ‡2 B. | Newstead, J. 41086. | M. May 3/17. |
| ‡2 B. | Read, G. N. 9811. | M. May 3/17. |
| ‡2 B. | Sallows, G. 9296. | M. May 3/17. |
| *2 B. | Seaber, L.-Cpl. Harold. 12385. | W. and M. May 5/17. |
| ‡2 B. | Seymour, L. S. 9497. | M. May 3/17. |
| 2 C. IX | Armitage, Ernest Harold. 41120. | M. May 3/17. |
| *2 C. | Baker, A. 34441. | M. May 3/17. |
| ‡2 C. | Baldwin, B. Wm. 35379. | M. May 3/17. |
| 2 C. | Bell, E. C. 35262. | M. May 3/17. |
| 2 C. IX | Bloom, L.-Cpl. Jack. 34455. | M. May 3/17. |
| 2 C. | Campling, A.-L.-Sergt. A. 40167. | M. May 3/17. |
| 2 C. | Carter, Arthur Geo. 35396. | M. May 3/17. |

**Essex Regiment—contd.**

*B.E.F.*

‡2 C. Chapman, W. 41249. M. May 3/17.
‡2 C. Claxton, A.-Cpl. J. R. 41074. M. May 3/17.
*2 C. L.G.S. Dowling, S. T. 40176. M. May 3/17.
2 C. IX Ellison, Chas. Arthur. 34490. K. May 3/17. Det.D./B.
‡2 C. IX Free, A. T. H. 35423. M. May 3/17.
2 C. XII Fuller, A. E. 35420. W. and M. May 3/17.
2 C. XI Herbert, Maurice. 35270. M. May 3/17.
2 C. IX Holben, Jas. 40272. M. May 3/17.
*2 C. IX Hudson, H. E. 35302. M. May 3/17.
‡2 C. Jackson, L.-Cpl. F. A. 35370. M. May 3/17.
2 C. Johnson, J. 35448. W. and M. April 9/17.
‡2 C. Lee, E. S. 35320. M. May 3/17.
2 C. Low, Cpl. George. 19191. M. May 3/17.
2 C. X Mendham, L.-Cpl. Harry C. 41097. M. May 3/17.
*2 C. IX Palmer, Thomas. 31209. M. May 3/17.
*2 C. Pavitt, J. 41099. M. May 3/17.
2 C. Peplow, W. W. 35463. M. April 11/17.
*2 C. Smith, W. H. 10775. M. May 3/17.
2 C. Tilbrook, Cpl. H. 23205. M. May 3/17.
2 D. Elliott, Paul. 15215. M. Oct. 23/16. R/Enq.
‡2 D. Fitzjohn, W. C. 19226. M. May 3/17.
*2 D. Hughes, F. 35308. K. May 10/17. Det.D./B.
2 D. XV Loughborough, Chas. 34531. M. May 3/17.
2 D. XV Mercer, R. W. 34541. M. May 3/17.
‡2 D. Monk, J. 34543. M. May 3/17.
2 D. North, A. F. 18960. W. and M. Oct. 28/16. R/Enq.
‡2 D. Redding, L.-Cpl. R. W. 30316. M. May 3/17.
2 D. Spooner, A. 35481. W. and M. April 9/17.
2 D. XIII Swan, Wm. 15954. K. April 9/17. Det.D./B.
‡2 ? Terry, P. G. 34586. M. May 3/17.
*2/7 C. Parry, A. 34555. W. and M. May 3/17.
‡9 **Clark, 2nd Lieut. S. A.** M. July 11/17.
9 **Derbyshire, 2nd Lieut. A.** W. and M. April 30/17.
9 C. **Rees, Lieut. A. M.** W. and M. Oct. 18/16.
9 **Savill, 2nd Lieut. R. J.** M. April 30/17.
9 **Yardley, 2nd Lieut. W.** W. and M. April 30/17.
9 A. Allen, L. W. 32897. M. April 30/17.
9 A. Day, A. J. 34821. M. April 30/17.
9 A. Firman, P. G. 26906. M. Unoff. K. April 30/17.
*9 A. IV Gale, W. 34906. W. and M. April 30/17.
9 A. II Holmes, W. C. 40688. K. April 9/17. Det.D./B.
9 A. II Jackson, A. 34832. M. April 30/17.
‡9 A. Leonard, A. E. 18039. W. and M. April 30/17.
9 A. I Leonard, Chas. Jas. 34835. W. and M. April 30/17.
9 A. I Thurgood, Stanley. 34139. W. and M. April 30/17.
9 A. IV Wapples, F. 43437. M. Oct. 18/16. R/Enq.
9 A. I White, L.-Cpl. John Wm. 35354. K. April 9/17. Det.D./B.
‡9 B. V Chapman, V. 31758. K. April 9/17. Det.D./B.
9 B. V Griggs, A. 35020. M. April 9/17.
9 B. Nicholls, C. 40882. M. April 28/17.
9 D. Adams, A. 19352. M. April 30/17.
9 D. Barley, Arthur. 40694. M. April 30/17.
9 D. XIII Bee, J. 43377. W. and M. Unoff. K. April 9/17.
*9 D. Burles, S. 23236. M. April 30/17.
‡9 D. Campion, A. 43381. W. and M. April 30/17.
9 D. XV Chaplin, G. 34113. M. April 30/17.
9 D. Christian, L.-Cpl. E. T. 738. (43541) M. April 30/17.
9 D. XVI Cooke, C. 40784. W. and M. April 30/17.
9 D. XIV Cox, C. 40783. M. April 30/17.

**Essex Regiment—contd.**

## *B.E.F.*

| | | |
|---|---|---|
| 9 D. | Davis, H. F. 40780. | M. April 30/17. |
| 9 D. | Griffiths, W. C. 29183. | M. April 30/17. |
| 9 D. XV | Hammond, A. E. V. 31621. | M. April 30/17. |
| 9 D. XVI | Twidale, T. 40803. | M. April 30/17. |
| 10 B. | Howe, E. H. 29382. | M. March 7/17. |
| 10 B. VIII | Moorcroft, F. T. 43160. | M. Oct. 21/16. R/Enq. |
| 10 C. IX | Blyth, G. F. A. 29302. | K. Feb. 5/17. Det.D./B. |
| 10 D. | Hunt, Cpl. Robert Arthur. 13365. | W. and M. Oct. 21/16. R/Enq. |
| 11 A. | Cook, C. F. 19147. | M. Oct. 15/16. |
| 11 A. | Edwards, Jack. 9725. | M. Oct. 15/16. R/Enq. |
| 11 A. | Game, A.-Sergt. H. 16778. | M. Oct. 15/16. R/Enq. |
| 11 A. I | Haywood, Wm. Arthur. 24596. | M. Oct. 15/16. R/Enq. |
| *11 A. | Hughes, Charles Wm. 16667. | W. and M. Oct. 15/16. R/Enq. |
| 11 A. | Woods, C. 41337. | M. April 22/17. |
| ‡11 B. | Ash, L.-Cpl. A. W. 34612. | M., bel. K. April 22/17. |
| ‡11 B. | Blake, R. J. 34786. | M., bel. K. April 21/17. |
| *11 B. | Curtis, Sergt. Bert. 40028. | W. and M. April 22/17. |
| 11 B. | Herrington, H. 978. | M. April 22/17. |
| 11 B. | Ince, H. 28239. | M. April 22/17. |
| ‡11 B. | Perkins, A. G. 32407. | W. and M. April 22/17. |
| ‡11 B. | Richer, H. 34798. | M. April 22/17. |
| *11 B. VII | Starling, Fredk. 32422. | M. April 22/17. |
| *11 B. | Watson, J. H. 20940. | M. Oct. 14/16. R/Enq. |
| 11 C. X | Gardener, Stanley Percival. 32399. | W. Unoff. M. April 22/17. |
| 11 C. IX | Keeley, L.-Cpl. E. A. 20872. | M. Sept. 15/16. R/Enq. |
| 11 C. | Millward, J. 43162. | M. Mar. 23/17. |
| 11 C. IX | Waite, Edw. 40017. (Fr. 4th, 3778.) | K. Oct. 15/16. Det D./B. R/Enq. |
| 11 C. | Way, G. 28215. | M. Oct. 15/16. R/Enq. |
| ‡11 C. IX | Woodcock, A. 28209. | M. Oct. 15/16. R/Enq. |
| 11 D. XIV | Birchmore, L.-Cpl. T. J. 13157. | M. Oct. 15/16. R/Enq. |
| 11 D. | Ford, H. 34662. | M. April 22/17. |
| ‡11 D. | Goodwin, C. 13725. | W. and M. April 22/17. |
| 11 D. | Griffiths, J. M. 21789. | M. Oct. 15/16. R/Enq. |
| *11 D. XIII | Hewes, Thos. Herbert. 33978. | M. April 22/17. |
| 11 D. | Mouatt, A. T. 15948. | M. April 22/17. |
| 11 D. XIII | Mumford, C. J. 40955. | M. April 22/17. |
| 11 D. | Picking, J. 23166. | M. April 22/17. |
| 11 D. | Russell, H. B. 34795. | M. April 22/17. |
| 11 D. XIII | Schofield, Fredk. Chas. 3/1108. | W. and M. April 22/17. |
| *11 D. | Thompson, Frederick Wm. 23204. | M. May 3/17. |
| 11 D. XIII | Turner, S. R. 34764. | W. and M. April 22/17. |
| 11 D. | Walker, L.-Cpl. H. W. 34799. | M. April 22/17. |
| *11 D. | Whybird, L.-Cpl. A. 10487. | M. Oct. 15/16. R/Enq. |
| 11 D. | Worledge, Frederick. 32204. | M. April 22/17. |
| 12 B. | Bateman, Ernest. 17673. (Fr. H.Q.) | M. April 11/17. |
| 12 C. I.T.M. | Grisdale, Matthew. 27005. (Fr. 12 Essex.) | K. May 1/17. Det.D./B. |
| 13 | **Barrett, 2nd Lieut. J. A.** | M. April 28/17. |
| 13 | **Brown-Paterson, M.C., 2nd Lieut. W.** | M. April 28/17. |
| 13 | **Clarke, Capt. J. J. G.** | M. April 28/17. |
| 13 | **Ibbotson, 2nd Lieut. R.** (Fr. 5th.) | M. April 28/17. |
| 13 | **Mason, 2nd Lieut. D. H.** | M. April 28/17. |
| 13 | **Ritson, 2nd Lieut. C. W.** | K. April 23/17. Det.D./B. |
| 13 | **Vowles, 2nd Lieut. S. F.** (Fr. 3rd.) | M. April 28/17. |
| 13 A. II | Adams, F. W. 29029. | M. April 28/17. |
| 13 A. | Barker, H. 31632. | M. April 28/17. |
| 13 A. or B. | Barnes, Arthur. 26653. | M. April 28/17. |
| 13 A. | Batman, Cpl. W. 21766. | M. April 28/17. |

Essex Regiment—contd.

*B.E.F.*

13 A. Bayford, J. 31451. M. April 28/17.
13 A. Bendall, Sergt. H. 12069. M. April 28/17.
13 A. Bettles, G. J. 43465. M. April 28/17.
13 A. Bird, F. 24084. M. April 28/17.
13 A. IV Blowers, H. A. 7987. M. April 28/17.
13 A. Brewster, Percy. 32737. M. April 28/17.
13 A. I Bridges, L.-Cpl. Thos. Jos. 9454. M. April 28/17.
13 A. Brown, L.-Cpl. C. 13493. M. April 28/17.
13 A. Buckman, Chas. 23972. M. April 28/17.
13 A. Bugg, H. 19369. M. April 28/17.
13 A. Cain, J. 29205. M. April 28/17.
‡13 A. IV Chandler, H. 17220. K. Nov. 13/16. Det.D./B. R/Enq.
13 A. I Chapman, Cecil. 13997. M. April 28/17.
13 A. III Clay, Arthur. 29171. M. April 28/17.
13 A. Compton, H. W. 43538. M. April 30/17.
13 A. II Cox, Richard. 13756. M. April 28/17.
13 A. I Cracknell, Wm. Stowell. 31525. M. April 28/17.
13 A. Crowe, E. E. 29177. M. April 28/17.
13 A. Daniels, E. A. 19254. M. April 28/17.
13 A. Foard, A. 8755. M. April 28/17.
13 A. I Harding, E. E. 3254. M. April 28/17.
*13 A. Hardwick, D. 13785. M. May 3/17.
13 A. IV Harlow, Ernest. 33905. M. April 28/17.
13 A. or H.Q. Hayward, Bertram Bernard. 31664. M. April 28/17.
13 A. III Higgins, John. 28309. M. April 28/17.
13 A. Holland, L.-Cpl. W. T. J. 31529. M. April 28/17.
13 A. II Homewood, Sergt. Paul. 17336. M. April 28/17.
13 A. Howard, J. D. 31728. M. April 28/17.
13 A. III Howarth, Fred. Jas. 23658. M. April 28/17.
13 A. Howson, N. 32616. M. April 28/17.
13 A. Kerrison, F. E. 41299. M. April 28/17.
13 A. III Mack, O. C. 28502. M. April 28/17.
13 A. McWalters, P. 32642. M. April 28/17.
13 A. Morsley, S. 27935. M. April 28/17.
13 A. IV Munday, Sidney. 29200. M. April 28/17.
13 A. Norgate, A.-Sergt. H. O. 41291. M. April 28/17.
13 A. Peacock, H. 35141. M. April 28/17.
13 A. Playle, C. C. 32496. M. April 28/17.
13 A. Plomer, E. R. 29199. M. April 28/17.
13 A. Roast, Jas. 23706. M. April 28/17.
13 A. Root, G. E. 32838. M. April 28/17.
13 A. Rugg, Arthur Hy. Wm. 8035. M. April 28/17.
13 A. Skinner, C. J. 33158. M. April 28/17.
13 A. L.G.S. Slate, L.-Cpl. F. C. 17327. M. April 28/17.
13 A. II Smith, L.-Cpl. E. G. 21421. M. April 28/17.
13 A. Stone, S. 35117. M. April 28/17.
13 A. Street, Wm. James. 13701. M. April 28/17.
13 A. III Stroud, Fred. 35116. M April 28/17.
13 A. Suckling, L.-Cpl. Geo. 13354. M. April 28/17.
*13 A. Twitchett, Thos. Jas. 31865. M. April 28/17.
13 A. Tye, A.-Cpl. H. 41296. M. April 28/17.
13 A. Underlin, W. F. 23221. M. April 28/17.
13 A. Wagg, L.-Cpl. W. 41298. M. April 28/17.
13 A. III Warner, A.-Cpl. Fredk. 14444. M. April 28/17.
13 A. I Whitwell, C. H. 21574. M. April 28/17.
13 B. Bailey, W. J. 41429. M. April 28/17.
13 B. V Bateman, Edgar. 28083. M. April 28/17.
13 B. VIII Bateman, E. C. 28403. K. Nov. 13/16. Det.D./B. R/Enq

**Essex Regiment—contd.**

*B.E.F.*

13 B. VII Beadle, L.-Cpl. Thos. 31574. M. April 28/17.
13 B. Berisford, L.-Cpl. F. 13816. M. April 28/17.
13 B. Bullen, C. F. 19750. M. April 28/17.
13 B. Burgess, L.-Cpl. F. E. 17584. M. April 28/17.
13 B. V Clark, L.-Cpl. H. 17570. K. July 28/16. Det.D./B.
13 B. Clarke, J. W. 31601. M. April 28/17.
13 B. VII Cooper, W. L. 17681. M. April 28/17.
13 B. VIII Davey, Chas. Ernest. 41433. (Late 3 Cambs. Regt., 6645.) M. April 28/17.
13 B. VI Golding, A. W. 35130. M. April 28/17.
13 B. Hammond, A. 31568. M. April 28/17.
13 B. Keeley, L.-Cpl. R. J. 41411. M. April 28/17.
*13 B. Leeder, G. W. 28047. M. Nov. 13/16. R/Enq.
13 B. Lowe, D. E. 41436. M. April 28/17.
13 B. VII Maber, C. T. 43074. K. Nov. 13/16. Det.D./B.
*13 B. Orton, Wm. Charles. 18863. M. Nov. 13/16. R/Enq.
13 B. Parker, T. H. 41417. M. April 28/17.
13 B. V Ransom, E. 11052. M. Feb. 19/17.
13 B. Saville, E. 28451. M. April 28/17.
13 B. Simmonds, L.-Cpl. A. W. 17550. M. April 28/17.
13 B. Smith, C. E. 31546. M. April 28/17.
13 B. Sparrow, W. S. 41424. M. April 28/17.
13 B. Swannell, F. T. 17549. M. April 28/17.
13 B. Tebbutt, D. 41467. M. April 28/17.
13 B. V Thompson, C. 32627. M. April 28/17.
13 B. Tomlin, G. 29241. M. April 28/17.
13 B. V Turvey, F. G. 29206. M. April 28/17.
13 B. L.G.S. Wildbore, Isaac. 41427. M. April 28/17.
13 B. Yarham, L.-Cpl. E. 31612. M. April 28/17.
13 C. L.G.S. Barnes, C. E. 31466. M. April 28/17.
13 C. Bearman, W. 31656. M. April 28/17.
13 C. L.G.S. Bonfield, John. 18109. M. April 28/17.
13 C. Boon, J. 41500. M. April 28/17.
13 C. L.G.S. Boulton, L.-Cpl. Stephen. 18076. M. April 28/17.
13 C. Brace, H. 32586. M. April 28/17.
13 C. Brown, A. C. 30255. M. April 28/17.
13 C. IX Byrne, W. 35281. M. April 28/17.
13 C. Clegg, A. 32620. M. April 28/17.
13 C. Cooper, H. G. 41317. M. April 28/17.
13 C. IX Cotten, J. 21516. M. April 28/17.
13 C. Cousins, A.-Cpl. R. C. 18276. M. April 25/17.
13 C. XI Daniells, Rube Jos. 18175. M. April 28/17.
13 C. X Dawkins, G. 32588. M. April 28/17.
13 C. De Negri, W. G. 21482. M. April 28/17.
13 C. XII Felstead, Ernest. 28821. M. April 28/17.
13 C. Foreman, L.-Cpl. A. 41508. M. April 28/17.
13 C. Francis, W. J. 31497. M. April 28/17.
13 C. Frost, P. E. 43099. M. April 28/17.
13 C. L.G.S. Good, J. W. 18051. M. April 28/17.
13 C. XI Greff, H. 35424. M. April 28/17.
13 C. XI Hammerton, T. 18957. M. April 28/17.
13 C. Hayward, Sergt. Thos. 30990. M. April 28/17.
13 C. IX Hinton, S. G. 31653. M. April 28/17.
13 C. X Holt, E. J. 28679. M. April 28/17.
13 C. Hoskyn, A. E. S. 18119. M. April 28/17.
13 C. XII Jolly, Wm. Henry. 19420. M. April 28/17.
13 C. X Ketley, Lawrence J. 43100. M. April 28/17.
13 C. XII Lane, Wm. 17375. M. April 28/17.
13 C. Lawrence, A. 32584. M. April 28/17.

**Essex Regiment**—contd.

## *B.E.F.*

13 C. Mansfield, L.-Cpl. A. 15527. M. April 28/17.
13 C. Maskell, S. G. 29209. M. April 28/17.
13 C. XII Middleditch, Wm. 32579. M. April 28/17.
13 C. Osgodby, A. C. 35140. M. April 28/17.
13 C. Pointer, J. 31602. M. April 28/17.
13 C. IX Raven, F. 43028. M. April 28/17.
13 C. Roscoe, H. 18647. M. April 28/17.
13 C. Rozee, W. J. 17221. M. April 28/17.
13 C. H.Q. Skeet, Henry Jas. 31106. M. April 28/17.
13 C. XI Smith, A. 29210. M. April 28/17.
13 C. IX Smith, Sergt. Hamilton Barnabus. 43634. M. April 28/17.
13 C. Toynbee. P. 43085. M. April 28/17.
13 C. XI Walters, Alfred. 31471. M. April 28/17.
13 C. VI Whitmore, W. E. 31609. M. April 28/17.
13 C. Wilson, H. 32591. M. April 28/17.
13 C. Womack, A. A. 27919. M. April 28/17.
13 C. XII Woods, F. 43133. M. April 28/17.
13 D. XIV Badrick, C. 41485. M. April 28/17.
13 D. Bayford, J. 26755. M. April 28/17.
13 D. Billing, F. W. 20843. M. April 28/17.
13 D. XV Bonnick, A. A. 43201. M. April 28/17.
13 D. Booth C. F. 24621. M. April 28/17.
13 D. L.G.S. Boulton, L.-Cpl. Wm. 18354. M. April 28/17.
13 D. Buck, G. 19870. M. April 28/17.
13 D. XV Burgess, B. L. 31565. M. April 28/17.
13 D. Byford, E. 24728. M. April 28/17.
13 D. Byford, H. 23220. M. April 28/17.
13 D. Cain, T. A. 29204. M. April 28/17.
13 D. Chatwell, E. A. 29188. M. April 28/17.
13 D. Cockerill, G. P. 29217. M. April 28/17.
13 D. Coe, C. 29222. M. April 28/17.
13 D. Collingwood, Wm. Chas. 18678. M. April 28/17.
13 D. Collins, J. 41316. M. April 28/17.
13 D. XIII Collins, W. 21821. M. April 28/17.
13 D. Davies, D. 26735. M. April 28/17.
13 D. Dillon, H. 8782. M. April 28/17.
13 D. XIV Garwood, James. 20859. M. April 28/17.
13 D. George, T. W. 29198. M. April 28/17.
13 D. XIII Giles, Sabel J. 41499. M. April 28/17.
13 D. Harvey, E. 31498. M. April 28/17.
13 D. Jacobs, J. 18616. M. April 28/17.
13 D. Johnson, Cyril. 29142. M. April 28/17.
13 D. Lancaster, F. 18857. M. April 28/17.
13 D. XIII Lee, Geo. 31652. M. April 28/17.
13 D. Livermore, E. 10702. M. April 28/17.
13 D. Lodge, George William. 43127. (1590) M. April 28/17.
13 D. Lodge, W. G. 23219. M. April 28/17.
13 D. XIV Morgan, L.-Cpl. H. B. 43111. M. April 28/17.
13 D. O'Hare, J. 32638. M. April 28/17.
13 D. XIV Padley, C. W. 31109. M. April 28/17.
13 D. Perkins, J. W. 29189. M. April 28/17.
13 D. XIII Pye, L.-Cpl. L. G. 41446. M. April 28/17.
13 D. Ratledge, Fred. 29218. M. April 28/17.
13 D. XVI Roberts, George. 31331. M. April 28/17.
13 D. Roberts, H. 10378. M. April 28/17.
13 D. Rout, Wm. H. 41490. M. April 28/17.
‡13 D. Siequien, T. 21566. M. April 28/17.
13 D. Smith, L.-Cpl. J. G. 18656. M. April 28/17.

**Essex Regiment**—contd.

## *B.E.F.*

| | | |
|---|---|---|
| 13 D. | Starling, J. H. 41328. | M. April 28/17. |
| 13 D. XV | Toyer, E. 31837. | M. April 28/17. |
| 13 D. | Viles, G. F. 18923. | M. April 28/17. |
| 13 D. XVI | Weston, J. C. G. 41481. | M. April 28/17. |
| 13 D. XIII | White, Geo. 41461. | M. April 28/17. |
| 13 D. | Witherell, Sergt. A. 19332. | M. April 28/17. |
| 13 D. | Withers, Wm. 31144. | M. April 28/17. |
| 13 D. | Woods, E. F. 41496. | M. April 28/17. |
| 13 D. | Wooller, A. J. 21619. | M. April 28/17. |
| 13 D. XIV | York, Alfred Ernest. 29215. | M. April 28/17. |
| *13 ? M.G.S. | Livings, D. 17595. | M. Nov. 13/16. R/Enq. |
| 13 ? Gren. Co. | Musgrove, H. 17749. | M. Nov. 13/16. R/Enq. |

## *E.E.F.*

| | | |
|---|---|---|
| 4 | **Gidley, Lt. F. W.** (Fr. 1st.) | M. Mar. 27/17. |
| 4 | **Sweet, Lieut. F. Gordon.** (Fr. 3rd.) | K. Mar. 27/17. Det.D./B. |
| 4 | **Vincent, 2nd Lieut. W. Morris.** | K. March 26-27/17. Det.D./B. |
| 4 A. | Abrams, W. 200335. (1804.) | M. Mar. 27/17. |
| 4 A. | Arkend, Isadore. 200653. (2549.) | M. Mar. 27/17. |
| 4 A. II | Aylett, Chas. 201293. (Late 3980.) | M. Mar. 27/17. |
| 4 A. | Aylett, E. W. 200305. (1746.) | W. and M. Mar. 26/17. |
| 4 A. L.G.S. | Bull, Frank H. 200320. (Late 1780) | W. and M. Mar. 26/17. |
| 4 A. | Clements, L.-Cpl. H. 200076. (1169.) | W. and M. Mar. 26/17. |
| 4 A. | Coleman, R. J. 200375. | M. Mar. 27/17. |
| 4 A. | Elliott, F. T. 200218. (1555.) | W. and M. Mar. 26/17. |
| 4 A. | Elliott, R. T. 200264. (1657.) | W. and M. Mar. 26/17. |
| 4 A. | Emberson, R. W. 200763. | M. Mar. 27/17. |
| 4 A. | Harding, L.-Cpl. Fredk. John. 200953. (Late 3260.) | M. Mar. 27/17. |
| 4 A. | Kewley, John Fredk. 200623. (2480.) | W. and M. Mar. 26/17. |
| 4 A. | Lincoln, F. 200130. | W. and M. Mar. 26/17. |
| 4 A. | Middleditch, H. 200705. (2706.) | W. and M. Mar. 26/17. |
| 4 A. II | Morris, R. G. F. 200187. (1470.) | M. Mar. 27/17. |
| 4 A. | Park, R. W. 200585. | W. and M. Mar. 26/17. |
| 4 A. | Poulton, W. S. 200061. (1040.) | W. and M. Mar. 26/17. |
| 4 A. | Scott, Robt. 201090. (3487.) | M. Mar. 27/17. |
| 4 A. | York, W. J. 200180. (Late 1448.) | M. Mar. 27/17. |
| 4 B. | Baker, J. 201232. (Late 3648.) | M. Mar. 27/17. |
| 4 B. VIII | Beard, Cpl. F. H. 200453. | M. Mar. 27/17. |
| 4 B. VI | Bond, A. G. 200234. (1583.) | M. Mar. 27/17. |
| 4 B. VI | Brown, H. 200475. (2164.) | M. Mar. 27/17. |
| 4 B. | Burgess, Ivor S. 200543. | M. Mar. 27/17. |
| 4 B. | Courtman, Robt. 200686. (2637.) | W. and M. Mar. 26/17. |
| 4 B. VII | Dawson, Ed. Chas. 200532. (2277.) | W. and M. Mar. 26/17. |
| 4 B. | Drakeford, C.-Q.-M.-S. Harold G. 200051. (Late 895.) | M. Mar. 27/17. |
| 4 B. | Ellis, G. H. 201424. | M. Mar. 27/17. |
| 4 B. | Folkes, Joe. 200374. (1893.) | W. and M. Mar. 26/17. |
| 4 B. VI | Forte..s, Bernard. 201039. (3406.) | M. Mar. 27/17. |
| 4 B. | French, Reginald. 200482. (2179.) | W. and M., bel. K. Mar. 26/17. |
| 4 B. | Harris, Percy Henry. 201644. (5480.) | W. and M., bel. K. Mar. 26/17. |
| 4 B. | Hircock, P. W. 200508. (2225.) | M. Mar. 27/17. |
| 4 B. | Howell, J. H. 200582. (3395.) | W. and M. Mar. 26/17. |
| 4 B. | Howes, Sgt. G. R. 200068. (Late 1087) | M. Mar. 27/17. |
| 4 B. | Lawrence, Archie. 200467. | M. Mar. 27/17. |
| 4 B. | Layton, F. G. 200366. | M. Mar. 27/17. |
| 4 B. VII | Rix, L.-Cpl. F. W. 200235. | M. Mar. 27/17. |
| 4 B. | Rose, Edgar Conal Gordon. 201024. (Late 3373.) | M. March 27/17. |

**Essex Regiment—contd.**

## *E.E.F.*

4 B. Stiff, H. 200891. W. and M. **March 26/17.**
4 B. Trundle, Cpl. W. T. 200717. M. **Mar. 27/17.**
4 C. Bird, J. 200915. W. and M. **Mar. 26/17.**
4 C. Clark, W. 200944. W. and M. **Mar. 26/17.**
4 C. Cook, A. M. 200676. (2615.) W. and M. **Mar. 26/17.**
4 C. Davies, T. E. 200248. (Late 1620.) W. and M. **Mar. 26/17.**
4 C. Ellis, George. 200581. W. and M. **Mar. 26/17.**
4 C. Hill, R. 201179. (3589.) W. and M. **Mar. 26/17.**
4 C. King, A. J. 200356. W. and M. **Mar. 26/17.**
4 C. Lunn, R. H. 200835. (Late 3053.). M. **Mar. 27/17.**
4 C. Marshall, J. 201126. (3528.) M. **Mar. 27/17.**
4 C. Palfrey, Sergt. H. J. 201117. M. **Mar. 27/17.**
4 C. Sloan, Wm. John. 200780. W. and M. **Mar. 26/17.**
4 C. Smith, Jas. 201414. W. and M. **Mar. 26/17.**
4 C. Vandy, Victor Stanley. 200193. (Late 1481.) M. **Mar. 27/17.**
4 C. Western, R. 201613. (5449.) M. **Mar. 27/17.**
4 D. Andrew, Geo. J. 200969. K. **March 26/17.** Det.D./B.
4 D. Ashwell, A. J. 200961. (3273.) M. **Mar. 27/17.**
4 D. Baldwin, W. J. 201382. M. **Mar. 27/17.**
4 D. Beesley, Wm. 200492. (2199.) W. and M. **April 19/17.**
4 D. Burbeck, J. 201157. M. **Mar. 27/17.**
4 D. Bygrave, E. L. 201429. W. and M. **Mar. 26/17.**
4 D. Deed, P. W. 200287. (Late 1716.) M. **Mar. 27/17.**
4 D. Hawkes, Sergt. H. C. 201092. (3489.) W. and M. **Mar. 26/17.**
4 D. Ladham, A. 200144. (1364.) M. **Mar. 27/17.**
4 D. Newman, Chas. 200900. (Late 3175.) W. and M. **Mar. 26/17.**
4 D. Oakley, F. 200592. W. and M. **Mar. 26/17.**
4 D. Palmer, W. 200786. W. and M. **Mar. 26/17.**
4 D. Poulton, Alf. Victor. 200322. (1783.) W. and M. **Mar. 26/17.**
4 D. Pratt, J. W. 200959. W. and M. **Mar. 26/17.**
4 D. Shaw, S. J. 201260. (Late 3698.) W. and M. **Mar. 26/17.**
4 D. Stokes, Wm. Jas. 200562. W. and M. **Mar. 26/17.**
4 D. Thorogood, H. W. 201265. (Late 3704.) W. and M. **Mar. 26/17.**
4 D. Traylor, L.-Sgt. C. H. 200037. (631.) M. **March 27/17.**
4 D. Woof, Cpl. John Thos. 201107. (3504.) M. **Mar. 27/17.**
4 ? Ambrose, G. 201148. M. **Mar. 27/17.**
4 ? Baker, T. A. 200637. M. **Mar. 27/17.**
4 ? **Sig. S.** Bellamy, L.-Cpl. W. J. 200229. (Late 1576.) M. **Mar. 27/17.**
4 ? Bleaney, B. 201383. M. **Mar. 27/17.**
4 ? **Sig. S.** Brewer, Chas. 200773. (Late 2905.) W. and M. **Mar. 26/17.**
4 ? Broad, G. 201063. M. **Mar. 27/17.**
4 ? Brown, W. 200077. W. and M. **Mar. 26/17.**
*4 ? Calver, W. C. 201230. W. and M. **Mar. 26/17.**
4 ? Canning, J. 201388. M. **Mar. 27/17.**
4 ? Cawker, S. 201019. W. and M. **Mar. 26/17.**
4 ? Cornish, E. 201158. M. **Mar. 27/17.**
4 ? Crabbe, W. R. 200146. W. and M. **Mar. 26/17.**
4 ? Ennis, F. 201166. W. and M. **Mar. 26/17.**
4 ? Farr, L.-Cpl. W. 201118. W. and M. **Mar. 26/17.**
4 ? Geyton, H. T. 200458. M. **Mar. 27/17.**
4 ? Gladden, J. 200795. W. and M., bel. K. **Mar. 26/17.**
4 ? Goodwin, G. 200951. W. and M. **Mar. 26/17.**
4 ? Green, A. 200395. M. **Mar. 27/17.**
4 ? Hermitage, J. 201224. W. and M. **Mar. 26/17.**
4 ? Holt, H. 200387. W. and M. **Mar. 26/17.**

**Essex Regiment**—contd.

## *E.E.F.*

| | | | |
|---|---|---|---|
| 4 | ? | Howard, C. H. 201627. | M. **Mar. 27/17.** |
| 4 | ? | Hyde, W. 200837. | M. **Mar. 27/17.** |
| 4 | ? | Jenkins, J. 201624. | W. and M. **Mar. 26/17.** |
| 4 | ? | Johnson, A. C. 201277. | W. and M. **Mar. 26/17.** |
| 4 | ? | Lugsden, F. 201140. | M. **Mar. 27/17.** |
| 4 | ? | McMasters, G. A. 200361. | M. **Mar. 27/17.** |
| 4 | ? | Marshall, J. 201126. | M. **Mar. 27/17.** |
| 4 | ? | Mugford, P. C. 200769. | W. and M. **Mar. 26/17.** |
| 4 | ? | Myers, W. S. 200998. | W. and M. **Mar. 26/17.** |
| 4 | ? | Oswald, D. 200831. | M. **Mar. 27/17.** |
| 4 | ? | Perry, A. T. 200244. | W. and M. **Mar. 26/17.** |
| 4 | ? | Poole, H. 201000. | M. **Mar. 27/16.** |
| 4 | ? | Poultney, W. A. 201018. | W. and M. **Mar. 26/17.** |
| 4 | ? | Prior, G. 201193. | W. and M. **Mar. 26/17.** |
| 4 | ? | Ratford, M. C. 200923. | W. and M. **Mar. 26/17.** |
| 4 | ? | Reed, R. 200117. | W. and M. **Mar. 26/17.** |
| 4 | ? | Robinson, W. 200343. | W. and M., bel. K. **Mar. 26/17.** |
| 4 | ? | Sampson, F. 200747. | W. and M. **Mar. 26/17.** |
| 4 | ? | Sanderson, H. C. 200934. | W. and M. **Mar. 26/17.** |
| 4 | ? | Sargeant, H. 200858. | M. **Mar. 27/17.** |
| 4 | ? | Senior, P. 201222. | M. **Mar. 27/17.** |
| 4 | ? | Sharp, G. 201196. | M. **Mar. 27/17.** |
| 4 | ? | Sharpe, A. 201203. | M. **Mar. 27/17.** |
| 4 | ? | Simpson, Cpl. A. E. 200546. | W. and M. **Mar. 26/17.** |
| 4 | ? | Smith, Cpl. S. 201101. | W. and M. **Mar. 26/17.** |
| 4 | ? | Smoothy, W. 200636. | M. **Mar. 27/17.** |
| 4 | ? | Staines, F. 200306. | M. **Mar. 27/17.** |
| 4 | ? | Stringer, R. W. 201472. | W. and M. **Mar. 26/17.** |
| 4 | ? | Sturges, W. A. 200928. | M. **Mar. 27/17.** |
| 4 | ? | Talbot, F. 200219. | W. and M. **Mar. 26/17.** |
| 4 | ? | Taylor, H. 201208. | W. and M. **Mar. 26/17.** |
| 4 | ? | Timms, F. J. 201146. | W. and M. **Mar. 26/17.** |
| 4 | ? | Vincent, H. 200639. | M. **Mar. 27/17.** |
| 4 | ? | Vonneck, W. E. 200957. | W. and M. **Mar. 26/17.** |
| 4 | ? | Waite, V. R. E. 200560. | W. and M. **Mar. 26/17.** |
| 4 | ? | Warman, G. 200254. | M. **Mar. 27/17.** |
| 4 | ? | Webb, A. 200743. | W. and M. **Mar. 26/17.** |
| 4 | ? | Wellington, Sgt. D. S. 200255. | M. **Mar. 27/17.** |
| 4 | ? | Wilson, S. J. 200473. | W. and M. **Mar. 26/17.** |
| 4 | ? | Windust, J. J. 200538. | W. and M. **Mar. 26/17.** |
| 4 | ? | Wood, G. J. 201271. | M. **Mar. 27/17.** |
| 4 | ? | Wood, Cpl. J. 201107. | M. **Mar. 27/17.** |
| 5 | | **Beard, 2nd Lieut. E. C.** | M. **Mar. 26/17.** |
| 5 | | **Gould, Capt. C. A.** | M. **Mar. 26/17.** |
| 5 | | **Wilson, 2nd Lieut. C. O.** | M. **Mar. 26/17.** |
| 5 | A. | Beere, E. 251113. | M. **Mar. 26/17.** |
| 5 | A. II | Clarke, F. 251195. | W. and M. **Mar. 26/17.** |
| 5 | A. | Day, Alfred E. 250863. (Late 3483.) | W. and M. **Mar. 26/17.** |
| 5 | A. | Everard, Sidney F. 250126. (Late 1554.) | K. **Mar. 26/17.** Det.D./B. |
| 5 | A. | Humphreys, Sgt. P. R. 250408. (Late 2288.) | W. and M. **Mar. 26/17.** |
| 5 | A. | Jarvis, A. 250079. (1367.) | W. and M. **Mar. 26/17.** |
| 5 | A. | Keymer, C. H. 250525. (Late 2548.) | M. **Mar. 26/17.** |
| 5 | A. | Prior, W. G. 251373. | W. and M. **Mar. 26/17.** |
| 5 | A. | Ralph, L.-Cpl. Fred. 250328. (Late 2101.) | M. **Mar. 26/17.** |
| 5 | A. | Scotney, A. G. 251122. (Late 3896). | W. and M. **Mar. 26/17.** |

**Essex Regiment—contd.**

## *E.E.F.*

| | | |
|---|---|---|
| 5 A. | Wright, Percy Wm. 250463. (Late 2401.) | W. and M. **Mar. 26/17.** |
| 5 B. | Bambridge, H. 251287. | W. and M. **Mar. 27/17.** |
| 5 B. | Carr, L.-Cpl. Ernest Wm. 250197. (1772.) | W. and M. **Mar. 27/17.** |
| 5 B. | Davidson, Thomas. 257378. (Late 4312.) | M. **Mar. 26/17.** |
| 5 B. | Gray, W. C. 251118. | M. **Mar. 26/17.** |
| 5 B. | Halls, Sgt. H. H. 250005. (Late 109.) | W. and M. **Mar. 26/17.** |
| 5 B. | Langley, L.-Sergt. A. E. 250084. | W. and M. **Mar. 26/17.** |
| 5 B. | Mann, Sergt. A. 250357. | K. **Mar. 26/17.** Det.D./B. |
| 5 B. | Theadham, Geo. 250871. (3498.) | W. and M. **Mar. 26/17.** |
| 5 C. | Buckingham, P. 250580. (Late 2717.) (Also known as Buckham.) | M. **Mar. 26/17.** |
| 5 C. | Hyndes, A. E. 250440. (Late 2354.) | W. and M. **Mar. 26/17.** |
| 5 C. L.G.S. | Joy, Tom. 250263. (Late 1930.) | W. and M. **Mar. 26/17.** |
| 5 C. | Little, A. 250728. (3152.) | M. **Mar. 26/17.** |
| 5 C | Munson, F. 250592. (Late 2767.) | M. **Mar. 26/17.** |
| 5 C. | Salmon, A. 250185. (Late 1724.) | M. **Mar. 26/17.** |
| 5 C. | Smith, A. E. 251170. (3969.) | M. **Mar. 26/17.** |
| 5 C. | Smith, A. W. 250407. (2286.) | K. **Mar. 26/17.** Det.D./B. |
| 5 C. | Tansley, P. E. 251227. | W. and M. **Mar. 26/17.** |
| 5 D. XIV | Bell, A. W. 250530. (Late 2557.) | W. and M. **Mar. 26/17.** |
| 5 D. | Eve, F. F. 250290. (2006.) | M. **Mar. 26/17.** |
| 5 D. | Millar, W. Leslie. 250454. (Late 2386.) | W. and M. **Mar. 26/17.** |
| 5 D. | Moseley, W. 250600. (2791.) | M. **Mar. 27/17.** |
| 5 D. | Partridge, C. W. 250654. (2933.) | W. and M. **Mar. 26/17.** |
| 5 D. | Stone, H. C. 250931. (Late 3600.) | M. **Mar. 26/17.** |
| 5 ? | Arnold, W. 250299. | W. and M **Mar. 26/17.** |
| 5 ? | Bailey, E. A. 251728. | M. **Mar. 26/17.** |
| 5 ? | Boreham, B. 251034. | W. and M. **Mar. 26/17.** |
| 5 ? | Brazier, C 250272. | M. **Mar. 26/17.** |
| 5 ? | Buller, R. 250717. | M. **Mar. 26/17.** |
| 5 ? | Clark, E. H. 250754. | M. **Mar. 26/17.** |
| 5 ? | Cook, E. C. 250500. | W. and M. **Mar. 26/17.** |
| 5 ? | Cutmore, F. 252681. | M. **Mar. 26/17.** |
| 5 ? | Cutter, F. M. 250791. | W. and M. **Mar. 26/17.** |
| 5 ? | Darbey, H. E. 251064. | M. **Mar. 26/17.** |
| 5 ? | Davidson, T. 251378. | W. and M. **Mar. 26/17.** |
| 5 ? | Deards, T. 251368. | W. and M. **Mar. 26/17.** |
| 5 ? | Devenish, J. 250057. | W. and M. **Mar. 26/17.** |
| 5 ? | Dunn, A. W. 251277. | W. and M. **Mar. 26/17.** |
| 5 ? | Earey, H. 251183. | M. **Mar. 26/17.** |
| 5 ? | Emery, E. 250503. | M. **Mar. 26/17.** |
| 5 ? | Everett, E. H. 250196. | W. and M. **Mar. 26/17.** |
| 5 ? | Grove, H. 250335. | M. **Mar. 26/17.** |
| 5 ? | Hibburt, G. 251735. | W. and M. **Mar. 26/17.** |
| 5 ? | Hoslett, H. 251194. | M. **Mar. 26/17.** |
| 5 ? | Howard, W. 250755. | M. **Mar. 26/17.** |
| 5 ? | Hubbard, L. A. 250649. | M. **Mar. 26/17.** |
| 5 ? | King, T. W. 250094. | W. and M. **Mar. 26/17.** |
| 5 ? | Malyon, F. C. 250957. | W. and M. **Mar. 26/17.** |
| 5 ? | Mills, F. J. 251222. | M. **Mar. 26/17.** |
| 5 ? | Murray, Cpl. J. 251339. | W. and M. **Mar. 26/17.** |
| 5 ? | Neary, J. 252534. | M. **Mar. 26/17.** |
| 5 ? | Olley, F. G. 251089. | W and M. **Mar. 26/17.** |
| 5 ? | Patient, F. 250761. | M. **Mar. 26/17.** |
| 5 ? | Perrin, H. F. 250512. | M. **Mar. 26/17.** |

**Essex Regiment—contd.**

## *E.E.F.*

| | | | |
|---|---|---|---|
| 5 ? | | Potter, S. S. 251224. | M. **Mar. 26/17.** |
| 5 ? | | Pullen, O. 251189. | W. and M. **Mar. 26/17.** |
| 5 ? | | Rainbird, A.-Cpl. H. F. W. 251338. | M. **Mar. 26/17.** |
| 5 ? | | Rouse, R. 250755. | M. **Mar. 26/17.** |
| 5 ? | | Seaborne, A. J. 250486. | W. and M. **Mar. 26/17.** |
| 5 ? | | Shead, L.-Cpl. A. 250877. | W. and M. **Mar. 26/17.** |
| 5 ? | | Simpson, C. 251096. | M. **Mar. 26/17.** |
| 5 ? | | Smith, T. W. 251242 | W. and M. **Mar. 26/17.** |
| 5 ? | | Succamore, E. 250639. | W. and M. **Mar. 26/17.** |
| 5 ? | | Thorpe, C. R. 251027. | M. **Mar. 26/17.** |
| 5 ? | | Turner, C. J. 250295. | M. **Mar. 26/17.** |
| 5 ? | | Wade, W. 250145. | W. and M. **Mar. 26/17.** |
| 5 ? | | Willshere, H. 251331. | M. **Mar. 26/17.** |
| 5 ? | | Wilson, B. F. 251168. | M. **Mar. 26/17.** |
| 6 B. | | **Clubb, Lieut. Howard Wm.** | M., bel. K. **Mar. 27/17.** |
| 6 | | **Tee, Capt. Eric Wm.** | W. and M. **Mar. 25/17.** |
| 6 A. | | Barry, E. G. 275667. (Late 3905.) | W. and M. **Mar. 27/17.** |
| 6 A. | | Cole, W. 275753. (4469.) | M. **Mar. 27/17.** |
| 6 A. | | Cook, Frank Machin. 276177. (6316.) | W. and M. **Mar. 27/17.** |
| 6 A. | | Croucher, Cpl. Harold G. 276135. (Late 6019.) | M. **Mar. 27/17.** |
| 6 A. | | Esmond, J. 275464. (3158.) | W. and M. **Mar. 27/17.** |
| 6 A. | | Gentry, G. H. 275382. (2370.) | M. **Mar. 27/17.** |
| 6 A. | | Hardes, Alfred Alex. 275465. (Late 3161.) | W. and M. **Mar. 27/17.** |
| 6 A. | | Hunt, F. H. C. 275997. (Late 5659.) | M. **Mar. 27/17.** |
| 6 A. | | McGrath, W. 275469. | W. and M. **Mar. 27/17.** |
| 6 A. | | Mitchell, (?) L.-Cpl. J. A. 275275. (Late 1960.) | W. and M. **Mar. 27/17.** |
| 6 A. | | Pascoe, R. T. 275791. (Late 4640.) | M. **Mar. 27/17.** |
| 6 A. | | Salmon, Philip. 275408. (Late 2667.) | W. and M. **Mar. 27/17.** |
| 6 A. | II | Urry, E. A. 275741. (Late 4252.) | M. **Mar. 27/17.** |
| 6 A. | | White, F. J. 275595. (Late 3597.) | W. and M. **Mar. 27/17.** |
| 6 B. | | Bryant, Herbert Fredk. 275797. (Late 4688.) | W. and M. **Mar. 27/17.** |
| 6 B. | | Dear, Wm. 276517. (Late 7410.) | M. **Mar. 27/17.** |
| 6 B. | VIII | Deas, L.-Cpl. J. G. 275978. | M. **Mar. 27/17.** |
| 6 B. | | Elliott, Geo. 275996. | M. **Mar. 27/17.** |
| 6 B. | | Frakes, L.-Cpl. A. 275115. | W. and M. **Mar. 26/17.** |
| *6 B. | | Halsey, H. 276179. (6350.) | W. and M. **Mar. 27/17.** |
| 6 B. | VI | McGuiness, W. 275155. (1527.) | W. and M. **Mar. 26/17.** |
| 6 B. | | Mansell, S. J. 275241. (Late 1779.) | W. and M. **Mar. 27/17.** |
| 6 B. | | Munns, W. 276528. | W. and M. **Mar. 26/17.** |
| 6 B. | | Parker, Arthur Chas. 275937. (Late 5475.) | W. and M. **Mar. 26/17.** |
| 6 B. | | Saunders, Joseph. 277379. (Late 8649.) | W. and M. **Mar. 26/17.** |
| 6 B. | | Sealey, R. W. 275313. (Late 2098.) | M. **Mar. 27/17.** |
| 6 B. | Sig. S. | Sharp, W. G. 275936. (Late 5467.) | M. **Mar. 27/17.** |
| 6 B. | | Simmonds, H. 275035. | M. **Mar. 27/17.** |
| 6 B. | | Towns, L.-Sergt. J. T. 275303. (Late 2084.) | W. and M. **Mar. 26/17.** |
| 6 B. | | Voisey, D. C. 275281. | M. **Mar. 27/17.** |
| 6 B. | | Whitbread, W. 275621. (Late 3700.) | M. **Mar. 26/17.** |
| 6 B. | | Young, Joseph. 276107. (5949.) | M. **Mar. 27/17.** |
| 6 C. | | Downham, E. 276492. (7379.) | W. and M. **Mar. 27/17.** |
| 6 C. | | Moore, W. W. 275185. (Late 1605.) | W. and M. **Mar. 26/17.** |
| 6 C. | | Rix, P. 275453. | W. and M. **Mar. 26/17.** |
| 6 C. | | Stewart, G. W. 275766. (4515.) | W. and M. **Mar. 26/17.** |
| 6 D. | | Austin, C.-S.-M. W. G. 275024. (448) | W. and M. **Mar. 26/17.** |

**Essex Regiment**—contd.

## *E.E.F.*

| | | |
|---|---|---|
| **6 D.** | Bedford, Geo. Herbert. 270478. (Late 7363, fr. A. Co.) | M. **Mar. 27/17.** |
| **6 D.** | Linklet, A. 276561. | M. **Mar. 27/17.** |
| **6 D.** | Munn, L.-Cpl. B. 275084. | M. **April 22/17.** |
| **6 D.** | Tavener, W. C. 275608. (3673.) | M. **Mar. 27/17.** |
| **6 ?** | Ayling, J. F. 276073. | M. **Mar. 27/17.** |
| **6 ?** | Barlow, A. J. 275320. | W. and M., bel. K. **Mar. 27/17.** |
| **6 ?** | Clark, Cpl. L. N. 275214. | W. and M. **Mar. 27/17.** |
| **6 ?** | Edney, W. E. 275135. | W. and M. **Mar. 27/17.** |
| **6 ?** | Ellis, A. R. 276048. | W. and M. **Mar. 26/17.** |
| **6 ?** | Fallack, F. R. 275429. | M. **Mar. 27/17.** |
| **6 ?** | Freeman, R. 275499. | W. and M. **Mar. 27/17.** |
| **6 ?** | Gebbs, L.-Cpl. A. 275410. | W. and M. **Mar. 27/17.** |
| **6 ?** | Horsnell, H. W. 275895. | W. and M. **Mar. 27/17.** |
| **6 ?** | Hurle, G. 275994. | W. and M. **Mar. 26/17.** |
| **6 ?** | Miles, W. F. 275373. | W. and M. **Mar. 26/17.** |
| **6 ?** | Miller, H L. 276544. | M. **Mar. 27/17.** |
| **6 ?** | **Paice, Sergt. F. C. 1158.** | **D/W. Mar. 29/17, Det.D./B.** |
| **6 ?** | Petty, F. A. 275718. | W. and M. **Mar. 27/17.** |
| **6 ?** | Poulter, B. P. 275870. | M. **Mar. 27/17.** |
| **6 ?** | Rowley, F. 275685. | W. and M. **Mar. 27/17.** |
| **6 ?** | Sheppard, S. J. 276130. | W. and M. **Mar. 26/17.** |
| **6 ?** | Skinner, L.-Cpl. E. 275423. | M. **Mar. 27/17.** |
| **6 ?** | Upex, J. A. E. 276208. | W. and M. **Mar. 27/17.** |
| **6 ?** | Vane, Cpl. A. 275043. | W. and M. **Mar. 27/17.** |
| **6 ?** | Wedge, H. J. 275587. | W. and M., bel. K. **Mar. 27/17.** |
| **6 ?** | Wells, S. R. 276169. | M. **Mar. 27/17.** |
| **7 C.** | **Gill, 2nd Lieut. W. G. O.** | W. and M., bel. K. **Mar. 27/17.** |
| **7** | **Gould, 2nd Lieut. R. E.** | M. **Mar. 27/17.** |
| **7** | **Hetherington, Lieut. Guy.** | W. and M. **Mar. 27/17.** |
| **7 A.** | Brooks, D. 300992. (3985.) | M. **Mar. 27/17.** |
| **7 A.** | Cocks, E. F. 300735. (Late 3439.) | M. **Mar. 27/17.** |
| **7 A. Sig. S.** | Groome, C. 300821. (Late 3633.) | M. **Mar. 27/17.** |
| **7 A.** | Harrall, C. A. F. 300346. (Late 2490.) | M. **Mar. 27/17.** |
| **7 A.** | Hurley, G. 300810. (Late 3610.) | M. **Mar. 27/17.** |
| **7 A.** | Wood, A. J. 300918. | M. **Mar. 27/17.** |
| **7 B.** | Robinson, A. H. 300407. (Late 2624.) | M. **Mar. 27/17.** |
| **7 B.** | Rolph, W. A. 301198. (4343.) | M. **Mar. 27/17.** |
| **7 C.** | Ames, Geo. 300065. (Late 1704.) | M. **Mar. 27/17.** |
| **7 C.** | Bancroft, W. E. 300712. (3386.) | M. **Mar. 27/17.** |
| **7 C.** | Carter, A. H. 300554. (Late 2980.) | M. **Mar. 27/17.** |
| **7 C. IX** | Cheshire, A. E. 300498. (Late 2824.) | M. **Mar. 27/17.** |
| **7 C. IX** | Christie, Albert Edw. 300891. (3764.) | M. **Mar. 27/17.** |
| **7 C. XII** | Hall, Gilbert. 301028. (Late 4061.) | M. **March 27/17.** |
| **7 C.** | Hopkins, Cpl. C. W. 300131. (Late 1930.) | M. **Mar. 26-27/17.** |
| **7 C. X** | Valens, A. 300967. (Late 3926.) | M. **Mar. 27/17.** |
| **7 C. XII** | Willsher, H. J. 300768. | M. **Mar. 27/17.** |
| **7 D.** | **Bettinson, G. 300859. (Late 3695.)** | M. **Mar. 27/17.** |
| **7 D.** | Disney, Geo. T. 300214. (2129.) | M. **Mar. 27/17.** |
| **7 D.** | Jarman, J. 300241. (Late 2184.) | M., bel. K. **Mar. 27/17.** |
| **7 D.** | Nother, A. G. 300692. (Late 3332.) | M. **Mar. 27/17.** |
| **7 D. XIV** | Stamp, W. C. 300935. (3844.) | M. **Mar. 27/17.** |
| **7 ?** | Auger, L.-Cpl. B. 301095. | M. **Mar. 27/17.** |
| **7 ?** | Beeton, F. 301097. | M. **Mar. 27/17.** |
| **7 ?** | Bowden, H. 301134. | M. **Mar. 27/17.** |
| **7 ?** | Butler, C. W. 300732. | M. **Mar. 27/17.** |
| **7 ?** | Crease, H. D. 300623. | M. **Mar 27/17.** |
| **7 ?** | Crowe, B. 300284. | M., bel. K. **Mar. 27/17.** |

**Essex Regiment**—contd.

*E.E.F.*

| | | |
|---|---|---|
| 7 ? | Dellar, D. D. 300258. | M. Mar. 27/17. |
| 7 ? | Frost, A. 301068. | M. Mar. 27/17. |
| 7 ? | Gunn, T. S. 300608. | M. Mar. 27/17. |
| 7 ? | Kent, W. H. 300965. | M., bel. K. Mar. 27/17. |
| 7 ? | Lockwood, C. 300157. | M. Mar. 27/17. |
| 7 ? | Louis, A. 300322. | M. Mar. 27/17. |
| 7 ? | Lusher, H. G. 300916. | M. Mar. 27/17. |
| 7 ? | Monk, G. C. 300328. | M. Mar. 27/17. |
| 7 ? | Shipp, W. J. 300685. | M. Mar. 27/17. |
| 7 ? | Webb, G. 301032. | M. Mar. 27/17. |
| 7 ? | Whiting, L.-Cpl. E. 300373. | M. Mar. 27/17. |

## ESSEX YEOMANRY.

*B.E.F.*

| | | |
|---|---|---|
| A. Squad. | Tibbenham, Trumpeter Arthur Thos. 80797. (Late 3rd, No. 2029.) | M. April 14/17. |
| B. | Bassett, G. 80444. | M. April 11/17. |
| B. | Stowell, Trumpeter Arthur. 80785. 2015.) | W. and M. April 11/17. |
| B. | Warren, L.-Cpl. Frank Ernest. 80185 | W. and M. April 11/17. |
| C. | **Dunmow Troop** Matthams, D. 80242. (2015.) | M. April 11/17 |
| ? | Anderson, S. A. 81018. | M. April 11/17. |
| ? | Baines, W. H. 80982. | M. April 11/17. |
| ? | Bayman, F. W. 80668. | M. April 11/17. |
| ? | Harvey, E. A. 80268. | M. April 11/17. |
| ? | Matthams, D. T. 80240. | M. April 11/17. |
| ? | Smith, Sergt. A. E. 80329. | M., bel. K. April 11/17. |
| ? | Smith, B. 80631. | M., bel. K. April 11/17. |
| ? | Steward, C. 80613. | W. and M., bel. K. April 11/17. |
| ? | Steward, C. W. 81194. | M. April 11/17. |

## ROYAL FLYING CORPS.

*B.E.F.*

| | | |
|---|---|---|
| *1 Squad. | **Anderson, Lieut. R. W. L.** | M. June 11/17. |
| ‡1 | **Atkins, 2nd Lieut. G. C.** | M. June 19/17. |
| 1 | **Cole, 2nd Lieut. M. G.** | M. May 18/17. |
| 1 | **Drummond, Lt. L. (Fr. 1st Canadian R.E.)** | M. May 18/17. |
| ‡1 | **Lloyd, 2nd Lieut. R. S.** | M. June 18/17. |
| *1 | **McFerran, Lieut. T. M.** | M. June 21/17. |
| 1 | **Welch, 2nd Lieut. H. (Fr. R.F.A.)** | M. March 28/17. |

**Flying Corps, Royal—contd.**

## *B.E.F.*

| | | |
|---|---|---|
| 2 | **Brown, 2nd Lieut. A. R.** | M. **April 6/17.** |
| 2 | **Byrne, 2nd Lieut. E.** (Fr. Gordons.) | M. **Mar. 11/17.** |
| 2 | **Croker, 2nd Lt. F. R.** (Fr. 6 Lancs. Fus.) | M. **April 27/17.** |
| 2 | **Rowe, 2nd Lt. B. F.** (Fr. 1 R. Fus.) | M. **June 1/17.** |
| 2 | **Stonier, Lt. W. J.** (Fr. Bedfords.) | M. **April 27/17.** |
| 2 | **Whitaker, Capt. V. J.** (Fr. 3 Lincs.) | M. **April 6/17.** |
| 3 | **De Ross, 2nd Lieut. A. G. S.** | K. **Feb. 14/17.** Det.D./B. |
| 3 | **Young, 2nd Lt. Francis Chisholm.** | K. about **Feb. 14/17.** Det.D./B. |
| 3 | Morgan, Cpl. A. S. 4834. (Att. Fr. S.A. Sig. Co. R.E.) | M. **April 22/17.** |
| 4 | **Fletcher, 2nd Lt. G. H.** (Fr. 1 W. Yorks.) | M. **June 2/17.** |
| 4 | **McNamara, 2nd Lieut. J. C.** | M. **June 3-4/17.** |
| 5 | **Allan, 2nd Lieut. L. E.** (Fr. West & Cumb. Yeo.) | M. **April 26/17.** |
| 5 | **Hope, Lt. H. B. T.** (Fr. 3/4 Northants.) | M. **April 26/17.** |
| 6 | **Durkin, 2nd Lt. F. V.** (Fr. 7 Worc.) | M. **June 7/17.** |
| 6 | **Halliday, Lt. M. F. J.** (Fr. 1 Glos.) | M. **June 7/17.** |
| 6 | **Phillipps, Lieut. A. J. C. E.** | M. **June 7/17.** |
| 7 | **Gaulter, Lieut. V.** | M. **May 7/17.** |
| 7 | **Jackson, 2nd Lt. G. W.** (Fr. 7th. North. Fus.) | M. **May 7/17.** |
| ‡7 | **Simon, Lt. G. P.** (Fr. R.G.A.) | M. **June 27/17.** |
| *7 | **Vipond, 2nd Lieut. F. E.** (Fr. 9th Manchesters.) | M. **June 27/17.** |
| 8 | **Hatch, Lieut. G.** (Fr. 17 Londons.) | M. **April 6/17.** |
| 8 | Langridge, Cpl. E. 1908. | M. **April 6/17.** |
| *9 | **Allen, M.C., Capt. A. S.** (Fr. 18 Canadians.) | M. **April 30/17.** |
| *9 | **Barlow, Lieut. H. C.** (Fr. Lancs. Fus.) | M. **June 18/17.** |
| *9 | **Bean, 2nd Lieut. B. H.** (Fr. 6 Welsh Fus.) | M. **June 28/17.** |
| 9 | **Cramb, 2nd Lieut. W. B.** (Fr. A. & S.H.) | M. **April 14/17.** |
| *9 | **Ellis, Lieut. R. W.** | M. **June 18/17.** |
| 9 | **Freemantle, 2nd Lieut. R. P. C.** | M. **April 30/17.** |
| 9 | **Graves, Lt. C. L.** (Fr. Canadian Local Forces.) | M. **April 24/17.** |
| 9 | **Matthews, Lt. F. A.** (Fr. Sussex.) | M. **April 24/17.** |
| 9 | **Sherman, 2nd Lieut. P.** | M. **April 30/17.** |
| 10 | **Roux, 2nd Lieut. F.** | M. **April 26/17.** |
| 11 | **Clifton, 2nd Lieut. W. G. T.** (Fr. Ox. and Bucks.) | M. **Mar. 31/17.** |
| 11 | **Horncastle, M.C., 2nd Lt. L. M.** (Fr. 1st Wilts.) | M. **May 20/17.** |
| 11 | **Hudson, 2nd Lieut. T. J.** | M. **May 20/17.** |
| *11 | **MacBrayne, 2nd Lieut. D. C. H.** | M. **June 21/17.** |
| ‡11 | **Robertson, Capt. C. E.** | M. **July 12/17.** |
| 11 | **Tolhurst, Lieut. B. J.** | M. **April 22/17.** |

**Flying Corps, Royal—contd.**

## *B.E.F.*

| | | |
|---|---|---|
| 11 | **Turner, Lieut. W. G. D.** | **M. May 24/17.** |
| 11 | Clarkson, Sergt. Albert. 3049. | **M. Sept. 30/16. R/Enq.** |
| 11 | Gosnay, 2nd A.M. Hubert Victor. 61870. (A Flight.) | **M. Mar. 24/17.** |
| 11 | Hadlow, 2nd A.M. F. 2632. (Fr. 2nd London.) | **M. April 1/17.** |
| 11 | Wood, 2nd A.M. G. 15275. (Late 61869.) | **M. April 6/17.** |
| 12 | **Davies, 2nd Lieut. D. E.** | **M. April 29/17.** |
| 12 | **Rathbone, Lt. G. H.** (Fr. 9 Canadians) | **M. April 29/17.** |
| 12 | **Thomson, Lieut. T.** | **M. April 25/17.** |
| 12 | **Turnbull, 2nd Lieut. Alec. M.** | **M. April 25/17.** |
| 13 | **Evans, Lieut. H. H.** (Fr. 2 C.M.R.) | **K. April 5/17. Det.D./B.** |
| 13 | **Powell, Lt. P. J. G.** (Fr. A.S.C.) | **M. April 2/17.** |
| 13 | **Thorburn, Capt. James.** (Fr. R.G.A.) | **M. Feb. 11/17.** |
| 13 | Bonner, Obs. Percy. 1897. (C Flight.) | **M. April 2/17.** |
| ‡13 | Stewart, Cpl. G. 3223. | **M. April 11/17.** |
| *15 | **De Conway, 2nd Lt. J.** (Fr. Lovats Scouts.) | **M. June 15/17.** |
| 15 | **Sayer, 2nd Lieut. J. H.** | **M. April 3/17.** |
| 15 | Walker, 2nd Cl. Air Mech. J. 28707. | **M. April 12/17.** |
| ‡16 | **Franklin, Lieut. R. V.** | **K. June 24/17. Det.D./B.** |
| 16 | **Knight, Lt. O. R.** (Fr. 4 W. Surreys) | **M. April 6/17.** |
| 16 | **Lawrence, 2nd Lt. N. A.** (Fr. R. Fus.) | **M. April 30/17.** |
| 16 | **McKissock, Lieut. W. E.** | **K. June 1/17. Det.D./B.** |
| 16 | **Munn, 2nd Lieut. L. V.** (Fr. 6th Leicesters.) | **M. (W.O.L. Feb. 23/17.)** |
| 16 | **Stout, 2nd Lieut. G. R. Y.** | **M. April 30/17.** |
| 18 | **Hunt, 2nd Lieut. E. W. A.** | **M. May 1/17.** |
| 18 | **Miller, 2nd Lieut. G. B.** | **M. May 1/17.** |
| 18 | **Todd, M.C., 2nd Lt. A.** (Fr. 4th D.L.I.) | **M. April 12/17.** |
| 18 | **Walton, Lt. O. T.** (Fr. 3 S. Lancs.) | **M. April 12/17.** |
| 18 | **Waters, 2nd Lieut. H. E.** | **M. June 2/17.** |
| 18 | Beebee, Cpl. Alfred. 14956. (C. Flight) | **M. April 29/17.** |
| 18 | Burgess, Sergt Henry Philip. 19135. | **M. Mar. 11/17.** |
| 18 | Russell, Sergt. S. 9701. (Fr. E. Kent.) | **M. May 7/17.** |
| 18 | Stead, Sergt. G. 2119. | **M. April 29/17.** |
| 19 | **Applin, 2nd Lieut. R.** | **M. April 29/17.** |
| 19 | **Capper, Lieut. E. W.** (Fr. Montgomery Yeo.) | **M. April 14/17.** |
| 19 | **Davidson, M.C., Capt. D. A. L.** | **M. April 30/17.** |
| ‡19 | **Lowe, 2nd Lieut. M.** | **M. June 27/17.** |
| 20 | **Anderson, Lieut. W.** | **M. March 17/17.** |
| 20 | **Blackwood, Capt. John.** | **M. Jan. 25/17.** |
| ‡20 | **Crafter, M.C., Lt. J.** (Fr. 20 Lond.) | **M. July 8/17.** |
| 20 | **Cubbon, Capt. F. R.** (Fr. 72 Punjabis.) | **M. June 9/17.** |
| 20 | **Hume, Lieut. Ronald.** (Fr. 20th R. Fus.) | **M. April 6/17.** |
| 20 | **Marshall, 2nd Lieut. B. S.** | **M. June 7/17.** |
| 20 | **Smith, 2nd Lieut. R.** (Fr. 3rd K.O.Y.L.I.) | **M. April 6/17.** |
| ‡20 | Aldred, Sergt. B. 77449. | **M. May 23/17.** |
| ‡20 | Lloyd, 2nd Air Mech. C. P/11192. | **M. June 7/17.** |
| ‡20 | Worthing, 2nd Cl. Air Mech. G. 78285. | **M. May 5/17.** |
| 21 | **Gee, 2nd Lieut. G. R. D.** | **M. June 4/17.** |

Flying Corps, Royal—contd.

## B.E.F.

| | | |
|---|---|---|
| 22 | **Harris, 2nd Lieut. H.** | M. June 5/17. |
| 22 | **Loveland, Lt. H.** (Fr. 78 Canadians.) | K. April 2/17. Det.D./B. |
| 22 | **Stewart, 2nd Lieut. J. D. M.** | M. April 26/17. |
| 23 | **Cheatle, 2nd Lieut. C. C.** | M. May 5/17. |
| ‡23 | **Clark, 2nd Lieut. W. H.** | M. July 6/17. |
| 23 | **Elsley, Lieut. L.** | M. April 5/17. |
| 23 | **Garrett, 2nd Lieut. H. T.** | M. May 20/17. |
| 23 | **Higginbottom, 2nd Lt. F.** (Fr. 9th Cheshires.) | M. April 5/17. |
| 23 | Abrahams, Sgt. Clarence. 6969. | M. May 19/17. |
| 25 | **Bates, 2nd Lieut. A. H.** | M. April 13/17. |
| 25 | **Boultbee, Lt. A. E.** (Fr. Northants.) | M. March 17/17. |
| *25 | **Ferriman, Lieut. F. S.** (Fr. Ox. & Bucks.) | M. June 7/17. |
| 25 | **Pollard, 2nd Lt. G. H.** (Fr. 9 A. & S.H.) | M. June 7/17. |
| 25 | **Severs, 2nd Lieut. A. G.** | M. Mar. 28/17. |
| 25 | **Woollen, 2nd Lieut. D. C.** | M. April 13/17. |
| ‡25 | Barnes, Sergt. W. A. 61925. | M. April 13/17. |
| 25 | King, Air Mech. F. 61783. | M. Mar. 17/17. |
| ‡25 | Sturrock, L.-Cpl. C. 1888. (Fr. Black Watch.) | M. May 28/17. |
| ‡27 | **Palmer, 2nd Lieut. G. H.** | M. July 14/17. |
| 27 | **Proud, 2nd Lt. J. R. S.** (Fr. 7 R. W. Kents.) | M. April 6/17. |
| 27 | **Wedderspoon, Lieut. J. H. B.** (Fr. R.F.A.) | M. April 6/17. |
| ‡29 | **Bird, 2nd Lieut. D. J. de A.** | M. June 27/17. |
| 29 | **Gaskian, 2nd Lt. C. S.** (Fr. R.F.A.) | M. May 7/17. |
| *29 | **Harper, Lieut. G. P.** | M. June 23/17. |
| ‡29 | **Holt, Capt. W. P.** | M. June 24/17. |
| 29 | **Jennings, Capt. Alex.** (Fr. R.F.A.) | M. April 7/17. |
| 29 | **Pascoe, 2nd Lieut. E. J.** | M. April 14/17. |
| 29 | **Rogers, 2nd Lieut. C. V. de B.** | M. April 21/17. |
| 29 | **Sadler, 2nd Lt. F.** (Fr. 9 D.L.I.) | M. April 21/17. |
| 29 | **Sloan, 2nd Lieut. C. R.** | M. May 12/17. |
| ‡29 | **Winterbotham, Lieut. F. W.** | M. July 13/17. |
| ‡34 | Lewis, Sergt. G. 78492. | M. May 24/17. |
| 35 | **Cotterill, Lt. H. G. K.** (Fr. R.F.A.) | M. June 6/17. |
| 35 | **Devenish, Lt. G. W.** (Fr. R.F.A.) | M. June 6/17. |
| 40 | **Allcock, Capt. W. T. L.** | M. June 5/17. |
| 40 | **Barwell, Capt. F. L.** (Fr. 16 Lond.) | M. April 29/17. |
| 40 | **Brewis, Lieut. J. A.** | M. April 29/17. |
| 40 | **Pell, 2nd Lieut. H. S.** | M. April 6/17. |
| 40 | **Sinclair, Lieut. D. M. F.** | M. Mar. 30/17. |
| ‡41 | **Sturgess, 2nd Lieut. T. M.** | M. June 24/17. |
| ‡41 | **Thompson, Lieut. W. G.** | M. July 14/17. |
| 42 | **Baylis, 2nd Lieut. C. J.** | M. about June 7/17. |
| 42 | **Jacot, 2nd Lieut. E.** | M. June 16/17. |
| 43 | **Blackburn, 2nd Lieut. H. D.** | M. April 5/17. |
| 43 | **Fenton, 2nd Lieut. A. H.** | M. Mar. 4/17. |
| 43 | **Frew, 2nd Lieut. J. G. H.** | M. April 16/17. |
| 43 | **Gagne, 2nd Lieut. J.** | M. May 24/17. |
| 43 | **Goode, Lieut. G. M.** | M. May 24/17. |
| 43 | **Jackson, Lt. J. B.** (Fr. 12 R. Scots.) | M. June 7/17. |

Flying Corps, Royal—contd.

## *B.E.F.*

| | | |
|---|---|---|
| 43 | **Knox, 2nd Lt. C. D.** (Fr. 10 Suffolks.) | M. Mar. 17/17. |
| 43 | **Lownds, Lieut. Reginald H.** | M. March 17/17. |
| 43 | **Rutter, M.C., Capt. D. C.** | M. June 7/17. |
| 43 | Russell, 1st Cl. Air Mech. F. 1130. (A. Flight.) | M. April 16/17. |
| 43 | **Wood, 2nd Lieut. P. L.** | M. Mar. 4/17. |
| 43 | Moult, 2nd Cl. Air Mech. A. 77562. | M. April 28/17. |
| 45 | **Blake, Lieut. J. E.** | M. April 6/17. |
| 45 | **Brayshay, Capt. W. S.** (Fr. A.S.C.) | M. April 6/17. |
| 45 | **Campbell, Lieut. C. St. G.** | M. April 6/17. |
| 45 | **Carey, 2nd Lieut. A. S.** | M. May 27/17. |
| •45 | **Caulfield, 2nd Lieut. T. St. G.** | M. June 16/17. |
| 45 | **Edwards, Capt. D. W.** (Fr. A.S.C.) | M. April 6/17. |
| ‡45 | **Fotheringham, Lt. J. B.** (Fr. 20 Canadians.) | M. July 7/17. |
| ‡45 | **Gleed, 2nd Lieut. J. V. A.** | M. July 7/17. |
| 45 | **Marshall, 2nd Lieut. J. A.** (Fr. Hunts. Cyclist Bn.) | M. April 6/17. |
| 45 | **Metheral, Lieut. T. A.** | K. June 5/17. Dest.D./B. |
| 45 | **Mills, Lieut. W. L.** (Fr. R.F.A.) | M. May 9/17. |
| ‡45 | **Synder, Lieut. F. C. H.** (Fr. 25 Res. Canadians.) | M. July 7/17. |
| 45 | **Truscott, M.C., Lt. Francis G.** (Fr. 6th Suffolks.) | M. April 6/17. |
| ‡45 | Cook, Sergt. E. A. 1920. | M. June 5/17. |
| •45 | Shaw, 2nd Cl. Air-Mech. 46969. | M. June 5/17. |
| ‡45 | Thompson, 2nd Cl. Air Mech. S. 77921. | M. June 5/17. |
| 46 | **Long, 2nd Lt. C. P.** (Fr. R.E.) | K. April 13/17. Det.D./B. |
| 46 | **Stephen, 2nd Lieut. J. P.** | K. May 23/17. Det.D./B. |
| 48 | **Berry, 2nd Lt. O. W.** (Fr. K.O.S.B.) | M. April 8/17. |
| ‡48 | **Clarke, 2nd Lieut. H. C.** | M. July 6/17. |
| 48 | **Clifford, 2nd Lieut. W. J.** | M. April 25/17. |
| 48 | **Cull, Flt.-Com. A. Tulloch.** (Fr. 3rd Seaforths.) | M. May 11/17. |
| ‡48 | **Farnes, 2nd Lt. H. C.** (Fr. K.R.R.C.) | M. July 6/17. |
| 48 | **Lovell, Lieut. L. G.** | M. April 11/17. |
| 48 | **Owen, Lieut. T. J.** | K. April 8/17. Conf. and Det. R/Enq. |
| ‡48 | **Smither, 2nd Lieut. H.** | M. July 6/17. |
| 48 | **Tomkies, Lt. H. L.** (Fr. 17 Sherwds.) | M. April 25/17. |
| 48 | Trusson, 1st Cl. Air Mech. Arthur. 40181. (Fr. 11th Hussars.) | M. May 11/17. |
| 53 | **Adams, 2nd Lieut. T.** | M. May 12/17. |
| 53 | **Kelly, 2nd Lt. O. R.** (Fr. 20 Northd. Fus.) | M. May 12/17. |
| 54 | **Duxbury, 2nd Lt. H. C.** | M. May 11/17. |
| 54 | **Pixley, Capt. R. G. M.** | M. June 4/17. |
| ‡55 | **Battersby, Lt. P. W.** (Fr. W. Som. Yeo.) | M. July 7/17. |
| 55 | **Evans, 2nd Lieut. Bernard.** | M. April 8-10/17. |

**Flying Corps, Royal**—contd.

*B.E.F.*

| | | | |
|---|---|---|---|
| ‡55 | | **Fitzherbert, Capt. W. W.** | M. **July 7/17.** |
| 55 | | **Greg, Capt. A. T.** (Fr. Cheshires.) | K. **April 23/17.** Det.D./B. |
| 55 | | **Holroyde, Lieut. J. S.** (Fr. E. Yorks.) | M. **May 10/17.** |
| 55 | | **Honer, Lt. D. J.** (Fr. R.F.A.) | M. **June 4/17.** |
| 55 | | **Jeffery, 2nd Lieut. R. E.** | M. **May 25/17.** |
| ‡55 | | **Matheson, Lieut. A. P.** | M. **July 13/17.** |
| ‡55 | | **Oliver, Lieut. F. L.** (Fr. Somerset L.I.) | M. **July 13/17.** |
| 55 | | **Palmer, 2nd Lieut. P. R.** | M. **May 25/17.** |
| 55 | | **Pitt, 2nd Lieut. B. W.** | M. **May 10/17.** |
| 55 | | Bond, 1st Cl. Air Mech. W. 19789. | M. **May 10/17.** |
| *55 | B. | Cluney, George. 13342. (Fr. 2 S. Lancs.) | M. **June 4/17.** |
| 56 | | **Chaworth-Musters, Lieut. R. M.** | M. **May 7/17.** |
| *56 | | **Coles, Lieut. W. T.** | M. **June 17/17.** |
| *56 | | **Hamer, Lieut. H.** | K. **June 6/17.** Det.D./B. |
| 56 | | **Kay, 2nd Lieut. M. A.** | M. **April 30/17.** |
| ‡56 | | **Spearpoint, 2nd Lieut. H. G.** | M. **June 17/17.** |
| 57 | | **Gillespie, 2nd Lt. G. W.** (Fr. 9th Middlesex.) | M. **April 13/17.** |
| *57 | | **McNaughton, Capt. N. G.** | M. **June 24/17.** |
| 57 | | **Margerison, Lieut. T.** | M. **April 13/17.** |
| 57 | | **Margoliouth, 2nd Lieut. A. H.** | M. **April 2/17.** |
| *57 | | **Mearms, Lieut. A. H.** (Fr. Black Watch.) | M. **June 24/17.** |
| 57 | | **Ormerod, 2nd Lt. A.** (Fr. R.F.A.) | M. **April 13/17.** |
| 57 | | **Sworder, Lieut. H. P.** (Fr. W. Surrey) | M. **April 2/17.** |
| 57 | | Sibley, 2nd Cl. Air Mech. R. 77252. | W. and M. **April 13/17.** |
| 59 | | **Bailey, Lieut. C. F.** | M. **April 6/17.** |
| 59 | | **Boyd, 2nd Lt. P. B.** (Fr. Gordons.) | M. **April 13/17.** |
| 59 | | **Chalk, Lt. W. J.** (Fr. 11 Canadians.) | M. **April 13/17.** |
| 59 | | **Cooksey, 2nd Lieut. K. B.** | M. **April 8/17.** |
| 59 | | **Day, Lieut. W. L.** | M. **April 6/17.** |
| 59 | | **Horne, Lieut. H. G. M.** | M. **April 13/17.** |
| 59 | | **Morris, Flt.-Lt. G. T.** (Fr. Ayrshire Yeo.) | K. **April 11/17.** Det.D./B. |
| 59 | | **Ray, 2nd Lt. P. O.** (Fr. 8 Black Watch.) | M. **April 13/17.** |
| 59 | | **Souter, Lieut. J. M.** | K. **April 11/17.** Det.D./B. |
| 59 | | **Stuart, Capt. J.** (Fr. 1 Innis. Fus.) | M. **April 13/17.** |
| 59 | | **Tanfield, 2nd Lt. A. H.** (Fr. 1 R. Warwicks.) | M. **April 13/17.** |
| 59 | | **Wood, Lt. M. H.** (Fr. 4th Lincs.) | M. **April 13/17.** |
| 59 | | Barrie, Vincent, N., 2nd Cl. A.M. 40213. | M. **April 6/17.** |
| 59 | | Jones, 2nd Cl. A.M. Reg. Handsford. 44854 | M. **April 8/17.** |
| ‡60 | | **Adam, 2nd Lieut. A. R.** (Fr. 6th Seaforth Highlanders.) | M. **July 3/17.** |
| 60 | | **Chapman, 2nd Lieut. L. C.** | M. **April 14/17.** |
| 60 | | **Cock, 2nd Lieut. John H.** | M. **April 14/17.** |
| 60 | | **Elliott, Lieut. J. McC.** | M. **April 16/17.** |
| 60 | | **Grandin, 2nd Lieut. R. J.** (Fr. A.S.C.) | M. **May 18/17.** |
| 60 | | **Joyce, 2nd Lieut. Philip S.** | M. **Mar. 6/17.** |
| *60 | | **Lloyd, Lieut. D. R. C.** | M. **June 16/17.** |
| 60 | | **Milot, Major J. A.** | M. **April 8/17.** |
| *60 | | **Murray, Lieut. D. C. G.** | M. **June 27/17.** |
| 60 | | **Phalen, 2nd Lieut. R. V.** | M. **May 28/17.** |
| 60 | | **Robertson, 2nd Lieut. D. N.** | M. **April 16/17.** |

**Flying Corps, Royal—contd.**

*B.E.F.*

| | | |
|---|---|---|
| 60 | **Williams, 2nd Lieut. V. F.** | **M. April 2/17.** |
| 66 | **Roberts, Lt. R. M.** (Fr. K.O.Y.L.I.) | **M. May 28/17.** |
| *66 | **Shirley, 2nd Lieut. A. V.** (Fr. Welsh Horse.) | **M. June 8/17.** |
| 70 | **Adams, 2nd Lieut. V. H.** | **M. May 4/17.** |
| 70 | **Butler, Lieut. H.** (Fr. Yorks.) | **M. March 25/17.** |
| 70 | **Chuter, Lieut. H. A.** (Fr. R. Fus.) | **M. March 25/17.** |
| 70 | **Gayner, 2nd Lieut. W. J.** (Fr. 4th Som. L.I.) | **M. May 9/17.** |
| 70 | **Harley, Lieut. J.** | **M. June 3/17.** |
| 70 | **Henderson, Capt. E. J.** | **M. March 25/17.** |
| 70 | **Norris, 2nd Lt. L. A.** (Fr. R.E.) | **M. March 25/17.** |
| 70 | **Swann, Lieut. G. W.** | **M. March 24/17.** |
| 70 | **Ward-Price, Lt. L.** (Fr. R. H. Guards.) | **M. March 25/17.** |
| ‡70 | **Watlington, 2nd Lt. H. J.** | **M. July 6/17.** |
| 70 | Bond, 2nd Cl. Air Mech. W. J. 77683. | **M. April 24/17.** |
| 70 | Breakfield, 2nd Cl. Air Mech. George D. 25156. | **M. May 9/17.** |
| ‡70 | Giles, 2nd Cl. Air Mech. A. 61924. | **M. June 3/17.** |
| 70 | Pearce, Chas. R. 23042. (B. Flight). (Fr. 1st C.D.A. Col.) | **D. Aug. 24/16. Det.D./B.** |
| 100 | **Holmes, Lieut. Thos. G.** | **M. May 6/17.** |
| *100 | **Lockhart, Lt. W. E.** (Fr. Canad. Engineers.) | **K. June 12/17. Det.D./B.** |
| 100 | Ekins, 2nd Cl. Air Mech. A. W. 46133. | **M. May 6/17.** |
| 14 Wing | **Reeves, Flt.-Lt. F. Pember.** (Fr. 6th Squad R.N.A.S.) | **M. June 6/17.** |
| ? | **Bacon, 2nd Lieut. L. G.** | **M. May 5/17.** |
| ? | **Brichta, Lt. G. J. C.** (Fr. 2nd Canadian Mounted Rifles.) | **K. Mar. 6/17. Det.D./B.** |
| ? | **Edwards, 2nd Lieut. E. L.** (Fr. 2 Welsh Regt.) | **M. May 1/17.** |
| ‡? | **Eyre, Flt.-Lt. C. A.** (Fr. R.N.A.S.) | **M. July 7/17.** |
| ? | **Gilson, 2nd Lt. A. I.** | **M. March 17/17.** |
| ? | **Halse, 2nd Lieut. C. H.** | **M. April 24/17.** |
| ? | **Harley, 2nd Lieut. F. W.** (Fr. 7th Black Watch.) | **M. June 3/17.** |
| ? | **Howard, 2nd Lieut. J. K.** (Fr. 5th Sherwoods.) | **M. Feb. 11/17.** |
| ? | **Johnston, 2nd Lieut. H. A.** | **M. Mar. 11/17.** |
| ‡22 Wing | **Kent, Sub-Lt. R. L.** (Fr. R.N.A.S., 10 Sq.) | **M. July 11/17.** |
| ‡? | **McGowan, M.C., Lt. J. C.** (Fr. Scottish Horse.) | **M. July 7/17.** |
| ? | **Muir, 2nd Lieut. J. H.** | **M. April 7/17.** |
| ? | **Murray, Lt. A. A.** (Fr. 49 Canadians) | **K. Mar. 19/17. Det.D./B.** |
| ‡? 11 Wing | **Parker, Sub-Lt. L. H.** (Fr. R.N.A.S., 10 Sq.) | **M. June 15/17.** |
| ? | **Pepler, Lieut. S. J.** | **K. Mar. 6/17. Det.D./B.** |
| *? | **Powell, 2nd Lieut. C. H.** | **M. June 15/17.** |
| ? | **Radcliffe, Lieut. G. A.** (Fr. A. & S. Highlanders.) | **M., bel. K. April 25/17.** |
| ? | **Rimer, 2nd Lieut. J. C.** | **M. March 17/17.** |
| ‡? 22 Wing | **Saunders, Flt.-Sub-Lt. R. G.** | **M. June 24/17.** |
| ? | **Simpson, Capt. F. J.** (Fr. 1 Canadian Mounted Rifles.) | **K. Mar. 12/17. Det.D./B.** |

Flying Corps, Royal—contd.

*B.E.F.*

? Smith, Flt.-Sub-Lt. H. L. (10 Wing.) (Fr. R.N.A.S.) M. May 24/17.
*? Thayre, M.C., Capt. F. J. H. M. June 9/17.
? Webb, 2nd Lieut. T. M. May 10/17.
? White, 2nd Lieut. B. W. (Fr. 1 Liverpools.) M. April 8/17.
? William, M.C., Capt. W. G. B. M. May 12/17.
*20 Balloon Co. Wickson, Capt. E. A. (Fr. Canadians.) K. June 16/17. Det.D./B.

*BALKANS.*

47 C. Flight Clutterbuck, 2nd Air Mech. G. 41410. K. Feb. 27/17. Det.D./B.

*E.E.F.*

14 Squad. Bevan, Capt, Frank H. V. M. April 19/17.
? Robertson, Lt. J. R. (Fr. F. & F. Yeo.) M. May 12/17.
? Williamson, M.C., Capt. Chas. K. Mar. 27/17. Det.D./B.

GLOUCESTERSHIRE REGIMENT.

*B.E.F.*

1 B. VI Holland, E. H. 2299. M. Sept. 8-9/16. R/Enq.
*4 A. I Thatcher, A. 200673. W. and M. April 24-25/17.
4 C. XII Gladwell, H. H. 33186. M. April 24/17.
4 D. Furneaux, Hewin Jas. 201548. M. April 24-25/17.
4 D. Theobald, C.-S.-M. A. 200070. M. April 24-25/17.
4 D. Workman, F. A. 202548. M. April 24-25/17.
2/4 D. XVI Bevan, J. 235004. M. April 8/17.
6 A. L.G.S. Abbott, Hy. 266835. (5217.) M. April 24/17.
6 A. Creech, R. 203079. M. April 24/17.
6 A. II Lewis, G. H. 33568. M. April 24/17.
6 A. IV Pates, Chas. D. 266959. M. April 24/17.
6 A. L.G.S. Stanley, Leslie. 267085. (5513.) M. April 24/17.
*6 B. V Benton, J. H. 33170. W. and M. April 24/17.
2/6 D. Perring, John. 4762. M. Sept. 6/16.
8 A. M.G.S. Evans, P. J. 27723. M. Nov. 18/16.
*8 A. I Newton, C. 37178. M. Nov. 18/16. R/Enq.
8 A. Symes, F. A. 26336. M. Nov. 18/16. R/Enq.
*8 B. Williams, A.-Sergt. T. J. 37227. M. Nov. 18/16. R/Enq.
8 C. Cordell, A. 20408. M. Nov. 18/16. R/Enq.
‡8 C. Robinson, T. J. 37195. W. and M. Nov. 18/16. R/Enq.
10 B. XVI Clarke, James John. 22954. M. Sept. 9/16.
12 Burgess, 2nd Lieut. W. T. M May 8/17.
12 B. Merrell, 2nd Lieut. A. W. M. May 8/17.
12 B. Parr, M.C., Capt. W. W. M. May 8/17.
12 Ryde, 2nd Lieut. J. T. (Fr. 1 Beds.) W. and M. May 8/17.
12 A. II Bater, J. H. 22809. M. May 8/17.
‡12 A. Bath, Sergt. A. 32512. M. May 8/17.
12 A. IV Battie, Wm. John. 37815. M. May 8/17.

**Gloucestershire Regiment—contd.**

## *B.E.F.*

| | | |
|---|---|---|
| ‡12 A. | Beadle, Cpl. B. 16726. | M. May 8/17. |
| 12 A. I | Bendall, L.-Cpl. Alb. Edw. 27909. | M. May 8/17. |
| *12 A. IV | Bennett, J. 37866. | M. May 8/17. |
| ‡12 A. | Biddle, O. 28420. | W. and M. May 3/17. |
| ‡12 A. | Butten, F. 32323. | M. May 8/17. |
| 12 A. or B. | Carter, Sgt. Maurice. 37843. | M. May 8/17. |
| ‡12 A. | Cox, S. A. Y. 16485. | M. May 8/17. |
| 12 A. III | Durrant, L.-Cpl. Montague. 37863. | M. May 8/17. |
| ‡12 A. | Evans, W. J. 37690. | M. May 8/17. |
| ‡12 A. | Freeman, C. 37861. | M. May 8/17. |
| ‡12 A. M.G.S. | Gerrish, J. W. J. 27903. | M. May 8/17. |
| ‡12 A. | Gowen, F. 16753. | M. May 8/17. |
| 12 A. I | Grant, Albert John. 37242. | M. May 8/17. |
| ‡12 A. | Haworth, W. 37608. | W. and M. May 8/17. |
| *12 A. | Hitchings, Chas. Wm. 22600. | W. and M. May 8/17. |
| 12 A. | Hunt, W. T. 25217. | M. May 8/17. |
| 12 A. III | Johnson, A. W. 37860. | M. May 8/17. |
| ‡12 A. | Joyce, F. C. 31133. | M. May 8/17. |
| 12 A. | Knapp, T. G. 32527. | M. May 8/17. |
| ‡12 A. | Lamb, E. G. 14093. | M. May 8/17. |
| 12 A. I | Manison, J. 32520. | M. May 7/17. |
| *12 A. I | Martin, C. H. 27910. | W. and M. May 8/17. |
| ‡12 A. | Powell, H. J. 24679. | M. May 8/17. |
| *12 A. I | Quarterly, Wm. 37644. | M. May 8/17. |
| ‡12 A. | Radway, H. 30070. | M. May 8/17. |
| ‡12 A. | Roberts, E. E. 18848. | M. May 8/17. |
| 12 A. | Roberts, John. 33577. | M. May 8/17. |
| *12 A. | Shepherd, Wm. James. 30779. | M. May 8/17. |
| ‡12 A. | Smith, G. 18850. | M. May 8/17. |
| ‡12 A. | Smith, W. G. 37599. | M. May 8/17. |
| ‡12 A. | Spearing, E. R. 36586. | M. May 8/17. |
| 12 A. | Stokes, S/B. Donald Morley. 14172. | M. May 8/17. |
| ‡12 A. IV | Taylor, E. G. 23532. | M. May 8/17. |
| ‡12 A. | Tidball, C. 33593. | M. May 8/17. |
| *12 A. | Todd, William Richard. 37859. | M. May 8/17. |
| 12 A. IV | Willis, G. 26814. | M. May 8/17. |
| ‡12 B. | Apperley, R. W. 13850. | M. May 8/17. |
| ‡12 B. | Banwell, W. H. 18836. | M. May 8/17. |
| ‡12 B. | Carter, W. 37817. | M. May 8/17. |
| ‡12 B. | Dobson, Cpl. J. 18706. | M. May 8/17. |
| 12 B. | Easton, Robert. 37699. | K. Feb. 25/17. Det.D./B. |
| 12 B. | Evans, Cpl. J. W. 14442. | M. May 8/17. |
| 12 B. VI | Harper, E. 21172. | M. May 8/17. |
| ‡12 B. | Heyden, A. 25211. | M. May 8/17. |
| 12 B. VII | Hines, Fred. Chas. 22264. | M. May 8/17. |
| ‡12 B. | Hinks, G. 33591. | M. May 8/17. |
| ‡12 B. | Norman, G. H. 14364. | M. May 8/17. |
| ‡12 B. | Parkins, T. 33595. | M. May 8/17. |
| ‡12 B. | Rescarla, G. 24143. | M. May 8/17. |
| ‡12 B. | Shore, C. 24906. | M. May 8/17. |
| ‡12 B. | White, L.-Cpl. W. T. 11850. | M. May 8/17. |
| 12 B. VI | Williams, Fred. 32141. | M. May 8/17. |
| ‡12 B. | Wood, J. 32140. | W. and M. May 3/17. |
| ‡12 C. | Barry, R. 37816. | M. May 8/17. |
| ‡12 C. | Barton, A. 28249. | M. May 8/17. |
| ‡12 C. | Breen, J. 37834. | M. May 8/17. |
| ‡12 C. | Brett, F. J. 14849. | W. and M. May 8/17. |
| ‡12 C. | Brown, J. 37874. | M. May 8/17. |

**Gloucestershire Regiment—contd.**

## *B.E.F.*

‡12 C. Browning, H. 203381. M. May 8/17.
12 C. Chappell, Cpl. F. H. 14479. W. and M. May 8/17.
‡12 C. Desmond, G. G. 203386. M. May 8/17.
12 C. X Evans, Herbert Chas. 27284. M. May 8/17.
12 C. Fisher, E. 14663. W. and M. May 8/17.
‡12 C. Fletcher, F. 16528. M. May 8/17.
*12 C. Green, Geo. Peter. 37849. M. May 8/17.
‡12 C. Holder, H. 28286. M. May 8/17.
12 C. X Hooper, L.-Cpl. Albt. Lawson. 31931. M. May 8/17.
‡12 C. Lewis, Reginald John. 14342. W. and M. May 8/17.
‡12 C. McKillop, D. 37838. M. May 8/17.
12 C. XI Parsons, Harold J. 14920. W. and M. May 8/17.
12 C. Rawlins, L.-Sergt. Albert. 20535. M. May 8/17.
12 C. XII Skinner, Reginald. 31285. W. and M. May 8/17.
*12 C. X Starbuck, Cpl. S. A. 32522. M. May 8/17.
12 C. IX Whiting, J. H. 37828. M. May 8/17.
12 C. Williams, E. 14579. W. and M. Sept. 3/16.
‡12 C. IX Williams, Frederick. 36786. M. May 8/17.
12 D. Brown, W. A. H. 16656. M. May 8/17.
12 D. XIII Gibbins, Herbert H. 29383. W. and M. May 8/17.
‡12 D. Green, A. F. 19217. W. and M. May 8/17.
‡12 D. Keyte, J. W. 32526. M. May 8/17.
12 D. XIV Salisbury, F. E. 37269. W. and M. May 8/17.
12 D. Summers, L.-Sgt. E. H. 31924. W. and M. May 8/17.

## *BALKANS.*

2 C. Mott, L.-Cpl. Henry John. 22328. M. April 25/17.
2 ? Kemp, L.-Cpl. A. 8991. W. and M. Dec. 7/16.
Davis, A. H. 29252. M. April 25/17.
9 A. II Norman, Cyril Gilbert. 17739. M. April 25/17.
9 A. Ogden, E. 16916. M. April 25/17.
*9 A. Reynolds, Frank. 16874. W. and M. April 25/17.
9 A. IV Wood, George. 37026. M. April 25/17.
9 A. Wothers, J. 15962. M. April 24/17.
9 B. VIII Barton, S. 27938. K. April 25/17. Det.D./B.
9 B. Norburn, W. E. 12485. M. May 9/17.
9 B. V Wootton, L.-Cpl. E. 15505. M. April 25/17.
9 C. Cawler, L.-Cpl. Howard. 27911. M. May 9/17.
9 C. XI Morris, E. E. 29425. M. May 8-9/17.
9 C. Read, E. G. 31843. M. May 9/17.
9 D. XIV Clements, J. 27947. M. May 8-9/17.
*9 D. M.G.S. Crossley, C. 16859. M. May 9/17.
*9 D. XVI Harris, James. 12978. M. May 9/17.
*9 D. Moore, W. 21618. M. May 9/17.
*9 D. XVI Smith, T. 28533. M. May 9/17.
9 ? Beale, Cpl. E. 13139. M. April 25/17.
*9 ? Bullock, L.-Cpl. L. J. 27947. M. May 9/17.
‡9 ? Freeman, F. 28213. W. and M. April 25/17.
9 ? Hale, Cpl. G. 20179. M. April 25/17.
*9 ? Holmes, J. T. 17107. M. May 9/17.
9 ? Howes, W. S. 17214. M. April 25/17.
*9 ? Jones, E. 24583. M. May 9/17.
*9 ? Page, C. 12974. M. May 9/17.
*9 ? Smith, W. G. 12806. M. May 9/17.
9 ? Stallard, L.-Cpl. C. A. 20773. (Fr. 3) M. April 25/17.
*9 ? Tanner, E. 29823. M. May 9/17.
9 ? Withers, Walter. 26207. (Fr. 16th.) M. April 25/17.

**Gloucestershire Regiment—contd.**

## *PERSIAN GULF.*

| | | |
|---|---|---|
| 7 A. | Bodman, M. 28712. | M. Feb. 10/17. |
| 7 A. | Brooker, G. 10310. | M. Feb. 10/17. |
| 7 A. | Cartwright, Thos. 31625. | M. Feb. 10/17. |
| 7 A. | Coggins, W. A. 25710. | M. April 21/16. R/Enq. |
| 7 A. | Cowles, D. 25040. | K. Feb. 10/17. Det.D./B. |
| *7 A. | Roper, Ernest Chas. 28444. | K. Feb. 10/17. Det.D./B. |
| 7 A. IV | Smith, E. G. 11883. | K. Feb. 10/17. Det.D./B. |
| 7 B. | Barton, J. H. 29315. | D/W. Feb. 3/17. Det.D./B. |
| 7 B. | Buswell, Harry. 28274. | M. Feb. 10/17. |
| 7 B. | Flatman, Cpl. Wm. 22254. | D/W. Feb. 26/17. Det.D./B. |
| *7 B. | Harper, R. 27907. | W. and M. Feb. 25/17. |
| ‡7 B. | Johnstone, R. E. 29426. | K. Jan. 29/17. Det.D./B. |
| 7 B. | Willmott, Jos. Maurice. 26393. | K. Dec. 15/16. Det.D./B. |
| 7 D. | Gale, L.-Cpl. A. 3314. | W. and M. Feb. 25/17. |
| 7 ? | Box, J. 31623. | M. Feb. 10/17. |
| 7 ? | Bradford, A. 20473. | M., bel. K. Mar. 30/17. |
| 7 ? | Challinor, A. 31542. | W. and M. Jan. 25/17. |
| 7 ? | Colley, Cpl. A. 23045. | M. Feb. 10/17. |
| 7 ? | Corrie, E. V. 21385. | K. Sept. 30/16. Det.D./B. |
| 7 ? | Davis, Charles. 24233. | K. Feb. 18/17. Det.D./B. |
| 7 ? | Harper, R. F. 27907. | W. and M. Feb. 25/17. |
| 7 ? | Marmont, C. E. 23413. | M. Feb. 10/17. |
| 7 ? | Simms, F. A. 26700. | W. and M. Jan. 25/17. |
| 7 ? | Turner, Cpl. A. T. 10677. | W. and M. Feb. 25/17. |

## GORDON HIGHLANDERS.

## *B.E.F.*

| | | |
|---|---|---|
| 1 | **Lee, 2nd Lieut. S. E.** | M. April 11/17. |
| 1 A. | Manson, G. A. C. 11351. | M. April 9-11/17. |
| ‡1 B. VI | Simpson, Robert. 11690. | M. May 14/17. |
| 1 C. | Bruce, L.-Cpl. W. 43259. | M. April 9-11/17. |
| ‡1 C. XII | Campbell, Alex. 11368. | Unoff. M. June 18/17. |
| 1 C. | Hay, Geo. 40341. | M. April 9-11/17. |
| 1 C. | Meiklejohn, J. 15015. | W. and M. April 9-11/17. |
| 1 C. X | Webster, Geo. P. 14994. | M. May 11/17. |
| 1 D. Gren. S. | Anderson, David W. 43359. | K. April 7/17. Det.D./B. R/Enq. |
| 1 D. | Anderson, A.-Cpl. J. 9975. | M. April 9-11/17. |
| 1 Sig. S. | Seller, William. 40158. | M. April 9-11/17. |
| 2 | **Ferguson, 2nd Lt. D. F.** | M. May 7/17. |
| 2 C. | **Gordon, Capt. M. L.** | W. and M. May 7/17. |
| ‡2 A. | Shirra, Henry. 40606. | M. May 7/17. |
| ‡2 A. | Towns, R. 43010. | M. May 7/17. |
| 2 B. | Allan, William. 43389. | M. May 7/17. |
| *2 B. VI | Anley, Geo. 946. | M. May 7/17. |
| *2 B. VII | Johnstone, L.-Cpl. Jas. 9654. | M. May 7/17. |
| 2 B. VII | Mackenzie, Donald. S/17446. | M. May 7/17. |
| ‡2 B. | Nugent, Sergt. C. 8807. | M. May 7/17. |
| 2 C. | Docherty, L.-Cpl. J. 7637. | M. Mar. 30/17. |
| ‡2 C. L.G.S. | Scott, James. 43124. | M. May 7/17. |
| 2 D. | Gammach, A. 40067. | M. April 2/17. |
| ‡2 D. | Murray, L.-Cpl. J. 12610. | M. May 7/17. |
| ‡2 ? I.T.M. | Kennedy, Robt. 43541. (20 Bgde.) | W. and M. June 7/17. |

**Gordon Highlanders—contd.**

*B.E.F.*

4 A. I Grant, T. S. M. 202122. W. and M. April 23/17.
4 A. II Millar, Bandsman David. 406. M. April 23/17.
4 A. Ogg, Wm. 201907. (5048.) M. April 23/17.
‡4 A. Sutherland, A. 200478. M. April 23/17.
4 B. V Bruce, Andrew Mitchell. 241336. M. April 23/17.
‡4 B. Cowan, F. F. 202530. M. April 23/17.
4 B. VI Cowie, David Cassie. 210520. M. April 23/17.
4 B. VII Craigmyle, Douglas. 201786. W. and M. April 23/17.
*4 B. VIII Geddes, Cpl. Alex. 200090. M. April 23/17.
4 B. McDonald, G. 201411. W. and M. April 9/17.
4 B. VI Reid, Sgt. Sidney Francis Gerald. 201409. (4113.) M. April 23/17.
‡4 B. VI Ross, David. 202703. M. April 23/17.
4 C. Barclay, A. 202601. M. April 9/17.
*4 C. XII Catto, Alex. 202632. M. April 23/17.
*4 C. Orr, Robt. S/40826. (Fr. Lovat Scouts and Camerons.) M. April 23/17.
‡4 C. Reith, A. C. 201605. M. April 23/17.
*4 C. IX Scholefield, Jas. W. 202719. M. April 23/17.
‡4 C. Tough, W. 8957. M. April 23/17.
‡4 D. XIV Burnett, Cpl. Alexander. 201406. M. April 23/17.
*4 D. XIV Butcher, Ernest Chas. S/40795. M. April 23/17.
‡4 D. Carnwath, J.. 202769. M. April 23/17.
‡4 D. Carter, W. 13230. M. April 23/17.
*4 D. Finlayson, C. 14052. M. April 23/17.
4 D. XIII Grimes, Jos. Holder. 202523. M. April 23/17.
‡4 D. Harm, E. 13375. M. April 23/17.
4 D. XIV Jamieson, Wm. 202573. M. April 23/17.
‡4 D. Lind, R. G. F. 201058. M. April 23/17.
‡4 D. McKay, J. 200546. M. April 23/17.
*4 D. XIV Simpson, Leith. 201373. M. April 23/17.
4 D. Sutherland, Alex. G. 201135. (Snip. S.) M. April 23/17.
4 D. XIV Watt, David. 201580. M. April 23/17.
4 D. M.G.S. Watt, John S. 3496. W. and M. Nov. 15/16.
4 D. Webster, Arthur K. 201865. (Snip. S.) W. and M. April 23/17
5 A. III Anderson, L.-Cpl. John. 26000. M. May 16/17.
‡5 A. Beveridge, G. A. S. 263001. W. and M. May 16-17/17.
5 A. Cruickshank, G. 241095. M. April 9-10/17.
5 A. I Gardner, Thomas. R. 260056. M. May 3/17.
‡5 A. Hay, Sergt. S. 240072. M. May 16/17.
5 A. II Insch, James. 1530. K. Nov. 13/16. Conf. and det.
5 A. Rae, George S. 240304. M. May 16/17.
*5 A. II Reid, Chas. 242425. (5607.) K. May 16/17. Det.D./B.
*5 A. I Smith, Peter. 241181. M. May 16/17.
‡5 B. Bowie, A. C. 242158. W. and M. May 16/17.
‡5 B. Cunningham, J. 260098. M. May 16/17.
‡5 B. Ingram, R. 260094. M. May 16/17.
‡5 B. Munro, J. S. 242223. M. May 16/17.
‡5 B. Ritchie, J. 242224. W. and M. May 16-17/17.
5 B. VIII Roxburgh, Wm. 260087. W. and M. May 16/17.
‡5 B. Turnbull, D. 260081. M. May 16/17.
*5 B. VIII Turner, S/B. A. 241627. K. May 16-17/17. Det.D./B.
‡5 C. X Chalmers, Sgt. Chas. Tait. 240197. W. and M. May 16-17/17.
‡5 C. McDonald, A. 240989. M. May 16/17.
5 C. XII Reilly, Robert. 17483. M. May 16/17.
*5 C. XII Walsh, Geoffrey. 242118. M. May 16/17.
5 D. Cruden, J. 241481. M. April 9-11/17.
‡5 D. Methven, James A. 240648. M. April 19/17.

**Gordon Highlanders.—contd.**

*B.E.F.*

| | | | |
|---|---|---|---|
| ‡5 D. | | Norrie, C. 241043. | M. April 23/17. |
| 6 A. | | Fordun, A. 276988. | M. April 23/17. |
| 6 A. | | Gibson, F. 266816. | M. April 9/17. |
| *6 A. I | | Glendinning, John Riddell. 285021. | M. Unoff. W. May 16/17. |
| ‡6 A. | | Green, W. 265729. | M. May 16/17. |
| 6 A. | | Knight, J. 266811. | M. April 9/17. |
| 6 A. | | Lister, T. 5709. | M. April 23/17. |
| 6 A. | | Lyall, W. 265039. | M. April 9/17. |
| ‡6 A. | | McGuire, A. 5325. | W. and M. April 23/17. |
| 6 A. | | Mackenzie, R. 265447. | M. April 23/17. |
| 6 A. | L.G.S. | McQueen, Jas. Neil. 266999. | M. April 23/17. |
| ‡6 A. | | McRae, J. 285029. | M. April 23/17. |
| 6 A. | | McWilliam, J. 265768. | M. April 23/17. |
| ‡6 A. | | Nuttall, N. 15983. | M. May 16/17. |
| 6 A. | | Priest, Andrew. 266312. | M. April 23/17. |
| 6 A. | | Richardson, F. G. 266862. | W. and M. April 23/17. |
| 6 A. | | Thomson, J. 266172. | M. April 23/17. |
| 6 A. | | Wilson, A. 285038. | M. April 23/17. |
| ‡6 B. | | Davies, J. 292456. | M. May 16/17. |
| ‡6 B. | | Esslemont, J. 265727. | M. May 16/17. |
| 6 C. | | Brodie, Jas. 285046. | W. and M. April 23/17. |
| 6 C. | | Bruce, J. 265779. | M. April 23/17. |
| 6 C. | | Gaunt, L. Wm. 266658. | M. April 23/17. |
| ‡6 C. | | Murray, T. 266903. | M. April 9/17. |
| 6 C. | IX | Rae, Thomas. 267005. | W. and M. April 9/17. |
| 6 C. | XI | Shirran, L.-Cpl. John. 266263. | M. May 16/17. |
| ‡6 C. | | Sim, A. 291095. | M. May 16/17. |
| 6 C. | | Watt, Wm. 285138. | M. April 23/17. |
| 6 C. | | Williamson, T. 266663. | M. April 9/17. |
| 6 D. | XV | Graham, W. A. 285092. (Fr. 2/8th.) | M. April 23/17. |
| 6 D. | XIII | Low, John. 285095. (Fr. A. & S. High. 4214 and 301834.) | M. April 23/17. |
| 6 D. | XV | MacKeand, Tom. 285105. | M. April 23/17. |
| 6 D. | | Masson, J. L. 266409. | W. and M. April 23/17. |
| ‡6 D. | | Milne, L.-Cpl. W. 265117. | M. April 9/17. |
| 6 D. | | Milne, Cpl. Walter. 265399. | M. April 23/17. |
| 6 D. | | Petrie, J. 266927. | M. April 23/17. |
| 6 D. | | Potts, A. 266913. | M. Mar. 5/17. |
| 6 D. | | Robertson, G. 266926. | M. Mar. 5/17. |
| 6 D. | | Tough, G. 266204. (12002.) | M. April 9/17. |
| 7 | | **Hillas, Capt. A. B. E.** | M. April 23/17. |
| 7 | | **McTavish, 2nd Lt. J. D.** | W. and M. April 23/17. |
| 7 A. | | **Miller, 2nd Lieut. E. G.** | K. April 23/17. Det.D./B. |
| 7 A. | IV | Henderson, Robert. 292329. (5847.) | K. April 23/17. Det.D./B. |
| 7 A. | | O'Donnell, J. J. 292287. | M. April 23/17. |
| 7 A. | IV | Rutherford, Harry W. 310039. | W. and M. April 23/17. |
| 7 A. | IV | Shaw, A. 40679. | M. April 23/17. |
| 7 A. | | Wyllie, S. A. 292493. | M. April 23/17. |
| ‡7 B. | | Burness, J. A. 290477. | W. and M. April 23/17. |
| 7 B. | | Esson, L.-Cpl. W. 290401. | M. April 23/17. |
| *7 B. or C. | | Henderson, Jas. 310077. | W. and M. April 23/17. |
| *7 B. | | Morrison, Wm. 292467. (6311.) | W. and M. April 23/17. |
| 7 B. | | Stephen, L.-Cpl. A. 290626. | M. April 23/17. |
| 7 B. | | Stewart, Sgt. Robert C. | M. April 23/17. |
| 7 C. | X | Baillie, Sam. S/40687. | M. April 23/17. |
| *7 C. | XII | Bain, L.-Cpl. John. 310250. | M. April 23/17. |
| 7 C. | X | Cumming, Jas. 292604. | M. April 23/17. |

**Gordon Highlanders—contd.**

*B.E.F.*

| | | |
|---|---|---|
| 7 C. IX | Frew, J. 310354. | W. and M. **April 23/17.** |
| 7 C. | McRobbie, L.-Cpl. J. 292188. | M. **April 23/17.** |
| 7 C. | O'May, Daniel. 310367. | M. **April 23/17.** |
| 7 C. | Rennie, L.-Cpl. E. 291002. | M. **April 23/17.** |
| 7 D. XVI | Massie, J. Gordon. 291624. | M. **April 23/17.** |
| 7 D. | Stewart, D. 291043. | M. **April 23/17.** |
| 7 ? | Milne, L.-Cpl. John. 3718. | K. **Nov. 13/16.** Det.D./B. |
| 8/10 B. VII | Canning, John. S/10630. | W. and M. **April 9-10/17.** |
| ‡8/10 B. | Grant, J. 11984. | M. **April 9-10/17.** |
| 8/10 B. | McFarlane, J. C. 40473. | M. **April 9-10/17.** |
| 8/10 B. | Strang, R. 13478. | M. **April 9-10/17.** |
| ‡8/10 B. | Stuart, L. A. 40438. | W. and M. **April 28/17.** |
| *8/10 B. V | Wilson, Gideon. 43008. | M. **April 9-10/17.** |
| 8/10 C. IX | Gray, W. T. 15048. | K. **April 9/17.** Det.D./B. |
| 8/10 D. | Sim, A. 5963. | M. **April 23-24/17.** |
| 9 | **MacWhirter, M.C., Major T.** | M. **April 27/17.** |
| ‡16 D. | Myron, J. 266433. | M. **May 16/17.** |

# FOOT GUARDS

## 1. COLDSTREAM.

*B.E.F.*

| | | |
|---|---|---|
| 1 2 | Ashburn, T. G. 15167. | M. **Sept. 15/16.** R/Enq. |
| 1 3 | Cardy, F. R. 15422. | M. **Sept. 15/16.** R./Enq. |
| 1 3 | Overton, G. G. 15626. | M. **Sept. 15/16.** R/Enq. |
| 1 3 IX | Robinson, Arthur. 13648. | K. **Sept. 15/16.** Det.D./B. |
| 1 3 | Whitehead, A. B. 14289. | K. **Sept. 15/16.** Det.D./B. R/Enq. |
| 2 1 I | Masters, Sidney. 15770. | M. **Sept. 14-16/16.** R/Enq. |
| 2 1 | Moody, W. J. 16221. | M. **Sept. 14-16/16.** R/Enq. |
| 2 1 I | Picking, Joseph. 15051. | M. **Sept. 14-16/16.** R/Enq. |
| 2 3 XI | Parnell, Alfred A. 10824. | M. **Sept. 14-16/16.** R./Enq. |
| 2 4 | Long, Harry. 17457. | W. and M. **Sept. 21-26/16.** R/Enq. |
| 3 1 II | Fripp, W. 15206. | M. **Sept. 15/16.** R/Enq. |
| 3 3 | Bowdler, Henry Arnold. 16491. | M. **Sept. 25/16.** R./Enq. |
| 3 3 | Dewhurst, E. 16352. | K. **Sept. 15/16.** Det.D./B. |

## 2. GRENADIERS.

*B.E.F.*

| | | |
|---|---|---|
| 1 1 II | Haughton, R. 25523. | K. **Nov. 29/16.** Det.D./B. |
| 1 1 III | Holloway, L.-Cpl. W. 23897. | M. **Sept. 14-16/16.** R/Enq. |
| ‡2 | **Blackwood, 2nd Lt. Lord Basil.** | M. **July 3/17.** |
| ‡2 | **Gunnis, 2nd Lt. I. Fitz G. S.** | M. **July 3-4/17.** |
| 2 2 | Hammond, Wm. 24998. | M. **Sept. 25/16.** R./Enq. |
| 2 3 IX | Eustace, L.-Cpl. Geo. 15521. | K. **Sept. 15/16.** Det.D./B. |
| ‡2 3 IX | Neville, John. 17465. | W. and M. **Sept. 25/16.** R/Enq. |
| 2 4 XIII | Johnson, Alfred. 24456. | K. **Sept. 25/16.** Det.D./B. |
| 3 1 IV | Staunton, Wm. 19213. | K. **Sept. 14/16.** Det.D./B. |

**Guards, Foot—contd.**

**2. Grenadiers—contd.**

## *B.E.F.*

| | | |
|---|---|---|
| 3 1 II | Watson, Fredk. James. 23761. | K. Sept. 14-17/16. Det.D./B. |
| 3 2 VI | Hilton, Frank. 23424. | M. Sept. 14-17/16. R/Enq. |
| 3 2 | Kitchiner, L.-Cpl. H. 20552. | M. Sept. 14-17/16. R/Enq. |
| 3 2 VIII | Reece, L.-Cpl. Reginald. 22004. | M. Sept. 14-17/16. R/Enq. |
| 3 3 | Mitchell, T. 10608. | M. Sept. 14-17/16. R/Enq. |
| 3 4 XV | England, Ralph. 24714. | M. Sept. 14-17/16. R/Enq. |
| 3 4 XIII | Rogers, J. J. 23810. | M. Sept. 14-17/16. R/Enq. |
| 4 2 | Chainey, W. J. 25019. | M. Sept. 25/16. R/Enq. |
| 4 2 | Chetwyn, Ernest. 24337. | M. Sept. 25/16. R/Enq. |
| *4 3 XII | Wright, W. H. 21275. | W. and M. Sept. 16/16. R/Enq. |
| 4 4 XV | Cooke, W. 22771. | K. Sept. 28/16. Det.D./B. |
| 4 4 | Holden, George. 25527. | M. Mar. 11/17. |

### 3. IRISH.

## *B.E.F.*

| | | |
|---|---|---|
| 1 3 | Brien, Con. 6336. | M. Sept. 17/16. R/Enq. |
| *1 4 | Leydon, Frank. 9765. | M. Sept. 17/16. R/Enq. |
| 2 2 VIII | Cummins, John. 8139. | K. Sept. 13/16. Det.D./B. R/Enq. |
| 2 4 | Ryan, John. 5472. | M. Sept. 15/16. R/Enq. |

### 4. SCOTS.

## *B.E.F.*

| | | |
|---|---|---|
| 1 B. | Chappell, L.-Cpl. Joseph. Robt. 8771. | M. Sept. 15/16. R/Enq. |
| 1 B. | Graham, Thomas. 183376. | M. Sept. 15/16. R/Enq. |
| 2 | **Chapman, 2nd Lt. David A. J.** | K. Sept. 15/16. Det.D./B. |
| 2 G. X | Clement, Elliott. 14652. | M. Sept. 25/16. R/Enq. |
| 2 H. | Watson, Edmund. 14278. | M. Sept. 25/16. R/Enq. |
| ‡2 ? | Barclay, Thos. 7063. | K. Sept. 25/16. Det.D./B. |

### 5. WELSH.

## *B.E.F.*

| | | |
|---|---|---|
| 1 1 IV | Jones, Dennis Lloyd. 2284. | W. and M. Sept. 16/16. R/Enq. |
| 1 1 | Jones, John. 1067. | M. Nov. 19/16. R/Enq. |
| 1 2 VIII | Evans, D. T. 1822. | M. Dec. 5/16. |
| 1 4 | Evans, Harold. 2579. | M. Mar. 6/17. |

### 6. MACHINE GUN GUARDS.

## *B.E.F.*

| | | |
|---|---|---|
| *2nd Bgde. Coldstream S. | Green, Thos. B. 12429. | K. Sept. 15/16. Det.D./B. |

## HAMPSHIRE REGIMENT.

### *B.E.F.*

| | | | |
|---|---|---|---|
| ‡1 B. | | Collins, F. 22470. | M. May 11/17. |
| 1 B. V | | Vince, John Henry. 19550. | M. Oct. 23/16. R/Enq. |
| 1 C. X | | Earl, Chas. 22513. | W. and M. Oct. 23/16. R/Enq. |
| 1 D. XIV | | Waterman, C. C. 25057. | K. April 10/17. Det.D./B. R/Enq. |
| 2 | | **Snyder, 2nd Lieut. L.** | M. April 23/17. |
| *2 W. | | Andrews, T. C. 29759. | M. April 23/17. |
| 2 W. III | | Gollop, W. H. S. 32640. | W. and M. April 23/17. |
| 2 W. III | | Hockings, F. C. 29625. | W. and M. April 23/17. |
| *2 W. I | | Kite, John. 16910. | W. and M. April 23/17. |
| 2 W. | | Loveday, J. W. 242465. | M. April 23/17. |
| 2 W. II | | Samphier, Wm. G. 20399. | M. April 23/17. |
| 2 W. | | Stancombe, A. J. 33407. | M. April 23/17. |
| 2 W. | | Warne, Percy Fredk. 9467. | D/W. April 23/17. Det.D./B. |
| 2 W. | | Wright, Walter. 17014. | M. April 23/17. |
| 2 X. | | Clifford, S/B. W. 27380. (Fr. H.Q.) | M. April 23/17. |
| 2 X. | | Emery, W. 27648. | M. April 23/17. |
| *2 X. | | Harris, A. T. 17540. (Fr. 1 Dorsets.) | K. Dec. 12/16. Det.D./B. |
| 2 X. | | Harris, D. 13535. | M. April 23/17. |
| 2 X. | | Hollis, J. W. 12026. | M. April 23/17. |
| 2 X. | | Ives, A. 26550. | M. April 23/17. |
| 2 X. | | Parker, L.-Sergt. H. J. 29555. | M. April 23/17. |
| 2 X. | | Smith, P. A. 29573. | M. April 23/17. |
| 2 X. | | Spencer, J. 17078. | M. April 23/17. |
| 2 X. | | Stone, W. L. 29606. | M. April 23/17. |
| 2 Y. | | Anderson, L.-Cpl. Jas. 29499. | M. April 23/17. |
| 2 Y. XI | | Baiden, Conrad. 29502. | W. and M. Oct. 20/16. R/Enq. |
| 2 Y. | | Bongers, Oscar Leon. 31652. | M. April 23/17. |
| ‡2 Y. | | Chappell, Edw. 17845. (Fr. 177 R.E.) | M. Unoff. W. Oct. 18/16. R/Enq. |
| 2 Y. X | | Clarke, Robt. 31668. | M. April 23/17. |
| 2 Y. | | Collopy, John. 9454. | M. April 23/17. |
| 2 Y. | | Davis, Alfred. 7467. | M. April 23/17. |
| ‡2 Y. | | Forrester, J. A. 24647. | M. April 23/17. |
| 2 Y. X | | Goree, W. G. 31582. | M. April 23/17. |
| 2 Y. | | Gould, Reg. J. 18566. | M. April 23/17. |
| 2 Y. X | | Goulding, E. C. 24656. | M. April 23/17. |
| 2 Y. | | Holman, Sergt. V. 9589. | M. April 23/17. |
| ‡2 Y. | | Iken, H. 21852. | M. April 23/17. |
| 2 Y. II | | Quennell, Leonard. 31764. | M. April 23/17. |
| 2 Y. | | Stephenson, J. 15931. | M. April 23/17. |
| 2 Y. | | Taylor, A. 9664. | M. April 23/17. |
| 2 Y. X | | Watts, Ernest. 24987. | M. April 23/17. |
| 2 Z. | | Bishop, T. 27251. | M. April 23/17. |
| 2 Z. | | Boswell, H. 25821. | M. April 23/17. |
| 2 Z. | | Bull, R. J. 10821. | M. Oct. 18/16. |
| 2 Z. | | Chapman, Douglas Alb. 3/4277. | M. April 23/17. |
| 2 Z. or H.Q. | | Clements, W. 10984. | M. April 23/17. |
| 2 Z. XIV | | Cooper, E. 10833. | W. and M. April 23/17. |
| 2 Z. | | Creswell, L.-Cpl. W J. 10835. | M. Oct. 18/16. R/Enq |
| 2 Z. | | Freemantle, F. 27317. | M. April 23/17. |
| 2 Z. | | Gannaway, A. 24616. | M. April 23/17. |
| 2 Z. | | Hampson, L.-Cpl. T. 17917. | W. and M. April 23/17. |
| 2 Z. XIV | | Haskett, Fred Thos. 25425. | M. April 23/17. |
| 2 Z. | | Hastings, Harold. 14400. | W. and M. April 23/17. |
| 2 Z. | | Heath, B. 27262. | M. April 23/17. |
| 2 Z. | | Hestall, G. 13697. | M. April 23/17. |

**Hampshire Regiment—contd.**

## *B.E.F.*

2 Z. Kind, S. H. 31834. M. April 23/17.
2 Z. XV Larkin, Sergt. Percy. 8345. M. April 23/17.
2 Z. XIII McLeod, John A. 23127. M. April 23/17.
2 Z. Mills, A.-Cpl. A. J. 4080. (Fr. 3rd.) M. April 23/17.
2 Z. Misselbrook, F. 478. (Fr. 3rd.) M. April 23/17.
2 Z. XIV Northover, Hubert Claude. 29814. M. April 23/17.
2 Z. Palmer, H. 31773. K. April 14/17. Det.D./B.
2 Z. Quelch, A.-Cpl. P. E. 14345. M. April 23/17.
2 Z. XIII Tilley, John Wm. 27374. M. April 23/17.
2 Z. Warr, W. H. 24696. M. April 23/17.
2 ? I.T.M. Walsh, Edward. 9879. (88 Bgde. 1 Batty.) K. Sept. 18/16. Det.D./B.
14 A. I Chapman, A. E. 15713. M. Sept. 4/16. R/Enq.
14 B. Carter, Robt. 21662. M. Sept. 3/16. R/Enq.
*14 B. VIII Stares, Chas. Henry. 12829. M. Sept. 3/16. R/Enq.
14 B. Merchant, L.-Cpl. Bartley. 20893. M. Sept. 3/16. R/Enq.
14 B. Stephens, L.-Sgt. A. 5143. M. Sept. 3/16. R/Enq.
14 B. Vincent, Walter. 15457. M. Sept. 3/16. R/Enq.
14 B. Wells, Mathias. 15044. M. Sept. 3/16. R/Enq
14 C. Budden, L.-Cpl. H. J. 12880. M. Sept. 3/16. R/Enq.
14 C. Cranstone, Albert. 12894. M. Sept. 3/16. R/Enq.
14 C. Prior, Hugh. 12993. M. Sept. 3/16. R/Enq
14 C. Pullen, Wm. G. 12995. M. Sept. 3/16. R/Enq.
‡14 D. XV Dudley, Henry J. 13955. M. Sept. 3/16. R/Enq.
14 D. XIV Gillingham, A. 13997. M. Sept. 3/16. R/Enq.
*14 D. Holloway, Sig. W. G. 14435. M. Sept. 3/16. R/Enq.
14 D. Johnson, J 13996. M. Sept. 3/16. R/Enq.
14 ? M.G.S. Fuller, George W. 19510. M. Sept. 3/16. R/Enq.
14 ? Jackson, Norman Edw. 29634. (Fr. 9.) M. Sept. 3/16.
14 ? M.G.S. Pullman, Peter. 8469. M. Sept. 3/16. R/Enq.
15 A. or B. Hinton, Albert Edward. 29662. M. Sept. 15/16. R/Enq.
15 B. Cook, A. 20980. M. Sept. 15/16.
‡15 C. X Hedges, Jas. R. 26998. M. June 7/17.
‡15 C. XII Hymas, Leonard. 27048. M. July 7/17.
15 C. Richardson, George. 18832. W. and M. Oct. 7/16.
15 C. Tilbury, Joseph S. 24716. M. Oct. 7/16. R/Enq.

## *BALKANS.*

‡10 **Bennett, Lieut. G. T.** M. May 31/17.
10 C. Cooper, A. W. 18079. M. Dec. 7/15. R/Enq.
12 **Gibaud, 2nd Lieut. E. J.** M. April 24-25/17.
12 **Tidy, 2nd Lieut. Percy E.** W. and M. April 24-25/17.
12 A. Burton, W. 3742. M. April 25/17.
12 A. Campden, A. J. 25481. K. April 25/17. Det.D./B.
12 A. Cooper, H. 13039. M. April 25/17.
12 A. IV Goldie, W. 32019. M. April 24-25/17.
12 A. Knight, John. 13840. M. April 24-25/17.
12 A. Rickman, B. G. 15398. M. April 24-25/17.
12 B. Cambridge, Sergt. Jas. H. 3/4894. M. April 24-25/17.
12 B. Feltham, H. 8829. M. April 25/17.
12 B. Hawthorne, Edgar Thos. 31946. M. April 25/17.
12 B. Hunt, A. R. 25654. M. April 25/17.
12 B. Hunt, P. E. 21514. M. April 25/17.
12 B. VIII Mason, H. 25680. M. April 24-25/17.
12 B. Meredith, Sergt. R. V. 13770. M. April 25/17.
12 B. Perham, H. E. 32324. M. April 24-25/17.
12 B. Rendell, Arthur. 31974. M. April 24/17.
12 B. Walker, Alb. Edw. 13320. M. April 24-25/17.

**Hampshire Regiment—contd.**

## *BALKANS.*

| | | |
|---|---|---|
| 12 B. | Wilkes, Albert. 13758. | M. **April 25/17.** |
| ‡12 C. | Evans, John. 13442. | M. **April 24-25/17.** |
| 12 C. | Gladdis, C. H. 25446. | M. **April 24-25/17.** |
| 12 C. IX | McGuirk, Wm. 256840. | M. **April 24-25/17.** |
| 12 D. M.G.S. | Manning, Frank E. C. 13609. | M. **April 24-25/17.** |
| 12 D. XIII | Moore, Samuel. 13582. | M. **April 25/17.** |
| 12 D. M.G.S. | Neale, T. 13579. | M. **April 24-25/17.** |
| 12 D. | Payne, Walter. 13274. | W. and M. **April 24-25/17.** |
| 12 D. | Pearce, G. 13555. | W. and M. **April 24-25/17.** |
| 12 D. | Perks, L.-Cpl. Harold J. 31943. | W. and M. **April 24-25/17.** |
| 12 D. | Smith, John. 15387. | W. and M. **April 24-25/17.** |
| 12 D. XV | Stokes, Morris Kew. 32002. | W. and M. **April 24-25/17.** |
| 12 D. | Vellender, F. G. 13812. | W. and M. **April 24-25/17.** |
| 12 D. | Wood, L.-Cpl. R. 8159. | M. **April 25/17.** |
| 12 D. M.G.S. | Woodward, Herb. B. 13279. | M. **April 24-25/17.** |
| 12 D. | Worgan, Edward. 13168. | W. and M. **April 25/17.** |
| 12 ? | Bailey, L.-Cpl. R. 15441. | M. **April 24-25/17.** |
| 12 ? | Bowler, L.-Cpl. W. R. 15705. | M. **April 24-25/17.** |
| 12 ? | Bromley, F. 13434. | M. **April 24-25/17.** |
| 12 ? | Earley, F. J. 202421. | M. **April 24-25/17.** |
| 12 ? | Griffiths, T. 13650. | M. **April 24-25/17.** |
| 12 ? | Hancox, G. 13034. | M. **April 24-25/17.** |
| 12 ? | Howard, W. 23435. | M. **April 24-25/17.** |
| 12 ? | Hunt, F. 11626. | M. **April 24-25/17.** |
| *12 ? | Joyce, J. L. 25065. | M. **April 24/17.** |
| 12 ? | Moth, Sergt. F. E. 4884. | M. **April 24-25/17.** |
| 12 ? | Nolan, G. 31937. | M. **April 24-25/17.** |
| 12 ? | Pettifer, L.-Cpl. S. A. 13496. | M. **April 24-25/17.** |
| 12 ? | Porter, L.-Cpl. W. A. 13200. | M. **April 24-25/17.** |
| 12 ? | Robertson, W. 13005. | W. and M. **April 24-25/17.** |
| 12 ? | Robinson, G. 13418. | M. **April 24-25/17.** |
| 12 ? | Sayer, T. O. 12108. | W. and M. **April 24-25/17.** |
| 12 ? | Ware, S. 25032. | W. and M. **April 24-25/17.** |
| 12 ? | Webb, F. H. 13329. | M. **April 24-25/17.** |
| 12 ? | Wilson, L.-Cpl. E. 31942. | M. **April 24-25/17.** |
| 12 ? | Wright, D. 13730. | M. **April 24-25/17.** |

## *E.E.F.*

| | | |
|---|---|---|
| 8 | **Attfield, 2nd Lt. S. H.** (Fr. 1 W. Surrey.) | W. and M. **April 19/17.** |
| 8 | **Hills, 2nd Lt. Arthur Hyde.** | W. and M. **April 19/17.** |
| 8 | **King, 2nd Lieut. R. D.** | M. **April 19/17.** |
| 8 | **Pakeman, Lieut. H.** | M. **April 19/17.** |
| 8 | **Ratsey, 2nd Lieut. S. G.** | M. **April 19/17.** |
| 8 | **Seely, Capt. Chas. G.** | W. and M. **April 19/17.** |
| 8 A. | Bartlett, L.-Cpl. T. 330273. | M. **April 19/17.** |
| 8 A. | Cooke, L. L. 331497. (3483.) | M. **April 19/17.** |
| 8 A. | Crabbe, Archibald Beaconsfield. 330714. | W. and M. **April 19/17.** |
| 8 A. | Hart, W. G. 331029. (Late 2714.) | M. **April 19/17.** |
| 8 A. | Hawes, Chas. 330811. (2395.) | M. **April 19/17.** |
| 8 A. | Hickens, Wm. 330836. | M. **April 19/17.** |
| 8 A. | Holmes, Sgt. W. 330426. (1774.) | W. and M. **April 19/17.** |
| 8 A. | Knight, C. E. 330617. | M. **April 19/17.** |
| 8 A. | Moth, F. C. 330997. (2676.) | M. **April 19/17.** |
| 8 A. | Parrett, F. 331530. | M. **April 19/17.** |
| 8 A. | Phillips, G. Ernest. 331117. | M. **April 19/17.** |
| 8 A. | Russell, T. I. 330209. | M. **April 19/17.** |
| 8 A. | Smith, W. S. 331548. (Late 3534.) | M. **April 19/17.** |

**Hampshire Regiment—contd.**

*E.E.F.*

| | | |
|---|---|---|
| 8 A. | Trueman, L.-Cpl. E. 330393. | M. April 19/17. |
| 8 A. IV | Ward, F. W. J. 330509. | M. April 19/17. |
| 8 A. | White, H. N. 331249. | M. April 19/17. |
| 8 B. | Airey, Rich. 331559. | M. April 19/17. |
| 8 B. | Baker, Hubert Geo. 331006. (2687.) | M. April 19/17. |
| 8 B. | Britton, O. W. F. 330183. | M. April 19/17. |
| 8 B. | Butcher, W. H. 330492. | M. April 19/17. |
| 8 B. | Cassford, Fred G. 330769. | M. April 19/17. |
| 8 B. | Childs, C. H. 330588. | M. April 19/17. |
| 8 B. | Giles, F. N. W. 331411. | M. April 19/17. |
| 8 B. | Hall, A. W. 331266. | M. April 19/17. |
| †8 B. Sig. S. | Hapgood, H. S. 330876. | K. April 19/17. Det.D./B. |
| 8 B. | Heath, Harry Charlie. 331120. (2837) | M. April 19/17. |
| 8 B. | Ives, G. A. 330691. | M. April 19/17. |
| 8 B. | Jones, H. W. 331507. | M. April 19/17. |
| 8 B. | Matthews, Thos. Edw. 330127. | M. April 19/17. |
| 8 B. | Plumridge, L.-Cpl. E. 330435. (2178.) | M. April 19/17. |
| 8 B. | Pritchett, Robt. Geo. 330531. (Late 1948.) | M. April 19/17. |
| 8 B. | Simmonds, W. H. 330717. | M. April 19/17. |
| 8 B. | Smith, F. 330549. (1974.) | M. April 19/17. |
| 8 B. | Stone, Charlie. 331086. (2792.) | M. April 19/17. |
| 8 B. | Thompson, R. W. 330827. | M. April 19/17. |
| 8 B. | Warren, E. S. 330271. | M. April 19/17. |
| 8 B. | White, Arthur Henry. 331301. | M. April 19/17. |
| 8 B. | White, D. A. 331219. | M. April 19/17. |
| 8 B. | Willis, L.-Cpl. Geo. Bolton. 331441. | M. April 19/17. |
| 8 B. | Witham, H. G. 331310. (3120.) | M. April 19/17. |
| 8 C. | Allen, W. S. J. 331118. (Late 2835.) | M. April 19/17. |
| 8 C. | Baskett, W. G. 331244. | M. April 19/17. |
| 8 C. | Coxhead, A. N. 330947. | W. and M. April 19/17. |
| 8 C. | Daniel, Wallace, H. J. 330984. (Late 2658.) | W. and M. April 19/17. |
| 8 C. L.G.S. | Dodsworth, Harry. 330582. (Late 2019.) | M. April 19/17. |
| 8 C. | Finlay, Colin Douglas. 330309. | M. April 19/17. |
| 8 C. | Gilbert, R. J. 330342. | M. April 19/17. |
| 8 C. | Hacker, F. 331359. (3178.) | W. and M. April 19/17. |
| 8 C. | Hill, W. 331133. | M. April 19/17. |
| 8 C. | Hookey, W. J. 331708. | W. and M. April 19/17. |
| 8 C. | Lane, Cpl. W. J. 330394. | M. April 19/17. |
| 8 C. | Legg, E. C. 331084. | W. and M. April 19/17. |
| 8 C. | Mann, W. G. 331374. (3194.) | M. April 19/17. |
| 8 C. | Munday, E. 330899. | M. April 19/17. |
| 8 C. | Parkinson, A. J. 330920. (2572.) | M. April 19/17. |
| 8 C. XI | Pepper, A. 330432. (1781.) | W. and M. April 19/17. |
| 8 C. | Sillence, Walter. 331169. (Late 2910.) | M. April 19/17. |
| 8 C. | Singleton, J. 331129. | M. April 19/17. |
| 8 C. | Twitchen, Percy E. 331550. (1702.) | M. April 19/17. |
| 8 C. | Warell, Sergt. Harold. 330294. | M. April 19/17. |
| 8 C. | Watts, V. 330816. | W. and M. April 19/17 |
| 8 C. | Webster, Sgt. B. 331286. (3093.) | M. April 19/17. |
| 8 C. | Wheeler, A. 330195. (1356.) | W. and M. April 19/17. |
| 8 C. | Wolfe, Cpl. F. 330706. | M. April 19/17. |
| 8 D. | Bartlett, Jas. R. 330561. | W. and M. April 19/17. |
| 8 D. | Bennett, B. G. 330973. | M. April 19/17. |
| 8 D. | Bettenson, R. J. 330818. (2405.) | M. April 19/17. |
| 8 D. XVI | Carpenter, T. J. 331508. | M. April 19/17. |

**Hampshire Regiment—contd.**

### *E.E.F.*

| | | |
|---|---|---|
| 8 D. | Catlow, Thos. 331176. (2918.) | M. April 19/17. |
| 8 D. | Caws, Sergt. Ernest Hy. 330041. | M. April 19/17. |
| 8 D. | Churchill, E. A. 330525. | M. April 19/17. |
| 8 D. | Corney, H. 330626. | M. April 19/17. |
| 8 D. XVI | Dimmick, E. 330970. | M. April 19/17. |
| 8 D. | Dunning, F. 331110. (2826.) | M. April 19/17. |
| 8 D. | Harris, L.-Cpl. J. H. 331354. (3172.) | M. April 19/17. |
| 8 D. | Lacey, A. J. 331108. | M. April 19/17. |
| *8 D. | Merriott, Chas. Geo. 331147. | W. and M. April 19/17. |
| 8 D. | Richards, A. 331015. | M. April 19/17. |
| 8 D. | Rowe, E. H. 330795. | M. April 19/17. |
| 8 D. | Shepherd, Walter. 331531. | M. April 19/17. |
| 8 D. XIII | Shilton, L.-Cpl. F. 330522. | M. April 19/17. |
| 8 D. XIII | Smith, J. E. 330644. (Late 2126.) | M. April 19/17. |
| 8 D. | Stone, W. 330809. | M. April 19/17. |
| 8 D. | Vale, Albert. 330840. | M. April 19/17. |
| 8 D. | White, H. F. 330679. (2173.) | M. April 19/17. |
| 8 D. | Winsor, P. L. 331177. (2919.) | M. April 19/17. |
| 8 ? | Andrews, J. A. 331298. | M. April 19/17. |
| 8 ? | Ash, C. G. 330109. | M. April 19/17. |
| 8 ? | Bartlett, E. J. 331054. | M. April 19/17. |
| 8 ? | Batchelor, E. E. 330657. | M. April 19/17. |
| 8 ? | Board, H. R. 330451. | M. April 19/17. |
| 8 ? | Bone, G. F. 331188. | M. April 19/17. |
| 8 ? | Brooks, D. R. 330750. | M. April 19/17. |
| 8 ? | Bryant, G. 331510. | M. April 19/17. |
| 8 ? | Burrows, H. G. 331069. | M. April 19/17. |
| 8 ? | Butler, J. 330902. | M. April 19/17. |
| 8 ? | Calley, W. V. P. 330623. | M. April 19/17. |
| 8 ? | Chambers, Bert Frank. 331509. (Late 3495.) | M. April 19/17. |
| 8 ? | Chiverton, F. 330187. | M. April 19/17. |
| 8 ? | Church, A. D. 330541. | M. April 19/17. |
| 8 ? | Clarke, W. 330213. | M. April 19/17. |
| 8 ? | Cooper, H. E. 330957. | M. April 19/17. |
| 8 ? | Cornwell, F. W. 331251. | M. April 19/17. |
| 8 ? | Dallimore, E. A. 33282. | M. April 19/17. |
| 8 ? | Dennett, G. A. 331042. | M. April 19/17. |
| 8 ? | Dennis, A. A. 330066. | M. April 19/17. |
| 8 ? | Dibbins, W. T. 330592. | M. April 19/17. |
| 8 ? | Downer, L.-Cpl. R. 330516. | M. April 19/17. |
| 8 ? | Edwards, W. 331072. | M. April 19/17. |
| 8 ? | Elliott, E. C. 331037. | M. April 19/17. |
| 8 ? | Eyers, E. 331091. | M. April 19/17. |
| 8 ? | Farr, D. 331418. | M. April 19/17. |
| 8 ? | Floyd, H. 330122. | M. April 19/17. |
| 8 ? | Freemantle, P. 331512. | M. April 19/17. |
| 8 ? | Foyle, L.-Cpl. A. H. 331340. | M. April 19/17. |
| 8 ? | Fraser, B. W. 331073. | M. April 19/17. |
| 8 ? | Gardner, A. C. 331184. | M. April 19/17. |
| 8 ? | Gritt, L. 331076. | M. April 19/17. |
| 8 ? | Griffen, C. F. 331475. | M. April 19/17. |
| 8 ? | Hall, G. 330758. | M. April 19/17. |
| 8 ? | Hamblin, A. J. 331082. | M. April 19/17. |
| 8 ? | Hatherall, L.-Cpl. H. 331378. | M. April 19/17. |
| 8 ? | Hayden, L.-Cpl. W. 330586. | M. April 19/17. |
| 8 ? | Hayes, L.-Cpl. A. G. 331389. | M. April 19/17. |
| 8 ? | Hayles, J. 330566. | M. April 19/17. |
| 8 ? | Hemmings, F. 331302. | M. April 19/17. |

**Hampshire Regiment—contd.**

## *E.E.F.*

| | | |
|---|---|---|
| 8 ? | Herrington, S. 330410. | W. and M. April 19/17. |
| 8 ? | Hill, T. 331397. | M. April 19/17. |
| 8 ? | Hoare, C. 331260. | M. April 19/17. |
| 8 ? | Horsecroft, C. 330201. | M. April 19/17. |
| 8 ? | House, W. 331431. | M. April 19/17. |
| 8 ? | Hunt, H. A. C. 330135. | M. April 19/17. |
| 8 ? | Hunt, R. 331461. | M. April 19/17. |
| 8 ? | Hurst, R. 331038. | M. April 19/17. |
| 8 ? | James, L. V. F. 330099. | M. April 19/17. |
| 8 ? | Jones, C. H. 330995. | M. April 19/17. |
| 8 ? | Kinch, V. J. 330971. | M. April 19/17. |
| 8 ? | Legg, J. 330344. | M. April 19/17. |
| 8 ? | Leggatt, J. 331541. | M. April 19/17. |
| 8 ? | Littlefield, F. 331182. | M. April 19/17. |
| 8 ? | Lovegrove, J. B. 330694. | M. April 19/17. |
| 8 ? | Morey, Sergt. J. 330476. | M. April 19/17. |
| 8 ? | Moylan, J. W. 330933. | M. April 19/17. |
| 8 ? | Murray, G. B. 330988. | M. April 19/17. |
| *8 ? | Newlands, L. 331140. | M. April 19/17. |
| 8 ? | Newman, E. F. 330584. | M. April 19/17. |
| 8 ? | Osman, F. 330478. | M. April 19/17. |
| 8 ? | Parker, G. 331216. | M. April 19/17. |
| 8 ? | Payne, T. 331013. | M. April 19/17. |
| 8 ? | Phillips, E. 330411. | M. April 19/17. |
| 8 ? | Philpott, W. J. 331064. | M. April 19/17. |
| 8 ? | Pidgeon, F. G. 330682. | M. April 19/17. |
| *8 ? | Pike, W. 331236. | M. April 19/17. |
| 8 ? | Primmer, E. G. 330151. | M. April 19/17. |
| 8 ? | Richards, A. C. 330649. | M. April 19/17. |
| 8 ? | Ricketts, F. T. 330912. | M. April 19/17. |
| 8 ? | Rogers, P. A. G. 331039. | M. April 19/17. |
| 8 ? | Scammell, C. F. 331173. | M. April 19/17. |
| 8 ? | Scorell, H. W. 330485. | M. April 19/17. |
| 8 ? | Sibbick, A. L. 330577. | M. April 19/17. |
| *8 ? | Silsbury, W. 330390. | M. April 19/17. |
| 8 ? | Slade, D. 331050. | M. April 19/17. |
| 8 ? | Smith, Sergt. C. 330641. | M. April 19/17. |
| 8 ? | Spencer, A. 331221. | M. April 19/17. |
| 8 ? | Squires, A. T. 331545. | M. April 19/17. |
| 8 ? | Stephens, H. 331500. | M. April 19/17. |
| *8 ? | Stocks, T. 330846. | M. April 19/17. |
| *8 ? | Street, V. 330391. | M. April 19/17. |
| 8 ? | Summerfield, J. 330884. | M. April 19/17. |
| 8 ? | Sutton, H. 331402. | M. April 19/17. |
| 8 ? | Taylor, L.-Cpl. W. 331401. | M. April 19/17. |
| 8 ? | Trowbridge, W. M. 331005. | M. April 19/17. |
| 8 ? | Tuck, B. 330591. | M. April 19/17. |
| 8 ? | White, L.-Sergt. J. W. 330439. | M. April 19/17. |
| 8 ? | Worboys, T. C. 331562. | M. April 19/17. |
| 8 ? | Young, A. W. 330731. | M. April 19/17. |
| 8 ? | Young, E. G. 330289. | M. April 19/17. |

## *PERSIAN GULF.*

| | | |
|---|---|---|
| 4 A. | Avery, C. W. 3244. | M. Jan. 21/17. |
| 4 A. | Hallett, W. 204117. | W. and M. Feb. 23-24/17. |
| 4 B. | Clifford, W. 204108. | W. and M. Feb. 23-24/17. |
| 4 B. | Cox, L.-Cpl. Percival Wm. 202988. | W. and M. Feb. 23-24/17. |
| 4 B. | Gill, L.-Cpl. F. 3415. (Fr. 2/4th.) | M. Jan. 21/16. |
| 4 B. | Pearce, Geo. Wm. 3400. (Fr. 2/4th.) | M. Jan. 21/16. R/Enq. |

**Hampshire Regiment—contd.**

## *PERSIAN GULF.*

| | | |
|---|---|---|
| 4 B. | Robinson, C. A. 4029. | K. Feb. 23-24/17. Det.D./B. |
| 4 C. | Chalk, G. 202253. | W. and M. Feb. 23-24/17. |
| 4 C. | Compton, Roy. 202004. (4481.) | M. Feb. 23-24/17. |
| 4 C. | Cool, Henry Wm. 201145. | W. and M. Feb. 23-24/17. |
| 4 C. | Fullbrook, John. 200359. | M. Feb. 23-24/17. |
| 4 C. | Lampert, O. 201580. (4007.) | W. and M. Feb. 23-24/17. |
| 4 C. | Lawrence, F. 201006. (3134.) | W. and M. Feb. 23-24/17. |
| 4 C. | Pulleyblank, Walter Edw. 203279. | M. Feb. 23-24/17. |
| 4 D. | Tigwell, G. 2051. | M. Jan. 21/16. |
| 4 ? | Applegate, S. 200821. | M. Feb. 23-24/17. |
| 4 ? | Bulpit, Alfred. 2623. | M., bel. K. Jan. 21/16. R/Enq |
| 4 ? | Cox, H. 200214. | M. Feb. 23-24/17. |
| 4 ? | Crook, C. 201990. | W. and M. Feb. 24/17. |
| 4 ? | Grist, F. 204115. | W. and M. Feb. 23-24/17. |
| 4 ? | Hughes, A. 201536. | W. and M. Feb. 23-24/17. |
| 4 ? | Kent, W. A. 2659. | M. Jan. 21/16. |
| 4 ? | Rennoldson, L.-Cpl. E. J. H. 204158. (Fr. 5th, 3456.) | M. Feb. 23-24/17. |
| 4 ? | Sharland, Cpl. A. 200219. | W. and M. Feb. 23-24/17. |
| 4 ? | Slack, W. 203287. | M. Feb. 23-24/17. |
| 4 ? | Smith, Cpl. O. J. 203071. | M. Feb. 23-24/17. |
| 4 ? | Starling, E. 204138. | W. and M. Feb. 23/17. |
| 4 ? | Weller, F. 203103. | M. Feb. 23-24/17. |
| 4 ? | Woodland, F. 201979. | M. Feb. 23-24/17. |

## HEREFORDSHIRE REGIMENT.

## *E.E.F.*

| | | |
|---|---|---|
| 1 | **Whittaker, 2nd Lt. W. H.** | W. and M. Mar. 27/17. |
| 1 A. | Wargent, Sergt. C. W. 235098. (1068.) | W. and M. Mar. 26/17. |
| 1 B. V | Barnett, L.-Cpl. R. W. 235244 (1381.) | W. and M. Mar. 26/17. |
| 1 B. | Dunn, W. H. 235468. | W. and M. Mar. 26/17. |
| 1 B. VII | Fell, Richard M. L. 236374. (Late 3723.) | W. and M. Mar. 26/17. |
| 1 C. IX | Brimfield, Harry. 236478. | W. and M. Mar. 26/17. |
| 1 C. XII | Caines, A. 236502. (Late 3929.) | M. Mar. 27/17. |
| 1 C. | Evans, L.-Cpl. W. A. 237103. (Late 5526.) | W. and M. Mar. 26/17. |
| 1 C. | Holloway, F. R. 4187. | W. and M. Mar. 26/17. |
| 1 C. | Matthews, P. A. 235582. | W. and M. Mar. 26/17. |
| 1 C. X | Porter, Leonard. 236108. | M. Mar. 27/17. |
| 1 C. | Stone, W. G. 235654. (Late 2196.) | M. Mar. 26/17. |
| 1 C. X | Tanswell, H. 235343. | M. Mar. 26/17. |
| 1 ? | Bushnell, J. H. 235646. | M. Mar. 26/17. |
| 1 ? | Churnside, Sergt. C. 235421. | W. and M. Mar. 27/17. |
| 1 ? | Clarke, H. 235497. | M. Mar. 27/17. |
| 1 ? | Collins, T. G. 236139. | M. Mar. 27/17. |
| 1 ? | Dance, W. E. 236460. | M. Mar. 27/17. |
| 1 ? | Davis, L.-Cpl. O. 236248. | W. and M. Mar. 26/17. |
| 1 ? | Donovan, A. E. 236623. | W. and M. Mar. 26/17. |
| 1 ? | Fletcher, Sgt. E. A. G. 235600. | M. Mar. 27/17. |
| 1 ? | Hall, W. 237039. | M. Mar. 27/17. |

**Herefordshire Regiment**—contd.

## *E.E.F.*

1 ? Hargest, R. 235469. W. and M. **Mar. 26/17.**
1 ? Harris, C.-Q.-M.-S. J. F. 235335. M. **Mar. 26/17.**
1 ? Hilton, G. 236065. W. and M. **Mar. 26/17.**
1 ? Nicholls, W. T. 236620. M. **Mar. 27/17.**
1 ? Pope, Cpl. G. 235381. W. and M. **Mar. 26/17.**
1 ? Savory, W. E. 235763. W. and M. **Mar. 27/17.**
1 ? Smith, Sergt. W. 235424. M. **Mar. 27/17.**
1 ? Taylor, Sergt. G. R. 236242. W. and M. **Mar. 26/17.**
1 ? Walker, J. 236092. W. and M. **Mar. 26/17.**
1 ? Withington, T. H. 235757. W. and M. **Mar. 26/17.**

# HIGHLAND LIGHT INFANTRY.

## *B.E.F.*

2 **Miller, 2nd Lieut. G. B.** W. and M. **May 1/17.**
2 A. Aitken, Jas. 28250. (H.Q. Sig.) M. **April 28/17.**
2 A. L.G.S. Bennett, Thomas. 30576. W. and M. **April 28/17.**
‡2 A. L.G.S. Brenner, Wm. 25822. M. **April 28/17.**
2 A. II Brooks, Chas. 353025. (Fr. 5 R. Scots.) M. **April 28/17.**
2 A. Bourne, W. 25822. M. **April 28/17.**
‡2 A. Eastwood, F. 32789. M. **April 28/17.**
2 A. Fleming, Wm. 353017. (42744.) M. **April 28/17.**
*2 A. IV L.G.S. Gibson, John. 7918. W. and M. **April 28/17.**
2 A. III Grant, Cpl. John. 35143. M. **April 28/17.**
‡2 A. Henderson, J. 11749. M. **April 28/17.**
2 A. I McEwan, John. 41063. M. **April 28/17.**
2 A. McGlinchey, James. 32891. M. **April 28/17.**
2 A. II McKay, James. A/9022. M. **April 28/17.**
2 A. McKinnon, D. 13085. M. **April 28/17.**
2 A. I McMecking, L.-Cpl. Wm. 35161. W. and M. **April 28/17.**
2 A. III Mulligan, James. 19290. M. **April 28/17.**
2 A. II Nunneley, L.-Cpl. John Cecil. 35168. Unoff. W. and M. **April 30/17.**
2 A. Smith, D. S. 353026. (Fr. R. Scots.) M. **April 28/17.**
2 A. Stewart, A. 31102. M. **April 28/17.**
2 A. Sig. S. Timilty, L.-Cpl. Jos. 3022. W. and M. **April 28/17.**
2 B. Cameron, H. J. 353031. M. **April 28/17.**
2 B. Cameron, J. A. 30563. M. **April 28/17.**
‡2 B. Egan, W. 23723. M. **April 28/17.**
*2 B. Gaines, Herbert E. 29478. M. **Nov. 13/16.** R/Enq.
2 B. Hutton, J. 353042. M. **April 28/17.**
2 B. V Jackson, W. H. 2079. M. **April 28/17.**
‡2 B. Jobes, R. 21458. M. **April 28/17.**
‡2 B. McCove, W. 17220. M. **April 28/17.**
2 B. Peacock, W. 30868. M. **April 23/17.**
2 B. Watson, J. 7689. M. **April 28/17.**
2 C. Curry, R. 1012. M. **April 28/17.**
*2 C. Harris, Harry. 353051. (Erroneously known as 42780.) (Fr. 9th.) M. **April 28/17.**
2 C. Luke, James. 35279. W. and M. **April 28/17.**
2 C. Pickford, W. H. 21600. M. **Nov. 13/16.** R/Enq.
2 C. XI Wharton, W. B/21149. M. **April 28/17.**
2 D. XIII Aitchison, Jas. 42896. M. **April 28/17.**

**Highland Light Infantry—contd.**

*B.E.F.*

| | | |
|---|---|---|
| 2 D. XIII | Aitken, Arthur. 4436. | W. and M. April 28/17. |
| *2 D. | Douglas, L.-Cpl. Gordon. 35103. | W. and M. April 28/17. |
| 2 D. | Harris, Gaby. 31695. | W. and M. April 28/17. |
| 2 D. | Hutton, L.-Cpl. G. 7452. | M. April 28/17. |
| 2 D. XIV | Kennedy, Geo. M. 21035. | W. and M. April 28/17. |
| ‡2 D. | McAllister, J. 7042. | M. April 28/17. |
| 2 D. XV | McAuslan, John. 35120. | M. April 28/17. |
| 2 D. | Miller, J. 35282. | M. April 28/17. |
| 2 D. | Neill, J. 30571. | M. April 23/17. |
| 2 D. XIV | Rae, Alex. 8808. | M. April 28/17. |
| ‡2 D. | Rae, J. 8784. | M. April 28/17. |
| 2 D. XVI | Reid, John H. 2856. | M. April 28/17. |
| 2 D. XV | Scott, Wm. 42883. | M. April 28/17. |
| 2 D. | Toner, Arthur. 14660. | W. and M. April 28/17. |
| 2 ? L.G.S. | Batchelor, Robt. 21153. | M. April 28/17. |
| 9 | **Maitland, 2nd Lieut. A.** | M. May 20/17. |
| 9 A. | Board, Sergt. Wm. 330244. | M May 20/17. |
| ‡9 A. | Breslin, W. 332938. | W. and M. May 20/17. |
| 9 A. II | Brown, Alex. 332914. | M. May 20/17. |
| 9 A. II | Christie, John. 332915. | M. May 20/17. |
| 9 A. III | Clarkson, L.-Cpl. Arthur John. 5128 | W. and M. Nov. 2/16. R/Enq. |
| ‡9 A. IV | Duthie, Ernest R. 332131. | M. May 20/17. |
| ‡9 A. | Gibson, W. 332405. | W. and M. May 20/17. |
| ‡9 A. | Gordon, C. 333958. | M. May 20/17. |
| 9 A. III | Gordon, Charles. 241745. (4454.) | Unoff. M. May 20/17. |
| *9 A. | Hardie, Thos. 330718. (2807.) | M. May 20/17. |
| ‡9 A. II | McClusky, John. 332917. | W. and M. May 20/17. |
| ‡9 A. | McCrone, A.-L.-Cpl. A. 331565. | M. May 20/17. |
| ‡9 A. | McIntosh, A.-L.-Cpl. J. 330309. | M. May 20/17. |
| *9 A. II | Mitchell, Wm. G. 333099. | M. May 20/17. |
| *9 A. L.G.S. | Ross, John. 332260. | M. May 20/17. |
| *9 A. I | Smith, Thos. John. 330413. | M. May 20/17. |
| *9 A. II | Ward, Neil. 333119. (1625.) | M. May 20/17. |
| *9 A. I | Weir, Anthony Thomson. 330931. | M. May 20/17. |
| 9 B. | Burnett, Hendry. 332089. | M. May 20/17. |
| ‡9 B. | Davidson, T. 333123. | M. May 20/17. |
| *9 B. VIII | Donnachie, Saml. 332381. | M. May 20/17. |
| ‡9 B. | Dunlop, R. 331321. | M. May 20/17. |
| *9 B. VI | McCuish, John. 333820. | M. May 20/17. |
| ‡9 B. | Mudd, T. 332642. | M. May 20/17. |
| 9 B. VIII | Munn, Andrew. 331979. | M. May 19/17. |
| ‡9 B. | Thomson, J. 332016. | M. May 20/17. |
| *9 C. IX | Charlton, Robt. Malcolm. 333365. | W and M. May 20/17. |
| ‡9 C. | Creaney, J. 331471. | M. May 20/17. |
| ‡9 C. | Ferguson, A. M. 331522. | W. and M. May 20/17. |
| ‡9 C. | Geddes, A.-L.-Cpl. R. T. 331411. | M. May 20/17. |
| 9 C. IX | McMillan, Malcolm. 5038. | W. and M. Nov. 1/16. R/Enq. |
| ‡9 D. | McLean, A.-L.-Cpl. A. 332228. | W. and M. May 20/17. |

**Highland Light Infantry—contd.**

## *B.E.F.*

‡9 D. V Speight, W. E. 333197. M. May 20/17.
‡9 D. Watson, J. H. 332824. M. May 20/17.
10 Scott, Capt. A. M. April 24/17.
10/11 A. Bradshaw, J. 10237. M. April 11/17.
10/11 A. Byers, Wm. 38246. M. April 23/17.
10/11 A. II Carmichael, Wm. 31595. M. April 23/17.
*10/11 A. I Castle, L.-Cpl. H. 41868. W. and M. April 24/17.
10/11 A. Dundas, D. 26484. M. April 11/17.
10/11 A. Harper, S. 41874. M. Mar. 29/17.
10/11 A. Hughes, John. 21173. M. April 24/17.
‡10/11 A. McClure, C. 42418. W. and M. April 23/17.
10/11 A. McDermott, T. 41573. M. Mar. 29/17.
10/11 A. McGhie, J. 42414. M. April 23/17.
10/11 A. IV McKenzie, Wm. 42451. M. April 11/17.
10/11 A. I McLachlan, A. 42416. W. and M. April 24/17.
10/11 A. Malcolm, J. 42433. M. April 23/17.
10/11 A. I Milligan, J. 40065. W. and M. April 11/17.
10/11 A. Reid, Robt. 28010. M. April 23/17.
10/11 B. Beresford, A. 41089. M. April 11/17.
10/11 B. Blain, W. 32919. M. April 11/17.
10/11 B. V Donaldson, Colin. 38158. M. April 23/17.
10/11 B. McAuley, H. 42511. M. April 23/17.
10/11 B. McFarlane, A. 40747. M. April 11/17.
10/11 B. Riggens, W. 17360. M. April 11/17.
10/11 B. Tinto, L.-Cpl. J. 21247. M. April 11/17.
10/11 B. V Weatherstone, W. 42490. W. and M. May 9/17.
10/11 C. Austin, R. 22314. M. April 11/17.
10/11 C. Battersby, F. 181. M. April 24/17.
10/11 C. Conley, A. 38169. M. April 24/17.
*10/11 C. IX Donnelly, Joseph. 1759. M. April 23/17.
‡10/11 C. Fraser, Alick. 40460. Unoff. M. April 11/17.
10/11 C. L.G.S. Gray, Wm. 40137. (1588.) W. and M. April 11/17.
10/11 C. Inglis, Geo. 24885. M. April 11/17.
‡10/11 C. Johnstone, J. 38199. W. and M., bel. K. April 23/17.
10/11 C. Kinniburgh, John. 41873. M. April 11/17.
10/11 C. L.G.S. Latimer, J. 40476. M. April 23/17.
10/11 C. McGuinness, D. 38173. M. April 23/17.
10/11 C. X McIntyre, Daniel. 305. M. April 11/17.
10/11 C. Mayo, J. 41920. M. April 23/17.
10/11 C. XI Sinclair, Dugald. 38062. W. and M. April 23/17.
10/11 C. XII Weston, F. H. 41132. M. April 11/17.
*10/11 D. XV Bayliss, W. F. 41613. W. and M. April 11/17.
10/11 D. Hill, S. or H. 38069. M. April 23/17.
10/11 D. XV Lawrence, Geo. M. 33216. M. April 23/17.
10/11 D. McCallum, James. 18169. M. April 11/17.
10/11 D. XIII O'Hare, John. 928. M. April 24/17.
10/11 D. Skivington, P. 38091. M. April 24/17.
‡10/11 D. Spowart, W. 8648. W. and M. April 11/17.

**Highland Light Infantry—contd.**

## *B.E.F.*

11 C. Donnelly, J. 1679. M. April 23/17.
12 A. Rae, J. 41442. M. April 9-11/17.
12 B. Bateman, Ernest. 17673. (Fr. H.Q.) M. April 9-11/17.
12 B. VII Rawson, L.-Cpl. Robt. 26534. M. Aug. 13/16.
12 B. VI Wilson, George. 4043 M. April 23/17.
12 C. IX Cooper, John. 10298. M. April 9-11/17.
‡12 C. Forrester, J. 17952. W. and M. April 25/17.
12 C. XII Irving, David. 41719. W. and M. April 8-11/17.
12 C. IX Jaques, F. G. 28997. M. April 25/17.
12 C. X Lawson, George E. 42596. W. and M. April 10/17.
12 C. Lawson, J. 7386. M. April 25/17.
12 C. IX Lay, W. 20016. M. April 25/17.
12 C. X McCandlish, John. 11866. M. Sept. 25/16.
‡12 C. McDonald, A. 22385. W. and M. April 11/17.
12 C. McDougall, W. 25770. M. April 9-11/17.
12 C. XII McNaught, Peter. 41807. W. and M. April 11/17.
12 C. XII Murray, F. 23468. W. and M. April 23/17.
12 C. Simpson, H. 40478. M. April 25/17.
12 C. IX Stewart, Wm. 41786. M. April 9-11/17.
12 ? Kirkland, L.-Cpl. Jas. 40339. K. April 23/17. Det.D./B.
15 A. Brown, L.-Cpl. Wm. 982. M. April 3/17.
‡16 A. IV Haldane, Geo. Goodall. 33431. W. and M. Nov. 18/16. R/Enq.
‡16 A. Miller, J. 27305. M. Nov. 18/16.
16 B. Cheyne, Cpl. James H. 14707. W. and M. Nov. 18/16.
16 B. VII Ferguson, Andrew. 1693. W. and M. Nov. 18/16.
16 B. VI Lunney, John. 30275. W. and M. Nov. 18/16.
‡16 B. Scott, Alex. 43081. K. Nov. 18/17. Det.D./B.
•16 B. V Welsh, Geo. B. 43116. M. Nov. 18/16. R/Enq.
‡16 C. Clark, W. 27485. W. and M. April 14/17.
16 C. XI Fairlie, Duncan. 26690. M. Nov. 18/16. R/Enq.
16 C. X Grant, Willie. 33125. M. April 14/17.
•16 C. McDonald, Donald. 14571. M. Nov. 18/16. R/Enq.
‡16 C. Milligan, L.-Cpl. Robt. C. 14760. M. Nov. 18/16. R/Enq.
‡16 C. Muir, William. 20715. M. Nov. 18/16. R/Enq.
16 C. Thomson, L.-Cpl. John. 12658. M. Nov. 18/16. R/Enq.
16 D. Cassidy, William John. 4324. M. Nov. 18/16. R/Enq.
16 D. Fleming, James. 33425. M. Nov. 18/16. R/Enq.
16 D. XVI Gray, Harry. 43182. (Late 1557.) M. Nov. 18/16. R/Enq.
•16 D. Hamilton, Archibald. 43180. M. Nov. 18/16. R/Enq.
16 D. McCartney, Patrick. 5763. M. Nov. 18/16.
16 D. McDermid, L.-Cpl. Dan. 14686. M. Nov. 18/16.
16 D. XIV MacDonald, Duncan. 35671. W. Unoff. M. Feb. 5/17.
16 D. XIV Macfarlane, Cpl. Peter. N. 43173. M. Nov. 18/16. R/Enq.
16 D. Middleton, John. 27361. M. Nov. 18/16. R/Enq.
16 D. XV Robertson, Jas. 43188. M. Nov. 18/16. R/Enq.
16 D. XIII Ross, George. 41029. M. Nov. 18/16. R/Enq.
16 D. XIII Young, George. 43151. M. Nov. 18/16. R/Enq.
16 ? Smith, A. F. 14505. D/W. April 15/17. Det.D./B.
17 A. Andrews, Robt. 41586. K. Feb. 13/17. Det.D./B.
17 B. McBride, T. 34061. M. April 1/17.
17 B. Roy, Alex. 33368. M. Nov. 18/16. R/Enq.
17 D. Bryson, James. 41055. M. Nov. 18/16. R/Enq.
17 D. XV Greive, Walter. 30180. W. and M. April 1/17.
‡18 Y. Bone, J. 35308. M. May 1/17.

**Highland Light Infantry—contd.**

## *E.E.F.*

| | | |
|---|---|---|
| 7 | **Lamb, 2nd Lieut. G. B.** | M. **April 26/17.** |
| 7 ? | Fitzpatrick, G. 280247. | M. **April 19/17.** |
| 7 ? | Logan, J. 280715. | M. **April 19/17.** |
| 7 ? | Rowden, J. 282550. | M. **April 19/17.** |

## *PERSIAN GULF.*

| | | |
|---|---|---|
| 1 A. | **Balfour, Capt. J. A.** | K. **Jan. 11/17.** Det.D./B. R/Enq. |
| 1 A. | Armstrong, L.-Cpl. W. 20420. | W. and M. **Jan. 9-11/17.** |
| 1 A. | Cooper, H. 21060. | M. **Dec. 22/16.** |
| 1 A. | Dodds, J. W. 7821. | M. **Mar. 8/16.** R/Enq. |
| 1 A. | Gray, Thomas. 1097. | W. and M. **Jan. 9-11/17.** |
| 1 A. | Watson, C. 20402. | W. and M. **Jan. 9-11/17.** |
| 1 A. | Young, J. E. 20403. | M. **Dec. 22/16.** |
| 1 B. VI | Campbell, D. 28509. | M. **Jan. 9-11/17.** |
| 1 B. | Gallacher, Patrick. 7310. | M. **Jan. 11/17.** |
| 1 B. VI | Gushlow, A.-L.-Sergt. G. 11819. | M. **April 18/16.** R/Enq. |
| 1 B. VIII | Henry, Alexander G. 26669. | M. **Jan. 9-11/17.** |
| 1 B. VII | Lang, John. 8160. | M. **Jan. 11/17.** |
| 1 B. VII | McDade, Wm. 1251. | M. **Jan. 9-11/17.** |
| 1 B. | McPhail, D. 26956. | W. and M. **Jan. 9-11/17.** |
| 1 B. | Mack, David. 25006. | M. **Jan. 9-11/17.** |
| 1 B. | Mallin, Hugh. 18164. | M. **Jan. 9-11/17.** |
| 1 B. VII | Morrison, William. 30427. | W. and M., bel. K. **Jan. 9-11/17.** |
| 1 C. | Dillon, Jack G. C. 30423. | W. and M. **Jan. 9-11/17.** |
| 1 C. | Thayne, L.-Sergt. Robert. 9849. | W. and M. **Jan. 9-11/17.** |
| 1 D. | Ward, Sergt. Wm. A. 16232. | M. **Jan. 9-11/17.** |
| 1 ? | Cochrane, A. 9120. | M. **Jan. 9-11/17.** |
| 1 ? | Dineen, C. 31422. | M. **Jan. 9-11/17.** |
| 1 ? | Eddington, F. 11121. | W. and M. **Jan. 9-11/17.** |
| 1 ? | Ferguson, A. 11445. | M. **Jan. 9-11/17.** |
| 1 ? | Gilchirst, J. 21332. | M. **Jan. 9-11/17.** |
| 1 ? | Green, H. 5398. | W. and M. **Jan. 9-11/17.** |
| 1 ? | Haughey, Cpl. B. 33296. | M. **Jan. 9-11/17.** |
| 1 ? | Hornsby, A. 20375. | M. **Dec. 22/16.** |
| 1 ? | Polland, H. 19846. | W. and M. **Jan. 9-11/17.** |
| 1 ? | Porteous, C. 25936. | M. **Jan. 11/17.** |
| 1 ? | Prete, F. 35429. | W. and M. **Jan. 9-11/17.** |
| 1 ? | Roberts, J. 8847. | W. and M. **Jan. 9-11/17.** |
| 1 ? | Shaw, L.-Cpl. A. 23125. | W. and M., bel. K. **Jan. 9-11/17.** |
| 1 ? | Shaw, A. 20041. | M. **Jan. 9-11/17.** |
| 1 ? | Spiller, L. W. 20394. | M. **Nov. 23/16.** |
| 1 ? | Taylor, T. 8504. | W. and M., bel. K. **Jan. 9-11/17.** |
| 1 ? | Whitten, Sergt. J. 8605. | W. and M., bel. K. **Jan. 9-11/17.** |
| 1 ? | Whitworth, Sergt. W. 11969. | W. and M. **Jan. 9-11/17.** |

**HOUSEHOLD BATTALION.**

## *B.E.F.*

| | | |
|---|---|---|
| | **Bridgeman, Lieut. H. H. O.** | M. **May 11/17.** |
| | **Tyrwhitt-Drake, 2nd Lt. D'V. Y.** | M. **May 3/17.** |
| | **Williams, 2nd Lieut. S. D.** | M. **May 3/17.** |
| 1 I | Barnes, Geo. Ernest. 2151. | M. **May 11/17.** |

**Household Battalion**—contd.

## *B.E.F.*

| | | | |
|---|---|---|---|
| ‡ | 1 I | Butchers, Geo. Fredk. 1761. | M. **May 3/17.** |
| | 1 I | Carier, H. 1737. | M. **May 11/17.** |
| | 1 | Colchester, C. F. 394. (Life Gds. Co.) | W. Unoff. M. **Mar. 14/17.** |
| | 1 | Cooper, Albert Rich. 151. | M. **May 3/17.** |
| • | 1 III | Eyden, Jas. White. [illegible]5. | M. **May 3/17.** |
| ‡ | 1 I | Flowers, E. W. 1117. | M. **May 3/17.** |
| | 1 IV | Griffiths, Cpl. Albert W. 744. | M. **May 3/17.** |
| | 1 III | Holman, W. 39. | M. **May 11/17.** |
| • | 1 II | McMurdo, Thos. 184[illegible] | M. **May 3/17.** |
| | 1 IV | Musselle, Fred. 1448. | M. **May 11-12/17.** |
| ‡ | 1 IV | Nicholls, Cpl. Thos. Wm. 1963. | M. **May 3/17.** |
| ‡ | 1 I | Taylor, J. W. 60. | W. and M. **May 3/17.** |
| | 1 I | Wale, Alec. 67. | W. and M. **May 3/17.** |
| | 1 I | Weller, Cpl. Alfred Jas. 66. | W. and M. **May 3/17.** |
| | 1 IV | Whitehead, E. G. 2123. | M. **May 3/17.** |
| | 1 IV | Wood, Alfred. 113. | M. **May 3/17.** |
| | 2 V | Barrington, Thos. Edw. 2088. | M. **May 3/17.** |
| • | 2 V | Bertram, Geo. 1870. | M. **May 3/17.** |
| ‡ | 2 V | Ford, G. William. 415. | M. **May 3/17.** |
| | 2 VIII | Hawthorn, John. 1850. | M. **May 11/17.** |
| • | 2 VIII | Jones, James. 1922. | M. **May 3/17.** |
| | 2 | McSharry, Francis. 1836. | M. **May 11/17.** |
| • | 2 V | Mellor, Frank. 2156. | M. **May 3/17.** |
| ‡ | 2 VII | Pollitt, Cpl. Stanley. 1569. (Fr. 2nd Life Guards.) | K. **May 3/17.** Det.D./B. |
| | 2 VI | Pryke, G. S. 1967. | M. **May 3/17.** |
| | 3 XII | Belchamber, Wm. 1458. | M. **May 3/17.** |
| | 3 IX | Bewley, Wilson. 2060. | M. **May 3/17.** |
| | 3 IX | Carter, Frank. 2045. | M. **May 3/17.** |
| | 3 XII | Clinker, Jas. 1471. | M. **May 3/17.** |
| | 3 | Corcoran, Joe. 1060. | M. **May 3/17.** |
| | 3 IX | Culmer, George E. 730. | M. **May 3-4/17.** |
| ‡ | 3 | Davies, L.-Cpl. Joseph. 2099. | M. **May 3/17.** |
| • | 3 X | Gott, Chas. Henry. 773. | M. **May 3/17.** |
| ‡ | 3 IX | Groves, Tpr. Harry. 1896. | M. **May 3/17.** |
| | 3 X | Hackett, J. 782. | M. **May 3/17.** |
| | 3 X | Herriett, Chas. 2093. | M. **May 3/17.** |
| | 3 X | Holmes, Albert Edward. 779. | M. **May 3/17.** |
| | 3 IX | Jennings, A. G. 747. | M. **May 3/17.** |
| | 3 XI | Mann, Joseph. 822. | M. **May 3/17.** |
| • | 3 X | Mason, Tom. 1682. | M. **May 3/17.** |
| | 3 IX | Meekings, Herbert John. 825. | M. **May 3/17.** |
| | 3 X | Mitchell, Chas. D. 1936. | M. **May 3/17.** |
| | 3 XI | Morris, Cpl. Leonard. 824. | M. **May 3/17.** |
| | 3 IX | Mullane, L.-Cpl. John Francis. 1249. | K. **May 20/17.** Det.D./B. |
| | 3 XII | Newell, Albert Edward. 1814. | M. **May 3/17.** |
| | 3 XV | Patterson, A. D. 1718. | K. **April 11/17.** Det.D./B. |
| | 3 XII | Rawson, R. F. 1430. | M. **May 2/17.** |
| | 3 IX | Seep, F. H. 846. | W. and M. **April 11/17.** |
| | 3 | Sellers, Cpl. of Horse, Edw. 1051. | M. **May 3/17.** |
| | 3 X | Sharples, J. C. 1614. (Fr. 2nd Life Guards.) | M. **May 3/17.** |
| | 3 IX | Starkey, Thos. George. 753. | M. **May 3-4/17.** |
| • | 3 IX | Strong, Walter N. 1584. | M. **May 3/17.** |
| | 3 X | Sykes, Tom Eric. 2044. | M. **May 3/17.** |

**Household Battalion**—contd.

## *B.E.F.*

| | | | |
|---|---|---|---|
| | 3 X | Watson, E. 805. | M. May 3/17. |
| | 3 XII | Webb, Claude Geo. 899. | M. May 3/17. |
| | 4 XIV | Hing, Harry Ellis. 1123. (Fr. 2nd Life Guards, 3813.) | D/W. April 11/17. Det.D./B. |
| • | 4 XIII | Horne, J. B. 1072. | M. May 11/17. |
| | 4 XVI | Miller, T. L. F. 2136. | M. May 11/17. |
| • | H.Q. | Tooth, Bert. 531. | W. Unoff. M. May 3/17. |
| | ? | Ball, F. A. 1660. (Fr. R.H.G.) | W. Unoff. M. April 11/17. |
| ‡ | ? | Bennett, E. 1036. | W. and M. May 3/17. |
| ‡ | ? | Butterfield, A. J. 1409. | M. May 3/17. |
| ‡ | ? | Cooper, S. A. 2077. | M. May 3/17. |
| ‡ | ? | Dewey, F. 1462. | M. May 3/17. |
| ‡ | ? | Dyer, V. 767. | M. May 3/17. |
| ‡ | ? | Firth, T. H. 1688. | M. May 3/17. |
| ‡ | ? | Hoade, L.-Cpl. J. T. 746. | M. May 5/17. |
| ‡ | ? | Hodgetts, W. 444. | M. May 5/17. |
| ‡ | ? | Hodgkiss, T. 88. | M. May 5/17. |
| ‡ | ? | Holloway, O. W. 1777. | M. May 5/17. |
| ‡ | ? | Ibbottson, G. H. 2047. | M. May 5/17. |
| ‡ | ? | Jenkins, J. S. 1491. | M. May 5/17. |
| ‡ | ? | McInnes, A. 1932. | W. and M. May 3/17. |
| ‡ | ? | Marshall, W. 1852. | M. May 3/17. |
| ‡ | ? | Mennell, W. E. 473. | M. May 3/17. |
| ‡ | ? | Moore, S. C. 2022. | M. May 11/17. |
| ‡ | ? | O'Neill, P. 1860. | M. May 3/17. |
| ‡ | ? | Parris, W. L. 1808. | W. and M. May 3/17. |
| ‡ | ? | Read, E. J. 841. | M. May 3/17. |
| ‡ | ? | Shipton, J. R. 829. | M. May 3/17. |
| ‡ | ? | Simmonds, H. C. 1785. | M. May 3/17. |
| ‡ | ? | Tucker, E. C. 2173. | M. May 3/17. |
| ‡ | ? | Vines, W. 2033. | M. May 3/17. |
| ‡ | ? | West, Cpl. F. J. 712. | M. May 3/17. |
| ‡ | ? | Whiteman, E. M. 1780. | M. May 3/17. |
| ‡ | ? | Williams, W. J. 2052. | M. May 3/17. |

## HUSSARS.

### *B.E.F.*

| | | | |
|---|---|---|---|
| ‡3 | ? | Feleter, J. 23100. | M. May 20/17. |
| ‡3 | ? | Swift, L.-Cpl. W. 10748. | M. May 20/17. |
| *4 | B. III | Hall, Gilbert Sidney. 40161. | M. May 23/17. |
| 10 | A. | Simpkin, M.C., Sgt. J. W. R. 591. | D/W. April 12/17. Det.D./B. R/Enq. |
| 10 | ? | Ransome, J. 28901. | W. and M. April 11/17. |
| 15 | B. | Handscombe, Fred Wyatt. 5924. | M. April 8/17. |

### *E.E.F.*

| | | | |
|---|---|---|---|
| 13 | ? | Redman, R. G. 41502. | M., bel. drowned April 15/17. "Cameronia." |

**Hussars—contd.**

## *PERSIAN GULF.*

| | | |
|---|---|---|
| 13 | **Clarkson, 2nd Lieut. J. O. P.** | K. **Mar. 10/17.** Det.D./B. |
| 13 D. | Wren, Trumptr. Frank. 7003. | W. and M. **March 5/17.** |
| ‡13 ? | Mason, Reuben. 6791. | K. **Mar. 5/17.** Det.D./B. |
| 13 ? | Spicer, J. 6010. | W. and M. **Mar. 5/17.** |

# INDIAN ARMY.

## *B.E.F.*

### DECCAN HORSE.

| | | |
|---|---|---|
| 20 ? | **Lawford, Lieut. E. E.** | M. **June 13/17.** |

## *PERSIAN GULF.*

### BURMA INFANTRY.

| | | |
|---|---|---|
| 93 ? | **Pearson, Lt. Jas. B.** (Fr. I. A. Res.) | M. **Mar. 25/17.** |

### GURKHA RIFLES.

| | | |
|---|---|---|
| 8 | **Nelson, 2nd Lt. Ernest B.** (Fr. Q. Victoria's Own Corps of Guides.) | D/W. **Mar. 15/17.** Det.D./B. |

### MAHRATTAS.

| | | |
|---|---|---|
| 105 | **Chitty, Col. E. R. J.** | W. and M. **Mar. 25/17.** |

### PUNJABIS.

| | | |
|---|---|---|
| 27 | **Le Mesurier, 2nd Lt. Arthur Edwd.** | M. **Mar. 9/17.** |

### SIKHS.

| | | |
|---|---|---|
| 36 | **Cunningham, Lt. Chas. Stewart.** | K. **Feb. 1/17.** Det.D./B. |
| 36 | **Mitchell, 2nd Lieut. J. H.** | M., bel K. **Feb. 1/17.** |
| 47 | **Southern, 2nd Lt. Hugh.** (Fr. 35th.) | M. **April 17-18/16.** R/Enq. |

# ROYAL INNISKILLING FUSILIERS.

## *B.E.F.*

| | | |
|---|---|---|
| 1 | **Hall, Lieut. M. W. F.** | M. **May 19/17.** |
| 1 | **Hermges, 2nd Lieut. A. C. G.** | M. **May 19/17.** |
| 1 | **Osman, Capt. E. E.** | K. **May 19-20/17.** Det.D./B. |
| 1 A. III | Fettes, Cpl. Geo. 9854. | M. **Jan. 28/17.** |
| 1 A. or C. | Goldman, H. A. 40519. (Fr. 12th Londons, 5674.) | M. **Jan. 28/17.** |
| *1 A. | Houston, Alex. 9494. | K. **Jan. 27/17.** Det.D./B. R/Enq. |
| 1 A. III | Jamieson, Robert. 4723. (Fr. 3rd.) | M. **Jan. 27/17.** |
| 1 A. | McGonigle, C.-S.-M. David. 9535. | W. and M. **Jan. 27/17.** |

**Inniskilling Fusiliers, Royal—contd.**

## *B.E.F.*

| | | | |
|---|---|---|---|
| 1 A. | | McLoughlin, W. 3598. | M. Oct. 11/16. |
| 1 B. | VI | Goldman, Sam. 12899. (Fr. 6th.) | M. Jan. 27/17. |
| 1 B. | | McCormick, Thomas. 17796. | W. and M. Jan. 27/17. |
| ‡1 B. | | Taylor, J. 4548. | M. May 19/17. |
| ‡1 C. | | Bekett, C. A. 41107. | M. May 19/17. |
| *1 C. | X | Bevan, John. 29871. | M. May 19/17. |
| *1 C. | X | Brown, Cpl. Jas. 43339. | M. May 19/17. |
| *1 C. | IX | Browne, C. 29930. | M. May 19/17. |
| ‡1 C. | XII | Buckle, A. 43377. (Erroneously known as 40053.) (6 Lond., 5835) | M. May 19/17. |
| 1 C. | IX | Burgess, G. 323077. (Fr. 6 Londons, 6085.) | W. and M. Jan. 28/17. |
| ‡1 C. | | Bush, J. 7/26539. | M. May 19/17. |
| ‡1 C. | | Clare, W. 41103. | M. May 19/17. |
| *1 C. | XII | Connor, David. 25277. (Fr. 2nd.) | M. May 19/17. |
| *1 C. | XI | Cranston, George. 14264. | M. May 23/17. |
| ‡1 C. | | Delaney, A. 29849. | M. May 19/17. |
| ‡1 C. | X | Eckett, Charles. 41107. | M. May 19/17. |
| *1 C. | | Foster, L.-Cpl. Andrew. 3302. | M. May 19/17. |
| ‡1 C. | | Gilligan, T. 28439. | M. May 19/17. |
| *1 C. | XI | Hall, E. H. 43448. | M. May 19/17. |
| 1 C. | XII | Harradine, Herbert. 43386. | M. May 19/17. |
| 1 C. | | Harvey, Cecil H. 43385. (Fr. 6th London, 1916.) | Unoff. M. abt. May 14/17. |
| 1 C. | IX or XI | Hay, J. 3/12902. | M. Jan. 28/17. |
| *1 C. | X | Hook, A. F. 2/41068. | M. May 19/17. |
| *1 C. | | Kerr, Cpl. Geo. 27143. (Fr. 4th.) | M. May 19/17. |
| ‡1 C. | | Leckey, W. J. 29904. | M. May 19/17. |
| *1 C. | XII | McCarthy, Daniel. 3166. (Fr. 4th.) | M. May 19/17. |
| ‡1 C. | | McCrory, Sergt. Frank. 1635. | M. May 19/17. |
| ‡1 C. | | McDaid, R. 29702. | M. May 19/17. |
| ‡1 C. | | McLaughlin, A. 29794. (Fr. 4th.) | M. May 19/17. |
| ‡1 C. | | McManus, J. 19030. | M. May 19/17. |
| ‡1 C. | | McMeekin, W. 29232. (Fr. 4th.) | M. May 19/17. |
| ‡1 C. | | McSherry, W. 4245. | M. May 19/17. |
| ‡1 C. | | Mullan, Joseph. 4183. | M. May 19/17. |
| ‡1 C. | | Mullen, J. 29447. | M. May 19/17. |
| ‡1 C. | | Patton, L.-Cpl. S. 8854. | M. May 19/17. |
| ‡1 C. | | Reilly, E. 10964. | M. May 19/17. |
| *1 C. | XI | Russell, H. 10188. | M. May 19/17. |
| 1 C. | XI | Russell, Harry Nash. 471468. (Fr. 12th London, 4199.) | W. and M. Jan. 28/17. |
| ‡1 C. | | Rutherford, G. 11598. | M. May 19/17. |
| *1 C. | XI | Scott, A. J. 43403. | M. May 19/17. |
| ‡1 C. | XII | Sheehan, Edward. 25859. | M. May 19/17. |
| *1 C. | XI | Slow, E. 43418. | M. May 19/17. |
| *1 C. | X | Sly, W. 41073. | M. May 19/17. |
| ‡1 C. | | Tohill, F. 3246. (Fr. 4th.) | M. May 19/17. |
| *1 C. | | Tubb, Sergt. Jas. Leicester. 43461. | M. May 19/17. |
| ‡1 C. | X | Wells, A. C. 41110. | M. May 19/17. |
| ‡1 D. | | Allen, C. R. 43432. | W. and M. May 19/17. |
| ‡1 D. | | Bond, A.-C.-S.-M. F. P. 8781. | W. and M. May 19/17. |
| 1 D. | XIV | Dixon, Arthur. 27780. | M. Jan. 28/17. |
| ‡1 D. | | Farrell, J. 29927. | W. and M. May 19/17. |
| 1 D. | | Felton, Joseph. 24754. | W. and M. Jan. 27/17. |

**Inniskilling Fusiliers, Royal—contd.**

*B.E.F.*

‡1 D. Graham, J. 4/29917. M. May 19/17.
‡1 D. Hardman, R. 5/16628. M May 19/17.
‡1 D. XV Keates, Frederick Wm. 41099. M. May 19/17.
*1 D. XIII Lamb, F. A. 43452. M. May 19/17.
*1 D. XIV Lott, Arthur. 41046. M. May 19/17.
‡1 D. McAtear, J. 24155. W. and M. May 19/17.
*1 D. Marshall, James. 29916. W. and M. May 19/17.
‡1 D. XIII Owers, Joseph. 43457. M. May 19/17.
‡1 D. Philpott, W. H. 43458. (40127.) M. May 19/17.
*1 D. XV Wilkinson, John. 26841. M. May 19/17.
‡1 D. Yates, C. 43413. M. May 19/17.
1 ? Noad, L.-Cpl. Chas. S. 43395. (Fr. 6th London, 6021.) Unoff. M. abt. May 14/17.
1 ? Porter, J. A. 29952. K. April 24/17. Det.D./B.
‡1 ? Swain, H. B. 322950. (Fr. 6 Lond.) M. May 19/17.
2 A. Preston, L.-Cpl. John. 7084. M. Nov. 23/16. R/Enq.
2 B. VII Baxter, P. 40724. D/W. April 2/17. Det.D./B.
2 B. VII Charles, Arthur L. 40727. M. April 1/17.
2 C. Sanderson, C. A. 374458. (Fr. 8th Londons.) M. April 1/17.
2 ? Chesham, Archibald Frank. 371691. (Formerly 3972, 8 Londons.) K. April 1/17. Det.D./B.
7 A. Henderson, P. 23078. W. and M. Sept. 9/16. R/Enq.
7 D. XIII Bell, Thomas. 43299. M. Sept. 9/16. R/Enq.
*7 D. Blakley, Cpl. Bertie. 9437. W. and M. Sept. 9/16. R/Enq.
7 D. M.G.S. Crowley, Wm. 28701. W. and M. Sept. 9/16. R./Enq.
7 D. Smith, M. 43281. W. and M. Sept. 7/16. R/Enq.
‡8 A. Dillon, Thomas. 26153. W. and M. Sept. 9/16. R/Enq.
‡8 D. Cody, John Maurice. 129482. M. Sept. 9/16. R/Enq.
*8 D. McCauley, Bernard. 20543. W. and M. Sept. 9/16. R/Enq.
8 D. Murphy, P. J. 20675. M. Sept. 9/16. R/Enq.
‡8 D. Ponfield, A. G. 28245. M. Sept. 9/16. R/Enq.
8 ? I.T.M. Asple, Michael. 40321. (49 Bgde.) M. Mar. 7/17.
*11 C. McKay, L.-Cpl. Alex. 17390. M. Sept. 15/16. R/Enq.

*BALKANS.*

*5 ? Smith, Michael. 43281. W. and M. Sept. 7/16

**ROYAL IRISH FUSILIERS.**

*B.E.F.*

1 **Armstrong, Lieut. G. C. S. (Fr. 3rd.)** K. May 3/17. Conf. and Det.D./B.
1 **Cullen, Lieut. G. S. Y.** K. April 11/17. Det.D./B.
‡1 **Fitt, 2nd Lieut. N. E. L.** M. June 24/17.
‡1 **Kisly, 2nd Lieut. F. P.** M. June 21/17.

**Irish Fusiliers, Royal—contd.**

## *B.E.F.*

| | | | |
|---|---|---|---|
| 1 | | **McGibney, 2nd Lieut. F. G.** | K. May 3/17. Det.D./B. |
| 1 | | **Sheridan, 2nd Lieut. H. H.** | W. and M. May 3/17. |
| *1 | A. | Byrne, Ben. 13860. | M. Dec. 10/16. R/Enq. |
| 1 | A. I | Byrne, Simon. 21740. | M. May 3/17. |
| 1 | A. | Cassidy, T. 2821. | M. April 11/17. |
| 1 | A. I | Devlin, Patrick J. 21054. | M. Oct. 29/16. |
| 1 | A. or B. | Donaghy, Edward. 23452. | M. April 11/17. |
| 1 | A. III | Donaghy, Patrick J. 3846. | W. and M. April 15/17. |
| 1 | A. | Doyle, D. 3843. | M. April 11/17. |
| 1 | A. | Ennis, Sergt. Michael. 15951. | M. Oct. 12/16. R/Enq. |
| *1 | A. III | Holmes, L.-Cpl. William. 5812. | M. May 3/17. |
| 1 | A. II | Johnson, George. 14903. | M. May 3/17. |
| 1 | A. | McIntyre, M. 18110. | M. Oct. 12/16. R./Enq. |
| ‡1 | A. | McLean, G. H. 17822. | M. May 3/17. |
| ‡1 | A. | McMahon, Fetherston. 3528. | M. May 3/17. |
| 1 | A. | O'Hagan, James. 12972. | M. April 11/17. |
| 1 | A. | O'Keefe, Patrick. 10987. | M. Oct. 12/16. R/Enq. |
| ‡1 | A. | Quinn, Jas. Andrew. 11441. | M. May 3/17. |
| 1 | A. | Reilly, Peter. 7046. | M. Oct. 12/16. R/Enq. |
| 1 | A. L.G.S. | Skelton, Frank. 23566. | W. and M. May 3/17. |
| *1 | A. I | Taylor, Cpl. Percy. 18891. | M. May 3/17. |
| *1 | A. or B. | Tierney, James. 9075. | M. May 3/17. |
| ‡1 | A. | Walsh, P. 3669. | W. and M. May 3/17. |
| 1 | B. | Anderson, Joseph. 23514. | M. April 11/17. |
| 1 | B. | Brompton, J. 16481. | M. April 11/17. |
| 1 | B. M.G.S. | Gallagher, Thos. J. 20937. | W. and M. May 3/17. |
| 1 | B. | Gibney, B. 24640. | W. and M. April 9/17. |
| *1 | B. III | Holmes, L.-Cpl. A. 11097. | M. May 3/17. |
| ‡1 | B. | Kavanagh, C. 21768. | M. May 10/17. |
| 1 | B. VII | Lennon, James. 5979. | W. and M. May 3/17. |
| 1 | B. | O'Hara, Michael. 24624. | W. and M. April 9/17. |
| ‡1 | B. | O'Keefe, A. 19992. | W. and M. May 3/17. |
| 1 | B. or D. | Seymour, Robt. 24648. | M. April 11/17. |
| *1 | B. VI | Wallace, L.-Cpl. P. 10513. | M. May 3/17. |
| ‡1 | C. | Aiken, J. 24176. | M. May 3/17. |
| ‡1 | C. | Bradley, T. 2887. | M. May 3/17. |
| 1 | C. | Brady, T. 25042. | M. April 11/17. |
| 1 | C. | Brien, L.-Cpl. W. 24876. | M. April 11/17. |
| 1 | C. X | Connolly, George Hny. 40091. | M. April 11/17. |
| 1 | C. | Croly, W. 11334. | W. and M. April 11/17. |
| ‡1 | C. | Gray, J. 24299. | M. May 3/17. |
| 1 | C. | Hagger, Cpl. W. 9475. | M. April 11/17. |
| 1 | C. | Howes, A. 18991. | M. April 11/17. |
| 1 | C. | Johnstone, P. 25208. | W. and M. April 11/17. |
| 1 | C. | Larkin, P. 2505. | M. April 11/17. |
| *‡1 | C. | Lavery, F. 20571. | M. May 3/17. |
| 1 | C. | Lawler, W. 43109. | M. April 11/17. |
| ‡1 | C. | McKenna, L. 23424. | M. April 11/17. |
| 1 | C. | Maguire, J. 23900. | M. April 11/17. |
| 1 | C. | Maguire, J. 10967. | M. April 11/17. |
| 1 | C. IX | O'Brien, L.-Cpl. W. 24876. | M. April 11/17. |
| 1 | C. | Stewart, Wm. 24200. | M. May 3/17. |
| *1 | D. XVI | Banyard, L.-Cpl. Arthur C. 22222. | W. and M. May 3/17. |
| 1 | D. XVI | Follis, Samuel. 4749. | M. April 11/17. |
| 1 | D. | Foy, P. 17863. | M. April 11/17. |
| 1 | D. | Juett, Cpl. Geo. Henry. 22719. | W. and M. May 3/17. |
| *1 | D. XIV | Kenlock, S. 15677. | W. and M. April 11/17. |
| 1 | D. | McCaffrey, J. 24162. | W. and M. April 11/17. |

**Irish Fusiliers, Royal**—contd.

## *B.E.F.*

| | | |
|---|---|---|
| 1 D. | McDonnell, J. 3937. | M. April 11/17. |
| 1 D. XIV | McGanhey, Patrick Jas. 16331. | W. and M. April 11/17. |
| 1 D. XIV | McGill, James. 20230. | M. April 11/17. |
| 1 D. | McLintock, R. 3622. | M. April 11/17. |
| 1 D. | Moore, J. 24400. | M. April 11/17. |
| 1 D. | Porter, W. 19849. | W. and M. April 11/17. |
| 1 D. XV | Price, L.-Cpl. Wm. 18962. | W. and M. April 11/17. |
| *1 D. XV | Redmond, Edward. 9147. | K. April 11/17. Det.D./B. R/Enq. |
| 1 D. XVI | Robinson, David. 40140. (Fr. 8th Hussars.) | K. April 11/17. Det.D./B. |
| 1 D. XIII | Stanbridge, Henry. 9264. | W. and M. April 11/17. |
| *7 | **Wray, Lieut. P. H.** | K. June 7/17. Det.D./B. |
| 7 A. | McKinley, R. 3527. | M. Sept. 9/16. |
| 7 B. | Graham, Robert. 12752. | M Sept. 5/16. R/Enq. |
| *7 B. IV | Hamilton, L.-Cpl. James. 23814. | W. and M. Sept. 9/16. R/Enq. |
| 7 B. V | Moore, Samuel. 21646. | M. Sept. 5/16. R/Enq. |
| 8 | **McMillan, 2nd Lt. E. J.** (Fr. 4th.) | M. Jan. 12/17. |
| 8 A. | Hanley, P. 3676. | M. Sept. 6/16. R/Enq. |
| ‡11 A. I | Gaynor, Michael. 3361. | M. Oct. 12/16. R/Enq. |

## *BALKANS.*

| | | |
|---|---|---|
| 5 C. XI | McKay, John. 12751. | M. before April 8/17. |
| 5 ? | Tennent, J. 16980. | M. before April 8/17. |

# ROYAL IRISH REGIMENT.

## *B.E.F.*

| | | |
|---|---|---|
| 2 B. VII | Cash, John. 5080. | W. and M. July 14/16. R/Enq. |
| 2 B. | Coonan, E. 6405. | M. July 14/16. R/Enq. |
| ‡2 B. | Powell, Benjamin. 11615. | W. and M. Sept. 3/16. R/Enq. |
| *2 C. | Cotter, Cpl. Patrick. 10545. | M. Sept. 3/16. R/Enq. |
| ‡2 C. X | O'Brien, John. 8087. | M. Sept. 3/16. |
| ‡2 ? | McCarthy, P. 10336. | M. June 7/17. |
| ‡2 ? | Murphy, Patrick. 11538. | M. June 7/17. |
| 6 | **Henna, 2nd Lieut. J. R.** | K. Sept. 9/16. Det.D./B. |
| ‡6 A. | Doherty, George. 2312. | W. and M. Sept. 9/16. R/Enq. |
| 6 A. | Early, J. 5419. | M. April 5/17. |
| 6 A. | O'Rourke, James. 7788. | M. April 5/17. |
| 6 B. | Quinn, T. 3608. | M. April 5/17. |
| 6 C. IX | Fanning, John. 9754. | M. Sept. 9/16 |
| 6 D. Pioneer S. | Murray, Joseph. 9715. | W. and M. Sept. 3/16. |
| 6 D. | Ryan, Patrick. 9872. | W. and M. Sept. 9/16. R/Enq. |

## *BALKANS.*

| | | |
|---|---|---|
| 1 C. M.G.S. | Billingsley, Sydney E. 8189. | W. and M. Mar. 6/17. |

## ROYAL IRISH RIFLES.

### B.E.F.

| | | |
|---|---|---|
| 1 A. II | Browne, Richard. 1401. | W. and M. Oct. 23-26/16. R/Enq. |
| 1 A. II | Knott, John. 43150. | M. May 3/17. |
| 1 A. | Read, J. 8735. | M. April 16/17. |
| 1 D. | Gracie, Sergt. John. 6573. | K. Oct. 26/16. Det.D./B. |
| 1 D. | Hughes, Gerald. 43856. (Fr. 22 Lond.) | M. Nov. 15/16. |
| 1 D. XIII | McComb, Thos. 8850. | K. Oct. 26/16. Det.D./B. |
| *1 D. | Sweeny, Robert. 9592. | M. Mar. 5-10/17. |
| 2 C. | Craig, S. 5373. | M. April 16/17. |
| 2 C. | Rooney, E. 7566. | M. April 16/17. |
| ‡2 D. | McDowell, W. 8799. | W. and M. May 17/17. |
| 7 | **Scollard, M.C., Capt. D.** | K. April 20/17. Det.D./B. |
| 7 A. | McPhillips, Joseph. 3930. | M. Sept. 9/16. |
| 7 A. | Murphy, C.-S.-M. Wm. Joseph. 748. | M. Sept. 9/16. R/Enq. |
| ‡7 B. VII | Jew, Harold. 3840. | M. June 8/17. |
| 7 B. | McClimond, J. 5421. | M. Sept. 9/16. |
| 7 C. | Daly, D. 8421. | M. Mar. 8/17. |
| 7 D. | Cain, A. 41909. (Fr. Northants, 202512.) | M. April 21/17. |
| 7 D. | Willmett, G. A. 4222. | M. April 20/17. |
| ‡8 B. | Martin, Walter. 42104. | M. June 7/17. |
| ‡14 A. I | Knight, L. J. 2192. | M. June 9/17. |

### BALKANS.

| | | |
|---|---|---|
| 6 A. | McCann, John. 2305. | M. April 24/17. |
| 6 A. | Martin, J. 11191. | W. and M. April 28/17. |
| 6 ? | Bell, P. 7384. | W. and M. (rep. Feb. 8/17.) |

## EAST KENT REGIMENT.

### B.E.F.

| | | |
|---|---|---|
| 1 | **Bullock, 2nd Lieut. T. E. G.** | W. and M. April 22/17. |
| 1 | **Davis, 2nd Lieut. P. W. T.** | M. March 30/17. |
| ‡1 | **Harrington, 2nd Lieut. T. F.** | W. and M. June 24/17. |
| *1 B. | Armstrong, B. 12863. | M. Mar. 30/17. |
| *1 B. | Bradford, L.-Cpl. Charlie. 1060. | M. Sept. 15/16. R/Enq. |
| 1 B. | Brown, C. J. 9393. | M. Sept. 6/16. |
| 1 B. | Calver, Bertram John. 6048. | W. and M. Sept. 25/16. R/Enq. |
| 1 B. V | Crampton, Wm. Booth. 15505. (Fr. R.W. Kent.) | M. Sept. 15/16. |
| 1 B. | Cullen, A. 8407. | M. Mar. 30/17. |
| 1 B. | Garner, H. 10416. | M. Sept. 15/16. R/Enq. |
| 1 B. VI | Tilley, George. G/12777. | M. Mar. 30/17. |
| 1 C. XII | Harding, A. E. 8818. | M. Sept. 9/16. R/Enq. |
| 1 C. | Hughes, J. J. G/12833. | W. and M. April 15/17. |
| 1 C. | Smith, John. 15741. (1767.) | M. Mar. 30/17. |
| 1 C. X | Tomkin, P. 15791. | M. Mar. 30/17. |
| 1 D. | Carter, J. 12901. | M. Mar. 30/17. |
| 6 | **Dinsmore, 2nd Lt. J. H.** (Fr. Div. Staff.) | M. May 3/17. |
| 6 | **Forster, 2nd Lieut. R. L. F.** | M. May 3/17. |
| 6 | **King, 2nd Lieut. E. A.** (Fr. 4th.) | M. May 3/17. |

**Kent Regiment, East—contd.**

## *B.E.F.*

| | | |
|---|---|---|
| 6 | **Kirkpatrick, 2nd Lieut. A.** | M. **May 3/17.** |
| 6 | **Warnington, 2nd Lieut. C.** | M. **May 3/17.** |
| ‡6 A. | Allen, L.-Cpl. S. 13700. | M. **May 3/17.** |
| 6 A. | Andrews, Lawrence B. 19016. | M. **May 3/17.** |
| 6 A. II | Bailey, W. T. 11431. | K. **April 9/17.** Det.D./B. |
| ‡6 A. | Banks, A. A. 9816. | M. **May 3/17.** |
| ‡6 A. | Barden, L. C. 107. | M. **May 3/17.** |
| 6 A. II | Bennett, Fred. Chas. 18838. | M. **May 3/17.** |
| 6 A. L.G.S. | Berry, Albert Ernest. 13633. | M. **May 3/17.** |
| ‡6 A. | Bradshaw, A. 17668. | M. **May 3/17.** |
| *6 A. III | Brown, J. 13670. (Fr. 9 Entrench. Batt.) | M. **May 3/17.** |
| ‡6 A. I | Brown, Percy Edward. G/13076. | M. **May 3/17.** |
| 6 A. L.G.S. | Cavalier, E. S. 8062. | M. **May 3/17.** |
| *6 A. L.G.S. | Cottingham, John Albert. 8491. | M. **May 3/17.** |
| 6 A. II | Dagg, L.-Cpl. C. C. 18748. | M. **May 3/17.** |
| ‡6 A. | Dellar, H. 13586. | M. **May 3/17.** |
| 6 A. II | Hayes, Patrick. 18853. | M. **May 3/17.** |
| ‡6 A. | Hazelden, F. 18941. | W. and M. **May 2/17.** |
| ‡6 A. | Howard, T. 18851. | M. **May 3/17.** |
| ‡6 A. | Hunt, A. 15758. | M. **May 3/17.** |
| ‡6 A. | Jeffery, L.-Cpl. R. 13095. | M. **May 3/17.** |
| ‡6 A. | Jenner, J. 13651. | M. **May 3/17.** |
| ‡6 A. | Jupp, J. H. 18205. | M. **May 3/17.** |
| 6 A. I | Keen, Albert J. 13722. | W. and M. **May 2/17.** |
| ‡6 A. | Kendrick, A.-Cpl. H. 1317. | M. **May 3/17.** |
| 6 A. III | Knight, Chas. John Thos. 13592. | M. **May 3/17.** |
| ‡6 A. | Ladd, J. R. 13688. | M. **May 3/17.** |
| ‡6 A. I | Lashmar, Cpl. H. G. 13580. | M. **May 3/17.** |
| 6 A. | Lewis, E. C. 9900. | M. **May 3/17.** |
| ‡6 A. | Marah, W. A. 8311. | M. **May 3/17.** |
| 6 A. | Moore, Cpl. Percy. 13669. | M. **May 3/17.** |
| ‡6 A. | Moore, Cpl. W. 115. | M. **May 3/17.** |
| ‡6 A. | Orgrave, L.-Cpl. F. S. 6802. | W. and M. **May 3/17.** |
| ‡6 A. | Osborne, W. T. 13648. | M. **May 3/17.** |
| ‡6 A. | Pain, Sergt. A. T. 13579. | M. **May 3/17.** |
| 6 A. IV | Passant, L.-Cpl. T. A. 20852. | Unoff. M. **May 3/17.** |
| 6 A. or C. IX | Reader, W. 13660. | M. **May 3/17.** |
| ‡6 A. | Rich, A. 13637. | M. **May 3/17.** |
| ‡6 A. | Simpson, H. 13174. | M. **May 3/17.** |
| 6 A. I | Stansell, Robt. 19040. | M. **May 3/17.** |
| ‡6 A. | Styles, W. R. 18611. | M. **May 3/17.** |
| ‡6 A. | Thomas, L.-Cpl. E. S. 10226. | M. **May 3/17.** |
| *6 A. IV | Thorpe, Thos. Vaughan. 15760. | M. **May 3/17.** |
| *6 A. III | Twaite, George. 19051. | W. and M. **May 3/17.** |
| ‡6 A. | Tyler, A. H. 13176. | M. **May 3/17.** |
| 6 A. L.G.S. | Vining, Cecil H. E. 13089. | W. and M. **May 3/17.** |
| ‡6 A. | Willis, W. 3955. | M. **May 3/17.** |
| *6 A. I | Winter, Richard A. 18742. | M. **May 3/17.** |
| ‡6 B. | Allan, T. H. 13622. | M. **May 3/17.** |
| ‡6 B. | Barden, W. J. 20219. | M. **May 3/17.** |
| 6 B. | Beeching, L.-Cpl. Arthur. 257. | M. **May 3/17.** |
| ‡6 B. | Box, J. A. 19044. | M. **May 3/17.** |
| ‡6 B. | Brown, A. J. 13426. | M. **May 3/17.** |
| *6 B. V | Bullen, T. T. 17593. | W. and M. **May 3/17.** |
| 6 B. VIII | Burnap, Richd. John. G/20123. | M. **May 3/17.** |
| *6 B. L.G.S. | Coleman, L.-Cpl. Philip. 3062. | M. **May 3/17.** |

**Kent Regiment, East—contd.**

## *B.E.F.*

‡6 B. Colley, J. 6984. M. May 3/17.
6 B. VIII Dawes, T. J. 18967. M. May 3/17.
‡6 B. VI Denne, D. 20109. M. May 3/17.
6 B. VIII Dyer, Cpl. Frank Ernest. 4338. M. May 3/17.
‡6 B. Ferneley, E. 13698. M. May 3/17.
‡6 B. Harris, T. 18953. M. May 3/17.
6 B. VIII Hill, H. 19021. M. May 3/17.
‡6 B. Johnson, J. T. 18948. M. May 3/17.
‡6 B. Knight, E. 13656. M. May 3/17.
‡6 B. Lawrence, R. 20031. M. May 3/17.
6 B. V Lyle, T. G. 13413. M. May 3/17.
6 B. North, Charles G. A. 500. W. and M. Oct. 7/16. R/Enq.
‡6 B. Pearce, T. E. 13420. M. May 3/17.
‡6 B. Poole, H. E. 13692. M. May 3/17.
‡6 B. Roberts, E. 9911. W. and M. May 3/17.
‡6 B. Rose, G. P. 13573. M. May 3/17.
6 B. VI Russell, F. E. 10118. M. May 8/17.
‡6 B. VIII Saggers, Sergt. A. A. 7793. M. May 3/17.
*6 B. VIII Seymour, A. 11689. M. May 3/17.
‡6 B. Shearman, J. 11092. M. May 3/17.
6 B. Snashall, G. J. 13643. M. May 3/17.
6 B. VIII Tegg, Wm. Richard. 19043. M. May 3/17.
‡6 B. Tompkins, W. 13602. M. May 3/17.
6 B. VIII Triggs, F. J. D. 20174. M. May 3/17.
*6 B. VI Waller, J. H. 13184. M. May 3/17.
*6 B. VIII Welch, Wm. 272. M. May 3/17.
‡6 B. VI White, N. E. G/20177. M. May 3/17.
‡6 B. Wiffen, E. 20183. M. May 3/17.
‡6 B. Woodland, E. 10135. M. May 3/17.
6 B. Wyeth, Jn. Thos. 8930. M. May 3/17.
6 C. XII Abell, Richard. 8373. W. and M. Oct. 7/16. R/Enq.
6 C. IX Apps, E. T. 8166. M. May 3/17.
‡6 C. Bates, C. W. 13116. M. May 3/17.
6 C. M.G.S. Blatchley, Edwin. G/18983. M. May 3/17.
‡6 C. Blott, H. W. 10225. M. May 3/17.
‡6 C. XI Brown, J. 13100. M. May 3/17.
6 C. IX Bryant, Alfred. 8508. M. May 3/17.
6 C. Butler, Harry. 9729. K. Oct. 7/16. R/Enq.
*6 C. XII Cheeseman, Charles. G/18965. M. May 3/17.
6 C. XII Clover, S. G. 18976. M. May 3/17.
6 C. XII Coffield, Ernest. 18845. M. May 3/17.
*6 C. XI Coomber, Harold. 13619. M. May 3/17.
6 C. X Curtiss, Robt. 20940. M. May 3/17.
‡6 C. Dounham, L.-Cpl. W. 18958. M. May 3/17.
6 C. Garley, G. E. 18822. M. May 3/17.
6 C. IX Gilbert, T. 18966. M. May 3/17.
‡6 C. IX Harris, Percy. 13122. M. May 6/17.
6 C. IX Harrison, Herbert. 701. K. May 1/17. Det.D./B.
‡6 C. Hawkins, Walter H. 1105. M. May 3/17.
6 C. Head, C. 13671. M. May 3/17.
‡6 C. Hinkley, J. 13681. M. May 3/17.
*6 C. XII Johnson, L.-Cpl. Johnson Harry. 8824. M. May 3/17.
‡6 C. Knott, W. C. 546. M. May 3/17.
6 C. IX London, A. 13136. W. and M. May 2/17.
‡6 C. Mills, H. 4339. M. May 3/17.
‡6 C. Mitchell, G. W. 8465. M. May 3/17.

**Kent Regiment, East—contd.**

## *B.E.F.*

| | | |
|---|---|---|
| **6 C.** | Potts, G. 13626. | M. **May 3/17.** |
| ***6 C. IX** | Saffery, J. 20167. | M. **May 3/17.** |
| **6 C. X** | Solly, L.-Cpl. G. C. L. 3960. | W. and M. **April 9/17.** |
| **‡6 C.** | Terry, H. 5246. | M. **May 3/17.** |
| **6 C.** | Triptree, L.-Cpl. A. G. 7914. | M. **May 9/17.** |
| **‡6 C.** | Weaver, R. 13599. | M. **May 3/17.** |
| **6 C.** | Whale, R. F. 7068. | M. **May 3/17.** |
| **‡6 C.** | Wickham, Sergt. W. E. 13557. | M. **May 3/17.** |
| **6 C. XII L.G.S.** | Wood, L.-Cpl. Ernest. 5870. | M. **May 3/17.** |
| **6 C. X** | Wright, Bertie Reginald. 20905. | M. **May 3/17.** |
| **‡6 C.** | Wyatt, W. 2849. | M. **May 3/17.** |
| **‡6 D. XV** | Arnott, H. W. 13717. | M. **May 3/17.** |
| **6 D. XVI** | Bridges, L. A. F. 19007. | M. **May 3/17.** |
| ***6 D. XV** | Briscoe, S. 13733. | M. **May 3/17.** |
| **‡6 D.** | Bulgin, Sergt. W. A. 9747. | M. **May 3/17.** |
| **6 D. XV** | Campbell, Cyril Raymond. 13709. | M. **May 3/17.** |
| **‡6 D.** | Cooper, F. 1040. | M. **May 3/17.** |
| ***6 D. XVI** | Davidson, W. G. 20941. | M. **May 3/17.** |
| **‡6 D.** | Hall, F. 9144. | M. **May 3/17.** |
| ***6 D. XIII** | Hawksbee, W. 19052. | M. **May 3/17.** |
| **6 D. XVI** | Inwood, Geo. 20912. | M. **May 3/17.** |
| ***6 D. XV** | Jacklin, W. T. 19003. | W. and M. **April 1/17.** |
| **6 D.** | Jenner, T. C. 13131. | M. **April 9/17.** |
| **‡6 D.** | Kerrison, R. H. 1064. | M. **May 3/17.** |
| **‡6 D.** | Lovell, H. J. 13689. | M. **May 3/17.** |
| **‡6 D.** | Manning, W. 13593. | M. **May 3/17.** |
| **6 D. L.G.S.** | Martinne, Rich. A. 19024. | M. **May 3/17.** |
| **‡6 D.** | Matthews, A. E. 13635. | M. **May 3/17.** |
| **‡6 D.** | Miller, J. T. 2524. | M. **May 3/17.** |
| **6 D. XVI** | Molyneux, Norman. 20934. | M. **May 3/17.** |
| **‡6 D.** | Pettman, A. L. 15771. | M. **April 9/17.** |
| ***6 D. XIV** | Pitts, Wm. 2853. | M. **May 3/17.** |
| **‡6 D.** | Riches, F. G. 7654. | M. **May 3/17.** |
| **6 D. XIII** | Roberts, Emrys Jones. 13708. | M. **May 3/17.** |
| **‡6 D.** | Ruddle, W. H. 13714. | M. **May 3/17.** |
| **‡6 D. XV** | Sayer, F. H. 18936. | M. **May 3/17.** |
| **6 D. XVI** | Shoebridge, Alfred. 20948. | M. **May 3/17.** |
| **6 D. XIV** | Thomsett, W. 18940. | M. **May 3/17.** |
| **‡6 D.** | Turner, G. 18930. | M. **May 3/17.** |
| **‡6 D.** | Turner, S. J. 20946. | M. **May 3/17.** |
| ***6 D.** | Warman, Thos. 13629. | Unoff. M. **May 3/17.** |
| **‡6 D.** | Witch, P. C. 13611. | M. **May 3/17.** |
| **7** | **Butler, 2nd Lieut. J. W.** | M. **May 3/17.** |
| **7** | **Cheesman, 2nd Lieut. A. A.** | M. **May 3/17.** |
| **7** | **Church, 2nd Lieut. G. W.** | W. and M. **May 3/17.** |
| **7** | **Hilder, 2nd Lieut. H. S.** | M. **May 3/17.** |
| **7 B.** | **Johnston, 2nd Lieut. S. B.** | M. **May 28/17.** |
| **7** | **Lane, 2nd Lieut. J. E.** (Fr. 4th.) | W. and M. **May 3/17.** |
| **7 A.** | Akehurst, W. 20185. | M. **May 3/17.** |
| ***7 A. II** | Apps, L.-Cpl. E. 15735. | M. **May 3/17.** |
| **‡7 A.** | Barsley, C. H. J. 15547. | M. **May 3/17.** |
| **7 A. III** | Bentley, Roland Cunard. G/20056. | M. **May 3/17.** |
| ***7 A.** | Blackburn, Cecil John. 15822. | M. **May 3/17.** |
| **7 A. III** | Blackwell, Jack E. 20041. | M. **May 3/17.** |
| **‡7 A. III** | Bowkett, R. C. 20040. | M. **May 3/17.** |
| ***7 A. III** | Brown, L.-Cpl. C. D. 7033. | M. **May 3/17.** |
| **7 A. I** | Brown, Fred. 12990. | M. **Nov. 18/16. R/Enq.** |

**Kent Regiment, East—contd.**

*B.E.F.*

‡7 A. II Calfe, R. C. 19160. M. May 3/17.
7 A. Casserley, Walter S. 19173. M. May 3/17.
7 A. IV Churchward, W. 17661. W. and M. May 3/17.
‡7 A. Clackett, A. E. 9511. M. May 3/17.
7 A. Corke, James. 1956. M. May 3/17.
‡7 A. Denning, J. H. H. 19176. M. May 3/17.
‡7 A. III Farrell, Patrick. 13214. M. May 3/17.
7 A. Gibson, L.-Cpl. Percy Jas. 15603. M. May 3/17.
‡7 A. Golding, J. 10911. W. and M. May 3/17.
‡7 A. Goldsmith, V. A. 20815. M. May 3/17.
•7 A. IV Gratton, W. 13492. M. May 3/17.
7 A. Hardie, B. 19178. M. May 3/17.
•7 A. I Heading, Wm. 11282. M. Oct. 18/16.
7 A. L.G.S. Hurst, L.-Cpl. A. E. 20816. M. May 3/17.
•7 A. I.T.M. Kidd, Frank. 13228. (55 Bgde.) M. May 3/17.
7 A. III Laker, W. H. 9334. M. May 5/17.
7 A. II Luck, L.-Cpl. Arch. Edwd. 20562. M. May 3/17.
7 A. McDonald, John. 13234. M. May 3/17.
•7 A. II Mekins, L. 13235. M. May 3/17.
•7 A. IV Ormerod, Robt. Briggs. 19133. M. May 3/17.
7 A. Pott, L.-Cpl. E. H. G. 19123. M. May 3/17.
‡7 A. Ribchester, L.-Cpl. J. 20918. M. May 3/17.
‡7 A. M.G.S. Sammon, M. J. 13246. M. May 3/17.
‡7 A. Shaill, A. 13247. M. May 3/17.
‡7 A. Shoebridge, H. 18868. M. May 3/17.
7 A. II Smith, Arthur. G/19152. M. May 3/17.
‡7 A. I Stevens, C. 20818. W. and M. May 3/17.
7 A. II Stiles, Hy. Rich. G/19151. M. May 3/17.
‡7 A. Taken, J. 2278. M. May 3/17.
7 A. I Taylor, Arthur Cecil. 19194. M. May 3/17.
‡7 A. II Walbancke, Richard. 19192. M. May 3/17.
7 A. IV Ward, James Henry. 17660. M. May 3/17.
7 A. IV Winterflood, W. 17676. M. May 3/17.
‡7 B. Allen, G. 15534. M. May 27/17.
7 B. VIII Anderson, Percy Oswald Robt. 20850 M. May 3/17.
•7 B. VII Andrews, Henry Jesse. 15536. M. May 3/17.
7 B. Angus, Norman M. 20833. M. May 3/17.
7 B. VII Arnold, Percy W. 12981. M. Nov. 18/16. R/Enq.
‡7 B. Baldock, W. 4916. M. May 3/17.
•7 B. VII Baylay, Chas. 20847. M. May 3/17.
‡7 B. Bergin, W. 13197. M. May 3/17.
‡7 B. Brookes, H. 8124. M. May 3/17.
‡7 B. Camburn, L.-Cpl. F. 11404. M. May 3/17.
‡7 B. Chambers, J. 18039. M. May 3/17.
‡7 B. VIII Cornhill, Arthur John. 10230. M. Nov. 18/16. R/Enq.
7 B. Corrie, Ernest G. 20848. M. May 3/17.
•7 B. V Darvill, Charles Henry. 7321. W. and M. Nov. 18/16. R/Enq.
7 B. V Dixon, MacDonald. G/15821. W. and M. May 3/17.
•7 B. M.G.S. Ezard, Jack. 13212. M. May 3/17.
‡7 B. Fannon, J. 13213. M. May 3/17.
•7 B. VII Fillary, T. V. 18011. M. May 3/17.
7 B. VII French, Oxley. 15596. M. May 3/17.
7 B. VIII Fyson, Geo. P. 18186. M. May 3/17.
7 B. Green, Fred. 1290. W. and M. Nov. 18/16.
7 B. Huntly, L.-Sergt. P. H. 1682. M. May 3/17.
‡7 B. Johnston, P. 13393. M. May 3/17.
‡7 B. Kelly, H. 11628. M. May 3/17.

**Kent Regiment, East—contd.**

*B.E.F.*

‡7 B. Kingsford, Cpl. A. 5335. M. May 3/17.
‡7 B. Lawrence, R. 1311. M. May 3/17.
7 B. V Lewin, Harry F. 19130. M. May 3/17.
‡7 B. Linkins, C. 20806. M. May 3/17.
‡7 B. McDermott, J. 13233. M. May 3/17.
‡7 B. Morris, G. 1428. M. May 3/17.
7 B. Mortimer, Angus Norman. 20833. M. May 3/17.
7 B. L.G.S. Murray, P. S. 20843. W. and M. May 3/17.
‡7 B. Myhil, S. 13239. M. May 3/17.
7 B. V Odd, Frank Alfred. 20858. M. May 3/17.
‡7 B. Powell, C. H. 15665. M. May 3/17.
7 B. VII Pyett, Geo. Henry. 10330. M. May 3/17.
‡7 B. Richards, C. 18584. M. May 3/17.
‡7 B. Salvage, L.-Cpl. J. 18675. M. May 3/17.
‡7 B. Selling, C. 5141. M. May 3/17.
‡7 B. Stanford, J. 18873. M. May 3/17.
‡7 B. Stringer, B. 13250. M. May 3/17.
7 B. Stuckey, Ralph H. 20820. M. May 3/17.
7 B. VII Thorns, H. C. G/19164. M. May 3/17.
7 B. V Tingcombe, Geo. C. 19153. M. May 3/17.
‡7 B. Venton, F. 9181. M. May 3/17.
‡7 B. Watson, R. I. 18662. M. May 3/17.
‡7 B. Weaver, A. G. 18206. M. May 3/17.
*7 B. VIII Welband, Norman Kennington. 15708. M. May 3/17.
‡7 B. Wells, E. G. 18676. M. May 3/17.
*7 B. VIII Williams, E. 18080. M. May 3/17.
7 B. VIII Wood, Herbert Trevor. 20839. M. May 3/17.
7 B. VIII Woodland, H. 15718. (Late 2240 Kent Cyclists.) K. Nov. 18/16. Det.D./B. R/Enq
‡7 C. Adams, W. A. 18686. M. May 3/17.
7 C. L.G.S. Aitken, L.-Cpl. W. W. G/731. W. and M. May 3/17.
7 C. Andrews, A. J. 15535. M. May 3/17.
‡7 C. Austin, J. 17571. M. May 3/17.
7 C. M.G.S. Bartle, F. H. G/19195. M. May 3/17.
‡7 C. Best, E. E 10348. M. May 3/17.
‡7 C. Blewitt, F. 18681. M. May 3/17.
‡7 C. Bridge, R. 18695. M. May 3/17.
‡7 C. Bridger, W. J. 13011. M. May 3/17.
‡7 C. Brown, F. 10148. M. May 3/17.
7 C. L.G.S. Browne, A. V. 13786. M. May 3/17.
7 C. L.G.S. Carr, L.-Cpl. Chas. Thos. G/3663. W. and M. May 3/17.
7 C. X Chapman, Sergt. A. H. R. 2258. M. May 3/17.
‡7 C. Chapman, J. 10142. M. May 3/17.
*7 C. IX Christmas, H. 20312. M. May 3/17.
7 C. L.G.S. Cleaver, Stanley M. 13193. W. and M. May 3/17.
‡7 C. Copping, T. 1582. M. May 3/17.
7 C. XII Cox, Harry. 10743. M. May 3/17.
‡7 C. Dowsing, H. 2728. M. May 3/17.
‡7 C. IX Flint, S. 10167. M. May 3/17.
7 C. XII Hetherington, Wm. Jas. 20011. (Fr. 5th, No. 2819.) M. May 3/17.
‡7 C. Howlett, A. 10315. M. May 3/17.
‡7 C. XII Morgan, J. H. 15649. M. May 3/17.
‡7 C. Murch, L.-Cpl. H. W. 749. M. May 3/17.
‡7 C. Newman, C. W. 10234. M. May 3/17.
‡7 C. Newport, C. 2508. M. May 3/17.
*7 C. XI Offord, E. L. 2905. W. and M. May 3/17.

**Kent Regiment, East—contd.**

## *B.E.F.*

| | | | |
|---|---|---|---|
| ‡7 C. | | Page, A. 3788. | M. May 3/17. |
| ‡7 C. | | Parker, R. C. 678. | M. May 3/17. |
| 7 C. | | Piper, Ernest Geo. 15659. | M. May 3/17. |
| 7 C. | XI | Player, H. J. 17950. | M. May 3/17. |
| ‡7 C. | | Stedman, L.-Sergt. A. 513. | M. May 3/17. |
| ‡7 C. | | Stonebridge, A. 10201. | M. May 3/17. |
| ‡7 C. | | Tomsett, A. 10405. | M. May 3/17. |
| ‡7 C. | | Vidler, S. 15702. | M. May 3/17. |
| ‡7 C. | | Vinall, E. T. 10426. | M. May 3/17. |
| ‡7 C. | | Weaver, L.-Sergt. H. 803. | M. May 3/17. |
| ‡7 C. | M.G.S. | White, James Alexander. 20008. | M. May 3/17. |
| ‡7 C. | | Wiles, P. N. 18677. | M. May 3/17. |
| 7 C. | | Willett, Herbert Walter. 2227. | M. May 3/17. |
| 7 C. | XI | Wilson, L.-Cpl. Clement. 8556. | M. May 3-4/17. |
| 7 C. | | Wood, Herbert. 729. | M. May 3/17. |
| 7 D. | XVI | Arnold, Ernest Fred. 20016. | W. and M. May 3/17. |
| 7 D. | XVI | Coomer, Chas. Alb. 12182. | M. May 3/17. |
| 7 D. | | Cranston, Sergt. W. V. 1959. | M. May 3/17. |
| 7 D. | M.G.S. | Dudson, Albert. 15581. | M. May 3/17. |
| ‡7 D. | | Ennis, J. 13274. | W. and M. May 3/17. |
| *7 D. | M.G.S. | Holdstock, S. J. 13042. | M. May 3/17. |
| ‡7 D. | | Moore, A. E. 17697. | M. May 3/17. |
| 7 D. | XVI | Nutt, P. J. G/20827. | W. and M. May 3/17. |
| 7 D. | | Pattenden, G. T. 18092. | W. and M. May 3/17. |
| ‡7 D. | | Smith, A. E. 15684. | W. and M. May 3/17. |
| 7 I.T.M. | | Keen, L. F. 1256. (55 Bgde.) | M. Nov. 22/16. |
| *8 C. | | **Carlos, 2nd Lieut. E. S.** | K. June 14/17. Det.D./B. |
| 8 B. | | Kitchen, Jas. Duthie. 12544. | M. April 16/17. |
| 8 D. | XV | Baker, John. 8690. | M. Sept. 5/16. R/Enq. |
| ‡8 D. | XVI | Parrott, Geo. Fredk. 5432. | M. June 15/17. |
| 8 ? | | Coeshall, L. 12164. | M. April 16/17. |

## *BALKANS.*

| | | |
|---|---|---|
| ‡2 ? | Carr, Cpl. G. 8657. | W. and M. May 19/17. |
| ‡2 ? | Martin, S. 7899. | W. and M. May 19/17. |

## *PERSIAN GULF.*

| | | |
|---|---|---|
| 5 A. | Emery, Sergt. F. 242823. (6051.) | W. and M. Mar. 9/17. |
| 5 ? | Brice, A. 241907. | W. and M. Feb. 12/17. |
| 5 ? | Goldup, A. 1520. | M., bel. K. Dec. 17/16 |
| 5 ? | Johncey, M. 241210. | W. and M. Mar. 9/17. |
| 5 ? | Wickens, C.-S.-M. A. F. 170. | K. Feb. 24/17. Det.D./B. |

# ROYAL WEST KENT REGIMENT.

## *B.E.F.*

| | | | |
|---|---|---|---|
| 1 A. | III | Graham, Ivie Campbell. G/7612. | W. and M. Feb. 10/17. |
| 1 B. | VI | Clibbons, Wm. George. 6393. | W. and M. July 22/16. R/Enq. |
| 1 B. | | Peacock, L.-Cpl. Percy. 16055. (Fr. 12th E. Surrey.) | M. July 22/16. R./Enq. |
| 1 B. | | Robinson, S. H. 8948. (Fr. 1 W. Surrey.) | M. Sept. 3/16. R/Enq. |

**Kent Regiment, Royal West—contd.**

## *B.E.F.*

| | | |
|---|---|---|
| **1 C. L.G.S.** | **Hibben, A. 9086.** | **M. July 22/16. R./Enq.** |
| **1 C. X** | Johnson, Richard Edwin. 10557. | W. and M. Unoff. K. **April 9/17.** Conf. and Det. |
| **1 C. X** | **Pepper, Bertram L. 7224.** | **K. Sept. 11/16. Det.D./B.** |
| **1 C.** | Pickering, Jas. Shackleton. 5927. | **M. Sept. 4/16. R/Enq.** |
| **1 C.** | Whitehead, C. 16025. | **M. April 9/17.** |
| **1 D.** | Pye, Wm. 475. | W. and M. **July 22/16. R/Enq.** |
| **6** | **Williams, Capt. E. T.** | M. **May 3/17.** |
| **6 A.** | Andrews, R. 4957. | M. **July 3/16. R./Enq.** |
| ***6 A.** | Andrews, L.-Cpl. Wm. 2295. | M. **May 3/17.** |
| **‡6 A.** | Burt, Cpl. A. E. 10987. | M. **May 3/17.** |
| **‡6 A.** | Childs, J. 11421. | M. **May 3/17.** |
| **‡6 A.** | Comerford, F. 11059. | M. **May 3/17.** |
| ***6 A. I** | Connolly, Wm. Patrick. 23232. | M. **May 3/17.** |
| **6 A. I** | Cooper, A.-Cpl. A. G. 3042. | M. **May 3/17.** |
| **6 A. II** | Field, A. 11024. | M. **May 3/17.** |
| ***6 A.** | Goff, Albert. 10116. | M. **May 3/17.** |
| **6 A.** | Goldsmith, Geo. Fredk. G/6698. | M. **Oct. 7/16. R/Enq.** |
| **‡6 A. III** | Groombridge, S. 6168. | M. **May 3/17.** |
| **6 A.** | Hall, Cpl. Wm. Herbert. 3920. | M. **May 3/17.** |
| **6 A. II** | Hills, James. 17610. (Fr. W. Surreys) | M. **May 2/17.** |
| **‡6 A.** | Jewiss, G. C. 8790. | M. **May 3/17.** |
| **6 A.** | Martin, Geo. 11934. | M. **May 3/17.** |
| **‡6 A.** | Muncy, Cpl. H. 823. | M. **May 3/17.** |
| **‡6 A.** | Nightingale, Wm. Arthur. 6803. | M. **May 3/17.** |
| ***6 A.** | Pratt, J. 9336. | W. and M. **May 3/17.** |
| ***6 A. or C.** | Reed, Sergt. Edward. 6785. | M. **May 3/17.** |
| **‡6 A.** | Simmons, E. 4980. | M. **May 3/17.** |
| **‡6 A.** | Slythe, V. 11106. | M. **May 3/17.** |
| **6 A. I** | Stapleton, Fredk. 17896. | M. **May 3/17.** |
| **6 A.** | Tuley, William. 10842. | M. **July 3/16. R/Enq.** |
| **‡6 A.** | Vayce, C. 17397. | M. **May 3/17.** |
| **6 A.** | Wheeler, Cpl. E. 126. | M. **July 3/16. R./Enq.** |
| ***6 A.** | Wise, Sergt. F. A. 10696. | M. **May 3/17.** |
| **‡6 B.** | Arnold, L.-Sergt. F. 4110. | M. **April 9/17.** |
| **6 B.** | Bannister, Geo. 10728. | M. **April 9/17.** |
| **‡6 B.** | Bloomfield, H. 15233. | M. **May 3/17.** |
| **‡6 B.** | Bullen, S. S. 17593. | W. and M. **May 3/17.** |
| **6 B. VII** | Card, L.-Cpl. Fred. 3885. | M. **May 3/17.** |
| **‡6 B.** | Chamberlain, E. 14553. | M. **Oct. 7/16. R/Enq.** |
| ***6 B. VIII** | Green, J. G/2852. | M. **May 3/17.** |
| **‡6 B.** | Hills, T. 12814. | M. **May 3/17.** |
| **‡6 B.** | Langridge, G. 19283. | M. **May 3/17.** |
| ***6 B. V** | Mansfield, Reginald. 23083. | M. **May 3/17.** |
| **‡6 B.** | Milledge, L.-Cpl. T. A. 13033. | M. **May 3/17.** |
| **‡6 B.** | Moat, J. F. G. 15459. | M. **May 3/17.** |
| **6 B. V** | Pizzey, L.-Cpl. T. G. 9397. | M. **May 3/17.** |
| **‡6 B.** | Quinnell, A.-Cpl. W. 6551. | M. **May 3/17.** |
| **6 B.** | Reed, Herbert George. 391. | M. **July 3/16. R./Enq.** |
| **6 B. VI** | Roberts, L.-Cpl. J. E. 24735. | W. and M. **May 3/17.** |
| **6 C.** | Blaine, A. J. 15872. | M. **Oct. 7/16. R/Enq.** |
| **‡6 C. XI** | Clifton, W. E. 25103. | M. **May 3/17.** |
| **6 C. XI** | Davies, Geo. 17803. | W. Unoff. M. **April 9/17.** |
| **6 C. IX** | Denyer, A. E. 17610. | M. **May 3/17.** |
| **6 C. XII** | Elvin, R. 10995. | M. **July 3/16. R/Enq.** |

**Kent Regiment, Royal West—contd.**

*B.E.F.*

‡6 C. Haddon, F. 17751. M. May 3/17.
‡6 C. Halsey, R. 18937. M. May 3/17.
‡6 C. Kirkpatrick, J. 17838. M. May 3/17.
‡6 C. Middleton, A.-Cpl. S. 11251. M. May 3/17.
6 C. X Newstead, Thomas. 10785. M. Oct. 7/16. R/Enq.
6 C. Norris, Cpl. Alfred. 101. M. May 3/17.
‡6 C. Polley, A. 14774. M. May 3/17.
6 C. X Ruck, Wm. John. 17545. M. May 3/17.
6 C. X Smith, L.-Cpl. Chas. Wm. 12821. K. Oct. 7/16. Det.D./B.
‡6 C. Taylor, H. 18922. M. May 3/17.
6 C. XI Weller, C. L. 2129. M. April 9/17.
‡6 C. Wheaday, A. 19285. M. May 3/17.
‡6 D. Bennett, J. 17781. M. May 3/17.
‡6 D. Card, D. E. F. 14706. M. May 3/17.
6 D. Dawes, A. 13309. M. Oct. 7/16. R/Enq.
‡6 D. Eley, R. 16706. M. May 3/17.
‡6 D. Embleton, A. 984. M. May 3/17.
‡6 D. Handley, F. 18946. M. May 3/17.
•6 D. XV Mills, L.-Cpl. G. 15451. M. May 3/17.
6 D. XIII Nye, J. 7834. M. May 3/17.
‡6 D. Pocock, H. 5417. M. May 3/17.
6 D. Smith, E. J. 3471. M. Oct. 7/16. R/Enq.
6 D. Taylor, Mark. 24915. M. May 3/17.
6 D. XIV Wrighton, Albert. 14575. M. April 9/17.
6 ? Wheal, J. H. 10658. M. May 3/17.
7 **Corley, 2nd Lieut. E. C.** K. Feb. 23/17. Det.D./B.
‡7 A. Bailey, R. 18808. M. May 3/17.
‡7 A. Chaffer, W. 25342. M. June 1/17.
7 A. Gearing, Thomas. 2244. W. and M. May 3/17.
•7 A. I Hill, G. W. 1018. M. May 3/17.
•7 A. Lettington, F. 4036. M. May 3/17.
7 A. III Melloy, Patrick. 18558. M. Feb. 14/17.
•7 A. Nind, A. 9604. M. June 1/17.
7 A. I Olney, E. W. 24630. K. Mar. 22/17. Det.D./B.
7 A. Sims, W. 11198. M. Sept. 30/16. R./Enq.
7 B. Blundell, R. 3904. M. Nov. 18/17.
7 C. or D. Luckman, L.-Cpl. W. 2098. W. and M. May 3/17.
•7 C. XII Monckton, L.-Cpl. Oswald. 1681. M. June 3/17.
‡7 C. Orpwood, W. 11407. M. June 3/17.
•7 C. IX Smorthit, Wm. Fredk. 5481. M. June 3/17.
7 D. XVI Allen, F. J. W. 24497. M. May 3/17.
•7 D. XV Birkenfield, Cpl. Wm. 23636. M. May 3/17.
‡7 D. Brown, G. 1990. M. May 3/17.
7 D. XVI Buckley, R. 23623. W. and M. May 3/17.
‡7 D. Evans, A. 24604. M. May 3/17.
7 D. Gillard, A. 24554. W. and M. May 3/17.
7 D. Lang, Sergt. Geo. 525. (Late C.-S.-M.) M. May 3/17.
•7 D. XV Lewis, F. D. 24864. M. May 3/17.
‡7 D. XIII Life, S. 24561. M. May 3/17.
‡7 D. Link, H. 23625. M. May 3/17.
‡7 D. Mallyon, L. 23588. M. May 3/17.
‡7 D. Parker, W. 10264. M. May 3/17.
‡7 D. Parkinson, W. 17510. M. May 20/17.
•7 D. XIV Pearce, Geo. H. 12118. M. Nov. 18/16. R/Enq.

**Kent Regiment, Royal West**—contd.

## *B.E.F.*

| | | |
|---|---|---|
| *7 D. | Prentice, Cpl. Geo. 18803. | M. Nov. 18/16. R/Enq. |
| ‡7 D. | Pritchard, I. 25263. | M. May 3/17. |
| ‡7 D. | Springett, Albert. 12830. | M. Nov. 18/16. R/Enq. |
| ‡7 D. | Taylor, H. G. 2944. | M. Nov. 18/16. R/Enq. |
| ‡7 D. | Thayre, L.-Cpl. C. 3265. | W. and M. May 3/17. |
| ‡7 D. | Wellington, H. 24804. | M. May 3/17. |
| ‡7 D. | Woodger, A. 12134. | W. and M. May 3/17. |
| *8 C. | Sergeant, Alfred H. 15901. | K. April 11/17. Det.D./B. |
| 10 A. | Abbott, J. 9033. | M. Sept. 17/16. R./Enq. |
| *10 B. | Burton, L.-Cpl. F. 24246. | W. Unoff. M. June 7/17. |
| ‡11 A. | Clark, Wm. Alfred. 10594. | M. Oct. 7/16. R/Enq. |
| 11 A. | Green, W. 18259. | M. Oct. 7/16. R./Enq. |
| 11 A. II | Lucking, Henry Gordon. 8161. | M. Sept. 15/16. R/Enq. |
| ‡11 A. II | Powell, Edward Norman. 8055. | K. April 8/17. Det.D./B. |
| ‡11 A. M.G.S. | Whiteman, Chas. W. 18543. | K. June 7/17. Det.D./B. |
| ‡11 A. or B. | Williams, Charles. 10845. | M. Sept. 15/16. R/Enq. |
| 11 B. | Crane, A. W. 327. | K. Sept. 15/16. Det.D./B. R/Enq. |
| *11 D. XIII | Cawley, H. F. 18355. | M. Oct. 7/16. R/Enq. |
| ‡11 D. XI | Philpott, H. 18481. | W. Unoff. M. June 7/17. |
| ‡11 ? I.T.M. | Crockford, L.-Cpl. Vernon. Geo. 9457. (122 Bgde.) | W. and M. Sept. 15/16. R/Enq. |

## *E.E.F.*

| | | |
|---|---|---|
| *2/4 A. I | Norris, F. C. 201015. | K. April 19/17. Det.D./B. |
| *2/4 A. III | Webb, E. 200168. (1282.) | W. and M. April 19/17. |
| 2/4 A. | Yorke, L.-Cpl. E. 200858. (2453.) | M. April 19/17. |
| 2/4 C. | Markwich, H. 1967. | K. April 19/17. Det.D./B. |
| 2/4 ? | Bance, T. 201012. | M. April 19/17. |

## KING EDWARD'S HORSE.

## *B.E.F.*

| | | |
|---|---|---|
| B. Squad. | Coombes, Sgt.-Maj. Val. H. 493. | M., bel. K. Mar. 22/17. |
| B. | Emond, G. 1030. | M. Mar. 22/17. |

## KING'S ROYAL RIFLE CORPS.

## *B.E.F.*

| | | |
|---|---|---|
| 1 A. | Coombes, W. 18600. | M. Feb. 17/17. |
| 1 A. | Day, H. A. 203118. | M. Feb. 17/17. |
| 1 A. or B. | Ford, Edw. Geo. 35536. | M. May 3/17. |
| 1 A. or D. | Mintern, Charles L. 35620. | M. April 29/17. |
| 1 A. IV | Perkins, L.-Cpl. H. L. R/2845. | M. Feb. 17/17. |
| 1 A. II | Phillips, W. R/5080. | K. Feb. 17/17. Det.D./B. |
| 1 A. I | Read, E. T. 35598. | M. April 29/17. |
| 1 A. II | Rice, William. 35691. | M. April 29/17. |

**King's Royal Rifle Corps—contd.**

## *B.E.F.*

| | | | |
|---|---|---|---|
| 1 B. or D. | Knight, H. 1224. | M. April 14/17. |
| 1 B. VII | Mahoney, A. 35741. | M. May 3/17. |
| 1 B. | Tabor, H. 2022. | M. May 3/17. |
| *1 C. | Broad, Oliver Wm. 473. | M. Nov. 14/16. R/Enq. |
| ‡1 C. | Chapman, J. H. 35432. | M. April 29/17. |
| 1 C. | Davis, Charley. 9859. | M. Feb. 17/17. |
| 1 C. XII | Joy, Aubrey Henry. 203073. | K. Feb. 17/17. Det.D./B. |
| 1 C. IX | Sinclair, Jas. Malcolm. 27684. | K. Feb. 17/17. Det.D./B. R/Enq |
| 1 C. | Styles, L.-Cpl. R. J. V. 11901. | M. Feb. 17/17. |
| *1 C. | Toon, George Wm. 22011. | M. Nov. 14/16. R/Enq. |
| 1 C. IX | Turner, Sergt. Alex. Gedge. 9363. | M. Feb. 17/17. |
| *1 D. XVI | Baker, Sergt. E. W. Y/1701. | W. and M. April 29/17. |
| 1 D. | Bolton, F. 20992. | M. April 29/17. |
| 1 D. | Bursill, A. 10182. (Late 10183, 1st Fijian Rifles.) | K. Feb. 17/17. Det.D./B. |
| 1 D. | Crisp, F. J. 35629. | M. April 29/17. |
| 1 D. | Down, A. V. 37469. | M. April 29/17. |
| 1 D. XIV | Gerrard, Dudley S. R/25310. | M. Feb. 17/17. |
| 1 D. | Loveday, Jess. 32651. | M. April 29/17. |
| 1 D. | Oliver, Alf. T. 13136. | M. April 17/17. |
| *1 D. | Reed, Harry Vernon. 27479. | M. April 29/17. |
| 1 D. | Scholes, S. 10242. | M. Feb. 17/17. |
| 1 D. | Shone, C.-S.-M. Henry. 9640. | M. Mar. 10-14/17. |
| *1 D. XIV | Triance, A. E. 16589. | W. and M. April 29/17. |
| 1 D. | Wilson, J. 37459. | M. April 29/17. |
| ‡2 | **Abadie, D.S.O., Lt.-Col. R. N.** | M. July 10/17. |
| ‡2 | **Boucher, 2nd Lieut. A. G.** (Fr. 6th.) | M. July 10/17. |
| ‡2 | **Clinton, Capt. W. L.** | M. July 10/17. |
| ‡2 | **Gott, 2nd Lieut. W. H. E.** | M. July 10/17. |
| ‡2 | **Mills, Lieut. H. J. F.** | M. July 10/17. |
| ‡2 | **Munro, 2nd Lieut. B. C.** | M. July 10/17. |
| ‡2 | **Sheepshanks, 2nd Lieut. Wm.** | M. July 10/17. |
| ‡2 | **Taylor, 2nd Lieut. D. H.** | M. July 10/17. |
| ‡2 | **Ward, Capt. H. K.** (Fr. R.A.M.C.) | M. July 10/17. |
| *2 B. | Henderson, C. T. 22687. | M. Sept. 27/16. R/Enq. |
| 7 | **Herbertson, Lieut. A. H.** | M. May 16/17. |
| 7 A. II | Samuels, Louis. 20985. | M. Unoff. W. Sept. 15/16. R/Enq |
| 7 A. | Smith, L.-Cpl. Thos. 1528. | K. Sept. 15/16. Det.D./B. |
| 7 B. V | Crowther, J. 8958. | M. Sept. 15/16. R/Enq. |
| 7 C. | St. Pierre, E. C. F. 2601. | M. April 11/17. |
| 7 C. XI | Wilkes, John T. 16938. | M. April 11/17. |
| 7 D. Sig. S. | Blazeby, L. C. 19160. | M. April 10/17. |
| *7 D. | Thatcher, Cpl. Harry. 979. | M. May 15/17. |
| ‡7 D. | Wood, G. A. 9389. | M. May 16/17. |
| 8 | **Butcher, 2nd Lt. C. E.** (Fr. 4 R. Fus) | W. and M. May 3/17. |
| 8 A. | Benson, J. 24162. | W. and M. May 3/17. |
| ‡8 A. | Boyall, W. L. 12034. | W. and M. May 3/17. |
| ‡8 A. | Cavell, T. W. 32118. | W. and M. May 3/17. |
| ‡8 A. | Couzens, A. H. 20465. | W. and M. May 3/17. |
| ‡8 A. | Croucher, J. 32154. | W. and M. May 3/17. |
| ‡8 A. | Davenport, L.-Cpl. F. 155. | W. and M. May 3/17. |
| 8 A. II | Durrant, William. 31387. | W. and M. May 3/17. |
| 8 A. or C. | Greenhalgh, L.-Cpl. W. 11261. | W. and M. May 3/17. |
| 8 A. II | Guy, Anthony Clifford. 12532. | W. and M. May 3/17. |
| ‡8 A. | Howell, Sergt. G. H. 15740. | W. and M. May 3/17. |
| 8 A. IV | Jackson, Albert John. 36387. | W. and M. May 3/17. |
| 8 A. I | Jennings, A. F. 201109. | W. and M. May 3/17. |

**King's Royal Rifle Corps—contd.**

## *B.E.F.*

| | | |
|---|---|---|
| 8 A. | Lewinton, W. 429. (Comm. Sec. att. Signals.) | W. and M. May 3/17. |
| *8 A. | Lewis, Robt. 237. | W. and M. May 3/17. |
| ‡8 A. | Lightowler, H. J. 24165. | W. and M. May 3/17. |
| *8 A. III | Ringe, A. G. 12819. | W. and M. May 3/17. |
| 8 A. II | See, L.-Cpl. Charles. 37873. | M. May 3/17. |
| ‡8 A. | Shillan, A. R. 18734. | W. and M. May 3/17. |
| ‡8 A. | Slade, E. 370. | W. and M. May 3/17. |
| *8 A. | Smith, James. R/35723. | W. and M. May 3/17. |
| ‡8 A. | Spilsbury, R. 234. | W. and M. May 3/17. |
| 8 A. II | Stone, Robt. 36269. | W. and M. May 3/17. |
| ‡8 A. | Taylor, W. A. 36380. | W. and M. May 3/17. |
| *8 A. II | Toogood, T. W. 36239. | M. May 3/17. |
| *8 A. | Want, Arthur Herbert. 36280. | W. and M. May 3/17. |
| ‡8 A. | Wright, H. 15875. | W. and M. May 3/17. |
| *8 B. | Davis, L.-Cpl. Tom. 20074. | W. and M. May 3/17. |
| 8 B. or C. | Durrant, Thos. 1038. (Com. S.) | W. and M. May 3/17. |
| 8 B. or C. | Eastwood, Mark. 24254. | W. and M. May 3/17. |
| ‡8 B. | White, L. H. 10684. | W. and M. May 3/17. |
| *8 C. XII | Ashby, Cpl. H. H. 37047. | M. May 3/17. |
| 8 C. | Bailey, Robert. 30307. | M. May 3/17. |
| 8 C. | Berry, Thos. Neville. 33638. | M. May 3/17. |
| 8 C. or D. XI | Burgess, L.-Cpl. W. 15111. | M. May 3/17. |
| 8 C. or D. | Burnitt, L.-Cpl. Archie. R/21037. | M. May 3/17. |
| 8 C. X | Butler, Lionel G. 31610. | W. and M. May 3/17. |
| ‡8 C. | Charley, A. J. 16032. | W. and M. May 3/17. |
| ‡8 C. | Chuter, W. 32284. | M. May 3/17. |
| 8 C. XII | Coquard, Wm. 33619. | M. April 12/17. |
| 8 C. | Edkins, Frank E. 9698. | M. May 3/17. |
| ‡8 C. | Elks, E. 13094. | W. and M. May 3/17. |
| 8 C. X | Field, R. 27645. | W. and M. May 3/17. |
| ‡8 C. | Goring, G. H. 4441. | W. and M. May 3/17. |
| 8 C. | Hall, L.-Cpl. J. R. 4049. | M. May 3/17. |
| 8 C. or D. XV | Hawkes, J. R/31521. | W. and M. May 3/17. |
| ‡8 C. | Hertzberg, N. 1498. | M. May 3/17. |
| 8 C. XII | Jackson, Wm. R/33610. | M. May 3/17. |
| 8 C. | Jones, George. 11764. | M. May 3/17. |
| ‡8 C. | Kay, T. 14661. | M. May 3/17. |
| *8 C. | Kneller, H. J. 33611. | M. May 3/17. |
| *8 C. XI | Martin, G. 33630. | M. May 3/17. |
| 8 C. X | Matthews, Leonard John. 20889. | M. May 3/17. |
| ‡8 C. | Miller, W. R. 4875. | M. May 3/17. |
| ‡8 C. | Phillips, G. C. V. 6327. | M. May 3/17. |
| 8 C. X | Proctor, C. R/22099. | W. and M. May 3/17. |
| 8 C. X | Pybus, Ridley. 6237. | M. Sept. 15/16. |
| ‡8 C. | Rabbinsoitz, B. 29413. | W. and M. May 3/17. |
| 8 C. L.G.S. | Rudduck, Sergt. Chas. 18523. | M. May 3/17. |
| 8 C. X | Shaw, T. 33655. | M. May 3/17. |
| ‡8 C. | Sheran, J. 10701. | M. May 3/17. |
| *8 C. | Skinner, Albert John. R/36452. | M. May 3/17. |
| 8 C. XI | Standing, E. G. 29100. | M. May 3/17. |
| ‡8 C. | Steward, F. W. 11104. | M. May 3/17. |
| 8 C. XI | Wade, L.-Cpl. B. R/20282. | M. May 3/17. |
| *8 C. | Walker, Sergt. J. 5846. | M. May 3/17. |
| 8 C. or D. | Webb, W. 5274. | W. and M. May 3/17. |
| 8 C. L.G.S. | Wilson, Geo. Edw. R/22135. | M. May 3/17. |
| 8 D. XIV | Antliff, F. J. 32340. | M. May 3/17. |
| *8 D. | Bendall, W. 13041. | M. May 3/17. |

**King's Royal Rifle Corps—contd.**

*B.E.F.*

| | |
|---|---|
| 8 D. XIII Buckle, Bertram Reg. C/12151. | M. May 3/17. |
| 8 D. Burton, L.-Cpl. C. W. R/20063. | M. May 3/17. |
| 8 D. XIV Field, A. 33627. | M. May 3/17. |
| ‡8 D. XIII Garlick, F. 12375. | M. May 3/17. |
| 8 D. XV Groves, Herbt. John. C/6954. (Fr. 18th.) | M. May 3/17. |
| ‡8 D. Jordan, J. 29098. | M. May 3/17. |
| *8 D. Lane, E. 12419. | M. May 3/17. |
| *8 D. XIV Longbottom, Garnett. 20555. | M. Unoff. W. Sept. 15/16. R/Enq. |
| 8 D. XVI Outhwaite, Wallace. 30413. | M. May 3/17. |
| ‡8 D. Potter, L.-Cpl. J. J. 1962. | W. and M. May 3/17. |
| ‡8 D. XIV Pratt, J. W. 7350. | M. May 3/17. |
| 8 D. XV Rogers, Wm. Alfred. R/30454. | M. May 3/17. |
| ‡8 D. Smith, J. H. 12225. | M. May 3/17. |
| ‡8 D. Sowman, F. J. 27301. | M. May 3/17. |
| ‡8 D. XV Swanson, C. S. 36416. | M. May 3/17. |
| 8 D. XIII Wilkinson, L.-Cpl. H. S. 7878. | M. May 3/17. |
| 8 D. Winn, J. 9630. | M. Sept. 15/16. R/Enq. |
| 9 A. I Armorey, R. V. 21153. | K. Sept. 15/16. Det.D./B. R/Enq. |
| 9 B. VIII Bracey, P. 22062. | K. Sept. 15/16. Det.D./B. R./Enq. |
| 9 B. V Trendall, Wilfred. 20160. | M. April 9/17. |
| ‡9 C. IX McKenzie, F. C. R/21640. | M. May 26/17. |
| ‡10 B. Remington, A. 36721. | W. and M. April 4/17. |
| 10 D. XIV Back, Erroll. 15680. | W. and M. Sept. 3/16. R./Enq. |
| 10 D. XVI Ludbrook, W. R/32825. | M. Feb. 28/17. |
| *11 A. M.G.S. Pullen, S. A/200294. | K. April 4/17. Det.D./B. |
| *11 B. Bance, L.-Sergt. James. R/1809. | M. June 9/17. |
| 12 B. or C. Reynolds, T. J. 27321. | W. and M. Feb. 20/17. |
| 12 C. Moorby, J. W. 32193. | M. Feb. 15/17. |
| 12 C. Rumbol, G. 33119. | W. and M. Oct. 7/16. R./Enq. |
| ‡12 D. Dillon, H. 10492. | M. Sept. 18/16. |
| 13 A. I Atterton, Geo 33744. | M. April 10/17. |
| 13 A. Barden, P. 7918. | M. April 10/17. |
| 13 A. L.G.S. Barton, L.-Cpl. V. R. 4501. | W. and M. April 10/17. |
| 13 A. III Elliott, Saml. J. 33783. (Fr. H.Q. Snip. S.) | W. and M. April 23/17. |
| 13 A. Green, W. 30318. | M. April 10/17. |
| 13 A. Horton, S. 17179. | M. April 10/17. |
| 13 A. I Lee, Fredk. Geo. Robt. 33786. | K. April 10/17. Det.D./B. R/Enq. |
| 13 A. Longworth, G. 9257. | M. April 10/17. |
| 13 A. Thomas, J. 4734. | W. and M. April 10/17. |
| *13 B. VIII Baker, Ernest James. 33721. | K. April 10/17. Det.D./B. |
| 13 B. Blakeman, H. V. 16899. | M April 9-11/17. |
| 13 B. VIII Brown, Geo. Hen. 33719. | M. April 9-11/17. |
| 13 B. VIII Bugg, W. 33720. | W. and M. April 11/17. |
| 13 B. Burton, J. W. 3836. | M. April 11/17. |
| 13 B. VIII Franklin, C. R/37592. | M. April 9-11/17. |
| 13 B. VIII Gay, W. 33737. | M. April 9-11/17. |
| 13 B. VI Grundy, A. C. 6611. | M. April 9-11/17. |
| 13 B. VI Hall, J. 29642. | W. and M. April 23/17. |
| 13 B. VIII Mason, F. 33805. | W. and M. April 23/17. |
| 13 B. Underwood, J. B. 4647 | M. April 9-11/17. |
| 13 C. or D. Ball, Geo. Edgar. R/37899. | W. and M. April 23/17. |
| 13 C. X Clark, H. G. R/17912. | M. April 25/17. |
| 13 C. X Crane, W. E. 33729. | M. April 10/17. |

**King's Royal Rifle Corps—contd.**

## *B.E.F.*

| | | |
|---|---|---|
| 13 C. | Curtis, G. H. 34228. | M. April 11/17. |
| 13 C. XII | Pepper, G. A. 28067. | M. April 11/17. |
| 13 D. XV | Kenzie, Ernest Jas. R. R/37630. | W. and M. April 25/17. |
| ‡13 D. | Moxham, P. C. 602. (Fr. 6th.) | M. April 23/17. |
| *13 D. | Spencer, L. R/4414. | M. April 11/17. |
| 16 | **Allan, 2nd Lt. R. (Fr. 8 Scot. Rifles)** | W. and M. April 23/17. |
| 16 | **Forrest, 2nd Lieut. L. B.** | M. May 20/17. |
| '16 | **Peacocke, 2nd Lt. J.** (Fr. 3rd.) | M. May 20/17. |
| 16 A. I | Andrews, Horace Fredk. C/1770. | Unoff. M. May 20/17. |
| 16 A. | Barnett, Sidney. 3506. | W. and M. April 23/17. |
| ‡16 A. | Berridge, W. G. 3821. | W. and M. May 20/17. |
| *16 A. | Cameron, W. F. A/201257. | K. May 20/17. Det.D./B. |
| 16 A. IV | Chesman, L.-Cpl. John C. 20666. | W. and M. April 23/17. |
| *16 A. III | Collett, C. W. 27208. | W. and M. May 20/17. |
| *16 A. II | Cove, L.-Cpl. G. 201215. | M. May 20/17. |
| ‡16 A. IV | Gray, Alfred. 37219. | M. May 20/17. |
| 16 A. | Holmes, E. P. 19157. | M. April 23/17. |
| ‡16 A. | James, W. 28374. | M. May 20/17. |
| 16 A. II | Joynson, Wm. John. R/37226. | M. April 23/17. |
| ‡16 A. III | Kirk, Cyril. 978. | M. May 20/17. |
| 16 A. | Knowles, W. J. 36980. | W. and M. April 23/17. |
| 16 A. IV | Lamb, John. R/19642. | M. April 23/17. |
| 16 A. II | Ligate, C. 27263. | M. May 20/17. |
| 16 A. I | Lloyd, J. T. 20990. | W. and M. April 23/17. |
| 16 A. III | Mason, L.-Cpl. E. 21954. | W. and M. April 23/17. |
| 16 A. IV | Mogridge, L.-Cpl. Herb. Thos. 36211 | W. and M. May 20/17. |
| ‡16 A. | Mortley, H. 35621. | M. May 20/17. |
| ‡16 A. | Murray, R. V. 201242. | M. May 20/17. |
| 16 A. III | Osborn, T. S. R/36194. | M. April 23/17. |
| ‡16 A. | Parker, T. 436. | M. May 20/17. |
| ‡16 A. | Parker, W. J. 38247. | M. May 20/17. |
| 16 A. IV | Redhead, Jas. Wm. A/201212. | M. May 20/17. |
| ‡16 A. | Robinson, Sergt. J. 199. | M. May 20/17. |
| 16 A. or H.Q. | Ruddlesden, S/B. C. S. 928. | W. and M. May 20/17. |
| 16 A. I | Staal, Mark. 34074. | M. Feb. 26/17. |
| ‡16 A. | Stockill, J. 6153. | M. May 20/17. |
| ‡16 A. | Tooth, G. E. 34085. | W. and M. May 20/17. |
| 16 A. | Wellbeloved, S. 22143. | M. April 23/17. |
| 16 A. IV | Wilkes, Cpl. E. R/20172. | M. May 20/17. |
| *16 A. IV | Wood, George. R/36290. | M. May 20/17. |
| ‡16 A. | Wootton, J. J. 18632. | M. May 20/17. |
| 16 B. VII | Ainsworth, Tom. C/613. | W. and M. April 23/17. |
| 16 B. VI | Beaty, Sergt. W. E. C/556. | M. April 23/17. |
| ‡16 B. | Bedson, A. C. 1239. | M. May 20/17. |
| 16 B. | Biggs, A. R/36986. | M. April 23/17. |
| ‡16 B. | Bowen, A. 105. | M. May 20/17. |
| 16 B. | Bowman, H. F. 29430. | M. April 23/17. |
| 16 B. | Bowry, W. C. R/32023. | M. April 23/17. |
| ‡16 B. | Bungay, A. 14168. | M. May 20/17. |
| 16 B. M.G.S. | Butterworth, Cyril. C/7861. | M. April 23/17. |
| 16 B. | Cotton, T. W. 203145. | W. and M. April 23/17. |
| 16 B. VII | Forse, A. C. 16850. | M. April 23/17. |
| ‡16 B. VII | Greenhalgh, Cpl. Fred. 180. | M. April 23/17. |
| 16 B. VIII | Hann, Gilbert. R/33984. | K. April 23/17. Det.D./B. |
| 16 B. | Hurst, H. 36159. | M. April 23/17. |
| 16 B. | Liddle, Alan. 36150. | W. and M. April 23/17. |
| 16 B. | Lucas, Sergt. P. J. 36207. | M. April 23/17. |
| 16 B. VIII | Ludford, Chas. W. 30176. | M. April 23/17. |

**King's Royal Rifle Corps—contd.**

## *B.E.F.*

16 B. Morgan, L.-Cpl. G. 7006. M. April 23/17.
16 B. V Mountney, A. 141. M. April 23/17.
*16 B. Payne, Percy Chas. A/201163. M. May 20/17.
16 B. VI Riley, G. N. 36994. M. April 23/17.
16 B. VII Ritchie, T. R/5257. W. Unoff. M. April 23/17.
16 B. Roe, A. 8004. M. April 23/17.
16 B. Scandrett, F. 1448. M. April 23/17.
16 B. V Scott, J. M. R/36177. M. April 23/17.
16 B. Simmonds, W. 203313. M. April 23/17.
‡16 B. Simms, F. 201236. M. May 20/17.
16 B. Skilton, H. V. 30996. M. April 23/17.
16 B. Smith, David Daniel. 32231. M. April 23/17.
16 B. Storey, D. W. 20151. M. April 23/17.
‡16 B. Such, L.-Cpl. J. E. 2273. M. May 20/17.
16 B. Sutcliffe, H. 13202. M. April 23/17.
16 B. VIII Wilson, Fred E. 18710. M. Aug. 25/16. Det.D./B.
16 B. VII Winstone, George Henry. R/34101. M. Dec. 13/16.
16 B. VIII Young, Jas. Dyer. R/36188. M. April 23/17.
16 C. Bastock, Cpl. J. H. 36204. W. and M. April 23/17.
16 C. XII Brazier, L.-Cpl. C. A/203266. W. and M. April 23/17. (2nd Cas.)
16 C. XII Bristow, H. D. 792. M. April 23/17.
16 C. Coates, F. 8089. W. and M. April 23/17.
16 C. Cobden, Sergt. Wm. Jas. C/731. M. April 23/17.
16 C. Cutting, Arthur. C/1013. M. April 23/17.
16 C. X Donavan, Patrick Geo. 16663. Unoff. W. and M. Nov. 5/16.
16 C. Edmonds, L.-Cpl. J. 6946. M. April 23/17.
16 C. IX Edwards, Arthur John. 36172. M. April 23/17.
16 C. X Emerson, Arthur L. 13144. M. Nov. 5/16.
16 C. Fox, H. 12107. M. April 23/17.
16 C. Gaylor, G. 203197. M. April 23/17.
16 C. Hancock, Sergt. Reecie. 692. M. April 23/17.
16 C. XI Hepplestone, W. 1676. M. April 23/17.
16 C. XII Hills, Herbert. 203292. M. April 23/17.
16 C. Hinds, L.-Cpl. F. L. 396. W. and M. April 23/17.
16 C. King, L.-Cpl. E. C. P. Y/52. M. April 23/17.
16 C. Parsloe, R. 34043. M. April 23/17.
16 C. XII Peel, Norman. R/21404. W. and M. April 23/17.
*16 C. L.G.S. Postans, J. W. C/1409. W. and M. April 23/17.
16 C. XII Prior, Fredk. John. 34050. M. April 23/17.
16 C. Ramsey, G. 37012. M. April 23/17.
16 C. XII Salmon, H. A. R/34060. M. April 23/17.
16 C. Thorp, Chas. Jas. 34083. M. April 23/17.
16 C. XII Wells, Geo. W. 11686. W. and M. April 23/17.
*16 C. XI Whitworth, N. 12575. W. and M. April 23/17.
16 C. IX Williams, C. H. 234098. M. April 23/17.
16 C. X Willis, Edw. F. 12917. W. and M. April 23/17.
16 C. XII Wood, L.-Cpl. Walter Geo. R/37220 M. April 23/17.
*16 D. XIV Demery, A. E. 5059. W. and M. April 23/17.
‡16 D. Doody, G. 37232. M. May 20/17.
16 D. Eccles, Edward. 36987. M. May 20/17.
16 D. XIV Hague, J. 32788. W. and M. April 23/17.
‡16 D. Hancock, L.-Cpl. H. 990. M. May 20/17.
*16 D. XIII Hardiman, Wm. Thos. 203235. M. May 20/17.
16 D. XV James, Wm. Chas. 30227. M. May 20/17.
‡16 D. Jones, P. P. 865. M. May 20/17.
‡16 D. Lucas, B. S. 37227. M. May 20/17.
*16 D. XVI Mayfield, John Wm. R/36166. M. May 20/17.

King's Royal Rifle Corps—contd.

## *B.E.F.*

*16 D. XIV Mayo, A. J. 36227. M. May 20/17.
‡16 D. Pennington, A. S. 36155. M. May 20/17.
*16 D. XV Phillips, S. C. 19288. M. May 20/17.
16 D. Poole, F. E. 18927 M. Nov. 6/16.
*16 D. XIV Reed, L.-Cpl. Stanley. A/203255. M. May 20/17.
‡16 D. Robins, G. 34054. M. May 20/17.
*16 D. XIV Sibley, Cpl. Ben. C/303. M. May 20/17.
*16 D. XV Smith, L.-Cpl. J. C/350. M. May 20/17.
‡16 D. Till, H. 203283. M. May 20/17.
‡16 D. Walker, Cpl. R. 880. M. May 20/17.
16 D. XIII Wheeler, Henry Stanley. 34344. M. May 20/17.
16 D. XVI Zimmerman, Jos. C/6123. M. April 28/17.
‡16 ? Heath, F. 36214. W. and M. April 23/17.
‡16 ? Keegan, T. J. 34015. W. and M. April 23/17.
‡16 ? Stokes, H. G. 7595. W. and M. April 23/17.
17 A. Oxlade, A. A. R/17365. M. Sept. 3/16. R/Enq.
17 B. I.T.M. Blagdon, Wm. Chas. 3016. (117 Bgde.) M. Sept. 3/16. R/Enq
17 C. XI Ellis, Arthur. 4063. M. Sept. 3/16. R/Enq.
‡18 A. I.T.M. Battye, Harry. C/7452. (122 Bgde 1 Bty.) W. and M. Sept. 15/16. R/Enq.
‡18 A. II Holmes R. F. C/1253. M. June 7/17.
18 A. Pearson, Allen. C/7675. K. Sept. 15/16. Det.D./B.
‡18 C. Ford, Albert Edward. C/7612. W. and M. Sept. 15/16. R/Enq.
18 C. Hellowell, Ernest. 6638. M. Sept. 15/16. R./Enq.
*18 C. Wallis, Joseph. 6749. W. and M. Sept. 15/16. R/Enq.
‡18 D. XV Halls, L.-Cpl. Albert Daniel. 200844. M. June 14/17.
*18 D. XVI Spinks. C/6878. K. May 21/17. Det.D./B.
21 C. Postgate, Sid. 12971. W. and M. Sept. 15-17/16. R/Enq.
21 D. Hope, Charles. 19483. K. Sept. 15-17/16. Det.D./B. R/Enq.

# LANCASHIRE FUSILIERS.

## *B.E.F.*

1 **Rogers, 2nd Lieut. A. E.** M. May 3/17.
‡1 A. Bradbury, R. 25200. M. May 30/17.
1 A. III Butterworth, H. 202998. (Fr. 5th.) W. and M. April 25/17.
1 A. Cockerill, G. 35982. W. and M. April 25/17.
‡1 A. Graney, C. 9709. M. May 30/17.
‡1 A. Heap, W. 29988. M. May 30/17.
‡1 A. McGarry, Thos. 19213. M. Mar. 23/17.
‡1 A. Nield, J. 29680. M. May 30/17.
‡1 A. III Nuttall, A. 34551. M. May 30/17.
‡1 A. Owen, S. 5610. M. May 30/17.
‡1 A. Pollard, Thos. E. 2992. M. May 30/17.
1 A. Roden, J. 14602 W. and M. April 25/17.
‡1 A. I Sabine, Cpl. A. 1550. M. May 30/17.
‡1 A. Walker, G. F. 3528. M. May 30/17.
‡1 A. Wrigley, H. 41811. W. and M. May 30/17.
1 C. IX Brown, Robert. 28708. (Fr. 13th.) M. Feb. 28/17.
1 C. Johnson, James H. 20711. W. and M. Feb. 28/17.
‡1 C. Valentine, Samuel John. 38337. (Fr. 8th, 307865.) M. April 25/17.

**Lancashire Fusiliers—contd.**

*B.E.F.*

| | | | |
|---|---|---|---|
| 1 C. XI | Walker, Thos. 31126. | M. April 25/17. | |
| 1 D. XIII | Freeman, G. R. 20692. | M. Feb. 28/17. | |
| *1 D. XV | Kelleher, L.-Cpl. Jas. 21414. | M. May 30/17. | |
| ‡1 D. | Kelly, T. 21149. | W. and M. May 30/17. | |
| ‡1 D. | Marsh, F. 24575. | M. May 30/17. | |
| *1 D. XIII | Mooney, Joseph P. 35995. | M. May 30/17. | |
| ‡1 D. XIV | Taylor, Phil. 34461. | M. May 30/17. | |
| *1 D. XIV | Whittaker, L.-Cpl. W. H. 3866. | M. May 30/17. | |
| 2 | **Briggs, 2nd Lieut. E. M.** (Fr. 7th.) | M. May 3/17. | |
| 2 | **Concannon, 2nd Lieut. J.** | M. May 3/17. | |
| 2 | **Davenport, 2nd Lieut. R.** | M. May 3/17. | |
| 2 | **Norris, 2nd Lieut. B.** | M. May 3/17. | |
| 2 C. | **Slater, 2nd Lieut. J. E.** (Fr. 5 East Lancs.) | W. and M. May 3/17. | |
| 2 A. I | Batchelor, H. 25736. | M. May 3/17. | |
| ‡2 A. | Davies, L.-Cpl. W. 35898. (Fr. 3rd.) | M. May 30/17. | |
| ‡2 A. | Gaffney, H. 37548. | M. Oct. 23/16. | R/Enq. |
| ‡2 A. | Gilbert, Arthur Richard. 37082. | M. Oct. 12/16. | R/Enq. |
| 2 A. L.G.S. | Hill, L.-Cpl. D. 27937. | M. May 3/17. | |
| 2 A. I | Lomas, Herbert. 37407. | M. Oct. 12/16. | R/Enq. |
| 2 A. IV | Park, Harold. 20811. | M. May 3/17. | |
| 2 A. | Pearson, J. T. 3/21399. | M. Oct. 23/16. | R/Enq. |
| 2 A. L.G.S. | Perry, William. 2764. | M. Oct. 12/16. | R/Enq. |
| 2 A. | Spowage, G. H. 37468. | M. Oct. 12/16. | R/Enq. |
| ‡2 A. | Swarbrick, J. 3735. | M. May 3/17. | |
| *2 B. VIII | Avis, H. 24679. | M. May 3/17. | |
| ‡2 B. | Bagnall, S. 16411. (Fr. 18th.) | M. May 3/17. | |
| 2 B. L.G.S. | Breeze, E. C. 24447. | M. May 3/17. | |
| 2 B. VIII | Brown, L.-Cpl. A. 24490. | M. May 3/17. | |
| 2 B. | Brown, P. 37040. | M. Oct. 12/16. | R/Enq. |
| ‡2 B. | Calvert, G. E. 34714. (Fr. 13th.) | M. May 3/17. | |
| *2 B. | Clarke, R. 6975. (Fr. 12th.) | M. May 3/17. | |
| 2 B. VI | Clegg, J. T. 25240. | M. May 3/17. | |
| ‡2 B. | Clough, E. 24477. (Fr. 3rd.) | M. May 3/17. | |
| ‡2 B. | Clugston, C. 3/24524. | M. May 3/17. | |
| ‡2 B. | Cunliffe, J. 15341. (Fr. 20th.) | M. May 3/17. | |
| ‡2 B. | Curtis, A. H. 24094. (Fr. 3rd.) | M. May 3/17. | |
| ‡2 B. | Dagg, L.-Cpl. W. 7403. (Fr. 13th.) | M. May 3/17. | |
| ‡2 B. | Davidson, J. 24548. (Fr. 3rd.) | M. May 3/17. | |
| ‡2 B. | Dean, L.-Cpl. W. 24102. (Fr. 3rd.) | M. May 3/17. | |
| 2 B. VIII | Dunbavin, Thomas. 19304. | M. Oct. 23/16. | R/Enq. |
| 2 B. VI | Eatch, Ernest. 37074. | M. Oct. 23/16. | R/Enq. |
| 2 B. VI | Edwards, Chas. Kemble. 37829 | M. Dec. 7-23/16. | R/Enq. |
| ‡2 B. VIII | Farnworth, Thomas. 21162. | M. May 3/17. | |
| ‡2 B. | Farrell, T. 9660. (Fr. 10th.) | M. May 3/17. | |
| ‡2 B. | Fidler, H. 24459. (Fr. 3rd.) | M. May 3/17. | |
| ‡2 B. | Fleming, L. 3672. (Fr. 9th.) | M. May 3/17. | |
| ‡2 B. | Foster, L.-Cpl. H. 28170. (Fr. 4th.) | M. May 3/17. | |
| 2 B. VIII | Giddins, Cpl. Albert. 8435. | M. Oct. 12/16. | R/Enq. |
| *2 B. | Griffiths, Sergt. Frank. 2673. | M. May 3/17. | |
| ‡2 B. | Johnson, L.-Cpl. J. 6738. | M. May 3/17. | |
| ‡2 B. | Jones, L.-Cpl. O. S. V. 4485. | M. May 3/17. | |
| ‡2 B. | Leech, John. 21651. | M. May 3/17. | |
| ‡2 B. | Lomax, J. 202126. | M. May 3/17. | |
| *2 B. | Lovell, H. B. 238007. | M. May 3/17. | |
| ‡2 B. | Lumb, Sergt. J. W. 1326. | M. May 3/17. | |

Lancashire Fusiliers—contd.

*B.E.F.*

2 B. VII Mills, Wm. 4465. (Fr. 9th.) M. May 3/17.
2 B. Moores, Alfred. 15124. (Fr. 16th.) M. May 3/17.
‡2 B. Murphy, L.-Cpl. T. 2724. M. May 3/17.
‡2 B. Nuttall, F. 3/24461. M. May 3/17.
*2 B. Percy, John Robert. 37612. M. Oct. 23/16. R/Enq.
2 B. VI Pearson, Fred. 41485. M. May 3/17.
‡2 B. Potts, D. 22/33714. M. May 3/17.
‡2 B. V Rickard, J. H. 21/35161. M. May 3/17.
2 B. L.G.S. Reynolds, Frank. 24671. M. May 3/17.
2 B. L.G.S. Stott, David. 3/29445. M. Oct. 12/16. R/Enq.
‡2 B. Talks, J. 37924. M. May 3/17.
2 B. VIII Thomas, Joseph Wm. 238004. M. May 3/17.
*2 B. VII Walker, G. D. 38369. M. May 3/17.
‡2 B. Waring, E. 11/32215. M. May 3/17.
‡2 B. Westley, T. F. 238017. M. May 3/17.
2 B. VIII Wilkins, A. 37206. M. May 3/17.
2 B. VII Winstanley, J. E. 23770. M. May 3/17.
‡2 B. Wolstencroft, J. 4/28315. M. May 3/17.
*2 B. Wood, James. 3/18215. M. Oct. 12/16. R/Enq.
‡2 C. Ashworth, F. 32250. (Fr. 21st.) M. May 3/17.
‡2 C. Ault, W. 21038. (Fr. 9th.) M. May 3/17.
2 C. XII Barrett, John. 242995. W. and M. May 3/17.
2 C. XII Child, Ephraim. 22770. M. May 3/17.
*2 C. Child, Ronald J. 32476. K. April 9/17. Det.D./B.
‡2 C. Cleaver, L.-Cpl. C. F. 24192. (Fr. 3rd.) M. May 3/17.
‡2 C. Cocker, D. 37666. M. May 3/17.
‡2 C. Cocker, H. 24518. (Fr. 3rd.) M. May 3/17.
‡2 C. Couperthwaite, J. E. 20324. M. May 3/17.
*2 C. Curley, Sergt. John Thomas. 2/2872. M. May 3/17.
*2 C. Dawson, Thomas. 28242. M. May 3/17.
‡2 C. Eddleston, J. 26455. (Fr. 17th.) M. May 3/17.
*2 C. IX Johnson, G. W. 9244. M. May 3/17.
2 C. XI Joynson, William. 37673. W. and M. May 3/17.
2 C. X Langham, Harry. 37112. M. May 3/17.
*2 C. XII Leach, F. 32292. M. Oct. 12/16. R/Enq.
2 C. XI Lichtenstein, Monty. 20335. M. May 3/17.
2 C. McGrath, R. J. 5381. M. Oct. 12/16. R/Enq.
2 C. Maguire, E. 305996. (3343.) (Fr. 8th.) M. May 3/17.
‡2 C. Maines, T. 4440. M. May 3/17.
‡2 C. Mercer, J. 9387. M. May 3/17.
2 C. Mountford, George. 37132. M. Oct. 12/16.
‡2 C. Norman, Cpl. J. 3210. M. May 3/17.
2 C. Openshaw, Arthur. 37677. M. Oct. 23/16. R/Enq.
‡2 C. Parkinson, Cpl. J. 4/28339. M. May 3/17.
*2 C. IX Pearson, John. 10186. M. May 3/17.
‡2 C. Rosbotham, T. J. 37961. M. May 3/17.
‡2 C. Rush, A. 37951. M. May 3/17.
‡2 C. Short, W. H. 32520. M. May 3/17.
‡2 C. Shutt, J. 17/22209. M. May 3/17.
2 C. XII Spencer, Robt. 37864. M. May 3/17.
2 C. XI Standing, W. H. 35110. (Fr. 21st.) M. May 3/17.

**Lancashire Fusiliers**—contd.

*B.E.F.*

| | | |
|---|---|---|
| ‡2 C. | Sutcliffe, E. 37931. | M. May 3/17. |
| ‡2 C. | Thomas, L.-Cpl. H. 3/3136. | M. May 3/17. |
| 2 C. | Thorp, J. 37193. | M. May 3/17. |
| ‡2 C. | Tinker, Cpl. T. 552. | M. May 3/17. |
| 2 C. | Tucker, D.C.M., Cpl. Thomas. 552. | M. May 3/17. |
| 2 C. X | Turner, J. E. 37186. | M. Oct. 12/16. R/Enq. |
| *2 C. IX | Watson, W. 38383. | M. May 3/17. |
| 2 C. IX | Wharfe, Frank. 24017. | M. May 3/17. |
| 2 D. | Aspin, Cpl. James. 192. | M. Oct. 23/16. R/Enq. |
| 2 D. | Bowring, L. C. 2754. | M. April 11/17. |
| ‡2 D. | Eden, G. T. 22698. (Fr. 16th.) | M. May 3/17. |
| 2 D. | Gosling, Sig. Edwd. 5608. | M. May 3/17. |
| 2 D. XVI | Grundy, Herbert. 34712. (Fr. 13th.) | M. May 3/17. |
| *2 D. XV | Helliwell, J. W. 20344. | M. May 3/17. |
| 2 D. | Highcock, Jas. 26265. (Fr. 21st.) | W. and M. April 9/17. |
| ‡2 D. | Hodkinson, W. 25877. | M. May 3/17. |
| 2 D. | Kirkbride, C. 4679. | M. April 11/17. |
| *2 D. XV | Lumley, Josiah. 35780. | K. May 3/17. Det.D./B. |
| ‡2 D. XV | McDonald, John William. 5225. | M. Oct. 23/16. R/Enq. |
| 2 D. | Marsh, William. 37131. | M. Oct. 12/16. R/Enq. |
| ‡2 D. XIV | Parkinson, Frank. 22/32753. | M. May 3/17. |
| ‡2 D. | Scarisbrick, J. 20/31564. | M. May 3/17. |
| 2 D. | Simpson, Joseph. 37681. | M. Oct. 23/16. R/Enq. |
| *2 D. | Stainton, John. 38380. | M. May 3/17. |
| 2 D. | Street, Wm. Henry. 37680. (Late 3/6, 3895.) | M. Oct. 23/16. R/Enq. |
| *2 D. | Wilkinson, J. A. 36578. | M. May 3/17. |
| ‡2 D. XVI | Worsley, William. 12070. | M. May 3/17. |
| ‡2 D. XV | Wright, J. H. C. 37211. | M. Oct. 12/16. R/Enq. |
| 2 Pioneer | S. Dean, Ellis. 32485. | M. May 3/17. |
| 2 ? | Lewis, Arthur. 11. | K. Feb. 6/17. Det.D./B. |
| ‡5 C. IX | Jones, J. A. 235252. | W. Unoff. M. June 7/17. |
| 5 D. | Gordon, H. A. 201741. | M. April 14/17. |
| 2/5 W. | Lovell, H. 7652. (4356.) (Fr. E. Lancs.) | W. and M. Sept. 10/16. R/Enq. |
| 2/5 X. VIII | O'Rorke, Joseph. 2535. | W. and M. June 28/16 |
| 2/5 Y. | Schofield, Richard. 5255. | K. Sept. 9/16. Det.D./B. |
| 2/5 Y. | Wolstencroft, R. 202145. | W. and M. Jan. 8/17. |
| *2/5 W. IV | Buckley, James. 5260. (Fr. 6th, 11834.) | M. Sept. 9/16. R/Enq. |
| *3/5 | **Mackay, Capt. S. F. H.** (Fr. 2/5 E. Lancs.) | M. June 13/17. |
| 3/5 C. | Murphy, H. D. 203167. | M., bel. K. April 2/17. |
| 3/5 C. | Swift, Thomas. 203153. (6233.) | M., bel. K. April 2/17. |
| ‡6 C. | Bamford, W. 241981. | M. May 25/17. |
| *6 C. X | Maddock, Henrick. 242455. | M. May 3/17. |
| ‡2/6 A. | Laycock, A. 240800. | M. June 13-14/17. |
| ‡2/6 A. L.G.S. | Peak, L.-Cpl. J. G. 242142. | M. June 13/17. |
| ‡2/6 D. | Anderson, A. 241007. | M. June 13/17. |
| *2/6 D. XIII | Caley, Robert. 243127. | M. June 13/17. |
| 7 A. | Rowley, L.-Cpl. Geo. 282161. (5075.) (Fr. 3/5 Manchesters.) | M. April 13/17. |
| 7 D. XIV | Shaw, F. 281531. (4129.) | M. April 13/17. |
| 2/7 B. | Copestick, H. 281928. | M. April 18/17. |
| 2/7 B. | Stephens, W. B. 282274. (5200.) | M. April 18/17. |
| 2/7 C. | Evans, Harry. 281868. (Late 4687.) | M. April 18/17. |

**Lancashire Fusiliers—contd.**

*B.E.F.*

2/7 C. Simms, H. 281979. **M. April 18/17.**
2/7 C. Unsworth, W. 281065. **M. April 18/17.**
‡8 D. Chase, S. 306658. M. May 25/17.
8 D. XIV Edge, A. 31792. (Fr. 4th.) **M. May 3/17.**
‡2/8 A. Dixon, J. E. 307038. M. May 15/17.
9 W. Burns, James. 4404. M. **Sept. 26/16.** R/Enq.
9 W. Chapman, Fred. 22958. (Fr. 3rd.) M. **Sept. 26/16.** R/Enq.
9 W. M.G.S. Morgan, John J. 3057. M. **Sept. 26/16.**
*9 W. Poole, Lot. 27904. M. **Sept. 26/16.** R/Enq.
9 W. Robinson, Edwin. 27986. M. **Sept. 26/16.** R/Enq.
9 W. M.G.S. Robinson, J. W. 27809. M. **Sept. 26/16.**
9 W. Schofield, Robert. 36370. (Fr. 2/5.) M. **Sept. 26/16.** R/Enq.
9 X. Sanderson, Frank. 27821. M. **Sept. 26/16.**
‡9 X. Sowden, R. 36566. M. **Sept. 26/16.** R/Enq.
9 Y. Brennand, Eddwis. 9418. M. **Sept. 26/16.** R/Enq.
*9 Y. Cryer, Sergt. Liebig. 12695. W. and M. **Sept. 26/16.** R/Enq.
*9 Y. Heathcote, Maurice. 3555. M. **Sept. 26/16.** R/Enq.
9 Y. Robinson, Alfred Edgar. 36579. M. **Sept. 26/16.** R/Enq.
‡9 Y. X Stephen, Harold. 36380. M. **Sept. 26/16.**
9 Z. Laycock, Walter. 27691. M. **Sept. 26/16.** R/Enq.
9 Z. XVI Shannon, P. 27703. M. **Sept. 26/16.** R/Enq.
9 ? I.T.M. Cryer, John Henry. 12/9944. M. **Sept. 29/16.**
10 **Bingham, 2nd Lieut. B. A.** W. Unoff. M. **May 12/17.**
10 **Comyn, Major D. C. E. ff.** M., bel. K. **May 11/17.**
'10 **Harriss, Capt. R. E.** M., bel. K. **May 12/17.**
10 **Hastings, 2nd Lieut. J. L.** W. Unoff. M. **May 17/17.**
10 **Knight, 2nd Lieut. E. J.** (Fr. 7th.) M. **May 12/17.**
‡10 A. Bailey, Ernest. 37988. W. and M. **April 30/17.**
*10 A. III Beatson, L.-Cpl. Leonard Sydney. 25746. K. **May 13/17.** Det.D./B.
‡10 A. Clay, F. 22023. M. **May 12/17.**
‡10 A. Freedman, A. 30854. M. **May 12/17.**
‡10 A. Gill, J. E. 7743. M. **May 12/17.**
‡10 A. Grindrod, H. 24538. M. **May 12/17.**
10 A. I Jarvis, R. 24789. M. **May 12/17.**
10 A. L.G.S. Lee, Cpl. Ernest. 13422. W. Unoff. M. **May 12/17.**
‡10 A. II Lord, Samuel. 20055. M. **May 12/17.**
10 A. III Mersom, L.-Cpl. J. F. 39538. M. **May 12/17.**
*10 A. II Pearson, Sergt. E. H. 24784. W. and M. **12/17.**
*10 A. IV Smithies, Cpl. E. 33737. M. **May 12/17.**
*10 A. V Maskew, J. B. 38024. M. **May 12/17.**
‡10 A. Woolvin, L.-Cpl. E. 4955. M. **May 12/17.**
‡10 B. Boyes, H. 41979. M. **May 12/17.**
‡10 B. V Carter, Henry John. 41978. M. **May 12/17.**
10 B. VI Cheetham, J. M. 39563. M. **May 12/17.**
‡10 B. VIII Cunliffe, W. H. 38000. M. **May 12/17.**
‡10 B. Dabbs, E. 9163. M. **May 12/17.**
‡10 B. Davison, W. 34504. M. **May 12/17.**
‡10 B. Kenyon, W. 38020. M. **May 12/17.**
*10 B. Mooney, Henry. 4332. M. **May 12/17.**
‡10 B. Noble, Cpl. J. 39532. M. **May 12/17.**
‡10 B. Oates, F. A. 39554. M. **May 12/17.**
‡10 B. Pascall, Sergt. W. W. 24816. M. **May 12/17.**
‡10 B. Pickup, J. 38033. M. **May 12/17.**
‡10 B. Seed, Sergt. J. 24808. M. **May 12/17.**
‡10 B. Shepherd, W. 29794. M. **May 12/17.**
10 B. VIII Smith, Cpl. Fred. Rawlinson. 24793. M. **May 12/17.**
‡10 B. Taylor, F. 17981. M. **May 12/17.**

**Lancashire Fusiliers—contd.**

*B.E.F.*

*10 B. VIII Williams, J. 10008. — W. and M. 12/17.
10 C. Maude, John Chas. 13571. — W. and M. Oct. 8/16.
‡10 C. Roberts, R. 34843. — W. and M. Nov. 8/16. R/Enq.
10 C. IX Whatmough, Herbert. 24589. — M. May 12/17.
‡10 D. Allwood, S. 31474. — M. May 12/17.
‡10 D. Arrowsmith, J. 39929. — M. May 12/17.
10 D. XV Ashton, L.-Cpl. Wm. 28522. — M. May 12/17.
‡10 D. Boyle, Frank. 4327. — M. May 12/17.
10 D. XIV Coxon, John Henry. 25142. — M. May 12/17.
‡10 D. Davies, L.-Cpl. J. 5703. — M. May 12/17.
10 D. XV Holmes, L.-Cpl. John Percy. 39570. — M. May 12/17.
‡10 D. Horey, N. 13629. — M. May 12/17.
‡10 D. Hughes, A. 28145. — M. May 12/17.
10 D. XV Parkinson, Joseph. 24500. — M. May 12/17.
‡10 D. Shuttleworth, R. 35690. — M. May 12/17.
10 D. XIV Simpson, K. B. 15645. — M. May 12/17.
‡10 D. Stevens, R. 5327. — M. May 12/17.
‡10 D. Stott, T. 34954. — M. May 12/17.
10 D. XIV Stott, J. W. 20170. — K. May 12/17. Det.D./B.
‡10 D. Tempest, J. 34563. — M. May 12/17.
10 D. XIV Whitney, A. E. 41991. — M. May 12/17.
‡10 D. Widdowson, J. 19182. — M. May 12/17.
10 D. XV Wynn, Fredk. 19115. — M. May 5/17.
11 A. Ashton, William. 8745. — K. Oct. 7/16. Det.D./B.
‡11 A. Dean, Francis Ernest. 34682. — M. Oct. 21/16. R/Enq.
11 A. or B. Duckworth, Wm. 32236. — M. Oct. 2/16.
11 A. Fallon, Cpl. J. P. 28515. — W. and M. Oct. 21/16.
11 A. Tillotson, R. 5473. — M. Oct. 21/16. R/Enq.
11 A. I Worsley, Thomas. 34637. — M. Oct. 21/16. R/Enq.
11 B. Henigan, John. 28811. — M. Oct. 21/16.
11 C. Butler, J. H. 32251. — M. Oct. 21/16.
*11 C. Crabtree, Lewis. 27185. — W. and M. Oct. 21/16. R/Enq.
11 C. Rush, Alfred. 26882. — W. and M. Oct. 21/16.
‡11 D. Hooper, Thomas. 8940. — M. Oct. 21/16. R/Enq.
16 A. Emery, P. 31370. — M. April 1/17.
*16 C. XII Fairclough, Samuel. 31428. — K. Apr. 17/17. Det.D./B.
*16 C. Foster, Wm. 37781. — M. Nov. 23/16. R/Enq.
17 Y. XII Bradley, E. 34321. — M. April 12/17.
17 Z. Wilson, Sergt. J. H. 10539. — W. and M. April 14/17.
18 **Prescott, 2nd Lieut. R. J.** — M. April 15/17.
18 W. I Barrett, Thomas. 24614. — W. and M. April 15/17.
18 W. *Chafer, Harry. 22771. — M. April 15/17.
18 W. Chapman, A. 28762. — M. April 15/17.
18 W. Doherty, Sergt.-Maj. 16242. — W. and M. April 15/17.
18 W. II Farr, Alfred Sutton. 15912. — W. and M. April 15/17.
18 W. Gee, Cpl. H. 15747. — M. April 15/17.
18 W. Holyoak, T. W. 22794. — M. April 15/17.
18 W. Le Grice, W. 22800. — M. April 15/17.
18 W. IV Lee, Joseph Collis. 22799. — W. and M. April 15/17.
18 W. Philpots, J. 21226. — M. April 15/17.
18 W. Skerrington, G. 22703. — M. April 15/17.
‡17 W. Starchfield, Sergt. W. 14134. — M. May 6/17.
18 W. Wardle, Bandsman R. 16162. — W. Unoff. M. April 15/17.
18 Z. XIV Coote, Geo. 24884. — W. and M. April 15/17.
18 Z. Smart, W. H. 24615. — M. April 15/17.
18 Z. XIV Wilkinson, Ernest. 22708. — W. and M. April 14/17.
20 **Gibbons, 2nd Lieut. E. I.** — W. and M. April 29/17.
20 Y. Tonge, P. 35494. — W. and M. May 1/17.

Lancashire Fusiliers—contd.

## *BALKANS.*

| | | |
|---|---|---|
| 12 ? | Barrett, E. 21448. | W. and M. Sept. 14/16. |

## EAST LANCASHIRE REGIMENT.

### *B.E.F.*

| | | |
|---|---|---|
| ‡1 A. | Hartley, F. 36567. | M. May 11/17. |
| 1 A. | Hulse, E. 29295. | M. Oct. 18/16. R./Enq. |
| 1 A. | Pilling, Herbert. 26362. | M. Oct. 18/16. R/Enq. |
| 1 A. IV L.G.S. | Robson, E. 22660. | M. Oct. 18/16. R/Enq. |
| ‡1 C. X | Cowgill, W. 34324. | W. and M. May 11/17. |
| 1 D. XIII | Cocking, Percy. 18522. | W. and M. April 15/17. |
| 1 D. XIII | Nicholson, T. 11079. | W. and M. Aug. 27/16. R/Enq. |
| ‡1 D. XIII | Smith, Samuel. 29154. | M. Oct. 18/16. R/Enq. |
| ‡1 ? | Mansell, Joseph Martin. 29321. | D/W. Oct. 25/16. Det.D./B. |
| 2 A. IV | Shaw, James Albert. 12363. | K. Oct. 23/16. Det.D./B. R/Enq. |
| *2 A. | Thompson, G. 8907. | K. Mar. 4/17. Det.D./B. |
| 2 B. | Crowther, Wilfred. 22274. | M. Unoff. W. Mar. 4/17. |
| *2 B. | Dooley, Thomas. 23857. | M. Oct. 23/16. R/Enq. |
| 2 B. V | Pilling, Irvine. 28994. | M. Mar. 4/17. |
| 2 B. V | Wilkinson, Sergt. Harold Cecil. 18573. | K. Mar. 4/17. Det.D./B. |
| 2 C. X | Bowden, Joseph. 19427. | K. Aug. 28/16. Det.D./B. |
| 2 D. XV | Carlton, Lewis. 23837. | M. April 10/17. |
| 2 D. | Clayton, Harry. 18269. | M. April 10/17. |
| 2 D. | Cusse, L. V. 9711. | M. April 10/17. |
| 2 D. | Leary, R. 9273. | M. Mar. 4/17. |
| 2 D. | Marsden, A.-Sergt. H. 36601. | M. April 10/17. |
| 2 D. | Ratcliffe, Richard. 28676. | M. April 10/17. |
| 4 B. V | Battle, Jas. 202070. | M. April 24/17. |
| 4 B. | Bleasdale, J. 201818. | M. April 25/17. |
| 4 B. VIII | Pickup, Albert. 201976. (4670.) | M. April 25/17. |
| 4 C. | Lyons, L.-Cpl. P. 200703. (2588.) | M. April 24/17. |
| 4 C. | Stewart, H. 201930. | W. and M. April 24/17. |
| 5 A. | Ashton, G. 242752. | M. April 28/17. |
| 5 A. | Astin, Arthur. 241320. (3622.) | M. April 28/17. |
| 5 A. | Bentham, Richard. 241661. (4174.) | M. April 28/17. |
| 5 A. | Campion, L.-Cpl. W. E. 240754. | M., bel. K. April 28/17. |
| 5 A. | Clough, J. 241993. | M. April 28/17. |
| 5 A. | Cook, R. 240577. | M. April 28/17. |
| 5 A. | Greenwood, R. 241418. | M. April 28/17. |
| 5 A. | Hartley, R. 241273. | M. April 28/17. |
| 5 A. | Heys, R. H. 241677. | M. April 28/17. |
| 5 A. L.G.S. | Johnston, John Willie. 241637. | M. April 28/17. |
| 5 A. | Keys, W. 241626. | M. April 28/17. |
| 5 A. | Lowe, R. J. 241958. | M. April 28/17. |
| 5 A. | Whitehead, J. W. 241142. | M. April 28/17. |
| ‡5 B. | Barclay, J. 242567. | W. and M. May 31/17. |
| ‡5 D. | Harrison, Sgt. W. H. 241077. | W. and M. May 31/17. |
| 5 D. | Simpson, W. 241350. | M. May 31/17. |
| 7 B. | Wood, Percy. 29862. | M. June 7/17. |
| ‡7 C. | Harrison, G. W. 28573. | M. Mar. 19/17. |

**Lancashire Regiment, East—contd.**

*B.E.F.*

| | | |
|---|---|---|
| *7 C. | Stuttard, Harry. 23274. | M. Oct. 26/16. R/Enq. |
| 8 | **Burnett, Capt. I. A. K.** | W. and M. May 31/17. |
| 8 | **Edmondson, Capt. F.** | M. April 11/17. |
| 8 | **Forster, Capt. W. J.** | K. May 30-31/17. Det.D./B. |
| 8 | **Heard, 2nd Lieut. C. M.** | W. and M. April 10/17. |
| 8 | **Wright, Capt. E. M.** | M. April 11/17. |
| 8 A. I | Armstrong, Frank. 32194. | W. and M. April 23/17. R/Enq. |
| 8 A. | Banks, A. 28457. | M. April 28/17. |
| ‡8 A. | Davis, T. B. 34430. | M. April 28/17. |
| 8 A. II | Evans, Walker. 24692. | W. and M. April 28/17. |
| 8 A. II | Foulds, Robert. 29098. | M. April 11/17. |
| 8 A. | Hartley, F. W. 34185. | M. April 11/17. |
| 8 A. L.G.S. | Lindsay, Harold. 29110. | M. April 28/17. |
| 8 A. | Mashiter, L.-Cpl. Ernest. 23019. | M. April 28/17. |
| 8 A. III | Reid, Samuel. 29084. | W. and M. April 28/17. |
| 8 A. III | Roberts, John. 32231. | W. and M. April 28/17. |
| 8 A. II | Smith, Cpl. Richard. 18454. | W. and M. April 11/17. |
| ‡8 A. II | Stocks, Fred. 29554. | M. April 23/17. |
| *8 B. VII | Buck, Sydney. 203148. | M. May 31/17. |
| ‡8 B. | Butterworth, L.-Cpl. W. B. 23034. | W. and M. May 31/17. |
| ‡8 B. VI | Clayton, Wm. Lockwood. 37190. | W. and M. May 31/17. |
| 8 B. VI | Crook, James. 16491. | W. and M. Nov. 16/16. |
| 8 B. | Ellison, J. 26940. | M. April 11/17. |
| 8 B. | Flyn, J. 13666. | M. April 23/17. |
| 8 B. VII | Harris, L.-Cpl. H. S. 32248. | W. and M. April 11/17. |
| 8 B. | Neil, J. 14309. | M. April 11/17. |
| 8 B. | Oliver, F. W. 29135. | M. April 14/17. |
| 8 B. | Procter, A. E. 29468. | M. Jan. 15/17. |
| ‡8 B. | Richardson, L.-Cpl. J. 24009. | W. and M. April 28/17. |
| *8 B. VI | Riding, R. Homer. 28982. | W. and M. April 11/17. |
| 8 B. V | Roche, John Joseph. 29127. | M. April 11/17. |
| 8 B. | Simpson, A. 235032. | M. April 28/17. |
| 8 B. | Smith, F. 29556. | W. and M. April 11/17. |
| 8 B. VIII | Stockdale, Wm. 36979. | M. April 28/17. |
| 8 B. | Walker, G. P. 34507. | M. April 14/17. |
| *8 B. VI | Whittaker, Joseph. 27412. | M. May 31/17. |
| 8 C. | Atherton, R. 19683. | M. April 28/17. |
| 8 C. | Bowes, J. F. 29497. | M. April 11/17. |
| ‡8 C. | Coll, Rowland. 17984. | M. May 31/17. |
| ‡8 C. IX | Etherington, W. 29509. | W. and M. Nov. 16/16. R/Enq. |
| 8 C. XI | Graham, Rennie. 34440. | M. April 28/17. |
| ‡8 C. | Howarth, M. 10779. | M. April 28/17. |
| ‡8 C. XI | Ingham, Wm. 37050. | M. April 11/17. |
| 8 C. | Jepson, A. 235015. | M. April 10/17. |
| 8 C. | Lowe, W. 29539. | M. April 28/17. |
| 8 C. | McDermott, L.-Cpl. J. 23371. | M. April 28/17. |
| ‡8 C. | McGinty, J. 6508. | M. May 31/17. |
| 8 C. IX | Oakley, Harry. 17487. | M. April 28/17. |
| 8 C. XII | Richardson, Robt. 35288. | M. April 28/17. |
| 8 C. | Rossi, J. J. 28906. | M. April 28/17. |
| *8 C. | Smalley, Herbert. 37071. (Fr. 153rd Co., R.E.) | M. April 28/17. |
| 8 C. | Tyldesley, A. S. 37360. | M. April 23/17. |
| 8 D. | Blades, A. 18729. | M. April 11/17. |
| ‡8 D. | Cooper, W. A. 35044. | M. April 28/17. |
| ‡8 D. | Grady, Sergt. M. 16317. | W. and M. May 31/17. |
| 8 D. XV | Grogan, James. 37039. | W. and M. April 25/17. |
| ‡8 D. | Hall, R. 29145. | M. May 31/17. |

**Lancashire Regiment, East—contd.**

## *B.E.F.*

| | | |
|---|---|---|
| 8 D. XV | Hargreaves, G. 24655. | M. April 11/17. |
| 8 D. | Higson, A. 26984. | M. April 11/17. |
| 8 D. | Horner, J. 19690. | M. April 28/17. |
| ‡8 D. | Hoyle, J. W. 29773. | M. May 31/17. |
| 8 D. | Hutchinson, J. W. 37043. | M. April 11/17. |
| 8 D. | Lavelle, J. 37054. | M. April 11/17. |
| ‡8 D. | McClure, J. 21454. | M. May 31/17. |
| ‡8 D. | Peacock, G. L. 29114. | M. May 31/17. |
| *8 D. | Riley, L.-Cpl. John Jas. 235025. | M. May 31/17. |
| 8 D. XIII | Stott, Thomas. 37069. | M. April 11/17. |
| 8 D. XV | Tabron, Peter. 34688. | M. April 28/17. |
| ‡8 D. | Taylor, J. 37301. | M. May 31/17. |
| 8 D. | Wilkinson, R. 37070. | M. April 28/17. |
| 8 D. XIII | Williams, Thos. 37078. | M. May 31/17. |
| ‡8 ? M.G.S. | Lewis, Wm. 29536. | W. and M. May 31/17. |
| *11 Y. | Ward, Jas. 26961. | M. May 9/17. |

## *PERSIAN GULF.*

| | | |
|---|---|---|
| 6 A. | Laffy, John. 11319. | M. April 9/16. R/Enq. |
| 6 B. | Bunting, Arthur. 23428. | D/W. Feb. 10/17. Det.D./B. |
| 6 B. VI | Howarth, Geo. 27128. | K. Jan. 15/17. Det.D.B. |
| 6 C. | Ormerod, W. 19764. | W. and M. April 4/16. R/Enq. |
| 6 D. | Chapples, Sergt. Robert. 18817. | M. April 9/16. R./Enq. |
| 6 D. | Collinge, Arthur. 27398. | D/W. Feb. 26/17. Det.D./B. |
| 6 D. | Conway, John. 12043. | M. April 9/16. R./Enq. |
| 6 D. | Taylor, Arnold. 24299. | K. Mar. 9/17. Det.D./B. |
| 6 ? | Allen, Tom. 21848. | D/W. Feb. 8/17. Det.D./B. |
| ‡6 ? | Brightmore, S. 8268. | W. and M. April 30/17. |
| 6 ? | Hindle, J. 15916. | W. and M. Mar. 10/17. |
| 6 ? | Ollier, J. 6302. | M. Dec. 15/16. |

# LOYAL NORTH LANCASHIRE REGIMENT.

## *B.E.F.*

| | | |
|---|---|---|
| ‡1 | **Barrett, Lieut. R. C.** | M. July 10/17. |
| ‡1 | **Gifford, Lieut. G. A.** | M. July 10/17. |
| ‡1 | **Matthews, 2nd Lieut. S. E.** | M. July 10/17. |
| ‡1 | **Robb, Lt. H. A.** (Fr. 13 Sherwds.) | M. July 10/17. |
| ‡1 | **Shippard, 2nd Lieut. S. W.** | M. July 10/17. |
| 1 A. | Battersby, H. 23846. | M. Mar. 7/17. |
| 1 A. | Heron, Wm. R. 35966. | M. Feb. 25/17. |
| 1 A. III | Machin, Edward. 29657. | M. Feb. 24/17. |
| 1 B. VI | Hancock, Fredk. John. 26860. | K. Sept. 26/16. Det.D./B. R/Enq. |
| 1 B. | James, W. G. 26872. | M. Mar. 7/17. |
| 1 C. | Heaney, James. 26757. | M. Sept. 29/16. R/Enq. |
| 1 C. X | McNamara, Richard. 25380. | M. March 7/17. |
| 1 D. | Byrne, Charles. 26560. | M. Sept. 26/16. R/Enq. |
| 1 ? | Crawford, R. T. 26581. | W. and M., bel. K. Mar. 7/17. |
| ‡4 A. | Yates, P. 203465. | M. April 28/17. |
| 4 B. V | Crane, John. 2829. | W. and M. Sept. 9/16. R/Enq. |
| 4 B. XII | Martin, Tom. 6230. (Fr. 5 E. Lancs., 4655.) | W. and M. Sept. 8/16. R/Enq. |

**Lancashire Regiment, Loyal North—contd.**

## *B.E.F.*

| | | |
|---|---|---|
| 4 C. XI | Ingle, L.-Cpl. Harold. 6141. (Late 4425, 3/10 Manchs.) | M. Sept. 9/16. R/Enq. |
| 4 C. | Taylor, William. 4600. | M. Sept. 9/16. R/Enq. |
| 4 C. IX | Whinney, T. 6260. | W. and M. Sept. 9/16. R/Enq. |
| 4 C. XII | Wilson, Joseph. 4381. | M. Sept. 9/16. R/Enq. |
| 4 D. | Collier, S. 202740. | M. Sept. 9/16. |
| ‡4 D. | Donnelly, L.-Sergt. J. 202900. | M. May 19/17. |
| ‡5 | **Marseille, Capt. R. K. G.** | M. July 6/17. |
| ‡5 A. | Hodges, E. A. 243052. | M. June 3/17. |
| 7 A. | Colclough, George. 27479. | M. Nov. 14/16. R/Enq. |
| ‡7 A. | Delman, Cpl. W. L. 27291. | M. Nov. 8/16. R/Enq. |
| ‡7 A. | Price, L.-Cpl. Tom. 33662. | M. June 8/17. |
| *8 B. VII | Williams, Herbert. 27727. | K. June 7/17. Det.D./B. |
| 8 C. M.G.S. | Laurie, A. 29704. | K. Oct. 12/16. Det.D./B. |
| ‡8 D. | Geraghty, M. 29677. | M. June 2/17. |
| 9 ? | Savill, William. 23435. (Fr. 20th Manchesters.) | W. and M. Sept. 3/16. |
| 10 | **Roberts, 2nd Lieut. H. N.** | W. and M. April 28/17 |
| 10 | **Stonehouse, 2nd Lieut. R. A.** | M. April 28/17. |
| 10 A. | Ainsworth, E. 25362. | M. April 11/17. |
| 10 A. or C. | Austin, C. 27735. | W. and M. April 28/17. |
| 10 A. | Barrett, J. F. 33804. | W. and M. April 11/17. |
| 10 A. | Clarke, H. 31993. | M. April 11/17. |
| 10 A. II | Cottrell, Fred. S. 31998. | M. April 28/17. |
| 10 A. | Cox, Herbert. 35621. | W. and M. April 11/17. |
| ‡10 A. | Davis, L.-Cpl. W. 31826. | M. April 28/17. |
| ‡10 A. II | Denvir, John. 3/31935. | W. and M. April 11/17. |
| 10 A. | Erwood, Edward. 33132. | M. April 11/17. |
| 10 A. III | Fletcher, Ellis. 31938. | M. April 11/17. |
| ‡10 A. | Gent, G. 33199. | W. and M. April 28/17. |
| 10 A. | Lemon, Geo. Eyre. 33097. | W. and M. April 11/17. |
| 10 A. M.G.S. | Liddell, L.-Cpl. Frank. 17688. | M. Unoff. W. April 28/17. |
| 10 A. IV | Livingstone, William. 23357. | M. April 28/17. |
| ‡10 A. I | McCue, T. 200402. | M. April 28/17. |
| 10 A. II | Mason, Edw. 203475. | W. and M. April 11/17. |
| 10 A. | Ogden, H. 25682. | W. and M. April 16/17. |
| ‡10 A. III | Pearson, J. W. 203466. | M. April 28/17. |
| ‡10 A. | Pugh, J. 17025. | W. and M. April 28/17. |
| 10 A. III | Todd, L.-Cpl. John. 33932. | W. and M. April 11/17. |
| 10 A. IV | Wallwork, W. T. 19163. | W. and M. April 11/17. |
| *10 B. | Allen, L.-Cpl. Geo. 24651. | M. April 28/17. |
| 10 B. L.G.S. | Atkinson, F. 25237. | M. April 11/17. |
| ‡10 B. | Barnes, J. 15932. | W. and M. April 28/17. |
| 10 B. | Brade, J. 31794. | W. and M. April 11/17. |
| 10 B. | Briggs, G. H. 33945. | M. April 11/17. |
| 10 B. VII | Cheetham, Daniel. 32454. | W. and M. April 28/17. |
| 10 B. VI L.G.S. | Clarke, Thos. 25492. | M. April 28/17. |
| 10 B. VIII | Cooper, Sam. 24626. | M. April 11/17. |
| 10 B. M.G.S. | Crowhurst, J. J. 33119. | W. and M. April 28/17. |
| 10 B. | Currie, Cpl. A. 11195. | M. April 11/17. |
| 10 B. or C. | Davies, Sergt. Jas. 15143. | W. and M. April 11/17. |
| 10 B. | De Veto, Antony. 23348. | M. April 11/17. |
| ‡10 B. | Dunning, P. 17714. | M. April 28/17. |
| 10 B. VIII | Elliott, Robert. 32461. | M. April 11/17. |
| 10 B. | Fowler, Harry. 24670. | Unoff. M. Jan. 28/17. |
| 10 B. | Goodenough, Geoffrey Horwood. 33832. | M. April 28/17. |
| 10 B. | Harley, Wm. 25204. | M. April 28/17. |

**Lancashire Regiment, Loyal North—**contd.

*B.E.F.*

| | | |
|---|---|---|
| 10 B. | Hooper, Cpl. T. 18116. | M. April 11/17. |
| 10 B. | Koehler, C. 3277. (Late 1st.) | W. and M. Nov. 15/16. |
| 10 B. VIII | Leaver, James. 33198. | M. April 28/17. |
| ‡10 B. | McClellan, L.-Cpl. R. 24529. | M. April 28/17. |
| 10 B. | Partington, L.-Cpl. Herbert. 14408. | M. April 28/17. |
| ‡10 B. | Pitt, H. 33868. | M. April 28/17. |
| 10 B. | Skinner, Sydney. 27748. | W. Unoff. M. April 28/17. |
| 10 B. | Tatlock, Wm. 25236. | M. May 28/17. |
| ‡10 B. | Thomas, L.-Cpl. W. 33888. | M. April 28/17. |
| 10 B. | Tong, G. 16835. | W. and M. April 11/17. |
| 10 B. | Wallis, G. W. 33900. | M. April 11/17. |
| ‡10 B. | Walters, Albert Edward. 33898. | M. April 28/17. |
| 10 B. | Wilkinson, S. 27752. | W. and M. April 28/17. |
| ‡10 B. | Winwood, E. 24972. | M. April 28/17. |
| 10 C. X | Bardsley, T. 203439. | M. April 28/17. |
| ‡10 C. | Burke, J. 3744. | M. April 28/17. |
| 10 C. XI | Chester, Richard. 24022. | M. April 11/17. |
| ‡10 C. | Clifford, L.-Cpl. C. 13570. | M. April 28/17. |
| 10 C. | Costello, J. 22568. | M. April 11/17. |
| 10 C. | Daley, G. 22379. | M. April 11/17. |
| 10 C. L.G.S. | Dewhurst, James. 203436. | M. April 11/17. |
| ‡10 C. | Downs, A.-Cpl. T. 12746. | M. April 28/17. |
| 10 C. XI | Dunn, Cpl. Christopher. 21607. | W. and M. Nov. 15/16. |
| ‡10 C. | Flitcroft, H. 32030. | M. April 28/17. |
| ‡10 C. | Gillibrand, H. 17368. | M. April 28/17. |
| ‡10 C. | Greehalgh, W. 23694. | W. and M. April 28/17. |
| 10 C. | Haines, Arthur Henry. 35885. | M. April 11/17. |
| 10 C. XII | Hall, Richard Albert. 203432. (7210.) | M. April 28/17. |
| 10 C. | Hampson, H. 31942. | M. April 11/17. |
| 10 C. XI | Holt, Gordon. 31803. | W. and M. April 28/17. |
| ‡10 C. | Low, A. F. 33854. | M. April 28/17. |
| ‡10 C. X | Oddie, Alfred. 25278. | M. April 28/17. |
| ‡110 C. | Pantling, H. J. 35888. | M. April 28/17. |
| 10 C. X | Powell, Walter John. 35889. | M. April 28/17. |
| 10 C. or D. L.G.S. | Priestley, W. 27637. | M April 28/17. |
| 10 C. XII | Renison, E. H. 32478. | M. April 11/17. |
| ‡10 C. | Rimmer, J. 2698. | M. April 28/17. |
| ‡10 C. | Shawcross, T. 19498. | M. April 28/17. |
| ‡10 C. | Stagles, Cpl. J. H. 12935. | M. April 28/17. |
| ‡10 C. | Unsworth, J. 14394. | M. April 28/17. |
| ‡10 D. | Bond, A. 27589. | M. April 28/17. |
| ‡10 D. | Bond, R. 25350. | M. April 28/17. |
| 10 D. | Bowden, R. 203458. | W. and M. April 11/17. |
| 10 D. XV | Bradley, Sergt. Jas. Smyth. 33917. | M. April 28/17. |
| 10 D. | Bridges, L.-Cpl. W. 16881. | W. and M. April 11/17. |
| 10 D. | Colbert, L.-Cpl. P. 2638. | M. April 11/17. |
| 10 D. | Cuff, Richard. 11731. | •M. April 28/17. |
| ‡10 D. | Foley, H. J. 33226. | M. April 28/17. |
| 10 D. | Hadfield, H. 31860. | M. April 11/17. |
| ‡10 D. | Hambly, A. E. 33846. | M. April 28/17. |
| 10 D. | Keen, Fredk. 25724. | M. April 28/17. |
| 10 D. | McFarlane, L.-Cpl. Wm. 33927. | W. and M. April 11/17. |
| ‡10 D. XIII | Maddox, William. 33913. | M. April 28/17. |
| 10 D. | Makin, Sergt. Harold Prescott. 12976. | W. and M. April 11/17. |
| 10 D. | Maund, Albert. 33915. | M. April 27/17. |
| ‡10 D. | Mulroy, J. 25823. | M. April 28/17. |
| 10 D. | Pettigrew, L.-Cpl. T. 18466. | W. and M. April 11/17. |

**Lancashire Regiment, Loyal North—contd.**

## *B.E.F.*

| | | |
|---|---|---|
| 10 D. XIV | Swain, H. J. 33916. | W. and M. April 11/17. |
| ‡10 D. | Whatmouth, T. 266155. | W. and M. April 28/17. |
| ‡10 D. | Winwood, L.-Sergt. W. H. 34071. | M. April 28/17. |

## *BALKANS.*

| | | |
|---|---|---|
| 12 ? | Roberts, R. R. 265716. | M. April 1/17. |

## *PERSIAN GULF.*

| | | |
|---|---|---|
| 6 B. | Duxbury, Astley. 24991. | K. April 28/17. Det.D./B. |
| 6 D. | Desmond, A. P. 20837. | M. April 9/16. |
| 6 D. | Roberts, J. W. 21262. | M. April 9/16. R./Enq. |
| 6 D. | Sandwell, C. I. 20879. | M. April 9/16. R./Enq. |
| 6 D. | Tootell, Wasley. 20840. | M. April 9/16. R./Enq. |
| 6 D. | Waldron, R. 12511. | M. April 9/16. R/Enq. |
| 6 D. | Wareing, John. 21302. | M. April 9/16. R./Enq. |
| 6 ? | Ryan, J. 15345. | M. April 9/17. |
| 6 ? | Smith, Francis. 21040. | D. April 15/17. Det.D./B. |
| 6 ? | Stringfellow, Thos. 16276. | D/W. Mar. 10/17. Det.D./B. |

**SOUTH LANCASHIRE REGIMENT.**

## *B.E.F.*

| | | |
|---|---|---|
| 2 B. VIII | Clarke, Albert Morris. 22468. | M. Oct. 21/16. R/Enq. |
| *2 B. VII | Wise, R. 19530. | K. Oct. 21/16. Det.D./B. |
| 2 C. | Cuddick, S. 11721. (Fr. 8th.) | M. Oct. 21/16. R/Enq. |
| 4 | **Jacobs, 2nd Lieut. D.** | M. April 10/17. |
| 4 ? | Tasker, W. 5179. | M. Oct. 12/16. |
| 2/4 C. | Mayor, H. 201521. | M. April 10/17. |
| 2/5 | **Cocking, 2nd Lieut. J. O. C.** | M. April 10/17. |
| ‡2/5 B. | Leicester, Cpl. J. 241117. | M. May 13/17. |
| 2/5 C. | Mutch, R. 240740. | M. April 10/17. |
| ‡2/5 C. | Smith, Sergt. Thos. 240968. | M. July 2-3/17. |
| ‡2/5 D. | Travis, Sergt. J. 241057. | M. April 10/17. |
| 7 | **Cole, 2nd Lieut. W. N.** | M. Feb. 5/17. |
| ‡7 A. | Houghton, John. 16739. | M. Nov. 18/16. R/Enq. |
| 7 B. | Burton, John. 18587. | M. Feb. 5/17. |
| 7 B. | Conquest, A. G. 31695. | M. Nov. 18/16. |
| *7 B. VI | O'Brien, William. 10681. | M. May 19/17. |
| *7 B. VI | Piper, F. G. 31055. | M. May 19/17. |
| 7 B. | Poole, J. 15322. | M. Feb. 5/17. |
| ‡7 B. VIII | Thomas, Brindley. 34088. | W. Unoff. M. June 7/17. |
| ‡7 B. | Thorne, J. 14128. | M. May 19/17. |
| *7 B. M.G.S. | Yeadon, Sergt. T. P. 12735. | M. May 19/17. |
| ‡7 C. IX | Fairclough, J. 31816. | Unoff. M., bel. K. July 8/17. |
| 7 D. | Sudlow, R. 31774. (Late 4th, 4363.) | W. and M. Nov. 14/16. |
| 7 ? | Drye, John Wm. 34191. (Late W. Yorks. 12806.) | M. May 3/17. |
| *8 A. II | Ainsworth, J. W. 36009. | K. June 6/17. Det.D./B. |
| ‡8 A. | Grewer, R. 31939. | M. June 7/17. |
| 8 A. | Haworth, J. T. 29838. (Fr. M.G.C., No. 4586.) | M. Oct. 21/16. R/Enq. |
| ‡8 A. | Kenworthy, G. 31103. | M. June 7/17. |

Lancashire Regiment, South—contd.

## B.E.F.

| | | |
|---|---|---|
| ‡8 A. | Owen, W. J. 34225. | M. June 7/17. |
| ‡8 B. VIII | Bradley, Eli. 29756. | M. June 7/17. |
| 8 B. | Roberts, Herbert. 31119. | M. Feb. 18/17. |
| 8 B. | Thomas, J. L. 31131. | M. Oct. 21/16. |
| 8 C. XI | Glennon, T. 17990. | M. Feb. 18/17. |
| 8 ? | Smith, G. S. 15280. | M. Sept. 1/16. |

## PERSIAN GULF.

| | | |
|---|---|---|
| *6 | Caftarns, M.C., Capt. G. R. | K. Feb. 12/17. Det.D./B. |
| 6 | Fraser, 2nd Lieut. Alex. R. | D/W. April 26/17. Det.D./B. |
| 6 A. | Dinsmore, Cpl. A. 11799. | M. April 5/16. R/Enq. |
| 6 B. | Muir, A.-Cpl. James. 11038. | M. April 9/16. R/Enq. |
| *6 B. VIII | Sudworth, J. H. 26492. | W. and M. April 30/17. |
| 6 C. | Wilcock, James. 18579. | D/W. Feb. 14/17. Det.D./B. |
| 6 D. | Bryce, G. 26511. | D. Feb. 18/17. Det.D./B. |
| 6 D. | Cosgrove, P. 18616. | K. Feb. 12/17. Det.D./B. |

# KING'S OWN ROYAL LANCASTER REGIMENT.

## B.E.F.

| | | |
|---|---|---|
| 1 | Graham, Lieut. C. H. M. | K. April 11/17. Det.D./B. |
| 1 | Walker, 2nd Lieut. J. E. | W. and M. May 3/17. |
| 1 A. IV | Barker, Frank. 17246. | M. July 1/16. R./Enq. |
| 1 A. L.G.S. | Davies, J. 1634. | M. Oct. 23/16. R/Enq. |
| *1 A. | Edwards, Edward. 6003. | M. May 3/17. |
| 1 A. | Newton, Frank. 27276. | M. April 10/17. |
| 1 A. IV | Waites, Samuel F. 32810. | M. April 10/17. |
| 1 A. IV | Whiteway, Ben. 27633. | W. and M. May 3/17. |
| 1 B. VI | Abrahall, Geo. Albert. 26851. | M. May 3/17. |
| 1 B. VII | Cook, A. W. 32913. | M. May 3/17. |
| 1 B. or D. | Coyle, Bernard. 241791. (4384.) | M. May 3/17. |
| ‡1 B. | Hulme, Cpl. W. 32771. | W. and M. May 3/17. |
| 1 B. VIII | Rushton, Walter. 32874. | W. and M. April 11/17. |
| ‡1 B. | Smethurst, G. 24319. | W. and M. April 11/17. |
| ‡1 B. | Smith, C. 27075. | M. May 11/17. |
| 1 C. | Brown, Frank. 27953. | M. May 3/17. |
| *1 C. IX | Garlick, W. 24058. | W. and M. April 10/17. |
| ‡1 C. | Jenning, Wm. 27684. | K. May 3/17. Det.D./B. |
| 1 C. XII | Lees, Jas. 1906. | W. and M. April 12/17. |
| ‡1 C. X | Read, Harry. 33407. | M. May 3/17. |
| ‡1 C. | Reading, A. 27291. | M. May 3/17. |
| ‡1 C. | Richardson, O. 24596. | M. May 3/17. |
| *1 C. L.G.S. | Tillotson, J. W. 33404. | M. May 3/17. |
| ‡1 C. | Watson, T. 201858. | M. May 3/17. |
| ‡1 D. | Gray, G. 24231. | M. May 3/17. |
| ‡1 D. XVI | Hardern, D. H. 32168. | K. May 3/17. Det.D./B. |
| ‡1 D. | Mateer, C. 32087. | M. May 3/17. |
| 1 D. | Mawson, T. 24750. | W. and M. April 9/17. |
| ‡1 D. | Mitchell, Cpl. T. B. 32860. | W. and M. April 12/17. |
| ‡1 D. XIII | Walters, L.-Cpl. J. G. 14632. | K. May 3/17. Det.D./B. R/Enq. |
| 1 D. XIV | Whitehead, Ernest. 25628. | M. May 3/17. |

**Lancaster Regiment, King's Own Royal—contd.**

## *B.E.F.*

| | | | |
|---|---|---|---|
| 4 C. | | Grey, Ernest Albert. 4930. | K. Sept. 26/16. Det.D./B. |
| 4 C. IX | | Newby, L.-Cpl. Tom. 2953. | M. Dec. 23/16. R/Enq. |
| 4 D. | | Wilson, Allen. 2764. | M. Sept. 28/16. R/Enq. |
| 4 ? | | Shepherd, L.-Cpl. John Lyson. 200603. | W. and M. April 12/17. |
| 5 | | **Gregg, 2nd Lt. C. E.** | M. June 15/17. |
| 5 C. | | Hough, J. 241021. | W. and M. April 11/17. |
| 8 A. | | Bell, J. J. 201241. | M. April 26-30/17. |
| 8 A. | | Brown, J. 241968. | M. April 26-30/17. |
| ‡8 A. | | Gorton, J. 30044. | W. and M. April 9-12/17. |
| 8 A. | | Hill, Albert. 2750. | M. April 12/17. |
| 8 A. or D. | | Hussey, Fred. 22941. | W. and M. April 26-30/17. |
| *8 A. or D. | | James, Richard Henry. 201994. (4/5752.) | W. and M. May 16/17. |
| ‡8 A. | | McKeown, J. 30043. | W. and M. April 9-12/17. |
| 8 A. or C. | | Mitchell, J. 25039. | M. April 12/17. |
| 8 A. | | Nichols, A. E. 242453. | M. April 26-30/17. |
| ‡8 A. | | Pledger, D. 33485. | M. May 23/17. |
| 8 A. III | | Russell, Frank. 30195. | W. and M. April 26-30/17. |
| *8 B. V | | Dobson, John. 26648. | M. May 12/17. |
| 8 B. | | Felstead, J. 27572. | M. April 26-30/17. |
| 8 B. or C. | | Green, B. H. 24393. | W. and M. April 26-30/17. |
| ‡8 B. | | Healey, J. 27777. | W. and M. April 30/17. |
| ‡8 B. | | Hodgson, H. 23539. | W. and M., bel. K. April 9-12/17. |
| 8 B. or C. | | Leyland, Wm. 22976. | W. and M. April 9-12/17. |
| ‡8 B. | | Rawcliffe, R. 202410. | M. May 23/17. |
| ‡8 B. | | Roskell, A.-Cpl. W. 11538. | W. and M. May 12/17. |
| 8 C. or D. | | Carey, James. 15363. | M. April 26-28/17. |
| 8 C. or D. | | Eley, Thos. Herbert. 27767. | M. April 9-12/17. |
| 8 C. | | Haugh, R. 23168. | W. and M. 9-12/17. |
| 8 C. XII | | Laithwaite, Aloysius. 27598. | M. April 9-12/17. |
| *8 C. XII | | Lea, James. 27756. | M. May 12/17. |
| ‡8 C. | | Stopforth, R. 201771. | M. May 12/17. |
| 8 C. X | | West, R. 23355. | M. May 12/17. |
| *8 D. XIII | | Bennett, P. S. 27764. | M. May 12/17. |
| ‡8 D. | | Bottoms, W. J. 13636. | M. May 12/17. |
| 8 D. XIV | | Brooker, L.-Cpl. G. 9947. | M. April 26-30/17. |
| 8 D. | | Gough, W. 12121. | M. April 26-30/17. |
| 8 D. | | Lolley, Wm. 11979. | M. April 26-30/17. |
| ‡8 D. | | McLoughlin, M. 201874. | M. May 12/17. |
| 8 D. | | Meaden, Walter. 20211. | M. May 12/17. |
| 8 D. | | Seward, W. 17248. | M. April 9-12/17. |
| 8 D. XV | | Shaw, Fred. 27746. | M. April 9-12/17. |
| ‡8 D. | | Warner, A.-Sergt. H. 15328. | W. and M. April 26-30/17. |
| 8 D. XIV | | Wilson, John Wm. 33477. | M. May 12/17. |
| 8 D. XIV | | Yates, Robert. 27497. | M. April 12/17. |
| ‡8 ? | | Capstick, Thos. Edward. 32662. | K. June 16-20/17. Det.D./B. |
| 8 ? I.T.M. | | Walton, F. 27485. (76 Bde. 1 By.) | M. April 26-30/17. |
| *11 B. | | Cooke, John. 22415. | K. May 18/17. Det.D./B. |

## *BALKANS.*

| | | | |
|---|---|---|---|
| 2 ? | | Chamberlain, D. 20128. | M. Oct. 28/16. |
| *2 ? | | Cusack, H. 12751. | M. May 31/17. |
| *2 ? | | Holding, A/Cpl. J. 17590. | M. May 31/17. |

## *PERSIAN GULF*

| | | | |
|---|---|---|---|
| 6 1 | | Barrett, Fred. 11464. | M. April 9/16. R/Enq. |
| 6 1 IV | | Birkett, Robt. 25308. | W. and M. Feb. 9/17. |

**Lancaster Regiment, King's Own Royal—contd.**

*PERSIAN GULF.*

| | | |
|---|---|---|
| 6 1 II | McNally, T. 1096. | W. and M. Feb. 9/17. |
| 6 1 II | Reeves, John Edwin. 12777. | M. Dec. 20/16. |
| 6 1 | Rushton, L.-Cpl. Wm. 19034. | M. April 9/16. R./Enq. |
| 6 2 V | Bevins, Roger. 18743. | K. Feb. 9/17. Det.D./B. |
| •6 2 VIII | Dye, Bertram. 15544. | M. April 30/17. |
| 6 2 VI | McDermott, W. 20745. | W. and M. Feb. 9/17. |
| 6 2 | Morrell, Claude. 23275. | D/W. May 2/17. Det.D./B. |
| 6 2 VI | Richmond, L.-Cpl. Frank. 18847. | W. and M. Feb. 9/17. |
| 6 3 IX | Greenwood, Jos. Johnson. 24240. | D/W. Feb. 27/17. Det.D./B. |
| 6 3 XI | Whiteside, J. 19555. | W. and M., bel. K. Feb. 9/17. |
| 6 ? | Davis, J. 16933. | W. and M. Feb. 9/17. |
| 6 ? | Grisedale, W. 25326. | W. and M. Feb. 9/17. |
| 6 ? | Henderson, P. 18186. | W. and M. Feb. 9/17. |
| ‡6 ? | Hodgson, L. 20868. | M. April 30/17. |
| 6 ? | Johnson, J. 3755. | W. and M. Feb. 9/17. |
| 6 ? | Murray, E. 19147. | M. Feb. 9/17. |
| 6 ? | Rodda, J. 6788. | M. April 9/16. |
| 6 ? | Roe, S. 13184. | M. Feb. 9/17. |
| 6 ? | Tingle, H. 18965. | W. and M. Feb. 9/17. |
| 6 ? | Walmsley, W. 11399. | W. and M. Feb. 9/17. |

## DUKE OF LANCASTER'S OWN YEOMANRY.

*B.E.F.*

| | | |
|---|---|---|
| C. or D. Squad. III Troop | Whittaker, L.-Cpl. Harry. 110482. (Late 3831.) | W. and M. Mar. 24/17. |

## LANCERS.

*B.E.F.*

| | | |
|---|---|---|
| 12 ? | Sutton, J. 412. | W. and M. April 9/17. |
| 21 I | Lawrence, Sergt. W. 6444. | W. and M. April 6/17. |

## LEICESTERSHIRE REGIMENT.

*B.E.F.*

| | | |
|---|---|---|
| '1 | Stevens, Lieut. A. L. | M. April 18/17. |
| 1 A. or C. | Johnson, G. E. 23099. | W. and M. Sept. 27/16. |
| ‡1 B. V | Mace, Wm. Thos. 24999. | M. Sept. 15/16. R/Enq. |
| 1 C. | Phillips, Henry. 40929. | M. April 18/17. |
| 1 C. XII | Taylor, J. 27169. | M. April 18/17. |

**Leicestershire Regiment—contd.**

## *B.E.F.*

| | | |
|---|---|---|
| 1 D. | Harper, Thomas. 9525. | M. Sept. 15/16. R/Enq. |
| 1 D. | Thompson, H. L. 17924. | M. Sept. 15/16. R./Enq. |
| 1 D. | Wells, Harry. 11562. | M. Sept. 15/16. R/Enq. |
| ‡4 A. | Bailey, A. 201152. (Scout S.) | M. June 8/17. |
| 4 A. III | Clarke, W. J. 235014. | K. April 22/17. Det.D./B. |
| ‡4 B. | Bullock, L.-Cpl. 14376. | M. June 8/17. |
| 4 B. V | Corbridge, Edgar Cecil. 202050. (5906.) | M. April 22/17. |
| 4 B. V | Daines, E. 201449. | M. April 23/17. |
| 4 B. | Gooding, P. P. 235027. | M. April 22/17. |
| 4 B. | Hayes, J. W. 235033. | M. April 22/17. |
| 4 B. V | Kirkham, John. 200602. (3036.) | M. April 22/17. |
| 4 B. | Limb, E. V. 201552. | M. April 22/17. |
| 4 B. | Lord, E. 201641. | M. April 22/17. |
| 4 B. | Masters, E. J. 202916. | M. April 22/17. |
| 4 B. | Pick, J. W. 200943. | M. April 22/17. |
| ‡4 D. XVI | Topliss, W. 201440. | M. June 8/17. |
| 2/4 C. IX | Machin, George. 201931. (5761.) | Unoff. W. and M. April 2/17. |
| ‡5 B. VII | Hubbard, Fred. 242377. | M. June 8/17. |
| ‡5 C. XI | Beck, A. 241691. | M. June 8/17. |
| 2/5 A. | Skinner, J. A. 242345. | M. April 1/17. |
| 2/5 A. | Smith, W. 241101. (Late 3320.) | M. Mar. 31/17. |
| ‡2/5 B. | Thornton, Percy. 241267. | M. May 31/17. |
| ‡6 A. | Hunt, A. 8453. | W. and M. May 3/17. |
| *6 A. IV | Pickerin, R. 12942. | W. and M. Sept. 17/16. |
| *6 B. V | Bodicoate, G. W. 21108. | W. and M. May 3/17. |
| 6 B. V | Goodwin, G. S. 14614. | W. and M. May 3/17. |
| 6 B. V | Markham, W. 32967. | M. May 3/17. |
| 6 B. or D. | Rimmington, J. W. 10971. | M. May 3/17. |
| 6 B. VII | Smith, Wm. 27037. | W. and M. May 3/17. |
| 6 D. XIII | Barber, J. W. 16630. | M. May 3/17. |
| ‡6 D. XV | Clarke, John. 15289. | K. May 3/17. Det.D./B. |
| 6 D. | Dale, Sergt. H. F. 16248. | M. May 3/17. |
| ‡6 D. | Hutt, A. 10821. | M. May 3/17. |
| ‡7 B. | Hetherington, W. 29876. | M. May 3/17. |
| 7 B. | Jackson, Jas. 36088. | W. and M. May 3/17. |
| 7 B. M.G.S. | Richards, Sgt. Horace. 17224. | M. April 6/17. |
| ‡7 C. | Robinson, R. 12400. | M. May 3/17. |
| 8 | **Clarke, 2nd Lieut. F. W. H.** | M., bel. W. May 3/17. |
| *8 | **Haines, Lieut. F. P.** | M. June 16/17. |
| 8 | **Oliver, Lieut. (A.-Capt.) F. R.** | M. May 3/17. |
| 8 | **Pitts, 2nd Lieut. F. B.** (Fr. 3rd.) | W. and M. May 3/17. |
| ‡8 A. | Adams, J. 18440. | M. May 3/17. |
| ‡8 A. | Andrews, L.-Cpl. S. 33003. | M. May 3/17. |
| ‡8 A. | Archer, J. 25061. | M. May 3/17. |
| ‡8 A. | Baker, T. S. 25180. | M. May 3/17. |
| ‡8 A. | Ball, L.-Cpl. A. E. 33218. | M. May 3/17. |
| 8 A. | Ballard, L.-Cpl. L. 33006. | M. May 3/17. |
| ‡8 A. | Barnes, G. 11774. | M. May 3/17. |
| 8 A. IV | Bell, F. J. 37767. | M. May 3/17. |
| ‡8 A. | Black, Sergt. G. W. 18699. | M. May 3/17. |
| ‡8 A. | Brockhouse, J. 18025. | M. May 3/17. |
| ‡8 A. | Burdett, J. W. 22934. | M. May 3/17. |
| ‡8 A. | Burton, L.-Cpl. W. C. 12326. | M. May 3/17. |
| *8 A. III | Buswell, W. 33208. | M. May 3/17. |
| ‡8 A. III | Chambers, Sidney James. 25620. | M. May 3/17. |
| 8 A. III | Chapman, Albert. 33158. | M. May 3/17. |
| ‡8 A. | Clulow, L.-Cpl. A. V. 9331. | M. May 3/17. |

**Leicestershire Regiment—contd.**

*B.E.F.*

‡8 A. Davey, A. 33033. M. May 3/17.
*8 A. III Draper, William Cecil. 33168. M. May 3/17.
‡8 A. Ellis, G. A. 40124. M. May 3/17.
*8 A. IV Everitt, L.-Cpl. A. J. 33037. M. May 3/17.
8 A. I Ford, A. 200786. (3401.) M. May 3/17.
‡8 A. Freeman, B. E. 33170. M. May 3/17.
‡8 A. French, A. 33040. M. May 3/17.
‡8 A. Gibson, J. 40126. M. May 3/17.
‡8 A. Glover, W. R. 36765. M. May 3/17.
8 A. XI Goddard, Archie. 18607. M. May 3/17.
8 A. Hardy, W. T. 27005. M. May 3/17.
‡8 A. Harrison, Sergt. C. W. 19147. M. May 3/17.
8 A. III Heuson, L.-Cpl. J. A. 200875. M. May 3/17.
‡8 A. Hubbard, L.-Cpl. S. 20083. M. May 3/17.
‡8 A. James, Cpl. George. 19150. M. May 3/17.
‡8 A. Keller, F. 200144. M. May 3/17.
8 A. III Lewin, T. G. 26848. M. May 3/17.
8 A. M.G.S. McClellan, L.-Cpl. G. 15170. W. and M. May 3/17.
8 A. Page, G. H. 40139. W. and M. Sept. 25/16. R./Enq.
*8 A. Palmer, C.-S.-M. Alf. Edwin. 13062. W. and M. May 3/17.
‡8 A. Penfold, Sergt. R. C. 13017. M. May 3/17.
‡8 A. Philpot, W. 202061. M. May 3/17.
‡8 A. Poulton, J. A. 20548. M. May 3/17.
8 A. Ratcliffe, A. 200410. M. May 3/17.
‡8 A. Rolph, T. 33151. M. May 3/17.
‡8 A. Shaw, T. E. 3111. M. May 3/17.
‡8 A. Smith, B. E. 18535 M. May 3/17.
‡8 A. III Tutty, F. S. 20888. M. May 3/17.
‡8 A. Walsh, T. 36747. M. May 3/17.
‡8 A. White, L.-Cpl. C. H. 40146. M. May 3/17.
‡8 A. Whitney, C. 36656. M. May 3/17.
8 A. Whittaker, E. 36657. M. May 3/17.
8 A. Whittaker, Robinson. 36679. M. May 3/17.
‡8 A. Withnall, L.-Sergt. G. W. 15241. M. May 3/17.
‡8 A. Worthington, A. 40145. M. May 3/17.
‡8 A. Wright, J. 36036. M. May 3/17.
‡8 B. Barnes, J. A. 20569. M. May 3/17.
8 B. VIII Boulter, A. 28679. M. May 3/17.
‡8 B. Burnett, F. F. 19308. M. May 3/17.
‡8 B. Burnham, E. 23826. M. May 3/17.
8 B. Dakin, Wm. 21185. M. May 3/17.
8 B. or D. Faulkner, T. 20678. M. May 3/17.
‡8 B. Fleming, J. 37893. M. May 3/17.
*8 B. VI Gilliams, L.-Cpl. Harold Percy. 9089 M. May 3/17.
‡8 B. V Grain, John Ed. 32635. M. May 3/17.
‡8 B. VI Gribble, Geo. 32043. M. May 3/17.
8 B. Hackett, Chas. 17068. M. May 3/17.
8 B. Harrison, H. 27071. M. May 3/17.
‡8 B. Hitchin, M. 40907. M. May 3/17.
‡8 B. Holden, L.-Cpl. J. P. 24031. M. May 3/17.
‡8 B. Hunt, A. 9351. M. May 3/17.
8 B. Joslin, Fredk. (Tripie.) 33176. M. May 2/17.
8 B. Madder, H. F. 20243. M. May 3/17.
‡8 B. Messenger, E. G. 33180. M. May 3/17.
‡8 B. Moore, A. 23217. M. May 3/17.
8 B. M.G.S. Moore, L.-Cpl. S. 12484. M. May 3/17.
*8 B. Mowbray, Thomas. 20624. M. May 3/17.
‡8 B. Nicholls, B. C. 33063. M. May 3/17.

**Leicestershire Regiment—contd.**

## *B.E.F.*

| | | |
|---|---|---|
| ‡8 B. | Osborne, E. J. 33067. | M. May 3/17. |
| ‡8 B. or C. | Palmer, Wm. 40906. | W. and M. May 3/17. |
| ‡8 B. | Peppiatt, D. 33132. | M. May 3/17. |
| ‡8 B. | Pollard, J. 12781. | M. May 3/17. |
| 8 B. | Powell, John Humphrey. 12580. | M. May 3/17. |
| 8 B. VI | Ralph, Chas. 31652. | M. May 3/17. |
| ‡8 B. VIII | Read, John. 20556. | M. May 3/17. |
| ‡8 B. | Reeves, A.-Cpl. T. W. 43043. | M. May 3/17. |
| *8 B. | Ridgway, C. 23404. | M. May 3/17. |
| 8 B. | Rigby, A. 31187. | M. May 3/17. |
| ‡8 B. | Roberts, Cpl. H. 13182. | M. May 3/17. |
| ‡8 B. | Roberts, J. 33077. | M. May 3/17. |
| ‡8 B. | Roome, E. 11951. | M. May 3/17. |
| 8 B. VI | Rudkin, Sgt. John Arch. 201721. (5472.) | M. May 3/17. |
| 8 B. | Setterfield, A.-C.-S.-M. John. 8400. | M. May 13/17. |
| 8 B. | Sharp, Francis Eric. 32843. | M. May 3/17. |
| ‡8 B. | Shepherd, Alfred Benford. 21268. | M. May 3/17. |
| ‡8 B. | Smith, E. 36735. | M. May 3/17. |
| 8 B. VI | Smith, Gordon. 36733. | M. May 3/17. |
| ‡8 B. VIII | Smithson, J. H. 36734. | M. May 3/17. |
| ‡8 B. | Taylor, T. 36646. | M. May 3/17. |
| *8 B. | Waddington, Geo. Cowper. 20138. | W. and M. May 3/17. |
| ‡8 B. | Ward, F. 40910. | M. May 3/17. |
| *8 B. | Weston, Arthur. 12137. (Cook.) | M. May 3/17. |
| 8 B. or D. | Whittaker, Joseph. 11007. | M. May 3/17. |
| ‡8 B. | Wilkinson, L.-Cpl. H. G. 36400. | M. May 3/17. |
| ‡8 B. | Willis, H. "Mickey." 18693. | M. May 3/17. |
| ‡8 B. | Wright, O. 31695. | M. May 3/17. |
| 8 C. X | Bennett, C. 201792. (5578.) | M. May 3/17. |
| ‡8 C. | Clark, W. 33028. | M. May 3/17. |
| 8 C. | Copson, Pearcy Chas. 13014. | W. and M. May 3/17. |
| ‡8 C. | Evans, F. G. 21877. | M. May 3/17. |
| 8 C. L.G.S. | Evans, R. L. 37823. | M. May 3/17. |
| 8 C. IX | Garlick, C. G. 27141. | M. May 3/17. |
| ‡8 C. | Haseldine, E. 16804. | M. May 3/17. |
| 8 C. IX | Miller, A. F. 33189. | W. and M. May 3/17 |
| ‡8 C. | Morey, J. H. 33127. | M. May 3/17. |
| ‡8 C. | Noble, A.-Cpl. F. E. 11670. | M. May 3/17. |
| ‡8 C. | Phillips, A. 33131. | M. May 3/17. |
| ‡8 C. XI | Potts, A. 36396. | M. May 3/17. |
| ‡8 C. XII | Rogers, H. H. 36372. | M. June 16/17. |
| ‡8 C. | Seymour, A. K. 36397. | M. May 3/17. |
| ‡8 C. | Thornton, A.-Cpl. F. 18611. | M. May 3/17. |
| ‡8 C. | Wright, R. 30395. | M. May 3/17. |
| ‡8 D. | Allen, A. 14363. | M. May 3/17. |
| ‡8 D. | Almond, C. 33161. | M. May 3/17. |
| 8 D. | Andrews, Herbert Percy. 11605. | M. May 3/17. |
| ‡8 D. | Dugdale, J. 37797. | M. May 3/17. |
| ‡8 D. | Garrett, Cpl. E. 11503. | M. May 3/17. |
| ‡8 D. XIV | Hill, John C. 22933. | M. May 3/17. |
| 8 D. XV | Jordan, H. 27020. | M. May 3/17. |
| 8 D. XIV | Matthams, Fred. 33182. | M. May 3/17. |
| ‡8 D. | Slatter, J. 15942. | M. May 3/17. |
| 8 D. XIV | Taylor, William. 33280. | M. May 3/17. |
| 8 D. XV | Wareing, R. F. 33146. | M. May 3/17. |
| 8 D. XV | Wormald, Frank. 241990. (5514.) | M. May 3/17. |

Leicestershire Regiment—contd.

*B.E.F.*

| | | | |
|---|---|---|---|
| 9 | | **Boyd, 2nd Lt. C. G. (Fr. Notts & Derby.)** | W. Unoff. M. May 3/17. |
| 9 | | **Eales, 2nd Lieut. F. D. S.** | M. May 3/17. |
| 9 | A. | Bell, Cpl. Fredk. 16101. | M. May 3/17. |
| *9 | A. | Burden, W. 23137. | M. Sept. 25/16. R/Enq. |
| ‡9 | A. | Greenwood, J. 36706. | M. May 3/17. |
| 9 | A. IV | Hancox, F. 25574. | M. May 3/17. |
| ‡9 | A. | Hinks, J. W. 20115. | M. May 3/17. |
| ‡9 | A. | Kay, H. 12336. | M. May 3/17. |
| 9 | A. II | Kayley, James. 36616. | M. Unoff. W. May 3/17. |
| 9 | A. III or IV | King. Louis. 36507. | M. May 3/17. |
| ‡9 | A. | Kirby, L.-Cpl. J. T. 13102. | M. May 3/17. |
| ‡9 | A. | Lawrence, W. 25659. | M. May 3/17. |
| ‡9 | A. | Park, Cpl. T. 36661. | M. May 3/17. |
| ‡9 | A. | Ramsden, J. 40876. | M. May 3/17. |
| 9 | A. | Robinson, H. 40299. | M. May 3/17. |
| 9 | A. II | Rushton, L.-Cpl. Geo. 36482. | M. May 3/17. |
| ‡9 | A. | Sargent, Sergt. E. 11397. | M. May 3/17. |
| ‡9 | A. | Sheen, L.-Cpl. W. 16676. | M. May 3/17. |
| ‡9 | A. | Stanley, A. H. 40828. | M. May 3/17. |
| ‡9 | A. IV | Twells, Albert. 36513. | M. May 3/17. |
| ‡9 | A. | Wareham, A. 35646. | M. May 3/17. |
| ‡9 | B. | Abbott, G. A. 20826. | M. May 3/17. |
| *9 | B. | Barwell, E. 25613. | M. May 3/17. |
| 9 | B. VII | Bennett, G. 36486. | M. May 3/17. |
| ‡9 | B. | Blakesley, W. J. 16036. | M. May 3/17. |
| ‡9 | B. VI | Boys, Reginald Henry. 25222. | M. May 3/17. |
| ‡9 | B. | Chapman, W. 23087. | M. May 3/17. |
| ‡9 | B. | Clegg, F. 36699. | M. May 3/17. |
| ‡9 | B. | Daniels, F. 27244. | M. May 3/17. |
| 9 | B. VI | Driver, P. W. 24141. | M. May 3/17. |
| 9 | B. V | Dumelow, L.-Cpl. H. 21468. | M. May 3/17. |
| 9 | B. VIII | English, Stephen. 36673. | M. May 3/17. |
| ‡9 | B. | Freeman, R. 40092. | M. May 3/17. |
| ‡9 | B. | Guilliam, J. A. 23451. | M. May 3/17. |
| ‡9 | B. | McHugh, T. 36536. | M. May 3/17. |
| *9 | B. VIII | Mayoh, H. 33262. | M. May 3/17. |
| ‡9 | B. | Palfreyman, H. 11937. | M. May 3/17. |
| ‡9 | B. | Pearce, J. 25710. | M. May 3/17. |
| ‡9 | B. | Richardson, J. A. 25886. | M. May 3/17. |
| ‡9 | B. | Rogerson, Cpl. F. W. 36517. | M. May 3/17. |
| ‡9 | B. | Shepherd, H. 36495. | M. May 3/17. |
| ‡9 | B. | Sowter, F. H. 25048. | M. May 3/17. |
| *9 | B. VII | Spencer, William. 17422. | M. May 3/17. |
| ‡9 | B. | Wade, R. 22444. | M. May 3/17. |
| ‡9 | C. | Cooper, H. 14518. | M. May 3/17. |
| *9 | C. | Doughty, Sergt. Douglas. 14564. | M. May 3/17. |
| ‡9 | C. | Green, J. T. 40839. | M. May 3/17. |
| 9 | C. XII | Hewer, Reginald. 40235. | M. May 3/17. |
| 9 | C. | Hopkinson, A.-Sergt. W. J. 36516. | M. April 12/17. |
| 9 | C. X | Hubbard, Herbert. 40844. | M. May 3/17. |
| ‡9 | C. | Jacques, H. J. 20805. | M. May 3/17. |
| 9 | C. XII | Kelsey, Ernest H. C. 23281. | M. Sept. 25/16. R/Enq |
| ‡9 | C. | Martin, E. C. 21296. | M. May 3/17. |
| ‡9 | C. | Parkes, C. 14777. | M. May 3/17. |
| *9 | C. | Powers, Sergt. J. 14768. | W. and M. May 3/17. |
| 9 | C. XII | Young, Percy. 33150. | M. May 3/17. |
| ‡9 | D. | Ashworth, T. 36553. | M. May 3/17. |

**Leicestershire Regiment—contd.**

## B.E.F.

| | | |
|---|---|---|
| 19 D. | Clarke, Sergt. G. 11547. | K. May 3/17. Det.D./B. |
| 19 D. | Frary, J. H. 36599. | M. May 3/17. |
| 9 D. XIV | Hill, Cyril. 22603. | M. May 3/17. |
| 9 D. | Hubbard, Benj. Jas. 201483. (5008.) | M. May 3/17. |
| 19 D. | Jones, F. 40866. | M. May 3/17. |
| 9 D. XIV | Mansell, L.-Cpl. E. 24965. | M. May 3/17. |
| 19 D. XIV | Marsh, L.-Cpl. Herbert Golder. 36571. | W. and M. May 3/17. |
| 19 D. | Sills, C. E. 26636. | M. May 3/17. |
| 19 D. | Trow, B. 40892. | M. May 3/17. |
| 19 D. | Webb, A. E. 40900. | M. May 3/17. |

## E.E.F.

| | | |
|---|---|---|
| 2 ? | Smith, Sydney. 241083. | M., bel. drowned April 15/17. |

## PERSIAN GULF.

| | | |
|---|---|---|
| 2 | **Sowter, Lieut. V. H. E.** | D/W. April 23/17. Det.D./B. |
| 2 | **Swindells, 2nd Lt. C. G. R.** (Fr. 7th.) | M. Jan. 9/17. |
| 2 B. | Allen, Amos. 17566. | M. March 10/16. R./Enq. |
| 2 C. | Bullock, L. 6/10577. | M. Jan. 9/17. |
| 2 D. | Gough, J. E. 19442. (Fr. K.O.Y.L.I.) | M. April 6/16. R./Enq. |
| 2 D. XV | Hand, Reginald. 9581. | K. April 23/17. Det.D./B. |
| 2 D. | Harrison, Arthur. 28697. | M. Jan. 9/17. |
| 2 D. | Howe, A. 10413. | M. Jan. 9/17. |
| 2 D. | Ross, Thos. Arthur. 10/20227. | M. Jan. 9/17. |
| 2 D. XIV | Wright, G. H. 3/28675. | M. Jan. 9/17. |
| *2 ? | Bollands, F. 8280. | M. Mar. 9/17. |
| 2 ? | Buckingham, J. L. 19483. | W. and M. Mar. 8-10/16. |
| 2 ? | Middleton, L.-Cpl. H. 11919. | M. Feb. 1/17. |
| 2 ? | Riley, L. 40300. | M. April 15/17. |
| 2 ? | Spencer, H. 22490. (Fr. 10th.) | W. and M. Mar. 9/17. |

# LEINSTER REGIMENT.

## B.E.F.

| | | |
|---|---|---|
| 12 A. | Reynolds, L.-Cpl. James. 5316 | K. June 23/17. Det.D./B. |
| 2 C. | Merriman, T. 7974. | W. and M. April 12/17. |
| 2 C. | Ribbans, E. E. 5476. | M. April 12/17. |
| 2 D. XV | Kennedy, L.-Cpl. Patrick. 4755. | W. and M. Jan. 10/17. |
| 7 A. | McLaughlin, Thos. 1687. | W. and M. Sept. 3/16. |
| 7 D. XV | Leonard, James. 3174. | M. Sept. 9/16. R/Enq. |

## LINCOLNSHIRE REGIMENT.

### *B.E.F.*

| | | |
|---|---|---|
| ‡1 A. II | Spencer, William. 7907. | M. Sept. 25/16. R/Enq. |
| 1 B. | Broadbent, Leonard. 22632. | M. Sept. 25/16. R/Enq. |
| ‡1 ? | Borrill, H. 22570. | W. and M. April 11/17. |
| 2 W. | **Eld, Lieut. Arthur.** | K. April 18/17. Det.D./B. |
| 2 W. | Brace, W. 30951. | M. April 19/17. |
| 2 W. | Davies, W. 26920. | M. April 18/17. |
| ‡2 W. I | Dowse, J. H. 23108. | M. Oct. 23/16. R/Enq. |
| 2 W. | Ling, Herbert. 16635. | M. Oct. 23/16. R./Enq. |
| 2 W. | Michie, T. 33005. | M. April 19/17. |
| ‡2 W. III | Nicholson, Benjamin. 1378. | M. Oct. 23/16. R/Enq. |
| 2 W. IV | Tasker, E. 10346. | W. and M. April 19/17. |
| *2 W. | Taylor, W. 17008. | W. and M. Oct. 23/16. R/Enq. |
| 2 W. | Wedgbury, L.-Cpl. Harry J. 32807. | M. April 19/17. |
| 2 X. | Cambray, H. 27083. | M. Mar. 4/17. |
| 2 X. V | Dawson, Wm. 27169. | M. Mar. 4/17. |
| 2 X. | Hubbard, L.-Cpl. Charles R. 40245. | M. Mar. 4/17. |
| 2 X. | Moore, Cpl. Vincent Reg. 32798. | M. March 4/17. |
| *2 Y. XI | Thompson, Joseph. 22641. | M. Oct. 23/16. R/Enq. |
| 2 Z. XIV | Barker, A. 40302. | M. Mar. 4/17. |
| 2 Z. | Dennis, George F. 40240. | M. Mar. 4/17. |
| ‡2 Z. | Parker, T. C. 30977. | M. April 4/17. |
| *2 Z. | Taylor, John. 1943. | M. Oct. 23/16. R/Enq. |
| 4 A. M.G.S. | Stevenson, H. J. 201103. (3648.) | M. May 2/17. |
| ‡4 A. | Williamson, J. A. 201724. | M. May 2/17. |
| ‡4 B. V | Edwards, L.-Cpl. Ernest Albert. 201391. | M. June 8/17. |
| ‡4 B. VI | Johnson, Harry. 242250. | M. June 8/17. |
| ‡4 B. V | Mason, Harry. 200534. | M. June 8/17. |
| *4 B. | Robinson, J. H. 201488. | M. June 8/17. |
| ‡4 B. VI | Thornley, Frank. 201812. | M. June 8/17. |
| ‡4 B. VII | Tilley, J. H. 202111. | M. June 8/17. |
| ‡4 D. XV | Dixon, F. 201721. | M. June 8/17. |
| ‡4 D. L.G.S. | Pembleton, H. N. 202620. | M. June 8/17. |
| ‡4 D. XV | Sellars, L.-Cpl. Joseph. 201220. | M. June 8/17. |
| ‡4 D. | Sollom, G. 202621. | M. May 3/17. |
| ‡4 H.Q. | Fallows, Bert. 203214. (Scout.) | M. June 8/17. |
| ‡4 ? | Tutty, Christopher Leak. 202154. | M. June 8/17. |
| 2/4 C. | Whatmough, L.-Cpl. C. E. 201517. | W. and M. April 19/17. |
| 2/4 D. | Smith, E. 201611. | M. April 4/17. |
| 5 B. | Dixon, C. 242436. | M. April 20/17. |
| 5 C. | Field, G. 240720. | M. April 20/17. |
| 2/5 | **Walker, Lieut. J. W.** | W. and M. April 11/17. |
| 2/5 A. | Arkless, J. W. 241784. | M. April 11/17. |
| 2/5 A. | Baker, R. T. 241773. | M. April 11/17. |
| 2/5 A. | Bowins, T. 241514. | M. April 11/17. |
| 2/5 A. | Bracken, J. H. 241779. | M. April 11/17. |
| 2/5 A. | Brown, F. 241777. | M. April 11/17. |
| *2/5 A. I | Clarke, P. 4791. | W. and M. April 11/17. |
| 2/5 A. | Clarke, F. 241534. | W. and M. April 11/17. |
| 2/5 A. | Coates, T. W. 241790. (5475.) | M. April 11/17. |
| 2/5 A. | Crane, T. A. 242028. | W. and M. April 11/17. |
| ‡2/5 A. | Dromey, C.-S.-M. W. G. 5594. | M. April 11/17. |
| 2/5 A. | Ellwood, S. 241885. | M. April 11/17. |
| 2/5 A. | Foster, L.-Cpl. G. W. 240992. (3807) | M. April 11/17. |
| 2/5 A. | Greenstock, E. G. 242005. | M. April 11/17. |
| 2/5 A. I | Harding, J. H. 242193. (6239.) | Unoff. W. and M. April 11/17. |
| 2/5 A. III | Hardy, Harold. 242194. | M. April 11/17. |
| 2/5 A. | Hargreaves, J. 241894. | M. April 11/17. |

**Lincolnshire Regiment—contd.**

*B.E.F.*

| | | |
|---|---|---|
| 2/5 A. III | Innell, E. J. 242030. (6056.) | M. April 11/17. |
| *2/5 A. | Leeman, W. H. 240957. (Late 3733.) | M. April 11/17. |
| 2/5 A. IV | Lowery, L.-Cpl. John Wm. 241416. (Late 4641.) | M. April 11/17. |
| 2/5 A. II | Palmer, Joseph Rich. 241409. | M. April 11/17. |
| *2/5 A. I.T.M. | Read, Wm. Geo. 240774. (3219.) (177 Bgde.) | M. April 11/17. |
| 2/5 A. | Rose, L.-Cpl. C. 241398. | M. April 11/17. |
| 2/5 A. | Spencer, T. V. 242267. | *M. April 11/17. |
| ‡2/5 A. | Tranter, L.-Cpl. G. 241420. | M. April 11/17. |
| 2/5 A. | Wilkinson, G. F. 241930. | M. April 11/17. |
| 2/5 A. | Wilkinson, L.-Cpl. P. G. 240621. (2729.) | M. April 11/17. |
| 2/5 B. VII | Baker, G. H. 241475. (Late 4724.) | M. April 11/17. |
| 2/5 B. VII | Bycroft, Tom. 241905. (5909.) | M. April 11/17. |
| 2/5 B. VII | Chapman, Sniper C. 242189. (Late 6235.) | M. April 11/17. |
| 2/5 B. VIII | Cooper, Ralph. 241452. (4695.) | M. April 11/17. |
| 2/5 B. | Coulbeck, W. 240529. | M. April 11/17. |
| 2/5 B. | Doughty, L.-Cpl. H. 241470. | M. April 11/17. |
| 2/5 B. | Foster, L.-Cpl. H. 241195. | M. April 11/17. |
| 2/5 B. | Fox, L.-Cpl. Tom. 240920. | M. April 11/17. |
| 2/5 B. | Goodwin, Sergt. J. C. 240295. | M. April 11/17. |
| 2/5 B. | Hodson, E. 241913. | M. April 11/17. |
| 2/5 B. | Holland, A. D. 242048. | M. April 11/17. |
| 2/5 B. VII | Kerslake, H. 242031. (Late 6057.) | M. April 11/17. |
| 2/5 B. V | Lill, F. 241485. (4736.) | M April 11/17. |
| 2/5 B. VIII | Longhurst, A. 241991. | M. April 11/17. |
| 2/5 B. VIII | Munton, E. 241439. (4671.) | M. April 11/17. |
| 2/5 B. VIII | Pell, E. 241914. (Late 5921.) | M. April 11/17. |
| 2/5 B. | Phillipson, C. E. 241920. | M. April 11/17. |
| ‡2/5 B. VIII | Piper, Lewis John. 242071. (6110.) | M. April 11/17. |
| 2/5 B. | Pitt, J. W. 241830. | M. April 11/17. |
| 2/5 B. | Rouse, W. 240893. | M. April 11/17. |
| 2/5 B. | Simpson, Reginald Wm. 241450. (4691.) | M. April 11/17. |
| 2/5 B. | Smith, Sergt. C. H. 240004. | M. April 11/17. |
| 2/5 B. | Smith, J. W. 242200. | M. April 11/17. |
| 2/5 B. | Stanham, W. 240962. | M. April 11/17. |
| *2/5 B. | Winterbottom, Cpl. Albert. 240167. (1575.) | M. April 11/17. |
| 2/5 C. | Abbott, H. 241580. | M. April 11/17. |
| 2/5 C. | Adams, Albert Edward. 241969. (Late 5989.) | M. April 11/17. |
| 2/5 C. | Adams, J. 241967. | M. April 11/17. |
| 2/5 C. XI | Ballard, Wm. Thos. M. 242057. (Late 6089.) | M. April 11/17. |
| 2/5 C. | Barker, G. 241361. | M. April 11/17. |
| 2/5 C. | Best, Robt. C. 242081. (Late 6123.) | M. April 11/17. |
| 2/5 C. | Billingham, E. W. 241804. | M. April 11/17. |
| 2/5 C. | Chinnery, E. J. 242041. (Late 6073.) | M. April 11/17. |
| 2/5 C. | Cook, R. S. 241776. | M. April 11/17. |
| 2/5 C. XI | Cuthbert, Geo. Wm. 241814. (Late 5500.) | M. April 11/17. |
| 2/5 C. | Dennis, L.-Cpl. W. 241367. | M. April 11/17. |

**Lincolnshire Regt.—contd.**

## *B.E.F.*

2/5 C. Edwards, G. 241812. M. April 11/17.
2/5 C. IX Edwards, J. R. 241384. (4603.) M. April 11/17.
2/5 C. IX Farrow, H. W. 242086 (6128.) M. April 11/17.
2/5 C. IX Fawcett, Jack. 242145. (Late 6191.) M. April 11/17.
2/5 C. Garbutt, J. G. 241801. M. April 11/17.
2/5 C. XII Gillings, L.-Cpl. L. 241391. (Late 4610.) M. April 11/17.
2/5 C. IX Gloyn, H. E. 241397. (4616.) M. April 11/17.
2/5 C. XII Hawkins, Walter Sidney, 241941. (Late 5960.) M. April 11/17.
2/5 C. Hunt, L.-Cpl. Joseph Henry. 241348. (4563.) M. April 11/17.
2/5 C. Jackson, D. 241351. M. April 11/17.
2/5 C. Jones, F. 240072. M. April 11/17.
2/5 C. Kidd, L.-Cpl. A. E. 241803. M. April 11/17.
2/5 C. Kisby, L.-Cpl. C. B. 241593. M. April 11/17.
2/5 C. Knibbs, F. 241181. M. April 11/17.
2/5 C. Lamminan, L.-Cpl. B. 4864. M. April 11/17.
2/5 C. Lindley, C. H. 242156. M. April 11/17.
2/5 C. X McNay, Jas. 241877. M. April 11/17.
2/5 C. Markham, G. C. (Chris.) 241374. M. April 11/17.
2/5 C. X Mumby, W. H. 241602. (Late 4875.) M. April 11/17.
2/5 C. XI North, E. C. 241386. (4605.) M. April 11/17.
2/5 C. Nundy, D. 241377. (4594.) M. April 11/17.
2/5 C. Parkin, R. W. 242167. M. April 11/17.
2/5 C. Penrose, J. 241792. M. April 11/17.
2/5 C. Proctor, F. W. 241581. M April 11/17.
2/5 C. XI Ragan, Henry. 242073. (6112.) M. April 11/17.
2/5 C. Reed, L.-Cpl. Thos. 241370. (Late 4585.) M. April 11/17.
2/5 C. Robinson, T. 241362. M. April 11/17.
2/5 C. Rose, T. 241582. (4854.) M. April 10/17.
2/5 C. Sanderson, J. T. 241366. (4581.) M. April 11/17.
2/5 C. IX Saunders, A. J. 242172. (6218.) M. April 11/17.
2/5 C. IX Sawyer, L.-Cpl. Wm. 241599. (Late 4872.) M. April 11/17.
2/5 C. Scharde, Leonard. 242074. (6115.) M. April 9-11/17.
2/5 C. Scoithorne, R. 241588. M. April 11/17.
2/5 C. XII Sipling, L.-Cpl. F. 241596. (4869.) M. April 11/17.
2/5 C. Smith, Isaac Ernest. 240799. (Late 3280.) M. April 11/17.
2/5 C. Smith, J. T. 240597. M. April 11/17.
2/5 C. X Smith, L.-Cpl. Sidney B. 241345. (4559.) M. April 11/17.
2/5 C. Smith, W. 241590. M. April 11/17.
2/5 C. Snowshall, R. 242171. M. April 11/17.
2/5 C. Sparks, A. R. 242054. M. April 11/17.
2/5 C. Tavner, Clifford M. 242062. (6096.) M. April 11/17.
2/5 C. XII Taylor, Harold. 241353. M. April 11/17.
2/5 C. Taylor, Cpl. W. J. 240915. (3627.) M. April 11/17.
2/5 C. Thornton, Maurice. 240971. (3766.) M. April 11/17.
2/5 C. XI Vessey, Carey. 241395. (4614.) M. April 11/17.
2/5 C. Walker, Fredk. Chas. 241931. (Late 5950.) M. April 11/17.
2/5 C. Walker, Sgt. Harry T. 240925. (3656) M. April 11/17.
2/5 C. XII Walling, J. W. 242175. (6221.) M. April 11/17.
2/5 C. Walton, J. H. 241358. M. April 11/17.

**Lincolnshire Regiment—contd.**

## *B.E.F.*

| | | |
|---|---|---|
| **2/5 C. XII** | Watson, James. 241764. (5385.) | M. **April 11/17.** |
| **2/5 C.** | Whitfield, Chas. Willred. 241350. (Late 4565.) | M. **April 11/17.** |
| **2/5 C.** | Willson, Cpl. F. 240639. | **M. April 11/17.** |
| **2/3 C.** | Young, J. 241390. | M. **April 11/17.** |
| **7 A.** | Rodgers, G. 43154. | **M. April 23/17.** |
| **7 A. IV H.Q.** | Woods, A. E. 40129. | M. **April 22/17.** |
| **7 B. VIII** | Bradley, J. 27882. | W. and M. **April 23/17.** |
| **‡7 B.** | Kilminster, W. S. 18362. | W. and M. **April 23/17.** |
| **7 B.** | Oldman, C. 17906. | **M. April 22/17.** |
| **‡7 B.** | Woodward, J. 14508. | W. and M. **April 23/17.** |
| **7 C. X** | Howsam, C. R. 17986. | **M. April 23/17.** |
| **7 C. X** | Hurst, J. W. 28279. | M. **April 23/17.** |
| ***7 C. XI** | Leedham, Walter. 30900. | M. **May 15/17.** |
| **‡7 C.** | Todd, H. 14525. | W. and M. **April 23/17.** |
| **7 C. X** | Wilson, F. 22774. | W. and M. **April 23/17.** |
| **7 D. or H.Q.** | Dixon, Francis. 25895. | M. **April 23/17.** |
| **7 D. XVI** | Spratt, L.-Cpl. Fred. 19036. | W. and M. **April 23/17.** |
| **7 D. or H.Q.** | Young, A. B. 11770. | M. **April 22/17.** |
| **8** | **Posner, 2nd Lt. P. E.** (Fr. 3 S. Staffs) | W. and M. **April 28/17.** |
| **8 A. and B.** | **Rables-Rabbula, Capt. A. J.** | W. and M. **April 28/17.** |
| **8** | **Tedder, 2nd Lieut. O. S.** | M. **April 28/17.** |
| ***8 A. IV** | Archer, J. 25061. | M. **May 3/17.** |
| **8 A.** | Ashling, G. 40828. | W. and M. **April 9-12/17.** |
| **8 A. I** | Birkett, Thos., Edward. 14582. | M. **April 9-12/16.** |
| **‡8 A.** | Blythe, W. 16856. | M. **April 20-28/17.** |
| **8 A. or H.Q.** | Burn, L. 18916. (Sig. S.) | M **April 28/17.** |
| **‡8 A.** | Bush, W. J. 40008. | M. **April 20-28/17.** |
| **8 A.** | Christian Geo. 202414. (Fr. 4 Lincs.) | K. **April 20-28/17. Det.D./B.** |
| **‡8 A. II** | Cox, J. E. 40831. | M. **April 20-28/17.** |
| **‡8 A.** | Crow, J. 10275. | M. **April 20-28/17.** |
| **‡8 A.** | Dawson, D. M. C. 203103. | M. **April 26-28/17.** |
| **‡8 A.** | Fenn, R. J. 40828 | M. **April 20-28/17.** |
| **‡8 A.** | Gray, L.-Cpl. H. R. 1147. | M. **April 20-28/17.** |
| **‡8 A.** | Henden, H. 43293. | M. **April 20-28/17.** |
| **‡8 A.** | Henson, T. 16873. | M. **April 20-28/17.** |
| **8 A.** | Jones, Thomas. 32979. | M. **April 9-12/17.** |
| **8 A. III** | Liddell, Arthur. 32977. | M. **April 9-12/17.** |
| **‡8 A.** | Morriss, W. G. 25123. | M. **April 20-28/17.** |
| **‡8 A.** | Randall, G. 11953. | M. **April 20-28/17.** |
| **‡8 A.** | Rogers, V. G. 16707. | M. **April 20-28/17.** |
| **8 A. II** | Rush, W. J. 40008. | M. **April 17/17.** |
| **‡8 A.** | Twelves, W. J. 15652. | M. **April 20-28/17.** |
| **8 A. or B.** | **M.G.S.** White, Harold B. 10178. | M. **April 20-28/17.** |
| **8 B. V** | Atkinson, R. A. 27517. | M. **April 20-28/17.** |
| **‡8 B.** | Brace, G. 1706. | M. **April 20-28/17.** |
| **8 B. or H.Q.** | Cobley, W. 1633. (Sig. S.) | M. **April 28/17.** |
| **8 B. V** | Collins, John J. 13169. | M. **April 9-12/17.** |
| ***8 B. V** | Doncaster, H. 13545. | M. **April 20-28/17.** |
| **8 B. VIII** | Edge, Albert. 632. | M. **April 20-28/17.** |
| ***8 B. VIII** | Ellwood, Sergt. Arthur. 7/13006. | M. **April 28-29/17.** |
| **‡8 B.** | Forsyth, J. J. 27511. | M. **April 20-28/17.** |
| **‡8 B.** | Glaister, John Robert. 30581. | M. **April 20-28/17.** |
| **‡8 B.** | Graveling, E. 18290. | M. **April 20-28/17.** |
| **‡8 B.** | Grimstead, A. 1787. | M. **April 20-28/17.** |
| **‡8 B.** | Hayward, F. 10448. | M. **April 20-28/17.** |
| **‡8 B.** | Herrick, J. F. 40691. | M. **April 20-28/17.** |
| **8 B.** | Marshall, F. 9931. | M. **April 9-12/17.** |
| **‡8 B.** | Morton, Joseph. 23649. | M. **April 20-28/17.** |

**Lincolnshire Regiment—contd.**

## *B.E.F.*

| | | |
|---|---|---|
| *8 B. VIII | O'Kane, Edward. 30595. | M. April 20-28/17. |
| 8 B. | Pyrah, Sig. W. 15888. | M. April 9-12/17. |
| ‡8 B. | Simpson, J. B. 43314. | M. April 20-28/17. |
| ‡8 B. | Steward, G. R. 27417. | M. April 20-28/17. |
| ‡8 B. | Ullyatt, E. 40834. | M. April 20-28/17. |
| ‡8 C. | Allen, J. H. 27167. | M. April 20-28/17. |
| 8 C. X | Altoft, L.-Cpl. J. R. 27527. | M. April 20-28/17. |
| ‡8 C. | Bark, C. P. 17892. | M. April 20-28/17. |
| 8 C. | Clarke, L.-Cpl. T. 40840. | W. and M. April 9-12/17. |
| *8 C. IX | Cox, Harry. 27259. | M. April 23/17. |
| 8 C. | Dixon, Joseph. 26057. | M. April 20-28/17. |
| ‡8 C. | Fell, L.-Cpl. L. J. 18326. | M. April 20-28/17. |
| 8 C. XI | Fisher, W. S. 11/1752. | M. April 20-28/17. |
| 8 C. XI | Foat, Victor. 27187. | W. and M. April 20-28/17. |
| 8 C. | Fussey, George. 14475. | W. and M. April 20-28/17. |
| ‡8 C. | Gaskin, L.-Cpl. H. 17046. | M. April 20-28/17. |
| *8 C. XI | Herring, J. E. 2242. | M. April 20-28/17. |
| 8 C. XI | King, Sydney. 40857. | W. and M. April 20-28/17. |
| ‡8 C. | Pacey, J. H. 19262. | M. April 20-28/17. |
| 8 C. | Parish, Joseph. 2240. | M. April 20-28/17. |
| ‡8 C. | Pycroft, T. 27612. | M. April 20-28/17. |
| ‡8 C. | Raven, T. 18075. | W. and M. April 20-28/17. |
| 8 C. | Rowe, Sniper Arthur. 8564. (Fr. H.Q.) | M. April 20-28/17. |
| 8 C. | Spiers, Noel Thomas. 16682. | W. and M. April 20-28/17. |
| 8 C. | Taylor, L.-Cpl. J. T. 11889. | W. and M. April 9-12/17. |
| 8 C. X | Thornley, Alfred. 27589. | M. April 28/17. |
| ‡8 C. | Tindall, Cpl. H. 11809. | M. April 20-28/17. |
| *8 C. X | Twelvetree, E. 27610. | M. April 20-28/17. |
| 8 C. X | West, Fredk. John. 40848. | W. Unoff. M. April 20-28/17. |
| ‡8 C. | Whitfield, J. 27358. | W. and M. April 20-28/17. |
| 8 C. X | Windle, W. G. 3/26027. | M. April 20-28/17. |
| 8 D. | Ashton, Thomas. 43328. | M. April 20-28/17. |
| ‡8 D. | Bell, G. R. 12546. | M. April 20-28/17. |
| *8 D. | Brown, George. 11172. | M. April 11/17. |
| ‡8 D. | Cole, Arthur. 26437. | M. April 20-28/17. |
| ‡8 D. XVI | Cope, L.-Cpl. E. A. 14427. | M. April 20-28/17. |
| ‡8 D. XVI | Elsom, W. 27078. | M. April 20-28/17. |
| ‡8 D. | Hill, H. 13033. | M. April 20-28/17. |
| *8 D. | Hudgill, Arthur Jas. 13337. | M. April 20-28/17. |
| 8 D. XIV | Jones, Ernest Frank. 12204. | M. April 20-28/17. |
| ‡8 D. | King, Joshua. 18211. | M. April 20-28/17. |
| 8 D. | Merriman, A. 30905. | M. April 20-28/17. |
| ‡8 D. XV | Perry, F. 18233. | M. April 20-28/17. |
| ‡8 D. | Roberts, Albert H. 15548. | M. April 20-28/17. |
| 8 D. M.G.S. | Robinson, A. 16162. | M. April 20-28/17. |
| 8 D. | Robson, Thomas Albert. 30642. | M. April 20-28/17. |
| 8 D. | Stocks, L.-Cpl. John Henry 8571. | M. April 20-28/17. |
| 8 D. XVI | Taylor, W. 10/1486. | M. April 20-28/17. |
| ‡8 D. | Thompson, H. 17890. | M. April 20-28/17. |
| ‡8 D. | Turner, L.-Cpl. Edward. 19242. | M. April 20-28/17. |
| 10 | **Dickson, Lieut. E. D.** | M. April 28/17. |
| 10 | **Elsom, 2nd Lieut. H.** (Fr. 1st.) | M. April 28/17. |
| 10 | **Hendin, 2nd Lieut. H. P.** | M. April 28/17. |
| 10 | **Lavender, 2nd Lieut. J. E.** | M. April 28/17. |
| ‡10 A. | Adams, A. 40940. | M. April 28/17. |
| ‡10 A. | Adams, F. 43500. | M. April 28/17. |
| ‡10 A. | Aldus, R. 30745. | M. April 28/17. |

**Lincolnshire Regiment—contd.**

## *B.E.F.*

10 A. IV Allison, F. 30110. M. April 28/17.
‡10 A. Ancliffe, L. 203359. M. April 28/17.
‡10 A. III Bear, R. 1644. M. April 28/17.
*10 A. Bell, Albert. 203100. M. April 28/17.
‡10 A. Borman, L.-Cpl. T. 147. M. April 28/17.
‡10 A. Breakwell, J. H. 40922. M. April 28/17.
‡10 A. Chapman, G. 203399. M. April 28/17.
‡10 A. Chappell, L.-Cpl. F. 43548. M. April 28/17.
10 A. Chell, A. 40923. (Fr. 1 S. Staffs.) M. April 28/17.
‡10 A. Coulbeck, T. S. 1710. W. and M. April 28/17.
*10 A. IV Cross, F. H. 43543. (2141.) M. April 28/17.
‡10 A. Doughty, H. 40970. M. April 28/17.
10 A. II Douglas, Robt. 40926. M. April 28/17.
*10 A. Edwards, E. 203058. M. April 28/17.
‡10 A. Evans, C. W. G. 43556. M. April 28/17.
10 A. Evans, Fred. 32949. M. April 28/17.
‡10 A. Field, G. W. 43544. W. and M. April 28/17.
10 A. or C. Fitton, Walter R. 40971. (Fr. 1 N. Staffs, 24488.) M. April 28/17.
‡10 A. Flatters, E. 1951. M. April 28/17.
10 A. III Gray, H. 203307. M. April 28/17.
‡10 A. Green, Cpl. H. E. 32918. M. April 28/17.
*10 A. III Hanks, A. G. 43559. M. April 28/17.
‡10 A. Holmes, L.-Cpl. N. 43694. M. April 28/17.
‡10 A. III Ingram, Harry. 203072. M. April 28/17.
‡10 A. James, F. T. 202432. M. April 28/17.
‡10 A. Lambert, H. J. 202966. M. April 28/17.
‡10 A. Lewis, C. 40657. M. April 28/17.
10 A. IV Longbottom, Ernest. 40930. M. April 28/17.
*10 A. II Nelson, J. C. 1744. M. April 28/17.
‡10 A. Oldham, Joseph. 40932. M. April 28/17.
10 A. II Onslow, J. 202808. M. April 28/17.
10 A. Pacey, J. R. 28476. (Fr. 2nd & 3rd.) M. April 28/17.
‡10 A. Pearson, C. H. 27011. M. April 28/17.
‡10 A. Reynolds, J. W. 27782. M. April 28/17.
‡10 A. Sillitoe, Sergt. E. G. 41001. M. April 28/17.
10 A. IV Taylor, R. 40933. M. April 28/17.
*10 A. II Towl, T. 28460. M. April 28/17.
‡10 A. Turner, J. 200351. M. April 28/17.
‡10 A. Walker, E. 40949. M. April 28/17.
10 A. I Watson, John R. 1385. W. and M. April 28/17.
10 A. Williams, J. 43710. M. April 10/17.
‡10 A. Williams, W. 40947. M. April 28/17.
‡10 B. Allen, A. 203392. M. April 28/17.
‡10 B. Breedon, J. 203361. M. April 28/17.
‡10 B. Brooke, Sergt. R. J. 367. M. April 28/17.
‡10 B. Broughton, L.-Sergt. G. 40151. M. April 28/17.
10 B. Cheavin, Cpl. S. R. 1027. M. April 28/17.
‡10 B. Clark, L.-Cpl. A. V. 1746. M. April 28/17.
10 B. VII Clarke, L.-Cpl. Sigs. 1287. W. and M. April 28/17.
10 B. VIII Dolby, H. 25129. M. April 28/17.
‡10 B. Dunkley, T. F. 203404. M. April 28/17.
‡10 B. VIII Eagles, L.-Cpl. A. E. 40937. M. April 28/17.
10 B. V Gibbons, William. 40972. M. April 28/17.
10 B. Graham, E. 32997. K. April 28/17. Det.D./B. R/Enq.
‡10 B. VI Haigh, Fred. 40973. M. April 28/17.
10 B. VI Hammersley, A. 203407. M. April 28/17.

**Lincolnshire Regiment—contd.**

## *B.E.F.*

| | | |
|---|---|---|
| 10 B. VIII | Hogger, G. F. 18325. | M. April 28/17. |
| ‡10 B. | Horton, J. R. 203391. | M. April 28/17. |
| ‡10 B. | Howley, E. 40976. | M. April 28/17. |
| ‡10 B. | Hunt, F. 16176. | M. April 28/17. |
| ‡10 B. | Hyams, H. 203070. | M. April 28/17. |
| ‡10 B. | Johnson, G. 203371. | M. April 28/17. |
| 10 B. VIII | Kelford, F. J. 40593. | M. April 28/17. |
| ‡10 B. | Langdon, W. 43665. | M. April 28/17. |
| ‡10 B. | Large, L.-Cpl. J. 1702. | M. April 28/17. |
| ‡10 B. | Little, C. E. 370. | M. April 28/17. |
| ‡10 B. | Lund, G. 203352. | M. April 28/17. |
| *10 B. VIII | Main, Albert Edwd. 30749. | M. April 28/17. |
| ‡10 B. | Mather, Cpl. H. 32921. | M. April 28/17. |
| ‡10 B. | Merchant, C. W. H. 21341. | M. April 28/17. |
| *10 B. | Minter, E. 203112. | M. April 28/17. |
| ‡10 B. | Mocock, H. 30616. | M. April 28/17. |
| ‡10 B. | Nicholson, R. 30721. | M. April 28/17. |
| 10 B. V | Tayles, Edwin. 19139. | M. April 28/17. |
| ‡10 B. | Thomas, B. 41004. | M. April 28/17. |
| ‡10 B. | White, Sergt. G. D. 635. | W. and M. April 28/17. |
| *10 C. | Allen, Wm. 203115. | M. April 28/17. |
| 10 C. XI | Bilsby, F. 1376. | M. April 28/17. |
| 10 C. XI | Brown, Samuel. 30696. | M. April 28/17. |
| *10 C. or D. | Clewlow, Fredk. Geo. 203403. | M. April 28/17. |
| ‡10 C. | Dickinson, A.-Cpl. A. 640. | M. April 28/17. |
| ‡10 C. | Illsley, J. 203146. | M. April 28/17. |
| 10 C. XI | Ingham, Helliwell. 40981. | M. April 28/17. |
| *10 C. | Jenkins, Sergt. A. 599. | M. April 28/17. |
| 10 C. IX | Johnstone, H. 43578. | M. April 28/17. |
| 10 C. X | Kelsey, W. H. 26171. | M. April 20-28/17. |
| 10 C. IX | Moulson, Cpl. Norman. 32965. | M. April 28/17. |
| ‡10 C. | Noble, W. A. 1692. | M. April 28/17. |
| *10 C. | Paddon, Samuel Harding. 7750. | M. April 28/17. |
| ‡10 C. | Price, J. 40572. | M. April 28/17. |
| 10 C. | Riddington, Harry. 203420. | M. April 28/17. |
| *10 C. | Roe, Reuben. 203380. | M. April 28/17. |
| ‡10 C. | Rust, E. F. 1814. | M. April 28/17. |
| *10 C. XI | Sargent, George E. 40913. | M. April 28/17. |
| ‡10 C. | Taylor, G. H. 203094. | M. April 28/17. |
| *10 C. XI | Titherington, Rennie. 203158. | M. April 28/17. |
| ‡10 C. | Todd, W. 40991. | M. April 28/17. |
| ‡10 C. | Watson, T. W. 30690. | M. April 28/17. |
| ‡10 D. | Agate, C. E. 40951. | M. April 28/17. |
| ‡10 D. | Bird, W. F. 891. | M. April 28/17. |
| ‡10 D. | Bird, W. J. 40956. | M. April 28/17. |
| ‡10 D. | Briars, J. 40941. | M. April 28/17. |
| *10 D. XVI | Burke, L.-Cpl. Francis. 43423. | M. April 28/17. |
| 10 D. | Carter, Robt. 40963. (Fr. 1 N. Staffs, 24420.) | M. April 28/17. |
| 10 D. XV | Collins, H. 43621. | M. April 28/17. |
| 10 D. | Connelly, J. 203049. | M. April 28/17. |
| ‡10 D. | Cubley, A. 28434. | M. April 28/17. |
| ‡10 D. | Dewson, L.-Cpl. W. G. 253. | M. April 28/17. |
| 10 D. | Exton, E. 13720. | M. April 28/17. |
| ‡10 D. | Fenton, G. 203365. | M. April 28/17. |
| 10 D. XVI | Gittins, Sig. Harry. 808. | M. April 28/17. |
| *10 D. XV | Grice, Chas. 43622. | M. April 28/17. |
| 10 D. XIII | Gould, H. E. 876. | K. April 28/17. Det.D./B. |

**Lincolnshire Regiment—contd.**

*B.E.F.*

‡10 D. Gummery, E. J. 43494. M. April 28/17.
‡10 D. Hall, G. 30585. M. April 28/17.
‡10 D. Knowles, S. 975. M. April 28/17.
*10 D. Lightfoot, Willie. 40997. M. April 28/17.
‡10 D. Marriott, L.-Cpl. G. O. 1350. M. April 28/17.
10 D. XIII Marshall, L.-Cpl. John. 7941. M. April 28/17.
10 D. XIV Proudley, G. F. 1325. M. April 28/17.
10 D. Quance, Cpl. Ernest John. 882. M. April 28/17.
‡10 D. XV Robinson, Arthur Cecil Cavendish. 202919. M. April 28/17.
,10 D. Rylatt, Ellis Arthur. 40907. M. April 28/17.
‡10 D. Smith, G. 43427. M. April 28/17.
*10 D. Smith, Herbert. 14327. M. April 28/17.
‡10 D. Smith, J. 40675. M. April 28/17.
10 D. XV Thirkell, Wilfred Bell. 30678. M. April 28/17.
10 D. XVI Towers, Cpl. Richard. 1490. K. April 28/17. Det.D./B.
*10 D. XVI Webb, Cpl. James. 32931. D/W. April 9/17. Det.D./B.
10 D. XIII Welbourne, R. W. 1805. M. April 28/17.
10 D. XIV Williams, Cpl. Edgar. 32911. (Fr. Lancs. Fus.) M. April 28/17.
‡10 D. Winks, A. J. 1811. M. April 28/17.
10 ? H.Q. Roe, Sig. Fred. 71. Unoff. K. April 28/17. Conf. and Det.D./B.

## LINCOLNSHIRE YEOMANRY.

*E.E.F.*

? ? Dicker, Thos. Harry. 18533. M., bel. drowned April 15/17. "Arcadian."

## KING'S LIVERPOOL REGIMENT.

*B.E.F.*

1 C. **Bannatyne, Lieut. (A/Capt.) N. J.** Unoff. W. and M. May 3/17.
1 **Bland, Capt. P. R.** M. May 3/17.
1 A. Barlow, S. 52499. W. and M. April 28/17.
1 A. or B. Catherall, Cpl. A. 53015. M. May 3/17.
1 A. Draper, W. 202622. (Fr. 5th.) M. May 3/17.
‡1 A. Ellens, Jas. Chas. 47257. M. May 3/17.
‡1 A. Robinson, J. W. 56524. M. May 3/17.
1 B. VI Armstrong, Fred. 52489. M. May 3/17.
‡1 B. Callaghan, R. 8262. M. May 3/17.
1 B. Hoerty, H. 28193. M. Nov. 13-15/16. R/Enq.
*1 B. VII Roberts, Joseph. 32745. K. April 23/17. Det.D./B.
1 B. Perry, Edward Griffith. 26170. M. April 28/17.
1 B. VI Starkey, John. 52739. K. Nov. 13-15/16. Det.D./B.

Liverpool Regiment, King's—contd.

## B.E.F.

‡1 B. Walsh, F. 52761. M. May 3/17.
1 C. Brown, E. 25250. M. April 28/17.
1 C. Burgess, J. H. 38817. M. April 28/17.
1 C. Cunningham, H. 26967. M. April 28/17.
1 C. Habisreuter, A.-L.-Sergt. A. 28145. M. April 28/17.
‡1 C. Heasley, A. 9127. M. May 3/17.
1 C. Jennings, Drmr. M. P. 11265. M. April 24/17.
*1 C. IX Price, G. H. 41223. M. May 3/17.
1 C. Sparks, A.-Sergt. R. 9739. M. April 28/17.
1 D. L.G.S. Duckworth, Walter. 52573. (Fr. 2/10 Manchester, 3482.) M. May 8/17.
‡1 D. XIV Gill, Jas. Patrick. 28102. W. and M. May 3/17.
‡1 D. Harding, A. 30444. M. May 3/17. R/Enq.
‡1 D. Hodges, F. 37530. M. May 3/17.
‡1 D. Lees, Herbert. 52640. W. and M. May 3/17.
*1 D. XIII Moorcroft, John. 42865. M. May 3/17.
‡1 D. Parkes, E. 8985. M. May 3/17.
1 D. XIII Pritchard, Hugh Henry. 9978. M. May 3/17.
1 D. Riley, Jas. 27155. W. and M. Mar. 13/17.
1 D. Turner, L.-Cpl. Abraham. 52753. (Fr. 2/10 Manch., 2546.) M. May 3/17.
*1 ? I.T.M. Costigan, John Fred. 53018. (6 Bgde.) W. and M. April 28/17.
1 ? M.G.S Kelly, James P. 52638. (Fr. 2/10 Manchesters.) K. Nov. 13-15/16. Det.D./B.
‡1 ? I.T.M. Tovlan, Hugh. 37222. (6 Bgde.) M. April 28/17.
1 ? L.G.S. Watson, Walter William. 53178. K. Nov. 13-15/16. Det.D./B.
4 **Gaulter, 2nd Lt. Chas. P.** (Fr. 3rd.) K. Aug. 18/16. Det.D./B.
‡4 C. Skelly, G. 41885. M. May 20/17.
*4 C. X Tisdale, Ralph. 31187. W. Unoff. M. May 20/17.
‡5 A. IV Wilcox, Jas. 201519. (3922.) W. and M. Sept. 18/16.
‡6 B. Leigh, T. S. 241651. M. May 11/17.
6 B. VI Tyson, David Albert. 241876. M. May 11/17.
‡6 C. Clarke, L.-Cpl. A. J. 240483. M., bel. K. May 11/17.
7 A. Herring, G. J. 27466. M. Mar. 22/17.
7 A. IV Ratcliffe, Tom. 267870. (Fr. 4th, 6375.) M. April 23/17.
7 B. V Dagger, Richard. 5396. M. Sept. 25/16. R/Enq.
7 D. XV Hampson, John Wm. 6905. (Fr. 9th Manchesters, 3751.) M. Unoff. K. Sept. 17/16. R/Enq.
7 D. Sig. Love, H. 6903. W. and M. Sept. 25/16. R/Enq
‡7 ? Bradshaw, L.-Cpl. Wm. 269686. M. June 4/17.
‡2/7 A. Addy, W. H. 269558. M. May 7/17.
‡2/7 A. Causer, C. 267671. M. May 7/17.
‡2/7 A. Joynt, J. 269417. M. May 7/17.
‡2/7 A. Laws, H. 267681. M. May 7/17.
2/7 A. Middleton, Frank. 269640. (8364.) M. May 7/17.
‡2/7 A. Parry, L.-Cpl. R. T. 267555. M. May 7/17.
‡2/7 A. Partridge, J. 267669. M. May 30/17.
‡2/7 A. Toohey, J. P. 267529. M. May 7/17.
2/7 A. I Whalley, J. J. 204261. M. May 7/17.
‡2/7 A. Williams, A. A. M. 267468. (5767.) M. May 7/17.
‡2/7 A. Williams, J. 266171. M. May 7/17.
*8 A. I Buchanan, Lindsay Blair. 307845. (5859.) M. Unoff. W. Sept. 26-28/16. R/Enq.
*8 A. III Capon, S. 5863. M. Sept. 26-28/16. R/Enq.
‡8 A. IV Fogell, Wm. 6411. M. Sept. 26-28/16. R/Enq.
8 B. Roughley, Peter. 305083. (Late 1365.) M., bel. K. Feb. 22/17.

**Liverpool Regiment, King's—contd.**

*B.E.F.*

| | | |
|---|---|---|
| ‡8 C. | Ashton, F. 308090. | M. May 18/17. |
| 8 C. | Burns, James. 6032. (Fr. 5 Manc.) | M. Sept. 26/16. R/Enq. |
| 8 C. | Humphreys, T. C. 6049. | M. Sept. 26/16. R/Enq. |
| 8 D. XIII | Ford, Fredk. 6494. (Late 4602, 3/8 Manchesters.) | M. Sept. 28/16. R/Enq. |
| *2/8 C. IX | Smith, J. W. 306397. | W. and M. May 8/17. |
| 9 B. | Spelacy, Thomas. 2224. | M. Sept. 25/16. R/Enq. |
| 9 C. IX | Parratt, Joseph H. 331398. | M. Mar. 4/17. |
| ‡2/9 A. III | Henry, John. 331433. (4014.) | M. June 11/17. |
| 2/9 C. | Vining, F. 331193. | M. April 10/17. |
| ‡10 | **Blencowe, 2nd Lt. L. C.** | M., bel. K. June 29/17. |
| ‡10 | **Jowett, 2nd Lieut. A.** | M., bel. K. June 29/17. |
| 10 | **MacGilvray, 2nd Lt. J. D.** (Fr. 4th Camerons.) | M. Feb. 18/17. |
| *2/10 | **MacLaren, 2nd Lieut. D.** | M. June 29/17. |
| ‡2/10 C. | Collins, L.-Sergt. J. H. 356027. | Unoff. W. and M. June 29/17. |
| 2/10 C. | Costine, W. R. 357658. | M. April 10/17. |
| ‡2/10 C. | Davies, Wm. 358094. | Unoff. W. and M. June 29/17. |
| ‡2/10 C. | Mackenzie, Sergt. R. G. 355243. | M. Unoff. W. June 29/17. |
| ‡2/10 C. | Okell, Wm. Lee. 357828. | Unoff. W. and M. June 29/17. |
| 2/10 C. | Tyson, Sergt. F. J. 355602. (3476.) | M Feb. 18/17. |
| 2/10 D. | Greig, A. E. 356527. (5071.) | M. April 10/17. |
| 12 A. I | Gillett, Henry. 18134. | M. Sept. 15-16/16. R/Enq. |
| 12 A. | Hatton, T. L. 14746. | W. and M., bel. K. Mar. 15/17. |
| 12 A. | Hullock, P. 48817. | M. Mar. 28/17. |
| 12 A. | Nestor, Mickeal. 27032. | W. and M. Oct. 7/16. R/Enq. |
| 12 D. | Elliott, J. J. 35583. | W. and M. Oct. 8/16. R/Enq. |
| 12 D. XV | Heaton, Albert James. 14568. | M. Sept. 3/16. R/Enq. |
| ‡12 D. | Morgan, G. 48906. | M. May 9/17. |
| 12 D. | Phillips, R. E. 56090. | M. Mar. 28/17. |
| ‡12 ? M.G.S. | Burke, G. 18558. | K. Mar. 29/17. Det.D./B. |
| 13 | **Coates, Major H. E.** (Fr. 11th.) | K. May 3/17. Det.D./B. |
| 13 | **Innes, 2nd Lieut. A. J.** | M. May 3/17. |
| 13 | **Phillips, Lieut. J. A.** | W. and M. May 3/17. |
| *13 A. III | Bennett, Albert. 48666. | M. May 3/17. |
| ‡13 A. | Birtwell, W. 40580. | W. and M. May 3/17. |
| 13 A. III | Cox, Edward (Ted). 48685. | M. April 9/17. |
| *13 A. M.G.S. | Glover, L.-Cpl. Thomas. 52326. | M. May 3/17. |
| ‡13 A. | Hodson, J. E. 30752. | W. and M. May 3/17. |
| *13 A. L.G.S. | McCarty, L.-Cpl. J. 23772. | M. May 3/17. |
| 13 A. IV | Malcolm, G. A. 51551. | K. May 3/17. Det.D./B. |
| 13 A. I | Nuttall, John Edward. 41857. | M. April 13/17. |
| ‡13 A. | Sutherland, A. 14298. | M. May 3/17. |
| 13 A. | Taylor, Richard. 37080. | M. April 9/17. |
| ‡13 B. | Brophy, J. 58686. | W. and M. May 3/17. |
| ‡13 B. | Cheevers, Sergt. P. 14122. | M. May 3/17. |
| ‡13 B. | Dobson, E. 13185. | M. May 3/17. |
| ‡13 B. | Fazackerley, R. 46711. | M. May 3/17. |
| ‡13 B. | Fyles, W. 37019. | W. and M. May 3/17. |
| 13 B. VII | Gale, Thos. 35661. | M. May 11/17. |
| ‡13 B. | Harris, W. 48718. | W. and M. May 3/17. |
| *13 B. VIII | Harrison, Albert. 48717. | W. and M. May 3/17. |
| ‡13 B. VIII | Higgins, Jas. Henry. 42562. | M. May 3/17. |
| ‡13 B. | McFarrens, H. 58689. | M. May 3/17. |
| 13 B. V | Moore, M. 52421. | M. May 3/17. |
| ‡13 B. | Morris, C. 24487. | M. May 3/17. |
| 13 C. XI | Bentham, Robt. Geo. 58577. | M. May 3/17. |
| *13 C. IX | Dawson, Thos. 8585. | M. May 3/17. |

**Liverpool Regiment, King's—contd.**

## *B.E.F.*

*13 C. Kirky, Cpl. J. 22751. Unoff. W. and M. **May 3/17.**
13 C. X Leigh, J. 46786. M. **May 3/17.**
*13 C. M.G.S. Molyneaux, Cpl. Francis. 51848. W. and M. **May 3/17.** R/Enq.
‡13 C. Parkinson, P. G. 30102. M. **May 3/17.**
13 C. X Povey, C. 48755. K. **May 3/17.** Det.D./B.
13 C. XII Wilson, J. H. 48995. D/W. **April 11/17.** Det.D./B.
13 D. XV Adams, Albert. 22302. M. **May 3/17.**
13 D. XV Birchall, L.-Cpl. Frank. 24640. M. **May 3/17.**
*13 D. IV Cherrington, G. T. 48682. W. and M. **May 3/17.**
13 D. Hussey, A. 12762. M. **April 11/17.**
‡13 D. Jackson, L.-Cpl. F. 51790. M. **May 3/17.**
‡13 D. XIV Kerton, C. H. 48735. M. **May 3/17.**
13 D. XIII Lee, C. 48739. W. and M. **May 8/17.**
*13 D. XIV McLean, A. 52358. W. Unoff. M. **May 3/17.**
‡13 D. McMullin, J. 14516. W. and M. **May 3/17.**
‡13 D. Nelson, J. 41863. M. **May 3/17.**
‡13 D. Newman, H. 10675. M. **May 3/17.**
‡13 D. Nicholson, G. E. 48751. M. **May 3/17.**
13 D. XIII O'Hare, John P. 14318. M. **May 3/17.**
13 D. XV Rankin, R. 48377. M. **May 3/17.**
‡13 D. Tudor, Wm. Henry. 42422. W. and M. **May 3/17.**
‡13 D. Vogs, H. 27300. M. **May 3/17.**
13 D. XVI Wild, Herbert. 23668. M. **May 3/17.**
13 D. Winterbottom, Sergt. H. R. 22887. M. **May 3/17.**
13 ? Court, L.-Cpl. W. T. 51809. (Fr. 10) K. **May 8/17.** Det.D./B.
‡17 **Chavasse, Lieut. Aidan.** W. and M. **July 4/17.**
17 A. L.G.S. McCarthy, Dan. 24910. W. and M. **Oct. 12/16.** R/Enq.
17 B. VII Brown, John. 31091. M. **Oct. 12/16.** R/Enq.
17 B. Robinson, James. 31174. M. **Oct. 12/16.** R/Enq.
17 B. VI Smith, J. G. 58046. W. and M. **April 9/17.**
17 C. IX Charnock, John. 38132. M. **Oct. 12/16.** R/Enq.
17 D. Gibbins, Archer Amos. 51650. M. **Oct. 12/16.** R/Enq.
‡17 D. Warburton, W. C. 51671. M. **Mar. 8/17.**
18 **Ashcroft, 2nd Lieut. F.** K. **April 9/17.** Det.D./B.
18 **Coupe, 2nd Lieut. A.** K. **April 9/17.** Det.D./B.
18 **Ewing, 2nd Lieut. H. G.** M. **April 9/17.**
18 **Stewart, 2nd Lieut. J. N.** M. **April 14/17.**
18 2 M.G.S. Adams, W. E. 17242. K. **April 23/17.** Det.D./B.
18 2 Cooper, Chas. Wm. 57916. M. **April 23/17.**
*18 2 Jones, Sgt.-Maj. John Daniel. 17060. K. **April 23/17.** Det.D./B.
18 2 Langford, Henry Geo. 53115. W. and M. **Oct. 18/16.** R/Enq.
18 2 Reed, Patrick. 47477. W. and M. **April 9/17.**
18 2 VIII Robertson, James. 57566. M. **April 9/17.**
‡18 4 Hodgkinson, J. 57713. M. **April 23/17.**
18 4 Hollis, W. 17602. M. **April 23/17.**
19 3 Allen, Stanley H. 51684. M. **Oct. 12/16.** R/Enq.
19 3 XII Slupton, Fredk. Wm. 52086. M. **April 9/17.**
*19 3 IX Suggett, Wm. 57843. W. and M. **April 9/17.**
‡20 1 Bradbury, Jas. 49490. W. Unoff. M. **June 9/17.**
‡20 1 Sloan, D. 36949. W. and M. **April 9/17.**

## *BALKANS.*

14 A. Simcock, Wm. 21026. M. **Feb. 27/17.**
14 B. VI Hill, A. R. 24044. M. **Sept. 14/16.** R/Enq.

## *E.E.F.*

2 Garr. Bn. Gordon, H. 33321. M., bel. drowned **Feb. 20-24/17.**

## LONDON REGIMENT.

### *B.E.F.*

| | | | |
|---|---|---|---|
| 1 | | **Warren, 2nd Lieut. E. C.** | M., bel. W. **May 3/17.** |
| *1 | A. IV | Bishop, Eric Arthur. 225019. | K. **May 13/17.** Det.D./B. |
| 1 | A. IV | Brooker, L. V. G. 202290. (Late 5250) | M. **April 7/17.** |
| ‡1 | A. | Butcher, E. 202426. | M. **May 3/17.** |
| *1 | A. | Byhan, Percy. 3469. | M. **Oct. 2/16.** R/Enq. |
| ‡1 | A. | Carter, W. 202982. | M. **May 3/17.** |
| 1 | A. II | Cook, Thomas. 204112. | M. **May 3/17.** |
| ‡1 | A. | Currie, C. 203629. | M. **May 3/17.** |
| 1 | A. | Elbourn, Wm. 4334. | M. **Oct. 1-2/16.** |
| 1 | A. III | Hartfield, W. A. 203804. | M. **May 3/17.** |
| 1 | A. | Holliday, H. S. 301948. (Late 4639.) | M. **Oct. 7/16.** |
| 1 | A. L.G.S. | Hutchins, W. J. 203707. (7534.) | M. **April 7/17.** |
| 1 | A. or B. | Martin, A. 203385. | M. **May 3/17.** |
| ‡1 | A. | Starr, W. 202326. | M. **May 3/17.** |
| ‡1 | A. | Swain, Fredk. 203968. (8282.) | M. **June 16/17.** |
| 1 | A. or C. | Taylor, Alb. Victor. 203596. (7240.) | M. **May 3/17.** |
| ‡1 | B. | Ardley, J. W. 204029. | M. **May 3/17.** |
| *1 | B. VII | Bristow, William Leonard. 204602. | M. **May 3/17.** |
| 1 | B. VI | Brooker, Leslie. 5251. | M. **Sept. 15/16.** R/Enq. |
| ‡1 | B. | Coe, J. F. 204085. | M. **May 3/17.** |
| 1 | B. VII | Goodridge, A. G. 6993. | K. **Oct. 7/16.** Det.D./B. |
| 1 | B. VII | Graham, Charles. 4623. | K. **Oct. 1/16.** Det.D./B. R/Enq. |
| 1 | B. VI | Loton, Wm. 204069. (8390.) | M. **May 3/17.** |
| ‡1 | B. VI | Mitchell, Geo. Christopher. 6956. | M. **Oct. 2/16.** R/Enq. |
| 1 | B. VII | Orchard, Geo. 203397. (7035.) | M. **May 3/17.** |
| †1 | B. VII | Smith, John Lawrence. 225015. (5680.) | M. **June 16/17.** |
| ‡1 | B. VIII | Smith, J. T. 5441. | M. **Sept. 15/16.** R/Enq. |
| ‡1 | B. | Somers, E. 203337. | M. **May 3/17.** |
| ‡1 | B. | Thompson, L.-Cpl. W. G. 202979. | M. **May 3/17.** |
| 1 | B. VIII | Vidgen, Fred. 203217. (6820.) | M. **May 3/17.** |
| ‡1 | C. | Aldridge, A. 203006. | M. **May 3/17.** |
| ‡1 | C. | Binchford, Cpl. L. 200543. | M. **May 3/17.** |
| *1 | C. | Bowen, J. 203107. (6687.) | M. **May 3/17.** |
| 1 | C. IX | Brett, John Duncan. 232741. (5902.) | M. **May 3/17.** |
| 1 | C. X | Clarke, Arthur. 3878. | M. **Sept. 15/16.** R/Enq. |
| 1 | C. | Day, Arthur Ernest. 203315. (6993.) | M. **May 3/17.** |
| 1 | C. XII | Driscoll, D. 230952. | M. **May 3/17.** |
| ‡1 | C. | Frost, F. 203575. | M. **May 3/17.** |
| 1 | C. | Gane, W. J. 203897. | M. **April 9/17.** |
| 1 | C. | Gauld, Wm. 201976. (4684.) | M. **May 3/17.** |
| ‡1 | C. X | Hill, R. 201688. | M. **May 3/17.** |
| 1 | C. XII | Mote, J. B. 6211. | M. **Sept. 15/16.** R./Enq. |
| 1 | C. IX | Palmer, Arthur Alfred. 203586. (Fr. 10th, 7230.) | M. **May 3/17.** |
| ‡1 | C. | Peacock, A. E. 203886. | M. **May 15/17.** |
| *1 | C. | Reeve, A. G. V. 200267. | M. **May 3/17.** |
| 1 | C. | Riggs, Frederick. 8028. | M. **Oct. 7-8/16.** R/Enq. |
| ‡1 | C. | Simpson, W. L. 203280. | M. **May 3/17.** |
| ‡1 | C. | Wiseman, H. A. 203882. | M. **May 3/17.** |
| ‡1 | D. | Ainge, W. 204063. | M. **May 3/17.** |

**London Regiment—contd.**

## *B.E.F.*

1 D. XIII Barrow, Harry. 3185. K. April 9/17. Det.D./B.
‡1 D. Carl, J. W. 201636. M. May 3/17.
‡1 D. Conquest, W. G. 203995. M. May 3/17.
*1 D. XV Hallam, A. 203388. (7025.) M. May 3/17.
1 D. XVI Halls, Edward Chas. 203983. (8301.) M. May 3/17.
1 D. XVI Johnson, Francis Edward. 202392. (5438.) M. May 3/17.
‡1 D. Kaisser, S. L. 204072. M. May 3/17.
1 D. Kellow, Reginald. 200361. M. May 20/17.
‡1 D. Lock, J. 204041. M. May 3/17.
1 D. McIntosh, Alex. 202166. M. May 3/17.
1 D. Morlidge, Joseph. 203405. (7043.) M. May 3/17.
‡1 D. Nicholl, W. G. 204175. M. May 15/17.
1 D. M.G.S. Payne, A. J. 202026. (Late 4771.) K. Sept. 15/16. Det.D./B. R/Enq
1 D. XIV Potter, Fred. 4861. M. Sept. 15/16. R/Enq.
1 D. XVI Stokes, W. C. 4394. M. Oct. 7-8/16. R/Enq.
1 D. Williamson, Chris. 201724. (4298.) M. May 3/17.
1 ? Huckle, L.-Cpl. Harry A. 2798. K. Oct. 7-8/16. Det.D./B.
‡1 ? Lynn, Christopher Chas. 201165. (3430.) K. Mar. 19/17. Det.D./B.
‡2/1 A. III Allen, Sgt. Alb. Edw. 201545. M. June 16/17.
‡2/1 A. Baker, W. E. J. 202611. M. May 20/17.
‡2/1 A. III Blake, Thos. Lindsay. 204469. M. June 16/17.
‡2/1 A. Dowton, J. W. 204375. M. May 17/17.
‡2/1 A. IV Fisher, Harry. 201555. M. June 16/17.
‡2/1 A. Franklin, W. 204545. Unoff. M. June 16/17.
‡2/1 A. Hughes, A. 202610. M. May 20/17.
‡2/1 A. II Mackinnon, A. 204467. M. June 16/17.
‡2/1 A. Muscatt, W. H. J. 202586. M. June 16/17.
‡2/1 A. III Schofield, G. R. 20448. M. May 15/17.
‡2/1 A. Spear, M. 202776. M. May 17/17.
‡2/1 B. VI Clark, L.-Cpl. W. A. 203530. W. and M. June 16/17.
‡2/1 B. VII Foreman, Mark. 204325. M. June 16/17.
‡2/1 B. VI Holliday, Wm. Chas. 201118. (3330.) W. and M. June 16/17.
‡2/1 B. VII King, F. E. 202986. M. June 16/17.
‡2/1 B. V Marshall, Henry. 204344. M. June 16/17.
*2/1 B. Russell, Albert. 203387. M. May 3/17.
‡2/1 B. VI Scott, Henry John. 20455. M. June 16/17.
‡2/1 B. VII Smeaton, Albert Edw. 204476. M. June 8/17.
2/1 C. XI Champion, P. W. 203546. (7190.) W. and M. May 14/17.
‡2/1 C. Clark, L. W. 202672. M. May 14/17.
‡2/1 C. X M.G.S. Wiffen, Arthur Geo. 202490. (5593.) M. June 16/17.
‡2/1 D. XV Bodger, Thos. C. 201846. M. June 16/17.
‡2/1 D. Brown, Cpl. C. 201240. (3582.) M. June 15/17.
‡2/1 D. Fone, A. 203967. M. May 17/17.
‡2/1 D. XIII Griffin, C. H. 204359. (8710.) W. and M. June 16/17.
‡2/1 D. Hoe, Cpl. A. J. 202793. M. May 17/17.
‡2/1 D. Pilley, George. 202514. M. June 16/17.
‡2 **Harris, 2nd Lieut. H. M.** (Fr. London Yeo.) M. June 16/17.
2 **Heagerty, 2nd Lieut. R. B.** M., bel. W. May 3/17.
*2 **Henderson, Lieut. G. B.** M., bel. K. June 16/17.
*2 **Thompson, 2nd Lieut. R. S.** M. June 15/17.
2 A. Bignell, A. 233314. (7524.) M. May 3/17.
‡2 A. Cahill, E. G. 232977. M. May 3/17.
2 A. II Coomber, W. 232979. (6356.) M. May 3/17.

**London Regiment—contd.**

## *B.E.F.*

| | | |
|---|---|---|
| 2 A. IV | Finch, A. V. J. 232339. (5361.) | W. Unoff. M. May 3/17. |
| ‡2 A. | Harris, G. A. 233051. | M. May 3/17. |
| ‡2 A. | Martin, C. 232140. | M. May 3/17. |
| 2 A. II | Maulkerson, Jn. Thos. 233172. (6849) | M. May 3/17. |
| *2 A. | North, J. 233594. | M. May 3/17. |
| 2 A. II | Power, Chas. 231990. (4861.) | M. May 3/17. |
| 2 A. | Read, L.-Cpl. Arthur Geo. 230684. | M. May 3/17. |
| 2 A. or C. | Ridley, Fred. Wm. 232776. (5957.) | M. May 3/17. |
| *2 A. or C. | Salisbury, P. H. 233140. (6799.) | M. May 3/17. |
| *2 A. | West, Alfred. 234139. (8388.) | M. May 3/17. |
| 2 A. | Willey, C. E. 5012. | M. Jan. 14/17. |
| 2 A. I | Wood, G. 233197. (6883.) | M. May 3/17. |
| ‡2 B. VII | Adams, L.-Cpl. Frank. 280641. | Unoff. M. June 16/17. |
| 2 B. M.G.S. | Dennis, R. C. 232878. (6172.) | Unoff. M. May 3/17. |
| ‡2 B. | Hart, A. F. 232734. | W. and M. May 3/17. |
| 2 B. V | Howell, A. J. 234140. (7097.) | M. May 3/17. |
| 2 B. or D. | Kendall, Percy. 233530. (8074.) | M. May 3/17. |
| 2 B. VI | Radley, A. G. 233162. (6833.) | M. May 3/17. |
| *2 B. or C. L.G.S. | Ryall, W. 232200. (5192.) | M. May 3/17. |
| 2 B. VII | Tilyard, A. 7077. | M. May 3/17. |
| *2 B. V | Turner, Arthur. 233202. (6888.) | W. and M. May 3/17. |
| ‡2 B. | Wilks, A. 230042. | M. May 3/17. |
| 2 C. or D. | Clay, L.-Cpl. Ernest Wm. 230669. (2516.) | M. May 3/17. |
| ‡2 C. | Dormer, E. C. 233073. | M. May 3/17. |
| 2 C. or D. | English, H. J. 4670. | M. Sept. 15-19/16. R/Enq. |
| 2 D. | Baker, J. J. 4331. | M. Sept. 15-17/16. R/Enq. |
| *2 D. XIII | Baker, Wm. C. L. 7569. (Late 22nd.) | M. Sept. 15-17/16. R/Enq. |
| 2 D. XIV | Coult, Fredk. Wm. 233230. (6958.) | M. May 3/17. |
| ‡2 D. XIV | Farmer, H. W. 234134. (7090.) | W. and M. May 3/17. |
| 2 D. XIV | Heard, L.-Cpl. F. J. 233521. (8064.) | M. May 3/17. |
| 2 D. | High, J. 5908. | M. Sept. 15-17/16. R/Enq. |
| 2 D. M.G.S. | Holt, L.-Cpl. Jas. D. 5032. | M. Sept. 15-17/16. |
| *2 D. | Moore, M. A. 232172. | M. May 3/17. |
| 2 D. XIV | Parr, Arthur Geo. 233137. (6796.) | M. May 3/17. |
| ‡2 D. | Perrin, H. 232125. | M. May 3/17. |
| ‡2 D. | Reeves, E. 233562. | W. and M. June 12/17. |
| ‡2 D. | Reeves, E. F. 8111. | W. Unoff. M. May 3/17. |
| 2 D. | Roe, John Wm. 232770. (5945.) | W. and M. May 3/17. |
| ‡2 D. XV | Shelley, Wm. George. 3285. | M. Sept. 15-17/16. R/Enq. |
| ‡2 D. | Sparrow, Cpl. H. 230076. | M. May 3/17. |
| ‡2 D. | Wilkinson, T. 232783. | M. May 3/17. |
| *2/2 | **Evans, 2nd Lt. A. J.** (Fr. 19th.) | M. June 15/17. |
| *2/2 | **Hawkins, Capt. H. I.** | M. June 16/17. |
| ‡2/2 A. | Barton, C. J. 231313. | W. and M. May 15/17. |
| ‡2/2 A. | Buckley, E. 232470. | M. May 15/17. |
| ‡2/2 A. | Conway, A. C. 233670. | M. May 5/17. |
| ‡2/2 A. | Duck, E. W. 231718. | M. June 15/17. |
| ‡2/2 A. | Heath, L.-Cpl. W. G. 232613. | M., bel. K. May 15/17. |
| ‡2/2 B. | Bolton, A. J. 232632. | Unoff. M. June 16/17. |
| ‡2/2 B. | Dawe, L.-Cpl. W. C. 232702 | Unoff. W. and M. June 16/17. |
| ‡2/2 B. | Dowden, Charles. 232255. | Unoff. W. and M. June 16/17. |
| *2/2 B. | Duggan, William. 232281. | Unoff. W. and M. June 16/17. |
| ‡2/2 B. | Fletcher, G. 5686. | M. June 16/17. |
| ‡2/2 B. VIII | Ivers, E. 233757. | Unoff. M. June 16/17. |
| ‡2/2 B. VI | Knowles, S. 231526. | Unoff. M. June 16/17. |
| *2/2 B. | Sare, Sig. Ernest. 232683. (5814.) | Unoff. W. and M. June 16/17. |
| *2/2 B. VI | Scott, Cpl. E. S. 232331. | Unoff. W. and M. June 16/17. |
| ‡2/2 B. VIII | Smith, W. 232519. | Unoff. M. June 16/17. |

London Regiment—contd.

*B.E.F.*

*2/2 B. Trenchard, Sig. Jack. 231252. M. June 16/17.
‡2/2 B. Venables, L.-Cpl. E. 232410 Unoff. W. and M. June 16/17.
‡2/2 C. Clarke, L.-Cpl. C. E. 231112. Unoff. M. end June or early July/17.
‡2/2 C. Western, W. S. 472308. M. May 7/17.
‡2/2 D. XVI Durrant, Percy. 232365. M. June 16/17.
*2/2 D. XV Grant, William R. 233818. (8488.) W. and M. May 15/17.
‡2/2 D. XIV Jones, Sidney John. 232367. (5394.) Unoff. M. June 16/17.
‡2/2 D. Lambourn, E. 232611. W. and M. May 15/17.
‡2/2 D. XIV Parrish, George E. 233845. Unoff. M. June 16/17.
2/2 D. XV Pearman, W. 23244. W. and M. May 15/17.
*2/2 D. Stanton, Wm. 233810. W. Unoff. M. May 14/17.
‡2/2 D. Steggall, W. 203526. M., bel. K. May 15/17.
*2/2 D. XIII Stenner, R. F. 233836. (8510.) M., bel. K. May 12/17.
*2/2 D. Wallis, R. 233632. (8154.) W. and M. May 14/17.
‡2/2 ? Lipsham, A. F. 231652. W. and M. May 15/17.
‡2/2 ? Lungley, Arthur Fredk. 232408. Unoff. M. June 16/17.
3 A. I Admans, C. F. 201839. W. and M. May 3/17.
3 A. Bidewell, W. 4916. M. Sept. 10/16. R/Enq.
3 A. I Catton, Sydney. 200557. M. May 3/17.
3 A. III Faulkner, A. 4874. M. Sept. 13/16. R/Enq.
*3 A. IV Kinzett, Edward John. 2294. M. Oct. 8/16. R/Enq.
3 A. III Osmond, L.-Cpl. Geo. Jos. 200873. M. May 3/17.
3 A. IV Scully, A. 4621. M. Oct. 8/16. R/Enq.
3 A. IV Smith, Wm. John Robt. 5179. M. Oct. 8/16. R/Enq.
‡3 B. Bell, A. 252083. M. May 13/17.
3 B. VII Forster, Ernest. 252109. (Late 5013.) M. Sept. 20/16
3 B. Harris, B. D. 233408. M. May 3/17.
‡3 B. Kallmeier, L. 253126. M. May 13/17.
‡3 B. King, J. 251005. M. May 3/17..
3 B. VIII Sanford, J. 4956. W. and M. Oct. 8/16.
3 B. Weltner, J. 233630. M. May 4/17.
3 C. Nichols, L.-Cpl. Ht. Matthew. 200565 (Fr. 1st, 2257.) M. May 10/17.
‡3 D. Beevor, W. 252936. M. May 3/17.
‡3 D. Berwick, H. C. 253485. M. May 3/17.
*3 D. Burgess, S. 251986. M. May 10/17.
3 D. L.G.S. Dale, A. R. 252020. (4882.) M. May 3/17.
3 D. XIII Doe, S. Ernest. 251099. (3272.) M. May 10/17.
3 D. XV Hargrove, Geo. 251636. (4189.) M. May 5/17.
‡3 D. Harrington, L.-Cpl. E. J. 250141. M. May 4/17.
‡2/3 A. Elder, Arthur A. 252201. M. June 16/17.
‡2/3 B. Dimes, Albert Henry. 253364. (6892.) M. June 16/17.
‡2/3 C. X Hamilton, Chas. R. 252802. M. June 16/17.
‡2/3 D. Andrews, J. 252455. M. June 16/17.
‡2/3 D. Bayley, H. R. C. 252795. M. June 16/17.
‡2/3 D. Burrell, J. W. 252559. M. June 16/17.
‡2/3 D. XIV Gradley, Wm. Ernest. 252261. (5239.) M. June 16/17.
‡2/3 D. Killey, A. 252494. M. June 16/17.
‡2/3 D. XIII Merritt, Edward. 251588. M. June 16/17.
‡2/3 D. XV Stewart, Wm. J. 203927. (Late 8236, 1st Bn.) M. June 16/17.
‡2/3 D. Thackray, A. T. 203568. M. Unoff. W. June 15/17.
*4 **Bottomley, Capt. E. W.** M. June 15/17.
*4 **Monkman, 2nd Lieut. E. A.** M. June 15/17.
*4 **Parker, Capt. W. H.** M., bel. K. June 15/17.
*4 **Wheatley, 2nd Lieut. J. H. L.** M. June 15/17.

**London Regiment—contd.**

## *B.E.F.*

‡4 A. III Hearn, Arthur Alfred. 7028. M. Oct. 7/16. R/Enq.
4 A Herbert, S. E. 7027. (Fr. 3/3 R. Fus.) W. and M. **Sept. 9/16.**
*4 A. III Holl, J. 780337. (1979.) M. **May 6/17.**
4 A. Saville, Charles Cecil. 1827. M. **Sept. 9/16.**
*4 C. XII Allen, W. J. 283774. (7377.) Shell shock and Unoff. M. **May 11/17.**
4 C. Baker, E. 4581. M. **Sept. 21/16.** R/Enq.
*4 C. XII Brown, Thos. Henry. 281698. (4244.) M. **May 11/17.**
4 D. XV Ainsley, Leonard Crombie. 3326. M. **Sept. 9/16.**
4 D. Heddesheimer, Sgt. Ernest Geo. 2702 M. **Oct. 7/16.** R/Enq.
‡4 D. XIV Steggall, W. G. 245043. Unoff. M. **May 16/17.**
*2/4 **McDowell, 2nd Lieut. R.** M. **June 15/17.**
*2/4 **Stevenson, 2nd Lieut. E. A.** M. **June 15/17.**
*2/4 **Williams, 2nd Lt. S. M.** (Fr. 20th.) M. **June 15/17.**
*2/4 A. Barnard, Albert Henry. 282698. (5733.) M. **June 16/17.**
‡2/4 A. Burgess, A. 282418. M. **June 16/17.**
‡2/4 A. Rushman, W. T. 283831. M. **June 16/17.**
‡2/4 A. Waters, L.-Cpl. G. J. 281392. W. and M. **June 15/17.**
‡2/4 B. VIII Atkins, J. W. 283887. M. **June 16/17.**
‡2/4 B. Barnett, Herman. 282688. M. **June 16/17.**
‡2/4 B. V Blake, T. 282388. (3535.) M. **June 14-16/17.**
2/4 B. V M.G.S. Cole, Geo. Henry. 280661. (Late 2572.) M. **Oct. 7-10/16.**
‡2/4 B. V Hart, G. T. 282395. M. **June 16/17.**
‡2/4 B. Hart, Harry. 282658. M. **June 16/17.**
*2/4 B. VII Haynes, W. A. 282502. M. **June 15/17.**
*2/4 B. VI Howlett, W. S. 282482. K. **May 17/17.** Det.D./B.
‡2/4 B. Marsh, H. 282177. M. **June 16/17.**
‡2/4 B. Noah, James. 282494. M. **June 16/17.**
‡2/4 B. V Nunn, Thomas. 281498. M. **June 16/17.**
‡2/4 B. Palmer, Albert Oswald. 282656. (5680.) M. **June 16/17.**
‡2/4 B. V Simpkin, L.-Cpl. Alfred Henry. 282383. M. **June 16/17.**
‡2/4 B. VI Sweeney, J. 282386. (5333.) M. **June 16/17.**
‡2/4 B. VIII Taylor, Jas. 282496. M. **June 16/17.**
‡2/4 B. Thomas, L.-Cpl. W. M. 282663. (5687.) M. **June 16/17.**
*2/4 C. X Hamburg, Nathan. 283366. K. **May 14/17.** Det.D./B.
*2/4 D. XVI Bowers, B. 282585. M. **June 16/17.**
‡2/4 D. Burt, Will. 281480. M. **June 16/17.**
‡2/4 D. Butler, Cyril J. G. 225027. M. **June 16-17/17.**
‡2/4 D. Cobby, R. 282534. M. **June 16/17.**
‡2/4 D. XIV Collis, H. 283602. M. **June 16/17.**
‡2/4 D. Dansey, L. J. 282143. M. **June 16/17.**
‡2/4 D. Dulieu, H. 282233. M. **June 16/17.**
‡2/4 D. Ellis, Cpl. E. 282252. M. **June 16/17.**
‡2/4 D. L.G.S. Gowers, Arthur Sidney. 282542. Unoff. M. **June 16/17.**
‡2/4 D. Hastilow, S. 282144. M. **June 15/17.**
‡2/4 D. Keir, A. G. 282510. M. **June 16/17.**
‡2/4 D. Matthews, W. 282249. M. **June 16/17.**
‡2/4 D. Monk, Sgt. H. S. 282189. M. **June 16/17.**
*2/4 D. Parker, L.-Cpl. Albert. 282290. M. **June 16/17.**
*2/4 D. Payne, C.-S.-M. C. E. 280729. (2670.) M. **June 16/17.**
‡2/4 D. Penska, Wm. Chas. 282162. M. **June 16/17.**
‡2/4 D. XV Perrin, Walter Geo. 204296. M. **June 16/17.**
‡2/4 D. XVI Perry, Fredk. Walter. 282574. M. **June 16/17.**

**London Regiment—contd.**

## *B.E.F.*

‡2/4 D. XV Williams, A. 282206. — M. June 16/17.
‡2/4 ? Mullocks, Arthur Thos. 283434. (6998.) — M. June 16/17.
‡2/4 ? Sly, Herbert Jas. 283583. — Unoff. M. June 16/17.
‡5 **Harvey, Capt. B. S.** — K. July 1/16. Det.D./B. R/Enq.
5 A. III Anthony, P. L. 3722. — M. Oct. 9/16. R/Enq.
5 A. L.G.S. Clarke, F. B. 303281. (Late 5272.) — K. April 12/17. Det.D./B.
‡5 A. Cleminson, John. 10048. (Fr. 2/7th Essex.) — M. Oct. 9/16. R/Enq.
*5 A. IV Dixon, Leonard Wm. 4364. — M. Oct. 9/16. R/Enq.
,5 A. III Figgins, L.-Cpl. G. J. 2888. — K. Oct. 8/16. Det.D./B.
5 A. Newman, J. H. 10525. — M. Oct. 4/16. R/Enq.
5 B. Bradley, Walter. 10663. (3045, 2/7 Middlx.) — W. and M. Sept. 6-10/16. R/Enq.
,5 B. Cooper, J. B. 4788. — M. Oct. 9/16. R/Enq.
5 B. VII Crowter, H. W. 4744. — K. Oct. 9/16. Det.D./B.
5 B. V Dowell, Sidney Henry. 303457. — M. May 3/17.
*5 B. Eason, J. 10727. (Fr. 7 Middlesex, 2604.) — M. Sept. 6-10/16. R/Enq.
5 B. V Freeborn, John Gordon. 303458. (5470.) — M. May 3/17.
5 B. Gee, Ernest Edward. 10759. — M. Sept. 6-10/16. R/Enq.
5 B. VII Pearce, Francis Geo. 302993. — W. and M. May 3/17.
*5 B. VI Smith, A. 2420. — W. and M. Oct. 9/16. R/Enq.
5 B. VIII Smith, Arthur Geo. 303656. (5684.) — K. May 3/17. Det.D./B.
5 C. IX Baldock, Geo. Wm. 315002. — M. May 3/17.
*5 C. Fishwick, Edward Alfred. 304168. (10744.) — M. May 3/17.
5 C. Hatch, L.-Cpl. Leslie J. 302542. (4270.) — M. May 3/17.
5 C. Hutchinson, Ernest J. 10508. (Fr. 7, 4029.) — M. Sept. 6/16. R/Enq.
5 C. X Staniforth, Godfrey Douglas. 302045. — M. May 3/17.
‡5 C. Tyrell, J. B. 315059. — M. May 3/17.
5 C. Watson, Cpl. Francis Thos. 300494. (Late 675.) — M. Feb. 14/17.
‡5 C. XI Wooldridge, Lewis Rich. 2237. — M. Nov. 9/16. R/Enq.
5 C. Worthington, James. 315060. — M. May 3/17.
5 D. Backler, A. S. 10642. — K. Sept. 10/16. Det.D./B. R/Enq.
,5 D. I.T.M. Breeze, Fredk. H. 302595. (4363.) (169 Bgde.) — Unoff. W. and M. May 3/17.
5 D. XV Harland, Sgt. Geo. 304205. — M. May 3/17.
5 D. XV Key, H. 304242. (Fr. 2/7 Middlsx., 2065.) — M. May 3/17.
5 D. Knight, Ernest Thos. 315036. — Unoff. M. May 3/17.
*5 D. XIV Large, Henry. 303569. (5590.) — W. and M. May 3/17.
5 D. XIII Law, S. 315018. — M. May 3/17.
5 D. McNeice, Wm. 10539. — M. Oct. 9/16. R/Enq.
5 D. XV Melrose, Stanley Victor. 315019. — M. May 3/17.
5 D. Scarfe, H. M. 302068. — M. May 3/17.
5 D. Tarry, L.-Cpl. T. G. 4001. — M. Oct. 9/16. R/Enq.
‡5 D. Town, H. G. 302136. — M. May 3/16.
*5 D. M.G.S. West, Joseph J. 1920. — M. Oct. 8/16. R/Enq.
‡2/5 D. Phillips, Harry. 304601. — M. June 18/17.
‡2/5 D. Wastell, F. 302458. (4021.) — M., bel. K. June 17/17.
6 **Jameson, 2nd Lieut. C. M.** — W. and M. May 21/17.
‡6 A. IV Hate, B. F. (Fr. 3/6th.) — W. and M. Sept. 15/16. R/Enq.
6 A. Scholl, C. 4111. — M. Sept. 2/16.
6 A. I Smiles, Alfred John. 322657. (Late 5500.) — W. and M. Feb. 20/17.

**London Regiment—contd.**

## *B.E.F.*

‡6 B. Allen, H. J. 323587. M. May 21/17.
6 B. VI Martin, Thos. 4724. M. Sept. 15/16. R/Enq.
6 C. Barber, R. W. J. 1563. K. Sept. 15/16. Det.D./B. R/Enq.
6 C. Gullock, Geo. 320319. (1730.) W. and M. Feb. 20/17.
‡6 C. X Johnson, G. 322893. W. and M. June 8/17.
6 C. XI Such, Antony. 3344. W. and M. Sept. 15/16.
6 C. XII Theobald, Andrew Jas. 321046. (Late M. Feb. 20/17.
6 D. Bomb. Pl. Brooks, John. 3583. W. and M. Oct. 8/16. R/Enq.
‡6 D. XIII Claricoat, A. J. 323283. M. June 7/17.
*6 D. XIV Oliver, Dan Charlie. 4142. W. and M. Sept. 16/16. R/Enq.
6 D. XIV Pearce, Thos. Geo. 321428. (Late 3716.) M. Feb. 20/17.
6 D. XVI Thomas, Geoffrey Jos. 3646. W. and M. Sept. 15/16. R/Enq.
6 ? M.G.S. Knight, Reuben. 6350. K. Oct. 8/16. Det.D./B
2/6 **Clarke, 2nd Lieut. R. F.** M. May 21/17.
2/6 A. **Coldicott, 2nd Lt. H. E.** (Fr. 15th.) M. May 21/17.
2/6 **Hartley, Capt. W. J.** M. May 21/17.
2/6 **Johnson, 2nd Lieut. A. M. T.** M. May 21/17.
2/6 **Keller, Lieut. F. F.** M. May 21/17.
‚2/6 A. IV Alderton, J. 323694. M. May 21/17.
‡2/6 X. M.G.S. Barker, F. W. 321689. M. May 21/17.
‡2/6 A. Baxter, G. 322362. M. May 21/17.
2/6 A. III Carpenter, E. 323619. M. May 21/17.
*2/6 A. Childs, W. F. 323577. M. May 21/17.
*2/6 A. Colquohoun, A. W. 322509. (5322.) M. May 21/17.
‚2/6 A. Cook, Fred. Samuel. 322257. M. May 21/17.
2/6 A. III Cousins, F. 321985. M. May 22/17.
‡2/6 A. Drake, E. G. 322540. M. May 21/17.
‡2/6 A. Dwyford, F. G. 321460. M. May 21/17.
‡2/6 A. Ehrenberg, J. 322404. M. May 21/17.
‡2/6 A. Emery, E. T. 321981. M. May 21/17.
‚2/6 A. Fisher, James. 323702. M. May 21/17.
*2/6 A. III Germain, Sgt. Geo. 321058. (3105.) W. and M. May 21/17.
2/6 A. Goldacre, Geo. Edwin. 322269. M. May 21/17.
2/6 A. II Hayworth, C. 322493. M. May 22/17.
‡2/6 A. Hetherington, W. 322276. M. May 21/17.
2/6 A. Hillier, J. L. 320697. (2461.) M. May 21/17.
‡2/6 A. Hinton, A. F. 322418. M. May 21/17.
‡2/6 A. Jarvis, W. B. 322301. M. May 21/17.
*2/6 A. or D. Jones, Wm. 322370. (Snipers' S.) M. May 21/17.
*2/6 A. McCarron, J. 321900. M. May 21/17.
*2/6 A. II McDonald, W. H. 323573. M. May 21/17.
2/6 A. Miles, Cpl. E. H. 320968. M. May 22/17.
*2/6 A. Montandon, E. 322411. M. May 21/17.
‡2/6 A. Parker, Cpl. W. 320698. M. May 21/17.
‡2/6 A. Postle, A. F. 322417. M. May 21/17.
‡2/6 A. Quartley, F. C. 322978. M. May 21/17.
‡2/6 A. Ransome, A. 323356. M. May 21/17.
*2/6 A. II Raper, J. A. 323576. M. May 21/17.
*2/6 A. III Roberts, G. 322259. M. May 21/17.
‡2/6 A. Rowland, J. 320141. M. May 21/17.
*2/6 A. III Singer, Walter T. 321660. (4096.) M. May 21/17.
*2/6 A. Smith, Cpl. F. S. 320724. (2511.) M. May 21/17.
*2/6 A. II Taylor, Wm. George. 322406. M. May 22/17.
2/6 A. II Thomas, L.-Cpl. Fredk. Geo. 320604 M. May 21/17.
‡2/6 A. Tunmer, W. 321730. M. May 21/17.
2/6 A. Twyford, Frank Geo. 321460. (3765.) M. May 21/17.
‡2/6 A. Welford, L.-Sergt. J. B. 320979. M. May 21/17.

**London Regiment—contd.**

## *B.E.F.*

|  |  |  |
|---|---|---|
| ‡2/6 A. | West, H. T. 322361. | M. May 21/17. |
| ‡2/6 A. | Whiteley, E. S. 323701. | M. May 21/17. |
| ‡2/6 A. | Willcox, E. A. 320559. | M. May 21/17. |
| *2/6 B. VI | Bailey, Harry. 345007. | M. May 21/17. |
| 2/6 B. | Bain, Arch. Jas. 321720. (4184.) | M. May 21/17. |
| 2/6 B. | Bence, Cpl. Richard Jas. 321556. | M. May 21/17. |
| ‡2/6 B. | Biggs, W. H. 322177. | M. May 21/17. |
| *2/6 B. VIII | Bowley, C. H. 323627. | M. May 21/17. |
| ‡2/6 B. | Brightly, E. J. 323595. | M. May 21/17. |
| ‡2/6 B. VIII | Brown, C. R. 322380. | M. May 21/17. |
| 2/6 B. VII | Brown, Percy W. 322448. (5256.) | M. May 21/17. |
| ‡2/6 B. | Cotton, H. 322279. | M. May 21/17. |
| ‡2/6 B. | Cresswell, Cpl. A. T. M. 320775. | M. May 21/17. |
| 2/6 B. | Cue, Fredk. Arthur. 323624. | M. May 21/17. |
| ‡2/6 B. | Darwell, J. 322182. | M., bel. K. May 21/17. |
| ‡2/6 B. VIII | Dickinson, E. 321550. | M. May 21/17. |
| *2/6 B. VIII | Edwards, Sergt. Herbert Stanley. 320803. (2634.) | M. May 21/17. |
| *2/6 B. | Evans, Chas. Thos. 321852. | M. May 21/17. |
| 2/6 B. VIII | Farnes, Fredk. 322492. | M. May 21/17. |
| *2/6 B. | Gardner, Percy A. 322297. (5081.) | W. and M. May 21/17. |
| 2/6 B. VIII | Gray, Sergt. Victor Alexander. 320790. (2607.) | M. May 21/17. |
| ‡2/6 B. | Haynes, G. 323712. | W. and M. May 21/17. |
| *2/6 B. | Highlett, H. S. 322876. | M. May 21/17. |
| *2/6 B. | Hunter, S. 322294. | M. May 21/17. |
| ‡2/6 B. | Juler, F. 321546. | W. and M. May 21/17. |
| ‡2/6 B. | Martin, F. J. 322382. | W. and M. May 21/17. |
| *2/6 B. VIII | Massey, Charles. 321966. | M. May 21/17. |
| *2/6 B. VIII | Murray, Patrick. 323525. | M. May 21/17. |
| ‡2/6 B. | Patterson, G. 321750. | W. and M. May 21/17. |
| ‡2/6 B. | Pead, F. T. 322392. | M., bel. K. May 21/17. |
| 2/6 B. | Randall, Harry F. 321816. | M. May 21/17. |
| 2/6 B. VIII | Richards, Francis H. 345011. | M. May 21/17. |
| ‡2/6 B. | Ruse, E. R. 320861. | M., bel. K. May 21/17. |
| *2/6 B. | Smith, L.-Cpl. A. W. 320411. (1928.) | M., bel. K. May 21/17. |
| ‡2/6 B. | Spink, C. G. 322425. | M., bel. K. May 21/17. |
| *2/6 B. | Spriggs, Wm. 322285. (5068.) | M. May 21/17. |
| ‡2/6 B. | Thorne, L.-Cpl. L. S. 321034. | M. May 21/17. |
| *2/6 B. | Tye, L.-Cpl. E. 322491. (5303.) | W. and M. May 21/17. |
| *2/6 B. | Williams, A. H. 322282. | M. May 21/17. |
| ‡2/6 B. VIII | Williams, J. H. 322280. | M. May 21/17. |
| ‡2/6 B. | Wraith, Percy. 323601. | M. May 21/17. |
| *2/6 B. | Wright, Wilfred Wulstan. 345004. | M. May 21/17. |
| 2/6 B. VIII | Young, Charles H. 323403. | M. May 20/17. |
| 2/6 C. X | Ambrose, Albert G. 320725. | Unoff. M. May 21/17. |
| *2/6 C. | Halnon, A. 323975. | M. May 21/17. |
| *2/6 C. XI | Lowen, George. 324037. (8264.) | M. May 21/17. |
| *2/6 C. X | Partridge, A. S. 322322. | M. May 21/17. |
| *2/6 C. | Potter, Cpl. H. R. 320700. | M. May 21/17. |
| 2/6 C. XII | Thompson, Robt. Chas. 321761. (4250.) | W. and M. May 21/17. |
| *2/6 C. XI | Wiltshire, L.-Cpl. Huse Lindsay Phillips. 322429. | M. May 21/17. |
| ‡2/6 D. | Armston, B. C. 345006. | M. May 21/17. |
| ‡2/6 D. | Bindoff, P. E. 321854. | M. May 21/17. |
| ‡2/6 D. | Corp, L. G. 322008. | M. May 21/17. |
| *2/6 D. | Neal, Ernest. 321890. (4432.) | M. May 21/17. |

**London Regiment—contd.**

*B.E.F.*

‡2/6 D. Plummer, A. G. 323790. M. May 21/17.
*2/6 D. XVI Talbot, Hubert. 320194. M. May 21/17.
7 A. II Cole, Harry Wm. W. 7015. M. Oct. 7/16. R/Enq.
*7 A. III Costello, W. F. 352415. K. June 7/17. Det.D./B.
7 A. Harris, J. A. 1578. M. Oct. 7/16. R/Enq.
*7 A. Press, Cpl. H. 2104. W. and M. Oct. 7/16. R/Enq.
‡7 B. Crocker, C. 7019. M. Oct. 7/16. R/Enq.
‡7 B. VII Harvey, L. 353216. (6859.) K. June 7/17. Det.D./B.
7 B. Jackman, J. P. 7002. M. Oct. 7/16. R/Enq.
*7 B. V Scott, L.-Cpl. Albert. 1928. W. and M. Oct. 7/16. R/Enq.
7 B. Sears, Sergt. C. J. 2280. W. and M. Oct. 7/16. R/Enq.
7 C. Frost, John Henry. 351181. (Late 3441.) M. Sept. 15/16.
*7 C. X Jilbert, Wm. Francis. 6399. M. Sept. 15/16. R/Enq.
‡7 C. XI O'Brien, T. W. 354432. M. June 7/17.
7 D. XIII Bartlett, John. 7067. M. Oct. 7/16. R/Enq.
7 D. Eagles, Percy Geo. 6212. M. Oct. 7/16. R./Enq.
7 D. XIII Knightley, Ernest H. 1867. W. and M. Oct. 7/16.
*2/7 B. VIII Barker, Fredk. Thos. Stanly. 353962. (7835.) W. and M. May 23/17.
‡2/7 B. Bruty, C. H. 352601. M. May 23/17.
*2/7 B. VI Greenwood, J. T. 351266. W. and M. May 22/17.
‡2/7 B. Hill, D. E. 352706. M. May 23/17.
*2/7 D. Northam, L.-Cpl. A. R. 351102. M. May 23/17.
‡2/7 D. Wimbledon, C. 352276. M. May 23/17.
2/7 ? Bubear, G. 4871. K. Oct. 7/16. Det.D./B.
‡8 **Wakefield, 2nd Lieut. L. J.** W. and M. June 16/17.
‡8 1 III Aston, Sgt. William Arthur. 373411. W. and M. June 7/17.
8 1 I Beynon, W. 4101. K. Sept. 15/16. Det.D./B.
8 2 VIII Dawes, Albert. 4775. K. Oct. 9/16. Det.D./B.
*8 2 VII Harper, B. 373881. K. June 7/17. Det.D./B.
8 2 McGregor, W. M. 3709. M. Oct. 7/16. R/Enq.
‡8 2 VIII Pierce, L.-Cpl. 373446. M. June 7/17.
‡8 3 X Graham, A. 5640. M. June 7/17.
8 3 XII Kennison, C. J. 6453. M. Oct. 7/16. R/Enq.
*8 3 XI Merryweather, A. W. 5867. M. Oct. 7/16. R/Enq.
8 3 Pawle, L.-Cpl. Ernest S. 372053. (4476.) W. and M. Oct. 7/16. R/Enq.
*8 3 XII Pavey, Wm. J. 6464. W. and M. Oct. 7/16. R/Enq.
*8 3 L.G.S. Rawlinson, John Taylor. 6535. M. Oct. 7/16. R/Enq.
8 4 XIV Eastwell, Arthur Walter. 5760. M. Oct. 8/16. R/Enq.
*8 4 XV Gillman, Alfred J. 4510. M. Oct. 7/16. R/Enq.
8 4 Hardy, G. E. 3550. M. Oct. 8/16. R/Enq.
*8 4 XIV Hornsby, Edgar. 4965. M. Oct. 7/16. R/Enq.
8 4 Jepps, Walter. 2539. M. Oct. 8/16. R/Enq.
‡8 4 Keen, H. J. 4872. M. Oct. 7/16. R/Enq.
8 4 Lazzell, A. A. 5876. M. Oct. 7/16. R/Enq.
8 4 Martin, J. T. 4955. M. Oct. 8/16. R/Enq.
8 4 Nickie, C. 5933. M. Oct. 7/16.
‡8 4 Williams, Thos. Arthur. 5611. M. Oct. 8/16. R/Enq.
8 ? L.G.S. Beazeley, A. W. 4115. M. Oct. 7/16. R/Enq.
‡2/8 C. Hales, J. 5085. Unoff. M. June 17/17.
9 **Gibb, 2nd Lieut. W. I.** W. Unoff. M. April 14/17.
9 **Sim, 2nd Lieut. N. Y.** K. Sept. 9/16. Det.D./B.
9 A. Coppen, L.-Cpl. A. 393033. M. April 14/17.
9 A. Gibbons, C. R. 392748. M. April 14/17.
9 A. IV Smith, Syd. Harriss. 393823. (7780) K. April 14/17. Det.D./B.
9 A. IV Spencer, R. S. 391085. (Late 3743.) M. April 14/17.
9 B. V Barnes, Arth. Herbt. 392741. (6428.) K. April 14/17. Det.D./B.

London Regiment—contd.

*B.E.F.*

9 B. M.G.S. Barnes, G. H. 393593. (7487.) M. April 14/17.
9 B. VIII Blackburn, J. E. 394276. (Late 8513.) M. April 14/17.
9 B. V Burrows, G. H. 7893. W. and M. Sept. 9/16. R/Enq.
9 B. VI Carter, Matthew. 391659. (4689.) M. April 14/17.
9 B. Edwards, L.-Cpl. Leoline A. 7874. (Late 8th Middlesex, 3772.) M. Oct. 9/16. R/Enq.
9 B. L.G.S. Evans, A. 6434. K. April 14/17. Det.D./B.
9 B. VI Faulks, Edwin Alfred. 393275. (7058) K. April 14/17. Det.D./B. R/Enq.
9 B. V Gammie, John Henry. 5455. M. Oct. 9/16. R/Enq.
9 B. VIII George, H. W. 394343. D/W. May 14/17. Det.D./B.
9 B. Head, Cpl. A. E. 393905. M. April 14/17.
9 B. VI Howlett, P. A. 393244. (7023.) M. April 14/17.
9 B. Jackson, F. G. 392931. (6654.) M. April 14/17.
9 B. VI Jackson, Cpl. Harold Edw. 390748. (3143.) M. April 14/17.
9 B. King, E. E. 391784. M. April 14/17.
9 B. VI Lambert, Chris. 391784. (4909.) M. April 14/17.
9 B. VI Leach, J. R. 7499. K. April 14/17. Det.D./B.
9 B. VIII Peet, C. H. 392558. (6130.) M. April 14/17.
9 B. Reilly, Patrick. 393629. (7529.) M. April 14/17.
9 B. Seymour, Sergt. Reginald Q. 393894. (Late 7862.) M. April 14/17.
9 B. VII Smith, Stanley Ed. 392409. (5928.) M. April 14/17.
9 B. V Swan, Wm. Wilfrid. 393493. (Late 7387.) K. April 14/17. Det.D./B.
9 B. VII Tunnell, R. S. 392872. (Late 6587.) M. Unoff. K. April 14/17. Conf. and Det.D./B.
9 B. V Woodcock, J. E. 394300. (8537.) M. April 14/17.
9 C. XII Bernstein, Chas. Nathaniel. 393106. (Late 6859.) M. April 14/17.
9 C. XII Bouldstridge, Victor E. 392691. (Late 6376.) M. April 14/17.
9 C. XI Child, Harold Wm. 6051. M. Oct. 9/16. R/Enq.
9 C. Copestake, C. C. 6879. M. Jan. 26/17.
9 C. or D. Corrigan, G. 415135. (Fr. 1st Entrench. Bn.) W. and M. May 3/17.
9 C. Friday, Edward. 7155. K. April 14/17. Det.D./B.
9 C. Goodhind, Jeffery. 391195. M. April 14/17.
9 C. XI Hall, B. 7910. M. Oct. 9/16. R/Enq.
9 C. L.G.S. Kirkby, Geo. Wm. 393495. (Late 7024.) M. April 14/17.
9 C. Moynihan, G. T. 3364. K. Oct. 9/16. Det.D./B.
9 C. Soulby, C. 393797. M. April 14/17.
9 C. Spong, Stephen Thos. 393584. (Late 7478, fr. 12th.) W. and M. April 14/17.
9 C. IX Taylor, Geo. 392873. (6583.) W. and M. April 14/17.
9 C. IX Walden, George. 4183. K. July 1/16. Det.D./B. R/Enq.
9 C. X West, Wm. 393105. (Late 6858.) K. April 14/17. Det.D./B.
9 D. Beer, I. A. E. 392422. M. Mar. 26/17.
9 D. XVI Day, Vivian. 393379. (7165.) (Late 11th, 2843.) K. April 14/17. Det.D./B.
9 D. M.G.S. Durrant, Herbert F. 394338. (Late 8575.) M. Mar. 26/17.
9 D. Honess, F. 392853. (6564.) M. April 14/17.
9 D. Hunt, C. 4306. M. Oct. 9/16. R/Enq.
9 D. Johnson, A. F. 394294. M. April 14/17.
9 D. Sparrowhawk, W. E. 393130. M. April 14/17.
9 D. XIV Watson, Herbert Henry. 7655. W. and M. Oct. 9/16. R/Enq.

**London Regiment—contd.**

*B.E.F.*

‡2/9 D. Mersh, Wm. 415021. M. June 6/17.
‡2/10 D. Cornwal, J. 2537. W. and M. June 14/17.
‡2/10 D. Grimwood, W. 4200. W. and M. June 14/17.
‡2/10 D. XVI Wilby, W. 423115. M. June 14/17.
12 A. III Bowerman, Oswald G. 472606. (Late 5970.) W. and M. April 9/17.
12 A. II Dudman, Albert Victor. 6332. M. Oct. 7/16. R/Enq.
*12 A. II Goodwin, Harry Thos. 18/7921. (Late Northants, 5830.) M. Sept. 9/16. R/Enq.
12 A. II Stanley, A. J. 6281. M. Nov. 7/16. R/Enq.
12 A. L.G.S. Sutton, Wm. Conrad. 473402. (Late 7175.) K. April 9/17. Det.D./B.
12 A. IV Turner, Frank. 7949. W. and M. Oct. 7/16. R/Enq.
12 B. Clarke, F. 7849. M. Sept. 9/16. R./Enq.
12 C. XII Berry, John Leonard. 5260. M. Oct. 7/16. R/Enq.
12 C. X Bland, Herbert. 4322. K. Sept. 19/16. Det.D./B.
12 C. Woodwards, Ernest. 7573. (Late 2nd, 3185.) K. Oct. 7/16. Det.D./B.
12 D. XIV Duffin, Frank R. 6383. K. Oct. 7/16. Det.D./B.
12 D. XV Smith, R. E. 7957. M. Sept. 9/16. R/Enq.
‡12 D. XIII Toms, Philip Roy. 7304. (4605.) K. Sept. 9/16. Det.D./B.
12 D. Westfield, Fredk. C. 6318. M. Oct. 7/16. R./Enq.
*2/12 B. V Doody, Charles. 471903. K. June 13/17. Det.D./B.
13 A. Blundell, F. C. 1788. M. Jan. 19/17.
13 A. II Brown, Fredk. John. 7533. K. Sept. 26/16. Det.D./B. R/Enq.
13 A. or B. Hunter, B. S. 491837. M. April 9/17.
13 A. Thwaites, H. 7799. M. Jan. 19/17.
13 A. Whaley, H. G. 493654. M. April 7/17.
13 C. IX Cohen, S. 6310. K. April 9/17. Det.D./B.
13 C. IX Timbs, Charles A. 7591. W. and M. Sept. 9/16. R/Enq.
14 A. III Day, Stanley Albert. 7146. K. Sept. 9/16. Det.D./B. R/Enq.
*14 A. Norman, J. 513691. (7804.) M. May 10/17.
14 A. L.G.S. Wilson, Herbert. 5464. W. and M. Sept. 9/16. R/Enq.
14 B. VIII Beachey, Sergt. A. R. 511386. (4901.) W. and M. May 11/17.
14 B. VI Blackburn, John. 513157. (Late 8355) W. and M. April 9/17.
14 B. VII Curbutt, Frank. 512581. W. and M. May 11/17.
‡14 B. Ferguson, A. J. 514269. (8481.) W. and M. May 11/17.
‡14 B. Peachey, Sgt. A. R. 511386. W. and M. May 11/17.
14 B. V Riley, Sydney Thos. 514248. W. and M. May 11/17.
14 B. VII Walton, Thos. Edw. 514209. (8414.) M. May 11/17.
‡14 C. X Curtice, John K. 512790. Unoff. W. and M. June 27-28/17.
14 D. XV Aldous, C. L. 513787. W. and M. May 11/17.
14 D. XIII Bargman, W. J. 513563. W. and M. May 11/17.
14 D. XV Sword, Fred. 513308. (7348.) W. and M. May 11/17.
*15 **Moran, 2nd Lieut. J.** M. June 7/17.
15 A. IV Chenery, Ernest. 4815. M. Oct. 7/16. R/Enq.
15 A. II Conzina, A. 53071. M. Sept. 15/16. R/Enq.
*15 A. II Richards, Bernard. 532084. (4732.) M. June 7/17.
15 A. II Sharp, Thomas Paine. 6679. K. Oct. 7/16. Det.D./B.
15 A. Wombell, Jas. Horace. 3746. K. Oct. 7/16. Det.D./B. R/Enq.
‡15 B. VI Farrier, J. J. 533587. M. June 7/17.
‡15 B. VI Munro, Gordon. 531593. (4049.) M. June 7/17.
15 C. Couchman, A. G. 4432. M. Sept. 14/16. R/Enq.
15 D. Bell, Fredk. Donald Linnell. 3972. M. Oct. 7/16. R/Enq.
15 D. XIII Chandler, Albert Edward. 5605. M. Oct. 7/16. R/Enq.
‡15 D. Cronin, L.-Cpl. Gerald P. 532736. W. and M. June 7/17.
‡15 D. XV Davison, Robt. Wm. 534148. M. June 7/17.
15 D. XIII Freeston, G. B. 4712. M. Oct. 7/16. R/Enq.

**London Regiment—contd.**

## *B.E.F.*

‡15 D. Greenwood, L.-Cpl. Leslie Reg. 532786. — M. June 7/17.
15 D. XV Hinrick, Ernest. 6144. — M. Oct. 7/16. R/Enq.
‡15 D. XIV Simmonds, H. F. R. 533962. — M. since June 7/17.
15 D. XVI Snow, B. 5746. — M. Oct. 7/16.
16 **Betteridge, 2nd Lieut. J. H. (Fr. Border Regt.)** — K. April 14/17. Det.D./B.
16 **Gray, Lieut. C. P.** — M. April 14/17.
16 **Pickles, 2nd Lt. H.** (Fr. 4 Border.) — M. April 14/17.
16 A. Beavington, Sidney Jas., 5514. (Fr. 8th.) — W. and M. Oct. 9/16. R/Enq.
16 A. IV Glaisher, Frank Geo. 552349. (Late 5332.) — M. Unoff. K. April 14/17. Conf. and Det.D./B.
16 A. or B. McIntyre, Leslie. 554477. (8747.) — M. April 14/17.
16 A. Millen, Harry. 552609. — M. April 14/17.
‡16 A. III Rider, W. T. 553704. (7345.) — M. April 14/17.
16 A. Smith, Henry Sidney. 8891. (Fr. 2/8 Middlesex.) — M. Sept. 18/16. R/Enq.
16 A. III Tavendale, Jas. 552628. (Late 5737.) — M. April 14/17.
‡16 A. III Trewin, Fred. L. 551372. (4011.) — K. April 14/17. Det D./B. R/Enq.
16 A. IV Wareham, Bert. 552785. (5982.) — M. April 14/17.
*16 A. Wingfield, A. W. 4882. — K. Oct. 9/16. Det.D./B.
*16 B. or C. Amey, Walter. 4795. — M. Sept. 10/16. R/Enq.
*16 B. VI Branwhite, E. R. 6154. — M. Sept. 10/16. R/Enq.
16 B. VIII Bryen, Geo. Augustus. 550988. (Late 3432.) — M. April 14/17.
16 B. VI Carter, Harry Leslie. 551756. (Late 4546.) — M. April 14/17.
16 B. VII French, Jas. 553284. (6822.) — M. April 14/17.
16 B. Inns, W. H. 551913. — M. April 14/17.
16 B. VII Nichols, Rowland F. 552836. (Late 6059.) — M. April 14/17.
16 B. Rayner, E. J. 5407. — W. and M. Sept. 10/16. R/Enq.
16 B. Thynne, S. 553452. — M. April 14/17.
16 C. XI Druett, Sgt. Percy. 550209. (Late 1761.) — M. April 14/17.
16 C. IX Ell, L. V. 551893. (4750.) — M. April 14/17.
16 C. IX English, Henry. 552514. (5572.) — M. April 14/17.
16 C. XI Gregory, Norman Edgar. 4440. — K. Sept. 10/16. Det.D./B. R/Enq.
16 C. Jackson, John R. 551966. (4853.) — M. April 14/17.
16 C. X Jordan, H. 8854. (Fr. 2/8 Middlx., 4907.) — M. Sept. 10/16. R/Enq.
16 C. X Lancaster, E. E. 553961. (7605.) — M. April 14/17.
16 C. Rudall, W. H. 553540. — M. April 14/17.
16 C. IX Samuels, Cpl. Wm. Percival. 3426. — K. April 14/17. Det.D./B.
16 C. Trenge, A. 553493. — M. April 14/17.
16 C. Vince, L.-Cpl. J. 551929. — M. April 14/17.
16 D. XIV Beeching, A. E. 553054. (6503.) — M. April 14/17.
16 D. L.G.S. Crawford, Leonard. 552338. (Late 5135.) — M. April 14/17.
16 D. XV Dowden, W. T. 5701. — M. April 14/17.
16 D. XIV Gedge, Frank Herbt. 553286. (6825.) — M. April 14/17.
16 D. L.G.S. Port, Ernest. 552426. — M. Unoff. W. April 14/17.
16 D. XV Prince, E. N. 553438. (7603.) — M. April 14/17.
16 D. XIV Scowcroft, Jas. 553740. (Late 7381.) — K. April 14/17. Det.D./B.
16 D. Selliwood, W. H. 553886. — M. April 14/17.
‡16 D. Sillitoe, Cpl. John Thos. 554514. (8792.) — M. Sept. 10/16. R/Enq.
16 D. Smith, Arthur Beresford. 3650. — M. Sept. 10/16. R/Enq.

**London Regiment**—contd.

*B.E.F.*

*16 D. XIV West, L.-Cpl. E. H. 55394. M. April 14/17.
16 D. Whetburn, A. 550304. M. April 14/17.
16 D. Young, John Reginald. 552756. (Late 5935.) M. April 14/17.
17 A. Curtis, W. 6859. M. Oct. 1/16. R/Enq.
*17 A. III Goddard, H. A. 5656. M. Oct. 1/16. R/Enq.
17 A. or C. Heath, Samuel. 572372. (Late 5181) M. Oct. 1/16.
17 B. Corby, W. 573742. (Late 6966.) M. Oct. 1/16.
‡17 B. VII Davies, F. H. 572700. W. Unoff. M. June 9/17.
*17 B. Kiggins, J. 2662. M. Oct. 1/16. R/Enq.
*17 C. Blaine, Wm. 5693. M. Oct. 1/16. R/Enq.
17 C. Pankhurst, Percy. 6885. M. Oct. 1/16. R/Enq.
17 C. Wiles, W. J. 571041. (Late 3044.) M. Oct. 1/16.
*17 D. XIII Stanger, Charles. 1893. M. Oct. 1/16. R/Enq.
18 A. Fletcher, H. A. 593754. M. April 7/17.
18 A. Kemsley, R. 593502. M. April 7/17.
18 A. or B. Kirkham, Sergt. Alexander. 1777. M. April 4/17.
18 B. Carpenter, Sgt. Geo. 593401. (Late 6221.) Unoff. M. April 7/17.
18 B. Damen, E. W. S. 592885. W. and M. April 7/17.
18 B. or D. Elliott, W. 590373. (1727.) W. and M. April 7/17.
18 B. Gains, L.-Cpl. A. F. 593381. W. and M. April 7/17.
18 B. Gill, W. 593831. W. and M. April 7/17.
18 B. or D. Hall, Geo. Alfred. 594023. (6957.) M. April 7/17.
18 B. or D. XV Heath, Chas. Horace. 594193. (8021.) M. April 7/17.
18 B. King, W. A. 594246. (8081.) M. April 7/17.
18 B. Lambourn, E. C. 592238. (4663.) M. April 7/17.
18 B. Lemar, W. D. 593389. (6193.) M. April 7/17.
18 B. Meinke, W. 594174. W. and M. April 7/17.
18 B. Reeve, Wilfred Chas. 592059. (Late 4416.) M. April 7/17.
18 B. VIII Richman, W. R. 593679. (6586.) M. April 9/17.
18 B. VII Sindall, Sergt. T. R. 590037. (351.) W. and M. April 7/17.
18 B. Skinner, T. 590755. M. April 7/17.
18 B. Smith, James. 593697. (6605.) M. April 7/17.
18 B. Tindall, Sergt. T. R. 590037. W. and M. April 7/17.
18 B. VIII Wright, W. 593129. (5854.) M. April 7/17.
18 C. X Adams, H. G. 593891. (Late 6822.) W. and M. April 7/17.
18 C. Burt, L. 591350. M. April 7/17.
18 C. Dalton, W. 593638. M. April 7/17.
18 C. Holman, L.-Cpl. S. 590311. W. and M. April 7/17.
18 C. James, B. H. 591706. M. April 7/17.
18 C. X Nicholls, Chas. E. 591853. (Late 4144) M. April 7/17.
‡18 C. X Turner, Arthur Jesse. 591619. M. June 8/17.
18 C. X Woodrow, John Jas. 593882. (Late 6812.) W. and M. April 7/17.
18 D. XIII Mobbs, J. 590364. (1708.) M. April 7/17.
19 A. Moulton, G. R. 4138. M. Sept. 15/16. R/Enq.
*19 B. VIII Norman, Geo. 5710. M. Sept. 15/16. R/Enq.
19 B. VI Norris, Thos. Maurice. 5900. (Fr. K.R.R.C., 7164.) K. Sept. 15-16/16. Det.D./B.
19 B. Willcox, Wm. Fredk. 7181. M. Sept. 29/16.
‡19 C. XI East, Thomas. 3543. W. and M. Sept. 15/16. R/Enq.
*19 C. Tanner, Fredk. Geo. 595. (Transport Sec.) W. and M. Sept. 29/16. R/Enq.
20 C. Milgate, John Edwin. 3751. M. Oct. 1/16. R/Enq.
21 A. II Holl, E. 6768. M. Oct. 8/16. R/Enq.
21 A. III Killick, Alfred. 6939. K. Oct. 8/16. Det.D./B. R/Enq.

**London Regiment—contd.**

## *B.E.F.*

‡21 A. Kinnick, Alfred. 25353. — M. June 10/17.
21 A. IV Ramsell, G. 3639. — M. Oct. 8/16. R/Enq.
‡21 A. IV Woolley, J. L. 650848. — M. June 7/17.
‡21 B. VI Harrington, Robt. Jas. 652322. — M. June 7/17.
*21 B. Matthews, Fredk. 653155. (6669.) (Fr. 2/5 E. Surreys, 2543.) — W. and M. Oct. 8/16. R/Enq.
*21 C. XII Elsworth, Wm. Arthur. 651357. — K. June 7/17. Det.D./B.
21 C. Scarborough, E. 2633. — M. Sept. 15/16.
‡21 D. XV Moloney, A. 653336. — W. Unoff. M. June 7/17.
‡21 D. Parsons, Albert Edw 653411. — M. June 7/17.
21 D. Playle, L.-Cpl. Wallace. 3907. — W. and M. Oct. 8/16. R/Enq.
‡21 D. XIII Read, E. 653314. — M. June 7/17.
*21 D. XVI Tue, L.-Cpl. J. S. 652612. — M. June 7/17.
‡21 ? Milson, H. J. 651818. — M. July 10/17.
*22 B. VI Drew, W. H. 5248. — W. and M. Sept. 16/16. R/Enq.
22 C. IX Crane, Arthur Beams. 4736. — W. and M. Oct. 8/16. R/Enq.
22 C. XII Illman, H. T. 6172. — M. Oct. 8/16. R/Enq.
‡22 C. XII Simonds, J. 5273. — W. and M. Oct. 8/16. R/Enq.
22 D. Ravenscroft, Albert. 683144. (6211.) — M. Oct. 9/16. R/Enq.
23 A. I Collier, Alfred Wm. 7514. (Fr. 9th.) — M. Sept. 16/16. R/Enq.
23 A. I King, T. R. 5637. — K. Sept. 15/16. Det.D./B.
‡23 B. V Harding. 203261. — W. Unoff. M. June 7/17.
‡23 B. Heath, William. 4622. — M. Sept. 16/16. R/Enq.
23 B. VI Hind, L.-Cpl. Harry Victor. 2490. — K. Sept. 18/16. Det.D./B.
‡23 C. X Cain, Joseph. 703048. (6760.) — M. June 7/17.
23 C. Douthwaite, Arthur Geo. 3764. — M. Sept. 16/16. R/Enq.
23 C. XI Elliott, M. J 5024. — M. Unoff. W. Oct. 2/16.
‡23 C. L.G.S. Monk, Harry. 703574. — K. June 7/17. Det.D./B.
23 C. Poulter, E. 8035. — M. Oct. 2/16.
23 C. Wilmot, B. J. 4268. — M. Sept. 16/16. R/Enq.
‡23 D. XIII Berridge, F. A. 703344. — K. June 7-8/17. Det.D./B.
23 D. XIV Broad, Alex. Wm. Hry. 1876. — K. Sept. 16/16. Det.D./B.
23 D. XIV Hughes, Horace. 4804. — M. Sept. 16/16. R/Enq.
23 D. Oram, W. J. 1394. — M. Sept. 16/16. R/Enq.

## *BALKANS.*

2/13 A. Lamb, W. A. 3891. — M. Aug. 6/16. R./Enq. (French Cas.).
2/13 B. V Licquorish, Chas. Wm. 3697. — M. Aug. 6/16. R./Enq. (French Cas.).
‡2/13 ? Bytheway, A. A. 491772. — M. June 4/17.
*2/20 A. I Carter, Chas. Jas. 630838. (2589.) — W. and M. April 25/17.
2/20 A. Conley, Daniel. 632039. — M., bel. K. April 25/17.
2/20 A. II Ellis, Harry J. 632023. — M., bel. K. April 25/17.
2/20 A. III Ellis, John. 632029. — M., bel. K. April 25/17.
2/20 A. I Norris, G. S. 630328. — W. and M. April 23/17.
2/20 A. III Sadler, T. 632989. — M., bel. K. April 25/17.
2/20 A. II Silver, Louis. 633705. — M., bel. K. April 25/17.
2/20 A. IV Wade, Herbert. 633897. — M. April 25/17.
‡2/20 A. M.G.S. Watts, Frank Donald. 633855. — K. April 23/17. Det.D./B. R/Enq.
2/20 B. VIII Appleton, Wm. 633048. (6107.) — M. April 25/17.
2/20 B. VIII Goodwin, L.-Cpl. H. F. P. 632250. (Late 5037.) — M., bel. K. April 25/17.
2/20 B. VI Shone, C. 632781. — M. April 25/17.
2/20 D. XIII Ellinor, S. 633061. (Late 6121.) — M. April 25/17.
2/20 D. Rosenberg, J. 633710. (Late 7509.) — M. April 25/17.
2/20 ? Beadles, A. W. 633838. — M. April 25/17.
2/20 ? Coney, F. L. 632139. — M., bel. K. April 25/17.

**London Regiment**—contd.

## BALKANS.

| | | |
|---|---|---|
| **2/20 ?** | Hooks, F. 630033. | M., bel. K. **April 25/17.** |
| **2/20 ?** | Jordan, W. J. 632398. | M., bel. K. **April 25/17.** |
| **2/20 ?** | Nash, L.-Cpl. L. G. 631103. | M., bel. K. **April 25/17.** |
| **2/20 ?** | Snashull, F. G. 631948. | M., bel. K. **April 25/17.** |
| **2/20 ?** | Taffs, H. 632249. | W. and M. **April 23/17.** |
| **2/20 ?** | Walters, H. 632775. | M., bel. K. **April 25/17.** |
| **2/21 A. Sniper's S.** | Hill, Harry C. 4206. | W. and M. **Feb. 6/17.** |
| **2/21 D.** | Jones, W. C. 650763. (Late 2703.) | M. **Mar. 22/17.** |
| **2/22 D.** | Davies, Harry Maxwell. 683887. (Old No. 7012.) | W. and M. **Jan. 30/17.** |

## E.E.F.

| | | |
|---|---|---|
| **10** | **Ducane, 2nd Lieut. R. E. M.** | W and M. **April 19/17.** |
| **10 1** | Collins, J. 422213. (3983.) | W. and M. **April 19/17.** |
| **10 1** | Graham, Douglas. 424123. | M. **April 17/17.** |
| **10 1** | Hale, Alfred. 424125. | M. **April 19/17.** |
| **10 1** | Higdon, F. 421514. (2972.) | W. and M. **April 19/17.** |
| **10 1 L.G.S.** | Howard, C. H. 420924. (Late 2039) | W. and M. **April 19/17.** |
| **10 1** | Howes, John Jas. 421375. (2765.) | W. and M. **April 19/17.** |
| **10 1 III** | Lewis, Thos. 420698. (Late 1653.) | M. **April 19/17.** |
| **10 1** | Roach, W. F. 422025. (3669.) | M. **April 19/17.** |
| ***10 1 I** | Surgett, A. H. 421062. | W. and M. **April 19/17.** |
| **10 2** | Lewis, Jim. 422241. (4071.) | M. **April 19/17.** |
| **10 2** | Scanlan, W. 421692. (3210.) | W. and M. **April 19/17.** |
| **10 2** | Sharman, J. 421819. (3390.) | M. **April 19/17.** |
| ***10 3** | Chapman, G. F. 420673. | W. and M. **April 19/17.** |
| **10 3** | Hyde, J. F. 421008. (2180.) | W. and M. **April 19/17.** |
| **10 3** | Southgate, C. 421518. (2979.) | W. and M. **April 19/17.** |
| **10 3 IX** | Watts, Sgt. J. W. 420862. (Late 1917) | M. **April 19/17.** |
| **10 3** | Wright, Joe. 420348. | W. and M. **April 19/17.** |
| **10 4 XIV** | Coulton, J. W. 424098. | M. **April 19/17.** |
| **10 4 XIV** | Jefferies, G. S. 420088. | W. and M. **April 19/17.** |
| **10 4 XVI** | Pullen, H. 241816. (3385.) | W. and M. **April 19/17.** |
| **10 4 XV** | Savage, H. J. 422079. (3739.) | M. **April 19/17.** |
| **10 ?** | Clifford, L.-Cpl. H. V. 420836. | W. and M. **April 19/17.** |
| ***10 ?** | Clitheroe, L.-Cpl. G. E. 421629. | W. and M. **April 19/17.** |
| **10 ?** | Davies, E. 424167. | W. and M. **April 19/17.** |
| **10 ?** | Maxwell, A. O. 421804. | M. **April 19/17.** |
| **10 ?** | Wade, Cpl. Victor A. 420554. (Late 1385.) | M. **April 19/17.** |
| **10 ?** | Wilson, Jas. Harold. 421496. (2949.) | W. and M. **April 19/17.** |
| ***10 ?** | Woolacott, W. 420881. | W. and M. **April 19/17.** |
| **11** | **Gibson, Lieut. H. O. S.** | W. and M. **April 19/17.** |
| **11 A. III** | Aird, Cpl. W. G. 450098. | M. **April 19/17.** |
| ***11 A. IV** | Atkinson, Harold Jas. 453117. | M. **April 19/17.** |
| **11 A.** | Ayers, Edwin Chas. 451043. (Late 3141.) | M. **April 19/17.** |
| **11 A.** | Blair, Chas. Alex. 450243. (Late 1732.) | M. **April 19/17.** |
| **11 A. IV** | Broom, John. 453122. | M. **April 19/17.** |
| **11 A. IV** | Cohen, L.-Cpl. Fredk. Arthur. 450842. (2772.) | M. **April 19/17.** |
| **11 A. IV** | Drake, Cpl. Frank. 450710. (2528.) | M. **April 19/17.** |
| ***11 A. I** | Green, R. C. 451358. (3676.) | M. **April 9/17.** |
| **11 A.** | Joyce, J. H. 453121. (4342.) | W. and M. **April 19/17.** |
| **11 A.** | Sharp, Thos. 451577. (Late 4028.) | M. **April 19/17.** |
| **11 A.** | Wood, D. W. 453078. (2605.) (Fr. 12th.) | M. **April 19/17.** |
| **11 B. L.G.S.** | Barton, W. 451131. (Late 3314.) | M. **April 19/17.** |

**London Regiment**—contd.

## *E.E.F.*

11 B. V Carey, John Arber. 451063. (3182.) M. April 19/17.
11 B. L.G.S. Chester, W. J. 451053. (Late 3163) M. April 19/17.
11 B. Evans, Wm. Jas. 453096. M. April 19/17.
11 B. L.G.S. Hersant, R. 453109. W. and M. April 19/17.
11 B. Kick, W. C. 450244. (Late 1733.) W. and M. April 19/17.
11 B. VI Morton, H. R. 453080. M. April 19/17.
11 B. Partington, H. K. 453099. M. April 19/17.
11 B. Rollinson, G. 453100. M. April 19/17.
11 B. Schween, W. A. 451484. M. April 19/17.
11 B. V Tadd, Wm. Geo. 451336. (Late 3634.) W. and M. April 19/17.
11 B. Taylor, Sgt. Geo. 451552. (Late 3986) M. April 19/17.
11 B. VI Weeden, J. R. 453126. M. April 19/17.
11 B. VIII Woodger, Harold. 450043. (1116.) M. April 19/17.
11 B. V Woodward, J. 453102. M. April 19/17.
11 C. Almand, F. C. 451785. (Late 4349.) M. April 19/17.
11 C. X Callaghan, R. T. L. 452021. (4678.) M. April 19/17.
11 C. L.G.S. Feast, L.-Cpl. F. W. 450817. (Late 2724.) M. April 19/17.
11 C. X Gowrley, G. H. 453198. M. April 19/17.
11 C. XII Langdon, Robt. 450733. (Late 2564.) M. April 19/17.
11 D. XIV Chase, Arthur Cecil. 450598. (Late 2338.) M. April 19/17.
11 D. XIV Dyke, E. A. 451611. (Late 4072.) W. and M. April 19/17.
11 D. XV Greenwood, Alfred. 450764. M. April 19/17.
11 D. L.G.S. Gregory, S. H. 451280. (Late 3559.) W. and M. April 19/17.
11 D. Hurst, H. 451104. (3267.) W. and M. April 19/17.
11 D. XV Marks, Mortimer E. 451032. (Late 3117.) W. and M. April 19/17.
11 D. Miller, Stanley Geo. 450586. (2320.) M. April 19/17.
11 D. Moore, J. 451389. (3717.) M. April 19/17.
11 D. L.G.S. Nobbs, L.-Cpl. W. C. 451114. (3286.) M. April 19/17.
11 D. XIV Read, Walter. 451705. M. April 19/17.
11 D. XIV Rowley, E. 451371. M. April 19/17.
11 D. XV Shields, Alwynne Chas. 450825. (Late 2746.) M. April 19/17.
11 D. Snow, F. J. 451262. (Late 3531.) W. and M. April 19/17.
11 D. Streatfield, E. A. 450936. M. April 19/17.
11 D. Trenaman, E. B. 453090. W. and M. April 19/17.
11 D. XV Vail, H. 451553. (Late 3988.) M. April 19/17.
11 D. XIV Wilson, G. J. 450967. (Late 3009.) M. April 19/17.
11 D. XV Wilson, L.-Cpl. J. E. 450530. (Late 2240.) M. April 19/17.
11 D. XV Woodley, H. 452472. (5593.) K. May 19/17. Det.D./B.
11 ? Atkinson, H. J. 433117. M. April 19/17.
11 ? Barker, Henry. 451831. (Late 4419.) M. April 19/17.
11 ? Barnley, Cpl. S. C. 450436. W. and M. April 19/17.
11 ? Broom, J. 453122. M. April 19/17.
11 ? Crocker, A. H. 451030. W. and M. April 19/17.
11 ? Dobbs, J. 453197. M. April 19/17.
11 ? Downes, T. W. 51431. W. and M. April 19/17.
11 ? Ekers, A. 453202. M. April 19/17.
11 ? Gannon, J. J. 451780. W. and M. April 19/17.
11 ? Heading, L.-Cpl. J. A. R. 451612. M. April 19/17.
11 ? King, C. 453177. M. April 19/17.
11 ? Knight, R. H. H. 450451. M. April 19/17.
11 ? Lewis, A. E. 453215. M. April 19/17.
11 ? Pratten, R. J. 452023. M. April 19/17.

**London Regiment—contd.**

*E.E.F.*

| | | |
|---|---|---|
| **11 ?** | Smith, J. 453183. | M. April 19/17. |
| **11 ?** | Stout, C. 453133. | M. April 19/17. |
| **11 ?** | Vandover, T. W. 451839. | W. and M. April 19/17. |
| **11 ?** | Wale, R. 451235. | M. April 19/17. |
| **11 ?** | Wilkins, S. 451534. | W. and M. April 19/17. |
| **11 ?** | Worsell, J. 450464. | W. and M. April 19/17. |

## LONDON YEOMANRY (COUNTY OF)

*E.E.F.*

| | | |
|---|---|---|
| **2 A. Squad.** | Bookham, D. C. 11598. (3010.) | M. May 26/17. |

## LOTHIANS AND BORDER HORSE.

*B.E.F.*

| | | |
|---|---|---|
| **B. Squad.** | Watson, L.-Sergt. G. P. 120177. (1364.) | M. Mar. 22/17. |

## MACHINE GUN CORPS (INFANTRY).

*B.E.F.*

| | | |
|---|---|---|
| **‡2** | **Manger, 2nd Lieut. E.** | M. July 10/17. |
| **2 A.** | **Wilson, Lt. A. S. (Fr. 3 S. Lancs.)** | M. April 23/17. |
| **‡2 C. S.** | Hoyle, A. 63305. | Unoff. M. July 10/17. |
| **‡2 S S.** | Longbottom, F. 60726. | Unoff. M. July 10/17. |
| **2 D.** | Neal, J. H. 17030. | M. Sept. 9/16. R/Enq. |
| **‡6** | Bird, E. 16076. | M. April 28/17. |
| **6 2** | Brand, Ernest. 25776. | M. April 28/17. |
| **6 2 S.** | Bullock, W. A. 46805. | M. April 28/17. |
| **6** | Carnelly, John Henry. 30513. (Fr. 3 Dragoon Guards.) | M. April 11/17. |
| **‡6** | Claringbold, W. H. 58785. | M. April 28/17. |
| **6 2** | Garrett, A. G. 29404. | M. April 28/17. |
| **‡6** | Haman, J. 9203. | M. April 28/17. |
| ***6 2** | Harrow, John. 60900. | M. April 28/17. |
| ***6 3** | Williams, Wm. 11395. (Fr. 1 Liverpools.) | M. April 13/17. |
| **‡8** | Arrol, J. H. 51509. | M. April 11/17. |
| ***8 C.** | Read, Walter. 8276. | M. April 28/17. |

**Machine Gun Corps Infantry—contd.**

## *B.E.F.*

*8 Wilson, Ernest. 81366. — K. **April 10/17.** Det.D./B.
9 4 S. Axham, Wm. Geo. 84294. — M. **May 3/17.**
9 1 S. Burge, 2nd Gnr. 7607. (Fr. K.R.R.C.) — M. **Mar. 27/16.**
‡9 Dempster, W. 44664. — M. **May 3/17.**
‡9 McCarthy, G. 71922. — M. **May 3/17.**
10 Anders, H. 33728. — M. **April 23/17.**
‡10 Annis, J. 10459. — M. **May 3/17.**
11 Alesbrook, Geo. 29204. (Fr. 1st E. Lancs.) — W. and M. **April 19/17.**
11 3 Pike, George. 17997. — W. and M. **April 9/17.**
‡12 Batty, A. 35106. — M. **May 4/17.**
12 Denning, Sig. Reg. E. 67326. — M. **May 3/17.**
‡14 A. S. Davis, L.-Cpl. Arthur. 16798. — M. Nov. 18/16. R/Enq.
15 Gunn, John. 8394. — W. and M. **April 9/17.**
‡26 Brannen, J. 34414. — M. **May 3/17.**
‡26 Dymock, J. 17389. — M. **May 3/17.**
27 **Burrows, 2nd Lieut. W. G. R.** — M. **May 3/17.**
27 Atkinson, T. 36754. — W. Unoff. M. **May 3/17.**
27 1 S. Dawkins, Walter. 57577. — W. and M. **May 3/17.**
‡27 Dee, William J. 60097. — M. **May 3/17.**
27 Gorton, William. 60233. — K. **April 9/17.** Det.D./B.
‡27 Howes, R. 6493. — W. and M. **June 3/17.**
27 Johnston, Sergt. Edw. 18326. — M. **May 3/17.**
27 Loudon, Sergt. Alex. 18427. (Fr. 10 A. & S. Highlanders, 1804.) — W. and M. **May 3/17.**
‡27 Nesbit, R. 25165. — M. **May 3/17.**
27 1 S. Pritchard, G. R. 37080. — M. **May 3/17.**
‡27 Reeves, A. 60046. — W. and M. **June 3/17.**
27 Ward, Frank. 60381. — W. and M. **May 3/17.**
27 1 S. Welding, A. R. 12444. — W. and M. **May 3/17.**
*36 2 Rowley, Edward. 44217. — M. **May 3/17.**
‡41 Armstrong, A. 85060. — W. and M. **May 3/17.**
‡41 Holder, J. 44425. — W. and M. **May 3/17.**
‡41 Willford, J. H. 3291. (Fr. 7th K.R.R.C.) — W. and M. **May 3/17.**
42 Booth, E. 19850. — M. **April 9/17.**
43 Wileman, John. 44926. (Fr. 6th Leicesters.) — M. **Sept. 6/16.**
‡44 Sheppard, A. W. 59871. — W. and M. **April 27/17.**
‡45 Burke, P. 45280. — M. **April 23/17.**
‡45 Williams, J. T. 81811. — M. **April 23/17.**
‡46 Austin, C. E. 8925. — M. **April 11/17.**
‡46 Tanner, C. 41984. (Fr. 12 H.L.I.) — M. **April 11/17.**
46 2 Young, George. 41849. (Fr. K.O.S.B. att. 12 H.L.I.) — M. **April 11/17.**
‡50 Smith, J. 22040. — M **May 16/17.**
*51 Davies, Jas. Wilfred. 3642. — W. and M. **April 24/17.**
51 De Banks, H. 30483. — M. **April 23/17.**
‡51 Hart, A. W. 85369. — W. and M. **April 23/17.**
51 Meakins, Sergt. Cyril. 3635. — M., bel. K. **April 23/17.**
52 B. S. Cromarty, R. M. 68602. — W. and M. **April 24/17.**
52 McArthur, Sergt. A. J. 9627. — W. and M. **April 25/17.**
52 Snape, Thos. 3851. — M. **Nov. 2/16.**
52 C. S. Spence, A. 63134. — W. and M. **May 8/17.**
54 3 Rivett, Sergt. Geo. 4093. — M. **May 3/17.**
‡54 Trowell, F. 10914. — W. and M. **May 3/17.**
55 **Watson, 2nd Lieut. F.** — M. **May 3/17.**
55 C. Allan, Albert Edw. 37838. — W. and M. **May 3/17.**
55 Gristwood, L.-Cpl. Leo. Wm. 4176. — M. **May 3/17.**

**Machine Gun Corps (Infantry)—contd.**

*B.E.F.*

| | | |
|---|---|---|
| 55 | Harridy, David. 4555. | W. and M. **May 3/17.** |
| ,55 | Kyte, A. 83101. | K. **May 3/17.** Det.D./B. |
| ‡55 | Luttimore, F. 4180. | M. **April 3/17.** |
| ‡55 | Summers, F. 4217. | M. **May 3/17.** |
| ‡58 | Buswell, P. 49844. (Fr. 9 Cheshires) | K. **June 10/17.** Det.D./B. |
| 59 | Wilson, James S. 12126. | M. **Sept. 4/16.** |
| 63 | **Hipwell, 2nd Lieut. H. R.** (Fr. 4th Seaforths.) | M., bel. K. **April 24/17.** |
| 64 | **Bennett, Lt. V. R.** (Fr. 3 Sherwds.) | K. **April 10/17.** Det.D./B. |
| ‡69 | **Pain, Major William.** 35888. | K. **June 7/17.** Det.D./B. R/Enq. |
| *69 | Kirbyson, Edw. 12113. (Fr. 11 W. Yorks.) | Unoff. M. **June 10/17.** |
| ‡74 | Somerville, W. H. 8344. | M. **April 26/17.** |
| *76 18 | Mobey, George. 64450. | M. **April 26/17.** |
| ‡87 | Craig, J. 21336. | M. **April 24/17.** |
| ‡87 | Innes, A. 35585. | W. and M. **April 23/17.** |
| *88 | **Owen, 2nd Lt. R. F. L.** (Fr. Essex.) | K. **April 23/16.** Det.D./B. |
| ,88 | Culversbert, G. 72016. | M. **April 14/17.** |
| 88 | Forrest, Jas. 60674. | M. **April 14/17.** |
| 88 | Holdom, W. 71998. | M. **April 14/17.** |
| 88 | McFaddon, A. 71981. | M. **April 14/17.** |
| 88 | Oliver, Geo. 20685. | M. **April 14/17.** |
| ‡88 | Paterson, J. 23909. | W. and M. **April 23/17.** |
| 88 | Pratt, A. 43486. (Fr. 1 Essex.) | M. **Oct. 19/16.** |
| 88 | Riley, J. 37975. | M. **April 14/17.** |
| ,88 | Shergold, L.-Sergt. A. 21479. | M. **April 14/17.** |
| ,88 | Trayhorn, L.-Cpl. A. 21482. | M. **April 14/17.** |
| 88 | Whiteway, W. 21486. | M. **April 14/17.** |
| ,90 | Gray, W. 7289. | M. **April 23/17.** |
| 90 3 | Kelley, Geo. 71323. | W. and M. **April 23/17.** |
| ‡92 | Jennison, R. 70345. | M. **May 3/17.** |
| ‡92 | Kingsley, J. A. 85156. | M. **May 3/17.** |
| ,92 | Owen, L. G. 42843. | M. **May 3/17.** |
| ,92 | Richardson, Jackson. 82258. | K. **May 17/17.** Det.D./B. |
| *93 | Felton, W. 13290. | W. and M. **May 3/17.** |
| *94 | Dent, T. 25020. | M. **May 19/17.** |
| 98 | Burton, Zach. 82822. | M. **April 23/17.** |
| 98 | Neave, F. J. E. 70748. | M. **April 23/17.** |
| 99 | France, F. 18052. (Fr. 1 R. Berks) | W. and M. **April 29/17.** |
| 99 | Jarvis, W. E. 23563. (Fr. 23 R. Fus.) | K. **Feb. 17/17.** Det.D./B. R/Enq. |
| 99 1 S. | Lang, G. 46410. | W. and M. **Feb. 18/17.** |
| ‡100 | Hicks, Fred. 45714. | M. **May 20/17.** |
| ‡100 Y. D. | Marrow, Henry. 65298. | W. and M. **May 21/17.** |
| 103 | Foster, L. 44342. | W. and M. **April 29/17.** |
| ‡103 | Goodwin, J. 44669. | M. **April 29/17.** |
| 103 | Ganett, W. 46429. | W. and M. **April 30/17.** |
| ‡103 | McConway, M. 34630. | M. **April 28/17.** |
| ‡103 | Whitworth, J. 71006. | M. **April 29/17.** |
| 111 | **Robinson, Lt. C. A.** (Fr. 4 Innis. Fus.) | K. **April 9/17.** Det.D./B. |
| 111 | Hogben, W. S. 31243. | W. and M. **April 11/17.** |
| 111 4 | King, Fred. R/13176. (Fr. 13 K.R.R.C.) | W. and M. **April 23/17.** |
| *111 4 | Turner, A. R. 37646. (Fr. 13 K.R.R.C.) | W. and M. **April 24/17.** |
| 112 | Chant, W. 13767. | M., bel. K. **April 28/17.** |
| 112 | Richardson, Lewis Miller. 59933. | W. and M. **April 10/17.** |
| 113 | **Tanner, 2nd Lieut. E. G. C.** | K. **July 1/16.** Det.D./B. |
| 116 | Green, Geo. W. 28032. | M. **Sept. 3/16.** R/Enq. |

**Machine Gun Corps (Infantry)—contd.**

## *B.E.F.*

| | | |
|---|---|---|
| *124 | Bradley, T. 22456. (Fr. 32 R. Fus.) | K. Oct. 4/16. Det.D./B. R/Enq. |
| ‡142 A. | Spence, Harry. 26837. | M. June 9/17. |
| 143 6 S. | Falconbridge, L.-Cpl. Sidney Howard. 24400. (Fr. 7 Warwicks.) | K. Feb. 6/17. Det.D./B. |
| 149 | Walton, Joseph. 11785. | M. Nov. 14/17. |
| 150 | **Cummins, 2nd Lieut. A. E.** | M. April 23/17. |
| 150 | **Hall, 2nd Lieut. M. A.** | W. Unoff. M. April 23/17. |
| 150 | Jerome, G. H. 23481. | M. April 23/17. |
| 151 | Barnes, Wm. 70422. | W. and M. April 14/17. |
| 151 D. | Buller, C. 5820. | W. and M. April 14/17. |
| 152 | Bates, J. 43353. | M. April 23/17. |
| 152 | Campbell, Edward C. 73486. | M. April 23/17. |
| 152 | Clark, A. 73471. | M. April 23/17. |
| 152 | Connolly, J. 46440. | M. April 23/17. |
| 152 | Galbraith, J. 73491. | M. April 23/17. |
| 152 D. | Greer, Frank. 303122. (Fr. 8 A. & S. Highlanders.) | M. April 23/17. |
| 152 | Griffin, G. W. 68384. | M. April 23/17. |
| 152 | McGilp, A. 73484. | M. April 23/17. |
| 152 | McKinven, A. 73487. | M. April 23/17. |
| 152 | Maclean, D. 73488. | M. April 23/17. |
| 152 | McQueen, A. 23298. | M. April 23/17. |
| 152 D. | May, John. 73481. (Fr. A. & S.H.) | M. April 23/17. |
| ‡152 | Orr, J. C. 301896. (Fr. 8 A. & S. H.) | W. and M. April 23/17. |
| 152 | Pearson, L. 58572. | M. April 23/17. |
| 152 D. | Sellars, H. 43459. | M. April 23/17. |
| 152 | Smith, Robt. 60176. | M. April 23/17. |
| 152 | Stewart, Peter. 73494. (Fr. 8 A. & S. Highlanders, 1894.) | M. April 23/17. |
| *152 D. | Thorne, Harold. 81726. | M. May 16/17. |
| *152 D. | Towse, Thos. Haigh. 65899. | M. May 16/17. |
| 152 | Winter, J. 23716. | M. April 23/17. |
| 152 | Wood, E. 59435. | M. April 23/17. |
| ‡153 | Boyes, Sergt. J. 20168. | M. May 16/17. |
| ‡153 | Hitchin, R. J. 84373. | M. May 16/17. |
| ‡153 | Smith, S. F. 86002. | M. May 16/17. |
| *153 | Smith, Thomas Parker. 67130. | M. May 16/17. |
| ‡153 | Steel, F. W. 85997. | M. May 16/17. |
| 154 | Burgin, J. W. 44731. | M. April 23/17. |
| 169 | Talbot, Cedric Walter. 1338. (Fr. 5th Londons.) | W. and M. Sept. 9/16. R/Enq. |
| ‡174 | Gorrell, Edward. 202851. (Fr. 2/5 N. Staffs, 7316.) | M. May 8/17. |
| *189 | Graham, Walter. Z/3285. (Cl.) (Fr. R.N.D., Nelson.) | W. and M. April 24/17. |
| 190 | Barrett, John. 26518. (Fr. 10 Dub. Fus.) | M. Feb. 10/17. |
| ‡195 | Mead, Sergt. Sidney. 46676. | Unoff K. June 11/17. |
| ‡197 | Price, W. H. 86955. | K. June 8/17. Det.D./B. |
| *206 | Bindsey, C. 3179. | Unoff. M. June 15/17. |
| ‡206 | White, Percy Wilson. 55884. | Unoff. M. June 15/17. |
| 208 | Aylwin, E. 65473. | W. and M. May 3/17. |

**Machine Gun Corps (Infantry)—contd.**

## B.E.F.

| | | |
|---|---|---|
| 208 D. | Butler, Sergt. Henry. 45213. | W. and M. May 3/17. |
| ‡208 | Hunt, L.-Cpl. James. 86415. | K. May 3/17. Det.D./B. |
| ‡208 | Palmer, B. Terris. 65652. | K. May 3/17. Det.D./B. |
| *208 | Scott, W. C. 203945. (Fr. K.O.Y.L.I.) | M. May 5/17. |
| ‡208 | Turnbull, J. R. 242753. (Fr. 2/5th York & Lancs.) | M. May 3/17. |
| ‡208 | Wilson, P. 66301. | M. May 3/17. |
| *212 | **Anderson, Lieut. J. G.** | M. June 3/17. |
| 212 2 | Harewood, Thos. Hy. 86330. | M. May 4/17. |
| *213 | Gaulton, Harry George. 67811. | M. May 3/17. |
| *213 | Mortimer, L.-Cpl. D. 64454. | W. and M. May 3/17. |
| ‡213 | Perkins, F. E. 81491. | M. May 3/17. |

## BALKANS.

| | | |
|---|---|---|
| 65 | Sims, L.-Cpl. W. C. 13292. | W. and M. Jan. 6/17. |
| *78 | Sargent, Edgar Stanley. 33404. | W. and M. April 24/17. |
| 81 | McKenzie, J. 48856. | W. and M. Oct. 6/16. |
| ? | **Wakeley, 2nd Lieut. W. N.** | M. May 8-9/17. |
| *? | Craik, J. R. 33345. | M. |

## E.E.F.

| | | |
|---|---|---|
| 158 3 S. | Fletcher, Jack. 50390. | W. and M. Mar. 27/17. |
| *? | Chennell, R. 54076. | W. and M. April 19/17. |
| ? | Sandel, James. 57144. | M., bel. drowned Jan. 1/17. "Ivernia." |

## PERSIAN GULF.

| | | |
|---|---|---|
| 39 | Kirk, J. 61374. | M. Jan. 25/17. |
| 133 | **Bow, 2nd Lt. G. C.** (Fr. 7 A. & S. Highlanders.) | M. Mar. 25/17. |
| 133 | Bawn, W. 36886. | M. Mar. 25/17. |
| 133 | Forrest, Fred. 37483. | M., bel. K. Mar. 25/17. |
| 133 | Ling, J. 34244. | M. Mar. 25/17. |
| 133 | McDonald, R. 62194. | M. Mar. 25/17. |
| 133 | Reid, Henry Kidd. 31885. | M. Mar. 25/17. |
| ? | Cope, J. 9591. (Fr. 2 Leicesters.) | M. Feb. 11/17. |
| ? | Herd, Robt. 34278. | W. and M. Mar. 25/17. |
| ? | Kelly, Cpl. D. 62172. | W. and M. Mar. 25/17. |
| ? | Peters, L.-Cpl. W. 31902. | W. and M. Mar. 25/17. |

**MACHINE GUN CORPS (CAVALRY).**

## B.E.F.

| | | |
|---|---|---|
| 6 | Carnell, J. 50513. | M. April 11/17. |
| 8 Bgde. 8 Squad. | Plater, J. 51258. (Fr. 10 & 18 Hussars.) | W. and M. April 11/17. |

## MACHINE GUN CORPS (HEAVY).

### *B.E.F.*

| | | |
|---|---|---|
| C. 8 | **Toshack, 2nd Lt. T.** (Tank.) (Fr. 1 E. Yorks.) | M., bel. K. April 11/17. |
| ‡C. ? | Arnold, H. E. 75044. | M. April 23/17. |
| ‡C. ? | Gilmour, G. C. 522. | M. April 11/17. |
| ‡C. ? | Hagan, T. 945. | M. April 11/17. |
| ‡C. ? | Hillhouse, Sergt. R. 2258. | M. April 11/17. |
| ‡C. ? | McGillivray, R. 76679. | M. April 11/17. |
| D. 3 S. | Lawson, Andrew Charles. 32486. | M. Sept. 16/16. R/Enq. |
| D. 11 | **Davies, 2nd Lieut. H. P.** | M. April 24-25/17. |
| D. 11 | **Swears, Lt. H. M.** ("Dodo" Tank.) | M. April 8-9/17. |
| D. 11 I | Barrett, C. 76375. | M. April 11/17. |
| D. 11 | Cave, Thos. H/75328. | M. April 11/17. |
| D. 11 | Drummond, Angus McKay. 75921. | M. April 11/17. |
| D. 11 | Lord, Harry. 76782. | M. April 11/17. |
| ‡D. 11 | Robertson, Cpl. K. G. 23187. | M. April 11/17. |
| D. 12 II | Clayton, Oswald. 32139. | Unoff. M. May 3/17. |
| D. 12 | Shepherd, E. 32100. | M. May 3/17. |
| D. 12 | Thomson, J. H. 1945. | M. May 3/17. |
| ‡D. ? | Burton, F. 75334. | M. April 4/17. |
| ‡D. ? | Fisher, Cpl. G. C. 32262. | M. May 3/17. |
| D. ? | Gardner, Basil. 32210. | M. April 11/17. |
| ‡D. ? | Lean, Gnr. H. 2494. | W. and M., bel. K. April 11/17. |
| ‡D. ? | Thomas, Gnr. G. H. 75068. | M. May 3/17. |
| ? 11 | **Clarkson, 2nd Lieut. H.** | M. April 11/17. |
| ? 12 | **McCoull, Lieut. W. S.** | M. May 3/17. |

### *E.E.F.*

| | | |
|---|---|---|
| ? | Saunders, J. W. 40164. | M. April 18-23/17. |

## MANCHESTER REGIMENT.

### *B.E.F.*

| | | |
|---|---|---|
| 2 A. III | Broome, L. 46682. | M. April 4/17. |
| *2 A. L.G.S. | Halliwell, L.-Cpl. Geo. 15631. | W. Unoff. M. April 14/17. |
| 2 B. VIII | Billinge, T. 6718. | W. Unoff. M. April 14/17. |
| 2 B. | Howarth, Harry. 41454. | M. Nov. 18/16. R/Enq. |
| ‡2 B. or D. | Nalborough, L.-Cpl. Alfred. 2026. | M. Nov. 18/16. R/Enq. |
| ‡2 C. X | Bancroft, N. 29390. | M. April 2/17. |
| 2 C. XI | Harrop, John. 41464. | M. Nov. 13-15/16. R/Enq. |
| ‡2 C. | Wood, L.-Cpl. John. 7685. | M. Nov. 18/16. R/Enq. |
| *2 D. XV | Birch, William. 41359. | M. Nov. 18/16. R/Enq. |
| 2 D. XIII | Gee, James. 34671. | M. April 2/17. |
| ‡2 D. | Taylor, Lawrence. 41541. | M. Nov. 18/16. R/Enq. |
| ‡5 B. | Roberts, Tom. 202437. | M. June 8/17. |
| *2/5 B. | Gleave, Chas. 202532. | M. June 8/17. |
| ‡2/5 B. | Hirst, Thos. 202200. | M. June 8/17. |
| ‡7 A. | Malcolm, A.-Cpl. R. 276737. | W. and M. April 25/17. |
| 7 D. XIV | Myers, H. 276003. (3380.) | W. and M. May 13/17. |

**Manchester Regiment**—contd.

## *B.E.F.*

| | | |
|---|---|---|
| ‡2/7 B. | Eglin, Arthur. 2812. | M. May 3/17. |
| ‡2/7 D. | Jackson, A. C. 277136. | M. May 14/17. |
| ‡2/7 D.* | Kelly, T. 47616. | M. May 13/17. |
| ‡2/7 D. | Monk, Sergt. J. W. 275710. | M. May 14/17. |
| ‡2/7 D. | Swanbrick, H. 277551. | M. May 14/17. |
| ‡2/7 D. XVI | Mills, Samuel. 277644. | M. May 14/17. |
| ‡8 A. | Bretherton, H. 301998. | M. June 3/17. |
| ‡8 C. | O'Donnell, F. 300707. | M. May 30/17. |
| *2/8 | **Irlam, 2nd Lieut. G. A.** | K. June 18-20/17. Det.D./B. |
| 9 D. | Garside, Edwin. 351809. (3764.) | M. April 25/17. |
| 9 D. | Jevons, J. W. 351324. | M. April 25/17. |
| 9 D. XIII | Lord, S. 352320. (4877.) | M. April 25/17. |
| 9 D. | Potts, William. 351843. | M. April 26/17. |
| *2/9 A. | Wood, Cpl. Charlie. 350976. (2643.) | M. May 19/17. |
| 10 D. | Hamblett, J. E. 356590. | M. April 24/17. |
| 10 D. | McNulty, J. 375966. | M. April 24/17. |
| ‡2/10 C. | Clayton, Fred. 377436. | M. June 4/17. |
| ‡11 S. XIII | Evans, Joseph. 3584. | M. Sept. 29/16. R/Enq. |
| 11 S. | Jones, Charles. 3660. | M. Sept. 26-30/16. R/Enq. |
| 11 S. | Thomas, Walter. 2561. | M. Sept. 26-30/16. R./Enq. |
| 12 | **Doughty, 2nd Lt. G. H.** (Fr. 18th.) | M. April 25/17. |
| 12 A. I | Bywater, R. 41967. | M. April 25/17. |
| 12 A. | Chafer, D. 15715. | M. Aug. 26/16. |
| 12 A. IV | Darby, J. C. 41974. | M. April 25/17. |
| 12 A. I | Edwards, Wm. 48725. | M. April 25/17. |
| 12 A. | Gallagher, T. 46616. | M. April 25/17. |
| 12 A. | Hayes, G. 4315. | M. April 25/17. |
| 12 A. IV | Holt, Frank. 39692. | M. Feb. 8/17. |
| 12 A. | Jolly, Sergt. Arthur. 49195. | M. April 25/17. |
| ‡12 A. | Noble, Cpl. J. 3874. | W. and M. April 25/17. |
| 12 A. | Reid, Cpl. R. L. 4360. | M. April 25/17. |
| 12 A. | Stewart, A.-Sergt. J. 46554. | M. April 25/17. |
| 12 A. | Tindale, L.-Cpl. H. 3956. | M. Feb. 8/17. |
| 12 A. I | Walker, L.-Cpl. J. 8966. | W. and M. April 25/17. |
| 12 A. | Whitehead, J. 45377. | M. April 25/17. |
| 12 B. | Lambert, Alfred. 19429. | M. April 25/17. |
| 12 B. V | Metcalfe, F. 24704. | M. Oct. 31/16. |
| 12 B. | Spencer, J. E. 44542. | M. April 25/17. |
| ‡12 B. | Tennant, H. 46567. | W. and M. April 25/17. |
| 12 C. | Broughton, J. W. 46880. | M. Feb. 9/17. |
| 12 C. | Dolley, J. 48602. | M. April 25/17. |
| 12 C. X | Litchfield, Robt. 39712. | M. April 25/17. |
| 12 C. IX | Locker, F. 28868. | M. Nov. 13/16. |
| 12 C. XI | Spencer, George. 30750. | M. April 25/17. |
| 12 C. | Watson, W. 48605. | M. April 25/17. |
| 12 C. M.G.S. | Westwood, Albert Edward. 23322. | K. May 12/17. Det.D./B. |
| 12 D. XIV | Ahern, C. F. 46572. | W. and M. April 25/17. |
| 12 D. | Bradshaw, Cpl. R. 5620. | M. April 25/17. |
| 12 D. XVI | Dodds, Louis. 32496. | M. April 25/17. |
| 12 D. | Kelly, Albert. 39703. | M. Feb. 8/17. |
| 12 D. XIV | Naylor, John W. 41952. | M. April 25/17. |
| 12 D. XVI | Taylor, Albert. 46908. | M. Feb. 8/17. |
| *12 D. | Tunnicliffe, J. B. 5536. | M. April 25/17. |
| *12 D. XVI | Warburton, T. 46637. | K. Feb. 8/17. Det.D./B. |
| 16 A. | Ashton, Sergt. C. E. 7074. | M. April 23/17. |
| 16 A. | Boardman, E. 7436. | M. April 23/17. |
| 16 A. IV | Bowden, Cpl. Wm. 1473. | M. April 23/17. |

**Manchester Regiment**—contd.

## B.E.F.

16 A. Bush, E. H. 41821. M. April 23/17.
16 A. Davies, H. 32554. M. April 23/17.
16 A. Emerton, A. O. 41823. M. April 23/17.
16 A. Estill, C. H. 23082. M. April 23/17.
16 A. II Gardiner, Alfred Robt. 41828. M. April 23/17.
16 A. Gunn, A. E. 41856. M. April 23/17.
16 A. II Hindley, George. 25227. M. April 23/17.
16 A. IV Hockaday, Fred Lee. 17652. W. and M. April 23/17.
16 A. Kershaw, Sigr. Clifford. 47279. W. and M. April 23/17.
16 A. Mitchell, G. A. 40828. M. April 23/17.
‡16 A. Potts, I. 43032. M. April 23/17.
16 A. IV Shore, William. 25396. M. April 23/17.
16 A. III Stone, Reuben. 33502. W. and M. April 23/17.
16 A. Whitehead, J. 38738. M. April 23/17.
16 B. VI Dunkerley, Edward. 27421. M. April 23/17.
16 B. Sheard, Cpl. Geo. 6676. (Fr. H.Q.) M. April 23/17.
16 C. Billington, L.-Cpl. Harry. 19704. W. and M. April 23/17.
16 C. Edwards, J. 27185. M. April 23/17.
16 C. Mills, L.-Cpl. W. 6655. M. April 23/17.
16 C. Pearce, L.-Sergt. A. D. 1248. W. and M. April 23/17.
16 C. XII Ridgway, Alfred. 35587. M. April 23/17.
16 C. IX Stevens, Drum. Chas. Alfred. 723. M. April 23/17.
16 C. XI Worsley, L.-Cpl. Spencer Samuel. 7556. M. April 23/17.
‡17 A. III Blair, Fred. 47429. M. April 23/17.
‡17 A. Blythe, J. 35979. M. April 23/17.
*17 A. II Brookes, L.-Cpl. John Willie. 43217. M. April 23/17.
‡17 A. Cuerdon, F. J. 36152. M. April 23/17.
‡17 A. Dodds, G. A. 34281. M. April 23/17.
17 A. Dwyer, H. 34008. M. April 23/17.
‡17 A. Goddridge, F. 43230. M. April 23/17.
‡17 A. Loftus, T. 36937. M. April 23/17.
‡17 A. Marshall, C. 43423. M. April 23/17.
*17 A. I Oakenfull, F. 41689. W. and M. April 23/17.
‡17 A. Polken, James. 45006. W. and M. April 23/17.
17 A. Seaborn, L.-Cpl. Edward. 27606. M. April 23/17.
‡17 A. IV Shaw, L.-Sergt. Harry. 47314. M. April 23/17.
‡17 A. Simister, D. 47351. M. April 23/17.
‡17 A. Struttman, R. W. 45046. M. April 23/17.
‡17 A. Taylor, J. 44565. W. and M. April 23/17.
17 A. Sig. S. Tyldesley, W. G. 46598. M. April 23/17.
17 A. II Upton, Henry. 27586. M. April 23/17.
17 A. IV Utting, George. 39950. M. April 23/17.
‡17 A. Waller, Sergt. H. G. 8937. M. April 23/17.
17 A. IV Ward, Tom. 34153. M. April 23/17.
‡17 B. Baumber, A. 34820. M. April 23/17.
17 B. Bird, Sergt. Fred. 43151. M. April 23/17.
17 B. VIII Booth, T. 34439. M. April 23/17.
*17 B. VII Burton, Thomas. 34826. M. April 23/17.
‡17 B. Collinson, Cpl. Frank. 18346. W. and M. April 23/17.
‡17 B. Davies, J. W. 36277. M. April 23/17.
*17 B. M.G.S. Edwards, Alfred. 31181. M. April 23/17.
17 B. VIII Grognet, Wallace. 45057. M. April 23/17.
17 B. VII Hope, Albert. 33608. M. Oct. 12/16. R/Enq.
17 B. Hudspith, Jas. 39531. M. April 23/17.
17 B. VI Jones, Cpl. Owen. 8201. M. April 23/17.
17 B. VI Knight, Herbert E. 43422. M. April 23/17.
17 B. Ledger, Louis. 8712. M. April 23/17.

**Manchester Regiment—contd.**

## B.E.F.

17 B. VI O'Connor, Francis Patrick. 43198. M. April 23/17.
*17 B. Parker, C. F. 34307. M. April 23/17.
‡17 B. Roberts, V. H. 30218. M. April 23/17.
17 B. VIII Schofield, A. 39959. M. April 23/17.
‡17 B. Stevens, J. 47327. W. and M. April 23/17.
17 B. Sutton, Alfred. 47215. (Fr. H.Q. Sig. S.) M. April 23/17.
*17 B. Swales, L.-Cpl. A. 30494. M. April 23/17.
17 B. Tophill, Geo. Savigny. 9345. M. April 23/17.
*17 B. Tye, W. E. 43346. M. April 23/17.
17 B. Viner, Bernard. 33620. M. April 23/17.
‡17 B. Ward, A. W. 43343. M. April 23/17.
‡17 B. Webster, Sergt. F. 8347. M. April 23/17.
17 B. V Whittingham, G. 47346. M. April 23/17.
17 B. Willmott, Wm. Chas. 47284 M. April 23/17.
‡17 B. Wolstenholme, F. 25052. M. April 23/17.
17 B. Wright, J. 34544. M. April 23/17.
‡17 C. X Gray, Bertie. 43297. M. April 23/17.
‡17 C. Hall, Sergt. A. 43305. M. April 23/17.
17 C. Mort, John. 32390. M. Oct. 12/16. R/Enq.
17 C. Stafford, Wm. Ives. 45005. M. April 23/16.
‡17 C. Wilkinson, L.-Cpl. C. 47365. M. April 23/17.
17 D. XIII Aiken, Cpl. Joe. 8043. M. April 23/17.
17 D. Sig. S. Grange, Joseph. 36539. M. April 23/17.
‡17 D. Rostron, L.-Cpl. E. 34692. M. April 23/17.
‡17 D. Wilkinson, J. 47158. M. April 23/17.
17 D. XV Williams, Howell. 39963. W. and M. April 23/17.
18 **Eminten, 2nd Lieut. F. A.** M., bel. K. April 23/17.
18 **Gill, 2nd Lieut. N. B.** M., bel. K. April 23/17.
18 **Hague, 2nd Lt. J. H.** (Fr. 7th.) M. April 23/17.
18 **Martin, 2nd Lieut. G. S.** (Fr. 5th.) M. April 23/17.
18 B. **Maybury, 2nd Lieut. R.** (Fr. 6th.) M. April 23/17.
18 **Westphal, 2nd Lieut. B. A.** M., bel. K. April 23/17.
18 B. **Wyatt, 2nd Lieut. S. J. L.** K. April 23/17. Det.D./B.
18 A. II Devenport, John. 43889. M. April 23/17.
‡18 A. Haft, I. 47879. W. and M. April 23/17.
18 B. VI Baldwin, Mark. 43824. M. April 23/17.
18 B. VII Boldstridge, H. 7591. M. April 23/17.
18 B. VI Hobbs, Henry. 28210. K. April 23/17. Det.D./B.
18 B. VII Mayer, Amos. 21043. M. April 23/17.
*18 B. Roberts, L.-Cpl. Robert. 43723. W. and M. Oct. 12/16. R/Enq.
‡18 B. VI Robinson, W. 43821. M. Oct. 12/16. R/Enq.
‡18 B. Theaker, H. 44027. M. Oct. 12/16. R/Enq.
18 C. Burns, Thos. 44140. W. and M. April 23/17.
18 C. Carter, C. E. 43702. M. April 23/17.
18 C. Heaney, G. 43924. M. April 23/17.
18 C. XII Longley, John. 47882. M. April 23/17.
18 C. X Sayle, W. E. 47914. M. April 23/17.
18 C. XI Stamp, Ralph. 44130. M. April 23/17.
‡18 C. Stott, J. 36058. W. and M. April 12/17.
18 C. Williamson, A. T. 43697. M. April 23/17.
18 C. Withington, Wm. 43974. M. April 23/17.
18 C. Woodhouse, J. 34699. M. April 23/17.
18 D. Ashcroft, R. 43997. (Fr. 8 Manch., 3004.) K. Oct. 12/16. Det.D./B. R/Enq
18 D. Henstock, F. 48014. M. April 23/17.
18 D. XIII Hunter, Walter. 10129. M. April 23/17.
*18 D. Middleton, G. 44162. (5289.) W. and M. April 23/17.
18 D. XIII Mitchell, Daniel Smithies. 36279. M. April 23/17.

Manchester Regiment—contd.

*B.E.F.*

| | |
|---|---|
| 18 D. XIII Williams, Ralph. 44019. | M. April 23/17. |
| 19 A. Berwick, George. 47181. | W. and M. April 2/17. |
| 19 B. VII Every, Sigr. Ernest Chas. 41917. | K. April 2/17. Det.D./B. R/Enq. |
| 19 B. Mann, Walter. 12588. | M. April 23/17. |
| 19 B. Marriott, F. T. 41801. | M. April 2/17. |
| ‡19 B. V Nolan, George. 31389. | K. April 2/17. Det.D./B. |
| 19 B. Whiteley, J. H. 27268. | M. April 9/17. |
| 19 B. VII Williamson, Harry. 41800. | K. April 2/17. Det.D./B. |
| 19 C. L.G.S. Gannon, Jas. Thos. 40964. (Fr. 2/4 Leicester.) | W. and M. April 23/17. |
| 19 C. XI Lutton, Harry. 46719. | M. April 23/17. |
| 19 C. Perry, T. H. 41888. | K. April 23/17. Det.D./B. |
| 19 C. Thomson, Jas. Adie. 11944. | K. April 2/17. Det.D./B. |
| 19 C. M.G.S. Walton, Harry. 12559. | Unoff. M. about April 9/17. |
| 19 D. I.T.M. Turner, Jas. Edward. 12464. (21st Bgde.) | W. and M. April 9/17. |
| ‡20 A. Bolver, L. A. 40393. | W. and M. May 4/17. |
| 20 A. IV Chadwick, W. 40283. | W. and M. May 4/17. |
| 20 A. Conquest, W. A. 18430. (Sig. S.) | W. and M. May 4/17. |
| 20 A. Eyre, Sergt. E. 17617. | M. Unoff. K. Sept. 3/16. R/Enq. |
| ‡20 A. IV Gardner, B. 25216. (Fr. 12 R. Fus.) | M. Sept. 3/16. R/Enq. |
| *20 A. Gren. S. Heap, Arthur. 25091. (Fr. 1st E. Lancs.) | M. Sept. 3/16. R/Enq. |
| *20 A. Hirst, Frederick. 26900. | M. May 4/17. |
| ‡20 A. I Holden, Harold. 31399. | W. and M. May 4/17. |
| 20 A. M.G.S. Patterson, A.-Cpl. Alec. 17456. | W. and M. May 4/17. |
| 20 A. Smith, John. 31078. | M. Sept. 3/16. R/Enq. |
| ‡20 B. Day, Frederick. 26817. | M. May 11/17. |
| 20 B. King, P. A. 49519. | M. April 4/17. |
| 20 B. Lynch, James. 18330. | W. and M. Sept. 3/16. R/Enq. |
| 20 C. X Hart, H. C. 26042. (Fr. 9 L. N. Lancs.) | M. Sept. 3/16. R/Enq. |
| ‡20 C. Gren. S. Pendlebury, J. H. 18446. | W. and M. Sept. 3/16. R/Enq. |
| *21 A. Barnett, L.-Cpl. Charles Titus. 43530 (H.Q. Bombers.) | K. Nov. 26/16. Det.D./B. |
| 21 A. Boothman, L.-Cpl. Harold. 18531. | W. and M. May 11-15/17. |
| 21 A. Howlett, Thomas. 18622. | M. Mar. 25/17. |
| 21 A. M.G.S. Jagger, H. 18927. | M. Mar. 26/17. |
| 21 A. Otterenshaw, W. 18963. | M. Mar. 25/17. |
| 21 A. Sharpe, G. 35201. | M. Mar. 26/17. |
| 21 A. Taylor, Fred. 27481. | M. Mar. 25/17. |
| 21 A. Wray, J. H. 19717. | M. Mar. 29/17. |
| *21 B. V Ainsworth, James. 49553. | M. May 11-15/17. |
| ‡21 B. Ainsworth, S. 49571. | M. May 11-15/17. |
| ‡21 B. VI Barber, L.-Cpl. Thomas. 40633. | M. May 11/17. |
| ‡21 B. VI Brown, A. J. 49550. (Fr. 12th.) | M. May 11-15/17. |
| ‡21 B. Hartley, A. J. 49569. | M. May 11-15/17. |
| ‡21 B. Hayes, W. 49560. | M. May 11-15/17. |
| ‡21 B. Tasker, J. H. 40661. | M. May 11-15/17. |
| ‡21 B. Tonge, J. H. 202789. | W. and M. May 11-15/17. |
| *21 B. Warburton, Harry. 202636. | W. and M. May 11-15/17. |
| 21 C. Baker, A. 43628. | M. April 2/17. |
| ‡21 C. X Davies, Edwin. 30250. | M. May 11-15/17. |
| 21 C. XI Finch, W. F. 49592. | M. May 11-15/17. |
| ‡21 C. Heywood, L.-Cpl. T. 276897. | M. May 11-15/17. |
| *21 C. Hughes, L.-Cpl. Arthur. 43636. | M. Jan. 10-12/17. |
| 21 C. Lambert, C. 43507. | M. Mar. 29/17. |
| *21 C. XI Leaver, Sergt. Samuel H. 19178. | W. and M. May 11-15/17. |
| 21 C. X Shepperd, Jas. 45223. | W. and M. May 10-15/17. |

**Manchester Regiment—contd.**

## *B.E.F.*

| | | |
|---|---|---|
| 21 C. M.G.S. | Whittaker, L.-Cpl. J. T. 18759. | W. and M. Mar. 10/17. |
| *21 D. XIV | Davie, J. W. 43479. | M. May 11-15/17. |
| 21 D. XIII | Hallam, Leonard. 19400. | W. and M. Jan. 11/17. |
| 21 D. | Hanrahan, Joseph. 19399. | W. and M. Jan. 11/17. |
| 21 D. Sig. S. | Mycocks, Alfred. 18071. | M. May 11-15/17. |
| 21 D. XIII | Thomas, Herbert Austin. 32669. | M. May 11-15/17. |
| *21 D. | Thwaites, Sergt. J. H. 43528. | K. May 11-15/17. Det.D./B. |
| *21 D. | Turner, Jas. Henry. 11021. | W. and M. May 11-18/17. |
| ‡21 D. | Walsh, T. 17521. | M. May 11-15/17. |
| 21 D. XV | Westcombe, Herbert. 38455. | M. May 11-15/17. |
| ‡21 D. | Wright, L.-Cpl. E. 7668. | W. and M. May 11-15/17. |
| 22 | **Duguid, D.S.O., M.C., Capt. C. F.** | M., bel. K. May 13/17. |
| 22 | **Towers, 2nd Lieut. W. G.** (Fr. 4th.) | K. April 2/17. Det.D./B. |
| ‡22 A. | Fernley, R. 21654. | M. May 13/17. |
| *22 A. III | Martin, Frederick D. 20107. | W. and M. May 13/17. |
| 22 A. Sig. S. | Taylor, Thomas. 20124. | M. Mar. 14/17. |
| 22 B. | Jasper, G. S. 42016. | M. April 30/17. |
| 22 B. VIII | Jones, James. 47968. | M. April 30/17. |
| 22 B. | King, A. 44272. | M. April 30/17. |
| 22 B. | Whitehead, A. E. 49239. | M. April 30/17. |
| 22 C. XII | Airriss, G. F. 44317. | M. Mar. 14/17. |
| *22 C. | Beardsworth, Sergt. George. 10855. | W. and M. May 13/17. |
| 22 C. or D. | Bryan, Thomas. 10316. | M. May 9/17. |
| 22 C. XI | Coupe, Chas. Arthur. 43582. (Late 2927.) | M., bel. P. March 14/17. |
| 22 C. X | Harrington, Jas. 47091. | M. Mar. 14/17. |
| 22 C. IX | Jones, Gwilym Edw. 40752. | M. Mar. 14/17. |
| 22 C. | Levis, Harry. 43594. | M. Mar. 14/17. |
| 22 C. XII | McGarry, H. 35406. | M. Mar. 14/17. |
| 22 C. or D. | Sanderson, Thos. 40091. | W. and M. April 2/17. |
| 22 D. | Bell, W. 49081. | W. and M. April 2/17. |
| 22 D. XIII | Brett, John. 40693. | M. May 13/17. |
| 22 D. | Caugney, Wm. Henry. 43575. | W. and M. Jan. 11/17. |
| 22 D. XIII | Cook, Walter. 27413. | M. Mar. 14/17. |
| 22 D. XIV | Cooper, Charles. 49252. (? att. fr. 24th.) | W. and M. April 2/17. |
| 22 D. XV | Emmerson, Tom. 38926. | M. April 2/17. |
| *22 D. L.G.S. | Forrest, H. 14388. | W. and M. May 13/17. |
| 22 D. | Hamer, W. 2823. | W. and M. Mar. 28/17. |
| 22 D. XV | Handley, Joseph. 39987. | M. May 13/17. |
| ‡22 D. | Knott, J. T. 33046. | M. May 14/17. |
| ‡22 D. | Martindale, T. W. 46744. | M. May 13/17. |
| ‡22 D. | Morley, R. 2990. | M. May 13/17. |
| 22 D. XVI | Riley, E. 47647. | M. April 2/17. |
| 22 D. XIII | Rockliff, Frank Cyril. 18996. | M. Mar 14/17. |
| 22 D. | Russell, H. 27448. | M. Mar 14/17. |
| 22 D. | Smith, A. 49219. | M. April 2/17. |
| 22 D. XVI | Smith, L.-Cpl. Stanley. 43595. | W. and M. Mar. 14/17. |
| 22 D. | Smithson, W. 20951. | M. April 2/17. |
| ‡22 D. | Southwell, J. 29000. | M. May 13/17. |
| 23 X. | Geddes, J. 46861. | M. April 27/17. |
| 23 X. VIII | Monk, John. 38448. | M. April 27/17. |
| 24 C. or D. XII | Boardman, Edward. 31100. | W. and M. Dec. 6/16. |

## *BALKANS.*

| | | |
|---|---|---|
| 13 A. | Wolstenholme, J. 13514. | M. before May 1/17. |
| 13 ? | Johnson, C. H. 24235. | M. end April/17. |
| *13 ? | Oliver, J. H. 5094. | M., bel. K. April 24/17. |

**Manchester Regiment**—contd.

## *PERSIAN GULF.*

| | | |
|---|---|---|
| 1 | **Butterworth, Lt. B.** (Fr. 3rd.) | W. and M. **March 25/17.** |
| 1 1 | Brewer, L.-Cpl. W. 972. | M. **Feb. 9/17.** |
| 1 1 | Craven, J. 2849. | W. and M. **Mar. 25/17.** |
| 1 1 | Lee, John Wm. 32811. | K. **Jan. 9/17.** Det.D./B. |
| 1 2 VIII | Glynn, D. 32768. | W. and M. **Mar. 25/17.** |
| 1 2 | Nuttall, Sam. 33189. | W. and M. **Mar. 25/17.** |
| 1 2 V | Port, Wm. Henry. 2194. | W. and M. **Mar. 8/16.** R/Enq. |
| 1 2 VI | Ricketts, Walter. 33658. | M. **Mar. 25/17.** |
| 1 2 | Shoreman, J. 2412. | M. **Mar. 8/16.** |
| 1 2 V | Stafford, L. 33525. | W. and M. **Mar. 25/17.** |
| 1 3 XI | Borlase, Wm. 23933. | M. **Mar. 8/16.** R/Enq. |
| 1 3 XI | Cowan, G. H. 6959. | M. **Mar. 25/17.** |
| 1 3 | Giles, C. F. 9049. | W. and M. **Mar. 26/17.** |
| 1 3 IX | Igo, Thos. 23379. | W. and M. **Mar. 25/17.** |
| 1 3 | Jones, Arthur. 32226. | M. **Feb. 9/17.** |
| 1 3 | Wagstaffe, George. 36518. | W. and M. **Mar. 25/17.** |
| 1 3 IX | Winfield, W. 25015. (35045.) | W. and M. **Mar. 25/17.** |
| 1 4 | Archer, Geo. Wm. 7619. | K. **Jan. 9/17.** Det.D./B. |
| 1 4 | Berry, E. 33956. | M. **Feb. 9/17.** |
| 1 4 | Cadman, Cpl. Thos. Henry. 11185. | M. **Feb. 9/17.** |
| 1 4 XVI | Durr, P. 3170. (Fr. 11th.) | K. **Jan. 9/17.** Det.D./B. |
| 1 4 | Grady, Sergt. John. 1326. | W. and M. **Jan. 9/17.** |
| 1 4 | Hayes, S. 7486. | M. **Feb. 9/17.** |
| 1 4 | Houghton, Sgt. Joseph Edward. 1623 | M. **Jan. 9/17.** |
| 1 4 | Houghton, Joseph. 16645. | M. **Feb. 9/17.** |
| 1 ? | Acton, H. 37017. | M. **Mar. 25/17.** |
| 1 ? | Chadwick, G. 3980. | M. **Feb. 9/17.** |
| 1 ? | Coy, A. 1545. | W. and M. **Jan. 9/17.** |
| 1 ? | Cummins, Sergt. A. 1205. | W. and M. **Mar. 25/17.** |
| 1 ? | Fallows, W. 27176. | M. **Mar. 25/17.** |
| 1 ? | Farrell, J. 4881. | W. and M. **Jan. 9/17.** |
| 1 ? | Garland, H. 2938. | M. **Mar. 25/17.** |
| 1 ? | Gastell, Sergt. H. 7630. | M. **Mar. 25/17.** |
| 1 ? | Grayson, T. 1953. | W. and M. **Mar. 25/17.** |
| 1 ? | Jackson, S. 2031. | M. **Mar. 25/17.** |
| 1 ? | Jennings, R. 27348. | W. and M. **Jan. 9/17.** |
| 1 ? | Marland, G. 23649. | W. and M. **Mar. 25/17.** |
| 1 ? | Moyland, T. 1054. | M. **Mar. 8/16.** R/Enq. |
| 1 M.G.S. | Newman, C. 2377. | W. and M. **Mar. 8/16.** R/Enq. |
| 1 ? | Rogers, T. 2795. | M. **Mar. 25/17.** |
| 1 ? | Sharkey, F. 9110. | W. and M. **Mar. 25/17.** |
| 1 ? | Slowcroft, Joseph. 29988. | W. and M. **Mar. 25/17.** |
| 1 ? | Tierney, L.-Cpl. P. 1266. | W. and M. **Mar. 26/17.** |
| 1 ? | Young, F. 30764. | W. and M. **Mar. 25/17.** |

## MIDDLESEX REGIMENT.

## *B.E.F.*

| | | |
|---|---|---|
| 1 A. I | Bell, Thos. Wm. 41631. | M. **April 23/17.** |
| *1 A. | Butt, L.-Cpl. H. 41547. | M. **April 23/17.** |
| ‡1 A. | Feline, C. S. 34889. | K. **April 18/17.** Det.D./B. |
| 1 B. VI | Fitch, Edw. Geo. 41562. | M. **April 23/17.** |
| *1 B. VI | Fuller, J. 33470. | M. **April 23/17.** |

**Middlesex Regiment—contd.**

*B.E.F.*

| | | |
|---|---|---|
| 1 C. | Fenwick, Herbert. 43769. (Late 8, 5633.) | M. Nov. 2/16. R/Enq. |
| 1 C. | Harris, Arthur. 40164. | M. April 23/17. |
| ‡1 C. | Millership, J. W. 50975. | M. April 23/17. |
| ‡1 C. | Murrell, H. A. G. 34845. | M. April 23/17. |
| *1 C. X | Parrott, J. 34848. | Unoff. M. April 17/17. |
| 1 C. or D. | Jordan, Sergt. J. 10261. | M. April 24/17. |
| 1 C. XII | Rainbow, G. 6083. | M. April 23/17. |
| ‡1 C. XII | Samuel, Geo. Henry. 953? | M. April 23/17. |
| 1 C. XI | Samuels, P. 43528. | M. April 23/17. |
| *1 C. | Young, L.-Cpl. H. F. 9084. | M. April 23/17. |
| *1 D. | Lucas, P. 16896. | M. April 23/17. |
| 1 D. XV | Thomas, Albert. 8937 | M. April 23/17. |
| ‡2 A. | Comben, L.-Cpl. Hen. Frank. 8974. | M. May 5-6/17. |
| 2 A. | Fullex, A. M. 40421. | M. Oct. 30/16. |
| ‡2 A. | Hales, F. 6071. | M. May 5-6/17. |
| *2 C. IX | Smith, J. 23712. | M. May 5-6/17. |
| 2 D. XIII | Brotherton, J. 1369. | M. Oct. 23/16. R/Enq. |
| 2 D. M.G.S. | McLarty, John. 17576. | M. Oct. 23/16. R/Enq. |
| *2 ? | Howson, George A. 50842. | W. and M. April 11/17. |
| *3 A. | Jepp, William. 14903. | K. May 27/17. Det.D./B. |
| 4 | **Dawson, Major A. G.** | K. April 23/17. Det.D./B. R/Enq. |
| 4 B. | **Hooke, 2nd Lieut. A. D.** | M., bel. P. April 28/17. |
| ‡4 A. | Adams, A. 40475. | M. April 28/17. |
| 4 A. | Adams, Edw. Ernest. G/28306. | M. April 28/17. |
| ‡4 A. | Allen, S. 50525. | M. April 28/17. |
| ‡4 A. | Barker, G. 50534. | M. April 28/17. |
| 4 A. | Barker, Thos. 40478. | M. April 28/17. |
| ‡4 A. | Barry, R. 11146. | M. April 28/17. |
| 4 A. I | Beard, Alfred. 22224. (Fr. 6th.) | M. April 28/17. |
| 4 A. | Berryman, Dmr. Fredk. W. 40480. | M. April 11/17. |
| 4 A. | Blackwell, L.-Cpl. J. 14749. | M. April 24/17. |
| 4 A. | Boshier, Arthur Chas. 203286. | M. April 28/17. |
| 4 A. I | Brett, P. H. 50539. | M. April 24/17. |
| *4 A. IV | Brockman, Albert. 40914. | M. April 28/17. |
| 4 A. IV | Broom, Wm. Geo. 50538. | M. April 28/17. |
| *4 A. | Brown, T. 203034. | M. April 28/17. |
| ‡4 A. II | Button, A. H. 23088. | M. April 28/17. |
| 4 A. I | Connell, Frank. 22243. | M. April 28/17. |
| 4 A. | Cook, Walter Jas. 43050. | M. April 28/17. |
| 4 A. | Corder, F. J. 34096. | M. April 28/17. |
| ‡4 A. III | Cornwall, J. 50545. | M. April 28/17. |
| 4 A. | Edwards, A. 40476. | M. April 11/17. |
| 4 A. IV | Frew, L.-Cpl. James. 1342. (Known as James Ramsay.) | M. April 28/17. |
| 4 A. I | Griffin, Alf. Hry. 40895. | M. April 28/17. |
| 4 A. I | Harman, W. Fred. 50562. | M. April 28/17. |
| 4 A. | Harris, Thomas Wm. 205222. | M. April 28/17. |
| 4 A. | Loeber, A. 40196. | M. April 10/17. |
| ‡4 A. | McMullen, A. A. 202985. | M. April 28/17. |
| ‡4 A. | Marley, T. 50580. | M. April 28/17. |
| *4 A. | Merlin, Gerald. 40990. | M. April 28/17. |
| 4 A. I | Miller, John. 50575. | M. April 28/17. |
| *4 A. IV | Mitchell, Chas. Gordon. 43070. | M. April 28/17. |
| ‡4 A. | Oliver, G. 40985. | M. April 28/17. |
| 4 A. IV | Patmore, Cecil John. 2743. | M. April 24/17. |
| ‡4 A. | Sewell, T. H. 50590. | M. April 28/17. |
| 4 A. IV | Simpson, Harold. G/50586. | K. April 11/17. Det.D./B. |
| 4 A. I | Smith, L.-Cpl. Aurania Phillip. 50587 | M. April 28/17. |

Middlesex Regiment—contd.

## B.E.F.

|  |  |  |
|---|---|---|
| 4 B. VI | Alefounder, Alex. 9861. | M. April 28/17. |
| 4 B. VIII | Allen, C. 50528. | M. April 28/17. |
| ‡4 B. | Best, C. R. 3006. | M. April 28/17. |
| 4 B. | Billing, Fredk. Reg. 3504. | M. April 28/17. |
| ‡4 B. | Birkett, A. 6104. | M. April 28/17. |
| 4 B. | Blencowe, A. 3507. | M. April 10/17. |
| 4 B. or D. | Brammer, H. B. 13334. | M. April 11/17. |
| 4 B. | Clark, R. C. 203177. | M. April 28/17. |
| 4 B. VI | Clarke, Fredk. Wm. 42474. | M. April 11/17. |
| 4 B. VI | Cleaver, S. 3433. | W. and M. April 28/17. |
| ‡4 B. | Edgeley, B. 43056. | M. April 28/17. |
| 4 B. or D. | Ellis, Jas. 33329. | M. April 28/17. |
| 4 B. VII | Franklin, George. 40505. | M. April 28/17. |
| ‡4 B. | Godfrey, W. A. 40513. | M. April 28/17. |
| *4 B. | Goodwin, J. W. 5875. | M. April 28/17. |
| ‡4 B. | Head, J. 2983. | M. April 28/17. |
| 4 B. | Higgs, T. A. 40964. | M. April 28/17. |
| *4 B. | Howard, Edward Stanley. 14386. | M. April 28/17. |
| ‡4 B. | Huckett, E. 201231. (4014.) | M. April 28/17. |
| 4 B. | Hufford, W. H. 13080. | M. April 28/17. |
| ‡4 B. | Livesley, Sergt. T. 8849. | M. April 28/17. |
| *4 B. | Nessling, Charles. 203180. (7966.) | M. April 28/17. |
| 4 B. VIII | Orrom, H. L. 50651. | M. April 28/17. |
| ‡4 B. VIII | Rollings, A. J. 2955. | M. April 28/17. |
| ‡4 B. | Stevens, C. P. 40972. | M. April 28/17. |
| 4 B. VIII | Thorn, F. 40974. | M. April 28/17. |
| 4 B. V | Thresh, Alb. Edw. 23000. | M. April 27/17. |
| 4 B. | Tobyn, S. 29636. | M. April 10/17. |
| ‡4 B. | Truin, F. 22956. | M. April 28/17. |
| 4 B. | Weatherley, Sergt. F. G. 8498. | M. April 28/17. |
| *4 C. | Adams, L.-Cpl. B. 50937. | M. April 28/17. |
| 4 C. | Ball, Albert Geo. 50642. | M. April 28/17. |
| 4 C. | Baron, T. Storke. 33079. | M. April 10/17. |
| ‡4 C. | Carley, W. A. 40951. | W. and M. April 28/17. |
| 4 C. IX | Edwin, E. E. 40917. | M. April 11/17. |
| ‡4 C. | Gilligan, L.-Cpl. K. S. 606. | W. and M. April 28/17. |
| 4 C. | Hart, James. 15514. | M. April 28/17. |
| 4 C. | Kimmins, C. A. 204777. (5031.) | M. April 28/17. |
| ‡4 C. | Lowe, Sergt. J. 9232. | W. and M. April 28/17. |
| *4 C. IX | Matthews, L.-Cpl. A. J. 43069. | W. and M. April 28/17. |
| ‡4 C. | Moore, J. 204098. | M. April 28/17. |
| ‡4 C. | Simons, A. 43077. | M. April 28/17. |
| 4 C. | Skinner, H. 40894. | M. April 10/17. |
| 4 C. IX | Thompson, J. 40976. | M. April 28/17. |
| 4 D. L.G.S. | Cox, Alfred Edwin. 11023. | W. and M. April 28/17. |
| ‡4 D. | Enderby, M. S. 202907. | M. April 28/17. |
| *4 D. | Gray, G. 13253. | W. and M. April 28/17. |
| *4 D. | Hull, A.-Sergt. A. 12343. | M. April 28/17. |
| 4 D. | Lawson, A. 1595. | W. and M. April 28/17. |
| ‡4 D. XVI | North, F. A. W. 3286. | M. April 28/17. |
| *4 D. XIV | Peacock, Edgar Archibald. 20215. | M. April 28/17. |
| 4 D. L.G.S. | Pickton, L.-Cpl. W. 43071. | M. April 11/17. |
| 4 D. | Potter, D. 20340. | M. April 11/17. |
| 4 D. L.G.S. | Ruff, F. 10917. | W. and M. April 28/17. |
| 4 D. XVI | Snow, G. H. 40555. | K. Nov. 18/16. Det.D./B. |
| 4 D. | Swan, W. 32666. | M. April 11/17. |
| 4 D. | Thurston, L.-Cpl. Wm. 11221. | W. and M. April 28/17. |
| 4 ? | Church, Sidney John. 8820. | M. April 23/17. |

**Middlesex Regiment—contd.**

## *B.E.F.*

| | | | |
|---|---|---|---|
| 4 | ? | Waller, W. 13211. (7921.) (Fr. 1st.) | M. April 28/17. |
| 7 | A. | **Bishop, 2nd Lt. S. J. W.** (Fr. 4th Essex.) | M., bel. K. May 3/17. |
| 7 | | **Hartley, 2nd Lieut. R. H.** | M., bel. K. May 3/17. |
| 7 | | **Kemp, 2nd Lieut. B. A.** | M., bel. K. May 3/17. |
| 7 | | **Smith, 2nd Lieut. C. M.** (Fr. 7th Essex.) | M., bel. K. May 3/17. |
| 7 | | **Wright, 2nd Lieut. B.** | M., bel. K. May 3/17. |
| 7 | | **Wright, 2nd Lieut. H. W.** | M. May 3/17. |
| ‡7 | A. | Barker, F. 203416. | M. May 3/17. |
| 7 | A. III | Blick, Sergt. Gilbert. R. 200413. | M. May 3/17. |
| ‡7 | A. II | Bowler, R. 203421. | W. and M. May 3/17. |
| *7 | A. I | Jauncey, John. 3681. | M. Oct. 4/16. R/Enq. |
| *7 | A. II | Leonard, Wm. 205076. | M. May 31/17. |
| 7 | A. III | Mockford, Herbert. 2623. | M. Sept. 16/16. R/Enq. |
| 7 | A. I | Owens, Joseph John E. 201956. | M. May 3/17. |
| *7 | A. | Pullum, T. E. 15465. | M. May 3/17. |
| 7 | A. M.G.S. | Smith, John Fredk. 5383. | M. Sept. 16/16. R/Enq. |
| 7 | A. III | Staggs, G. R. 200971. (3544.) | M. May 3/17. |
| 7 | A. | Thomas, James. 16510. | M. May 3/17. |
| 7 | A. | Wyatt, W. H. 202499. | W. and M. April 9/17. |
| ‡7 | B. V | Barlow, L.-Cpl. Wm. 11818. | M. May 3/17. |
| 7 | B. VII | Dickeins, Henry Chas. Thos. 5550. | M. Sept. 16/16. R/Enq. |
| ‡7 | B. | Johnson, A. 201793. | M. May 3/17. |
| ‡7 | B. | Luckman, W. 200302. | M. May 3/17. |
| 7 | B. | Mulvey, John. 41798. | K. April 15/17. Det.D./B. |
| 7 | B. | Russell, Sgt. Chas. William. 4948. | K. Oct 7/16. Det.D./B. R/Enq. |
| ‡7 | B. | Shipp, J. 200390. | M. May 3/17. |
| 7 | C. L.G.S. | Bates, A. J. 203919. | W. and M. May 3/17. |
| 7 | C. X | Emery, William. 203996. | M. May 3/17. |
| ‡7 | C. | Fish, A. N. 203432. | M. May 3/17. |
| 7 | C. IX | Gibbons, Thomas B. 203435. (9021.) | M. May 3/17. |
| 7 | C. | Gould, L.-Cpl. A. 201127. (3815.) | M. May 3/17. |
| 7 | C. | Jarvis, L.-Cpl. H. W. C. 200144. | M. Oct. 10/16. |
| ‡7 | C. | Jones, A. 200616. | M. May 3/17. |
| 7 | C. L.G.S. | Mann, Josiah Hy. 204024. | M. May 3/17. |
| ‡7 | C. | Mitchell, T. 201703. | M. May 3/17. |
| 7 | C. XI | Muggeridge, Ed. J. 203959. | M. May 3/17. |
| 7 | C. XI | Munks, John. 201047. | M. May 3/17. |
| *7 | C. | Newling, Cpl. Chas. Hy. Quibel. 200323. (2112.) | M. May 3/17. |
| 7 | C. XI | Reeve, Wm. 201194. | M. May 3/17. |
| 7 | D. XIV | Andrews, L.-Sergt. Harold Sydney. 4778. | M. Oct. 4/16. R/Enq. |
| 7 | D. XIII | Ball, John Henry. 9506. | K. Oct. 1/16. Det.D./B. |
| 7 | D. XVI | Bambridge, G. H. 201256. (4058.) | M. May 3/17. |
| '7 | D. XIV | Barkway, Alan. 202638. | W. and M. May 3/17. |
| 7 | D. XIV | Berry, E. W. 202518. | W. and M. May 3/17. |
| ‡7 | D. | Camp, J. 202151. | W. and M. May 3/17. |
| 7 | D. XIV | Challis, Walter. 202208. | W. and M. May 3/17. |
| ‡7 | D. | Cridge, A. 203935. | M. May 3/17. |
| ‡7 | D. XVI | Curd, W. R. 5208. | K. Oct. 7/17. Det.D./B. |
| ‡7 | D. | Daynes, C. 204049. | M. May 3/17. |
| ‡7 | D. | Deacon, E. P. 202952. | M. May 3/17. |
| *7 | D. XIII | Fagg, A. E. 204090. | M. May 3/17. |
| ‡7 | D. | Golding, Frank Sidney. 15051. (Fr. 11th.) | M. May 3/17. |
| ‡7 | D. | Gordon, F. 202959. | M. May 3/17. |
| ‡7 | D. | Hartill, A. 202256. | M. May 3/17. |

**Middlesex Regiment—contd.**

## *B.E.F.*

‡7 D. Johnson, T. W. 202087. M. May 3/17.
‡7 D. Offley, A. 204029. M. May 3/17.
‡7 D. Pile, A. H. 202982. M. May 3/17.
‡7 D. Seabrooke, P. 15228. M. May 3/17.
‡7 D. Stenning, P. 202212. M. May 3/17.
‡7 D. Sutton, S. B. 202174. M. May 3/17.
7 D. Thitchener, C. S. 202958. W. and M. April 10/17.
7 D. XVI Weait, F. C. 205315. M. May 3/17.
*7 ? Broad, C. A. 205320. (34827.) (Fr. 16) M. May 31/17.
‡8 A. Chant, Chas. Walter. 241097. (4233) W. and M. May 19/17.
‡8 A. Curtis, W. 240258. M. May 19/17.
*8 A. II Hall, H. C. 242281. M. May 19/17.
8 A. Hughes, S/B. Fredk. Jas. 3703. M. Sept. 12/16. R/Enq.
*8 A. I King, G. W. 262997. M. May 19/17.
8 A. Meads, H. 4779. M. Sept. 12/16. R./Enq.
*8 A. II Woodroffe, A. S. 241335. (4770.) W. and M. May 19/17.
8 B. V Holmes, Leonard. 9501. (Fr. 19th Londons, 1566.) M. Sept. 15-16/16. R/Enq.
8 C. Stollard, Alf. Geo. 240702. W. and M. April 11/17.
‡8 C. Withers, J. 262905. M. May 3/17.
‡8 D. Gladdish, E. 240425. M. May 19/17.
‡8 D. Hammond, G. 241404. M. May 19/17.
*8 D. Jefferies, Bmr. Albert. 240153. M. May 19/17.
8 D. Moger, Arthur Wm. 263033. (3590.) M. May 19/17.
8 D. Pusey, A. J. 241279. W. and M. April 9/17.
‡8 D. Twinn, William Willis. 240516. M. May 19/17.
2/8 D. Mayes, L.-Cpl. William. 241293. (4634.) W. and M. April 10/17.
11 **Carter, 2nd Lieut. A. W.** M., bel. K. May 13/17.
11 **Towgood, 2nd Lieut. A. C. C.** M., bel. K. May 12/17.
11 A. IV Burgess, H. 22094. M. May 12/17.
11 A. Jones, Edward. 23738. M. May 12/17.
*11 A. IV Peacock, W. E. 42566. W. and M. May 12/17.
‡11 A. Walker, T. 2275. M. May 12/17.
‡11 A. Whelan, J. 8345. M. May 12/17.
11 B. Boyce, L.-Sergt. Albert H. 51178. W. and M. May 12/17.
*11 B. VII Cornish, E. 50104. M. May 12/17.
‡11 B. Powell, H. 11747. M. May 4/17.
‡11 B. Sessions, W. 9176. M. May 3/17.
11 B. L.G.S. Woodcock, George W. 40595. M. April 11/17.
‡11 C. Bentley, A. 12120. M. May 12/17.
‡11 C. Bodle, H. 50059. M. May 3/17.
‡11 C. Brown, Sergt. A. 5767. M. May 12/17.
‡11 C. Fuell, J. T. 42181. M. May 12/17.
‡11 C. Jarvis, J. 40602. M. May 12/17.
*11 C. X Moorhead, F. J. 50151. M., bel. K. May 4/17.
11 C. X Outram, G. 22184. M. April 9/17.
‡11 C. Turner, A. W. 71818. M. April 12/17.
‡11 C. XII Vincent, W. S. 8181. M. May 12/17.
‡11 C. White, J. 42625. M. May 12/17.
‡11 D. Franklin, H. 855. W. and M. April 11/17.
11 D. Keating, L.-Cpl. G. 11641. W. and M. April 10/17.
‡11 D. McIntosh, J. 42601. M. May 12/17.
11 D. XIV Sheffield, Herbert Archibald. 33882. K. April 9/17. Det.D./B.
‡11 D. XIV Stroulger, R. H. 34530. W. and M. May 5/17.
*11 ? Chapman, George. 1730. (Pioneer S.) M. April 10-11/17.
12 **Curtis, 2nd Lieut. E. St. G.** W. and M. May 3/17.
12 B. **Hotchkiss, 2nd Lieut. F. J. B.** W. Unoff. M. May 3-12/17.

**Middlesex Regiment—contd.**

## *B.E.F.*

| | | |
|---|---|---|
| 12 B. | **Pyman, Lieut. R. L.** (Fr. 5th.) | M. May 3/17. |
| 12 D. | **Walker, 2nd Lieut. W. H.** | M. May 3/17. |
| ‡12 A. | Abbs, W. 21725. | M. May 3/17. |
| 12 A. II | Beaty, T. H. 40041. (Fr. 10 R. Fus.) | Unoff. M. May 3/17. |
| *12 A. | Braithwaite, H. 6159. | M. May 3/17. |
| 12 A. III | Brock, John P. 40051. | M. May 3/17. |
| ‡12 A. | Chesterton, A. 2603. | M. May 3/17. |
| ‡12 A. | Church, E. 5686. | M. May 3/17. |
| 12 A. or D. XVI | Collins, L.-Cpl. Frank. 29336. (Fr. 6th.) | M. May 3/17. |
| ‡12 A. | Day, Robert. 20741. | M. May 3/17. |
| ‡12 A. | Dressler, G. 28188. | M. May 3/17. |
| ‡12 A. | Dunlop, J. 12465. | M. May 3/17. |
| ‡12 A. | Gilbert, L.-Cpl. H. 1312. | M. May 3/17. |
| *12 A. | Haggar, F. A. 26975. | M. May 3/17. |
| ‡12 A. | Haggar, J. 1147. (Fr. 14th.) | M. May 3/17. |
| ‡12 A. I | Howlett, Sigr. 5178. | Unoff. M., bel. P/W. May 3/17. |
| 12 A. | Hughes, R. 9521. | M. May 3/17. |
| ‡12 A. | Humphries, L.-Cpl. A. 2466. | M. May 3/17. |
| *12 A. II | Lancaster, Albert E. 40155. | M. May 3/17. |
| *12 A. III | Lansley, L.-Cpl. J. R. 40623. | M. May 3/17. |
| ‡12 A. | Marriott, C. 2592. | Unoff. M. May 3/17. |
| 12 A. | Marston, A. M. 11361. | W. and M. May 3/17. |
| ‡12 A. | Mason, L.-Cpl. A. 2177. | M. May 3/17. |
| ‡12 A. | Moules, F. 42285. | M. May 3/17. |
| 12 A. IV | Parker, Gilbert. G/40666. | W. and M. May 3/17. |
| ‡12 A. | Parsons, S. 40807. | M. May 3/17. |
| 12 A. | Paxton, Sergt. Geo. Jas. 3304. | W. and M. May 3/17. |
| ‡12 A. | Pease, J. H. 40630. | M. May 3/17. |
| ‡12 A. | Reeves, S. 2001. | M. May 3/17. |
| ‡12 A. | Roberts, H. C. 2196. | M. May 3/17. |
| ‡12 A. | Roff, L.-Cpl. H. T. 40642. | M. May 3/17. |
| ‡12 A. | Salter, W. 2557. | M. May 3/17. |
| ‡12 A. | Smith, J. 18018. | M. May 3/17. |
| 12 A. M.G.S. | Smith, Cpl. L. C. 7212. | M. May 3/17. |
| 12 A. III | Waters, A. 50773. | M. May 3/17. |
| ‡12 A. | Webber, W. L. 40052. | M. May 3/17. |
| ‡12 A. | Wheatley, L.-Cpl. H. 40640. | M. May 3/17. |
| ‡12 A. | Wilkinson, L.-Cpl. S. A. 2145. | M. May 3/17. |
| 12 A. I | Wiltshire, H. A. 22466. | M. May 3/17. |
| 12 A. | Woolf, Alfred. 40036. | W. and M. May 3/17. |
| 12 B. | Arnott, Fredk. John. 28993. | K. Feb. 19/17. Det.D./B. |
| ‡12 B. | Freeman, Cpl. B. 2102. | M. May 3/17. |
| ‡12 B. | Freeman, P. R. 40802. | M. May 3/17. |
| ‡12 B. | Gouldthorpe, P. 7085. | M. May 3/17. |
| ‡12 B. | Hallel, Leonard. 40091. | K. Sept. 26/16. Det.D./B. R/Enq. |
| 12 B. VI | Hatfield, L.-Cpl. H. J. 40656. (Fr. Middx. Yeo.) | M. May 3/17. |
| ‡12 B. | Hayward, F. 28273. | M. May 3/17. |
| 12 B. VIII | Healy, Andrew. 15759. | M. May 3/17. |
| ‡12 B. | Hedges, W. 34906. | M. May 3/17. |
| 12 B. M.G.S. | Heywood, F. 28273. | M. May 3/17. |
| ‡12 B. | Hodd, T. 8069. | M. May 3/17. |
| 12 B. | Kempley, A.-Sergt.-Maj. T. 2589. | M. May 3/17. |
| ‡12 B. VI | Pond, Francis. 42262. | M. May 3/17. |
| ‡12 B. VII | Poskitt, Wm. G/40093. (Fr. 31st R. Fus.) | M. Sept. 26/16. R/Enq. |
| 12 B. | Powell, John Wm. 40779. (Fr. H.Q.) | M. Feb. 17/17. |
| 12 B. | Quartly, A. 6229. | M. May 3/17. |

**Middlesex Regiment**—contd.

## *B.E.F.*

12 B. Smith, Percy Alfred. 3328. M. May 3/17.

‡12 B. Stride, W. 3550. M. May 3/17.

‡12 B. Sullivan, C. 42362. M. May 3/17.

‡12 C. Amos, Cpl. W. G. 15143. M. May 3/17.

12 C. L.G.S. Anns, Herb. Alf. 40761. M. May 3/17.

‡12 C. Attridge, Jas. Thos. 11346. M. May 3/17.

*12 C. XII Baker, G. F. 42293. M. May 3/17.

12 C. XI Bradford, W. T. 29038. M. May 3/17.

‡12 C. Calvert, A. 33920. M. May 3/17.

*12 C. Chandler, A. 29648. M. May 3/17.

‡12 C. Comer, L.-Cpl. W. 7129. M. May 3/17.

‡12 C. Cooper, J. 664. M. May 3/17.

12 C. IX Crekart, Leonard Jas. 28902. M. May 3/17.

12 C. IX Culvert, James. CS/33920. M. May 3/17.

12 C. Dallinger, Sig. H. 2032. W. and M. May 3/17.

12 C. X Deller, L.-Cpl. Henry Jas. 40760. M. May 3/17.

‡12 C. Dulake, A. 23532. M. May 3/17.

‡12 C. Fisher, J. 32370. M. May 3/17.

‡12 C. Fletcher, S. 22987. M. May 3/17.

‡12 C. Fuller, L.-Cpl. R. C. 6671. M. May 3/17.

12 C. XI Green, L.-Cpl. Edmund. 2847. M. May 3/17.

*12 C. Harlow, S. J. 33593. M. May 3/17.

12 C. M.G.S. Hawxwell, Chas. Baker. 28924. M. May 3/17.

‡12 C. M.G.S. Holmes, A. J. 33395. M. May 3/17.

12 C. Humphreys, L.-Sergt. G. G/6252. W. and M. May 3/17.

*12 C. XI Jones, H. W. 15878. M. May 3/17.

‡12 C. Kingston, L.-Cpl. A. 2693. M. May 3/17.

12 C. XII Knox, Herbert Frank. 40756. M. May 3/17.

‡12 C. M.G.S. Lacey, A. J. 1160. M. May 3/17.

‡12 C. XII Leaman, T. 11513. M. May 3/17.

12 C. Meadows, Wm. 1216. M. May 3/17.

‡12 C. Middleton, W. 3305. M. May 3/17.

‡12 C. Orledge, H. 40003. M. May 3/17.

‡12 C. IX Pooley, W. 29039. M. May 3/17.

‡12 C. Shephard, E. 1100. M. May 3/17.

‡12 C. XI Stevenson, A. G. 485. M. May 3/17.

12 C. M.G.S. Telling, L.-Cpl. A. J. 40700. M. May 3/17.

12 C. X Wiggins, B. A. G/40715. M. May 3/17.

12 C. Wilson, John Herbt. 40134. (Bn. Runner.) M. May 3/17.

‡12 C. Wright, H. G. 28016. M. May 3/17.

12 D. XV Baker, Malcolm. 5850. W. and M. May 3/17.

‡12 D. XIII Banbury, F. C. 33969. M. May 3/17.

12 D. XVI Bellingham, E. F. 40784. M. May 3/17.

‡12 D. Bannister, E. 32273. M. May 3/17.

‡12 D. Boardman, E. 32314. M. May 3/17.

‡12 D. Collins, Sergt. C. 6691 M. May 3/17.

‡12 D. Exton, L. 6774. M. May 3/17.

12 D. Fryer, Henry Thos. 32360. M. May 3/17.

12 D. XIII Gearing, E. G. 33822. M. May 3/17.

12 D. Goodall, Cpl. Henry Wm. 3223. W. and M. Sept. 26/16. R/Enq.

‡12 D. Hadley, E. 50888. M. May 3/17.

‡12 D. Halley, L.-Cpl. C. 1332. M. May 3/17.

12 D. XV Hocking, Percy. 40754. M. May 3/17.

‡12 D. Holland, L.-Cpl. R. S. 40740. M. May 3/17.

‡12 D. Humphries, B. 6832. M. May 3/17.

‡12 D. Hyde, C. 28966. M. May 3/17.

‡12 D. Jenkins, E. 1746. M. May 3/17.

**Middlesex Regiment—contd.**

## *B.E.F.*

| | | |
|---|---|---|
| *12 D. XV | Johnson, John. 5488. | M. **May 3/17.** |
| *12 D. | Humphreys, Albert. 6832. | W. and M. **May 3/17.** |
| 12 D. XVI | Kiddell, Edw. Jas. 40775. | W. and M. **May 3/17.** |
| 12 D. M.G.S. | Newman, A. E. G/32989. | M. Unoff. W. **May 3/17.** |
| 12 D. | Nicholson, Sergt. D. 3001. | M. **May 3/17.** |
| 12 D. XV | North, Geo. 43015. | M. **May 3/17.** |
| 12 D. | Robinson, G. A. 1340. | W. and M. **May 3/17.** |
| 12 D. XVI | Rowe, Sergt. W. J. 1986. | M. **May 3/17.** |
| ‡12 D. | Rumbelow, F. 29787. | M. **May 3/17.** |
| 12 D. XVI | Side, J. W. 2722. | Unoff. M. **May 3/17.** |
| 12 D. | Simpson, Douglas Macdonald. 12278. | M. **May 1-5/17.** |
| ‡12 D. | Turner, G. 34927. | M. **May 3/17.** |
| 12 D. | Webster, Sergt. Ernest Henry. 3249. | M. **May 3/17.** |
| 12 D. XV | White, H. C. 22754. | M. **May 3/17.** |
| 12 D. | Wightman, Hubert Douglas. 40773. | M. **May 3/17.** |
| ‡12 ? I.T.M. | Pickard, W. B. 40709. (54 Bde.) | M. **May 3/17.** |
| *13 | **Makeham, 2nd Lieut. E. N.** | M., bel. W. **June 13/17.** |
| ‡13 A. III | Antrobus, L.-Cpl. Alfred. 24174. | M. **June 10/17.** |
| ‡13 A. | Brien. 41881. | M. **June 10/17.** |
| ‡13 A. I | Enfield, G. 204471. | M. **June 10/17.** |
| ‡13 A. | Gordine, A. 961. | M. **June 10/17.** |
| *13 A. III | Hunt, Sidney. 241522. | Unoff. M. **June 9/17.** |
| 13 A. | Thompson, L.-Cpl. R. 13133. | W. and M. **April 15/17.** |
| ‡13 A. IV | Wilkinson, C. S. 42751. | W. Unoff. M. **June 9/17.** |
| 16 | **McCulloch, 2nd Lieut. K. L. M.** | M. **May 31/17.** |
| 16 | **Peake, 2nd Lt. J. L.** | M. **May 31/17.** |
| ‡16 A. | Badwell, L.-Sergt. Thos. Wm. 6629. | W. and M. **May 31/17.** |
| ‡16 A. | Baxter, C. J. 43316. | M. **May 31/17.** |
| *16 A. IV | Bradford, J. 6418. | M. **May 31/17.** |
| ‡16 A. | Butler, C. 5915. | M. **May 31/17.** |
| 16 A. | Coleman, G. A. 51419. | W. and M. **Feb. 28/17.** |
| 16 A. | Cummins, J. 6298. | W. and M. **Feb. 28/17.** |
| 16 A. | Evans, Alfred Sidney. 28279. | K. **April 23/17.** Det.D./B. |
| ‡16 A. | Hammond, E. J. 205337. | M. **May 31/17.** |
| 16 A. | Hoare, L.-Sergt. J. E. 43412. | M. **April 24/17.** |
| ‡16 A. | Hope, J. T. 205332. | M. **May 13/17.** |
| ‡16 A. I | Hughes, John. 3440. | M. **May 31/17.** |
| ‡16 A. | Hunn, W. T. E. 50809. | M. **May 31/17.** |
| ‡16 A. II | Knightley, Arthur. 205320. | M. **May 31/17.** |
| ‡16 A. III | Leppard, Sergt. Fred. Chas. 2291. | M. **May 31/17.** |
| ‡16 A. | Mason, E. 1227. | M. **May 31/17.** |
| ‡16 A. | Moule, G. 7616. | M. **May 31/17.** |
| *16 A. II | Newman, Cpl. A. 51104. | M. **May 31/17.** |
| ‡16 A. | Nowise, C. 5685. | M. **May 31/17.** |
| *16 A. | Pain, Cpl. Geo. Henry. 2088. | M. **May 31/17.** |
| *16 A. | Parker, A.-C.-S.-M. Hry. 8463. | M. **May 31/17.** |
| ‡16 A. | Price, A. H. 8506. | M. **May 31/17.** |
| ‡16 A. | Rider, J. 13389. | M. **May 31/17.** |
| ‡16 A. III | Rippingale, Arthur. 29981. | M. **May 31/17.** |
| *16 A. I | Wakerly, F. 50835. | M. **May 31/17.** |
| 16 A. | Wood, Edwin Jas. 40136. | M. **Feb. 28/17.** |
| ‡16 B. | Artus, A. 18330. | M. **May 31/17.** |
| *16 B. | Beecraft, Wm. Henry. 1352. | M. **May 31/17.** |
| *16 B. | Binder, Sgt. Arthur Robt. 1902. | W. and M. **May 31/17.** |
| *16 B. VIII | Bull, George. 204823. | M. **May 31/17.** |
| *16 B. V | Cox, Harry. 204814. (1911.) (Fr. 7th.) | M. **May 31/17.** |
| *16 B. V | Dewell, F. 205169. | M. **May 31/17.** |
| ‡16 B. | Gibson, L.-Cpl. B. 26347. | M. **May 31/17.** |
| ‡16 B. V | Goodwin, Bertram Geo. F/2469. | M. **May 30/17.** |

Middlesex Regiment—contd.

*B.E.F.*

‡16 B. Lucken, E. 3633. M. May 31/17.
*16 B. VIII Parsons, J. C. 1840. M. May 25-31/17.
‡16 B. Phillips, L.-Cpl. A. 17567. M. May 31/17.
‡16 B. Pope, Charles E. J. 40328. M. May 31/17.
‡16 B. VII Raymond, Cpl. Francis Henry. 2708. (Bomber.) W. and M. May 31/17.
‡16 B. Rayner, A. J. 43387. M. May 31/17.
*16 B. V Slinn, A. W. 34616. M. May 31/17.
*16 B. V Stenning, Cpl. S. 40336. M. May 30-31/17.
‡16 B. Wood, H. C. 40330. M. May 31/17.
‡16 C. Aylward, A. H. 34565. M. May 31/17.
*16 C. XII Barten, E. J. 200825. M. May 31/17.
‡16 C. Bodiam, E. J. 40358. M. April 23/17.
‡16 C. X Brookes, L.-Cpl. Chas. Jas. 40857. M. May 31/17.
*16 C. Bryant, L. 40858. M. May 31/17.
‡16 C. Cocoran, M. 43333. M. May 31/17.
‡16 C. Dalton, J. 40356. M. May 31/17.
16 C. Dutton, Arthur. 40834. (Fr. H.Q.) M. April 24/17.
*16 C. XI Flinn, G. 22806. M. May 31/17.
‡16 C. Fountain, B. 2604. M. May 31/17.
‡16 C. X Hutchinson, H. 40354. W. and M. May 31/17.
16 C. XVI Noble, H. 14132. M. Unoff. K. April 23/17.
‡16 C. Runeckles, A. 712. M. May 31/17.
‡16 D. Bedwell, H. 40872. M. May 31/17.
‡16 D. Bourne, G. 6784. M. May 10/17.
‡16 D. Brannon, J. 12417. M. May 31/17.
*16 D. Childs, W. 3208. M. May 31/17.
‡16 D. Crooks, J. J. 40379. M. May 31/17.
‡16 D. Davey, Sergt. Ernest. 1505. M. May 31/17.
‡16 D. Day, A. 23912. M. May 31/17.
*16 D. XIII Fogg, Cpl. E. 51082. M. May 31/17.
*16 D. XIII Johnstone, L.-Cpl. Joseph F. 51103 M. May 31/17.
‡16 D. XIII Golden, T. E. 29984. M. May 31/17.
‡16 D. X Hall, H. W. 23674. M. May 31/17.
‡16 D. Hayes, Sgt. Denzil Briscoe. 928. M. May 31/17.
‡16 D. XIII Haywood, L.-Cpl. L. 2809. W. and M. May 31/17.
‡16 D. Hedge, L.-Cpl. A. 2429. M. May 31/17.
‡16 D. Heiden, W. 202023. M. May 31/17.
‡16 D. Hostler, J. 29958. M. May 31/17.
‡16 D. Mayor, C. R. 43377. M. May 31/17.
*16 D. Partridge, Thos. Charles. 44384. M. May 31/17.
‡16 D. Rising, R. H. 203971. M. May 31/17.
‡16 D. Rogers, F. T. 6655. M. May 31/17.
‡16 D. XIII Rolfe, H. 43391. W. and M. May 31/17.
16 D. Shears, A. 43396. M. Feb. 28/17.
16 D. Unstead, Herb. 40377. M. April 23/17.
*16 D. XIII Wallace, John Reuben. 203862. (5005.) M. May 31/17.
‡16 D. XIII Weller, L.-Cpl. S. A. 40367. M. May 31/17.
‡16 D. Weller, L.-Cpl. W. F. 40376. M. May 31/17.
‡16 D. XV Wells, H. S. 43414. (5649.) M. May 31/17.
‡16 ? Clark, C. J. 51091. M. April 23/17.
‡16 ? Cross, F. J. 6210. W. Unoff. M. May 31/17.
*16 ? George, Peter Dennis. 205024. (4681) W. and M. May 31/17.
17 **Bonathon, 2nd Lieut. F. S.** W. and M. April 28/17.
17 B. **Dick, 2nd Lieut. N. B.** W. and M. April 28/17.
17 **Henderson, 2nd Lieut. A. R.** W. and M. April 28/17.
17 **Secrett, 2nd Lieut. A. G.** W. and M. April 28/17.

**Middlesex Regiment**—contd.

*B.E.F.*

17 A. M.G.S. Abear, J. L. 129. M. April 28/17.
‡17 A. Anderson, G. 41651. M. April 28/17.
17 A. Bailey, Sergt. J. A. 112. M. April 28/17.
‡17 A. Clark, G. E. F. 44050. M. April 28/17.
‡17 A. Collins, A. 202288. M. April 24/17.
‡17 A. Connell, R. 44089. M. April 24/17.
17 A. IV Davies, D. 2743. M. April 28/17.
17 A. I Divers, William. 5916. M. April 28/17.
‡17 A. Dunn, J. 6205. M. April 28/17.
‡17 A. Fox, S. J. 41668. M. April 28/17.
17 A. IV Frost, R. 202135. M. May 3/17.
17 A. Furneaux, L.-Cpl. Philip. F/704. M. April 28/17.
‡17 A. Gillett, W. H. 43645. M. April 28/17.
17 A. IV Grant, Geo. Edward. 34050. M. April 28/17.
17 A. Griffiths, Bandsman Frank K. 43657. M. April 28/17.
‡17 A. Harrington, H. 34293. M. April 28/17.
*17 A. Hennessey, A. J. 1449. M. Nov. 13/16. R/Enq.
‡17 A. Jempson, L.-Cpl. A. E. 41645. M. April 28/17.
‡17 A. IV Jenkins, L.-Sgt. Fredrics John. 5387 M. April 28/17.
‡17 A. Jones, W. 21002. M. April 28/17.
‡17 A. Levett, F. G. 24512. M. April 28/17.
‡17 A. McMillan, A. 24492. M. April 28/17.
‡17 A. Maynard, R. J. 24410. M. April 28/17.
‡17 A. I Nash, L.-Cpl. H. 14834. M. April 28/17.
*17 A. I Osborn, Fredk. Chas. 41632. M. April 28/17.
*17 A. III Parsons, E. S. 12171. M. April 28/17.
‡17 A. Peters, A. L. 1159. M. April 28/17.
‡17 A. Porter, W. F. 41647. M. April 28/17.
*17 A. IV Raymond, Fredk. Chas. 43978. M. April 28/17.
‡17 A. Ridgers, F. 43704. M. April 28/17.
17 A. IV Roffey, G. T. 50749. M. April 28/17.
*17 A. II Santer, W. 6109. M. April 28/17.
‡17 A. Sayers, E. J. 44150. M. April 28/17.
‡17 A. Shuter, L.-Cpl. H. E. 41658. M. April 28/17.
‡17 A. Smart, Sergt. F. W. 229. M. April 28/17.
17 A. Swann, Cpl. Thos. William. F/283. M. April 28/17.
‡17 A. Sweet, H. 41659. M. April 28/17.
‡17 A. Terry, C. 41635. M. April 28/17.
‡17 A. Tipping, J. 5563. M. April 28/17.
‡17 A. Try, L.-Cpl. C. A. 43859. M. April 28/17.
‡17 A. Tye, F. 44027. M. April 28/17.
‡17 A. I.T.M. Warren, G. H. 210. (6 Bgde.) M. April 28/17.
‡17 A. Webb, L.-Cpl. J. J. 5099. M. April 28/17.
‡17 A. M.G.S. Webb, Cpl. W. H. 1352. M. April 28/17.
*17 A. M.G.S. Willeats, F. 1335. M. April 28/17.
‡17 A. Wood, E. 43861. M. April 28/17.
‡17 A. Wood, G. G. 41662. M. April 28/17.
‡17 A. Wood, S. C. 41648. M. April 28/17.
‡17 B. Adams, F. 44153. M. April 28/17.
17 B. VIII Bigwood, W. G/43939. M. April 28/17.
*17 B. Brown, Fred Arthur Henry. 1219. M. April 28/17.
17 B. VII Chapman, Harry. 34339. M. April 28/17.
17 B. VII Chew, E. J. 34399. M. April 28/17.
‡17 B. Church, L.-Cpl. H. A. 43662. M. April 28/17.
17 B. Coen, Chas. J. Lawrence. 202852. (Fr. 7th, 7481.) M. April 28/17.
*17 B. Cole, Wm. J. 203035. M. April 28/17.
‡17 B. Cowhig, J. 34397. M. April 21/17.

**Middlesex Regiment—contd.**

*B.E.F.*

‡17 B. Davis, T. W. 203041. M. April 28/17.
‡17 B. Drew, W. 44105. M. April 28/17.
*17 B. V Emberson, L.-Cpl. Mark. 34190. M. April 28/17.
‡17 B. Evans, A. G. 26308. M. April 28/17.
‡17 B. Foster, B. 50728. M. April 23/17.
‡17 B. Gaylor, N. H. 34409. M. April 28/17.
17 B. VII Godfrey, E. G/43560. M. April 28/17.
17 B. V Gould, Wm. Chas. 34291. M. April 28/17.
17 B. V Green, Chas. Edw. 203188. M. April 28/17.
17 B. M.G.S. Greenwood, L.-Cpl. Chas. L. 43646. (Fr. 7th, 3384.) M. April 28/17.
17 B. V Hankins, W. 8186. M. April 28/17.
‡17 B. Harty, F. P. 43564. M. April 28/17.
‡17 B. Heslington, G. 2037. M. April 28/17.
‡17 B. Hitching, B. P. 44087. M. April 28/17.
*17 B. VIII Holliday, W. 203052. M. April 28/17.
17 B. Hollingsworth, Sgt. Leslie Wm. 34233. M. April 28/17.
‡17 B. Keasley, A. A. 43686. M. April 28/17.
‡17 B. Knight, G. A. W. 16533. M. April 28/17.
17 B. or D. Langley, H. 43906. M. April 28/17.
17 B. VIII Levey, W. H. 202916. (7591.) M. April 28/17.
‡17 B. VIII Lucas, James S. 43665. M. April 28/17.
‡17 B. Luxford, F. A. 203058. M. April 28/17.
17 B. VIII Marigold, L.-Cpl. F. 2976. M. April 28/17.
17 B. VI Monypenny, Geo. Francis. 203189. (7976.) M. April 28/17.
‡17 B. Mortimer, H. 43929. M. April 28/17.
‡17 B. Mortimer, J. J. 43570. M. April 28/17.
‡17 B. Moyse, L.-Cpl. A. 43900. M. April 28/17.
17 B. Pardoe, Cpl. Herbert Wm. 5. M. April 28/17.
‡17 B. V Pledger, L.-Cpl. W. G. 1782. M. April 28/17.
*17 B. VII Prior, Alfred Murray. 5107. M. April 28/17.
17 B. VIII Parker, Fredk. Moses. 203059. M. April 28/17.
17 B. VIII Ross, W. 203064. M. April 28/17.
17 B. VII Rowland, Walter Riches. 43716. M. April 28/17.
‡17 B. Ruff, J. L. 203065. M. April 28/17.
17 B. V Sapsworth, Wm. John. 203454. (42433.) M. April 28/17.
‡17 B. Scudder, L.-Cpl. T. E. 44086. M. April 28/17.
‡17 B. Sharman, S. R. 9707. M. April 28/17.
‡17 B. Sheate, C. T. 32537. M. April 28/17.
17 B. L.G.S. Sterne, L.-Cpl. F. 12041. M. April 28/17.
*17 B. VIII Walker, Frank. 201812. (5303.) M. April 28/17.
‡17 B. Warren, J. 44092. M. April 28/17.
17 B. VIII Wayland, A. C. 43655. M. Nov. 13/16. R/Enq.
17 B. V Webb, T. 44067. M. April 28/17.
17 B. VIII Wheeler, Cpl. Arthur. 203184. M. April 28/17.
17 B. V Wheeler, Ernest. 203071. M. April 28/17.
*17 B. VI Wilkinson, A. E. 43723. M. April 28/17.
‡17 C. Alderson, H. 1815. M April 28/17.
*17 C. X Anderson, E. J. 34772. M. April 28/17.
‡17 C. Appleton, B. 24460. M. April 28/17.
*17 C. XI Archer, J. 34263. M. April 28/17.
17 C. XI Attwell, Leonard Alfred. 27933. M. April 28/17.
*17 C. XI Backler, A. 24518. M. Nov. 13/16.
17 C. M.G.S. Bartram, F. W. 43544. M. April 28/17.
17 C. XII Bastin, Benj. 34030. M. April 28/17.

**Middlesex Regiment—contd.**

## *B.E.F.*

‡17 C. Beard, B. E. 34335. M. April 28/17.
17 C. Berry, A. B. 34207. M. April 28/17.
‡17 C. M.G.S. Bishopp, H. 43689. M. April 28/17.
17 C. XII Blyth, L.-Cpl. J. 34025. M. April 28/17.
17 C. IX Bones, Samuel. 34394. M. April 28/17.
17 C. XII Bradley, L.-Cpl. John Jas. 11078. M. April 28/17.
17 C. IX Bright, L. C. 34032. M. April 28/17.
•17 C. XII Buchall, Cpl. Clifford. 34026. M. April 28/17.
‡17 C. Burton, W. 34210. M. April 28/17.
‡17 C. Bushell, Cpl. C. 34026. M. April 28/17.
•17 C. IX Chambers, S. 34040. M. April 28/17.
‡17 C. Childs, C. 43670. M. April 28/17.
‡17 C. Clapton, L. 34038. M. April 28/17.
‡17 C. Clark, A. W. 44074. M. Dec. 13/16.
‡17 C. Clark, F. R. 29962. M. April 28/17.
‡17 C. Clements, R. 8674. M. April 28/17.
17 C. IX Courtney, L.-Cpl. Fredk. 50740. M. April 28/17.
17 C. XI Cox, W. G. 34712. M. April 28/17.
‡17 C. Curtis, A. 34041. M. April 28/17.
‡17 C. Denny, E. E. 43992. M. April 28/17.
‡17 C. Drackett, W. 15142. M. April 28/17.
•17 C. X Eady, Harold. 34003. M. April 28/17.
17 C. X Eve, A. 34222. M. April 28/17.
‡17 C. Everett, S. 34341. M. April 28/17.
17 C. IX Gill, L.-Cpl. T. E. 50421. M. April 28/17.
•17 C. X Goddard, L.-Cpl. W. J. 43680. M. April 28/17.
‡17 C. Hayles, H. 43022. M. April 28/17.
17 C. XII Hughes, Henry Jones. 2733. M. April 28/17.
‡17 C. Humphrey, H. 5773. M. April 28/17.
17 C. XI King, Arthur. 3649. M. April 28/17.
•17 C. X Kirk, Albert. 43955. M. April 28/17.
17 C. McKelvey, Sgt. G. H. J. 34199. M. April 28/17.
‡17 C. Mandall, R. 5852. M. April 28/17.
‡17 C. Marfin, L.-Cpl. H. W. 8850. M. April 28/17.
17 C. Matthews, L.-Cpl. W. C. 43944. M. April 28/17.
•17 C. X Murch, A. R. 43935. M. April 28/17.
17 C. X Osborne, P. 43936. K. Nov. 13/16. Det.D./B. R/Enq.
‡17 C. Pearce, G. F. 43708. M. April 28/17.
‡17 C. Pierce, A. J. 43960. M. April 28/17.
•17 C. X Polley, W. H. 43956. M. Nov. 13/16.
17 C. XII Riley, Alfred. 44011. M. April 25/17.
17 C. XII Russell, William John. 43894. M. April 28/17.
•17 C. X Shirvell, Sidney. 20934. M. April 28/17.
17 C. XI Sivil, Sergt. Thos. 40447. M. April 28/17.
17 C. X Smelt, Frank. 43722. M. April 28/17.
‡17 C. Smith, M. 16128. M. April 28/17.
•17 C. Veryard, Wm. Thos. 13166. M. April 28/17.
17 C. XII Walker, E. C. 6153. M. April 28/17.
17 C. X Wickenden, Stanley Wm. 50754. M. April 28/17.
‡17 C. Woolf, A. A. 50756. M. April 28/17.
‡17 D. Allsworth, W. 11532. M. April 28/17.
‡17 D. Bacon, H. W. 34088. M. April 28/17.
17 D. Bates, F. 20095. M. April 28/17.
‡17 D. Baucham, P. J. 34086. M. April 28/17.
•17 D. XIII Bell, F. 34089. M. April 28/17.
17 D. Blay, C. 872. M. April 28/17.
‡17 D. Bowcock, W. W. 34087. M. April 28/17.
‡17 D. Bremmer, H. G. 1702. M. April 28/17.

**Middlesex Regiment**—contd.

## *B.E.F.*

‡17 D. Brian, F. H. 9875. M. April 28/17.
17 D. XIV Bridgette, G. F. 9988. M. April 28/17.
‡17 D. Brown, W. H. 43949. M. April 28/17.
‡17 D. Burrows, L.-Cpl. F. A. 924. M. April 28/17.
‡17 D. Castle, J. T. 5474. M. April 28/17.
•17 D. XIII Caton, Frank. 34093. M. April 28/17.
‡17 D. Clapton, H. C. 34092. M. April 28/17.
‡17 D. Cobbold, W. 44013. M. April 24/17.
17 D. XV Cox, W. F. 43930. M. April 28/17.
•17 D. XVI Davies, Wm. Victor. 1169. M. April 28/17.
17 D. XVI Dyer, Charles Henry. 12. M. April 28/17.
‡17 D. Edmunds, Harold. 43896. M. April 28/17.
•17 D. XIV Edwards, L.-Cpl. J. R. 2913. M. April 28/17. R/Enq.
•17 D. XV Garrett, Cpl. E. A. 34048. M. April 27/17.
‡17 D. Hester, L.-Sergt. E. C. 5280 M. April 28/17.
17 D. XVI Hurman, Cpl. F. B. 959. M. April 28/17.
‡17 D. Kosh, A. H. 21727. M. April 28/17.
17 D. Lewis, J. 1158. M. April 28/17.
‡17 D. Newbutt, L.-Cpl. Derrick. 43857. M. April 28/17.
•17 D. XV Orsman, A. 26406. M. April 28/17.
‡17 D. Peterkin, E. S. 50747. M. April 28/17.
17 D. XVI Potter, Lionel. 43890. M. April 28/17.
17 D. XIII Rowland, Sergt. Geo. Fredk 837. M. April 28/17.
‡17 D. Saville, A. J. 44006. M. April 28/17.
17 D. Silcocks, E. L. 998. M. April 28/17.
17 D. XIV Slade, G. F. 203858. M. April 28/17.
17 D. XIII Spittle, G. W. 40978. M. April 28/17.
17 D. Spurgeon, Henry. 868. M. April 28/17.
•17 D. XV Storer, Jack. 5638. M. April 28/17.
•17 D. M.G.S. Thompson, P. 26395. M. April 28/17.
17 D. L.G.S. Willett, John Thos. 5481. M. April 28/17.
17 D. Windebank, Jack. 50755. M. April 28/17.
‡17 D. Wood, A. J. 43893. M. April 28/17.
17 D. XVI Young, Arthur G. 203075. M. April 28/17.
‡17 D. Youngs, S. B. 44012. M. April 28/17.
•17 ? M.G.S. Edwards, L.-Cpl. J. H. 2913. M. April 28/17.
17 ? I.T.M. Lee, T. 966. (6 Bgde.) W. Unoff. M April 28/17.
‡20 A. Hutcheson, L.-Sgt. E. 18617. M. May 22/17.
20 D. Hammans, Cpl. Harry. 51222. W. and M. May 5/17.
‡21 B. Dickinson, T. J. 41067. M. May 27/17.
‡23 A. Ashley, W. 29436. M. June 7/17.
‡23 A. Constable, W. G. 205036. M. June 7/17.
23 B. Hedges, Robt. A. 2392. M. Sept. 15/16. R/Enq.
‡23 B. Inglesby, A. 20239. M. June 7/17.
‡23 B. VIII Mills, R. 204497. M. June 7/17.
‡23 C. M.G.S. Ashby, W. F. 29436. M. June 7/17.
23 C. Bond, William. 9781. M., bel. K. Oct. 1/16. R/Enq.
‡23 D. Barnett, Frank. G.S./11574. M. June 7/17.

## *E.E.F.*

5 Cutter, H. A. F/3191. M., bel. drowned April 15/17. "Cameronia."
•5 ? Hayden, L.-Cpl. B. 15926. M., bel. drowned April 15/17.
•5 ? Sleap, Ernest. C.S./1604. M., bel. drowned April 15/17. "Cameronia."
2/9 **Snowden, Capt. Stanley.** K. April 13/17. Det.D./B.
2/10 A. King, A. 291871. (4870.) W. and M. Mar. 26/17.

**Middlesex Regiment—contd.**

*E.E.F.*

| | | |
|---|---|---|
| 2/10 A. | *Oakins, O. J. 291339. (3878.) | W. and M. April 19/17. |
| 2/10 B. | Bartley, A. H. 291407. (Late 3997.) | M. Mar. 26/17. |
| 2/10 B. V | Stevens, Frank. 293374. (2136.) | W. and M. April 19/17. |
| 2/10 B. | Sussex, Thos. Walter. 291825. (Late 4819.) | M. Mar. 26/17. |
| 2/10 B. VIII | Wilton, Arthur Edward. 293516. | W. and M. Mar. 26/17. |
| 2/10 B. VI | Young, L.-Cpl. Hy. Frank. 293329. (Late 683.) | M. Mar. 26/17. |
| 2/10 C. | Blake, J. 290190. (1491.) | W. and M. Mar. 26/17. |
| 2/10 C. XI | Lucas, Hubert Hy. 290832. (2666.) | M. Mar. 26/17. |
| 2/10 C. XII | Willis, E. 290803. (2606.) (Late D Co.) | M. April 19/17. |
| 2/10 C. | Young, Norman. 291887. | M. Mar. 26/17. |
| 2/10 C. IX | Young, Wm. Lionel. 293508. (Late 2950.) | M. Mar. 26/17. |
| 2/10 D. XVI | Grove, Basil Sydney Ernest. 291927. (Late 4932.) | K. April 19/17. Det.D./B. |
| 2/10 ? | Burgess, Sergt. G. R. 293420. | W. and M. Mar. 26/17. |
| 2/10 ? | Crawford, B. A. 291136. | W. and M. Mar. 26/17. |
| 2/10 ? | Harwood, A.-Cpl. F. C. 290333. | M. Mar. 26/17. |
| *2/10 ? | Hearn, W. 291937. | M. April 19/17. |
| 2/10 Sig. S. | Horswill, A. S. 290110. (Late 1319.) | M. Mar. 26/17. |
| 2/10 ? | Stephens, F. 293374. | W. and M. Mar. 26/17. |

**MONMOUTHSHIRE REGIMENT.**

*B.E.F.*

| | | |
|---|---|---|
| 2 D. XIV | Brown, Wm. Jas. 15939. | M. Jan. 27/17. |

**ROYAL MUNSTER FUSILIERS.**

*B.E.F.*

| | | |
|---|---|---|
| 1 W. | Atkins, L.-Sergt. Jas. Gilman. 4924. | K. Sept. 9/16. Det.D./B. |
| *1 W. | Cant, Wm. Henry. 10494. | M. Sept. 9/16. R/Enq. |
| 1 W. | Scannell, L.-Cpl. D. 6634. | W. and M. Sept. 9/16. R/Enq. |
| 1 W. | Turner, Jas. 6111. | M. Sept. 9/16. R/Enq. |
| 1 Y. | McCarthy, William. 2352. | M. Nov. 7/16 |
| 1 Z. | Hallissey, Patrick. 8752. | M. Sept. 9/16. R/Enq. |
| 1 Z. | Kelly, Francis. 5382. | W. and M. Sept. 9/16. R/Enq. |
| 2 C. | Russell, T. 6221. | M. Nov. 27/16. |
| 8 A. | Hussey, John. 3966. | M. Sept. 3/16. R/Enq. |
| 8 B. | Stack, L.-Cpl. Maurice Joseph. 1739. | M. Sept. 4/16. R/Enq. |
| 8 B. | Sullivan, Michael. 4118. | W. and M. Sept. 4/16. R./Enq. |

*BALKANS.*

| | | |
|---|---|---|
| 7 | Bagley, E. 13346. (Fr. 3 Dorsets.) | M. Dec. 7/16. R/Enq. |

## ROYAL NAVAL AIR SERVICE.

### *B.E.F.*

| | | |
|---|---|---|
| ‡? **Squad.** | **Ramsay, Flt.-Lieut. D. W.** | M. **June 7/17** |
| ‡4 **Squad. 4 Wing** | **Smith, Lt. L. H. Willard.** | M. **June 13/17.** |
| **11** | **Swinburne, Flt.-Sub.-Lt. T. R.** | M. **June 8/17.** |
| '? | **Moir, Flight Lieut., C.** | M. **May 15/17.** |
| •? | **Paine, Flt. Sub-Lieut. L. P.** | M. abt. **June 16/17.** |
| ? | **Roach, Flight Sub.-Lieut. E. D.** | M. **May 2/17.** |
| •? | **Stewart, Flt. Sub-Lt. W. Houston.** | M. **May 26/17.** |

### *BALKANS.*

| | | |
|---|---|---|
| **2 Wing** | **Perberdy, Flt. Sub.-Lt. Warner H.** | M. **Jan. 14/17.** |
| ‡? | **Marsh, Obs. Sub-Lieut. Leslie.** | M. **June 28/17.** |
| ‡? | **Maxwell, Sub.-Lt. J. E. (R.N.V.R.)** | M. **Mar. 30/17.** |
| ‡? | **Robinson, Flt.-Lieut. W. E.** | M. **May 8/17.** |

## ROYAL NAVAL DIVISION.

### *B.E.F.*

NOTE.—The letters in brackets, which follow after the numbers, refer to the place of enlistment.

**THE FOLLOWING ABBREVIATIONS ARE USED:—**

| | | | | | |
|---|---|---|---|---|---|
| Ch. ... | Chatham. | M. ... | Mersey. | W. .. | Wales. |
| B. ... | Bristol. | Ply.... | Plymouth. | So. ... | Southampton. |
| Cl. ... | Clyde. | Po. ... | Portsmouth. | | |
| L. ... | London. | T. ... | Tyneside. | | |

### 1st BRIGADE.

#### Drake Battalion.

| | | |
|---|---|---|
| ‡**A. I** | Brittain, Jas. Wilfred. R/111. | W. and M. **April 23/17.** |
| **A. II** | Campbell, Chas. Z/8283. (T.) | M. **April 16/17.** |
| **A. II** | Eaton, Hendel J. 2386. | M. **April 23/17.** |
| ‡**A. III** | Moran, Patrick. TZ/7392. | M. April 23/17. |
| '**A.** | Murchie, Archie. 4765. | M. **April 23/17.** |
| **B.** | Barnfather, Ernest. Z/7032. | M. **April 23/17.** |
| **B. M.G.S.** | Fyfe, Wm. Kemp. Z/3967. (Cl.) | W. Unoff. M. **April 23/17.** |
| **B.** | Mathews, P.O. Jas. Jos. Z/158. (M.) | W. and M. **April 23/17.** |
| **B. L.G.S.** | Meikle, Jas. 5940. | K. **April 23/17.** Det.D./B. |
| **B. VII** | Treves, A. F. L.Z/3968. | M. **April 23/17.** |
| **C.** | Burt, Robert. Z/6988. | M. **April 23/17.** |
| ·**C.** | McDonald, Angus. 6976. (Att. 8th Entrenching Bn.) | W. and M. **April 23/17.** |
| **C. IX** | Purseglove, Wm. K/525. (W.) | W. and M. **April 23/17.** |
| **C. X** | Walker, Wm. 440. (K.W.) | M. April 23/17. |
| **D. XV** | Hamblin, Ernest Wm. Z/1353. (B.) | W. and M. **April 23/17.** |
| **D. XVI** | Hetherington, P.O. Cyril Dudley. Z/2766. (T.) | W. and M. **April 23/17.** |

**Naval Division, Royal—contd.**

## *B.E.F.*

**1st Brigade—contd.**

**Drake Battalion—contd.**

| | | |
|---|---|---|
| *D. XVI | Miller, Percy Geo. R/194. | K. April 23/17. Det.D./B. |
| D. XVI | Parker, Harold. R/143. | W. and M. April 23/17. |
| D. XVI | Powell, James. Z/969. (W.) | M. Nov. 13/16. |
| D. | Rae, Wm. Robt. Jn. Z/5432. (Cl.) | W. and M. April 23/17. |
| D. XIII | Richardson, James. K/278. (W.) | M. April 23/17. |
| D. XVI | Smith, Albert. Z/268. (W.) | W. and M. April 23/17. |
| D. XIII | Thomson, Paul. Z/4785. (B.) | M. April 23/17. |
| D. | Wood, Geo. E. Z/2836. (L.) | W. and M. Feb. 4/17. |
| ? | Brown, Thomas Baird. Z/7558. (Cl.) | W. and M. Feb. 4/17. |
| ? | Brownbridge, Bernard. K.P./336. | W. and M. Feb. 4/17. |
| ? | Collins, Wm. Z/2001. (Cl.) | W. and M. Feb. 4/17. |
| ? | Dack, Maurice. Z/4526. (T.) | M. April 23/17. |
| ? | Laird, Alexander. Z/5021. (Cl.) | M. Feb. 4/17. |
| ? | Light, Charles. S.R./226. | W. and M. Feb. 17/17. |
| *? ? | Stokoe, L.S. Wm. Z/2921. | M. April 23/17. |
| ? | Wilson, P.O. James P. 2/3070. (Cl.) | W. and M. Feb. 17/17. |

**Hawke Battalion.**

| | | |
|---|---|---|
| A. L.G.S. | Brampton, Thos. E. Z/3981. (B.) | M. Feb. 3/17. |
| A. I | Peters, L/S. Andrew. Z/5347. (Cl.) | K. Nov. 14/16. Det.D./B. |
| B. VII | Jepson, Teddy. Z/5976. (T.) | M. Nov. 13/16. |
| ‡B. | Stables, Philip B. KW/335. | M. Nov. 13/16. R/Enq. |
| C. XII | Richardson, Harold Joseph. R/383. | M. Feb. 3/17. |
| C. IX | Smith, Robert. Z/3723. C.P. | M. Feb. 3/17. |
| C. | Swallow, Lawrence. Z/8873. (T.) | M. Feb. 3/17. |
| C. | Wright, Horace. 365. (R.) | M. Feb. 3/17. |
| D. XIV | Griffiths, John. Z/4319. (T.) | M. Feb. 3/17. |
| ? | Campbell, Robert. R/551. | M. April 23/17. |
| ? | Champneys, Robt. Potts. Z/1445. (T.) | M. Feb. 4/17. |
| ? | Hamilton, Robert. R/382. | M. Feb. 3/17. |
| ? | Jones, Dennis Owen. R/343. | K. April 18/17. Det.D./B. |
| ? | Richardson, Guy Bernard. L.Z./1329. (Fr. 11 En. Bn.) | K. Feb. 4/17. Det.D./B. |
| ? | Robinson, Benjamin. Z/840. (T.) | M. Feb. 3/17. |
| ? | Trott, Leslie. Z/1062. (L.) | W. and M. Feb. 4/17. |

**Hood Battalion.**

| | | |
|---|---|---|
| | **Bailey, Sub.-Lieut. D. F.** | W. Unoff. M. April 23/17. |
| A. III | Bennett, John Wm. Z/5863. | M. Nov. 13-14/16. R/Enq. |
| A. III | Bunting, (H.G.), Frank. KW/620. | M. Feb. 4/17. |
| A. IV | Dawson, Edward. Z/1781. (T.) | W. and M. Feb. 4/17. |
| A. II | Dixon, Walter Jas. Z/7927. (T.) | M. April 23/17. |
| A. L.G.S. | Titchener, Walter John. Z/416. (S.) | M. April 23/17. |
| C. | Monaghan, T. Z/2558. (Ty.) | M. April 23/17. |
| C. | Scott, Bertie Stewart. TZ/9659. | W. and M. April 23/17. |
| D. XIV | Baker, Francis Justin. Z/3225. (W.) | M. April 23/17. |
| D. IV | Goodison, Percy. 7155. | M. April 23/17. |
| *D. IV | Hughes, Wm. Edward. Z/740. (T.) | M. April 23/17. |
| ? | Bond, James Edw. Z/1283. (B.) | M. Feb. 4/17. |
| ? | Gibson, Edward. Z/1734. (T.) | M. Feb. 4/17. |
| ? | Rouse, Edw. Geo. Z/5119. (L.) | W. and M. Unoff. K. April 23/17. |
| *? | Simpson, John Robt. Z/8676. (T.) | M. April 23/17. |
| ? | Webster, Henry. Z/4114. (B.) | M. April 23/17. |

**Naval Division, Royal**—contd.

## *B.E.F.*

**1st Brigade**—contd.

### Nelson Battalion.

| | | |
|---|---|---|
| A. IV | Alder, P.O. James. Z/3641. (T.) | M. April 23/17. |
| A. IV | Bradburn, C. Z/3475. (B.) | M. April 23/17. |
| A. I | Lewington, Albert Wm. R/336. | W. and M. April 23/17. |
| A. I | Morrison, L/S. Wm. Thomson. Z/4283. (Cl.) | W. and M. April 23/17. |
| ‡B. VII | Boyle, Bernard. Z/24611. (Ch.) | M. Nov. 13/16. R/Enq. |
| B. VII | Loosemore, Richd. Morgan. Z/2485. (W.) | M. April 23/17. |
| B. V | McAuliffe, Edward. Z/7093. (T.) | M. Nov. 13/16. |
| C. XII | Dunnett, Chas. Wm. R/381. | M. April 23/17. |
| C. XI | Hockin, Leonard Wm. R/320. | M. April 24/17. |
| C. | Hurst, P.O. John. Z/3150. (T.) | W. Unoff. M. April 24/17. |
| C. X | March, George. Z/1359. | M. April 24/17. |
| C. XII | Neale, Geo. Wm. Z/836. (T.) (Fr. Collingwood Batt.) | W. and M. April 23/17. |
| C. | Slinn, R. 3743. | W. and M. April 23/17. |
| C. X | Taylor, Joseph Edwin. Z/814. (M.) | W. and M. April 24/17. |
| *C. IX | Turrell, Ernest Geo. R/355. | M. April 24/17. |
| D. XIII | Armstrong, Fred. Z/3635. (T.) | M. April 23/17. |
| D. XV | Bromley, Herbert. Z/638. (M.) | M. April 23/17. |
| D. XIII | Hubball, John James. R/71. | M. April 23/17. |
| ‡D. XV | Hutchinson, Henry. Z/5320. (T.) | M. April 23/17. |
| *D. ? | Kelly, John. 3304. | M. April 24/17. |
| D. | Lishman, Edward. Z/8168. (T.) | M. April 23/17. |
| D. XIII | Needham, Albert. Z/6680. (T.) | M. Feb. 3/17. |
| D. XIII | Webster, J. C. Z/9076. (B.) | M. April 24/17. |
| D. XIII | Williamson, Lawrence. 7290. | M. Nov. 13/16. R/Enq. |
| ? | Barker, Chris. Theodore. Z/3162. (L.) | M. April 23/17. |
| ? | Cunningham, John . Z/446. (M.) | M. April 23/17. |
| ? | Davison, Robert W. Z/1326. (T.) | M. Nov. 13/16. |
| ? | Garner, William. Z/5270. (T.) | M. April 23/17. |
| H.Q. | Graham, Wm. Lander. Z/3302. (Bomb. Pl.) | W. and M. Nov. 13/16. |
| ? | Hibberd, Wm. Neville. Z/5264. | K. Feb. 4/17. Det.D./B. |
| *? ? | Thompson, Walter. K.W./228. | M. April 23/17. |
| '? | Vaton, Etienne A. Z/5074. (L.) | K. Jan. 22/17. Det.D./B. |

## 2nd BRIGADE.

### Anson Battalion.

| | | |
|---|---|---|
| *B. VIII L.G.S. | Dewar, L.S. Robt. 1850. | M. Unoff. K. April 28/17. |
| C. XII | Proudlock, Wm. Z/3425. (Ty.) | M. Nov. 13/16. R/Enq. |
| C. IX | Rowett, E. Z/4701. (B.) | M. April 29/17. |
| ? | Foster, L.S. Ernest Walter. Z/356. (L.) (Fr. Nelson.) | M. April 23/17. |
| ? | Hughes, Wm. Hugh. Z/799. (M.) | W. Unoff. M. April 28/17. |

### Howe Battalion.

| | | |
|---|---|---|
| | **Sikes, Sub.-Lieut. R. H.** | K. April 24/17. Det.D./B. |
| | **Yeoman, Sub.-Lieut. W. R.** | W. and M. April 24/17. |
| A. I | Johnson, A. D. Z/1012. (B.) | M. April 25/17. |
| A. III | Wilson, Robert. Z/4173. (Cl.) | M. Feb. 17/17. |
| B. | Billen, J. H. R/251. | M. April 24/17. |

**Naval Division, Royal**—contd.

*B.E.F.*

**2nd Brigade**—contd.

**Howe Battalion**—contd.

| | | |
|---|---|---|
| B. | Cooper, Jas. Mason. Z/3453. | M. April 24/17. |
| B. | Rowe, Edwin. Z/1005. | K. Feb. 17/17. Det.D./B. |
| B. I | Webb, Arthur Claude. Z/4633. (T.) | W. and M. Feb. 17/17. |
| ‡D. XV | Macgregor, Andrew. Z/4190. (Cl.) | M. Nov. 13/16. R/Enq. |
| ? | Broadhead, Elijah. Z/6058. (T.) | W. and M. Feb. 17/17. |
| ? | Craig, P.O. Andrew. Z/2808. (Cl.) | M. Feb. 17/17. |
| ? | Duke, Wm. Thos. Z/6998. (T.) | W. and M. Feb. 17/17. |
| ? | Jennings, James. Z/8010. (T.) | M. Feb. 17/17. |
| ? | Ross, Robert. Z/2806. (Cl.) | W. and M. Feb. 17/17. |
| ? | Salt, Joseph H. Z/3355. | M. Feb. 17/17. |
| ? | Thacker, John. R/178. | M. Feb. 17/17. |
| ? | Walker, Jas. Wm. X/280. (K.) | K. Nov. 13/16. Det.D./B. |
| ? I.T.M. | Wheeler, L.S. Frank. Z/70. (M.) (189 Bgde.) | M. Nov. 14/16. |

**1st Marine Battalion.**

| | | |
|---|---|---|
| ‡ | **Holmes, 2nd Lieut. H. C.** | M. April 28/17. |
| | **Lion, Lieut. N. L.** | M. April 28/17. |
| | **Marsh, 2nd Lieut. F. S.** | M. April 28/17. |
| | **Platts, Lieut. E. L.** | M. April 28/17. |
| | **Robinson, Lt. Lawrence W.** | K. Feb. 17/17. Det.D./B. |
| | **Roe, 2nd Lieut. Cyril Gordon.** | M. April 28/17. |
| | **Upham, 2nd Lieut. H. E. R.** | K. Nov. 13/16. Det.D./B. R/Enq. |
| A. II | Andrews, Ed. Stanley. S/1172. (Ply.) | M. Feb. 17/17. |
| A. II | Annetts, Chris. G. 1616. | M. April 23/17. |
| A. | Austin, Chas. Norton. 16935. (Ch.) | M. Feb. 17/17. |
| A. | Bennett, Arthur. 1229. (Pl.) | M. April 28/17. |
| A. I | Best, Thos. James. 18158. | M. April 28/17. |
| A. I | Chambers, Wm. Thos. S/838. (Ch.) | M. April 28/17. |
| A. | Chandler, Wm. Richard. 1370. | M. April 28/17. |
| ‡A. I | Cooke, Arthur Edw. S/1669. (Ch.) | M. April 28/17. |
| A. I | Crawford, Alf. Geo. Thos. S/1621. (Po.) | M. April 28/17. |
| A. II | Fellingham, Cpl. Harry. 19815. (Ch.) | M. Feb. 17/17. |
| A. | Flanagan, Wilson. S/420. (Ch.) | M. Feb. 17/17. |
| A. IV | Furber, Chas. John. S/1080. (Ch.) | M. April 28/17. |
| •A. IV | Gray, Henry. S/18594. (Po.) | M. April 23/17. |
| •A. | Guy, Charles. 1681. | M. April 23/17. |
| A. IV | Hampshire, Tom. S/1298. (Ch.) | M. April 28/17. |
| A. I | Heath, L.-Cpl. Bert. 1792. (Ch.) | M. April 28/17. |
| A. | Higgs, Donald W. S/1683. (Po.) | M. April 28/17. |
| A. | Huckvale, John Chas. 1539. (Ply.) | M. April 28/17. |
| A. II | Johnson, Ernest J. S/55. (Ch.) | M. Feb. 17/17. |
| ‡A. IV | Mitchell, Ernest. S/863. (Ply.) | M. April 28/17. |
| A. L.G.S. | Monks, Harold. S/1514 (Ch.) | M. Feb. 17/17. |
| A. | Paterson, Alexander. S/606. (Ch.) | M. April 28/17. |
| A. | Smith, H. C. S/1246. | M. April 28/17. |
| •B. VII | Bird, E. 1618. (Po.) | M. April 27/17. |
| B. L.G.S. | Brewer, Wm. 17471. (Po.) | M. April 28/17. |
| B. | Britton George. 1651. (Ply.) | M. April 28/17. |
| •B. VI | Clarke, Geo. Wm. S/1544. (Ch.) | M. April 28/17. |
| •B. VI | Cox, Frederick Wm. S/410. | M. April 28/17. |
| B. VII | Davis, H. 228. | M. April 28/17. |
| B. | Dennett, Fredk. S/1588. (Po.) | M. April 28/17. |
| B. VII | Eames, L.-Cpl. Alfred Jas. S/1455. (Po.) | M. April 28/17. |

**Naval Division, Royal—contd.**

## *B.E.F.*

**2nd Brigade**—contd.

**1st Marine Battalion**—contd.

| | | |
|---|---|---|
| ‡B. VIII | Elliott, R. 1793. | Unoff. M., bel. K. **April 28/17.** Conf. and Det. |
| B. | Fisher, John. 12264. (Ply.) | M. **Nov. 13/16.** |
| B. VII | Foster, G. 1194. | M. **April 28/17.** |
| ‡B. V | Goodchild, Wm. Walter. S/153. (Ply.) | M. **April 28/17.** |
| B. VIII | Higgins, Albert Edw. S/1462. (Ch.) | M. **April 28/17.** |
| B. V | Hilton, G. 861. (Po.) | M. **April 28/17.** |
| ‡B. VII | Hodder, G. 1106. (Po.) | M. **April 28/17.** |
| B. VI | Humphreys, Frank. S/1428. (Pl.) | M. **April 28/17.** |
| •B. VI | Hutchings, Fredk. John. S/1415. (Po.) | M. **April 28/17.** |
| •B. | Keywood, George. 19598. | M. **April 28/17.** |
| B. VII | Lee, John. 1021. | M. **April 28/17.** |
| B. VII | Lewis, Sidney. 1518. | M. **April 28/17.** |
| B. VIII | Myerscough, John. 1361. (Pl.) | M. **April 28/17.** |
| B. VI | Neale, V. G. 1678. | M. **April 28/17.** |
| B. VIII | O'Hara, James. S/915. (Ch.) | M. **April 28/17.** |
| B. VII | Roe, S. H. 1599. | M. **April 28/17.** |
| B. VII | Staples, Robt. Jas. S/1431. (Ch.) | M. **April 28/17.** |
| B. | Stokes, Harold Chas. S/392. (Ch.) | M. **April 28/17.** |
| B. | Tilley, Cpl. Wm. J. A. 13677. (Ch.) | M. **April 28/17.** |
| B. V | Walker, W. 886. (Ch.) | M. **April 28/17.** |
| B. VIII | Whittaker, L.-Cpl. Henry Tattersall. S/1492. (Ch.) | M. **April 28/17.** |
| ‡C. | Barras, T. F. 16978. (Ply.) | M. **April 23/17.** |
| C. IX | Bate, Chas. H. S/1164. (Ply.) | M. **Feb. 17/17.** |
| C. | Brooke, Peter. 905. (Po.) | M. **April 28/17.** |
| •C. XI | Buckley, Basil. 1225. (Ch.) | M. **April 28/17.** |
| C. X | Bull, Philip Geo. 1729. (Po.) | M. **April 28/17.** |
| C. X | Buxton, L.-Cpl. Alfred. 587. (Ply.) | M. **April 28/17.** |
| C. XI | Daniels, W. F. S/1722. (Po.) | M. **April 28/17.** |
| C. | Eden, Cpl. Geo. Fredk. S/1270. (Po.) | M. **Feb. 17/17.** |
| C. | Forster, Wm. Robinson. 17539. | M. **April 28/17.** |
| C. IX | Garner, W. J. 6518. | M. **April 28/17.** |
| C. IX | Goodacre, G. 18877. (Ch.) | M. **April 28/17.** |
| C. | Green, Wm. John. 1635. | M. **April 28/17.** |
| C. IX | Hembury, Wm. Geo. S/1744. (Po.) | M. **April 28/17.** |
| ‡C. XII | Hodgetts, A. S/1565. (Po.) | M. **May 26/17.** |
| C. X | Irwin, John. 1735. | M. **April 28/17.** |
| C. XII | Jameson, Henry. S/1141. (Ch.) | M. **April 28/17.** |
| C. XII | Latham, Percy. 1870. (Ch.) | M. **April 28/17.** |
| C. XI | Lawrence, S. C. S/1745. (Po.) | M. **April 28/17.** |
| C. IX | Liggins, Regd. John. S/1375. (Po.) | M. **Feb. 17/17.** |
| C. | Lindsay, Wm. Edmund. 1418. | M. **April 28/17.** |
| C. X | Martin, Ernest Harold. S/1401. (Po.) | M. **April 28/17.** |
| C. L.G.S. | Milner, Robt. Victor. S/1284. (Ch.) | M. **April 28/17.** |
| C. | Morgan, J. A. 1598. (Ch.) | M. **April 28/17.** |
| C. X | Pickford, Wm. 1665. (Ch.) | M. **April 28/17.** |
| C. IX | Pritchard, F. E. 1051. (Pl.) | M. **April 28/17.** |
| C. XII | Rolfe, Wm. Calet. 18843. (Ch.) | M. **April 28/17.** |
| C. XII | Searle, James. 19834. (Ch.) | M. **April 28/17.** |
| C. X | Shaw, George. 16869. | M. **April 28/17.** |
| C. XII | Stagles, W. E. 19846. (Ch.) | M. **April 28/17.** |
| C. | Stapleton, John. 16946. (Po.) | M. **April 28/17.** |

**Naval Division, Royal—contd.**

## *B.E.F.*

**2nd Brigade—contd.**

**1st Marine Battalion—contd.**

| | | |
|---|---|---|
| C. | Unthank, Joseph. 17095. | Unoff. M. Nov. 13/16. |
| C. | Waldron, Albert. 15518. | M. April 28/17. |
| C. X | Woodham, Geo. 1276. | M. April 28/17. |
| ‡D. L.G.S. | Bradshaw, L.-Cpl. Edward. 16976. (Ply.) | M. April 28/17. |
| D. | Brett, Wm. E. 197870. (Ch.) | Unoff. M. end of April/17. |
| D. L.G.S. | Briggs, E. E. 16972. (Ply.) | M. April 28/17. |
| D. XV | Bulcock, J. 7508. | M. April 28/17. |
| D. | Chapman, A.-Sgt. Hy. Ellis. 15873. (Po.) | M. April 28/17. |
| D. XVI | Collett, Wm. Alfred. S/1902. | M. April 28/17. |
| ‡D. XVI | Culver, Horace. S/887. | M. April 28/17. |
| D. XIII | Harrington, Clifford Norton. 18809. (Ch.) | M. Feb. 17/17. |
| D. XVI | Hobbs, H. 1402. | M. April 28/17. |
| *D. XVI | Hunt, Henry. S/468. (Ch.) | M. April 28/17. |
| D. | Miller, Robt. Henry. 19811. (Ch.) | M. Nov. 13/16. |
| D. L.G.S. | Musson, Leonard. 1427. (S.) | M. April 28/17. |
| *D. XV | Temple, G. W. 7439. (Ch.) | M. April 28/17. |
| D. L.G.S. | Treacher, Thos. 18738. (Ch.) | M. Nov. 13/16. R/Enq |
| D. XVI | Trinder, T. 1819. | K. April 28/17. Det.D./B. |
| D. XIV | West, Albert Jas. S/1557. (Po.) | M. April 28/17. |
| *D. XIV | Whiting, Albert Edwin. 18469. (Po.) | M. April 28/17. |
| D. XIV | Yates, Percy. S/1528. (Pl.) | M. April 28/17. |
| ? | Bewley, A.-Cpl. J. R. 17442. (Ch.) | M. Feb. 17/17. |
| ? | Bruce, Harry E. 16361. (Ch.) | M. Feb. 17/17. |
| ? | Clark, Edw. Horace. 17165. (Po.) | M. April 28/17. |
| ? | Davis, Geo. Wm. S/1552. (Po.) | M. April 28/17. |
| ? | Finch, A.-Cpl. Frederick. 16828. (Ch.) | M. Feb. 17/17. |
| ? | Foster, Frederick. S/1228. (Ch.) | M. Feb. 17/17. |
| ? | Gunnall, Henry Jas. 1795. (Ch.) | M. April 28/17. |
| ? | Hinchcliff, Wm. Chas. S/551. (Ch.) | M. April 28/17. |
| ? | Hobbs, Reginald. 17634. (Ch.) | M. Feb. 17/17. |
| ? | Leggatt, A.-Cpl. Herb. S/297. (Ch.) | M. April 28/17. |
| *? | Pessol, L.-Cpl. Sam. 3362. (Ply.) | K. Feb. 17/17. Det.D./B. |
| ? | Sarson, P. 19404. | Unoff. M. April 27/17. |
| ? | Smallwood, Benjamin. 1237. (Po.) | M. April 28/17. |
| ? VII | Smith, Walter Chas. S/1294. (Ch.) | M. April 28/17. |
| ? | Smyth, Reg. Abbett. S/979. (Ch.) | M. Feb. 17/17. |
| ? | Treves, A. S/1467. (Ch.) | M. April 28/17. |
| ‡? | Willson, A.-Cpl. F. F. S/849. | M. April 28/17. |
| ? | Winders, Louis Albert. S/1680. (Ch.) | M. April 28/17. |

**2nd Marine Battalion.**

| | | |
|---|---|---|
| | **Burton-Fanning, Capt. N. E. E.** | M. April 28/17. |
| | **Campbell, Capt. J.** | M. April 28/17. |
| | **Hardy, 2nd Lieut. P. E. R.** | M. April 28/17. |
| | **Lake, 2nd Lieut. W. A.** | M. April 28/17. |
| | **Markham, Lieut. H. E.** (Fr. Collingwood Bn.) | M. April 26/17. |
| | **Walker, 2nd Lieut. D. H.** | M. April 28/17. |
| A. | Ballance, L.-Cpl. Robt. S/605. (Po.) | M. April 28/17. |
| A. I. | Barlow, C. H. 677. | M. April 28/17. |
| ‡A. III | Beaumont, Leonard. 18474. | M. April 28/17. |
| A. | Branson, Wm. Hay. 332. | M. April 28/17. |
| *A. II | Brassington, J. T. S/1551. | M. April 28/17. |

**Naval Division, Royal**—contd.

## *B.E.F.*

**2nd Brigade**—contd.

**2nd Marine Battalion**—contd.

‡A. II Bromfield, S. F. 1624. M. April 28/17.
A. IV Churchill, Wm. Chas. S/1557. (Po.) M. April 28/17.
*A. II Clarke, George. 18473. M. April 28/17.
A. Davis, T. S/1664. (Po.) M. April 28/17.
A. II Elmes, P.O. J. R. 1560. (S.) M. April 28/17.
A. III Exley, Edward. 1279. M. April 28/17.
A. Fawcett, Sig. Harry. S/1280. (Po.) M. April 28/17.
A. Flear, Frank Cyril. S/1662. (Po.) M. April 28/17.
A. I Green, George Wm. 1566. M. April 28/17.
A. Hacking, P.O. Robt. S/671. M. April 28/17.
A. IV Holder, Alfred H. F. F. S/1899. (Ch) M. April 28/17.
‡A. II Holdsworth, Cpl. T. 1251. M. April 28/17.
A. III Hulton, Chas. A. 1898. (Ch.) M. April 28/17.
*A. Jarvis, Allen. 877. M. April 28/17.
A. I Joyce, Chas. Wilford. S/887. (Po.) W. Unoff. M. April 28/17.
A. L.G.S. Kearney, John. S/1072. (Ply.) M. April 28/17.
A. L.G.S. Lawley, W. 18172. (Po.) M. April 28/17.
A. III Matthews, Samuel. S/1467. (Po.) M. April 28/17.
A. II Myers, S. S/693. M. April 28/17.
A. IV Panter, Percy Thos. S/1720. (Ch.) M. April 28/17.
A. IV Pardington, Fred Bernard. 1713. M. April 28/17.
A. I Pearce, Albert W. 1291. (Po.) M. April 28/17.
A. I Pippard, V. R. 18598. M. April 28/17.
A. III Pocok, Walter H. S/1230. (Ply.) M. April 28/17.
A. III Poynter, Stephen Geo. S/1707. (Ply.) M. April 28/17.
*A. Price, Sydney. S/676. M. April 28/17.
A. III Rhodes, W. H. 1201. (Po.) M. April 28/17.
A. II Riddeough, Frank. 1275. (Po.) M. April 28/17.
A. Robinson, A.-Cpl. Thos. S/116. M. April 28/17.
A. Roser, Frederick A. 1688. (Ply.) M. April 28/17.
A. I Ryding, C. S/879. M. April 28/17.
A. IV Seward, L. 11661. (Po.) Unoff. M. April 28/17.
A. I Sexton, L.-Cpl. C. J. S/858. (Ch.) M. April 28/17.
*A. III Shilling, L.-Cpl. George. 16376. M. April 28/17.
A. Smith, A. H. S/1107. (Ply.) M. April 28/17.
A. II Spratt, David Jn. 17330. (Ply.) M. April 28/17.
A. IV L.G.S. Steele, A. 18643. (Po.) M. April 28/17.
A. Sullivan, L.-Sgt. Thos. 1211. (Ply.) M. April 28/17.
A. III Wardleworth, Joseph. 1733. (Ch.) M. April 28/17.
A. II Webster, Wm. S/1168. (Ply.) M. April 28/17.
A. I Wilcock, E. 1462. (Ply.) M. April 28/17.
A. IV Willman, J. E. 1310. (Ply.) M. April 28/17.
B. VII Blackamore, Thos. Hy. S/79. (Po.) M. April 28/17.
B. VII Bohan, John. S/1216. (Po.) M. April 28/17.
B. L.G.S. Bracey, Albert. S/1131. (Ply.) M. April 28/17.
B. VIII Bradshaw, Jn. Hy. S/1351. (Po.) M. April 28/17.
B. VIII Brookes, T. S/711. M. April 28/17.
B. Broom, Alfred. S/480. (Ply.) M. April 28/17.
B. Caine, J. P. 1213. M. April 28/17.
B. VII Carruthers, L.-Cpl. Bertie. 632. M. April 28/17.
B. Cole, Theodore. 486. (Po.) M. April 28/17.
B. Cox, Wm. Geo. Clifford. 1604. M. April 28/17.
B. VIII Dimsdale, T. 846. (S.) M. April 28/17.
B. L.G.S. Edwards, Horace. S/1163. M. April 28/17.

**Naval Division, Royal—contd.**

*B.E.F.*

**2nd Brigade—contd.**

**2nd Marine Battalion—contd.**

| | | |
|---|---|---|
| B. | Forder, Hry. W. S/1533. (Ply.) | M. April 28/17. |
| B. | Gandy, Geo. Richard. S/689. (Po.) | M. April 28/17. |
| B. L.G.S. | Gray, Joseph. S/285. (Po.) | M. April 28/17. |
| B. | Harris, Sydney. 1077. | M. April 28/17. |
| B. VI | Harrod, J. W. S/1260. (Ply.) | M. April 28/17. |
| B. VI | Hartland, Harold. S/1818. (Ch.) | M. April 28/17. |
| B. | Holmes, David. 16408. (Ply.) | *M. April 28/17. |
| B. L.G.S. | Homer, T. 767. (Po.) | M. April 28/17. |
| B. L.G.S. | Hunt, W. E. P/18467. | M. April 24/17. |
| B. VI | Jackson, Harry. 942. | M. April 28/17. |
| B. VIII | Jay, Henry. 775. | M. April 28/17. |
| B. VII | Jenkins, Alfred E. S/1227. (Po.) | M. April 28/17. |
| B. VI | Johnson, Ed. S/744. (Po.) | M. April 28/17. |
| B. VI | Jones, Wm. S/951. (Ply.) (Real name McBride.) | M. April 28/17. |
| B. | Lanigan, Peter. 841. | M. April 28/17. |
| B. VIII | Lines, Thos. Chas. S/1597. (Ply.) | M. April 28/17. |
| B. VIII | Matthews, Jas. Edwin. 1612. (Ply.) | M. April 28/17. |
| B. | Matthews, J. 16087. | M. April 28/17. |
| B. VIII | Murphy, Thos. S/141. (Ply.) | M. April 28/17. |
| *B. VI | Neville, Harold Wm. S/1404. (Po.) | M. April 28/17. |
| ‡B. | Newman, Wm. 1651. (Po.) | M. April 28/17. |
| *B. | Nuttall, L.-Cpl. Cliff. 266. | M. April 28/17. |
| B. VIII | O'Brien, A.-Sgt. Patrick. 16032. (Ply.) | M. April 28/17. |
| B. | Pratt, Edwin Norman. 1409. (Ch.) | M. April 28/17. |
| B. VI | Radford, Wm. John. S/1703. (Po.) | M. April 28/17. |
| B. VIII | Richardson, George. S/987. (Po.) | M. April 28/17. |
| B. VI | Richens, P.O. Francis Wilmott. 1698. | M. April 28/17. |
| *B. VI | Rogers, H. 18619. (Po.) | M. April 28/17. |
| B. VI | Rouse, Robert. 796. | M. April 28/17. |
| B. VII | Stone, William. 1149. (Po.) | M. May 4/17. |
| ‡B. | Taylor, Sergt. C. H. 315. | M. April 28/17. |
| B. VI | White, H. L. S/822. | M. April 28/17. |
| B. VII | Wilkinson, Wm. Herbt. S/898. (Ply.) | M. April 28/17. |
| C. XI | Andrews, Frank. S/1470. | M. April 28/17. |
| C. V | Bean, W. Henry. 1125. (Po.) | M. April 28/17. |
| C. | Beresford, Cpl. J. R. W. 348. | M. April 28/17. |
| C. | Brennan, Patrick. 1074. (Ply.) | M. April 28/17. |
| C. IX | Buckley, B. S/246. (Ply.) | M. April 28/17. |
| C. XII | Burrows, E. H. S/1484. (Ply.) | M. April 28/17. |
| C. X | Butt, E. E. 1612. | M. April 28/17. |
| C. | Chambers, L.-Cpl. A. H. Gilbert. 16471. (Po.) | M. April 28/17. |
| ‡C. L.G.S. | Clarkson, Fred. 1057. (Po.) | M. April 28/17. |
| *C. IX | Curtis, Ernest. S/1694. (Po.) | M. April 28/17. |
| C. X | Edgell, Cyril J. S/1713. (Po.) | M. April 28/17. |
| C. X | Farmer, George. S/1553. (Po.) | M. April 28/17. |
| C. X | Gibson, Geo. Young. S/1010. (Po.) | M. April 28/17. |
| C. L.G.S. | Goninon, Wm. 1624. (Po.) | M. April 28/17. |
| *C. IX | Green, John. 1456. (Ply.) | M. April 28/17. |
| C. XII | Greening, Leonard. 1258. | M. April 28/17. |
| C. IX | Harding, Ewart F. S/1662. (Ch.) | M. April 28/17. |
| C. XII | Harris, Sergt. F. 12443. (Ply.) | M. April 28/17. |
| C. X | Heath, Leonard C. S/1176. (Po.) | M. April 28/17. |

**Naval Division, Royal**—contd.

## *B.E.F.*

**2nd Brigade**—contd.

**2nd Marine Battalion**—contd.

| | | | |
|---|---|---|---|
| **C. XI** | Hornby, Wm. Albert. 17593. (Ply.) | **M. April 28/17.** | |
| **C.** | Inchley, Percy C. S/1686. (Ply.) | **M. April 28/17.** | |
| **C. L.G.S.** | Jackson, Edwin. 1144. | **M. April 28/17.** | |
| **•C. XI** | Jenkins, Harold. 1025. | **M. April 28/17.** | |
| **C. XII** | Jones, Cpl. Frank. S/307. (Ply.) | **M. April 28/17.** | |
| **•C. IX** | Jones, Sam. S/189. (Ply.) | **M. April 28/17.** | |
| **C.** | Kyle, James. 1749. (Ply.) | **M. April 28/17.** | |
| **C. IX** | Landers, Bruce. S/146. | **M. April 28/17.** | |
| **C. XII** | Lane, G. 1472. (Po.) | **M. April 28/17.** | |
| **C. XI** | Lee, Geo. 1696. (Ply.) | **M. April 28/17.** | |
| **C. IX** | Long, James. S/1569. | **M. April 28/17.** | |
| **C. IX** | McDowell, Jos. Patrick. 17427. (Ply.) | **M. April 28/17.** | |
| **‡C. XII** | Mackenzie, L.-Cpl. Ian. S/1425. (Po) | **K. April 28/17.** | Det.D./B. |
| **C. X** | Macnamara, John Jos. S/1141. | **M. April 28/17.** | |
| **C. IX** | Moore, Arthur. S/1422. (Ch.) | **M. April 28/17.** | |
| **C. XI** | Moyle, Conrad. S/1554. (Ply.) | **M. April 28/17.** | |
| **C. IX** | Parvin, W. G. 1718. (Ply.) | **M. April 28/17.** | |
| **C. XII** | Paull, W. G. 1704. (Po.) | **M. April 28/17.** | |
| **C. XII** | Platten, R. J. S/911. | **M. April 28/17.** | |
| **C.** | Powell, Geo. Chas. 1875. | **M. April 28/17.** | |
| **C. IX** | Price, Chas. Thos. S/1486. (Po.) | **M. April 28/17.** | |
| **•C. XI** | Pritchard, F. S. 1694. | **M. April 28/17.** | |
| **C. IX** | Pugh, Albert Charles. 1643. | **M. April 28/17.** | |
| **C. X** | Rackley, Herbert. 1589. (Ply.) | **M. April 28/17.** | |
| **C. IX** | Rich, Sergt. Gerald Jas. 14525. | **M. April 28/17.** | |
| **C. X** | Rowley, Chas. C. Z/1377. (Ply.) | **M. April 28/17.** | |
| **C.** | Scratcherd, L.-Sergt. E. 14374. | **M. April 28/17.** | |
| **C. XII** | Smith, Thomas. 1198. | **M. April 28/17.** | |
| **•C. IX** | Stafford, W. E. 1689. (Ply.) | **M. April 28/17.** | |
| **C.** | Thompson, Wm. Slagg. S/885. (Ply.) | **M. April 28/17.** | |
| **C. IX** | Vicars, Thos. S/1140. (Ply.) | **M. April 28/17.** | |
| **C. XII** | Vinall, Wm. Thos. 18223. (Po.) | **M. April 28/17.** | |
| **C. XI** | Walters, E. W. S/1746. (Po.) | **M. April 28/17.** | |
| **C. XII** | Watson, G. C. H. S/1398. (Ply.) | **M. April 28/17.** | |
| **C. X** | Whalley, John. S/1348. (Po.) | **M. April 28/17.** | |
| **C. XII** | Wheelhouse, Jn. Hry. S/1345. (Po.) | **M. April 20/17.** | |
| **C. X** | Williamson, Stanley. S/1389. (Po.) | **M. April 28/17.** | |
| **‡C. L.G.S.** | Wood, A. 16503. (Ply.) | **M. April 28/17.** | |
| **‡C. IX** | Woods, John Ed. 1199. (Po.) | **M. April 28/17.** | |
| **‡C. XII** | Woodwards, W. J. S/1699. (Ply.) | **M. April 28/17.** | |
| **D. L.G.S.** | Agar, Geo. Atkin. S/1307. (Po.) | **M. April 28/17.** | |
| **D.** | Aslett, Geo. Henry. 1662. | **M. April 28/17.** | |
| **•D. L.G.S.** | Baker, Harry. S/304. (Ply.) | **M. April 28/17.** | |
| **D. XV** | Benson, Clarence. 1203. (Po.) | **M. April 28/17.** | |
| **D.** | Clayton, L.-Cpl. Fred. S/769. | **M. April 28/17.** | |
| **D. XVI** | Coate, Herbert. 1755. | **K. May 26/17.** | Det.D./B. |
| **D. XIII** | Cooper, Cyril Victor. S/1495. (Po.) | **M. April 28/17.** | |
| **•D.** | Corrigan, Patrick. 496. | **M. April 28/17.** | |
| **D.** | Cousins, A.-Cpl. Fredk. W. 16365. | **M. April 28/17.** | |
| **D. XIV** | Culverwell, L.-Cpl. Cecil. 15984. (Ply.) | **M. April 28/17.** | |
| **D.** | Cuthro, Jas. 1446. | **M. April 28/17.** | |
| **D. XVI** | Eatwell, Francis E. 17027. | **M. April 28/17.** | |
| **D.** | Farnworth, Amos. S/937. (Ply.) | **M. April 28/17.** | |
| **D. XV** | Fish, W. S/706. (Po.) | **M. April 28/17** | |

**Naval Division, Royal—contd.**

## *B.E.F.*

**2nd Brigade—contd.**

### 2nd Marine Battalion.

| | | |
|---|---|---|
| D. XVI | Francis, Richard D. 1428. (Po.) | M. April 26/17. |
| D. XV | Goodall, Geo. W. S/180. (Ply.) | M. April 28/17. |
| D. | Griswald, J. N. 18541. (Po.) | M. April 28/17. |
| D. | Hancock, Cpl. Edwin John. 17601. (Po.) | M. April 28/17. |
| D. | Harding, Geo. 1128. (Po.) | M. April 28/17. |
| D. XIII | Hatch, D. S/1259. (Po.) | M. April 28/17. |
| D. | Hazlehurst, Alfred. S/603. (Ply.) | M. April 28/17. |
| D. XV | Hermon, Fredk. Chas. S/1479. (Po.) | M. April 28/17. |
| D. XVI | Holdsworth, J. W. 1450. | M. April 26/17. |
| D. L.G.S. | Howie, Robt. A. 18283. | M. April 28/17. |
| D. XIV | Humber, J. 1433. | M. April 28/17. |
| D. | Hunt, John Chas. 13889. | M. April 28/17. |
| D. | Hurst, Herbert. 221. | M. April 28/17. |
| D. XIV | Hutchings, Alfred Jas. 1857. (Ch.) | M April 28/17. |
| D. XVI | Illingworth, Harold. S/937. (Po.) | M. April 28/17. |
| D. XVI | Joyner, Harold W. S/1044. (Po.) | M. April 28/17. |
| D. XIV | Kefford, W. J. 1476. (Ch.) | M. April 28/17. |
| D. XV | Lincoln, Alfred John. 1492. (Po.) | M. April 28/17 |
| D. XVI | Lowe, R. W. 1245. (Ply.) | M. April 28/17. |
| D. XIII | Lyttleton, Fred. 479. (Ply.) | M. April 28/17 |
| D. XIV | Magennis, Wm. S/1368. (Po.) | M. April 28/17. |
| D. | Maidens, R. 1315. (Po.) | M. April 28/17. |
| D. XVI | May, Cecil. 1533. (Po.) | M. April 28/17. |
| D. XIV | Morgan, P. J. 1643. (Ply.) | M. April 28/17. |
| D. XVI | Nutter, T. W. A. 17156. | M. April 28/17. |
| D. XV | Robertson, John A. 16607. | M. April 28/17. |
| D. XIII | Saunders, Jas. S/332. | M. April 28/17. |
| D. XV | Sawyer, J. 1766. | M. April 28/17. |
| ‡D. | Shergold, Fred Chas. S/1312. (Po.) | M. April 28/17. |
| ‡D. | Stocks, Chas. Ernest. 1728. | M. April 28/17. |
| D. XIII | Swain, C. 18829. (Ply.) | M. April 26/17. |
| D. XIII | Temple, A.-Sergt. Jos. Geo. 18499. (Po.) | M. April 28/17. |
| D. XVI | Thompson, Walter. S/1328. (Ply.) | M. April 28/17. |
| D. XV | Tremlett, C. C. 1749. | M. April 28/17. |
| D. XV | Walters, L. F. J. S/1746. (Po.) | M. April 28/17. |
| D. XV | Waterhouse, Leonard. 1292. | M. April 28/17. |
| D. XV | Wheeler, Albert. 1453. (Ply.) | W. Unoff. M. April 24/17. |
| D. | Wheeler, John. 1700. | M. April 28/17. |
| ? | Brough, J. H. 313. | M. April 28/17. |
| ? | Coleman, Clifford. 18561. | M. Nov. 13/16. R/Enq. |
| ? L.G.S. | English, H. S/8841. (Po.) | M. April 28/17. |
| ? | Hayles, Col.-Sergt. G. S. 14072. | M. April 28/17. |
| ? | Holt, Albert Robert. 16274. (Ply.) | M. April 28/17. |
| ? | Lambert, Edw. S/396. (Po.) | M. April 28/17. |
| ‡? | McMullen, Dennis. S/1621. (Ply.) | M. April 28/17. |
| ? I.T.M. | Murphy, W. 1150. (Ply.) (189 Bgde.) | M. April 28/17. |
| ? | Sanders, A/Sergt. John Mark. 14813. (Ply.) | M. April 28/17. |
| ? | Stolberg, Chas. 19478. (Ch.) | M. April 28/17. |
| ? | Thompson, Josiah. 1246. (Ply.) | M. April 28/17. |
| ? | Tuppen, Alfred Jos. Hy. S/1221. | M. April 28/17. |
| ? | Wakeham, Richard. 7915. (Ply.) | M. April 28/17. |
| ? | Walker, Thos. S/954. (Ply.) | K. Nov. 13/16. Det.D./B. |
| ? | Williams, A. S/1325. (Ply.) | M. April 28/17. |
| ? | Williams, Benjamin W. 1320. | M. April 28/17. |

## NEWFOUNDLAND REGIMENT.

### *B.E.F.*

| | | |
|---|---|---|
| 1 | **Alcock, 2nd Lieut. A.** | M., bel. K. April 14/17. |
| 1 | **Gardner, 2nd Lieut. C.** | M. April 14/17. |
| 1 | **Holloway, Lieut. R. P** | M., bel. K. April 14/17. |
| 1 | **Outerbridge, Lieut. Norman A.** | W. and M. April 14/17. |
| 1 | **Rowsell, M.C., Capt. R. S.** | W and M. April 14/17. |
| 1 | **Smith, 2nd Lieut. S. R.** | M. April 14/17. |
| 1 | **Stephenson, 2nd Lieut. J. S.** | M. April 14/17. |
| 1 A. | Adams, W. 2306. | M. April 14/17. |
| 1 A. | Blackmore, E. 1578. | M. April 14/17. |
| 1 A. | Clarke, W. J. 2574. | M. April 14/17. |
| 1 A. | Cranford, J. F. 2221. | M. April 14/17. |
| 1 A. | Frampton, H. 2198. | M. April 14/17. |
| 1 A. | Hewlett, A. 2333. | M. April 14/17. |
| 1 A. | Hoddinot, Sergt. L. 2234. | M. April 14/17. |
| 1 A. | Hollett, G. 1799. | M. April 14/17. |
| 1 A. | Ivany, L.-Cpl. W. C. 1201. | M. April 14/17. |
| 1 A. | Keats, W. 203. | M. April 14/17. |
| 1 A. | Keefe, S. 2043. | M. April 14/17. |
| 1 A. | Keeping, J. G. 2917. | M. April 14/17. |
| 1 A. | March, Cpl. C. L. 86. | M. April 14/17. |
| 1 A. | Martin, L. 2682. | M. April 14/17. |
| 1 A. | Mifllen, Cpl. C. J. 2963. | M. April 14/17. |
| 1 A. | Penney, C.-S.-M. A. J. 6. | M. April 14/17. |
| 1 A. | Penton, I. 2589. | M. April 14/17. R/Enq. |
| 1 A. | Piercey, B. 421. | M. April 14/17. |
| 1 A. | Polfrey, P. 2582. | M. April 14/17. |
| 1 A. | Reilly, P. 2902. | M. April 14/17. |
| 1 A. | Richards, L.-Cpl. F. McN. 8. | M. April 14/17. R/Enq |
| 1 A. | Rose, G. 2919. | M. April 14/17. |
| 1 A. | Ryan, B. 123. | M.. April 14/17. |
| 1 A. | Sherran, Cpl. N. 2458. | M. April 14/17. |
| 1 A. | Sinnott, S. 2089. | M. April 14/17. |
| 1 A. | St. John, J. 2493. | M. April 14/17. |
| 1 A. | Stone, H. 2099. | M. April 14/17. |
| 1 A. | Tarrant, E. 2446. | M. April 14/17. |
| 1 A. | Taylor, L.-Cpl E. F. 2525. | M. April 14/17. |
| 1 A. | Tucker, J. 2684. | M. April 14/17. |
| 1 A. | Vokey, H. 2614. | M. April 14/17. |
| 1 A. | Wills, C. 2681. | M. April 14/17. |
| 1 B. | Abbott, B. 2020. | M April 14/17. |
| 1 B. | Attwood, G. 1525. | M. April 14/17. |
| ‡1 B. | Ball, M. 2814. | M. April 14/17. |
| 1 B. | Bastow, A. C. 2750. | M. April 14/17. |
| 1 B. | Bennett, P. F. 770. | M. April 14/17. |
| 1 B. | Blackhall, Sergt. J. 1738. | M. April 14/17. |
| 1 B. | Brown, R. 2197. | M April 14/17. |
| 1 B. | Butler, J. 1289. | M. April 14/17. |
| 1 B. | Cake, A. E. 2463. | M. April 14/17. |

**Newfoundland Regiment**—contd.

*B.E.F.*

| | | |
|---|---|---|
| 1 B. | Carroll, B. 1903. | M. April 14/17. |
| 1 B. | Clark, W. 2268. | M. April 14/17. |
| 1 B. | Collins, J. 567. | M. April 14/17. |
| 1 B. | Cook, E. 2229. | M. April 14/17. |
| 1 B. | Crane, L.-Cpl. N. 363. | M. April 14/17. |
| 1 B. | Cuff, H. 524. | M. April 14/17. |
| 1 B. | Dawe, W. 184. | M. April 14/17. |
| 1 B. | Elsworth, J. 2469. | M. April 14/17. |
| 1 B. | Follett, A. 2920. | M. April 14/17. |
| 1 B. | Gallant, M. 2293. | M. April 14/17. |
| 1 B. | Groves, D. 1724. | M. April 14/17. |
| 1 B. | Hann, B. 1255. | M. April 14/17. |
| 1 B. | Hartley, Cpl. Arthur. Percy. 174. | M. April 14/17. |
| 1 B. | Holmes, A. 2551. | M. April 14/17. |
| 1 B. | Hussey, H. 2255. | M. April 14/17. |
| 1 B. | Janes, E. 2450. | M. April 14/17. |
| 1 B. | Jesseau, L.-Cpl. A. 249. | M. April 14/17. |
| ‡1 B. | Kean, W. 2599. | M. April 14/17. |
| 1 B. | King, Herbert H. 1981. | M. April 14/17. |
| 1 B. | King, W. J. 2430. | M. April 14/17. |
| ‡1 B. | Lane, G. 1482. | M. April 14/17. |
| 1 B. | Le Drew, H. 2633. | M. April 14/17. |
| 1 B. | Leonard, J. 2865. | M. April 14/17. |
| 1 B. | Luft, W. A. 1598. | M. April 14/17. |
| 1 B. | McKay, M. J. 1509. | M. April 14/17. |
| 1 B. | Madore, G. A. 1458. | M. April 14/17. |
| 1 B. | Martin, R. B. 2936. | M. April 14/17. |
| 1 B. | Meadus, C. J. 1015. | M. April 14/17. |
| 1 B. | Mercer, W. 2615. | M. April 14/17. |
| 1 B. | Mesher, C. A. 1727. | M. April 14/17. |
| 1 B | Morgan, G. 2867. | M. April 14/17. |
| 1 B. | Moulton, H. 2859. | M. April 14/17. |
| 1 B. | Pennell, C. 1428. | M. April 14/17. |
| 1 B. | Penney, A. J. 2696. | M. April 14/17. |
| 1 B. | Pretty, J. 2276. | M. April 14/17. |
| 1 B. | Rowsell, G. 1466. | M. April 14/17. |
| 1 B. | Skeans, F. 2267. | M. April 14/17. |
| 1 B. | Skinner, L.-Cpl. E. 2929. | M. April 14/17. |
| 1 B. | Smyth, T. 523. | M. April 14/17. |
| 1 B. | Stratton, F. 2715. | M. April 14/17. |
| 1 B. | Thompson, J. 139. | M. April 14/17. |
| 1 B. | Tilley, L.-Cpl. H. 307. | M. April 14/17. |
| 1 B. | Way, N. 2883. | M. April 14/17. |
| 1 C. | Bishop, C. G. 2524. | M. April 14/17. |
| 1 C. | Bollard, G. E. 2334. | M. April 14/17. |
| 1 C. | Booth, Sgt. John. 2405. | M. April 14/17. |
| 1 C. | Boyd, A. 2745. | M. April 14/17. |
| 1 C. | Brown, L.-Cpl. J. 2564. | M. April 14/17. |
| 1 C. | Caldwell, Sergt. E. C. 636. | M. April 14/17. R/Enq. |
| 1 C. | Chater, W. 2379. | M. April 14/17. |
| 1 C. | Cook, Cpl. A. S. 876. | M. April 14/17. |
| 1 C. | Crane, J. 2313. | M. April 14/17. |
| 1 C. | Cummings, A. 815. | M. April 14/17. |
| 1 C. | Delaney, B. 2775. | M. April 14/17. |
| 1 C. | Dicks, B. 2828. | M. April 14/17. |
| 1 C. | Dicks, J. A. 2390. | M. April 14/17. |
| 1 C. | Earls, J. J. 2747. | M. April 14/17. |
| 1 C. | Francis, A. E. 2918. | M. April 14/17. |

**Newfoundland Regiment**—contd.

## *B.E.F.*

1 C. Fudge, J. 2839. M. April 14/17.
1 C. Gear, Sergt. J. J. 695. M. April 14/17.
1 C. Gradner, F. 2475. M. April 14/17.
1 C. Haliday, A. 1885. M. April 14/17.
1 C. Harris, W. G. 2817. M. April 14/17.
1 C. Heath, Thos. 1666. M. April 14/17. R/Enq.
1 C. Hudson, L. G. 2214. M. April 14/17.
1 C. Hurley, R. J. 2982. M. April 14/17.
1 C. Hynes, L. E. 806. M. April 14/17.
1 C. Jackman, Cpl. A. 533. M. April 14/17. R/Enq
1 C. Jacobs, H. G. 2253. M. April 14/17.
1 C. Jones, H. 2783. M. April 14/17.
1 C. Kavanagh, E. 2548. M. April 14/17.
1 C. Kearley, W. J. 2372. M. April 14/17.
1 C. Knee, M. 2342. M. April 14/17.
1 C. Manuel, Cpl. A. 721. M. April 14/17.
1 C. Marks, L. 2961. M. April 14/17.
1 C. Marshall, J. H. 2432. M. April 14/17.
1 C. Martin, N. 2877. M. April 14/17.
1 C. Masters, W. 2797. M. April 14/17.
1 C. Mercer, P. 2374. M. April 14/17.
1 C. Moore, D. J. 741. M. April 14/17.
1 C. Moore, J. F. 2778. M. April 14/17.
1 C. Myers, C. 2601. M. April 14/17.
1 C. Neville, W. J. 376. M. April 14/17.
1 C. Normore, L. 2425. M. April 14/17.
1 C. Noseworthy, W. 2383. M. April 14/17.
1 C. O'Brien, J. J. 1378. M. April 14/17.
1 C. Patey, W. 1875. M. April 14/17.
1 C. Reid, J. H. 2414. M. April 14/17.
1 C. Rideout, G. 1595. M. April 14/17.
1 C. Ridout, T. 2455. M. April 14/17.
1 C. Ring, T. J. 2364. M. April 14/17.
1 C. Rose, P. 2474. M. April 14/17.
1 C. Rowsell, L.-Cpl. H. 2724. M. April 14/17.
1 C. Smith, Cpl. D. 2546. M. April 14/17.
1 C. Smith, W. H. 2868. M. April 14/17.
1 C. Snow, C. 2616. M. April 14/17.
1 C. Vaughan, J. 800. M. April 14/17.
1 C. Stead, J. 2487. M. April 14/17.
1 C. Stick, E. M. 2145. M. April 14/17.
1 C. Whelan, L.-Cpl. J. M. 2754. M. April 14/17.
1 C. Wiseman, C. 2000. M. April 14/17.
1 D. Bannister, Cpl. Whitfield. 889. M. April 14/17.
1 D. Bellows, L. 903. M. April 14/17.
1 D. Bennett, L.-Cpl. H. 910. M. April 14/17.
1 D. Benoit, W. 2683. M. April 14/17.
1 D. Beson, Sergt. P. 2232. M. April 14/17.
1 D. Colbourne, L.-Cpl B. S. 1675. M. April 14/17.
1 D. Collins, G. W. 2448. M April 14/17.
1 D. Connors, D. 649. M. April 14/17.
1 D. Costello, J 2593. M. April 14/17.
1 D. Coughlan, Louis. 2256. M. April 14/17.
1 D. Crocker, J. 2418. M. April 14/17.
1 D. Curtis, A. 2449. M. April 14/17.
1 D. Curtis, L.-Cpl. V. C. 2939. M. April 14/17.
1 D. Donnelly, W. 2163. M. April 14/17.

**Newfoundland Regiment**—contd.

*B.E.F.*

| | | |
|---|---|---|
| 1 D. | Doody, Cpl. M. A. 1982. | M. April 14/17. |
| 1 D. | Eddy, A. 2384. | M. April 14/17. |
| 1 D. | Frew, Cpl. M. 2246. | M. April 14/17. |
| 1 D. | Grouchy, Sergt. H. W. 2025. | M. April 14/17. |
| ‡1 D. | Halfyard, S. 2544. | M. April 14/17. |
| 1 D. | Harding, E. W. 2949. | M. April 14/17. |
| 1 D. | Harvey, H. 2336. | M. April 14/17. |
| 1 D. | Hayse, P. J. 2355. | M. April 14/17. |
| 1 D. | Healey, J. J. 2748. | M. April 14/17. |
| 1 D. | Hearn, A. 1024. | M. April 14/17. |
| 1 D. | Hynes, W. P. 2726. | M. April 14/17. |
| 1 D. | Johnston, G. 1930. | M. April 14/17. |
| 1 D. | Jordan, L.-Cpl. T. J. 1752. | M. April 14/17. |
| 1 D. | Keefe, A. 1971. | M. April 14/17. |
| 1 D. | Knowling, W. A 1693. | M. April 14/17. |
| 1 D. | Le Grow, R. 1972. | M. April 14/17. |
| 1 D. | McLean, Cpl. D. 2892. | M. April 14/17. |
| 1 D. | Manuel, H. 1838. | M. April 14/17. |
| 1 D. | Moakler, Sergt. J. P. 1766. | M. April 14/17. |
| 1 D. | Murray, A. 2733. | M. April 14/17. |
| 1 D. | Mutford, H. G. 2464. | M. April 14/17. |
| 1 D. | Neville, Cpl. R. 1080. | M. April 14/17. |
| 1 D. | Newell, Cpl. K. S. 1692. | M. April 14/17. |
| 1 D. | O'Rourke, Cpl. J. 1975. | M. April 14/17. |
| 1 D. | Oake, W. D. 1919. | M. April 14/17. |
| 1 D. | Osmond, A. F. 1131. | M. April 14/17. |
| 1 D. | Pearce, H. 1394. | M. April 14/17. |
| 1 D. | Power, F. 2652. | M. April 14/17. |
| 1 D. | Richards, D. 1082. | M. April 14/17. |
| 1 D. | Small, Cpl. T. 1389. | M. April 14/17. |
| 1 D. | Snow, J. 2703. | M. April 14/17. |
| 1 D. | Squires, K. 2055. | M. April 14/17. |
| 1 D. | Taylor, R. H. 1973. | M. April 14/17. |
| 1 D. | Thomas, Cpl. F. G. 1784. | M. April 14/17. |
| 1 D. | Vaters, J. E. 973. | M. April 14/17. |
| 1 D. | Verge, A. J. 1925. | M. April 14/17. |
| 1 D. | Woods, J. S. 2146. | M. April 14/17. |
| 1 D. | Wooldridge, J. H. 1993. | M. April 14/17. |

## NEW ZEALAND.

### AUCKLAND INFANTRY BATTALION.

*B.E.F.*

| | | |
|---|---|---|
| 1 6 | Perkins, R. S. B. 12/2080. | K. Sept. 26/16. Det.D./B. |
| *1 15 IX | Edmett, Eric Geoffrey. 24/1650. | W. and M. June 7/17. |
| ‡1 ? | Scanlon. 12/2106. | K. May 8/17. Det.D./B. (2nd cas.) R/Enq. |
| 2 3 | Adams, Leslie. 13/2994. | K. Oct. 15/16. Det.D./B. |
| 2 3 | Eoy, Jos. Michael. 24003. | M. Feb. 21/17. |
| 2 3 | Hopewell, L.-Cpl. Wilfred Vernon. 18801. | M. Feb. 21/17. |
| 2 3 | Price, S. 24051. | M. Feb. 21/17. |

**New Zealand—contd.**

**Auckland Infantry Battalion**—contd.

*B.E.F.*

| | | |
|---|---|---|
| ‡2 3 | Smith, Ernest Albert. 20436. | W. Unoff. M. **June 8/17.** |
| 2 6 | Butler, E. A. O. 14385. | M. **Feb. 21/17.** |
| 2 6 | Johnston, Robert. 241696. | M. **Feb. 21/17.** |
| 2 6 | Williamson, Harold Jas. 24/1866. | M., bel. W. **Feb. 21/17.** |
| 2 15 | Carr, Alex 21207. | M. **Feb. 21/17.** |
| 2 16 | McCabe, Geo. T. 13/3055. | M. **Feb. 26/17.** |
| ‡2 16 XIV | Norman, Arthur Henry. 18438. | M. **June 7/17.** |
| 2 16 | Webb, Robt. Byam. 25624. | M. **Feb. 21/17.** |
| ‡2 ? | Sullivan, A.-Cpl. Thos. Griffiths. 12/633. | M. **Feb. 21/17.** |

**CANTERBURY INFANTRY BATTALION.**

*B.E.F.*

| | | |
|---|---|---|
| ‡1 ? | Hay, Sergt. G. 6/58. | M. **Feb. 18/17.** |
| 2 1 | Hayman, L.-Cpl. Leslie. 6/3736. | D/W. **Oct. 1/16.** Det.D./B. |
| 2 2 | McDonald, Hugh David. 6/3798. | D/W. **Oct. 1/16.** Det.D./B. R/Enq |
| 2 12 | Larsen, A. 10240. | K. **Sept. 21/16.** Det.D./B. |
| 2 13 | Roper, Len. B. 6/3853. | K. **Oct. 1/16.** Det.D./B. |
| 2 ? | Derungs, Leonard Reg. 6/4022. | K. **Oct. 1/16.** Det.D./B. R/Enq. |
| 2 ? | Thoumine, David Edw. 10405. | K. **Oct. 1/16.** Det.D./B. |
| ‡2 ? | Whittaker, A. E. 6/4376. | M., bel. K. **June 7/17.** |

**MACHINE GUN CORPS.**

*B.E.F.*

| | | |
|---|---|---|
| ‡Sect. 3 | **Watson, 2nd Lieut. F. W.** | K. **June 7/17.** Det.D./B. |
| ‡ | Land, L.-Cpl. Edward. 23/477. | W. Unoff. M. **June 7/17.** |

**OTAGO INFANTRY BATTALION.**

*B.E.F.*

| | | |
|---|---|---|
| 1 4 | Joss, Chas. 83302. | M., bel. K. **Sept. 27/16.** Conf. and Det.D./B. |
| 1 10 | Finlayson, K. C. 8/918. | K. **Sept. 25/16.** Det.D./B. |
| 1 14 | Porter, Cpl. David. 8/2099. | K. **Sept. 27/16.** Det.D /B. |
| 1 14 | Walker, Joseph. 8/2168. | K. **Sept. 27/16.** Det.D./B. |
| 1 ? | Nelson, Wm. Peter. 23598. | K. **Sept. 27/16.** Det.D./B. |
| 2 ? | Bunting, Benjamin Harold. 13416. | K. **Oct. 1/16.** Det.D./B. |
| 2 ? | O'Connor, Percy Michael. 11095. | M., bel. K. **Sept. 15/16.** Conf. and Det.D./B. |

**OTAGO MOUNTED RIFLES.**

*E.E.F.*

| | | |
|---|---|---|
| *? | Bushell, Bmbr. D. F. W. 9/437. | K. **Mar. 27/17.** Det.D./B. |

New Zealand—contd.

## 3rd RIFLE BRIGADE.

### B.E.F.

| | | |
|---|---|---|
| 2 C. XI | Boyce, D. S. 24/694. | K. Sept. 15/16. Det.D./B. |

## WELLINGTON INFANTRY BATTALION.

### B.E.F.

| | | |
|---|---|---|
| 1 ? | Jones, Arthur Baynard. 11/325. | D/W. Oct. 30/16. Det.D./B. |
| 2 ? | McInnes, Cpl. H .A. 23861. | K. May 1/17. Det.D./B. |

## NORFOLK REGIMENT.

### B.E.F.

| | | |
|---|---|---|
| 1 | **Magnay, Capt. J. C. F.** | K. April 23/17. Conf. and Det.D./B. |
| ‡1 A. | Beales, C. 29510. | M. May 9/17. |
| ‡1 A. | Clarke, B. A. 16720. | M. May 14/17. |
| ‡1 A. | Daniels, C.-S.-M. J. J. 8665. | M. May 9/17. |
| 1 A. | Guyett, W. 43218. | M. April 23/17. |
| 1 A. | Smart, T. 43348. | M. April 28/17. |
| 1 A. I | Swann, P. W. 43297. | M. April 23/17. |
| 1 B. | Ainsworth, J. 13015. | M. April 23/17. |
| 1 B. VIII | Baxter, H. 6959. | M. April 23/17. |
| 1 B. V | Burnell, Alfred Wm. 13254. | M. May 9/17. |
| 1 B. VIII | Collison, T. W. 23346. | M. Unoff. W. Feb. 26/17. |
| 1 B. | Drew, W. 26474. | M. April 23/17. |
| 1 B. | Fox, H. 19173. | M. April 23/17. |
| *1 B. VII | Harvey, F. 26506. | K. April 23/17. Det.D./B. |
| 1 B. | Harvey, H. 29531. | M. April 23/17. |
| 1 B. | Howlett, Richd. Chas. 23600. | M. April 23/17. |
| 1 B. | Hunt, A. 19045. | M. April 23/17. |
| 1 B. | Matthews, L.-Cpl. F. 6861. (Fr. 3rd) | M. April 23/17. |
| 1 B. | Moore, Sergt. A. 10069. (Fr. 3rd.) | M. April 23/17. |
| 1 B. | Tidman, Percy. 16925. | W. and M. April 23/17. |
| 1 B. V | Vincent, Arth. Thos. 242565. (27002.) | W. and M. April 19/17. |
| 1 C. | Balls, Sergt. Walter. 3/8169. | W. and M. May 9/17. |
| ‡1 C. | Lyon, R. 26334. | M. May 18/17. |
| 1 C. | Williamson, G. A. 43392. | M. May 9/17. |
| ‡1 D. | Arnup, Sergt. H. 6662. | W. and M. April 23/17. |
| *1 D. | Burgess, L.-Sergt. H. 17210. | M. April 23/17. |
| 1 D. XVI | Carter, Richard. 15784. | M. April 23/17. |
| 1 D. XVI | Chapman, Donald Alf. 25649. | W. and M. April 23/17. |
| 1 D. | Farrow, F. 20948. | M. April 23/17. |
| 1 D. XII | Fitt, L.-Cpl. H. E. 9672. | M. April 23/17. |
| 1 D. | Olby, Sergt. J. 5936. | M. April 23/17. |
| ‡1 D. | Turner, L.-Cpl. F. 3/17318. | M. May 9/17. |
| 7 | **Dover, 2nd Lieut. W.** (Fr. 5th.) | W. and M. April 28/17. |
| 7 A. I | Adcock, A. S. 17683. | M. Oct. 12/16. R/Enq. |
| *7 A. II | Boughen, Wilfred James. 18360 | M. April 9/17. |
| *7 A. I | Ockenden, G. W. 26530. | K. April 9/17. Det.D./B. |
| *7 B. VI | Eaglestone, E. 22561. | W. and M. Oct. 12/16. R/Enq. |
| 7 B. VII | Gladden, L.-Cpl. F. 5520. | W. and M. Oct. 12/16. R/Enq. |

**Norfolk Regiment—contd.**

## *B.E.F.*

| | | |
|---|---|---|
| 7 B. VI | Newton, R. 40472. | M. April 28/17. |
| ‡7 B. | Nice, H. 16472. | W. and M. May 5/17. |
| 7 B. VII | Warnes, G. 10115. | W. and M. Oct. 12/16. R/Enq. |
| 7 C. XII | Bangay, Cpl. Wm. 7868. | M. April 28/17. |
| ‡7 C. | Beresford, J. W. 43051. | M. April 28/17. |
| 7 C. XI | Billing, Wm. Jas. 23490. | M. Oct. 12/16. R./Enq. |
| 7 C. XII | Blackburn, L.-Cpl. G. 19522. | M. April 28/17. |
| ‡7 C. | Brewster, W. 40639. | W. and M. May 7/17. |
| *7 C. | Brown, L.-Cpl. G. 29775. | M. April 28/17. |
| ‡7 C. | Brown, R. C. 40626. | M. April 28/17. |
| 7 C. | Capes, Herbert. 15200. | M. Aug. 12/16. R/Enq. |
| *7 C. | Carter, E. 40642. | M. April 28/17. |
| ‡7 C. | Couzens, A. 18196. | M. April 28/17. |
| ‡7 C. IX | Davis, Geo. 202772. (Fr. 4th.) | M. April 28/17. |
| ‡7 C. | Dix, B. 202793. | M. April 28/17. |
| ‡7 C. | Duroe, J. 40542. | W. and M. May 7/17. |
| 7 C. | Goreham, Arthur. 202130. | M. April 28/17. |
| ‡7 C. | Greenacre, H. 3/7048. | M. April 28/17. |
| ‡7 C. XII | Jones, T. C. 202759. | M. April 28/17. |
| ‡7 C. | Lamb, H. J. 203510. | M. April 28/17. |
| ‡7 C. | Lenney, G. 43652. | M. April 28/17. |
| ‡7 C. | Mayes, F. 29728. | M. April 28/17. |
| 7 C. X | Meyrick, G. B. 26391. | K. April 29/17. Det.D./B. |
| 7 C. | Naughton, Henry. 7551. | M. April 28/17. |
| 7 C. XII | Roberts, F. W. 202145. | W. and M. April 28/17. |
| ‡7 C. | Sewell, C. 17897. | M. April 28/17. |
| 7 C. IX | Ward, J. 18263. | M. Oct. 12/16. R/Enq. |
| ‡7 C. | Watson, H. 26534. | M. April 28/17. |
| 7 D. XV | Brown, Cpl. Matthew. 29770. | K. April 28/17. Det.D./B. |
| ‡7 D. XVI | Bryant, George Ernest. 23789. | M. April 28/17. |
| *7 D. IV | Clarke, Thos. 22401. | W. and M. April 28/17. |
| ‡7 D. | Everall, B. 40576. | W. and M. April 27/17. |
| ‡7 D. | Parsons, S. 24008. | M. April 28/17. |
| 7 D. XIII | Pawley, H. 43696. | M. April 28/17. |
| ‡7 D. | Ramm, L.-Cpl. W. 203509. | M. April 28/17. |
| ‡7 D. | Revell, L.-Cpl. H. 43032. | W. and M. April 28/17. |
| ‡7 D. | Rogers, B. J. 202164. | M. April 28/17. |
| 7 D. XIII | Rollin, B. W. W. 29688. | M. April 28/17. |
| ‡7 D. | Saunders, D. H. 40702. | W. and M. April 28/17. |
| 7 D. | Sayer, Harold C. W. 19960. | W. and M. April 28/17. |
| 7 D. XVI | Smith, A.-Sergt. Frank Herbt. 43037. | W. and M. April 28/17. |
| ‡7 D. | Whaley, A. E. 20207. | M. April 28/17. |
| ‡7 D. | Woodhouse, S. 43047. | M. April 28/17. |
| 8 B. | Boughton, Sidney. 20413. | M. Mar. 10/17. |
| 8 B. | Chaplin, Thos. Charlish. 24145. | M. Oct. 5/16. |
| 8 B. VII | Marjoram, A. 17053. | K. Feb. 17/17. Det.D./B. |
| ‡8 D. | Norman, J. 40021. | M. May 17/17. |
| ‡8 H.Q. | Burden, Fred. 43568. | M. Oct. 5/16. R/Enq. |
| 9 A. | **Graham, Capt. D. C.** | M., bel. K. April 28/17. |
| 9 A. or D. | Aldis, H. V. 16465. | M. Sept. 15/16. |
| 9 A. or C. | Bircham, Victor S. 40190. | M. Oct. 18/16. R/Enq. |
| 9 A. III | Bullen, T. G. 40196. | M. May/17. 2nd Cas. |
| 9 A. | Chaplin, E. A. 24262. | M. Oct. 18/16. R/Enq. |
| 9 A. | Croxen, Geo. A. 40200. (5033.) | M. Oct. 18/16. R/Enq. |
| *9 A. II | Edwards, Alan Hugh. 25919. | K. Oct. 18/16. Det.D./B. R/Enq. |
| 9 A. | Suffling, Henry Geo. 16476. | M. Sept. 15/16. R/Enq. |
| 9 B. | Batson, L.-Cpl. B. C. 40036. | M. Oct. 18/16. R/Enq. |

**Norfolk Regiment**—contd.

## *B.E.F.*

| | | |
|---|---|---|
| 9 C. IX | Hiscock, T. G. 26329. | K. April 23/17. Det.D./B. |
| ‡9 C. | Rudrum, A. B. 40101. | M. Oct. 18/16. R/Enq. |
| ‡9 D. | Kenny, F. J. W. 18198. | M. Sept. 15/16. R/Enq. |

## *E.E.F.*

| | | |
|---|---|---|
| 4 | **Porter, 2nd Lt. A. J. (Fr. 1st.)** | W. and M. April 19/17. |
| 4 | **Thurgar, Lieut. Ralph Wm.** | W. and M. April 19/17. |
| 4 A. | Bond, J. A. 203621. | M. April 19/17. |
| 4 A. | Childs, R. 201358. (5725.) | M. April 19/17. |
| *4 A. | Davidson, Wm. 203622. | W. and M. April 19/17. |
| 4 A. | Doggett, L.-Cpl. W. A. 200372. | M. April 19/17. |
| 4 A. | Fisher, Cecil H. 201155. (5046.) | M. April 19/17. |
| 4 A. | Frost, G. H. 200533. | M. April 19/17. |
| 4 A. | Graver, L.-Cpl. W. H. 200039. (Late 1323.) | K. April 19/17. Det.D./B. |
| 4 A. | Gurney, Albert. 201278. | M. April 19/17. |
| 4 A. | Harvey, Thos. 203313. (8816.) | M. April 19/17. |
| 4 A. | Marrison, H. 200880. (4360.) | W. and M. April 19/17. |
| 4 A. Sig. S. | Mason, W. H. 200086. | M. April 19/17. |
| 4 A. | Neale, Wm. 200539. (2896.) | M. April 19/17. |
| 4 A. | Read, H. 200586. (3009.) | M. April 19/17. |
| 4 A. | Rudman, Wm. 203315. (8818.) | M. April 19/17. |
| 4 B. VIII | Bird, Ronald Stanley. 200807. (Late 3695.) | M. April 19/17. |
| 4 B. | Boocock, Wm. 202865. (8367.) | M. April 19/17. |
| *4 B. VIII | Edwards, S. A. 200746. | W. and M. April 19/17. |
| 4 B. | Gates, L.-Cpl. F. 200484. (Late 2756.) | K. April 19/17. Det.D./B. |
| 4 B. | Haines, Sergt. G. 200874. | W. and M. April 19/17. |
| 4 B. VII | Hales, Regd. A. 200994. (Late 4644). | M. April 19/17. |
| 4 B. | Hewett, Cpl. C. E. 200217. (2320.) | W. and M. April 19/17. |
| 4 B. L.G.S. | Hewitt, J. 201288. (Late 5645.) | M. April 19/17. |
| 4 B. VIII | Jenkins, Wm. H. 203305. (8808.) | M. April 19/17. |
| 4 B. | Lovick, A. R. 200973. (Late 4606.) | M. April 19/17. |
| 4 B. | McInerney, Edw. Jas. 201353. (5718) | M. April 19/17. |
| *4 B. | Mason, Sydney. 200489. (2771.) | W. and M. April 19/17. |
| 4 B. VIII | Matthews, T. 203308. | M. April 19/17. |
| 4 B. | Moore, G. W. 202876. (Late 8378.) | M. April 19/17. |
| 4 B. | Neville, Sergt. F. C. 200709. (3438.) | W. and M. April 19/17. |
| 4 B. | Power, F. J. 200246. | M. April 19/17. |
| 4 B. | Sadd, J. P. 200126. | M. April 19/17. |
| 4 B. | Sargeant, Harry. 200504. (2806.) | W. and M. April 19/17. |
| *4 B. | Savage, Donald John. 200425. | W. and M. April 19/17. |
| 4 C. | Brown, Cpl. E. F. 201476. | M. April 19/17. |
| 4 C. XII | Chadwick, Harry. 202860. (8362.) | K. April 19/17. Det.D./B. |
| *4 C. | Green, Thomas. 203628. | W. and M. April 19/17. |
| 4 C. | Niland, Martin. 201302. (5659.) | M. April 19/17. |
| *4 C. XII | Noure, M. 202890. (8392.) (Fr. A.S.C.) | W. and M. April 19/17. |
| 4 C. | Pattinson, C.-S.-M. H. R. 200010. (Late 287.) | M. April 19/17. |
| 4 C. | Pitcher, M. F. 201171. | M. April 19/17. |
| *4 D. | Abbott, E. 201060. (4749.) | W. and M. April 19/17. |
| 4 D. | Aggas, F. S. 201118. | M. April 19/17. |
| 4 D. | Curtis, Robert. 200850. | M. April 19/17. |
| 4 D. | Dack, C. 200150. | W. and M. April 19/17. |
| 4 D. | Elsey, Sergt. D. J. 200005. | W. and M. April 19/17. |
| 4 D. | Frost, W. 201511. (5932.) | M. April 19/17. |
| 4 D. | Hull, Geo. 201424. (Late 5803.) | M. April 19/17. |
| *4 D. | Hurrell, P. R. 200501. (2802.) | K. April 19/17. Det.D./B. |

Norfolk Regiment—contd.

## *E.E.F.*

| | | | |
|---|---|---|---|
| *4 | D. XV | Law, Fred. 203333. (8836.) | W. and M. April 19/17. |
| 4 | D. | McCree, H. H. 201478. (5897.) | M. April 19/17. |
| *4 | D. | Oldham, A. E. 202891. | W. and M. April 19/17. |
| 4 | D. | Pickles, W. 202861. (8363.) | M. April 19/17. |
| 4 | D. | Pond, L.-Cpl. Herbert Horace. 200585. (3607.) | W. and M. April 19/17. |
| 4 | D. | Read, C. R. 201021. | K. April 19/17. Det.D./B. |
| 4 | D. XV | Rock, A. 203335. | M. April 19/17. |
| 4 | ? | Atherton, S. W. 200673. | M. April 19/17. |
| 4 | ? | Balls, H. 200806. | M. April 19/17. |
| 4 | ? | Barnard, G. Z. 200399. | M. April 19/17. |
| 4 | ? | Barnard, R. R. 200237. | M. April 19/17. |
| 4 | ? | Batty, J. 202671. | M. April 19/17. |
| 4 | ? | Beaty, G. W. 203439. | M. April 19/17. |
| 4 | ? | Bedwell, J. F. 200172. | M. April 19/17. |
| 4 | ? | Beeton, R. V. 201095. | M. April 19/17. |
| 4 | ? | Bell, W. L. 200436. | M. April 19/17. |
| 4 | ? | Bennell, A. J. 201485. | M. April 19/17. |
| 4 | ? | Birch, H. 201366. | M. April 19/17. |
| *4 | ? | Bird, Cpl. A. W. 200508. | W. and M. April 19/17. |
| *4 | ? | Bloomfield, H. F. 200863. | W. and M. April 19/17. |
| 4 | ? | Brown, L. 201348. | M. April 19/17. |
| 4 | ? | Browne, E. A. 201460. | M. April 19/17. |
| *4 | ? | Burke, M. 203630. | W. and M. April 19/17. |
| 4 | ? | Caines, A. G. 200084. | M. April 19/17. |
| *4 | ? | Carey, Sgt. J. H. 201257. | W. and M. April 19/17. |
| *4 | ? | Chapman, R. 200917. | W. and M. April 19/17. |
| *4 | ? | Chilvers, Sgt. P. 200284. | W. and M. April 19/17. |
| 4 | ? | Cockaday, A. E. 201347. | M. April 19/17. |
| 4 | ? | Cursons, S. E. 200924. | M. April 19/17 |
| 4 | ? | Davis, J. H. 201364. | M. April 19/17. |
| 4 | ? | Dawson, Cpl. W. 200480. | M. April 19/17. |
| 4 | ? | Daynes, S. J. 201451. | M. April 19/17. |
| 4 | ? | Dewing, Cpl. R. J. 200707. | M. April 19/17. |
| 4 | ? | Docking, H. J. 200190. | M. April 19/17. |
| *4 | ? | Dresh, J. T. 201345. | W. and M. April 19/17. |
| 4 | ? | Dunnett, P. A. 200462. | M. April 19/17. |
| *4 | ? | Ely, A. 200326. | W. and M. April 19/17. |
| *4 | ? | Feltham, J. E. 200733. | W. and M. April 19/17. |
| 4 | ? | Forster, J. 200695. | M. April 19/17. |
| 4 | ? | Franklin, F. W. 200336. | M. April 19/17. |
| 4 | ? | Hannant, L.-Cpl. G. C. 200374. | M. April 19/17. |
| 4 | ? | Hardment, F. 200669. | M. April 19/17. |
| 4 | ? | Harris, H. 203318. | M. April 19/17. |
| *4 | ? | Haward, S. A. 200747. | W. and M. April 19/17. |
| 4 | ? | Hingley, F. A. 202883. | M. April 19/17. |
| 4 | ? | Howes, A. 203453. | M. April 19/17. |
| *4 | ? | Howlett, L.-Cpl. Regd. Coleman. 200839. | W. and M. April 19/17. |
| 4 | ? | Jillings, W. 200793. | M. April 19/17. |
| *4 | ? | Kirby, G. 200102. | W. and M. April 19/17. |
| *4 | ? | Land, E. 201043. | W. and M. April 19/17. |
| *4 | ? | Law, T. 203333. | W. and M. April 19/17. |
| 4 | ? | Laws, W. 201162. | M. April 19/17. |
| 4 | ? | Lee, A. J. 201407. | M., bel. K. April 19/17. |
| 4 | ? | Lincoln, C. 200176. | M. April 19/17. |
| 4 | ? | McCann, W. T. B. 201311. | M. April 19/17. |
| 4 | ? | Marshall, F. F. 200379. | M. April 19/17. |
| 4 | ? | Marshall, T. W. 202886. | M. April 19/17. |

**Norfolk Regiment**—contd.

## *E.E.F.*

| | | |
|---|---|---|
| *4 ? | Martin, J. W. 202885. | W. and M. April 19/17. |
| *4 ? | Matthams, S. J. 201414. | W. and M. April 19/17. |
| *4 ? | Meale, H. 200488. | W. and M. April 19/17. |
| *4 ? | Neville, Sgt. T. 200709. | W. and M. April 19/17. |
| *4 ? | Norgate, Cpl. H. 200056. | W. and M. April 19/17. |
| *4 ? | Orvice, G. A. G. 200700. | W. and M. April 19/17. |
| 4 ? | Palmer, W. N. 200848. | M. April 19/17. |
| 4 ? | Parker, A. T. 201158. | M. April 19/17. |
| 4 ? | Pye, J. A. 200800. | M. April 19/17. |
| 4 ? | Rackham, R. 200835. | M. April 19/17. |
| *4 ? | Reeve, A. J. C. 200875. | W. and M. April 19/17. |
| 4 ? | Richardson, C. 202893. | M. April 19/17. |
| 4 ? | Rudling, J. J. 200956. | M. April 19/17. |
| 4 ? | Shackson, J. W. 201294. | M. April 19/17. |
| 4 ? | Shaw, J. 200495. | M. April 19/17. |
| 4 ? | Sinfield, H. 201415. | M. April 19/17. |
| 4 ? | Slater, F. J. 200959. | M. April 19/17. |
| *4 ? | Smith, F. G. 200547. | W. and M. April 19/17. |
| 4 ? | Smith, W. 201499. | M. April 19/17. |
| *4 ? | Tooke, E. R. 201061. | W. and M. April 19/17. |
| *4 ? | Walker, L.-Sergt. A. 201063. | W. and M. April 19/17. |
| 4 ? | Watts, R. 200861. | M. April 19/17. |
| 4 ? | Wells, Cpl. F. C. 201256. | M. April 19/17. |
| 4 ? | Youngman, W. 200123. | M. April 19/17. |
| 5 | **Beck, Capt. Evelyn.** | W. and M. April 19/17. |
| 5 | **Birkbeck, Capt. G. W.** | W. and M. April 19/17. |
| 5 | **Cubitt, Capt. E. H.** | W. and M. April 19/17. |
| 5 | **Grissell, D.S.O., Lt.-Col. B. S.** (Fr. 1) | W. and M. April 19/17. |
| 5 | **Harper, 2nd Lieut. R. C. M.** (Fr. Res. Officers.) | W. and M. April 19/17. |
| 5 | **Joseph, 2nd Lieut. W. G. A.** (Fr. 1 Gar. Batt. Northants.) | W. and M. April 19/17. |
| 5 | **Levy, 2nd Lieut. J.** (Fr. 4th.) | W. and M. April 19/17. |
| 5 | **Plaistowe, 2nd Lieut. R. R.** | W. and M. April 19/17. |
| 5 A. | Brown, F. W. 240751. (3341.) | M. April 19/17. |
| 5 A. | Bulley, W. 242537. (270261.) | M. April 19/17. |
| *5 A. | Channell, Cpl. H. 240390. (2521.) | W. and M. April 19/17. |
| 5 A. | Chapman, R. J. 241185. | M. April 19/17. |
| 5 A. | Curson, Bertie T. 240350. (2424.) | M. April 19/17. |
| 5 A. | Curson, L.-Cpl. Walter Harold. 240105. (1715.) | M. April 19/17. |
| 5 A. | Eaglo, Sidney. 240505. | M. April 19/17. |
| 5 A. | Fisher, Sgt. Joseph. 240304. (Late 2320.) | M., bel. K. April 19/17. |
| 5 A. | Gillings, Cpl. Arthur Wm. 240018. | W. and M. April 19/17. |
| 5 A. | Harmer, E. 241090. | W. and M. April 19/17. |
| *5 A. | Howard, J. J. 240083. (1624.) | W. and M. April 19/17. |
| 5 A. | Jonas, R. W. 240916. (4303.) | W. and M. April 19/17. |
| 5 A. | Newson, W. 240658. (3066.) | M. April 19/17. |
| 5 A. | Southgate, Sgt. A. L. 240700. (3173.) | W. and M. April 19/17. |
| 5 A. | Spurgeon, Frank Basil. 240881. (4218.) | W. and M. April 19/17. |
| 5 A. | Stone, G. E. R. 240882. | M. April 19/17. |
| 5 A. | Tiptod, L.-Cpl. R. 240662. | M. April 19/17. |
| *5 A. | Tooke, A. E. 240685. (3130.) | W. and M. April 19/17. |
| 5 A. | Woods, Sidney Saml. 240050. (1503.) | M. April 19/17. |
| *5 B. | Cash, Victor J. 241064. (4842.) | W. and M. April 19/17. |
| *5 B. M.G.S. | Dewing, John. 240233. (2116.) | W. and M. April 19/17. |
| 5 B. | English, S. H. 240451. | M. April 19/17. |

**Norfolk Regiment**—contd.

## *E.E.F.*

| | | |
|---|---|---|
| 5 B. | Gibson, Sidney. 240942. | M. April 19/17. |
| 5 B. | Hastings, Sergt. A. 240038. (1241.) | W. and M. April 19/17. |
| 5 B. | Horsley, R. A. 241148. | M. April 19/17. |
| 5 B. | Ogilvy, C.-Q.-M.-S. A. G. 240473. | M. April 19/17. |
| 5 B. | Wardale, J. W. 240768. (Late 3388.) | M. April 19/17. |
| 5 B. | Wier, G. W. 240821. | M. April 19/17. |
| 5 C. | Allenbury, H. J. 241563. | M. April 19/17. |
| 5 C. | Bird, Cpl. C. 240548. (2846.) | W. and M. April 19/17. |
| 5 C. | Bird, Sergt. F. 240129. (1819.) | W. and M. April 19/17. |
| 5 C. M.G.S. | Bird, Sgt. H. W. 240546. (Late 2844.) | M. April 19/17. |
| 5 C. | Bolton, Cecil J. 240638. (3023.) | M. April 19/17. |
| 5 C. | Brackenbury, G. 240279. | M. April 19/17. |
| 5 C. | Brooks, Sgt. W. C. 240347. (2420.) | M. April 19/17. |
| 5 C. | Brunning, L.-Cpl. G. 240870. | M. April 19/17. |
| 5 C. | Budds, W. Gladstone. 240924. (4323.) | M. April 19/17. |
| 5 C. | Clarke, Sgt. P. 240108. (1735.) | M. April 19/17. |
| 5 C. XI | Creasy, L.-Cpl. T. J. 240197. | W. and M. April 19/17. |
| *5 C. | Cubitt, George P. 242488. | W. and M. April 19/17. |
| 5 C. | Cutting, W. J. 240506. | M. April 19/17. |
| 5 C. | Dix, R. G. 241048. (4980.) | M. April 19/17. |
| 5 C. | Dunthorne, R. 242336. | M. April 19/17. |
| 5 C. or D. | Edwards, E. R. 240592. | M. April 19/17. |
| 5 C. | Fisher, Sgt. E. H. 240310. (Late 2332) | M. April 19/17. |
| *5 C. IX | Grief, Cpl. Hugh Edw. 240816. (3478.) | W. and M. April 19/17. |
| 5 C. | Hacon, Alfred. 240915. (Late 4301.) | M. April 19/17. |
| 5 C. X | Hensby, Fredk. 242519. | M. April 19/17 |
| 5 C. IX | Hudson, A. 242462. | M. April 19/17. |
| 5 C. | Jordan, W. 240356, | M. April 19/17. |
| 5 C. | Lines, F. 240132. | M. April 19/17. |
| 5 C. | Porter, Sig. Bertie Wm. 240857. (4168.) | W. and M. April 19/17. |
| 5 C. | Rudran, C. J. 240107. (1730.) | M. April 19/17. |
| 5 C. | Smalls, Ivo. 240652. (5053.) | M. April 19/17. |
| 5 C. | Tee, Joseph. 242563. | M. April 19/17. |
| *5 C. | Todd, Sergt. L. R. 241029. | M. April 19/17. |
| 5 C. | Turner, R. A. 241089. (4940.) | M., bel. K. April 19/17. |
| *5 C. | Vurley, F. J. 240742. (3316.) | W. and M. April 19/17. |
| 5 C. | Woods, Ernest John. 240378. (2500.) | W. and M. April 19/17. |
| 5 D. | Atherton, L.-Cpl. Edward. 242456. | M. April 19/17. |
| 5 D. | Barnes, F. 240157. | M. April 19/17. |
| 5 D. | Burnett, T. H. 242538. (26958.) | M. April 19/17. |
| 5 D. | Butcher, C. E. 240677. | M. April 19/17. |
| 5 D. XV | Curson, Stanley. 241175. | M. April 19/17. |
| 5 D. | Eglington, Edw. John. 240793. (3433) | W. and M. April 19/17. |
| 5 D. | Flerty, Henry. 240641. (Late 3038.) | M. April 19/17. |
| 5 D. XV | Gooch, A. 242312. (Late 7805.) | M. April 19/17. |
| 5 D. | Griffin, W. 240457. (2672.) | M. April 19/17. |
| 5 D. | Harrison, L.-Cpl. G. 240459. (2676.) | M. April 19/17. |
| 5 D. | Hastings, B. 240043. (1395.) | W. and M. April 19/17. |
| 5 D. | Howes, A. W. 240319. (Late 2345.) | M. April 19/17. |
| 5 D. | Moore, E. R. 240084. | M. April 19/17. |
| 5 D. | Postle, E. C. 240383. | M. April 19/17. |
| 5 D. XIII | Sadler, J. T. 240091. | M. April 19/17. |
| 5 D. | Spooner, Clarence. 240781. (Late 3410.) | M. April 19/17. |
| 5 D. | Warner, W. F. 241177. | M. April 19/17. |
| 5 D. | Warnes, Cpl. Horace. 240158. | M. April 19/17. |

**Norfolk Regiment**—contd.

## *E.E.F.*

| | | |
|---|---|---|
| 5 ? | Abel, E. A. 240984. | M. April 19/17. |
| 5 ? | Anderson, C. 241083. | M. April 19/17. |
| 5 ? | Aspin, J. 242447. | M. April 19/17. |
| 5 ? | Atmore, W. 240959. | M. April 19/17. |
| 5 ? | Bacon, E. 240536. | M. April 19/17. |
| 5 ? | Bailey, G. W. 240973. | M. April 19/17. |
| 5 ? | Bunger, H. 240908. | M., bel. K. April 19/17. |
| 5 ? | Beales, A. H. 242535. (26985.) | M. April 19/17. |
| 5 ? | Beckett, C.-S.-M. C. 240014. | M. April 19/17. |
| 5 ? | Blake, J. R. 240167. | M. April 19/17. |
| 5 ? | Bland, A. • 241070. | M. April 19/17. |
| 5 ? | Bliss, R. T. 240093. | M. April 19/17. |
| 5 ? | Bocking, H. 240194. | M. April 19/17. |
| 5 ? | Bonnett, Cpl. R. 240287. | M., bel. K. April 19/17. |
| 5 ? | Brock, G. 241113. | M. April 19/17. |
| 5 ? | Brown, W. 242340. | M. April 19/17. |
| 5 ? | Brunning, W. H. 241131. | M. April 19/17. |
| 5 ? | Buck, W. J. 240373. | M. April 19/17. |
| 5 ? | Burrell, E. 240871. | M. April 19/17. |
| 5 ? | Busby, B. 240159. | M. April 19/17. |
| 5 ? | Callaghan, D. 242449. | M. April 19/17. |
| 5 ? | Catchpole, L.-Sergt. A. A. 240186. | W. and M. April 19/17. |
| 5 ? | Cator, H. 241196. | M. April 19/17. |
| 5 ? | Cletharoe, A. W. R. 240202. | M. April 19/17. |
| *5 ? | Corley, J. 241024. | W. and M. April 19/17. |
| *5 ? | Cossey, J. 241178. | W. and M. April 19/17. |
| 5 ? | Creasey, C. R. 240196. | M. April 19/17. |
| 5 ? | Crown, W. 240161. | M., bel. K. April 19/17. |
| *5 ? | Dann, S. 240394. | W. and M. April 19/17. |
| 5 ? | Daws, J. 240035. | M. April 19/17. |
| 5 ? | Day, J. W. 240949. | M. April 19/17. |
| 5 ? | Dixon, H. D. 242544. (26925.) | M. April 19/17. |
| 5 ? | Edgely, V. 240025. | M. April 19/17. |
| 5 ? | Eke, F. J. 240792. | M. April 19/17. |
| 5 ? | Ellis, W. 240172. | M. April 19/17. |
| 5 ? | Fickling, A. 240022. | M. April 19/17. |
| 5 ? | Foyster, T. A. 242339. | M. April 19/17. |
| *5 ? | Funnell, L.-Cpl. E. T. 240596. | W. and M. April 19/17. |
| 5 ? | Furze, S. H. 242491. | M. April 19/17. |
| 5 ? | Goodson, F. J. 27046. | M. April 19/17. |
| *5 ? | Grief, Cpl. E. H. 240816. | W. and M. April 19/17. |
| 5 ? | Grimes, T. 240354. | M. April 19/17. |
| 5 ? | Groom, W. 240047. | M. April 19/17. |
| 5 ? | Hall, R. W. 240850. | W. and M. April 19/17. |
| *5 ? | Harden, E. G. 241043. | W. and M. April 19/17. |
| 5 ? | Harper, T. 242485. | M. April 19/17. |
| 5 ? | Harrison, R. 240626. | M. April 19/17. |
| *5 ? | Hendry, F. 240460. | W. and M. April 19/17. |
| 5 ? | Howard, A. E. 240947. | M. April 19/17. |
| 5 ? | Howman, B. 240504. | M. April 19/17. |
| 5 ? | Hudland. 242474. | M. April 19/17. |
| 5 ? | Jackson, H. R. 241108. | M. April 19/17. |
| 5 ? | Jarvis, R. 240557. | M. April 19/17. |
| 5 ? | Johnson, G. 242463. | M. April 19/17. |
| 5 ? | Kent, F. A. 241027. | M. April 19/17. |
| *5 ? | Kent, W. 240853. | W. and M. April 19/17. |
| 5 ? | Knights, G. 242506. | M. April 19/17. |
| 5 ? | Lake, A. R. 241066. | M. April 19/17. |
| *5 ? | Lambert, E. S. 241062. | W. and M. April 19/17. |

**Norfolk Regiment—contd.**

## *E.E.F.*

| | | |
|---|---|---|
| 5 ? | Land, Cpl. C. E. 240803. | M. **April 19/17.** |
| 5 ? | Large, A. G. 240512. | M. **April 19/17.** |
| 5 ? | Leeder, N. 240195. | M. **April 19/17.** |
| *5 ? | Loan, E. A. H. 240741. | W. and M. **April 19/17.** |
| 5 ? | Lyst, A. 242345. | M. **April 19/17.** |
| 5 ? | McNicholas, P. 242451. | M. **April 19/17.** |
| 5 ? | Maycroft, G. 241081. | M. **April 19/17.** |
| *5 ? | Mayes, F. 240470. | W. and M. **April 19/17.** |
| *5 ? | Merrison, L.-Cpl. P. 240695. | W. and M. **April 19/17.** |
| 5 ? | Mitchell, Cpl. H. J. 240188. | M. **April 19/17.** |
| *5 ? | Moore, H. 242558. | W. and M. **April 19/17.** |
| 5 ? | Moore, W. J. C. 240322. | M., bel. K. **April 19/17.** |
| 5 ? | Newell, W. H. 241012. | M. **April 19/17.** |
| 5 ? | Newstead, A. B. 240513. | M. **April 19/17.** |
| 5 ? | Oxborough, G. 241091. | M. **April 19/17.** |
| 5 ? | Parker, E. G. 240878. | M. **April 19/17.** |
| *5 ? | Pinchin, Cpl. J. 240309. | W. and M. **April 19/17.** |
| 5 ? | Pitcher, C. 240717. | M. **April 19/17.** |
| 5 ? | Pitcher, R. 241067. | M. **April 19/17.** |
| ;5 ? | Pitcher, W. J. 240948. | M. **April 19/17.** |
| *5 ? | Platten, J. 240219. | W. and M. **April 19/17.** |
| 5 ? | Proudfoot, S. E. 241122. | M. **April 19/17.** |
| 5 ? | Ramm, W. P. 240981. | M. **April 19/17.** |
| 5 ? | Rasberry, R. W. 241007. | M. **April 19/17.** |
| 5 ? | Reynolds, J. E. 240694. | M. **April 19/17.** |
| 5 ? | Robinson, Sgt. J. W. 240585. | M., bel. K. **April 19/17.** |
| 5 ? | Roy, B. 240432. | M. **April 19/17.** |
| 5 ? | Rudd, L. W. 242323. | M. **April 19/17.** |
| *5 ? | Rudrum, A. G. 240220. | W. and M. **April 19/17.** |
| 5 ? | Rusted, A. 240607. | W. and M. **April 19/17.** |
| *5 ? | Seals, R. W. 240789. | W. and M. **April 19/17.** |
| 5 ? | Smith, H. 242326. | M. **April 19/17.** |
| 5 ? | Smith, S. 240424. | M. **April 19/17.** |
| 5 ? | Smitn, L.-Cpl. T. J. 240530. | M. **April 19/17.** |
| *5 ? | Smith, W. 241150. | W. and M. **April 19/17.** |
| 5 ? | Snelling, H. W. 240267. | M. **April 19/17.** |
| ‡5 ? | Sparkes, E. W. 240453. | W. and M. **April 19/17.** |
| 5 ? | Staff, F. H. 242509. | M. **April 19/17.** |
| 5 ? | Stearman, M. 240698. | M. **April 19/17.** |
| *5 ? | Steggles, A. C. 240748. | W. and M. **April 19/17.** |
| *5 ? | Sussums, H. 242519. | W. and M. **April 19/17.** |
| 5 ? | Strangleman, C. 240807. | M. **April 19/17.** |
| *5 ? | Thompson, H. R. 240861. | W. and M. **April 19/17.** |
| 5 ? | Till, J. 27037. | M. **April 19/17.** |
| *5 ? | Tuck, C. J. 241154. | W. and M. **April 19/17.** |
| 5 ? | Tuddenham, Sergt. W. S. 240150. | M. **April 19/17.** |
| 5 ? | Tullett, L.-Cpl. A. W. 241564. | M. **April 19/17.** |
| *5 ? | Vincent, A. T. 242565. | W. and M. **April 19/17.** |
| 5 ? | Ward, H. 241063. | M. **April 19/17.** |
| 5 ? | Ward, R. H. 242317. | M. **April 19/17.** |
| 5 ? | Watkins, L.-Sergt. J. A. 242498. | M. **April 19/17.** |
| 5 ? | Watson, E. 240221. | M. **April 19/17.** |
| ‡5 ? | Watts, W. 240542. | W. and M. **April 19/17.** |
| 5 ? | Webster, C. R. 240543. | M. **April 19/17.** |
| *5 ? | Welham, C.-S.-M. B. 240493. | W. and M. **April 19/17.** |
| *5 ? | Whiffen, A. E. J. 240378. | W. and M. **April 19/17.** |
| 5 ? | White, J. 242480. | M. **April 19/17.** |
| 5 ? | Woodcock, F. H. 242511. | M. **April 19/17.** |
| 5 ? | Wright, C. A. 241020. | M. **April 19/17.** |

**Norfolk Regiment**—contd.

## *E.E.F.*

| | | |
|---|---|---|
| 5 ? | Wright, R. C. 241093. | M. April 19/17. |
| *5 ? | Wright, R. W. 240497. | M., bel. K. April 19/17. |

## *PERSIAN GULF.*

| | | |
|---|---|---|
| *2 A. | Ames, A. G. 26082. | D/W. Mar. 6/17. Det.D./B Basra. |
| *2 B. | Knights, R. G. 7491. | K. Feb. 24/17. Det.D./B. |
| 2 D. | Baldwin, F. A. 25928. | W. and M. Feb. 24/17. |
| *2 D. | Turvey, Geo. Wilfred. 23569. | K. Feb. 24/17. Det.D./B. |
| 2 ? | Childs, B. W. 15712. (Fr. 10th.) | M., bel. D/Dis. May 22/16. |
| 2 ? | Nash, G. 14216. | M. Feb. 24/17. |
| 2 ? | Wiffin, C. 24031. | M. Feb. 24/17. |

# NORTHAMPTON REGIMENT.

## *B.E.F.*

| | | |
|---|---|---|
| ‡1 | **Airth, 2nd Lieut. E. C.** | M. July 10/17. |
| ‡1 | **Aylett, M.C., Capt. E. R. C.** | M. about July 10/17. |
| ‡1 | **Chisholm, 2nd Lieut. D. C.** | M. July 10/17. |
| ‡1 | **Hayes, Capt. E. D.** | M. July 10/17. |
| ‡1 | **Needham, 2nd Lieut. R. P.** | M. July 10/17. |
| ‡1 | **Saxton, 2nd Lieut. R. C.** | M. July 10/17. |
| ‡1 | **Smith, 2nd Lieut. G. H.** | M. July 10/17. |
| ‡1 | **Tollemache, Col. the Hon. D. P.** (Fr. 7th Hussars.) | M. July 10/17. |
| 1 B. | Greeves, H. 43319. | M. Sept. 9/16. R/Enq. |
| 2 A. | Chapman, G. E. 10379. | W. and M. Mar. 4/17. |
| 2 A. L.G.S. | Lane, A. W. 16874. | W. and M. Mar. 4/17. |
| 2 A. | Thomas, F. 30633. | W. and M. Mar. 4/17. |
| 2 A. IV | Wilson, A. R. 14552. | W. and M. Mar. 4/17. |
| 2 C. H.Q. | Summerlin, F. C. 9739. | M. Mar. 4/17. |
| 2 D. XVI | Garrett, James. 16908. | M. Mar. 4/17. |
| 2 D. | Horton, F. 27151. | M. April 26/17. |
| *2 ? | Boreham, D. S. 26533. | K. Mar. 7/17. Det.D./B. |
| ‡2 ? | Sherdel, Geo. 22430. (14967.) (Fr. M.G.C.) | M. April 26/17. |
| 6 A. | Balderson, Arthur W. 10920. | W. and M. Feb. 17/17. |
| 6 A. II | Bass, Alfred Henry. 26792. | K. Feb. 17/17. Det.D./B. |
| 6 A. | Moore, S. G. 17643. | W. and M. Feb. 17/17. |
| *6 B. VI | Beetson, Ernest. 30938. | W. and M. May 3/17. |
| 6 B. | Brooks, E. 14794. | M. May 3/17. |
| ‡6 B. | Burchnell, G. 3/10467. | M. May 3/17. |
| 6 B. VIII | Coxhill, L.-Cpl. H. 18423. | M. May 3/17. |
| 6 B. VII | Dean, W. A. 25447. | M. Feb. 17/17. |
| ‡6 B. | Dixon, F. C. 27942. | M. May 3/17. |
| 6 B. VIII | Dunn, G. J. 28270. | M. Feb. 17/17. |
| 6 B. VI | Emerton, Arthur Wm. 30928. | M. May 3/17. |
| ‡6 B. | Furness, R. 22554. | M. May 3/17. |
| 6 B. | Garton, Frank. 43091. | M. May 3/17. |
| 6 B. M.B.S. | Holmes, Cpl. H. T. 13038. | M. May 3/17. |
| ‡6 B. | Hutson, H. 18814. | M. May 3/17. |
| 6 B. | Lawrence, Percy Goodwin. 43160. (Fr. Bedfords.) | W. and M. Mar. 19-20/17. |

**Northampton Regiment—contd.**

## *B.E.F.*

| | | |
|---|---|---|
| ‡6 B. V | Neville, Horace. 24248. | K. **Feb. 17/17.** Det.D./B. |
| 6 B. VI | Orton, Walter. 17866. | M. **Feb. 17/17.** |
| ‡6 B. | Pell, C. A. 31123. | M. **May 3/17.** |
| ‡6 B. | Purser, H. 14011. | M. **May 3/17.** |
| 6 B. | Rogers, L.-Cpl. A. T. 14836. | M. **Feb. 17/17.** |
| 6 B. V | Savings, Edward Chas. 31017. | M. **May 3/17.** |
| 6 B. VI | Silsby, H. 25437. | M. **May 3/17.** |
| 6 B. | Walker, J. 20367. | M. **Mar. 20/17.** |
| 6 C. XII | Brigstock, W. J. 27703. | K. **Mar. 20/17.** Det.D./B. |
| ‡6 C. | Drage, L.-Cpl. W. G. 43065. | M. **May 3/17.** |
| 6 C. | Frisby, Harold. 15966. | M., bel. K. **Feb. 17/17.** |
| 6 C. X | Gough, C. J. 30030. | M. **May 3/17.** |
| ‡6 C. | Hobbs, L. 40021. | M. **May 3/17.** |
| ‡6 C. | Howes, H. 20479. | M. **May 3/17.** |
| 6 C. IX | Loasby, Frank. 18875. | M. **May 3/17.** |
| *6 C. IX | Maber, Wm. Chas. 40067. | M. **May 3/17.** |
| 6 C. X | Pettit, George. 30904. | M. **May 5/17.** |
| ‡6 C. | Scott, L. 43235. | M. **May 3/17.** |
| 6 C. X | Smith, L.-Cpl. Geo. Hry. 18247. | M. **Feb. 17/17.** |
| 6 C. M.G.S. | Willmer, L.-Cpl. F. 1590. | M. **May 3/17.** |
| 6 D. | Archer, Harry. 13444. | W. and M. **Feb. 17/17.** |
| 6 D. | Chambers, H. J. 27863. | M. **Feb. 17/17.** |
| 6 D. XIII | Clarke, F. 17894. | M. **Feb. 17/17.** |
| 6 D. XIV | Payne, J. 43207. | M. **Feb. 17/17.** |
| 6 D. XV | Sells, L. 43231. | M. **Feb. 17/17.** |
| 6 D. XIII | Taylor, John. 22067. | M. **Feb. 17/17.** |
| 6 D. XVI | Timms, W. J. 32297. | W. and M. **Mar. 20/17.** |
| *6 D. XIV | Yeomans, A. 43292. | M. **May 3/17.** |
| ‡6 ? | Savill, F. 24775. | M. **June 3/17.** |
| ‡6 ? | Tillett, W. 27051. | M. **May 3/17.** |
| 7 A. I | Howe, Herbert. 28077. | M. **April 17/17.** |
| 7 A. | Roberts, G. 27592. | M. **April 17/17.** |
| ‡7 C. | Bliss, Edward Thos. 28312. | W. and M. **June 16/17.** |

## *E.E.F.*

| | | |
|---|---|---|
| 4 | **Bishop, Lieut. R. B.** | W. and M. **April 19/17.** |
| 4 | **Hird, 2nd Lt. C. (Fr. 8 W. Riding.)** | W. and M. **April 19/17.** |
| 4 | **Leadbitter, 2nd Lieut. G. G.** | M. **April 19/17.** |
| 4 | **Lines, 2nd Lieut. S. J.** | W. and M. **April 19/17.** |
| 4 | **Murray, Capt. R. L.** | W. and M. **April 19/17.** |
| 4 A. | Dean, Geo. 203454. | M. **April 19/17.** |
| 4 A. | Martin, F. G. 203464. | M. **April 19/17.** |
| 4 A. II | Sharpe, B. 200554. (2721.) | M. **April 19/17.** |
| 4 A. | Waters, L.-Cpl. F. H. 200328. | M. **April 19/17.** |
| 4 B. | Finch, Fredk. 200788. | M. **April 19/17.** |
| 4 B. VIII | Jordan, A.-L.-Cpl. F. J. 201366. (5191.) | W. and M. **April 19/17.** |
| 4 B. | Parker, R. 200214. (1851.) | W. and M. **April 19/17.** |
| 4 B. | Sargent, Herbt. Spencer. 200762. | W. and M. **April 19/17.** |
| 4 B. | Spencer, Samuel. 200997. (4140.) | W. and M. **April 19/17.** |
| 4 B. | Tompkins, L.-Sergt. Herbert. 200465. | M. **April 19/17.** |
| 4 C. | Avery, Frank Wm. 200103. (1371.) | W. and M. **April 19/17.** |
| 4 C. IX | Butchard, A. 200413. (Late 2432.) | M. **April 19/17.** |
| 4 C. | Coombs, Bernard. 200080. | M. **April 19/17.** |
| 4 C. | Labrum, J. 201059. | M. **April 19/17.** |
| 4 C. | Rodwell, Cpl. A. 200169. (1708.) | W. and M. **April 19/17.** |
| 4 C. | Thorpe, John. 201392. (5221.) | W. and M. **April 19/17.** |
| 4 C. | Vickery, W. 203500. | M. **April 19/17.** |

**Northampton Regiment—contd.**

## *E.E.F.*

| | | |
|---|---|---|
| 4 D. | Billingham, William. 200546. | W. and M. April 19/17. |
| 4 D. | Chapman, G. 200809. (3760.) | W. and M. April 19/17. |
| 4 D. | Coles, F. 200502. (2603.) | W. and M. April 19/17. |
| 4 D. L.G.S. | Hatfield, Sergt. A. E. 201323. | M. April 19/17. |
| 4 D. | Moore, Wm. 200028. (247.) | M. April 19/17. |
| 4 D. | Payne, Cpl. B. T. 200109. (1392.) | M. April 19/17. |
| 4 D. | Perkins, E. 201443. | W. and M. April 19/17. |
| 4 D. | Pickbourne, L.-Cpl. W. S. 200390. | M. April 19/17. |
| 4 D. | Roberts, F. F. J. 203308. | W. and M. April 19/17. |
| 4 D. | Smith, H. 200739. | M. April 19/17. |
| 4 D. XV | Smith, J. T. 201458. | W. and M. April 19/17. |
| 4 D. | Swann, L.-Sergt. Harry Wm. 200198. | M. April 19/17. |
| 4 D. | Whitehead, Leonard. 203313. | W. and M. April 19/17. |
| 4 D. | Wild, A.-L.-Sergt. E. S. 201325. (5148.) | W. and M. April 19/17. |
| 4 ? | Adcock, A. E. 203321. | M. April 19/17. |
| 4 ? | Allan, E. 200991. | M. April 19/17. |
| 4 ? | Allen, J. B. 200424. | M. April 19/17. |
| 4 ? | Andrews, L.-Cpl. A. 201012. | M. April 19/17. |
| 4 ? | Asbrey, W. W. 200283. | W. and M. April 19/17. |
| 4 ? | Bailey, A. T. 201452. | M. April 19/17. |
| 4 ? | Barnes, G. H. 201040. | W. and M. April 19/17. |
| 4 ? | Bates, A. E. 201117. | M. April 19/17. |
| 4 ? | Bates, E. 201506. | M. April 19/17. |
| 4 ? | Bird, H. 200302. | M. April 19/17. |
| 4 ? | Bishop, O. 201412. | M. April 19/17. |
| 4 ? | Bland, A. E. 201085. | W. and M. April 19/17. |
| 4 ? | Boon, A. J. 201154. | M. April 19/17. |
| 4 ? | Boon, F. 200821. | W. and M. April 19/17. |
| 4 ? | Bosworth, W. C. 200961. | M. April 19/17. |
| 4 ? | Boulter, W. G. 201256. | M. April 19/17. |
| 4 ? | Bree, A. 200533. | M. April 19/17. |
| 4 ? | Burton, C. 200950. | M. April 19/17. |
| 4 ? | Busby, A. E. 200891. | M. April 19/17. |
| 4 ? | Church, T. W. 200957. | M. April 19/17. |
| 4 ? | Clarke, R. A. 201056. | W. and M. April 19/17. |
| 4 ? | Clarke, R. H. 201251. | M. April 19/17. |
| 4 ? | Cobb, Cpl. W. 200256. | M. April 19/17. |
| 4 ? | Crane, P. 200838. | M. April 19/17. |
| 4 ? | Crofts, E. P. 200306. | M. April 19/17. |
| 4 ? | Dickenson, A. 203289. | M. April 19/17. |
| 4 ? | Fairey, W. F. 201035. | M. April 19/17. |
| 4 ? | Finch, J. 38861. | M., bel. drowned April 15/17. "Arcadian." |
| 4 ? | Freeman, E. J. 200301. | W. and M. April 19/17. |
| 4 ? | Gilbert, T. 201462. | W. and M. April 19/17. |
| 4 ? | Ginns, Cpl. E. 200292. | M. April 19/17. |
| 4 ? | Glover, C. E. 200725. | M. April 19/17. |
| 4 ? | Hale, O. 201115. | W. and M. April 19/17. |
| 4 ? | Haseldine, H. 200693. | M. April 19/17. |
| 4 ? | Helms, A. 200429. | M. April 19/17. |
| 4 ? | Hollis, A. 201190. | W. and M. April 19/17. |
| 4 ? | Holmes, John. 202203. | W. and M. April 19/17. |
| 4 ? | Houghton, P. 200694. | M. April 19/17. |
| 4 ? | Howe, A. 201312. | W. and M. April 19/17. |
| 4 ? | Keller, H. 200862. | M., bel. K. April 19/17. |
| 4 ? | Leaton, L.-Cpl. W. 200790. | W. and M. April 19/17. |
| 4 ? | Lewis, H. E. 201534. | W. and M. April 19/17. |
| 4 ? | Lilley, H. 200632. | M. April 19/17. |

**Northampton Regiment**—contd.

*E.E.F.*

| | | | |
|---|---|---|---|
| 4 | ? | Lilley, W. A. 203300. | M. April 19/17. |
| 4 | ? | McKenzie, R. A. B. 201434. | M. April 19/17. |
| 4 | ? | Marks, B. 201091. | M. April 19/17. |
| 4 | ? | Martin, J. T. 201022. | M. April 19/17. |
| 4 | ? | Mayes, T. B. 203301. | M. April 19/17. |
| 4 | ? | Morris, A. 200398. | M. April 19/17. |
| 4 | ? | Newman, Cpl. F. 200058. | W. and M. April 19/17. |
| 4 | ? | Nightingale, T. W. 201915. | M. April 19/17. |
| 4 | ? | Norton, A. 200503. | M. April 19/17. |
| 4 | ? | Nunley, L. 200689. | M. April 19/17. |
| 4 | ? | Panter, A. 200738. | W. and M. April 19/17. |
| 4 | ? | Panter, S. E. 200189. | W. and M. April 19/17. |
| 4 | ? | Parker, H. W. 200823. | M. April 19/17. |
| 4 | ? | Parsons, A. W. 200908. | M. April 19/17. |
| 4 | ? | Penrose, A. 201533. | M. April 19/17. |
| 4 | ? | Pulley, T. 200492. | M. April 19/17. |
| 4 | ? | Rigby, C. 200021. | W. and M. April 19/17. |
| 1 | ? | Roberts, T. G. 201148. | W. and M. April 19/17. |
| 4 | ? | Rodgers, H. 200334. | M. April 19/17. |
| 4 | ? | Rudlands, F. 200826. | M. April 19/17. |
| 4 | ? | Shaw, L.-Cpl. T. A. 201456. | M. April 19/17. |
| 4 | ? | Sheppard, S. F. 201004. | M. April 19/17. |
| 4 | ? | Shorey, E. J. 200663. | W. and M. April 19/17. |
| 4 | ? | Smith, E. 200382. | W. and M. April 19/17. |
| 4 | ? | Smith, A.-L.-Cpl. H. W. 200320. | M. April 19/17. |
| 4 | ? | Smith, J. 201072. | W. and M. April 19/17. |
| 4 | ? | Stubley, O. C. 200710. | M. April 19/17. |
| 4 | ? | Sturgess, J. 200897. | M. April 19/17. |
| 4 | ? | Tarlton, Sergt. W. 200423. | M. April 19/17. |
| 4 | ? | Tarry, W. 200210. | W. and M. April 19/17. |
| 4 | ? | Tottingham, A. G. 200896. | M. April 19/17. |
| 4 | ? | Walker, W. L. 201135. | W. and M. April 19/17. |
| 4 | ? | Ward, G. S. 201389. | M. April 19/17. |
| 4 | ? | Ward, W. 200990. | M. April 19/17. |
| 4 | ? | Watkins, T. W. 201173. | M. April 19/17. |
| 4 | ? | Webb, A. E. 200442. | W. and M. April 19/17. |
| 4 | ? | Wheeler, J. W. 203317. | M. April 19/17. |
| 4 | ? | Wood, Sergt. J. 200039. | W. and M. April 19/17. |

**NORTHAMPTONSHIRE YEOMANRY.**

*B.E.F.*

| | | | |
|---|---|---|---|
| 1 | A. Sqd. 4 Trp. | Smith, H. H. 145274. (984.) | M. April 11/17. |
| 1 | B. Squad | Child, Walter. 145372 | W. and M. April 11/17. |
| 1 | B. | Lathbury, A. R. 145457. (1229.) | M April 11/17. |
| 1 | ? | Skears, J. 145984. | M April 11/17. |

## NORTHUMBERLAND FUSILIERS.

### *B.E.F.*

| | | |
|---|---|---|
| 1 Y. | **Bucknall, Capt. W. H. C.** | K. May 3/17. Det.D./B. |
| 1 Z. | **Passingham, 2nd Lieut. E. G.** | M. May 3/17. |
| 1 W. | Calthorpe, J. 38378. | W. and M. April 9/17. |
| •1 W. III | Cudmore, A. 34596. | M. May 3/17. |
| 1 W. II | Matthews, Wm. 266007. (Late 6th, 4497.) | W. Unoff. M. May 3/17. |
| •1 W. | Stobbs, A.-Sergt. Albert. 9841. | W. and M. May 3/17. |
| ‡1 X. | Mason, M. 426. | M. May 3/17. |
| ‡1 X. | Walker, S. 36268. | M. May 3/17. |
| ‡1 X. | Walton, A. 36266. | M. May 3/17. |
| 1 Y. | Beavon, W. 40143. | W. and M. April 23/17. |
| ‡1 Y. | Broadley, G. 242337. | M. May 6/17. |
| 1 Y. XI | Brown, Jonathan Geo. Arnold, 3812. (Late 2nd.) | W. and M. April 9/17. 2nd Cas. |
| ‡1 Y. | Chadwick, L.-Cpl. C. 38421. | M. May 3/17. |
| 1 Y. | Cooper, J. 6380. | M. April 13/17. |
| ‡1 Y. | Frater, J. 24243. | M. May 3/17. |
| •1 Y. | Martin, Wm. 200140. | M. May 3/17. |
| 1 Y. | Ruddy, P. 17115. | W. and M. April 9/17. |
| 1 Y. | Wilson, Thos. 27/761. (Fr. 27th.) | W. and M. April 13/17. |
| 1 Z. | Bailly, L.-Cpl. A. C. 34438. | M. Mar. 21/17. |
| 1 Z. XIV | Barbour, Robert. 46871. | M. May 10/17. |
| 1 Z. XIV | Bickerton, Geo. Wright. 34443. | M. May 3/17. |
| 1 Z. XIV | Caddell, Hugh. 46870. | M. May 10/17. |
| ‡1 Z. | Johnson, J. 36248. | M. May 3/17. |
| 1 Z. L.G.S. | McCormack, Wm. 9282. | M. May 10/17. |
| 1 Z. | MacDonald, J. 46897. | M. April 9/17. |
| 1 Z. XVI | Potter, W. E. A. 8589. | M. Mar. 21/17. |
| ‡1 Z. | Silvers, Cpl. A. 8055. | M. May 10/17. |
| 1 Z. XVI | Thomson, John N. 46811. | M. Mar. 21/17. |
| 1 Z. | Wanless, Thos. 27410. | M. April 9/17. |
| 4 B. VI | Beattie, Fred. 2703. | M. Sept. 15/16. R/Enq. |
| 4 C. L.G.S. | Marples, Wm. 3441. | K. Nov. 15/16. Det.D./B. |
| 4 D. XV | Bush, James. 5073. | M. Oct. 30/16. R/Enq. |
| 4 D. | Cook, Fred. 9023. | M. Sept. 15/16. R/Enq. |
| ‡5 | **Clephan, 2nd Lt. W. R.** (Fr. 6th.) | M. July 7/17. |
| 5 A. | Gaunt, J. W. 242093. | M. April 20/17. |
| 5 A. | Reynolds, J. 263033. | M. April 20/17. |
| 5 B. VIII | Bills, Samuel Geo. 5631. | M. Nov. 14/16. R/Enq. |
| 5 B. | Ogden, Arthur. 241936. (Late 6698.) | M. Nov. 14/16. |
| 5 B. | Rush, John Thomas. 3678. | M. Nov. 14/16. |
| 5 B. | Stocks, C. 7115. | M. Nov. 14/16. R/Enq. |
| 5 C. X | Hemming, Walter Jas. 242105. (6876.) | W. and M. April 18/17. |
| ‡6 | **Aldrich, 2nd Lt. F. P.** (Fr. 4th.) | M. July 6/17. |
| 6 B. | Bellaby, W. 257251. | M. Nov. 27/16. |
| 6 B. VII | Slight, David. 4165. | M. Sept. 15/16. R./Enq. |
| 6 D. | Boylan, J. 267246. | M. April 16/17. |
| 6 D. XV | Deedman, H. P. 266657. | M. April 16/17. |
| 6 D. | Gray, Ivan. 265434. | M. April 16/17. |
| 6 D. | Hargreaves, S. 235280. | M. April 16/17. |
| 7 B. | **Brooke-Booth, 2nd Lieut. Baron.** | K. Oct. 1/16. Det.D./B. R./Enq. |
| 7 | **Swinney, 2nd Lieut., J. H. C.** | M., bel. P. April 16/17. |
| 7 A. | Brodie, V. F. 7012. | M. Nov. 14/16. R/Enq. |
| ‡7 A. I | Dunn, Sergt. George. 1157. | M. Nov. 14/16. R/Enq. |
| 7 A. | Sim, W. 290972. | M. April 15/17. |
| 7 B. VI | Darvell, E. 7023. | W. and M. Nov. 14/16. R/Enq |
| •7 B. | Taylor, L.-Cpl. Wm. 3508. | M. Sept. 15/16. R/Enq. |
| 7 B. VIII | Turner, Robt. 5636. | M. Nov. 14/16. |

**Northumberland Fusiliers—contd.**

*B.E.F.*

| | | |
|---|---|---|
| 7 B. VIII | White, S. 291764. (5647 & 19120.) | M. Nov. 14/16. R/Enq. |
| 7 D. XIII | Bell, Wm. 291883. | M. April 17/17. |
| ‡7 D. XIV | Edwards, T. 291100. (3695.) | M. April 17/17. |
| ‡7 D. | Ryan, James F. 46100. | M. April 17/17. |
| ‡7 D. XV | Smith, Thos. 290795. | M. April 16/17. |
| *8 W. | Barnatt, Joseph. 20760. | M. Sept. 26/16. R/Enq. |
| 8 W. | Castle, A. 22371. | M. Sept. 26/16. R/Enq. |
| 8 X. VII | Mayne, J. G. 20574. | W. and M. Sept. 26/16. R/Enq. |
| 8 X. | Morton, L.-Cpl. Lewis Arth. 18335. | M. Sept. 26/16. R/Enq. |
| 8 X. V | Robinson, Albert. 18412. | M. Sept. 26/16. R/Enq. |
| ‡8 X. VI | Weeks, Albert. 18541. | M. Sept. 26/16. R/Enq. |
| 8 X. VII | Wright, Edward. 18135. | M. Sept. 26/16. R/Enq. |
| 8 Y. X | Bolton, Edward. 17429. | W. and M. Sept. 26/16. R/Enq. |
| 8 Y. | Grant, T. B. 7554. | M. Sept. 26/16. R/Enq. |
| 8 Y. IX | Joyce, Robert. 17456. | M. Sept. 26/16. R/Enq. |
| ‡9 A. | Duffy, James. 188. | M. Feb. 8/17. |
| 9 B. VIII | Derby, L.-Cpl. Wm. Stanley. 22/848 | W. and M. April 23/17. |
| ‡9 B. | Hodgson, J. 22074. | M., bel. K. May 23/17. |
| ‡9 B. | Soulsby, W. 12172. | K. April 23/17. Det.D./B. |
| 9 B. | Yearham, Cpl. T. W. 14737. | M. April 23/17. |
| 9 C. | Comery, J. L. 13052. | M. April 23/17. |
| 9 C. | Offord, L. C. 44742. | M. April 23/17. |
| *10 A. II | Theobald, Tom. 4998. | M. Sept. 26/16. R/Enq. |
| 10 B. | McPhee, Thomas. 13826. | W. and M. Sept. 25/16. R/Enq |
| *10 C. XI | Bell, Fred. 40231. | M. June 10/17. |
| ‡11 B. VIII | Reed, Thos. 7255. | M. June 7/17. |
| *12 | **Queen, 2nd Lieut. J.** | W. and M. June 16/17. |
| 12 A. | Goodson, G. W. 46127. | M. April 14/17. |
| ‡12 A. III | Patterson, Thos. Wm. 33910. | M. June 16/17. |
| ‡12 A. | Ward, Wm. Geo. 46147. | M. June 16/17. |
| ‡12 B. V | Buck, H. 35241. | M. June 16/17. |
| ‡12 B. VII | Wilkinson, C. 45735. | M. June 16/17. |
| ‡12 C. XI | Brown, Robt. L. 46134. | M. June 16/17. |
| ‡12 C. XI | Ketcher, Harold Edwin. 35259. | M. June 16/17. |
| 12 D. XV | Hodgson, John. 35347. | W. and M. April 12/17. |
| ‡12 D. | Marshall, John Lindsay. 33899. | M. June 16/17. |
| *13 | **Duncan, Lieut. J. D. P.** | W. and M. June 16/17. |
| *13 | **Reidy, Capt. F. J.** | M., bel. K. June 16/17. |
| ‡13 A. III | Weddle, James. 5989. | M. June 16/17. |
| ‡13 B. | Conway, Sergt. Daniel. 5261. | M. June 16/17. |
| ‡13 C. XIII | Batch, C. W. 349. | M. June 16/17. |
| ‡13 C. XI | Dixon, Cpl. John. 37772. | M. June 16/17. |
| ‡13 C. X | Stebbins, Herbert. 30/337. | M. June 16/17. |
| 13 D. XVI | Carr, E. 46444. | W. and M. April 2/17. |
| ‡13 D. M.G.S. | Graham, H. 6146. | M. Unoff. W. June 16/17. |
| ‡13 D. XVI | Hudson, W. 32/420. | M. June 16/17. |
| ‡13 D. XIII | Pennington, Cpl. J. 35380. | M. June 16/17. |
| ‡14 A. | Madge, H. T. 45478. | M. June 2/17. |
| ‡14 A. II | Sumner, Christopher. 22809. | M. June 2/17. |
| ‡15 D. XV | Noake, Alfred. 39738. | M. April 1/17. |
| 16 A. I | Boulter, Herbert. 34345. | M. Feb. 10/17. |
| 16 A. | Fox, R. E. 40388. | M. Feb. 10/17. |
| 16 B. VIII | Plummer, Arthur. 34356. | M. Feb. 13/17. |
| 16 B. | Winn, H. 1. | W. and M. April 10/17. |
| 16 C. | Willis, Fred. 31/115. (Fr. A. Co.) | M. Feb. 10/17. |
| ‡16 D. XVI | Barker, Tom. 44119. | M. June 5/17. |
| 16 D. XVI | Stevenson, Wm. 1350. | K. April 2/17. Det.D./B. |

**Northumberland Fusiliers—contd.**

## *B.E.F.*

*20 A. II Allen, Ernest. 34927. Unoff. W. and M., bel. D/W. **June 7/17.**
‡20 A. I Bainbridge, John. 33798. M. **June 5/17.**
‡20 A. Barker, L.-Cpl. J. 37440. M. **June 5/17.**
‡20 A. III Cockburn, William. 48023. M. **June 5/17.**
*20 A. I Collins, Edgar Harold. 38581. M. **June 5/17.**
‡20 A. Dixon, T. 684. M. **June 5/17.**
‡20 A. Glentworth, J. N. 38577. M. **June 5/17.**
20 A. Green, L.-Cpl. R. 5614. M. **April 27-28/17.**
‡20 A. Hadden, E. C. 37298. M. **June 5/17.**
‡20 A. Hawley, G. 39523. M. **June 5/17.**
‡20 A. Noble, W. S. 1531. M. **June 5/17.**
20 A. I Parker, E. 38567. M. Unoff. K. **April 9/17.**
‡20 A. Pollard, C. 15080. M. **June 5/17.**
‡20 A. Pye, R. 38569. M. **June 5/17.**
‡20 A. IV Roy, Wm. 35466. M. **April 28/17.**
‡20 A. Scholes, T. H. 35643. M. **June 5/17.**
‡20 A. Smith, L.-Cpl. E. G. 44106. M. **June 5/17.**
‡20 A. Stiven, H. J. 205. M. **June 5/17.**
‡20 A. III Turnbull, Harry. 22/333. M. **June 5/17.**
‡20 B. VI Aylward, Edward. 47748. M. **June 5/17.**
‡20 B. VII Barnett, T. H. 43145. M. **June 5/17.**
‡20 B. Cass, A. 48032. M. **June 5/17.**
‡20 B. Collin, Sergt. W. 42505. M. **June 5/17.**
‡20 B. Crame, G. W. 13221. M. **June 5/17.**
‡20 B. VI Davis, Fred. 50257. M. **June 5/17.**
‡20 B. Dixon, John Robert. 21/1005. M. **June 5/17.**
*20 B. Fox, John Thos. 8317. M. **April 9/17.**
‡20 B. Heron, J. T. 414. M. **June 17/17.**
‡20 B. Holman, W. 47111. M. **June 5/17.**
‡20 B. V Joyce, Robert. 38620. M. **June 5/17.**
‡20 B. McGrory, W. 220. M. **June 5/17.**
‡20 B. Mallinson, L.-Cpl. C. 36219. M. **June 5/17.**
‡20 B. VII Robinson, James. 20611. M. **June 5/17.**
‡20 B. Taylor, G. W. 37382. M. **June 5/17.**
‡20 C. Atherton, G. 136. W. and M. **June 5/17.**
‡20 C. Branton, G. 48006. M. **June 5/17.**
‡20 C. III Chapman, Walter. 47103. M. **June 5/17.**
‡20 C. IX Clark, Cpl. John Henry. 35460. M. **June 5/17.**
‡20 C. Claxton, L. W. 48025. M. **June 5/17.**
‡20 C. Gibson, J. 37296. M. **June 5/17.**
*20 C. IX Harker, Richard. 1460. M. **April 9/17.**
‡20 C. XI Harrison, Roger. 37485. M. **June 5/17.**
‡20 C. Hill, T. C. 37472. M. **June 5/17.**
‡20 C. IX Hilton, Edgar W. 36231. M. **June 5/17.**
‡20 C. Hunter, Cpl. G. E. 1627. M. **June 5/17.**
*20 C. IX Leese, A. 50263. M. **June 5/17.**
20 C. IX Lowther, B. 47120. K. **April 27/17.** Det.D./B.
‡20 C. Nee, J. 1190. M. **June 5/17.**
‡20 C. O'Brien, J. 48349. M. **June 5/17.**
‡20 C. Walker, F. 36151. M. **June 5/17.**
‡20 C. Warner, J. 37431. M. **April 9/17.**
‡20 D. Allan, M. 475. W. and M. **June 5/17.**
‡20 D. Black, William. 43092. M. **June 5/17.**
‡20 D. Boothby, J. 47764. M. **June 5/17.**
*20 D. Burke, W. H. 36162. M. **April 27-28/17.**
‡20 D. Goldie, L.-Sergt. J. 1566. M. **June 5/17.**
‡20 D. Harrison, Cpl. Cairns. 22/1013. M. **June 5/17.**

Northumberland Fusiliers—contd.

## *B.E.F.*

‡20 D. McBride, R. 37512. M. June 5/17.
‡20 D. Orr, David. 20/863. M. June 5/17.
20 D. Rawnsley, Arthur. 524. (Fr. 9th.) M. Nov. 11/16. R./Enq.
‡20 D. Robson, Cpl. G. 1363. M. June 5/17.
‡20 D. Scotchbrook, T. N. 36155. M. June 5/17.
‡20 D. Sonter, J. R. 48355. M. June 5/17.
‡20 ? Colling, J. 47781. (Fr. R.E.) M. June 5/17.
‡21 A. Campbell, W. 37233. M. June 5/17.
‡21 A. Conway, G. R. 117. M. June 5/17.
‡21 A. Farrow, J. H. 35930. M. June 5/17.
‡21 A. Gee, F. A. 47820. M. June 5/17.
‡21 A. Gibbons, E. 48365. M. June 5/17.
‡21 A. Hunt, G. 32036. M. June 5/17.
21 A. Lawrence, W. 39359. M. April 7-9/17.
‡21 A. O'Donnell, J. 1724. M. June 5/17.
‡21 A. Ridge, T. 79. M. June 5/17.
‡21 A. Robson. 32116. M. June 5/17.
21 A. Rogers, J. W. 595. M. April 9/17.
‡21 A. Ryans, H. 204102. M. June 5/17.
21 A. Shiell, L.-Cpl. R. D. 37197. M. April 9/17.
*21 A. I Trainor, W. 39183. K. April 8-9/17. Det.D./B.
‡21 A. Watts, J. 33659. M. June 5/17.
‡21 B. Andrews, F. 35530. M. June 5/17.
‡21 B. Brown, J. F. 39021. M. June 5/17.
*21 B. VI Culverhouse, P. 47789. M. June 5/17.
‡21 B. Davidson, J. G. 204144. M. June 5/17.
‡21 B. V Duckworth, J. H. 39028. M. June 5/17.
‡21 B. Spratt, R. P. 37201. M. June 5/17.
‡21 B. VI Stubbs, Richd. Mark. 37251. M. June 5/17.
‡21 B. V Wilkin, Thos. 35953. M. May 6/17.
‡21 C. Atherton, J. 984. M. June 5/17.
‡21 C. Croft, J. 31465. M. June 5/17.
21 C. IX Duke, Geo. Isaac. 48046. M. April 9/17.
‡21 C. Mitchinson, A. 1093. M. June 5/17.
‡21 C. X Newell, Henry. 48420. M. June 5/17.
‡21 C. or D. Potter, Sergt. John. 35539. M. June 5/17.
‡21 C. Reynolds, F. 17822. M. June 5/17.
21 C. Weddell, Sgt. Thos. 1020. M. April 9/17.
‡21 D. Clennell, John. 38517. M. June 5/17.
‡21 D. Collingwood, A.-Cpl. J. 1696. M. June 5/17.
‡21 D. XVI Collins, Joseph. 44131. W. and M. June 5/17.
‡21 D. XIII Cook, George W. H. 48033. M. June 5/17.
‡21 D. Dyer, E. W. 47794. M. June 5/17.
‡21 D. Harrison, T. B. 1360. M. June 5/17.
‡21 D. XIV Holmes, Frank. 35937. M. June 5/17.
‡21 D. XIII Hood, John. 1590. M. June 5/17.
‡21 D. Hutchinson, A.-Cpl. C. 39171. M. June 5/17.
‡21 D. Ling, G. E. 31931. M. June 5/17.
‡21 D. McNichol, J. 35963. M. June 5/17.
‡21 D. XIII Riddle, William. 4312. M. June 5/17.
‡21 D. Roddam, A.-Sergt. E. R. 19486. M. June 5/17.
‡21 D. Storey, J. J. 119. M. June 5/17.
‡22 A. I Bainbridge, Geo. 200593. M. June 5/17.
‡22 A. Bell, Cpl. George. 504. M. June 5/17.
‡22 A. III Crossley, Herbert. 34996. M. June 5/17.
‡22 A. Goldsbury, Charles. 46110. M. June 5/17.
‡22 A. IV Knapton, Fred. 374. (Fr. 29th.) M. June 5/17.

**Northumberland Fusiliers—contd.**

## *B.E.F.*

‡22 A. Preston, L.-Cpl. Thomas. 1493. M. June 5/17.
‡22 A. I Smith, Norman. 46115. M. June 5/17.
‡22 A. Stephenson, L.-Cpl. Herbert. 21/1707. M. June 5/17.
‡22 A. I Webster, F. H. 46109. M. June 5/17.
*22 B. Bell, John D. 35011. W. Unoff. M. June 5/17.
‡22 B. Clasper, John. 291645. M. June 5/17.
*22 B. VI Harris, Fred. Thos 47194. M. April 9/17.
‡22 B. VI Harris, Joseph W. 200211. M. June 5/17.
‡22 B. Hedly, Matthew. 1369. M. June 5/17.
‡22 B. Potts, G. 34117. M. April 9/17.
‡22 B. V Priestley, Edmund. 47374. M. May 6/17.
‡22 B. V Stanton, Charles Bertrand. 34018. M. June 5/17.
‡22 B. Swaine, Benjamin. 36018. M. June 5/17.
‡22 B. VII Weighill, William. 36130. M. June 5/17.
‡22 B. V. Wilson, Featherstone. 36131. M. June 5/17.
‡22 C. IX Burt, R. A. 1167. M. June 5/17.
‡22 C. IX Edwards, Thomas. 75. M. June 5/17.
‡22 C. X Eyre, Albert. 13156. M. June 5/17.
‡22 C. VIII Graham, A.-L.-Sergt. Robt. 21/919 M. June 5/17.
‡22 C. Hutchinson, Alex. 21/1504. M. June 5/17.
‡22 C. Price, J. 6439. M. June 5/17.
‡22 D. Bilclough, L.-Cpl. Wm. 22/922. M. June 5/17.
‡22 D. XIII Marshall, H. 47326. M. June 5/17.
22 D. Quinn, C. 1002. M. April 9/17.
22 D. XIII Scott, W. F. 38284. K. April 9/17. Det.D./B.
22 D. Taylor, W. 38294. M. April 9/17.
‡22 D. Thompson, James Joseph. 38295. M. April 27/17.
22 D. Thompson, J. S. 34994. M. April 9/17.
22 D. Trusler, L. 204148. M. April 9/17.
23 **Jamieson, 2nd Lieut. J.** M., bel. W. April 29/17.
23 C. **Menzies, 2nd Lieut. H.** W. and M. April 29/17.
23 **Philip, 2nd Lieut. D. C.** M., bel. W. April 29/17.
23 **Watson, 2nd Lieut. J. L.** M., bel. W. April 27/17.
23 A. or D. Clarke, Henry Cecil. 40680. M. Feb. 11/17.
23 A. Dillon, R. 38072. M. Feb. 11/17.
23 A. Garbutt, John. 47506. M. April 9/17.
23 A. Grant, Cpl. Thomas. 180. M. Feb. 11/17.
23 A. Hart, J. Harold. 38077. M. Feb. 11/17.
23 A. Melville, J. 177. (Fr. 20th.) M. April 9/17.
23 A. III Robinson, Sgt. Albert. 19/1682. W. and M. Feb. 11/17.
23 A. or B. West, Harry. 1524. M. April 27/17.
23 A. II Yule, L.-Cpl. James. 46368. W. and M. April 9/17.
23 B. V Adam, R. J. 35031. M. April 29/17.
‡23 B. Atkinson, F. 31391. M. April 29/17.
23 B. Baxter, Sig. S. E. 47078. M. April 29/17.
‡23 B. Birchmore, N. B. 47452. M. April 29/17.
‡23 B. Blakewell, A.-Cpl. H. 444. M. April 29/17.
23 B. V Blench, Robert. 16/549. M. April 29/17.
‡23 B. Collins, A.-Cpl. S. 40808. M. April 29/17.
23 B. V Colton, Martin Luther. 204881. M. April 29/17.
‡23 B. Cope, J. 38036. M. April 29/17.
‡23 B. Cotton, M. L. 204881. M. April 29/17.
*23 B. or D. Curtis, L.-Cpl. A. 46382. M. April 29/17.
‡23 B. Dunn, J. H. 47453. M. April 29/17.
23 B. L.G.S. Foster, A. E. 38041. M. April 29/17.
‡23 B. Irving, J. 38104. M. April 29/17.
*23 B. V Mathews, Fred. 20717. Unoff. M., bel. P/W. May 3/17.

**Northumberland Fusiliers**—contd.

## B.E.F.

23 **B. VI** Matthews, Walter W. 35023. M. **April 29/17.**
23 **B. VIII** Ogden, Sergt. John. 40835. M. **April 29/17.**
‡23 **B.** Patchett, A. 40776. M. **April 29/17.**
*23 **B. VII** Read, Alf. Henry. 46352. M. **April 29/17.**
23 **B.** Read, Percy. 19660. M. **April 29/17.**
23 **B.** Reveley, Geo. 1092. M. **April 29/17.**
23 **B.** Sheville, Alfred. 47450. M. **April 29/17.**
23 **B. VI** Stalker, Geo. Henry. 38050. M. **April 29/17.**
23 **B. VIII** Sugden, E. W. 40740. M. **April 29/17.**
23 **B. V** Walker, Geo. 47436. M. **April 29/17.**
23 **B.** Watson, Cpl. John. 1493. M. **April 29/17.**
23 **B.** Wilkinson, Walter J. 39350. W. and M. **April 29/17.**
‡23 **C.** Brisley, L. A. 47469. M. **April 29/17.**
23 **C. XII** Eccles, W. 212. M. **April 29/17.**
*23 **C. XII** McGuigan, Thomas. 10417. W. and M. **April 9/17.**
‡23 **C. IX** Morgan, J. L. 47439. K. **April 29/17.** Det.D./B. R/Enq.
‡23 **C.** Murray, P. 34712. M. **April 29/17.**
23 **C.** Sharp, George. 22/1490. M. **April 29/17.**
‡23 **C.** Smith, R. B. 18955. M. **April 29/17.**
‡23 **C.** Thompson, H. 16340. M. **April 29/17.**
‡23 **C.** Tweedy, J. 23067. M. **April 29/17.**
‡23 **D.** Barker, D. W. 11155. M. **April 29/17.**
‡23 **D.** Beddoes, F. H. 37955. M. **April 29/17.**
23 **D.** Robson, Joseph. 37973. M. **Feb. 11/17.**
*23 **?** Edwards, Henry John. 47803. (Late R.E.) M. **April 28/17.**
24 **C.** **Baker, 2nd Lieut. D. J.** M. **April 28/17.**
24 **A. M.G.S.** Appleyard, Harold. 41514. M. **April 28/17.**
24 **A.** Blain, Wm. Thos. 23187. M. **April 28/17.**
24 **A.** Ferry, R. F. 47361. M. **April 28/17.**
‡24 **B.** Barstow, G. 285088. M. **April 28/17.**
‡24 **B.** Bishop, E. 285080. M. **April 28/17.**
24 **B.** Boughton, Albert Hy. 285081. (35817.) M. **April 28/17.**
‡24 **B.** Curry, J. 25/814. M. **April 28/17.**
‡24 **B.** Dobson, M. O. 285099. M. **April 28/17.**
24 **B.** Flatley, T. 242. M. **April 28/17.**
24 **B.** Harrison, H. 44162. M. **April 28/17.**
24 **B.** Hill, H. H. 42398. M. **April 28/17.**
*24 **B.** Jackson, Chas. 24181. M. **April 28/17.**
24 **B.** Jackson, Cpl. Robert. 37635. M. **April 28/17.**
*24 **B.** Johnson, L.-Cpl. Wm. 19171. M. **April 28/17.**
‡24 **B.** Kay, Harry. 34165. M. **April 28/17.**
24 **B.** McDowell, Jas. 1117. (Fr. 27th.) M. **April 28/17.**
‡24 **B.** McKenna, J. 13163. M. **April 28/17.**
24 **B.** Nalton, J. E. 44183. M. **April 28/17.**
24 **B.** Parker, H. 44191. M. **April 9/17.**
24 **B.** Ryles, Joseph E. 24104. M. **April 28/17.**
‡24 **B.** Scott, D. 34180. M. **April 28/17.**
*24 **B.** Starkie, James. 45695. M. **April 28/17.**
24 **B.** Stephen, W. 37662. M. **April 9/17.**
‡24 **B.** Tones, G. 42509. M. **April 28/17.**
24 **B.** Wedgebury, A. 41659. M. **April 28/17.**
24 **B. M.G.S.** West, Willie. 41563. M. **April 28/17.**
24 **B.** Wilson, G. 45555. M. **April 28/17.**
24 **B.** Wray, J. 35709. M. **April 28/17.**
‡24 **C.** Boyle, R. 904. M. **April 28/17.**
24 **C. or D.** Buckley, D. 35063. M. **April 28/17.**

**Northumberland Fusiliers—contd.**

## *B.E.F.*

| | | |
|---|---|---|
| 24 C. or D. | Bunnyan, James. 45665. | M. April 28/17. |
| *24 C. XII | Coates, John. 45719. | K. April 9/17. Det.D./B. |
| ‡24 C. | Dyer, E. E. 36024. | M. April 28/17. |
| 24 C. M.G.S. | Horner, Chas. Fredk. 44163. | M. April 28/17. |
| 24 C. | Hunter, Herbert. 44153. | M. April 9/17. |
| 24 C. M.G.S. | Murty, Thomas. 41542. | W. and M. April 9/17. |
| 24 C. XII | Needham, George Harold. 44184. | M. April 28/17. |
| 24 C. XII | Wood, J. C. 41496. | M. April 28/17. |
| 24 D. XIII | Dunion, L.-Cpl. James. 42372. | M. April 28/17. |
| ‡24 D. | Ferguson, J. G. 22128. | W. and M. April 28/17. |
| 24 D. XV | Grant, Peter. 42386. | M. April 28/17. |
| 24 D. XIII | Hall, George. 11646. | M. April 28/17. |
| ‡24 D. | Harvey, G. 44164. | W. and M. April 28/17. |
| 24 D. | Hilditch, J. 35061. | M. April 28/17. |
| 24 D. | Hogg, R. 16258. | M. April 28/17. |
| ‡24 D. L.G.S. | Holloway, L.-Cpl. F. 24/1110. | M. April 28/17. |
| *24 D. | Holmes, Walter. 36044. | M. April 28/17. |
| ‡24 D. | Jacklin, W. 285123. | M. April 28/17. |
| 24 D. | Johnson, A. A. 285125. (Late 4 York & Lancs. Entrench. Batt., 6119.) (Erroneously known as 35861.) | M. April 28/17. |
| 24 D. XVI | Keen, John Conibeare. 47856. | M. April 28/17. |
| ‡24 D. | Kehoe, Cpl. D. 1469. | M. April 28/17. |
| ‡24 D. XVI | Limback, R. J. 47867. | M. April 28/17. |
| ‡24 D. | Lodge, G. 48249. | M. April 28/17. |
| ‡24 B. | McCutcheon, J. 47892. | M. April 28/17. |
| 24 D. XV | Maughan, Sergt. John. 517. | M. April 28/17. |
| 24 D. | Peat, Joseph G. 35065. | M. April 28/17. |
| 24 D. | Preston, W. G. 35091. | M. April 28/17. |
| 24 D. | Saddington, T. 1498. | M. April 9/17. |
| 24 D. XV | Tomlinson, Harry. 36034. | M. April 28/17. |
| *24 D. | Walker, Clarence Edward. 36058. | M. April 28/17. |
| ‡24 D. | Ward, W. B. 36057. | M. April 28/17. |
| 24 D. XVI | Winder, Herbert. 41587. | M. April 9/17. |
| 24 D. | Wood, Arthur. 35101. | M. April 28/17. |
| 24 D. | Young, Thomas. 36060. | M. April 28/17. |
| 24 ? I.T.M. | Hall, Lewis. 22915. (36776.) (103 Bgde.) | W. Unoff. M. April 28/17. |
| 25 | **Cox, 2nd Lieut. P. C.** | M. April 28/17. |
| 25 | **Mitchell, 2nd Lieut. W.** | M. April 28/17. |
| 25 | **Prudham, 2nd Lieut. T. P.** | M. April 28/17. |
| 25 | **Wheeler, 2nd Lieut. H. G.** | M. April 28/17. |
| 25 A. IV | Cutler, J. J. 47051. | M. April 28/17. |
| 25 A. | Dungworth, H. 35132. | M. April 28/17 |
| ‡25 A. | Errington, C.-S.-M. A. 42503. | M. April 28/17. |
| 25 A. | Newton, J. 35117. | M. April 28/17 |
| 25 A. IV | North, A. W. 46969. | M. April 28/17 |
| 25 A. | Pentland, Cpl. John. 525. | M. April 28/17 |
| ‡25 A. | Spencer, A. N. 46989. | M. April 28/17. |
| ‡25 A. II | Stubbs, Willie. 34918. | M. April 9/17. |
| *25 A. I | Thomas, Edmund Wm. 47953. | K. Mar. 14/17. Det.D./B. |
| ‡25 A. | Watkinson, J. H. 38797. | M. April 28/17. |
| 25 A. | Williams, H. 40636. | M. April 28/17 |
| 25 B. | Boxall, H. 47017. | M. April 9/17. |
| 25 B. | Davison, Thos. 35544. (Officers' Mess) | M. April 9/17. |
| 25 B. | Dixon, Richard. 24718. | M. April 28/17. |

**Northumberland Fusiliers—contd.**

## *B.E.F.*

| | | | | |
|---|---|---|---|---|
| ‡25 | B. | | Donnelly, D. 924. | M. April 28/17. |
| 25 | B. | VIII | Haithwaite, Clifford. 38825. | M. April 28/17. |
| 25 | B. | VIII | Hobbs, Alfred Thos. John. 47012. | M. April 28/17. |
| ‡25 | B. | | Kilpatrick, H. J. 420. | M. April 28/17. |
| 25 | B. | | Lowes, L.-Sergt. R. 42511. | M. Mar. 18/17. |
| 25 | B. | | Otter, Harry. 35118. | M. April 28/17. |
| 25 | B. | V | Penfound, Tom F. 47002. | M. April 28/17. |
| ‡25 | B. | | Spence, H. 14638. | M. April 28/17. |
| 25 | B. | | Surtees, T. 235133. | M. April 9/17. |
| ‡25 | B. | | Tester, F. 235164. | M. April 28/17. |
| •25 | B. | | Tolan, Richard. 39521. | M. April 28/17. |
| ‡25 | B. | | Walton, J. 47014. | M. April 28/17. |
| 25 | C. | | Brannan, James. 30/155. | M. April 28/17. |
| 25 | C. | X | Doyle, Charles. 34078. | M. April 28/17. |
| ‡25 | C. | | Ewins, R. P. 47056. | M. April 28/17. |
| 25 | C. | X | Hirst, Chas. 34902. (Late 19th W. Yorks, 29628.) | M. April 9/17. |
| 25 | C. | XII | Johnson, Willie. 44470. | M. April 28/17. |
| ‡25 | C. | | McGrevy, Cpl. J. 1175. | M. April 28/17. |
| ‡25 | C. | | March, W. 1131. | M. April 28/17. |
| 25 | C. | | Marshall, Allan. 35115. | M. April 28/17. |
| •25 | C. | XII | Meehan, John. 1091. | M. April 28/17. |
| 25 | C. | | North, J. 38900. | M. April 28/17. |
| 25 | C. | L.G.S. | O'Connor, Arthur. 1194. | M. April 28/17. |
| 25 | C. | | Pedder, A. 44475. | M. April 28/17. |
| 25 | C. | | Reed, T. 441. | M. April 28/17. |
| •25 | C. | XII | Smith, Maurice Victor. 235148. | Unoff. K. April 28/17. Det.D./B. |
| 25 | C. | | Williams, T. 48144. | M. April 28/17. |
| 25 | D. | XIV | Brown, Fredk. Stannard. 47387. | W. and M. April 28/17. |
| 25 | D. | XV | Culver, G. S. 47779. | K. Mar. 26/17. Det.D./B. |
| 25 | D. | XIV | Dickinson, Henry G. R. 47800. | K. April 9/17. Det D./B. |
| 25 | D. | XVI | Hardisty, G. J. 50201. | M. April 28/17. |
| 25 | D. | | Hinchcliffe, Wm. H. 47393. | M. April 28/17. |
| ‡25 | D. | | Jennings, Silias H. 38950. | M. April 28/17. |
| 25 | D. | XIV | Mills, L.-Cpl. Fred. 35568. | M. April 28/17. |
| 25 | D. | | Parkin, John. 35119. | M. April 28/17. |
| 25 | D. | | Quinn, C. 34905. | M. April 9/17. |
| •25 | D. | XIII | Scott, Hugh. 4797. | K. April 28/17. Det.D./B. |
| •25 | D. | | Shepherd, Louis Armstrong. 42513. | W. and M. April 28/17. |
| ‡25 | D. | | Siddall, W. 35121. | W. and M. April 28/17. |
| •25 | D. | XIII | Smith, T. 35706. | M. April 28/17. |
| 25 | D. | | Stamper, R. D. 44506. | M. April 9/17. |
| ‡25 | ? | | Bailey, H. 35135. | M. April 28/17. |
| ‡25 | ? | | Barker, W. 235129. | M. April 28/17. |
| ‡25 | ? | | Cowe, D. W. 27679. | M. April 28/17. |
| 25 | ? | | France, William. 27642. | M. April 28/17. |
| 25 | ? | | Green, Ernest E. 30066. | M. April 28/17. |
| 25 | ? | | Hindmarsh, W. 43178. | M. April 28/17. |
| 25 | ? | | Murrie, John Wm. Cowell. 43300. | M. April 28/17. |
| ‡25 | ? | | Sharman, H. 35133. | M. April 28/17. |
| •25 | ? | | Slater, Clayton. 351. | M. April 28/17. |
| ‡25 | ? | | Toogood, G. W. 27815. | M. April 28/17. |
| 25 | ? | | Wood, Harry. 35709. | M. April 28/17. |
| 25 | ? | | Wright, Harry. 33704. | M. April 28/17. |
| 26 | A. | | Rayer, C. 47556. | M. April 9/17. |
| •26 | A. | | Richardson, A. J. 285142. | W. and M. April 28/17. |
| 26 | A. | IX | Sutcliffe, Sig. Herb. 48303. | K. April 9/17. Det.D./B. |
| ‡26 | B. | VII | Kossick, Laurence. 36325. | M. June 5/17. |

**Northumberland Fusiliers—contd.**

## *B.E.F.*

:26 C. Layton, H. R. 34203. M. April 9/17.
26 C. X Wilson, Wm. 235275. M. April 9/17.
‡26 D. XIV Smith, Wm. Ernest. 34857. M. June 5/17.
26 D. Sutcliffe, J. 48304. M. April 9/17.
26 D. Westwood, A. 37610. M. April 9/17.
‡26 D. Whalley, J. A 36311. W. Unoff. M. June 5/17.
27 **Westhorp, 2nd Lieut. W. H.** K. April 28/17. Det.D./B.
‡27 A. Carran, W. 100. M. April 28/17.
27 A. Dilcock, H. 44241. M. April 9/17.
‡27 A. Edwards, T. W. 44243. M. April 28/17.
‡27 A. Fisher, J. 292694. M. April 28/17.
:27 A. Flay, J. C. 44246. M. April 9/17.
27 A. Foster, J. E. 44245. M. April 9/17.
*27 A. IV McMahon, Wm. 42418. M. April 28/17.
27 A. M.G.S. Moultrie, Wm. 41051. M. April 9/17.
‡27 A. O'Connor, J. 34235. M. April 28/17.
27 A. III Preston, Norman. 45986. W. and M. April 28/17.
‡27 A. Thompson, L.-Cpl. J. 40988. M. April 28/17.
27 A. Warren, Ben. 35794. M. April 28/17.
27 A. York, Matthew. 1467. (Fr. 16th.) M. April 9/17.
‡27 B. V Bell, J. E. 202898. M. April 28/17.
27 B. V Bickerdike, Jacob. 21245. M. April 28/17.
27 B. M.G.S. Brown, John T. 810. M. April 28/17.
27 B. Clayford, W. 40934. M. April 9/17.
*27 B. Douglas, George. 240856. M. April 28/17.
27 B. V Edmonds, Chas. E. 34674. M. April 9/17.
‡27 B. Fawcett, M. 34214. M. April 28/17.
‡27 B. Fenwick, J. 240766. M. April 28/17.
‡27 B. Ferguson, J. 50291. M. April 28/17.
27 B. VII Foster, Craven. 40950. M. April 28/17.
*27 B. M.G.S. Hall, J. R. 40954. M. April 28/17.
*27 B. Hall, V. 50296. M. April 28/17.
‡27 B. Hinds, Cpl. F. 998. M. April 28/17.
‡27 B. Kane, W. 40941. M. April 28/17.
27 B. VIII Keppie, Cyclist Walter. 37908. M. April 28/17.
27 B. or D. Oddy, Edgar. 50278. M. April 28/17.
‡27 B. Perry, G. E. 203264. M. April 28/17.
‡27 B. Pyke, T. 47901. M. April 28/17.
‡27 B. Rodgers, P. 42429. M. April 28/17.
:27 B. Senior, J. 44206. M. April 9/17.
27 B. VII Turner, J. H. 21217. M. April 28/17.
27 B. V Vayro, Jas. 48277. M. April 9/17.
27 B. Watson, J. 34683. M. April 9/17.
27 B. Wright, Beaumont. 201342. M. April 9/17.
‡27 B. Wright, F. W. 35796. M. April 28/17.
‡27 C. Batchelor, C. H. 806. M. April 25/17.
*27 C. X Cawthorne, William. 40930. M. April 25/17.
‡27 C. Gleeson, A.-Cpl. W. 40967. M. April 25/17.
‡27 C. Hall, J. 41036. M. April 25/17.
27 C. XII Harrison, Geo. 50297. M. April 26/17.
27 C. XI Hebert, W. G. 203425. M. April 9/17.
‡27 C. Keritzer, L.-Cpl. F. 6910. M. April 25/17.
27 C. X McCabe, J. 21051. (103 Bgde., Sap. Co.). M. April 25/17
27 C. XII Morgan, Frank. 1421. M. April 25/17.
27 C. Newton, Geo. Armstrong. 48198. M. April 26/17.
‡27 C. Patterson, L.-Cpl. W. H. 580. M. April 25/17.
*27 C. X Simpson, Arthur. 47947. M. April 28/17.

Northumberland Fusiliers—contd.

## *B.E.F.*

27 C. IX Singleton, John. 42441. — M. April 9/17.
27 C. Smith, H. H. 44207. — M. April 9/17.
27 C. Whiteley, Leonard. 41061. — M. April 25/17.
27 C. Wilkinson, Sergt. J. 738. — M. April 25/17.
27 D. Chenery, Albert Ernest. 40965. — M. April 28/17.
‡27 D. Drury, A. 22852. — M. April 25/17.
27 D. Hatfield, W. 35777. — M. April 28/17.
‡27 D. Nash, J. 24939. — M. April 27/17.
‡27 D. Palmer, L.-Cpl. J. W. 864. — M. April 28/17.
27 D. XIII Place, I. R. 25184. — M. April 28/17.
27 D. Thompson, H. M. 25036. — M. April 28/17.
27 D. XIII Wharton, Thos. 23538. — M. April 28/17.

## *BALKANS.*

2 A. Moffatt, L.-Cpl. Thos. M. 3422. — M. Jan. 1/17.
2 D. Hall, Hugh. 751. — W. and M. Sept. 10/16, R/Enq.

# OXFORDSHIRE AND BUCKINGHAMSHIRE LIGHT INFANTRY.

## *B.E.F.*

*2 A. II Burden, Edward Dickens. 9320. — M. Unoff. W. Nov. 13-14/16. R/Enq.
2 A. Claydon, W. 23097. — W. and M. April 28/17.
2 A. II Farr, T. W. 24512. — M. Nov. 13/16. R/Enq.
2 A. I Jane, L. P. 33203. — W. and M. April 28/17.
2 A. III Lewis, Tom. 17821. — M. April 28/17.
2 A. Thompson, W. 26025. — M. April 17/17.
2 B. VI Cannam, G. E. 16638. — K. April 28/17. Det.D./B.
2 B. Goss, F. 24863. — M. April 28/17.
2 B. Holker, W. 26028. — K. April 14/17. Det.D./B.
2 B. Lovell, S. 21350. — M. April 28/17.
2 B. VII Marshall, G. 33218. — M. April 28/17.
2 B. Morley, B. 23017. — M. April 28/17.
2 C. XII Boswell, H. 16396. — M. April 28/17.
2 C. Challis, H. C. 22440. — M. April 28/17.
2 C. IX Child, Fred. Wm. 25951. — W. and M. April 28/17.
2 C. Dyer, A. G. 24359. — M. April 28/17.
*2 C. XI High, John. 16500. — M. April 28/17.
‡2 C. Sainsbury, J. 18707. — W. and M. April 28/17.
‡2 C. XI Sleath, J. 21816. — M. April 28/17.
*2 C. L.G.S. Williams, Percy. 22587. — M. Nov. 13/16.
2 D. Hoare, H. 20981. — M. April 28/17.
2 D. Withall, F. C. 33293. — M. April 30/17.
2 ? I.T.M. Hardwick, Albert. 25903. — M. May 1/17.
4 **Taylor, 2nd Lieut. H. S.** — M. April 28/17.
4 **Tilley, 2nd Lieut. A. H.** — M. April 7/17.
‡4 C. Paxton, L.-Cpl. H. 201378. — W. and M. May 21/17.
4 D. XV Aries, G. H. 202153. — M. April 19/17.
4 D. XIV Bowler, Cpl. A. 202537. — M. April 19/17.
4 D. Russell, W. E. 203400. — M. April 4/17.

**Oxfordshire and Buckinghamshire Light Infantry**—contd.

## *B.E.F.*

| | | |
|---|---|---|
| 2/4 C. | Harris, Cpl. F. A. 201083. | M. April 28/17. |
| 2/4 C. IX | Shepherd, Jn. Hy. 200361. | M. April 28/17. |
| 2/4 D. XIV | Covey, Stanley Geo. Dade. 200445. (2266.) | M. April 28/17. |
| 2/4 D. | Hutchings, L.-Cpl. G. E. 200190. | M. April 28/17. |
| 2/4 D. | Thomas, A. 203756. | M. April 28/17. |
| 5 | **Bulmer, 2nd Lieut. J. L.** | M. May 3/17. |
| 5 | **Harper, 2nd Lieut. C. C.** (Bombing Officer.) | M. May 3/17. |
| 5 A. I | Angus, G. 23841. | M. May 3/17. |
| 5 A. | Ayres, G. W. 32621. | M. May 3/17. |
| 5 A. | Bailey, B. A. 32944. | M. May 3/17. |
| 5 A. III | Baughan, L.-Cpl. E. A. 23791. | M. May 3/17. |
| 5 A. | Bird, Sergt. H. G. 10156. | M. May 3/17. |
| *5 A. II | Bishop, Chas. Oscar. 22319. | M. May 3/17. |
| 5 A. II | Bristow, George. 22245. | W. and M. May 3/17. |
| ‡5 A. | Brown, W. 32561. | M. May 3/17. |
| 5 A. I | Clack, H. T. 202111. | Unoff. M. May 3/17. |
| ‡5 A. | Clifford, J. W. 16619. | M. May 3/17. |
| 5 A. III | Durose, Thomas. 23859. | M. May 3/17. |
| ‡5 A. | Eaton, A. 16708. | M. May 3/17. |
| 5 A. II | Green, L.-Cpl. Geoffrey Wm. 200535. | M. May 3/17. |
| 5 A. III | Heath, F. L. 32605. | W. and M. May 3/17. |
| 5 A. | Howe, Albert Victor. 26398. | M. May 3/17. |
| 5 A. | Janes, Claud. 265935. | M. May 3/17. |
| 5 A. | Lively, E. 10269. | M. May 3/17. |
| 5 A. II | Minns, H. W. 202132. | M. May 3/17. |
| ‡5 A. | Nelmes, S. 9672. | M. May 3/17. |
| *5 A. III | Reneher, W. 18457. | M. May 3/17. |
| ‡5 A. | Richards. 202233. | M. May 3/17. |
| ‡5 A. | Rivers, H. F. 19446. | M. May 3/17. |
| 5 A. | Robinson, C. 33113. | M. May 3/17. |
| 5 A. I | Rockley, Geo. 32573. | M. Unoff. K. May 3/17. |
| 5 A. | Smith, L.-Cpl. Gerald. 32617. | W. and M. Sept. 15/16. R/Enq. |
| 5 A. IV | Stanford, Lewis. 12349. | M. May 3/17. |
| 5 A. III | Starner, Sydney Alfred. 202754. | M. May 3/17. |
| ‡5 A. | Steptoe, Douglas. 10804. | M. May 3/17. |
| 5 A. | Umney, Bertie David. 12249. | W. and M. May 3/17. |
| 5 A. | White, Geo. 15177. | M. May 3/17. |
| 5 A. IV | Withey, Edw. 32620. | M. May 3/17. |
| 5 A. III | Woodford, B. 23168. | M. May 3/17. |
| 5 B. VII | Angell, L.-Sgt. Richd. Sydney. 11543. | W. and M. May 3/17. |
| *5 B. | Brown, Cpl. Frank Lincoln. 10444. | M. May 3/17. |
| 5 B. | Bushnell, Sergt. A. H. 201703. | M. May 3/17. |
| ‡5 B. | Clements, J. G. 200577. | M. May 3/17. |
| 5 B. VI | Duckering, R. 20735. | M. May 3/17. |
| 5 B. | Fradgley, J. G. 19430. | W. and M. Sept. 16/16. R/Enq. |
| 5 B. V | Freeman, Harry Wm. 22976. (Fr. H.Q.) | M. May 3/17. |
| ‡5 B. | Giles, R. R. 202343. | M. May 3/17. |
| ‡5 B. | Halloran, E. 24424. | M. May 3/17. |
| 5 B. VI | Harper, H. 25966. | M. May 3/17. |
| 5 B. VIII | Hatton, Walter Jas. 26340. | M. May 3/17. |
| ‡5 B. | Plumb, A. 17448. | M. May 3/17. |
| 5 B. or D. | Smith, A. 22106. | M. May 3/17. |
| *5 C. XII | Batson, A. 24457. | M. May 3/17. |
| 5 C. | Bray, Sgt. Edgar Hy. 202967. | M. May 3/17. |
| 5 C. or D. | Carter, R. R. 24600. | M. May 3/17. |
| ‡5 C. | Cooper, G. 27533. | M. May 3/17. |

**Oxfordshire and Buckinghamshire Light Infantry—contd.**

*B.E.F.*

| | | |
|---|---|---|
| **5 C. IX** | Cross, L.-Cpl. Percy. 17104. | **M. May 3/17.** |
| ***5 C. XI** | Eldridge, Herbert. 266065. | **M. May 3/17.** |
| **‡5 C.** | Elliott, J. S. 12967. | M. May 3/17. |
| **5 C. XI** | Gibson, A. 32600. | **M. May 3/17.** |
| **‡5 C. XII** | Harris, W. J. 32813. | M. May 3/17. |
| **‡5 C.** | Hempel, J. W. 17734 | M. May 3/17. |
| **‡5 C.** | Hindo, F. 26406. | M. May 3/17. |
| **5 C. XI** | Horne, Albert Job. 20853. | **M. May 3/17.** |
| **5 C. X** | Oliver, Albert Edward. 32709. | **M. May 3/17.** |
| **5 C. IX** | Pearson, Cpl. M. G. 200171. | W. and M. **May 3/17.** |
| **5 C. XI** | Perry, Gilford. 12055. | **M. May 3/17.** |
| **5 C. XI** | Smith, Albert C. 32878. | **M. May 3/17.** |
| **5 C.** | Smith, Cpl. Frank Gilbert. 16017. | M. May 3/17. |
| **‡5 C.** | Spriggs, F. 200340. | M. May 3/17. |
| **‡5 C. IX** | Tapley, L.-Cpl. W. H. 10657. | M. May 3/17. |
| ***5 C. X** | Thorne, J. 265677. (2344.) | **M. May 3/17.** |
| **5 C. XI** | Waddup, F. 22712. | **M. May 3/17.** |
| ***5 C. XII** | Whitaker, F. 266531. | **M. May 3/17.** |
| ***5 C. X** | Wilson, F. 266211. | M. Unoff. K. **May 3/17.** |
| **‡5 C. XII** | Wilson, Henry. 18918. | M. May 3/17. |
| **‡5 C. X** | Witherall, Percy Augustus. 16233. | **M. May 3/17.** |
| ***5 C. IX** | Wood, Chas. B. 22916. | **M. May 3/17.** |
| **5 D. XIII** | Bagwell, E. 33091. | **M. May 3/17.** |
| **5 D. XIV** | Biswell, W. E. 265495. | M. May 3/17. |
| **5 D. XIII** | Blay, Sidney. 26372. | M. May 3/17. |
| **5 D. XIV** | Burfoot, Percy Albert. 10849. | **M. May 3/17.** |
| **‡5 D.** | Cherry, L.-Cpl. F. 24903. | M. May 3/17. |
| **‡5 D.** | Crook, G. 20836. | M. May 3/17. |
| **5 D.** | Davey, Sig. Harry. 22352. | **M. May 3/17.** |
| **‡5 D.** | Dover, S. D. V. 27221. | M. May 3/17. |
| **5 D. XVI** | Edens, Percival E. 201496. | **M. May 3/17.** |
| **5 D. XIII** | Faulkner, Albert. 16687. | **M. May 3/17.** |
| ***5 D. L.G.S.** | Guest, J. 18126. | **M. May 3/17.** |
| **5 D. XIV** | Hipwell, G. W. 11894. | **M. May 3/17.** |
| **‡5 D.** | Jeffries, E. 17233. | M. May 3/17. |
| **‡5 D.** | Kitchen, A. W. 202789. | M. May 3/17. |
| **‡5 D.** | Lewis, A. W. 201739. | M. May 3/17. |
| **‡5 D.** | Lisseter, F. H. 11024. | M. May 3/17. |
| **‡5 D.** | Ludlow, H. 202767. | M. May 3/17. |
| **‡5 D.** | Mashford, J. R. 16649. | M. May 3/17. |
| **‡5 D.** | Mitchell, R. C. 32521. | M. May 3/17. |
| **5 D. XIII** | Pearman, Frank Valentine. 24272. | M. May 3/17. |
| **5 D.** | Pickton, Henry. 26585. | **M. May 3/17.** |
| **‡5 D.** | Pratt, W. 17369. | M. May 3/17. |
| **‡5 D.** | Rickard, J. H. 203199. | M. May 3/17. |
| ***5 D. L.G.S.** | Smart, F. W. 32523. | **M. May 3/17.** |
| **‡5 D.** | Surman, E. 8357. | M. May 3/17. |
| **‡5 D.** | Toy, J. A. 21369. | M. May 3/17. |
| **‡5 D.** | Turner, F. 267146. | M. May 3/17. |
| ***5 D.** | Waddup, Frank. 16473. | **M. May 3/17.** |
| **5 D. XVI** | West, Gordon. 25812. | **M. May 3/17.** |
| **5 D.** | White, L.-Cpl. A. G. 266358. | **M. May 3/17.** |
| **5 D.** | White, George Henry. 202769. | **M. May 3/17.** |
| **6 C. XII** | Pratt, Maurice John. 32839. (Fr. Ox. Hussars, 2246.) | W. and M. **Oct. 7/16. R/Enq.** |

**Oxfordshire and Buckinghamshire Light Infantry—contd.**

## *B.E.F.*

### Buckinghamshire Battalion.

| | | |
|---|---|---|
| 1 C. | Hayman, J. W. 266865. (Late 4764.) | D/W. **April 7/17.** Det.D./B. |
| 1 D. | Cross, L.-Cpl. Francis. 265897. (2688.) | M. **Mar. 10/17.** |

## *BALKANS.*

| | | |
|---|---|---|
| 7 | **Baker, Lieut. C. P.** | M. **May 9/17.** |
| 7 | **Pickford, 2nd Lt. Herbert T. R.** | W. and M. **April 24/17.** |
| 7 | **Steele, Lieut. F. A. Durno.** | M. **May 8-9/17.** |
| 7 A. | Acton, L.-Cpl. B. 26310. | M. **May 9/17.** |
| *7 A. | Allen, L.-Cpl. Albert. 13869. | M., bel. K. **May 9/17.** |
| 7 A. III | Cushing, Chas. A. 26500. | M. **May 9/17.** |
| 7 A. | Harding, H. 26397. | M. **May 9/17.** |
| 7 A. | Harrison, S. H. 11929. | M. **May 9/17.** |
| 7 A. | Howe, C. E. 27420. | M. **May 9/17.** |
| 7 A. | Ogle, W. G. A. 26546. | M. **May 9/17.** |
| 7 A. | Porter, W. G. 13035. | M. **May 9/17.** |
| 7 A. | Puttick, G. A. 27444. | M. **May 8-9/17.** |
| 7 A. | Selwyn, J. T. 26559. | M. **May 9/17.** |
| *7 A. | Sirrett, Seragt. G. A. 13397. | M., bel. K. **May 9/17.** |
| 7 A. | Spencer, James. 20803. | M. **May 9/17.** |
| 7 B. | Atkins, Fredk. Jas. 13260. | M. **May 9/17.** |
| 7 B. | Bugby, Geo. 13333. | M. **May 9/17.** |
| 7 B. | Carter, John. 21799. | M. **May 9/17.** |
| 7 B. | Clarke, A. 13632. | M. **May 9/17.** |
| 7 B. | Corps, Henry Wm. 27384. | M. **May 9/17.** |
| 7 B.* | Croton, W. 16728. | M. **May 9/17.** |
| 7 B. VIII | Dawburn, L. P. 27396. | M. **May 9/17.** |
| 7 B. | Ewers, Wm. Geo. 23640. | M. **May 9/17.** |
| 7 B. | Flut, Harry. 24688. | M. **May 9/17.** |
| 7 B. | Gillard, L.-Cpl. G. 19593. | M. **May 8-9/17.** |
| 7 B. | Gower, F. C. 27412. | M. **May 9/17.** |
| 7 B. | Jeffrey, Arthur W. 13045. | M. **May 9/17.** |
| 7 B. | Lord, V. G. 12702. | M. **May 9/17.** |
| 7 B. | Piggott, E. 24191. | M. **May 9/17.** |
| *7 B. | Rensch, Arthur Chas. 27453. | M., bel. K. **May 9/17.** |
| 7 B. | Tack, Cpl. A. E. 13382. | M., bel. K. **May 9/17.** |
| 7 B. | Wisson, J. T. 12821. | M. **May 9/17.** |
| 7 B. | Woods, T. C. 13829. | M. **May 9/17.** |
| 7 C. X | Arnold, John Jas. 26488. | M. **May 9/17.** |
| 7 C. | Brown, F. 16954. | M. **May 9/17.** |
| *7 C. | Chadwick, T. 26907. | M. **May 9/17.** |
| 7 C. | Dunlin, Tom. 28483. | M. **May 9/17.** |
| 7 C. | Gilder, G. W. 23194. | M. **May 9/17.** |
| 7 C. | Hawes, E. G. 16729. | M. **May 9/17.** |
| 7 C. IX | King, Sergt. F. J. 14109. | M. **May 9/17.** |
| 7 C. IX | Mackey, Albert Wm. 26538. | M. **May 9/17.** |
| 7 C. | Mills, H. L. 26539. | M. **May 9/17.** |
| 7 C. IX | Morris, H. R. 22811. | M. **May 9/17.** |
| 7 C. | Piercy, W. F. 12660. | M. **May 9/17.** |
| 7 C. | Saunders, Ernest. 22692. | M. **May 9/17.** |
| 7 C. | Ward, E. 27332. | M. **May 9/17.** |
| 7 C. | Watson, Harold Jos. 15407. | M. **May 9/17.** |
| 7 D. XIII | Barfoot, Cpl. C. 11822. | M. **April 25/17.** |
| *7 D. XV | Barlow, B. 23229. | W. and M. **April 25/17.** |
| 7 D. | Box, T. 27335. | M. **April 24-25/17.** |
| 7 D. XIV | Cole, R. 26501. | M. **April 25/17.** |
| 7 D. M.G.S. | Feathers, Alf. Lenard. 26512. | K. **May 9/17.** Det.D./B. |

**Oxfordshire and Buckinghamshire Light Infantry—contd.**

## *BALKANS.*

7 D. XIII Freeman, Edw. H. 10976. M. April 24-25/17.
7 D. XVI French, A. G. 12838. M. May 9/17.
*7 D. XIV Geary, Sergt. J. R. 13249. M., bel. K. May 9/17.
7 D. XIV Harding, Cpl. A. L. 22867. M. April 25/17.
7 D. Harding, Wallace F. 12620. M. April 25/17.
7 D. Henson, Harold. 27417. M. May 9/17.
7 D. XVI Lightman, Chas. Hayden. 27435. M. May 9/17.
7 D. XV Mitchell, C. E. 14012. K. April 28/17. Det.D./B.
‡7 D. XIV Price, W. E. 26551. W. and M. April 25/17.
7 D. XV Schaffer, Cpl. Chris. Jas. 26561. M. May 9/17.
7 D. Smith, G. W. 26560. M. April 25/17.
*7 D. XVI Taifsom-Shepherd, A. R. 27577. W. and M. May 9/17.
7 D. Thornton, Bugler C. G. 12250. M. April 25/17.
7 D. M.G.S. Williams, A. J. 26580. M. May 9/17.
7 ? Barnes, A. 10817. M. May 9/17.
7 ? Beeching, T. C. 26489. M. May 9/17.
*7 ? Boyde, Cpl. G. 14115. M., bel. K. May 9/17.
*7 ? Bradshaw, Sergt. H. 15511. M., bel. K. May 9/17.
*7 ? Bucknall, T. 11353. M., bel. K. May 9/17.
7 ? Dorrington, W. 23701. M. May 9/17.
*7 ? Eustace, Sergt. R. 13837. M., bel. K. May 9/17.
7 ? Gibbs, F. 27414. M. May 9/17.
7 ? Gilmartin, L.-Cpl. A. 14050. M. May 9/17.
7 ? Gowers, H. 26515. M. May 9/17.
7 ? Hall, W. J. 8598. M. May 9/17.
7 ? Hancox, C. 24667. M. April 25/17.
7 ? Harman, E. W. 13701. M. May 9/17.
7 ? Holland, A. 12604. M. May 9/17.
*7 ? Ison, L.-Cpl. C. J. 14112. M., bel. K. May 9/17.
*7 ? Jennings, C. 14374. M., bel. K. May 9/17.
7 ? Joyce, H. 12933. M. May 9/17.
7 ? Lewis, G. E. 24214. M. May 9/17.
*7 ? Maxworthy, W. 15028. M., bel. K. May 9/17.
*7 ? Millington, Sergt. J. 17444. M., bel. K. May 9/17.
*7 ? Morgan, E. 15083. M., bel. K. May 9/17.
7 ? Pearce, F. J. 15095. M. May 9/17.
7 ? Pimm, Sergt. D. 9581. M. May 9/17.
*7 ? Siggs, Sergt. A. 13857. M., bel. K. May 9/17.
7 ? Swain, A. C. 12941. M. May 9/17.
7 ? Timmins, A. 24171. M. May 9/17.
7 ? Tooley, W. J. 13221. M. May 9/17.
7 ? Trinder, R. 14492. M. May 9/17.
7 ? Turnock, J. 13087. M. May 9/17.
7 ? Watts, S. 17300. M. May 9/17.
*7 ? Webb, F. G. 13835. M. May 9/17.
7 ? Wood, E. 18187. M. May 9/17.
*8 D. Bowns, L.-Cpl. J. 16174. W. and M. May 8/17.
8 D. M.G.S. Robbins, L.-Cpl. Wm. Fredk. 21257. M. May 8-9/17.
*8 ? Harriss, J. 16406. M. April 24-25/17.

## *PERSIAN GULF.*

1 R. Williams, C. A. 8353. W. and M. Dec. 1/15.

## RIFLE BRIGADE.

### B.E.F.

| | | |
|---|---|---|
| 1 A. II | Ashwell, Frank. B/203591. | W. and M. May 4/17. |
| 1 A. | Coaker, A. A. 27707. | M. April 9/17. |
| ‡1 A. | Dawkins, J. 355. | W. and M. May 4/17. |
| 1 A. III | Hines, Herbert Chas. 20896. | W. and M. April 9/17. |
| 1 A. I | Leary, Dennis. 17711. | M. May 12/17. |
| 1 A. | Lowry, R. R. 27732. | W. and M. April 10/17. |
| 1 A. L.G.S. | Moat, C. S/8519. | M. Oct. 18/16. R/Enq. |
| 1 A. I | Peters, Chas. Oldridge. S/27735. | W. and M. April 9/17. |
| 1 A. III | Wheeler, G. S/30890. | W. and M. April 12/17. |
| 1 B. | Barnes, Walter. 203531. | M. Oct. 19/16. R./Enq. |
| 1 B. VII | Brooks, J. R. S/25815. | W. and M. April 9/17. |
| 1 B. | Darling, W. J. 16784. | M. April 15/17. |
| 1 B. | Kelly, Arthur George. 11123. | W. and M. Oct. 19/16. R/Enq. |
| 1 B. VIII | White, Wm. A. B/203556. | M. Oct. 23/16. R./Enq. |
| *1 C. XI | Barnes, Henry Wm. 30702. | K. May 11/17. Det.D./B. |
| 1 C. | House, C. 17784. | W. and M. April 9/17. |
| *1 C. X | Hurley, L.-Cpl. Michael Thos. 17823. | M. Oct. 18/16. R/Enq. |
| 1 C. | Johnson, Jos. Freeman. G/42329. | M. April 23/17. |
| *1 C. IX | Lewis, H. S/24227. | K. April 9/17. Det.D./B. |
| 1 C. | Simmons, Harry Daniel. S/23787. | M. April 9/17. |
| 1 C. | Wardell, Geo. 8662. | M. May 9/17. |
| *1 I. | Arthur, J. S/25749. | W. and M. May 5/17. |
| 1 I. XIII | Collett, Wm. Reuben. 20722. | M. May 12/17. |
| 1 I. XIV | Gamble, J. B/203476. | W. and M. May 11/17. |
| 1 I. | Haggett, A.-Sergt. S. 4534. | W. and M. April 9/17. |
| ‡1 I. | Hughes, E. S. 21084. | M. May 11/17. |
| 1 I. | Ingle, Thos. 17764. | M. Oct. 18/16. |
| 1 I. XIV | Prince, W. B/200576. | M. May 11/17. |
| 1 I. | Taylor, A. E. 17826. | M. Oct. 19/16. R/Enq. |
| ?‡ I. XV | Town, Henry Gilbert. 302136. | M. May 3/17. |
| 1 I. L.G.S. | Yeomans, Clement Harold. 203409. (Fr. K.R.R.C.) | M. Oct. 19/16. |
| 2 A. | Atkins, A. 16437. | M. Oct. 23/16. R/Enq. |
| 2 A. | Beasley, John. S/16536. | K. Oct. 22-24/16. Det.D./B. |
| 2 A. I | Harrison, Horace. 8210. | M. Oct. 23/16. R./Enq. |
| 2 A. III | Holding, H. Leo. S/19003. | K. Nov. 12/16. Det.D./B. |
| ‡2 A. | Price, E. C. 11448. | W. and M. April 22/17. |
| 2 A. IV | Simmonds, Sidney Henry. S/26869. | W. and M. Mar. 4/17. |
| 2 B. V. | Becken, Henry. 19721. | M. Oct. 23/16. R/Enq. |
| *2 B. V | Carey, R. S/13624. | M. Oct. 23/16. R/Enq. |
| 2 B. VI | McIntosh, Jas. Alex. 14873. | M. Oct. 23/16. R/Enq. |
| 2 B. VII | Peerless, E. J. S/27351. | D. of exhaustion Mar. 16/17. Det.D./B. |
| 2 B. | Phillips, B. G. S/16505. (Fr. 10.) | M. April 4/17. |
| 2 C. | Allman, A.-Cpl. Walter Arthur Saml. S/16528. | M. Oct. 23/16. R/Enq |
| 2 D. | McKiernan, J. 19432. | M. Oct. 23/16. |
| ‡2 D. XVI | Moore, L. S. 19875. | M. Oct. 23/16. R/Enq. |
| ‡2 D. M.G.S. | Rice, J. A. 14693. | M. Oct. 23/16. R/Enq. |
| 2 ? | Oake, Cpl. Walter John. S/25423. | K. Oct. 22/16. Det.D./B. |
| 3 B. V | Orchard, Richard R. 15839. | W. and M. Sept. 1/16. R/Enq. |
| ‡3 C. XI | Sains, A. J. 30771. | W. Unoff. M. June 7/17. |
| *3 D. XV | Radcliffe, Harold. 2224. | K. June 13/17. Det.D./B. |
| ‡3 D. | Stanley, W. S/31365. | W. Unoff. M. June 8/17. |
| 7 A. IV | Batts, W. 15794. | W. and M. Sept. 15/16. R/Enq. |
| ‡7 A. II | Levenson, Harry. 11583. | M. Sept. 15/16. R/Enq. |
| 7 A. I | Tallett, H. 28577. | K. April 11/17. Det.D./B. |
| ‡7 B. | Dodsworth, Geo. Albert. S/16025. | M. Sept. 15/16. R/Enq. |
| 7 C. IX | Crickenden, H. 26321. | W. Unoff. K. May 3/17. |

**Rifle Brigade—contd.**

## *B.E.F.*

| | | |
|---|---|---|
| 7 D. | Robson, Geo. 20558. (Fr. 9 K.R.R.C.) | K. Sept. 15/16. Det.D./B. R/Enq. |
| 8 | **Oakley, 2nd Lieut. H. B.** | M. May 3/17. |
| 8 | **Reed, 2nd Lieut. F. W. C.** | M. May 3/17. |
| 8 A. I | Baker, Percy Alf. S/14467. | K. Sept. 15/16. Det.D./B. R/Enq. |
| 8 A. IV | Farley, Albert Fred. 12795. | M. May 3/17. |
| ‡8 A. | Inskip, J. 28941. | M. May 3/17. |
| ‡8 A. | Jobson, B. 12647. | M. May 3/17. |
| 8 A. | Monk, E. W. H. 5212. | M. Sept. 15/16. R/Enq. |
| 8 B. V | Bull, John Wm. S/17451. | M. May 3/17. |
| ‡8 B. | Campbell, E. E. 26225. | M. May 3/17. |
| *8 B. V | Forder, Albert Fredk. 26518. | M. May 3/17. |
| 8 B. VII | Hanchard, Albert W. 20564. | M. May 3/17. |
| 8 B. VII | Potter, Sidney Chas. 18486. | K. April 11/17. Det.D./B. |
| ‡8 B. | Scott, W. E. 15202. | M. May 3/17. |
| ‡8 B. | Spurrier, A. 8536. | W. and M. May 3/17. |
| ‡8 C. | Barber, E. 8439. | M. May 3/17. |
| ‡8 C. | Barton, C. S. 17967. | W. and M. May 3/17. |
| *8 C. X | Baverstock, Cpl. Sid. Geo. 5664. | W. and M. May 3/17. |
| 8 C. X | Brown, T. S/18576. | M. May 3/17. |
| *8 C. XII | Cecil, L.-Cpl. A. 23971. | M. May 3/17. |
| 8 C. XII | Chapman, Wm. Henry. 13758. | W. and M. May 3/17. |
| ‡8 C. | Jones, J. R. 24005. | M. May 3/17. |
| *8 C. X | Lee, L.-Cpl. E. S. 28434. | W. and M. May 3/17. |
| 8 C. IX | Lockyer, Albert Wm. 25242. | W. and M. May 3/17. |
| ‡8 C. | McGinlay, L.-Sergt. J. P. 9782. | W. and M. May 3/17. |
| 8 C. XII | Smith, G. 3/26064. | M. May 3/17. |
| 8 C. X | Suffield, R. 23280. | M. May 3/17. |
| 8 C. XII | Webster, Cecil. 15084. | M. May 3/17. |
| 8 D. XV | Bates, Cpl. Cyril Chas. S/6372. | K. May 3/17. Det.D./B. |
| 8 D. | Birkett, A. E. S/20742. | M. May 3/17. |
| *8 D. XVI | Bloxham, Sergt. H. S/25869. | M. May 3/17. |
| ‡8 D. | Brooks, A. E. 27674. | W. and M. May 3/17. |
| ‡8 D. | Buchanan, A. L. 21645. | M. May 3/17. |
| 8 D. XV | Crooks, Frank. 27531. | M. May 3/17. |
| ‡8 D. | Freedman, S. 16135. | W. and M. May 3/17. |
| ‡8 D. | Furley, A. F. 12795. | M. May 3/17. |
| ‡8 D. | Green, G. 26995. | M. May 3/17. |
| 8 D. XIV | Hanson, G. S/25268. | M. May 3/17. |
| 8 D. XVI | Kemp, A.-Cpl. G. 5394. | M. May 3/17. |
| 8 D. XIV | Longman, R. J. 19501. | M. May 3/17. |
| *8 D. | Missen, A.-Cpl. H. 7639. | W. and M. May 3/17. |
| ‡8 D. | Nicholls, G. 20367. | M. May 3/17. |
| ‡8 D. | Sands, Frank. 1791. | M. May 3/17. |
| 8 D. XIV | Seabrook, Cpl. Fred. 6477. | M. May 3/17. |
| ‡8 D. | Selzer, Cpl. C. W. H. 6140. | M. May 3/17. |
| *8 D. XVI | Shepherd, Arthur. S/26267. | M. May 3/17. |
| 8 D. XVI | Smith, John Alf. 26268. | W. and M. May 3/17. |
| ‡8 D. | Stanley, Cpl. F. J. 831. | M. May 3/17. |
| *8 D. XVI | Thompson, Wm. John. 16490. | W. and M. May 3/17. |
| 8 D. XVI | Ward, L.-Cpl. R. S/5552. | W. and M. May 3/17. |
| 8 D. | Weed, A. 5977. | M. May 3/17. |
| ‡8 D. | Wickens, W. 10453. | M. May 3/17. |
| *8 D. XIII | Withey, A. G. S/26277. | M. May 3/17. |
| ‡8 D. | Wright, E. G. 26023. | M. May 3/17. |
| *8 ? | Parker, A. E. 26254. | K. April 11/17. Det.D./B. |
| *8 ? Sig. S. | Pert, Leonard Harry. S/17986. | K. May 3/17. Det.D./B. |
| 9 | **Howatt, 2nd Lt. W. H.** (Fr. 7 Scot. Rifles.) | W. and M. May 3/17. |
| 9 | **Plater, Lt. R. H.** (Fr. A.S.C.) | W. and M. May 3/17. |

**Rifle Brigade—contd.**

## *B.E.F.*

| | | |
|---|---|---|
| 9 | **Statham, 2nd Lt. A. Y.** (Fr. 3/5 E. Surreys.) | W. and M. **May 3/17.** |
| 9 A. | **Wade, 2nd Lieut. G. E. A.** | W. and M. **May 3/17.** |
| 9 C. | **Wheatley, 2nd Lieut. W. C.** | W. and M. **May 3/17.** |
| 9 A. | Andrews, Fredk. Geo. S/28459. | M. **May 3/17.** |
| ‡9 A. | Battman, J. W. 30426. | M. **May 3/17.** |
| 9 A. IV | Bottrell, Herbert Wm. 10955. | M. **May 3/17.** |
| ‡9 A. | Davies, W. 130. | M. **May 3/17.** |
| 9 A. | Eaton, George. 26095. | M. **May 3/17.** |
| ‡9 A. | Edgington, H. S. 28464. | M. **May 3/17.** |
| 9 A. | Ellis, Jas. 18252. | M. **May 3/17.** |
| *9 A. I | Elton, R. 28915. | M. **May 3/17.** |
| 9 A. II | Flanders, A.-Cpl. J. P. 593. | M. **May 3/17.** |
| ‡9 A. IV | Greenfield, Walter Gilbert. 7546. | M. **May 3/17.** |
| 9 A. II | Griffin, W. H. S/25931. | W. and M. **May 3/17.** |
| 9 A. III | Griffiths, A. S. 3/26100. | M. **May 3/17.** |
| ‡9 A. | Hill, W. 29536. | M. **May 3/17.** |
| 9 A. III | Jackson, E. T. H. S/26110. | M. **May 3/17.** |
| *9 A. I | Janes, Charles John. S/28379. | M. **May 3/17.** |
| ‡9 A. | Lande, A. 2848. | M. **May 3/17.** |
| ‡9 A. | Leahy, W. J. P. 17470. | M. **May 3/17.** |
| 9 A. IV | Lilliott, F. L. 56. | M. **May 3/17.** |
| ‡9 A. IV | Pamment, J. 203113. | W. and M. **May 3/17.** |
| 9 A. II | Savory, A. E. S/30457. | M. **May 3/17.** |
| ‡9 A. | Smith, Sidney Charles. 22221. | M. **May 3/17.** |
| 9 A. | Tester, L.-Cpl. Wilfred E. S/26136. (Fr. H.Q. Bomb. S.) | M. **May 3/17.** |
| *9 A. | Thomas, Arthur Geo. 6714. | M. **May 3/17.** |
| 9 A. IV | Tivey, Wm. Robt. 17338. | W. and M. **May 3/17.** |
| 9 A. IV | Trice, Wm. Walter. 18519. | M. **May 3/17.** |
| ‡9 A. | Watts, E. A. 29478. | M. **May 3/17.** |
| 9 B. | Carrier, Sergt. Frank. S/30417. | M. **May 3/17.** |
| *9 B. VII | Chapple, Arthur. 26031. | M. **May 3/17.** |
| ‡9 B. | Davis, E. S/130. | M. **May 3/17.** |
| '9 B. V | Griffiths, Geo. Hy. 15489. | M. **May 3/17.** |
| ‡9 B. | Hall, G. S. 4901. | M. **May 3/17.** |
| ‡9 B. VI | Hurley, A. 26044. | Unoff. M. or K. **May 3/17.** |
| ‡9 B. V | Jackson, Charles. 18521. | M. **May 3/17.** |
| 9 B. VI | Lamy, Edward S. 10166. | W. and M. **Sept. 15/16. R/Enq.** |
| ‡9 B. | McCarthy, E. C. 1679. | M. **May 3/17.** |
| ‡9 B. | Martin, F. W. 19592. | M. **May 3/17.** |
| '9 B. V | Pearce, T. J. S/28313. | M. **May 3/17.** |
| ‡9 B. | Rhyump, John. 10103. | M. **Sept. 15/16.** R/Enq. |
| 9 B. VII | Snelling, F. M. S. 200702. | M. **May 3/17.** |
| ‡9 B. | Terry, J. W. T. 266. | M. **May 3/17.** |
| *9 B. VII | Thompson, James. 7832. | M. **May 3/17.** |
| ‡9 B. | Thomson, A.-Cpl. J. 7832. | M. **May 3/17.** |
| 9 B. | Togwell, Wm. Henry. S/26564. | M. **May 3/17.** |
| ‡9 B. | Wicks, L.-Cpl. W. E. 3664. | M. **May 3/17.** |
| ‡9 B. | Williams, T. J. 687. | M. **May 3/17.** |
| 9 B. | Woodward, E. E. S/28474. | M. **May 3/17.** |
| ‡9 B. | Woof, P. 30463. | W. and M. **May 3/17.** |
| 9 C. IX | Baldwin, E. 30411. | M. **May 3/17.** |
| 9 C. L.G.S. | Child, Regd. H. 24271. | M. **May 3/17.** |
| 9 C. H.Q. | Dessent, T. B/2995. (Bomb. S.) | M. **May 3/17.** |
| 9 C. XI | Devine, D. W. 30385. | M. **May 3/17.** |
| 9 C. | Esfall, Percy. 526164. | M. **May 3/17.** |
| ‡9 C. | Hawker, Sergt. R. 30415. | M. **May 3/17.** |
| 9 C. IX | Hope, Albert. 3375. | M. **May 3/17.** |

**Rifle Brigade—contd.**

## *B.E.F.*

| | | |
|---|---|---|
| †9 C. XII | Lewis, Edward. 8444. | W. and M. **May 3/17.** |
| 9 C. | Marshall, T. 333. | M. **May 3/17.** |
| 9 C. L.G.S. | Morris, Paul. 10080. | M. **May 3/17.** |
| †8 C. | Nicholls, J. W. 29543. | M. **May 3/17.** |
| 9 C. XI | Paxton, Robert. B/203009. | M. **May 3/17.** |
| †9 C. | Pearce, W. 29539. | M. **May 3/17.** |
| 9 C. XI | Redwood, Fredk. 23956. | M. **May 3/17.** |
| *9 C. IX | Ribbans, Fredk. Wm. 30405. | M. **May 3/17.** |
| 9 C. XII | Risley, F. T. S/18520. | K. **May 3/17.** Det.D./B. |
| 9 C. X | Simmonds, Stanley E. 30398. | M. **May 3/17.** |
| 9 C. | Smith, Henry Wm. S/8932. | M. **May 3/17.** |
| †9 C. | Thompson, L. 12635. | M. **May 3/17.** |
| 9 C. IX | Williams, L. G. S/16193. | M. **May 3/17.** |
| 9 C. X | Winn, A. E. 30400. | M. **May 3/17.** |
| †9 D. | Baker, F. B. 29533. | W. and M. **May 3/17.** |
| 9 D. | Barber, J. Z/387. | M. **April 9/17.** |
| †9 D. | Creed, Sergt. B. F. 3247. | W. and M. **May 3/17.** |
| †9 D. | Doyle, M. K. 26092. | M. **April 23/17.** |
| 9 D. | Greenslade, A. A. S/28130. | W. and M. **May 3/17.** |
| 9 D. XIII | Leary, J. 16435. | M. **May 3/17.** |
| †9 D. | Liddle, R. H. 9918. | W. and M. **May 3/17.** |
| †9 D. | McMorrow, M. 1372. | M. **May 3/17.** |
| 9 D. XV | Phillips, E. A. 18434. | W. and M. **May 3/17.** |
| 9 D. | Sewell, Percy. 3162. | M. **Sept. 15/16.** R/Enq. |
| 9 D. | Taylor, S. S/13037. | M. **May 3/17.** |
| *9 D. XIV | Watts, L.-Cpl. O. W. 12706. | Unoff. M. **May 3/17.** |
| *9 ? L.G.S. | Mauktelow, G. M. 18659. | Unoff. W. and M. **May 3/17.** |
| 10 C. | Atherley, Thos. Walter. B/200040. | M. **Feb. 19/17.** |
| 10 D. | Craven, L.-Cpl. James. 1251. | M. **Sept. 3/16.** R/Enq. |
| 10 D. XIII | Downs, A. B. 5766. | M. **Feb. 19/17.** |
| 10 D. XV | Gillingham, H. 20337. | M. **Feb. 19/17.** |
| 10 D. | Greenner, Alfred Albert. 23725. | M. **Feb. 19/17.** |
| †10 D. XIV | Hoare, Charles. 15377. | M. **Sept. 18/16.** R/Enq. |
| 10 D. | Williams, A. 1400. | M. **Feb. 19/17.** |
| 11 | **Hepburn, 2nd Lt. A. M.** (Fr. 6th.) | K. **Sept. 3/16.** Det.D./B. |
| 11 A. I | Carpenter, Cpl. H. F. S/26424. | M. **Feb. 14/17.** |
| 11 A. III | Duce, A. B. S/21351. | W. and M. **Feb. 16/17.** |
| 11 A. | Engwell, Frank. 5772. | W. and M. **Sept. 26/16.** R/Enq. |
| 11 A. | Lewis, H. G. 13070. | M. **Sept. 3/16.** R/Enq. |
| 11 A. | Merrill, F. 12708. | M. **Sept. 3/16.** R/Enq. |
| 11 A. | Noakes, Fred Chas. 26413. | M. **Feb. 24/17.** |
| 11 A. | Rofe, Thos. Wm. 18993. | M. **Feb. 15/17.** |
| 11 A. | Wallace, Percy. 18990. | K. **April 5/17.** Det.D./B. |
| 11 A. I | Wicker, H. 14991. | M. **Sept. 3/16.** R/Enq. |
| 11 B. V | Almond, Wm. Edward. 27565. | M. **Feb. 17/17.** |
| 11 B. VIII | Gillingham, W. 18988. | M. **Feb. 15/17.** |
| 11 B. | Prigmore, T. C. 37. | W. and M. **Sept. 18/16.** R./Enq. |
| 11 B. | Teat, L.-Cpl. Enos Schofield. 5786. | M. **Feb. 17/17.** |
| †11 C. | Marsh, C. G. 2256. | W. and M. **Sept. 18/16.** R/Enq. |
| 11 D. | Chittenden, E. G. S/27682. (Fr. 8.) | M. **Feb. 16/17.** |
| 11 D. | Williams, E. 29879. | W. and M. **Mar. 30/17.** |
| 12 | **Bailey, 2nd Lt. Anthony Drummond.** (Fr. 8 Sherwoods.) | K. **Dec. 16/16.** Det.D./B. |
| *12 A. III | Everest, G. 19528. | W. and M. **Oct. 7/16.** R/Enq. |
| 12 A. | Legg, L.-Cpl. E. J. S/1873. | W. and M. **Oct. 7/16.** |
| 12 A. | Rodwell, Percy Lewis. 21811. | M. **Oct. 7/16.** R/Enq. |
| 12 B. | Atkins, F. W. 17531. | M. **Oct. 7/16.** R/Enq. |
| 12 B. VII | Bird, G. C. 21006. | M. **Oct. 7/16.** R/Enq. |
| *12 B. | Goodwin, Edgar Arthur. 20385. | W. and M. **Oct. 7/16.** R/Enq. |

**Rifle Brigade**—contd.

*B.E.F.*

| | | |
|---|---|---|
| 12 B. | Sharp, W. 6294. | K. Sept. 5/16. Det.D./B. |
| 12 C. L.G.S. | Coe, Percy Wm. S/14418. | K. Sept. 5/16. Det.D./B. |
| 12 D. | Seymour, Thos. Samuel. 20915. | K. Oct. 7/16. Det.D./B. R/Enq. |
| 13 | **Hobday, 2nd Lieut. W. E.** | W. and M. April 10/17. |
| 13 | **Johnson, 2nd Lieut. F. B.** | M. May 31/17. |
| 13 A. | Bear, E. G. 16194. | M. April 23/17. |
| 13 A. | Callaghan, W. 2165. | W. and M. April 23/17. |
| 13 A. II | Coventry, Geo. O. S/21978. | M. April 11/17. |
| 13 A. | Croxford, J. 3767. | W. and M. April 23/17. |
| 13 A. or B. | Earlen, G. 24975. | M. April 11/17. |
| 13 A. or D. | Edwards, E. G. S/23451. | M. April 11/17. |
| 13 A. III | Evans, W. H. S/28613. | W. and M. April 27/17. |
| 13 A. | Fletcher, W. 28614. | M. April 11/17. |
| 13 A. II | Jackson, Fredk. John. 203218. | M. April 11/17. |
| 13 A. II | Jewell, Fred. Wm. 203283. | W. and M. April 11/17. |
| 13 A. I | Langrish, Thomas. 16206. | M. April 11/17. |
| 13 A. L.G.S. | Lovelock, W. 6445. | W. and M. April 23/17. |
| 13 A. | Medlock, H. 27430. | W. and M. April 11/17. |
| 13 A. III | Shapley, Chas. 15074. | W. and M. April 11/17. |
| 13 A. II | Still, H. J. S/27114 | M. April 11/17. |
| 13 A. or B. | Tollett, G. A. B/203623. | W. and M. April 23/17. |
| ‡13 B. | Bowden, Ernest. S/15491. | K. Nov. 14/16. Det.D./B. R/Enq. |
| 13 B. VI | Claridge, George B. S/23345. | W. and M. April 11/17. |
| 13 B. VII | Driver, John Wm. S/28629. | W. and M. April 23/17. |
| 13 B. | Duffy, B. 3416. | M. April 11/17. |
| 13 B. VI | Ellwood, H. S/23591. | K. April 11/17. Det.D./B. |
| 13 B. VIII | Gray, Jas. A. 420469. (B/203201.) | W. and M. April 23/17. |
| 13 B. | Hills, A.-Sergt. W. 3971. | W. and M. April 23/17. |
| 13 B. VI | McAuliffe, Michael. 558. | M. April 11/17. |
| 13 B. VII | Moreton, F. N. B/203286. | W. and M. April 11/17. |
| 13 B. V | Richardson, Sidney Alfred. S/21408. | W. and M. April 11/17. |
| 13 B. | Smith, J. 15537. | M. April 28/17. |
| 13 B. | Tesseyman, J. W. 30988. | M. April 28/17. |
| 13 B. | Thomas, Daniel. 3227. | M. April 11/17. |
| 13 B. | Thornley, J. 7354. | M. April 11/17. |
| 13 B. | Webb, C. 30139. | W. and M. April 23/17 |
| 13 B. | Werlander, H. 30839. | M. April 28/17. |
| 13 C. XII | Bennett, L.-Cpl. W. E. 7768. | M. April 28/17. |
| *13 C. | Birch, George. 2205. | M. May 31/17. |
| ‡13 C. XII | Butzbach, L.-Cpl. Arthur Stanley. 200796. | M. May 30/17. |
| ‡13 C. | Clark, H. 6868. | M. May 31/17. |
| *13 C. X | Crake, S. G. 423686. | M. June 1/17. |
| ‡13 C. | Crane, A.-Sergt. P. 24294. | M. May 31/17. |
| 13 C. | Crees, Sergt. Fredk. S/4435. | M. April 28/17. |
| ‡13 C. | Daniels, A. 19696. | W. and M. May 31/17. |
| 13 C. X. | Doswell, H. S/1159. | W. and M. April 11/17. |
| ‡13 C. | Field, L.-Cpl. W. 6735. | M. May 31/17. |
| ‡13 C. | Hussey, A. 423708. (Fr. 2/10 Londons, 6698.) | W. and M. May 31/17. |
| ‡13 C. | Jane, E. E. 200825. | W. and M. May 31/17. |
| *13 C. | Job, H. 423704. (6694.) | W. and M. May 31/17. |
| 13 C. | Moss, Sergt. J. 27345. | M. April 28/17. |
| 13 C. IX | Pearce, Edwin Wellesley. 17226. | M. April 28/17. |
| ‡13 C. XI | Richards, Harry. 30833. | W. and M. May 31/17. |
| *13 C. IX | Sargent, George Ernest. 17212. | W. and M. May 31/17. |
| 13 C. | Scothern, L.-Cpl. H. 9140. | M. April 28/17. |
| 13 C. | Scott, Daniel. 3/30834. | M. April 28/17. |

**Rifle Brigade—contd.**

## *B.E.F.*

| | |
|---|---|
| ‡13 C. XI Smallman, Chas. Alf. S/30857. | M. May 31/17. |
| 13 C. Smith, H. W. 4483. | M. April 28/17. |
| ‡13 C. XII Smith, J. 15982. | W. and M. May 31/17. |
| 13 C. XII Squires, A. J. 2407. | M. April 28/17. |
| *13 C. XI Swain, Henry. 30852. | W. and M. May 31/17. |
| 13 C. IX Turnbull, Wm. 27469. | M. April 11/17. |
| *13 C. or D. Warner, Sgt. Horace. 203313. | W. and M. May 31/17. |
| 13 C. Webster, Sidney T. 15837. | M. April 11/17. |
| ‡13 C. White, A.-Cpl. S. 871. | M. May 31/17. |
| ‡13 C. Wiles, A. E. 20674. | W. and M. May 31/17. |
| 13 D. Boddy, E. 4058. | M. April 11/17. |
| 13 D. Methven, W. J. 21920. | M. April 11/17. |
| 13 D. Price, C. H. S/3885. | W. and M. April 11/17. |
| 13 D. XV Shirley, Henry. S/21953. | M. April 11/17. |
| 13 D. XIV Williams, Lewis John. 203312. | W. and M. April 9/17. |
| 13 D. Winnett, W. A. 20679. | M. April 11/17. |
| 13 D. XV Workman, Sgt. Fredk. S/29449. | M. May 3/17. |
| 13 ? Sill, Henry Beck. 203304. (Late K.R.R.C.) | K. Nov. 14/16. Det.D./B. |
| 13 ? Verlander, Harry. S/30839. | M. April 28/17. |
| 16 **McLehose, 2nd Lieut. J. C.** | K. Feb. 13/17. Det.D./B. |
| 16 A. Crimmin, A.-Cpl. Albt. Hy. P/1204. | M. Sept. 3/16. R/Enq. |
| 16 A. I Finch, H. C. 14545. | M. Sept. 3/16. R/Enq. |
| 16 A. I Gapper, Henry Martin. 6270. | M. Sept. 3/16. R/Enq. |
| 16 A. Osborne, Jas. J. 14514. | M. Sept. 3/16. R/Enq. |
| 16 A. Passmore, S. 53. | M. Sept. 3/16. R/Enq. |
| 16 A. Springbeth, Harold. 17606. | M. Sept. 3/16. R/Enq. |
| ‡16 A. IV White, Harry Douglas. S/16300. | K. Sept. 3/16. Det.D./B. |
| *16 A. Woollard, James R. S/16430. | M. Sept. 3/16. R/Enq. |
| ‡16 B. Cove, Harry. 309. | M. Sept. 3/16. R/Enq. |
| ‡16 B. VIII Cross, C. S/16907. | K. Oct. 7/16. Det.D./B. |
| 16 B. VII Davis, J. W. 374. | M. Sept. 3/16. R/Enq. |
| 16 B. VIII Farrow, Wm. Mark. S/17517. | M. Sept. 3/16. R/Enq. |
| 16 B. Rawlings, G. 251. | M. Sept. 3/16. R/Enq. |
| ‡16 B. Redstone, G. S/18356. | K. Oct. 21/16. R/Enq. |
| 16 B. Williams, W. J. 1282. | M. Sept. 3/16. R/Enq. |
| 16 C. XI David, A. 18317. | M. Feb. 14/17. |
| 16 C. Graham, J. 13795. | M. Sept. 3/16. R./Enq. |
| 16 C. XI Woodward, Augustus. 529. | M. Sept. 3/16. R/Enq. |
| 16 D. XVI Carvell, H. W. 17556. | M. Feb. 14/17. |
| 16 D. XVI Harris, Gordon. 14268. | M. Feb. 14/17. |
| ‡16 D. James, G. A. 1320. | M. Sept. 3/16. R/Enq. |
| ‡16 D. Miles, Wm. George. 890. | M. Sept. 3/16. R/Enq. |
| 16 D. XVI Underwood, W. E. 13973. | M. Sept. 3/16. R/Enq. |

## *BALKANS.*

| | |
|---|---|
| 4 B. V Gomme, Sergt. G. 3083. | M. May 8/17. |

## *E.E.F.*

| | |
|---|---|
| 19 ? Judd, E. H. 3671. | M., bel drowned, Jan. 1/17. "Ivernia." |
| 19 ? Shaw, Philip John. 3572. | M., bel drowned, Jan. 1/17. "Ivernia." |
| 20 ? Rawlings, H. 2294. | M., bel drowned, Jan. 1/17. "Ivernia." |
| 21 ? Dennis, Harry S. 209680. | M., bel. drowned April 15/17. |

## ROYAL ARMY MEDICAL CORPS.

### *B.E.F.*

| | | |
|---|---|---|
| **10 F. Amb.** | Manning, John Thos. 90695. | K. April 13/17. Det.D./B. |
| **10 Fld. Amb.** | Taylor, W. 77481. | K. April 12/17. Det.D./B. |
| **50 F.A. A. Sec.** | Williams, Sergt. Wm. Thos. 35593. | M. April 24/17. |
| **72 ?** | Phillips, F. A. J. 52010. | M. May 4/17. |
| **2/3 S. Midland Fld. Amb. B. Sec.** | Stone, Alfred Edward. 439417. | M. April 22/17. |

### *BALKANS.*

| | | |
|---|---|---|
| **78 Fld. Amb.** | **Gedge, Rev. Basil Johnson.** | D/W. April 26/17. Det.D./B. |

### *E.E.F.*

| | | |
|---|---|---|
| **?** | **Daly, C.M.G., Col. Thos.** | M., bel. drowned April 15/17. "Arcadian" |
| **?** | **Grier, Lieut. William.** | M., bel. drowned April 15/17. "Arcadian." |
| **?** | Jones, A. T. 90102. | M., bel. drowned April 15/17. |
| **‡?** | Rose, Stephen Geo. 104573. | M., bel. Drowned, April 15/17. |

### *PERSIAN GULF.*

| | | |
|---|---|---|
| **39 Fld. Amb. C. Sec.** | Brady, J. 31021. | K. Mar. 8/17. Det.D./B. |

## ROYAL FUSILIERS.

### *B.E.F.*

| | | |
|---|---|---|
| **1 B. VI** | Coe, J. 204085. (8408.) | M. May 3/17. |
| **1 C. Sig. S.** | King, F. 4293. | K. April 10/17. Det.D./B. R/Enq. |
| **1 Sig. S.** | Martin, A. G. 5910. | K. Feb. 8/17. Det.D./B. |
| **2** | **Daniell, 2nd Lieut. G. F. B.** | K. April 24/17. Det.D./B. |
| **2 W. or X.** | Ashdown, Alfred Wykes. 19478. (Fr. 26th.) | M. April 24/17. |
| **2 W. or X.** | Curtis, A. 11379. | M. April 24/17. |
| **2 W. I** | Day, H. G. 1047. | W. and M. April 24/17. |
| **2 W. or X.** | Ellery, Fredk. Chas. 8231. (Fr. 3.) | W. and M. April 24/17. |
| **2 W. or X.** | Goble, F. T. 41296. (Fr. H.Q.) | M. April 24/17. |
| ***2 W. IV** | Harris, Sergt. B. W. 53057. | W. and M. April 24/17. |
| **2 W. II** | Hayward, W. J. 15850. | M. Feb. 28/17. |
| **‡2 W.** | Howell, W. 16629. | M. April 24/17. |
| **2 W. IV** | Merritt, Thos. 41309. | M. April 24/17. |
| **2 W. or X.** | Pascho, L.-Cpl. Leonard. 16748. | M. April 24/17. |
| ***2 W. or X.** | Puddephat, G. 12143. | M. April 24/17. |
| **‡2 W.** | Self, H. 29246. | W. Unoff. M. April 24/17. |
| **‡2 W.** | Smith, E. 12573. | W. and M. April 24/17. |
| **2 W. IV** | Toser, T. 219. | M. Feb. 28/17. |

**Royal Fusiliers—contd.**

## *B.E.F.*

2 W. IV Vear, Edgar Wm. 62278. K. Feb. 28/17. Det.D./B.
2 W. or Y. Warman, L.-Cpl. Ernest Petley. 53284. M. April 24/17.
2 W. IV Wright, Edgar R. 15438. W. and M. Feb. 28/17.
‡2 X. Alder, Steph. John. 32650. M. April 24/17.
‡2 X. Block, F. 53107. M. April 24/17.
2 X. VII Edwards, Ernest. 7147. M. Feb. 28/17
‡2 X. Ilsley, A. 53537. M. April 24/17.
‡2 X. Knight, P. 19784. M. April 24/17.
2 X. L.G.S. Lee, L.-Cpl. S. J. 10264. W. and M. April 24/17.
‡2 X. Light, W. 53129. M. April 24/17.
‡2 X. Lindrop, W. 1757. M. April 24/17.
2 X. V Luton, L.-Cpl. P. 8158. M. April 24/17.
*2 X. VI Macpherson, Cyril. 47979. M. April 24/17.
*2 X. Mann, W. G. 34427. M. April 24/17.
‡2 X. Murritt, T. 41309. M. April 24/17.
2 X. V Pearce, H. 52280. M. April 24/17.
2 X. Taylor, Tom W. 12854. M. July 1/16. R/Enq.
2 X. V Tuckfield, Sgt. John Wm. 53103. M. April 24/17.
2 X. Wayland, B. 16697. W. and M. Feb. 28/17.
2 X. VIII Welham, Frank Cecil. 53292. (Form. 1889.) M. April 24/17.
‡2 X. White, H. 62282. M. April 24/17.
2 X. Whiterod, Arch. 35158. M. Feb. 28/17.
2 X. VIII Wiggins, J. W. 9579. W. Unoff. M. April 24/17.
2 X. VII Williams, V. 11831. W. and M. April 24/17.
2 Y. Abel, L.-Cpl. Elijah 24572. M. Feb. 28/17.
2 Y. XI Daniels, O. F. 1543. M. Feb. 28/17.
*2 Y. XI Gurr, F. W. 53155. M. April 24/17.
2 Y. Hellmund, L.-Cpl. Reg. 3304. M. May 11/17.
‡2 Y. Higgins, H. 25601. M. April 24/17.
*2 Y. X Hitchen, A. W. 53065. M. May 11/17.
*2 Y. XII Jackson, H. 56247. M. May 27/17.
‡2 Y. XI Martin, Wm. Alfred. 53156. M. May 11/17.
2 Y. Mead, Hugh. 37205. M. Feb. 28/17.
2 Y. Moore, Leonard Chas. 52297. M. April 24/17.
‡2 Y. Nice, F. 37269. M. April 24/17.
2 Y. XIII Pratt, L.-Cpl. J. W. 18022. M. April 24/17.
2 Y. X Quy, Fredk. Geo. 19661. M. May 11/17.
2 Y. X Rumbold, Wm. Phillip. 23800. M. May 11/17.
*2 Y. XI Strange, Geo. Stephen. 39606. M. May 11/17.
‡2 Y. Trash, E. 53056. M. May 11/17.
2 Y. Wheeler, R. A. 62288. M. Feb. 28/17.
2 Y. Wood, L.-Cpl. E. J. 9450. M. Feb. 28/17.
2 Z. Bastick, L.-Cpl. Arthur. 11089. M. Feb. 28/17.
2 Z. Brookes, D. 14396. W. and M. April 24/17.
‡2 Z. Broom, T. 21364. M. April 24/17.
‡2 Z. Clarke, L.-Cpl. G. 51572. M. April 24/17.
2 Z. XVI Clark, Henry Daniel. 13978. M. Feb. 28/17.
2 Z. XIII Craske, G. T. 51582. W. and M. Feb. 28/17.
2 Z. Fitch, G. 42241. W. and M. Feb. 28/17.
*2 Z. Foster, John. 53167. M. April 24/17.
‡2 Z. Grant, M. 26793. M. May 29/17.
2 Z. XIII Hall, Fred. 8568. M. April 24/17.
2 Z. XVI Jolly, F. 53063. W. and M. April 24/17.
2 Z. XIV Jones, Fred. Geo. 51569. M. Feb. 28/17.
‡2 Z. Lutch, T. 6859. M. April 24/17.
2 Z. Palmer, L.-Cpl. Percy. 53075. M. April 24/17.

**Royal Fusiliers—contd.**

## *B.E.F.*

| | | | |
|---|---|---|---|
| ‡2 | Z. | Penfold, E. 41153. | W. and M. April 24/17. |
| ‡2 | Z. | Tedder, W. 14078. | W. and M. April 24/17. |
| 2 | H.Q. | Woods, Cpl. Fred. 13873. | M. Feb. 28/17. |
| *2 | ? | Tucker, Harry. 39525. | W. and M. April 24/17. |
| 4 | Z. | **Cheshire, Lieut. E. C.** | M. May 3/17. |
| 4 | | **Hiddingh, Lieut. S. vande P.** | K. May 3/17. Det.D./B. |
| 4 | | **Nicholson, 2nd Lieut. B. H. (Fr. 6th.)** | M. May 3/17. |
| 4 | W. | **Parr, 2nd Lieut. W. A.** | W. Unoff. M. May 3/17. |
| 4 | | **Parsons, 2nd Lieut. A. E.** | M. May 3/17. |
| *4 | | **Snaith, 2nd Lieut. W. E.** | K. May 3/17. Det.D./B. |
| *4 | W. IV | Baker, Cpl. C. W. 8787. | M. May 3/17. |
| 4 | W. or Y. M.G.S. | Benford, Alfred. G/20422. | M. May 3/17. |
| ‡4 | W. | Bowd, Cpl. F. 24196. | M. May 3/17. |
| 4 | W. IV | Brooker, T. C. W. 63002. | M. May 3/17. |
| 4 | W. | Cole, Sergt. H. J. 8791. | M. May 3/17. |
| ‡4 | W. | Cooper, L.-Cpl. G. 52235. | M. May 3/17. |
| 4 | W. II | Drage, L.-Cpl. G. J. 54842. | M. May 3/17. |
| ‡4 | W. | Fox, G. 55261. | M. May 3/17. |
| *4 | W. | Gammon, P. 52497. | W. and M. May 3/17. |
| ‡4 | W. | Hankins, H. 65319. | M. May 3/17. |
| 4 | W. | Harding, Geo. Victor. 228029. | M. Unoff. D/W. May 3/17. |
| ‡4 | W. | Hartley, F. E. 9548. | M. May 3/17. |
| 4 | W. | Hodgkin, Cpl. Enoch. 660. | M. April 13/17. |
| ‡4 | W. | Holland, J. 36782. | M. May 3/17. |
| ‡4 | W. | Hutchinson, T. 47158. | M. May 3/17. |
| 4 | W. III | Johnson, A. H. 54847. | W. and M. May 3/17. |
| 4 | W. II | Jupp, Fred. 36774. | M. May 3/17. 2nd Cas. |
| ‡4 | W. II | King, A. W. 65253. | M. May 3/17. |
| *4 | W. | Laithwaite, Cpl. Wm. 9283. | M. May 3/17. |
| ‡4 | W. | Lee, W. 65317 | M. May 3/17. |
| 4 | W. | Lockett, Cpl. F. 9751. | M. April 9/17. |
| *4 | W. III | Love, P. G. 41303. | W. and M. May 3/17. |
| ‡4 | W. | Maynard, J. 228016. | M. May 3/17. |
| 4 | W. | Morley, C. G/65261. | M. May 3/17. |
| 4 | W. | Moss, Arthur. 65254. | M. May 3/17. |
| ‡4 | W. IV | Neetley, W. 9412. | M. May 3/17. |
| 4 | W. | Padgett, W. Jas. 65255. | M. May 3/17. |
| ‡4 | W. | Pryor, A. 65311. | M. May 3/17. |
| ‡4 | W. I | Richardson, A. L. 24209. | M. May 3/17. |
| 4 | W. | Ridge, J. 10223. | M. Mar. 27/17. |
| ‡4 | W. | Smith, G. 63711. | M. April 9/17. |
| 4 | W. IV | Stannard, Fred. 52689. | M. May 3/17. |
| 4 | W. | Stevens, G. H. 47189. | M. May 3/17. |
| 4 | W. I | Trood, T. 14646. | M. May 3/17. |
| ‡4 | W. II | Wakelin, Evan. 65258. | M. May 3/17. |
| 4 | W. I | Watkins, A. W. 47985. | W. and M. May 3/17. |
| 4 | W. | Williams, J. Harold. 9896. | M. May 5/17. |
| 4 | X. VII | Ancell, Geo. H. 55123. | M. April 13/17. |
| ‡4 | X. VIII | Bailey, William. 11619. | M. May 3/17. |
| 4 | X. | Cawthra, E. 55140. | M. April 13/17. |
| 4 | X. | Collins, Charles. 1899. | K. April 9/17. Det.D./B. |
| 4 | X. | Davey, F. J. 50996. | M. May 3/17. |
| 4 | X. | Ellison, H. 55158. | M. April 13/17. |
| ‡4 | X. | Hobson, H. A. 20846. | M. May 3/17. |
| 4 | X. or Z. | Rendall, Carl Edw. Adolphus. 22658. | M. May 3/17. |
| *4 | X. or Z. | Revell, W. 34899. | M. May 3/17. |
| ‡4 | X. VII | Roberts, Chas. 65272. | K. May 8/17. Det.D./B. |

Royal Fusiliers—contd.

*B.E.F.*

4 X. Wilson, E. A. 55325. M. May 3/17.
4 Y. XII Bell, Bernard. 62163. M. May 3/17.
4 Y. XII Bell, C. D. 9782. M. May 3/17.
*4 Y. X Bright, R. E. 49972. M. May 3/17.
‡4 Y. Capel, C. 9619. M. May 3/17.
*4 Y. X Cumplen, Wm. Chas. 4308. M. May 3/17.
‡4 Y. Eales, H. 55151. M. May 3/17.
‡4 Y. Elmer, Y. 65269. M. May 3/17.
‡4 Y. Farrar, R. P. 52933. M. May 3/17.
4 Y. IX Foster, A. G. 16859. M. May 3/17.
‡4 Y. Freeman, S. 55066. M. May 3/17.
4 Y. Fricker, T. 618. M. April 13/17.
*4 Y. VIII Green, Geo. F. 10615. M. May 3/17.
4 Y. XII Gurr, W. Henry. 24455. M. May 3/17.
‡4 Y. Guy, T. 44193. M. May 3/17.
4 Y. V Hardy, G. 48482. M. May 3/17.
4 Y. XI Hardy, S. G. 62216. M. May 3/17.
‡4 Y. Henson, R. 16691. M. May 3/17.
‡4 Y. Hicks, R. F. 42506. M. May 3/17.
‡4 Y. Hitt, J. 48000. M. May 3/17.
‡4 Y. Hunt, W. 52510. M. May 3/17.
‡4 Y. Hulme, J. 9279. M. May 3/17.
4 Y. XII Leppard, Cpl. Leslie Paul. 24017. M. May 3/17,
*4 Y. L.G.S. Lucas, Ernest Freeman. 24599. K. April 13/17. Det.D./B.
1 Y. X L.G.S. Nevill, A. 9645. M. May 3/17.
4 Y. Newton, Sig. J. T. 11445. (Fr. H.Q.) M. April 13/17.
‡4 Y. Pittman, J. 10363. M. May 3/17.
4 Y. X Pook, Harold Alfred. 228019. (Late 4 Sussex. 201853.) M. May 3/17.
‡4 Y. Porter, L.-Cpl. B. 1511. M. May 3/17.
4 Y. or Z. Richardson, Stanley H. 63642. M. May 3/17.
*4 Y. XII Rose, G. W. G/65275. M. May 3/17.
‡4 Y. Ruddem, S. 53366. M. May 3/17.
4 Y. Smith, Albert Edw. Ernest. 27677. M. May 3/17.
*4 Y. IX Smith, S. 55059. M. May 3/17.
4 Y. Tidman, L.-Sergt. G. H. 10870. W. and M. April 13/17.
‡4 Y. Woolridge, L. 9158. M. May 3/17.
‡4 Z. L.G.S. Bennett, Cpl. G. 4226. K. April 9/17. Det.D./B.
‡4 Z. Bishop, A.-Cpl. J. 2552. M. May 3/17.
*4 Z. Bishop, A.-Sergt. J. A. 14801. M. May 3/17.
*4 Z. XIII Brashier, Sidney. 50570. M. May 3/17.
‡4 Z. Brennan, L.-Cpl. J. 14927. M. May 3/17.
4 Z. Broughton, Wm. Edward. 24587. M. April 13/17.
*4 Z. XVI Carter, L.-Cpl. Geo. 12284. M. May 3/17.
*4 Z. XVI Dalton, Sergt. H. W. 53285. M. May 3/17.
4 Z. Daniels, Jas. 53291. M. April 9/17.
4 Z. XV Evans, L.-Cpl. Fredk. Thos. 14425. K. Aug. 16/16. Det.D./B.
*4 Z. Groves, Walter L. S/2889. M. May 3/17.
*4 Z. XIV Hartley, Wm. P. 45877. M. May 3/17.
4 Z. Holden, G. 16599. M. April 13/17.
4 Z. Jones, Sergt. Richard. 8727. M. Unoff. K. May 3/17.
4 Z. XIV Kember, Lewis. 52522. M. April 14/17.
4 Z. XIV Kenton, H. 52520. M. May 3/17.
4 Z. XIV King, H. H. 3273. M. Unoff. K. May 3/17.
‡4 Z. Kinghorn, K. 53304. M. May 3/17.
*4 Z. XIII Landberges, Geo. Wm. 32601. M. May 6/17.
‡4 Z. XV Lawson, Cpl. C. E. 17598. W. and M. May 3/17.

Royal Fusiliers—contd.

## B.E.F.

4 Z. XVI McDonald, J. 11514. M. May 3/17.
4 Z. XIV Mawer, Harry. 53307. M. May 3/17.
4 Z. XIV Pay, Arthur John. 34625. W. and M. May 3/17.
4 Z. XIII Quaife, Douglas Walter. 50292. M. May 3/17.
‡4 Z. Ratcliffe, H. 44310. M. May 3/17.
‡4 Z. XIV Sansom, L.-Cpl. F. 14230. M. May 3/17.
4 Z. XIII Shackleton, Robert. 65277. M. May 3/17.
4 Z. Stanford, A. 52548. M. April 13/17.
4 Z. XV Willcox, Wortley Harold. 2475. M. May 3/17.
‡4 Z. Waby, F. 52748. M. May 3/17.
‡4 Z. Wright, H. 18020. M. May 3/17.
*2/4 B. VIII Minet, C. W. 283353. M. June 16/17.
‡2/4 B. Twitchin, G. H. 283829. (8032.) M. June 16/17.
‡2/4 D. Cook, J. 282258. M. June 16/17.
*2/4 ? Skinner, A. 282214. Unoff. M. May 16/17.
7 **Juniper, 2nd Lieut. J. H.** M., bel. K. April 29/17.
7 **Randall, Lieut. E. W.** K. April 23/17. Det.D./B.
*7 **Wood, Lieut. P. B.** (Fr. 5th.) K. April 23/17. Det.D./B.
7 A. I Batchelor, W. 46670. D/W. Feb. 22/17. Det.D./B.
7 A. I Baxter, A. H. 62929. M. April 23/17.
‡7 A. II Bradley, A. J. T. 65430. W. and M. May 31/17.
7 A. I Butcher, Frank. 53100. (Fr. 19, 12, and 5 Bns.) M. April 23/17.
7 A. IV Castle, A. H. 48414. M. April 23/17.
‡7 A. II Fowler, A. 15883. M. April 29/17.
7 A. III Leeds, Robt. Temple. 62959. M. April 23/17.
7 A. IV Maley, D. 61304. M. Feb. 7/17.
7 A. IV Mantle, F. J. G/32524. M. April 23/17.
7 A. III Miller, Oliver. 62957. M. April 23/17.
*7 A. Pearce, R. 62953. M. April 29/17.
7 A. IV Perry, Sidney Thos. 63392. K. April 15/17. Det.D./B
7 A. IV Platten, P. C. 61074. M. April 29/17.
7 A. III Rodgers, Wm. 23237. M. Nov. 13/16.
7 A. II Skillman, Stanley Winterbourn. 52738. M. April 23/17.
7 B. VII Bryant, W. 16119. M. April 23/17.
7 B. VI Charlick, Ernest H. R. 62920. (Fr. 3rd W. Surreys.) M. April 23/17.
*7 B. VII Chase, Fredk. Wm. 49729. M. April 23/17.
7 B. V Gordon, G. A. 44167. M. April 29/17.
7 B. Hanley, A. 48424. M. April 23/17.
7 B. VI Helden, F. C. 25258. M. Nov. 13/16.
‡7 B. Kennington, W. J. 29658. M. April 23/17.
7 B. VII Perkins, R. W. 62915. W. Unoff. M. April 23/17.
7 B. Read, J. T. 26246. M. April 23/17.
7 B. Selwood, T. J. 62742. M. April 23/17.
*7 B. VIII Stroud, J. 29086. M. April 29/17.
7 B. VII Sutton, Frank. 3102. M. April 23/17.
7 B. VIII Tourle, E. 60997. W. and M. April 23/17.
*7 B. VII Wraight, W. 34774. W. and M. April 29/17.
7 C. Akehurst, Wm. Hry. 61028. M. April 23/17.
7 C. XI Baulcomb, Chas. Hy. 61029. M. April 23/17.
7 C. XI Boughey, Walter. 52361. M. April 29/17.
7 C. IX Collett, Alfred E. 26838. M. Nov. 13/16. R/Enq.
*7 C. XI Dawkins, Ernest E. A. 48004. M. April 23/17.
7 C. IX Giddings, A. G. G/24911. W. and M. April 23/17.
7 C. XI Glanfield, G. 21881. M. April 29/17.
7 C. XI Gutteridge, H. D. G/27949. W. and M. Feb. 5/17.

**Royal Fusiliers—contd.**

## *B.E.F.*

7 C. Harrison, Cpl. H. 3624. **M. April 23/17.**
7 C. IX Hawkins, L.-Cpl. E. 26705. M. **April 23/17.**
7 C. Huntingford, James. 52378. **M. April 23/17.**
7 C. XII Keefer, L. E. 61284. **M. Feb. 6/17.**
7 C. Kettle, C. W. 26789. **M. April 23/17.**
7 C. XII Lovelock, Wm. Richard. G/25383. W. Unoff. M. **April 23/17.**
7 C. X Middleton, Chas. 22195. **M. April 23/17.**
7 C. XI Norris, Henry. 48417. M. **April 23/17.**
7 C. Pascoe, W. 26729. **M. April 23/17.**
7 C. X Rattledge, Jas. Arthur. 422643. (8234.) M. **April 23/17.**
*7 C. X Reed, Wm. 62763. W. and M. **April 23/17.**
7 C. Sheffield, Cpl. H. 52392. W. and M. **April 23/17.**
7 C. Simpson, L.-Cpl. E. 28949. **M. April 23/17.**
7 C. Smith, F. J. 3097. M. **April 23/17.**
7 C. XI Swan, L.-Cpl. Ernest Alfred. 26750. M. **April 23/17.**
7 C. Tee, Cpl. C. A. 61250. **M. April 23/17.**
7 C. Wadey, Fred John. 17188. (62947, 3rd R.W. Surrey.) **M. April 23/17.**
7 C. Willis, A.-Sergt. Albert. 14880. M. **April 23/17.**
7 C. Wingrove, C. 27991. M. **April 23/17.**
7 D. Bigg, W. C. 52478. **M. April 23/17.**
7 D. XVI Boreham Wm. 18663. M. **April 23/17.**
*7 D. XIII Burton, Albert. Hry. 62937. W. and M. **April 23/17.**
7 D. XIV Bushell, John Wm. Chas. 20086. **M. April 23/17.**
7 D. XVI Cook, E. 61044. (late Middx.) M. **April 23/17.**
7 D. XV Craddock, William. 26957. W. and M. **April 23/17.**
‡7 D. XIII Creech, A. N. 61040. K. **April 28/17.** Det.D./B.
7 D. XVI Cross, Albert John. 27573. M. **April 23/17.**
‡7 D. Danahar, D. 4711. M. **May 28/17.**
*7 D. XVI Edwards, Wm. Richard. 8146. W. and M. **April 23/17.**
7 D. Hitchings, A. G. 62940. **M. April 23/17.**
*7 D. L.G.S. Hoffman, Sidney. 17025. W. and M. **Feb. 11/17.**
7 D. Howlett, A. 29048. **M. April 28/17.**
7 D. XIV Kidd, Geo. Fredk. 35935. M. **April 23/17.**
‡7 D. Low, L.-Cpl. M. 51295. W. and M. **April 23/17.**
7 D. XV Marsh, L.-Cpl. Wm. C. 51306. W. and M. **April 17/17.**
7 D. Rose, W. J. 61339. **M. April 23/17.**
7 D. Small, I. 62768. M. **April 23/17.**
7 D. Small, R. E. 24423. (Sig. S.) **M. April 23/17.**
7 D. XVI Smith, R. 44165. M. **April 23/17.**
7 D. XVI Spring, Wm. Francis. 11101. M. **April 23/17.**
7 D. Stocker, James. 44166. **M. April 23/17.**
‡7 D. Wates, J. J. 29091. M. **May 28/17.**
7 D. Winfield, C. 62941. **M. April 23/17.**
7 D. Winfield, P. C. 39338. (Fr. 3rd W. Surrey.) **M. April 23/17.**
7 D. XVI Woodward, Alfred Barnes. 62942. M. **April 18/17.**
8 **Backlake, Lieut. B. A.** M., bel. K. **May 3/17.**
8 **Lethbridge, Lieut. C. A.** W. and M. **May 3/17.**
8 **Turney, Major R. W.** (Fr. 6th.) M. **May 3/17.**
8 **Withall, 2nd Lieut. John.** (Fr. 6th.) K. **Oct. 7/16.** Det.D./B.
‡8 A. Arnold, H. E. 10520. M. **May 3/17.**
8 A. Ashby, L.-Cpl. Raymond. P.S./10544 M. **Oct. 7/17.** R/Enq.
*8 A. or B. Askew, Arthur. 47201. M. **May 3/17.**
‡8 A. Bevis, R. 12674. * M. **Sept. 18/16.**
*8 A. or C. Cunliffe, Wallace. 7804. M. **May 3/17.**
8 A. II Dewhirst, W. Horace L. 10136. M. **Oct. 7/16.** R/Enq.

**Royal Fusiliers—contd.**

## *B.E.F.*

| | | |
|---|---|---|
| 8 A. II | Gladman, Archbald Fred. 60646. | M. May 3/17. |
| *8 A. L.G.S. | Grimes, Geo. Wm. 55318. | W. and M. May 3/17. |
| 8 A. III | Nash, Rufus. 47236. | M. May 3/17. |
| *8 A. II | Roberts, L.-Sergt. Ben. 41453. | M. May 3/17. |
| *8 A. or B. Bomb. S. | Robinson, Arthur. 10184. | W. and M. Oct. 6/16. R/Enq. |
| 8 A. III | Tadd, Walter Ford. 26308. | M. May 3/17. R/Enq. 2nd Cas. |
| ‡8 B. | Bath, G. 60419. | M. May 3/17. |
| ‡8 B. | Beardwell, T. 60437. | M. May 3/17. |
| ‡8 B. | Collins, L.-Cpl. C. 8587. | M. May 3/17. |
| 8 B. VI | Dixon, E. A. 49737. | M. May 3/17. |
| 8 B. VIII | Dwight, J. 60675. | M. May 3/17. |
| ‡8 B. | Evans, E. 60679. | M. May 3/17. |
| ‡8 B. VII | Gater, M. F. St. B. 55322. | M. May 3/17. |
| ‡8 B. | Gidman, L.-Cpl. E. 18114. | M. May 3/17. |
| ‡8 B. | Gilbert, H. 50759. | M. May 3/17. |
| ‡8 B. | Gilchrist, A. 55321. | M. May 3/17. |
| 8 B. | Hall, Robert Evelyn. 42858. | M. May 3/17. |
| ‡8 B. | Hubbard, W. 209. | M. May 3/17. |
| ‡8 B. | Hutley, J. 27777. | M. May 3/17. |
| 8 B. VI | Jarrett, L.-Cpl. Cavendish. 60686. | M. May 3/17. |
| ‡8 B. | Kidsley, H. 10805. | M. May 3/17. |
| 8 B. VIII | Knight, L.-Cpl. Ernest Henry. 60690. | M. May 3/17. |
| 8 B. V | Nunn, Sergt. Harry. 29170. | M. May 3/17. |
| *8 B. VII | Owens, Hugh Pugh. 60632. | M. May 3/17. |
| 8 B. V | Pentecost, B. W. R. 41362. | M. May 3/17. |
| ‡8 B. | Roberts, L.-Sergt. B. 47453. | M. May 3/17. |
| ‡8 B. | Roberts, J. 47695. | M. May 3/17. |
| 8 B. L.G.S. | Robinson, L.-Cpl. Cecil. 5545. | M. May 3/17. |
| ‡8 B. | Skilton, P. 50428. | M. May 3/17. |
| 8 B. VI | Smith, Fred. Dresser. 60706. | W. and M. May 3/17. |
| 8 B. V | Suter, Sergt. A. J. 60704. (Fr. 6th Sussex, 448.) | M. May 3/17. |
| 8 B. VIII | Tickner, Edwd. Jackson. 60709. | M. May 3/17. |
| 8 B. V | Wainwright, Leslie. 23228. | M. May 3/17. |
| 8 B. VII | Wardley, Sydney. 60712. | M. May 3/17. |
| 8 B. VIII | Wight, J. D. G/60676. | M. May 3/17. |
| 8 C. X | Ames, Sidney H. G/60665. | W. and M. May 3/17. |
| *8 C. XII | Bullock, Wm. Edward. 23624. | K. May 3/17. Unoff. P/W. Conf. and Det. |
| ‡8 C. | Craig, J. 49733. | W and M. May 3/17. |
| 8 C. | Curtis, Thos. Henry. 55298. | M. May 3/17. |
| ‡8 C. | Drummond, J. 4991. | M. May 3/17. |
| ‡8 C. | Fischer, T. 10540. | W. and M. May 3/17. |
| 8 C. | Helliwell, Fred. 10652. | M. May 3/17. |
| 8 C. | Hudson, Archluss. 60454. | M. May 3/17. |
| 8 C. IX | Mansell, William 10353. | W. and M. May 3/17. |
| ‡8 C. | Pledge, J. 50475. | M. May 3/17. |
| ‡8 C. | Price, W. 55303. | M. May 3/17. |
| ‡8 C. IX | Pybus, Harold. 5128. | M. Oct. 7/16. R/Enq |
| 8 C. X | Rands, Oliver Francis. 3177. | M. May 3/17. |
| *8 C. IX | Rowell, Joseph. 47246. | M. May 3/17. |
| ‡8 C. | Sawyer, W. 60656. | W. and M. May 3/17. |
| ‡8 C. | Stead, C. 60728. | M. May 3/17. |
| 8 C. XI | Swetnam, F. 14375. | M. May 3/17. |
| 8 C. | Topley, Sergt. James. 682. | M. May 3/17. |
| 8 C. IX | Williamson, Harold. 47446. | M. May 3/17. |
| 8 D. XIII | Dunn, Wm. Fredk. 47205. | M. May 3/17. |

**Royal Fusiliers—contd.**

*B.E.F.*

‡8 D. Fry, A. 60736. M. May 3/17.
‡8 D. Kevelle, A. 26859. M. May 3/17.
8 D. XVI Mabbott, P. 12786. (Fr. H.Q.) M. May 3/17.
‡8 D. Northern, S. 41347. M. May 3/17.
8 D. XV Rye, L.-Cpl. W. E. 60701. K. April 7/17. Det.D./B.
‡8 D. XV Smith, George. 8224. M. May 3/17.
8 D. XV Veness, W. S. 60730. M. May 3/17.
8 D. L.G.S. Weeden, K. 24665. W. and M. May 3/17.
8 D. XIV Weller, W. 55307. M. May 3/17.
8 ? M.G.S. Chapman, L.-Cpl. Ed. S. 16334. K. Oct. 7/16. Det.D./B.
*8 ? I.T.M. Hercock, Sidney. 9833. (36 Bde.) M. May 2/17.
*8 ? Hopes, Sniper Wm. 10121. K. April 9/17. Det.D./B.
8 ? Jones, Robert. 24765. W. and M. Sept. 15-17/16.
*8 ? Morris, Arthur. 36437. (Fr. 8th.) M. Oct. 7/16. R/Enq.
9 A. **Fraser, 2nd Lieut. D. C.** K. May 3/17. Det.D./B.
‡9 A. Brownscombe, L.-Sgt. G. 60389. M. May 3/17.
‡9 A. Bye, A. 6501. M. May 3/17.
9 A. Cater, F. W. 60458. M. May 3/17.
9 A. IV Dixon, Geo. G/36168. M. Oct. 7/16. R/Enq.
‡9 A. Dyer, W. 62440. M. May 3/17.
9 A. II Edwards, John Francis. 22638. M. May 3/17.
‡9 A. III Funnell, A. 5372. M. May 3/17.
9 A. II Golding, W. J. 60504. M. May 3/17.
9 A. III Hiscocks, Alfred Richard. M. May 3/17.
9 A. I Hodson, Fredk. Richard. 52873. M. May 3/17.
‡9 A. Holliday, J. 5208. M. May 3/17.
9 A. III Kent, Chas. Albt. 24940. M. May 3/17.
‡9 A. Knight, J. 52877. M. May 3/17.
9 A. Laycock, T. H. 27426. M. Oct. 7/16. R/Enq.
‡9 A. Marron, J. 55341. M. May 3/17.
9 A. or B. I Middleton, E. F. 60465. M. May 3/17.
9 A. or B. VII Middleton, Jack. 26360. M. May 3/17.
*9 A. L.G.S. Neill, James, P. S. 10576. M. May 8/17.
9 A. I Orton, Regd. 52885. M. May 3/17.
9 A. L.G.S. Pinnock, Cpl. Henry. 7014. M. May 3/17.
9 A. I. Pratt, Alfred Chas. 60592. Unoff. M. May 3/17.
9 A. III Reed, Chas. 4/60508. M. May 3/17.
‡9 A. Sherston, R. 60467. M. May 3/17.
9 A. I Tidman, J. 9726. M. May 3/17.
9 A. I Turrell, Wm. Jesse. G/37156. M. May 3/17.
‡9 A. Wadham, G. 55349. M. May 3/17.
‡9 A. Withers, C. 10494. M. May 3/17.
*9 B. VIII Becker, Wm. 62069. M. May 3/17.
*9 B. VII Booth, F. S. G/52850. W. and M. May 3/17.
9 B. VII Bristow, W. R. 839. W. and M. May 3/17.
9 B. Histed, Chas. Albert. 48551. M. May 3/17.
‡9 B. Hover, L.-Sergt. H. 18857. M. May 3/17.
9 B. Hudson, G. W. 62592. M. May 3/17.
9 B. VIII Hyde, G. E. 55333. M. May 3/17.
‡9 B. VII Johnson, A. 50126. M. May 3/17.
*9 B. VIII Lawson, David. 55335. M. May 3/17.
9 B. V Marra, L.-Cpl. Wm. 9715. M. Oct. 7/16. R/Enq.
‡9 B. Moreley, L. 25315. M. May 3/17.
‡9 B. Nash, A. 50260. M. May 3/17.
9 B. Nash, L.-Cpl. F. J. 15572. M. Oct. 7/16. R/Enq.
9 B. L.G.S. Neeves, Ivor Stanley. 20175. M. May 5/17.
‡9 B. Pearson, L.-Cpl. C. 11647. M. May 3/17.
‡9 B. Pickles, E. 55342. M. May 3/17.

**Royal Fusiliers—contd.**

## *B.E.F.*

| | | |
|---|---|---|
| *9 B. | Sandy, L.-Cpl. A. E. 49871. | K. May 3/17. Det.D./B. |
| *9 B. VII | Scopes, Albert Edwd. 62357. | M. May 3/17. |
| *9 B. | Spriggs, Alf. Wm. 55345. | M. May 3/17. |
| *9 B. | Warrilow, J. 10994. | W. and M. April 9/17. |
| *9 B. | Westlake, Bert. 28257. | W. and M. May 3/17. |
| 9 B. V | Wragg, Herbert Samuel. 27145. | M. Oct. 7/16. R/Enq. |
| ‡9 C. X | Rayment, Jas. 65235. | W. and M. May 3/17. |
| 9 C. L.G.S. | Travis, Harry. 4769. | M. April 9/17. |
| 9 D. XIII | Applewhite, Wm. Edgar. 53336. | K. May 3/17. Det.D./B. |
| 9 D. | Boldick, Jos. 9351. | M. Oct. 7/16. R/Enq. |
| 9 D. XIII | Copeland, A. E. G/62412. | M. May 3/17. |
| 9 D. XV | Graysmark, Fredk. 62588. | W. and M. May 3/17. |
| ‡9 D. XIII | Henchcliffe, W. 9273. | M. May 3/17. |
| ‡9 D. | Pluck, L.-Sergt. D. 1149. | M. May 3/17. |
| ‡9 D. | Small, S. 23757. | M. May 3/17. |
| *9 D. XVI | Walsh, P. 65239. | W. and M. May 3/17. |
| 9 D. | Webb, Ernest. 60590. | M. May 3/17. |
| *9 I.T.M. | Nightingale, Geo. 60482. (36 Bde.) | M. May 3/17. |
| 10 A. L.G.S. | Davies, L.-Cpl. G. H. 1431. (Fr. H.Q.) | W. and M. April 10-11/17. |
| 10 A. | Gibson, Cpl. Allan Leslie. 93. (Fr. H.Q. Bomb.) | M. April 23/17. |
| ‡10 A. | Jackson, J. 54801. | M. April 26/17. |
| 10 A. I | Tassell, Fredk. Noel. G/47636. | M. April 11/17. |
| 10 B. | Atkinson, Cpl. F. E. 61873. (Late Sergt.) (Fr. W. Kent.) | M. April 11/17. |
| 10 B. VII | Booker, S. 52112. | W. and M. April 10/17. |
| ‡10 B. | Bowdidge, R. J. 339. | W. and M. April 10/17. |
| 10 B. | Croucher, W. J. 21081. | M. April 10/17. |
| 10 B. | Dean, C. 1360. | W. and M. April 10/17. |
| 10 B. VI | Duffey, J. 16641. | M. April 10/17. |
| 10 B. | Hart, E. 42247. | M. April 10/17. |
| 10 B. VIII | Miller, Mark Wm. 5301. | W. and M. April 10/17. |
| 10 B. VII | Parsloe, F. H. 37852. | W. and M. April 23/17. |
| ‡10 B. | Spencer, Cpl. A. A. 533. | M. April 11/17. |
| 10 B. | Tee, Wm. 42778. | W. and M. April 9/17. |
| 10 B. VII | West, Geo. F. 34706. | W. and M. April 9/17. |
| 10 C. IX | Barltrop, Rdby. 61844. | M. April 10/17. |
| 10 C. Sig. S. | Bash, Leon. 1602. | M. April 12/17. |
| 10 C. IX | Lewis, Henry. 5137. | M. Nov. 18/16. R/Enq. |
| ‡10 C. IX | Marton, Cpl. W. A. 772. | Unoff. M., bel. K. April 10/17. |
| 10 C. | Stanborough, R. 10147. | M. April 10/17. |
| 10 C. XII | Thomas, L.-Cpl. C. F. 1371. | M. Unoff. W. April 10/17. |
| 10 C. X | Yeomans, Albert. 5351. | M. April 11/17. |
| 10 D. | Adam, H. 48287. | M. April 10/17. |
| 10 D. XII | Chalfoner, L.-Cpl. Douglas Geo. 927. | W. and M. April 23/17. |
| 10 D. | Hayes, J. 42622. | M. April 11/17. |
| 10 D. | Hourigan, L.-Cpl. Jeremiah. 6705. | M. April 10/17. |
| 10 D. | Jukes, Sidney Frank. 8677. | W. and M. April 10/17. |
| 10 D. | Wilkinson, Geo. 1162. | M. April 11/17. |
| 10 ? | Pleasance, L.-Sergt. W. F. 9561. | M. April 23/17. |
| 11 B. | **Neate, Capt. N. R.** | M. May 3/17. |
| 11 A. II | Berry, John William. 10150. | M. Feb. 10/17. |
| 11 A. | Howells, W. A. 2098. | M. Feb. 10/17. |
| 11 A. | Lomax, Sergt. Horatio Nelson. 7354. | M. Feb. 10/17. |
| 11 A. II | Newman, Walter Sidney. 60377. | M. Feb. 10/17. |

**Royal Fusiliers—contd.**

*B.E.F.*

11 A. III Steward, Frank. 60325. M. Feb. 17/17.
11 B. Adams, Alfred Geo. 7498. M. Sept. 26/16.
‡11 B. Arnold, W. 26270. M. May 3/17.
11 B. Anstiss, L.-Cpl. J. 12282. M. May 3/17.
11 B. VII Badger, Harold Douglas. 7526. M. May 3/17.
‡11 B. Birch, A. 24714. M. May 3/17.
11 B. V Bowman, R. 51780. M. May 3/17.
11 B. M.G.S. Bradbury, Percy Ed. 2070. M. May 3/17.
11 B. VIII Cousins, W. S. 51805. M. Feb. 17/17.
‡11 B. Dickens, F. 55325. W. and M. May 3/17.
‡11 B. Snip. S. Dominey, Herb. Wm. 7549. M. May 3/17.
11 B. M.G.S. Ferris, Franc's Wm. 2034. M. May 3/17.
*11 B. VIII Fleming, A. D. 7569. M. May 3/17.
‡11 B. Guirey, Sergt. T. 18166. M. May 3/17.
11 B. M.G.S. Hall, F. R. 10663. M. May 3/17.
11 B. Kirkland, Sergt. Geo. 51786. W. and M. Feb. 17/17.
11 B. VIII Page, Walter. 51739. M. May 3/17.
11 B. Redman, Albert. 14277. W. and M. Sept. 25-26/16. R/Enq.
‡11 B. VIII Steel, Ernest Edw. 17889. (Trans. Sec.) M. May 3/17.
‡11 B. Symons, L. A. 7968. M. May 3/17.
‡11 B. Thomas, C. 16461. M. May 3/17.
11 B. V Twine, Jas. 51743. M. Feb. 17/17.
11 B. VIII Uden, A. E. 60333. W. and M. Feb. 17/17.
11 B. M.G.S. Vowell, Peter Guthrie. G/51719. (Fr. K.R.R.C.) M. Feb. 17/17.
*11 B. V Walker, E. 7712. M. May 5/17.
11 B. M.G.S. Wing A. 51744. M. Feb. 17/17.
‡11 B. Wood, L.-Sergt. J. 7716. M. May 3/17.
‡11 C. Gall, H. 18642. M. May 3/17.
‡11 C. Holland, Cpl. T. 9432. M. May 3/17.
11 C. XI Rogers, Richard Jas. 50415. M. May 3/17.
11 D. XIV Birt, J. 35892. K. Feb. 17/17. Det.D./B.
11 D. Corden, L.-Cpl. Jas. Arthur. 2652. M. Feb. 17/17.
‡11 D. M.G.S. Frammingham, W. J. 50396. M. May 3/17.
‡11 D. Frost, L.-Cpl. H. B. 23492. M. May 3/17.
11 D. XVI Humphreys, L.-Cpl. W. 7945. W. and M. Feb. 17/17.
11 D. XV Jones, J. H. 28008. W. and M. Sept. 26/16.
11 D. XV Roberts, P. 41814. M. Feb. 17/17.
11 D. Sayer, D. 5460. K. Feb. 17/17. Det.D./B.
11 D. Williams, L.-Cpl. Wm. Arthur. 8255 W. and M. Feb. 17/17.
12 1 Clark, Percy Thos. 6002. M. Sept. 4/16. R/Enq.
‡12 3 X Miller, G. W. 63552. W. Unoff. M. June 10/17.
12 4 XV Bolton, Sidney. 9169. M. Jan. 26/17.
‡12 4 XV Peacock, F. M. 2256. W. and M. June 14-15/17.
‡12 4 Wilsdon, C. W. 65464. W. Unoff. M. June 10/17.
13 **Bayley, 2nd Lieut. R. J.** M., bel. K. April 29/17.
13 **Jefferys, 2nd Lieut. H. L.** M. April 28/17.
13 **Yandle, 2nd Lieut. T.** M. April 10/17.
13 A. Aikman, W. 62979. M. April 23/17.
13 A. Atkins, E. 228120. M. April 23/17.
13 A. IV Bangs, G. W. 51449. M. April 24/17.
13 A. Boyce, Wm. M. D. 21411. (H.Q. Runner.). M. April 10/17.
13 A. Broadley, H. 51588. M. April 10-11/17.
13 A. Cole, Claud. 61486. M. April 23/17.
13 A. Cunningham, J. 51617. M. April 24/17.
13 A. Dewberry, Sergt. A. 61477. M. April 10-11/17.

**Royal Fusiliers—contd.**

## *B.E.F.*

13 A. III Doubleday, S. 11137. M. April 10-11/17.
13 A. Ealey, S. T. 65006. M. April 28/17.
13 A. or C. Emsden, A. W. 228128. M. April 28/17.
13 A. Entwhistle, A. 51595. M. April 28/17.
13 A. Errington, T. W. G/65141. M. April 23/17.
13 A. IV Gray, Wm. R. 51456. M. April 10-11/17.
13 A. Harris, A. 43908. M. April 23/17.
13 A. Hazelden, W. 61379. M. April 10-11/17.
13 A. Joyce, F. G/65162. M. April 23/17.
13 A. Judd, Walter. 5977. M. April 10/17.
13 A. I Kirk, A. 51441. K. April 9/17. Det.D./B.
13 A. I Martin, Frank. 41225. M. April 23/17.
‡13 A. Middleton, G. H. 61397. W. and M. April 10-11/17.
13 A. IV Oakden, Thos. 8917. W. and M. April 11/17.
13 A. Pater, W. H. 61418. M. April 23/17.
13 A. I Robbins, W. 48549. M. April 23/17.
13 A. III Soards, Arthur E. 11167. M. April 23/17.
13 A. II Wallbank, Arthur. 3244. M. April 10-11/17.
13 A. IV Ward, Fred. 51439. M. April 23/17.
13 A. III Weldon, Sidney. G/61441. M. April 10-11/17.
13 A. Wonnacott, W. 65052. M. April 24/17.
13 B. Adlam, J. A. Y. 8500. M. April 29/17.
13 B. VI Andrews, Arthur Fredk. 6401. W. and M. April 10-11/17.
13 B. Bartlett, J. W. 51483. M. April 10-11/17.
13 B. Batzer, R. H. 65165. M. April 28/17.
13 B. Bovingdon, F. 228123. M. April 28/17.
13 B. L.G.S. Bowen, Fredk. Wm. 63610. W. and M. April 10-11/17.
13 B. VIII Brace, A. E. G/2620. M. April 28/17.
13 B. Brown, Cpl. Geo. Arthur. G/2533. M. April 28/17.
13 B. Carlin, J. J. 51406. M. April 28/17.
13 B. Carlo, E. V. 228125. (65077.) (Fr. 1 Londons.) M. April 23/17.
13 B. V Goodman, Frank. 11220. M. April 24/17.
13 B. VI Holness, A. H. 9382. M. April 23/17.
13 B. VII Inskip, Edward Robert. 65107. M. April 24/17.
13 B. Kilcoyne, A. L. 65035. M. April 24/17.
13 B. Ladd, Chas. Wm. 51471. M. April 24/17.
13 B. McCarthy, L.-Cpl. John. 12179. M. April 28/17.
‡13 B. Miles, G. 26274. W. and M. April 10-11/17.
13 B. Morrice, A. H. 5623. W. and M. April 10-11/17.
13 B. Neaves, J. 55227. M. April 28/17.
13 B. Nuttram, G. W. 62889. M. April 28/17.
13 B. Ormering, Theodore C. R. 22227. M. April 28/17.
13 B. V Phillips, A.-S.-M. Arhtur Wm. G/4090. M. April 23/17.
13 B. Pluck, Thos. Jas. 61771. M. April 28/17.
13 B. VII Portnow, Wm. J. 20289. W. and M. April 9/17.
13 B. VI Robinson, Gilbert. 65045. M. April 24/17.
13 B. Rowe, Ernest Leslie. 4726. M. April 28/17.
*13 B. Skinner, J. 22211. W. and M. April 10/17.
13 B. Smith, F. H. 228139. M. April 28/17.
‡13 B. Sullivan, P. J. 25851. W. and M. April 10-11/17.
13 B. VIII Thompson, Harvey. 48545. M. April 24/17.
13 B. Wilkinson, R. H. S. 51433. M. April 10-11/17.
13 C. XI Anderson, G. H. 51438. W. and M. April 10-11/17.
*13 C. XI Baron, W. 61761. K. April 11/17. Det.D./B.
13 C. Bell, Thomas A. 57395. M. April 28/17.
13 C. Bell, T. A. 62990. M. April 28/17.

Royal Fusiliers—contd.

*B.E.F.*

| | | |
|---|---|---|
| 13 C. XI | Broad, Geo. 11125. | W. Unoff. M. April 10/17. |
| 13 C. | Brown, W. A. 61360. | M. April 28/17. |
| 13 C. or D. | Catling, Fredk. Chas. 9672. | M. Nov. 16/16. |
| 13 C. | Clover, S. 11106. | M. April 24/17. |
| 13 C. | Day, H. H. 228111. | M. April 28/17. |
| ‡13 C. | Evans, Cpl. J. 51584. | W. and M. April 11/17. |
| *13 C. | Howson, George A. 62902. | W. and M. April 11/17. |
| 13 C. | Kensett, L.-Cpl. Henry Jas. 5388. | M. April 10-11/17. |
| ‡13 C. | Leroy, E. L. 61385. | W. and M. April 10-11/17. |
| 13 C. IX | Manktelow, A. W. J. G/61309. | W. Unoff. M. April 23/17. |
| 13 C. XII | Strickson, Sergt. J. W. 1109. | K. April 10/17. Det.D./B. |
| 13 C. | Sutton, L.-Cpl. James. 11165. | M. April 10-11/17. |
| 13 C. IX | Warren, Wm. Ernest. 61822. | W. and M. April 28/17. |
| 13 C. X | Watts, Wm. 898. | W. and M. April 10-11/17. |
| 13 C. | Webb, J. 61825. | M. April 28/17. |
| 13 C. | Wells, W. 63605. | M. April 10-11/17. |
| 13 C. XI | Wolstenholme, Sgt. W. 61472. (Late 21636 and 13065, 13 E. Surreys and Suffolks.) | K. April 9/17. Det.D./B. |
| ‡13 D. XIV | Amos, E. A. 61827. | K. April 10-11/17. Det.D./B. R/Enc |
| 13 D. | Baker, Joseph Henry. 61036. | M., bel K. April 24-29/17. |
| 13 D. | Baugh, A. 62982. (Fr. 6th.) | M. April 29/17. |
| 13 D. XVI | Brimstead, Frank. G/61362. | M. April 26/17. |
| 13 D. | Bussell, David Lewis Roy. 65024. | M. April 29/17. |
| 13 D. | Cowell, L.-Cpl. Alf. John. 228151. (3692.) (Fr. Londons.) | M. April 29/17. |
| 13 D. M.G.S. | Edwards, Jos. E. 24250. | M. April 29/17. |
| 13 D. | Fuell, W. 9681. | M. April 10-11/17. |
| 13 D. | Gee, A. 65150. | M. April 29/17. |
| ‡13 D. XVI | Gibbins, F. 7860. | Unoff. W. and M. April 29/17. |
| 13 D. XIV | Gibson, P. J. A. 10957. | W. Unoff. M. April 29/17. |
| 13 D. XVI | Ibberson, Geo. 47808. | M. April 29/17. |
| 13 D. | Jeffreys, J. 18998. | M. April 10-11/17. |
| 13 D. L.G.S. | Kelsey, F. 63273. | W. Unoff. M. April 10-11/17. |
| 13 D. | Knight, W. R. 4199. | M. April 10-11/17. |
| 13 D. XIII | Lewis, Peter. G/63268. (1066, 4th R. Fus.) | W. Unoff. M. April 10-11/17. |
| 13 D. XVI | Peters, W. C. G/61436. | W. and M. April 10/17. |
| 13 D. | Plowman, A. E. 65041. | M. April 29/17. |
| 13 D. | Puttock, C. P. 228155. | M. April 28/17. |
| ‡13 D. XV | Rewell, T. G. 41261. | K. April 10/17. Det.D./B. |
| 13 D. | Richardson, F. 55233. | M. April 29/17. |
| 13 D. | Robinson, Edward Ernest. 65140. | M. April 28/17. |
| 13 D. XV | Ruewell, T. G/41261. | M. April 10-11/17. |
| 13 D. XV | Stenning, J. 61830. | W. Unoff. M. April 24/17. |
| 13 D. | Terry, E. W. 41265. | M. April 23/17. |
| 13 D. | Tillyard, W. 15617. | K. April 24/17. Det.D./B. |
| 13 D. XV | Whitaker, J. G/51610. | W. Unoff. M. April 26/17. |
| 13 ? | Bovingdon, Frank. 65075. | M. April 28/17. |
| 13 ? | Crudgington, Harry. 204250. (Fr. Londons, 8593.) | M. April 24/17. |
| ‡13 ? L.G.S. | Curl, Cpl. T. 6242. | W. Unoff. M. April 25/17. |
| 13 ? | Gregory, Herbert. 65135. (Fr. 2nd Middlx., 35382.) | K. April 29/17. Conf. and Det. |
| 13 ? | Harris, H. J. 65034. | M. April 29/17. |
| 13 ? | Schiff, B. 204187. (Late 1 Lond., 1/8523.) | M. April 28/17. |

**Royal Fusiliers**—contd.

*B.E.F.*

| | | |
|---|---|---|
| 13 ? | Wilson, Fredk. Wm. 22814. (Fr. 1 Londons, wrongly known as 65096.) | M. April 24/17. |
| 17 | **Brodie, 2nd Lieut. S. E.** | W. and M. April 16/17. |
| 17 B. VIII | Marriner, J. T. 1907. | M. April 28/17. |
| 17 B. V | Marsh, L.-Cpl. James. 8098. | M. April 28/17. |
| 17 B. V | Western, L.-Cpl. Chas. Jos. 7062. | M. April 28/17. |
| 17 C. IX | Black, Joseph. 51644. | M. Feb. 10/17. |
| ‡17 D. | Slade, Cpl. J. 1885. | W. and M. April 28/17. |
| 17 D. | Town, Cpl. F. W. 966. | W. and M. April 16/17. |
| 17 ? I.T.M. | Gane, Sergt. Francis Grant. 354. (5th Bdge.) | M. April 28/17. |
| 18 A. | White, L. 61456. | M. April 23/17. |
| 20 | **Bulbeck, Lt. H. E.** | K. Nov. 6/16. Det.D./B. |
| *20 A. IV | Bartram, Frank. 10164. | K. April 16/17. Det.D./B. R/Enq. |
| 20 A. III | Hastings, Wm. Chas. 53207. | M. April 16/17. |
| 20 A. II | Laver, Edw. Rawlings. 62841. | W. and M. April 14/17. |
| 20 A. IV | Miles, Cpl. O. 51259. | K. April 16/17. Det.D./B. |
| 20 B. VII | Bishop, F. A. 62811. | W. and M. April 16/17. |
| ‡20 B. | Field, Alfred. 63504. | M. May 20-24/17. |
| 20 B. VI | Goldman, J. S. 52825. | W. and M. April 16/17. |
| ‡20 B. | Gosling, H. 42243. | M. May 20/17. |
| *20 B. VII | Lippy, L.-Cpl. T. 166220. | K. April 16/17. Det.D./B. |
| 20 B. | Sellen, Geo. Russell. G/62854. | M. April 16/17. |
| *20 B. M.G.S. | Steel, Leonard Stanley. 3285. | K. April 16/17. Det.D./B. |
| 20 B. V | Stevens, Ellis. 29857. | M. May 20/17. |
| 20 C. X | Burrows, Harold Cyril. 25049. | M. May 20/17. |
| ‡20 C. | Hardy, J. 24741. | M. May 20/17. |
| ‡20 C. | Ives, C. W. 63626. | M. May 20/17. |
| 20 C. | Roberts, Cpl. B. 5542. | M. May 6/17. |
| 20 C. | Slatter, Sergt. Arthur Albert. 26603. | W. and M. May 20/17. |
| *20 C. XI | Thompson, Alfred. 60941. | M. May 20/17. |
| *20 C. IX | Thrower, Edwin. 41986. | M. May 20/17. |
| *20 D. | Burley, Geo. Jos. 228057. (Fr. 1st London.) | M. May 20/17. |
| ‡20 D. XV | Cunliffe, L.-Cpl. T. G. 47369. | W. and M. May 20/17. |
| ‡20 D. | Fripp, L.-Cpl. E. 14234. | W. and M. May 20/17. |
| 20 D. XIII | Payne, Wm. Chas. 53254. | M. May 16/17. |
| 20 D. | Stubbs, Wm. Lionel. G/63674. | M. April 16/17. |
| ‡20 D. | Tassall, W. H. 62858. | M. May 20/17. |
| 20 ? M.G.S. | Irwin, Percy. 16645. | K. April 16/17. Det.D./B. |
| 22 | **Perraton, 2nd Lieut. F. M.** | M. April 29/17. |
| 22 | **Simons, Capt. Leon.** | M. Feb. 17/17. |
| 22 | **Saword, 2nd Lieut. R.** | M. April 29/17. |
| 22 | **Stevenson, 2nd Lieut. F.** | M. April 27/17. |
| 22 A. | Allen, L.-Cpl. E. 47858. | M. Feb. 17/17. |
| 22 A. | Bartlett, L.-Cpl. Richard L. W. 51986. | W. and M. Feb. 17/17. |
| 22 A. or B. L.G.S. | Batting, Cpl. Horace John. 48283. | M. April 29/17. |
| 22 A. IV | Bonner, Horace Jack. 51988. | M. Feb. 17/17. |
| 22 A. | Bright, A. G. 16614. | M. Feb. 17/17. |
| 22 A. or D. | Brittain, E. 50961. | M. April 29/17. |
| *22 A. | Chittenden, Cpl. Ernest Sydney. 48365. (1203.) | M. April 29/17. |
| ‡22 A. | Cooper, H. 1511. | W. and M. April 20/17. |
| ‡22 A. | Durrant, Cpl. E. F. 7743. | M. April 29/17. |
| 22 A. II | Easton, Walter John. 1256. | W. and M. Feb. 17/17. |
| 22 A. or D. | Finer, L.-Cpl. Horace Jas. 1372. | W. and M. April 29/17. |

**Royal Fusiliers—contd.**

## *B.E.F.*

| | | |
|---|---|---|
| *22 A. | Gilford, W. 15368. | M. April 29/17. |
| 22 A. L.G.S. | Hennessey, Sergt. Herbert W. 1233. | M. Feb. 21/17. |
| 22 A. | Perkins, Thomas. 50047. | M. Feb. 17/17. |
| 22 A. or D. | Regan, Wm. Daniel. 5575. | M. April 29/17. |
| 22 A. | Smith, Sergt. T. 413. | M. Feb. 17/17. |
| 22 A. | Starkey, Edw. Arthur. 51996. | M. Feb. 17/17. |
| 22 A. II | Ward, L. J. 51253. | K. Feb. 17/17. Det.D./B. |
| 22 A. or B. | Wright, L.-Cpl. S. H. 47857. | M. Feb. 17/17. |
| ‡22 B. | Amer, C. 1508. | M. April 29/17. |
| 22 B. VII | Benn, G. V. 16856. | M. May 29/17. |
| 22 B. | Brickell, P. H. 23473. | M. April 29/17. |
| 22 B. V | Cole, C. V. 41291. | M. April 29/17. |
| ‡22 B. | Downs, L.-Cpl. J. H. 47482. | M. April 29/17. |
| *22 B. V | Goodwin, Sgt. Fredk. 1305. | M. April 28/17. |
| ‡22 B. | Guilford, W. 15368. | M. April 29/17. |
| 22 B. or D. | Hardy, L.-Cpl. W. J. 53098. | M. April 29/17. |
| 22 B. | Harrington, Walter. 1860. | W. and M. July 28/16. |
| ‡22 B. | Hollway, Miller W. 43732. | M. April 29/17. |
| ‡22 B. | Langley, John Harry. 4575. | M. April 29/17. |
| *22 B. | Larkin, Thos. 47021. | M. April 29/17. |
| 22 B. or C. | Lucking, George E. 27985. | M. May 3/17. |
| 22 B. | Middleton, L.-Cpl. Barham. 49387. | M. April 29/17. |
| *22 B. | Rogerson, Sgt. Robt. Hry. 1556. | M. April 29/17. |
| 22 B. V | Stride, William Owen. 46716. | M. May 3/17. |
| *22 B. L.G.S. | Trafford, Thos. John. 50316. | M. April 29/17. |
| 22 B. VI | Walker, L.-Sgt. Lionel Bertram. 1666 | M. Feb. 17/17. |
| ‡22 B. | Worrall, F. 20764. | M. April 29/17. |
| 22 C. XII | Evans, Chas. Wm. H. 23270. | W. and M. Feb. 17/17. |
| *22 C. | Evans, Sgt. E. A. 11805. | W. and M. April 29/17. |
| 22 C. | Fuller, W. 61537. | M. Feb. 17/17. |
| 22 C. or D. | Jackson, A. G/51993. | M. April 29/17. |
| 22 C. M.G.S. | Loker, L.-Cpl. A. 3325. | W. and M. Feb. 17/17. |
| 22 C. IX | Milne, J. W. 51966. | M. Feb. 17/17. |
| 22 C. X | Neale, H. C. 25539. | K. Feb. 17/17. Det.D./B. |
| *22 C. | Orders, L.-Cpl. Archibald. 34737. | M. April 29/17. |
| 22 C. | Outram, Alex. Robert. 51968. | M. Feb. 17/17. |
| 22 C. or D. | Sibson, G. 23479. | M. April 29/17. |
| 22 C. | Stanborough, Sgt. Ernest G. 483. | M. Feb. 17/17. |
| 22 C. | Staples, A. H. 1601. | M. Feb. 17/17. |
| 22 C. IX | Tarr, J. R. 51978. | M. Feb. 17/17. |
| ‡22 C. | Walton, F. 48291. | M. April 29/17. |
| ‡22 C. | Webb, J. 11075. | M. May 3/17. |
| 22 D. | Blundell, L.-Cpl. Geo. K/684. | M. April 29/17. |
| 22 D. | Bryan, Cpl. A. 25005. | W. and M. April 29/17. |
| ‡22 D. | Crane, Sergt. E. 717. | W. and M. April 29/17. |
| ‡22 D. | Fuller, E. A. 9665. | M. April 29/17. |
| 22 D. XIV | Le Grove, Ben. 62490. | M. Feb. 17/17. |
| ‡22 D. | Leney, R. A. 61542. | M. May 3/17. |
| 22 D. XIV | Manchester, L.-Cpl. 6014. | W. and M. April 29/17. |
| 22 D. | Roberts, L.-Cpl. E. 8156. | M. April 29/17. |
| ‡22 D. | Smith, J. 53092. | W. and M. April 29/17. |
| ‡22 D. | Turner, J. H. 9578. | M. April 29/17. |
| 22 D. XIV | Veglio, Ralph Vincent. 770. | M. April 29/17. |
| ‡22 D. | Woolford, S. A. 2121. | M. April 29/17. |
| 22 D. XIV | Workman, Leslie. 62501. | W. and M. April 29/17. |
| 23 | **Burgess, 2nd Lieut. R. C.** | M. May 3/17. |
| 23 A. | Andrews, Geo. Jas. 63057. | M. Feb. 17/17. |
| 23 A. III | Barker, L.-Cpl. Alfred Alex. 47530. | K. May 3/17. Det.D./B. |
| ‡23 A. | Brockley, L.-Cpl. G. 9164. | M. May 3/17. |

**Royal Fusiliers—contd.**

*B.E.F.*

| | | | |
|---|---|---|---|
| 23 A. or C. | Gregg, Cpl. Bert E. 6990. | M. May 3/17. | |
| ‡23 A. IV | Haslam, Cpl. Clifford. 7688. | K. April 29/17. | Det.D./B. |
| 23 A. | Johnson, T. 17810. | M. Feb. 17/17. | |
| 23 A. III | Main, R. 4528. | M. Feb. 18/17. | |
| ‡23 A. | Merricks, F. 27545. | M. May 3/17. | |
| ‡23 A. | Neale, E. W. 21620. | M. May 3/17. | |
| *23 A. III | Pryke, B. J. 27204. | M. May 3/17. | |
| *23 A. | Rhodes, Harry Steer. 223. | M. May 3/17. | |
| ‡23 A. | Stepney, L.-Cpl. J. 1579. | M. May 3/17. | |
| ‡23 A. III | Welch, Percy David. 61757. | M. May 3/17. | |
| 23 A. | Willott, Harold. 5966. | K. Jan. 28/17. | Det.D./B. |
| 23 B. VIII | Ashman, L.-Cpl. L. 60920. | M. May 3/17. | |
| 23 B. V | Beales, C. E. C. 37355. | K. Feb. 17/17. | Conf. and Det. |
| 23 B. VIII | Bibby, Chas. 3888. | M. May 3/17. | |
| 23 B. VI | Coey, V. J. G/51268. | M. May 3/17. | |
| .23 B. VI | Golds, L.-Cpl. L. H. G/61643. | M. May 2-3/17. | |
| 23 B. | Goodrum, Sidney George. 63088. | W. and M. May 3/17. | |
| 23 B. VI | Hague, Wm. 4721. | K. May 3/17. | Det.D./B. |
| *23 B. VII | Harber, R. W. 49639. | M. May 3/17. | |
| *23 B. VI | Horsfall, John. 4193. | M. May 3/17. | |
| ‡23 B. V | Laycock, Sergt. Percy Guy Dinham. 1281. | M. May 3/17. | |
| ‡23 B. | Martin, E. 1793. | M. May 3/17. | |
| *23 B. or C. | Rait, Douglas. 1656. | M. May 3/17. | |
| 23 B. VIII | Thomson, L.-Cpl. Wm. 1234. | W. and M. Feb. 17/17. | |
| 23 B. L.G.S. | Walsh, John. 47826. | M. May 3/17. | |
| 23 B. | Watkin, Rex. 20870. | W. and M. Feb. 17/17. | |
| *23 B. V | Wild, Albert Henry. 1496. | M. Nov. 14/16. | R/Enq. |
| 23 B. VII | Wright, Cpl. Geo. Fredk. 20295. | M. May 3/17. | |
| 23 C. XI | Britten, H. A. 3779. | K. Nov. 13/16. | Det.D./B. |
| *23 C. | Brown, L.-Cpl. James. 1513. | M. May 3/17. | |
| 23 C. X | Hutt, Claud S. 63157. | K. Feb. 17/17. | Det.D./B. R/Enq. |
| *23 C. XI | James, L.-Cpl. B. C. 63067. | M. May 3/17. | |
| ‡23 C. | Mayhew, C. N. 26231. | M. May 3/17. | |
| 23 C. IX | Prescott, Cpl. J. 25563. | Unoff. M. May 3/17. | |
| 23 C. X | Ryan, J. D. 32591. | W. and M. Feb. 17/17. | |
| 23 C. IV | Sexton, L.-Cpl. Eric John. 8143. | M. May 3/17. | |
| ‡23 C. | Walker, A. J. 37418. | M. May 3/17. | |
| 23 C. | White, Basil S. 50193. | W. and M. Feb. 17/17. | |
| 23 D. XVI | Carter, Ernest Alf. 1946. | M. May 3/17. | |
| 23 D. | Cochrane, Thomas. 63124. | M. Feb. 17/17. | |
| *23 D. XV | Davies, M.M., L.-Cpl. A. E. 1861. | Unoff. K. May 3/17. | |
| ‡23 D. | Fuller, V. H. 1506. | M. May 3/17. | |
| 23 D. XVI | Hayward, Cpl. James. 6184. | M. May 3/17. | |
| 23 D. XIV | Jinks, L.-Cpl. Wm. Henry. 2870. | M. May 3/17. | |
| 23 D. XIII | Mickleburgh, S. G. 49778. | M. Feb. 17/17. | |
| 23 D. L.G.S. | Miller, G. 61658. | M. May 3/17. | |
| 23 D. XIII | Morris, Charles. 11295. | M. April 14/17. | |
| ‡23 D. | Polson, L.-Cpl. J. P. 10009. | M. May 3/17. | |
| ‡23 D. XIII | Rawlings, A. 42221. | M. May 3/17. | |
| ‡23 ? | Gilbert, A. 63152. (Fr. W. Surreys.) | M. April 23/17. | |
| ‡23 ? | Lloyd, Chas. Edward. 4665. | K. Nov. 13/17. | Det.D./B. |
| 23 L.G.S. | Philpot, Thos. Harold. 10933. | K. Nov. 13/16. | Det.D./B. |
| 24 | **Barnes, 2nd Lt. V. K.** (Fr. 1st.) | M. April 27-30/17. | |
| ‡24 A. | Bain, D. 3633. | M. April 30/17. | |
| ‡24 A. | Barrowman, Robert Wishart. 2174. | K. April 30/17. | Det.D./B. |
| 24 A. | Bennett, Sgt.-Maj. Donald A. 2593. | M. April 14/17. | |

Royal Fusiliers—contd.

*B.E.F.*

| | | |
|---|---|---|
| 24 A. or C. | Butler, C. 60885. | M. April 30/17. |
| ‡24 A. | Campbell, G. 3870. | M. April 30/17. |
| ‡24 A. | Ward, A. E. 51222. | W. and M. April 30/17. |
| 24 A. | Wood, Benjamin. 3619. | M. April 30/17. |
| 24 B. | Collins, A. J. 61630. | W. and M. April 22/17. |
| 24 B. VI | Dolding, Cpl. Robert. 60858. | M. April 29/17. |
| 24 B. VII | Garnish, T. 51222. | W. and M. April 29/17. |
| ‡24 B. | Gillingham, H. 61161. | M. April 29/17. |
| 24 B. V | Godfrey, E. A. 60808. | M. April 29/17. |
| ‡24 B. | Haines, A. 60862. | M. April 29/17. |
| ‡24 B. | Kearns, L.-Cpl. S. C. 1394. | M. April 29/17. |
| *24 B. VIII | Levett, A. G. 61201. | M. April 29/17. |
| ‡24 B. V | Mann, Henry M. 52101. | W. and M. April 29/17. |
| 24 B. | Oram, G. 27167. | M. Nov. 13/16. R/Enq. |
| ‡24 B. | Sharpe, E. G. 61616. | M. April 29/17. |
| ‡24 B. | Smith, Sigr. Yorke. 2261. | M. Nov. 13/16. R/Enq. |
| 24 B. VIII | Taylor, Sgt. Walter Prince. 3063. | M. April 29/17. |
| ‡24 B. | Van Thal, M. J. 20110. | M. April 29/17. |
| ‡24 B. | Woodbridge, L.-Cpl. H. 9500. | W. and M. April 29/17. |
| 24 C. | Margetson, G. E. 52044. | M. April 14/17. |
| 24 C. | Turner, F. E. 27555. | M. Nov. 13/16. R/Enq. |
| 24 D. XV | Bowden, J. 47693. | M. April 29/17. |
| 24 D. XIV | Moon, Cpl. Chas. George. 2739. | M. April 30/17. |
| ‡24 D. | Philpott, W. J. 27521. | M. April 29/17. |
| 24 D. XV | Reeve, W. T. 61221. | M. April 29/17. |
| ‡24 D. XV | Walters, Fredk. B. 60850. (Fr. 4/10 Middlesex, 4781.) | M. Nov. 13/16. R/Enq. |
| 26 | Addis, 2nd Lieut. D. M. | W. Unoff. M. June 7/17. |
| ‡26 A. | Botterill, John G. 52718. | K. June 15/17. Det.D./B. |
| ‡26 A. III | Dudgeon, Alb. Jos. 19032. | K. June 17/17. Det.D./B. |
| ‡26 A. | King, L.-Cpl. E. P. 52706. | M. June 7/17. |
| 26 A. | Patman, Reg. Bernard. 2354. | K. Oct. 7/16. Det.D./B. R/Enq. |
| ‡26 A. M.G.S. | Taylor, Harold A. 19411. | K. June 7/17. Det.D./B. |
| 26 B. VIII | Hill, L.-Cpl. C. L. 19467. | W. and M. Sept. 15-18/16. R/Enq. |
| ‡26 B. M.G.S. | Parsons, F. A. 60069. | M. June 7/17. |
| ‡26 C. X | Collison, Percy. 52967. | M. June 7/17. |
| 26 C. XI | Webster, C. S. 20326. | K. Sept. 15-18/16. Det.D./B. R/Enq. |
| *26 C. XI | Westwood, L.-Cpl. Denis Augustus. 19825. | K. Sept. 15-18/16. R/Enq. |
| 26 D. XVI | Adams, H. Leslie. 8960. | M. Sept. 15-18/16. R/Enq. |
| 26 D. Sig. S. | Lee, A. C. 19765. | K. Sept. 15-18/16. Det.D./B. R/En |
| 26 D. Snip. S. | Weetman, Harry. 8961. | M. Sept. 15-18/16. R/Enq. |
| *26 H.Q. Snip. S. | Moore, Alf. Geo. 41851. | K. June 7/17. Det.D./B. |
| *32 A. | Brent, James. 21359. | M. Oct. 7/16. R/Enq. |
| ‡32 A. II | Smithyes, L.-Cpl. W. R. 22057. | M. June 7/17. |
| 32 B. VIII | Boughtwood, E. 21752. | M. Sept. 15/16. |
| 32 B. | Burns, James. 16497. | M. Oct. 4-10/16. |
| 32 B. VI | Holterman, F. 21173. (Sniping S.) | W. and M. Oct. 4-10/16. R/Enq. |
| 32 B. VI | Smith, Sergt. Hugh. 17957. | K. Oct. 4/16. Det.D./B. R/Enq. |
| ‡32 C. VII | Faithfull, Ferdinand Alb. 22451. | M. June 7/17. |
| *32 D. | Owen, G. 20847. | M. Oct. 4-10/16. R/Enq. |
| 32 D. | Pile, H. 20659. | W. and M. Sept. 15/16. |
| ‡33 ? | Carter, James. 16040. | M. Unoff. W. May 23/17. |

## ROYAL SCOTS.

### B.E.F.

| | | |
|---|---|---|
| 2 | **Darker, 2nd Lt. N. C.** | M. May 3/17. |
| 2 | **Halcrow, 2nd Lt. T. T.** | M. May 3/17. |
| ‡2 A. | Bonner, A. 31976. | M. May 3/17. |
| ‡2 A. | Bryce, Cpl. G. 8504. | M. May 3/17. |
| 2 A. | Collins, Henry. 29595. | Unoff. M. May 3/17. |
| 2 A. | Collins, John. 26957. | M. April 9/17. |
| 2 A. III | Donaldson, Matthew. 40660. | M. April 23/17. |
| ‡2 A. IV | Fiddes, L.-Cpl. Henry S. 43018. | M. May 3/17. |
| ‡2 A. | Fleming, E. 18501. | M. May 3/17. |
| ‡2 A. | Gallacher, J. 34614. | M. May 3/17. |
| ‡2 A. | Kirkland, P. 39699. | M. May 3/17. |
| *2 A. III | McCann, Patrick. 34278. | M. May 3/17. |
| ‡2 A. | McLean, J. 11027. | M. April 15/17. |
| ‡2 A. | Moore, C. 4036. | M. May 3/17. |
| ‡2 A. | Moynagh, C.-Q.-M.-S. J. 7661. | M., bel. K. May 3/17. |
| 2 A. L.G.S. | Pitts, Sam. 26319. | M. May 3/17. |
| *2 A. II | Robertson, Sgt. George. 302630. (5290.) | M. May 3/17. |
| 2 A. III | Sinclair, Jn. 24181. | W. and M. May 3/17. |
| 2 A. | Stewart, Sgt. Daniel. 35649. | W. and M. May 3/17. |
| 2 A. I | Telfer, W. C. 34532. | M. May 3/17. |
| 2 A. I | Wands, Walter. 34397. | Unoff. M. May 3/17. |
| *2 B. V | Angus, John. 40377. | M. May 3/17. |
| 2 B. VIII | Bain, Cairns. 30048. | W. and M. May 3/17. |
| ‡2 B. | Balgowan, A. 251062. | M. May 3/17. |
| 2 B. VI | Boss, Alex. 34187. | M. May 3/17. |
| ‡2 B. VII | Brebner, J. 14240. | M. May 3/17. |
| 2 B. V | Edwards, Sgt. Alex. 9141. | M. May 3/17. |
| 2 B. L.G.S. | Ferguson, Robt. 40384. (Fr. 7th.) | W. and M. May 3/17. |
| 2 B. | Grant, Robert. 34952. | M. May 3/17. |
| ‡2 B. | Henderson, A. 275475. | M. May 3/17. |
| ‡2 B. | Hennessey, T. 34951. | M. May 3/17. |
| 2 B. VI | Holmes, John. 275903. | M. May 3/17. |
| ‡2 B. | Hunter, L.-Cpl. T. 16278. | M. May 3/17. |
| *2 B. V | Kemp, L.-Cpl. Robert. 20794. | M. May 3/17. |
| *2 B. VIII | McArthur, Duncan. 251130. | W. and M. May 3/17. |
| *2 B. V | McDonald, William. 21031. | M. May 3/17. |
| 2 B. VII | McFetridge, David. 34290. | M. May 3/17. |
| ‡2 B. | Morrison, A. 38067. | M. May 3/17. |
| ‡2 B. | Murray, Cpl. A. 28161. | M. May 3/17. |
| ‡2 B. | Newsome, Wm. 30970. | M. Nov. 13/16. R/Enq. |
| ‡2 B. | Olive, J. 8690. | M. Nov 13/16. R/Enq. |
| 2 B. | Potts, Joseph. 34912. | K. April 10/17. Det.D./B. R/Enq |
| ‡2 B. | Powers, H. 8530. | M. May 3/17. |
| ‡2 B. | Shoesmith, L.-Cpl. C. 11641. | W. and M. May 3/17. |
| ‡2 B. | Traynor, J. 20786. | W. and M. May 3/17. |
| *2 B. M.G.S. | Wilson, John A. 29860. | M. Nov. 13/16. R/Enq. |
| 2 B. | Wright, H. 9583. | W. Unoff. M. May 3/17. |
| *2 C. X | Aird, John. 250976. | Unoff. W. and M. May 3/17. |
| ‡2 C. | Barclay, R. 250834. | M. May 3/17. |
| *2 C. XI | Beveridge, Stephen Tait. 201121. (4271.) | M. May 3/17. |
| 2 C. X | Brown, Andrew D. 201119. (Fr. 4th, 4268.) | M. May 3/17. |
| ‡2 C. | Clay, H. 200753. | M. May 3/17. |
| ‡2 C. | Cunningham, D. 34633. | M. May 3/17. |
| 2 C. L.G.S. | Dougherty, L.-Cpl. J. G. 2744. | W. and M. Nov. 13/16. |
| 2 C. XII | Fraser, L.-Cpl. Wm. 276206. | M. May 3/17. |

**Scots, Royal—contd.**

## *B.E.F.*

2 C. XII Gill, J. 202513. M. May 3/17.
2 C. X Hart, Charlie. 34040. M. May 3/17.
‡2 C. Hart, J. 34168. W. and M. April 9/17.
‡2 C. Johnston, W. 22178 M. May 3/17.
‡2 C. Kidd, D. 301027. M. May 3/17.
2 C. XII Love, Francis. 34720. M. April 9-10/16.
‡2 C. X McAllister, J. 12369. M. May 3/17.
‡2 C. McInroy, L.-Cpl. D. 21707. M. May 3/17.
2 C. Mackintosh, John. 20818. K. April 19/17. Det.D./B.
2 C. X Milne, Archibald. 23044. W. and M Nov. 13/16.
‡2 C. Milton, J. 33496. M. May 3/17.
2 C. Riddle, Sergt. Chas. 250037. W. and M. May 3/17.
*2 C. XI Ross, Colin. 33324. M. May 3/17.
2 C. X Russell, Cpl. F. 20357. M. May 3/17.
*2 C. X Shiels, Thos. 201026. M. May 3/17.
2 C. XII Smith, Sig. G. 24033. W. and M. April 23/17.
*2 D. XVI Bethune, David. 9889. M. May 3/17.
‡2 D. Boyle, J. 43183. M. May 3/17.
‡2 D. Broom, J. 43185. M. May 3/17.
‡2 D. Carroll, Fred. Jas. 11549. M. May 3/17.
2 D. XIV Davie, David. 34507. M. May 3/17.
2 D. Edwards, David. 31412. M. May 3/17.
2 D. Hislop, L.-Cpl. James. 2760. W. and M. Nov. 13/16.
*2 D. XV McCann, J. 40421. M. May 3/17.
‡2 D. McKay, L.-Cpl. W. 23490. M. May 3/17.
2 D. XIII Mackenzie, L.-Cpl. Robt. 20916. M. April 23/17.
‡2 D. McNab, D. 31315. M. May 3/17.
2 D. XVI McNicol, Donald. 38189. M. May 3/17.
‡2 D. Muir, T. 39268. M. May 3/17.
‡2 D. Thomson, A. 39022. M. May 3/17.
‡2 D. Thorburn, Wm. 16629. M. May 3/17.
‡2 ? Stark, J. 2975. W. and M. Oct. 24/16.
*2 ? L.G.S. Thomson, W. 43110. K. June 4/17. Det.D./B.
5 Y. XI Teale, Albert Rayner. 251571. (4325) M. Jan. 16-18/17.
‡8 A. III Aithie, Jas. 43118. M. May 16/17.
‡8 A. Lowrie, Cpl. P. 325185. M. May 16/17.
‡8 A. Waller, J. 325754. M. May 16/17.
*8 B. Delargy, E. 335727. M. Feb. 15/17.
9 **Cook, 2nd Lieut. H.** (Fr. 4th.) K. April 23/17. Det.D./B.
9 A. Allan, L.-Cpl. J. 351268. M. April 22/17.
‡9 A. Baillie, John. 352961. K. April 23-26/17. Det.D./B.
9 A. II Berman, Manuel. 352504. (5835.) M. Mar. 28/17.
‡9 A. Flynn, C. 325605. W. and M. April 21/17.
9 A. or D. Kirkhope, Walter D. 351207. M. April 12/17.
*9 A. IV Millar, Bandsman Tom. 351267. M. April 22/17.
9 A. Muir, D. 352340. M. April 23/17.
9 A. IV Simpson, Wm. 352237. W. and M. April 21/17.
9 A. Snodgrass, Robt. 352495. M. April 22/17.
9 A. II Wallace, Walter Geo. 352978. M. April 23/17.
9 B. VI Anderson, David. 352297. Unoff. K. April 23/17. Conf. and Det.D./B.
9 B. VII Birrell, L.-Cpl. J. P. 350829. W. and M. April 23/17.
9 B. VII Cruikshank, G. 351371. W. and M. April 23/17.
*9 B. Douglas, J. 352383. W. and M. April 22/16.
9 B. Forsyth, Cpl. A. L. 350123. (1362.) W. and M. April 23/17.
9 B. Landesborough, Alex. 351701. (4785.) M. April 23/17.

**Scots, Royal—contd.**

## *B.E.F.*

|  |  |  |
|---|---|---|
| ‡9 B. VII | Mathieson, Alex. 352539. (5935.) | M. April 23/17. |
| ‡9 B. | Rigby, J. 330660. | M. April 23/17. |
| 9 B. VI | Rigby, James. 370106. | M. April 23/17. |
| 9 B. VI | Sellar, Robt. J. 351033. (3439.) | M. April 23/17. |
| 9 C. IX | Buchanan, Tom. 353003. | W. and M. April 23/17. |
| 9 C. XII | Fenton, Wm. 351786. (4977.) | M. April 23/17. |
| 9 C. | Hempseed, Sgt. Robt. Banks. 250159 (1441.) | M. April 23/17. |
| 9 C. X | Linklater, Alex. E. 351895. (5160.) | W. and M. April 23/17. |
| 9 C. | McAlpine, Kenneth, 300654. | W. and M. April 23/17. |
| 9 C. XII | Strachan, Alex. 352521. (5917.) | W. and M. April 23/17. |
| 9 D. XIV | Coop, John. 352191. | M. April 23/17. |
| 9 D. | Elrick, Cpl. C. 350326. | W. and M. April 9/17. |
| 9 D. M.G.S. | Shingler, L.-Cpl. R. 352533. | W. and M. April 9/17. |
| 9 D. XIII | Wilcock, Arthur. 352597. | M. April 23/17. |
| 11 | **Sandilands, 2nd Lt. J. G.** | M., bel. K. March 21/17. |
| 11 | **Waddell, 2nd Lieut. J. H.** | W. and M. June 5/17. |
| ‡11 A. | Burgoyne, A. 16663. | W. and M. April 7/17. |
| ‡11 A. | Dunbar, D. 301542. | M. May 3/17. |
| 11 A. I | Duncan, Alex. 40360. | Unoff. M., bel. K. April 8/17. |
| •11 A. | Gavin, William. 13392. | M. May 3/17. |
| ‡11 A. | Louie, T. 14153. | M. May 3/17. |
| 11 A. | McDonald, W. J. 43022. | M., bel. K. Mar. 22/17. |
| ‡11 B. | Haggart, R. 39601. | M. May 3/17. |
| ‡11 B. VII | Ness, Jas. 27065. | M. May 3/17. |
| ‡11 B. | Park, J. 36114. | M. May 3/17. |
| ‡11 B. | Scott, L.-Cpl. J. M. 29746. | M. May 3/17. |
| ‡11 B. | Tolmie, G. 39098. | M. May 3/17. |
| 11 C. X | Anderson, J. H. 41199. | M. April 12/17. |
| ‡11 C. | Anderson, T. 41196. | M. April 9/17. |
| 11 C. XI | Bradshaw, Cpl. Alfred. 21123 | M. Mar. 21/17. |
| ‡11 C. | Hamilton, T. 35951. | M. May 3/17. |
| 11 C. X | Hislop, James. 41223. | W. and M. April 9/17. |
| 11 C. | Little, George. 13314. | M., bel. K. Mar. 21/17. |
| •11 C. X | Mack, John. 34380. | M. May 3/17. |
| 11 C. | Meek, Jas. 16897. | M. April 12/17. |
| 11 C. XI | Millar, Sig. Jas. A. 39545. | W. and M. April 9/17. |
| •11 C. XII | Montgomery, Murdo. 38627. | M. May 3/17. |
| 11 C. | Sealey, D. 40344. | W. and M. Mar. 21/17. |
| 11 C. XI | Wright, L.-Cpl. David. 21130. | W. and M. April 12/17. |
| 11 D. XVI | Comrie, L.-Cpl. Robert. 34655. | M., bel. K. Mar. 21/17. |
| 11 D. | Dodd, R. 20606. | M. Mar. 21/17. |
| 11 D. | Greig, D. 25813. | M., bel. K. Mar. 21/17. Conf. Det.D./B. |
| 11 D. | Millar, Benjamin. 22935. | M. Mar. 21/17. |
| 11 D. | Paxton, Sergt. G. 15993. | M., bel. K. Mar. 21/17. |
| 11 D. | Russell, Frank. 12331. | W. and M. July 19/16. R/Enq. |
| 11 D. XIII | Wotherspoon, Thos. | M. July 14/16. R/Enq. |
| 12 | **Henderson, 2nd Lt. W. J.** (Fr. 4th.) | M. May 3/17. |
| 12 | **Macouat, 2nd Lieut. J.** | W. Unoff. M. April 12/17. |
| 12 A. | **Neill, 2nd Lieut. D. T.** (Fr. 7th.) | M. May 3/17. |
| 12 | **Ritchie, Capt. R. R.** (Fr. 9 Scot. Rfls) | K. May 3/17. Det.D./B. |
| •12 A. | Anderson, Sgt. Alexander. 13391. | M. May 3/17. |
| •12 A. III | Bowie, Robert. 33299. | M. May 3/17. |
| 12 A. II | Cooper, Robert S. 40870. | M. May 3/17. |
| 12 A. H.Q. Orderlies | Dalloway, Arthur. 11431. | W. and M. April 9/17. |
| 12 A. I | Dornion, Charles. 40336. | M. May 3/17. |
| ‡12 A. | Gibson, R. 40688. | M. May 3/17. |

Scots, Royal—contd.

*B.E.F.*

| | | |
|---|---|---|
| ‡12 A. | Gray, J. 38713. | M. May 3/17. |
| 12 A. IV | Jacobs, L.-Cpl. J. 24472. | W. and M. April 12/17. |
| ‡12 A. | McCamley, P. 36650. | M. May 3/17. |
| ‡12 A. | McGregor, C.-S.-M. A. 11201. | W. and M. April 12/17. |
| 12 A. IV | MacIntosh, Willie. 31956. | M. May 3/17. |
| ‡12 A. | Miller, J. 38717. | M. May 3/17. |
| 12 A. IV | Morrison, R. B. 38761. | M. May 3/17. |
| ‡12 A. | Robertson, A. 43304. | W. and M. April 12/17. |
| ‡12 A. | Rummery, Sergt. C. 40244. | K. May 3/17. Det.D./B. |
| ‡12 A. | Simpson, A. 40710. | M. May 3/17. |
| 12 A. III | Spaven, Thomas. 43278. | M. April 12/17. |
| ‡12 A. | Stewart, W. 27511. | M. May 3/17. |
| 12 A. III | Thomson, John M. 40123. | W. and M. May 3/17. |
| 12 A. III | Trail, David. 30066. | M. May 3/17. |
| ‡12 B. | Bole, W. 34707. | M. May 3/17. |
| ‡12 B. | Clancey, L.-Cpl. J. 10890. | W. and M. April 9/17. |
| 12 B. VI | Horne, Andrew. 39646. | M. April 12/17. |
| 12 B. VI | Howden, Jas. 40761. (Fr. 5th.) | M. April 12/17. |
| ‡12 B. | Lindsay, D. 39614. | M. May 3/17. |
| 12 B. | McEvoy, Sergt. G. H. 14537. | M. April 9/17. |
| 12 B. | McLean, A. 27469. | M. April 12/17. |
| ‡12 B. VI | McNair, David. 41472. | M. May 3/17. |
| 12 B. V | McTaggart, Alex. 41466. | M. May 3/17. |
| 12 B. VI | Millar, Fredk. R. 39376. | M. May 3/17. |
| 12 B. | Paterson, Robert. 41474. | M. May 3/17. |
| 12 B. | Pendrick, Thos. E. 40855. | W. and M. April 12/17. |
| *12 B. V | Robertson, Geo. 27887. | Unoff. M. May 3/17. |
| ‡12 B. | Seacy, G. 11515. | M. May 3/17. |
| *12 B. VII | Slesson, Duncan Sherrif. 43532. | M. May 3/17. |
| 12 C. | Ayton, W. 40743. | M. April 12/17. |
| 12 C. | Killeen, J. 26254. | W. and M. April 12/17. |
| ‡12 C. | Mitchell, S. S. 39624. | W. and M. April 9/17. |
| 12 C. X | Neill, Thomas. 38411. | W. and M. April 12/17. |
| 12 C. | Smith, Thomas. 26668. | M. April 12/17. |
| ‡12 D. XVI | Donn, George (real name Ryrie). 275. | M. June 6/17. |
| 12 D. | Hare, W. 23627. | M. April 12/17. |
| *12 D. | Lister, George S. 40039. | M. May 3/17. |
| ‡12 D. | Lowe, J. 39619. | W. and M. April 12/17. |
| 12 D. | Perry, Thomas. 40776. | M. April 12/17. |
| 12 D. XIII | Rowntree, Wm. Norman. 40485. | M. April 12/17. |
| 13 | **Adamson, Lieut. R. T. A.** | K. April 23/17. Det.D./B. |
| 13 | **Davies, Lieut. G. V. F.** | M. April 23/17. |
| 13 | **Gellatly, 2nd Lieut. R.** | M. April 23/17. |
| 13 | **Maclachlan, 2nd Lt. K. G.** (Fr. 8th.) | M. April 23/17. |
| 13 | **Mungall, 2nd Lieut. R.** | M. April 13/17. |
| 13 | **Salveson, 2nd Lt. E. T. S.** (Fr. 7th.) | M. April 23/17. |
| 13 | **Smith, 2nd Lt. C. H.** (Fr. 9th.) | M. April 23/17. |
| 13 C. | **Stewart, Lieut. G. L.** | K. April 9/17. Det.D./B. |
| 13 | **Woodrow, 2nd Lieut. W. D.** | W. Unoff. M. April 23/17. |
| 13 A. | Bell, A. 16146. | W. and M. April 11/17. |
| 13 A. I | Drummond, Alex. 41258. | M. Aprril 23/17. |
| 13 A. III | Fairnington, W. 33339. | M. April 23/17. |
| 13 A. III | Fearnley, John. 41137. | W. and M. April 11/17. |
| ‡13 A. I | Moffat, John. 15826. (Fr. 12th Bn.) | M. Sept. 15/16. R/Enq. |
| 13 A. M.G.S. | Peel, Thos. G. 21072. | M. April 23/17. |
| 13 A. | Smellie, Alex. 16921. | K. April 23/17. Det.D./B, |
| 13 A. I | Wyllie, Alfred. 31463. | M. April 9/17. |

**Scots, Royal—contd.**

## *B.E.F.*

13 B. V Craig, Robert. 38234. M. April 23/17.
13 B. Hagan, W. 15123. M. April 11/17.
13 B. VI Moffat, Ben. 40092. M. April 23/17.
13 B. VI Paterson, John. 27835. M. Sept. 15/16. R/Enq.
13 B. Rae, L.-Cpl. John. 40097. M. April 23/17.
13 B. Williams, Albert H. 40093. M. April 23/17.
13 C. Cantley, R. 38643. M. April 23/17.
13 C. XII Langley, Frank. 41376. (Wrongly known as 47510.) W. Unoff. M. April 11/17.
13 C. McArthur, Jas. 41290. (Fr. 3rd R. Scots Fus., 19130.) K. April 23/17. Det.D./B.
13 C. XII Macfarlane, H. M. 27643. M. April 11/17.
13 C. Mason, F. 39544. M. April 23/17.
13 C. Paterson, Sgt. John McKinlay. 18297 M. April 23/17.
13 C. Simpson, Wm. 38820. M. April 23/17.
13 C. XI Tunnoch, David. 41282. M. April 23/17.
13 C. Williamson, J. 39209. M. April 23/17.
13 D. XIV Archer, David. 26889. M. April 11/17.
13 D. M.G.S. Glennie, George D. 16126. M. April 23/17.
13 D. XV Thompson, James. 41117. M. April 23/17.
13 D. Watson, A. 30700. M. April 23/17.
15 D. **Bone, 2nd Lieut. J. Craigie.** M. April 28/17.
15 **Croneen, 2nd Lieut. L.** M. April 28/17.
15 **Munro, 2nd Lieut. J. D.** M. April 28/17.
15 **Wilson, 2nd Lt. A. C.** (Fr. 3rd.) M. April 28/17.
‡15 A. Anderson, J. 47472. M. April 28/17.
‡15 A. Beaven, L.-Cpl. H. G. 7369. M. April 28/17.
‡15 A. Bell, D. 43441. W. and M. April 28/17.
‡15 A. III Brindley, Jas. Marshall. 22106. M. April 28/17.
‡15 A. Brown, J. 32967. W. and M. April 28/17.
‡15 A. Chapman, H. 18697. M. April 28/17.
*15 A. II Chisholm, Rodrick. 30428. W. and M. April 28/17.
‡15 A. Cooper, G. 18193. M. April 28/17.
‡15 A. Crichton, T. 21129. W. and M. April 28/17.
15 A. Doherty, G. 43516. M. April 9/17.
‡15 A. Findlater, G. 39384. M. April 28/17.
‡15 A. Foley, W. 43591. M. April 28/17.
*15 A. Gibson, John R. S. 31549. M. April 28/17.
‡15 A. Sap. Co. Grant, Jas. 43392. M. April 28/17.
‡15 A. Hogg, Cpl. Thos. 43485. M. April 28/17.
‡15 A. Hollawell, E. 47431. M. April 28/17.
15 A. or D. Hutchinson, L.-Cpl. Jas. 21616. M. April 28/17.
‡15 A. Leeming, W. 47429. M. April 24/17.
15 A. or B. II Letton, Sgt. Wm. Henry. 19540. M. May 28/17.
15 A. McEwen, John. 43414. M. April 28/17.
*15 A. II McClymont, Peter. 31492. M. April 28/17.
‡15 A. Mitchell, J. 18179. M. April 28/17.
‡15 A. Narrie, W. 24663. M. April 28/17.
‡15 A. Scott, G. 26425. M. April 28/17.
15 A. II Scott, Geo. 26354. M. April 28/17.
‡15 A. Shearer, L.-Cpl. T. 26944. M. April 28/17.
‡15 A. Smith, Harold. 27199. M. April 9/17.
‡15 A. Stewart, J. 47455. M. April 9/17.
*15 A. I Stuart, Roderick. 2276. K. April 28/17. Det.D./B.
*15 A. II Tong, W. Herbert. 47428. W. Unoff. M. April 18-24/17.
*15 A. I Ward, Dan. 33423. M. April 28/17.
15 A. III Wilson, L.-Cpl. Andrew. 23980. M. April 28/17.

**Scots, Royal—contd.**

*B.E.F.*

15 B. VII Andrews, James. 30188. M. April 28/17.
15 B. V Baxendale, Cpl. Harry. 39378. M. April 28/17.
15 B. Baxter, W. 20120. M. Unoff. W. April 28/17.
15 B. VI Baxter, William. 39473. M. April 28/17.
‡15 B. Boyle, J. 43650. W. and M. April 28/17.
‡15 B. Bundy, W. 34498. M. April 24/17.
15 B. VII Campbell, A. 47464. (Fr. 2/7, 270011.) M. April 28/17.
15 B. VI Carrington, Alfred. 30183. M. April 28/17.
‡15 B. Christison, W. 43663. W. and M. April 23/17.
•15 B. V Collins, Peter. 30585. W. and M. April 28/17.
‡15 B. Cosgrove, J. 19170. W. and M. April 28/17.
•15 B. L.G.S. Dickson, J. R. 34453. M. April 28/17.
•15 B. VII Davidson, Peter. 26974. M. April 28/17.
15 B. VII Douglas, Norman. 17357. M. April 28/17.
15 B. VIII Fair, L.-Cpl. G. 30608. M. April 28/17.
‡15 B. Ferguson, M. S. 47467. (Late 2/7, 270016.) M. April 28/17.
•15 B. Flannery, Michael. 12737. M. April 28/17.
‡15 B. Forsyth, T. 33970. M. April 28/17.
‡15 B. Goodwin, Edw. 17387. M. April 28/17.
‡15 B. VII Halkett, David. 30638. M. April 28/17.
•15 B. Hamilton, L. 43596. M. April 28/17.
15 B. VI Hughes, Thomas. 18692. M. April 28/17.
‡15 B. Ireland, R. 29640. M. April 28/17.
15 B. M.G.S. Johnson, L.-Cpl. A. 18691. M. April 28/17.
‡15 B. Kinnock, G. 21623. M. April 28/17.
‡15 B. Leisham, W. 22396. M. April 28/17.
15 B. V McGuingan, Arthur. 19305. M. April 28/17.
•15 B. VIII McKay, D. 43411. M. April 28/17.
‡15 B. McPherson, C. 2563. M. April 28/17.
•15 B. V Mahon, W. 31417. M. April 28/17.
‡15 B. Massey, L.-Cpl. T. 20997. M. April 28/17.
15 B. VII Mitchell, Alex. 39388. M. April 28/17.
‡15 B. Paton, J. 43430. M. April 28/17.
15 B. VIII Pearson, L.-Cpl. J. 43629. M. April 28/17.
•15 B. VIII Reid, C. 43471. M. April 28/17.
‡15 B. Stewart, W. 34477. M. April 28/17.
‡15 B. Temple, F. 47435. M. April 28/17.
‡15 B. Tilney, E. 21480. M. April 28/17.
‡15 B. Wallbanks, W. 34419. M. April 28/17.
‡15 B. Walsh, J. 27209. M. April 28/17.
‡15 B. Warren, S. 22410. M. April 28/17.
15 B. or H.Q. Williams, Hugh. 17507. (Sig. S.) M. April 28/17.
15 B. VI Winton, John. 29855. M. April 28/17.
‡15 C. Alexander, J. 30711. M. April 28/17.
‡15 C. Burns, T. 43447. W. and M. April 28/17.
‡15 C. Craig, J. 17805. M. April 28/17.
‡15 C. Donnelly, S. 24748. W. and M. April 28/17.
15 C. XI Dunlop, Cpl. Harry. 18147. M. April 28/17.
15 C. Farrell, Wm. 18244. M. July 1/16. R/Enq.
‡15 C. IX Gorrie, Andrew. 34100. M. April 28/17.
15 C. X Gray, J. 31146. M. April 28/17.
15 C. Greenlaw, Sergt. Jas. 19489. M. April 28/17.
‡15 C. Haldane, J. 31491. M. April 24/17.
‡15 C. Keenan, R. 43609. M. April 28/17.

**Scots, Royal**—contd.

## *B.E.F.*

15 C. X Leeming, W. 270056. M. April 28/17.
15 C. McDonald, Archibald. 30725. M. April 9/17.
15 C. McDonald, T. 12989. M. April 9/17.
15 C. McGlashan, C. 43370. M. April 28/17.
15 C. IX McManus, L.-Cpl. Bernard Vincent. 43509. M. April 28/17.
15 C. Myers, F. 26695. M. Mar. 8/17.
15 C. or D. IX Proctor, John J. 32344. M. April 28/17.
*15 C. X Purves, William. 18079. M. April 28/17.
*15 C. IX Saunders, L.-Cpl. Harry. 43477. M. April 28/17.
‡15 C. Scholield, Joseph Henry. 18236. M. April 28/17.
‡15 C. Shanks, R. 19367. M. April 28/17.
15 D. XIV Adams, John. 39422. M. April 28/17.
‡15 D. Barton, L.-Cpl. J. 43493. W. and M. April 28/17.
15 D. Brierley, Harold. 17840. M. April 28/17.
*15 D. Brunton, Andrew. 13582. M. April 28/17.
15 D. Bryce, Sergt. Wm. 13187. M. April 28/17.
*15 D. XVI Combe, George H. 43584. M. April 28/17.
*15 D. XVI Davidson, Charles. 29841. W. and M. April 28/17.
15 D. Doyle, Fred. 17874. M. April 28/17.
*15 D. Duncan, John. 29722. (Fr. 14th.) M. April 28/17.
‡15 D. Farquhar, R. 34045. M. April 28/17.
*15 D. Flett, Joseph. 29926. M. April 28/17.
15 D. XIII Fraser, C. 20143. M. April 28/17.
‡15 D. XIII Geoghegan, Alfred. 24682. M. April 28/17.
‡15 D. Gibson, F. 21135. M. April 28/17.
‡15 D. Goodear, W. 17888. M. April 28/17.
‡15 D. Graham, T. 21014. M. April 28/17.
15 D. XIV Grant, James. 13203. M. April 28/17.
15 D. M.G.S. Hughes, Philip. 17918. M. April 28/17.
15 D. Inglis, John. 12258. M. April 28/17.
‡15 D. Kane, T. 34140. M. April 28/17.
15 D. Key, W. S. 43550. M. April 28/17.
‡15 D. Lauder, J. 16644. M. April 28/17.
*15 D. M.G.S. Leather, Sgt. H. 43638. W. and M. April 28/17.
15 D. XVI Lyon, Robt. 18067. M. April 28/17.
15 D. McArthur, J. 19834. M. April 28/17.
*15 D. XV McCafferty, William. 34427. M. April 28/17.
‡15 D. McCarlie, R. 39151. M. April 28/17.
15 D. XIV McCracken, Jas. 17963. M. April 28/17.
‡15 D. McGeechan, C. 26817. M. April 28/17.
*15 D. McKay, L.-Cpl. Archibald. 20404. M. April 28/17.
‡15 D. McWalter, D. 23308. M. April 28/17.
‡15 D. Mahoney, Jas. 17950. M. April 28/17.
‡15 D. Masterton, R. 43619. M. April 28/17.
‡15 D. Meldrum, Robert. 3232. K. April 28/17. Det.D./B.
‡15 D. Munro, D. 43548. M. April 28/17.
‡15 D. Parkes, G. 18591. M. April 28/17.
‡15 D. Pickin, Fred. 43530. M. April 28/17.
‡15 D. Proctor, R. 43457. M. April 28/17.
*15 D. XV Reid, L.-Cpl. Geo. 20704. K. April 28/17. Det.D./B.
‡15 D. Rennie, J. 17993. M. April 28/17.
‡15 D. Ritchie, R. 11730. M. April 28/17.
‡15 D. Ritchie, T. 34370. M. April 28/17.
*15 D. Shaw, A. 18356. M. April 28/17.
*15 D. XV Soutar, Peter. 30319. M. April 28/17.

Scots, Royal—contd.

*B.E.F.*

15 D. Standerwick, Frank. 18020. M. April 28/17.
‡15 D. Steel, H. 29837. M. April 28/17.
‡15 D. Thomas, J. 18026. M April 28/17.
‡15 D. Walker, Cpl. J. 18031. M. April 28/17.
15 D. XIII Young, Archibald. 23003. M. April 28/17.
16 **MacKenzie, 2nd Lt. W. S.** (Fr. 4th.) M. April 28/17.
16 A. Christie, George. 43810. M. April 28/17.
16 A. IV Colvin, A.-Cpl. Jas. 19737. M. April 28/17.
‡16 A. Cross, T. 270155. (47344.) M. April 28/17.
16 A. I Davidson, Alex. 43874. M. April 28/17.
16 A. I Douglas, George. 18568. M. April 28/17.
‡16 A. Fraser, W. A. 38663. M. April 28/17.
16 A. Ingram, T. 43733. M. April 9/17.
16 A. III Jenkinson, James. 301140. M. April 28/17.
16 A. IV Joures, Robert. 330355. M. April 28/17.
16 A. II Kelly, Jas. 38056. M. April 28/17.
16 A. Luke, James. 31889. M. April 28/17.
16 A. II McCall, John. 38357. M. April 28/17.
16 A. McConnochie, A. 34225. M. April 28/17.
16 A. McFarlane, A. 38813. M. April 28/17.
16 A. McGuire, Jas. 43882. M. April 28/17.
16 A. III McLeod, Neil M. 41242. M. April 28/17.
16 A. III McMahon, Thos. 38543. M. April 28/17.
16 A. McMillan, R. 19858. M. April 28/17.
16 A. Morris, A.-Cpl. Robert E. 23489. M. April 9/17.
16 A. III Murie, John. 38682. M. April 28/17.
16 A. Newlands, John. 38667. M. April 28/17.
16 A. Paterson, R. L. 18885. M. April 7/17.
16 A. Quinn, J. 38819. M. April 28/17.
16 A. III Richardson, Sergt. James. 43809. M. April 28/17.
16 A. II Simpson, Cpl. Christopher. 19361. M. April 28/17.
16 A. III Sponder, Sergt. W. H. 18922. M. April 28/17.
16 A. White, John M. 41248. M. April 28/17.
16 B. Chisholm, R. 31411. M. April 7/17.
16 B. VIII Cochrane, R. 38647. M. April 28/17.
16 B. V Coyle, Albert. 33934. M. April 28/17.
16 B. V Gibson Geo. 29417. M. May 28/17.
16 B. VIII Halton, W. 43534. M. April 28/17.
16 B. VII Hay, James G. 41235. M. April 28/17.
16 B. V Knox, William. 38672. M. April 28/17.
*16 B. McDade, Joseph. 15208. M. April 9/17.
16 B. McDonald, R. 33009. M. April 28/17.
16 B. VII McIntosh, Walter. 38811. M. April 28/17.
16 B. VIII McIntosh, Wm. 33699. M. April 28/17.
16 B. VIII Scoon, James R. 19916. M. April 9/17.
‡16 B. Walkinshaw, E. 19948. M. April 28/17.
16 C. XI Clapperton, John. 43582. M. April 28/17.
16 C. Hardie, T. 34731. M. April 9/17.
16 C. McKechnie, J. 39436. M. April 28/17.
16 C. Reynolds, J. 43759. M. April 9/17.
16 C. Vance, Cpl. Matthew. 43225. M. April 28/17.
*16 D. Ferguson, A.-C.-S.-M. Wm. Urquhart. 19471. M. April 28/17.
16 D. Hatley, J. 19326. M. April 9/17.
16 D. Howarth, D. 39322. M. April 28/17.
16 D. XVI Livie, David. 33001. M. April 28/17.
16 D. XIV Mackay, Sergt. George. 19845. M. April 28/17.

**Scots, Royal—contd.**

## *B.E.F.*

| | | |
|---|---|---|
| 16 D. | McShane, B. 33017. | M. April 28/17. |
| 16 D. XIII | Mathison, Wm. 19994. | M. April 28/17. |
| 16 D. XV | Norwood, C. H. 47354 (or 270142.) | M. April 7/17. |
| 16 D. XIV | Thom, William. 18427. | M. April 28/17. |
| 16 D. XIV | Wagstaff, W. A. 270090. (47408.) | M. April 28/17. |
| 16 ? | Aird, L.-Cpl. J. 43715. | M. April 28/17. |
| 16 ? | Bain, Thos. C. 351395. (Fr. 9 D. Co.) | M. April 28/17. |
| 16 ? | Braid, G. 34297. | M. April 28/17. |
| 16 ? | Brennan, L.-Cpl. J. 43694. | M. April 28/17. |
| ‡16 ? | Cargill, C. 39167. | M. April 28/17. |
| 16 ? | Gilchrist, H. 38530. | M. April 28/17. |
| 16 ? | Knowles, J. T. 39357. | M. April 28/17. |
| 16 ? | McKenzie, Wm. 43888. (Fr. 4th.) | M. April 28/17. |
| 16 ? | McNaught, L.-Cpl. J. 34407. | M. April 28/17. |
| *16 ? | Madden, J. 38549. | K. April 9/17. Det.D./B. |
| 16 ? | Neilson, A. 43791. | M. April 28/17. |
| 16 ? | Paton, G. 43883. | M. April 28/17. |
| 16 ? | Rocks, J. 43725. | M. April 28/17. |
| 16 ? | Scanton, J. 14092. | M. April 28/17. |
| 16 ? | Skelland, R. 18646. | M. April 28/17. |
| 16 ? | Smith, T. 27964. | M. April 28/17. |
| 16 ? | Watson, P. 19951. | M. April 28/17. |
| 16 ? | Wishart, L.-Cpl. W. 43760. | M. April 28/17. |

## *E.E.F.*

| | | |
|---|---|---|
| 4 A. I | Angus, Francis Jas. 200238. (1593.) | W. and M. April 19/17. |
| 4 A. III | Fyall, John C. K. 200190. | M. April 19/17. |
| 4 A. L.G.S. | Lusk, Robert. 201143. | W. and M. April 19/17. |
| 4 D. | Kemp, C.-Q.-M.-S. Jas. 200075 (Late 1207.) | M. April 19/17. |
| 4 ? | McKay, J. 275298. | M. April 19/17. |
| 4 ? | Rorrison, Q.-M.-S. J. 200006. | M. April 19/17. |
| 7 1 II | Alexander, John. 201426. (Fr. 4th.) | M. April 19/17. |

### ROYAL SCOTS FUSILIERS.

## *B.E.F.*

| | | |
|---|---|---|
| 1 | **Davidson, 2nd Lieut. G. P.** | M., bel. K. May 3/17. |
| 1 | **Henderson, 2nd Lieut. A.** | W. and M. May 3/17. |
| 1 | **Newbigging, 2nd Lt. A. T.** (Fr. 3rd.) | M., bel. K. May 3/17. |
| 1 | **Petter, 2nd Lieut. H. R.** | W. and M. May 3/17. |
| 1 | **Robertson, 2nd Lieut. W.** | W. and M. May 3/17. |
| 1 A. II | Adam, Norman. 33489. | M. May 3/17. |
| ‡1 A. | Abbishaw, H. H. 19147. | M. June 5/17. |
| ‡1 A. | Brenan, J. 20851. | M. May 3/17. |
| ‡1 A. | Capel, Sergt. W. 16459. | W. and M. May 3/17. |
| ‡1 A. | Charlton, L.-Cpl. G. 16033. | W. and M. May 3/17. |
| ‡1 A. | Fleming, D. 27190. | M. May 3/17. |
| 1 A. or B. | Galbraith, S/B. Hugh Harris. 28211. | W. and M. May 5/17. |
| ‡1 A. | Harkness, G. 40920. | M. May 3/17. |
| *1 A. III | Kelly, Jas. 25433. | M. May 3/17. |
| *1 A. IV | Paterson, L.-Cpl. Wm. 35044. | K. May 3/17. Det.D./B. |

**Scots Fusiliers, Royal—contd.**

## *B.E.F.*

1 A. IV Richardson, Douglas. 27353. M. May 3/17.
1 A. III Ruxton, James. 23427. M. Mar. 22/17.
‡1 A. Spiers, R. 25095. M. May 3/17.
‡1 A. Taylor, W. 40961. M. May 3/17.
‡1 A. Tough, J. 41072. M. May 3/17.
‡1 A. Young, W. 28909. M. May 3/17.
*1 B. Burgoyne, Cpl. A. 11237. M. May 4/17.
1 B. Burns, W. 20987. M. April 27/17.
1 B. VII Dickie, John. 25515. M. May 3/17.
‡1 B. Gray, W. 33565. W. and M. May 3/17.
*1 B. VII Haggarty, John. 12129. W. and M. May 6/17.
‡1 B. Hodson, H. 19711. W. and M. May 3/17.
‡1 B. Jack, D. 23131. M. May 5/17.
‡1 B. Kerr, S. 40914. W. and M. May 3/17.
‡1 B. Lithgow, T. 13284. M. May 5/17.
1 B. VI McIntosh, James. 33573. M. May 3/17.
‡1 B. Middlemass, J. 27277. M. May 3/17.
‡1 B. Murray, J. 41021. M. May 3/17.
‡1 B. Northover, C. 20009. W. and M. May 3/17.
1 B. VI Pittendrich, Robert. 33552. W. and M. May 3/17.
‡1 B. Scullin, H. 24345. W. and M. May 3/17.
‡1 B. Shorrock, H. 19611. W. and M. May 3/17.
*1 B. VII Wilson, Alexander. 41060. M. May 3/17.
‡1 B. Wilson, J. 41059. M. May 3/17.
‡1 C. or D. Anderson, L.-Sgt. Alexander. 43000. (Fr. 10th R. Scots.) M. May 3/17.
1 C. Boland, E. 40927. M. May 22/17.
*1 C. IX Brown, James. 33596. M. May 3/17.
1 C. Cartwright, Wm. 17944. M. May 3/17.
‡1 C. Clements, Sergt. T. 8895. W. and M. May 3/17.
‡1 C. Colquhoun, J. 23778. M. May 3/17.
‡1 C. Conboy, J. 11278. M. May 3/17.
1 C. Gordon, L.-Cpl. T. J. 40214. M. May 3/17.
*1 C. Guyan, James. 25415. M. May 3/17.
‡1 C. Hodgson, R. 15221. M. May 3/17.
1 C. X Johnstone, Jas. 28388. M. May 3/17.
1 C. XI Leslie, E. 32883. M. May 3/17.
1 C. X McNae, John C. 40946. W. and M. May 3/17.
1 C. XI McPhee, John. 25917. M. May 3/17.
‡1 C. Malcolm, J. 19735. M. May 3/17.
‡1 C. Marshall, G. 43104. W. and M. May 3/17.
‡1 C. Millar, J. 14186. M. May 3/17.
1 C. Nicol, Sgt. J. 43077. (Fr. 10 R. Scots) M. Nov. 13/16. R/Enq
‡1 C. Peter, J. 32871. W. and M. May 3/17.
*1 C. IX Trotter, L.-Cpl. David. 11804. M. May 3/17.
‡1 D? Anderson, J. 40925. M. May 3/17.
‡1 D. Baptie, G. 33560. M. May 3/17.
1 D. Blackhall, Jas. 40812. W. and M. May 3/17.
1 D. XIII Boyd, L.-Cpl. David. 32840. M. May 3/17.
1 D. Burnside, L.-Cpl. Geo. 24484. M. May 3/17.
*1 D. XV Graham, Andrew. 41002. M. May 3/17.
1 D. Inglis, S/B. John. 17919. M. May 3/17.
1 D. XIII Lindsay, L.-Cpl. Jas. 25451. M. May 3/17.
1 D. XIV McLeod, John. 33602. M. May 3/17.
*1 D. Myles, Alex. 32866. M. May 3/17.
‡1 D. Napier, A. 33566. M. May 3/17.
1 D. XIII Phillips, Thomas. 24655. M. May 3/17.
‡1 D. Reilly, J. 7706. M. May 3/17.
1 D. XVI Turner, Andrew. 41056. M. May 3/17.

**Scots Fusiliers, Royal—contd.**

*B.E.F.*

| | | |
|---|---|---|
| *1 ? | Mackenzie, Jas. Stephenson. 35066. | M. May 30/17. |
| ‡1 ? | Parker, J. 15340. | M. May 3/17. |
| ‡1 ? | Sellars, R. 32127. | M. June 2/17. |
| 2 | **Campbell, 2nd Lt. T. S.** (Fr. 5th.) | M. April 23/17. |
| 2 | **Sinclair, 2nd Lt. E. A.** (Fr. 5th.) | M. April 23/17. |
| 2 | **Trench, 2nd Lt. D.** (Fr. 4th.) | D/W. April 23/17. Det.D./B. |
| 2 A. | Carruthers, T. 40644. | M. April 23/17. |
| 2 A. | Colston, J. 43327. | M. April 23/17. |
| 2 A. | Dinwoodie, G. 24739. | W. and M. April 23/17. |
| 2 A. I | Dye, L.-Cpl. John. 40649. | M. April 23/17. |
| 2 A. | Edgar, Jas. 40545. | M. April 23/17. |
| ‡2 A. | Forrest, Henry. 23595. | M. April 23/17. |
| 2 A. | Graham, J. 33471. | M. April 23/17. |
| 2 A. | Graham, R. 43329. | M. April 23/17. |
| 2 A. | Hogg, W. 33457. | M. April 23/17. |
| 2 A. | Hyslop, R. 40687. | M. April 23/17. |
| 2 A. I | Jamieson, J. 40561. | W. and M. April 23/17. |
| 2 A. or B. | McCrimmon, Duncan. 40289. (Late 2/4 R. Scots. 3238.) | M. Oct. 16/16. R./Enq. |
| 2 A. | McDowall, G. 34995. | M. April 23/17. |
| 2 A. | McGaw, G. 40547. | M. April 23/17. |
| 2 A. | McGregor, D. 40291. | M. April 7/17. |
| 2 A. | McNair, G. 33461. | M. April 23/17. |
| 2 A. | Mitchell, H. 33482. | M. April 23/17. |
| 2 A. | O'Neill, J. 43372. | M. April 23/17. |
| 2 A. IV | Pringle, Robert. 34991. | M. April 23/17. |
| 2 A. | Proudfoot, Cpl. Js 23535. | M. April 23/17. |
| *2 A. I | Reilly, W. 40774. | K. April 23/17. Det.D./B. |
| *2 A. | Robertson, A. 23031. | M. April 23/17. |
| 2 A. IV | Robertson, L.-Cpl. John. 40320. | M. April 23/17. |
| 2 A. III | Smith, John. 33464. | M. April 23/17. |
| 2 A. | Welsh, W. 40541. | M. April 23/17. |
| 2 B. | Barclay, Hendry. 40387. | M. April 23/17. |
| 2 B. | Barr, M. 40621. | M. April 23/17. |
| 2 B. | Birnie, W. 6130. | M. April 23/17. |
| 2 B. | Boyd, R. 34968. | M. April 7/17. |
| 2 B. VIII | Brown, Peter. 28811. | M. April 23/17. |
| 2 B. VIII | Buchanan, Robert. 28733. | W. and M. April 23/17. |
| 2 B. | Cameron, N. 17281. | M. April 23/17. |
| 2 B. | Creamer, John. 28579. | M. April 23/17. |
| 2 B. | Darrie, J. 40576. | M. April 23/17. |
| 2 B. | Dinnie, L.-Cpl. J. 17699. | M. April 23/17. |
| 2 B. | Douglas, P. 34800. | M. April 23/17. |
| 2 B. | Earl, M. 41122. | M. April 23/17. |
| 2 B. VI | Given, Wm. 41112. | M. April 23/17. |
| ‡2 B. | Graham, J. 40669. | M. April 23/17. |
| 2 B. VI | Haggart, John. 28774. | M. April 23/17. |
| 2 B. VI | Harkess, G. L. 34830. | M. April 23/17. |
| 2 B. V | Hyslop, James Brodie. 40749. | M. April 23/17. |
| 2 B. VI | Innes, Cpl. Charles S. 40235. | M. April 23/17. |
| 2 B. VIII | Jarvis, R. B. 29900. | M. April 23/17. |
| 2 B. | Jeffs, Wm. John. 41102. | M. April 23/17. |
| 2 B. | Johnston, A. 20723. | M. April 23/17. |
| 2 B. | Kelly, J. 34944. | W. and M. April 23/17. |
| ‡2 B. L.G.S. | Lees, Geo. Kenyon. 40262. | K. April 23/17. Det.D./B. R/Enq. |

**Scots Fusiliers, Royal—contd.**

## *B.E.F.*

| | | |
|---|---|---|
| 2 B. VI | Lennox, Hugh. 28620. | W. and M. **April 23/17.** |
| 2 B. VIII | Lowe, Robert. 34797. | M. **April 7/17.** |
| 2 B. | McFeat, J. 41138. | M. **April 23/17.** |
| 2 B. VIII | McLeay, L.-Cpl. Alex. 34827. | K. **April 23/17.** Det.D./B. |
| 2 B. | McParland, P. 40451. (Late 2784, H.L.I.) | M. **Oct. 16/16.** R/Enq. |
| 2 B. | Martin, J. 22929. | W. and M. **April 23/17.** |
| 2 B. | Monaghan, B. 23682. | M. **April 23/17.** |
| 2 B. | Pickles, A.-Cpl. A. 7942. | M. **April 23/17.** |
| 2 B. | Risk, L.-Cpl. Alfred. 40381. | M. **April 23/17.** |
| 2 B. | Saunders, Sig. Thomas. 29897. | M. **April 23/17** |
| 2 B. | Smith, O. 20932. | M. **April 23/17.** |
| 2 B. VIII | Steel, Cpl. James. 40608. | M. **April 23/17.** |
| 2 B. | Taylor, H. 7018. | M. **April 23/17.** |
| 2 B. VI | Welsh, John. 28782. | M. **April 23/17.** |
| 2 C. XI | Arlette, A. M. 40616. | M. **April 23/17.** |
| 2 C. | Lamont, D. 7971. | M. **April 23/17.** |
| 2 C. L.G.S. | McCalden, Lawrence. 40406. | W. Unoff. M. **April 23/17.** |
| 2 C. | Middlemass, W. 28713. | M. **April 23/17.** |
| 2 C. | Nisbet, J. 17826. | M. **April 23/17.** |
| ‡2 C. | Smart, James. 40338. | W. and M. **April 23/17.** |
| 2 D. | Buchanan, J. 40623. | M. **April 23/17.** |
| 2 D. XIII | Compton, Harvy. 40646. | M. **April 23/17.** |
| 2 D. | Fisher, Jas. 40744. | M. **April 23/17.** |
| D. | Gardner, W. 40746. | M. **April 23/17.** |
| 2 D. | Hodgson, T. 40565. | M. **April 23/17.** |
| 2 D. | Kean, R. 40443. | W. and M. **April 23/17.** |
| 2 D. XIII | Low, John. 40757. | M. **April 23/17.** |
| 2 D. | McGinnes, J. 41116. | M. **April 23/17.** |
| 2 D. XIV | Renwick, Adam. 40551. | M. **April 23/17.** |
| 2 D. | Stark, J. M. 40325. | W. and M. **April 23/17.** |
| 2 D. | Wodehouse, J. 28788. | M. **April 23/17.** |
| **6/7 D.** | **Whitelaw, 2nd Lieut. J. W.** | M. **April 11/17.** |
| ‡6/7 A. | Brown, J. 27602. | M. **April 23/17.** |
| 6/7 A. | Dufton, L. 40125. | M. **April 11/17.** |
| 6/7 A. | Goldthorpe, A. 40132. | M. **April 11/17.** |
| ‡6/7 A. | Isherwood, L.-Cpl. W. 18024. | M. **April 23/17.** |
| 6/7 A. | Kilmartin, William. 20214. | M. **April 11/17.** |
| 6/7 A. | Lewis, S. 23455. | M. **April 11/17.** |
| 6/7 A. | Parker, G. 17194. | M. **April 11/17.** |
| 6/7 A. | Ritchie, George. 43258. | M. **April 11/17.** |
| 6/7 A. | Sneddon, J. 29205. | M. **April 11/17.** |
| 6/7 A. | Stephenson, E. 40153. | W. and M. **April 11/17.** |
| 6/7 A. | Taylor, G. 11826. | W. and M. **Sept. 15/16.** |
| 6/7 B. VI | Finningham, Jas. 34921. | M. **April 11/17.** |
| ‡6/7 B. | Fullarton, Sgt. T. 5413. | M. **April 24/17.** |
| *6/7 B. VIII | Grier, Richard. 20628. | M., bel. K. **April 21/17.** |
| 6/7 B. | Howarth, William. 15477. | W. and M. **April 11/17.** |
| ‡6/7 B. | McCafferty, E. 6850. | M., bel. K. **April 21/17.** |

**Scots Fusiliers, Royal—contd.**

## *B.E.F.*

‡6/7 B. McKie, H. 40036. M. April 23/17.
6/7 B. VI McLarty, John. 19643. M. April 20/17.
‡6/7 B. McMahon, J. 20425. M. April 23/17.
6/7 B. Simpson, L.-Sergt. J. 13139. M. April 11/17.
*6/7 B. VII Smith, F. 40058. Unoff. M. April/17.
6/7 C. X McCallum, Archie. 29843. M. April 11/17.
‡6/7 C. Mallon, F. 25980. M. April 23/17.
6/7 C. X Munn, Wm. 29845. M. April 11/17.
6/7 C. or D. Robertson, Wm. 43244. W. and M. April 10/17.
6/7 D. XV Frisken, Cpl. James. 29953. W. and M. April 11/17.
*6/7 D. Donnelly, John. 17036. M. April 11/17.
6/7 D. Hedley, Sgt. D. 16986. M. April 11/17.
6/7 D. McNair, A. 20989. W. and M. April 11/17.
6/7 D. Mailer, John Hodgson. 29234. K. April 11/17. Conf. and Det.D./B.

## *E.E.F.*

4 Logan, 2nd Lieut. J. M. April 19/17.
4 A. Brown, James. 201617. (Late 9703.) M. April 19/17.
4 A. L.G.S. Campbell, Sergt. A. 200322. M. April 19/17.
4 A. Murray, Hugh. 241253. M. April 19/17.
4 A. Norris, Geo. Fredk. 201715. (9827.) M. April 19/17.
4 B. Richardson, Chas. Edward. 201426. M. April 19/17.
4 C. Breckenridge, Wm. 200790. M. April 19/17.
4 C. IX Duncan, Douglas Greig. 202871. M. April 19/17.
*4 C. XII Gaunt, J. 203211. M., bel. K. April 19/17.
4 C. McGibbon, Archibald. 202894. M. April 19/17.
4 C. Robertson, Dan. 202925. (11887.) M. April 19/17.
4 C. Taylor, John. 200159. D/W. April 20/17. Det.D./B.
4 D. Todhunter, R. 203201. M. April 19/17.
4 ? Allan, M. 201174. M. April 19/17.
4 ? Barclay, William. 203358. M. April 19/17.
*4 ? Beggs, R. 205133. M. April 19/17.
4 ? Boyd, T. 201152. M. April 19/17.
*4 ? Campbell, M. 203368. M. April 19/17.
‡4 ? Clinie, Sergt. G. 200796. M. April 19/17.
4 ? Drummond, R. 200674. M. April 19/17.
4 ? Forsyth, J. 202876. M. April 19/17.
*4 ? Geddes, W. 203360. M. April 19/17.
4 ? Gibson, J. 202976. M. April 19/17.
4 ? Gibson, W. 203328. M. April 19/17.
4 ? Gow, E. 202881. M. April 19/17.
‡4 ? Harrison, C. 203207. M. April 19/17.
*4 ? Kennedy, W. 203336. M. April 19/17.
4 ? McKechnie, J. 203014. M. April 19/17.
4 ? McQueen, Sergt. G. 240027. M. April 19/17.
*4 ? Merry, J. 241293. M., bel. K. April 19/17.
4 ? Miller, T. 200973. M. April 19/17.
‡4 ? Morrison, R. 200977. M. April 19/17.
4 ? Munro, L.-Cpl. R. M. 200268. M. April 19/17.
4 ? Murray, David L. 202896. M. April 19/17.
4 ? Ritchie, Andrew. 202344. W. and M. April 19/17.
*4 ? Scott, A. 241306. W. and M. April 19/17.
4 ? Stewart, T. 203017. M. April 19/17.
4 ? Templeton, S. 200809. M. April 19/17.

Scots Fusiliers, Royal—contd.

*E.E.F.*

| | | |
|---|---|---|
| 5 | **Kennedy, Capt. Walter Douglas.** | M. **April 19/17.** |
| 5 | **McBeth, 2nd Lt. J. D. G.** | W. and M. **April 19/17.** |
| 5 | **McKenzie, Lieut. R. P.** | M. **April 19/17.** |
| 5 B. | Chapman, L.-Cpl. A. 241545. (Late 3959.) | M. **April 19/17.** |
| 5 B. or C. | Greenaway, George. 241541. (Late 4185.) | M. **April 19/17.** |
| 5 B. | Hardy, C. T. 201350. (9291.) (Fr. 4.) | M. **April 19/17.** |
| 5 B. | Sandeman, Sgt. Jas. 241169. (9350.) | W. and M. **April 19/17.** |
| 5 B. | Westhorpe, Bert. 201476. (9433.) | M. **April 19/17.** |
| 5 D. | Rollo, Robt. 240695. (7812.) | W. and M. **April 19/17.** |
| 5 ? | Garner, G. H. 201344. | W. and M. **April 19/17.** |
| ‡5 ? | Gordon, D. M. 202381. | M. **June 5/17.** |
| 5 ? | Greenway, G. 241541. | M. **April 19/17.** |
| 5 ? | Hendrie, Sergt. J. 240045. | W. and M. **April 19/17.** |
| 5 ? | McDerment, D. 240565. | M., bel. K. **April 19/17.** |
| 5 ? | McKenzie, R. 240556. | M. **April 19/17.** |
| *5 ? | Malley, J. 241233. | M. **June 5/17.** |
| *5 ? | Mason, H. 201403. | M. **June 5/17.** |
| 5 ? | Mathers, G. 241386. | M. **April 19/17.** |
| 5 ? | Simpson, D. 241403. | M. **April 19/17.** |
| 5 ? | Stewart, A.-Cpl. J. 240233. | M. **April 19/17.** |

## KING'S OWN SCOTTISH BORDERERS.

*B.E.F.*

| | | |
|---|---|---|
| 1 A. IV | Dunbar, Wm. 25069. | M. **April 23/17.** |
| 1 A. | Harriman, G. W. 25603. | M. **April 23/17.** |
| 1 A. IV | Harrison, W. 16932. | W. and M. **April 23/17.** |
| ‡1 A. | Hunter, Sergt. J. 7458. | M. **April 16/17.** |
| 1 A. IV | McGarry, James. 21883. | W. and M. **April 23/17.** |
| 1 A. | Moore, H. 13122. | M. **April 23/17.** |
| 1 A. | Rigg, F. 18333. | M. **April 23/17.** |
| 1 A. III | Stewart, Cpl. John. 7811. | W. and M. **April 23/17.** |
| 1 B. V | Graham, J. 6342. | M. **April 23/17.** |
| 1 B. | Labourn, L.-Cpl. W. 21191. | M. **April 23/17.** |
| 1 B. V | Thomson, Wm. 25039. | W. and M. **April 23/17.** |
| 1 B. VI | Webb, Samuel. 12870. | W. and M. **Jan. 29/17.** |
| 1 C. | Dickson, T. 15772. | M. **April 23/17.** |
| 1 C. X | Hammond, Geo. 41106. | M. **April 23/17.** |
| 1 C. X | McDonald, Robt. 40516. | K. **April 23/17.** Det.D./B. |
| 1 C. IX | Ritchie, John M. 25804. | M. **April 23/17.** |
| 1 D. | Anderson, T. 18115. | M. **April 23/17.** |
| 1 D. | Jackson, J. H. 9335. | M. **April 23/17.** |
| D. XVI | McGuire, James. 25823. | M. **April 23/17.** |
| 1 D. | Wylie, James. 16348. | M. **Jan. 30/17.** |
| 1 ? | Elkins, J. 28598. | K. **Jan. 28/17.** Det.D./B. |
| *2 A. II | Argent, John. 28623. | K. **April 9/17.** Det.D./B. |
| 2 A. II | Fussey, A. S. 40065. | K. **Sept. 25/16.** Det.D./B. |
| *2 A. IV | Lough, Thos. F. 16702. | M. **May 8/17.** |
| 2 B. VII | Cunningham, John. 23422. | K. **May 15/17.** Det.D./B. |
| 2 B. VIII | Neve, Sydney Valentine. 22133. | K. **Sept. 3/16.** Det.D./B. |
| ‡2 B. | Robertson, A. 21615. | W. and M. **May 8/17.** |

**Scottish Borderers, King's Own—contd.**

## *B.E.F.*

| | | |
|---|---|---|
| ‡2 B. | Rolland, J. 28705. | M. May 8/17. |
| ‡2 B. | Scott, R. 29368. | M. May 8/17. |
| ‡2 C. | Coppins, A. 14151. | W. and M. May 8/17. |
| ‡2 C. | Gould, R. 44072. | M. May 8/17. |
| ‡2 C. | Graham, P. 16712. | M. May 8/17. |
| 2 C. X | Steele, Adam. 12937. | M. May 8/17. |
| 2 D. XIII | Ball, L. A. 18611. | M. July 23/16. R/Enq. |
| 2 D. M.G.S. | Cairns, T. G. 40890. | M. May 9/17. |
| •2 D. XV M.G.S. | Dow, A. 40370. | M. May 9/17. |
| 2 D. XIII | Edgar, L.-Cpl. Walter. 25283. | D/W. April 26/17. Det.D./B. |
| ‡2 D. | Woodcock, Sergt. H. 11755. | M., bel. K. May 13/17. |
| 2 ? | Campbell, James. 40088. (Fr. 7/8th.) | W. and M. April 24/17. |
| 2 ? | O'Brien, Peter. 26415. | K. May 3/17. Det.D./B. |
| 6 | **Campbell, Lt. J. B.** (Fr. 5th.) | M. May 3/17. |
| 6 C. | **Lawrie, 2nd Lieut. J. A.** | M. May 3/17. |
| 6 | **Little, 2nd Lieut. J. R.** | M. May 3/17. |
| 6 | **Lushington, 2nd Lieut. P. J. W.** | M. May 3/17. |
| 6 | **McLaren, Lieut. D.** (Fr. 3rd.) | M. May 3/17. |
| 6 | **Reid, 2nd Lieut. G.** | M. May 3/17. |
| 6 | **Reid, Lieut. T. M.** | M. May 3/17. |
| 6 | **Scott, 2nd Lt. A. H.** (Fr. 4th.) | M. May 3/17. |
| ‡6 A. | Adamson, W. 22741. | M. May 3/17. |
| 6 A. III | Alexander, Thos. 25812. | M. May 3/17. |
| ‡6 A. | Amers, R. 11637. | W. and M. May 3/17. |
| ‡6 A. | Campbell, G. 20443. | M. May 3/17. |
| ‡6 A. | Clegg, P. 22340. | M. May 3/17. |
| ‡6 A. | Cochrane, William. 27217. | M. May 3/17. |
| 6 A. II | Conington, Walter. 12065. | M. May 3/17. |
| ‡6 A. | Douglas, G. 19971. | M May 3/17. |
| 6 A. IV | Duff, John. 23577. | M. May 3/17. |
| ‡6 A. | Dunse, G. 25451. | M. May 3/17. |
| ‡6 A. | Forrest, L. 40633. | W. and M. May 3/17. |
| ‡6 A. | Hamilton, T. 27126. | M. May 3/17. |
| 6 A. | Hanson, Percy. 20072. | M. May 3/17. |
| ‡6 A. III | Hare, Arthur D. 22468. | W. Unoff. M. June 2/17. |
| •6 A. | Hogg, Sgt. Robt. 7791. | W. and M. May 3/17. |
| 6 A. or C. | Hutchinson, Albert. 24270. | M. May 3/17. |
| 6 A. or B. | Hutchison, A.-Cpl. Wm. 41025. | M. May 3/17. |
| ‡6 A. | Johnstone, W. 24903. | M. May 3/17. |
| ‡6 A. | Law, A. G. 28112. | M. May 3/17. |
| ‡6 A. | Lawrie, R. 27200. | M. May 3/17. |
| •6 A. III | Lockhart, John. 24909. | Unoff. W. and M. May 3/17. |
| ‡6 A. | McFadyean, H. 24005. | M. May 3/17. |
| 6 A. | Martin, L.-Cpl. Walter. 20954. | M. May 3/17. |
| ‡6 A. | Maxwell, S. 22770. | M. May 3/17. |
| 6 A. | Minford, L.-Cpl. John. 14443. | M. May 3/17. |
| •6 A. I | Mundell, Robt. 29991. | W. and M. May 3/17. |
| •6 A. III | Patterson, Robt. Gordon. 20988. | W. and M. May 3/17. |
| ‡6 A. III | Reid, J. 27191. | M. May 3/17. |
| ‡6 A. | Sharkey, W. 27680. | M. May 3/17. |
| •6 A. | Simpson, J. 23876. | W. and M. April 9/17. |
| ‡6 A. L.G.S. | Turner, Eric. 22341. | M. May 3/17. |
| ‡6 A. | White, G. P. 12153. | M. May 3/17. |
| 6 A. Sig. S. | Wilding, J. W. 15444. | M. May 3/17. |
| ‡6 A. | Wyllie, R. 20361. | M. May 3/17. |
| ‡6 B. | Allison, A. 24751. | M. May 3/17. |

**Scottish Borderers, King's Own—contd.**

*B.E.F.*

‡6 B. Amos, T. 29665. M. May 3/17.
6 B. V Arres, Alex. 201334. (8368.) M. May 3/17.
‡6 B. Bell, L.-Cpl. Wm. 22946. M. May 3/17.
‡6 B. Bold, Cpl. Andrew. 22553. M. May 3/17.
6 B. Bottomley, L.-Cpl. J. P. 18187. M. May 3/17.
6 B. VI Breckenridge, L.-Cpl. John. 40560. M. May 3/17.
*6 B. Brown, David. 16035. M. May 3/17.
‡6 B. Carlin, N. 26685. M. May 3/17.
6 B. Clerk, Jas. S 25680. M. May 3/17.
6 B. VII Crabtree, Jas. 18762. M. May 3/17.
*6 B. VII Craig, D. 23788. M. May 3/17.
‡6 B. Craig, J. 7896. M. May 3/17.
‡6 B. Crawford, H. 26335. M. May 3/17.
‡6 B. Crichton, G. 40997. M. May 3/17.
6 B. V Currie, Robert. 26677. M. May 3/17.
6 B. VIII Dalgliesh, Wm. 23489. M. May 3/17.
‡6 B. Donachie, H. 25727. M. May 3/17.
‡6 B. Duff, J. 16760. W. and M. May 3/17.
6 B. Dunsmore, L.-Cpl. David. 43105. M. May 3/17.
6 B. VII Firth, A. 19932. M. May 3/17.
‡6 B. Garrick, A. 29569. M. May 3/17.
6 B. or C. Gray, John. 27835. M. April 9/17.
6 B. Henderson, William. 29428. M. May 3/17.
‡6 B. Hermiston, M. 201456. M. May 3/17.
6 B. VI Hume, T. 20078. M. May 3/17.
6 B. VI Inglis, John. 19731. M. May 3/17.
6 B. Jardine, L.-Cpl. 25587. M. May 3/17.
‡6 B. Lang, J. 14531. M. May 3/17.
‡6 B. Leiper, G. 19701. M. May 3/17.
6 B. Leith, Duncan. 27608. (Fr. Entrench. Battn.) M. May 3/17.
‡6 B. McAdie, J. 27438. M. May 3/17.
6 B. VIII McCredie, James. 24657. M. May 3/17.
‡6 B. McLaughlan, R. 12459. M. May 3/17.
‡6 B. Marshall, E. 16769. M. May 3/17.
‡6 B. Moffat, T. 200779. M. May 3/17.
6 B. VIII Paterson, Cpl. Geo. 24893. M. May 3/17.
‡6 B. Redpath, A. 29669. M. May 3/17.
‡6 B. Richardson, S. 20829. M. May 3/17.
‡6 B. Rickard, A.-Cpl. W. 19113. M. May 3/17.
6 B. V Roberts, Allan. 40557. M. May 3/17.
‡6 B. Robson, Act.-C.-S.-M. T. 18687. M. May 3/17.
‡6 B. Simpson, A.-Cpl. J. 24885. M. May 3/17.
*6 B. V Smith, Edward. 240289. M. May 3/17.
6 B. Strachan, C. 29463. M. May 3/17.
‡6 B. Thompson, L.-Cpl. F. 22332 M. May 3/17.
‡6 B. Waddell, L.-Sergt. J. 14291. M. May 3/17.
6 B. VIII Wark, Wm. S. 27230. M. May 3/17.
6 B. V Watson, Chas. 41054. M. May 3/17.
‡6 B. Wood, R. A. 29628. M. May 3/17.
‡6 C. Ashmead, William. 43033. M. May 3/17.
‡6 C. Ballantyne, A. 29995. M. May 3/17.
6 C. IX Beattie, Cpl. W. C. 29354. M. May 3/17.
‡6 C. Bray, L. 26978. M. May 3/17.
‡6 C. Brown, A. 27210. M. May 3/17.
6 C. IX Brown, W. R. 24887. M. May 3/17.
6 C. L.G.S. Calvert, Edgar. 40653. M. May 3/17.

**Scottish Borderers, King's Own—contd.**

## *B.E.F.*

‡6 C. Christie, L.-Cpl. G. 44003. M. May 3/17.
‡6 C. Cowan, A. 24808. M. May 3/17.
6 C. X Dinan, James. 27151. M. May 3/17.
‡6 C. Dorey, J. 25646. M. May 3/17.
6 C. Sig. S. Edward, George S. M. 41018. M. May 3/17.
‡6 C. Ferguson, L.-Cpl. W. 23840. M. May 3/17.
6 C. X Fitzpatrick, J. 27162. M. May 3/17.
‡6 C. Henderson, C. 27829. M. May 3/17.
6 C. Gallacher, Jas. 9634. M. May 3/17.
6 C. XI Gallantry, Andrew. 27248. M. May 3/17.
6 C. XI Gillies, Murdoch. 25369. M. May 3/17.
*6 C. Hamill, John. 27218. M. May 3/17.
6 C. IX Irvine, James. 25289. M. May 3/17.
‡6 C. Jack, Wm. 25409. M. May 3/17.
‡6 C. Jackson, A. 26348. M. May 3/17.
‡6 C. Jones, W. 21934. M. May 3/17.
6 C. XII Kelting, Arthur. 41034. W. and M. May 3/17.
*6 C. Lees, H. A. S. 18867. M. May 3/17.
‡6 C. Little, A.-Cpl. J. 16094. W. and M. May 3/17.
6 C. X McAllister, Alex. 27160. M. May 3/17.
‡6 C. McDavid, L.-Sergt. J. 240203. M. May 3/17.
‡6 C. Mackay, R. A. 26935. M. May 3/17.
‡6 C. McKie, A. 22947. M. May 3/17.
6 C. X MacKinnon, Andrew. 29571. M. May 3/17.
‡6 C. McRobert, R. 11940. M. May 3/17.
‡6 C. Moonan, J. 40621. M. May 3/17.
‡6 C. Patterson, A. 24992. M. May 3/17.
‡6 C. Paterson, J. 40620. M. May 3/17.
‡6 C. Pringle, R. 23866. M. May 3/17.
6 C. IX Reid, J. G. 18783. M. May 3/17.
6 C. XI Rettie, John. 25861. M. May 3/17.
6 C. X Robson, Wm. 5875. M. May 3/17.
‡6 C. Roy, W. 24923. M. May 3/17.
6 C. Seggie, Cpl. Tom. 17895. M. May 3/17.
‡6 C. Stein, Sergt. G. 12837. M. May 3/17.
‡6 C. Swan, J. 41048. M. May 3/17.
6 C. X Vance, Wm. 27165. M. May 3/17.
6 C. XI Walker, Robt. 27171. M. May 3/17.
6 C. XII Watson, Finlay. 19713. M. May 3/17.
6 C. L.G.S. Williamson, H. 43061. M. May 3/17.
‡6 C. Williamson, Sergt. J. 10900. M. May 3/17.
‡6 C. Wilson, C. 8459. M. May 3/17.
‡6 C. Wylie, W. 40153. M. May 3/17.
*6 D. Buckley, Sig. Frank. 19997. W. and M. May 3/17.
‡6 D. Carney, James. 21088. Unoff. M. about May 7/17.
‡6 D. Fraser, H. 27186. M. May 3/17.
6 D. Ker, J. 24953. M. Mar. 31/17.
6 D. Pearson, A.-Cpl. T. 17732. M. April 1/17.
*6 ? L.G.S. Johnston, L.-Cpl. Leslie. 4126. M. May 3/17.
7/8 A. I Allan, Thos. 40710. M. April 9-12/17.
7/8 A. IV Bird, W. A. 21444. M. April 9-12/17.
7/8 A. Black, R. 40702. M. April 9-12/17.
7/8 A. II Blaen, Sergt. J. 29309. Unoff. M. April 9-12/17.
7/8 A. or C. Campbell, H. 27736. (Fr. Fife & Forfar Yeo.) M. April 9-12/17.
7/8 A. III Cooper, Sig. Alfred. 28638. M. April 9-12/17.
7/8 A. III Docherty, L.-Cpl. Hugh. 15619. K. Sept. 15/16. Det.D./B.

**Scottish Borderers, King's Own—contd.**

## *B.E.F.*

| | | |
|---|---|---|
| 7/8 A. I | Duncan, Wm. 27778. | M. April 9-12/17. |
| 7/8 A. | Fleming, Alexander. 27399. | M. April 9-12/17. |
| 7/8 A. | Paton, Robt. 15919. | M. April 9-12/17. |
| 7/8 A. | Scott, Thomas. 15893. | W. and M. April 9-12/17. |
| 7/8 A. | Scullin, L.-Cpl. F. 11136. | M. April 9-12/17. |
| 7/8 A. | Telfer, Jas. 29939. | M. April 23/17. |
| 7/8 B. | Blakeman, Sig. Basil. 15782. | M. April 9-12/17. |
| 7/8 B. | Burrows, T. 29897. | M. April 9-12/17. |
| 7/8 B. VI | Denholm, William. 29523. | M. April 9-12/17. |
| 7/8 B. VI | Graham, James. 29346. | M. April 9-12/17. |
| *7/8 B. | Hadfield, Tom. 29906. | K. April 23/17. Det.D./B. |
| 7/8 B. VI | Manterfield, W. 29910. | M. April 9-12/17. |
| 7/8 B. V | Morrison, Jas. B. 23431. | M. April 9-12/17. |
| 7/8 B. VII | Oldfield, Harry. 29907. | M. April 9-12/17. |
| 7/8 B. V | Richmond, Will. 14369. | M. April 9-12/17. |
| 7/8 C. VI | Stevenson, J. W. 29911. | M. April 9-12/17. |
| 7/8 C. IX | Partridge, Sam. 29892. | M. April 9-12/17. |
| 7/8 C. X | Walter, Clement H. 29853. | M. April 9-12/17. |
| 7/8 D. XIII | Easterbrook, Roy. 27828. | M. April 9-12/17. |
| 7/8 D. | Hall, Cpl. Robt. Allen. 8192. | K. April 9-12/17. Det.D./B. |
| 7/8 D. | Haywood, A. 40267. (Late 2/7 R. Scots, 3742.) | M. Unoff. K. Sept. 15/16. R/Enq. |
| 7/8 D. | Maskery, L.-Cpl. Wm. John. 18287. | M. April 9-12/17. |
| 7/8 D. | Miller, W. B. 44131. | M. April 9-12/17. |
| 7/8 D. | Mundell, J. 40225. | M. April 9-12/17. |
| 7/8 D. XIV | Stewart, D. 41079. | M. April 9-12/17. |
| 7/8 D. | Watt, Andrew. 44147. | M. April 9-12/17. |
| 8 A. | Ballingall, W. 27769. | M. April 9-12/17. |
| 8 B. | Burnett, D. 29945. | M. April 9-12/17. |
| 8 B. | Morrin, L.-Cpl. T. 29302. | M. April 9-12/17. |

## *E.E.F.*

| | | |
|---|---|---|
| 4 | **Forrest, Major W. T.** | W. and M. prev. rep. K. April 19/17. |
| *4 A. | Bell, Willie. 200157. (8113.) | M. April 19/17. |
| 4 A. L.G.S. | Brockie, Walter. 200384. (Late 6489.) | W. and M. April 19/17. |
| *4 A. | Brockie, Wm. R. 200693. (7143.) | M. April 19/17. |
| *4 B. | Coulter, Ralph. 200766. (7284.) | M. April 19/17. |
| 4 B. | Dolan, M. 240222. (1347.) | M April 19/17. |
| 4 B. | Dunn, C. 200206. (4420.) | W. and M. April 19/17. |
| 4 B. | Hogg, Robt. 200773. (7308.) | M. April 19/17. |
| *4 B. | Maxwell, Matthew. 240616. (2207.) | M. April 19/17. |
| 4 B. | Watson, Geo. 200269. | K. April 19/17. Det.D./B. |
| *4 B. | Welsh, James. 201222. (8215.) | W. and M. April 19/17. |
| *4 C. XI | Peart, Edward. 201649. | M. April 10/17. |
| 4 D. | Callander, L.-Cpl. Wm. 201061. | M. April 19/17. |
| *4 D. | Ford, John. 200285. | M. April 19/17. |
| 4 D. | Frier, Robt. 201541. | W. and M. April 19/17. |
| 4 D. XVI | Murray, Jas. 200941. (7667.) | M. April 19/17. |
| 4 ? | Bainbridge, Harold. 201642. (9281.) | W. and M. April 19/17. |
| ‡4 ? | Brinkworth, Chas. F. 201707. (9346.) | K. April 19/17. Det.D./B. |
| 4 ? | Coulter, R. 200766. | M. April 19/17. |
| *4 ? | Craig, J. A. 201455. | W. and M. May 31/17. |
| 4 ? M.G.S. | Cunningham, W. 200571. (6857.) | M. April 19/17. |
| 4 ? | Dongal, L.-Cpl. W. 200254. | W. and M. April 19/17. |

**Scottish Borderers, King's Own—contd.**

*E.E.F.*

4 ? Ferguson, Thos. Funnahill. 201832. (Fr. 5th, No. 9471.) M. April 19/17.
4 ? Ford, J. 200285. M. April 19/17.
4 ? Galbraith, W. 201307. M. April 19/17.
4 ? Halliday, A. 241069. M. April 19/17.
4 ? Hope, G. 200672. M. April 19/17.
4 ? Lough, J. 241647. M. April 19/17.
*4 ? Lough, R. 200822. W. and M. April 19/17.
4 ? McAllister, Sergt. T. 241056. M. April 19/17.
4 ? Murray, J. 200941. M. April 19/17.
4 ? White, R. R. 200758. M. April 19/17.
5 **Gibb, 2nd Lieut. R. A.** M. April 19/17.
5 **Henery, 2nd Lieut. H. W. L.** K. April 19/17. Det.D./B
5 **McLeod, Lieut. Geo. C.** W. and M. April 19/17.
5 A. Litterick, R. 240562. M. April 19/17.
*5 A. Sig. S. Mabon, John. 200403. W. and M. April 19/17.
5 A. Smith, Jas. 240027. (2117.) W. and M. April 19/17.
5 B. Croall, R. 240959. (2904.) M. April 19/17.
5 B. Foley, James. 240172. (Late 1228.) M. April 19/17.
5 C. XII Bell, Wm. John. 241004. (4228.) M. April 19/17.
5 C. Black, David. 240577. (Late 2025.) M. April 19/17.
5 C. McCormick, A. 240715. (2324.) M. April 19/17.
5 C. XI Rothery, Cpl. J. 241075. M. April 19/17.
5 D. XVI Jolly, Ernest Geo. 201807. (9446.) M. April 19/17.
5 D. XVI Little, Frank. 241173. M. April 19/17.
5 D. XIII Murray, John. 240892. (2758.) M. April 19/17.
5 D. Richardson, Arthur. 241073. (4345.) M. April 19/17.
5 ? Adie, J. 201789. M. April 19/17.
5 ? Ashburner, L.-Cpl. J. 240299. M. April 19/17.
*5 ? Bain, J. 201604. W. and M. April 19/17.
5 ? Boyle, J. 240494. M. April 19/17.
5 ? Carson, W. 241510. M. April 19/17.
5 ? Charteris, E. 241278. M. April 19/17.
5 ? Cockburn, D. 201768. M. April 19/17.
*5 ? Cowan, Cpl. T. 240017. W. and M. April 19/17.
*5 ? Dalziel, J. C. 241634. W. and M. April 19/17.
5 ? Dickson, J. 240075. M. April 19/17.
*5 ? Douglas, E. 201806. W. and M. April 19/17.
5 ? Evans, Sergt. G. 201786. M. April 19/17.
5 ? Gilbertson, Cpl. J. 240168. M. April 19/17.
*5 ? Gouldie, L.-Cpl. A. M. 240536. W. and M. April 19/17.
5 ? Gregor, W. 201741. M. April 19/17.
5 ? Hughes, T. 241256. M. April 19/17.
5 ? Jackson, J. 201679. M. April 19/17.
5 ? James, W. 201752. W. and M. April 19/17.
5 ? Jardine, W. 241214. M. April 19/17.
5 ? Kerr, J. 201709. M. April 19/17
*5 ? Knowles, R. 240912. W. and M. April 19/17.
5 ? Laird, A. 201647. M. April 19/17.
5 ? McLauchlan, E. 240620. M. April 19/17.
5 ? Murchie, T. 240390. M. April 19/17.
5 ? Murray, W. 240324. M. April 19/17.
*5 ? Nicol, L.-Cpl. J. 240360. W. and M. April 19/17.
*5 ? Porteous, R. 201838. W. and M. April 19/17.
5 ? Richardson, Cpl. J. 240438. M. April 19/17.
5 ? Richardson, J. 240844. M. April 19/17.
5 ? Steel, H. 241054. M. April 19/17.

**Scottish Borderers, King's Own—contd.**

***E.E.F.***

| | | |
|---|---|---|
| 5 ? | Telfer, J. 241128. | M. April 19/17. |
| 5 ? | Wallace, J. 240718. | M. April 19/17. |
| 5 ? | Wilson, J. 241628. | M. April 19/17. |

**SCOTTISH RIFLES.**

***B.E.F.***

| | | |
|---|---|---|
| 1 D. | **Newlands, 2nd Lieut. S. L. L.** | M., bel. P/W. May 27/17. |
| ‡1 A. | Aspley, W. 17898. | M. May 20/17. |
| 1 A. | Bennett, A. 43008. | M. April 23/17. |
| *1 A. III | Brannan, Sigr. Anthony. 19735. | M. May 20/17. |
| ‡1 A. | Catchesides, J. 12081. | M. May 20/17. |
| ‡1 A. | Coates, J. 40474. | W. and M. May 27/17. |
| ‡1 A. | Cummins, J. 41077. | M. May 27/17. |
| ‡1 A. | Galloway, Charles. 40503. | W. and M. May 20/17. |
| 1 A. II | Jackson, John. 26025. | K. April 16/17. Det.D./B. |
| ‡1 A. | Jamieson, A. 28661. | M. May 20/17. |
| ‡1 A. | Kelly, S. 8069. | M. May 20/17. |
| *1 A. I | Kerr, William J. 23586. | M. May 20/17. |
| ‡1 A. I | Knight, J. 41384. | M. May 27/17. |
| ‡1 A. | McAllister, H. 3686. | M. May 27/17. |
| ‡1 A. | Smith, J. 27786. | W. and M. May 20/17. |
| *1 A. I | Stewart, Wm. 23163. | W. and M. May 20/17. |
| ‡1 A. | Walker, J. 40415. | W. and M. May 20/17. |
| ‡1 A. | Ward, J. 11092. | M. May 27/17. |
| 1 B. VI | Bullock, Wm. 41026. | M. April 14/17. |
| *1 B. V | Dean, Octavius. 40343. | M. May 16/17. |
| *1 B. VIII | Himsworth, Harry. 41063. | M. May 27/17. |
| *1 B. V | Lancaster, Wm. 41385. | M. May 16/17. |
| *1 B. V | McCrossman, Walter. 41393. | M. May 16/17. |
| ‡1 B. | McFarlane, J. 27631. | M. May 16/17. |
| ‡1 B. or C. | Noble, Charles. 8453. | M. May 20/17. |
| ‡1 B. V | Paterson, William A. 40322. | Unoff. M. June 23/17. |
| *1 B. V | Preston, Sergt. John. 18802. | K. May 20/17. Det.D./B. |
| *1 B. VI | Ramsay, George. 23198. | M. May 15/17. |
| ‡1 B. | Reascod, L.-Cpl. C. 41491. | M. May 16/17. |
| *1 B. VIII | Taylor, Willis. 41064. | M. May 27/17. |
| ‡1 C. XII | Barrow, James. 30162. | M. May 27/17. |
| 1 C. X | Highet, L.-Cpl. Thos. 30163. | M. May 20/17. |
| *1 C. | Murray, J. 30152. | M. May 20/17. |
| *1 C. XII | Perrons, L.-Cpl. W. H. 17555. | M. May 20/17. |
| ‡1 C. | Porter, J. 40987. | M. May 27/17. |
| ‡1 C. X | Rycroft, Leonard. 40371. | W. and M. May 20/17. |
| ‡1 C. | Thomson, R. 43240. | M. May 27/17. |
| *1 C. X | Walters, A. 41009. | W. and M. May 21/17. |
| ‡1 D. | Bathgate, J. 40332. | M. May 20/17. |
| 1 D. XV | Bell, Thomas. 43219. | M. Oct. 29/16. R/Enq. |
| 1 D. XIV | Bolger, C. 23017. | M. Oct. 29/16. |
| *1 D. XIII | Davie, Allan Ramsay. 40303. | Unoff. M. Oct. 29/16. |
| 1 D. | Dickson, H. 27196. | W. and M. April 16/17. |
| ‡1 D. XIII | Douglas, Wat. 43126. | M. May 27/17. |
| ‡1 D. | Gilchrist, W. 30105. | M. May 27/17. |

**Scottish Rifles—contd.**

## *B.E.F.*

1 D. XIII Houghton, Cpl. B. 40351. (Late 2/9 R. Scots, 2751.) M. Unoff. W. Oct. 29/16. R/Enq.
‡1 D. Kinnison, W. 20903. M. May 27/17.
*1 D. XVI McLachlan, Walter. 27462. M. May 20/17.
1 D. McMillan, William. 22456. M. Oct. 29/16. R/Enq.
1 D. Murray, John. 43028. M. Oct. 29/16. R./Enq.
‡1 D. XIV Robbie, A. 30301. M. May 27/17.
‡1 D. Robertson, Cpl. A. C. D. 41439. M. May 27/17.
1 D. Simm, A. 10698. M. April 16/17.
1 D. Stewart, Thos. 40409. M. Oct. 29/16. R/Enq.
‡1 D. Stuart, A.-Cpl. J. 40422. M. May 27/17.
*1 D. XV Thomson, Matthew Sillan. 26700. M. May 27/17.
‡1 D. XVI Walker, David. 31728. M. May 27/17.
‡2 A. Barr, O. 15863. W. and M. May 5-6/17.
2 C. XII Hope, L.-Cpl. Harry. 15794. M. Oct. 23/16. R./Enq.
*2 C. or D. Howieson, Joseph. 40074. W. and M. May 5-6/17.
‡2 D. Blackhurst, J. 41243. M. May 5-6/17.
*2 D. XIV Campbell, Walter B. 41216. M. Unoff. W. May 5-6/17.
2 D. Goode, Cpl. T. 9200. M. May 5/17.
‡2 D. Lincoln, A. 8735. M. May 5-6/17.
‡2 D. McKinley, F. 41293. M. May 5/17.
‡2 D. Smith, T. 25645. M. May 5-6/17.
2 D. XIV Strolin, Fred. 25939. W. and M. Oct. 23/16. R/Enq.
2 D. XIV Stuart, R. 30172. M. May 5-6/17.
2 ? Tonner, Michael. 40031. K. Nov. 14/16. Det.D./B.
5 **Owen, 2nd Lt. J.** W. Unoff. M., bel. K. May 20/17.
5 A. Leggate, Wm. 238008. M. Feb. 14/17.
5 A. MacIsaac, Geo. I. 210229. (6631.) M. Feb. 14/17.
*5 C. XI Farish, Alfred. 200725. (7820.) W. Unoff. M. May 3/17.
5 D. Church, Albert Edward. 3604. M. Oct. 29/16. R/Enq.
5 D. Meikle, James. 201184. (Late 9212.) M. Oct. 29/16. R/Enq.
5 D. XIV Walker, L.Cpl. & S/B. Herbert Chas. 202388. M. April 14/17.
5 D. Webster, Wm. C. 1973. M. Nov. 6/16.
‡5 ? Ashton, W. Hay. 200493. (7086.) M. April 23/17.
5 ? M.G.S. Kinghorn, Thos. A. 200716. (7796.) K. April 23/17. Det.D./B. R/Enq.
*5 ? McGovern, L.-Cpl. Patrick. 1243. K. Oct. 28/16. Det.D./B.
*5/6 A. IV Berrie, Cpl. Wm. 200199. W. and M. May 20/17.
*5/6 A. IV Cameron, Wm. 201707. M. May 20/17.
‡5/6 A. Coe, H. 240956. M. May 20/17.
*5/6 A. III Dagg, L.-Cpl. John Hunter. 200516. (6511.) M. May 20/17.
*5/6 A. II Edwards, Alfred. 241109. M. May 27/17.
5/6 A. Kirkland, Cpl. Jack. 240267. (1947.) M. April 14/17.
‡5/6 A. Luke, G. B. 200729. M. May 27/17.
*5/6 A. II McDonald, William. 202276. (1528.) M. May 27/17.
*5/6 A. McLachlan, Robert. 201582. W. and M. May 3/17.
‡5/6 A. Ralston, R. 240522. W. and M. May 20/17.
‡5/6 A. Reilly, J. 203912. M. May 20/17.
*5/6 A. III Spencer, Hedley. 241028. M. May 20/17.
5/6 A. IV Storrie, L.-Cpl. John. 240363. M. May 20/17.
*5/6 A. IV Turner, Robert. 203809. (1527.) M. May 20/17.
‡5/6 A. Woodburn, James. 30069. M. May 27/17.
‡5/6 B. Arnott, W. 202150. M. May 27/17.
‡5/6 B. Barr, J. 200704. M. May 27/17.
*5/6 B. V Beighton, H. 241165. W. and M. May 20/17.
*5/6 B. VIII Bennett, James. 265273. (1567.) M. May 20/17.
‡5/6 B. Duff, R. 202260. M. May 27/17.

Scottish Rifles—contd.

*B.E.F.*

‡5/6 B. VI Dunlop, A. 200781. W. and M. May 20/17.
‡5/6 B. Gabriel, J. 29136. M. May 20/17.
‡5/6 B. Gilroy, J. 202282. W. and M. May 20/17.
*5/6 B. V Horsburgh, Alex. 202501. M. May 20/17.
‡5/6 B. Hughes, W. E. L. 241230. M. May 20/17.
*5/6 B. V Johnston, Gavin. 203910. (1538.) M. May 20/17.
*5/6 B. VIII Laing, John. 202337. W. and M. May 20/17.
‡5/6 B. Mills, G. 201646. M. May 20/17.
‡5/6 B. Robertson, J. 202224. M. May 20/17.
5/6 B. VIII Sproule, Wm. Alex. 20064. M. May 20/17.
*5/6 B. V White, Cpl. Robert. 200678. (7707.) W. and M. May 20/17.
‡5/6 C. Gray, J. L. 201688. M. May 20/17.
5/6 C. Krause, R. 202477. M. April 14/17.
5/6 C. Law, T. 240727. M. April 14/17.
*5/6 C. IX Stewart, Wm. 202190. (1362.) M. May 27/17.
5/6 D. XV Baynes, T. W. W. 202761. W. and M. April 14/17.
*5/6 D. XIII Collier, Vincent. 201797. (1718.) M. May 27/17.
5/6 D. Crawford, David. 202701. (2448.) W. and M. April 14/17.
*5/6 D. XIV Crombie, R. G. 202368. (1914.) W. and M. May 20/17.
5/6 D. XIII Cumming, E. 202254. W. and M. April 14/17.
*5/6 D. XV Gill, John. 30101. M. May 27/17.
‡5/6 D. Hall, P. 202778. M. May 20/17.
5/6 D. XIV Lawrie, Alex. 202391. W. and M. April 14/17.
‡5/6 D. Levick, R. 265546. M. May 20/17.
5/6 D. XV Robertson, Peter. 202294. W. and M. April 14/17.
‡5/6 D. Rodgers, A. 41480. M. May 20/17.
‡5/6 D. Sloan, J. 240807. M. May 20/17.
5/6 D. XVI Steele, W. 202308. W. and M. April 14/17.
‡5/6 ? Cooper, T. 201430. W. and M. May 20/17.
5/6 ? Wilkie, Alex. Stewart. 203916. (Fr. 5th. 1544.) M. April 14/17.
6 B. Clements, R. 241241. W. and M. April 14/17.
6 D. Jardine, D. B. 240112. W. and M. April 14/17.
9 **Boyd, 2nd Lieut. D. T.** M. May 3/17.
‡9 A. Bannon, J. 27819. W. and M. April 12/17.
9 A. I Darroch, Sig. Joseph. 24756. M. April 12/17.
‡9 A. Gillespie, W. 25100. M. May 3/17.
‡9 A. Grant, Daniel. 266396. W. Unoff. M. May 3/17.
9 A. Kerry, A. 17337. M. April 12/17.
*9 A. II Kirkcaldy, R. 28036. D/W. April 12/17. Det.D./B. R/Enq.
9 A. I Nugent, James. 7840. M. May 3/17.
9 A. Stoba, Robert. 40958. M. Unoff. W. April 9/17.
‡9 A. Tanner, J. 23696. M. May 3/17.
9 A. IV Watson, Wm. 40527. M. April 9-12/17.
9 B. VIII Gold, John. 19882. M. May 3/17.
*9 B. VII Laidlaw, Cpl. Robert. 30334. M. May 3/17.
*9 B. V Love, Wm. 25625. M. May 3/17.
9 B. McEwan, A. 43469. M. April 9/17.
*9 B. VII McGee, P. 26197. W. Unoff. M. May 3/17.
‡9 B. McKay, R. 239065. M. May 3/17.
*9 B. V McMeekin, Jas. 28402. K. April 9/17. Det.D./B.
‡9 B. McMillan, D. 7792. M. May 3/17.
9 B. VII McMurtrie, Tom. 41178. M. May 3/17.
9 B. V Rankin, Cpl. Fraser. 25821. M. April 11-12/17.
‡9 B. VII Scott, Sam. 238064. M. May 3/17.
*9 B. VIII Thompson, David. 266207. (3113.) M. May 3/17.
9 B. or D. VIII Wilson, A. M. 28040. M. May 3/17.

**Scottish Rifles—contd.**

## *B.E.F.*

‡9 B. Windle, Cpl. R. 18097. M. May 3/17.
‡9 C. Adam, Cpl. W. 30345. M. May 3/17.
‡9 C. Alston, A. 240449. M. May 3/17.
*9 C. Bannan, Joseph. 12256. M. May 3/17.
9 C. XI Barnes, Cpl. J. M. 265817. M. May 3/17.
‡9 C. Baverstock, C. 18288. M. May 3/17.
‡9 C. Betts, Cpl. Frederick. 10671. W. and M. April 12/17.
‡9 C. Bradshaw, W. 32904. M. May 3/17.
‡9 C. Cuthbertson, Cpl. W. 43372. M. May 3/17.
9 C. X Dalrymple, M. D. 4168. M. April 21/17.
9 C. Fairbairn, Peter. 30377. M. May 3/17.
‡9 C. Findlay, J. 7553. M. May 3/17.
‡9 C. Findlay, J. 11186. M. May 3/17.
9 C. IX Flannigan, Thos. W. Unoff. M. April 30/17.
9 C. XI Ford, John. 41480. W. Unoff. M. April 13/17.
‡9 C. Hamilton, C. 30364. M. May 3/17.
9 C. Hart, William. 30366. M. May 3/17.
9 C. IX Henry, Joe. 8907. M. May 3/17.
‡9 C. Logan, A. 40615. M. May 3/17.
‡9 C. IX McLeod, W. 25635. W. and M. April 12/17.
‡9 C. McCoombe, J. 40940. M. May 3/17.
‡9 C. McGrannaghan, J. 40948. M. May 3/17.
‡9 C. MacIntyre, A. 201102. M. May 3/17.
9 C. Matheson, Duncan. 40951. (Fr. H.Q.) M. April 12/17.
‡9 C. Marshall, L.-Sergt. A. 11932 M. May 3/17.
‡9 C. Morrison, R. 28667. M. May 3/17.
*9 C. X O'Neill, John. 8194. M. May 3/17.
9 C. X Robertson, John. 2845. Unoff. W. and M. April 30/17.
‡9 C. Rooney, J. 9906. M. May 3/17.
‡9 C. Spence, R. 17818. M. May 3/17.
*9 C. X Taylor, Archibald Auburn. 30360. M. May 3/17.
9 D. Bolstar, Cpl. J. 23697. M. May 3/17.
*9 D. XVI Craik, Cpl. J. 24768. M. May 3/17.
9 D. Eyres, Ernest. 14477. M. May 8-9/17.
‡9 D. Gentles, G. 27855. M. May 3/17.
‡9 D. XVI McCallum, William. 13470. W. and M. April 12/17.
‡9 D. McCulloch, D. 11779. M. May 3/17.
‡9 D. McLaughlin, W. 17445. M. May 3/17.
‡9 D. Miller, W. 43281. M. May 3/17.
‡9 D. Mullen, T. 24735. M. May 3/17.
‡9 D. Nicol, W. 240415. M. May 3/17.
‡9 D. Orr, A. 30513. M. May 3/17.
‡9 D. Robb, W. 43553. M. May 3/17.
‡9 D Watt, L.-Cpl. G. 43342. M. May 3/17.
10 A. Douglas, W. 200071. M. April 23-26/17.
†10 A. Grimlay, P. 23793. M. April 24/17.
10 A. M.G.S. Lawson, Mathew. 18396. W. and M. April 24/17.
10 A. I Terrace, L.-Cpl. Wm. Eglinton. 41145 W. and M. April 9/17.
10 B. Ewing, L.-Cpl. A. 12658. M. Mar. 24/17.
*10 B. VIII McParlane, James. 23051. M. April 26/17.
10 C. Adams, Alfred (Scout). 13822. M. Sept. 25/16. R/Enq.
‡10 D. Clark, G. 40255. M. April 24/17.
10 D. XV Boyle, Andrew. 28715. M. Mar. 24/17.
10 D. XIV Collins, Hugh. A/7665. W. and M. April 24/17.
10 D. King, M. 18374. M. April 23-26/17.
10 D. XVI Moyes, Jas. H. 25509. M. April 23-26/17.
‡10 D. Russell, J. 41324. M. April 24/17.

Scottish Rifles—contd.

## BALKANS.

| | | |
|---|---|---|
| 11 | **Cooper, Lieut. O. H. D.** (Fr. 6th H.L.I.) | W. and M. **May 8-9/17.** |
| 11 | **Hepner, 2nd Lieut. H.** | M. **May 9/17.** |
| ‡11 | **McGhee, Capt. H.** | K. **May 8/17.** Conf. and Det.D./B |
| 11 | **Mitchell, Lieut, J. M.** | M. **May 9/17.** |
| 11 1 II | Bonner, Alex. 26596. | M. **May 8-9/17.** |
| 11 1 II | Kerr, Joseph. 7879. | W. and M. **May 8-9/17.** |
| *11 1 II | Neilson, J. S. 24806. | W. and M. **June 3/17.** |
| 11 1 I | White, John. 20050. | M. **May 8-9/17.** |
| 11 1 I | Young, L.-Cpl. Alex. 14675. | M. **May 8-9/17.** |
| 11 2 VIII | McDougall, Frank. 26207. | W. and M. **May 8-9/17.** |
| 11 2 | Neison, Thos. 28374. | M. **May 8-9/17.** |
| *11 3 | Bain, Alexander. 26667. | W. and M. **May 8-9/17.** |
| 11 3 | Smith, John. 14628. | W. and M. **May 8-9/17.** |
| 11 4 | McGucken, Michael. 14512. | M. **May 8-9/17.** |
| 11 4 XV | Reid, D. 27540. | M. **May 8-9/17.** |
| 11 4 XIII | Rhinds, John. 28453. | M. **May 8-9/17.** |
| 11 ? | Boak, J. 30522. | M. **May 8-9/17.** |
| 11 ? | Bonner, A. 14518. | W. and M. **May 8-9/17.** |
| 11 ? | Burns, R. 30543. | W. and M. **May 8-9/17.** |
| 11 ? | Clark, R. 19652. | M. **May 8-9/17.** |
| 11 ? | Cooper, F. 8579. | M. **May 8-9/17.** |
| 11 ? | Edgley, A. 17503. | M. **May 8-9/17.** |
| 11 ? | Eyre, E. 14477. | M. **May 8-9/17.** |
| 11 ? | Finch, F. 23568. | M. **May 8-9/17.** |
| 11 ? | Gallagher, D. 15408. | M. **May 8-9/17.** |
| 11 ? | Gemmell, J. 14429. | M. **May 8-9/17.** |
| 11 ? | Hails, M. 14445. | M. **May 8-9/17.** |
| *11 ? | Hall, Cpl. J. 25544 | W. and M. **June 3/17.** |
| 11 ? | Hastings, H. 28169. | M. **May 8-9/17.** |
| *11 ? | Hunter, L.-Cpl. W. 15434. | W. and M. **June 3/17.** |
| 11 ? | Kelly, J. 4964. | M. **May 8-9/17.** |
| 11 ? | Little, G. 28284. | W. and M. **May 8-9/17.** |
| 11 ? | Loyden, M. 26607. | W. and M. **May 8-9/17.** |
| 11 ? | McDonald, J. 28599. | W. and M. **May 8-9/17.** |
| 11 ? | McLatchie, J. 14427. | W. and M. **May 8-9/17.** |
| ‡11 ? | Marshall, R. 28359. | W. and M. **May 8-9/17.** |
| 11 ? | Mathie, J. 23121. | W. and M. **May 8-9/17.** |
| 11 ? | Nelson, A.-Sergt. T. 11828. | M. **April 24-25/17.** |
| 11 ? | Parker, J. 28664. | M. **May 8-9/17.** |
| 11 ? | Quinn, F. 28353. | M. **May 8-9/17.** |
| 11 ? | Robertson, J. 28131. | M. **May 8-9/17.** |
| 11 ? | Simpson, D. 14435. | W. and M. **May 8-9/17.** |
| 11 ? | Smith, W. 14951. | M. **May 8-9/17.** |
| 11 ? | Wilson, W. 28451. | M. **May 8-9/17.** |
| 11 ? | Wyness, J. 25762. | M. **May 8-9/17.** |

## E.E.F.

| | | |
|---|---|---|
| 8 Y. X | Aitken, A. 291125. | M. **April 19/17.** |
| 8 Y. IX | Hannah, Wm. 202971. | M. **April 19/17.** |
| 8 Y. XI | Naylor, Arthur. 290407. (7656.) | M. **April 19/17.** |
| 8 Z. | Martin, Arthur. 290707. (374.) | M. **April 19/17.** |
| 8 ? | Baxter, W. 291247. | M. **April 19/17.** |

**Scottish Rifles—contd.**

## *E.E.F.*

| | | |
|---|---|---|
| 8 ? | Day, P. 203019. | M. April 19/17. |
| ‡8 ? | Dunbar, J. 203001. | M. April 19/17. |
| 8 ? | Lynch, H. 291579. | M. April 19/17. |
| 8 ? | McDermott, J. 291608. | M. April 19/17. |
| 8 ? | Monaghan, J. 203076. | M. April 19/17. |
| 8 ? | Taylor, L.-Cpl. H. 290249. | M. April 19/17. |
| 8 ? | Thompson, A. 290479. | M. April 19/17. |

# SEAFORTH HIGHLANDERS.

## *B.E.F.*

| | | |
|---|---|---|
| 2 | **Dawson, 2nd Lieut. Wm.** | M. April 11/17. |
| 2 C. | **Grove, Lieut. P. C.** | K. April 11/17. Det.D./B. |
| 2 | **Macauley, 2nd Lieut. B. W.** | M. May 3/17. |
| 2 C. | **Macmillan, 2nd Lieut. R. A. C.** | K. April 11/17. Det.D./B. |
| 2 A. | Bruce, Robert. 14943. | M. April 11/17. |
| 2 A. | Burns, Joseph. 6114. | M. July 1/16. R/Enq. |
| *2 A. | Gentles, Wm. S/1649. | M. April 11/17. |
| ‡2 A. | Hague, H. J. 5582. | M. May 3/17. |
| 2 A. | Lewis, Wm. Henry. 7640. | M. May 3/17. |
| ‡2 A. | McIver, J. 17592. | M. May 3/17. |
| 2 A. IV | McNeill, Michael. 40618. | M. April 11/17. |
| 2 B. | Cameron, Sgt. Allen. 40521. | K. April 11/17. Det.D./B. |
| 2 B. | Dawson, C. 40528. | W. and M. April 11/17. |
| 2 B. | Ewen, L.-Sergt. George. 43088. | K. April 11/17. Det.D./B. |
| *2 B. VII | Galbraith, J. Magill. S/40512. | K. April 11/17. Det.D./B. |
| ‡2 B. | Graham, K. 16327. | M. May 3/17. |
| 2 B. | Laing, Sergt. Joseph. 1183. | W. and M. April 11/17. |
| 2 B. | McDonald, Angus. 7138. | M. April 11/17. |
| 2 B. | McGillivray, J. 7854. | M. April 11/17. |
| 2 B. | McIntosh, T. 10444. | W. and M. April 11/17. |
| 2 B. | MacKay, Christopher G. 16373. | W. and M. April 11/17. |
| ‡2 B. | McNaughton, W. 10228. | M. April 11/17. |
| ‡2 B. XIII | Montgomery, L.-Cpl. A. 40511. | M. May 3/17. |
| 2 B. VI | Nicolson, Cpl. Robert. 10252. | M. April 11/17. |
| 2 B. | Pollock, A. 147. | W. and M. April 11/17. |
| 2 B. or D. | Wardrop, Angus. 40636. | M. May 3/17. |
| 2 B. | Work, W. 13696. | M. April 11/17. |
| 2 C. | Beattie, W. 43120. | M. April 11/17. |
| ‡2 C. | Bews, J. 14935. | M. May 3/17. |
| 2 C. X | Fletcher, David. 8835. | W. and M. April 11/17. |
| 2 C. | Greenock, James. S/16286. | M. May 3/17. |
| ‡2 C. | Kennedy, D. 450. | M. May 3/17. |
| 2 C. IX | McAllister, Wm. John. 10608. | W. and M. April 11/17. |
| ‡2 C. XII | McLeod, James. 5360. | M. May 3/17. |
| ‡2 C. | Mitchell, G. 43155. | M. May 3/17. |
| 2 C. | Morris, J. 43185. | M. April 11/17. |
| 2 C. IX | Murray, Thos. 10776. | M. Oct. 14/16. R/Enq. |
| ‡2 C. | Rankin, D. 7887. | M. May 3/17. |
| ‡2 C. | Scott, L.-Cpl. D. 9554. | M. May 3/17. |
| ‡2 C. | Wilson, Sergt. J. 10458. | M. May 3/17. |
| ‡2 D. | Anderson, J. 10655. | M. May 3/17. |

**Seaforth Highlanders—contd.**

## *B.E.F.*

| | | | |
|---|---|---|---|
| ‡2 D. | | Bloomfield, P. E. 10646. | M. May 3/17. |
| ‡2 D. | | McCaskie, Cpl. J. 7142. | M. May 3/17. |
| ‡2 D. | | McDonald, L.-Cpl. J. 5391. | M. May 3/17. |
| ‡2 D. | | McLeod, J. 7438. | M. May 3/17. |
| 2 D. | XV | Mitchell, Jas. S/43093. | M. May 3/17. |
| ‡2 D. | | Pow, R. 273. | M. May 3/17. |
| ‡2 D. | | Shepherd, E. 9896. | M. May 3/17. |
| ‡2 D. | XV M.G.S. | Sinclair, L.-Cpl. A. A. 7448. | M. May 3/17. |
| 2 D. | | Wilson, L.-Cpl. John. 5705. | M. May 3/17. |
| 2 H.Q. Sig. | | Sadler, W. 10221. | M. April 11/17. |
| ‡4 1 | | Cronin, C. 200694. | M. May 3/17. |
| *4 1 | | Foster, John Francis. 200754. | M. April 23-24/17. |
| ‡4 1 | | Henderson, T. R. 40829. | M. April 23-24/17. |
| 4 2 | | Alston, James. 202438. | W. Unoff. M. April 22-24/17. |
| 4 3 | X | Sneddon, Wm. 202270. (Fr. 4th.) | M. April 23/17. |
| 5 A. | | Banks, G. 241998. | M. April 9/17. |
| 5 B. | L.G.S. | Glover, L.-Cpl. G. 241327. (Late 4759.) | W. and M. April 9/17. |
| 5 C. | | Hamill, J. 241056. | M. April 9/17. |
| ‡6 A. | II | Adams, James. 285251. | M. May 12-16/17. |
| ‡6 A. | | Anderson, A. L. 285243. | M. May 12-16/17. |
| *6 A. | II | Fraser, S. 267406. | M. May 11-16/17. |
| 6 A. | II | Fowler, L.-Cpl. W. L. B. 265632. | W. and M. May 12-16/17. |
| ‡6 A. | | Heggie, W. 285109. | M. May 12-16/17. |
| *6 A. | I | Hilton, Alfred. 1978. | M. May 15-16/17. |
| ‡6 A. | II | Hunter, Robt. 285029. (Fr. A. & S. Highlanders.) | M. May 12-16/17. |
| 6 A. | IV | Milligan, A. W. 266903. | W. and M. May 12-16/17. |
| 6 A. | IV | Moir, Wm. 276407. | M. April 9/17. |
| ‡6 A. | | Morrison, M. 267468. | M. May 12-16/17. |
| ‡6 A. | | Muschamp, J. C. V. 265605. | M. May 12-16/17. |
| *6 A. | II | Neilson, Alex. 285078. | W. and M. May 12-16/17. |
| ‡6 A. | | Steele, O. 266616. | M. April 23-25/17. |
| ‡6 A. | | Walker, A. 265407. | M. April 23-25/17. |
| 6 A. | IV | Young, Wm. 267474. | W. and M. May 12-16/17. |
| ‡6 C. | | McDonald, Archibald. 41017. | W. and M. May 12-16/17. |
| 6 C. | | Munro, G. 285478. | W. and M. April 9/17. |
| 6 C. | XII | Murfitt, L.-Sergt. A. 265628. | K. May 14-16/17. Det.D./B. |
| *6 D. | XIV | Cormack, F. S. 235030. | K. May 15/17. Det.D./B. |
| 7 A. | I | Kinninburgh, L.-Cpl. Thos. 9714. | W. and M. April 9/17. |
| 7 C. | IX | Brine, L.-Cpl. Hume McKenzie. 12647 | M. Oct. 12/16. R/Enq. |
| ‡7 C. | | Scorgie, A. 9450. | M. May 8/17. |
| 7 C. | XI | Smith, George. 11149. | M. Oct. 14/16. R/Enq. |
| ‡7 C. | | Stevenson, R. 5788. | M. May 8/17. |
| ‡7 D. | | Cooper, A. 8654. | W. and M. May 2/17. |
| 7 D. | | Cowe, John. 6670. | M. May 1/17. |
| 7 D. | XIII | Mitchell, Cpl. Gideon Gray. 1182. | M. May 2/17. |
| ‡7 D. | | Thomas, W. 12777. | M. April 30/17. |
| ‡8 | | **Mackenzie, 2nd Lt. A.** (Fr. 3rd.) | M. July 8/17. |
| ‡8 A. | III | Lamb, William. 10799. | K. April 9/17. Det.D./B. |
| 8 B. | | Clark, Wm. 8985. | K. April 24/17. Det.D./B. |
| 8 B. | | Martin, W. 40904. | M. April 23/17. |
| ‡8 C. | X | Corden, Isaac. 12757. | K. April 23/17 Conf. and Det.D./B. |

## BALKANS.

| | | |
|---|---|---|
| ‡1 Garr. A. | Millar, J. 17481. | M. June 20/17. |
| ‡1 „ A. II | Morrison, L.-Cpl. Geo. 15197. | M. June 20/17. |
| ‡1 „ B. | Wilson, Sergt. Jas. 17093. (Fr. H.L.I., 27690.) | M. June 20/17. |
| ‡1 „ C. XI | Dishart, John. 15301. | M. June 20/17. |
| ‡1 „ ? | Callaghan, P. 17766. | M. June 20/17. |
| ‡1 „ ? | Campbell, K. 17485. | M. June 20/17. |
| ‡1 „ ? | Campbell, N. 7096. | M. June 20/17. |
| ‡1 „ ? | Craig, J. 15343. | M. June 20/17. |
| ‡1 „ ? | M.G.S. Craig, John. 15342. | M. June 20/17. |
| ‡1 „ ? | Hadfield, S. 15545. | M. June 20/17. |
| ‡1 „ ? | Kimble, A. 14799. | M. June 20/17. |
| ‡1 „ ? | McDowell, J. 14610. | M. June 20/17. |

## PERSIAN GULF.

| | | |
|---|---|---|
| 1 A. | Campbell, Kenneth McIntyre. 9057. | M. April 22/16. |
| 1 A. II | Russell, Wm. S/11780. | D/W. Jan. 25/17. Det.D./B. |
| ‡1 B. | Bailey, F. W. 10063. | W. and M. April 22/17. |
| 1 C. | McDougall, D.C.M., L.-Cpl. Wm. 798. | K. Feb. 22/17. Det.D./B. |
| 1 C. | Rae, David. 10269. | M. Jan. 7/16. R/Enq. |
| 1 ? | Donnelly, F. 8098. | W. and M. April 22/16. |
| ‡1 ? | Graham, A. 7237. | M. April 21/17. |
| 1 ? | Haston, A. 4254. | W. and M. April 24/16. |
| 1 ? | Robertson, E. 13265. | M. Mar. 30/17. |

# SHERWOOD FORESTERS.

## B.E.F.

| | | |
|---|---|---|
| 1 A. or D. | Adams, B. W. 13645. | W. and M. Mar. 4/17. |
| 1 A. | Mossop, W. 73146. | W. and M. Nov. 10/16. |
| 1 A. | Saint, M. 71188. | W. and M. Mar. 4/17. |
| 1 A. | Thomas, E. 51945. | W. and M. Mar. 4/17. |
| 1 B. | Baxter, L.-Cpl. H. 24706. | M. Mar. 4/17. |
| 1 B. V | Bye, L.-Cpl. Harry. 32472. | W. and M. Unoff. K. Mar. 4/17. Conf. and details. |
| 1 B. VII | Shadlock, A. E. 80051. | W. and M. April 13/17. |
| 1 C. | Bosworth, L.-Cpl. Edwin. 71170. | W. and M. Mar. 4/17. |
| 1 C. XI | Leedham, Ernest. 58709. | W. and M. April 14/17. |
| 1 C. | Mazillins, H. E. 80025. | M. April 5/17. |
| 1 C. | Swann, J. H. 05610. | M. April 5/17. |
| 1 C. X | Taylor, Wallace Hry. 78254. | M. April 14/17. |
| 1 D. | Colves, F. 10131. | W. and M. Mar. 4/17. |
| 1 D. XVI | Hallam, A. 43680. | M. Mar. 4/17. |
| *1 H.Q. | Bird, J. E. 10404. | M. May 5/17. |
| 2 C. | Cutts, F. 24347. | W. and M. Sept. 13/16. |
| 2 D. | Brown, Sidney. 18554. | M. Sept. 15/16. |

**Sherwood Foresters—contd.**

*B.E.F.*

| | | |
|---|---|---|
| 2 D. | Hatfield, L.-Cpl. Frank. 34407. | W. and M. Oct. 11/16. |
| ‡2 D. | Slaney, John. 70688. (Fr. 6th.) | W. and M. Oct. 16/16. R/Enq. |
| 2 D. | Williams, John. 57241. | M. Sept. 15/16. R./Enq. |
| ‡5 | **Coles, Capt. H. J.** | W. and M. June 30—July 3/17. |
| ‡5 C. | **Loney, 2nd Lieut. R.** | W. and M. June 30—July 3/17. |
| ‡5 | **Martin, 2nd Lieut. R. F.** | M. July 1/17. |
| 5 | **Stone, Capt. A.** | M. April 29/17. |
| ‡5 C. | Till, G. 201363. | M. April 29/17. |
| ‡5 C. | Spray, J. W. 203459. | M. April 29/17. |
| ‡5 D. | Lilley, Thos. Arthur. 2403. | Unoff. M. July 1/17. |
| 2/5 | **Alliban, Lieut. W. B.** | M. May 4/17. |
| 2/5 A. II | Sainsbury, Geo. Harvey. 202974. (6521.) | M. May 4/17. |
| ‡2/5 B. | Cockroft, F. 202363. | M. May 4/17. |
| ‡2/5 B. | Eaton, H. 201878. | M. May 5/17. |
| 2/5 B. VI | Jones, Chas. 202849. | W. and M. May 5/17. |
| 2/5 B. | Keeling, Cpl. Alfred. 200926. | M. May 5/17. |
| 2/5 B. VI | Lewis, Arthur Gordon. 202892. | W. and M. May 5/17. |
| ‡2/5 B. | Potter, Sergt. R. J. 200206. | W. and M. May 3/17. |
| ‡2/5 B. | Smith, E. 202040. | M. May 5/17. |
| 2/5 B. VI | Taylor, Wm. 202120. | W. and M. May 5/17. |
| 2/5 B. | Wood, L.-Cpl. J. 200854. | M. May 3/17. |
| 2/5 C. IX | Bedding, L.-Cpl. Walter Richard. 202848. | M. May 3-4/17. |
| ‡2/5 C. | Guinan, M. J. 201866. | M. May 4/17. |
| ‡2/5 C. | Lewis, L.-Cpl. H. 201944. | M. May 4/17. |
| 2/5 D. | Andrews, F. D. 202809. (6354.) | M. Unoff. K. May 5/17. |
| ‡2/5 D. | Bailey, F. J. 201182. | M. May 4/17. |
| ‡2/5 D. | Caulton, L. 202024. | M. May 4/17. |
| ‡2/5 D. | Dickson, O. B. 203556. | W. and M. May 5/17. |
| 2/5 D. | Ecol, Wm. Henry. 203538. | M. May 5/17. |
| 6 | **Brown, Lieut. C. A.** | W. and M. April 23/17. |
| ‡6 | **Dolley, 2nd Lieut. R. C. F.** | M. July 1/17. |
| 6 C. XI | Birley, B. 240392. | M. April 23/17. |
| 2/6 A. | Bayston, F. 241901. | M. April 7/17. |
| 2/6 A. | Wildgoose, Cpl. Rich. 241620. | W. and M. April 27/17. |
| 2/6 C. XV | Old, Sergt. Charles. 2705. | Unoff. W. and M. April 21/17. |
| ‡2/6 D. | Lomas, C.-S.-M. S. H. 241062. | W. and M. April 27/17. |
| 2/6 D. | Piller, F. 242181. (5945.) | M. April 27/17. |
| ‡7 A. | Harvey, C. C. 269807. | M. May 19/17. |
| ‡7 B. V | Baird, William. 8411. | W. and M. Oct. 12/16. R/Enq. |
| *7 D. L.G.S. | Knight, Jas. Chas. 269848. (20636.) | K. May 15/17. Det.D./B. |
| 2/7 | **Downer, 2nd Lt. F. (Fr. 5 Manc.)** | M. April 2/17. |
| 2/7 C. X | Turton, L.-Cpl. Chas. Saml. 265663. (Late 2761.) | W. and M. April 2/17. |
| 2/7 C. IX | Whittaker, Herbert. 266872. (5431.) | M. April 2/17. |
| 8 | **Duff, M.C., 2nd Lieut. W. P.** | M. April 23/17. |
| 8 | **Hopkinson, 2nd Lieut. E.** | M. about April 23/17. |
| *8 A. II | Harrison, L.-Cpl. Henry. 305299. | W. and M. May 30/17. |
| 8 C. | Allwood, Horace. 305549. | M. April 23/17. |
| 8 C. X | Barrett, Sig. Geo. Wm. 307528. | M. April 23/17. |
| 8 C. XII | Barwise, W. 307666. | M. April 23/17. |
| 8 C. | Bowler, J. 305135. | M. April 23/17. |
| 8 C. | Boyce, W. 306963. | M. April 23/17. |
| 8 C. | Bramley, W. 306019. | M. April 23/17. |

**Sherwood Foresters—contd.**

## *B.E.F.*

8 C. IX Brotherhood, N. B. 307617. M. April 23/17.
8 C. Brown, C. 307612. M. April 23/17.
8 C. XII Buzan, H. E. 307559. M. April 23/17.
8 C. Calvert, H. 307548. M. April 23/17.
8 C. Clougher, J. 307609. M. April 23/17.
8 C. Cobb, W. C. 305333. M. April 23/17.
8 C. L.G.S. Curtis, Sergt. John Wm. 305401. (2250.) M. April 22/17.
8 C. IX Ellis, Alfred. 306955. M. April 23/17.
8 C. IX Farrand, F. 307655. (6702.) M. April 23/17.
8 C. IX Frost, John Ernest. 306021. (3246.) M. April 23/17.
8 C. IX Gammage, Fredk. 305874. (2989.) M. April 23/17.
8 C. XI Garbett, G. 305026. M. April 23/17.
8 C. L.G.S. Goodacre, E. 306098. M. April 23/17.
8 C. Graham, L.-Cpl. J. 305258. M. April 23/17.
8 C. XII Hewson, E. R. 307696. (6268.) M. April 23/17.
8 C. XII Hinchley, L.-Cpl. J. 307675. M. April 23/17.
8 C. Hitchcock, E. 307560. M. April 23/17.
8 C. X Hodgkinson, Sam. 307587. M. April 23/17.
8 C. X Holwell, James. 305848. M. April 23/17.
8 C. Jones, T. H. 267165. M. April 23/17.
8 C. Kirkwood, Samuel. 307626. M. April 23/17.
8 C. Lee, T. 307698. M. April 23/17.
8 C. IX Mallinson, V. 307583. (20069.) M. April 23/17
8 C. Marshall, J. 306408. M. April 23/17.
8 C. Miller, G. 305715. M. April 23/17.
8 C. Moore, W. 307627. M. April 23/17.
8 C. IX Morley, H. A. 307589. M. April 23/17.
8 C. XII Osborne, L.-Cpl. C. 305200. M. April 23/17.
8 C. Partridge, J. H. 307064. M. April 23/17.
8 C. Peatfield, J. 305288. M. April 23/17.
8 C. Phillips, F. 307664. M. April 23/17.
8 C. Proctor, A. 307569. M. April 23/17.
8 C. XII Rawding, Harry. 70030. M. April 23/17.
8 C. XI Robinson, E. 307519. M. April 23/17.
8 C. Sansom, Sergt. H. 307068. M. April 23/17.
8 C. Scott, R. 13356. M. April 23/17.
8 C. Smedley, Saml. 305205. M. April 23/17.
8 C. Smith, B. 305535. M. April 23/17.
8 C. IX Smith, F. 18071. M. April 23/17.
8 C. X Smith, Geo. H. 70053. M. April 23/17.
8 C. Steele, W. 306132. M. April 23/17.
8 C. IX Street, Cpl. Wm. 305595. M. April 23/17.
8 C. Toplis, B. 307561. M. April 23/17.
8 C. Vacey, L.-Cpl. R. 305887. M. April 23/17.
8 C. Wall, C. 307562. M. April 23/17.
8 C. Ward, L.-Cpl. W. 306349. M. April 23/17.
8 C. White, J. W. 305726. M. April 23/17.
8 C. XII White, W. H. 307358. (20023.) M. April 23/17.
8 C. Willmott, L. S. 306395. M. April 23/17.
‡2/8 A. Buxton, C. O. 306326. M. April 29/17.
‡2/8 A. Cook, F. 306858. M. April 27/17.
2/8 A. Corbett, G. 305765. (2783.) M. and W. April 27/17.
2/8 A. I Dixon, John Wm. 307189. M. April 27/17.
‡2/8 A. Eyley, L.-Sergt. A. 305967. M. April 27/17.
2/8 A. III Harrison, L.-Cpl. Simon. 306280. M. April 27/17.
2/8 A. III Laver, Arthur. 307005. M. April 27/17.
‡2/8 A. II Spencer, A. 307470. K. April 27/17. Det.D./B.
*2/8 A. III Thompson, Fredk. 306532. W. and M. April 27/17.

**Sherwood Foresters—contd.**

## *B.E.F.*

|  |  |  |
|---|---|---|
| 2/8 B. | McDermott, Victor E. 307207. (Late 5868.) | K. April 7/17. Det.D./B. |
| 2/8 B. VII | Poole, J. W. 305341. (2008.) | M. April 7/17. |
| 2/8 B. | Reeves, W. 307175. | M. April 7/17. |
| 2/8 B. VII | Rose, F. 307389. (6099.) | M. April 7/17. |
| 2/8 B. | Tombs, G. H. 307347. | M. April 7/17. |
| 9 B. | Burrows, J. 22680. | M. Sept. 26/16. R/Enq. |
| ‡9 C. XII | Goatham, Stanley W. 269860. | K. April 24/17. Det.D./B. |
| ‡9 D. XV | Smith, Samuel Henry. 28648. | K. June 10/17. Det.D./B. |
| 9 D. XIV | Youson, G. 13122. | W. and M. Sept. 26/16. R/Enq. |
| ‡9 ? | Barker, W. 71022. | M., bel. K. June 7/17. |
| 10 A. | Beckett, W. H. 50417. | M. April 23/17. |
| 10 A. | Lowe, L.-Cpl. F. 22193. | M. April 23/17. |
| 10 B. | Baxter, G. 31852. | W. and M. April 23/17. |
| 10 B. VI | Bradley, John Wm. 54133. | W. and M. April 23/17. |
| 10 B. V | Dorn, C. H. 19716. | W. and M. April 23/17. |
| 10 B. | Ryan, Sergt. J. 14951 | W. and M. April 23/17. |
| 10 B. M.G.S. | Scott, L.-Cpl. W. 25860. | M. April 23/17. |
| 10 B. VII | Self, W. J. 58959. | W. and M. April 23/17. |
| 10 D. XVI | Ackstine, Solomon. 80076. | M. April 23/17. |
| 10 D. | Green, Sig. J. W. 49398. | M. April 23/17. |
| ‡11 A. II | Cox, H. 71853. | M. June 7/17. |
| 11 A. III | Parnham, Ernest. 32216. | M. Oct. 1/16. R./Enq. |
| ‡11 A. II | Steeper, C. 71844. | M. June 7/17. |
| ‡11 C. XII | Brown, Herbert J. 73202. | W. and M. Oct. 1/16. R/Enq. |
| ‡11 C. | Pumley, B. 71814. | M. June 7/17. |
| *‡11 C. X | Rockley, G. 57678. | W. Unoff. M. June 7/17. |
| 11 C. XII | Wragg, George. 70545. | W. and Unoff. M. April 9/17. |
| ‡11 D. XV | Crozier, Percy. 45645. | M. June 7/17. |
| ‡12 D. XVI | Plucknett, Wm. Geo. 76486. | K. June 8/17. Det.D./B. |
| ‡15 W. II | Brown, G. E. 27856. | M. May 15-16/17. |
| ‡15 W. | Eaton, K. 33017. | M. May 15-16/17. |
| ‡15 W. | Gregory, Sergt. A. 28279. | M. May 15-16/17. |
| 15 W. II | Sylvester, Tom. 31222. | W. and M. May 15-16/17. |
| 15 X. | Brooks, Sgt. Walter. 24113. | M., bel. K. May 9/17. |
| ‡15 X. | Burton, S. 23862. | M. May 15-16/17. |
| ‡15 X. | Hinton, L.-Cpl. W. 24005. | W. and M. May 9/17. |
| ‡15 X. | Renshaw, R. 31413. | W. and M. May 15-16/17. |
| 15 X. | Rowley, Sergt. W. 82007. | M. May 15-17/17. |
| ‡16 A. | Charles, B. 70555. | M. May 28/17. |
| 16 B. VIII | Taylor, Fred. 26497. | M. Oct. 9/16. R/Enq. |
| 16 C. XI | Brewin, Cpl. H. J. 19343. | M. Oct. 9-10/16. R/Enq. |
| 16 C. | Holmes, J. 70129. | M. Oct. 8-10/16. R./Enq. |
| 16 C. | Plant, Harold. 26534. | M. Sept. 3/16. R/Enq. |
| 17 A. | Shaw, Cpl. Henry Basil. 27557. | M. Sept. 3/16. R/Enq. |
| 17 A. | Thacker, Sgt. John Albert. 27524. | M. Sept. 3/16. R/Enq. |
| 17 B. | Hunt, L.-Cpl. Frederick. 28068. | M. Sept. 3/16. R/Enq. |
| ‡17 B. VI | Pickin, Phillip. 18711. (Fr. 13th.) | M. Sept. 3/16. R/Enq. |
| 17 B. | Sharpe, Wm. 42786. | M. Sept. 3/16. R/Enq. |
| 17 B. or C. | Smith, Albert. 28173. | M. Sept. 3/16. R/Enq. |
| 17 C. | Bardill, Percy. 31999. | M. Sept. 3/16. R/Enq. |
| 17 C. | Mills, Harry. 30636. | M. Sept. 3/16. R/Enq. |
| *17 C. XI | Orr, Frank James. 26956. | M. Sept. 3/16. R/Enq. |
| 17 C. L.G.S. | Peet, James John. 28500. | M. Sept. 3/16. R/Enq. |
| 17 C. X | Phillips, R. B. 31288. | M. Sept. 3/16. R/Enq |
| 17 D. | Heath, Thos. Percival. 28795. | M. Sept. 3/16. R/Enq. |
| 17 D. XIII | Trivett, Charles R. 13708. | M. Sept. 3/16. R/Enq. |
| 17 D. XIV | Wilcox, Cpl. Ernest. 30556. | W. and M. Sept. 3/16. R/Enq. |

**SHERWOOD RANGERS (Nottinghamshire Yeomanry.)**

*BALKANS.*

? **Squad.** Morris, G. L. 2653. W. and M. **Oct. 7/16.**

**SHROPSHIRE LIGHT INFANTRY.**

*B.E.F.*

‡1 **Davies, 2nd Lieut. J. G.** W. and M. **June 1/17.**
1 A. IV Cooper, J. E. 22484. K. **April 18/17.** Det.D./B.
‡1 A. Gibson, C. 18822. M. **June 1/17.**
‡1 A. Hallam, J. 33185. M. **June 1/17.**
‡1 A. I Link Cpl. Francis. 23601. (Fr. 3 Herefords.) M. **June 1/17.**
‡1 A. I Mather, William. 203792. W. and M. **June 1/17.**
‡1 A. Mather, W. 204497. M. **June 1/17.**
‡1 A. Mellon, Thomas. 27048. K. **May 29/17.** Det.D./B.
‡1 A. Morris, L.-Cpl. W. E. 12970. M. **June 4/17.**
•1 A. Owens, Albert Victor. 204449. M. **June 1/17.**
‡1 B. Leighton, T. 18216. M. **June 1/17.**
‡1 C. XII Lawens, Robert. 27064. M. **June 1/17.**
‡1 C. Sambrook, C. 21316. M. **June 1/17.**
‡1 C. Titley, G. 23626. M. **June 1/17.**
1 D. XV Butler, E. W. 18994. M. **Sept. 18/16.** R/Enq.
•1 D. XIV Caswell, Cpl. Isaac. 18674. M. **June 1/17.**
‡1 D. XIV Chappell, H. 24373. M. **June 1/17.**
‡1 D. Pearce, T. 11437. W. and M. **Sept. 18/16.** R/Enq.
5 **Lee, 2nd Lieut. P. W.** K. **April 8/17.** Det.D./B.
5 A. Bullock, Sergt. Wm. 11045. W. and M. **Sept. 16/16.** R/Enq.
‡5 A. Lloyd, Richard. 6446. W. and M. **Sept. 16/16.** R/Enq.
5 B. Fryer, F. W. 8795. M. **May 3/17.**
•5 B. VIII Sale, Wm. 24376. M. **May 3/17.**
5 C. Aldred, W. G. 20821. W. and M. **April 8/17.**
5 C. X Potter, J. 20836. W. and M. **Mar. 19/17.**
5 C. Walker, R. 26212. W. and M. **Sept. 16/16.** R/Enq.
•5 D. Jones, Arthur. 10921. W. and M. **May 3/16.** R/Enq
‡5 D. Lawley, A.-Cpl. J. 11508. W. and M. **May 3/17.**
‡5 ? Rookes, Jas. Herbert. 204115. (2/4 Glosters, 201109.) K. **April 27/17.** Det.D./B.
7 A. III Burgoyne, L.-Cpl. Wm. Leonard. 18690. W. and M. **May 3/17.**
7 A. Daniels, Wilfred. 26305. M. **Nov. 13/16.** R/Enq.
7 A. Gould, L.-Cpl. S. 24310. M. **April 9/17.**
7 A. II James, L.-Cpl. R. H. 20992. W. and M. **Mar. 9/17.**
7 B. Edwards, E. 13634. W. and M. **April 9/17.**
•7 B. Edwards, William Hy. 23735. M. **Nov. 13/16.** R/Enq.
7 B. Hull, R. 26992. M. **May 5/17.**
7 B. VII Morgate, Cpl. F. 20355. M. **April 9/17.**
7 B. VII Murray, Harry. 22495. M. **April 9/17.**
7 B. Roberts, W. H. 26346. M. **Nov. 13/16.** R/Enq.
7 B. VII Rowley, W. Harry. 24742. W. and M. **April 9/17.**
‡7 B. Taylor, Cpl. W. 26986. W. and M. **May 3/17.**
•7 C. Andrews, W. C. 22109. M. **May 3/17.**
7 C. XI Bowen, L.-Cpl. Chas. 14740. Unoff. M. **May 3/17.**
7 C. Steadman, C. 14069. K. **Nov. 13/16.** Det.D./B. R/Enq.
7 D. Davies, E. G. 19728. W. and M. **April 9/17.**

**Shropshire Light Infantry**—contd.

## *BALKANS.*

| | | |
|---|---|---|
| 8 C. | **Ebdon, 2nd Lt. W. S.** (Fr. 11 Glos.) | M. **May 15/17.** |
| 8 C. XII* | Gough, Alan. 24047. | K. **April 25/17.** Det.D./B. |

## *E.E.F.*

| | | |
|---|---|---|
| 2 Y. X | Bennett, James. 7364. | *M., bel. drowned **Feb. 20-24/17.** |
| ? | **Skinner, Major J. S.** | M., bel. drowned **Feb. 20-24/17.** |

## SOMERSET LIGHT INFANTRY.

## *B.E.F.*

| | | |
|---|---|---|
| 1 | **Bailey, 2nd Lt. R. H. D.** (Fr. 8th.) | M. **May 3/17.** |
| 1 | **Massie, 2nd Lieut. S. E.** | M. **May 9/17.** |
| ‡1 A. | Bumford, A.-Cpl. E. 12247. | M. **May 3/17.** |
| ‡1 A. | Jones, F. J. 7066. | M. **May 3/17.** |
| 1 A. | Watts, Frank H. 26755. | M. **May 3/17.** |
| ‡1 C. | Crosby, G. 5600. | M. **May 3/17.** |
| ‡1 C. | Henwood, E. 19926. | W. and M. **April 9/17.** |
| 1 C. XI | Kynaston, Albert. 26809. | M. **April 10/17.** |
| 1 H.Q. Sig. S. | Mills, Wm. Francis. 34190. | M. **May 3/17.** |
| 6 A. | Richardson, James. 20055. | W. and M. **Sept. 16/16. R/Enq.** |
| 6 B. | Ralph, George. 14893. | M. **Sept. 16/16.** R/Enq. |
| 6 B. | Sandford, Fred. 10401. | W. and M. **Sept. 16/16.** R/Enq. |
| 6 C. | Ballam, L.-Cpl. H. 10930. | W. and M. **Sept. 16/16.** R/Enq. |
| ‡6 C. | Preece, E. T. 20364. | M. **Sept. 4-6/16.** R/Enq. |
| *6 C. | Tilley, J. T. 7260. (Fr. 3rd.) | W. and M. **Sept. 16/16.** R/Enq. |
| 7 A. I | Gregory, W. 21280. | M. **Oct. 1/16.** R/Enq. |
| 7 B. | Drayton, A. 14886. | M. **April 12/17.** |
| 7 B. VIII | Eason, Charles. 19951. | K. **Oct. 1/16.** Det.D./B. |
| ‡7 D. | Dare, B. J. 26888. | W. and M. **April 8/17.** |
| ‡7 D. | Harp, S. 17354. | M. **May 3/17.** |
| ‡7 D. | Minshall, L.-Cpl. J. 10015. | M. **May 3/17.** |
| 7 D. XVI | Odams, L.-Cpl. C. 14936. | K. **Sept. 16/16.** Det.D./B. R/Enq. |
| 7 D. XIV | Rainey, Ernest. 27205. | M. **April 4/17.** |
| 8 | **Vaughan, 2nd Lt. L. H.** (Fr. 4th.) | K. **April 24/17.** Det.D./B. |
| 8 A. or D. | Ashman, Sergt. A. S. 11202. | W. and M. **April 28/17.** |
| 8 A. | Ashworth, S. 15059. | M. **April 28/17.** |
| 8 A. | Bagge, J. 20993. | M. **April 28/17.** |
| 8 A. | Barber, G. 26012. | M. **April 23/17.** |
| 8 A. | Bennett, A.-Cpl. S. 12357. | M. **April 28/17.** |
| 8 A. III | Brown, G. 15768. | M. **April 23/17.** |
| 8 A. | Butt, D. 17612. | M. **April 28/17.** |
| ‡8 A. | Down, J. 18821. | W. and M. **April 28/17.** |
| 8 A. | Fellows, L.-Cpl. W. 6515. | M. **April 23/17.** |
| 8 A. II | Gale, Alfonso. 26651. | M. **April 28/17.** |
| 8 A. II | Geach, Cpl. Wm. Arthur. 15203. | W. and M. **April 28/17.** |
| 8 A. | Gray, H. 26614. | M. **April 28/17.** |
| 8 A. | Haskell, A. J. 26123. | M. **April 28/17.** |
| ‡8 A. | Hitchcock, L.-Cpl. W. 14174. | M. **April 28/17.** |
| 8 A. or B. | Hodder, Reginald. 17524. | M. **April 28/17.** |
| 8 A. | Horton, W. E. 26060. | M. **April 28/17.** |
| 8 A. | Patch, A. 30200. | M. **April 28/17.** |
| 8 A. | Rendell, W. A. 15066. | M. **April 28/17.** |

**Somerset Light Infantry—contd.**

## *B.E.F.*

| | | |
|---|---|---|
| 8 A. I | Shipp, Henry. 32199. | M. April 28/17. |
| ‡8 A. | Stone, W. 20650. | M. April 28/17. |
| 8 A. | Tanner, Cpl. A. W. 18878. | W. and M. April 28/17. |
| 8 A. M.G.S. | Taylor, L.-Cpl. W. C. 16030. | M. Unoff. K. April 28/17. |
| 8 A. I | Veysey, Richard. 27752. | M. April 28/17. |
| 8 A. I | White, George. 32213. | M. April 23/17. |
| 8 B. | Allard, H. 19950. | M. April 23/17. |
| 8 B. | Baker, James. 11142. | M. April 28/17. |
| 8 B. | Breedon, L.-Cpl. G. W. 15413. | M. April 28/17. |
| 8 B. | Brown, E. S. 30035. | M. April 28/17. |
| 8 B. | Brown, R. 19639. | M. April 28/17. |
| 8 B. | Carpenter, F. 34223. | M. April 23/17. |
| 8 B. | Channon, C. W. 30050. | M. April 23/17. |
| 8 B. | Dyer, F. J. 31955. | M. April 28/17. |
| 8 B. | Gardiner, W. 25458. | M. April 9-12/17. |
| 8 B. | Heal, R. G. 29990. | M. April 28/17. |
| 8 B. | Hines, W. E. 32184. | M. April 28/17. |
| 8 B. | Hiscocks, E. J. 19758. | M. April 23/17. |
| 8 B. | Hodges, W. J. 34238. | M. April 23/17. |
| 8 B. VIII | Jarvis, N. 29989. | M. April 28/17. |
| 8 B. | Luxon, R. 30034. | M. April 28/17. |
| ‡8 B. | Marsh, L.-Cpl. W. 8475. | W. and M. April 23/17. |
| 8 B. | Marsh, L.-Cpl. W. R. 14775. | M. April 24/17. |
| 8 B. | Masterson, McL. 15698. | M. April 23/17. |
| 8 B. | Moriarty, James H. 29965. | M. April 23/17. |
| 8 B. | Robertson, N. W. 18969. | M. April 28/17. |
| 8 B. | Russell, A. 26574 | M. April 23/17. |
| 8 B. | Salter, G. 25511. | M. April 23/17. |
| 8 B. | Thomas, Sergt. E. G. 16984. | M. April 23/17. |
| 8 B. | Wood, F. S. 26557. | M. April 23/17. |
| 8 C. | Bindon, L.-Cpl. W. J. 9610. | M. April 28/17. |
| 8 C. | Call, F. M. H. 26578. | M. April 28/17. |
| 8 C. | Cox, L.-Cpl. F. H. 21519. | M. April 28/17. |
| 8 C. | Day, J. J. 34322. | M. April 28/17. |
| 8 C. Gren. Sec. | Dean, W. J. 15207. | M. April 9-12/17. |
| ‡8 C. | Fenton, Sergt. H. 19137. | W. and M. April 23/17. |
| 8 C. | Gay, F. 21777. (Fr. 3rd.) | M. April 28/17. |
| 8 C. | Hannam, R. H. J. 20500. | M. April 28/17. |
| 8 C. | Heathman, F. 21561. | M. April 28/17. |
| 8 C. IX | Murley, Joseph. 26405. | M. April 28/17. |
| *8 C. XII | Potter, A. J. 16130. | W. and M. April 28/17. |
| 8 C. IX | Powell, G. W. 27665. | M. April 28/17. |
| 8 C. XII | Ryman, George E. 34349. | M. April 28/17. |
| 8 C. | Tipper, W. H. 32240. | M. April 28/17. |
| 8 C. IX | Watchorn, W. 27684. | M. April 28/17. |
| 8 C. | Williams, F. J. 26213. | M. April 28/17. |
| 8 D. XIII | Ashford, T. 26344. | W. and M. April 23/17. |
| 8 D. | Brooks, E. J. 20801. | M. April 28/17. |
| 8 D. XVI | Court, Edwin Henry. 21719. | M. April 28/17. |
| 8 D. XVI | Dyer, A. 16009. | M. April 9-12/17. |
| ‡8 D. | Freegard, L.-Cpl. C. 13298. | M. April 11/17. |
| 8 D. | Hunter, J. G. 15676. | M. April 23/17. |
| 8 D. | Lampard, John F. H/15607. | W. and M. April 28/17. |
| 8 D. XIV | Pannell, W. 29982. | M. April 28/17. |
| 8 D. | Seaward, R. A. 30003. | M. April 28/17. |
| ‡8 D. | Speller, Cpl. Fred. 5705. | W. and M. April 28/17. |
| 8 D. XIII | Turner, Albert H. 27676. | M. April 28/17. |
| 8 H.Q. Snip. S. | Back, H. J. 29980. | M. April 28/17. |

**Somerset Light Infantry—contd.**

## *B.E.F.*

| | | |
|---|---|---|
| 8 H.Q. | Baker, E. J. 30037. | M. April 23/17. |
| 8 H.Q. Sig. S. | Beere, C. R. 11968. | M. April 28/17. |
| 8 H.Q. | Edwards, E. H. 19145. | M. April 23/17. |
| 8 H.Q. | Gardner, S. M. 19934. | M. April 28/17. |
| 8 Sig. H.Q. | Hole, Alb. Ernest. 21745. | M. April 23/17. |
| 8 H.Q. | Johnson, Frederick. 15420. | M. April 28/17. |
| 8 H.Q. | Lee, Sergt. J. H. 5538. | M. April 23/17. |
| 8 H.Q. | Longman, G. E. 32191. | M. April 28/17. |
| *8 H.Q. XI | Meggison, Joseph. 15856. (Fr. C.) | W. and M. April 11/17. |
| 8 H.Q. | Storey. 27627. | M. April 28/17. |
| 8 ? | Trim, L.-Cpl. Ernest Frank. 12156. (Fr. H.Q. Co.) | M. April 28/17. |
| 8 H.Q. | Waite, T. 13903. | M. April 28/17. |

## *E.E.F.*

| | | |
|---|---|---|
| 12 ? | Brooks, E. 290029. | M., bel. drowned Feb. 20-24/17. |

## *PERSIAN GULF.*

| | | |
|---|---|---|
| ‡4 ? | Smith, Sergt. Geo. Chas. 203116. (30325.) | Accid. K. May 4/17, near Khandalla, India. Conf. and Dets. asked. |
| 5 Sig. S. | Carey, L.-Cpl. Chas. Cyril. 2133. | M., bel. K. Jan. 26/17. |

**NORTH STAFFORDSHIRE REGIMENT.**

## *B.E.F.*

| | | |
|---|---|---|
| 1 | **Ryley, Lieut. D. A. G. B.** | M. Feb. 11/17. |
| 1 B. | Crawford, Harry. 28620. | M. Sept. 1/16. R/Enq. |
| 1 D. | Llewellyn, L.-Cpl. W. 11185. | M. Feb. 11/17. |
| 1 ? I.T.M. | Wilkinson, L.-Cpl. Alfred Jas. 7941. (72 Bgde.) | M. Nov. 26/16. |
| 2 A. IV | Benjamin, Fredk. 34795. | Unoff. M. April 23/17. |
| 5 | **Butterfield, 2nd Lieut. C. W.** | M., bel. K. May 11/17. |
| ‡5 | **Graham, Major C. E.** (Fr. 2nd Borders.) | W. and M. July 1-5/17. |
| ‡5 | **Green, 2nd Lieut. B.** | M., bel. K. July 1/17. |
| ‡5 | **Greeves, 2nd Lieut. J.** | M. July 1/17. |
| ‡5 | **Johnson, 2nd Lieut. R. F.** | M. July 1/17. |
| ‡5 | **Lowe, M.C., 2nd Lieut. J. E.** | M. July 1/17. |
| ‡5 | **Masefield, 2nd Lieut. C. J. B.** | M. July 1/17. |
| *5 | **Rayner, Capt. B. H.** | M., bel. K. June 14/17. |
| ‡5 | **Ross, 2nd Lieut. P. B.** | M. July 1/17. |
| ‡5 | **Scrivener, Capt. A. F.** | M. July 1/17. |
| 5 A. III | Smith, A. 6416. | K. Mar. 14/17. Det.D./B. |
| 5 B. | Brookes, J. 201584. | M. Mar. 4/17. |
| 5 B. VIII | Hulme, Chas. Jos. 202360. (6505.) | M. Mar. 14/17. |
| 5 C. | Wilshaw, L.-Cpl. Fred. 201199. (Late 4546.) | W. and M. Mar. 14/17. |
| 5 D. | Barker, J. 203146. | M. Mar. 14/17. |
| 5 D. | Bennett, E. 202330. | M. Mar. 14/17. |
| 5 D. XIII | Jones, Aaron. 201829. (5571.) | M. Mar. 14/17. |
| 5 D. | Lockett, A. 202018. | M. Mar. 14/17. |
| 5 D. | Mansell, P. 201774. | W. and M. Mar. 14/17. |
| 5 D. | Stevenson, J. 201549. | M. Mar. 14/17. |

**Staffordshire Regiment, North—contd.**

## *B.E.F.*

5 D. XV Webster, J. 3837. K. Mar. 14/17. Det.D./B.
‡5 ? Clarke, F. W. 2359. M. Oct. 13/16.
*2/5 A. Breeze, H. 201281. (4668.) M. May 8/17.
2/5 A. Carr, Frank. 7348. M. May 8/17.
*2/5 A. Coles, T. 202684. M. May 8/17.
‡2/5 A. Huggett, A. J. 202652. M. May 8/17.
‡2/5 D. Plant, Edward. 201045. (4287.) M. June 14/17.
6 **Canby, Lieut. R. L.** M., bel. K. May 8/17.
‡6 A. Armshaw, G. 242345. M. May 25/17.
‡6 A. Atkins, C. 241318. M. May 25/17.
‡6 A. Gooch, F. 242626. M. May 25/17.
*6 A. I Lofts, Cecil C. 241305. M. May 25/17.
‡6 A. Moss, J. 242593. M. May 25/17.
‡6 A. Perry, A. 241777. M. May 25/17.
‡6 A. IV Staniforth, J. 241858. W. and M. May 24/17.
‡6 A. Upton, J. 240950. M. May 3/17.
‡6 B. Bradford, J. 242555. M. May 25/17.
‡6 B. V Liddle, A.-Sergt. L. S. 240327. M. May 21/17.
‡6 B. VII Lockley, H. G. 242590. M. May 25/17.
‡6 B. Merrick, A. 240162. M. May 24/17.
‡6 B. V Pellington, F. 242472. M. May 25/17.
‡6 B. Smith, J. 241141. M. May 25/17.
‡6 C. Arrowsmith, E. 241822. W. and M. May 24/17.
‡6 C. Baker, P. 241195. (4052.) M. May 25/17.
*6 C. Bevington, Sholto. 242619. M. May 25/17.
*6 C. X Clarke, Cpl. Wm 240561. M. May 25/17.
‡6 C. XI Fearn, George. 242539. W. and M. May 24/17.
*6 C. XII Fox, H. 241779. W. and M. May 24/17.
‡6 C. L.G.S. Gask, A. H. 241376. W. and M. May 25/17.
‡6 C. Hill, W. 240879. M. May 25/17.
‡6 C. Kelly, T. 242330. M. May 25/17.
‡6 C. Kinnersley, H. C. 241885. M. May 25/17.
‡6 C. Preston, A. 241289. M. May 25/17.
*6 C. IX Rhodes, E. 242546. M. May 24/17.
‡6 C. Robinson, J. 242497. M. May 25/17.
*6 C. IX Rodgers, A. 242477. W. and M. May 24/17.
‡6 C. Selvey, H. 241342. M. May 25/17.
‡6 C. Slater, A. 241355. W. and M. May 6/17.
‡6 C. Smith, G. H. 240232. M. May 25/17.
‡6 C. XI Sutton, William J. 240769. W. and M. May 24/17.
*6 C. L.G.S. Walker, L.-Cpl. Michael Arthur. 240791. W. and M. May 24/17.
‡6 D. Ashmole, C. 240811. M. May 25/17.
‡6 D. Bennett, J. W. 241288. M. May 25/17.
‡6 D. Davies, T. B. 241292. (4033.) M. May 25/17.
‡6 D. Eardley, J. H. 242583. W. and M. May 25/17.
‡6 D. M.G.S. Follows, Geo. Robt. 240304. (2166) M. May 25/17.
‡6 D. Hawkeswell, Cpl. G. 241208. M. May 25/17.
‡6 D. Hodson, Cpl. W. 240050. W. and M. May 24/17.
‡6 D. Husbands, J. H. 242625. M. May 25/17.
‡6 D. Marshall, J. T. 242316. W. and M. May 24/17.
‡6 D. Phillips, J. 242566. W. and M. May 24/17.
‡6 D. Riddle, F. J. 242417. W. and M. May 24/17.
‡6 D. Wood, T. 241445. M. May 25/17.
‡2/6 A. Burton, Cpl. A. 241650. M. May 8/17.
*2/6 A. Dale, Cpl. Stephens. 241736. M. May 8/17.
‡2/6 A. Housego, A. J. 242250. M. May 8/17.

**Staffordshire Regiment, North—contd.**

## *B.E.F.*

*2/6 A. Lewis, J. H. 242045. M. May 8/17.
‡2/6 A. Locker, C. A. 241734. M. May 8/17.
‡2/6 A. Lucas, J. 240974. M. May 8/17.
‡2/6 A. Palmer, L.-Cpl. F. A. 241718. M. May 8/17.
‡2/6 A. Pritchard, W. 241568. M. May 8/17.
‡2/6 A. Ratcliffe, Cpl. W. 211657. M. May 8/17.
‡2/6 A. Smithard, W. 240980. M. May 8/17.
2/6 A. I Turner, Geo. James. 242268. M. May 8/17.
‡2/6 A. Vernon, A.-Cpl. Horace. 241611. M. May 8/17.
‡2/6 B. Amos, W. B. 241545. M. May 8/17.
‡2/6 B. Cartlidge, H. 241462. M. May 8/17.
‡2/6 B. Chester, L. H. B. 242120. M. May 8/17.
2/6 B. Dowell, L.-Cpl. R. 241072. M. May 8/17.
‡2/6 B. Roberts, L. B. 242114. M. May 3/17.
‡2/6 B. Topley, Cpl. T. W. 241073. M. May 3/17.
2/6 B. VII Wardle, John Thos. 242673. K. May 9/17. Det.D./B.
*8 **Shackleton, 2nd Lt. R.** (Fr. 2nd.) W. and M. June 8/17.
8 A. Boote, David. 18239. M. Nov. 18-19/16. R/Enq.
8 A. III Cook, Thomas H. 13663. M. Nov. 18/16.
‡8 A. I Edgeley, Charles. 40504. M. Nov. 18-19/16. R/Enq.
8 A. Hancock, Ralph. 40457. (Fr. 5th.) M. Nov. 18-19/16. R/Enq.
‡8 A. Jones, E. 40519. M. Nov. 18-19/16. R/Enq.
‡8 A. Parr, Benjamin. 13224. M. Nov. 18/16. R/Enq.
‡8 A. Sandbach, W. 18553. M. Nov. 18-19/16. R/Enq.
‡8 B. V Archer, L.-Cpl. Ernest Harry. 17333. Unoff. M. June 8/17.
8 C. Brookes, Sergt. L. A. 14211. M. Nov. 18-19/16. R/Enq.
‡8 C. Hill, John. 11790. M. Nov. 18-19/16. R/Enq.
8 C. Johnson, W. H. 17315. M. Nov. 18/16.
8 C. Moston, Harry. 19332. M. Nov. 18-19/16.
‡8 D. Bromley, Leonard. 18406. Unoff. M. about Oct. 18/16.
8 D. Burton, Vincent. 12403. M. Nov. 18-19/16. R/Enq.
*8 D. Copestake, Sigr. Harold. 12496. M. Nov. 18-19/16. R/Enq.
8 D. Goodwin, H. 40453. M. Nov. 18-19/16. R/Enq.
8 D. Heath, W. 13148. M. July 29-31/16. R/Enq.
‡8 D. XIII Jackson, L.-Cpl. Wm. Edwin. 40480 M. Nov. 18-19/16. R/Enq.
*8 D. Williams. Edward. 14202. M. Nov. 18-19/16. R/Enq.
9 C. IX Taylor, F. 13553. M. April 19/17.
9 D. XIII Bailey, Wm. 12031. M. April 26/17.
9 D. Felton, F. 28816. M. April 26/17.
‡9 D. Leese, A. E. 13372. M., bel. K. May 27/17.

## *E.E.F.*

‡? Ellis, Edwin. 39316. M., bel. drowned, April 15/17.

## *PERSIAN GULF.*

7 A. Barnett, Samuel. 6543 M. Jan. 25/17.
7 A. Davis, Richard. 8251. M. Mar. 10/17. R/Enq.
7 A. Gorman, T. 7922. W. and M. April 5/16.
7 A. Harvey, Jack. 19206. W. and M. Jan. 25/17.
7 A. Hopkins, James. 11/18588. M. Jan. 25/17.
7 A. Insley, L.-Cpl. Geo. 10241. W. and M. Feb. 25/17.
7 A. III Le Doux, James. 14301. W. and M. Jan. 25/17.
7 A. Powell, Sergt. G. T. 16776. M. Jan. 25/17.
7 A. Shenton, William. 14182. W. and M. Jan. 25/17.
7 A. Simpson, Joseph Wm. 10328. W. and M. Jan. 25/17.
7 A. Smith, C. R. 27191. M. Jan. 25/17.
7 A. Smith, L.-Cpl. John C. 10018. M. Mar. 25/17.
7 B. Duff, A.-C.-S.-M. J. 7677. K. Jan. 26/17. Det.D./B.

**Staffordshire Regiment, North—contd.**

## *PERSIAN GULF.*

| | | |
|---|---|---|
| 7 B. | Gater, L.-Cpl. J. W. 15771. | K. Mar. 25/17. Det.D./B. |
| 7 B. | Harrison, F. 25606. | M. Mar. 25/17. |
| 7 B. | James, W. 23046. | M. Jan. 25/17. |
| 7 B. | Talbot, J. 22551. | M. Jan. 27/17. |
| 7 C. | Allman, Stanley. 8853. | M. Mar. 25/17. |
| 7 C. | Beardsley, W. 26807. | M. Jan. 25/17. |
| 7 C. | Bull, Richard. 23211. | W. and M. Feb. 25/17. |
| 7 C. | Dolby, L.-Cpl. T. C. 23220. | M. Jan. 25/17. |
| 7 C. XII | Glover, E. 26320. | W. and M. Jan. 25/17. |
| 7 C. | Gough, Alfred. 18133. | M. Mar. 25/17. |
| 7 C. | Hodgkinson, A. 11370. | W. and M. Jan. 25/17. |
| 7 C. | Lawson, John. 11/16569. | M. Jan. 25/17. |
| 7 C. XII | Mellor, Cpl. H. 13916. | W. and M. Jan. 25/17. |
| 7 C. | Powell, G. 17618. | M. Jan. 25/17. |
| 7 C. | Skelding, L.-Cpl. Harold. 12854. | M. Jan. 25/17. |
| 7 D. | Brown, F. 10700. | M. Mar. 25/17. |
| 7 D. | Gadd, G. E. 27038. | D/W. March 9/17. Det.D./B. |
| 7 D. | Warham, John. 16931. | W. and M. April 9/16. R/Enq. |
| 7 ? | Adams, J. 11/19046. | M. Mar. 25/17. |
| 7 ? | Binns, A. E. 25671. | W. and M. Feb. 25/17. |
| 7 ? | Butcher, Arthur. 25678. | M. Jan. 25/17. |
| 7 ? | Davies, J. 13200. | M. Jan. 25/17. |
| 7 ? | Eaton, H. 12574. | W. and M. Jan. 25/17. |
| 7 ? | Edge, Arthur. 7583. (Fr. 4th.) | W. and M. April 9/16. |
| 7 ? | Elkin, E. 9202. | M. Jan. 25/17. |
| 7 ? | Gerrity, L.-Cpl. J. 16937. | M. Mar. 25/17. |
| 7 ? | Hammersley, A. 27936. | M. Jan. 25/17. |
| 7 ? | Hancock, T. 11459. | W. and M. April 9/16. |
| 7 ? | Hopwood, F. 23347. (Fr. 3rd.) | M. Jan. 25/17. |
| 7 ? | Hunt, H. 27752. | M. Jan. 25/17. |
| 7 ? | Iball, J. 7806. | M. Dec. 18/16. |
| 7 ? | Layton, H. 9653. | M. Mar. 25/17. |
| 7 ? | Measham, W. H. J. 24740. | M. Jan. 25/17. |
| 7 ? | Mountford, E. 8/12798. | M. Jan. 25/17. |
| 7 ? | Page, B. H. 8742. | M. Mar. 25/17. |
| 7 ? | Steadman, J. C. 15671. | M. Jan. 25/17. |
| 7 ? | Tye, A. 19374. | M. Jan. 25/17. |

**SOUTH STAFFORDSHIRE REGIMENT.**

## *B.E.F.*

| | | |
|---|---|---|
| 1 A. I | Death, Wm. Henry. 32593. | M. Mar. 28/17. |
| ‡1 A. | Drinkell, C. E. 25070. | M. May 12/17. |
| ‡1 A. | Fletcher, R. A. 15128. | M. May 15/17. |

**Staffordshire Regiment, South—contd.**

*B.E.F.*

| | | |
|---|---|---|
| 1 A. | Glover, G. 17072. | M. Mar. 28/17. |
| 1 A. II | Green, A. 40091. | M. Mar. 28/17. |
| ‡1 A. | Hall, A. C. 21032. | M. May 12/17. |
| ‡1 A. | Hartshorn, J. G. 17275. | M. May 12/17. |
| 1 A. | Hayward, Sergt. A. 8724. | M. Mar. 28/17. |
| ‡1 A. | Jobber, C. 10236. | M. May 13/17. |
| 1 A. | Malia, S/B. Edward. 10622. | M. Mar. 28/17. |
| ‡1 A. III | Morris, Thomas. 18126. | M. May 12/17. |
| 1 A. I | Moule, Cpl. H. L. 32497. | M. Mar. 28/17. |
| 1 A. | Moulton, J. 40074. | M. Mar. 28/17. |
| 1 A. I | Parsons, Cpl. J. R. 22696. | W. and M. May 12/17. |
| ‡1 A. | Penny, D. 10755. | M. May 12/17. |
| 1 A. | Perry, W. T. 11033. | M. Mar. 28/17. |
| ‡1 A. | Pinnock, L.-Cpl. H. 32538. | M. May 12/17. |
| ‡1 A. I | Poole, Edward. 31214. | M. May 12/17. |
| 1 A. | Pritchard, W. 31188. | M. Mar. 28/17. |
| *1 A. II | Sharman, Jos. Jas. 23105. | M. May 12/17. |
| 1 A. | Thorley, L.-Cpl. E. 40065. | M. Mar. 28/17. |
| ‡1 A. | Vaughan, H. 18946. | M. May 12/17. |
| ‡1 A. | Whiteside, T. W. C. 40628. | W. and M. May 12/17. |
| ‡1 B. | Beck, J. E. 31025. | M. May 13/17. |
| 1 B. VIII | Hammonds, W. 32607. | M. Jan. 11/17. |
| 1 B. | Marshall, J. 32611. | M. Jan. 11/17. |
| 1 B. | Morgan, J. E. 17946. | W. and M. May 13/17. |
| 1 B. | Owen, W. J. 40150. | M. May 15/17. |
| 1 C. XI | Rumbles, Fred. 40145. | W. and M. Jan. 11/17. |
| ‡1 D. | Horton, J. 12869. | M. May 12/17. |
| *1 D. XIII | Ingram, E. 19661. | M. May 12/17. |
| ‡1 D. | Marshall, W. 23073. | M. May 12/17. |
| ‡1 D. XIII | Pitt, Albert Osmond. 32651. | W. and M. May 12/17. |
| *1 D. XV | Richardson, Adam. 31765. | M. May 12/17. |
| ‡1 D. | Sharpe, W. 24383. | M. May 12/17. |
| *1 D. | Stubbs, L.-Cpl. A. E. 20063. | W. and M. May 12/17. |
| 2 | **Smith, 2nd Lt. J. S. (Fr. 5th.)** | K. April 23/17. Det.D./B. |
| 2 | **Tate, Capt. H. G.** | M. Feb. 17/17. |
| 2 | **Wilmot, 2nd Lieut. E. S.** | M. Nov. 13-15/16. |
| 2 A. or C. | Aggett, L.-Cpl. George. 10287. | M. April 28/17. |
| 2 A. | Allen, E. 11290. | M. April 28/17. |
| 2 A. | Ashbrook, E. 12866. | M. April 28/17. |
| 2 A. | Ashby, Sig. E. L. G. 9466. | M. May 3/17. |
| 2 A. IV | Bagnall, Cpl. W. 40317. | M. Feb. 17/17. |
| 2 A. III | Chappell, E. H. 43004. | W. and M. April 28/17. |
| 2 A. III | Fielding, Walter. 32459. | M. April 28/17. |
| 2 A. | Goodwin, L.-Cpl. A. 30260 | M. Feb. 17/17. |

**Staffordshire Regiment, South—contd.**

## *B.E.F.*

| | | |
|---|---|---|
| 2 A. III | Jones, A. 29876. | W. and M. April 28/17. |
| 2 A. IV | Jones, Albert Edward. 40396. | M. Feb. 17/17. |
| 2 A. | Keenan, M. 29735. | M. Feb. 17/17. |
| ‡2 A. | Mildoon, J. 18778. | M. May 3/17. |
| ‡2 A. | Neil, F. 9612. | M. May 3/17. |
| 2 A. | Nolan, Jas. 32058. | W. and M. April 28/17. |
| 2 A. L.G.S. | Penrice, D. A. 14807. | W. Unoff. M. April 28/17. |
| 2 A. | Phillips, F. 19518. | M. Mar. 31/17. |
| 2 A. III | Powell, Thos. 32136. | M. April 28/17. |
| 2 A. | Proud, W. 404c5. | M. Mar. 31/17. |
| *2 A. | Robinson, Cpl. Sydney Chas. 40408. | M. May 3/17. |
| 2 A. | Sharp, G. 266'0. | M. Feb. 17/17. |
| ‡2 A. IV | Sheldon, Fred. 32130. | W. and M. April 28/17. |
| 2 A. IV | Slack, C. J. 32292. | M. Feb. 17/17. |
| ‡2 A. | Stott, Gilbert. 31977. | M. May 3/17. |
| 2 B. VII | Barber, Cpl. A. G. 24405. | W. and M. April 28/17. |
| 2 B. | Bryan, Cpl. John. 18839. | M. April 28/17. |
| ‡2 B. | Clayton, F. 31960. | M. April 28/17. |
| 2 B. VIII | Cosgriff, Thomas. 11306. | M. April 28/17. |
| 2 B. or C. | Eyre, J. T. 9546. | M. April 28/17. |
| 2 B. | Harvey, R. 40360. | M. April 28/17. |
| 2 B. | Hill, Ernest. 32974. | M. April 28/17. |
| 2 B. V | Hutchinson, R. 30961. | W. and M. April 28/17. |
| 2 B. VII | Rooley, Gibson. 32983. | M. April 28/17. |
| *2 B. | Ward, John. 9398. | M. Nov. 13-15/16. R/Enq. |
| 2 B. | Wood, W. 9229. | M. April 28/17. |
| 2 C. | Armstrong, Ernest. 9214. | M. Feb. 17/17. |
| *2 C. XII | Banks, P. 32450. | Unoff. M. April/17. |
| 2 C. | Bird, L.-Cpl. A. 40569. | M. Feb. 17/17. |
| 2 C. | Blewitt, H. 30226. | M. Feb. 17/17. |
| 2 C. or D. | Bramley, Thos. Clifford. 40571. | M. April 28/17. |
| ‡2 C. | Chaplin, T. 28238. | W. and M. April 28/17. |
| ‡2 C. X | Collinson, Sgt. Joseph Albin. 40539. | K. April 18/17. Det.D./B. |
| 2 C. | Edwards, J. 30364. | M. April 28/17. |
| 2 C. | Fellows, J. T. 18123. | M. Nov. 13-15/16. R/Enq. |
| ‡2 C. | Fewtrell, S. L. 26767. | M. May 3/17. |
| 2 C. | Horton, F. A. 23963. | M. April 28/17. |
| 2 C. | Millard, G. E. 17902. | M. April 28/17. |
| 2 C. | Mitchell, T. H. 40375. | M. Feb. 17/17. |
| 2 C. | Osborne, Cpl. B. 19891. | M. April 28/17. |
| 2 C. IX | Parish, Walter. 31858. | M. April 28/17. |
| 2 C. | Perks, W. 15495. | M. April 28/17. |
| 2 C. or H.Q. L.G.S. | Riley, T. G. 31717. | M. May 3/17. |
| ‡2 C. IX | Roebuck, Joseph Alfred. 9510. | M. Nov. 13-15/16. R/Enq. |
| 2 C. XII | Rollinson, Mark. 15461. | M. April 28/17. |
| 2 C. | Russell, T. 17100. | M. April 28/17. |
| 2 C. | Taylor, L.-Cpl. G. W. 9591. | M. April 28/17. |
| *2 C. IX | Thomason, Wm. 20720. | W. and M. April 28/17. |

**Staffordshire Regiment, South—contd.**

*B.E.F.*

2 C. XII Williams, F. C. 28527. M. Feb. 17/17.
2 D. Atkin, A. 32296. M. April 28/17.
2 D. Attwood, J. 31297. M. April 28/17.
2 D. Bartholomew, Edgar. 32967. M. April 28/17.
*2 D. XIII Borrill, H. 32486. M. April 28/17.
2 D. Brown, J. E. 26515. M. April 28/17.
2 D. Brown, L.-Cpl. P. 40330. M. April 28/17.
2 D. Brudenell, Harry. 40328. M. Feb. 17/17.
2 D. Cooper, J. 32298. M. April 28/17.
2 D. XV Evans, Bert. 25039. M. April 28/17.
2 D. Gall, F. 32489. M. April 28/17.
2 D. Garton, H. 32300. M. April 28/17.
2 D. Hall, J. 24411. M. April 28/17.
2 D. Harris, Edw. 15382. M. April 28/17.
2 D. Henley, J. 16370. M. April 28/17.
2 D. Hill, E. 31711. M. April 28/17.
2 D. XIII Hoggard, John Hry. 32304. M. April 28/17.
2 D. Holden, L.-Cpl. J. 16721. M. April 28/17.
2 D. XV Hughes, Wm. 25474. M. April 28/17.
2 D. Hyde, A. 31967. M. April 28/17.
2 D. Jackson, W. 17154. M. Nov. 13-15/16. R/Enq.
2 D. Johnson, G. H. 31712. M. April 28/17.
‡2 D. Jones, L.-Cpl. F. 21304. W. and M. April 28/17.
‡2 D. Kennedy, C. W. 32490. W. and M. April 28/17.
2 D. XIII Mantle, Fredk. 32101. M. April 28/17.
2 D. Maynard, J. T. 32305. M. April 28/17.
2 D. Mears, E. 19930. M. April 28/17.
2 D. XV Mole, Harry. 11442. M. April 28/17.
2 D. Moorhouse, G. 40379. M. April 28/17.
2 D. Pearson, Thos. H. 22725. M. April 28/17.
2 D. XVI Reynolds, George. 11652. M. Feb. 17/17.
2 D. Simpson, F. 32481. M. April 28/17.
2 D. Squires, G. 12175. M. April 28/17.
*2 D. Sap. Pl. Stevenson, Thos. 12492. M. April 28/17. R/Enq.
2 D. Targett, A. E. 23626. M. April 28/17.
2 D. Vickers, A. 28548. M. April 28/17.
2 D. Whitehouse, J. W. 19016. M. April 28/17.
‡2 D. XIII Williams, L.-Cpl. Joseph Henry. 13548. W. and M. April 28/17.
*2 ? I.T.M. Jones, H. H. 20122. W. and M. April 28/17.
‡4 A. Angell, G. 19081. M. May 27/17.
5 A. Busby, F. W. 203201. M. Mar. 14/17.
5 A. Davies, J. J. 200630. M. Mar. 14/17.
5 B. VI Brown, Henry W. 200934. W. and M. Mar. 14/17.
5 B. V Pyatt, Wm. 202963. (Late 3276.) W. and M. May 14/17.
5 C. XI Moule, H. 201990. (Late 1964.) M. Mar. 14/17.
‡5 C. L.G.S. Simpson, W. A. 203269. M. June 28/17.
‡6 B. VII Hall, W. 242597. Unoff. M. July 1/17.
‡6 B. V Thompson, B. 241789. Unoff. M. July 1/17.
‡6 C. Lowe, W. H. 240922. M. May 25/17.
‡6 C. Orton, A. 241730. M. May 25/17.
‡6 C. Plant, W. 241006. M. May 25/17.
‡6 C. XI Poulton, S. 240819. M. May 25/17.
*6 C. Taverner, W. 241957. M. May 25/17.
2/6 A. Thornton, C. 241776. M. April 27/17.
2/6 B. Careless, Lyons Wm. 241525. (4943.) M. April 11/17.
‡2/6 D. Noble, J. W. 25109. M. May 23/17.
8 **Bourne, 2nd Lieut. A. S.** W. and M. April 23/17.

**Staffordshire Regiment, South—contd.**

*B.E.F.*

| | | |
|---|---|---|
| 8 | **Browne, 2nd Lieut. A. J. H.** | W. and M. **April 23/17.** |
| 8 | **Cotterell, 2nd Lieut. R. V.** (Fr. 5th.) | K. **April 23/17. Conf. and Det.** |
| 8 | **Stephens, 2nd Lieut. J. S.** | W. and M. **April 23/17.** |
| 8 A. | Adkin, E. 3/31706. | M. **April 23/17.** |
| 8 A. | Bellamy, G. E. 43051. | M. **April 23/17.** |
| 8 A. | Biddulph, Cpl. A. 43037. | M. **April 23/17.** |
| 8 A. | Carson, G. 43068. | M. **April 23/17.** |
| 8 A. II | Coleman, W. 40437. | W. and M. **April 23/17.** |
| *8 A. II | Fitchett, Frank. 43081. | M. **May 27/17.** |
| ‡8 A. | Harris, G. E. 13593. | M. **April 23/17.** |
| 8 A. | Hodgson, T. W. 3/31878. | M. **April 23/17.** |
| ‡8 A. | Johnson, T. 28464. | M. **April 23/17.** |
| 8 A. | Neale, W. E. 23172. | M. **April 23/17.** |
| 8 A. | Sanderson, A. E. 28466. (Fr. 4th.) | M. **April 23/17.** |
| 8 A. IV | Sindall, G. F. 31718. (Fr. 3rd.) | M. **April 23/17.** |
| 8 A. II | Stockley, J. 3/31887. | W. and M. **April 23/17.** |
| 8 A. | Ward, J. 40535. | W. and M. **April 23/17.** |
| 8 A. | Wootton, L.-Cpl. W. 13437. | M. **April 23/17.** |
| 8 A. I | Wright, W. 40529. | W. and M. **April 23/17.** |
| 8 B. | Williams, Frank. 29676. | M. **April 23/17.** |
| 8 C. | Beesley, Sergt. H. 11/19432. | M. **April 23/17.** |
| 8 C. | Bolton, T. 3/31872. | M. **April 23/17.** |
| 8 C. X | Caddick, Joseph. 31873. (Fr. 3rd.) | W. and M. **April 23/17.** |
| 8 C. X | Chamberlain, H. 43003. | W. and M. **April 23/17.** |
| 8 C. XI | Crisp, Walter Joseph. 14260. | K. **April 23/17. Det.D./B.** |
| 8 C. | Davies, R. A. 3/31874. | M. **April 23/17.** |
| 8 C. | Davies, S. 3/18337. | M. **April 23/17.** |
| ‡8 C. | Eglington, E 11/12018. | W. and M. **April 23/17.** |
| 8 C. IX | Evans, Sidney. 20446. (Fr. 11th.) | M. **April 24/17.** |
| 8 C. | Gold, Chas. Thos. 20456. (Fr. 11th) | M. **April 23/17.** |
| 8 C. XII | Green, Horace. 43137. | M. **April 23/17.** |
| 8 C. X | Hammond, Sidney. 28450. (Fr. 3rd.) | M. **April 23/17.** |
| 8 C. XI | Handley, Jos. Wm. 11/24861. | M. **April 23/17.** |
| 8 C. | Harding, A. 40476. | M. **April 23/17.** |
| 8 C. | Heath, T. W. 10/13277. | M. **April 23/17.** |
| 8 C. | Hunt, J. 24912. (Fr. 11th.) | M. **April 23/17.** |
| ‡8 C. IX | James, J. T. 40480. | W. and M. **April 23/17.** |
| 8 C. | Keightley, Thos. 43145. (Fr. 11th, 21101.) | M. **April 23/17.** |
| 8 C. XII | Kempin, Wm. 40484. | W. and M. **April 23/17.** |
| ‡8 C. | McDonough, T. 3/30570. | W. and M. **April 23/17.** |
| 8 C. X | Mace, W. J. 31356. (Fr. 3rd.) | M. **April 23/17.** |
| *8 C. XII | Mitchell, R. 18661. | W. and M. **April 23/17.** |
| 8 C. | Morris, Percy. 8/13445. | M. **April 23/17.** |
| 8 C. | Murfin, A. 40492. | M. **April 23/17.** |
| 8 C. | Parton, J. T. 30579. (Fr. 3rd.) | M. **April 23/17.** |
| 8 C. | Pearson, N. 30674. (Fr. 3rd.) | M. **April 23/17.** |
| 8 C. XI | Portman, Wm. 31884. (Fr. 3rd.) | M. **April 23/17.** |
| ‡8 C. | Richards, E. 11/18834. | W. and M. **April 23/17.** |
| *8 C. X | Sedgley, Alfred. 13910. | W. and M. **April 23/17.** |
| 8 C. XII | Whitton, John. 43169. | M. **April 23/17.** |
| 8 C. | Williamson, Joseph. 43172. | M. **April 23/17.** |
| 8 C. XII | Witham, J. 43171. | M. **April 23/17.** |
| 8 D. | Bailey, E. 3/31603. | M. **April 23/17.** |
| 8 D. | Downing, G. B. 30556. | M. **April 23/17.** |
| 8 D. XV | Ellis, L.-Cpl. George. 43186. | M. **April 23/17.** |
| 8 D. | Holmes, F. 3/30542. | M. **April 28/17.** |
| 8 D. | Horne, L.-Sgt. R. E. 11/19720. | M. **April 23/17.** |
| 8 D. XV | Lonsdale, S. 25108. (Fr. 11th.) | M. **April 23/17.** |

**Staffordshire Regiment, South—contd.**

*B.E.F.*

| | | |
|---|---|---|
| *8 D. XV | Price, John Thomas. 30460. | M. April 23/17. |
| 8 D. | Weaver, John. 11857. (Fr. 11th.) | M. April 23/17. |
| 8 D. XVI | West, H. 43218. | M. April 23/17. |
| 8 D. | Woodthorpe, F. J 26966. | M. April 23/17. |
| *8 ? | Thompson, Ernest. 31622. | M. Feb. 25/17. |

## STAFFORDSHIRE YEOMANRY.

*E.E.F.*

| | | |
|---|---|---|
| ? Squad. | Chilton, F. J. 300359. | M. April 17/17. |

## SUFFOLK REGIMENT.

*B.E.F.*

| | | |
|---|---|---|
| 2 | **Pryke, 2nd Lieut. A.** | W. and M. April 11/17. |
| 2 W. | Adey, A.-Sergt. J. 19438. | M. May 1/17. |
| ‡2 W. | Bryant, Sergt. Arthur. 8486. | K. June 18/17. Det.D./B. |
| 2 W. | Masterson, W. 34577. | M. April 28/17. |
| *2 W. | Sibering, A.-Sergt. A. 19009. | M. May 1/17. |
| 2 X. | Gordon, A. 50668. | M. April 28/17. |
| 2 X. or Y. Snip. S. | Mynott, Edward Geo. 28844. | M. April 11/17. |
| ‡2 Y. | Balls, V. 12898. | M. April 11/17. |
| 2 Y. | Benson, A.-Sergt. N. 19157. | M. May 1/17. |
| 2 Y. XI | Cawthorne, F. W. 40759. | K. April 9/17. Det.D./B. |
| 2 Y. XI | Cullingford, Geo. 13296. | W. and M. April 11/17. |
| *2 Y. XII | Fisher, Ernest James. 30727. | M. April 11/17. |
| ‡2 Y. | Laws, F. 40736. | M. April 11/17. |
| 2 Y. | Stubbings, Sergt. William. 12831. | M. Nov. 13/16. R/Enq. |
| ‡2 Y. | Wright, J. 44077. | M. April 11/17. |
| 2 Z. XVI | Bowyer, Harry. 40744. | W. and M. April 11/17. |
| ‡2 Z. | Southgate, A. 19019. | W. and M. April 11/17. |
| ‡4 A. | Cornell, O. 201784. | W. and M. April 23/17. |
| *4 A. I | Crack, H. S. 201917. | M. April 23/17. |
| ‡4 A. | Gibson, W. J. 200877. | M. April 23/17. |
| 4 A. | Mabbutt, F. 201762. | M. April 23/17. |
| *4 A. | Mattin, S. 200897. | M. April 23/17. |
| ‡4 A. I | Morgan, J. W. 201431. | W. and M. April 23/17. |
| 4 A. IV | Patman, Wm. 202207. | W. and M. April 23/17. |
| 4 A. L.G.S. | Ratcliffe, S. J. 200357. | M. April 23/17. |
| *4 A. | Smith, A. 202214. | M. April 23/17. |
| 4 A. | Sterry, A. D. 202937. (Late 6525.) | M. April 23/17. |
| *4 A. II | Wall, Tom. H. 201227. (3817.) | M. April 23/17. |
| *4 B. | Aldous, L.-Cpl. L. 201214. | M. April 23/17. |
| *4 B. VII | Bates, F. 202372. | K. April 23/17. Det.D./B. |
| 4 B. | Brown, O. W. 201487. | M. April 23/17. |
| *4 B. | Calver, J. 202361. | M. April 23/17. |
| 4 B. | Cooper, J. 201133. | M. April 23/17. |

**Suffolk Regiment—contd.**

*B.E.F.*

| | | | |
|---|---|---|---|
| 4 B. | | Crick, A. 202127. | M. April 23/17. |
| 4 B. | | Davison, J. W. 238026. | M. April 23/17. |
| 4 B. | | Garrett, T. F. 200048. | M. April 23/17. |
| 4 B. | | Guttward, F. W. 202313. | M. April 23/17. |
| 4 B. | | Gooch, J. 201978. | M. April 23/17. |
| 4 B. | VI | Gray, John. 202250. (5439.) | W. and M. April 23/17. |
| 4 B. | | Hawthorne, T. 202364. | M. April 23/17. |
| 4 B. | | Hines, L.-Cpl. P. 201361. | M. April 23/17. |
| 4 B. | | Jones, C. 201880. | M. April 23/17. |
| *4 B. | VIII | King, A. 201912. (6105.) | W. and M. April 23/17. |
| 4 B. | L.G.S. | Page, J. 201121. (3051.) | W. and M. April 23/17. |
| 4 B. | VI | Peck, Jas. Robt. 201864. (Late 6051.) | M. April 23/17. |
| 4 B. | | Scarff, W. C. 200640. | M. April 23/17. |
| 4 B. | | Taylor, A. 202128. | M. April 23/17. |
| 4 B. | | Trowell, R. J. B. 200737. | M. April 23/17. |
| ‡4 C. | | Alsop, J. G. 202255. | M. April 23/17. |
| 4 C. | | Baldwin, S. W. 200766. | M. April 23/17. |
| 4 C. | | Barker, L.-Cpl. E. 201385. | M. April 23/17. |
| 4 C. | | Beales, B. 202139. | M. April 23/17. |
| 4 C. | XII | Breed, L.-Cpl. E. 201305. | M. April 23/17. |
| 4 C. | | Brooke, A.-L.-Cpl. H. T. 202346. | M. April 23/17. |
| 4 C. | | Clifton, C. 202415. | M. April 23/17. |
| 4 C. | XII | Cocker, Cpl A. W. 200267. (1762.) | M. April 23/17. |
| 4 C. | | Cole, G. 201939. | M. April 23/17. |
| 4 C. | | Cook, A.-L.-Cpl. C. 201287. | M. April 23/17. |
| 4 C. | X | Cowles, F. H. J. 200280. (1788.) | M. Unoff. K. April 23/17. |
| 4 C. | | Cutter, Sidney. 201938. (5126.) | M. April 23/17. |
| 4 C. | | Dawson, J. K. 3786. | M. Nov. 2/16. |
| 4 C. | | Dew, A. C. 201941. | M. April 23/17. |
| 4 C. | | Everson, Sergt. A. 200732. | M. April 23/17. |
| 4 C. | | Farrow, E. H. 200849. | M. April 23/17. |
| 4 C. | | Fisher, A.-L.-Cpl. M. 200970. | M. April 23/17. |
| 4 C. | XI | Forrester, Alfred. 201805. | M. April 23/17. |
| 4 C. | XI | Goode, Wm. Chris. 201942. (Late 5130 and 4017.) | M. April 23/17. |
| 4 C. | X | Johnson, B. W. A. 201706. (4983.) | M. April 23/17. |
| 4 C. | XI | Lewis, A.-L.-Cpl. Harry. 201373. (4157.) | M. April 23/17. |
| 4 C. | | Lovick, B. F. 202252. | M. April 23/17. |
| 4 C. | XII | Mayes, R. 201760. (5039.) | M. April 23/17. |
| 4 C. | | Moyes, S. F. 200847. | M. April 23/17. |
| 4 C. | | Overton, R. H. 201679. | M. April 23/17. |
| 4 C. | | Phillips, C. 201949. | M. April 23/17. |
| 4 C. | | Prentice, Cpl. E. 200704. | M. April 23/17. |
| 4 C. | | Race, J. 202258. | M. April 23/17. |
| 4 C. | XI | Riss, E. G. 200738. | M. April 23/17. |
| 4 C. | XII | Roper, W. H. 200622. | M. April 23/17. |
| ‡4 C. | | Smith, G. 201246. | M. April 23/17. |
| 4 C. | | Smy, Cpl. R. 200462. (2113.) | M. April 23/17. |
| 4 C. | | Snowden, Sergt. F. L. 201827. | M. April 23/17. |
| 4 D. | | Bennett, R. F. 201439. | M. April 23/17. |
| 4 D. | | Bond, C. 201819. | M. April 23/17. |
| 4 D. | | Breed, W. 201644. | M. April 23/17. |
| ‡4 D. | | Bridge, E. 201816. | W. and M. April 17/17. |
| 4 D. | | Brinkley, W. A. 202266. | M. April 23/17. |
| 4 D. | | Bunn, C. 201669. | M. April 23/17. |
| 4 D. | | Collins, L.-Cpl. Bevis C. 202175. | M. April 23/17. |
| 4 D. | | Dawson, J. 201717. | M. April 23/17. |

**Suffolk Regiment—contd.**

## *B.E.F.*

| | | |
|---|---|---|
| 4 D. | Dean, A. V. 201713. | M. April 23/17. |
| 4 D. | Ellwood, J. 202179. | M. April 23/17. |
| 4 D. XV | Filby, Sergt. William. 200084. | M. April 23/17. |
| 4 D. XVI | Gallant, A. G. 202416. (5614.) | M. April 23/17. |
| 4 D. | Hales, A/L.-Cpl. A. 200696. | M. April 23/17. |
| 4 D. | Hayden, J. 201700. | M. April 23/17. |
| 4 D. | Houghton, A. E. 202544. | W. and M. April 28/17. |
| 4 D. | King, F. 202157. | M. April 23/17. |
| 4 D. | Mickleburgh, A/L.-Cpl. G. 202202. | M. April 23/17. |
| 4 D. | Nixon, Sergt. H. 200488. (2160.) | M. April 23/17. |
| 4 D. | Pickett, Albert John. 202002. (5191.) | W. and M. April 23/17. |
| ‡4 D. | Pilbrow, Cpl. W. 200988. | W. and M. April 23/17. |
| 4 D. | Poole, A. 201999. (5188.) | M. April 23/17. |
| 4 D. | Purkis, L.-Cpl. A. 201802. | M. April 23/17. |
| 4 D. | Smith, L. G. 202215. | M. April 23/17. |
| 4 D. | Smith, Cpl. T. 200990. | M. April 23/17. |
| 4 D. | Webb, L.-Sergt. H. 200641. | M. April 23/17. |
| 7 | **Elvey, 2nd Lieut. C. L.** | K. about April 9/17. Det.D./B. |
| ‡7 A. | Adcock, H. 202280. | M. April 28/17. |
| 7 A. | Bassett, John. 20196. | W. and M. April 28/17. |
| ‡7 A. | Bayles, L.-Cpl. W. A. 13455. | W. and M. April 28/17. |
| ‡7 A. | Chaston, J. 18352. | M. April 28/17. |
| ‡7 A. | Clark, D. A. 202013. | M. April 28/17. |
| 7 A. | Frost, S. G. 30871. | M. April 28/17. |
| 7 A. | Harold, W. G. 201602. | M. Unoff. W. April 28/17. |
| 7 A. | Morley, L.-Cpl. Chas. 16053. | W. and M. April 28/17. |
| 7 A. or D. | Potter, F. E. 9218. | M. Oct. 12/16. R/Enq. |
| 7 A. | Ramplay, Herbert Victor. 24821. | W. and M. April 28/17. |
| *7 A. L.G.S. | Rice, A. E. 40587. | Unoff. M. April 28/17. |
| *7 A. | Smallwood, Anthony. 201630. | M. April 28/17. |
| 7 A. L.G.S. | Smith, Geo. Wm. 43043. | M. April 28/17. |
| ‡7 A. | Stebbings, W. A. 43059. | W. and M. April 28/17. |
| 7 A. I | Wills, Stephen. 12304. | M. Oct. 12/16. R/Enq. |
| ‡7 B. | Bishop, J. 20640. | M. April 28/17. |
| 7 B. V | Boutherway, F. W. 201579. (Fr. 4th, 4656.) | W. and M. April 28/17. |
| 7 B. VI | Brunning, S. C. S. 40977. | M. April 28/17. |
| 7 B. IV | Fisk, A. G. 8401. (Fr. 3rd.) | M. April 28/17. |
| 7 B. | Gardiner, Sigr. Chas. 13060. (Fr. H.Q.) | M. April 28/17. |
| ‡7 B. | Gosling, G. 15191. | M. April 28/17. |
| 7 B. or C. | Manning, Wm. Frank. 14169. | M. April 28/17. |
| 7 B. VII | Morton, R. J. 40704. | W. and M. April 28/17. |
| 7 B. VI | Parker, W. J. 40714. | M. April 28/17. |
| 7 B. | Peasey, L.-Cpl. V. H. 12989. | M. Oct. 12/16. R/Enq. |
| ‡7 B. | Rance, J. 241786. | M. April 28/17. |
| ‡7 B. | Read, H. B. 50582. | W. and M. April 28/17. |
| ‡7 B. | Sharman, A. 18996. | M. April 28/17. |
| ‡7 B. | Sheppard, L.-Cpl. T. 40589. | M. April 28/17. |
| 7 C. IX | Ainsworth, Fred. 19362. | W. and M. April 28/17. |
| 7 C. IX | Barber, W. J. 17589. | M. April 28/17. |
| 7 C. IX | Barton, E. S. 20026. | M. April 28/17. |
| 7 C. IX | Bell, F. 40954. | M. April 28/17. |
| ‡7 C. | Blundell, R. 50575. | M. April 28/17. |
| ‡7 C. | Bull, L.-Cpl. F. 30808. | M. April 28/17. |
| 7 C. XI | Buttress, L.-Cpl. Robert. 26770. | M. April 28/17. |
| ‡7 C. | Carter, H. 12122. | M. April 28/17. |
| 7 C. | Chambers, John. 43037. | W. Unoff. M. April 28/17. |

**Suffolk Regiment**—contd.

## *B.E.F.*

| | | |
|---|---|---|
| 7 C. | Copping, Samuel Oscar. 15316. | M. April 28/17. |
| 7 C. | Crofts, Rupert Edwin. 24891. (Fr. H.Q.) | M. April 28/17. |
| ‡7 C. | Fairweather, W. C. 43177. | W. and M. April 28/17. |
| 7 C. | Greatrix, P. W. 40628. | M. April 28/17. |
| 7 C. XII | Horrex, Geo. 13826. | M. April 28/17. |
| *7 C. L.G.S. | Howard, Harry. 43184. | M. April 28/17. |
| 7 C. XI | Howlett, Frank. 43185. | M. April 28/17. |
| ‡7 C. | Howlett, H. 34389. | M. April 28/17. |
| 7 C. IX | Leek, Claud, 43195. (Late 2294.) | M. Oct. 12/16. R/Enq. |
| ‡7 C. IX | Page, Cpl. Jas. 9500. | M. April 28/17. |
| 7 C. | Peck, Arthur Stanley. 8606. | M. April 28/17. |
| 7 C. XI | Prankard, Chas. 50599. | M. April 29/17. |
| 7 C. | Rolfe, William. 24961. | M. Oct. 12/16. R/Enq. |
| ‡7 C. | Sapey, E. 43209. | M. April 28/17. |
| 7 C. X | Skinner, W. G. 203831. | K. April 28/17. Det.D./B. |
| 7 C. X | Smith, L.-Cpl. Chas. Wm. 18851. | M. April 28/17. |
| 7 D. XIV | Elwell, J. G. 40659. | W. and M. April 28/17. |
| 7 D. | Howard, G. W. 26833. | M. Oct. 12/16. |
| 7 D. | Langley, E. 18332. | M. Oct. 12/16. R/Enq. |
| ‡7 D. | Mitchell, J. D. 43264. | W. and M. April 28/17. |
| 7 D. | Nicholls, Harry. 203000. (Fr. 4th.) | W. and M. April 28/17. |
| ‡7 D. | Websdale, S. D. 15859. | W. and M. April 28/17. |
| ‡7 D. | Wythe, A. 43286. | W. and M. April 28/17. |
| *7 ? | Elston, Geo. Jas. 19299. | K. April 28/17. Det.D./B. |
| 8 | **Row, Lieut. J. E.** | K. Oct. 20/16. Det.D./B |
| 8 B. | Brame, L.-Sergt. Frank. 14571. | M. Feb. 17/17. |
| 8 C. | Grimsey, L.-Cpl. Fredk. Walter. 13007. | M. Sept. 28/16. R/Enq. |
| 8 C. | Nobbs, George Wm. Arthur. 24999. | M. Sept. 28/16. R/Enq. |
| 9 A. | Brooks, E. C. 17801. | W. and M. Sept. 13-16/16. R/Enq. |
| 9 B. | Vincent, H. 28739. | M. April 26/17. |
| ‡9 C. | Reeman, Harry. 17876. | M. Sept. 13-16/16. R/Enq. |
| ‡9 C. | Reeman, Cpl. Thos. 13852. | M. Sept. 13-16/16. R/Enq. |
| ‡9 C. | Roe, Jas. 13306. | M. Sept. 13-16/16. R/Enq. |
| 9 D. | Emmens, Wm. Henry. 15096. | M. Sept. 13-16/16. R/Enq. |
| 11 | **Grand, 2nd Lieut. H. S.** | K. April 28/17. Det.D./B. |
| 11 | **Hunt, 2nd Lieut. J. W. R.** | M. April 28/17. |
| 11 | **Sheen, 2nd Lieut. C.** | D/W. May 3/17. Det.D./B. |
| 11 A. | Batchelor, A. E. 9687. | M. April 28/17. |
| 11 A. | Bilham, L.-Cpl. Wm. Charles. 13819. | K. April 28/17. Det.D./B. |
| 11 A. | Cherry, Sergt. Sydney Harry. 50457. | M. April 28/17. |
| 11 A. | Cragg, E. 24816. | M. April 28/17. |
| 11 A. | Daniels, Wm. F. 21007. | M. April 28/17. |
| 11 A. | Dyson, A. R. 9765. | M. April 28/17. |
| 11 A. II | Edwards, Ernest John. 43476. | M. April 28/17. |
| 11 A. | Elliott, H. 5234. | M. April 28/17. |
| 11 A. | Farrow, L.-Cpl. L. G. 18777. | M. April 28/17. |
| 11 A. | Felton, F. H. D. 24853. | M. April 28/17. |
| 11 A. | Free, A. 8938. (Fr. 3rd.) | M. April 28/17. |
| 11 A. IV | Gedge, A. 17518. | M. April 28/17. |
| 11 A. | Hale, Sig. J. 18718. | M. April 28/17. |
| 11 A. | Hawkins, E. 43489. | M. April 28/17. |
| 11 A. II | Jepson, Wm. Livesey. 41132. | M. April 28/17. |
| 11 A. IV | Kerry, C. 34991. | M. April 28/17. |
| 11 A. | Missen, A. 18367. | M. April 28/17. |
| 11 A. IV | Nunn, Albert. 9597. | M. April 23/17. |
| 11 A. | Parr, T. K. 3/9788. | M. April 28/17. |
| 11 A. II | Pittman, J. 41136. | M. April 28/17. |

**Suffolk Regiment—contd.**

*B.E.F.*

11 A. Rogers, A. 43514. M. April 28/17.
11 A. Stevens, L.-Sergt. C. W. 17203. M. April 28/17.
11 A. II Watson, R. 16419. M. April 28/17.
11 A. Welch, S. 16375. M. April 28/17.
11 A. Willingham, Cpl. W. 43388. M. April 28/17.
11 A. Willis, F. 25119. M. April 28/17.
11 A. Woods, F. 23750. M. April 28/17.
11 A. York, L.-Cpl. H. 43529. M. April 28/17.
11 B. Askew, H. 14419. M. April 28/17.
11 B. Barber, Sergt. Soloman. 16606. M. April 28/17.
11 B. Barlow, L.-Cpl. W. 24220. M. April 28/17.
11 B. VIII Browne, Cpl. E. F. 43399. M. April 28/17.
11 B. Byham, F. 14302. M. April 28/17.
11 B. Checksfield, C. H. 43466. M. April 9/17.
11 B. Curry, Sidney. 19111. M. April 21/17.
11 B. Dennis, W. 28331. M. April 28/17.
11 B. Devey, Fred J. 41144. M. April 28/17.
11 B. VI Durham, G. W. 23496. M. April 28/17.
11 B. Edge, W. J. E. 41143. M. April 28/17.
11 B. Goldsmith, L.-Cpl. Arthur. 13422. M. April 28/17.
11 B. Hancock, H. B. 24422. M. April 28/17.
11 B. Hepher, J. W. 23971. M. April 28/17.
11 B. Hunt, L.-Cpl. G. 13544. M. April 28/17.
11 B. Kester, E. 15218. M. April 28/17.
11 B. Linford, A.-Sergt. A. A. 15663. M. April 28/17.
11 B. Long, H. 17511. M. April 28/17.
11 B. VIII Lush, R. 43498. M. April 28/17.
11 B. Mannall, R. 20813. M. April 28/17.
11 B. Medcalf, A. W. 16820. M. April 28/17.
11 B. VI Patterson, George. 25238. K. April 28/17. Det.D./B.
11 B. VI Peacock, V. 15906. M. April 9/17.
11 B. Phillips, A. J. 26873. M. April 28/17.
11 B. V Smith, J. W. C. 35079. M. April 28/17.
11 B. VI Waring, T. H. 41148. M. April 28/17.
11 B. Willis, W. 34778. M. April 28/17.
11 C. Bowles, G. 9132. M. April 28/17.
11 C. Daines, Wm. 24160. M. April 28/17.
11 C. Hardy, S. 26293. M. April 28/17.
11 C. Hurley, Cpl. E. 43491. M. April 28/17.
11 C. Pettitt, W. C. 13606. M. April 27/17.
11 C. Rignall, A. B. 14774. M. April 28/17.
11 C. XI Tynet, T. 27669. M. April 27-28/17.
11 D. Brown, C. A. 16123. M. April 28/17.
11 D. XVI Catchpole, J. 24830. M. April 28/17.
11 D. Cooper, A. J. 22263. M. April 28/17.
11 D. M.G.S. Cornwell, Percy. 15894. M., bel. K. April 28/17.
11 D. XIII Downing, Fred. 20447. M. April 9/17.
11 D. Fiske, A. 18961. M. April 28/17.
11 D. Flagg, S. 16277. M. April 28/17.
11 D. Hayes, Frank. 41158. M. April 28/17.
11 D. XVI Hollingworth, Geo. Wm. 41159. M. April 28/17.
11 D. I.T.M. Hopkin, L.-Cpl. Oliver. 16336. (101 Bgde.) M. April 9/17.
11 D. Johnson, J. A. 16914. M. April 28/17.
11 D. Kirby, J. 15881. M. April 28/17.
11 D. Nash, J. A. 26311. M. April 28/17.
11 D. Neal, Cpl. N. 16248. M. April 28/17.
11 D. Palmer, C. W. 18212. M. April 28/17.
11 D. Porter, W. 16257. M. April 28/17.

**Suffolk Regiment**—contd.

*B.E.F.*

| | | |
|---|---|---|
| 11 D. | Rose, E. 24800. | M. April 9/17. |
| 11 D. XVI | Runnacles, L.-Cpl. H. 12080. | M. April 23/17. |
| 11 D. | Smith, A. 23487. | M. April 28/17. |
| 11 D. XIII | Smith, H. 235222. | M. April 28/17. |
| 11 D. XV | Thomson, A. W. 50686. | M. April 28/17. |
| 11 D. | Vernham, H. C. 24813. | M. April 28/17. |
| 11 D. | White, G. 34159. | M. April 28/17. |
| 11 D. | Wright, W. 34855. | M. April 28/17. |
| ‡12 A. | Barham, V. 27593. | M. May 6/17. |
| ‡12 A. | Blott, H. V. 17517. | M. May 6/17. |
| 12 A. | Carter, Wm. Jas. 20791. | M. May 6/17. |
| 12 A. | Cunningham, T. E. 22467. | M. May 6/17. |
| ‡12 A. | Day, S. R. 20660. | M. May 6/17. |
| 12 A. H.Q. | Elias, H. R. 27010. | M. May 6/17. |
| ‡12 A. | Hack, A. 27627. | M. May 6/17. |
| ‡12 A. | Hancock, E. S. 27327. | M. May 6/17. |
| ‡12 A. III | Holley, Geo. Fredk. 22428. | M. May 6/17. |
| ‡12 A. | Houlding, S. 50418. | M. May 6/17. |
| 12 A. | Maloney, Anthony. 22008. | M. May 6/17. |
| 12 A. | Marsh, Cpl. Hy. Baker. 22427. | M. May 6/17. |
| ‡12 A. | Moore, S. E. 22440. | M. May 6/17. |
| ‡12 A. | Nicholls, E. 34393. | M. May 6/17. |
| ‡12 A. | Pettitt, W. 27650. | M. May 6/17. |
| ‡12 A. | Porter, H. 16821. | M. May 6/17. |
| 12 A. I | Wilding, Samuel. 28606. | M. May 6/17. |
| ‡12 A. | Wolfe, F. C. 31482. | M. May 6/17. |
| ‡12 D. | Hanger, F. 41034. | M. May 6/17. |
| 12 D. | Heald, Alfred Richard. 27489. (Police Staff.) | M. May 6/17. |
| ‡12 D. | North, F. H. 22300. | M. May 6/17. |
| 12 D. XIV | Simpson, G. H. 41042. | M. May 6/17. |

*E.E.F.*

| | | |
|---|---|---|
| *5 D. | Blythe, Harry. 240653. (2561.) | W. and M. April 19/17. |
| *5 ? | Smith, H. W. 241330. | W. and M. April 19/17. |
| *15 ? | Perry, H. 320903. | M. May 25/17. |

**EAST SURREY REGIMENT.**

*B.E.F.*

| | | |
|---|---|---|
| 1 | **Bigger, 2nd Lieut. J. A. W.** | M. May 8/17. |
| 1 | **Gashion, 2nd Lieut. S. M.** | M. May 8/17. |
| 1 | **Hyde-Edwards, 2nd Lieut. C.** | M., bel. W. May 8/17. |
| 1 | **Mobbs, 2nd Lieut. E. T.** | M. May 8/17. |
| 1 | **Strong, 2nd Lieut. O. A.** | M. May 8/17. |
| 1 | **Sullivan, Capt. E. G.** | M., bel. K. May 8/17. |
| 1 1 IV | Austin, L.-Cpl. Edwin. 11577. | M. May 8/17. |
| ‡1 1 | Ayres, J. A. 10678. (Snip. S.) | M. May 8/17. |
| ‡1 1 | Bailey, A. 25728. | M. May 8/17. |
| ‡1 1 | Baker, L.-Cpl. G. 25718. | M. May 8/17. |
| ‡1 1 | Balchin, E. 30719. | M. May 8/17. |
| ‡1 1 | Baldwin, G. 16980. | M. May 8/17. |

Surrey Regiment, East—contd.

*B.E.F.*

| | | |
|---|---|---|
| 1 1 III | Brandon, John George. 25717. | M. May 8/17. |
| ‡1 1 | Burr, A. 10747. | M. May 8/17. |
| ‡1 1 | Butler, Cpl. A. 10415. | M. May 8/17. |
| ‡1 1 | Challis, W. 30209. | M. May 8/17. |
| *1 1 IV | Clarke, L.-Cpl. Harold Victor 31186 | M. May 9/17. |
| ‡1 1 L.G.S. | Cooke, L.-Cpl. W. 15. | W. and M. May 8/17. |
| ‡1 1 | Cooper, Sergt. D. W. 7564. | M. May 8/17. |
| ‡1 1 | Crawley, C. 9222. | W. and M. May 8/17. |
| ‡1 1 | Culver, A. 30899. | M. May 8/17. |
| 1 1 IV | Dicks, John Henry. 31072. | M. May 8/17. |
| ‡1 1 | Downing, H. 25752. | M. May 8/17. |
| *1 1 IV | Dowsing, H. S. D. 25754. | M. June 9/17. |
| ‡1 1 | Dunkley, V. 32367. | M. May 8/17. |
| 1 1 | Forder, G. 6265. | W. and M. Sept. 25/16. R/Enq. |
| ‡1 1 | Gill, M. 32480. | M. May 8/17. |
| 1 1 III | Godfrey, L.-Cpl. Fred. 33389. | M. May 8/17. |
| 1 1 I | Harwood, Cpl. W. J. 17719. | M. May 8/17. |
| 1 1 IV | Humphreys, Hy. Francis. 10640. | M. May 8/17. |
| *1 1 IV | Hunt, Harry J. 25721. | M. May 8/17. |
| 1 1 IV | Ironside, Douglas. 30644. | M. May 8/17. |
| ‡1 1 | Jordon, A. 9450. | M. May 8/17. |
| 1 1 | Jude, H. 17798. (Fr. 4th.) | M. Sept. 5/16. R/Enq. |
| ‡1 1 | Lane, A. W. 31017. | M. May 8/17. |
| 1 1 | Le Bretton, Walter C. 11860. | M. May 8/17. |
| 1 1 II | Martin, L. 7623. | M. May 8/17. |
| ‡1 1 | Minns, J. 25720. | M. May 8/17. |
| ‡1 1 | Panton, T. 10422. | M. May 8/17. |
| 1 1 III | Potter, Albert. 1669. | W. and M. May 8/17. |
| ‡1 1 | Read, B. 32688. | M. May 8/17. |
| ‡1 1 | Roughman, W. 26767. | M. May 8/17. |
| 1 1 L.G.S. | Saunders, Wm. Hry. 10876. | M. May 8/17. |
| *1 1 L.G.S. | Searle. Fred. 7744. | M. May 8/17. |
| ‡1 1 | Seymour, H. 31062. | M. May 8/17. |
| ‡1 1 | Shuffell, M. 30832. | M. May 8/17. |
| ‡1 1 | Spiers, T. 2345. | M. May 8/17. |
| *1 1 III | Squibb, L. W. 30786. | M. May 8/17. |
| *1 1 III | Stone, W. J. 32745. | M. May 8/17. |
| ‡1 1 | Thomas, A. 31051. | M. May 8/17. |
| *1 1 I | Thomasson, W. 14837. | M. May 8/17. |
| ‡1 1 | Townsend, D. 442. | M. May 8/17. |
| ‡1 1 | Trimm, C. 11601. | M. May 8/17. |
| 1 1 II | Turner, L.-Cpl. Chas. Bert. 31045. | M. May 8/17. |
| ‡1 1 | Waller, G. 30696. | M. May 8/17. |
| ‡1 1 M.G.S. | Walton, W. 17134. | M. May 8/17. |
| ‡1 1 | Ward, H. 32405. | M. May 8/17. |
| *1 1 | Warren, John Henry. 14449. | M. May 8/17. |
| ‡1 1 | Westwood, W. 9738. | M. May 8/17. |
| ‡1 1 | Wilkinson, A. 10331. | M. May 8/17. |
| ‡1 1 | Wilmer, S. 31053. | M. May 8/17. |
| 1 1 III | Wilmore, L.-Cpl. E. Alfred. 18997. | M. May 8/17. |
| 1 1 I | Wright, F. W. 32735. | M. May 8/17. |
| 1 2 | Ashton, S/B. Henry Geo. 28024. | M. May 8/17. |
| 1 2 V | Barrett, Fred. 17808. | M. May 8/17. |
| ‡1 2 | Brown, A. 32463. | M. May 8/17. |
| ‡1 2 VIII | Challenger, Walter Ernest. 31146. | M. May 8/17. |

**Surrey Regiment East—contd.**

## *B.E.F.*

| | | |
|---|---|---|
| 1 2 VIII | Colborn, Wm. 10911. | M. May 8/17. |
| ‡1 2 | Donoghue, J. 64466. | M. May 8/17. |
| ‡1 2 | Edwards W. 25743. | M. May 8/17. |
| ‡1 2 L.G.S. | Elliot, Sidney. 30992. | M. May 8/17. |
| 1 2 VI | Finney, J. J. 21072. | M. May 8/17. |
| 1 2 | Firmin. 30773. | M. May 8/17. |
| 1 2 VII | Geale, W. G. 28035. | M. May 8/17. |
| ‡1 2 | Gennery, L.-Cpl. E. 5744. | M. May 8/17. |
| ‡1 2 | Handley, F. 10854. | M. May 8/17. |
| 1 2 VI | Heath, G. H. 31008. | Unoff. W. and M. May 8/17. |
| ‡1 2 | James, J. 337. | M. May 8/17. |
| *1 2 VII | Jenkins, S. W. 31080. | M. May 8/17. |
| 1 2 VII | Johnson, A. M. 10737. | M. May 8/17. |
| ‡1 2 | Josland, A. 31012. | M. May 8/17. |
| ‡1 2 | Lamb, W. 20384. | M. May 8/17. |
| *1 2 | Nash, Percy John. 31161. | M. May 8/17. |
| *1 2 or 3 | Poplett, L.-Cpl. Harold H. 28003. (Fr. 5th.) | W. and M. May 8/17. |
| 1 2 V | Reeves, W. G. 4860. | M. May 8/17. |
| ‡1 2 | Road, E. 7367. | M. May 8/17. |
| *1 2 VIII | Simmer, L.-Cpl. A. J. 16121. | M. May 8/17. |
| 1 2 L.G.S. | Smith, Arthur H. 31067. | M. May 8/17. |
| 1 2 II | Smith, Wm. Jas. 31042. | M. May 8/17. |
| *1 2 | Steadman, J. G. 1935. | M. May 8/17. |
| ‡1 2 | Stemp, J. 32531. | M. May 8/17. |
| ‡1 2 | Swift, C. 14876. | M. May 8/17. |
| 1 2 | Tippins, Cpl. Chas. Jas. 11153. | M. May 8/17. |
| ‡1 2 | Townsend, F. 32655. | M. May 8/17. |
| *1 2 VII | Tugwell, H. 19525. | M. May 8/17. |
| 1 2 | Wallis, S/B. Wm. Geo. 8175. (Fr. H.Q.) | M. May 8/17. |
| ‡1 2 | Watts, F. 31056. | M. May 8/17. |
| 1 2 M.G.S. | Wells, P. 28009. | M. May 8/17. |
| ‡1 2 | Willmott, H. 7177. | W. and M. May 8/17. |
| 1 2 VII | Woodward, J. 30778. | M. May 8/17. |
| *1 3 X | Adams, W. 30764. | M. May 8/17. |
| ‡1 3 | Baigent, F. 6616. | M. May 8/17. |
| 1 3 IX | Bareham, Fred. Percy. 32453. | M. May 8/17. |
| *1 3 XII | Becker, James. 32455. | M. May 8/17. |
| ‡1 3 Sig. S. | Bird, Henry Arthur. 4705. | M. May 8/17. |
| *1 3 XII | Bory, Chas. Alex. 17946. | M. May 8/17. |
| ‡1 3 | Bradley, E. 6267. | M. May 8/17. |
| 1 3 XII L.G.S. | Budden, Herbert. 33391. | M. May 8/17. |
| ‡1 3 | Butler, F. 11745. | M. May 8/17. |
| ‡1 3 | Carter, E. 25723. | M. May 8/17. |
| *1 3 X | Carter, Walter. 10682. | M. May 8/17. |
| 1 3 IX | Clifton, C. A. 30765. | M. May 8/17. |
| 1 3 IX | Compton, Percy. 32278. | M. May 8/17. |
| ‡1 3 | Cooper, E. 7007. | M. May 8/17. |
| ‡1 3 | Curtis, A. 25737. | M. May 8/17. |
| *1 3 L.G.S. | Durrant, L.-Cpl. Frank Edwin. 3533. | M. May 8/17. |
| ‡1 3 | Ells, E. 31073. | M. May 8/17. |
| 1 3 | Franklin, S/B. Ernest Albert. 9662. | M. May 8/17. |
| *1 3 L.G.S. | Fuller, George. 4570. | M. May 8/17. |
| ‡1 3 | Giddon, T. 5440. | M. May 8/17. |
| ‡1 3 | Gray, E. 16138. | M. May 8/17. |

**Surrey Regiment, East**—contd.

## *B.E.F.*

1 3 XII Guy, T. E. 14884. M. May 8/17.
‡1 3 Harris, G. 32489. M. May 8/17.
*1 3 XI Hedges, S. A. 17465. M. May 8/17.
1 3 L.G.S. Hutton, Walter Jas. 16237. M. May 8/17.
‡1 3 Irons, A. 20889. M. May 8/17.
‡1 3 Jenkins, A. 10727. M. May 8/17.
‡1 3 Jones, R. 33396. M. May 8/17.
‡1 3 Kerry, A. 20417. M. May 8/17.
‡1 3 Kittle, R. 10695. M. May 8/17.
‡1 3 Lucas, L. 31174. M. May 8/17.
‡1 3 Matthews, C. 31160. M. May 8/17.
1 3 L.G.S. Maughan, W. J. 10732. M. May 8/17.
‡1 3 XII Miles, L. F. 10956. M. May 8/17.
1 3 Monk, L.-Cpl. Robt. Chas. 32387. M. May 8/17.
‡1 3 Mortimer, A. 20849. M. May 8/17.
1 3 Muggeridge, W. H. 31070. M. May 8/17.
1 3 X Overs, E. F. 25180. M. May 8/17.
*1 3 XI Poplett, H. 31030. M. May 8/17.
‡1 3 Price, F. J. 10175. M. May 8/17.
‡1 3 Quinn, W. 33390. M. May 8/17.
‡1 3 Reid, L.-Cpl. W. 32390. M. May 8/17.
‡1 3 Rolls, T. 10739. M. May 8/17.
1 3 X Seymour, L.-Cpl. J. 32523. M. May 8/17.
‡1 3 X Shingler, Horace. 10202. M. May 8/17. R/Enq. (2nd cas.)
1 3 Small, L.-Cpl. E. 11414. M. May 8/17.
1 3 L.G.S. Smallpiece, Harry. 4212. M. May 8/17.
‡1 3 Smith, William. 28065. M. Sept. 3/16. R/Enq.
1 3 X Speechley, Jonathan. 30785. M. May 8/17.
‡1 3 Stroud, A. 30733. M. May 8/17.
*1 3 Sturgess, Sergt. Geo. 8677. M. May 8/17.
1 3 or 4 Taylor, Chas. 17199. M. May 8/17.
1 3 X Turner, Arthur. 11004. M. May 8/17.
1 3 Walker, L.-Cpl. Arthur Percy. 5622. M. May 8/17.
1 3 XII Walker, R. H. 31185. M. May 8/17.
‡1 3 Wenham, L.-Cpl. R. 31180. M. May 8/17.
1 3 X Williams, Sig. H. 10661. M. May 8/17.
‡1 3 Witney, E. 32737. M. May 8/17.
‡1 3 Wood, F. 32735. M. May 8/17.
‡1 3 Wood, J. 3088. M. May 8/17.
*1 4 Adey, John Fredk. 8157. M. May 8/17.
1 4 XVI Allson, W. 14446. M. April 23/17.
‡1 4 Breedon, P. 31140. M. May 8/17.
‡1 4 Brookes, L.-Cpl. J. 25859. M. May 8/17.
1 4 XVI Brookes, L.-Cpl. J. 28079. M. May 8/17.
‡1 4 Brown, A. 8453. M. May 8/17.
1 4 XV Brown, A. J. 25751. M. May 8/17.
‡1 4 Cackett, H. 4827. M. May 8/17.
1 4 XV Chilver, F. 31068. M. May 8/17.
1 4 XIV Cobb, L.-Cpl. Frank Churchill. 31171. M. May 8/17.
1 4 XVI Cokeeffe, Charles. 32508. M. May 8/17.
‡1 4 Cooper, Sergt. G. 10006 M. May 8/17.
1 4 L.G.S. Dimon, P. J. 28045. M. May 8/17.
*1 4 L.G.S. Emery, Ernest Peter. 10723. M. May 8/17.
‡1 4 Evans, H. 4824. M. May 8/17.

**Surrey Regiment, East—contd.**

## *B.E.F.*

| | | | |
|---|---|---|---|
| ‡1 4 | | Evans, W. 32478. | M. May 8/17. |
| ‡1 4 | | Foley, V. 33398. | M. May 8/17. |
| 1 4 | XIII | Foreman, Fred. 7132. | M. May 8/17. |
| ‡1 4 | | Goulding, L.-Cpl. J. 1206. | M. May 8/17. |
| ‡1 4 | | Griffiths, L.-Cpl. G. 7408. | M. May 8/17. |
| ‡1 4 | | Harris, L.-Cpl. H. 6452. | M. May 8/17. |
| ‡1 4 | | Harvey, Fredk. Wm. 9893. | M. May 8/17. |
| 1 4 | XV | Haynes, F. R. 30613. | M. May 8/17. |
| 1 4 | | Heasman, W. G. 30607. | M. May 8/17. |
| ‡1 4 | | Holmwood, H. 30608. | M. May 8/17. |
| ‡1 4 | | Homewood, E. 22974. | M. May 8/17. |
| ‡1 4 | | Langley, J. 33394. | M. May 8/17. |
| ‡1 4 | | Lidbury, W. 30711. | M. May 8/17. |
| ‡1 4 | | McGourty, P. 32744. | M. May 8/17. |
| ‡1 4 | | McMullen, H. 32507. | M. May 8/17. |
| ‡1 4 | | Martin, L.-Cpl. E. 1874. | M. May 8/17. |
| 1 4 | | Mason, V. 17720. | M. May 8/17. |
| ‡1 4 | | Mitchell, H. 32395. | M. May 8/17. |
| ‡1 4 | | O'Keefe, W. 32308. | M. May 8/17. |
| ‡1 4 | | Parker, S. 10480. | M. May 8/17. |
| 1 4 | XVI | Peckham, Fred. 25747. | M. May 8/17. |
| ‡1 4 | | Pitt, F. 30667. | M. May 8/17. |
| 1 4 | | Redman, E. C. G. 31162. | M. May 8/17. |
| •1 4 | XIV | Reynolds, P. 32389. | M. May 6/17. |
| ‡1 4 | | Roberts, F. 10064. | M. May 8/17. |
| ‡1 4 | | Skipper, A. 23088. | M. May 8/17. |
| ‡1 4 | L.G.S. | Slaughter, F. 7271. | M. May 8/17. |
| 1 4 | | Smith, Frank. 22664. | M. May 8/17. |
| ‡1 4 | | Smith, G 31060. | M. May 8/17. |
| ‡1 4 | | Smith, W. 11620. | M. May 8/17. |
| 1 4 | | Spong, L.-Cpl. V. 22181. | M. May 8/17. |
| •1 4 | XIV | Toogood, Thos. Wm. 22254. | M. May 8/17. |
| ‡1 4 | | Tracey, Cpl. J. 10611. | M. May 8/17. |
| ‡1 4 | | Whibley, G. 18238. | M. May 8/17. |
| 1 4 | L.G.S. | Wiffin, B. H. 18258. | M. May 8/17. |
| 1 4 | XIV | Wolstenholme, Harry. 33436. | M. May 8/17. |
| •1 4 | XV | Wyeth, H. 8611. | M. May 8/17. |
| 1 ? | | Mumford, Alfred Fredk. 19222. | M. May 8/17. |
| 7 | | **Adams, 2nd Lieut. G. A.** | M., bel. W. **April 9/17.** |
| 7 | | **Hovenden, 2nd Lieut. A. L.** | M. May 3/17. |
| 7 | | **Leach, Capt. E. S. W.** | K. May 3/17. Det.D./B. |
| ‡7 | A. II | Fisher, Albert. 32625. | K. April 30/17. Det.D./B. |
| 7 | A. II | Kington, Matthew Hy. 24353. | M. May 3/17. |
| 7 | A. IV | Mount, L.-Cpl. Percy Victor. 23256. | M. April 9/17. |
| •7 | A. I | Sellberg, Leonard. 19361. | M. May 3/17. |
| ‡7 | A. | Staner, S. 3095. | M. May 3/17. |
| 7 | A. | Treadle, G. 23442. | W. Unoff. M. May 1/17. |
| 7 | B. | Bennett, Henry. 16142. (Known as "Bunny"). | M. May 3/17. |
| 7 | B. | Morris, W. 6763. | M. April 9/17. |
| ‡7 | B. | Riley, W. 17167. | M. April 9/17. |
| •7 | B. V | Smith, H. H. 31377. | M. May 3/17. |
| ‡7 | B. | Taylor, A. 24365. | M. May 3/17. |

**Surrey Regiment, East—contd.**

*B.E.F.*

| | | |
|---|---|---|
| *7 B. | Taylor, V. J. 11539. | M. May 3/17. |
| 7 C. XI | Carter, J. 21467. | M. May 3/17. |
| ‡7 C. | Cole, I. 17388. | M. May 3/17. |
| 7 C. X | Coulotock, L.-Cpl. H. 16295. | M. May 3/17. |
| 7 C. XI | Dixon, L.-Cpl. C. 10631. | M. May 3/17. |
| 7 C. X | Farmer, H. 23951. | M. May 3/17. |
| 7 C. X | Green, Geo. Thos. 24828. | M. May 3/17. |
| ‡7 C. | Harford, L.-Cpl. P. 10710. | M. May 3/17. |
| ‡7 C. | Hooks, W. 6805. | M. May 3/17. |
| *7 C. X | Lester, L.-Cpl. W. N. 1652. | M. May 3/17. |
| ‡7 C. | Mitchell, A.-Sergt. W. 477. | M. May 3/17. |
| 7 C. X | Nash, G. 11162. | M. May 3/17. |
| ‡7 C. | Neary, L.-Cpl. W. 10694. | M. May 3/17. |
| ‡7 C. | Price, Sergt. W. 9736. | M. May 3/17. |
| ‡7 C. | Rose, A. 15870. | M. May 3/17. |
| 7 C. X | Rulton, A. 4573. | M. May 3/17. |
| 7 C. | Self, Cecil George. 24818. | M. May 3/17. |
| ‡7 C. | Spittle, G. 14912. | M. May 3/17. |
| *7 C. M.G.S. | Swan, Jos. Fredk. 15969. | M. May 3/17. |
| ‡7 C. | Thripp, A. 11104. | M. May 3/17. |
| ‡7 C. | Towler, A. E. 4271. | M. May 3/17. |
| ‡7 C. | Walter, J. 11317. | M. May 3/17. |
| ‡7 C. X | Wilmot, Wm. John. 21913. | M. May 3/17. |
| ‡7 C. | Woolley, A. G. 24822. | M. May 3/17. |
| 7 D. XVI | Amor, Cpl. C. E. 11944. | M. May 3/17. |
| ‡7 D. | Banham, D. 20641. | M. May 3/17. |
| *7 D. XIV | Bowring, Hry Frank. 32610. | M. May 3/17. |
| ‡7 D. | Bradley, L.-Cpl. A. 7182. | M. May 3/17. |
| *7 D. XVI | Bridcutt, C. 21459. | M. May 3/17. |
| ‡7 D. | Fane, S. D. 32626. | M. May 3/17. |
| ‡7 D. | George, W. H. 6142. | M. May 3/17. |
| 7 D. XIV | Hemmings, G. F. J. 22250. | M. May 3/17. |
| ‡7 D. | *Hills, A. 14683. | M. May 3/17. |
| 7 D. | Howard, Sergt. S. J. 367. | M. May 3/17. |
| ‡7 D. | Hunt, G. E. 23383. | M. May 3/17. |
| ‡7 D. | Letts, P. F. 32828. | M. May 3/17. |
| 7 D. XVI | Sherriff, F. E. 17778. | M. May 3/17. |
| 7 D. XIV | Waller, Albert. 21912. | M. May 3/17. |
| 7 D. L.G.S. | Wheaton, J. 15528. | M. May 3/17. |
| 8 A. | **Brown, 2nd Lieut. H. V.** | M. May 3/17. |
| 8 | **Seater, 2nd Lieut. P. J.** | M. May 3/17. |
| 8 A. or B. | Allen, L.-Sergt. Alexander. 5594. | W. and M. May 3/17. |
| 8 A. III | Amess, L.-Sgt. Fred. Chas. 8247. | M. Sept. 30/16. R/Enq. |
| 8 A. or B. | Balls, J. 4951. | M. May 3/17. |
| 8 A. or C. | Cockerell, W. 28404. | W. and M. May 3/17. |
| *8 A. or B. | Crouch, G. A. 4714. | W. and M. May 3/17. |
| *8 A. III | Crouch, W. H. G. 4706. | M. May 3/17. |
| *8 A. or C. | Derriman, Leonard. 21782. | M. May 3/17. |
| *8 A. or B. | Eastman, W. 8679. | W. and M. May 3/17. |
| 8 A. IV | Ede, A. 23241. | W. Unoff. M. May 3/17. |
| ‡8 A. | Gearan, Sergt. D. 11834. | M. May 3/17. |
| 8 A. III | Harber, Francis David. 30462. | M. May 3/17. |
| *8 A. or C. | Hudson, J. H. 23255. | W. and M. May 3/17. |
| *8 A. or C. | Johnson, T. 28299. (11318.) | W. and M. May 3/17. |
| 8 A. | King, William. 28412. | W. and M. Sept. 30/16. R/Enq. |
| 8 A. II | Loasby, F. 17972. | W. and M. May 3/17. |
| 8 A. III | McKenzie, Thos. 4777. | M. May 3/17. |
| ‡8 A. I | Rix, L.-Cpl. Wm. Archer G/4931. | M. May 3/17. |
| *8 A. or C. | Rowe, Cpl. Fred. 5296. | M. May 5/17. |

**Surrey Regiment, East—contd.**

## *B.E.F.*

| | | |
|---|---|---|
| 8 A. I | Self, Wm. John. 28411. (Fr. 15th Middlesex.) | M. Sept. 30/16. |
| *8 A. IV | Souster, W. 25633. | K. May 2/17. Det.D./B. |
| 8 A. or B. L.G.S. | Tyler, L. Cpl. Geo. 30840. | M. May 3/17. |
| 8 A. or B. | Wallace, J. F. 202598. | W. and M. May 3/17. |
| 8 A. | Whelan, T. 28397. | M. Sept. 30/16. R/Enq. |
| 8 B. or C. X | Alston, Alfred A. 23279. | M. May 3/17. |
| 8 B. VIII | Ambler, L.-Cpl. Henry. 15947. | M. May 3/17. |
| ‡8 B. | Baker, W. E. 32331. | M. May 3/17. |
| 8 B. or C. L.G.S. | Beswick, J. C. 5166. | M. May 3/17. |
| 8 B. VII | Blackmore, Wm. 24299. | M. May 3/17. |
| *8 B. VII | Blake, Wm. Arthur. 31111. | M. May 3/17. |
| 8 B. L.G.S. | Bridgland, Jn. Wm. 17398. | M. May 3/17. |
| 8 B. or D. | Brown, L.-Cpl. Geo. Victor. 25670. | W. and M. May 1-5/17. |
| ‡8 B. | Caplin, W. 28212. | M. May 3/17. |
| 8 B. or D. | Childs, L.-Cpl. Basil. 4000. | M. May 3/17. |
| 8 B. L.G.S. | Coppard, Cecil Trayton. 28112. | M. May 3/17. |
| ‡8 B. | Cranstone, A. 30405. | M. May 3/17. |
| ‡8 B. | Darrington, R. 3571. | M. May 3/17. |
| *8 B. or D. | Fryer, E. A. 22570. | M. May 3/17. |
| ‡8 B. or C. L.G.S. | Gates, Thos. 32249. | M. May 3/17. |
| ‡8 B. | Griggs, C. 22906. | M. May 3/17. |
| 8 B. | Grimshaw, Fred. 9535. | M. May 3/17. |
| ‡8 B. I.T.M. | Haisman, Geo. 28341. (55 Bgde.) (Fr. 13 Middlesex, 22105.) | W. and M. May 3/17. |
| ‡8 B. | Harris, G. 22907. | M. May 3/17. |
| 8 B. VI | Hicks, E. T. 202612. | M. May 3/17. |
| ‡8 B. | Hider, W. 33492. | W. and M. May 3/17. |
| *8 B. or D. | Holloway, Charles. 24298. | M. May 3/17. |
| *8 B. | Holt, H. 25626. | W. and M. May 3/17. |
| 8 B. or C. X | Johnston, A. J. 30372. | W. and M. May 3/17. |
| ‡8 B. | Jones, T. 25155. | W. and M. May 3/17. |
| 8 B. or C. XI | Joseph, L.-Cpl. S. H. 11798. | W. and M. May 3/17. |
| ‡8 B. | Kelly, J. 7677. | W. and M. May 3/17. |
| ‡8 B. V | Keyworth, J. 8962. | M. May 3/17. |
| 8 B. or D. | Knight, A. 6208. | M. May 3/17. |
| ‡8 B. | Knight, L.-Cpl. E. 5036. | M. May 3/17. |
| ‡8 B. | Lanson, L. 3152. | M. May 3/17. |
| *8 B. or D. | Litton, A. H. 23732. | M. May 3/17. |
| 8 B. VIII | Mounty, Joe. 31091. | M. May 3/17. |
| 8 B. or C. | Owen, Jn. Chas. 19218. | M. May 3/17. |
| 8 B. or C. | Pestell, A. W. 32349. | Unoff. M. May 3/17. |
| 8 B. VI | Potts, Samuel Hayden. 31094. | M. May 3/17. |
| ‡8 B. VIII | Roberts, F. 31134. | M. May 3/17. |
| *8 B. or D. | Rosam, A. 22421. | M. May 3/17. |
| 8 B. or D. | Salmon, L. W. 31096. | W. and M. May 3/17. |
| *8 B. | Soames, Sergt. Tom. 28252. | M. May 3/17. |
| ‡8 B. | Stevens, J. 23271. | M. May 3/17. |
| 8 B. or C. | Thomas, James Albert. 5122. | M. May 3/17. |
| *8 B. VIII | Toms, J. E. 30847. | M. May 3/17. |
| 8 B. or C. | Turnbull, Sgt. Alexander. 28427. | W. and M. May 3/17. |
| *8 B. or D. M.G.S. | Walker, Wright. 25654. | M. May 3/17. |
| *8 B. or C. | Wallace, Jas. Hay. 1880. | W. and M. May 3/17. |
| 8 B. M.G.S. | Watling, G. 20076. | M. May 3/17. |
| ‡8 B. VII | White, T. W. 25668. | M. May 5/17. |
| 8 B. VI | Wood, C. A. 28176. | M. May 3/17. |
| 8 B. V | Woolgar, Sydney. 31108. | M. May 3/17. |

**Surrey Regiment, East—contd.**

## *B.E.F.*

‡8 B. Woolnough, C. 28461. M. May 3/17.
*8 C. or D. Blackledge, L.-Cpl. Albert Wm. 8516. W. and M. May 3/17.
*8 C. or D. Burdock, Wm. 30410. M. May 1-5/17.
‡8 C. Chapman, Sergt. G. 8638. M. May 1-5/17.
*8 C. or D. Clark, W. H. G/25645. W. and M. May 3/17.
‡8 C. Cooper, A. 5191. M. May 3/17.
*8 C. Davies, W. H. 28366. M. May 3/17.
‡8 C. Ford, J. 28239. M. May 3/17.
*8 C. X Gillam, Fred. 30380. W. and M. May 3/17.
8 C. Hargrave, Sergt. F. S. 6687. M. May 3/17.
*8 C. XI Hartland, Wm. 25171. M. May 3/17.
‡8 C. King, E. 31090. W. and M. May 3/17.
8 C. Largent, William. 5225. M. May 3/17.
‡8 C. Middleton, J. 28342. M. May 3/17.
*8 C. XI Mills, Robert. 39398. M. May 3/17.
8 C. X Neale, Francis Leopold. 30382. M. May 3/17.
‡8 C. Parsons, W. G. 28246. M. May 3/17.
*8 C. Phillips, Cuthbert. 31123. M. May 1-5/17.
‡8 C. Pratt, T. 28273. M. May 3/17.
*8 C. L.G.S. Shires, H. G/25188. W. and M. May 3/17.
‡8 C. Stoneybridge, J. 28285. M. May 1-5/17.
‡8 C. Trezise, J. 30164. M. May 3/17.
‡8 C. Tunmore, S. 5120. M. May 3/17.
8 D. Cumming, A. S. 32301. M. May 3/17.
8 D. XV Day, William. 10639. M. May 3/17.
‡8 D. Easum, T. 31414. M. May 3/17.
‡8 D. Foord, W. 22903. M. May 3/17.
8 D. XIV Frost, Chas. Philip. 20421. M. Sept. 30/16. R/Enq.
‡8 D. Gilbert, J. 22905. M. May 3/17.
‡8 D. Harrison, R. 2794. W. and M. May 20/17.
8 D. XV Horton, G. H. 30440. M. May 3/17.
‡8 D. Knapp, E. G. T. 19232. M. May 3/17.
‡8 D. Martin, D. W. 5487. M. May 3/17.
*8 D. XVI Mason, A. V. 22429. M. May 3/17.
8 D. XIII Miles, Charles. 32346. M. May 3/17.
8 D. XIII Morris, T. H. 22443. M. May 3/17.
8 D. Munro, Walter H. 18963. M. May 3/17.
‡8 D. Murphy, J. 17301. M. May 3/17.
*8 D. XV Nicholls, Wm. David. 32347. M. May 3/17.
‡8 D. Oram, H. 24306. M. May 3/17.
‡8 D. Parks, H. 30432. M. May 3/17.
‡8 D. Sinden, A. 22929. M. May 3/17.
‡8 D. Smith, E. 8202. M. May 3/17.
8 D. XV Stow, Walter. 30155. M. May 3/17.
‡8 D. Truss, A. 5863. M. May 3/17.
8 D. XVI Warner, P. F. 30852. M. May 3/17.
*8 D. XV Washington, L.-Cpl. A. 2398. M. May 3/17.
‡8 D. Willmott, C. 25192. W. and M. May 3/17.
‡8 ? Jones, H. E. 7176. W. and M. May 3/17.
*8 ? I.T.M. Neville, John Richard. 4444. (55 Bgde.) M. May 3/17.
*8 ? Northfield, T. S. 18061. M. May 8/17.
*9 B. VI Holder, Henry. 20597. K. June 12/17. Det.D./B.
9 D. Beadle, Wm. 4125. M. Aug. 16/16. R/Enq.
‡12 B. VI Fookes, Edw. Bernard. 14523. M. June 7/17.
‡12 B. Osborne, S. 16300. M., bel. K. Sept. 10/16.
‡12 B. Scobell, L.-Cpl. Thos. Henry. 14204 M. Sept. 15/16. R/Enq.
12 C. XI Keefe, Harold John. 17272. M. Sept. 15/16. R/Enq.

Surrey Regiment, East—contd.

## *B.E.F.*

| | | |
|---|---|---|
| 12 D. XIV | Fisher, Herbert F. 14241. | M. Sept. 15/16. R/Enq. |
| 13 B. | Mills, 2nd Lieut. T. B. | M. May 24/17. |
| 13 A. III | Chowney, H. A. 25708. | K. April 24/17. Det.D./B. |
| 13 C. | Clark, W. 13774. | M. Mar. 16/17. |
| 13 C. XII | Edwards, W. A. 25691. | W. and M. April 24/17. |
| ‡13 D. | Leakey, S. 16022. | K. Sept. 15/16. Det.D./B. |

## *BALKANS.*

| | | |
|---|---|---|
| 2 A. | Wiggins, Wm. 14911. | M. Jan. 26/17. |
| 2 D. XIV | Radford, L.-Cpl. F. 18063. | M. April 25/17. |
| 2 ? | Blythe, T. B. 12005. | M. Jan. 26/17. |

## ROYAL WEST SURREY REGIMENT.

## *B.E.F.*

| | | |
|---|---|---|
| 1 A. I | Ainsworth, Chas. 4111. | W. and M. April 23/17. |
| ‡1 A. II M.G.S. | Arnold, L.-Cpl. W. J. 10903. | M. April 23/17. |
| ‡1 A. | Balchin, E. 13372. | M. April 23/17. |
| ‡1 A. | Barnes, H. 1112. | M. April 23/17. |
| 1 A. | Boulter, Ernest. 8749. | M. April 23/17. |
| ‡1 A. | Bullock, W. 7106. | M. April 23/17. |
| 1 A. M.G.S. | Cackett, Alfred Edw. 1289. | M. April 23/17. |
| 1 A. III | Curtis, Arthur Leonard. 9693. | M. April 23/17. |
| 1 A. | Cutts, A. 5385. | M. Aug. 24/16. |
| •1 A. II | Daborn, Ben. 37895. | M. April 23/17. |
| ‡1 A. | Dudley, A. 10349. | M. April 23/17. |
| 1 A. III | Eales, W. 37075. | M. April 23/17. |
| 1 A. IV | Forbes, L.-Cpl. A. G. 37080. | W. and M. April 23/17. |
| ‡1 A. | Foy, E. 37904. | M. April 23/17. |
| ‡1 A. | Fry, Sergt. W. 22478. | M. April 23/17. |
| ‡1 A. | Gilbert, J. 773. | M. April 23/17. |
| 1 A. | Goodridge, Walter. 8230. | M. April 23/17. |
| 1 A. I | Goodwin, H. G. 24628. | M. April 23/17. |
| ‡1 A. | Green, B. 1840. | M. April 23/17. |
| ‡1 A. | Green, G. 37079. | M. April 23/17. |
| ‡1 A. | Green, H. 11377. | M. April 23/17. |
| ‡1 A. | Grevitt, T. 8360. | M. April 23/17. |
| ‡1 A. | Hazel, H. 12314. | W. and M. April 23/17. |
| 1 A. | Jenkins, Sig. and L.-Cpl. Thos. 10607 | W. and M. April 23/17. |
| ‡1 A. | King, C. 21978. | M. April 23/17. |
| ‡1 A. | McKenzie, R. 14611. | M. April 23/17. |
| 1 A. I | MacMullan, L.-Cpl. Jas. 22495. | W. and M. April 23/17. |
| 1 A. I | Mann, A. H. 22506. | M. April 23/17. |
| ‡1 A. | Martin, Alfred. 577. | M. April 23/17. |
| 1 A. I | Menchen, Jas. 24395. | M. April 23/17. |
| 1 A. I | Moulder, W. E. 18703. | M. April 23/17. |
| ‡1 A. | New, A. 37012. | M. April 23/17. |
| ‡1 A. | Ormiston, A. 18776. | M. April 23/17. |
| ‡1 A. | Skelton, R. 24462. | M. April 23/17. |
| 1 A. II | Smith, Frank. 37953. | M. April 23/17. |
| ‡1 A. | Snelling, Sergt. H. 9765. | M. April 23/17. |
| 1 A. III | Southon Albert Geo. 37950. | M. April 23/17. |

**Surrey Regiment, Royal West—contd.**

## *B.E.F.*

| | | |
|---|---|---|
| 1 A. | Taylor, James. 8637. | M. April 23/17. |
| 1 A. II | Thomson, L.-Cpl. R. 4873. | M. April 23/17. |
| 1 A. | Verdon, Albert Edw. 10363. | M. April 23/17. |
| 1 A. or D. | Walden, Wm. Arthur. 37189. | M. April 23/17. |
| 1 A. | Ward, L.-Cpl. W. J. 2376. | M. April 23/17. |
| 1 A. II | Webb, F. J. 9262. | M. April 23/17. |
| ‡1 A. IV | White, Leonard. 37198. | W. and M. May 20/17. |
| ‡1 A. | Wollard, H. 13266. | M. April 23/17. |
| ‡1 A. | Woodruff, W. 15998. | M. April 23/17. |
| 1 A. I | Woods, W. Bowman. 8070. | M. April 23/17. |
| 1 A. or D. L.G.S. | Wright, John. 731. | M. April 23/17. |
| ‡1 B. | Anderson, L.-Cpl. C. 9765. | M. April 23/17. |
| 1 B. or D. | Bance, Sergt. C. 9685. | W. and M. April 23/17. |
| ‡1 B. | Boss, A. 16055. | M. April 23/17. |
| ‡1 B. | Brightwell, J. 14577. | M. April 23/17. |
| 1 B. L.G.S. | Butcher, Tom. 11030. | M. April 23/17. |
| 1 B. VIII | Caws, Gordon Frank. 37056. | M. April 23/17. |
| 1 B. VI | Cooke, G. S. 37051. | Unoff. M. April 23/17. |
| 1 B. V | Downes, L.-Cpl. R. E. 24456. | M. April 23/17. |
| 1 B. V | Fisher, Arthur. 6786. | M. April 23/17. |
| •1 B. | Freer, Wm. 18844. | M. April 23/17. |
| •1 B. VI | Garner, A. 13721. | M. April 23/17. |
| •1 B. | Garnham, E. A. 13621. | K. May 20/17. Det.D./B. |
| ‡1 B. | Goddard, J. 37908. | W. and M. April 23/17. |
| ‡1 B. VIII | Heasman, William. 37177. | M. April 23/17. |
| •1 B. or C. | Hicks, Bandsman Jos. 10075. | M. April 23/17. |
| 1 B. V | Hother, W. 2190. | W. and M. May 30/17. |
| ‡1 B. | Kemp, A. 24459. | M. April 23/17. |
| 1 B. VIII | Linford, L.-Cpl. Alb. 21980. (Fr. 17 Lancers.) | M. April 23/17. |
| ‡1 B. | Miller, Sigr. E. 4310. | M. April 23/17. |
| •1 B. VII | Mills, Reginald G. 37135. | W. and M. April 23/17. |
| ‡1 B. | Oakley, F. 22508. | M. April 23/17. |
| 1 B. VII | Over, Frank. 6665. | M. April 23/17. |
| ‡1 B. | Rawlings, John Edward. 14577. | M. April 23/17. |
| 1 B. | Richardson, A. 9220. | M. April 23/17. |
| 1 B. or D. M.G.S. | Simpson, L.-Cpl. J. A. 3789. | Unoff. M. April 23/17. |
| ‡1 B. | Simpson, W. 201828. | M. April 23/17. |
| ‡1 B. | Symes, P. 7004. | W. and M. April 23/17. |
| ‡1 B. | Tidy, F. 37058. | M. April 23/17. |
| ‡1 B. | Underwood, R. 37960. | M. April 23/17. |
| ‡1 B. | Wales, T. 682. | W. and M. April 23/17. |
| 1 B. or D. | Watts, R. P. 13243. | M. April 23/17. |
| ‡1 B. | West, A. 24432. | W. and M. April 23/17. |
| •1 B. VI | Westby, Ben. Spriggs. 37195. | M. April 23/17. |
| ‡1 B. | Westrop, A. 15461. | M. April 23/17. |
| ‡1 B. | White, H. 37187. | M. April 23/17. |
| 1 B. | Williams, Cpl. W. 911. (H.Q. Sig.) | M. April 23/17. |
| ‡1 C. | Adam, C. 6762. | M. April 23/17. |
| ‡1 C. | Austin, B. 12939. | M. April 23/17. |
| ‡1 C. | Bailey, J. C. 205319. | M. May 20/17. |
| 1 C. XI | Baker, Alfred Chas. 14534. | M. April 23/17. |
| ‡1 C. | Baker, Cpl. E. 22481. | M. April 23/17. |
| 1 C. XI | Baker, F. A. 22536. | M. April 23/17. |
| •1 C. L.G.S. | Barber, L.-Cpl. F. 8409. | M. April 23/17. |
| ‡1 C. | Blackman, Albert. 205270. (Fr. 4.) | M. May 20-22/17. |
| ‡1 C. | Blythin, C. 18814. | M. May 23/17. |
| ‡1 C. | Brookes, H. 37030. | M. April 23/17. |

**Surrey Regiment, Royal West—contd.**

*B.E.F.*

1 C. L.G.S. Brooks, Sergt. Percy. 10237. M. April 23/17.
‡1 C. IX Bulgen, Cpl. A. A. 22483. M. April 23/17.
1 C. L.G.S. Bullimore, W. 15016. (Fr. H.Q.) M. April 23/17.
*1 C. Cox, L.-Cpl. Walter Stanley. 7510. M. April 23/17.
1 C. XI Downing, P. 14627. M. April 23/17.
‡1 C. Evans, T. 18837. M. April 23/17.
*1 C. XII Farminer, Arthur John. 205260. M. May 20/17.
*1 C. X Goodall, Albert Edwd. 205238. (Fr. 4th.) W. and M. May 20/17.
1 C. or D. L.G.S. Goodwin, L.-Cpl. Tom. 24446. M. April 23/17.
‡1 C. Green, Cpl. C. 3703. M. April 23/17.
‡1 C. Griggs, S. 13727. M. April 23/17.
*1 C. IX Hall, W. J. 8069. M. April 23/17.
1 C. X Hardy, Geo. G 15018. M. April 23/17.
1 C. Hillier, H. G. G/14996. M. April 23/17.
‡1 C. Hockey, Ernest. 15029. M. April 23/17.
‡1 C. Hudson, Edward. 10159. (Fr. 3rd.) M. April 23/17.
‡1 C. X Jarvis, L.-Cpl. Willby. 10601. M. April 23/17.
‡1 C. Kemp, J. 6191. M. April 23/17.
1 C. IX Lacy, Charlie Albert. 15010. M. April 23/17.
‡1 C. Littlefield, E. 37931. M. April 23/17.
*1 C. XII Lunn, William F. 11214. M. April 23/17.
*1 C. May, Cpl. H. 10672. M. April 23/17.
1 C. XI Mayo, T. W. 3639. M. April 23/17.
*1 C. IX Mitchell, A. 15004. M. April 23/17.
1 C. Newby, J. W. 24477. M. April 23/17.
1 C. O'Donoghue, W. 6179. M. April 23/17.
‡1 C. XII Pacey, W. W. 15038. Unoff. M. April 23/17.
*1 C. X Parvin, Albert. 15011. W. and M. May 20/17.
‡1 C. Peters, L.-Cpl. C. 27152. M. April 23/17.
‡1 C. Pierce, A. 3811. M. April 23/17.
‡1 C. Radley, L.-Cpl. E. 9933. W. and M. April 23/17.
‡1 C. Rivett, A. 577. M. April 23/17.
1 C. Rugman, F. C. 15025. W. and M. April 23/17.
*1 C. Sheffield, Herbert. 10858. M. April 23/17.
*1 C. XI Singleton, W. 21872. M. April 23/17.
‡1 C. Smith, Sergt. F. 8144. W. and M. April 23/17.
1 C. XI Smith, F. W. 7752. M. April 23/17.
‡1 C. Smith, R. 24408. M. May 20/17.
‡1 C. Spawton, F. 2917. M. April 23/17.
‡1 C. Stuart, F. 24412. M. April 23/17.
‡1 C. Tribe, A. 15012. M. April 23/17.
‡1 C. Worrall, Thomas. 5600. M. April 23/17.
‡1 D. Algar, B. 5550. M. April 23/17.
‡1 D. Allen, C. 37021. M. April 23/17.
‡1 D. Arnold, A. 4226. M. April 23/17.
‡1 D. Atkins, Cpl. J. 6805. M. April 23/17.
‡1 D. Brooks, G. 37878. M. April 23/17.
1 D. XIV Cantle, A. E. 14615. M. April 23/17.
‡1 D. Caraher, T. 22106. M. April 23/17.
‡1 D. Chamberlain, L.-Cpl. W. 11057. M. April 23/17.
*1 D. Clayton, L.-Cpl. T. 6769. M. April 23/17.
‡1 D. Coe, F. 37054. M. April 23/17.
1 D. XVI Cooper, T. 9960. M. April 23/17.
‡1 D. Davie, J. E. 14621. M. April 23/17.
*1 D. Dobson, F. 9833. M. April 23/17.
1 D. XVI Donkin, Harold A. B. 18971. D. pneumonia Dec. 22/16. Det. of illness. R/Enq.
1 D. Dowler, B. 9178. M. April 23/17.

Surrey Regiment, Royal West—contd.

*B.E.F.*

‡1 D. Dunn, H. 22484. M. April 23/17.
1 D. XVI Dye, Henry Laurence. 6756. M. April 23/17.
1 D. XVI Earl, John. 11235. M. April 23/17.
‡1 D. Faggetter, A. W. 2018. M. April 23/17.
1 D. XVI Finch, L.-Cpl. Wm. Fredk. 37900. W. and M. April 23/17.
‡1 D. Fordham, F. 13284. M. April 23/17.
1 D. XIV Foster, Fredk. Chas. 22502. W. and M. April 23/17.
‡1 D. Franklin, E. 37902. M. April 23/17.
1 D. Freeman, C. 11779. M. April 24/17.
1 D. L.G.S. Friday, Cpl. J. T. 4784. M. April 23/17.
1 D. XIII Furner, F. W. 40004. M. April 23/17.
‡1 D. Gardiner, W. 11311. M. April 23/17.
1 D. XVI Gotts, John. 24489. M. April 23/17.
1 D. XV Grant, L.-Cpl. Edward. 14633. M. April 23/17.
1 D. XVI Gray, Joseph. 13383. M. Nov. 5/16.
‡1 D. Gyatt, P. 37091. M. April 23/17.
1 D. Haime, Chas. Henry. 7134. M. April 23/17.
1 D. XV Harvey, Wm. Arthur. 13235. M. April 23/17.
*1 D. Howes, F. G. S. 6879. M. April 23/17.
*1 D. Jenner, L.-Cpl. Percy John. 7342. M. April 23/17.
‡1 D. Jennings, Cpl. A. 10809. M. April 23/17.
‡1 D. Johns, S. 9416. M. April 23/17.
‡1 D. Johnson, L.-Cpl. W. 6355. M. April 23/17.
1 D. XVI McDonald, P. 37134. M. April 23/17.
1 D. XV Manfield, Horace 7219. M. April 23/17.
1 D. XIII Moore, A. E. 37938. M. April 23/17.
1 D. XVI Moore, L.-Cpl. E. 24484. M. April 23/17.
1 D. XVI Morris, L.-Cpl. Chas. 18593. M. April 23/17.
1 D. XV Newman, Arthur Edward. 3979. M. April 23/17.
‡1 D. Page, A. 3992. W. and M. April 23/17.
‡1 D. Peters, Cpl. T. 11365. M. April 23/17.
1 D. XVI Pockham, A.-Sergt. H. 309. M. April 23/17.
‡1 D. Reader, W. 22186. M. April 23/17.
‡1 D. Richardson, E. 18831. M. April 23/17.
1 D. Rouse, P. 4868. M. April 23/17.
‡1 D. Shepherd, L.-Cpl. B. 5947. M. April 23/17.
‡1 D. Slater, C. 18721. M. April 23/17.
‡1 D. Smart, W. 11027. M. April 23/17.
‡1 D. Smith, F. 16060. M. April 23/17.
1 D. Smith, G. H. 37173. M. April 23/17.
1 D. Smith, Cpl. Stanley Geo. 22487. M. April 23/17.
1 D. XIV Swatridge, Wm. Geo. 4742. M. April 23/17.
1 D. XVI Terry, Walter Henry. 8037. M. April 23/17.
1 D. Towers, D. 37958. M. April 23/17.
1 D. XV Wakeham, Reginald Geo. Fred. 12931. M. April 23/17.
1 D. XVI Walker, Wilfred Russell. 18797. M. April 23/17.
‡1 D. Watford, Sergt. W. 9702. M. April 23/17.
‡1 D. Webb, George Alex. 22206. M. April 23/17.
1 D. Williams, Sgt. Geo. Fred. 6592. M. April 23/17.
1 D. XIII Wise, Cpl. E. W. 6622. M. April 23/17. 2nd Cas.
‡1 D. XIII Wood, Ernest. 8449. W. and M. Nov. 3/16.
1 D. XVI Worsfold, L.-Cpl. F. 37197. W. Unoff. M. April 23/17.
1 D. XVI Wright, Cpl. Simon H. 37018. M. April 23/17.
‡2 A. Stroud, M.M., H. J. 6995. M. May 14/17.
‡2 B. Eaton, L.-Cpl. G. 9700. M. May 12/17.
2 B. V Nutkins, W. 17780. (Fr. 9 E. Surrey) M. Sept. 6/16. R/Enq.
2 B. VIII Sherwood, J. F. G. 12988. W. and M. April 2/17.
*2 B. V Thomas, Edwin. G/22476. M. May 12/17.

**Surrey Regiment, Royal West—contd.**

## *B.E.F.*

2 C. XII Foreman, C. 359. (H.Q. Snip. S.) K. April 2/17. Det.D./B.
2 D. Crabb, W. 22457. (Late 9th Lancers.) M. Mar. 14/17.
‡2 D. Pailthorpe, F. 39363. M. May 12/17.
6 Maisey, 2nd Lieut. A. G. W. and M. May 13/17.
*6 A. III Alderdice, Norman H. 6613. W. and M. May 12/17.
‡6 A. IV Brade, A. E. 8184. W. and M. May 12/17.
‡6 A. Butcher, Cpl. A. 145. M. May 12/17.
6 A. II Cackett, Jack. 5664. M. May 12/17.
‡6 A. Duce, Joseph. 9219. M. May 12/17.
*6 A. Durrant, Sergt. Thomas. 8086. W. and M. May 12/17.
‡6 A. Edwards, L.-Cpl. E. T. 35. M. May 12/17.
6 A. I Foote, Ernest John. 22588. M. May 12/17.
‡6 A. Guiver, F. 40161. M. May 12/17.
‡6 A. Harlow, A. 40152. W. and M. May 12/17.
‡6 A. Lewis, H. 7699. M. May 12/17.
6 A. II Luckett, J. A. 13489. W. and M. May 12/17.
*6 A. II Metcalfe, Fred. 9244. W. and M. May 12/17.
‡6 A. Mills, Cpl. C. 40109. M. May 12/17.
*6 A. IV Nash, E. C. 13890. M. May 12/17.
‡6 A. III Roberts, Saml. E. Percy. 22772. W. and M. May 12/17.
6 A. II Smalley, Arthur Innes. 13770. M. May 12/17.
‡6 A. Smith, L.-Cpl. F. J. 6777. M. May 12/17.
‡6 A. Stock, J. 13292. M. May 12/17.
‡6 A. II Tobey, Ernest Arthur. 9183. M. May 12/17.
6 A. II Way, Herbt. G/22205. M. May 12/17.
6 B. VIII Brown, R. J. 8119. M. May 12/17.
‡6 B. Bullock, G. A. 22229. M. May 12/17.
‡6 B. VII Burden, C. 12149. W. and M. May 12/17.
6 B. Emmett, C. 18687. W. and M. April 9/17.
6 B. Jenner, Cpl. Arthur Philip. 22551. M., bel. K. April 9/17.
‡6 B. V Jones, L.-Cpl. W. 22617. M. May 12/17.
6 B. VII Kau, Joseph. 22776. W. Unoff. M. May 12/17.
*6 B. V Knight, Ernest. 10712. W. and M. Unoff. K. April 9/17.
‡6 B. V Middleton, Alan Reg. 22783. M. May 12/17.
‡6 B. Skinner, F. E. 22774. W. and M. May 12/17.
6 C. XII Breese, Wm. 13584. M. April 7/17.
6 C. IX Collins, Wm. 22135. W. and M. April 10/17.
6 C. XII Washbrook, G. 14295. M. April 7/17.
6 C. L.G.S. Williams, L.-Cpl. Ernest. 1995. W. and M. April 9/17.
6 C. Wurdle, W. T. 14252. W. and M. April 7/17.
6 D. Denny, L.-Cpl. Wm. Jas. G. 8/359. M. April 10/17.
‡6 D. Page, L.-Cpl. A. G. 40121. M. May 3/17.
‡7 A. I Brock, C. 22003. M. May 3/17.
7 A. III Copeland, F. 21150. (Fr. Middlesex.) K. Sept. 28/16. Det.D./B.
7 A. III Gibson, F. A. 37910. M. May 3/17.
7 A. M.G.S. Housden, Albert. 6096. W. and M. May 3/17.
7 A. Lane, T. 21756. W. and M. May 3/17.
‡7 A. Phipps, C. 13238. M. May 3/17.
‡7 A. Sirett, W. 1243. M. May 3/17.
*7 A. III Spriggs, Thos. Wm. 24653. M. May 3/17.
7 A. I.T.M. Thake, C. 11891. (55 Bgde.) W. and M. Nov. 10/16.
‡7 B. Crane, A.-Cpl. Frank. 3580. M. May 3/17.
7 B. VIII Day, H. G. J. 21154. (Fr. 15 Middx.) M. Sept. 28/16. R./Enq.
7 B. or C. Farrow, C. G. 9096. W. and M. Feb. 24-27/17.
7 B. V Greenwood, Charles. 37743. W. and M. May 3/17.
7 B. V Massey, Wm. Geo. 14228. M. Feb. 24-27/17.
7 B. Rice, Harry. 14940. (Fr. R. Fus.) M. Feb. 24-27/17.
7 B. M.G.S. Ryde, S. A. 21199. W. and M. Feb. 24-27/17.

**Surrey Regiment, Royal West—contd.**

*B.E.F.*

‡7 B. Saggers, Alfred. 11875. M. May 3/17.
7 B. Spencer, W. J. 8335. K. Sept. 28/16. Conf. and det.
7 B. Strange, Wm. 20217. M. Sept. 28/16. R/Enq.
‡7 B. Taylor, Percy T. 14189. M. May 3/17.
7 B. VI Wildman, Thos. G/14913. M. Feb. 24-27/17.
7 B. Woodruff, Frederick. 13653. M. Feb. 24-27-17.
7 C. XI Brooks, Sydney Jas. 18227. M. May 3/17.
*7 C. X Fisher, Cpl. Wm. Robert. 5525. M. Sept. 28/16. R/Enq.
‡7 C. Gallier, F. 5101. M. May 3/17.
*7 C. Hayward, P. 21168. M. Sept. 28/16. R/Enq.
7 C. Rapley, H. 6977. M. Nov. 18/16. R/Enq.
7 C. XI Smith, G. 7017. M. Sept. 28/16. R/Enq.
*7 C. Spiers, Geo. 5903. M. Sept. 28/16. R/Enq.
*7 C. X Wild, J. 13404. M. Nov. 18/16. R/Enq.
7 D. M.G.S. Barnes, R. H. 21135. (Fr. Middlx.) M. Feb. 24-27-17.
*7 D. Fedarb, F. T. 10482. M. Sept. 28/16. R/Enq.
7 D. Hughes, James E. 220832. M. Feb. 24-27/17.
‡7 D. Jennings, Ashwell Robt. 11827. M. Sept. 28/16. R/Enq.
7 D. XIII Joyce, R. E. 37769. K. Feb. 24-27/17. Det.D./B.
7 D. XIII Mitchell, L.-Cpl. John Wm. 39072. M. Feb. 24-27/17.
7 D. Peters, J. E. 7733. (Fr. 10th.) M. Sept. 28/16. R./Enq.
7 D. XVI Thomas, Leslie Edw. 8698. M. Nov. 18/16. R/Enq.
‡7 D. Tuffnail, L.-Cpl. L. 37826. M. May 3/17.
‡7 D. XVI Weldon, Francis. 22064. M. May 3/17.
8 A. Miers, J. 6014. M. April 15/17.
8 B. VI Bennifer, Thos. 9260. W. and M. May 19/17.
8 C. Hammond, A. 2574. M. April 15/17.
8 C. XI Smith, C. W. 18180. M. Sept. 4/16. R/Enq.
10 A. IV Attree, Cpl. G. 5125. M. Feb. 24/17.
10 A. Beadell, H. 21868. M. Feb. 24/17.
10 A. Hart, A. 21822. M. Feb. 24/17.
10 A. III Millea, A. 21832. M. Feb. 24/17.
10 A. Roberts, Fred. 10432. M. Sept. 15-17/16. R./Enq.
10 B. VII Hageman, A. W. N. 7467. W. and M. Sept. 15-17/16. R/Enq.
‡10 D. Banks, H. 27705. W. and M. June 6-7/17.
10 D. Champion, A. 12729. M. Feb. 24/17.
10 D. Paxman, Cpl. F. 13409. M. Feb. 24/17.
10 D. XVI Saunders, T. R. 21851. M. Feb. 24/17.
‡10 I.T.M. Banks, James. 17453. (124 Bgde.) W. and M. June 7/17.
‡11 B. Barnwell, Wm. John. 11112. M. June 7/17.
‡11 ? Fenton, Reg. Gilbert. 11221. K. June 10/17. Det.D./B.
18 4 Evans, E. 53100. M. April 23/17.
18 4 Hodgkinson, J. 57713. M. April 23/17.

*E.E.F.*

2/4 A. L.G.S. Allen, Edw. Wm. Herbert. 201782. (4028.) W. and M., bel. K. Mar. 26/17.

# ROYAL SUSSEX REGIMENT.

## B.E.F.

| | | |
|---|---|---|
| 2 A. III | Archer, Charles. 8625. | W. and M. **July 23/16.** R./Enq. |
| 2 C. XI | Robinson, Eli. 852. | W. and M. **Sept. 9/16.** R/Enq. |
| 2 D. XIII | Blake, F. W. 5447. | M. **Sept. 9/16.** R/Enq. |
| 2 D. | Purser, S. 17739. | M. **Mar. 14/17.** |
| ‡7 | **Willard, Lieut. A. E.** | M. **July 3/17.** |
| ‡7 B. | Aukett, J. F. 5378. | M. **May 3/17.** |
| 7 B. VI | Cate, J. 1768. | M. **April 9/17.** |
| 7 B. VII | Covell, A. J. 9094. | K. **April 9/17.** Det.D./B. |
| ‡7 B. | Dewley, W. G. 13149. | M. **May 3/17.** |
| ‡7 B. | Gell, W. H. 3577. | M. **May 3/17.** |
| ‡7 B. | Hawkins, T. F. 13393. | M. **May 3/17.** |
| ‡7 C. | Deadman, A. C. 8369. | M. **May 3/17.** |
| ‡7 C. X | Flecknoe, L.-Cpl. Geo. Fredk. 18026 | M. **May 3/17.** |
| ‡7 C. | George, W. 177. | M. **May 3/17.** |
| ‡7 C. | Ratcliffe, A. 5905. | M. **May 3/17.** |
| 7 C. X | Richardson, L.-Cpl. W. 8138. | M. **May 3/17.** |
| 7 C. L.G.S. | Taylor, G. H. 9610. | M. **May 3/17.** |
| ‡7 D. | Coltman, V. J. 14120. | M. **May 3/17.** |
| 7 D. XV L.G.S. | Fitt, Thomas. 18088. | M. **April 9/17.** |
| 7 D. XVI | Funnell, L.-Cpl. A. W/18091. | M. **May 3/17.** |
| ‡9 C. XII | Dennis, John. 53. | M. **June 6-11/17.** |
| ‡9 D. XV | Puttock, J. 6658. | W. **June 23/17.** Unoff. D/W. **June 26.** Conf. and Details. |
| 11 A. I | Coward, W. 3895 | M. **Sept. 3/16.** R/Enq. |
| *11 A. | Smith, H. 4872. | M. **Sept. 3/16.** R/Enq. |
| 11 B. V | Astley, Cpl. Edwin. 15131. | M. **Oct. 21/16.** |
| 11 B. | Burgess, J. C. D. 294. | M. **Sept. 3/16.** R/Enq. |
| 11 B. | Jocelyn, H. 323. | M. **Sept. 3/16.** R/Enq. |
| *11 B. VI | Whane, E. 15287. | K. **Feb. 13/17.** Det.D./B. |
| *11 C. X | Bowers, G. 5777. | M. **Oct. 21/16.** R/Enq. |
| 11 C. | Burr, Ernest Wm. 3936. | M. **Sept. 3/16.** R/Enq. |
| 11 D. | Catt, L.-Cpl. A. G. 909. | M. **Sept. 3/16.** R/Enq. |
| 11 D. XIV | Delpine, S. V. 3753. | M. **Sept. 3/16.** R./Enq. |
| 11 D. | Ellis, Richard. 788. | M. **Sept. 3/16.** R/Enq. |
| *12 | **Sheppard, 2nd Lieut. F. W.** | M. **June 12/17.** |
| 12 A. | Searle, Fred. 15588. | K. **Oct. 21/16.** Det.D./B. R/Enq. |
| *12 D. XIV | Whiting, L.-Cpl. A. H. 17927. (1499) | M. **Sept. 3/16.** R/Enq. |
| 13 B. | Bagot, Fred. Spencer Welesley. 4138 | K. **Oct. 21/16.** Det.D./B. |

## E.E.F.

| | | |
|---|---|---|
| 4 A. II | Mears, John. 200444. (2105.) | M. **Mar. 26/17.** |
| 4 B. | Cooper, E. 200885. | M. **Mar. 26/17.** |
| 4 B. VII | Fuller, John Richd. 200277. (Late 1792.) | M. **Mar. 26/17.** |
| 4 B. | Ingram, Geo. Catland. 201166. (3628.) | M. **Mar. 26/17.** |
| 4 B. VI | Lisher, Christopher. 200701. (2671.) | W. and M. **Mar. 26/17.** |
| 4 B. V | Miles, Jas. 201197. (Late 3690.) | W. and M. **Mar. 26/17.** |
| 4 B. VIII | Walder, A. E. 200526. (Late 2263.) | M. **Mar. 26/17.** |
| 4 C. | Florance, J. C. 200841. (3099.) | M. **Mar. 26/17.** |
| 4 C. | Miles, A. 200170. (1568.) | W. and M. **April 19/17.** |
| 4 C. | Smart, Walter. 201443. (4105.) | W. and M. **Mar. 26/17.** |
| 4 D. XIV | Crook, E. G. 201282. (3859.) | M. **Mar. 26/17.** |
| 4 D. XV | Crook, H. 200993. (3360.) | M. **Mar. 26/17.** |
| 4 D. | Davis, Tom. 200614. (2470.) | M. **Mar. 26/17.** |
| 4 D. | Dawes, Alfred C. 201043. (Late 3429) | K. **Mar. 26/17.** Det.D./B. |
| 4 D. XIII | Dell, Reg. Chas. 200569. (2557.) | M. **Mar. 26/17.** |
| 4 D. | Hammond, G. A. 200034. | W. and M. **Mar. 26/17.** |

**Sussex Regiment, Royal—contd.**

*E.E.F.*

| | | |
|---|---|---|
| 4 D. | Laker, A. F. 200328. (1880.) | M. Mar. 26/17. |
| 4 D. | Novell, P. R. 200325. (Late 1874.) | M. Mar. 26/17. |
| 4 D. XVI | Phipps, G. 200212. (1650.) | W. and M. Mar. 26/17. |
| 4 D. | Warren, A. H. 201012. (3588.) | M. Mar. 26/17. |
| 4 D. | Wicking, Wilfred R. 200966. (Late 3317.) | W. and M. Mar. 26/17. |
| 4 ? | Allen, Reg. Chas. 200505. (Late 2221) | M. Mar. 26/17. |
| 4 ? | Beer, G. 200421. | W. and M. Mar. 26/17. |
| 4 ? | Burcher, Frank. 200047. | W. and M. Mar. 26/17. |
| 4 ? | Burgess, P. 200804. | M. Mar. 26/17. |
| 4 ? | Carpenter, L.-Cpl. E. 200655. | M. Mar. 26/17. |
| 4 ? | Champ, V. 200586. | M. Mar. 26/17. |
| 4 ? | Crouch, A. 200381. | W. and M. Mar. 26/17. |
| 4 ? | Davis, A. 201428. | W. and M. Mar. 26/17. |
| 4 ? | Gasson, E. J. 200814. | M. Mar. 26/17. |
| 4 ? | Gray, J. W. 201390. (Late 4032.) | M. Mar. 26/17. |
| 4 ? | Grinyer, T. 200674. | M. Mar. 26/17. |
| 4 ? | Hills, S. 200592. | W. and M. Mar. 26/17. |
| 4 ? | Hother, H. 201073. | W. and M. Mar. 26/17. |
| 4 ? | Izard, J. W. 201157. | M. Mar. 26/17. |
| 4 ? | Kerr, R. 200343. | M. Mar. 26/17. |
| 4 ? | Knight, H. 200538. | M. Mar. 26/17. |
| 4 ? | Merter, L. C. 200710. | W. and M. Mar. 26/17. |
| 4 ? | Morley, W. 201182. | W. and M. Mar. 26/17. |
| 4 ? | Oates, J. 201416. | W. and M. Mar. 26/17. |
| 4 ? | Read, C. 200338. | M. Mar. 26/17. |
| 4 ? | Rishman, A. 200259. | M. Mar. 26/17. |
| 4 ? | Sanders, H. 200156. | M. Mar. 26/17. |
| 4 ? | Sayers, A. 201099. | W. and M. Mar. 26/17. |
| 4 ? | Scutt, H. 201892. | W. and M. May 7/17. |
| 4 ? | Sloman, F. J. 200178 | M. Mar. 26/17. |
| 4 ? | Stamp, V. 200230. | M. Mar. 26/17. |
| 4 ? | Stemp, G. 200845. | W. and M. Mar. 26/17. |
| 4 ? | West, A. 201115. | M. Mar. 26/17. |
| 4 ? | Wicking, Theodore. 200924. | M. Mar. 26/17. |
| 2/4 C. | Burt, Cpl. Stanley W. 200401. (2017.) | M., bel. K. Mar. 26/17. |

**TRENCH MORTAR BATTERIES.**

**A. ARTILLERY.**

*B.E.F.*

| | | | |
|---|---|---|---|
| 31 Div. | X. Batty. | Boully, 2nd Lieut. F. C. | M. July 10/17. |
| 24 | Z. | Humphreys, Ben. 109331. (Fr. C/106th Bgde. R.F.A.) | K. Oct. 23/16. Det.D./B. |
| 25 | W. | Pardhy, Gnr. M. M. 79880. | W. and M. Oct. 10/16. |
| 131 | V. | Howarth, J. T. 117372. | M. May 13/17. |
| 61 | ? | Cooper, F. 64361. | W. and M. Mar. 2/16. |

*BALKANS.*

| | | | |
|---|---|---|---|
| 60 Div. | X. Batty. | Williams. 2902. | K. Oct. 8/16. Det.D./B. (French Cas.) |

V

**Trench Mortar Batteries—contd.**

**B. INFANTRY.**

*N.B.—These names also appear under their respective regiments.*

***B.E.F.***

| Bgde. | Batty. | Name | Casualty |
|---|---|---|---|
| 5 | 2 | Gane, Sgt. Francis Grant. 354. (Fr. 17 R. Fus.) | M. April 28/17. |
| 5 | 2 | Hardwick, Albert. 25903. (Fr. 2 Ox. & Bucks.) | M. May 1/17. |
| 6 | ? | Barnes, Edward Arthur. 52501. (Fr. 1st Liverpools, 4779.) | W. and M. April 28/17. |
| •6 | ? | Costigan, John Fred. 53018. (Fr. 1st Liverpools.) | W. and M. April 28/17. |
| •6 | ? | Jones, H. H. 20122. (Fr. 2 S. Staffs.) | W. and M. April 28/17. |
| 6 | ? | Lee, T. 966. (Fr. 17th Middlesex.) | W. and M. April 28/17. |
| 6 | ? | Mooney, J. W. 52673. (Fr. 1st Liverpools.) | W. Unoff. M. April 28/17. |
| ‡6 | | Tovlan, H. 37222. (Fr. 1 Liverpools.) | M. April 28/17. |
| ‡6 | | Warren, G. H. 210. (Fr. 17 Middlesex.) | M. April 28/17. |
| 8 | ? | Holmes, Geo. Foden. 27971. (Fr. 8 E. Yorks.) | M. May 3/17. |
| 10 | | Grant, D. H. 2332. (Fr. 2nd Seaforths.) | M. April 11/17. |
| 12 | | Grisdale, Matthew. 27005. (Fr. 12 Essex, C. Co.) | K. May 1/17. Det.D./B. |
| ‡20 | | Kennedy, Robt. 43541. (Fr. 2 Gordons.) | W. and M. June 7/17. |
| 21 | ? | Turner, Jas. Edward. 12464. (Fr. 19 Manchs.) | W. and M. April 9/17. |
| 26 | ? | Wrigley, Chas. Kemble. 7148. (Fr. 4 S.A.Inf.) | W. and M. April 9/17. |
| 32 | ? | Kay, Cyril. 19319. (Fr. 9 W. Yorks.) | W. and M. Jan. 19/17. |
| 34 | ? | Cryer, John Henry. 12/9944. (Fr. 9 Lancs. Fus.) | M. Sept. 29/16. |
| •36 | ? | Hercock, Sidney. 9833. (Fr. 8 R. Fus.) | M. May 2/17. |
| 36 | ? | Nightingale, Geo. 60482. (Fr. 9 R. Fus.) | M. May 3/17. |
| 49 | ? | Asple, Michael. 40321. (Fr. 8 Innis. Fus.) | M. March 7/17. |
| 50 | •? | Kitching, H. 12454. (Fr. 7 Yorks.) | W. and M. Feb. 8/17. |
| 54 | ? | Leach, L.-Cpl. E. C. 19968. (Fr. 7 Bedfords.) | M. Feb. 17/17. |
| ‡54 | | Pickard, W. B. 40709. | M. May 3/17. |
| ‡55 | | Haisman, Geo. 28341. (Fr. 8 E. Surrey.) | W. and M. May 3/17. |
| 55 | ? | Keen, L. F. 1256. (Fr. 7 E. Kents.) | M. Nov. 22/16. |
| •55 | ? | Kidd, Frank. 13228. (Fr. 7th E. Kents.) | M. May 3/17. |
| •55 | ? | Neville, John Richard. 4444. (Fr. 8 E. Surreys) | M. May 3/17. |

**Trench Mortar Batteries—contd**

**B. Infantry—contd.**

*B.E.F.*

| Bgde. | Batty. | | |
|---|---|---|---|
| 55 | ? | Thake, C. 11891. (Fr. R.W. Surreys.) | W. and M. **Nov. 19/16.** |
| 70 | 1 | Dwight, Harry Bygrave. 31846. (Fr. 11 Sherwds.) | Unoff. M. **April 9/17.** |
| 72 | ? | Wilkinson, L.-Cpl. Alf. Jas. 7941. (Fr. 1 N. Staffs.) | M. **Nov. 26/16.** R/Enq. |
| 76 | 1 | Walton, F. 27485. (Fr. 8 K.O.R.L.) | M. **April 26-30/17.** |
| 86 | ? | Murphy, Owen. 20189. (Fr. 1 Dublin Fus.) | W. and M. **Feb. 28—Mar. 1/17.** |
| 87 | ? | Morley, H. Wm. 23646. (Fr. 1st Borders.) | M. **April 23/17.** |
| 88 | ? | Walsh, Edward. 9879. (Fr. 2 Hants.) | K. **Sept. 18/16.** Det.D./B |
| ‡92 | 2 | Richardson, Harold. 103. (Fr. 11 E. Yorks.) | M. **May 3/17.** |
| *101 | ? | Hopkin, L.-Cpl. Oliver. 16336. (Fr. 11 Suffks.) | M. **April 9/17.** |
| 103 | 1 | Hall, Lewis. 37676. (Fr. 24 North. Fus.) | W. Unoff. M. **April 28/17.** |
| 111 | ? | **Palmer, 2nd Lt. E. C. H.** (Fr. 13th R. Fus.) | W. Unoff. M. **April 23/17.** |
| 112 | | Humphries, Percy. 14608. (Fr. 11 Warwick.) | M. Unoff. K. **April 9/17.** |
| 117 | ? | Blagdon, Wm. Chas. 3016. (Fr. 17 K.R.R.C.) | M. **Sept. 3/16.** R/Enq. |
| ‡122 | 1 | Battye, Harry. C/7452. (Fr. 18 K.R.R.C.) | W. and M. **Sept. 15/16.** R/Enq. |
| ‡122 | | Crockford, L.-Cpl. Vernon Geo. 9457. (Fr. 11 W. Kents.) | W. and M. **Sept. 15/16.** R/Enq. |
| ‡124 | | Banks, Jas. 17453. (Fr. 10th W. Surrey.) | W. and M. **June 7/17.** |
| 124 | ? | Island, Cyril. 12759. (Fr. 21 K.R.R.C.) | K. **Oct. 7/16.** Det.D./B. R./Enq |
| 146 | ? | Geldard, W. 3372. (Fr. 7 W. Yorks.) | W. and M. **Sept. 3/16.** R/Enq. |
| 150 | | **Luckhurst, 2nd Lt. W. H.** (Fr. Yorks.) | W. and M. **April 24/17.** |
| 150 | | Leppington. W. 240786. (Fr. 5 Yorks.) | M. **April 25/17.** |
| 154 | | Aldcroft, J. 350890. (Fr. 9 R. Scots.) | M. **April 23/17.** |
| 164 | D. | Meadowcraft, W. 2781. (Fr. 2/5 Lancs. Fus.) | M. **Sept. 9/16.** |
| 169 | | Breeze, Fredk. H. 302595 (4363.) (Fr. 5 D. Lond.) | W. and M. **May 3/17.** |
| *177 | ? | Read, Wm. Geo. 240874. (3219.) (Fr. 2/5 Lincs.) | M. **April 11/17.** |
| *187 | ? | Fell, Cpl. F. 240276. (Fr. 2/5 York & Lancs.) | W. and M. **May 3/17.** |
| *187 | ? | Gill, J. 121624. (Fr. 2/5 K.O.Y.L.I.) | M. **May 3/17.** |

**Trench Mortar Batteries—contd.**

**B. Infantry—contd.**

## *B.E.F.*

| Bgde. | Batty. | | |
|---|---|---|---|
| *187 | ? | Parker, J. W. 241050. (Fr. 2 York & Lancs.) | W. and M. **May 3/17.** |
| 189 | | Murphy, W. 1150 (Pl.) (Fr. 2 R.M.B., R.N.D.) | M. **April 28/17.** |
| 189 | ? | Wheeler, L.S. Frank. Z/70. (M.) (Fr. Howe Bn. R.N.D.) | M. **Nov. 14/16.** |
| *197 | ? | Evans, G. 241252. (Fr. 2/5 K.O.Y.L.I.) | W. and M. **May 3/17.** |
| ? | | **Brogden, 2nd Lt. F. N.** (Fr. 8 E. Yorks.) | M., bel. K. **May 3/17.** |
| ? | ? | Murphy, Owen. 20189. (Fr. 1 Dublin Fus.) | W. and M. **Feb. 28—March 1/17.** |

## SOUTH WALES BORDERERS.

## *B.E.F.*

| | | |
|---|---|---|
| 2 | **Clarke, 2nd Lt. H. Y. Chatfield.** | W. and M. **April 23/17.** |
| 2 | **Davies, Capt. B. J.** | M., bel. K. **May 19/17.** |
| 2 | **Harries, 2nd Lieut. J. E.** | M., bel. K. **April 23/17.** |
| 2 | **Hopkins, 2nd Lieut. D. J.** | M., bel. K. **April 23/17.** |
| 2 A. | Atkins, W. D. 10920. | M. **April 23/17.** |
| 2 A. | Blackwood, W. 40625. | M. **April 23/17.** |
| 2 A. II | Bradbury, E. 40651. | M. **April 23/17.** |
| 2 A. | Bramley, A. T. 40652. | M. **April 23/17.** |
| 2 A. III | Button, Herbert Victor. 44215. | M. **April 23/17.** |
| 2 A. | Croudace, T. 35383. | M. **April 23/17.** |
| 2 A. | Davies, L.-Cpl. David Jas. 10523. | M. **April 23/17.** |
| *2 A. III | Halliday, G. 44412. | K. **April 13/17.** Det.D./B. |
| ‡2 A. IV | Hobby, Sergt. Hry. John. 10368. | W. and M. **April 23/17.** |
| 2 A. | Holt, G. A. 263013. | M. **April 23/17.** |
| 2 A. | Hooper, F. 263014. | M. **April 23/17.** |
| 2 A. I | Parker, Wm. Elliot. 40571. | M. **April 23/17.** |
| 2 A. | Richards, B. E. 39619. | M. **April 23/17.** |
| 2 A. | Rushforth, Sidney W. 40643. (Late Bedfords.) | M. **April 24/17.** |
| 2 A. | Walwyn, Geo. Valantine. 25535. | M. **April 23/17.** |
| 2 A. | Wilkins, A. H. 40801. | M. **April 23/17.** |
| 2 A. | Wills, Cpl. T. E. 9975. | W. and M. **April 23/17.** |
| *2 B. VII | Atack, E. B. 40550. | W. and M. **April 23/17.** |
| ‡2 B. | Cottenham, E. B. 45250. | W. and M. **April 23/17.** |
| ‡2 B. | Crook, G. H. B. 45245. | W. and M. **April 23/17.** |
| 2 B. | Crook, P. J. 45246. | M. **April 23/17.** |
| 2 B. V | Edwards, Sidney Jas. 44222. | M. **April 23/17.** |
| ‡2 B. VII | Giblin, L.-Cpl. Austin. 39556. | M. **May 19/17.** |
| 2 B. | Griffiths, A.-Sergt. E. 18490. | M. **April 23/17.** |
| 2 B. | Hutchings, W. 39570. | M. **April 23/17.** |
| 2 B. | Jones, Alf. 35732. (Fr. Welsh Fus.) | M. **April 23/17.** |
| 2 B. VII | Jones, William. 40005. | W. and M. **Jan. 28/17.** |

**Wales Borderers, South—contd.**

*B.E.F.*

2 B. VII Owen, G. 40573. W. and M. **April 23/17.**
2 B. Price, D. James. 12080. M. **Jan. 27/17.**
2 B. III Whittaker, Norman. 40619. W. and M. **April 23/17.**
‡2 B. Whyatt, Ambrose. 45178. M. **May 19/17.**
2 B. Wilson, Cpl. Henry. 40002. W. and M. **April 23/17.**
‡2 B. VI Woods, Walter. 37118. W. and M. **April 23/17.**
2 C. Beaty, J. S. 33091. M. **April 23/17.**
2 C. Bradbury, C. T. 34232. M. **April 23/17.**
‡2 C. IX Bradshaw, Horace Jas. 40586. W. and M. **April 23/17.**
2 C. X Evans, J. 39554. M. **April 23/17.**
2 C. IX Fitzhugh, W. 42596. M. **April 23/17.**
2 C. X Heels, Jonathan. 40785. M. **April 23/17.**
2 C. XI Johnson, Herbert Wm. 45257. M. **April 23/17.**
2 C. Meikle, J. 26478. M. **April 23/17.**
2 C. Norris, Brien Wm. 40607. W. and M. **April 23/17.**
‡2 C. Pembridge, Cpl. P. 21380. W. and M. **April 23/17.**
2 C. IX Pinnock, Wm. Adams. 40620. M. **April 23/17.**
2 C. Sanderson, Sergt. Stanley Geo. 9329. W. and M. **July 1/16.** R./Enq.
2 C. XI Smith, Arthur. 40611. M. **April 23/17.**
‡2 C. Smith, J. 45259. W. and M. **April 23/17.**
2 C. Tarrant, P. W. 40770. M. **April 23/17.**
‡2 C. Tickle, Cpl. E. C. 26634. W. and M. **April 23/17.**
2 D. XV Ashton, T. 28299. W. and M. **April 23/17.**
‡2 D. Barron, A. 40587. M. **May 19/17.**
*2 D. XIV Bourne, Jas. 37638. M. **May 19/17.**
*2 D. XIV Bowles, E. 40662. M. **May 19/17.**
2 D. XIV Caines, F. H. 44712. M. **May 19/17.**
*2 D. XIII Callow, T. 40780. M. **May 19/17.**
*2 D. XIII Collister, Alfred N. 26240. M. **May 19/17.**
‡2 D. Cottrell, Wm. Jas. 13317. M. **May 19/17.**
‡2 D. XV Henwood, Percy. 44396. M. or K. **May 19/17.**
‡2 D. Hubert, A. L. 202490. M. **May 19/17.**
2 D. Hull, E. D. 40794. M. **May 19/17.**
‡2 D. King, A. 45205. M. **May 19/17.**
2 D. Morgan, L.-Cpl. Wm. Jas. 11996. M. **July 1/16.** R/Enq.
‡2 D. New, T. J. 22518. M. **May 19/17.**
‡2 D. Playle, Cpl. C. 202448. M. **May 19/17.**
2 D. XVI Pownall, L.-Cpl. Thomas. 40059. M. **Jan. 27/17.**
*2 D. VI Sage, Frank Edward. 40759. M. **May 19/17.**
*2 D. XIV Schofield, Cpl. W. 33645. M. **May 19/17.**
‡2 D. Scott, W. 25299. M. **May 19/17.**
‡2 D. Sewell, W. 40756. M. **May 19/17.**
*2 D. Silvester, J. E. 25886. M. **May 19/17.**
*2 D. Snelling, Cpl. Tom. 45170. M. **May 19/17.**
‡2 D. Taylor, G. 40664. M. **May 19/17.**
‡2 D. Taylor, W. 40653. M. **May 19/17.**
‡2 D. Thomas, J. 44255. M. **May 19/17.**
*2 D. XIII Thomas, J. F. 40037. M. **May 19/17.**
2 D. XIV Watson, Bernard. 15251. M. **April 23/17.**
‡2 D. Weller, F. G. 44256. M. **May 19/17.**
5 ? Andrews, F. J. 17553. (Fr. 8 N. Staffs. Fr. Middlesex.) M. **July 30/16.**
‡12 A. Bardwell, H. 35401. M. **May 6/17.**
*12 A. Knight, Arthur. 23526. M. **May 6/17.**
12 B. Chard, A.-C.-S.-M. S. F. 23353. M. **April 21/17.**
12 B. Pollard, H. 39942. M. **April 21/17.**
12 C. IX Williams, J. C. H. 39955. M. **May 6/17.**

Wales Borderers, South—contd.

## BALKANS.

*8 D. XVI Hill, F. H. 17702. M. May 9/17.

## E.E.F.

### Brecknockshire Battalion.

1 ? Skan, Frank Ronald. 2534 M. July 4/15, near Aden.

## PERSIAN GULF.

*4 A. Arthur, R. 27039. M. April 30/17.
*4 A. III Barttey, John. 33639. M. April 30/17.
4 A. I Evans, Sidney. 23267. M. April 30/17.
*4 A. Jones, Thos. Seth. 15331. M. April 30/17.
4 A. Lane, Arthur Jas. 26872. M. April 30/17.
4 A. Long, Walter. 20300. M. April 30/17.
4 A. Lucas, F. 26936. M. April 30/17.
*4 A. Mapstone, E. 13884. M. April 30/17.
*4 A. Norris, G. B. 26637. M. April 30/17.
*4 A. Snell, T. 27646. M. April 30/17.
*4 A. Steptoe, H. 22918. M. April 30/17.
4 A. Stevens, H. 22834. M. April 30/17.
*4 A. Taker, James. 22779. M. April 30/17.
*4 B. VIII Bond, Robert Alfred. 28388. M. April 30/17.
*4 B. John, B. 27111. M. April 30/17.
4 B. Jones, Daniel. 12599. M. Feb. 3/17.
4 B. Matterface, A. 22926. M. April 30/17.
*4 B. Newman, John. 26941. M. April 30/17.
4 C. James, A.-Sergt. Wm. 12839. M. April 30/17.
*4 D. XIV Bent, F. H. 22958. M. April 30/17.
*4 D. XV Bowkett, J. 27513. M. April 30/17.
4 D Grimley, J. T. 27641. M. April 30/17.
*4 D. Humphrey, A. E. 12120. M April 30/17.
*4 D. Iball, A.-Cpl. Geo. 26903. M. April 30/17.
*4 D. XIV Owen, D. A. 27024. M. April 30/17.
*4 D. Scotts, Joe. 17533. M. April 30/17.
*4 D. Shelford. A. 12142. M. April 30/17.
*4 D. Sill, Ernest. 26922. M. April 30/17.
4 D. Strauther, Geo. Henry. 19755. M. April 9/16. R./Enq.
*4 D. Thomas, L.-Cpl. J. W. 4/13216. M. April 30/17.
*4 D. XV Watts, P. V. 22879. M. April 30/17.
‡4 D. XV Williams, G. E. 36592. K. April 30/17. Det.D./B.
*4 ? Arnold, D. 12277. M. April 30/17.
*4 ? Ashman, A. 26852. M. April 30/17.
*4 ? Ashwell, W. 12101. M. April 30/17.
*4 ? Barlow, Sergt. G. 12243. M. April 30/17.
*4 ? Bowgen, E. J. 22882. M. April 30/17.
*4 ? Burton, J. J. 27624. M. April 30/17.
*4 ? Carlyle, Sergt. T. 6822. M. April 30/17.
*4 ? Carr, Cpl. W. L. 25851. M. April 30/17.
4 ? Chelton, J. 48561. M. Feb. 15/17.
*4 ? Clarke, W. F. 27483. M. April 30/17.
*4 ? Copperwaite, W. 12108. M. April 30/17.
*4 ? Daniels, L.-Cpl. J. W. 34676. M. April 30/17.
*4 ? Davies, H. 28395. M. April 30/17.
*4 ? Davies, Cpl. T. 12391. M. April 30/17.
*4 ? Dearden, S. 27559. M. April 30/17.
*4 ? Duggan, S. 26603. M. April 30/17.
*4 ? Edwards, E. 27760. M. April 30/17.
*4 ? Finch, H. W. 9095. M. April 30/17.

**Wales Borderers, South—contd.**

## *PERSIAN GULF.*

| | | |
|---|---|---|
| 4 ? | Finch, J. 8903. | M. **Feb. 3/17.** |
| *4 ? | Forrester, D. A. 28403. | M. **April 30/17.** |
| *4 ? | Furness, J. 25522. | M. **April 30/17.** |
| 4 ? | Gasheel, T. 33949. | W. and M. **Feb. 15/17.** |
| *4 ? | Gateley, A. W. 27659. | M. **April 30/17.** |
| *4 ? | Goodhead, J. W. 26907. | M. **April 30/17.** |
| *4 ? | Hacker, G. 26851. | M. **April 30/17.** |
| 4 ? | Harris, G. W. 22935. | D/W. **Jan. 17/17. Det.D./B.** |
| *4 ? | Hilton, A. 26470. | M. **April 30/17.** |
| *4 ? | Hockley, W. G. 26909. | M. **April 30/17.** |
| *4 ? | Houlgraye, W. 37051. | M. **April 30/17.** |
| *4 ? | Howle, W. D. 27525. | M. **April 30/17.** |
| *4 ? | Howley, A.-Sergt. C. 27007. | M. **April 30/17.** |
| 4 ? | Jeffreys, R. 3/27488. | M., bel. K. **Dec. 20/16.** |
| 4 ? | Jones, L.-Cpl. D. B. 26572. | W. and M. **Feb. 15/17.** |
| *4 ? | Jones, D. 35519. | M. **April 30/17.** |
| *4 ? | Jones, D. J. 27778. | M. **April 30/17.** |
| *4 ? | Jones, D. J. 28426. | M. **April 30/17.** |
| *4 ? | Jones, S. 12332. | M. **April 30/17.** |
| 4 ? | Kay, A. 25547. | M. **May 24/16.** |
| *4 ? | Kelly, J. W. 19801. | M. **April 30/17.** |
| *4 ? | Lane, A. G. 26872. | M. **April 30/17.** |
| *4 ? | Lewis, L.-Cpl. Henry Frank. 10805. | M. **April 30/17.** |
| *4 ? | Lewis, J. H. 28429. | M. **April 30/17.** |
| *4 ? | Lumb, L.-Cpl. G. 34685. | M. **April 30/17.** |
| *4 ? | McCullock, D. 27017. | M. **April 30/17.** |
| *4 ? | McFarlane, T. 14196. | M. **April 30/17.** |
| *4 ? | Mason, A. 27787. | M. **April 30/17.** |
| *4 ? | Meadows, Sergt. Z. 27792. | M. **April 30/17.** |
| *4 ? | Meredith, L.-Cpl. J. C. 13110. | M. **April 30/17.** |
| *4 ? | Milner, J. 33873. | M. **April 30/17.** |
| *4 ? | Moffat, R. 19769. | M. **April 30/17.** |
| *4 ? | Morgan, W. L. 26275. | M. **April 30/17.** |
| *4 ? | Morgan, W. L. 26273. | M. **April 30/17.** |
| *4 ? | Norris, Sidney. 26873. | M. **April 30/17.** |
| *4 ? | Oakley, S. 14219. | M. **April 30/17.** |
| *4 ? | Owen, G. 33661. | M. **April 30/17.** |
| *4 ? | Owen, J. A. 28437. | M. **April 30/17.** |
| *4 ? | Piper, T. 13231. | M. **April 30/17.** |
| *4 ? | Pope, W. F. 26811. | M. **April 30/17.** |
| *4 ? | Proud, P. 12132. | M. **April 30/17.** |
| *4 ? | Ralph, V. J. 12138. | M. **April 30/17.** |
| *4 ? | Roberts, C. 27645. | M. **April 30/17.** |
| *4 ? | Roberts, W. A. 27809. | M. **April 30/17.** |
| *4 ? | Saxon, H. 19583. | M. **April 30/17.** |
| *4 ? | Shaw, S. 19688. | M. **April 30/17.** |
| *4 ? | Steele, L.-Cpl. E. 27033. | M. **April 30/17.** |
| *4 ? | Stephens, W. A. 18154. | M. **April 30/17.** |
| *4 ? | Stirk, A.-Cpl. P. 34695. | M. **April 30/17.** |
| *4 ? | Thompson, T. 27040. | M. **April 30/17.** |
| *4 ? | Trevan, Cpl. T. H. 34698. | M. **April 30/17.** |
| *4 ? | Wardle, A.-Sergt. T. J. 19735. | M. **April 30/17.** |
| *4 ? | Weston, W. J. 25995. | M. **April 30/17.** |
| *4 ? | Whitehead, A.-Cpl. J. 26991. | M. **April 30/17.** |
| *4 ? | Wild, A.-Cpl. J. 34699. | M. **April 30/17.** |
| *4 ? | Williams, C. 12301. | M. **April 30/17.** |
| *4 ? | Williams, C. 26117. | M. **April 30/17.** |
| 4 ? | Williams, E. 28451. | W. and M. **Feb. 15/17.** |
| *4 ? | Williams, T. 27355. | M. **April 30/17.** |

**Wales Borderers, South**—contd.

## *PERSIAN GULF.*

| | | | |
|---|---|---|---|
| *4 ? | | Williams, W. 14084. | M. April 30/17. |
| *4 ? | | Willson, J. E. 37660. | M. April 30/17. |
| *4 ? | | Wright, J. 27044. | M. April 30/17. |

## ROYAL WARWICKSHIRE REGIMENT.

## *B.E.F.*

| | | | |
|---|---|---|---|
| 1 | | **Cox, Capt. G. W.** | K. May 3/17. Det.D./B. |
| 1 | | **Devis, Lieut. Francis.** | K. April 1/17. Det.D./B. |
| 1 | | **Iles, 2nd Lieut. P. H.** | W. and M. April 11/17. |
| 1 | | **Lowder, 2nd Lieut. N. R.** | M. May 3/17. |
| ‡1 | A. I | Ash, Arthur Douglas. 16124. | K. April 11/17. Det.D./B. |
| 1 | A. I | Austin, L.-Cpl. W. 10190. | M. April 11/17. |
| 1 | A. I | Billingham, A. 1388. | K. April 11/17. Det.D./B. |
| 1 | A. | Burnett, S. 10637. | M. May 3/17. |
| 1 | A. II | Cross, G. W. 21345. | M. April 11/17. |
| 1 | A. | Fevers, William. 6377. | M. April 11/17. |
| 1 | A. | Murphy, W. 27384. | W. and M. May 3/17. |
| 1 | A. | Perks, A. 9007. | M. April 11/17. |
| 1 | A. I | Ponney, A. 23058. | K. April 11/17. Det.D./B. |
| 1 | A. III | Rollins, H. 18001. | M. April 11/17. |
| *1 | A. II | Smith, Herbert Jas. 16547. | M. May 3/17. |
| 1 | A. | Tedds, Joe. 4479. | M. April 11/17. |
| 1 | A. | Underwood, Cpl. Saml. Joseph. 7408. | W. and M. April 11/17. |
| 1 | A. | Watson, Sergt. A. 4594. | M. May 3/17. |
| 1 | B. | Astill, A.-Sergt. A. 9500. | M. May 3/17. |
| 1 | B. | Carter, A.-Cpl. B. 27052. | M. May 3/17. |
| 1 | B. VI | Fincham, Albert Thos. 16922. | M. May 3/17. |
| 1 | B. | Gee, J. 23964. | M. May 3/17. |
| 1 | B. | Gill, L.-Sergt. Joshua Thos. 1422. | M. May 3/17. |
| 1 | B. | Hardman, W. 10665. | M. May 3/17. |
| 1 | B. | Mawson, M. W. 11428. | M. May 3/17. |
| 1 | B. VI | Moore, Thos. 17989. | M. May 3/17. |
| 1 | B. VI | Moseley, Wm. 28336. | M. May 3/17. |
| 1 | B. VI | Palmer, L.-Cpl. A. C. 985. | M. May 3/17. |
| 1 | B. | Parker, S. 14841. | M. May 3/17. |
| 1 | B. | Parry, E. H 16683. | M. May 3/17. |
| 1 | B. | Pask, T. 27574. | M. May 3/17. |
| 1 | B. VIII | Smith, James. 17491. | W. and M. May 3/17. |
| 1 | B. | Taylor, A. H. 7951. | M. May 3/17. |
| 1 | B. | Tyler, F. 9740. | M. May 3/17. |
| 1 | B. | Webb, Robt. 27601. | M. Oct. 23/16. R/Enq. |
| 1 | B. | Wheeler, Ernest. 28305. | M. May 3/17. |
| 1 | B. | Youens, H. 10885. | M. May 3/17. |
| 1 | C. | Bently, J. T. 16472. | M. May 3/17. |
| ‡1 | C. IX | Chinn, J. 27870. | M. May 3/17. |
| 1 | C. | Collett, J. T. 10024. | M. May 3/17. |
| 1 | C. | Havard, Sergt. G. 4883. | M. April 11/17. |
| 1 | C. | Kemp, B. T. 16671. | M. May 3/17. |
| 1 | C. | Lewis, Arthur. 16139. | M. May 3/17. |
| 1 | C. | Lincoln, R. M. 1652. | M. May 3/17. |
| ‡1 | C. | Lolley, William. 13270. | M. Oct. 12/16. R/Enq. |

**Warwickshire Regiment, Royal**—contd.

*B.E.F.*

1 C. Luntley, C. 23281. M. May 3/17.
1 C. Marriott, E. A. 1264. M. April 11/17.
1 C. XII Marshall, W. 19604. M. May 3/17.
1 C. Matthews, H. 5335. M. May 3/17.
1 C. Miller, W. 13360. M. May 3/17.
1 C. Nelson, H. 27914. M. May 3/17.
1 C. X Robinson, Wm. 16034. M. May 3/17.
1 C. Shrewsbury, H. 27897. M. May 3/17.
1 C. Timms, W. G. 21403. M. May 3/17.
‡1 C. Truby, Alfred William. 19169. M. Oct. 23/16. R/Enq.
1 C. Walker, C. G. 27901. (5446.) W. and M. April 11/17.
1 C. XI Watts, E. 18650. M. May 3/17.
‡1 C. IX Welch, Wm. Alfred. 19602. K. June 6/17. Det.D./B. R/Enq.
1 C. Whitehead, C. H. 27913. M. May 3/17.
1 D. Adamson, A. 27293. M. May 3/17.
1 D. XIII Addenbrooke, Harry. 21078. M. May 3/17.
1 D. Adkins, A. G. 21450. M. May 3/17.
1 D. Alcocks, F. 30428. M. May 3/17.
1 D. Anderton, J. 27687. M. May 3/17.
1 D. Bainkworth, F. G. 28245. M. May 3/17.
1 D. XIII Bird, H. 1786. M. May 3/17.
1 D. XV Brinkworth, Frank Geo. 28245. M. May 3/17.
1 D. Brown, A. B. 7366. M. May 3/17.
1 D. Brown, A. F. 10942. M. May 3/17.
1 D. Burnett, D. 402. M. May 3/17.
1 D. Chance, T. 267672. (Fr. 7th.) M. May 3/17.
1 D. Francis, Harry. 4979. M. May 3/17.
1 D. Hand, W. 27038. M. May 3/17.
1 D. Hatfield, P. G. 267622. M. May 3/17.
1 D. Jones, W. 7125. M. May 3/17.
1 D. XIII Jones, W. E. 23086. M. May 3/17.
1 D. Muggleston, E. 1596. M. May 3/17.
1 D. Oates, L.-Cpl. Alfred. 27570. (Fr. 10th S. Staffs.) M. Oct. 12/16. R/Enq.
1 D. Peet, C. W. 22170. M. May 3/17.
1 D. Such, J. 21864. M. May 3/17.
1 D. XIII Timmins, Ernest. 28371. M. May 3/17.
1 D. Turrell, L.-Cpl. J. 8942. M. May 3/17.
1 D. Wade, W. H. 18458. M. May 3/17.
‡1 D. XIII Welch, Charles. 10830. M. May 3/17.
1 D. Yetman, R. E. 18652. M. May 3/17.
2 A. **Burrell, 2nd Lieut. F. G.** M. May 5/17.
2 **Heatherington, 2nd Lt. E. or H.** M. May 4/17.
2 **Lister, 2nd Lt. H. H. H.** M. May 4/17.
2 **Ring, Lt. N. A. M.** (Fr. 3rd.) M. May 4/17.
2 A. IV Addison, H. 1686. M. May 13/17.
2 A. II Atkins, E. 609. M. May 4/17.
2 A. Bakewell, Alb. Edgar Sam. 16687. W. and M. May 4/17.
‡2 A. Barker, R. 26983. M. May 4/17.
2 A. IV Codd, A. 26992. M. May 4/17.
‡2 A. Coleman, W. 10515. M. May 4/17.
2 A. III Coles, G. 23698. M. April 4/17.
2 A. Cooper, Cpl. A. 1479. M. Sept. 3/16. R/Enq.
2 A. L.G.S. Cooper, H. 26993. M. May 4/17.
*2 A. I Fiddis, Alex. Thos. 23700. W. and M. May 4/17.
2 A. III Green, L.-Cpl. A. F. 1765. M. May 3/17.
‡2 A. Johnson, W. 15355. M. May 4/17.
2 A. Knight, Joseph Wilfred. 178. Unoff. M. May 4/17.

**Warwickshire Regiment, Royal—contd.**

## *B.E.F.*

| | | |
|---|---|---|
| *2 A. | Nutt, George Edwards. 4790. | M. May 4/17. |
| ‡2 A. | Rawlings, B. T. J. 19483. | M. May 4/17. |
| 2 A. IV | Roberts, H. C. 23707. | M. May 4/17. |
| ‡2 A. | Scrivens, A. 7944. | M. May 4/17. |
| 2 A. I | Sharp, J. 26980. | W. and M. May 4/17. |
| 2 A. I | Starling, Geo. Baron. 23605. (Fr. R.E., 2057.) | M. May 4/17. |
| ‡2 A. III | Stevens, T. 26968. | M. May 4/17. |
| *2 A. II | Stubbs, Wm. 4700. | M. May 4/17. |
| *2 A. III | Wallace, H. 1023. | M. May 13/17. |
| 2 A. I | Ward, J. 27021. | W. and M. May 4/17. |
| ‡2 A. | Waters, G. 11623. | M. May 4/17. |
| ‡2 A. | Webb, W. 18112. | M. May 4/17. |
| 2 A. II | Wingfield, Albert. 709. | W. and M. May 13/17. |
| *2 B. VII | Andrews, Wm. Geo. 23687. | M. May 4/17. |
| ‡2 B. | Beswick, W. 17344. | M. May 4/17. |
| 2 B. VI | Bidgood, L.-Cpl. Wm. Henry. 23676. | M. May 4/17. |
| 2 B. VIII | Bowen, Cpl. W. R. 15589. | M. May 4/17. |
| 2 B. VIII | Child, George Andrew. 23632. | W. and M. May 4/17. |
| *2 B. VII | Chinery, George. 27257. | M. May 4/17. |
| 2 B. VI | Davidson, L.-Cpl. W. 23622. | M. April 4/17. |
| ‡2 B. | Felton, G. E. 2969. | M. May 4/17. |
| *2 B. or D. | Guest, Harry. 3320. | W. and M. May 4/17. |
| 2 B. V | Humphries, Cpl. Wm. Ernest. 15879 | M May 4/17. |
| 2 B. V | Lamboll, Fredk. 18702. | M. May 4/17. |
| ‡2 B. | Padbury, S. 21915. | M. May 4/17. |
| *2 B. V | Randell, Walter Jas. 27160. | M. May 4/17. |
| *2 B. V | Vear, Harry. 27073. | M. May 4/17. |
| 2 B. VIII | Walker, Robt. 1582. | M. May 4/17. |
| *2 B. | Wood, C. H. 10466. | M. May 4/17. |
| ‡2 C. | Ashford, G. H. 22456. | M. May 4/17. |
| ‡2 C. IX | Balls, S. 27108. | M. May 4/17. |
| *2 C. | Bott, Geo. W. 15286. | M. May 4/17. |
| *2 C. IX | Broadbent, W. Fred. 10430. | M. Sept. 3/16. R/Enq. |
| *2 C. X | Ellis, Wm. Alfred. 23624. | M. May 4/17. |
| *2 C. | German, Ernest J. 23652. | M. May 4/17. |
| 2 C. X | Hannibal, F. 1145. | W. and M. May 4/17. |
| *2 C. L.G.S. | Hickman, L.-Cpl. F. R. 4866. | M. May 4/17. |
| ‡2 C. | Johnson, W. 27054. | M. May 4/17. |
| *2 C. XI | Medley, L.-Cpl. John Wm. 27032. | M. May 4/17. |
| ‡2 C. | Nicholson, Cpl. G. 27147. | W. and M. May 4/17. |
| ‡2 C. | Parkes, C. S. 27033. | M. May 4/17. |
| ‡2 C. | Pooley, B. 27242. | M. May 4/17. |
| *2 C. | Sandall, Harry. 27173. | M. May 4/17. |
| ‡2 C. | Shufflebotham, E. 1645. | M. May 4/17. |
| ‡2 C. | Sparks, E. 27113. | W. and M. May 13/17. |
| 2 C. L.G.S. | Welbourn, Jacob. 27213. | M. May 4/17. |
| ‡2 D. | Balcombe, R. 23556. | M. May 3/17. |
| *2 D. XIV | Chambers, Frank. 27102. | M. May 4/17. |
| 2 D. | Connell, F. W. 4661. | M. May 4/17. |
| 2 D. | Downes, F. E. 19364. | M. May 4/17. |
| ‡2 D. XVI | Ellis, Clifford. 23643. | M. May 4/17. |
| ‡2 D. L.G.S. | Greenway, S. 4397. | M. May 4/17. |
| 2 D. Gren. S. | Harris, Fred. 29987. (22940.) | M. May 4/17. |
| ‡2 D. XIV | Hill, A. 30035. | M. Sept. 3/16. R/Enq. |
| ‡2 D. | Horton, F. 9808. | M. May 4/17. |
| ‡2 D. | Lane, H. 27092. | M. May 4/17. |
| *2 D. XIII | Meech, Reginald Wm. 1352. | M. May 4/17. |
| ‡2 D. | Payne, W. J. H. 10336. | M. May 4/17. |

**Warwickshire Regiment, Royal—contd.**

*B.E.F.*

| | | |
|---|---|---|
| 2 D. XIV | Perkins, T. 14453. | M. May 4/17. |
| 2 D. XVI | Powis, Chas. 3327. | K. May 13/17. Det.D./B. |
| ‡2 D. XVI | Rodwell, L.-Cpl. F. G. 29939. | M. May 4/17. |
| 2 D. | Rowley, A. E. 13032. | M. May 4/17. |
| 2 D. | Senior, Cpl. Wm. 10775. | M. May 4/17. |
| 2 D. XV | Sharratt, L.-Cpl. J. 1716. | M. May 4/17. |
| ‡2 D. | Spofford, C. 1153. | M. May 4/17. |
| ‡2 D. | Steadman, B. 3497. | M. May 4/17. |
| 2 D. | Taylor, G. W. 22092. | W. and M. May 4/17. |
| ‡2 D. | Teare, J. 30038. | M. May 13/17. |
| 2 D. | Watts, Frank A. 22093. | W. and M. May 4/17. |
| 2 ? | Rostin, L.-Cpl. A. B. 1037. (Fr. H.Q. Staff.) | K. Dec. 25/16. Det.D./B. |
| 2 ? | Webster, Reginald Ernest. (Formerly 22962, 2/9 Ox. & Bucks). 29984. | W. and M. Sept. 3/16. R/Enq. |
| 5 | **Orton-Smith, 2nd Lt. G. E.** (Fr. 6) | M. March 2/17. R./Enq. |
| *5 C. XI | Evans, Horace John. 201774. | M. May 9/17. |
| ‡6 A. II | Ball, G. 200684. (Fr. 5th.) | M. June 19/17. |
| ‡6 A. II | Lombard, Ernest. 242732. | M. June 19/17. |
| ‡6 A. II | Shenton, F. 202963. (Fr. 5th.) | M. June 19/17. |
| ‡6 A. II | Wilson, John Arthur. 242193. (20355) | M. June 1/17. |
| 6 B. VI | Marshall, Christopher Jn. 20886. | M. Feb. 4/17. |
| 6 B. VII | Pearce, Cpl. Fredk. John. 20826. | M. Feb. 4/17. |
| ‡6 D. XVI | Rogers, Cpl. Herbert Chas. 201291. | M. June 19/17. |
| ‡2/6 A. IV | Shock, Chas. 240070. | M. June 19/17. |
| 2/7 A. | Shaw, J. 258365. | W. and M. April 9/17. |
| 2/7 B. | Gillespie, James. 267237. (Late 5622.) | M. April 9/17. |
| 2/7 C. | Bond, John F. 217966. | M. April 9/17. |
| *8 | **Cooper, 2nd Lieut. W. E.** | K. abt. June 18/17. Det.D./B. |
| ‡10 A. | Bracey, F. 1173. | M. June 7/17. |
| ‡10 A. | Dooley, Chas. Henry. 27326. | M. Nov. 18/16. R/Enq. |
| 10 B. | Leigh, J. 27372. | W. and M. Nov. 18/16. |
| ‡10 C. XI | Thornhill, Chas. Henry. 17749. | K. Nov. 18/16. Det.D./B. |
| 10 C. X | Wood, Edward. 27443. | W. and M. Nov. 18/16. R/Enq. |
| 10 C. XI | Wright, Fredk. 27435. | M. Nov. 18/16. R/Enq. |
| ‡10 D. | Chipman, G. 1423. | M. May 10/17. |
| *10 D. XIII | Hodkinson, Alfred. 17559. | M. May 10/17. |
| ‡10 D. | Hopkins, F. W. 20957. | M. May 10/17. |
| ‡10 D. | Litherland, H. 15739. | M. May 10/17. |
| ‡10 D. | Lucas, T. 5511. | M. May 10/17. |
| 11 | **Shaw, Lieut. R.** | M., bel. W. April 28/17. |
| ‡11 A. | Bellamy, H. 28547. | M. April 23/17. |
| 11 A. II | Brown, Frank. 20991. | M. April 29/17. |
| *11 A. or D. | Davis, J. 1996. | W. and M. April 10/17. |
| 11 A. | Dawes, S. W. 306237. | M. April 29/17. |
| 11 A. | Fuller, T. 8724. | M. April 29/17. |
| 11 A. | Greenwood, Willie. 23309. | M. April 29/17. |
| 11 A. II | Haynes, Arthur. 267598. | M. April 29/17. |
| 11 A. | Johnson, J. 8805. | M. April 29/17. |
| 11 A. or D. | Jones, Sidney Fred. 23082. | M. April 29/17. |
| ‡11 A. | Lafford, F. C. 27801. | W. and M. April 10/17. |
| 11 A. | Mullaley, T. 11766. | M. April 29/17. |
| 11 A. | Pitcher, L.-Cpl. B. 9249. | K. April 9/17. Det.D./B. |
| ‡11 A. | Potter, L.-Sergt. A. A. 8794. | W. and M. April 23/17. |
| 11 A. | Povey, F. 23314. | M. April 29/17. |
| 11 A. I | Radburn, J. 28544. | M. April 29/17. |
| 11 A. | Ross, A. 20966. | M. April 29/17. |
| 11 A. | Taylor, D. 18808. | M. April 29/17. |
| 11 A. | Waters, C. 267952. | M. April 29/17. |

**Warwickshire Regiment, Royal—contd.**

## *B.E.F.*

| | | |
|---|---|---|
| 11 A. I | Williams, A. J. 27820. | M. April 29/17. |
| 11 B. V | Abbotts, E. 27847. | M. April 29/17. |
| 11 B. VI | Allcott, Jas. 11297. | M. April 29/17. |
| 11 B. | Badger, Sergt. W. E. 10650. | W. and M. April 11/17. |
| 11 B. | Barnett, H. 17846. | M. April 29/17. |
| 11 B. VII | Brinsley, Geo. 27786. | M. April 29/17. |
| 11 B. | Curtis, J. 9518. | M. April 29/17. |
| 11 B. | Goodall, Herbert. 240552. | M. April 29/17. |
| 11 B. | Hopkinson, Geo. 27548. (Fr. 2/8 Sherwood Foresters.) | M. April 29/17. |
| 11 B. VI | Jackson, Cyril. 17844. | M. April 29/17. |
| 11 B. | Laugher, F. 267054. | M. April 29/17. |
| 11 B. V | McCarthy, Alfred. 20597. | M. April 29/17. |
| 11 B. | Saunders, G. W. 9021. | M. April 29/17. 2nd Cas. |
| 11 B. | Smith, M. 23091. | M. April 29/17. |
| 11 B. | Spencer, Elliott. 20228. | M. April 29/17. |
| ‡11 B. | Vaughan, J. 18002. | W. and M. April 25/17. |
| 11 B. V | Williams, Wm. 27843. | M. April 29/17. |
| 11 B. | Williamson, W. 7863. | M. April 29/17. |
| 11 B. | Wright, H. 27212. | M. April 29/17. |
| 11 C. | Andrews, J. G. P. 1582. | M. April 27/17. |
| 11 C. | Bromwich, Harry. 21085. | M. April 27/17. |
| ‡11 C. | Davies, W. 4385. | M. April 28/17. |
| 11 C. X | Gregory, L.-Cpl. Harold. 20661. | K. April 28/17. Det.D./B. |
| ‡11 C. IX | Henshall, A. E. 27784. | M. Nov. 14-16/16. R/Enq. |
| ‡11 C. XI | Hughes, Henry. 22580. | M. April 28/17. |
| 11 C. I.T.M. | Humphries, Percy. 14668. (112 Bde) | M. Unoff. K. April 9/17. |
| 11 C. X | Melton, J. J. 21716. | M. April 29/17. |
| ‡11 C. | Player, W. J. 266975. | D/W. April 24/17. Det.D./B. |
| ‡11 C. | Plowman, E. 30225. | W. and M. April 23-29/17. |
| 11 C. IX | Small, Ernest. 22739. | K. April 11/17. Det.D./B. |
| 11 C. | Wilson, A. 5068. | M. April 29/17. |
| ‡11 D. | Adams, Sergt. E. 8097. | M. April 24/17. |
| 11 D. | Balding, J. 4277. | M. Aug. 10-11/16. |
| 11 D. | Barnett, L.-Cpl. Regd. 12364. | M. April 29/17. |
| 11 D. XIV | Brookes, L.-Cpl. Fred. Geo. 7987. | M. April 29/17. |
| 11 D. | Chapman, W. 22762. | M. April 29/17. |
| 11 D. | Cox, L.-Cpl. J. 17714. | M. April 11/17. |
| 11 D. | Driver, P. J. 14968. | M. April 29/17. |
| 11 D. | Featherstone, W. 7958. | M. April 29/17. |
| 11 D. XIV | Fisher, James. 19439. | K. April 11/17. Det.D./B. |
| 11 D. XVI | Griffin, L. 241444. (Fr. 2/6th.) | M. April 29/17. |
| 11 D. | Mouzer, A. J. 19435. | M. April 29/17. |
| 11 D. XI | Robertson, Harry Thos. 7819. | M. April 29/17. |
| 11 D. | Simms, Fred Thos. 16/1739. | M. April 29/17. |
| 11 D. | Thornley, F. E. 15466. | M. April 29/17. |
| ‡11 D. | Weaver, Cpl. A. J. 7890. | M. April 11/17. |
| ‡11 D. | White, J. 18367. | W. and M. April 28/17. |
| 11 D. XIII | Wilkins, Joseph. 17598. | M. April 29/17. |
| ‡14 | **Ivens, 2nd Lieut. J. P.** | M. June 25/17. |
| ‡14 A. or C. | Brittain, H. A. 16760. | M. June 3/17. |
| 14 A. III | Craddock, W. 1318. | W. and M. Sept. 3/16. R./Enq. |
| 14 B. | Moon, A. 17033. | M. Sept. 3/16. R/Enq. |
| 14 B. | Raymond, A. S. 30226. (Fr. 2/1 Hants Cyclists.) | M. Sept. 3/16. R/Enq. |
| 14 B. | Sice, Wm. Chas. 1338. | W. and M. Sept. 3/16. R/Enq. |
| 14 C. | Kemp, G. 15281. | M. Sept. 3/16. |
| *14 D. XIV | Storer, Ernest. 28438. | W. and M. May 7/17. |
| *14 ? | Pritchard, F. H. 21959. | K. May 18/17. Det.D./B. |

**Warwickshire Regiment, Royal—contd.**

*B.E.F.*

*15 A. IV Bridge, Cpl. Joseph Reg. 1374. M. May 9/17.
‡15 A. Chapple, W. E. 14/1454. M. May 9/17.
‡15 A. Hemming, J. 22770. M. May 9/17.
‡15 A. Headra, P. 1766. W. and M. May 9/17.
*15 A. III Hill, A. 240620. (2746.) M. May 9/17.
15 A. Hobbs, W. H. B. 28570. W. and M. May 9/17.
15 A. McMillan, Sergt. Wm. 88. M. May 9/17.
‡15 A. Percival, P. J. 22787. M. May 9/17.
‡15 A. Pratt, S. 12636. M. May 9/17.
*15 B. V Chapman, Cpl. Arthur. 14896. W. and M. May 9/17.
*15 B. V Freeman, S. 19581. M. May 9/17.
15 C. X Burn, J. E. 16/261. M. May 9/17.
15 C. L.G.S. Connell, F. 18765. M. May 9/17.
*15 C. Davis, Jas. 23561. W. and M. May 9/17.
‡15 C. Deeley, A. J. 1237. M. May 9/17.
‡15 C. X Edwards, L.-Cpl. Fredk. Jas. 19393 M. May 9/17.
*15 C. XI Elmore, J. H. 1945. (Fr. 16th.) M. May 9/17.
*15 C. XI Gray, Victor Lionel Jas. 241787. M. May 9/17.
‡15 C. Grazier, F. C. 1136. M. May 9/17.
‡15 C. XI Harper, John. 23568. M. May 9/17.
15 C. XII Mussellwhite, S. 28603. W. and M. May 9/17.
15 C. XI Mutlow, P. A. 1433. M. Unoff. W. May 9/17.
‡15 C. Penny, H. 18725. M. May 9/17.
15 C. IX Pittman, Sydney. 18690. M. May 9/17.
15 C. IX Rycroft, L. C. 1714. W. and M. May 9/17.
*15 C. X Thickett, Leonard. 16/1684. W. and M. May 9/17.
*15 C. XI Wilcox, David. 17370. M. May 9/17.
*15 C. XI Wood, H. 16/1783. M. May 9/17.
‡15 D. Beaumont, C. E. 988. M. May 9/17.
15 D. Chasey, H. 18748. W. and M. May 9/17.
15 D. XIII Collins, Arthur. 16200. M. May 9/17.
‡15 D. Davis, J. T. 3647. M. May 9/17.
15 D. L.G.S. Deacon, F. 968. W. and M. May 9/17.
‡15 D. Dutton, F. 17654. M. May 9/17.
*15 D. Godfrey, Harry. 1673. M. May 9/17.
‡15 D. Hartropp, W. H. 19257. M. May 9/17.
15 D. Hough, John. 28378. (Fr. H.Q.) M. May 9/17.
‡15 D. Howell, A. 1635. M. May 9/17.
15 D. XVI Lancaster, George. 28640. W. and M. May 9/17.
‡15 D. Macbeth, C. A. 28364. M. May 9/17.
‡15 D. XVI Padly, G. F. 28368. M. May 9/17.
*15 D. XV Rees, Timothy. 28630. M. May 9/17.
15 D. XV Sparrow, Alfred Wm. 20572. Unoff. W. and M. May 9/17.
15 D. XIII Stephens, F. W. 240050. M. May 9/17.
‡15 D. XIII Thomas, Percy George. 23578. M. May 9/17.
‡15 D. Williams, J. 28379. M. May 9/17.
16 A. Smout, L.-Cpl. A. H. 1278. W. and M. May 9/17.
16 B. VI Hopkins, L.-Cpl. A. J. 3241. M. April 16/17.
16 B. Kelly, Frank. 383. M. April 16/17.

*PERSIAN GULF.*

*9 B. Lees, W. 12653. K. Jan. 25/17. Det.D./B.
9 C. Lander, W. 2848. (Fr. B.) M. July 8/16.
9 D. Broadmoor, Sergt. G. H. 3943. K. Jan. 25/17. Det.D./B. R./Enq
9 D. Croft, Cpl. A. B. 12103. M. Jan. 25/17.
9 D. XIV Neighbour, C. 18446. K. Jan. 25/17. Det.D./B.
9 D. Perry, W. H. 16727. M. Jan 25/17.
9 ? Ansell, F. J. 13053. M. Jan 25/17.

**Warwickshire Regiment, Royal—contd.**

## *PERSIAN GULF.*

| | | |
|---|---|---|
| 9 ? | Brookes, W. 10741. | W. and M. April 19/16 |
| *9 ? | Clark, R. 10858. | M. Jan 25/17. |
| 9 ? | Kenning, G. 17044. | M. Jan 25/17. |
| 9 ? | Marles, F. E. 16766. | M. Jan 25/17. |
| *9 ? | Milnthorpe, H. 12574. | M. Jan 25/17. |

## WARWICK YEOMANRY.

## *E.E.F.*

| | | |
|---|---|---|
| D. Squad. | Waters, L.-Cpl. Rowland Wm. 1976. | K. April 19/17. Det.D./B. |

## ROYAL WELSH FUSILIERS.

## *B.E.F.*

| | | |
|---|---|---|
| ‡1 A. | Bacon, H. 24809. | M. May 15/17. |
| *1 A. II | Bailey, W A. 19308. | M. May 15/17. |
| *1 A. IV | Davies, David. 53958. | M. May 4/17. |
| 1 A. II | Edwards, D. J. 53959. | M. May 4-5/17. |
| ‡1 A. | Thomas, W. 53923. | W. and M. May 4/17. |
| 1 A. L.G.S. | Wild, W. K. 52064. | M. May 4/17. |
| ‡1 A. | Wilkinson, F. 52670. | M. May 4/17. |
| *1 A. L.G.S. | Williams, W. Rees. 12293. | W. and M. Sept. 3/16. R/Enq. |
| 1 B. VI | Acton, Cpl. Fredk. 53705. | W. and M. May 14/17. |
| *1 B. VII | Birchall, Richard. 53771. | M. May 14/17. |
| *1 B. Bomb. S. | Brazendale. 53772. | M. May 4/17. |
| 1 B. VII | Brownsey, L.-Cpl. A. H. 56608. | M. Sept. 3/16. R/Enq. |
| 1 B. | Jones, Wm. 5498. | W. and M. Sept. 3/16. R/Enq. |
| *1 B. V | Lloyd, Thomas J. 31596. | W. and M. May 3/17. |
| *1 B. IV | Lord, Sniper Thomas 63306. | M. May 14/17. |
| ‡1 B. | Morgan, R. 53802. | M. May 14/17. |
| ‡1 B. | Pugh, R. J. 55073. | M. May 14/17. |
| *1 B. VII | Rose, Stanley. 43617. | W. and M. May 14/17. |
| ‡1 B. or D. | Ward, R. 56651. | M. May 14/17. |
| 1 B. VIII | Williams, Alfred. 53981. | M. May 4/17. |
| 1 B. VII | Williams, T. G. 45157. | W. and M. May 4/17. |
| ‡1 C. | Aird, W. 6494 | W. and M. May 4/17. |
| *1 C. | Bayliss, Eden Thomas. 9623. | W. and M. May 4/17. |
| ‡1 C. | Collins, J. 63596. | M. May 4/17. |
| ‡1 C. | Crowther, J. T. 23861. | M. May 15/17. |
| ‡1 C. | Griffiths, T. H. 53821. | W. and M. May 4/17. |
| ‡1 C. | Griffiths, W. 44195. | M. May 15/17. |
| ‡1 C. | Hunt, J. 4919. | M. May 4/17. |
| 1 C. | James, W. 9374. | M. Mar. 30/17. |
| *1 C. XI | Jones, Edward. 36798. | M. May 15/17. |
| 1 C. | Jones, H. G. 53824. | M. Feb. 26/17. |
| ‡1 C. X | Kerams, Ernest. 267178. (4973.) | M. May 4/17. |
| 1 C. | Llewellin, Jas. 53831. | M. Feb. 27/17. |

**Welsh Fusiliers, Royal—contd.**

*B.E.F.*

| | | |
|---|---|---|
| 1 C. or D. | MacAllister, J. P. 30074. | M. Sept. 3/16. R./Enq. |
| ‡1 C. | Pilling, George. 23811. | M. May 4/17. |
| ‡1 C. | Poynton, W. 53727. | M. May 15/17. |
| ‡1 C. | Roberts, E. E. 53732. | M. May 5/17. |
| ‡1 C. | Sullivan, R. 5733. | M. May 15/17. |
| ‡1 C. | Taylor, Cpl. J. H. 5277. | W. and M. May 15/17. |
| ‡1 D. | Edwards, H. W. 53693. | M. May 5/17. |
| 1 D. XIII | Griffiths, Evan. 40813. | M. Sept. 3/16. |
| 1 D. XIV | Hurst, James. 207245. | W. and M. May 14/17. |
| 1 D. XV | Jones, Jas. Thos. 53715. | W. and M. May 5/17. |
| 1 D. XV | Keyes, L.-Cpl. Chas. 266079. | W. and M. May 15/17. |
| ‡1 D. | Roberts, J. F. 11430. | W. and M., bel. K. May 5/17. |
| ‡1 D. | Watkins, G. 56650. | M. May 15/17. |
| 2 C. | **Conning, Lieut. T. R.** | M. May 27/17. |
| 2 | **Lewis, 2nd Lt. W. O.** (Fr. 4th.) | W. and M. May 27/17. |
| 2 | **Orme, Lt. E. L.** (Fr. 3rd.) | W. and M. May 27/17. |
| *2 B. | **Phillips, 2nd Lieut. A.** | K. April 23/17. Det.D./B. |
| 2 | **Richards, 2nd Lt. J. D. M.** | M., bel. K. May 27/17. |
| ‡2 | **Williams, 2nd Lieut. T. B.** | M., bel. K. May 27/17. |
| *2 A. I | Bolton, Walter. 52214. | M. May 27/17. |
| ‡2 A. or B. VIII | Cohen, Maurice. 63170. | M. May 27/17. |
| ‡2 A. | Collier, F. 18350. | M. May 27/17. |
| ‡2 A. IV | Davies, William Jones. 44275 | M. May 27/17. |
| ‡2 A. | Evans, E. 291469. | M. May 27/17. |
| ‡2 A. M.G.S. | Evans, R. 54117. | W. Unoff. M. May 27/17. |
| ‡2 A. | Griffiths, G. E. 18380. | M. May 27/17. |
| ‡2 A. | Hawkins, B. 12121. | M. May 27/17. |
| *2 A. IV | Jones, Emrys Owen. 201385 | M. May 27/17. |
| ‡2 A. or D. L.G.S. | Jones, J. Rowland. 27998. | M. May 27/17. |
| ‡2 A. | Miller, W. 56238. | M. May 27/17. |
| ‡2 A. | Morgan, H. 54603. | M. May 27/17. |
| ‡2 A. | Parry, Sergt. N. J. 10567. | M. May 27/17. |
| ‡2 A. II | Pugh Lawrence. 56222. | M. May 27/17. |
| ‡2 A. | Sprosten, G. 37062. | M. May 27/17. |
| ‡2 A. II | Sturk, William Deacon. 22150. | M. May 27/17. |
| *2 A. | Wood, L.-Cpl. Wm. Ernest. 28057. | M. May 27/17. |
| 2 B. VII | Briggs, A. 27058. | M. Nov. 5/16. R/Enq. |
| ‡2 B. | Facer, J. 56232. | M. May 27/17. |
| ‡2 B. | Hampson, A. 56242. | M. May 27/17. |
| ‡2 B. VIII | Ibberson, Arthur. 56235. | M. May 27/17. |
| 2 B. VIII | Owen, Frank R. 29610. | M. May 27/17. |
| ‡2 B. | Parry, J. 16262. | M. May 27/17. |
| *2 B. VIII | Parry, Cpl. Richards. 55017. | M. May 27/17. |
| 2 B. | Rogers, Percy. 54109. | M. Nov. 5/16. R/Enq. |
| ‡2 C. | Battye, A. 56257. | M. May 27/17. |
| ‡2 C. | Bond, J. 266868. (Fr. 6th.) | M. May 27/17. |
| *2 C. XI | Charles, R. 291522 | M. May 27/17. |
| *2 C. | Davies, A. E. 54607. | M. Unoff. K. May 27/17. |
| *2 C. X | Evans, Edward David. 292592. | M. May 27/17. |
| ‡2 C. | Garth, A. E. 41759. | M. May 27/17. |
| ‡2 C. | Hughes, E. 56259. | M. May 27/17. |
| ‡2 C. | Hughes, L.-Cpl. H. 54596. | M. May 27/17. |
| ‡2 C. | Jones, R. 266622. (Fr. 6th.) | M. April 27/17. |
| ‡2 C. | Jones, T. 56248. | M. May 27/17. |
| ‡2 C. IX | Marsh, Fred. 36496. | M. May 27/17. |
| ‡2 C. | Parnell, R. B. 54101. | M. May 27/17. |
| ‡2 C. | Ratcliffe, J. 56252. | M. May 27/17. |
| *2 C. X | Trippier, J. 63048. | M. May 27/17. |
| ‡2 D. | Cadman, L.-Cpl. H. 8239. | M. May 27/17. |

**Welsh Fusiliers, Royal—contd.**

## *B.E.F.*

| | | |
|---|---|---|
| ‡2 D. | Dean, S. 39026. | M. May 27/17. |
| 2 D. XV | Evans, J. 55608. | W. and M. April 23/17. |
| ‡2 D. | Flint, G. 30665. | M. May 27/17. |
| ‡2 D. | Higham, J. 28949. | M. May 27/17. |
| ‡2 D. | Jones, J. T. 55230. | M. May 27/17. |
| ‡2 D. | Rillington, C. 54453. | M. April 23/17. |
| ‡2 D. | Traverse, W. 241699. | M. May 27/17. |
| *4 A. IV | Gould, W. R. 235023. | M. May 2/17. |
| ‡4 B. | Draper, H. S. 203318. | M. May 27/17. |
| ‡4 C. XI | Cresswell, W. 202075. | W. Unoff. M. May 28/17. |
| ‡4 C. | Hughes, J. 200911. | M. May 27/17. |
| ‡9 A. I | Tomlinson, Jonathan Harold. 63047. | M. June 7/17. |
| *10 A. IV | Davies, T. E. 45030 | W. and M. May 5/17. |
| 10 B. | Edwards, Roger. 54713. | M. Nov. 13/16. R/Enq. |
| 10 B. | Evans, I. 54714. | M. Nov. 13/16. |
| 10 B. V | Jones, Lewis Rich. 54738. | M. Nov. 13/16. |
| ‡10 B. | Price, W. L. 55075. | W. and M. April 8-11/17. |
| 10 B. | Reed, J. 54968. | M. April 8-11/17. |
| 10 B. | Roberts, R. 28541. | M. Nov. 13/16. |
| 10 C. | Abercrombv, L.-Sergt. Fred. 57032. (1471.) | W. and M. April 8-11/17. |
| 10 C. | Catling, G. 55555. | M. April 8-11/17. |
| 10 C. IX | White, A. 56031. | M., bel. K. April 8-11/17. |
| ‡10 D. | Jones, T. 33746. | W. and M. May 14/16. |
| ‡10 D. | Sheppard, W. J. 27046. | M. April 30/17. |
| 10 D. XIII | Walley, Victor Lee. 54437. | M. Nov. 13/16. R/Enq. |
| 10 ? | Cross, L.-Cpl. Albert Ed. 56011. | K. April 8-11/17. Det.D./B. |
| 14 | **James, 2nd Lt. E. L. (Fr. 2nd.)** | M. Feb. 18/17. |
| 14 A. III | Bentley, F. 55320. | W. and M. Feb. 18/17. |
| 14 C. | Brees, D. C. 55318. | M. Feb. 18/17. |
| 14 C. XII | Evans, L.-Cpl. William. 56870. | W. and M. Feb. 18/17. |
| 14 C. XII | Thomson, D. 26717. | M. Feb. 18/17. |
| 14 D. L.G.S. | Jones, Charles. 23134. | M. Feb. 18/17. |
| ‡15 B. | Evans, L. A. 55981. | M. May 6/17. |
| ‡15 B. | Hughes, H. M. 55404. | M. May 6/17. |
| ‡17 A. | Meredith, A.-Cpl. W. H. 25786. | M. Oct. 9/16. R/Enq. |
| 19 A. | Jones, David. 28381. | M. May 6/17. |
| ‡19 A. | Ruddock, H. 45507. | M. May 6/17. |
| 19 A. | Walsh, L.-Cpl. W. 45505. | W. and M. April 21/17. |
| ‡19 C. | Lilley, Sergt. W. 45662. | M. May 6/17. |

## *BALKANS.*

| | | |
|---|---|---|
| 11 ? | Mee, R. 35528. | M. Feb. 21/17. |

## *E.E.F.*

| | | |
|---|---|---|
| 3 4 | Lowe, Chas. 63686. | M., bel. drowned April 15/17, "Arcadian." |
| 5 | **Jones, 2nd Lt. E. Llewellyn Hustler.** (Fr. 12th.) | K. Mar. 26/17. Det.D./B. |
| 5 | **Thomas, 2nd Lieut. E. L.** | W. and M. Mar. 26/17. |
| 5 A. I | Hughes, Robert. 241092. (3194.) | W. and M. Mar. 26/17. |
| 5 A. | Jones, L.-Cpl. Edw. Parry. 240969. (2942.) | W. and M. Mar. 26/17. |
| 5 A. | Slater, J. 242953. (37200.) | W. and M. Mar. 26/17. |
| 5 A. | White, Alb. Edw. 266133. (3456.) | W. and M. Mar. 26/17. |
| 5 A. | Williams, T. 241884. (4494.) | W. and M. Mar. 26/17. |
| 5 C. | Edwards, R. T. 241604. (3892.) | K. Mar. 26/17. Det.D./B. |
| 5 C. | Johnson, R. 3434. | M. Mar. 26/17. |

**Welsh Fusiliers, Royal**—contd.

## *BALKANS.*

5 D. Ellis, J. D. 241341. (3589.) M. Mar. 26/17.
5 D. Foulkes, John. 201125. (8549.) W. and M. Mar. 26/17.
5 D. Griffith, W. 201354. (9188.) (Fr. 4th) M. Mar. 26/17.
5 D. Wheeler, W. E. 241229. W. and M. Mar. 26/17.
5 D. Williams, W. 241333. (3579.) M. Mar. 26/17.
5 ? Butler, J. W. 240802. W. and M. Mar. 26/17.
5 ? Catherall, E. G. 241382. W. and M. Mar. 26/17.
5 ? Davies, A. 240894. W. and M. Mar. 26/17.
5 ? Davies, A. 240634. (2216.) W. and M. Mar. 26/17.
5 ? Ellis, R. 241181. W. and M. Mar. 26/17.
5 ? Foulkes, J. 241448. W. and M. Mar. 26/17.
5 ? Griffiths, T. 241397. W. and M. Mar. 26/17.
5 ? Hands, J. 241692. W. and M. Mar. 26/17.
5 ? Harrington, J. 241381. W. and M. Mar. 26/17.
5 ? Hayes, Wm. Henry. 240341. (1221.) W. and M. Mar. 26/17.
5 ? Jones, T. J. 3269. M. Mar. 26/17.
5 ? Lloyd, A.-Sergt. T. 265677. W. and M. Mar. 26/17.
5 ? Millington, A. 241498. W. and M. Mar. 26/17.
5 ? Owen, H. 266378. W. and M. Mar. 26/17.
5 ? Roberts, D. O. 241112. W. and M. Mar. 26/17.
5 ? Sleigh, J. 241373. W. and M. Mar. 26/17.

## *E.E.F.*

‡5 ? Vernon, George Arthur. 242740. M., bel. drowned, April 15/17.
5 ? Wood, H. 242759. M. Mar. 26/17.
6 A. Jones, Hugh. 266715. W. and M. Mar. 26/17.
6 A. IV Williams, Thos. Wm. 267403. (5276.) W. and M. Mar. 26/17.
6 ? Jones, J. R. 266589. W. and M. Mar. 26/17.
6 ? Jones, J. S. 291399. W. and M. Mar. 26/17.
6 ? Newsham, C. R. 5247. M. Mar. 26/17.
6 ? Pierce, R. 266446. W. and M. Mar. 26/17.
6 ? Williams, E. 4155. M. Mar. 26/17.
6 ? Williams, W. 265359. W. and M. Mar. 26/17.
7 A. Bardsley, W. B. 291816. (4915.) W. and M. Mar. 26/17.
7 A. Dykes, Moses. 906. M., bel. K. Mar. 26/17.
7 A. III Jones, Evan Thos. 291390. W. and M. Mar. 26/17.
7 A. Jones, John Fredk. 290081. (716.) W. and M. Mar. 26/17.
7 A. IV Jones, Thomas. 291193. W. and M. Mar. 26/17.
7 A. III Jones, T. H. 290939. (3408.) W. and M. Mar. 26/17.
7 A. Lloyd, W. 291605. W. and M. Mar. 26/17.
7 A. Moss, S. 291863. W. and M. Mar. 26/17.
7 A. Wood, L.-Cpl. Hy. Edw. 291082. (4915.) W. and M. Mar. 26/17.
7 B. Davies, Evan Thos. 291175. (3921.) W. and M. Mar. 26/17.
7 B. Davies, L.-Cpl. G. O. 290261. W. and M. Mar. 26/17.
7 B. Gwynn, H. H. 291116. (3837.) M. Mar. 26/17.
7 B. Hodge, T. E. 290955. (3532.) W. and M. Mar. 26/17.
7 B. Jarvis, S. 290291. (1100.) W. and M. Mar. 26/17.
7 B. Jones, J. C. 291291. (4067.) M. Mar. 26/17.
7 B. Price, Cpl. Evan. 290899. (3413.) W. and M. Mar. 26/17.
7 B. Roberts, Thos. 291382. (4200.) W. and M. Mar. 26/17.
7 B. VI Woods, John. 291207. (3966.) W. and M. Mar. 19/17.
7 C. Pugh, Hugh. 291412. (4240.) W. and M. Mar. 26/17.
7 C. Williams, R. 290539. (2751.) W. and M. Mar. 26/17.
7 D. Barnshaw, T. 291866. (Late 4967.) W. and M. Mar. 26/17.
7 D. Jones, Jas. Owen. 291407. (4305.) W. and M. Mar. 26/17.
7 D. Jones, R. Wm. 291199. W. and M. Mar. 26/17.
7 D. Lloyd, Abel. 291479. (4322.) W. and M. Mar. 26/17.

**Welsh Fusiliers, Royal**—contd.

## *E.E.F.*

| | | |
|---|---|---|
| 7 D. XVI | Lloyd, Evan. 291538. | W. and M. Mar. 26/17. |
| 7 D. XIV | Mills, G. M. 290991. | W. and M. Mar. 26/17. |
| 7 D. | Owen, E. 290637. (2909.) | W. and M. Mar. 26/17. |
| 7 D. | Tudor, W. 291251. (4019.) | M. Mar. 26/17. |
| 7 D. XIV | Williams, Ellis. 291240. (4006.) | W. and M. Mar. 26/17. |
| 7 ? | Bailey, J. 4909. | M. Mar. 26/17. |
| 7 ? | Ball, G. 4913. | M. Mar. 26/17. |
| 7 ? | Bevan, T. 290897. | W. and M. Mar. 26/17. |
| 7 ? | Cawley, Robert. 291873. (4974.) | W. and M. Mar. 26/17. |
| 7 ? | Davies, J. 4047. | W. and M. Mar. 26/17. |
| 7 ? | Evans, G. 291083. | W. and M. Mar. 26/17. |
| 7 ? | Evans, T. 291530. | W. and M. Mar. 26/17. |
| 7 ? | Evans, Cpl. W. 290285. | W. and M. Mar. 26/17. |
| 7 ? | Griffiths, T. 290662. | W. and M. Mar. 26/17. |
| 7 ? | Hughes, E. 291405. | W. and M. Mar. 26/17. |
| 7 ? | Hughes, W. 4014. | W. and M. Mar. 26/17. |
| 7 ? | Jones, A. 3074. | M. Mar. 26/17. |
| 7 ? | Jones, H. 290514. | W. and M. Mar. 26/17. |
| 7 L.G.S. | Jones, Sergt. Hugh. 290532. | W. and M. Mar. 26/17. |
| 7 ? | Lewis, R. 737. | W. and M. Mar. 26/17. |
| 7 ? | Lloyd, W. P. 3357. | M. Mar. 26/17. |
| 7 ? | Longman, E. 1069. | M. Mar. 26/17. |
| 7 ? | Miller, J. 291712. | W. and M. Mar. 26/17. |
| 7 ? | Morgan, J. 290276. | W. and M. Mar. 26/17. |
| •7 ? | Owen, Sergt. T. 290428. (2535.) | K. Mar. 26/17. Det.D./B. |
| 7 ? | Owen, W. M. 291202. | W. and M. Mar. 26/17. |
| •7 ? | Pearson, S. 291080. | M. Mar. 26/17. |
| 7 ? | Phillips, P. 290435. | W. and M. Mar. 26/17. |
| 7 ? | Powell, Sergt. J. 290254. | W. and M. Mar. 26/17. |
| 7 ? | Powell, T. W. 291717. | W. and M. Mar. 26/17. |
| 7 ? | Pryce, J. O. 4112. | M. Mar. 26/17. |
| 7 ? | Roberts, D. 291701. | W. and M. Mar. 26-27/17. |
| 7 ? | Roberts, D. J. 290913. | W. and M. Mar. 26/17. |
| 7 ? | Smith, S. C. 291894. | W. and M. Mar. 26/17. |
| 7 ? | Smith, W. O. 4023. | M. Mar. 26/17. |
| 7 ? | Thomas W. 290353. | W. and M. Mar. 26/17. |
| 7 ? | Wilding, D. 291288. | W. and M. Mar. 26/17. |
| 7 ? | Williams, H. 291010 | W. and M. Mar. 26/17. |
| 7 ? | Williams, J. 1114. | M. Mar. 26/17. |
| ? ? | Rohun, Sergt. Edward. 19466. | M., bel. drowned April 15/17. "Arcadian." |

## *PERSIAN GULF.*

| | | |
|---|---|---|
| 8 A. or D. | Edwards, Wm. 17951. | M. April 7/16. |
| 8 B. VIII | Davies, B. F. 24361. | W. and M. Feb. 3/17. |
| 8 B. | Griffiths, Arthur. 12637. | M. April 5/16. |
| 8 C. | Hudson, Wm. Thos. 46113. | M. Dec. 20/16. |
| 8 D. | Walker, Arthur. 19919. | K. Feb. 15/17. Det.D./B. |

## WELSH REGIMENT.

### *B.E.F.*

| | | |
|---|---|---|
| **2 B. VII** | Herbert, Henry. 44652. | M. **Sept. 8/16.** R/Enq. |
| **2 B.** | • Rees, E. 39050. | M. **Sept. 8/16.** R/Enq. |
| **2 D.** | Banks, T. 11861. | W. and M. **Sept. 8/16.** R/Enq |
| **9 A. IV** | Slack, John Ed. 16990. | M. **Nov. 12/16.** |
| **10 C.** | Eamor, E. J. 47599. | M. **Mar. 23/17.** |
| **13 C.** | Morris, Cpl. Gwilym. 57223. | M. **May 30/17.** |
| **15 B. V** | Edwards, L.-Cpl. David John. 30213. | M. **April 30/17.** |
| **15 B. VI** | Hughes, Wm. 54595. | M. **April 30/16.** |
| **15 B.** | Read, L.-Cpl. F. C. 47734. | M. **April 30/17.** |
| **15 B.** | Tomkins, G. 54284. | M. **April 28/17.** |
| **15 B. VI** | Watson, Alfred Valient. 47766. | M. **April 30/17.** |
| **15 C. X** | Lewis, David. 54277. | M. **April 30/17.** |
| **16** | **Jones, 2nd Lt. J. B.** | M. **June 6/17.** |
| ***16 D. XVI** | Gillett, Marshall C. 23974. | K. **July 10/17.** Det.D./B. |

### *BALKANS.*

| | | |
|---|---|---|
| ***1** | **Simpson, 2nd Lieut. D.** | M., bel. K. **June 2/17.** |
| ***1 A.** | Harris, E. S. 50968. | M., bel. K. **May 31/17** |
| **‡1 D.** | Jones, Sergt. D. E. 28178. | M. **June 2/17.** |
| **‡1 D. XV** | Walsh, H. H. 58614. | M. **June 2/17.** |
| **‡1 ?** | Bowden, J. 241715. | M. **June 2/17.** |
| **‡1 ?** | Dance, A. 40754. | M., bel. K. **May 31/17.** |
| **‡1 ?** | John, E. D. 48082. | M., bel. K. **May 31/17.** |
| **‡1 ?** | Lewis, W. 21503. | M., bel. K. **May 31/17.** |
| **‡1 ?** | Luke, J. 10618. | M., bel. K. **May 31/17.** |
| **‡1 ?** | Maynes, W. 38066. | M., bel. K. **May 31/17.** |
| **‡1 ?** | Morris, E. 38603. | M. **June 2/17.** |
| **‡1 ?** | Smith, C. 15057. | M., bel. K. **May 31/17.** |

### *E.E.F.*

| | | |
|---|---|---|
| **4 A.** | **Williams, 2nd Lt. O. E.** (Fr. Imp. Camel Corps.) | K. **April 19/17.** Det.D./B. |
| **4 A.** | Evans, Isaiah. 200278. (Late 775.) | W. and M. **Mar. 26/17.** |
| **4 A.** | George, W. E. 2519. | M. **Mar. 26/17.** |
| **4 A.** | Griffiths, Cpl. Evan Rowland. 200662 | W. and M. **Mar. 26/17.** |
| **4 A.** | Griffiths, P. 200115. | W. and M. **Mar. 26/17.** |
| **4 A.** | Shaw, Ben. 201069. (Late 4463.) | W. and M. **Mar. 26/17.** |
| **4 A.** | Walters, G. 5526. | M. **Mar. 26/17.** |
| **4 C.** | Cornock, J. 201478. (Late 5637.) | W. and M. **Mar. 26/17.** |
| **4 C.** | Meredith, A. 201754. (6105.) | W. and M. **Mar. 26/17.** |
| **4 C.** | Picton, Sgt. W. G. 200110. (457.) | M. **Mar. 26/17.** |
| **4 C.** | Vaughan, J. 201765. (6107.) | M. **Mar. 26/17.** |
| **4 D.** | Duggan, Harry. 201688. (Late 6004.) | W. and M. **Mar. 26/17.** |
| **4 D.** | Morris, P. J. 201802. | W. and M. **Mar. 26/17.** |
| **4 D.** | Tobin, Maurice. 202584. (38677.) | W. and M. **Mar. 26/17.** |
| **4 ?** | Davies, B. J. 6161. | M. **Mar. 26/17.** |
| **4 ?** | Davies, A.-Cpl. D. W. 200821 | W. and M. **Mar. 26/17.** |
| **4 ?** | Davis, E. E. 201480. | W. and M. **Mar. 26/17.** |
| **4 ?** | Davies, A.-Cpl. G. 200838. | W. and M. **Mar. 26/17.** |
| **4 ?** | Griffiths, A.-Cpl. D. 200715. | W. and M. **Mar. 26/17.** |
| **4 ?** | Jones, L. R. 201820. | W. and M. **Mar. 26/17.** |
| **4 ?** | Lewis, W. J. 200629. | W. and M. **Mar. 26/17.** |
| **4 ?** | Morgan, L. F. 201819. | W. and M. **Mar. 26/17.** |
| **4 ?** | Owen, T. 4/6021. | M. **Mar. 26/17.** |
| **4 ?** | Rees, D. 200667. | W. and M. **Mar. 26/17.** |
| **4 ?** | Roberts, W. H. 4/5931. | M. **Mar. 26/17.** |
| **4 ?** | Thomas, D. M. 4/5935. | M. **Mar. 26/17.** |
| **4 ?** | Thomas, G. 6146. | M. **Mar. 26/17.** |

**Welsh Regiment—contd.**

## *E.E.F.*

| | | |
|---|---|---|
| 4 ? | Walters, J. 201326. | W. and M. Mar. 26/17. |
| 2/4 | **Bryant, 2nd Lt. Fredk. Jas. Mansel.** | K. Mar. 26/17. Det.D/B. |
| 5 | **Davis, Lieut. Cecil.** | W. and M. Mar. 26/17. |
| 5 A. | Edwards, R. 241143. (3314.) | K. Mar. 26/17. Det.D./B. |
| 5 B. | Baker, E. J. 5395. | M. Mar. 26/17. |
| 5 B. | Clark, Sgt. J. 240660. (2111.) | W. and M. Mar. 26/17. |
| 5 B. | Morgan, J. H. 241660. (5427.) | W. and M. Mar. 26/17. |
| 5 B. | Morris, Evan. 5592. | M. Mar. 26/17. |
| 5 B. | Morris, L.-Cpl. T. J. 240305. (1475.) | W. and M. Mar. 26/17. |
| 5 B. | Onion, J. A. 240148. (794.) | M. Mar. 26/17. |
| 5 B. | Rees, W. T. 241131. (Late 2938.) | W. and M. Mar. 26/17. |
| 5 C. | Baker, Sigr. E. J. 241378. (3377.) | M., bel. K. Mar. 26/17. |
| *5 C. | Brady, John. 240997. (2704.) | W. and M. Mar. 26/17. |
| 5 C. | Davies, Luther E. 241226. (3078.) | M. Mar. 26/17. |
| 5 C. | Jones, E. R. 240476. (Late 1803.) | W. and M. Mar. 26/17. |
| 5 C. X L.G.S. | Morgan, H. 241487. (5023.) | W. and M. Mar. 26/17. |
| 5 C. | Pearson, Sgt. Jas. Henry. 241435. | W. and M. Mar. 26/17. |
| 5 C. | Quick, Norman Edw. 240930. | W. and M. Mar. 26/17. |
| 5 C. | Williams, Edward. 242129. (Fr. Liverpools.) | M. Mar. 26/17. |
| 5 C. | Williams, L.-Cpl. W. 240704. (1318.) | W. and M. Mar. 26/17. |
| 5 D. | Bartlett, Chas. 241726. | W. and M. Mar. 26/17. |
| 5 D. | Davies, David Thos. 240631. | W. and M. Mar. 26/17. |
| 5 D. | Davies, W. D. 241689. | W. and M. Mar. 26/17. |
| 5 D. | Davies, Wm. Jas. 240586. | W. and M. Mar. 26/17. |
| 5 D. | Jones, T. H. 242013. (Late 6062.) | W. and M. Mar. 26/17. |
| 5 D. | Morris, Evan. 240869. (2675.) | W. and M. Mar. 26/17. |
| *5 D. | Thomas, L.-Sergt. Tom Owen. 240596. | W. and M. Mar. 26/17. |
| 5 ? | Arkell, E. J. 241836. | W. and M. Mar. 26/17. |
| 5 ? | Bailey, T. P. 1222. | M. Mar. 26/17. |
| 5 ? | Bracey, F. H. 1744. | M. Mar. 26/17. |
| 5 ? | Bradfield, W. J. 6056. | M. Mar. 26/17. |
| 5 ? | Butler, F 241175. | W. and M. Mar. 26/17. |
| 5 ? | Coles, E. J. 5299. | M. Mar. 26/17. |
| 5 ? | Davies, B. 3484. | M. Mar. 26/17. |
| 5 ? | Davies, J. 2951. | M. Mar. 26/17. |
| 5 ? | Davies, J. 240977. | M. Mar. 26/17. |
| 5 ? | Davies, W. H. 4729. | M. Mar. 26/17. |
| 5 ? | Evans, G. J. 5715. | M. Mar. 26/17. |
| 5 ? | Evans, O. 240462. | W. and M. Mar. 26/17. |
| 5 ? | Evans, R. 3020. | M. Mar. 26/17. |
| 5 ? | Griffiths, I. 241790. | M. Mar. 26/17. |
| 5 ? | Hatter, F. J. 241731. | W. and M. Mar. 26/17. |
| 5 ? | King, E. 240487. | W. and M. Mar. 26/17. |
| 5 ? | Lewis, D. P. 3052. | W. and M. Mar. 26/17. |
| 5 ? | Pitt, H. T. 241291. | W. and M. Mar. 26/17. |
| 5 ? | Powell, E. J. 3373. | M. Mar. 26/17. |
| 5 ? | Rendall, A. 241253. | M., bel. K. Mar. 26/17. |
| 5 ? | Skillicorn, F. 240868. | W. and M. Mar. 26/17. |
| 5 ? | Squires, L. E. 241774. | M. Mar. 26/17. |
| 5 ? | Stacey, C. H. 3416. | M. Mar. 26/17. |
| 5 ? | Thomas, G. 2295. | M. Mar. 26/17. |
| 5 ? | Thomas, H. J. 240677. | W. and M. Mar. 26/17. |
| 5 ? | Thomas, P. 241544. | M. Mar. 26/17. |
| 5 ? | Thomas, R. L. 5996. | M. Mar. 26/17. |
| 5 ? | Williams, J. 241295. | W. and M. Mar. 26/17. |
| 7 C. | Passmore, W. 240555. (1945.) | W. and M. Mar. 25/17. |

Welsh Regiment—contd.

## *PERSIAN GULF.*

| | | |
|---|---|---|
| 8 ? | Banwell, J. 24959. | M. June 12/16. |
| ‡8 ? | Evans, O. 44563. | M. Mar. 27/17. |
| ‡8 ? | Hillman, E. 11278 | M. Mar. 27/17. |
| ‡8 ? | Tullett, Cpl. G. 8929. | M. Mar. 27/17. |

## WEST RIDING REGIMENT (DUKE OF WELLINGTON'S).

## *B.E.F.*

| | | |
|---|---|---|
| 2 | **Belshall, 2nd Lt. S. A.** | M. May 3/17. |
| 2 | **Cunningham, Capt. K. E.** | W. and M. May 3/17. |
| 2 | **Heale, M.C., Capt. G. R. C.** | W. and M. Unoff. K May 3/17. |
| 2 | **Lambert, 2nd Lt. P. E.** | W. and M. May 3/17. |
| 2 | **Vices, 2nd Lieut. H. L.** | M. May 3/17. |
| ‡2 A. | Aedy, L. 235184. | M. May 3/17. |
| 2 A. IV | Ainley, Fred. 18063. | K. Oct. 12/16. Det.D./B. |
| 2 A. III | Banks, J. M. 265311. | M. May 3/17. |
| ‡2 A. I | Barrett, William. 235272. | M. May 3/17. |
| ‡2 A. | Beasty, T. 10662. | M. May 3/17. |
| ‡2 A. | Buckley, J. 18132. | M. May 3/17. |
| ‡2 A. | Butler, S. 11394. | M. May 3/17. |
| ‡2 A. | Clark, J. 26753. | M. May 3/17. |
| ‡2 A. | Cripps, Chas. Edwin. 17260. | M. May 3/17. |
| *2 A. I | Currie, John. 17867. | M. May 3/17. |
| 2 A. III | Curtis, Fredk. Chas. 235015. (24966.) | M. May 3/17. |
| ‡2 A. | Dawson, C. 16193. | M. May 3/17. |
| 2 A. IV | Dosser, Herbert. 24303. | M. May 3/17. |
| ‡2 A. | Emmott, W. 14068. | M. May 3/17. |
| *2 A. III | Firth, R. J. 235200. | M. May 3/17. |
| 2 A. III | Fox, Robert. 24312. | M. May 3/17. |
| ‡2 A. | Garrett, H. 24936. | M. May 3/17. |
| 2 A. III | Gill, Arthur. 19702. | M. May 3/17. |
| 2 A. | Goldsbrough, Fred. 19961. | M. Oct. 12/16. R/Enq. |
| ‡2 A. | Gray, J. W. 18764. | M. May 3/17. |
| ‡2 A. | Gunson, A.-Sergt. C. 235226. | M. May 3/17. |
| ‡2 A. | Hardwick, S. 10507. | M. May 3/17. |
| ‡2 A. | Harrison, A. 9472. | M. May 3/17. |
| *2 A. | Harrison, L.-Cpl. John Wm. 11235. | M. May 3/17. |
| 2 A. I | Hind, Sergt. Harold. 16655. | M. May 3/17. |
| ‡2 A. | Larrington, F. 18906. | M. May 3/17. |
| ‡2 A. | McDalienson, A. 23799. | M. May 3/17. |
| 2 A. L.G.S. | Mellor, Fredk. Wm. 14956. | M. May 3/17. |
| ‡2 A. | Moore, A. 24305. | M. May 3/17. |
| ‡2 A. | O'Rourke, T. 10550. | M. May 3/17. |
| ‡2 A. | Parker, R. 202954. | M. May 3/17. |
| ‡2 A. | Parker, Sergt. William. 10454. | M. May 3/17. |
| 2 A. III | Parkinson, C. 28939. | M. May 3/17. |
| ‡2 A. | Parkinson, D. 23716. | M. May 3/17. |
| 2 A. | Pyle, John George. 23845. | M. May 3/17. |
| ‡2 A. | Rothery, A. 201585. | M. May 3/17. |
| 2 A. | Sharpe, B. 26742. | W. and M. April 11/17. |
| ‡2 A. | Shaw, G. L. 204622. | M. May 3/17. |

**West Riding Regiment (Duke of Wellington's)—contd.**

*B.E.F.*

‡2 A. Shinn, L.-Cpl. A. E. 16528. M. May 3/17.
‡2 A. Simister, Cpl. W. 24438. M. May 3/17.
*2 A. or D. Simmons, L.-Cpl. H. C. 8968. M. May 3/17.
‡2 A. Simpson, J. R. 28745. M. May 3/17.
‡2 A. Slater, A. 200603. M. May 3/17.
‡2 A. Smith, A. 235218. M. May 3/17.
‡2 A. Smith, Cpl. D. 10882. M. May 3/17.
*2 A. IV Smith, Norman. 203060. M. May 3/17.
‡2 A. Sykes, Frank. 200205. M. May 3/17.
*2 A. Thorpe, Ben. 26742. M. April 9/17.
‡2 A. Turner, J. 26758. M. May 3/17.
2 A. Turton, Harold. 203893. (8172.) (Fr. 4th.) W. and M. May 3/17.
‡2 A. Walker, H. 28787. M. May 3/17.
‡2 A. Whiteley, Jas. Gordon. 28729. M. May 3/17.
‡2 A. Whittaker, H. 17033. M. May 3/17.
‡2 A. Wilson, A. 15687. M. May 3/17.
‡2 A. III Wimpenny, John. 13143. M. May 3/17.
2 A. IV Wood, George. 19178. M. May 3/17.
*2 B. or C. Barraclough, Norman. 29869. (Fr. 3.) M. May 3/17.
*2 B. VIII Barrett, Townend. 13549. M. May 3/17.
‡2 B. Barry, W. 23321. M. May 3/17.
2 B. Bentley, George. 14211. M. May 3/17.
‡2 B. Blythe, H. 15519. M. May 3/17.
2 B. L.G.S. Booth, L.-Cpl. Herbert. 16150. M. May 3/17.
*2 B. VII Bottomley, E. 28814. M. May 3/17.
‡2 B. Bowers, Cpl. C. H. 201109. M. May 3/17.
2 B. VII Broadbent, Harold. 19701. M. Oct. 12/16.
‡2 B. Burklen, C. F. 14293. M. May 3/17.
‡2 B. Carr, T. 9679. M. May 3/17.
2 B. Chaytor, Joseph. 6624. M. May 3/17.
2 B. V Clark, Frank. 28774. M. April 11/17.
‡2 B. Coleman, T. 18595. M. May 3/17.
*2 B. VII Conkerton, Clarence. 24391. M. May 3/17.
‡2 B. Corry, N. 235277. M. May 3/17.
‡2 B. Craddock, W. 235279. M. May 3/17.
‡2 B. Craven, F. 10553. M. May 3/17.
‡2 B. Credie, Fred. 16469. M. May 3/17.
2 B. VI Dawson, John William. 18609. W. and M. April 11/17.
2 B. VIII Dewhirst, Lewis. 18804. M. May 3/17.
2 B. VI Drinkwater, John. 16839. M. May 3/17.
‡2 B. Ellis, L. 17648. M. May 3/17.
2 B. V Emmott, Harold. 235281. M. May 3/17.
‡2 B. Flannagan, T. 24074. M. May 3/17.
‡2 B. Foye, T. 11759. M. May 3/17.
‡2 B. Hallas, E. C. 24940. M. May 3/17.
2 B. VII Hartley, John. 24941. M. May 3/17.
2 B. VIII Heaton, John Wm. 28836. M. May 3/17.
‡2 B. Helliwell, Cpl. W. 18385. M. May 3/17.
‡2 B. Heywood, John. 19658. M. May 3/17.
‡2 B. Hird, F. 12324. M. May 3/17.
2 B. VII Hobson, Edward. 28786. M. May 3/17.
2 B. VIII Horsfall, J. H. 24245. M. May 3/17.
2 B. Lawton, Frank. 10736. M. Oct. 12/16. R/Enq.
‡2 B. Loader, H. 235206. M. May 3/17.
‡2 B. VI Lottey, Harold Edwin. 24247. M. May 3/17.
2 B. or C. Lowe, Walter. 28949. M. May 3/17.
2 B. VIII Mamwell, John Edwin. 18400. M. May 3/17.
2 B. V Moorhouse, H. 265327. M. May 3/17.

**West Riding Regiment (Duke of Wellington's)—contd.**

*B.E.F.*

| | | |
|---|---|---|
| 2 B. VII | Naylor, Wm. 235213. | M. May 3/17. |
| 2 B. | Nichol, L.-Cpl. P. S. 24956. | W. and M. April 11/17. |
| 2 B. V | Patrick, J. W. 24341. | M. May 3/17. |
| 2 B. V | Pickles, Leonard. 13737. | M. May 3/17. |
| 2 B. VI | Quarmby, George. 24256. | M. April 11/17. |
| 2 B. | Reid, Sergt. John F. 9820. | M. May 3/17. |
| 2 B. VI | Rogers, Henry. 24260. | M. April 11/17. |
| *2 B. VI | Settle, Herbert. 23721. | M. May 3/17. |
| ‡2 B. | Shaw, J. E. 29372. | M. May 3/17. |
| ‡2 B. | Smelt, T. F. M. 9365. | M. May 3/17. |
| *2 B. VII | Stimpson, J. R. 28745. | M. May 3/17. |
| ‡2 B. | Stone, L.-Cpl. F. 24434. | M. May 3/17. |
| B. | Stott, F. 19935. | M. April 11/17. |
| ‡2 B. | Stubbs, James. 12380. | M. May 3/17. |
| *2 B. V | Taylor, Arthur John. 24414. | M. May 3/17. |
| 2 B. V | Thomas, George. W. 24949. | M. May 3/17. |
| 2 B. | Thompson, R. 29461. | M. May 3/17. |
| 2 B. | Watson, Ernest. 28932. | K. April 9/17. Conf. and Details. |
| *2 B. V | Wheelwright, Walker. 29046. | M. May 3/17. |
| ‡2 B. | Whiteside, J. T. 16201. | M. May 3/17. |
| ‡2 B. | Williams, A. 10625. | M. May 3/17. |
| ‡2 B. | Winn, R. 28837. | M. May 3/17. |
| ‡2 C. | Allan, H. E. 24369. | M. May 3/17. |
| 2 C. I | Bearton, A.-L.-Cpl. Percy Wm. 235237. | M. May 3/17. |
| ‡2 C. | Benson, Harry. 18702. | M. May 3/17. |
| ‡2 C. | Bentley, H. 10478. | M. May 3/17. |
| 2 C. X | Blamires, Harold. 23763. | M. April 11/17. |
| ‡2 C. | Bland, A. 235243. | M. May 3/17. |
| ‡2 C. | Bostock, W. 10643. | M. May 3/17. |
| ‡2 C. | Brittain, G. 24959. | M. May 3/17. |
| ‡2 C. XI | Crisp, William. 23776. | M. Oct. 12/16. R/Enq. |
| 2 C. | Darby, H. E. 18720. | W. and M. May 3/17. |
| ‡2 C. | Day, A. 202565. | M. May 3/17. |
| ‡2 C. | Drake, L. 18388. | M. May 3/17. |
| ‡2 C. | Duffy, J. 235249. | M. May 3/17. |
| ‡2 C. | Elsworth, J. E. 28855. | M. May 3/17. |
| 2 C. XI | Flack, Charles. 242397. | M. May 3/17. |
| ‡2 C. | Green, A. 203693. | M. May 3/17. |
| ‡2 C. | Harrison, A.-Cpl. F. E. 24322. | M. May 3/17. |
| ‡2 C. | Hewitt, Wm. Henry. 12395. | M. May 3/17. |
| ‡2 C. | Hudson, A. 24324. | M. May 3/17. |
| ‡2 C. | Javerley, G. W. 24325. | M. May 3/17. |
| ‡2 C. | Joynson, A. 16328. | M. May 3/17. |
| ‡2 C. | Mitchell, G. A. 268003. | M. May 3/17. |
| 2 C. IX | Morton, Frank. 19618. | M. May 3/17. |
| ‡2 C. | Preston, J. 14630. | M. May 3/17. |
| 2 C. | Townsley, Walter. 24951. | W. and M. April 11/17. |
| ‡2 C. XI | Whitaker, J. 300185. | M. May 3/17. |
| 2 C. | White, J. A. 23690. | W. and M. April 11/17. |
| 2 C. | Williams, J. T. 16268. | M. Oct. 12/16. R/Enq. |
| ‡2 C. | Wilson, G. 12788. | M. May 3/17. |
| 2 D. XV | Atkinson, W. 24026. | M. May 3/17. |
| 2 D. XVI | Baldwin, T. 267218. | M. May 3/17. |
| *2 D. XV | Bewsher, R. 24486. | M. May 3/17. |
| ‡2 D. | Bolderstone, H. 19984. | M. May 3/17. |
| *2 D. XIII | Brady, Thomas. 29463. | M. May 3/17. |
| *2 D. XV | Brighton, W. 235189. | M. May 3/17. |
| ‡2 D. | Browning, G. D. 17609. | M. May 3/17. |

**West Riding Regiment (Duke of Wellington's)—contd.**

*B.E.F.*

2 D. Canavan, Francis. 24496. M. May 3/17.
2 D. XIII Chapelow, John. 235195. M. May 3/17.
2 D. XV Crabtree, Fred. 18337. M. May 3/17.
2 D. XIII Dixon, L.-Cpl. Frank. 23811. M. May 3/17.
‡2 D. Eastwood, R. 14949. M. May 3/17.
2 D. Evitt, Fred. 18857. M. May 3/17.
‡2 D. Fawcett, R. 24506. M. May 3/17.
*2 D. XV Firth, G. 24234. M. May 3/17.
*2 D. Foster, Stanley. 28830. M. May 3/17.
2 D. Grainger, John. 11498. M. May 3/17.
2 D. XIII Green, John Israel. 300008. M. May 3/17.
‡2 D. Green, J. T. 24938. M. May 3/17.
‡2 D. Greenwood, J. 202348. M. May 3/17.
‡2 D. Halpine, W. 24511. M. May 3/17.
2 D. XIII Hartley, Herbert. 24244. M. May 3/17.
*2 D. XIII Harvey, L.-Cpl. A. E. 16657. M. May 3/17.
‡2 D. Healey, A. 15364. M. May 3/17.
*2 D. Hickman, Archie. 10760. M. May 3/17.
2 D. XV Higgitt, Peter. 23328. M. May 3/17.
‡2 D. Hill, G. 202802. M. May 3/17.
‡2 D. Hillas, L.-Cpl. J. 24240. M. May 3/17.
‡2 D. Holdsworth, J. H. 18184. M. May 3/17.
2 D. Holloway, C. H. 235204. M. May 3/17.
‡2 D. Hudson, J. W. 14839. M. May 3/17.
‡2 D. Humphries, Sergt. E. V. 8690. M. May 3/17.
2 D. XIII Jackson, James. 28746. M. May 3/17.
2 D. XV Jackson, Tom. 24269. M. May 3/17.
‡2 D. Jackson, W. 23590. M. May 3/17.
2 D. XVI Jay, Bertie. 235291. Unoff. M. end April or early May/17.
2 D. XV Jordan, T. 24401. M. May 3/17.
2 D. Kenworthy, Cpl. Geo. Edw. 11226. M. May 3/17.
‡2 D. Lavin, J. 11422. M. May 3/17.
‡2 D. Lawless, J. 29140. M. May 3/17.
2 D. Leak, Joseph. 267903. (1597.) M. May 3/17.
‡2 D. Limmer, B. 2679. M. May 3/17.
‡2 D. Lister, A. 13032. M. May 3/17.
‡2 D. Lyons, R. 15350. M. May 3/17.
‡2 D. McAvan, Sergt. B. 12257. M. May 3/17.
2 D. McGrath, James. 21639. M. May 3/17.
*2 D. McShane, Cpl. James. 23832. M. May 3/17.
‡2 D. Major, J. E. 17427. M. May 3/17.
*2 D. Midgley, Willie. 12808. W. and M. Oct. 12/16. R/Enq.
2 D. XIV Midwood, Henry. 23686. M. May 3/17.
‡2 D. Moore, W. 29211. M. May 3/17.
*2 D. Moreton, Sgt. David John. 17717. M. May 3/17.
*2 D. XVI Pickard, F. 10556. W. and M. Oct. 23/16. R/Enq.
‡2 D. Pickles, C. 20463. M. May 3/17.
‡2 D. Ricketts, J. 10720. M. May 3/17.
‡2 D. *Riley, J. 12258. M. May 3/17.
2 D. XIV Riley, Wm. 235215. M. May 3/17.
2 D. XV Senior, J. F. 17897. M. May 2/17.
‡2 D. Smith, Arthur. 8880. M. May 3/17.
2 D. Smith, Wm. 28851. M. May 3/17.
‡2 D. Snowden, T. 23764. M. May 3/17.
‡2 D. Stones, J. 10699. M. May 3/17.
‡2 D. Sutcliffe, T. 24984. M. May 3/17.
2 D. XIV Taylor, Cpl. Fred. 24986. M. May 3/17.
‡2 D. Truelove, F. 267906. M. May 3/17.
2 D. Walker, Arthur. 24224. M. May 3/17.

**West Riding Regiment (Duke of Wellington's)**—contd.

*B.E.F.*

‡2 D. Wallis, H. 268005. M. May 3/17.
2 D. Waugh, Cpl. Andrew. 24389. M. May 3/17.
‡2 D. Wilson, F. H. 14900. M. May 3/17.
‡2 D. Windle, A. 14290. M. May 3/17.
‡2 D. Yeadon, J. 267910. M. May 3/17.
4 A. II Bancroft, Sergt. Wilfred. 3060. M. Sept. 3/16.
4 A. III Baxter, H. 4755. M. Sept. 3/16. R/Enq.
4 A. II McEwen, John. 6763. (Fr. 7 North. Fus., No. 3111.) M. Sept. 3/16. R/Enq.
4 A. Smith, Landa. 5906. M. Sept. 3/16. R/Enq.
4 A. Teal, George. 2221. M. Sept. 3/16. R/Enq.
4 B. Fisher, L.-Cpl. J. 2510. M. Sept. 3/16. R/Enq.
4 B. VIII Gill, Miles. 4534. W. and M. Sept. 3/16. R/Enq.
*4 B. V Hirst, Albert. 2167. M. Sept. 3/16. R/Enq.
*4 B. VI Nicholls, Samuel. 5629. M. Sept. 3/16. R/Enq.
4 B. Smith, Charles Henry. 4513. M. Sept. 3/16. R/Enq.
4 B. VIII Thompson, Sergt. Herbert. 2446. M. Sept. 3/16. R/Enq.
4 C. XI Earnshaw, Walter. 6677. M. Sept. 17/16. R/Enq.
4 C. Kelly, Cpl. Geo. Harry. 4148. M. Sept. 17/16. R/Enq.
4 D. XIV Furness, A. 5799. M. Sept. 3/16. R/Enq.
4 D. XIV Gooch, Jas. Hy. 2179. M. Sept. 3/16. R/Enq.
*4 D. Riley, Edmund. 5653. M. Sept. 3/16. R/Enq.
4 D. XIII Stubbs, Chas. Edward. 6803. M. Sept. 3/16. R/Enq.
*4 ? O'Hara, Michael James. 5634. K. Sept. 3/16. Det.D./B.
2/4 **Peskett, 2nd Lieut. G. E. H.** M. May 3/17.
‡2/4 A. Bentley, C. 235048. M. May 3/17.
‡2/4 A. Blakey, F. 200940. M. May 3/17.
2/4 A. I Brown, W. A. 204421. (29095.) M. May 3/17.
‡2/4 A. Butler, S. 10160. M. May 3/17.
2/4 A. I Calvert, H. 15848. M. May 3/17.
‡2/4 A. Greenwood, D. 201282. M. May 3/17.
‡2/4 A. Hodgson, J. L. 201861. M. May 3/17.
‡2/4 A. Holroyd, W. 202071. M. May 3/17.
2/4 A. Stockton, Ben. 201249. M. May 3/17.
2/4 A. III White, Chas. Fred. 202214. (4897.) M. May 3/17.
‡2/4 A. Wortley, J. H. 204411. M. May 3/17.
‡2/4 B. Ashforth, C. 202238. M. May 3/17.
‡2/4 B. Broadbent, G. 202518. M. May 3/17.
‡2/4 B. Drake, W. 202305. M. May 3/17.
‡2/4 B. Furness, H. 235064. M. May 3/17.
2/4 B. Greenwood, J. T. 202514. M. May 3/17.
2/4 B. Haw, Cpl. James. 201439. M. May 3/17.
‡2/4 B. Hepworth, S. 202480. M. May 3/17.
‡2/4 B. Hirst, Dmr. J. W. 201397. M. May 3/17.
‡2/4 B. McHugh, J. 201469. M. May 3/17.
‡2/4 B. Ruddy, J. 201171. M. May 3/17.
‡2/4 B. Smith, W. H. 202129. M. May 3/17.
2/4 B. VIII Wells, Gilbert. 202574. M. May 2/17.
2/4 B. Wilson, L.-Sergt. Fred. 201681. M. May 3/17.
‡2/4 B. Wood, R. 202422. M. May 3/17.
‡2/4 B. Young, L.-Cpl. A. 201194. M. May 3/17.
‡2/4 C. Bloomer, A. 202021. M. May 3/17.
‡2/4 C. IX Brookes, William. 202022. M. May 3/17.
‡2/4 C. Brown, Thomas. 21020. M. May 3/17.
‡2/4 C. Bulmer, J. W. 200941. M. May 3/17.
‡2/4 C. Carter, A.-L.-Sergt. H. E. 201310. M. May 3/17.
2/4 C. IX Cotton, C. A. 202501. M. May 3/17.
2/4 C. Cox, Norman. 201303. M. May 3/17.

**West Riding Regiment (Duke of Wellington's)—contd.**

*B.E.F.*

|  |  |  |
|---|---|---|
| ‡2/4 C. X | Gray, Harry. 200794. | M. May 3/17. |
| 2/4 C. XI | Griffiths, A.-L.-Cpl. Joseph. 300027. | M. Unoff. K. May 3/17. |
| *2/4 C. X | Hill, Frank. 238021. | M. May 3/17. |
| ‡2/4 C. | Hinchcliffe, A. 235049. | M. May 3/17. |
| 2/4 C. IX | Jones, G. W. 238022. | M. May 3/17. |
| ‡2/4 C. | Martin, F. 201556. | M. May 3/17. |
| 2/4 C. IX | Oddy, Edgar. 202555. | M. May 3/17. |
| ‡2/4 C. | Riley, Sergt. W. 201312. | M. May 3/17. |
| ‡2/4 C. XI | Robertson, Sergt. Charlie. 201523. (3771.) | M., Inf. K. May 3/17. |
| ‡2/4 C. | Robinson, C. 12753. | M. May 3/17. |
| ‡2/4 D. | Broadbent, J. 202001. | M. May 3/17. |
| *2/4 D. XIII | Chapman, Sgt. E. H. 201311. | M. May 3/17. |
| *2/4 D. XIV | Goode, Fred. 202015. | M. May 3/17. |
| 2/4 D. L.G.S. | Haigh, E. B. 202338. | M. May 3/17. |
| ‡2/4 D. XVI | Hall, George. 202317. | M. May 3/17. |
| ‡2/4 D. | Halstead, W. 201414. | M. May 3/17. |
| 2/4 D. L.G.S. | Hartley, P. 201266. | M. May 3/17. |
| ‡2/4 D. | Hughes, F. 201632. | M. May 3/17. |
| ‡2/4 D. | Hurrell, W. 202557. | M. May 3/17. |
| ‡2/4 D. | Murgatroyd. 201164. | M. May 3/17. |
| ‡2/4 D. | Oakes, S. 200194. | M. May 3/17. |
| ‡2/4 D. | Richardson, L.-Cpl. H. 201597. | M. May 3/17. |
| ‡2/4 D. | Riley, Sergt. H. 200053. | M. May 3/17. |
| ‡2/4 D. | Shearer, A.-Cpl. D. A. 202075. | M. May 3/17. |
| ‡2/4 D. XVI | Southwell, W. H. 202537. | M. May 3/17. |
| 2/4 D. XIV | Turner, Chas. Percy. 202339. | M. May 3/17. |
| *2/4 D. | Wilson, Ernest. 202016. | M. May 3/17. |
| ‡2/4 D. | Wray, H. 201050. | M. May 3/17. |
| 5 A. | Deans, John W. 7102. | M. Sept. 3/16. R/Enq. |
| *5 A. IV | Goodall, Edward. 5892. | M. Sept. 3/16. R/Enq. |
| 5 A. | Smith, Arthur. 4427. | W. and M. Sept. 3/16. R/Enq. |
| 5 A. II | Speight, J. W. 3793. | W. and M. Sept. 3/16. R/Enq. |
| 5 A. I | Williams, Allan. 5990. | M. Sept. 3/16. R./Enq. |
| 5 B. | Brook, Willie. 5664. | M. Sept. 3/16. R/Enq. |
| 5 B. L.G.S. | Hellawell, Wilfred. 4698. | M. Sept. 3/16. R/Enq. |
| 5 B. VI | Shaw, Ernest. 5648. | M. Sept. 3/16. R./Enq. |
| 5 C. | Farrar, J. E. 7753. | M. Mar. 20/17. |
| 5 D. | Gill, Wilfred. 3934. | M. Sept. 19/16. R/Enq. |
| *2/5 | **Ridley, M.C., Lieut. P. R.** (Fr. Northern Cyclists.) | W. and M. May 3/17. |
| 2/5 | **Sykes, 2nd Lieut. and A./Cpt. E. T.** | W. and M. May 3/17. |
| *2/5 A. or B. VII | Anderson, Walter. 242770. | M. May 3/17. |
| 2/5 A. | Ball, Harry. 240575. (3104.) | M. May 3/17. |
| ‡2/5 A. | Bamforth, S. 242868. | M. May 3/17. |
| ‡2/5 A. | Banks, J. R. 241511. | M. May 3/17. |
| ‡2/5 A. | Bassingdale, E. 241787. | M. May 3/17. |
| 2/5 A. | Battye, Joseph. 241823. (5270.) | M. May 3/17. |
| 2/5 A. | Brook, Sergt. H. 240082. (1902.) | M. May 3/17. |
| ‡2/5 A. | Brooke, I. 241058. | M. May 3/17. |
| ‡2/5 A. | Clarke, L.-Cpl. P. S. 241554. | M. May 3/17. |
| 2/5 A. II | Coleman, F. H. 242798. | M. May 3/17. |
| ‡2/5 A. | Crabtree, A. 263031. | M. May 3/17. |
| *2/5 A. | Crabtree, Fred. 241553. | M. May 3/17. |
| ‡2/5 A. | Durskin, Cpl. J. 240216. | M. May 3/17. |
| *2/5 A. | Earnshaw, H. 241542. | M. May 3/17. |
| ‡2/5 A. | Elliott, J. G. 241185. | M. May 3/17. |
| 2/5 A. | Ellis, S/B. Harry. 241547. (4949.) | M. May 3/17. |

**West Riding Regiment (Duke of Wellington's)—contd.**

## *B.E.F.*

| | | |
|---|---|---|
| ‡2/5 A. | Garside, T. H. 241814. | M. May 3/17. |
| 2/5 A. IV | Garthwaite, Jas. 300059. | M. May 3/17. |
| ‡2/5 A. | Haigh, J. 240133. | M. May 3/17. |
| ‡2/5 A. | Hale, F. 242781. | M. May 3/17. |
| 2/5 A. II | Hale, H. B. 241943. (5415.) | Unoff. M. May 3/17. |
| 2/5 A. | Hall, Frank. 242781. (16092.) | M. May 3/17. |
| ‡2/5 A. | Hardy, Cpl. H. 240288. | M. May 3/17. |
| *2/5 A. I | Harvey, John Walter. 241374. (4588) | M. May 3/17. |
| ‡2/5 A. | Hey, Sergt. N. 240621. | M. May 3/17. |
| ‡2/5 A. | Hirst, F. 242017. | M. May 3/17. |
| *2/5 A. III | Hobson, Fred. 241778. (5219.) | M. May 3/17. |
| 2/5 A. | Holmes, Drmr. Harry. 241538. (4939.) | M. May 3/17. |
| 2/5 A. I | Hopkinson, J. W. 241828. (5275.) | M. May 3/17. |
| 2/5 A. | Horsfield, Stanley. 241536. | M. May 3/17. |
| *2/5 A. I | Kaye, Joe. 240246. (2383.) | M. May 3/17. |
| 2/5 A. II | Kenworthy, John. 241799. | M. May 3/17. |
| ‡2/5 A. | Kilburn, W. 241586. | M. May 3/17. |
| ‡2/5 A. | Kramer, A. 241582. | M. May 3/17. |
| ‡2/5 A. | Lee, J. 263062. | M. May 3/17. |
| ‡2/5 A. | Lemon, H. 240609. | M. May 3/17. |
| ‡2/5 A. | Lewis, W. 241519. | M. May 3/17. |
| ‡2/5 A. | Linton, E. 241121. | M. May 3/17. |
| ‡2/5 A. | Lodge, L.-Cpl. H. 241083. | M. May 3/17. |
| ‡2/5 A. | Lodge, J. 242026. | M. May 3/17. |
| ‡2/5 A. | Lowery, T. 242768. | M. May 3/17. |
| *2/5 A. III | Mackinan, A. 240029. (5738.) | M. May 3/17. |
| ‡2/5 A. | Mallinson, W. 241791. | M. May 3/17. |
| ‡2/5 A. | Marriott, J. G. 241543. | M. May 3/17. |
| ‡2/5 A. | Martin, E. 241085. | M. May 3/17. |
| ‡2/5 A. | Mathers, S. 263025. | M. May 3/17. |
| *2/5 A. | Milnes, Herbert. 241825. (5272.) | M. May 3/17. |
| ‡2/5 A. | Moorhouse, H. 241528. | M. May 3/17. |
| ‡2/5 A. | Morgan, L.-Cpl. J. C. 240572. | M. May 3/17. |
| 2/5 A. II | Oates, Fred. 241822. | M. May 3/17. |
| 2/5 A. II | O'Brien, Sgt. Joseph. 240944. (3758.) | M. May 3/17. |
| 2/5 A. | Parker, Richard. 241946. | M. May 3/17. |
| ‡2/5 A. | Parkin, Richard. 241545. (4946.) | M. May 3/17. |
| 2/5 A. II | Ramsden, Harry. 241525. (4922.) | M. May 3/17. |
| ‡2/5 A. | Roberts, W. 240631. | M. May 3/17. |
| 2/5 A. | Roebuck, Lawrence C. 241061. (3940) | M. May 3/17. |
| ‡2/5 A. | Rothwell, J. T. 241780. | M. May 3/17. |
| 2/5 A. | Sandford, Fred. 241540. | W. and M. May 3/17. |
| ‡2/5 A. | Smith, W. 240997. | M. May 3/17. |
| ‡2/5 A. | Sykes, E. 240730. | M. May 3/17. |
| ‡2/5 A. | Taylor, N. 241546. | M. May 3/17. |
| ‡2/5 A. | Thornton, H. 241533. | M. May 3/17. |
| 2/5 A. | Tinker, Percy. 242008. | M. May 3/17. |
| ‡2/5 A. | Townend, L. 242009. | M. May 3/17. |
| ‡2/5 A. | Ward, A. 240861. | M. May 3/17. |
| ‡2/5 A. | Watson, W. 241362. | M. May 3/17. |
| ‡2/5 A. | West, L.-Cpl. E. 241526. | M. May 3/17. |
| ‡2/5 A. | Wheelhouse, N. 240160. | M. May 3/17. |
| ‡2/5 A. | Wilcock, W. 240989. | M. May 3/17. |
| ‡2/5 A. | Wilds, F. 240322. | M. May 3/17. |
| 2/5 A. I | Wilkinson, Ronald. 242812. (8263.) | M. May 3/17. |
| ‡2/5 A. | Wilson, A. H. 242796. | M. May 3/17. |
| ‡2/5 A. | Woodhead, F. 241520. | M. May 3/17. |
| ‡2/5 B. | Allen, F. 241785. | M. May 3/17. |
| 2/5 B. VI | Allen, James Ernest. 241962. | M. May 3/17. |

**West Riding Regiment (Duke of Wellington's)—contd.**

## *B.E.F.*

‡2/5 B. Bamforth, B. 241783. M. May 3/17.
2/5 B. VI Battye, Walter. 241773. (5213.) M. May 3/17.
‡2/5 B. Beaumont, L. 242023. M. May 3/17.
‡2/5 B. Blackburn, W. M. 241846. M. May 3/17.
‡2/5 B. Booth, F. 242018. M. May 3/17.
‡2/5 B. Bracken, T. 241600. M. May 3/17.
‡2/5 B. Broadbent, S. H. 241859. M. May 3/17.
2/5 B. V Brook, Arthur. 241793. (5235.) M. May 3/17.
‡2/5 B. Bull, A. 241790. M. May 3/17.
‡2/5 B. Calvert, L.-Cpl. J. W. 240820. M. May 3/17.
‡2/5 B. Creaton, L.-Cpl. H. E. 241598. M. May 3/17.
2/5 B. Crowther, Cpl. Hubert. 241797. M. May 3/17.
*2/5 B. Dewhirst, G. D. 240678. (3311.) M. May 3/17.
‡2/5 B. Fisher, A. 20534. M. May 3/17.
‡2/5 B. Gray, W. 15346. M. May 3/17.
‡2/5 B. Greaves, J. 241577. M. May 3/17.
‡2/5 B. VII Green, G. 241782. (5223.) M. May 3/17.
2/5 B. VIII Gunn, Harold. 241601. (5010.) M. May 3/17.
‡2/5 B. Haigh, W. 241833. M. May 3/17.
‡2/5 B. Hamer, T. 240673. M. May 3/17.
‡2/5 B. Hanson, C. 241556. M. May 3/17.
‡2/5 B. Hanson, E. 240565. M. May 3/17.
‡2/5 B. Herbert, F. A. 241120. M. May 3/17.
2/5 B. or D. XV Hirst, Sig. H. 241784. (5225.) M. May 3/17.
‡2/5 B. Holmes, G. F. 241976. M. May 3/17.
2/5 B. Ibbotson, J. 241966. M. May 3/17.
‡2/5 B. Jackson, H. N. 241594. M. May 3/17.
‡2/5 B. Keighley, H. 240845. M. May 3/17.
*2/5 B. or D. Kershaw, L.-Cpl. Sig. Arth. 240720 M. May 3/17.
‡2/5 B. Loader, G. H. 240235. M. May 3/17.
*2/5 B. Midgley, Herbert. 241604. (5013.) M. May 3/17.
2/5 B. VI Nicholson, L.-Cpl. Herbert. 235084. M. May 3/17.
‡2/5 B. Pinkey, Sergt. T. 240818. M. May 3/17.
‡2/5 B. Poulson, E. 241777. M. May 3/17.
2/5 B. VI Rees, L.-Cpl. J. W. 235096. M. May 3/17.
2/5 B. V Shaw, E. 242797. Unoff. M. May 3/17.
2/5 B. Sykes, Sergt. Stanley. 240672. (3301.) M. May 3/17.
2/5 B. VI Taylor, Albert 241987. M. May 3-4/17.
2/5 B. Watson, Norman. 241574. M. May 3/17.
‡2/5 C. Armitage, H. V. 241906. M. May 3/17.
‡2/5 C. Barrow, W. H. 241751. M. May 3/17.
‡2/5 C. Beecham, G. 241644. M. May 3/17.
2/5 C. Bennett, L.-Cpl. Harry. 240690. (3338.) M. May 3/17.
‡2/5 C. Berridge, G. H 241631. M. May 3/17.
2/5 C. XI Boothroyd, Percy. 241924. (5393.) M. May 3/17.
‡2/5 C. Buckley, L.-Cpl. J. W. 241933. M. May 3/17.
‡2/5 C. Cassidy, W. 240791. M. May 3/17.
‡2/5 C. Cheetham, A. 241940. M. May 3/17.
‡2/5 C. Coupland, R. 241649. M. May 3/17.
‡2/5 C. Dyson, T. 241896. M. May 3/17.
‡2/5 C. Field, S. 240770. M. May 3/17.
2/5 C. XII Fitz-John, L.-Cpl. A. 242801. (16113) Unoff. M. May 3/17.
‡2/5 C. Gledhill, L.-Cpl. R. R. 241894 M. May 3/17.
2/5 C. IX Goddard, L.-Cpl. Brandon. 241934. (5404.) M. May 3/17.
‡2/5 C. Goldsborough, H. 241905. M. May 3/17.
‡2/5 C. Grant, F. 241955. M. May 3/17.
‡2/5 C. Hague, W. 241005. M. May 3/17.

**West Riding Regiment (Duke of Wellington's)—contd.**

*B.E.F.*

| | |
|---|---|
| ‡2/5 C. Hampshire, L. 241893. | M. May 3/17. |
| ‡2/5 C. Harpin, H. R. 240317. | M. May 3/17. |
| ‡2/5 C. Harrison, F. H. 241068. | M. May 3/17. |
| 2/5 C. XII Hawksworth, Norman. 241071. (3958.) | M. May 3/17. |
| 2/5 C. XI Hemingway, Harry. 241931. (5400.) | M. May 3/17. |
| ‡2/5 C. Hill, E. 241595. | M. May 3/17. |
| 2/5 C. IX Hollingworth, J. H. 240837. (3563) | M. May 3/17. |
| ‡2/5 C. Holroyd, H. 241055. | M. May 3/17. |
| ‡2/5 C. Houghland, Cpl. T. 241201. | M. May 3/17. |
| *2/5 C. XI Jepson, P. 241954. | M. May 3/17. |
| 2/5 C. XII Kaye, Cpl. H. 240260. | M. May 3/17. |
| 2/5 C. X Lamb, A. 242700. (16102.) | M. May 3/17. |
| *2/5 C. X Littlewood, Frank. 241936. (5406.) | M. May 3/17. |
| ‡2/5 C. Lockwood, L.-Cpl. John Edward. 241381. (4601.) | M. May 3/17. |
| *2/5 C. Lodge, Wm. 240233. (2351.) | M. May 3/17. |
| ‡2/5 C. Marsh, L.-Cpl. J. W. 241957. | M. May 3/17. |
| 2/5 C. Sig. S. Marshall, L.-Cpl. Joe. 240785. (3478.) | M. May 3/17. |
| ‡2/5 C. May, L.-Cpl. W. 240735. | M. May 3/17. |
| 2/5 C. XII Mellor, Arthur. 241610. (5020.) | Unoff. M. May 3/17. |
| ‡2/5 C. Moxon, D. 241863. | M. May 3/17. |
| ‡2/5 C. XII Ness, Douglas. 241705. (5204.) | M. May 3/17. |
| ‡2/5 C. O'Hanlon, L.-Cpl. E. 241747. | M. May 3/17. |
| ‡2/5 C. Oldroyd, H. 235086. | M. May 3/17. |
| *2/5 C. IX Parr, John Wm. 241074. (3967.) | M. May 3/17. |
| 2/5 C. IX Pilsworth, Willie. 241721. | M. May 3/17. |
| ‡2/5 C. Pinkney, W. R. 242792. | M. May 3/17. |
| ‡2/5 C. Roebuck, C. 241645. | M. May 3/17. |
| ‡2/5 C. Rothery, Sergt. T. 241075. | M. May 3/17. |
| ‡2/5 C. Rowe, H. 241661. | M. May 3/17. |
| ‡2/5 C. Russell, A. 241854. | M. May 3/17. |
| 2/5 C. XI Rylance, Ernest. 240733. | M. May 3/17. |
| ‡2/5 C. Seed, H. 235067. | M. May 3/17. |
| ‡2/5 C. Shindler, C. 235095. | M. May 3/17. |
| ‡2/5 C. Tate, W. 241613. | M. May 3/17. |
| 2/5 C. Tindall, L.-Cpl. Jas. 241621. (5032.) | M. May 3/17. |
| *2/5 C. IX Turner, Chas. 241858. (5314.) | M. May 3/17. |
| ‡2/5 C. Turner, E. A. 241641. | M. May 3/17. |
| ‡2/5 C. Vickers, J. E. 241734. | M. May 3/17. |
| *2/5 C. X Webster, C. W. 241743. (5175.) | M. May 3/17. |
| ‡2/5 C. Westerby, J. J. 241711. | M. May 3/17. |
| ‡2/5 C. Wilkinson, W. 241618. | M. May 3/17. |
| ‡2/5 D. Alderson, N. 241021. | M. May 3/17. |
| ‡2/5 D. Allpress, H. 241008. | M. May 3/17. |
| *2/5 D. XIV Armistead, D. 241717. (5142.) | M. May 3/17. |
| ‡2/5 D. Battye, D. 241606. | M. May 3/17. |
| ‡2/5 D. Beard, H. 241724. | M. May 3/17. |
| 2/5 D. Beardsell, Sergt. Percy. 240653. (3271.) | M. May 3/17. |
| *2/5 D. Bentley, Irvin. 241708. | M. May 3/17. |
| 2/5 D. XIII Bownes, Sergt. W. H. 240708. (3370.) | M. May 3/17. |
| 2/5 D. XIII Brunt, Sergt. F. C. 240706. (3367) | M. May 3/17. |
| ‡2/5 D. Curtois, H. 241700. | M. May 3/17. |
| ‡2/5 D. Fisher, H. 241040. | M. May 3/17. |
| 2/5 D. XIV Hellawell, Ernest. 241930. (5399.) | Unoff. M. May 3/17. |

**West Riding Regiment (Duke of Wellington's)**—contd.

## *B.E.F.*

‡2/5 D. Johnson, T. C. 241745. M. May 3/17.
‡2/5 D. Knapton, A. 241739. M. May 3/17.
‡2/5 D. Mosley, L.-Cpl. A. 241890. M. May 3/17.
2/5 D. XIII Oates, Cpl. C. R. 240087. (3832.) M. May 3/17.
‡2/5 D. Piggott, H. 241720. M. May 3/17.
2/5 D. XIII Shearsmith, Sidney. 241634. M. May 3/17.
*2/5 D. XIV Stockdale, Joseph. 240952. M. May 3/17.
*2/5 D. XIII Sykes, Walter. 241619. (5388.) M. May 3/17.
‡2/5 D. Taylor, A. E. 241001. M. May 3/17.
*2/5 D. Walter, F. W. 241684. (5104.) M. May 3/17.
‡2/5 D. Watson, J. W. 235104. M. May 3/17.
‡2/5 D. XIII Wear, Frank. 241690. M. May 3/17.
‡2/5 D. Webster, H. 240142. (2091.) M. May 3/17.
*2/5 D. Webster, Sergt. Sam. 240761. W. and M. May 3/17.
‡2/5 D. Weir, F. 241660. M. May 3/17.
‡2/5 D. White, H. 241086. M. May 3/17.
2/5 D. Wilkinson, Jos. Auckland. 241673. (5092.) M. May 3/17.
‡2/5 D. Wilson, F. 235103. M. May 3/17.
6 **Stockdale, 2nd Lieut. W.** M., bel. K. May 3/17.
6 C. Hodgson, E. 4026. M. Mar. 12/17.
6 C. Rouse, H. 6085. M. Mar. 12/17.
2/6 **Holroyd, 2nd Lt. C.** M. May 2/17.
2/6 A. Ayrton, Sergt. H. 266192. M. May 3/17.
‡2/6 A. Barker, R. 265297. M. May 3/17.
2/6 A. I Bridge, Arthur. 265177. (1806.) W. and M. May 3/17.
‡2/6 A. Escott, W. 300053. M. May 3/17.
2/6 A. II Foulger, Marlton Harry. 29049. M. May 3/17.
‡2/6 A. Graham, H. 266039. M. May 3/17.
‡2/6 A. Lee, S. 265985. M. May 3/17.
*2/6 A. II Lund, Arthur. 267201. M. May 3/17.
2/6 A. Maudsley, Sergt. Herbert. 265693. M. May 3/17.
2/6 A. III Shaw, Fred. 268364. (8559.) M. May 3/17.
‡2/6 A. Spedding, Cpl. W. H. 265402. M. May 3/17.
2/6 A. Sig. S. Wilson, Cpl. Harold. 265721. M. May 3/17.
‡2/6 B. Athorn, G. 265047. M. May 3/17.
‡2/6 B. Barker, G. 267047. W. and M. May 3/17.
‡2/6 B. Barker, H. 267285. M. May 3/17.
‡2/6 B. Beevers, C. H. 267173. M. May 3/17.
‡2/6 B. Brotherton, B. 267167. M. May 3/17.
2/6 B. V Goodall, Wm. 268390. M. May 3/17.
‡2/6 B. Johnson, W. 300069. M. May 3/17.
‡2/6 B. VII Kighley, L. A. 22820. M. May 3/17.
‡2/6 B. Lovell, A. H. 267672. M. May 3/17.
‡2/6 B. Lund, E. 265956. M. May 3/17.
‡2/6 B. Mawson, J. H. 267183. M. May 3/17.
*2/6 B. Metcalfe, George. 266960. M. May 3/17.
2/6 B. Moreland, Thos. 266900. M. May 3/17.
2/6 B. Murphy, L.-Cpl. C. 5049. M. May 3/17.
‡2/6 B. Newns, Sergt. C. W. 265925. M. May 3/17.
‡2/6 B. V Petty, W. 266446. M. May 3/17.
‡2/6 B. Read, T. 266952. M. May 3/17.
*2/6 B. or C. Roberts, A. 268370. M. May 3/17.
*2/6 B. VII Smith, John. 266752. (4416.) M. May 3/17.
‡2/6 B. Walton, J. T. 265399. M. May 3/17.
2/6 B. or D. Woodhead, E. 266127. (3365.) M. May 3/17.
‡2/6 C. Atkins, J. R. 267101. M. May 3/17.

**West Riding Regiment (Duke of Wellington's)**—contd.

*B.E.F.*

| | | |
|---|---|---|
| ***2/6 C.** | Barrett, L.-Sgt. Albert Nathan. 266414. (3813.) | M. **May 3/17.** |
| ***2/6 C. or D.** | Brook, Norman. 267682. (6118.) | M. **May 3/17.** |
| **‡2/6 C.** | Capstick, H. 267088. | M. **May 3/17.** |
| ***2/6 C. X** | Exley, Alfred. 305789. | M. **May 3/17.** |
| ***2/6 C. IX** | Forrest, H. B. 267045. | M. **May 3/17.** |
| **‡2/6 C.** | Gornall, E. 266380. | M. **May 3/17.** |
| **‡2/6 C.** | Greenwood, J. E. 268342. | M. **May 3/17.** |
| **‡2/6 C.** | Heldon, Cpl. A. 266047. | M. **May 3/17.** |
| **‡2/6 C.** | Kaye, J. 266224. | M. **May 3/17.** |
| **‡2/6 C.** | Lupton, J. 266102. | M. **May 3/17.** |
| **‡2/6 C.** | Marshall, W. 266350. | M. **May 3/17.** |
| ***2/6 C. XII** | Mellor, George. 18178. | M. **May 3/17.** |
| **‡2/6 C.** | Metcalfe, N. S. 268341. | M. **May 3/17.** |
| ***2/6 C. or D.** | Mitchell, Lewes Percy 268345. | M. **May 3/17.** |
| ***2/6 C.** | Mosley, James. 267094. (4984.) | M. **May 3/17.** |
| **‡2/6 C.** | Ormondroyd, S. 267233. | M. **May 3/17.** |
| **‡2/6 C.** | Patchett, J. E. 300074. | M. **May 3/17.** |
| **‡2/6 C.** | Ralph, H. 265425. | M. **May 3/17.** |
| **‡2/6 C.** | Sherwin, A. 267050. | M. **May 3/17.** |
| **‡2/6 C.** | Smith, Sergt. A. C. 265075. | M. **May 3/17.** |
| **‡2/6 C.** | Smith, A. V. 266141. | M. **May 3/17.** |
| **‡2/6 C.** | Smith, E. 266041. | M. **May 3/17.** |
| **2/6 C.** | Sugden, Charles. 267081. | M. **May 3/17.** |
| ***2/6 C. XI** | Sykes, Willie. 300081. | M. **May 3/17.** |
| **2/6 C. X** | Talbot, Gordon. 267083. | M. **May 3/17.** |
| **‡2/6 C.** | Walker, Sergt. Robt. E. 265035. (935.) | M. **May 3/17.** |
| **‡2/6 C.** | Walker, R. H. 268667. | M. **May 3/17.** |
| **‡2/6 C.** | Winterburn, Cpl. W. 265798. | M. **May 3/17.** |
| **‡2/6 C.** | Yeadon, H. 22787. | M. **May 3/17.** |
| **‡2/6 C.** | Yeadon, H. 265790. | M. **May 3/17.** |
| **‡2/6 D.** | Chapman, L.-Cpl. J. 266305. (3635) | M. **May 3/17.** |
| **‡2/6 D.** | Cookson, J. 267150. | M. **May 3/17.** |
| ***2/6 D. XIV** | Graham, Bertie. 267029. (4902.) | M. **May 3/17.** |
| ***2/6 D. XIV** | Graham, Lincoln. 265815. | M. **May 3/17.** |
| **‡2/6 D.** | Lambert, H. 250007. | M. **May 3/17.** |
| **2/6 D. XVI** | Mitchell, Wm. 205085. (1600.) | M. **May 3/17.** |
| **‡2/6 D.** | Nicholson, J. 267105. | M. **May 3/17.** |
| **‡2/6 D.** | Nixon, T. 17408. | M. **May 3/17.** |
| **‡2/6 D.** | Phillips, L.-Cpl. H. 266026. | M. **May 3/17.** |
| ***2/6 D. XIII** | **Pickles, Sgt.** John. 265890. (3001.) | M. **May 3/17.** |
| ***2/6 D. XV** | Pole, W. 205331. | M. **May 3/17.** |
| **‡2/6 D.** | Shackleton, A. 267059. | M. **May 3/17.** |
| ***2/6 D.** | Simpson, L.-Cpl. T. H. 20007. | M. **May 3/17.** |
| **‡2/6 D. XVI** | Veal, Frederick Horsfall. 268381. | Unoff. K. **May 3/17.** Det.D./B. |
| **‡2/6 D.** | Whiteoak, D. 267248. | M. **May 3/17.** |
| **7 B. VIII** | **Dunn, James.** 2474. | M. **Sept. 18/16.** R/Enq. |
| **‡7 B.** | Kiddy, J. A. 305013. | M. **May 14/17.** |
| **‡7 B.** | Metcalfe, L.-Sergt. R. 305254. | M. **May 14/17.** |
| **2/7 ,** | **Marler, 2nd Lieut. E.** (Fr. 6th.) | M. **May 3/17.** |
| **2/7 A.** | **Street, 2nd Lieut. H. F.** | M. **May 3/17.** |
| **‡2/7 A.** | Beaumont, A. 306870. | M. **May 3/17.** |
| **‡2/7 A.** | Booth, S. 205565. | M. **May 3/17.** |
| **2/7 A. I** | Enderby, H. 208433. | W. and M. **May 14/17.** |
| **2/7 A. I** | Fletcher, Walter. 306504. | M. **May 3/17.** |
| **‡2/7 A.** | Forshew, T. H. 306364. | M. **May 3/17.** |
| **‡2/7 A. III** | Greenwood, Harry. 306877. (4451.) | M. **May 3/17.** |

**West Riding Regiment (Duke of Wellington's)—contd.**

*B.E.F.*

‡2/7 A. Haley, Cpl. F. 306662. M. May 3/17.
2/7 A. Kershaw, Arthur. 306500. M. May 3/17.
2/7 A. IV Land, Fred. 306675. W. and M. May 3/17.
2/7 A. II Parkinson, L.-Cpl. Ernest. 12711. M. May 3/17.
2/7 A. IV Read, Fred. 306493. (3977.) M. May 3/17.
‡2/7 A. Robinson, C. 306878. M. May 3/17.
2/7 A. Walker, W. M. 306501. (3987.) M. May 3/17.
‡2/7 A. Whitworth, F. 306034. M. May 3/17.
2/7 A. M.G.S. Wilkinson, Charlie. 306667. (4185.) M. May 3/17.
‡2/7 A. II Winpenny, Arthur. 306777. (4307.) M. May 3/17.
‡2/7 B. Bartle, F. de F. 306527. M. May 3/17.
‡2/7 B. Biddles, J. H. 306600. M. May 3/17.
*2/7 B. V Cockroft, Willie. 306790. (4325.) M. May 3/17.
2/7 B. VI Durrans, Arthur. 306585. W. and M. May 3/17.
*2/7 B. Flynn, Frank. 306523. (4016.) W. and M. May 3/17.
*2/7 B. Foley, Leonard. 268402. W. and M. May 14/17.
‡2/7 B. Langton, H. 306933. M. May 3/17.
‡2/7 B. McHugh, Stephen. 29506. M. May 3/17.
2/7 B. Metcalfe, Sergt. Reg. Jos. 1352. M. May 12/17.
2/7 B. M.G.C. Orr, L.-Sergt. H. 305971. (2854.) M. May 3/17.
‡2/7 B. Skeldon, T. 306050. M. May 3/17.
‡2/7 B. Thompson, F. 306602. M. May 3/17.
‡2/7 C. Barrett, F. W. R. 308129. M. May 3/17.
*2/7 C. Baxter, Henry. 267644. (6011.) W. and M. May 3/17.
‡2/7 C. XII Brearley, L.-Cpl. Ewart H. 306984. (4472.) M. May 3/17.
2/7 C. IX Breeze, W. E. 306958. W. and M. May 3/17.
2/7 C. X Caulton, David. 306722. (4244.) W. and M. May 3/17.
‡2/7 C. Clayton, J. W. 306813. M. May 3/17.
‡2/7 C. Coulton, G. 306722. W. and M. May 3/17.
*2/7 C. Daley, John. 305919. (2768.) W. and M. May 3/17.
2/7 C. Godber, Harold. 306948. (4538.) M. May 3/17.
2/7 C. IX Greenwood, J. 306624. (4137.) W. and M. May 3/17.
2/7 C. X Hey, L.-Cpl. Laurence. 306910. W. and M. May 3/17.
‡2/7 C. Lumb, W. 306851. M. May 3/17.
2/7 C. XII Nimmo, Fredk. Geo. 307593. (29564 and 5977.) W. and M. May 3/17.
‡2/7 C. Noble, W. 308090. M. May 3/17.
2/7 C. X Plews, T. G. 306972. (4570.) W. and M. May 3/17.
*2/7 C. IX Redman, Lewis. 307609. W. and M. May 3/17.
‡2/7 C. Smith, J. 268432. M. May 3/17.
*2/7 C. XII Smith, Sam. 306550. (4051.) W. and M. May 3/17.
‡2/7 C. XI Tidswell, Harry. 306805. M. May 3/17.
‡2/7 C. Turner, J. 267821. M. May 3/17.
‡2/7 D. XIII Berry, Sigr. Fred. 306556. W. and M. May 3/17.
*2/7 D. Bill, Samuel. 305383. (1620.) W. and M. May 3/17.
‡2/7 D. Brown, F. 306572. M. May 3/17.
‡2/7 D. Fowler, J. H. 308107. M. May 3/17.
‡2/7 D. Gilbert, J. 306344. M. May 3/17.
‡2/7 D. Haigh, Cpl. A. 306560. W. and M. May 3/17.
*2/7 D. XV Heald, Edgar. 306235. M. May 3/17.
‡2/7 D. Kimpton, F. 306137. M. May 3/17.
‡2/7 D. Lucas, J. 308103. M. May 3/17.
‡2/7 D. XIII Lumb, Willie. 4411. M. May 3/17.
‡2/7 D. Naylor, G. 306052. M. May 3/17.
‡2/7 D. Neale, C. 306752. M. May 3/17.
2/7 D. XVI Oakes, John. 308135. M. May 3/17.

**West Riding Regiment (Duke of Wellington's)**—contd.

## *B.E.F.*

| | | |
|---|---|---|
| ‡2/7 ? | Sunderland, E. 306917. | M. May 3/17. |
| 8 | **Harris, 2nd Lieut. R. H.** | K. Sept. 28/16. Det.D./B. |
| 8 W. | Killen, F. 10663. | M. April 29/17. |
| 8 W. II | Myers, J. 24058. | M. April 29/17. |
| *8 X | Craven, Fredk. Cecil. 19302. | M. Sept. 29-30/16. R/Enq. |
| 8 X. VII | Halfacre, Frank H. 15695. | W. and M. Unoff. K. Sept. 14/16. R/Enq. |
| *8 X. V | Jackson, Ernest. 11890. | M. Sept. 14/16. R/Enq. |
| 8 X. VI | Pilling, L.-Cpl. R. 18418. | M. Jan. 17/17. |
| ‡8 X. V | Walker, Rowland. 14256. | M. Sept. 14/16. R/Enq. |
| 8 Y. XII | Chester, Thos. Wilfred. 24009. (Fr. 6.) | M. Jan. 16/17. |
| 8 Y. | Constantine, J. 10770. | M. Sept. 29-30/16. R./Enq. |
| 8 Z. | Head, J. 24267. | M. April 11/17. |
| 9 C. | **Chapman, Lieut. A. A.** | M., bel. K. April 22-27/17. |
| 9 | **Hatherell, 2nd Lieut. E. J.** | M. April 25/17. |
| 9 | **Smith, 2nd Lieut. J. S. A.** | M. April 25/17. |
| 9 A. I | Balmford, Willie. 24638. | M. April 25/17. |
| 9 A. | Balmforth, S. 12619. | M. April 25/17. |
| 9 A. | Booth, A. 24645. | M. April 25/17. |
| 9 A. | Bradford, J. C. 20301. | M. April 25/17. |
| 9 A. | Brearley, H. 23589. | M. April 25/17. |
| 9 A. | Broadwith, Arthur. 23565. | M. April 25/17. |
| 9 A. | Constantine, L.-Cpl. Arnold. 12923. | M. April 25/17. |
| 9 A. | Craven, G. F. 24543. | M. April 25/17. |
| 9 A. | Daykin, L.-Cpl. J. H. 22928. | M. April 25/17. |
| 9 A. | Dobson, F. 23325. | M. April 25/17. |
| 9 A. IV | Field, Harry. 23640. | M. April 25/17. |
| 9 A. IV | Harrison, Cpl. F. 24602. | M. April 25/17. |
| 9 A. | Harrison, F. 18772. | M. April 25/17. |
| 9 A. | Hayes, F. 24620. | M. April 25/17. |
| 9 A. | Knowles, R. 12899. | M. April 25/17. |
| 9 A. M.G.S. | Laycock, Wm. 18867. | M. April 25/17. |
| 9 A. | Luntley, J. 23512. | M. April 25/17. |
| 9 A. | Melvin, Frank. 24675. | M. April 25/17. |
| 9 A. III | Metcalfe, John Fairburn. 23573. | W. and M. April 24/17. |
| 9 A. IV | Mitchell, William. 12721. | M. April 25/17. |
| 9 A. | Parkinson, R. 28823. | M. April 25/17. |
| 9 A. II | Rhodes, James. 23583. | M. April 25/17. |
| 9 A. II | Smith, Fred. 235307. | M. April 25/17. |
| 9 A. | Wallis, L. W. 300126. | M. April 25/17. |
| 9 A. IV | Wright, Clarence Victor. 24701. | W. and M. April 25/17. |
| 9 B. | Baxter, B. 23563. | M. April 25/17. |
| 9 B. VIII | Bedford, George. 24641. | M. April 25/17. |
| 9 B. VIII | Crawshaw, Ralph. 29245. | M. April 25/17. |
| 9 B. V | Gledhill, Edwin. 24819. | M. April 25/17. |
| 9 B. VII | Greason, Chas. Wm. 23734. | M. April 25/17. |
| 9 B. VIII | Halliday, Cpl. Arthur. 17518. | M. April 25/17. |
| 9 B. V | Oldfield, Tom. 20087. | W. and M. April 25/17. |
| 9 B. VII | Sefton, Walter. 24687. | M. April 25/17. |
| 9 B. | White, G. E. 28840. | M. April 25/17. |
| *9 C. XI | Bird, James. 29477. | M. April 25/17. |
| ‡9 C. | Collinge, R. J. 15018. | M. April 25/17. |
| 9 C. XI | Cunliffe, Wilfred. 29473. | W. and M. April 25/17. |
| 9 C. | Happs, Matthew Percy. 300194. | M. April 25/17. |
| 9 C. XI | Robertshaw, Rowland. 235301. | W. and M. April 25/17. |
| ‡9 C. XI | Schofield, Charles Wm. 24838. | K. April 25/17. Det.D./B. |
| *9 C. XI | Thornton, Harold. 29402. | W. and M. April 25/17. |
| 9 C. XI | Wilson, Wm. 24842. | W. and M. April 25/17. |
| 9 D. XIV | Backhouse, L.-Cpl. A. L. 24605. | M. April 25/17. |

X

**West Riding Regiment (Duke of Wellington's)—contd.**

*B.E.F.*

| | | | |
|---|---|---|---|
| 9 D. | | Brook, T. 24810. | M. April 25/17. |
| 9 D. | | Chapman, H. 29353. | M. April 25/17. |
| 9 D. | XIV | Child, Wm. 23547. | M. April 25/17. |
| 9 D. | XVI | Clark, Jos. Henry. 23629. | M. April 25/17. |
| 9 D. | XVI | Duckworth, Arthur W. 20002. | M. April 25/17. |
| 9 D. | XIII | Hodgson, Albert. 16213. | M. April 25/17. |
| 9 D. | | Normanton, Willie. 14132. | M. April 25/17. |
| 9 D. | L.G.S. | Northey, William H. 20118. | W. and M. April 25/17. |
| 9 D. | XIII | Paucher, Joseph. 29678. | M. April 28/17. |
| 9 D. | XIII | Radcliffe, Handel. 24578. | M. April 25/17. |
| 9 D. | | Ratcliffe, C. 13191. | M. April 25/17. |
| 9 D. | XVI | Schofield, Sam. 20391. | M. April 25/17. |
| 9 D. | XIV | Senior, Jas. 300101. (6347.) | M. April 25/17. |
| ‡9 D. | | Smith, J. 20430. | M. April 25/17. |
| 9 D. | XV | Smith, John. 15421. | M. April 25/17. |
| 9 D. | | Thorp, H. 235312. | M. April 25/17. |
| 9 D. | | Tinker, Fred. 23602. | M. April 25/17. |
| 9 D. | XIV | Tordoff, Joe. 24629. | M. April 25/17. |
| 9 D. | | Wellwood, J. 12597. | M. April 25/17. |
| 9 D. | | Wilkinson, W. H. 23562. | M. April 25/17. |
| 10 A. | II | Cawthra, Harold I. 24994. | K. May 23/17. Det.D./B. |
| ‡10 A. | I | Seed, Francis. 29244. | M. June 7/17. |
| ‡10 A. | | Stewart, Cpl. John. 11214. | M. June 22/17. |
| ‡10 D. | | Peacock, Sergt. George. 12120 | W. and M. June 7/17. |

**WILTSHIRE REGIMENT.**

*B.E.F.*

| | | | |
|---|---|---|---|
| ‡1 D. | XIII | Austin, L.-Cpl. Frank. 25027. | M. June 5/17. |
| ‡1 D. | | Meadows, L.-Cpl. J. 29554. | M. June 5/17. |
| ‡1 D. | | Prosser, Sergt. H. 6972. | M. June 11/17. |
| *1 D. | | Rose, Henry Jas. 29758. | M. June 7/17. |
| ‡1 D. | | Tree, Sergt. A. 29557. | M. June 7/17. |
| ‡1 H.Q. | Snip. | Leak, Eric Raymond. 33005. | M. June 7/17. |
| 2 A. | | Angell, A. J. 33216. | M. April 9/17. |
| 2 A. | | Bendall, Wm. 7378. | M. Oct. 18/16. R/Enq. |
| 2 A. | | Gullis, Sergt. W. 18226. | W. and M. April 9/17. |
| 2 A. | | King, Sergt. S. H. 5881. | M. Oct. 18/16. R/Enq. |
| ‡2 A. | | Needham, W. 26923. | W. and M. April 9/17. |
| 2 A. | II | Steele, Harry Bertram. 25499. | M. Oct. 18/16. R./Enq. |
| 2 B. | L.G.S. | Butchers, F. W. 29891. | W. and M. April 9/17. |
| 2 C. | IX | Reed, William Henry. 26818. | M. April 9/17. |
| 2 D. | XIV | Beck, Hedley. 26734. | W. Unoff. M. April 9/17. |
| 2 D. | XIV | Burrough, L.-Cpl. W. 8360. | K. April 9/17. Det.D./B. |
| ‡2 D. | | Lawrence, W. J. 18227. | W. and M. April 9/17. |
| ‡2 D. | XIV | Lever, W. G. 23750. | W. and M. Oct. 18/16. R/Enq. |
| 2 D. | | Purnell, H. H. 9539. | M. Oct. 18/16. R/Enq. |
| 2 D. | | Udle, E. 13611. | M. April 9/17. |
| 2 D. | XV | Ward, Alfred Marshall. 26616. | M. April 9/17. |
| ‡6 C. | XI | Hockin, Geo. Henry. 31691. | M. June 7/17. |

**Wiltshire Regiment—contd.**

## *BALKANS.*

| | | |
|---|---|---|
| 7 | **Bartram, 2nd Lieut. H. F.** | M. April 24-25/17. |
| 7 | **Hayward, Lt. E. H.** (Fr. 2nd.) | M. April 24-25/17. |
| 7 | **Osborn, Capt. G. A. C.** | M. April 24/17. |
| 7 A. | Ainger, W. T. 32348. | M. April 24-25/17. |
| 7 A. | Bick, C. A. 12307. | M. April 24-25/17. |
| 7 A. | Brown, A. H. 2246. | M. April 24-25/17. |
| 7 A. | Bryant, A. G. 12477. | M. April 24-25/17. |
| 7 A. | Bull, L.-Cpl. Geo. 12262. | M. April 24/17. |
| 7 A. | Cooper, V. G. 12352. | M. April 24-25/17. |
| 7 A. | Creedy, A. 32349. | M. April 24-25/17. |
| 7 A. | Diaper, Chas. 12279. | M. April 24-25/17. |
| 7 A. | Diaper, E. J. 12278. | M. April 24-25/17. |
| 7 A. | Elliott, Ernest. 12425. | M. April 24-25/17. |
| 7 A. | Fergusson, A. 22037. | M. April 24-25/17. |
| 7 A. M.G.S. | Flambard, L.-Cpl. F. W. 10714. | M., bel. K. April 24-25/17. |
| 7 A. | Higgs, Sergt. E. 482. | M. April 24-25/17. |
| 7 A. | Hobbs, Thos. 21365. | M. April 24-25/17. |
| 7 A. | Knight, F. 12367. | M. April 24-25/17. |
| 7 A. | Lodge, E. W. 12853. | M. April 24-25/17. |
| 7 A. | Orchard, C. 12454. | M. April 24-25/17. |
| 7 A. | Pill, Sergt. P. H. 12333. | M. April 24-25/17. |
| 7 A. | Poole, Sergt. W. 8780. | M. April 24-25/17. |
| 7 A. | Porter, S. H. 12419. | M. April 24-25/17. |
| 7 A. M.G.S. | Potter, J. 10754. | M. April 24-25/17. |
| 7 A. | Prince, Fredk. 32437. | K. April 25/17. Det.D./B. |
| 7 A. | Rose, G. H. 12225. | M. April 23-23/17. |
| 7 A. | Weston, A. P. 12298. | M. April 24-25/17. |
| 7 A. | Wilson, Alfred Jas. 32435. | M. April 24-25/17. |
| 7 A. | Wilson, Howard Edw. 16045. | M. April 24-25/17. |
| 7 A. | Winslow, Cpl. J. F. 12358. | M., bel. K. April 25-25/17. |
| 7 B. VIII | Bolwell, Geo. Edwd. 10598. | M. April 24-25/17. |
| 7 B. V | Cook, Thomas. 14348. | M. April 25/17. |
| 7 B. | Hawkins, Albert. 18630. | M. April 24-25/17. |
| 7 B. M.G.S. | Hogg, C. L. 17097. | W. and M. April 24-25/17. |
| 7 B. | Holland, G. 14398. | M. April 24-25/17. |
| 7 B. | Izzard, H. 32352. | M. April 24-25/17. |
| 7 B. | Line, Richard. 14432. | M. April 24-25/17. |
| 7 B. | Ludlow, L.-Cpl. R. 12446. | M. April 24/17. |
| 7 B. | Rowley, Paul Edwd. 19319. | M. April 24-25/17. |
| 7 B. | Watson, E. E. 14530. | M. April 24/17. |
| 7 C. | Briggs, Sergt. Homer. 14043 | W. and M. April 25/17. |
| 7 C. M.G.S. | Burton, J. A. 16048. | M. April 24-25/17. |
| 7 C. M.G.S. | Featherstone, Robert. 33086. | M. April 24-25/17. |
| 7 C. | Froud, Horace. 26415. (Wiring S.) | M. April 24-25/17. |
| 7 C. | Howse, C. 25521. | M. April 24/17. |
| 7 C. | Knibbs, David. 14426. | W. and M. April 24-25/17. |
| 7 C. | Long, C. J. 20636. | M. April 24-25/17. |
| 7 C. | McKenna, Arthur. 33081. | M. April 24-25/17. |
| 7 C. IX | Noon, Leslie J. N. 13817. (Fr. Ox. and Bucks. 14707.) | M. April 25/17. |
| 7 C. | Rowlands, L.-Sergt. E. T. L. 13566. | W. and M. April 24-25/17. |
| 7 C. | Walker, P. 14020. | M. April 24-25/17. |
| 7 C. | Walton, Wallace. 15056. | M. April 24-25/17. |
| 7 C. | White, L.-Cpl. F. R. 25519. | M. April 24-25/17. |
| 7 C. | White, S. 13865. | M. April 24-25/17. |
| 7 D. | Baker, E. 14326. | M. April 24-25/17. |
| 7 D. | Baldwin, John Henry. 13802. | M. April 24-25/17. |
| 7 D. | Burnell, F. W. 13859. | M. April 24-25/17. |
| 7 D. | Burnell, H. 14303. | M. April 24-25/17. |

**Wiltshire Regiment—contd.**

## *BALKANS.*

| | | |
|---|---|---|
| 7 D. | Darling, A. L. 19472. | W. and M. **April 24-25/17.** |
| 7 D. | Doughty, Cpl. W. J. 12435. | W. and M. **April 24-25/17.** |
| 7 D. | Dunn, H. R. 14039. | M. **April 24-25/17.** |
| 7 D. | Grace, W. A. 25623. | M. **April 24-25/17.** |
| 7 D. | Grounds, Thos. 16097. | W. and M. **April 24-25/17.** |
| 7 D. | Guest, M. G. 15000. | M. **April 24-25/17.** |
| 7 D. | Turton, Len. 14037. | M. **April 24-25/17.** |
| 7 D. | Wade, C. 14519. | M. **April 24-25/17.** |
| 7 D. | Warner, Arthur W. 16030. | M. **April 24-25/17.** |
| *7 ? | Ashe-Everest, J. 22127. | M. **April 24-25/17.** |
| 7 ? | Beaven, Sergt. H. S. 8420. | M. **April 24-25/17.** |
| 7 ? | Besent, J. J. 17122. | M., bel. K. **April 24-25/17.** |
| 7 ? | Clarke, W. G. 12339. | M. **April 24-25/17.** |
| 7 ? | Cole, C. J. 26062. | W. and M. **April 24-25/17.** |
| 7 ? | Comley, J. G. 12474. | M. **April 24-25/17.** |
| 7 ? | Cooper, A. F. 25605. | M. **April 24-25/17.** |
| 7 ? | Doggett, F. W. 12249. | M., bel. K. **April 24-25/17.** |
| 7 ? | Gee, W. O. 12294. | M. **April 24-25/17.** |
| 7 ? | Gregory, J. O. 14093. | M. **April 24-25/17.** |
| 7 ? | Grist, Cpl. M. G. 15000. | W. and M. **April 24-25/17.** |
| 7 ? | Hanson, A. 25651. | M. **April 24-25/17.** |
| 7 ? | Hopkins, F. 14405. | M. **April 24-25/17.** |
| 7 ? | Hunt, L.-Cpl. F. F. 32380. | M. **April 24-25/17.** |
| 7 ? | Jennings, A. W. 12338. | M. **April 24-25/17.** |
| 7 ? | Long, W. 14437. | M. **April 24-25/17.** |
| 7 ? | Macfarlane, J. 33088. | M. **April 24-25/17.** |
| 7 ? | Newland, F. 24453. | M. **April 24-25/17.** |
| 7 ? | Noon, L.-Cpl. A. J. 12342. | M. **April 24-25/17.** |
| 7 ? | Palmer, E. F. 13549. | M. **April 24-25/17.** |
| 7 ? | Pegler, E. 12292. | M. **April 24-25/17.** |
| 7 ? | Penn, F. W. 14030. | M. **April 24-25/17.** |
| 7 ? | Pickett, S. G. 12399. | M. **April 24-25/17.** |
| 7 ? | Puttick, H. E. 23747. | M. **April 24-25/17.** |
| 7 ? | Smith, G. J. 14485. | M. **April 24-25/17.** |
| 7 ? | Smith, J. 14210. | M. **April 24-25/17.** |
| 7 ? | Spriggs, J. 14499. | W. and M. **April 24-25/17.** |
| 7 ? | Stone, H. 14496. | M. **April 24-25/17.** |
| 7 ? | Sumbler, A. J. 12390. | M. **April 24-25/17.** |
| 7 ? | Thompson, L.-Cpl. R. 19527. | M. **April 24-25/17.** |
| 7 ? | Tottle, W. H. 17021. | M. **April 24-25/17.** |
| 7 ? | Turtle, G. A. 14512. | M. **April 24-25/17.** |
| 7 ? | Walmesley, Sergt. A. G. 13803. | M. **April 24-25/17.** |
| 7 ? | Watts, G. R. 18618. | M. **April 24-25/17.** |
| 7 ? | Weston, G. 12408. | M. **April 24-25/17.** |
| 7 ? | Wyvell, A. J. 26061. | W. and M. **April 24-25/17.** |

## *PERSIAN GULF.*

| | | |
|---|---|---|
| 5 | **Brown, Capt. Eric F.** | D/W. **April 1/17.** Det.D./B. |
| 5 A. | Hall, C. J. 24483. | W. and M. **Jan. 25/17.** |
| 5 A. | Hurlestone, John R. 21123. | K. **Jan. 16/17.** Det.D./B. |
| 5 A. | Moore, Patrick. 23286. | W. and M. **Jan. 25/17.** |
| 5 B. | Penny, S. 20951. | M. **April 9/16.** R/Enq. |
| 5 B. | Waldron, A. H. 19520. | M. **April 9/16.** R/Enq. |
| 5 C. | Beasley, L.-Cpl. W. 18777. | K. **April 5/16.** Det.D./B. |
| 5 C. | Lewis, H. A. 11192. | K. **Feb. 4/17.** Det.D./B. |
| 5 C. | Macey, P. 26105. | M. **Jan. 14/17.** |
| 5 D. XVI | Axford, W. V. 12482. | K. **Jan. 25/17.** Det.D./B. |
| 5 D. | Hall, Charles. 13874. | W. and M. **April 25/16.** R/Enq. |

**Wiltshire Regiment**—contd.

## *PERSIAN GULF.*

5 ? Amor, Cpl. J. A. C. 9690. M. Dec. 23/16.

5 ? Baker, H. 23119. W. and M. Jan. 26/17.

5 ? Bull, L. 24158. W. and M. Jan. 25/17.

5 ? Smith, W. G. 26283. M. Jan. 25/17.

5 ? Wilder, George. 3/88. M. April 9/16. R/Enq.

5 ? Williamson, Henry Albert. 20868. M. April 9/16. R/Enq.

## WORCESTERSHIRE REGIMENT.

## *B.E.F.*

1 **Marrs, 2nd Lieut. F. M.** M. Mar. 4/17.

1 A. III Abbiss, J. 36566. W. and M. Mar. 4/17.

1 A. Bracey, H. R. 30458. M. Mar. 4/17.

1 A. Emms, Joseph Richard. 9014. W. and M. Mar. 4/17.

1 A. I Neil, Percy. 42674. W. and M. Mar. 4/17.

1 B. VIII Rushbrook, Alfred. 40512. K. March 4/17. Det.D./B.

1 B. VI Salter, Samuel Henry. 36441. K. March 4/17. Det.D./B.

1 C. Durham, Cpl. Alfred. 24235. M. Mar. 4/17.

1 C. Edwards, E. C. 42658. M. Mar. 4/17.

1 C. Everill, J. 36404. M. Mar. 4/17.

1 C. Harrison, W. R. 26208. M. Mar. 4/17.

1 C. Lane, Robert Hry. 36489. W. and M. Mar. 4/17.

1 C. Morris, A. E. 26279. M. Mar. 4/17.

1 C. IX Partridge, Rupert. 31259. M. March 4/17.

1 D. XIV Denslow, Arthur Ernest. 36415. M. March 4/17.

1 D. Geere, G. 9237. M. Mar. 4/17.

1 D. Hawkins, Cpl. C. 9624. W. and M. Mar. 4/17.

1 D. XVI Jasper, F. 36436. M. Mar. 4/17.

1 D. L.G.S. Lampitt, L.-Cpl. J. 17251. W. and M. Mar. 4/16.

1 D. XIV Payne, Wm. 30951. M. Mar. 4/17.

1 D. Prosser, H. 19717. W. and M. Mar. 4/17.

1 D. XV Rankin, Cpl. Jerimiah. 10662. W. and M. Mar. 4/16.

1 D. Ridley, F. 40576. M. Mar. 4/17.

2 **Mason, 2nd Lieut. V. G.** W. Unoff. M. May 20/17.

*2 A. or B. II Goldingay, Wm. 8419. W. and M. May 21/17.

*2 A. Hingley, Joseph. 22334. W. and M. May 21/17.

‡2 A. Hyde, A. 33386. M. May 14/17.

‡2 A. Knight, W. 26096. W. and M. May 21/17.

‡2 A. Moore, A. 9036. M. May 14/17.

*2 A. IV Pearse, Albert. 203229. M. May 21/17.

‡2 A. Rogers, J. E. 27740. M. May 21/17.

*2 A. III Smith, G. 33382. M. May 21/17.

2 A. Waters, S. C. 202328. M. May 14/17.

‡2 B. Belcher, I. 19444. M. May 21/17.

*2 B. VIII Bond, F. 23873. M. Nov. 5/16. R/Enq.

‡2 B. Buckley, J. W. 40776. M. May 21/17.

*2 B. Busby, L.-Cpl. C. 6919. M. May 21/17.

*2 B. VI Colpman, F. 42540. M. May 21/17.

2 B. VI Cowles, L.-Cpl. R. W. 24887. M. Feb. 27/17.

‡2 B. Cunningham, D. C. 34628. M. May 21/17.

‡2 B. Dixon, L.-Cpl. J. 6943. W. and M. May 21/17.

‡2 B. Evans, W. J. 203196. M. May 21/17.

‡2 B. Garlick, G. F. 7994. M. May 21/17.

**Worcestershire Regiment—contd.**

## *B.E.F.*

| | | |
|---|---|---|
| *2 B. VI | Gregory, G. 33411. | M. May 21/17. |
| ‡2 B. | Griffin, L.-Cpl. J. 6129. | W. and M. May 21/17. |
| ‡2 B. | Griffiths, G. E. 12490. | M. May 21/17. |
| *2 B. | Grover, Sergt. J. G. 10862. | M. May 21/17. |
| ‡2 B. | Hadley, E. C. 33202. | M. May 21/17. |
| ‡2 B. | Halford, L.-Cpl. H. 15044. | M. May 21/17. |
| 2 B. V | Harris, F. 33179. | M. May 21/17. |
| *2 B. V | Holt, Harry. 35287. | M. May 21/17. |
| ‡2 B. | Hughes, E. 40782. | M. May 21/17. |
| 2 B. | Laken, J. 33342. | M. Feb. 27/17. |
| ‡2 B. | Lavis, J. H. 203118. | M. May 21/17. |
| *2 B. | Lester, S. 29867. | M. May 21/17. |
| 2 B. VIII | Marsh, Sergt. John Wm. 12604. | M. May 20/17. |
| ‡2 B. VI | Minchin, Benjamin T. 19564. | M. May 21/17. |
| 2 B. | Poppy, L. 203253. | M. May 20/17. |
| ‡2 B. | Roberts, F. G. 36637. | M. May 21/17. |
| *2 B. VII | Robbins, H. C. 31419. | M. May 21/17. |
| 2 B. V | Sarney, E. W. 203130. | M. May 21/17. |
| ‡2 B. | Scarratt, S. 33367. | M May 21/17. |
| ‡2 B. | Sendall, C. J. 40253. | W. and M. May 21/17. |
| ‡2 B. | Stark, L.-Cpl. E. A. 29973. | M May 21/17. |
| ‡2 B. | Stephenson, F. J. 42551. | M. May 21/17. |
| ‡2 B. | Stride, C. 21038. | M. May 21/17. |
| *2 B. L.G.S. | Thomas, F. E. 31438. | M. May 21/17. |
| ‡2 B. VI | Turner, Joe. 37946. | M May 21/17. |
| ‡2 B. V | Vincent, F. 31007. | M. May 21/17. |
| *2 B. L.G.S. | Wildgust, H. 39616. | M. May 21/17. |
| ‡2 B. | Wilkes, T. 14588. | M. May 21/17. |
| ‡2 B. VI | Williams, E. F. 37782. | M. May 21/17. |
| 2 B. VII | Williams, Richard James. 26827. | W. and M. Mar. 1/17. |
| *2 C. XI | Battle, George. 24890. | M. May 21/17. |
| ‡2 C. | Boardman, J. 40774. | W. and M. May 21/17. |
| *2 C. XII | Clifford, H. 16557. | M. May 21/17. |
| ‡2 C. | Farley, A. 20605. | M. May 21/17. |
| ‡2 C. | Fincher, A. 27231. | W. and M. May 21/17. |
| 2 C. X | Greick, Marks. 42543. | M. Nov. 2/16. |
| ‡2 C. | Gwynn, W. F. 21582. | M. May 21/17. |
| ‡2 C. | Heritage, A. 202755. | M. May 21/17. |
| ‡2 C. X | Insall, J. 19333. | M. May 21/17. |
| ‡2 C. | Jones, G. 23386. | M. May 21/17. |
| ‡2 C. XII | Major, Edward. 30772. | M. May 21/17. |
| ‡2 C. | Noble, A. 40752. | M. May 21/17. |
| *2 C. X | Pepper, E. F. 26094. | M. May 20/17. |
| ‡2 C. | Roberts, Cpl. T. 6734. | M. May 21/17. |
| ‡2 C. | Sheward, L.-Cpl. A. 15359. | M. May 21/17. |
| ‡2 C. | Stanley, J. 8982. | M. May 21/17. |
| ‡2 C. | Taylor, L.-Cpl. A. 7777. | M. May 21/17. |
| ‡2 C. | Thompson, J. 203138. | M. May 21/17. |
| ‡2 C. | Turner, A. H. 35281. | M. May 21/17. |
| *2 C. IX | Whatmore, M. 37759. | M. May 21/17. |
| ‡2 C. X | Willetts, Jas. 203064. | M. May 21/17. |
| ‡2 D. XIII | Bethell, A. 21674. | Unoff. M. or K. May 21/17. |
| ‡2 D. | Botts, J. 23429. | M. May 21/17. |
| ‡2 D. | Danks, T. 40753. | M. May 21/17. |
| 2 D. XV | Dawes, Cpl. F. 9137. | W. and M. May 21/17. |
| *2 D. XIII | Milner, A. E. 9117. | M. May 21/17. |
| ‡2 D. | Silver, G. 31773. | M. May 21/17. |
| ‡2 D. | Tull, H. E. 35478. | M. May 21/17. |
| *2 D. XIV | Veale, Arthur J. 203247. | W. and M. May 21/17. |

**Worcestershire Regiment—contd.**

*B.E.F.*

| | | |
|---|---|---|
| ‡2 D. XV | Westwood, Arthur. 27581. | M. May 21/17. |
| ‡2 D. | Woodyatt, Geo. 31245. | M. May 21/17. |
| ‡3 B. | Cross, F. G. 40833. | M. June 2/17. |
| 4 | **Bateman, 2nd Lt. H. H.** (Fr. 14th.) | M. April 23/17. |
| 4 | **Edwards, 2nd Lt. E.** | K. May 31/17. Det.D./B. |
| 4 | **Holland, 2nd Lt. E. H.** | M. April 23/17. |
| 4 W. | **Nicholson, 2nd Lieut. G. D. Lothian.** | M. April 23/17. |
| '4 | **Pitt, 2nd Lieut. W. H.** | M. April 23/17. |
| '4 | **Wetherhead, 2nd Lieut. S. E. W.** | K. April 23/17. Det.D./B. |
| ‡4 W. | Bagley, G. 40375. | M. May 31/17. |
| 4 W. or Z. IV | Barrett, J. F. 23057. | W. and M. Nov. 18/16. |
| *4 W. | Clarke, R. 25314. | M. May 31/17. |
| ‡4 W. | Edwards, G. F. 36399. | M. May 31/17. |
| 4 W. | Goodman, E. 40542. | M. April 23/17. |
| 4 W. | Healey, F. 36511. | M. April 23/17. |
| '4 W. III | Hunt, Harry. 25471. | W. and M. April 23/17. |
| 4 W. | Hyde, A. 30795. | M. April 23/17. |
| ‡4 W. | Loveday, F. 40329. | W. and M. April 23/17. |
| ‡4 W. | Morris, G. W. 37418. | M. May 31/17. |
| '4 W. III | Pople, C. 40544. | M. April 23/17. |
| ‡4 W. | Smith, W. D. 40548. | M. May 31/17. |
| 4 W. | Saunders, A. 25033. | M. April 23/17. |
| ‡4 W. | Stephenson, S. 35309. | W. and M. April 23/17. |
| ‡4 W. | Stevens, G. E. 6/9792. | M. May 30/17. |
| '4 W. | Wood, J. 27714. | W. and M. April 28/17. |
| *4 W. IV | Woodhouse, Harry. 23357. | M. April 23/17. |
| ,4 W. | Yardley, E. 26090. | M. April 23/17. |
| 4 X. | Barker, L.-Cpl. V. A. 40640. | M. April 23/17. |
| '4 X. VI | Black, F. W. 5509. | M. April 23/17. |
| 4 X. | Brownswood, C. 25384. | M. April 23/17. |
| 4 X. VII | Craddock, Jas. 20990. | W. and M. April 24/17. |
| *4 X. VIII | Dix, Fredk. Horace. 37496. | K. May 31/17. Det.D./B. |
| 4 X. VII | Dodds, William. 203124. | M. April 23/17. |
| ‡4 X. | Dufty, H. H. 39736. | M. Nov. 26/16. |
| 4 X. | Gennard, Lewis. 22073. | W. and M. Oct. 18/16. |
| '4 X. VII | Hunt, L.-Cpl. Cecil George. 22925. | M. April 23/17. |
| ‡4 X. | Hurley, P. L. 35426. | M. May 31/17. |
| 4 X. | Lauder, A. 40651. | M. April 23/17. |
| '4 X. | Parry, S. 30222. | M. April 23/17. |
| 4 X. | Polhill, Bertie Albert. 8378. | M. April 23/17. |
| ‡4 X. VIII | Rowland, G. E. 37550. | M. June 6/17. |
| 4 X. VII | Smith, H. 200357. (Fr. 7th.) | M. April 23/17. |
| 4 X. | Sullivan, W. 21013. | M. April 23/17. |
| ‡4 X. | Taylor, W. 19090. | W. and M. April 23/17. |
| 4 X. | Teale, W. 36559. | M. April 23/17. |
| ‡4 X. | Thompson, J. 33430. | W. and M. April 23/17. |
| 4 Y. | Bailey, J. E. 20484. | M. April 23/17. |
| 4 Y. IX | Cullen, A. J. 40357. | W. and M. April 23/17. |
| 4 Y. IX | Dench, Jas. Alf. Richd. 40358. | W. Unoff. M. April 23/17. |
| 4 Y. | Dyer, Sergt. S. 19477. | M. April 23/17. |
| ‡4 Y. | Goodyer, J. 24204. | W. and M. April 23/17. |
| *4 Y. XI | Hudson, Percy Harold. H/40318. | M. April 23/17. |
| 4 Y. | Mullard, Wm. Edw. 9010. | M. April 23/17. |
| ,4 Y. | Randall, E. A. 40422. | M. April 23/17. |
| 4 Y. IX | Taylor, Alfred. 22998. | W. and M. Oct. 18/16. |
| 4 Y. | Wainwright, H. 22084. | M. April 23/17. |
| 4 Z. XIII | Clark, Harry. 40460. | W. and M. April 23/17. |
| ‡4 Z. | Howard, L.-Cpl. J. 33083. | W. and M. April 23/17. |

**Worcestershire Regiment—contd.**

## *B.E.F.*

| | | |
|---|---|---|
| ‡4 Z. | Humphries, G. 38141. | W. and M. April 23/17. |
| 4 Z. XIV | Pinkney, L.-Cpl. J. H. 25357. | M. April 23/17. |
| 4 Z. XIV | Summerton, Wm. 40294. | M. April 23/17. |
| 4 Z. XVI | Wittenham, H. 36917. | M. April 23/17. |
| ‡4 ? | Everton, F. 40384. | W. and M. April 23/17. |
| ‡4 ? | Jones, N. 34129. | M. April 23/17. |
| ‡4 ? | Milnes, F. 27406. | M. April 28/17. |
| 7 A. | Milward, W. 203837. | M., bel. K. April 13/17. |
| 7 B. | Arnold, Tom. 203150. | M. April 25/17. |
| 7 B. V | Vaughan, J. H. 203458. | M. April 25/17. |
| 7 B. VIII | White, Ernest. 203781. | M. April 25/17. |
| ‡7 C. | Baker, C. 203693. | M. May 27/17. |
| ‡7 C. | Davies, G. 36544. | M. May 27/17. |
| ‡7 C. | Goddard, E. 203198. | M. May 27/17. |
| 7 C. | Gordon, A. 203726. | M. April 25/17. |
| 7 C. | Millerchip, B. 201707. | M. April 25/17. |
| 7 C. XII | Silvester, J. T. 200133. | M. April 24/17. |
| ‡7 C. | Steventon, J. 201645. | M. May 27/17. |
| 7 C. | Stringer, Edward. 200264. | M. April 25/17. |
| 7 D. XVI | Apperley, H. 203813. | M. April 25/17. |
| 7 D. | Harris, F. B. 203728. | M. April 25/17. |
| *7 D. XVI | Hill, W. G. 202176. | W. and M. April 23/17. |
| 7 D. | Hill, W. 201079. | M. April 25/17. |
| 7 D. | Hopcutt, F. 203832. | M. April 25/17. |
| 7 D. | Mayall, W. 200758. | M. April 25/17. |
| 7 D. | Round, D. 201744. | M. April 25/17. |
| 7 D. | Shepherd, Alfred. 200291. | M. April 25/17. |
| 8 | **Richards, Lieut. A. G.** | W. and M. April 24/17. |
| 8 C. | Bishop, J. A. 241634. | M. April 24/17. |
| 8 C. | Hughes, J. 241046. | M. April 24/17. |
| 8 C. | King, L.-Cpl. F. J. 240159. | M. April 24/17. |
| 8 C. | Pugh, A. A. 241053. | M. April 24/17. |
| 8 C. | Stanton, H. 241563. | M. April 24/17. |
| 8 D. XIII | Allsopp, W. 241552. (4550.) | M. April 23/17. |
| 8 D. | Ballard, A. 240101. | M. April 24/17. |
| 8 D. XVI | Banbury, C. S. 241742. | M. April 24/17. |
| 8 D. | Bastable, Cpl. S. J. 241648. | M. April 24/17. |
| 8 D. | Baylis, P. 242634. | M. April 24/17. |
| 8 D. | Bourne, A. 240642. | M. April 24/17. |
| 8 D. XIV | Burgess, Fred Arthur. 242655. | M. April 24/17. |
| 8 D. XV | Coux, F. 242632. | M. April 24/17. |
| 8 D. | Cox, L. A. 240985. | M. April 24/17. |
| 8 D. XIV | Hopkins, Hy. Harvey. 242628. | M. April 24/17. |
| 8 D. | Houghton, Cpl. B. 240580. | M. April 24/17. |
| 8 D. | Mews, Dennis. 240555. | M. April 24/17. |
| 8 D. | Moore, A. 242582. | M. April 24/17. |
| 8 D. | Penney, L.-Cpl. T. 241037. | M. April 24/17. |
| 8 D. | Radcliffe, H. 242624. | M. April 24/17. |
| 8 D. | Skidmore, B. 241656. | M. April 24/17. |
| 8 D. | Smith, W. 241596. | M. April 24/17. |
| 8 D. | Spiers, T. 240667. | M. April 24/17. |
| 8 D. | Tranter, G. H. 241814. | M. April 24/17. |
| 8 D. | Wagstaffe, J. Bentley. 240727. (2938.) | M. April 24/17. |
| 8 D. | Watkins, E. 242268. | M. April 24/17. |
| 8 D. XIII | Westwood, S. 241764. | M. April 24/17. |
| 10 D. X | Amos, L.-Cpl. R. S. 39911. | M. Feb. 10/17. |
| 10 D. | Brown, Robt. Crister. 39938. | M. Nov. 18/16. R/Enq. |
| 10 D. XV | Goode, A. S. 40809. | W. and M. Feb. 11/17. |
| 10 D. | Hall, R. 30904. | W. and M. April 2/17. |

**Worcestershire Regiment—contd.**

## *B.E.F.*

10 D. XV Johnson, Robert. 39989. — M. Nov. 18/16.
‡10 D. Gren. Pl. Parton, N. A. 39869. — M. Nov. 18/16. R/Enq.
10 D. XVI Rushton, L.-Cpl. J. V. 27464. — M. Feb. 11/17.
10 D. XIII M.G.S. Taylor, Vincent. 22784. — M. Feb. 11/17.
10 D. XV Wakelin, A. 39908. — W. and M. Feb. 11/17.
12 Day, 2nd Lieut. G. H. (Fr. 7th.) — M., bel. K. April 24/17.
14 Pioneer A. Sadler, Geo. Hy. 24734. — D/W. May 2/17. Det.D./b.
14 „ D. Dalton, Walter Thomas. 35952. — M. Feb. 4/17.

## *BALKANS.*

11 1 II Bridges, Ernest Geo. 27408. — M. April 24-25/17.
11 1 Bruton, C. 17120. — M. April 25/17.
11 1 Gemmell, John. 38349. — M. April 24-25/17.
11 1 I Harris, James. 22789. — M. April 24-25/17.
11 1 Hartwell, J. 17853. — M. April 24-25/17.
11 1 I Jones, Geo. Fred. 19313. — M. April 24-25/17.
11 1 Jones, L.-Cpl. Ivor. 18316. — M. April 24-25/17.
11 1 Marshall, G. 17374. — M. April 24-25/17.
11 1 I Nicklin, John E. 30515. — M. April 24-25/17.
11 1 IV Pugh, Chas. 30688. — M. April 24-25/17.
11 1 Richards, C.-Q.-M.-S. Thos. John. 19661. — M. April 24-25/17.
11 1 Russell, Cpl. A. G. 17112. — M. April 24-25/17.
11 2 V Allen, William. 24570. — M. April 24-25/17.
11 2 Farrington, Sergt. A. E. 15855. — M. April 24-25/17.
11 2 Harper, A. E. 34776. — M. April 24-25/17.
11 2 VI James, G. H. 30996. — M. April 24-25/17.
11 2 VII Meecham, Arthur J. 34058. — M. April 24-25/17.
11 2 VII Mills, W. 34059. — M. April 24/17.
11 2 Pardoe, L.-Cpl. F. G. 31231. (Fr. 4 Entrench. Batt.) — M. April 24-25/17.
*11 2 VIII Pearson, Joseph. 30215. — M. April 24/17.
11 2 VI Shaw, Cpl. G. D. 27133. — K. April 20/17. Det.D./B.
11 3 Allery, Chas. Herbert. 34800. — M. April 24-25/17.
11 3 Badger, Sergt. W. 9579. — K. April 24/17. Det.D./B.
11 3 M.G.S. Bradshaw, H. 17734. — M. April 24-25/17.
*11 3 XI Cole, S. E. 30219. — M. April 24-25/17.
11 3 X Ealey, G. 34731. — M. April 24/17.
11 3 X Farrant, E. G. 30822. — M. April 24-25/17.
11 3 Glass, Heber Stanley. 38371. — M. April 24-25/17.
11 3 XI Johnson, Aaron. 18176. — M. April 24-25/17.
11 3 Lee, Ernest. 22200. — M. April 24-25/17.
11 3 X Moore, Arthur. 29824. — M. April 24-25/17.
11 3 X Newman, Walter. 27598. — M. April 24-25/17.
11 3 IX Patrick, T. A 18019. — M. April 24/17.
11 3 X Radford, W. W. 34816. — M. April 24-25/17.
11 3 Tinsley, Albert. 17722. — M. April 24/17.
11 3 Yates, H. 16103. — M. April 24-25/17.
11 4 Bedhall, Frank. 31152. — M. April 24-25/17.
11 4 XV Collins, W. J. 30814. — K. April 22/17. Det.D./B.
11 4 Lear, Horace. 34083. — M. April 24-25/17.
11 4 Newman, Wm. A. 20233. — M. April 24-25/17.
11 4 Palmer, Albert Victor. 22042. — M. April 24-25/17.
11 4 XIII Quittenden, Arthur. 15909. — M. April 24-25/17.
11 ? Banner, G. H. 18180. — M. April 24-25/17.
11 ? Butler, B. 31176. — M. April 24-25/17.
11 ? Chatham, N. 29565. — M. April 24-25/17.
*11 ? Chown, H. C. 34827. — M. April 24-25/17.

**Worcestershire Regiment—contd.**

## *BALKANS.*

11 ? Cuff, W. 24899. M. April 24-25/17.
11 Trans. S. Edwards, Fredk. 29902. M. April 23/17.
11 ? Farmer, D. 22628. M. April 24-25/17.
11 ? Franklin, J. H. 34737. M. April 24-25/17.
11 ? Griffiths, H. 16041. M. April 24-25/17.
11 ? Hartwell, D. I. 17853. M. April 24-25/17.
11 ? Haynes, L.-Cpl. E. 17103. M. April 24-25/17.
11 ? Jackson, L. 27412. M. April 24-25/17.
11 ? Leitch, R. 38354. M. April 24-25/17.
11 ? Lewis, Sergt. H. G. 17102. M. April 24-25/17.
11 ? Lymer, A. 23062. M. April 24-25/17.
11 ? Palmer, G. J. 36376. M. April 24-25/17.
11 ? Phœnix, F. 31024. M. April 24-25/17.
*11 ? Powell, H. 9400. M. April 24-25/17.
11 ? Pruden, J. 13203. M. April 24-25/17.
11 ? Randall, C. I. 18119. M. April 24-25/17.
11 ? Renovitch, P. 29938. M. April 24-25/17.
11 ? Smith, D. 28773. M. April 24-25/17.
11 ? Smith, T. 30032. M. April 24-25/17.
11 ? Stanford, J. 15892. M. April 24-25/17.
11 ? Trinder, R. W. 17165. M. April 24-25/17.
11 ? Weeks, W. A. 29854. M. April 24-25/17.

## *E.E.F.*

9 ? Merry, Samuel. 8711. (Fr. 1st and 2nd.) M., bel. drowned April 15/17. "Arcadia."
9 ? Packwood, Albert. 8708. M., bel. drowned April 15/17.

## *PERSIAN GULF.*

9 A. Hart, Arthur Thos. 20725. M. Jan. 25/17.
9 A. Holloway, E. J. 18674. M. Jan. 25/17.
9 A. Smith, A. 30532. M. Jan. 25/17.
9 A. Terry, Sergt. W. H. H. 6990. M. Jan. 25/17.
9 B. Brookes, Arthur. 30454. M. Jan. 25/17.
9 B. Howell, Clarence. 30582. M. Jan. 25/17.
9 B. Hughes, H. 27167. M. Jan. 25/17.
9 B. Westwood, J. 30885. M. Jan. 25/17.
9 B. Woolams, T. 8136. M. Jan. 25/17.
9 C. Bray, Archibald Edgar. 14146. M. Jan. 25/17.
9 C. XII Workman, W. 27350. M. Jan. 25/17.
9 D. XIV Baxter, David. 22293. M. April 20/16. R/Enq.
9 D. Bridgwater, B. F. 27024. M. Jan. 25/17.
9 D. XVI Harper, W. 11798. (Fr. 7 N. Staffs) M. April 5/16. R/Enq.
9 ? Bullivant, C. 31393. M. Jan. 25/17.
9 ? Carman, A. 10144. M. Jan. 25/17.
9 ? Clasper, A. E. 23166. M. Jan. 25/17.
9 ? Dowdeswell, H. 27199. M. Jan. 25/17.
9 ? Edwards, A. 31699. M. Jan. 25/17.
9 ? Fowler, Frank. 30269. K. Jan. 25/16. Det.D./B.
9 ? McFaul, L.-Sergt. J. P. F. 38026. M. Jan. 25/17.
9 ? Price, F. J. 21022. M. Jan. 25/17.
9 ? Read, Act.-Sergt. J. 14089. M. Jan. 25/17.
9 ? Rudge, A. E. 20930. M. Jan. 25/17.
*9 ? Seeney, W. 140372. M., bel. K. May 13/17.

## WORCESTER YEOMANRY.

### *E.E.F.*

| | | |
|---|---|---|
| ? | Blount, Charlie. 2975. | M. April 23/16. |
| ? | Forgham, Fred. S. 2999. | M. April 23/16. |

## YORKSHIRE REGIMENT.

### *B.E.F.*

| | | |
|---|---|---|
| 2 A. | Bryon, Ralph. 36047. | M. Oct. 18/16. |
| 2 A. IV | Child, W. J. M. 36052. | W. and M. Oct. 18/16. R/Enq. |
| 2 A. | Ginger, Wm. Fredk. 42347. | M. April 2/17. |
| 2 A. III | Myers, John Wm. 27342. (Fr. 11th.) | W. Unoff. M. Aug. 17/16. |
| 2 A. L.G.S. | Rutherford, S. H. 36213. | W. and M. April 2/17. |
| 2 B. | Barff, R. 7729. | M. Mar. 31/17. |
| 2 B. | Bell, T. 30574. | M. Mar. 31/17. |
| 2 B. VIII | Carey, A. H. 42307. | K. April 2/17. Det.D./B. |
| 2 B. V | Carter, G. 42293. | M. Mar. 31/17. |
| 2 B. VI | Davey, W. 42315. | W. and M. April 2/17. |
| 2 B. | Gill, L.-Cpl. R. 30579. | M. Mar. 31/17. |
| 2 B. VI | Gray, W. 36306. | M. Mar. 31/17. |
| 2 B. VI | Groves, W. 42342. | M. Mar. 31/17. |
| 2 B. | Horner, L.-Cpl. E. 8239. | W. and M. Mar. 31/17. |
| 2 B. VII | Robinson, C. D. 32974. | W. and M. Mar. 31/17. |
| 2 B. | Smith, I. 235299. | W. and M. April 24/17. |
| 2 B. | Smith, J. 10823. | M. Mar. 31/17. |
| 2 B. | Stephenson, J. R. 30727. | M. April 2/17. |
| 2 B. | Sutton, Harry. 33470. | M. April 2/17. |
| 2 B. VII | Tooke, Cpl. Wm. 24559. | M. Mar. 31/17. |
| 2 C. | Butler, B. 235276. | M. April 24/17. |
| 2 C. IX | Hodgson, Jos. 16164. | M. April 9/17. |
| 2 C. | Key, S. 36275. | M. April 9/17. |
| 2 C. XI | Wilson, George. 36294. | M. Oct. 18/16. |
| 2 C. | Wright, E. H. 33242. | M. April 2/17. |
| 2 D. | Brunskill, R. W. 38485. | M. April 2/17. |
| 2 D. XIV | Cook, Sgt. Ernest. 20563. | W. and M. April 9/17. |
| 4 | **Scarth, 2nd Lieut. J. H.** | M., bel. K. April 24/17. |
| 4 W. | Bell, R. D. 203107. (7697.) | W. and M. April 23/17. |
| 4 W. II | Cooksey, Alfred. 235197. | M. April 23/17. |
| 4 W. | Cracknell, R. J. 235044. | M. April 23/17. |
| 4 W. | Davis, A. 235046. | M. April 23/17. |
| 4 W. I | Frow, Chas. Hen. 241773. (Late 5th, 5804.) | M. April 23/17. |
| 4 W. | Graves, T. 235052. | M. April 23/17. |
| 24 W. | Sharples, R. 235110. | W. and M. April 23/17. |
| 24 W. | Smith, Cpl. G. 203204. | W. and M. April 23/17. |
| 4 W. | Sowerby, J. 201108. | M. April 23/17. |
| 24 W. | Swatman, T. 201415. | W. and M. April 23/17. |
| 4 W. | Whittaker, Geo. 235111. (8675.) | M. April 23/17. |
| 4 X. | Bellchamber, A. E. 202221. | M. April 23/17. |
| 24 X. | Bottomley, G. A. 235125. | W. and M. April 23/17. |
| 24 X. | Cole, E. T. 203000. | W. and M. April 23/17. |

**Yorkshire Regiment—contd.**

*B.E.F.*

4 X. Sig. S. Conroy, John. 201252. (4040.) — **M. April 23/17.**
‡4 X. VII Dodds, William. 203124. (7714.) — **M. April 23/17.**
4 X. Etherington, H. 203134. — **M. April 23/17.**
4 X. VII Felton, H. 203196. (8013.) — **M. April 23/17.**
•4 X. Foster, F. 202281. (6165.) — **M. April 23/17.**
4 X. L.G.S. Gill, James. 4047. — **M. Sept. 15/16.**
4 X. V Gillis, Joseph. 235140. — **W. and M. April 23/17.**
4 X. V Goulden, G. 30463. — **W. and M. April 23/17.**
4 X. Mann, R. 201186. — **M. April 23/17.**
•4 X. Miller, A. 202251. — **M. April 23/17.**
4 X. Oliver, Joseph Thos. 203085. (7675.) — W. and M. **April 23/17.**
•4 X. L.G.S. Peacock, John Geo. 200582. (2502.) — Unoff. M. **April/17.**
•4 X. V Scott, Fredk. Chas. 39197. — W. and M. **April 25/17.**
4 X. Smelt, Tom. 240294. (8772.) — **M. April 23/17.**
4 Y. Bailey, A. 202339. — **M. April 23/17.**
•4 Y. Barnett, S. 202226. — **M. April 23/17.**
‡4 Y. Brightley, A. 202991. — W. and M. **April 23/17.**
4 Y. Cooper, A. 201615. — **M. April 23/17.**
4 Y. Eades, R. W. 8659. — **M. April 23/17.**
4 Y. Goldby, J. W. 200663. — **M. April 23/17.**
4 Y. XII Humphries, Samuel. 260033. — **M. April 23/17.**
4 Y. Jamieson, J. 200438. — **M. April 23/17.**
4 Y. XII Knaggs, J. E. 235112. — **M. April 23/17.**
4 Y. XII Lewes, W. M. 203041. (7631.) — **M. April 23/17.**
4 Y. XII McIntyre, James. 201461. (4396.) — W. and M. **April 23/17.**
4 Y. Mee, Albert. 5255. — W. and M. **Sept. 15-17/16. R./Enq.**
4 Y. Simpson, J. 201509. — **M. April 23/17.**
4 Y. X Weighell, Sydney Jas. 200943. (3401.) — **M. April 23/17.**
4 Z. Candler, L.-Cpl. T. 200245. — **M. April 23/17.**
4 Z. Dunn, O. E. 201685. — **M. April 28/17.**
4 Z. VIII Evans, Jack. 235166. — W. and M. **April 23/17.**
4 Z. XIV Goodwin, W. 202284. (6168.) — **M. April 17/17.**
‡4 Z. Harrison, Sergt. W. G. 2906. — **M. April 23/17.**
4 Z. Hart, Tom. 200208. (1606.) — **M. April 23/17.**
•4 Z. Houghton, G. 235171. — **M. April 23/17.**
4 Z. XVI Matthews, C. A. 203077. (7667.) — **M. April 23/17.**
4 Z. XIII Miller, Stephen J. 203167. (7757.) — **M. April 23/17.**
4 Z. Pearson, A. 203180. (7770.) — **M. April 23/17.**
4 Z. Plews, G. 202958. — **M. April 23/17.**
4 Z. Richardson, G. 203182. — **M. April 23/17.**
4 Z. L.G.S. Smith, Jos. Fredk. 201143. (3875.) — **M. April 23/17.**
4 Z. Townsend, W. F. 202266. — **M. April 23/17.**
‡4 ? L.G.S. Hodgson, Jas. Richard. 200793. (3065.) — W. and M. **Sept. 15/16. R/Enq.**
•4 ? Maltby, William. 9034. — **M. Dec. 16/16.**
2/4 W. Swatman, L.-Cpl. Thomas. 4306. — W. and M. **April 23/17.**
‡5 **Carry, 2nd Lieut. E. G. Stewart.** — **M. June 27/17.**
5 **Whitehead, 2nd Lieut. F. B** — W. and M. **April 23/17.**
5 A. Allison, Sergt. T. 241531. — **M. April 23/17.**
5 A. Archer, W. 243250. — **M. April 23/17.**
5 A. Atkinson, R. 13663. — **M. April 23/17.**
5 A. Balson, T. 243252. — **M. April 23/17.**
5 A. Beaumont, Tom. 29159. — **M. April 23/17.**
5 A. Bennett, D. 243253. — **M. April 23/17.**
5 A. I Bowling, Dudley Gowen. 240789. — **M. April 23/17.**
5 A. Cattle, Cpl. H. 241101. — **M. April 23/17.**
5 A. Coates, H. 243255. — **M. April 23/17.**
5 A. Codling, Cpl. G. T. 241266. — **M. April 23/17.**
5 A. III Cook, W. 5686. — **M. April 23/17.**

Yorkshire Regiment—contd.

## *B.E.F.*

| | | |
|---|---|---|
| 5 A. III | Dullard, Jos. 243256. | M. April 23/17. |
| 5 A. | Ede, W. 8482. | M. April 23/17. |
| ‡5 A. | Fortune, D. J. 201848. | W. and M. April 23/17. |
| 5 A. | Galilee, Fred. 200815. | M. April 23/17. |
| 5 A. | Granger, C. E. 201616. (4689.) | M. April 23/17. |
| 5 A. L.G.S. | Hakes, L.-Cpl. Herbert C. 18495. | M. April 23/17. |
| 5 A. | Horton, F. 240558. | M. April 23/17. |
| 5 A. | King, T. 243277. (5723.) | W. and M. April 23/17. |
| ‡5 A. | Leonard, J. W. 240460. | W. and M. April 23/17. |
| 5 A. IV | Lintern, Cpl. Geo. 241040. | M. April 23/17. |
| 5 A. III | Marshall, C. L. 242472. | M. April 23/17. |
| 5 A. | Mun-oe, W. 243296. | M. April 23/17. |
| ‡5 A. | Pinkney, W. 21052. | M. April 23/17. |
| ‡5 A. | Riddle, W. 242494. | M. April 23/17. |
| 5 A. IV | Quintern, Cpl. G. E. 241040. (3153.) | M. April 23/17. |
| 5 A. III | Richmond, Percy Stuart. 242493. | M. April 23/17. |
| ‡5 A. | Simpson, G. A. 241346. | M. April 23/17. |
| ‡5 A. | Smith, H. 240287. | M. April 23/17. |
| ‡5 A. | Spurgin, F. 242505. | M. April 23/17. |
| 5 A. | Stephenson, Thos. Hy. 20257. (Fr. 2.) | M. April 24/17. |
| ‡5 A. | Stockdale, W. H. 201837. | M. April 23/17. |
| ‡5 A. | Vasey, Cpl. T. H. 240622. | M. April 23/17. |
| ‡5 A. | Waites, Sergt. G. 240645. | M. April 23/17. |
| *5 A. IV | Wright, C. E. 33298. | M. April 23/17. |
| 5 B. | Clarke, Cpl. E. 201549. | M. April 23/17. |
| *5 B. | Poole, W. A. 20571. | M. April 23/17. |
| 5 C. IX | Frost, Sergt. Harry. 240691. (2378.) | M. April 23/17. |
| 5 C. | Maloney, P. 3822. | W. and M. Sept. 15/16. R/Enq. |
| ‡5 C. | Wood, C. H. 240591. | M. April 23/17. |
| 5 D/. | Hebron, G. 201816. | M. April 23/17. |
| 5 D. | Iley, W. 14241. | M. April 23/17. |
| 5 I.T.M. | Leppington, W. 240786. (150 Bgde.) | M. April 23/17. |
| 6 A. | Harper, Henry. 3/8063. | M. Sept. 30/16. R/Enq. |
| 6 B. | Jowett, William. 10516. | M. Sept. 30/16. R/Enq. |
| 6 B. VII | McGeachy, Wm. 8189. | M. Feb. 8/17. |
| 6 C. or D. | Otterson, L.-Cpl. Jas. 18497. | M. Sept. 30/16. R/Enq. |
| *6 D. | Bartrom, John. 18773. | M. Sept. 15/16. R/Enq. |
| 6 D. | Bateman, R. 11092. | W. and M. Jan. 17/17. |
| 6 D. | Smithson, C. E. 18839. | M. Sept. 30/16. R/Enq. |
| 7 | **Croft, Capt. R. W. S.** | K. May 12/17. Det.D./B. |
| 7 C. | **Roper, 2nd Lieut. G. S. R.** | K. May 12/17. Det.D./B. |
| *7 | **Thacker, 2nd Lieut. W. A.** | K. May 12/17. Det.D./B. |
| 7 A. or C. | Buck, Act.-Sergt. A. 12615. | W. and M. Feb. 8/17. |
| 7 A. | Clemmet, L.-Cpl. J. T. 21098. | M. Jan. 17/17. |
| ‡7 A. | Cundall, C. 26713. | M. April 25/17. |
| 7 A. Snip. S. | Hall, T. 13686. | W. and M. Feb. 8/17. |
| ‡7 A. | Hughes, T. 12760. | M. April 23/17. |
| 7 A. I | Iredale, Thos. Beaumont. 28794. | W. and M. May 14/17. |
| 7 A. II | Moore, T. H. 38781. | W. and M. May 13/17. |
| 7 A. | Pattison, Sergt. 17849. | K. Nov. 5/16. Det.D./B. |
| 7 A. | Reader, L.-Cpl. H. 12026. | M. Nov. 6/16. |
| *7 A. III | Young, Harry. 27018. | K. Feb. 2/17. Det.D./B. |
| 7 B. VI | Boyes, Sgt. Wm. 20643. | M. Feb. 8/17. |
| 7 B. | Dutton, W. J. 18423. | M. April 23/17. |
| ‡7 B. | Golightly, Thos. 39167. | M. May 14/17. |
| ‡7 B. | Graham, William. 38581. | M. May 14/17. |
| 7 B. Snip, S. | Haigh, A/Cpl. Harold. 25732. | W. and M. Feb. 8/17. |
| 7 B. | Smith, Cpl. J. 10063. | M. Nov. 5/16. |
| 7 C. X | Easby, Cpl. J. W. 24370. | W. and M. May 13/17. |

**Yorkshire Regiment—contd.**

***B.E.F.***

| | | |
|---|---|---|
| 7 C. | Gent, Wm. H. 18112. | W. and M. Feb. 8/17. |
| ‡7 C. | Gilstin, James. 13596. | W. and M. May 13/17. |
| ‡7 C. XII | Harrison, Thos. 235247. | W. and M. May 13/17. |
| 7 C. M.G.S. | Jeffery, J. 28089. | W. and M. Feb. 8/17. |
| 7 C. | Just, W. 235248. | M. May 14/17. |
| *7 C. Bomb. S. | Linley, Cpl. Wm. 11844. | W. and M. May 13/17. |
| 7 C. X | Payne, W. Albert. 27906. | W. and M. Feb. 8/17. |
| ‡7 C. XI | Pollard, W. 29108. | M. May 13/17. |
| *7 C. XII | Robinson, Ernest. 39208. | M. May 13/17. |
| *7 C. | Rutherford, T. H. 39207. | M. May 13/17. |
| ‡7 C. | Sykes, James. 29160. | M. May 13/17. |
| *7 C. XI | White, Albert E. 14831. | W. Unoff. M. May 13/17. |
| ‡7 D. XV | Gibson, Jas. R. 3704. | Unoff. M. May 11/17. |
| ‡7 D. | McGrath, S. G. 201218. | M. April 22/17. |
| 7 D. | Lord, L.-Cpl. Jas. 38869. | M. April 25/17. |
| 7 D. | Mulligan, Andrew. 15009. | W. and M. Feb. 8/17. |
| ‡7 D. XIV | Pearl, A. E. 235259. | M. May 12/17. |
| ‡7 D. | Roper, A. 39138. | M. April 22/17. |
| 7 D. | Willis, L.-Cpl. Alex. 13688. | M. Feb. 8/17. |
| 7 ? I.T.M. | Kitching, H. 12454. (50 Bdge.) | W. and M. Feb. 8/17. |
| ‡8 A. III | Wright, T. D. 42621. | Unoff. W. and M. June 7/17. |
| 8 B. VI | Thorne, J. 28918. | M. Oct. 8/16. R/Enq. |
| ‡9 A. I | Good, Arthur. 41578. | M. June 7/17. |
| ‡9 A. I | Swales, James. 30366. | W. and M. June 7/17. |
| ‡9 A. | Slater, L.-Cpl. C. H. 17784. | W. and M. Oct. 7/16. R/Enq. |
| *9 A. IV | Studham, James. 16248. | M. June 7/17. |
| 9 A. | Thornton, W. 38242. | M. April 10/17. |
| 9 A. | Wilson, T. H. 38521. | M. April 10/17. |
| 9 B. VII | Alexander, Keith. 26607. | M. Sept. 23/16. R/Enq. |
| 9 B. | Postill, Harold. 30359. | M. Oct. 7/16. R/Enq. |
| ‡9 B. VIII | Rhodes, John. 260015. | M. June 7/17. |
| *9 B. | Shaw, Fred. 28757. | M. June 7/17. |
| *9 D. | Petty, John. 28326. | M. Oct. 7/16. R/Enq. |
| ‡9 D. XIII | Turton, Harry. 38047. | M. June 7/17. |
| ‡9 D. | Waugh, Sergt. Septimus. 17906. | K. June 7/17. Det.D./B. |
| 10 B. VIII | Purcell, Fred. 41831. | W. and M. April 11/17. |
| 10 B. VI | Ward, Jas. 41841. | M. April 11/17. |
| 10 C. XII | Coxon, Cpl. Albert. 20935. | W. and M. April 11/17. |
| 10 C. XI | Jones, B. J. 38726. | W. and M. April 11/17. |
| *10 C. M.G.S. | Knowles, F. H. 33213. | K. April 11/17. Det.D./B. |
| 10 D. XVI | Postgate, Thos. 19543. | W. and M. April 11/17. |
| 10 D. XV | Williams, Sig. Claude Henry. 260022. (Late 8651.) | M. April 11/17. |
| 10 ? | Curtis, H. 33119. (Late 6397, 2/4 Norfolk, att. 4th Northd. Fus.) | M. Sept. 23/16. R/Enq. |
| *13 H.Q. | Butterfield, Arthur. 9766. | Unoff. M., bel. K. June 1-15/17. |

**EAST YORKSHIRE REGIMENT.**

***B.E.F.***

| | | |
|---|---|---|
| 1 A. | Clark, Wm. 17011. (Fr. 8th.) | M. Sept. 16/16. |
| 1 A. L.G.S. | Hales, A.-L.-Cpl. James. 15248. | M. April 9/17. |
| 1 A. | Lilley, T. 25592. | M. April 9/17. |

**Yorkshire Regiment, East—contd.**

## *B.E.F.*

| | | |
|---|---|---|
| ‡1 A. | Pea, Alfred. 277880. | M. Sept. 16/16. R/Enq. |
| 1 A. | Perry, R. 13799. | M. April 9/17. |
| ‡1 A. L.G.S. | Skinn, C. 27879. | M. April 9/17. |
| 1 A. | Smith, H. W. 201538. (Fr. 4th.) | W. and M. April 9/17. |
| 1 B. VII | Baker, Frank. 18314. (Fr. W. Yorks, No. 31484.) | W. and M. Sept. 25/16. R/Enq. |
| 1 B. | Cartledge, L.-Cpl. George. 27887. | M. Sept. 16/16. R/Enq. |
| 1 B. VIII | Davidson, A. 31527. | M. April 9/17. |
| 1 B. | Hardwick, D. 31247. | M. April 9/17. |
| 1 B. | Tasker, R. H. 21728. | M Sept. 16/16. R/Enq. |
| 1 B. | Walshaw, L.-Cpl. W. 9537. | M. Sept. 16/16. R/Enq. |
| 1 C. IX | Collins, A.-Sergt. J. B. 9307. | K. Sept. 25/16. Det.D./B. |
| 1 C. XI | Denton, Thomas. 7456. | K. April 9/17. Det.D./B. |
| 1 C. | Potter, A. 8124. | M. April 9/17. |
| 1 C. IX | Sawford, John. 28016. | W. and M. April 9/17. |
| 1 C. | Sharp, C. 31170. (W. Yorks, 25406.) | M. Sept. 16/16. R/Enq. |
| 1 D. XIV | Buckley, John. 31122. | W. and M. April 9/17. |
| 1 D. XV | Dixon, Walter. 27828. | M. April 9/17. |
| ‡1 D. | Emerson, J. Wm. 31509. | M. April 9/17. |
| 1 D. XIII | Pashby, W. 23663. | M. April 9/17. |
| 1 D. | Shenmeld, H. 7638. | W. and M. April 9/17. |
| 1 D. XIII | Tuke, Alfred. 27860. | M. April 9/17. |
| 1 D. XVI | Yates, Charles. 37340. | M. April 9/17. |
| 4 | **Cowl, 2nd Lieut. J. D.** | M. April 23/17. |
| ‡4 | **Duggleby, 2nd Lieut.** | M. June 28/17. |
| 4 | **Earle, 2nd Lieut. W. A.** | M. April 23/17. |
| 4 | **Green, 2nd Lieut. N. W.** | M. April 23/17. |
| ‡4 | **Linsley, 2nd Lieut. F.** | M. June 28/17. |
| 4 | **Lofthouse, Lieut. G. H.** | M. April 23/17. |
| ‡4 | **Morrill, Capt. T. J.** | M. June 28/17. |
| 4 | **Peer, 2nd Lieut. E. F.** | M. April 23/17. |
| 4 A. III | Abbott, Tom. 203318. (8119.) | M. April 23/17. |
| 4 A. | Allerston, C. L. 200966. | M. April 23/17. |
| 4 A. I | Boothby, H. S. 203475. (8227.) | M. April 23/17. |
| 4 A. | Bridge, Robert. 202056. | M. April 23/17. |
| 4 A. | Brown, O. 203075. | M. April 23/17. |
| 4 A. | Charlesworth, J. H. 200896. | M. April 23/17. |
| 4 A. | Charlton, James. 203116. (Fr. Yorks Hussars, 6974.) | M. April 23/17. |
| 4 A. | Cockbill, W. 201063. | M. April 23/17. |
| 4 A. | Cook, A. 200782. | M. April 23/17. |
| 4 A. IV | Cooke, Harry Isitt. 200506. | M. April 23/17. |
| 4 A. | Dickenson, A. 201316. | M. April 23/17. |
| 4 A. II | Elliott, Andrew Maurice. 203082. | M. April 23/17. |
| ‡4 A. | Emmett, C.-S.-M. G. E. 200107. | M. April 23/17. |
| 4 A. | Fenton, T. 201068. | M. April 23/17. |
| 4 A. III | Galbraith, G. R. 201574. | M. April 23/17. |
| 4 A. II | Grassby, L.-Cpl. J. 3839. | M. April 23/17. |
| ‡4 A. | Grayburn, John. 4088. | M. Nov. 17/16. R/Enq. |
| 4 A. | Hague, H. 200863. (3001.) | M. April 23/17. |
| 4 A. | Holland, A. 201324. | M. April 23/17. |
| 4 A. | Hutchinson, C. E. 203108. | M. April 23/17. |
| 4 A. | Jordan, C. 201325. | M. April 23/17. |
| 4 A. | Lolley, Geo. Alf. 202799. | M. April 23/17. |
| 4 A. I | Morley, F. 200578. (2385.) | M. April 23/17. |
| 4 A. | Murrey, H. 201116. | M. April 23/17. |
| 4 A. | Nicholls, Sergt. J. W. 200119. | M. April 23/17. |
| ‡4 A. | Norton, W. 201790. | M. April 23/17. |
| 4 A. | Pinder, G. 200990. | M. April 23/17. |

**Yorkshire Regiment, East—contd.**

*B.E.F.*

| | | | |
|---|---|---|---|
| 4 A. | | Ralph, T. W. 203109. | M. April 23/17. |
| *4 A. | I | Reed, Edward. 201918. (5304.) | M. April 23/17. |
| 4 A. | | Roebuck, A. 201152. (3750.) | M. April 23/17. |
| 4 A. | I | Shaw, Harry. 202804. (6651.) | M. April 23/17. |
| 4 A. | | Spinks, G. R. 202880. | M. April 23/17. |
| 4 A. | | Stainton, John Wm. 201243. (3905.) | M. April 23/17. |
| 4 A. | | Teal, E. 201783. | M. April 23/17. |
| 4 A. | | Tindall, F. 201507. | M. April 23/17. |
| 4 A. | IV | Ulliott, Alva. 203477. | M. April 23/17. |
| *4 A. | II | Westoby, Harry. 200275. | M. April 23/17. |
| 4 A. | | Woodhall, Chas. Edw. 201173. | M. April 23/17. |
| 4 A. | | Wright, A. E. 201851. | M. April 23/17. |
| *4 A. | IV | Wright, Stanley. 201390. (4256.) | Unoff. M. April 23/17. |
| 4 B. | | Austin, W. 203576. | M. April 23/17. |
| 4 B. | VIII | Beaumont, Geo. 203514. | M. April 23/17. |
| 4 B. | VII | Best, E 200869. (3015.) | M. April 23/17. |
| 4 B. | | Bower, E. 202811. | M. April 23/17. |
| 4 B. | | Brackenbury, F. 201826. | M. April 23/17. |
| 4 B. | | Bray, J. 200579. | M. April 23/17. |
| 4 B. | VI | Broadbent, Thos. Hy. 202985. (6841.) | M. April 23/17. |
| 4 B. | | Brown, J. E. 201323. | M. April 23/17. |
| 4 B. | | Brown, Robt. 200504. (2262.) | M. April 23/17. |
| 4 B. | | Bullock, J. W. 202905. | M. April 23/17. |
| 4 B. | | Chalmers, Jas. 201688. (4819.) | M. April 23/17. |
| *4 B. | VIII | Corlett, L.-Cpl. Alex. Basil. 200175. | M. April 23/17. |
| 4 B. | | Corner, R. 200430. | M. April 23/17. |
| 4 B. | | Cowling, G. W. 200954. | M. April 23/17. |
| 4 B. | | Dick, A. 200732. | M. April 23/17. |
| 4 B. | | Farrah, Cpl. W. 200242. | M. April 23/17. |
| 4 B. | | Gosley, J. R. 203084. | M. April 23/17. |
| 4 B. | VII | Graham, C. A. 201614. | M. April 23/17. |
| 4 B. | | Grassby, L.-Cpl. J. E. 201199. | M. April 23/17. |
| 4 B. | | Hamshaw, J. 200305. | M. April 23/17. |
| 4 B. | | Hanson, A. E. 201334 | M. April 23/17. |
| 4 B. | | Horsley, W. 202865. | M. April 23/17. |
| 4 B. | | Jordan, G. 201313. | M. April 23/17. |
| 4 B. | | Kemp, C. 201751. | M. April 23/17. |
| 4 B. | | Kirkwood, F. A. 200572. | M. April 23/17. |
| 4 B. | VI | Lawrence, W. 201224. | M. April 23/17. |
| 4 B. | VIII | Markham, Geo. Emmerson. 201083. (3636.) | M. April 23/17. |
| 4 B. | | Mowforth, G. 202868. | M. April 23/17. |
| 4 B. | VI | Newstead, James. 202899. | M. April 23/17. |
| 4 B. | | Nudd, Sergt. W. 201487. | M. April 23/17. |
| 4 B. | V | Pearson, Herbert. 201593. | M. April 23/17. |
| 4 B. | | Pickering, G. 200281. | M. April 23/17. |
| 4 B. | | Polly, F. C. 200212. | M. April 23/17. |
| 4 B. | | Shaw, W. 200943. | M. April 23/17. |
| ‡4 B. | | Smith, L.-Cpl. E. 2892. | K. Sept. 15/16. Unoff. W. Sept. 18/1 Conf. asked. R/Enq. |
| 4 B. | | Trotter, E. 201899. | M. April 23/17. |
| 4 B. | VII | Wheelhouse, H. 203305. | W. and M. April 23/17. |
| 4 B. | | Wilby, T. M. 203058. | M. April 23/17. |
| 4 C. | | Allison, G. 202983. | M. April 23/17. |
| 4 C. | | Archer, H. A. 200883. | M. April 23/17. |
| 4 C. | | Barratt, G. W. 220074. | M. April 23/17. |
| 4 C. | | Belfield, W. H. 220134. | M. April 23/17. |
| 4 C. | | Bogg, L.-Cpl. Jas. Ernest. 200312. | K. April 23/17. Det.D./B |
| 4 C. | | Cameron, J. W. 203102. | M. April 23/17. |

**Yorkshire Regiment, East**—contd.

## *B.E.F.*

2/4 C. Chaplin, A. W. 202911. — W. and M. April 23/17.
4 C. Cullum, F. A. 220054. — M. April 23/17.
4 C. Cummongs, R. 201704. — M. April 23/17.
4 C. or D. Daines, A. B. 203007. (6863.) — M. April 23/17.
4 C. Gamwell, A. 200929. — M. April 23/17.
4 C. Garrick, H. 203148. — M. April 23/17.
4 C. Gorbett, G. 201537. — M. April 23/17.
4 C. Hall, F. C. 203201. — M. April 23/17.
4 C. IX Hammond, Harry. 220158. — M. April 23/17.
4 C. IX Harrison, Joseph. 201894. (5236.) — M. April 23/17.
4 C. Holliday, T. W. 220123. — K. April 23/17. Det.D./B.
4 C. Hopper, W. 203141. — M. April 23/17.
4 C. X Kippax, Dan. 202170. (5956.) — M. April 23/17.
4 C. Marshall, J. W. 201827. — M. April 23/17.
4 C. Mawer, H. 201820. — M. April 23/17.
4 C. XII Molyneux, Benjamin. 203070. — M. April 23/17.
4 C. Newman, L. 201315. — M. April 23/17.
4 C. Nicholson, F. R 203132. — M. April 23/17.
4 C. XII Norris, C. 201508. — M. April 23/17.
4 C. XI Parker, E. G. 203139. — M. April 23/17.
4 C. Reynolds, A. B. 200041. (541.) — M. April 23/17.
4 C. Reynolds, Cpl. E. 201118. (3704.) — M. April 23/17.
4 C. XII Siddle, John. 201191. (3828.) — M. April 23/17.
4 C. IX Smith, Oliver. 7992. — M. April 23/17.
4 C. Starkey, H. 203049. — M. April 23/17.
4 C. XII Thurston, W. 220047. — M. April 23/17.
4 C. Towers, Wm. 220147. (4706.) — M. April 23/17.
4 C. XII Walburn, Ivan. 203100. (6957.) — M. April 23/17.
4 D. XV Addison Harry. 200492. — M. April 23/17.
4 D. Branton, C. R. 200809. — M. April 23/17.
4 D. Crowhurst, A. 201400. — M. April 23/17.
4 D. Dent, Cpl. G. A. 201010. — M. April 23/17.
4 D. XIII Dukes, Stanley. 203004. — M. April 23/17.
2/4 D. Fincham, W. 202962. — Unoff. M. about July 3/17.
4 D. Glew, Sergt. A. 201565. — M. April 23/17.
4 D. Green, S. J. 202952. — M. April 23/17.
4 D. Habbershaw, Dennis. 201524. — M. April 23/17.
4 D. Harper, H. 200294. — M. April 23/17.
4 D. Hutchinson, G. 201636. — M. April 23/17.
4 D. McCrum, G. 203214. — M. April 23/17.
4 D. H.Q. Sigs. McDonald, L.-Cpl. Alex. 203156. (7014.) — M. April 23/17.
4 D. XV Mitchell, Eli. 201630. (4707.) — M. April 23/17.
4 D. Moor, A. 200763. — M. April 23/17.
4 D. Newell, L.-Cpl. A. 200780. — M. April 23/17.
4 D. Porter, H. 200735. — M. April 23/17.
4 D. Proudley, James. 4973. — M. April 23/17.
4 D. Scarsbrook, A. 203190. — M. April 23/17.
4 D. Schorah, J. 220143. — M. April 23/17.
4 D. Sherburn, W. 201737. — M. April 23/17.
2/4 D. XIII Smelt, W. 201411. — Unoff. M. June 27-29/17
4 D. Smith, Arthur. 203111. (6069 and formerly 3136, Yorks Hussars.) — M. April 23/17.
4 D. XVI Stephenson, Percy. 200898. (3096.) — M. April 23/17.
4 D. Stevenson, R. 220142. — M. April 23/17.
4 D. Taylor, A. 203051. — M. April 23/17.
4 D. Tindall, J. W. 220138. — M. April 23/17.
4 D. Tomlinson, A. 200713. — M. April 23/17.
4 D. Townend, A. 201528. — M. April 23/17.

**Yorkshire Regiment, East—contd.**

*B.E.F.*

4 D. Trowell, G. W. 201821. M. April 23/17.
4 D. Sig. S. Wallis, William. 220136. M. April 23/17.
4 D. Watts, H. P. 203061. M. April 23/17.
‡4 D. White, L.-Cpl. J. 200165. W. and M. April 23/17.
4 D. Wilkinson, W. 201434. M. April 23/17.
4 D. Winn, J. 20056. M. April 23/17.
*7 **Goldthorpe, 2nd Lieut. A. F.** K. May 12/17. Det.D./B
7 **Rerrie, M.C., Lt. E. S. (Fr. 3rd.)** W. and M. May 12/17.
*7 A. IV Benson, J. 201377. M. May 14/17.
‡7 A. Brand, H. E. 33456. M. May 14/17.
‡7 A. Colgrave, Cpl. M. 201670. M. May 13/17.
7 A. Crisp, C. 9012. M. April 24/17.
‡7 A. Dann, C. 32991. W. and M. May 13/17.
‡7 A. Farmes, J. 11591. M. May 13/17.
‡7 A. Hinchliffe, J. W. 203784. M. May 12/17.
*7 A. II Mills, Joseph. 30802. M. May 13/17.
*7 A. II Partington, J. 22640. K. May 12/17. Det.D./B.
7 A. II Pearson, James A. 35064. M. May 14/17.
‡7 A. Rusholme, W. A. 23643. M. May 14/17.
*7 B. Allison, Arthur. 33093. W. and M. May 12/17.
*7 B. Baren, T. 36662. W. and M. May 13/17.
‡7 B. Barnett, A.-Sergt. L. 11704. M. May 12/17.
7 B. Bateson, A. E. 33212. M. April 23/17.
*7 B. V Binnington, W. H. 24464. M. May 12/17.
*7 B. Brealey, A. 26002. Unoff. M. April 23—May 3/17.
‡7 B. Brealey, A. 467. M. May 12/17.
‡7 B. Burton, William. 16915. M. May 12/17.
7 B. Coupland, T. W. 22752. M. Nov. 8/16. R/Enq.
‡7 B. Cox, P. 16293. M. May 12/17.
7 B. Davis, Thomas. 13/1421. M. Nov. 5/16.
7 B. Eccles, Cpl. James. 6919. M. May 13/17.
*7 B. V Holdsworth, H. H. 13991. M. May 12/17.
7 B. Jameson, A. 28758. M. April 24/17.
7 B. VI Johnson, Albert. 28763. M. April 23/17.
7 B. Knaggs, John Wm. 22707. M. April 24/17.
‡7 B. Parkin, L.-Cpl. Willie. 7135. K. Nov. 5/16. Det.D./B. R/Enq.
‡7 B. Pyburn, J. 15116. M. May 12/17.
7 B. VI Roche, Patrick. 28283. M. April 23/17.
‡7 B. Rose, C. 27416. M. May 12/17.
7 B. Sillis, J. 23895. M. April 24/17.
7 B. Taylor, C. W. 28754. M. April 24/17.
‡7 B. Wiseman, J. G. 31218. M. May 12/17.
*7 B. VI Wood, Frederick. 61. (Fr. 14th.) M. May 12/17.
7 C. XII Armitage, C. 33422. W. and M. April 24/17.
7 C. Bailey, Cpl. J. 13053. M. Nov. 5/16. R/Enq.
7 C. Barber, F. V. 30928. M. Nov. 5/16. R/Enq.
7 C. Collins, J. 9/23094. K. Nov. 7/16. Det.D./B. R/Enq.
*7 C. Deake, Jabey B. 37867. M. May 12/17.
‡7 C. Ellis, J. R. 28335. W. and M. May 12/17.
‡7 C. Hunter, S. 33428. M. May 12/17.
7 C. Malone, J. 33116. M. May 12/17.
7 C. X Martin, W. E. 34262. M. May 13/17.
‡7 C. Normanton, E. 28322. M. May 13/17.
‡7 C. Throp, Samuel. 28309. M. May 12/17.
7 C. X Tythe, W. 34267. M. April 21/17.
‡7 C. Vant, Thomas. 28346. K. April 24/17. Det.D./B.
7 C. IX Westerdale, George Henry. M. April 9/17.
‡7 D. XIV Buttery, L.-Cpl. R. 24857. M. May 12/17.
‡7 D. Coils, William. 14165. M. May 12/17.

**Yorkshire Regiment, East—contd.**

*B.E.F.*

| | | |
|---|---|---|
| ‡7 D. | Conway, J. J. 16466. | W. and M. April 24/17. |
| 7 D. XIV | Dinsdale, Albert. 34949. | M. May 14/17. |
| ‡7 D. | Garfitt, W. 1115. | M. May 14/17. |
| 7 D. | Giblin, L.-Cpl. Ernest. 14360. | M. May 12/17. |
| ‡7 D. | Inglis, J. 1052. | M. May 12/17. |
| ‡7 D. | Lanham, G. 30887. | M. May 12/17. |
| ‡7 D. | Owen, P. E. 27718. | M. May 12/17. |
| 7 D. | Owens, Frank Ephraim. 12262. | M. May 12/17. |
| 7 D. XV | Parkinson, Walter E. 30903. | M. May 12/17. |
| ‡7 D. | Spittle, H. 34265. | M. May 12/17. |
| 8 | **Bibby, 2nd Lieut. J. M.** (Fr. Liverpools.) | M. May 3/17. |
| 8 | **Dalton, 2nd Lieut. H. M.** | M., bel. K. May 3/17. |
| 8 D. | **McIntyre, 2nd Lieut. F.** | M. May 3/17. |
| ‡8 A. | Appleyard. 32996. | M. May 3/17. |
| ‡8 A. | Boiks, G. 10/472. | M. May 3/17. |
| ‡8 A. | Cline, J. 28805. | M. May 3/17. |
| ‡8 A. II | Curtis, John Robert. 15744. | M. May 3/17. |
| ‡8 A. | Johnson, W. 9108. | M. May 3/17. |
| 8 A. III | King, C. E. 28802. | W. and M. May 3/17. |
| 8 A. I' | Parker, George W. 11259. | M. Nov. 13/16. R/Enq. |
| *8 A. IV | Pulford, G. R. 31318. (24511.) | W. and M. May 3-4/17. |
| *8 A. I | Rowe, Cpl. H. 18639. | W. and M. May 3-4/17. |
| ‡8 A. | Salmon, Sergt. Michael. 16483. | W. and M. May 3-4/17. |
| 8 A. I | Tulip, James. 33376. | M. May 3/17. |
| ‡8 A. | Walker, G. 21941. | M. May 3/17. |
| 8 A. | Wesson, Edward Sargison. 28804. | M. May 3/17. |
| ‡8 A. | Witty, E. 28477. | M. May 3/17. |
| 8 B. M.G.S. | Coe, Leonard. 31389. | M. May 3/17. |
| 8 B. | Hanson, O. H. 25116. | M. April 13/17. |
| ‡8 B. | Littledyke, G. 28530. | W. and M. May 11/17. |
| 8 B. V | McCann, J. R. 28440. | M. May 3/17. |
| ‡8 B. | Thorpe, A. 19862. | M. May 3/17. |
| ‡8 B. V | Warrener, L.-Cpl. W. F. 28457. | M. May 3/17. |
| *8 B. VIII | Wilson, T. W. 24891. | K. Mar. 15/17. Det.D./B. |
| ‡8 B. | Wood, F. 31431. | M. May 3/17. |
| ‡8 C. | Barrett, A. H. 28800. | W. and M. April 23/17. |
| 8 C. | Coventry, H. 14401. | M. May 3/17. |
| 8 C. | Lightfoot, J. 31409. | M. April 9-13/17. |
| 8 C. XII | McGaffin, Harry. 28533. | M. May 3/17. |
| ‡8 C. XI M.G.S. | Musson, Sidney. 8689. | W. and M. May 3/17. |
| ‡8 C. or D. | Ogilvy, Wm. Eyre. 31543. (38129.) | Unoff. M. June 10/17. |
| 8 C. XI | O'Shaughnessy, Percy. 28486. | W. and M. April 9-17. |
| 8 C. XI | Saul, James. 31286. | W. and M. April 9-13/17. |
| 8 D. XIV | Booth, Edw. 19945. | W. and M. April 9-13/17. |
| ‡8 D. | Clarke, T. C. 16942. | M. May 3/17. |
| *8 D. XIII | Coggrave, F. 5195. | M. Nov. 13/16. R/Enq. |
| 8 D. | Colling, Geo. 24821. | M. May 3/17. |
| 8 D. M.G.S. | Conmy, A. 28501. | M. May 3/17. |
| ‡8 D. | Foster, F. 201903. | M. May 3/17. |
| ‡8 D. | Horne, L.-Cpl. L. 27972. | M. May 3/17. |
| ‡8 D. | Wilson, J. 27305. | W. and M. May 3/17. |
| 8 ? I.T.M. | Holmes, Geo. Foden. 27071. (8th Bgde.) | M. May 3/17. |
| 10 | **Addy, Capt. J. C.** | M. May 3/17. |
| 10 | **Stringer, 2nd Lieut. D.** | W. and M. May 3/17. |
| 10 B. | **Webster, 2nd Lt. A. C.** (Fr. 4th.) | M. May 3/17. |
| 10 A. L.G.S. | Abba, Harold. 483. | M. May 3/17. |
| 10 A. | Atkinson, Bn. Bomber Frank. 197. (Fr. H.Q. Co.) | M. May 3/17. |

**Yorkshire Regiment, East—contd.**

## *B.E.F.*

| | | |
|---|---|---|
| ‡10 A. | Baker, F. 11963. (Fr. 7th.) | M. May 3/17. |
| ‡10 A. | Baker, H. 28036. | M. May 3/17. |
| *10 A. IV | Bancroft, David. 23939. | M. May 3/17. |
| 10 A. | Brown, Sigr. Herbert. 468. | M. May 3/17. |
| 10 A. I | Cain, W. 25392. (Fr. 3rd.) | M. May 3/17. |
| 10 A. II | Chapman, Alfred. 33213. | M. May 3/17. |
| ‡10 A. | Deighton, E. 3/26354. | M. May 3/17. |
| ‡10 A. | Ellis, S. 28050. | M. May 3/17. |
| 10 A. I | Elson, H. J. 37915. | M. May 3/17. |
| ‡10 A. | Forte, H. 220032. | M. May 3/17. |
| 10 A. | Harrison, Bomber Wilfred M. 503. | M. May 3/17. |
| *10 A. II | Heeson, W. E. 3/33095. | M. May 3/17. |
| 10 A. I | Kirkby, Fredk. Wm. 33115. | M. May 3/17. |
| 10 A. | Lee, Wm. 22121. | M. May 3/17. |
| 10 A. | Loughorn, Fred. 1184. | M. May 3/17. |
| ‡10 A. | Messenger, A. E. 1233. | M. May 3/17. |
| 10 A. III | Pinder, Noel Augustine. 27777. | M. May 3/17. |
| ‡10 A. | Nicholas, B. C. 30314. | M. May 3/17. |
| *10 A. | Stewart, Wm. 22914. (Fr. 3rd.) | M. May 3/17. |
| 10 A. | Turner, Cpl. Harold. 400. | M. May 3/17. |
| 10 A. IV | Tuxworth, John Percy. 399. | M. May 3/17. |
| ‡10 B. | Annis, R. E. 33345. (Fr. 3rd.) | M. May 3/17. |
| ‡10 B. | Bateman, H. 33105. (Fr. 3rd.) | M. May 3/17. |
| ‡10 B. | Baxter, J. 22035. | M. May 3/17. |
| ‡10 B. | Clark, J. W. 1286. | M. May 3/17. |
| 10 B. VIII | Cook, John Thos. 28046. | W. and M. May 3/17. |
| 10 B. V | Cresswell, Wm. Jos. 18994. | M. May 3/17. |
| ‡10 B. | Dunn, J. H. 37902. | M. May 3/17. |
| ‡10 B. | Eastwood, H. 36319. | M. May 3/17. |
| *10 B. VII | Fletcher, Z. 18906. | M. May 3/17. |
| ‡10 B. VIII | Fox, D. P. 220038. | M. May 3/17. |
| ‡10 B. | Frith, S. D. 6594. | M. May 3/17. |
| 10 B. V | Fussey, Harry. 33129. | M. May 3/17. |
| 10 B. VIII | Goldspink, Hy. Dalton. 28054. | M. May 3/17. |
| 10 B. V | Hotson, R. 21671. (Fr. 9th.) | M. May 3/17. |
| *10 B. | Jackson, L.-Cpl. Fredk. (Known as Peter.) 627. | M. May 3/17. |
| 10 B. V | Jagger, Frank. 18926. | M. May 3/17. |
| ‡10 B. | Jubb, R. 220041. | M. May 3/17. |
| ‡10 B. | McNally, Cpl. J. 220003. | M. May 3/17. |
| ‡10 B. VIII | Marritt, C. E. 220643. | M. May 3/17. |
| *10 B. | Martindale, Percy. 672. | M. June 22/17. |
| 10 B. VII | Matthews, George. [illegible] | M. Unoff. W. May 3/17. |
| *10 B. M.G.S. | Morley, Jos. Hry. 1380. | M. May 3/17. |
| ‡10 B. | Oldfield, F. 18745. | M. May 3/17. |
| 10 B. | Powell, T. A. 574. | M. May 3/17. |
| ‡10 B. | Runkee, C. 28234. | M. May 3/17. |
| 10 B. | Simpkins, C. 583. (Fr. H.Q.) | M. May 3/17. |
| 10 B. VIII | Smith, Arthur. 34990. | M. May 3/17. |
| 10 B. M.G.S. | Smith, L.-Cpl. Richard Henry. 1231. | M. May 3/17. |
| 10 B. VII | Southcott, S. C. 26084. (Fr. 9th.) | M. May 3/17. |
| *10 B. VIII | Summers, Herbert. 667. | M. May 3/17. |
| ‡10 B. | Walters, C. H. 18978. | M. May 3/17. |
| 10 B. V | Wilkes, Richard Edwin. 3/18898. (18998.) | M. May 3/17. |
| ‡10 B. | Winter, G. 1186. | M. May 3/17. |
| 10 C. | Balmforth, Christian. 35013. | M. May 3/17. |

**Yorkshire Regiment, East—contd.**

*B.E.F.*

‡10 C. Blackshaw, Cpl. S. 36356. M. May 3/17.
10 C. XI Coates, Edward J. 35028. K. May 3/17. Det.D./B.
‡10 C. Crowston, E. 1050. M. May 3/17.
*10 C. Dawson, A.-L.-Sgt. Ernest Wood. 92. M. May 3/17.
*10 C. Guest, W. Edward. 12033. (Fr. 7th.) M. May 3/17.
10 C. XI Haigh, Ernest Sylvester. 35084. M. May 3/17.
10 C. Harrison, F. W. 306. M. May 4-5/17.
*10 C. X Hawkins, B. W. 3/25365. M. May 3/17.
‡10 C. Holness, Albert. 36332. M. May 3/17.
‡10 C. Johnson, H. 532. M. May 3/17.
‡10 C. Linsley, R. 65. M. May 3/17.
‡10 C. Miller, E. 26583. M. May 3/17.
10 C. Schofield, Fred. 18919. M. May 3/17.
*10 C. Seckerson, L. 25353. M. May 3/17.
10 C. X Simon, H. S. 21806. (Fr. 9th.) M. May 3/17.
10 C. XI Spencer, George. 35073. M. May 3/17.
10 D. Cleary, Walter Jas. 958. M. May 3/17.
‡10 D. Clubley, Sergt. B. A. 723. M. May 3/17.
‡10 D. Keenan, L.-Cpl. B. 25371. M. May 3/17.
‡10 D. Kirkman, H. 118. M. May 3/17.
‡10 D. Lindley, G. E. 6652. (Fr. 2nd.) M. May 3/17.
10 D. XVI McBride, J. Taylor. 931. M. May 3/17.
*10 D. Pickles, John. 18902. (Fr. 3rd.) M. May 3/17.
‡10 D. Scrubbs, A. 26099. (Fr. 9th.) M. May 3/17.
11 **Ekins, 2nd Lieut. W. R. (Fr. 3rd.)** M. May 3/17.
11 **Hall, Lieut. A. B.** W. and M. May 3/17.
11 **Hutchinson, 2nd Lieut. B.** W. and M. May 3/17.
11 D. **Purll, 2nd Lieut. W. A. G.** M. May 3/17.
11 A. **Reeve, Capt. E. W.** M., bel. K. May 3/17.
11 **Staveley, Lieut. H. S.** W. and M. May 3/17.
11 **Woolcott, 2nd Lieut. R.** M. May 3/17.
‡11 A. Clare, J. E. 9867. M. May 3/17.
11 A. I Crossley, H. 36516. M. May 3/17.
11 A. Loftus, Cpl. Frank Leslie. 17596. M. May 3/17.
‡11 A. Sutton, A.-Cpl. H. 11980. M. May 3/17.
‡11 A. Willcox, A. 1219. M. May 3/17.
*11 B. Barker, George Thos. 1053. M. May 3/17.
11 B. VI Bocock, W. K. 28107. M. May 3/17.
*11 B. VIII Cooper, J. 36. (Fr. 14th.) M. May 3/17.
11 B. Farnill, Cpl. F. W. 728. M. May 3/17.
‡11 B. Golder, J. H. 3/26983. M. May 3/17.
11 B. VII Ingham, Charles R. 14187. M. May 3/17.
‡11 B. Newlove, J. 712. M. May 3/17.
‡11 B. Rogers, S. 14/83. M. May 3/17.
11 B. Shaw, Frank. 1089. M. May 3/17.
‡11 B. Thomas, A. K. 98. M. May 3/17.
‡11 B. Ward, A. 936. M. May 3/17.
11 C. Bennet, L.-Cpl. James. 36507. M. May 3/17.
‡11 C. Bishop, Cpl. W. 36482. M. May 3/17.
‡11 C. Briggs, G. E. 526. M. May 3/17.
‡11 C. Denman, W. 14/76. M. May 3/17.
*11 C. Duffy, James. 3/7253. M. May 3/17.
‡11 C. Edson, L.-Cpl. W. H. 25. M. May 3/17.
11 C. XII Evans, Harry G. 36462. M. May 3/17.
11 C. XI Farley, Wm. Dyer. 36454. M. May 3/17.
11 C. XI Farmer, F. 14/44. M. May 3/17.
11 C. Field, Richard. 934. M. May 3/17.
*11 C. IX Fulker, F. T. 37918. M. May 3/17.
*11 C. Hart, Sergt. R. E. 704. M. May 3/17.

**Yorkshire Regiment, East—contd.**

*B.E.F.*

11 C. X Heslop, G. H. 271. M. May 3/17.
*11 C. Jackson, Alfred. 1126. M. May 3/17.
‡11 C. Little, Septimus G. 28127. M. May 3/17.
‡11 C. Lockwood, E. A. 69. M. May 3/17.
11 C. Loft, Thomas. 1183. M. May 3/17.
‡11 C. Mallender, A. 1351. M. May 3/17.
11 C. X Morris, J. 19371. M. May 3/17.
*11 C. IX Ranby, L.-Cpl. H. 25536. M. May 3/17.
11 C. Raspin, L.-Cpl. F. 474. M. May 3/17.
‡11 C. I.T.M. Richardson, Harold. 103. (93 Bde. 2 Batty.) M. May 3/17.
*11 C. Robertson, James Henry. 1400. M. May 3/17.
‡11 C. Robinson, E. 28134. M. May 3/17.
11 C. Sills, Sig. H. 37338. M. May 3/17.
‡11 C. Storey, W. B. 10/1418. M. May 3/17.
11 C. Thurnell, A. R. 1270. M. May 3/17.
11 C. Turner, Jas. Harold. 1429. M. May 3/17.
‡11 D. Aisthorpe, F. T. 28141. M. May 3/17.
‡11 D. Ancliff, J. W. 28142. M. May 3/17.
‡11 D. Bales, A.-Sergt. J. H. 396. M. May 3/17.
*11 D. XVI Clarke, L.-Cpl. Chas. Fredk. 33062. M. May 3/17.
11 D. XVI Cleminson, A. E. 36424. M. May 3/17.
‡11 D. Elliott, A. E. 34632. M. May 3/17.
11 D. XV Evans, D. Campbell. 36433. M. May 3/17.
11 D. XV Fryer, C. J. 36435. M. May 3/17.
*11 D. XV Gardner, Cpl. W. K. 11/344. M. May 3/17.
‡11 D. Gould, A. E. 28147. M. May 3/17.
‡11 D. Grimwood, C. 706. M. May 3/17.
11 D. XV Hemming, Ed. Geo. 36539. M. May 3/17.
11 D. Hill, Harold. 28150. (Fr. 2/5 Linc.) M. May 3/17.
‡11 D. Ingram, E. 28151. M. May 3/17.
11 D. XIV Kennedy, H. 14/169. M. May 3/17.
‡11 D. Lee, F. 655. (Fr. 12th.) M. May 3/17.
11 D. Leonard, A. H. 28153. (Late 3rd Lincolns, 7940.) M. May 3/17.
‡11 D. Levesley, J. 684. M. May 3/17.
‡11 D. Ling, L.-Cpl. W. R. 50. M. May 3/17.
11 D. Mills, Sgt. Alfred. 11/605. M. May 3/17.
‡11 D. Nurse, C. 1065. M. May 3/17.
‡11 D. Parkinson, Cpl. E. 741. M. May 3/17.
11 D. XVI Russell, Fred. 36521. M. May 3/17.
‡11 D. Settrington, T. H. 26497. (Fr. 3rd.) M. May 3/17.
11 D. Smith, Fred. 1208. M. May 3/17.
11 D. Smith, Wm. Thomas. 1392. M. May 2/17.
11 D. Swinden, T. 612. M. May 3/17.
‡11 D. Thompson, G. L. 27289. M. May 3/17.
‡11 D. Thompson, H. 1268. M. May 3/17.
‡11 D. Thurloe, A.-L.-Cpl. R. F. 22500. M. May 3/17.
‡11 D. Watson, F. W. 1376. M. May 3/17.
11 D. XV Westcott, Harry. 36465. M. May 3/17.
‡11 D. Wilcox, A. 1219. M. May 3/17.
11 D. Willey, G. 1222. M. May 3/17.
‡11 H.Q. Bell, Sig. W. 36357. (Fr. D. Co.) M. May 3/17.
12 **Carrall, 2nd Lieut. J. E.** W. and M. May 3/17.
12 **Hall, 2nd Lieut. J. S.** M. May 3/17.
12 B. **Hignett, 2nd Lieut. W. R.** M. May 3/17.
12 **Holt, 2nd Lieut. W.** M. May 3/17.
12 **Jennings, 2nd Lieut. H. C.** M. May 3/17.
*12 A. Baron, J. W. 313. (Fr. 13th.) M. May 3/17.

**Yorkshire Regiment, East—contd.**

## *B.E.F.*

|  |  |  |  |
|---|---|---|---|
| ‡12 A. | Bethway, J. H. 28090. | M. May 3/17. | |
| 12 A. II | Bexfield, A. E. 13483. | M. May 3/17. | |
| ‡12 A. II | Braithwaite, J. W. 27077. | M. May 3/17. | |
| ‡12 A. | Brown, F. 57. | M. May 3/17. | |
| ‡12 A. | Brown, L.-Sergt. J. A. 220004. | M. May 3/17. | |
| 12 A. III | Craggy, Clarence Wm. 329. | M. Nov. 13/16. | R/Enq. |
| ‡12 A. | Dalton, I. J. 17945. | M. June 25/17. | |
| 12 A. | Edmunds, T. P. 510. | M. Nov. 13/16. | R/Enq. |
| ‡12 A. | Eley, E. 879. | M. May 3/17. | |
| *12 A. III | Ellis, F. 1446. (Fr. 10th.) | M. May 3/17. | |
| 12 A. II | Francis, Ernest Albert. 36559. | M. May 3/17. | |
| 12 A. | Freear, Richard O. 170. (Fr. 14th.) | M. Nov. 13/16. | |
| ‡12 A. | Jameson, J. W. 9912. | M. May 3/17. | |
| ‡12 A. | Kemp, G. W. 1454. | M. May 3/17. | |
| ‡12 A. | Lockwood, H. 28214. | M. May 3/17. | |
| 12 A. IV | Neall, George. 842. | M. May 3/17. | |
| ‡12 A. | Payne, S. H. 36616. | M. May 3/17. | |
| ‡12 A. | Spafford, E. 299. | M. May 3/17. | |
| 12 A. | Sutton, William. 36621. | M. May 3/17. | |
| 12 A. II | Swain, Robert. 36560. | M. May 3/17. | |
| 12 A. III | Turner, Joe. 36719. | M. May 3/17. | |
| *12 A. III | Wakefield, A. P. 36702. | M. May 3/17. | |
| 12 A. II | Warren, John B. 36693. | M. May 3/17. | |
| ‡12 A. II | Webb, Cpl. Fred Arthur. 16742. | M. May 3/17. | |
| 12 A. IV | Wilkinson, Tom. 166. (Fr. 14th.) | M. May 3/17. | |
| *12 A. | Wray, H. 481. | M. May 3/17. | |
| ‡12 B. | Anderson, T. 1156. | M. May 3/17. | |
| 12 B. VII | Brandon, E. 36577. | M. May 3/17. | |
| ‡12 B. | Bulman, Cpl. H. 1381. (Fr. 13th.) | M. May 3/17. | |
| 12 B. VI | Cooper, E. G. 25372. | M. May 3/17. | |
| 12 B. | Cullen, Thomas Hugh. 36726. | M. May 3/17. | |
| 12 B. VII | Dimmack, Joseph. 303. | M. May 3/17. | |
| ‡12 B. | Gregory, A.-Cpl. W. 7723. | M. May 3/17. | |
| ‡12 B. | Hill, Cpl. A. 36734. | M. May 3/17. | |
| ‡12 B. | Hodgson, J. A. 378. | M. May 3/17. | |
| 12 B. V | Johnson, Harold Wilfred. 36568. | M. May 3/17. | |
| 12 B. | Kirkwood, Ernest. 733. | M. May 3/17. | |
| 12 B. | Larvin, Thos. Henry. 783. | M. Nov. 13/16. | R/Enq. |
| 12 B. V | Marshall, Robt. 36723. | M. May 3/17. | |
| 12 B. | Moody, Harry. 36630. | M. May 3/17. | |
| 12 B. M.G.S. | Moulds, Alfred. 231. | M. May 3/17. | |
| 12 B. V | Needham, Robt. McCallum. 17925. | M. May 3/17. | |
| *12 B. VII | Norfolk, J. 36737. | M. May 3/17. | |
| 12 B. V | Osgerby, F. 222. (Fr. 14th.) | M. May 3/17. | |
| *12 B. VII | Peck, Ernest Tom. 33221. | M. May 3/17. | |
| 12 B. | Pindar, Cpl. Wm. 824. | M. May 3/17. | |
| 12 B. VIII | Potter, David. 33092. | M. May 3/17. | |
| ‡12 B. | Rogerson, F. 36576. | M. May 3/17. | |
| 12 B. | Russell, L.-Cpl. Charles 18469. | M. May 3/17. | |
| 12 B. VIII | Smith, Arthur. 33024. | M. May 3/17. | |
| 12 B. VI | Thornton, Thos. 33140. | M. May 3/17. | |
| *12 B. V | Tripcony, Ernest. 36721. | M. May 3/17. | |
| ‡12 B. | Wileman, P. 36684. | M. May 3/17. | |
| ‡12 B. | Wright, J. 35083. | M. May 3/17. | |
| 12 C. | Arnitt, Walter. 37871. | M. May 3/17. | |
| *12 C. or D. | Ashby, Harold. 21108. | M. May 3/17. | |
| ‡12 C. IX | Bamford, James Thos. 37872. | M. May 3/17. | |
| 12 C. IX | Barker, Joseph. 37873. | M. May 3/17. | |
| ‡12 C. | Blagg, H. 1470. | M. May 3/17. | |

**Yorkshire Regiment, East—contd.**

## B.E.F.

‡12 C. Bowran, H. J. 33470. M. May 3/17.
12 C. XII Bradshaw, L.-Cpl. F. 37350. M. May 3/17.
12 C. IX Bunford, Jas. Thos. 37872. M. May 3/17.
*12 C. IX Clapham, Harold. 38058. M. May 3/17.
‡12 C. Clements, J. E. 35209. M. May 3/17.
‡12 C. Coward, A. W. 37876. M. May 3/17.
12 C. XI Deakin, Wilfred. 19640. M. May 3/17.
‡12 C. Dyson, J. 914. M. May 3/17.
12 C. Easingwood, Sergt. Reginald. 316. M. May 3/17.
‡12 C. Farmery, J. 19113. M. May 3/17.
12 C. X Faulkner, Sergt. Harold. 1421. M. May 3/17.
‡12 C. Kemp, T. E. 19461. M. May 3/17.
12 C. Miner, A. 35055. M. May 3/17.
*12 C. Park, Cpl. Edward. 1177. W. and M. May 3/17.
12 C. XII Rojahn, J. 382. M. Nov. 13/16.
*12 C. IX Smith, Lawrence. 21539. M. May 3/17.
12 C. XI Turner, Fredk. 35076. M. May 3/17.
12 C. Turner, S. C. 28196. M. May 3/17.
‡12 C. Utton, H. W. 220013. M. May 3/17.
12 C. IX White, Lewis. 38055. M. May 3/17.
12 C. Willis, J. 4933. M. May 3/17.
12 C. IX Winterburn, Wm. Farrar. 38061. M. May 3/17.
12 D. XIII Ambler, Levi. 38047. M. May 3/17.
*12 D. XIV Bingham, George. 6444. M. April 23/17.
‡12 D. Bothamley, A. 35199. M. May 3/17.
‡12 D. Brookes, W. 1014. M. May 3/17.
12 D. Brumby, Jas. Harold. 38039. M. May 3/17.
*12 D. Bulcock, J. 36755. M. May 3/17.
12 D. Busby, J. 551. M. May 3/17.
‡12 D. Crabtree, W. J. 18994. M. May 3/17.
*12 D. Crabtree, Edgar. 36748. M. May 3/17.
12 D. XIV Cowe, Charles. 19926. M. May 3/17.
12 D. XVI Cox, Joseph James. 36549 M. May 3/17.
‡12 D. Cripps, W. P. 36603. M. May 3/17.
‡12 D. Dean, P. S. 36656. M. May 3/17.
12 D. XVI Doughty, L.-Cpl. Thos. Fredk. 36503 M. May 3/17.
12 D. XIII Freeman, F. L. 38041. M. May 3/17.
‡12 D. Gallaher, J. 6482. M. May 3/17.
*12 D. XIV Gill, Charles. 22064. M. May 3/17.
*12 D. Gray, Harry W. 25986. M. May 3/17.
‡12 D. Hall, G. 518. M. May 3/17.
12 D. Harris, W. 1323. W. and M. Nov. 13/16. R/Enq.
12 D. Harrison, Joshua. 1513. M. Nov. 13/16. R/Enq.
12 D. XIII Jebson, Sigr. John Harold. 34749. M. May 3/17.
‡12 D. Johnston, L.-Cpl. C. 1006. M. May 3/17.
12 D. XV Jones, Jas. 36680. M. May 3/17.
*12 D. XIII Larkin, Saml? 19417. M. May 3/17.
*12 D. XVI McConville, John. 36751. M. May 3/17.
‡12 D. Mercer, J. 37883. M. May 3/17.
*12 D. Mills, Albert. 38042. M. May 3/17.
12 D. Newman, Ernest. 38044. M. May 3/17.
‡12 D. Pashby, W. 21768. M. May 3/17.
‡12 D. Pooley, A. 25660. M. May 3/17.
‡12 D. Richardson, L.-Sergt. J. 180. M. May 3/17.
‡12 D. Sharp, L. G. 38045. (Fr. 3rd.) M. May 3/17.
*12 D. Scarborough, Walter. 23606. M. May 3/17.
‡12 D. Smith, J. T. 26004. M. May 3/17.
*12 D. Stamp, W. H. 24887. M. May 3/17.
‡12 D. Tasker, H. 1414. M. May 3/17.

**Yorkshire Regiment, East—contd.**

*B.E.F.*

| | | |
|---|---|---|
| 12 D. | Wales, W. S. 568. | M. Nov. 13/16. |
| 12 D. XV | Waller, H. 36008. | M. May 3/17. |
| 12 D. | Wallace, L.-Sergt. J. W. 1353. | M. May 3/17. |
| ‡12 D. | Waters, A. P. 772. | M. May 3/17. |
| 12 D. | Whitehead, Stanley. 396. | M. May 3/17. |
| ‡12 D. | Wood, A/Q.-M.-S. 6628. | M. May 3/17. |
| 13 | **Brown, 2nd Lieut. F. D.** | M. Mar. 8/17. |
| 13 A. | Farrah, J. Robert. 877. | W. and M. Nov. 13/16. R/Enq. |
| ‡13 A. | Stork, Thos. 889. | M. Nov. 13/16. R/Enq . |
| ‡13 B. or C. | Jackling, G. 22789. | W. and M. Nov. 5/16. R/Enq. |
| *13 B. | Lilley, S. 571. | M. Nov. 13/16. R/Enq. |
| 13 B. | Syph, J. 796. | M. Nov. 13/16. |
| 13 C. | Collinson, Wm. 1279. | M. Nov. 13/16. R./Enq. |
| ‡13 C. | Jennison, E. 1157. | M. Nov. 13/16. R/Enq. |
| ‡13 C. | Lane, Henry. 28068. (Fr. 4th, 1594.) | M. Nov. 13/16. R/Enq. |
| 13 C. | Midforth, F. W. 182. | M. Nov. 13/16. R/Enq. |
| 13 D. | Cropper, G. 28367. | M. Mar. 8/17. |
| ‡13 D. | Gledhill, J. H. 26181. | M. Nov. 13/16. R/Enq. |
| 13 D. | Kirman, H. S. 25020. | M. Mar. 8/17. |
| 13 D. | Livesey, R. 28742. | M. Mar. 8/17. |
| 13 D. XIV | Owen, J. H. 37277. | M. Mar. 8/17. |
| 13 D. | Richardson, Edward. 576. | M. Nov. 13/16. |
| 13 D. | Watson, F. 28734. | M. Mar. 8/17. |

*BALKANS.*

| | | |
|---|---|---|
| 2 | **Childerhouse, 2nd Lt. F. J.** (Fr. 9th Lincolns.) | K. Sept. 23/16. Unoff. P. Conf and Det. |
| 2 C. | Hughes, Cpl. Frank. 7904. | W. and M. April 11/17. |
| *2 D. | Ellis, T. 15731. | D. April 2/17. Det.D./B. |

*E.E.F.*

| | | |
|---|---|---|
| 5 A. | Foreman, S. S. 250219. | W. and M. Mar. 26/17. |

**WEST YORKSHIRE REGIMENT.**

*B.E.F.*

| | | |
|---|---|---|
| 1 A. III | Hollands, Lazarus. 29461. | K. May 30/17. Det.D./B |
| ‡1 A. | Riley, A. 38869. | M. May 24/17. |
| *1 A. II | Swithenbank, Wilfred. 38151. | M. May 24/17. |
| *1 A. I | Whitchurch, J. 47102. | M. May 27/17. |
| *1 C. | Crossland, Ernest. 18494. (Fr. H.Q.) | M. April 16/17. |
| 1 D. | Booth, F. 40740. | M. April 6/17. |
| 1 D. | Cooper, S/B. H. 33826. | M. April 16/17. |
| 1 D. | Fielding, L.-Cpl. W. 40726. | M. April 16/17. |
| *1 D. XIV | Gray, Sgt. Percy. 24337. | M. Sept. 18/16. R/Enq. |
| 1 D. | Kyman, H. 7613. | M. April 16/17. |
| 1 D. XIV | Stirk, Harry Binner. 34585. | M. April 16/17. |
| 1 D. | Stones, A. 19292. | M. April 16/17. |
| *1 ? | Lavender, Alfred. 13955. | K. Sept. 25/17. Det.D./B. |
| 2 B. | Purkiss, R. S. 8538. | W. and M. Mar. 4/17. |
| 2 D. | Pawson, R. 35127. | K. March 5/17. Det.D./B. |
| 5 | **Annesley, 2nd Lieut. E. G.** | M. May 3/17. |

**Yorkshire Regiment, West—contd.**

## *B.E.F.*

| | | |
|---|---|---|
| ‡5 B. | Flanagan, E. 201717. | M. May 3/17. |
| ‡5 B. | Godson, L.-Cpl. A. 201175. | M. May 3/17. |
| 5 C. | Armitage, Frank. 6347. | M. Sept. 28/16. R./Enq. |
| ‡5 C. | Child, J. 203065. (6424.) | M. April 13/17. |
| *5 C. | Franklin, Isaac. 201882. | M. May 3/17. |
| ‡5 C. | French, W. 200772. | M. May 3/17. |
| ‡5 C. | Geelan, J. 201903. | M. May 3/17. |
| ‡5 C. | Godson, E. 201473. | M. May 3/17. |
| *5 D. | Holmes, Cpl. H. B. 2247. | W. and M. Sept. 28/16. R/Enq. |
| 5 D. XIII | Pickles, Joseph Leonard. 5862. | M. Sept. 28/16. R/Enq. |
| 2/5 | Churchman, Lt. C. H. (Fr. 6th Suffolks.) | M. May 3/17. |
| 2/5 | Knowles, Capt. F. H. | M. May 3/17. |
| 2/5 A. | Wilson, 2nd Lt. A. | M. May 3/17. |
| ‡2/5 A. | Baines, L.-Cpl. A. 201671. | M. May 3/17. |
| ‡2/5 A. | Baul, E. 202050. | M. May 3/17. |
| 2/5 A. | Crampton, L.-Cpl. J. Tom. 201686. (4011.) | W. and M. May 3/17. |
| *2/5 A. I | Hirst, Walter. 40207. | Unoff. M. May 3/17. |
| ‡2/5 A. | Holmes, W. H. 200945. | M. May 3/17. |
| ‡2/5 A. | Horner, H. 201678. | M. May 3/17. |
| 2/5 A. I | Kershaw. 200265. | W. and M. May 3/17. |
| ‡2/5 A. | Leck, G. A. 201913. | W. and M. May 3/17. |
| ‡2/5 A. | Marshall, C. 202015. | M. May 3/17. |
| *2/5 A. | Mason, Sgt. Charlie. 200924. | W. and M. May 3/17. |
| ‡2/5 A. | Nicholls, G. 200312. | M. May 3/17. |
| *2/5 A. | Reddish, Wm. 201666. | M. May 3/17. |
| 2/5 A. | Redshaw, James. 201693. (4018.) | M. May 3/17. |
| ‡2/5 A. | Trowsdale, W. 201668. | M. May 3/17. |
| ‡2/5 A. | Woods, E. 200256. | M. May 3/17. |
| 2/5 B. | Abbott, Harold. 200557. (2163.) | M. May 3/17. |
| *2/5 B. | Abbott, Sgt. J. Wm. 200783. | W. and M. May 3/17. |
| ‡2/5 B. | Brown, W. 201728. | W. and M. May 3/17. |
| 2/5 B. | Dixon, Albert. 201940. | M. May 3/17. |
| ‡2/5 B. | Jackson, L. 201124. | M. May 3/17. |
| ‡2/5 B. | Judd, G. 201951. | M. May 3/17. |
| ‡2/5 B. | Kelly, W. 201103. | M. May 3/17. |
| ‡2/5 B. | Marshall, J. 201936. | M. May 3/17. |
| ‡2/5 B. | Marshall, T. 201187. | M. May 3/17. |
| 2/5 B. | Miller, A. 201346. (3401.) | M. May 3/17. |
| ‡2/5 B. | Moss, F. G. 201960. | M. May 3/17. |
| ‡2/5 B. | Pearson, P. 201722. | W. and M. May 3/17. |
| ‡2/5 B. | Postill, C. 201760. | M. May 3/17. |
| 2/5 B. | Prest, Robt. 201062. | M. May 3/17. |
| *2/5 B. VI | Reason, L.-Cpl. Harold. 201730. (4060.) | M. May 3/17. |
| ‡2/5 B. | Sanderson, H. 200689. | M. May 3/17. |
| ‡2/5 B. | Thompson, E. 200291. | M. May 3/17. |
| ‡2/5 C. | Andrews, W. 201874. | W. and M. May 3/17. |
| 2/5 C. | Biscombe, J. 201782. (4125.) | M. May 3/17. |
| ‡2/5 C. | Boughen, H. 201871. | M. May 3/17. |
| ‡2/5 C. | Boyes, H. 201193. | M. May 3/17. |
| ‡2/5 C. | Bratley, M. 202006. | M. May 3/17. |
| ‡2/5 C. | Capps, R. 200720. | M. May 3/17. |
| ‡2/5 C. | Carey, E. 201384. | W. and M. May 3/17. |
| ‡2/5 C. | Clarke, S. 201990. | M. May 3/17. |
| ‡2/5 C. | Dickenson, J. 202074. | M. May 3/17. |
| ‡2/5 C. | Doyley, H. 201891. | M. May 3/17. |

**Yorkshire Regiment, West—contd.**

## *B.E.F.*

‡2/5 C. Ellwood, W. 201792. M. May 3/17.

‡2/5 C. Featherstone, D. 200230. M. May 3/17.

‡2/5 C. XI Graham, E. A. 201505. W. and M. May 3/17.

‡2/5 C. Greenwood, R. 200647. M. May 3/17.

*2/5 C. XI Harrison, W. 201868. M. May 3/17.

‡2/5 C. Hay, C. 201870. M. May 3/17.

‡2/5 C. Head, L.-Cpl. F. 200210. M. May 3/17.

‡2/5 C. Hewson, A. 201982. M. May 3/17.

2/5 C. Hobson, Albert. 241961. M. May 3/17.

‡2/5 C. Holliday, J. W. 201877. M. May 3/17.

2/5 C. Horseman, L.-Cpl. Wm. Walter. 200917. M. May 3/17.

‡2/5 C. Hurst, D. 201994. M. May 3/17.

‡2/5 C. Hymas, L.-Cpl. C. 201014. M. May 3/17.

‡2/5 C. Lovett, G. 201995. M. May 3/17.

‡2/5 C. Marston, T. H. 201879. W. and M. May 3/17.

‡2/5 C. Michelson, J. 202123. M. May 3/17.

‡2/5 C. Milner, R. 201902. M. May 3/17.

‡2/5 C. Peckitt, H. 201988. M. May 3/17.

‡2/5 C. Rawson, A. 201905. M. May 3/17.

‡2/5 C. Rush, L. E. 201475. M. May 3/17.

2/5 C. Seymour, J. W. 201897. M. May 3/17.

‡2/5 C. Slater, Cpl. W. 200083. M. May 3/17.

2/5 C. Smith, Alfred. 201999. M. May 3/17.

‡2/5 C. Sparling, A. G. 202004. M. May 3/17.

‡2/5 C. Thompson, C. 202100. M. May 3/17.

‡2/5 C. Triffitt, J. F. 202080. M. May 3/17.

‡2/5 C. Usher, Cpl. G. 201774. M. May 3/17.

‡2/5 C. Walton, S. 201993. M. May 3/17.

‡2/5 C. Whitaker, S. 201989. M. May 3/17.

‡2/5 C. Wilcock, R. 200225. M. May 3/17.

‡2/5 C. Willey, L.-Cpl. J. 201776. M. May 3/17.

‡2/5 C. Wilson, C. 201893. M. May 3/17.

2/5 C. X Woolley, Lawrence. 200883. M. May 3/17.

2/5 D. Barrett, William Henry. 201847. M. May 3/17.

‡2/5 D. Brown, Sergt. G. 200963. W. and M. May 3/17.

‡2/5 D. Goundry, Sergt. O. 200904. W. and M. May 3/17.

‡2/5 D. Judson, Harold. 201556. (3786.) M. May 3/17.

‡2/5 D. Kirk, Cpl. H. C. 201152. M. May 3/17.

*2/5 D. Middlewood, B. 201224. M. May 3/17.

*2/5 D. Parkin, E. 202124. M. May 3/17.

‡2/5 D. Taylor, J. 201858. M. May 3/17.

‡2/5 D. Ward, J. 201389. M. May 3/17.

6 **Armistead, 2nd Lieut. T. E.** M., bel. K. May 3/17.

*6 **Jackson, 2nd Lieut. H. E.** M. June 12/17.

‡6 A. Bett, H. 242239. M. May 3/17.

6 A. Feather, Ernest. 5497. M. Sept. 3/16.

‡6 B. Bilborough, G. 242423. M. May 3/17.

*6 B. II Pinner, Charles. 242722. M. June 12/17.

‡6 B. V Whitehead, H. 240142. M. June 12/17.

6 C. Taylor, J. L. 6707. M. Mar. 12/17.

‡6 D. Biggins, L.-Cpl. W. 241027. M. May 3/17.

6 D. XVI Hubbard, Saml. 11599. (Fr. 8 Y. and L.) M. Sept. 3/16. R/Enq.

2/6 **Charlesworth, 2nd Lieut. G** M. May 3/17.

2/6 **Hall, 2nd Lieut. J. G.** M. May 3/17.

2/6 A. III Ambler, William. 242152. M. May 3/17.

‡2/6 A. Ashworth, J. 240817. M. May 3/17.

**Yorkshire Regiment, West—contd.**

## *B.E.F.*

| | | |
|---|---|---|
| 2/6 A. | Breaks, W. 242138. | M. May 3/17. |
| ‡2/6 A. | Brearton, W. 240898. | M. May 3/17. |
| 2/6 A. | Brook, Cyril. 241146. (3492.) | W. and M. May 3/17. |
| 2/6 A. | Charlesworth, James Hicks. 242380. | M. May 12/17. |
| ‡2/6 A. | Dixon, G. 242428. | M. May 3/17. |
| ‡2/6 A. | Fellows, W. 242388. | M. May 3/17. |
| *2/6 A. | Fletcher, L.-Cpl. John E. 241862. (4994.) | M. May 3/17. |
| ‡2/6 A. | Foster, M. 240254. | M. May 3/17. |
| 2/6 A. II | Frain, Joseph Ernest. 242431. (6080.) | M. May 3/17. |
| ‡2/6 A. II | Grayson, Charles. 242233. | M. May 3/17. |
| 2/6 A. | Hall, Wm. H. 242103. | M. May 3/17. |
| ‡2/6 A. | Hay, P. E. 242255. | W. and M. May 3/17. |
| 2/6 A. | Hensbey, L.-Cpl. John Jas. 240819. | M. May 3/17. |
| ‡2/6 A. | Jennings, J. 241867. | M. May 3/17. |
| ‡2/6 A. | Kirby, J. E. 242378. | M. May 3/17. |
| 2/6 A. IV | Lister, L.-Cpl. Alfred Taylor. 242154. | M. May 3/17. |
| ‡2/6 A. | Lund, R. 242236. | M. May 3/17. |
| ‡2/6 A. | McKeown, Frank. 242234. (5835.) | M. May 3/17. |
| ‡2/6 A. | Morrell, W. 242235. | M. May 3/17. |
| ‡2/6 A. | Morrison, J. 242365. | M. May 3/17. |
| ‡2/6 A. | Myers, E. 242385. | M. May 3/17. |
| ‡2/6 A. | Noble, R. 242246. | M. May 3/17. |
| *2/6 A. | North, Charles. 241864. | M. May 3/17. |
| 2/6 A. III | Pape, William. 242137. | M. May 3/17. |
| ‡2/6 A. | Parker, C. G. 241243. | M. May 3/17. |
| ‡2/6 A. | Petty, G. E. 241331. | M. May 3/17. |
| ‡2/6 A. | Pollard, J. W. 242241. | M. May 3/17. |
| 2/6 A. | Popple, W. 242368. | M. May 3/17. |
| ‡2/6 A. | Priestley, Greenwood. 242140. | M. May 3/17. |
| ‡2/6 A. | Prosser, W. 241284. | M. May 3/17. |
| ‡2/6 A. | Richardson, W. 242244. | M. May 3/17. |
| 2/6 A. I | Ripley, Thos. Edgar. 240851. (2941.) | M. May 3/17. |
| *2/6 A. I | Rodgers, Chas. 242161. | M. May 3/17. |
| 2/6 A. | Rotheray, Sergt. Percy. 240860. | K. May 3/17. Det.D./B. |
| 2/6 A. | Shaw, Sergt. Harold. 241117. | M. May 3/17. |
| 2/6 A. | Sturgeon, Walter. 241418. | M. May 3/17. |
| 2/6 A. I | Thompson, Luke. 4991. | M. May 3/17. |
| ‡2/6 A. | Tomlinson, F. 242158. | M. May 3/17. |
| ‡2/6 A. | Train, J. E. 242431. | M. May 3/17. |
| ‡2/6 A. | Train, W. 242288. | M. May 3/17. |
| ‡2/6 A. | Twivy, L.-Cpl. G. 241321. | M. May 3/17. |
| *2/6 A. | Walton, Frank. 240152. (1444.) | M. May 3/17. |
| ‡2/6 A. | Wells, F. 241896. | M. May 3/17. |
| ‡2/6 A. | White, D. 242247. | M. May 3/17. |
| ‡2/6 A. | Wiggott, F. 242167. | M. May 3/17. |
| 2/6 A. | Wilkinson, Arthur. 241366. (3970.) | M. May 3/17. |
| ‡2/6 B. | Broughton, E. 240209. | M. May 3/17. |
| 2/6 B. VIII | Cawthra, Walter. 241035. (3287.) | M. May 3/17. |
| ‡2/6 B. | Chapman, Sergt. G. 267467. | M. May 3/17. |
| ‡2/6 B. | Chester, H. 242038. | M. May 3/17. |
| ‡2/6 B. | Clark, J. 242031. | M. May 3/17. |
| ‡2/6 B. | Crampton, H. 242060. | M. May 3/17. |
| 2/6 B. | Firth, H. A. 240936. | W. and M. May 3/17. |
| 2/6 B. | Holdsworth, Cpl. G. 240560. | W. and M. May 3/17. |
| ‡2/6 B. | Horsfield, L.-Cpl. E. 242042. | W. and M. May 3/17. |
| ‡2/6 B. | Jackson, Cpl. A. 241340. | M. May 3/17. |
| ‡2/6 B. | Korwin, J. E. 242217. | M. May 3/17. |
| 2/6 B. VIII | Parkinson, Harry. 242010. | M. May 3/17. |

**Yorkshire Regiment, West—contd.**

## B.E.F.

‡2/6 B. Pickthall, W. 240750. M. May 3/17.
‡2/6 B. Pollard, A. 241436. M. May 3/17.
‡2/6 B. Rhodes, W. 240211. M. May 3/17.
2/6 B. Size, Harry. 242058. (5326.) M. May 3/17.
‡2/6 B. Smith, L. 242282. W. and M. May 3/17.
•2/6 B. VIII Snowden, Jack W. 242035. (5298.) M. May 3/17.
‡2/6 B. Tomlinson, A. 240951. M. May 3/17.
‡2/6 B. Wilson, J. H. 242291. M. May 3/17.
‡2/6 C. Brook, H. 241200. M. May 3/17.
‡2/6 C. Edwards, T. 240997. M. May 3/17.
•2/6 C. Ellison, Herbert A. 242447. M. May 3/17.
•2/6 C. Farrer, R. 241944. (5151.) M. May 3/17.
2/6 C. X Harrington, B. 242101. (5380.) M. May 3/17.
2/6 C. Hobson, H. 241961. Unoff. M. May 3/17.
‡2/6 C. Howland, R. 240852. M. May 3/17.
•2/6 C. Law, Walter. 241367. (3971.) M. May 3/17.
‡2/6 C. Speight, J. 241851. M. May 3/17.
‡2/6 C. Stocks, John. 240956. M. May 3/17.
2/6 C. L.G.S. Thompson, L.-Cpl. Robt. 241131. (3466.) M. May 3/17.
‡2/6 C. Thompson, W. 241298. M. May 3/17.
‡2/6 C. M.G.S. Thresh, Walter. 240969. M. May 3/17.
‡2/6 D. XIV Brook, J. W. 240753. M. May 3/17.
2/6 D. XIV Brooke, H. 242331. W. and M. May 3/17.
2/6 D. XIV Crompton, Percy. 242329. M. May 3/17.
‡2/6 D. XIV Dransfield, Joshua P. 242338. M. May 3/17.
‡2/6 D. Duffy, L.-Sergt. C. 241410. M. May 3/17.
‡2/6 D. Freeman, G. E. 241970. M. May 3/17.
•2/6 D. XIII Green, W. 241050. (3320.) M. May 3/17.
2/6 D. XVI Kay, A. 242372. (6016.) M. May 3/17.
‡2/6 D. Normington, F. 241453. M. May 3/17.
‡2/6 D. Rowley, F. 241991. M. May 3/17.
‡2/6 D. Simpson, H. 241995. M. May 3/17.
‡2/6 D. Turner, H. 242357. M. May 3/17.
‡2/6 D. Wallace, Sergt. W. 240170. M. May 3/17.
2/6 D. XIV Williams, R. G. 241990. (5233.) M. May 3/17.
7 B. Hallison, W. 268688. W. and M. April 10/17.
7 B. Thompson, C. 266035. W. and M. April 10/17.
7 C. I.T.M. Geldard, W. 3372. (Fr. 146 Bgde.) W. and M. Sept. 3/16. R/Enq.
2/7 **Hamilton, Lieut. Tom.** M. May 12/17.
2/7 A. IV Dunwell, Wilfred. 266440. (3871.) M. April 9/17.
2/7 A. Fields, Cpl. Arthur. 266281. W. and M. May 12/17.
•2/7 A. Fields, Cpl. Wm. Garnett. 266275. (3668.) M. May 12/17.
‡2/7 A. Hiley, T. 266936. M. May 12/17.
‡2/7 A. Mearis, F. B. 266271. M May 12/17.
‡2/7 B. Barraclough, L. 267721. M. May 12/17.
‡2/7 B. Burn, E. 266082. M. May 12/17.
‡2/7 B. Cowgill, S. P. 235184. M May 12/17.
2/7 B. VI Duxbury, R. 235186. M. May 12/17.
2/7 B. Fields, L.-Cpl. David. 266311. (3708.) M. May 12/17.
‡2/7 B. Gill, W. 235189. M. May 12/17.
‡2/7 B. Johns, B. 267146. M. May 12/17.
‡2/7 B. Kettlewell, G. 267001. M. May 12/17.
2/7 B. VII Mallinson, Willie. 268688. (Late 8181.) W. and M. April 10/17.
‡2/7 B. Metcalf, H. E. 266329. W. and M. May 12/17.
•2/7 B. VII Pilling, Joe. 235194. M. May 12/17.
2/7 B. Rowland, Thos. 267190 (5039.) M. May 12/17.

**Yorkshire Regiment, West—contd.**

## *B.E.F.*

‡2/7 B. Shaw, Alf. 47981. M. May 3/17.
2/7 B. VIII Smith, E. R. 268646. (8139.) M. May 12/17.
‡2/7 B. Ward, L.-Sergt. F. 266298. M. May 12/17.
2/7 B. V Woodmass, W. 267642. M. May 12/17.
*2/7 C. X Anderson, Wm. 266429. (3857.) M. April 10/17.
2/7 C. X Brear, H. V. 268654. (Late 8147.) M. April 10/17.
2/7 C. Cohen, H. 267300. M. April 10/17.
2/7 C. Dixon, W. 268558. M. April 10/17.
*2/7 C. Drake, E. 268656. M. April 10/17.
*2/7 C. Gadbury, L.-Cpl. W. H. D. 266438. M. April 10/17.
‡2/7 C. Hirst, Harry. 265978. (3297.) M. May 12/17.
*2/7 C. XI Hope, Thos. 265885. (3159.) M. April 10/17.
‡2/7 C. Hutchinson, John. 265059. M. May 2/17.
*2/7 C. X Jones, P. 267200. (5051.) M. April 10/17.
2/7 C. Lawson, Thos. Frankland. 265819. (Late 3057.) M. April 10/17.
2/7 C. IX Ledgard, Albert. 268650. (8143.) M. April 10/17.
2/7 C. IX Lee, James. 266431. M. May 12/17.
2/7 C. XI Mettrick, Sykes. 235206. M. April 10/17.
2/7 C. Pawson, A.-Sergt. P. 266370. M. April 10/17.
2/7 C. Potter, G. L. 266979. M. April 10/17.
2/7 C. IX Riley, L.-Cpl. Harry. 266149. M. May 12/17.
‡2/7 C. Rutherford, A. 267050. M. May 12/17.
2/7 C. Smithers, G. A. 235174. W. and M. April 11/17.
2/7 C. Stead, Harry. 266282. (3676.) W. and M. April 11/17.
2/7 C. X Stephenson, Thos. 235212. M. April 10/17.
*2/7 C. X Wardley, Albert. 268571. (8019.) M. April 10/17.
‡2/7 C. Woodhead, Sergt. G. 266352. M. May 12/17.
‡2/7 D. Barwick, E. 266490. M. May 12/17.
‡2/7 D. Broadley, J. 265808. M. May 12/17.
2/7 D. XIII Collins, Harry. 266145. M. May 12/17.
‡2/7 D. XVI Lewis, Ben. 267247. M. May 3/17.
‡2/7 D. Munton, Cpl. F. 266473. M. May 12/17.
2/7 D. XVI Spencer, Holdsworth. 269696. M. May 12/17.
2/7 D. XV Ward, Chas. Edward. 4976. M. Feb. 15/17.
8 A. Flint, J. 4637. (Fr. 5th.) M. Sept. 3/16. R/Enq
‡8 A. Foster, H. 305929. M. May 3/17.
‡8 A. Fox, G. H. 235227. M. May 3/17.
8 A. III Swale, Chas. Leopold. 4897. (Fr. 5th W. Yorks.) M. Sept. 3/16. R/Enq.
8 A. IV Ward, L.-Cpl. Herbert. 3922. M. Sept. 3/16. R/Enq.
8 B. VIII Hipkin, Arthur. 5033. W. and M. Oct. 4/16.
8 B. Rands, Charles. 4774. (Fr. 5th.) M. Sept. 3/16. R/Enq.
8 C. XII Taylor, Gilbert. 5024. (Fr. 5th.) M. Sept. 3/16. R/Enq.
‡2/8 A. Appleyard, F. 305138. M. May 3/17.
*2/8 A. Archer, Sgt. Ben. 305185. (1605.) M. May 3/17.
‡2/8 A. Blackburn, L.-Cpl. T. 305921. M. May 3/17.
*2/8 A. Broadley, W. J. 306705. (4657.) M. May 3/17.
‡2/8 A. Brook, S. 307012. M. May 3/17.
‡2/8 A. Burke, P. 306134. M. May 3/17.
2/8 A. Bush, Fred. 306706. (4568.) M. May 3/17.
2/8 A. IV Colburn, Jas. 306722. (4676.) M. May 3/17.
‡2/8 A. England, B. C. 305151. M. May 3/17.
2/8 A. Grant, J. 306651. (4572.) W. and M. May 3/17.
‡2/8 A. Hall, C. H. 235254. M. May 3/17.
2/8 A. Kingsley, John. 306711. M. May 3/17.
2/8 A. Kirkham, Harold. 307015. (5101.) M. May 3/17.

**Yorkshire Regiment, West—contd.**

## *B.E.F.*

2/8 A. or B. Medley, Ernest. 307736. — M. May 3/17.
2/8 A. or C. Mitchell, Harry. 306732. (4694.) — M. May 3/17.
‡2/8 A. Nield, C. 305982. — M. May 3/17.
‡2/8 A. Selby, R. 306969. — M. May 3/17.
*2/8 A. Shaw, T. 305925. — M. May 3/17.
‡2/8 A. Stead, S. 307751. — M. May 3/17.
*2/8 A. III Thompson, C. 306691. — M. May 3/17.
*2/8 A. Thornton, William. 305928. (3121.) — M. May 3/17.
‡2/8 A. Wade, L. 306750. — W. and M. May 22/17.
‡2/8 A. Ward, J. 307026. — W. and M. May 3/17.
‡2/8 A. White, P. 268103. — M. May 3/17.
2/8 A. III Wood, Wm. 306764. (4740.) — M. May 3/17.
2/8 B. Blackburn, Harry. 306987. (5061.) — M. May 3/17.
‡2/8 B. Brady, Sigr. J. 306051. — M. May 3/17.
2/8 B. V Furness, L.-Cpl. Jos. 306183. (3554.) — W. and M. May 3/17.
2/8 D. Wood, Sgt. Allan Whitaker. 305024. — W. and M. May 3/17.
9 A. Griffiths, John W. 12567. (Wrongly known as 13187.) — M. Sept. 27/16. R/Enq.
‡9 A. Huison, Walter. 37440. — K. June 14/17. Det.D.B.
9 A. Watson, Thomas Edward. 21082. — M. Sept. 26/16. R/Enq.
9 B. Barrett, Sylvester. 19130. — M. Sept. 27/16. R/Enq.
‡9 B. Darby, Philip Lancelot. 21021. — M. Sept. 14/16. R/Enq.
*9 B. VI Hobson, Harvey. 10510. — M. Sept. 27/16. R/Enq.
9 B. XI Maurice, B. 33972. — Unoff. W. and M. April 1/17.
9 B. Waterman, Charles L. 20141. — M. Sept. 27/16. R/Enq.
9 C. XI Harn, James Wm. 21878. — M. Sept. 14/16. R/Enq.
9 C. I.T.M. Kay, Cyril. 19319. (32 Bgde.) — W. and M. Jan. 19/17.
‡9 C. L.G.S. Town, Sydney. 18490. — W. and M. Sept. 14/16. R/Enq.
*9 D. Archer, Tom Burton. 15676. — W. and M. Sept. 14/16. R/Enq.
10 A. Barnfield, L.-Cpl. C. 13650. — M. April 23/17.
10 A. Barraclough, Arthur. 13097. — M. April 23/17.
10 A. Bell, W. 15386. — M. April 23/17.
10 A. Darwin. 2066. — M. April 23/17.
10 A. Ellis, G. W. 38502. — M. April 23/17.
10 A. Jarrett, H. 43090. — M. April 23/17.
*10 A. I Staniland, Sydney. 47064. — M. April 23/17.
10 A. II Taylor, Sergt. Alex. 12589. — W. and M. April 23/17.
10 A. Wilson, Cpl. A. 43105. — M. April 23/17.
‡10 B. Brooke, R. 13136. — M. May 12/17.
10 B. VIII Coote, Clifford. 24753. — W. and M. April 23/17.
10 B. VII Ferguson, Edw. 268500. — M. April 23/17.
10 B. VIII Gagen, J. R. 37352. — M. April 23/17.
‡10 B. VII Hollings, Clarance. 37397. — K. Feb. 15/17. Det.D./B.
*10 B. VI McEvoy, G. 235057. — K. April 23/17. Det.D./B.
10 B. V Middleton, Joe. 7679. — M. April 23/17.
10 B. Newbourn, W. 43108 — M. April 23/17.
10 B. VIII Stewart, J. 235051. — W. and M. April 23/17.
‡10 C. XII Turner, W. 29368. — W. and M. April 23/17.
10 D. Watson, Geo. Clifford. 43331. (Fr. 14 York & Lancs.) — M., bel. K. Mar. 9/17.
‡11 **Gill, 2nd Lieut. John I.** — W. and M. June 7/17.
11 **Harrison, M.C., 2nd Lieut. J.** — M., bel. K. May 3/17.
‡11 A. Wallbank, Leonard. 11472. — W. and M. June 7/17.
*11 A. or D. Wilson, Henry. 1307. (Fr. 18th.) — M. Oct. 7/16. R/Enq.
‡11 B. VI Bell, Jim. 19536. — M. June 8/17.
‡11 B. VII Marshall, Geo. 203387. — M. June 7/17.
‡11 B. Perfect A.-Sergt. E. D. 13096. — M. Unoff. W. June 7/17.
‡11 C. Marsh, Frank. 14368. — M. June 7/17.

**Yorkshire Regiment, West—contd.**

*B.E.F.*

| | | |
|---|---|---|
| 11 C. | Nightingale, Arthur. 43756. (Late 7th K.O.Y.L.I., 28243.) | W. and M. Oct. 7/16. R/Enq |
| ‡11 ? | Prince, C. 41108. | Unoff. M. June 7/17. |
| 12 | **Skeet, Capt. W. C.** | K. April 9/17. Det.D./B. |
| 12 | **Wooler, Capt. R. B.** (Fr. 11th.) | M. May 3/17. |
| 12 A. IV | Bradshaw, Cpl. Wm. 28014. | M. May 3/17. |
| ‡12 A. | Calvert, E. 17/544. | M. May 3/17. |
| 12 A. II | Cattle, John. 201239. | M. May 3/17. |
| ‡12 A. | Cuckson, H. 47970. | M. May 3/17. |
| 12 A. II | Firth, L.-Cpl. H. 17263. | M. May 3/17. |
| *12 A. | Gumbrell, Geo. E. 47232. | M. May 3/17. |
| ‡12 A. | Hillingsworth, D. H. 40664. | W. and M. May 3/17. |
| ‡12 A. | Hollingsworth, A.-Sergt. 22081. | K. May 3/17. Det.D./B. |
| 12 A. IV | Humphries, H. 47929. | M. May 3/17. |
| 12 A. I | Kelsey, Edgar. 37382. | K. May 9/17. Det.D./B. |
| 12 A. | Kent, T. H. 43698. | W. and M. April 13/17. |
| *12 A. | Newcomb, John. 40675. | M. May 3/17. |
| ‡12 A. II | North, Curtis. 25249. | K. April 9/17. Det.D./B. |
| ‡12 A. III | Robinson, Sgt. Leonard Alf. 43676. | K. April 9/17. Det.D./B. |
| 12 A. IV | Roebuck, J. 14379. | M. May 3/17. |
| ‡12 A. II | Thompson, Arthur Henry. 26129. | M. May 3/17. |
| ‡12 A. | Thompson, W. 201253. | M. May 3/17. |
| *12 A. | Wood, Henry Percy. 47040. | M. May 3/17. |
| ‡12 B. | Cooke, C. 235249. | M. May 10/17. |
| 12 B. VII | Donovan, Michael George. 46513. | W. and M. April 13/17. |
| 12 B. | Lamb, G. M. 38568. | M. April 9/17. |
| ‡12 B. | Lockhart, G. 40112. | M., bel. K. May 7/17. |
| ‡12 B. V | Wraith, A. 45930. | M. May 7/17. |
| 12 C. | Arundel, C. J. 9137. | W. and M. April 13/17. |
| ‡12 C. | Baxendale, C. 1537. | M. May 3/17. |
| 12 C. IX | Briggs, Frank Gledhill. 50455. | M. May 3/17. |
| 12 C. | Carter, W. 47291. | M. April 9/17. |
| 12 C. XI | Child, J. B. 23046. | M. April 13/17. |
| ‡12 C. | Evans, T. 15446. | M. May 3/17. |
| 12 C. | French, T. 10815. (Fr. 4th.) | W. and M. April 9/17. |
| 12 C. XI | Hall, Albert. 13461. | W. and M. May 3/17. |
| 12 C. | Kitching, W. 40644. | M. April 13/17. |
| *12 C. XII | McSherry, John. 50265. | M. May 3/17. |
| ‡12 C. | Priestley, H. 47262. | M. May 3/17. |
| 12 C. IX | Pullan, Arthur. 50518. | W. and M. May 3/17. |
| ‡12 C. | Scratchard, F. A. 24730. | W. and M. May 3/17. |
| 12 C. IX | Wood, E. 50259. | M. May 3/17. |
| *12 C. XI | Woodall, S. H. 50515. | M. May 3/17. |
| 12 D. XV | Dennison, Alfred. 37962. | M. April 12/17. |
| ‡12 D. | Gibson, J. 10756. | M. May 3/17. |
| *12 D. XIII | Kirk, L.-Cpl. Geo. M. 29556. | M. May 3/17. |
| 12 D. XVI | L.G.S. Machen, F. T. 50555. | M. May 3/17. |
| *12 D. | Morris, H. 50510. | M. May 3/17. |
| ‡12 D. XVI | M.G.S. Naylor, C. 50590. | M. May 3/17. |
| 15 | **Bicase, Capt. R. M. S.** | K. May 3/17. Det.D./B. |
| 15 | **Jennison, 2nd Lieut. J. L.** | M. May 3/17. |
| 15 | **Lisle, 2nd Lieut. J. W.** | M. May 3/17. |
| 15 D. | **Parkin, 2nd Lieut. A. S.** | M. May 3/17. |
| 15 | **Peck, 2nd Lieut. A. T.** | M. May 3/17. |
| 15 | **Scholes, 2nd Lieut. F. W.** | M. May 3/17. |
| 15 | **Thomas, 2nd Lieut. J. S.** | M. May 3/17. |
| *15 A. | Abraham, Cpl. Myer. 34185. | M. May 3/17. |
| 15 A. IV | Ainley, H. 24964 | M. May 3/17. |

Yorkshire Regiment, West—contd.

## B.E.F.

*15 A. or B. Batley, L.-Cpl. Clifford. 1399. M. May 3/17.
15 A. Bedford, Alfred. 34450. M. May 3/17.
‡15 A. Best, F. 36186. M. May 3/17.
15 A. Booth, L.-Cpl. Walter. 40141. M. May 3/17.
‡15 A. Carnes, Cpl. G. 173. M. May 3/17.
‡15 A. Chisholm, L.-Cpl. R. 32015. M. May 3/17.
‡15 A. Clark, W. H. 32333. M. May 3/17.
‡15 A. Derrett, C. 40358. M. May 3/17.
‡15 A. Duthoit, C. 36743. M. May 3/17.
15 A. Ellis, T. 33747. M. May 3/17.
*15 A. Ellison, Charles. 1258. M. May 3/17.
‡15 A. Gooder, G. 1456. M. May 3/17.
15 A. Harby, W. 40361. M. May 3/17.
15 A. Halliday, Cpl. Herbt. Edw. 32994. M. May 3/17.
‡15 A. Haynes, Sergt. H. C. 440. W. and M. May 3/17.
15 A. Heald, H. 36357. M. May 3/17.
15 A. Hemingway, Harry B. 36753. M. May 3/17.
‡15 A. Hudson, W. 32025. M. May 3/17.
15 A. III Johnson, Ernest. 24842. M. May 3/17.
15 A. Johnston, L.-Cpl. Ernest. 1179. M. May 3/17.
‡15 A. Jones, R. 40140. M. May 3/17.
‡15 A. Kelly, F. 242250. M. May 3/17.
‡15 A. Kirby, A. 38236. M. May 3/17.
15 A. III Lamplough, Fredk. C. 40514. M. May 3/17.
15 A. Linnecor, Leonard D. 38122. M. May 3/17.
15 A. Lister, Simeon. 38027. M. May 3/17.
‡15 A. McDowall, L. 1884. M. May 3/17.
15 A. II McKean, G. M. 45913. M. May 3/17.
‡15 A. Mellor, Sergt. H. 1104. M. May 3/17.
15 A. L.G.S. Nelsey, Herbert. 25312. M. May 3/17.
*15 A. or C. O'Grady, L.-Cpl. Thomas. 24986. M. May 3/17.
‡15 A. Olivant, L. 37961. M. May 3/17.
‡15 A. Saville, L.-Cpl. T. 33727. M. May 3/17.
*15 A. Skingley, Samuel. 33785. M. May 3/17.
‡15 A. Smith, S. 1849. M. May 3/17.
‡15 A. Taylor, E. 33474. M. May 3/17.
‡15 A. Taylor, W. 40143. M. May 3/17.
15 A. IV Teale, Jas. Alfred. 33691. M. May 3/17.
15 A. Townsley, Ernest. 32924. M. May 3/17.
15 A. II Varey, J. H. 33717. M. May 3/17.
*15 A. Walker, Albert. 38197. M. May 3/17.
15 A. White, Chas. 25148. M. May 3/17.
‡15 A. Wilkinson, Felix. 32626. M. May 3/17.
15 A. II Wright, W. H. 24933. M. May 3/17.
15 B. Airey, Sergt. Jas. Henry. 9. M. May 3/17.
15 B. Armitage, Walker. 1647. M. May 3/17.
‡15 B. Auden, A. 36941. M. May 3/17.
15 B. Barraclough, Haydn. 40524. M. May 3/17.
15 B. Batty, Edgar. 33760. M. May 3/17.
15 B. VI Beddow, Geo. R. G. 40349. M. May 3/17.
15 B. Brown, L.-Cpl. H. 1139. M. May 3/17.
15 B. Caisley, John W. 23234. M. May 3/17.
15 B. Chadwick, Fred. 28022. M. May 3/17.
15 B. Dalby, Geo. Hen. 27859. M. May 3/17.
‡15 B. Dennison, H. E. 32818. M. May 3/17.
‡15 B. Douglas, J. 8651. M. May 3/17.
15 B. Elliff, L.-Cpl. C. 23981. M. May 3/17.
*15 B. VIII England, Jonathan. 38232. M. May 3/17.

**Yorkshire Regiment, West—contd.**

## *B.E.F.*

| | | |
|---|---|---|
| ‡15 B. | Gledhill, O. 38417. | M. May 3/17. |
| *15 B. VII | Gray, Edwin. 181. (Fr. 19th.) | M. May 3/17. |
| 15 B. | Hall, Geo. W. 33077. | M. May 3/17. |
| 15 B. | Halstead, Geo. 38454. | M. May 3/17. |
| 15 B. | Harrison, Maurice. 40157. | M. May 3/17. |
| ‡15 B. | Hayhurst, S. 38239. | W. and M. May 3/17. |
| 15 B. | Higgins, John Jas. 28618. | M. May 3/17. |
| ‡15 B. | Hill, F. 38426. | W. and M. May 3/17. |
| *15 B. VI | Hills, Ernest. 35279. | M. May 3/17. |
| *15 B. VI | Hogg, Sergt. J. L. 468. | M. May 3/17. |
| ‡15 B. VI | Hornby, J. F. 20247. | M. May 3/17. |
| ‡15 B. | Hornsey, H. P. 32997. | W. and M. May 3/17. |
| ‡15 B. | Huby, H. 34164. | M. May 3/17. |
| 15 B. VIII | Hutchinson, Syd. 27872. | M. May 3/17. |
| *15 B. VII | Jackson, Bert. 32022. | M. May 3/17. |
| ‡15 B. | Jackson, L.-Cpl. H. S. 507. | M. May 3/17. |
| ‡15 B. | Kirk, J. R. 1243. | M. May 3/17. |
| ‡15 B. | Letby, Robert. 19780. | M. May 3/17. |
| ‡15 B. | Linsley, D. G. 1250. | M. May 3/17. |
| ‡15 B. | Lister, L. 32882. | M. May 3/17. |
| ‡15 B. XVI | Longstaff, Joe. 24236. | M. May 3/17. |
| ‡15 B. | Marshall, Walter G. 25992. | M. May 3/17. |
| 15 B. | Meeks, Walter E. 33762. | M. May 3/17. |
| 15 B. | Metcalfe, J. 33078. | M. May 3/17. |
| 15 B. | Moorby, Robert. 15/1117. | M. Unoff. W. May 3/17. |
| 15 B. | Pannett, A. 1361. | M. May 3/17. |
| ‡15 B. | Parkin, W. 1624. | M. May 3/17. |
| ‡15 B. | Perry, J. C. 40376. | M. May 3/17. |
| ‡15 B. | Pickles, Sergt. H. G. 721. | M. May 3/17. |
| 15 B. VI | Rollins, Ernest. 20379. | M. May 3/17. |
| 15 B. | Schofield, Snowden. 38032. | M. May 3/17. |
| 15 B. VIII | Walker, F. W. (Bob). 25569. | M. May 3/17. |
| *15 B. VI | Webster, Herbert. 33458. | M. May 3/17. |
| *15 B. | West, Arthur. 38061. | M. May 3/17. |
| 15 B. | Wilkinson, L.-Cpl. E. C. 36510. | M. May 3/17. |
| 15 C. | Benn, J. 29199. | M. May 3/17. |
| 15 C. XII | Boddy, Jas. Herbert Barker. 38563. | M. May 3/17. |
| *15 C. | Brown, Alfred. 38194. | M. May 3/17. |
| 15 C. L.G.S. | Bruines, B. 25334. | M. May 3/17. |
| ‡15 C. X | Butler, Harry. 1401. | M. May 3/17. |
| 15 C. | Culpan, L.-Cpl. Benjamin. 1582. | M. May 3/17. |
| 15 C. IX | Dalby, Arthur. 36864. | M. May 3/17. |
| 15 C. X | Dunwell, Clifford. 294. | M. May 3/17. |
| ‡15 C. | Eary, Sidney. 29964. | M. May 3/17. |
| ‡15 C. | Fenwich; J. W. 38269. | M. May 3/17. |
| ‡15 C. | Gallagher, J. 4/8539. | M. May 3/17. |
| ‡15 C. | Gravel, A. V. 32961. | M. May 3/17. |
| 15 C. | Holt, L.-Cpl. W. 1067. | M. May 3/17. |
| 15 C. XI | Hudson, Walter. 28686. | M. May 3/17. |
| 15 C. XI | Hughes, J. J. 40162. | M. May 3/17. |
| 15 C. | Jackman, Ingham. 40167. | M. May 3/17. |
| ‡15 C. | Kaye, G. 32411. | M. May 3/17. |
| ‡15 C. | Kitchen, T. 29193. | M. May 3/17. |
| 15 C. | Mills, Frank. 38545. | M. May 3/17. |
| ‡15 C. | Newman, G. 40534. | M. May 3/17. |
| ‡15 C. | Nicholson, A. 40529. | M. May 3/17. |
| *15 C. IX | Nicholson, W. 38078. | M. May 3/17. |
| 15 C. | Rauben, M. 33097. | K. May 3/17. Det.D./B. |
| ‡15 C. XII | Sutcliffe, Ernest. 24404. | M. May 3/17. |

Yorkshire Regiment, West—contd.

## B.E.F.

15 C. Sykes, L.-Cpl. W. C. 19/164. M. May 3/17.
‡15 C. Thompson, J. 38272. M. May 3/17.
‡15 C. Thorn, G. A. 9575. M. May 3/17.
15 C. IX Walker, John. 38442. M. May 3/17.
•15 C. or D. Westerman, Burnett. 1277. M. May 3/17.
15 C. Woffenden, E. 1003. M. May 3/17.
‡15 D. Arrowsmith, W. 27376. M. May 3/17.
•15 D. XV Backhouse, John Thos. 37041. M. May 3/17.
‡15 D. Blaze, W. 27368. M. May 3/17.
‡15 D. Booker, C. W. 40347. M. May 3/17.
15 D. XV Brown, Cpl. T. C. 24696. M. May 3/17.
‡15 D. Carr, W. 35623. M. May 3/17.
‡15 D. Cliff, A. 27317. M. May 3/17.
•15 D. Clough, Harold. 36346. M. May 3/17.
•15 D. XIV Culpan, Arthur. 38492. M. May 3/17.
‡15 D. Dickenson, E. 33429. M. May 3/17.
15 D. XVI Dickinson, Sydney. 277. M. May 3/17.
‡15 D. Dyson, J. 32655. M. May 3/17.
•15 D. XIII Edwards, A. L. 27345. M. May 3/17.
‡15 D. Ellis, E. 32962. M. May 3/17.
15 D. Ellis, John. 1945. M. May 3/17.
15 D. Ferrand, L.-Cpl. G. M. 15/325. M. end April/17.
‡15 D. Ford, W. 27042. M. May 3/17.
‡15 D. Gilmore, Arthur Henry. 29768. M. May 3/17.
15 D. XVI Haley, John. 36859. M. May 3/17.
‡15 D. Halstead, A. 36999. M. May 3/17.
‡15 D. Harper, E. 36846. M. May 3/17.
15 D. Haste, Sergt. J. 412. M. May 3/17.
15 D. Henry, Joseph. 537. M. May 3/17.
‡15 D. Hill, A. 1496. M. May 3/17.
15 D. Jones, David John. 15/1050. M. May 3/17.
‡15 D. Kitchen, R. 555. M. May 3/17.
‡15 D. Langstoff, J. 24236. M. May 3/17.
15 D. XIII Levi, H. 29527. M. May 3/17.
‡15 D. Mann, Cpl. J. A. 25277. M. May 3/17.
‡15 D. Medd, A. 33978. M. May 3/17.
•15 D. XIII Metcalfe, Clifford. 638. M. May 3/17.
‡15 D. Mitchell, J. E. 32906. M. May 3/17.
15 D. Morley, Fred. 32995. M. May 3/17.
15 D. XIV Naylor, Guy. 38434. M. May 3/17.
15 D. XVI Nelson, Sgt. Arthur. 1083. M. May 3/17.
‡15 D. Newton, H. 23849. M. May 3/17.
‡15 D. Outhwaite, R. 24496. M. May 3/17.
15 D. XIII Page, Wilfred. 31984. M. May 3/17.
‡15 D. Parker, W. B. 25732. M. May 3/17.
15 D. XV Philips, Wm. 27371. M. May 3/17.
‡15 D. Pickles, W. 722. M. May 3/17.
15 D. XIII Pollard, W. C. 38055. M. May 3/17.
‡15 D. Porter, D. 28707. M. May 3/17.
15 D. Potter, Sam. 1541. M. May 3/17.
‡15 D. Preston, H. 1032. M. May 3/17.
15 D. XII Roberts, F. 37976. M. May 3/17.
15 D. XV Robinson, Alfred. 37661. M. May 3/17.
15 D. XVI Sampson, Ernest Octavius. 37937. M. May 3/17.
‡15 D. XVI Sharlotte, William. 9701. M. May 3/17.
‡15 D. Stephenson, A. 34275. M. May 3/17.
‡15 D. Stephenson, G. R. 32611. M. May 3/17.
15 D. XIII Spencer, Percy. 27364. M. May 3/17.
15 D. XVI Taylor, Hubert. 34270. M. May 3/17.

**Yorkshire Regiment, West—contd.**

## *B.E.F.*

15 D. Taylor, J. E. 40176. M. May 3/17.
15 D. Tommis, Squire. 32188. M. May 3/17.
*15 D. Trendall, H. 34994. M. May 3/17.
‡15 D. Turkington, J. 914. M. May 3/17.
15 D. XIV Ward, Maurice. 36354. M. May 3/17.
‡15 D. Warren, T. 40131. M. May 3/17.
15 D. XV White, H. 38459. M. May 3/17.
‡15 D. Whitelow, H. 38261. M. May 3/17.
15 D. XVI Williamson, George. 38456. M. May 3/17.
‡15 D. Wroe, T. 38229. M. May 3/17.
‡15 ? Kelsey, H. 25312. M. May 3/17.
16 **Greville, 2nd Lieut. D. G. B.** M. May 3/17.
16 **Platnauer, 2nd Lieut. L. N.** W. and M. May 3/17.
‡16 A. Arkley, L.-Cpl. J. 4/8145. M. May 3/17.
16 A. III Blackburn, Alfred. 1640. M. Feb. 27/17.
16 A. Bradley, Jesse. 33324. (Fr. 3rd.) M. Feb. 27/17.
‡16 A. Corcoran, T. 32544. M. May 3/17.
‡16 A. Craig, A. 1734. M. May 3/17.
16 A. III Crookes, George. 20/359. M. Feb. 27/17.
‡16 A. Deighton, A. 1519. M. May 3/17.
‡16 A. Galenby, E. 388. M. May 3/17.
16 A. Gill, Chas. Henry. 13541. M. Feb. 27/17.
16 A. Gledhill, J. T. 40858. W. and M. Feb. 27/17.
‡16 A. Griffen, J. 41308. W. and M. May 3/17.
16 A. I Hall, Arthur. 37316. M. Feb. 27/17.
16 A. Hancon, D. 38320. W. and M. Feb. 27/17.
16 A. or B. M.G.S. Holdsworth, A. 40423. M. May 3/17.
16 A. Hughes, Bertram. 15136. M. Feb. 27/17.
16 A. Inman, Bandsman Sydney. 9606. M. Feb. 16/17.
16 A. IV Jaggar, Wilfred. 28892. K. Feb. 27/17. Det.D./B.
‡16 A. Lumb, M. 41309. M. May 3/17.
*16 A. Lumb, Mark. 43764. M. May 3/17.
16 A. Lynch, Joseph. 34004. M. Feb. 27/17.
16 A. Medley, Harry. 32335. M. Feb. 27/17.
16 A. Monkman, Harry. 32953. M. Feb. 27/17.
16 A. Morley, J. 32869. M. Feb. 27/17.
‡16 A. Morritt, W. 32852. M. May 3/17.
‡16 A. Owens, J. 40431. M. May 3/17.
16 A. IV Ratcliffe, S. 40196. M. May 3/17.
*16 A. IV Senior, Tom E. 32405. K. Feb. 27/17. Det.D./B.
16 A. I Shouksmith, Harold W. 40845. M. May 3/17.
16 A. IV Syson, G. 40440. M. Unoff. K. Feb. 27/17.
16 A. or C. Taylor, H. C. 18543. M. May 12/17.
16 A. I Tunstall, F. 40406. M. Feb. 27/17.
*16 A. White, Sig. H. 305244. Unoff. M. May 3/17.
16 A. or B. Wilks, Walter. 33061. M. Feb. 27/17.
16 B. VI Baldock, Claude Henry. 41713. M. May 3/17.
‡16 B. Barton, F. 19382. M. May 3/17.
16 B. VI Bell, Clifford. 38333. M. Feb. 27/17.
‡16 B. Bowring, S. 38056. M. May 3/17.
*16 B. VI Burns, B. 38644. M. May 3/17.
‡16 B. Feeney, J. 38811. M. May 3/17.
‡16 B. Flannery, F. 34128. M. May 3/17.
‡16 B. Garside, J. E. 32919. M. May 3/17.
‡16 B. Grist, C. 16201. W. and M. May 3/17.
16 B. Hale, Walter. 828. M. May 3/17.
16 B. Harsman, H. 36848. M. May 3/17.
‡16 B. Heyes, N. 9260. W. and M. May 3/17.
‡16 B. Hill, Sergt. George. 8420. M. May 3/17.

**Yorkshire Regiment, West—contd.**

## *B.E.F.*

16 B. VI Holmes, T. 300107. W. Unoff. M. May 3/17.
‡16 B. Horsman, H. 36848. M. May 3/17.
‡16 B. Jeffrey, T. F. 40824. M. May 3/17.
16 B. Lazarus, Louis. 8558. M. May 3/17.
16 B. McCormack, Cpl. Geo. 318. M. May 3/17.
16 B. Peck, J. W. R. 28690. M. Feb. 27/17.
‡16 B. Sloan, T. 22252. M. May 3/17.
‡16 B. Spencer, Sergt. A. 1231. M. May 3/17.
16 B. Wadsworth, L.-Cpl. Alfred. 32981. M. May 3/17.
*16 C. IX Askin, Arthur. 24872. M. May 3/17.
16 C. Bellamy, Frank. 41705. M. May 3/17.
‡16 C. Best, L.-Cpl. A. 20/249. M. May 3/17.
16 C. XII Bimrose, Alfred. 300105. M. May 3/17.
‡16 C. Braithwaite, M. 35628. M. May 3/17.
‡16 C. Brightman, Cpl. C. F. 40416. M. May 3/17.
‡16 C. Bruce, F. G. 1028. M. May 3/17.
‡16 C. Button, G. 38105. M. May 3/17.
‡16 C. Callaghan, G. 37918. M. May 3/17.
16 C. X Carter, J. 38796. M. May 3/17.
16 C. Cope, Sgt. Shoemaker Edw. 249. M. May 3/17.
*16 C. Crossland, L.-Cpl. Harry. 991. M. May 3/17.
‡16 C. Cummins, G. H. 17168. M. May 3/17.
‡16 C. Dalton, G. E. 9/21408. M. May 3/17.
‡16 C. Dane, Sergt. J. A. 821. M. May 3/17.
16 C. XI Dargue, L.-Cpl. Herbert. 1043. M. May 3/17.
‡16 C. Dawson, P. 28492. M. May 3/17.
16 C. XI Dent, L.-Cpl. Harry. 300113. M. May 3/17.
‡16 C. Drury, J. 24082. M. May 3/17.
‡16 C. Dutton, G. 1659. M. May 3/17.
16 C. IX Fallon, Chas. Hry. 18/554. M. May 3/17.
‡16 C. Fielding, F. 40225. M. May 3/17.
‡16 C. Flatter, J. C. 28497. M. May 3/17.
‡16 C. Fox, J. H. 38362. M. May 3/17.
‡16 C. Gibson, R. 38697. M. May 3/17.
‡16 C. Green, A. E. 23509. M. May 3/17.
16 C. IX Green, Wilfred. 24564. M. May 3/17.
16 C. Haigh, G. A. 1415. M. May 3/17.
‡16 C. Hanson, C. E. 1222. W. and M. May 3/17.
16 C. XII Hart, E. E. 20/20302. M. May 3/17.
*16 C. IX Hatfield, Herbert. 37553. M. May 3/17.
‡16 C. Heptinshall, Cpl. J. 1176. W. and M. May 3/17.
16 C. XI Holgate, A. 28522. M. May 3/17.
‡16 C. Jowett, C. 38783. M. May 3/17.
‡16 C. Laycock, H. 550. M. May 3/17.
‡16 C. Line, H. 36902. M. May 3/17.
‡16 C. Midgley, W. 32633. M. May 3/17.
‡16 C. Miller, F. H. 40827. M. May 3/17.
‡16 C. Murgatroyd, W. 38351. M. May 3/17.
16 C. Naylor, H. 36807. M. May 3/17.
16 C. X Parker, Harry. 38787. M. May 3/17.
‡16 C. Piggott, R. 29293. M. May 3/17.
16 C. XI Rhodes, Albert. 38782. M. May 3/17.
‡16 C. Sheldon, L.-Cpl. T. 23363. M. May 3/17.
‡16 C. Smith, F. 41710. M. May 3/17.
‡16 C. IX Smith, John Wm. 29327. M. May 3/17.
‡16 C. Smith, T. 1674. M. May 3/17.
‡16 C. Stephenson, C. W. 37458. M. May 3/17.
*16 C. IX Stockton, Chas. 13944. M. May 3/17.

**Yorkshire Regiment, West—contd.**

## *B.E.F.*

‡16 C. Sunderland, F. 19183. M. May 3/17.
‡16 C. Tillett, H. 32356. M. May 3/17.
‡16 C. Todd, W. E. 14/28171. M. May 3/17.
‡16 C. Taylor, A. 35568. M. May 3/17.
16 C. XI Valentine, L.-Cpl. G. H. 37459. M. May 4/17.
16 C. IX Waddington, J. 41712. M. May 3/17.
‡16 C. Wentworth, Sergt. J. 7372. M. May 3/17.
*16 D. Alcock, Wm. 33530. M. May 3/17.
‡16 D. XVI Bannister, A. W. 29288. M. May 3/17.
16 D. Bottomley, Wilfred Norman. 38370. W. and M. May 3/17.
‡16 D. Cowman, R. H. 38397. M. May 3/17.
‡16 D. Dawson, T. 38079. M. May 3/17.
16 D. XIV Dean, J. 23845. M. May 5/17.
16 D. XIV England, Wm. 21435. M. May 3/17.
16 D. Leonard, H. 38358. M. May 3/17.
16 D. Rappoport, Max. 32832. M. April 3/17.
16 D. Robinson, Horace. 1242. M. May 3/17.
‡16 D. Spencer, Sergt. F. W. 165. M. May 3/17.
16 D. Strawson, Sgt. H. 40441. (Late 4 Lincs., 3805.) M. May 3/17.
‡16 D. XIV Walker, Joe. 41673. M. May 3/17.
16 D. Woodward, S. 32895. M. May 3/17.
‡16 D. Wright, J. 28183. M. May 3/17.
‡16 D. Young, Cpl. A. 1491. M. May 3/17.
*17 W. II Atkinson, Jas. Henry. 41390. W. and M. May 27/17.
17 X. Goldthorpe, L. 38129. M. April 17/17.
17 X. Johnson, Sergt. G. 505. M. April 17/17.
17 X. Kaye, J. W. 38146. M. April 17/17.
17 X. Lambart, R. 43563. M. April 17/17.
17 X. VII Lawson, W. 41594. M. April 17/17.
17 X. VI Pasacovitch, Hyman. 41495. M. April 17/17.
17 X. Taggart, J. 41608. M. April 17/17.
17 X. Wilks, Willie. 41466. M. April 17/17.
*17 X. Wilson, John. 333. W. and M. April 17/17.
18 **Holt, 2nd Lieut. W.** M. May 3/16.
18 **Mansfield, 2nd Lieut. H. L.** W. and M. May 3/17.
*18 **Stall, 2nd Lieut. O. H.** M. July 2/17.
18 **Warner, 2nd Lieut. W. J.** W. and M. May 3/17.
18 A. Buckley, Percy. 40772. M. May 3/17.
‡18 A. Busfield, Cpl. R. 17239. M. May 3/17.
‡18 A. Bywater, W. 1460. M. May 3/17.
*18 A. Gentle, T. Harry. 37926. W. and M. May 3/17.
*18 A. III George, E. S. 47927. M. May 3/17.
‡18 A. Horley, H. 1201. M. May 3/17.
‡18 A. Horsefield, L.-Cpl. H. 25416. M. May 3/17.
‡18 A. Houghton, John Wm. 40481. M. May 3/17.
18 A. Jordan, Wm. 47994. M. May 3/17.
‡18 A. Leckenby, F. 34478. M. May 3/17.
‡18 A. Millward, G. 47997. M. May 3/17.
18 A. III Norton, Fredk. 300013. M. May 3/17.
*18 A. Petty, Sylvester. 39. K. Oct. 18/16. Det.D./B.
18 A. IV Richards, J. E. 300065. K. April 29/17. Det.D./B.
‡18 A. Smith, J. 1344. M. May 3/17.
18 A. IV Swallow, J. 300035. M. May 3/17.
18 A. I Tweedy, Herbert. 22951. M. May 3/17.
‡18 A. Wilson, J. 36790. M. May 3/17.
18 B. Bean, Herbert Walter. 33076. M. May 3/17.
18 B. Bell, A.-Cpl. Tom. 8292. (Fr. 2nd.) M. May 3/17.
‡18 B. Brayshaw, J. 41283. M. May 3/17.

**Yorkshire Regiment, West—contd.**

## *B.E.F.*

18 B. VII Broadley, John Ewart. 41287. M. May 3/17.
‡18 B. Buswell, F. V. 40453. W. and M. May 3/17.
‡18 B. Denton, L.-Sergt. T. W. 148. M. May 3/17.
*18 B. Dunn, J. 33364. M. May 3/17.
18 B. VII Ferguson, L.-Cpl. John. 12870. M. May 3/17.
18 B. Fisher, A. 40467. M. May 3/17.
18 B. Griffin, L.-Cpl. Alfred Ernest. 27285. M. May 3/17.
‡18 B. Hamilton, W. 20269. M. May 3/17.
*18 B. VII Hanson, Geo. James. 33422. W. and M. May 3/17.
18 B. Hawkridge, James. 33402. W. and M. May 3/17.
‡18 B. Housecroft, V. 26196. M. May 3/17.
‡18 B. Marshall, L. 335. M. May 3/17.
*18 B. Miller, Andrew. 34377. M. May 3/17.
‡18 B. Minns, Cpl. J. 7904. M. May 3/17.
‡18 B. Needham, S. O. 35270. M. May 3/17.
‡18 B. Norman, W. 40492. W. and M. May 3/17.
18 B. Payne, Fred. 34334. M. May 3/17.
‡18 B. Phillips, T. 1013. M. May 3/17.
18 B. Philpotts, Geo. 300059. M. May 3/17.
‡18 B. Pipe, H. 27487. M. May 3/17.
‡18 B. Poole, G. E. 47937. M. May 3/17.
18 B. Ragg, A. 40498. M. May 3/17.
‡18 B. Riley, Sergt. J. R. 9490. M. May 3/17.
18 B. VIII Shaw, Herbert. 40238. W. and M. May 3/17.
‡18 B. Shelton, E. 41277. M. May 3/17.
18 B. Spurr, Jack. 33114. W. and M. May 3/17.
‡18 B. Taylor, J. 40335. M. May 3/17.
‡18 B. Tempest, L.-Cpl. J. 24392. M. May 3/17.
‡18 B. Watson, D. 8787. M. May 3/17.
18 C. XI Adams, Percival Turvil. 47920. M. May 3/17.
18 C. Arundale, Geo. Amos. 33327. M. May 3/17.
‡18 C. Atkinson, P. F. 23933. M. May 3/17.
‡18 C. IX Barker, Arthur. 40265. M. May 3/17.
18 C. Binns, J. R. 33111. M. May 3/17.
‡18 C. Britton, C. 603. M. May 3/17.
‡18 C. Bryan, J. H. 528. M. May 3/17.
18 C. XII Cartlick, S. 38262. M. May 3/17.
‡18 C. Ellis, L. 41291. M. May 3/17.
18 C. Fearnside, W. E. 40271. M. May 3/17.
‡18 C. Godridge, W. H. 520. M. May 3/17.
18 C. Greetham, C. 300050. M. May 3/17.
‡18 C. Haynes, R. W. 33112. M. May 3/17.
18 C. Heeley, Robt. 18/639. W. and M. May 3/17.
18 C. IX Hindle, Chas. H. 48013. M. abt. May 3/17.
‡18 C. Hollingdrake, W. 709. M. May 3/17.
18 C. XI Hughes, Joseph Holmes. 300040. M. May 3/17.
‡18 C. Jackson, J. 12969. M. May 3/17.
18 C. Lee, Arthur. 40489. M. May 3/17.
‡18 C. Morony, T. 22751. M. May 3/17.
‡18 C. Nichol, L.-Cpl. H. H. 22908 M. May 3/17.
‡18 C. Parker, L.-Cpl. Tom. 8142. M. May 3/17.
18 C. XI Pearson, S. B. 23059. M. May 3/17.
*18 C. Richardson, Ernest. 300060. M. May 3/17.
*18 C. Simpson, George. 40502. M. May 3/17.
‡18 C. Study, Sergt. S. 40273. M. May 3/17.
‡18 C. Sturgeon, P. 47075. M. May 3/17.
‡18 C. Symons, F. W. H. 47075. M. May 3/17.
18 C. Thomas, F. E. 530. M. May 3/17.
*18 C. Thompson, Chas. Fred. 34383. M. May 3/17.

**Yorkshire Regiment, West—contd.**

## *B.E.F.*

| | | |
|---|---|---|
| ‡18 C. | Westwood, J. 22707. | M. May 3/17. |
| *18 D. | Anderton, John Wm. 34286. | W. and M. May 3/17. |
| 18 D. | Brunt, Arnold Vincent. 1331. | M. May 3/17. |
| ‡18 D. | Caygill, P. 40304. | M. May 3/17. |
| 18 D. XIII | Deas, William Selby. 41290. | M. May 3/17. |
| 18 D. XIII | Donnachie, Patrick. 41289. | M., bel. P/W. May 3/17. |
| ‡18 D. | Flatt, B. 41279. | M. May 3/17. |
| 18 D. | Jeffery, Arthur. 40786. | M. May 3/17. |
| *18 D. XIII | Luxford, Fred. 40232. | M. May 3/17. |
| ‡18 D. | Millington, C. 47977. | M. May 3/17. |
| *18 D. XV | Neal, Richard. 47935. | M. May 3/17. |
| ‡18 D. | Newsome, Jos. 27182. | M. May 3/17. |
| 18 D. XV | Rudstien, Solomon. 47940. | M. May 3/17. |
| ‡18 D. | Senior, F. 25565. | M. May 3/17. |
| ‡18 D. XIII | Shaw, Fred. 325344. | M. May 3/17. |
| 18 D. XIV | Spencer, Arthur. 300034. | M. May 3/17. |
| 18 D. XIII | Tiplady, Ronald. 40237. | W. and M. May 3/17. |
| *18 D. | Wall, G. 27332. | M. May 3/17. |
| 18 D. XV | Ward, John. 300037. | K. May 3/17. Det.D./B. |
| 18 D. XIII | White, J. E. 40816. | M. May 3/17. |
| ‡18 D. | Wilson, Fred. 300018. | M. May 3/17. |

## KING'S OWN YORKSHIRE LIGHT INFANTRY.

## *B.E.F.*

| | | |
|---|---|---|
| 2 A. | Benson, Robert. 42355. | M. Feb. 12/17. |
| *2 A. | Evans, Thomas. 35305. | M. Nov. 18/16. R/Enq. |
| 2 A. III | Gumby, H. 29611. | K. April 3/17. Det.D./B. |
| 2 A. M.G.S. | Hallas, John. 947. | Unoff. M. Nov. 18/16. |
| *2 A. I | Hopkins, John W. 31064. | M. Nov. 18/16. R/Enq. |
| 2 A. | Wilkinson, Will. 1386. | Unoff. M. April or May/15. (Sic.) |
| 2 B. VI | Binks, Mark. 16676. | M. April 14/17. |
| *2 B. | Cave, T. H. 42085. | M. Nov. 18/16. R/Enq. |
| 2 B. VII | Hirst, W. H. 35754. | M. Unoff. W. April 14/17. |
| 2 B. | Hodgson, J. A. 10048. | M. April 14/17. |
| 2 B. VI | King, H. 42336. | M. Feb. 12/17. |
| 2 B. VIII | Middleton, W. H. 38675. | M. April 14/17. |
| 2 B. | Morland, Ernest. 42351. | M. Feb. 12/17. |
| 2 B. VI | Morley, Lawrence. 13224. | M. April 14/17. |
| 2 B. VII | Rogerson, L.-Cpl. J. W. 10843. | M. April 14/17. |
| 2 B. | Smith, L.-Cpl. H. 35769. | M. April 14/17. |
| 2 B. V | Sykes, L.-Cpl. Clifford. 1626. | M. April 14/17. |
| 2 B. | Taylor, H. 13077. | M. April 14/17. |
| 2 B. | Watson, L.-Cpl. T. 23017. | M. April 14/17. |
| 2 C. IX | Alton, William. 34223. | W. and M. Feb. 10/17. |
| *2 C. | Brearley, J. 3/1511. | M. Nov. 18/16. R/Enq. |
| 2 C. | Breedon, Frank. 24624. | M. Feb. 12/17. |
| 2 C. IX | Brogden, J. T. 42153. | M. Feb. 12/17. |
| 2 C. | Burton, A. 42155. | M. Feb. 12/17. |
| 2 C. IX | Coates, Walter. 30976. | W. and M. Feb. 10/17. |
| ‡2 C. | Hurley, Herbert John. 23452. | M. Nov. 18/16. R/Enq. |
| 2 C. IX | Paget, C. 23319. | M. Nov. 18/16. |
| *2 C. | Roberts, L.-Cpl. Robert. 23335. | M. Nov. 18/16. R/Enq. |
| 2 C. | Shelcott, J. 22775. | M. Nov. 18/16. R/Enq. |
| 2 C. X | Snowdon, Wilfred. 42197. | M. Feb. 12/17. |

**Yorkshire Light Infantry, King's Own—contd.**

## *B.E.F.*

| | | |
|---|---|---|
| 2 C. | Thistleton, T. 42203. | M. Feb. 12/17. |
| ‡2 C. M.G.S. | Totts, A.-Cpl. A. R. 10092. | M. Nov. 18/16. R/Enq. |
| 2 C. | Waters, F. 42330. | M. Feb. 10/17. |
| *2 C. XII | Wilson, L. T. 11041. | M. Nov. 18/16. R/Enq. |
| 2 D. | Ainsworth, C. 35761. | M. Feb. 12/17. |
| 2 D. | Appleyard, G. 30942. | M. Feb. 12/17. |
| 2 D. XV | Oldroyd, James. 25814. | M. Nov. 18/16. R/Enq. |
| ‡2 D. | Woodhall, L.-Cpl. G. A. 23346. | K. April 14/17. Det.D./B. |
| 4 C. XI | Scott, A. J. 203285 (late 6877.) | M. April 10/17. |
| 2/4 | **Pickard, 2nd Lieut. R. G.** | D/W. Mar. 2/17. Det.D./B |
| 2/4 A. I | Armitage, Lawrence. 201532. (3966.) | M. ' Unoff. K. May 3/17. |
| ‡2/4 A. | Goodair, M. 201281. | M. May 3/17. |
| 2/4 A. II | Harper, H. 202364. | M. May 3/17. |
| 2/4 A. L.G.S. | Lisle, John. 202208. | M. May 3/17. |
| *2/4 A. IV | Lyon, Edgar. 202243. (5111.) | M. May 3/17. |
| ‡2/4 A. | Wilkins, A. W. 238004. | M. May 3/17. |
| ‡2/4 A. | Wilson, C. W. 202362. | M. May 5/17. |
| 2/4 B. V | Bonnington, J. 202445. | M. Mar. 14/17. |
| ‡2/4 C. | Davison, W. 202270. | W. and M. May 3/17. |
| ‡2/4 C. | Field, J. 202348. | M. May 3/17. |
| 2/4 C. | Ingham, Frank. 201089. | M. May 3/17. |
| ‡2/4 C. | Jackson, B. 201793. | M. May 3/17. |
| ‡2/4 D. | Smalley, H. 203937. | M. May 5/17. |
| 5 | **Moorcock, 2nd Lieut. F. A.** (Fr. 2nd.) | M. May 3/17. |
| *5 | **Pearson, 2nd Lieut. A.** | M. June 13/17. |
| 5 | **Pringle, 2nd Lieut. R. G.** (Fr. 8 H.L.I.) | M. April 23/17. |
| ‡5 C. X | Rothery, F. W/242978. | Unoff. M. June 22/17. |
| 2/5 | **Brewster, Lieut. B. S.** | M., bel. K. May 3/17. |
| ‡2/5 A. IV | Bilbrough, Percy. 21094. | M. May 3/17. |
| ‡2/5 A. | Brown, W. H. 13347. | M. May 3/17. |
| ‡2/5 A. | Chapman, W. 240535. | M. May 3/17. |
| 2/5 A. IV | Cowley, L.-Cpl. Herbert. 242161. | M. May 3/17. |
| 2/5 A. | Craythorne, John. (Sig. S.) | M. May 3/17. |
| *2/5 A. M.G.S. | Joplin, Walter Edward. 242055. | M. May 3/17. |
| ‡2/5 A. | Lindsay, A. 242016. | W. and M. May 3/17. |
| ‡2/5 A. | Seddon, Norman. 241412. | W. and M. May 3/17. |
| ‡2/5 A. | Smith, A. 21207. | W. and M. May 3/17. |
| 2/5 A. | Sutton, L.-Cpl. P. O. 242815. (Fr. H.Q.) | M. May 3/17. |
| ‡2/5 A. | Wadsworth, L.-Cpl. J. 11300. | M. May 3/17. |
| 2/5 A. | Walker, Sergt. John. 240480. | W. and M. May 3/17. |
| 2/5 B. | Anthony, A. 241422. | M. May 3/17. |
| ‡2/5 B. | Arnold, R. 242164. | M. May 3/17. |
| ‡2/5 B. | Crooks, L.-Cpl. B. 242780. | M. May 3/17. |
| ‡2/5 B. | Davison, S. 200878. | M. May 3/17. |
| 2/5 B. VII | Denton, John Sandeman. 242076. | M. May 3/17. |
| 2/5 B. | Hambrey, Sergt. Ernest Geo. 241118. | M. May 3/17. |
| 2/5 B. IX | Horn, Tom B. 24971. | W. and M. May 3/17. |
| *2/5 B. VII | Morley, J. A. 242807. | M. May 3/17. |
| ‡2/5 B. VIII | Romans, Ernest. 242375. | M. May 3/17. |
| 2/5 B. | Watson, Cpl. George. 3906. | M. Feb. 26/17. |
| ‡2/5 B. | Whitworth, H. P. 202246. | M. May 3/17. |
| *2/5 C. X | Ashton, Thos. 242107. | M. May 3/17. |
| ‡2/5 C. | Ball, L.-Cpl. J. 241447. | M. May 3/17. |
| ‡2/5 C. | Carrol, H. 41090. | M. May 3/17. |
| ‡2/5 C. | Clempson, J. W. 241393. | M. May 3/17. |
| ‡2/5 C. | Falkingham, W. 241318. | M. May 3/17. |

**Yorkshire Light Infantry, King's Own—contd.**

*B.E.F.*

*2/5 C. XII Groundwell, G. 200175. M. May 3/17.
2/5 C. Hall, L.-Cpl. Robt. J. 241747. M. May 3/17.
*2/5 C. XII Horsley, Horace. 242792. Unoff. W. and M. end April/17.
‡2/5 C. Jones, W. 263060. M. May 3/17.
‡2/5 C. Leadbeater, F. G. 240780. W. and M. May 3/17.
‡2/5 C. Levitt, C. S. 241080. M. May 3/17.
‡2/5 C. Lockwood, A. 241780. W. and M. May 3/17.
*2/5 C. IX Milner, Walter. 241968. W. and M. May 3/17.
‡2/5 C. Richardson, T. F. 202981. M. May 3/17.
‡2/5 C. Siswick, E. 202620. M. May 3/17.
‡2/5 C. Walker, J. 241150. W. and M. May 3/17.
2/5 C. Ward, E. 240868. M. Mar. 14/17.
2/5 D. Bridgman, R. 242773. M. May 3/17.
‡2/5 D. Cramp, J. 242147. W. and M. May 3/17.
*2/5 D. I.T.M. Evans, G. 241252. (187 Bgde.) W. and M. May 3/17.
2/5 D. Oldridge, T. H. 242035. M. Mar. 14/17.
‡2/5 D. Platts, Sergt. G. W. 240291. W. and M. May 3/17.
‡2/5 D. Scoltock, W. 241653. M. May 3/17.
2/5 D. Simpson, A. C. 241259. (Fr. H.Q.) W. and M. May 3/17.
*2/5 ? I.T.M. Gill, J. 241216. (187 Bgde.) M. May 3/17.
‡6 W. III Clark, S. C. 43060. K. May 10/17. Det.D./B.
6 W. Smith, J. 30905. M. April 10/17.
6 X. Ellis, L.-Cpl. A. 33214. M. April 9/17.
‡6 Y. Boothroyd, E. 33119. M. May 13/17.
6 Y. XI Hall, Arthur. 33930. M. May 13/17.
‡6 Y. XII Norcliffe, Sgt. Arthur. 10378. M. May 13/17.
6 Y. XI Redden, L.-Cpl. John. 34599. M. Sept. 16/16. R/Enq.
6 Y. Rowan, Edward. 24963. M. Sept. 16/16. R/Enq.
6 Y. IX Sampson, John. 42297. M. May 13/17.
6 Y. Wood, T. W. 40624. M. April 9/17.
6 Z. XIV Daines, Harry. 21565. M. April 10/17.
6 Z. XIV Fox, Tom. 26976. M. Sept. 15/16. R/Enq.
6 Z. France, Percy Birkett. 33143. M. April 10/17.
6 Z. Kelshaw, A. 18223. W. and M. Mar. 12/17.
6 Z. XVI Lawson, Wilfred. 3/2954. W. and M. Mar. 12/17.
6 Z. Middleton, R. H. 23014. M. Mar. 12/17.
6 Z. Thompson, E. 21487. W. and M. Mar. 12/17.
6 Gren. S. Foreman, G. 18212. K. Sept. 16/16. Det.D./B.
*7 B. VII Lister, L.-Cpl. Joseph. 35225. W. and M. Oct. 7/16. R/Enq.
‡7 C. Smith, H. H. 242133. M. May 3/17.
7 C. Sutherland, Norman M. 35479. M. Dec. 14/16.
‡7 ? Hook, J. 35204. M. April 27/17.
‡8 A. III Anderson, John. 38355. M. June 7/17.
8 A. Gill, Jesse. 35337. M. Jan. 23/17.
8 A. Shakespeare, E. 25072. M. Jan. 23/17.
‡8 B. V Brown, Reg. Harry. 35822. M. June 10/17.
‡8 B. V Haigh, Sydney. 34237. W. Unoff. M. June 8/17.
8 B. Walker, Fred. 13259. Unoff. M. July 1/16. R/Enq.
8 C. Kirton, J. 15449. M. Oct. 1/16. R/Enq.
‡8 C. Lazenby, Fred. 35566. M. June 9/17.
*8 D. Clark, F. 18803. W. and M. Oct. 1/16. R/Enq.
8 D. Graham, J. 38393. M. Oct. 1/16.
8 D. Hogg, Edward. 24915. M. Oct. 1/16. R/Enq.
8 ? Collins, P. 878. M. Oct. 1/16. R/Enq.
9 A. Cundill, Chas. 34871. M. Sept. 16/16.
9 A. IV Foster, A. 34936. W. and M. Sept. 16/16. R./Enq.
9 A. L.G.S. Heap, L.-Cpl. Arth. Maurice. 35734 D/W. May 1/17. Det.D./B.
9 A. Lazenby, A. 34930. M. Sept. 16/16. R/Enq.

**Yorkshire Light Infantry, King's Own—contd.**

*B.E.F.*

| | | |
|---|---|---|
| *9 A. | Nettleton, Sergt. C. E. 462. | K. April 9/17. Det.D./B. |
| 9 B. VII | Chambers, Geo. 34867. | M. Sept. 16/16. R/Enq. |
| ‡9 B. | Green, Sergt. W. J. W. 23612. | K. April 9/17. Det.D./B. |
| 9 B. | Harrison, L.-Cpl. G. R. 21230. | M. Sept. 16/16. R/Enq. |
| 9 B. V | Lawley, Sergt. Lionel. 16491. | M. Sept. 16/16. |
| 9 B. | Ogden, I. W. 34958. | M. Sept. 16/16. R/Enq. |
| 9 B. VIII | Richardson, L.-Cpl. Ernest. 19002. | M. Sept. 16/16. R/Enq. |
| 9 B. VII | Smith, L.-Cpl. Thos. 23989. | M. April 9/17. |
| 9 B. | Williamson, S. G. 42968. | W. and M. April 9/17. |
| 9 C. | Dean, J. 35728. | M. April 9/17. |
| 9 C. | Green, Albert. 18666. | W. and M. Sept. 16/16. R/Enq. |
| 9 C. M.G.S. | Lupton, A. W. 25801. | W. and M. April 12/17. |
| 9 C. IX | Roberts, Fred. Thos. 43636. | W. and M. April 9/17. |
| 9 C. X | Satchwell, Fred. 17115. | M. April 9/17. |
| 9 D. XIII | Alexander, D. C. 35401. (Fr. 17 Sherwoods.) | M. Sept. 16/16. R/Enq. |
| 9 D. | Cook, A. V. 44005. | W. and M. April 9/17. |
| 9 D. XVI | Cornish, Robt. Wm. 37641. | M. Sept. 16/16. R/Enq. |
| 9 D. XIII | Eldin, L.-Cpl. John. 26360. | W. and M. Sept. 16/16. R/Enq. |
| 9 D. XIV | Fisher, D. G. 40255. | M. April 28/17. |
| 9 D. | Smith, Albert. 24347. | M. Sept. 16/16. R/Enq. |
| 9 ? | Harker, Leonard. 37647. | M. Sept. 16/16. R/Enq. |
| 9 ? | Heath, A. 43627. | M. April 9/17. |
| 9 ? | Hewlett, Joseph. 16148. (Fr. 2nd Royal Fus.) | W. and M. Sept. 16/16. R/Enq. |
| 9 ? M.G.S. | Nelson, L.-Cpl. F. 14880. | K. April 9/17. Det.D./B. |
| 9 ? | Woodcock, Geo. 24180. | M. April 9/17. |
| 10 | **Winkworth, 2nd Lieut. C. H. C.** | K. Sept. 25/16. Det.D./B. |
| 10 A. I | Nicholson, Robt. Ernest. 35022. (Fr. 9 D.L.I.) | M. Sept. 25/16. R/Enq |
| 10 A. | Seymour, Thomas W. 34671. | M. Sept. 25/16. R/Enq. |
| 10 B. VIII | Hunter, Fred. 21376. | M. Sept. 26/16. R/Enq. |
| 10 B. | Reeder, H. 28076. | M. Mar. 1/17. |
| 10 B. VIII | Sugden, L.-Cpl. Alfred. 25551. | M. April 9/17. |
| ‡10 B. VIII | Talbot, Fred. 25234. | K. Sept. 25/16. Det.D./B. R/Enq. |
| 10 C. IX | Burns, R. 43463. | W. Unoff. M. April 9/17. |
| 10 C. XII | Damms, W. 28271. | M. April 11/17. |
| 10 C. X | Dean, E. W. 30060. | K. Oct. 16/16. Det.D./B. R./Enq. |
| 10 C. | Grundy, A. 37549. | M. Sept. 25/16. |
| *10 C. XI | Noble, Chas. H. 37611. (Fr. 5 W. Riding. 4489.) | M. Sept. 25/16. R/Enq. |
| 10 C. L.G.S. | Raynor, William. 28282. | M. April 9/17. |
| 10 C. | Scholes, James. 39683. | M. April 9/17. |
| 10 C. or D. | Sewell, Jas. 35051. | M. Sept. 25/16. R/Enq. |

**YORK & LANCASTER REGIMENT.**

*B.E.F.*

| | | |
|---|---|---|
| 2 | **Leach, 2nd Lieut. H. O.** | K. April 22/17. Det.D./B. |
| 2 A. | Cryer, G. A. 23158. | W. and M. Sept. 15/16. R/Enq. |
| 2 A. | Stamp, A. 7836. | W. and M. Sept. 25/16. R./Enq. |
| 2 B. | Davies, A. 1195. | M. April 22/17. |
| 2 B. | Finchett, John Thos. 31419. | W. and M. Oct. 12/16. R/Enq. |
| 2 B. | Holloway, B. 31389. | K. Oct. 12/16. R/Enq. |
| 2 B. | McLoughlin, W. 22855. | M. Oct. 12/16. R/Enq. |
| 2 B. | Norbury, Brierley. 26408. | M. April 22/17. |
| 2 B. | Platts, Arnold. 31387. (Fr. 3/4. 4868.) | M. Oct. 12/16. |
| 2 B. V | Seaton, F. 21783. | W. and M. April 22/17. |

York and Lancaster Regiment—contd.

*B.E.F.*

2 B. Tiler, Walter. 21328. K. April 14/17. Det.D./B.
‡2 B. White, John. 31055. M. Oct. 12/16.
2 B. Whitehouse, L.-Cpl. Jess. 9504. M. April 22/17.
‡2 C. Bailey, J. W. 241254. W. and M. May 3/17.
‡2 C. Campbell, S. 31122. M. April 15/17.
2 D. Bennett, G. 14/1204. M. Oct. 12/16. R/Enq.
‡2 D. L.G.S. Hind, B. 37987. K. April 15/17. Det.D./B.
2 D. Mickleweight, H. G. 20377. W. and M. April 22/17.
‡2 D. XVI Reilly, W. 2861. K. April 22/17. Det.D./B.
2 D. M.G.S. Stocks, William. 22746. M. Oct. 12/16. R/Enq.
‡2 D. Stubbs, L.-Cpl. P. 31458. M. Oct. 12/16.
‡4 A. Ball, A. R. 203887. M. June 12/17.
‡4 A. Bird, Cpl. W. H. 203128. M. June 12/17.
‡4 A. Gallagher, E. 200546. M. June 12/17.
*4 A. Goswell, F. J. 6585. M. Sept. 14/16. R/Enq.
‡4 A. Hayes, H. 203410. M. June 12/17.
‡4 A. Mills, A. 201977. M. June 12/17.
‡4 A. Parkin, F. 203142. M. June 12/17.
‡4 A. Ryan, J. H. 201813. M. June 12/17.
‡4 A. I Sewell, George. 235072. M. June 12/17.
‡4 B. VI Haywood, William. 200674. M. June 12/17.
‡4 B. VI Wood, Sergt. G. 200440. M. June 12/17.
‡4 D. XV Keyworth, J. 203385. M. June 12/17.
‡4 D. XV Oliver, L.-Cpl. Herbert Clarke. 200531. W. and M. June 12/17.
4 ? **Cliveley, 2nd Lieut. J. H.** W. and M. May 3/17
2/4 **Gale, Capt. W. N.** M. about May 3/17.
2/4 **Richardson, Major J. W.** W. and M. May 3/17.
‡2/4 A. Adcock, P. 204212. W. and M. May 3/17.
‡2/4 A. Armstrong, A. 201531. W. and M. May 3/17.
‡2/4 A. Batty, J. 202730. M. May 3/17.
‡2/4 A. Benstead, L.-Cpl. G. 202080. (5277.) M. May 3/17.
‡2/4 A. Edwards, A. 201607. M. May 3/17.
2/4 A. Hallatt, Randolph. 201663. W. and M. May 3/17.
2/4 A. II Harris, R. S. 201676. W. and M. May 3/17.
2/4 A. Hawkins, J. H. 200388. (1979.) M. May 3/17.
2/4 A. Higgins, W. F. 202377. (4901.) M. May 3/17.
‡2/4 A. Knoll, E. 201594. M. May 3/17.
‡2/4 A. Pickering, A. H. 201658. M. May 3/17.
2/4 A. IV Short, Cpl. F. 201575. M. May 3/17.
2/4 A. I Smith, W. H. 203033. (5840.) M. May 3/17.
‡2/4 A. Starkey, W. F. 202688. M. May 3/17.
‡2/4 A. Stevenson, Cpl. G. H. 201590. M. May 3/17.
*2/4 A. Warrington, F. 201579. M. May 3/17.
‡2/4 B. Batty, E. 201386. M. May 3/17.
2/4 B. VIII Bellairs, H. A. 202560. M. Mar. 12/17.
‡2/4 B. VIII Bellamy, L.-Sergt. Joe. 201107. M. May 3/17.
‡2/4 B. Brackenbury, L.-Cpl. H. 201074. M. May 3/17.
‡2/4 B. Crawshaw, W. 201198. M. May 3/17.
‡2/4 B. Henshaw, S. 204273. M. May 3/17.
‡2/4 B. Hewkin, E. 202388. W. and M. May 3/17.
‡2/4 B. M.G.S. Holland, Cpl. Donald Frazer. 201110. (3024.). M. Unoff. W. May 3/17.
*2/4 B. Matson, John Hry. 202317. (4790.) M. May 3/17.
‡2/4 B. Platts, B. 202380. M. May 3/17.
‡2/4 B. Smith, C. A. 202332. M. May 3/17.
2/4 B. Smith, George. 204254. (17064.) M. May 3/17.
‡2/4 B. Thackeray, F. 202375. M. May 3/17.
2/4 B. Wainwright, Sampson. 202661. M. May 3/17.
2/4 B. VI Wesley, Sergt. R. S. 200755. M. May 3/17.

York and Lancaster Regiment—contd.

*B.E.F.*

‡2/4 B. Wall, A. 202391. M. May 3/17.
‡2/4 B. Wigley, B. 202327. M. May 3/17.
*2/4 B. V Wildsmith, Joseph. 201517. M. May 3/17.
‡2/4 C. Bayliss, Cpl. Arthur. 201187. W. and M. May 3/17.
‡2/4 C. Bayliss, J. 204234. M. May 3/17.
2/4 C. XI Binks, L.-Cpl. H. 201207. M. May 3/17.
*2/4 C. IX Blackburn, Arnold. 201244. M. May 3/17.
*2/4 C. X Bradbury, Edgar F. 202594. M. May 3/17.
‡2/4 C. Chapman, W. H. 201192. M. May 3/17.
*2/4 C. Couldwell, A. 201204. M. May 3/17.
‡2/4 C. Cunnane, T. 202599. M. May 3/17.
‡2/4 C. Downing, W. H. 202788. M. May 3/17.
‡2/4 C. Drew, Sergt. E. 201239. M. May 3/17.
‡2/4 C. Etchells, J. 202598. M. May 3/17.
‡2/4 C. IX Ginever, J. N. 204399. M. May 3/17.
‡2/4 C. Glossop, R. H. 201212. M. May 3/17.
2/4 C. IX Goddard, John. 202590. (5176.) M. May 3/17.
‡2/4 C. Hampshire, S. H. 202766. M. May 3/17.
2/4 C. XI Hibberson, Geo. 201205. (3135.) M. May 3/17.
‡2/4 C. Hounslow, L. B. 202325. M. May 3/17.
‡2/4 C. Howson, T. 202459. M. May 3/17.
‡2/4 C. Kirby, W. 202601. M. May 3/17.
‡2/4 C. Lodge, C. 204279. M. May 3/17.
2/4 C. IX Reeder, L. K. 204261. M. May 3/17.
‡2/4 C. Sanderson, A. L. 201236. M. May 3/17.
2/4 C. X Scott, A. 201182. M. May 3/17.
‡2/4 C. Sheen, N. 204258. M. May 3/17.
2/4 C. X Southwell, Cpl. G. 201581. M. May 3/17.
*2/4 C. Simmonite, L.-Cpl. Jas. 201137. M. May 3/17.
2/4 C. IX Topham, Geo. Wm. 204374. (17216.) M. May 3/17.
‡2/4 C. Vickers, H. N. 201295. M. May 3/17.
2/4 C. Watkinson, Cpl. W. 201196. W. and M. May 3/17.
*2/4 C. Watson, Sig. W. F. 202420. M. May 3/17.
2/4 C. IX Wright, L.-Cpl. Thos. 201504. (3508.) M. May 4/17.
2/4 D. Abson, W. J. 202472. (5042.) W. and M. May 3/17.
2/4 D. XIV Ansell, Joseph. 204376 M. May 3/17.
‡2/4 D. Crisp, L.-Cpl. H. 202503. W. and M. May 3/17.
2/4 D. Elliott, L.-Cpl. D. 200988. (2866.) W. and M. May 3/17.
‡2/4 D. Frost, Maurice. 200858. M. May 3/17.
‡2/4 D. Haxby, C. 204263. M. May 3/17.
*2/4 D. Hill, A. 204395. W. and M. May 3/17.
2/4 D. Johnson, L.-Sergt. Wm. Geo. 200947. (2815.) M. May 3/17.
*2/4 D. Jolley, Harold Geo. 204375. (17219.) M. May 3/17.
2/4 D. XVI Kelly, J. H. 201638. (3683.) W. and M. May 3/17.
2/4 D. Lindley, John. 202477. W. and M. May 3/17.
‡2/4 D. Moseley, J. H. 202626. W. and M. May 3/17.
2/4 D. Pollard, A. 202623. (5215.) W. and M. May 3/17.
‡2/4 D. Ryalls, W. 202474. M. May 3/17.
‡2/4 D. Ward, M. 202510. M. May 3/17.
‡2/4 D. Williams, H. 201611. W. and M. May 3/17.
5 C. XII Beaulah, J. W. 242208. (6098.) W. and M. Sept. 20/16.
2/5 B. **Jenkins, 2nd Lieut. G. C.** M. May 3/17.
2/5 A. Adlington, Cpl. Wm. 241308. M. May 3/17.
*2/5 A. II Calladine, Ernest. 241347. (3803.) M. May 3/17.
‡2/5 A. Clinton, J. 241591. M. May 3/17.
‡2/5 A. Cook, V. 241899. M. May 3/17.
‡2/5 A. Crossland, N. 241666. M. May 3/17.
‡2/5 A. Featherstone, D. 241633. M. May 3/17.

**York and Lancaster Regiment—contd.**

## *B.E.F.*

| | | |
|---|---|---|
| *2/5 A. | Harper, L.-Sergt. Sidney. 240810. | W. and M. May 3/17. |
| 2/5 A. | Howcroft, Sergt. John. 241026. (3314) | W. and M. May 3/17. |
| ‡2/5 A. | Jepson, William. 241124. | W. and M. May 3/17. |
| ‡2/5 A. | Taylor, A. 241622. | M. May 3/17. |
| 2/5 B. | Crossland, L.-Cpl. Ernest. 241944. | M. May 3/17. |
| ‡2/5 B. | Hetherington, W. 242776. | W. and M. May 3/17. |
| ‡2/5 B. | Lockwood, S. 241798. | M. May 3/17. |
| ‡2/5 B. | Marsden, J. W. 241953. | W. and M. May 3/17. |
| 2/5 B. | Moseley, Cpl. Alf. 241048. (5531.) | W. and M. May 2-3/17. |
| 2/5 B. | Preston, Arthur. 240903. (3127.) | M. May 25/17. |
| ‡2/5 B. | Quinn, J. E. 240684. | W. and M. May 3/17. |
| 2/5 B. | Shearman, F. A. 241943. | M. May 3/17. |
| ‡2/5 B. | Wilson, H. 241849. | M. May 3/17. |
| ‡2/5 C. | Ferreday, Sgt. Frank. 241296. (3722) | M. May 3/17. |
| 2/5 C. | Harker, Geo. 242668. (16035.) | M. May 3/17. |
| ‡2/5 C. XII | Hutchinson, Geo. 242768. (16451.) | M. May 3/17. |
| 2/5 C. | Ince, Cpl. Frank. 240767. (2885.) | M. May 3/17. |
| 2/5 C. X | Kirby, L.-Cpl. C. H. 241256. | M. May 3/17. |
| ‡2/5 C. | Lowry, W. 241639. | M. May 3/17. |
| ‡2/5 C. | McHale, J. 241856. | M. May 3/17. |
| 2/5 C. XII | Madeley, Chas. Fred. 241821. (4641) | W. and M. May 3/17. |
| ‡2/5 C. | Pickering, George A. 241197. | M. May 3/17. |
| ‡2/5 C. | Pilley, F. 241058. | M. May 3/17. |
| ‡2/5 C. | Smith, L.-Cpl. W. 241000. | W. and M. May 3/17. |
| ‡2/5 C. | Spencer, B. 241864. | M. May 3/17. |
| *2/5 C. | Stoker, J. 242691. | M. May 3/17. |
| 2/5 C. XI | Thompson, L.-Cpl. Jn. Chas. 241281 (8705.) | M. May 3/17. |
| ‡2/5 C. | Walker, F. 241231. | M. May 3/17. |
| ‡2/5 C. | Wroe, G. 240915. | M. May 3/17. |
| ‡2/5 D. | Alker, E. V. 241960. | M. May 3/17. |
| 2/5 D. | Bluck, Fred. 241828. (4648.) | M. May 3/17. |
| *2/5 D. L.G.S. | Chadbund, L.-Cpl. J. T. 241166. | W. and M. May 3/17. |
| ‡2/5 D. | Hardy, L.-Cpl. R. 240841. | M. May 3/17. |
| *2/5 D. | Hughes, Alex. 242783. (16463.) | M. May 3/17. |
| 2/5 D. | Jaques, L.-Cpl. Tom. 240903. (3107.) | M. May 3/17. |
| ‡2/5 D. | Johnson, W. 241561. (4220.) | W. and M. May 3/17. |
| ‡2/5 D. | Meggitt, W. 241925. | W. and M. May 3/17. |
| 2/5 D. | Lockwood, Sergt. H. 241178. (3547.) | W. and M. May 3/17. |
| ‡2/5 D. | Park, G. W. 241825. | W. and M. May 3/17. |
| ‡2/5 D. | Quinlan, Joseph. 241547. | W. and M. May 3/17. |
| 2/5 D. XVI | Robinson, Thos. John. 242741. | M. May 3/17. |
| ‡2/5 D. | Staley, J. 241885. | W. and M. May 3/17. |
| ‡2/5 D. | Swindells, G. 241083. | M. May 3/17. |
| 2/5 D. | Taylor, L.-Cpl. Willie. 240758. | W. and M. May 3/17. |
| *2/5 ? I.T.M. | Fell, Cpl. F. 240276. (187 Bde.) | W. and M. May 3/17. |
| *2/5 ? I.T.M. | Parker, J. W. 241650. (187 Bde.) | W. and M. May 3/17. |
| 6 A. | Campbell, Arthur. 10585. | M. Sept. 29/16. R./Enq. |
| 6 A. | Judd, Chas. Jos. 31858. (Fr. Northants.) | M. Jan. 17/17. |
| 6 B. | Cooper, B. T. 31838. | M. Jan. 17/17. |
| 6 B. Trans. | S. Hirst, John. 3/4801. | W. and M. Jan. 17/17. |
| 6 C. | Goldsbrough, L.-Cpl. Harry. 39904. | M. Jan. 17/17. |
| 6 D. | Brownell, W. H. 17158. | M. Sept. 29/16. R/Enq. |
| 6 D. | Sefton, W. 10354. | M. Sept. 29/16. R/Enq. |
| 8 C. | Lucas, 2nd Lieut. E. H. A. | M. June 7/17. |
| ‡8 A. | Savage, Matthew. 32560. | W. and M. June 7/17. |
| ‡8 B. VI | Barker, A. 34361. | M. June 8/17. |

York and Lancaster Regiment—contd.

*B.E.F.*

| | | |
|---|---|---|
| *8 B. | Butler, Fred. 31245. (2329.) | K. Dec. 3/16. Det.D./B. |
| 8 C. | Turner, J. W. 1611. | M. April 9/17. |
| 8 D. | Evans, Sig. Ernest Edwin. 4769. | K. Mar. 15/17. Det.D./B. |
| 8 D. | Falding, Frank. 34255. | M. Sept. 29/16. R/Enq. |
| *8 D. | Geddie, C. 34858. | M. April 9/17. |
| ‡8 D. XIV | Haggas, L.-Cpl. T. 32747. | W. Unoff. M. June 7/17. |
| ‡8 D. | Holmes, E. J. 34756. | M. April 9/17. |
| 8 D. | Ingham, Lewis S. S. 38595. | M. April 9/17. |
| 8 D. | Jagger, A.-Cpl. E. 40137. | M. April 9/17. |
| 8 D. | Lindley, W. 37948. | M. April 9/17. |
| ‡8 D. XIV | Marshall, Fred. 201805. | M. June 7/17. |
| 8 D. | Mitchell, F. 31259. | M. April 9/17. |
| 8 D. | Neal, L.-Cpl. G. 34347. | M. April 9/17. |
| 8 D. | Phypers, Ernest Prior. 32234. | M. April 9/17. |
| 8 D. M.G.S. | Quincey, T. 34200. | M. April 9/17. |
| 8 D. | Smith, A. 34791. | M. April 9/17. |
| ‡8 D. XIV | Taylor, Sidney John Smith. 32678. | M. June 6/17. |
| ‡8 D. XV | Wallis, H. 201717. | M. June 7/17. |
| 8 D. M.G.S. | White, L.-Cpl. E. 34395. | M. Mar. 9/17. |
| 8 D. | Wilburn, Cpl. H. 19903. | M. April 9/17. |
| ‡9 A. III | Clegg, C. J. 40096. | Unoff. W. and M. June 7/17. |
| *9 A. III | Hall, E. A. 40512. | D/W. June 5/17. Det.D./B. |
| ‡9 C. | Payling, C. 14952. | M. June 26/17. |
| ‡9 C. | Walsh, T. 24329. | M. June 26/17. |
| 10 A. | Aram, L.-Cpl. H. 23764. | W. and M. April 21-28/17. |
| *10 A. I | Bailey, Jas. 21594. | M. April 9-12/17. |
| *10 A. I | Barnett, G. 32273. | M. April 21-28/17. |
| ‡10 A. | Blanch, E. 32376. | M. April 21-28/17. |
| 10 A. | Chapman, Ernest. 36207. | M. April 21-28/17. |
| 10 A. III | Dillon, John T. 32216. | M. April 28/17. |
| 10 A. L.G.S. | Eberlin, J. F. 22356. | M., bel. K. April 21-28/17. |
| ‡10 A. | France, Sergt. J. 19607. | M. April 21-28/17. |
| *10 A. | France, Wm. 34065. | M. April 21-28/17. |
| ‡10 A. | Ibbetson, A. 32347. | M. April 21-28/17. |
| 10 A. I | Ingham, Arthur. 23199. | M. April 21-28/17. |
| 10 A. | Johansen, Peter Frank. 32318. (73531) | M. April 21-28/17. |
| 10 A. III | Middleton, G. E. 22804. | M. April 21-28/17. |
| ‡10 A. | Rider, C. 32320. | M. April 22-28/17. |
| 10 A. | Shaw, Sgt. Frank. 4823. (Fr. H.Q. Sig. S.) | M. April 21-28/17. |
| 10 A. | Slater, Chas. 32381. | M. April 21-28/17. |
| ‡10 A. | Taylor, G. H. 40669. | M. April 21-28/17. |
| *10 A. | Watson, Chas. E. 32375. (Fr. 15 W. Yorks.) | M. April 21-28/17. |
| ‡10 A. | Wood, A. 32388. | M. April 21-28/17. |
| *10 B. | Bean, W. 25972. | M. April 21-28/17. |
| *10 B. | Booth, Sam. Clarence. 38783. | M. April 21-28/17. |
| 10 B. | Brown, J. 18551. | M. April 9-12/17. |
| ‡10 B. | Buttery, W. L. 200102. | M. April 21-28/17. |
| ‡10 B. | Cooper, T. F. 32355. | M. April 21-28/17. |
| 10 B. | Dean, L.-Cpl. J. W. 8971. | W. and M. April 9-12/17. |
| 10 B. | Drummond, H. 32281. | W. and M. April 9-12/17. |
| ‡10 B. | Eyre, J. C. 28251. | W. and M. April 9-12/17. |
| ‡10 B. | Farrell, M. 202197. | M. April 21-28/17. |
| 10 B. | Garratt, E. 32289. | W. and M. April 9-12/17. |
| ‡10 B. | Gold, W. 200879. | M. April 21-28/17. |
| ‡10 B. VIII | Holmes, George. 34129. | M. April 21-28/17. |
| 10 B. VI | Jackson, Firth. 24011. | M. April 21-28/17. |

**York and Lancaster Regiment—contd.**

## *B.E.F.*

| | | | |
|---|---|---|---|
| ‡10 B. | | Johnson, W. H. 32359. | M. April 21-28/17. |
| ‡10 B. | | Kennedy, L.-Cpl. T. 9853. | M. April 21-28/17. |
| ‡10 B. | | Lang, E. 32197. | M. April 21-28/17. |
| ‡10 B. | | Mellor, F. M. 19792. | M. April 21-28/17. |
| ‡10 B. | | Mills, L.-Cpl. A. F. S. 37480. | M. April 21-28/17. |
| 10 B. | | Richardson, L.-Cpl. Wm. 37540. | M. April 21-28/17. |
| ‡10 B. | | Ryles, P. 20323. | M. April 21-28/17. |
| ‡10 B. | | Scott, A. 202256. | M. April 21-28/17. |
| ‡10 B. | | Simms, H. 32374. | M. April 21-28/17. |
| 10 B. | VII | Sorbsy, L.-Cpl. Albert. 13063. | M. April 21-28/17. |
| ‡10 B. | | Swann, A. H. 31509. | M. April 21-28/17. |
| ‡10 B. | | Tankard, N. P. 32303. | M. April 21-28/17. |
| 10 B. | | Taylor, Henry. 32362. | M. April 21-28/17. |
| ‡10 B. | | Turnbull, H. L. 40471. | M. April 21-28/17. |
| 0 B. | | Ure, Leopold, J. D. 40673. | M. April 21-29/17. |
| 10 B. | | Vaughan, R. G. 40473. | W. and M. April 9-12/17. |
| 10 B. | VI | Vickers, L.-Cpl. Geo. 34166. | W. and M. April 9-12/17. |
| ‡10 B. | | Wadsworth, G. 38675. | M. April 21-28/17. |
| ‡10 C. | | Atkins, A.-Cpl. A. 14326. | M. April 21-28/17. |
| 10 C. | IX | Bloy, R. J. 32304. | M. April 21-28/17. |
| 10 C. | | Cromack, Joseph. 32346. | M. April 21-28/17. |
| 10 C. | | Downing, L.-Cpl. Alfred. 13644. | M. April 21-28/17. |
| 10 C. | | Gibbons, Arthur. 22683. | M. April 21-28/17. |
| ‡10 C. | | Hainsworth, L. 32326. | M. April 21-28/17. |
| ‡10 C. | | Hanson, E. 32168. | M. April 21-28/17. |
| 10 C. | X | Henson, J. J. 36218. | M. April 21-28/17. |
| *10 C. | | Lodge, F. 23546. | M. April 21-28/17. |
| ‡10 C. | | Mallinder, G. 22882. | M. April 21-28/17. |
| ‡10 C. | | Medcroft, W. 32308. | M. April 21-28/17. |
| *10 C. | | Petty, Sergt. Chas. Hry. 21393. | M. April 21-28/17. |
| ‡10 C. | | Roberts, H. 32299. | M. April 21-28/17. |
| *10 C. | | Rowan, Michael. 235238. (Late W. Yorks, 200791.) | M. April 21-28/17. |
| ‡10 C. | | Sewell, A. 32305. | M. April 21-28/17. |
| 10 C. | XI | Sewell, A. 235054. | M. April 21-28/17. |
| ‡10 C. | | Slade, Walter A. 38187. | M. April 21-28/17. |
| ‡10 C. | | Stenton, S. 34089. | M. April 21-28/17. |
| *10 C. | | Thorpe, Fred. 32301. | M. April 21-28/17. |
| 10 C. | | Watson, J. 40485. | M. April 21-28/17. |
| 10 D. | XIII | Bishop, Sergt. A. V. 2/10239. | M. April 21-28/17. |
| ‡10 D. | | Bland, F. 32149. | M. April 21-28/17. |
| ‡10 D. | | Carr, A. 137. | M. April 21-28/17. |
| *10 D. | XIII | Darbyshire, Wm. Wharton. 21407. | M. April 21-28/17. |
| 10 D. | | Dubber, Harry Chas. 20676. | M. April 21-28/17. |
| ‡10 D. | | Dunning, L.-Cpl. F. 19742. | M. April 21-28/17. |
| 10 D. | XIII | Greig, James. 20566. | M. April 21-28/17. |
| ‡10 D. | | Heath, H. 17927. | M. April 21-28/17. |
| ‡10 D. | | Kane, M. 32339. | M. April 21-28/17. |
| ‡10 D. | XIII | Northrop, Fred. 36248. | M. April 21-28/17. |
| ‡10 D. | | Scott, H. 34152. | M. April 21-28/17. |
| ‡10 D. | | Stevens, Sergt. W. 4440. | M. April 21-28/17. |
| 10 D. | XIII | Sutton, Bomber W. 17605. | W. and M. April 9-12/17. |
| ‡10 D. | | Thomas, R. 40682. | M. April 21-28/17. |
| ‡10 D. | | Thornley, J. 40522. | M. May 3/17. |
| ‡10 D. | | Tomlinson, John. 241494. | W. and M. April 28/17. |
| ‡10 D. | | Wilde, J. 40490. | M. April 21-28/17. |
| ‡10 D. | | Wiseman, G. R. 39003. | M. April 21-28/17. |
| ‡10 D. | | Wood, E. 40484. | M. April 21-28/17. |
| 10 ? | | Judge, J. 1562. | M. Mar. 30/17. |

**York and Lancaster Regiment—contd.**

## *B.E.F.*

| | | |
|---|---|---|
| 12 D. | Ibbitson, M. 16742. | M. Mar. 9/17. |
| ‡13 A. | Yates, W. 40498. | M. April 21-28/17. |
| ‡13 A. | Field, S. 31677. | M. May 8/17. |
| *13 C. X | Cresswell, L.-Cpl. G. 207. | M. May 20/17. |
| ‡13 C. | Elliott, A. 23188. | M. May 20/17. |
| ‡13 C. | Samson, R. T. 874. | M. May 3/17. |
| ‡13 C. | Smith, W. J. 1296. | W. and M. May 7/17. |
| ‡14 A. | Charlesworth, A. 29357. | M. May 7/17. |
| 14 A. | Giraud, Hervé. 927. | M. May 7/17. |
| 14 D. | Cahill, Wm. 3668. (Fr. 6th.) | M. Mar. 9/17. |
| *14 D. XVI | Wilson, John. 235149. | M. May 16/17. |

## *BALKANS.*

| | | |
|---|---|---|
| 1 | **Sussex, 2nd Lt. R. A.** (Fr. 4 W. Yorks.) | W. and M. March 20/17. |
| 1 A. | Hallam, W. H. 20450. | W. and M. Oct. 11/16. |
| 1 A. III | Raine, Joseph Dixon. 30041. | W. and M. Feb. 3/17. |
| 1 D. | David, L.-Sergt. C. 10114. | W. and M. Mar. 20/17. |
| 1 D. | Weston, T. W. W. 9791. | W. and M. Mar. 20/17. |
| 1 ? | Harris, S. 20589. | W. and M. Mar. 20/17. |
| 1 ? | Hinton, G. 13976. | W. and M. Mar. 20/17. |
| ‡1 ? | Hodgson, F. E. 27670. | M. June 26/17. |
| ‡1 ? | Jackson, T. 38417. | M. June 26/17. |
| 1 ? | Jenkinson, E. B. 10077. | M. Mar. 20/17. |

**THIS LIST CANCELS ALL PREVIOUS LISTS.**

# AUSTRALIAN BRANCH.

## British Red Cross

AND

## Order of St. John.

---

## AUGUST 1st, 1917.

# ENQUIRY LIST.

---

## MEDITERRANEAN, FRANCE AND BELGIUM.

54, VICTORIA STREET,
LONDON, S.W.

*Telephone: Victoria 8858.*

**The names with ‡ are New Enquiries; those with * have appeared in the Supplement of July 15th, 1917.**

# AUSTRALIAN IMPERIAL FORCES.

### 1st BATTALION A.I.F.

| Co. | | |
|---|---|---|
| C. | Ashford, E. 3228. | K. Nov. 5/16. Det.D./B. |
| | Bannan, Cpl. T. C. 802. | K. Nov. 5/16. Det.D./B. |
| | Boon, L.-Cpl. T. H. 1022. | D/W. April 11/17. Det.D./B. |
| | *Blake, F. G. 6471. | K. May 5-8/17. Det.D./B. |
| | Brombey, G. J. 3697. | W. and M. Nov. 5/16. |
| | *Brown, J. 5664. | K. April 9/17. Det.D./B. |
| | Budsworth, R. H. 18A. | W. and M. Nov. 5/16. |
| | *Charge, G. C. 5074. | K. April 9/17. Det.D./B. |
| C. | Clarkson, E. A. 5672. | M. Nov. 5/16. |
| | Constable, W. F. 392. | K. Nov. 5/16. Det.D./B. |
| | Cregan, C. A. 5668. | M. Nov. 5/16. |
| | *Davidson, W. A. 5995. | K. May 5-8/17. Det.D./B. |
| | Duggan, J. D. 3354. | K. Oct. 12/16. Det.D./B. |
| | Eather, T.-Sergt. F. 1462. | M. May 5-8/17. |
| | Farley, T. C. I. 3313. | M. Nov. 5/16. |
| B. | Flower, Sergt. R. O. 826. | K. Nov. 5/16. Det.D./B. |
| | Frost, A. 3318. | K. April 9/17. Det.D./B. |
| | ‡Gibson. 1037. | K. May 5/17. Det.D./B. |
| | Govers, A. 79. | K. Nov. 5/16. Det.D./B. |
| | *Green, F. 3746. | K. May 5/17. Det.D./B. |
| | ‡Graham, W. B. 3328. | K. Nov. 5/16. Det.D./B. |
| | ‡Huolohan, P. 3808. | K. May 9/17. Det.D./B. |
| | Jamieson, G. W. 2447 | K. Nov. 5/16. Det.D./B. |
| | Jeffery, A. 6028. | M. May 5-8/17. |
| A. | Johns, H. W. 4447. | D/W. Nov. 1/16. Det.D./B. |
| | *Jones, D. 6857. | K. May 5-8/17. Det.D./B |
| | Lake, L. C. 5733. | M. Nov. 5/16. |
| | *Loosemore, T. H. 6343. | K. April 17/17. Det.D./B. |
| | ‡McGlynn, D. F. 3417. | D/W. April 14/17. Det.D./B. |
| | McGregor, O. D. 5181. | M. Nov. 5/16. |
| | Mackley, T. 2492. | K. May 5-8/17. Det.D./B. |
| A. | *McLean, J. 6119. | W. and M. May 5-8/17. |
| | ‡McWaters, J. 6551. | K. April 9/17. Det.D/.B. |
| | Marshall, W. W. 5158. | M. May 5-8/17. |
| C. | Mason, Cpl. A. 3402. | M. Nov. 5/16. |
| | Miller, R. D. 5168. | M. Nov. 5/16. |
| C. | Morrison, L.-Cpl. J. G. 4038. | K. Nov. 5/16. Det.D./B. |
| A. | ‡Munday, B. J. 8096. | Unoff. M. April/17. |
| | Mundy, B. J. S. 7108. | M. May 5-8/17. |
| | ‡Norton, A. 1959. | K. May 6/17. Det.D./B. |
| | ‡O'Brien, D. M. 6549. | K. May 5-8/17. Det.D./B. |
| | Parkes, J. 3441. | K. May 5-8/17. Det.D./B. |
| | Parr, G. J. 726. | K. Nov. 5/16. Det.D./B. |
| C. | *Pearce, G. 6263. | K. May 5-8/17. Det.D./B. |
| | Penketh, N. D. 3444. | M. Nov. 5/16. |
| C. | Porter, W. F. 3809. | K. Nov. 5/16. Det.D./B. |

1st Battalion A.I.F.—contd.

| Co. | | |
|---|---|---|
| | Rankine, W. C. 5206. | M. Nov. 5/16. |
| | Rutherford, T. 5207. | K. Nov. 5/16. Det.D./B. |
| C. | ‡Savage, J. 6306. | K. May 5-8/17. Det.D./B. |
| | *Smith, H. H. 6085. | K. May 5-8/17. Det.D./B. |
| | Thorburn, M. K. 5239. | W. and M. Nov. 5/16. |
| | ‡Tideman, L. W. 5236. | K. Nov. 5/16. Det.D./B. |
| B. | Vandine, S. A. P. 5249. | W. and M. Nov. 5/16. |
| | Waghorn, C. A. 3933. | M. Nov. 5/16. |
| | Watts, J. W. 5265. | K. May 5-8/17. Det.D./B. |
| | ‡Whettem, R. 3518. | K. May 7/17. Det.D./B. |
| | *Woodland, S. W. F. 6781. | K. May 5-8/17. Det.D./B. |

2nd BATTALION A.I.F.

| | | |
|---|---|---|
| | Badewitz, J. C. 6468. | M. May 6/17. |
| | Chadban, H. 1926. | M. May 4/17. |
| | ‡Cooke, L.-Cpl. H. W. 2799. M.G.S. | K. April 9/17. Det.D/.B. |
| | Cornell, S. T. 5658. | K. April 9/17. Det.D./B. |
| | Davie, Sgt. W. C. 6027. | K. April 9/17. Det.D./B. |
| | Delmas, V. J. R. 2804. | M. May 5/17. |
| | Feeney, T. A. 3766. | M. May 5/17. |
| | ‡Hanlon, M. 4623. | K. Accid. June 17/17. Det.D./B. |
| A. | Harper, G. R. 2180. | K. Oct. 30/16. Det.D./B. |
| A. | ‡Harrison, B. W. 6270. | K. April 9/17. Det.D./B. |
| | Harrison, T. R. 6518. | K. April 9/17. Det.D./B. |
| | Hart, J. H. 6020. | K. April 9/17. Det.D./B. |
| | Howard, Cpl. L. 309. | K. April 9/17. Det.D./B. |
| | Hughes, S. S. 6762. | K. April 9/17. Det.D./B. |
| | *Knox, A. W. 7060. | K. May 6/17. Det.D./B. |
| | *McCarthy, L.-Cpl. O. F. 3569. | K. May 4/17. Det.D./B. |
| | ‡Mackay, A. R. 6057. | K. May 5/17. Det.D./B. |
| | Morrow, A. 1998. | D/W. Dec. 25/16. Det.D./B. |
| | *Mullaby, M. F. R. 6305. | D/W. April 15/17. Det.D./B. |
| | Murphy, C. J. 7006. | M. May 4/17. |
| | *Noakes, J. 4552. | K. April 20/17. Det.D./B. |
| | Paul, J. 5745. | K. May 4/17. Det.D./B. |
| | Perier. 122. | K. April 9/17. Det.D./B. |
| | Pleydell, B. 6815. | M. May 4/17. |
| | *Poole, L. G. 4000. | K. May 4/17. Det.D./B. |
| | Press, H. J. 4261. | M. May 4/17. |
| | ‡Scott, J. 4589. | K. April 9/17. Det.D./B. |
| | Smith, J. A. 7036. | M. May 4/17. |
| | *Smith, W. R. 5270A | D/W. Dec. 29/16. Det.D./B. |
| C. | Sumner, J. H. 4003. | D. Mar. 4/17. Det.D./B. |
| | Tweedie, W. A. 4373. | K. April 9/17. Det.D./B. |
| | Young, R. A. 6104. | K. May 4/17. Det.D./B. |

3rd BATTALION A.I.F.

| | | |
|---|---|---|
| | Anschau, Cpl. G. C. 244. | W. and M. May 5/17. |
| | Bailey, A. 5650. | K. April 18/17. Det.D./B. |
| | ‡Bean, J. S. 6459. | K. May 5/17. Det.D./B. |
| | ‡Beckhaus. 3694. | K. May 6/17. Det.D./B. |
| | Budge, J. 6233. | M. May 5/17. |
| | ‡Briggs, A. D. G. 4627. | K. April 6/17. Det.D./B. |

**3rd Battalion A.I.F.—contd.**

| Co. | Name | |
|---|---|---|
| | ‡Budd, W. A. J. 3711. | K. May 4/17. Det.D./B. |
| | Buttel. 5659. | K. April 9/17. Det.D./B. |
| | Clydesdale, A.-Sergt. W. C. S. 6981. | K. April 15/17. Det.D./B. |
| | *Cruickshank, A. 2589. | K. April 9/17. Det.D./B |
| | Earp, F. C. 3752. | K. May 5/17. Det.D./B. |
| | *Farrell, J. 4468. | D/W. May 7/17. Det.D./B. |
| | ‡Fielder, A. L. 6502. | W. and M. May 6/17. |
| D. | Fry, F. W. 3062. | K. April 15/17. Det.D./B. |
| | *Godart, T. B. 729. | W. and M. June 30/17. |
| | *Godson, J. H. 2654B. | K. May 6/17. Det.D./B. |
| | Halliday, J. McG. 3102. | M. April 15/17. |
| | Kelly, D. 5487. | D/W. Jan. 3/17. Det.D./B. |
| | *Lloyd, H. G. 6530. | K. April 9/17. Det.D./B. |
| | ‡Macdonald, R. G. 6540. | W. and M. May 7/17. |
| | ‡McGrath, L.-Sergt. H. T. J. 2149. | K. May 5/17. Det.D./B. |
| | Mackenzie, D. R. 2257A. | K. Nov. 4/16. Det.D./B. |
| | *Mahony, C. D. 5141. | W. and M. May 5/17. |
| | Mannell, E. J. 3145. | M. Feb. 28/17. |
| | Martin, F. H. 6425. | M. May 5/17. |
| C. | Mason, G. F. 4051. | K. Nov. 3/16. Det.D./B. |
| | *O'Connor, L.-Cpl. J. 359. | K. April 9/17. Det.D./B. |
| | *Osborne, J. 6554. | K. May 6/17. Det.D./B. |
| | Palmer, R. C. 4543. | K. April 9/17. Det.D./B. |
| | Reynolds, E. 2207. | K. Oct. 25/16. Det.D./B. |
| | Richards, C. 5731. | M. May 5/17. |
| | Richards, H. 6560. | K. April 9/17. Det.D./B. |
| | *Richards, U. M. 6342. | K. May 5/17. Det.D./B. R/Enq. |
| | Sanderson, I. E. 6566. | K. April 9/17. Det.D./B. |
| | *Shepherd, P. W. 2677. | K. May 5/17. Det.D./B. |
| | *Sinclair, N. R. J. 4299. | K. May 5/17. Det.D./B. |
| | Skelton, W. 6357. | M. May 5/17. |
| | Smith, W. B. 1625. | W. and M. May 5/17. |
| | *Stammers, W. 6105. | K. May 6/17. Det.D./B. |
| | ‡Stevens, A. 5229. | W. and M. May 6/17. |
| | *Swain, J. W. 5742. | K. May 5/17. Det.D./B. |
| | Tasker, C. R. 3233. | M. April 15/17. |
| | *Taylor, P. 6428. | K. May 4/17. Det.D./B. |
| | ***Tyson, Capt. J. G.** | K. May 3/17. Det.D./B. |
| | *Watson, Cpl. R. 2490. | K. May 5/17. Det.D./B. |

**4th BATTALION A.I.F.**

|  | |
|---|---|
| *Ackland, E. R. 6216. | K. May 6/17. Det.D./B. |
| *Adams, W. R. 911. | D/W. May 5/17. Det.D./B. |
| *Anderson, L.-Cpl. W. H. 1903. | K. May 5/17. Det.D./B. |
| Armstrong, A. B. 5649. | M. April 15/17. |
| Beattie, C. 6466. | M. April 15/17. |
| *Bell, J. R. 6232. | W. and M. April 15/17. |
| Boxshall, N. 4447. | M. April 15/17. |
| *Boyd, W. 649. | K. May 5/17. Det.D./B |
| Bradley, H. H. 4137. | K. April 15/17. Det.D./B. |
| *Brian, Sig. F. 6287. | K. May 5/17. Det.D./B. |
| *Bush, C. V. R. 387. | K. May 5/17. Det.D./B. |
| Campion, L.-Cpl. C. G. 619. | M. April 15/17. |
| Carter, S. J. 5059. | M. April 15/17. |
| Chauncey, Cpl. P. H. 1736. | M. April 15/17. |
| Colemann, H. W. 4472. | M. April 15/17. |

**4th Battalion A.I.F.—contd.**

**Co.**

| | |
|---|---|
| Cowell, H. E. 3722. | K. April 15/17. Det.D./B. R/Enq. |
| Crawford, H. S. 2587. | M. April 15/17. |
| *Davies, C. A. 6580. | K. May 8/17. Det.D./B. |
| Dickinson, H. F. 1112. | K. May 5/17. Det.D./B. R/Enq. |
| Dowling. 3076. | K. April 15/17. Det.D./B. |
| *Fleming, H. W. J. 3094. | K. May 6/17. Det.D./B. |
| Fletcher, A. E. 3749. | M. April 15/17. |
| Gane, N. H. 56. | M. April 15/17. |
| Gallagher, J. J. 234A. | M. April 15/17. |
| Gallagher, M. M. 233A. | M. April 15/17. |
| Gardiner, E. 1947. | M. April 15/17. |
| ‡Garvey, W. J. 767. | K. Jan. 3/17. Det.D./B. |
| Gay. 6274. | K. April 15/17. Det.D./B. |
| *Gilham, C. G. 5655. | D/W. May 23/17. Det.D./B. |
| Glyde, J. 6010. | M. April 15/17. |
| Gordon, E. 21. | K. April 15/17. Det.D./B. |
| Gorman, L. G. 219. | M. April 15/17. |
| *Grindley, R. 6734. | K. April 15/17. Det.D./B. |
| ‡Guy, F. W. 6269. | K. May 5/17. Det.D./B. |
| Hamilton, W. T. 6017. | M. April 15/17. |
| Harris, B. 2378. | K. April 15/17. Det.D./B. |
| Harris, L.-Cpl. R. 1368. | M. April 15/17. |
| Haughton. 4650. | K. April 18/17. Det.D./B. |
| Hawkes, H. C. 6497. | K. April 15/17. Det.D./B. |
| Hawtin, A. 6491. | M. April 15/17. |
| Hogan, W. J. 6494. | M. April 15/17. |
| Innes, H. G. 6135. | M. April 15/17. |
| Irwin, W. 439. | M. April 15/17. |
| *Jacob, C. G. 6378. | D/W. Mar. 6/17. Det.D./B. |
| Jarrett, T. G. 6499. | M. April 15/17. |
| Johnson, A. 6282. | M. April 15/17. |
| Johnston, J. G. 78. | K. Nov. 5/16. Det.D./B. |
| Jones, W. J. 4520. | K. May 5/17. Det.D./B. |
| Jones, L.-Cpl. J. J. 339. | K. April 15/17. Det.D./B |
| King, J. A. 6743. | M. April 15/17. |
| Mylan, W. H. 1592. | M. April 15/17. |
| O'Brien, H. E. 6143. | M. April 15/17. |
| Oswald, L.-Cpl. T. F. 3876. | M. April 15/17. |
| Page, A. W. 5754. | M. April 15/17. |
| Price, E. 2813. | M. April 15/17. |
| Ramsey, W. B. 6319. | K. April 15/17. Det.D./B. |
| Raymond, H. 5794. | M. April 15/17. |
| Regan, C. 714. | M. April 15/17. |
| Robertson, L. J. 6544. | K. April 15/17. Det.D./B. |
| Rooke, F. 3976. | K. Jan. 2/17. Det.D./B. |
| Rosser, W. 5766. | M. April 15/17. |
| *Rutherford, A. R. 3904. | K. May 7/17. Det.D./B. |
| Seers, G. 2831. | M. April 15/17. |
| Single, G, F. 6121. | M. April 15/17. |
| Smith, C. A. 3913. | M. April 15/17. |
| Stenning, W. J. 6797. | M. May 4/17. |
| Taylor, W. J. 3929. | M. April 15/17. |
| Thomson, J. 4632. | M. April 15/17. |
| *Tonkin, Lieut. | K. May 7/17. Det.D./B. |
| Turner, V. 161. | M. April 15/17. |
| *Twiss, J. E. 2853. | K. May 8/17. Det.D./B. |
| *Urquhart, A. 260. | K. April 30/17. Det.D./B. |
| *Waight. 6591. | K. May 5/17. Det.D./B. |
| Whiteley, D. G. 1194. | M. April 15/17. |

## 5th BATTALION A.I.F.

| Co. | Name | Status |
|---|---|---|
| | ‡Addis, T. M. 3680. | K. April 22/17. Det.D./B. |
| | Amery, D. B. 4969. | M. Dec. 11/16. |
| | Blackney, W. A. 6105. | D/W. Dec. 12/16. Det.D./B. |
| | Brown, M. R. 5664. | K. Nov. 2/16. Det.D./B. |
| | Cole. 6474. | W. Unoff. M. April 22/17. |
| | Collins, C. A. V. 4977. | K. Sept. 12/16. Det.D./B. |
| | ‡Dunbar. 6481. | K. April 22/17. Det.D./B. |
| | Farrell, E. W. K. 3277. | K. Mar. 3/17. Det.D./B. |
| B. | *Galvin, J. 6742. | W. Unoff. M. May 8/17. |
| | Haynes, L.-Cpl. R. 495. | K. May 9/17. Det.D./B. |
| | Heathcote, L.-Cpl. C. 3857. | K. Feb. 10/17. Det.D./B. |
| | Jovitt, J. 295. | D/W. Dec. 24/16. Det.D./B. |
| | *Lobb, A. J. 6770. | D/W. April 5/17. Det.D./B. |
| | Mackenzie, C. J. 4240. | M. April 17/17. |
| | Martin, J. H. 4257. (L.M.G.S.) | K. Mar. 2/17. Det.D./B. |
| | Norris, N. S. 3371. | M., 1916. |
| | *Parker, C. H. 6332. | D/W. Mar. 11/17. Det.D./B. |
| B. | ‡Paterson, G. W. 5422. | K. May 9/17. Det.D./B. |
| | Rialland, P. J. 6341. | K. Mar. 3/17. Det.D./B. |

## 6th BATTALION A.I.F.

| Co. | Name | Status |
|---|---|---|
| | Crosby, J. 3720. | M. Nov. 11/16. |
| | Gwen, H. B. 3319A. | K. Dec. 9/16. Det.D./B. |
| | Hart, I. D. 3778. | K. Nov. 27/16. Det.D./B. |
| | Jeffers, W. J. 4524. | M. Nov. 11/16. |
| | Johnston, A. 304. | K. Nov. 23/16. Det.D./B. |
| D. | Kirkness, C. Str. B. 3339. | K. April 17/17. Det.D./B. |
| | Marshall, T. A. 4543. | M. Nov. 11/16. |
| | Muller, G. A. 6323. | W. Unoff. M. Mar. 2/17. |
| | O'Callaghan, J. J. 4573. | M. Nov. 11/16. |
| | Wall, H. C. 496. | M. Nov. 11/16. |

## 7th BATTALION A.I.F.

| Co. | Name | Status |
|---|---|---|
| | Adkins, R. E. 4128. | K. Mar. 4/17. Det.D./B. |
| A. | ‡Fogarty, D. 2650B. | K. April 17/17. Det.D./B. |
| | Fraser, V. W. 5383. | K. Dec. 16/16. Det.D./B. |
| | *Hall, W. 897. | K. Mar. 4/17. Det.D./B. |
| | Noonan, E. 5807. | W. and M. Feb. 25/17. |
| D. | *O'Toole, D. T. 5736. | D/W. Mar. 2/17. Det.D./B. |

## 8th BATTALION A.I.F.

| Co. | Name | Status |
|---|---|---|
| | Firman, C. F. 1147. | M. May 8/17. |
| | Moore, A. N. 880. | K. Nov. 6/16. Det.D./B. |
| | Nicholls. 5736. | W. Unoff. M. April 17/17. |
| | ‡Slattery, W. J. 6347. | K. April 16/17. Det.D./B. |
| | ‡Stephens, G. E. 6600. | D/W. April 23/17. Det.D./B. |

## 9th BATTALION A.I.F.

| Co. | Name | |
|---|---|---|
| | *Alexander, A. 1305. | K. April 15/17. Det.D./B. |
| | Coe, A. J. 2613A. | D/W. Oct. 8/16. Det.D./B. |
| | Creed, L. A. 2605. | M. May 7/17. |
| | Downs, H. 5976. | M. May 7/17. |
| | Dunne, B. J. 6009. | W. and M. Feb. 25/17. |
| | Elston, G. E. 6017. | M. May 7/17. |
| | *Ford, G. W. 1947. | K. Feb. 23/17. Det.D./B. |
| | *Gilvear, A. A. 4496. | K. May 7/17. Det.D./B. |
| | Hearn, A. A. 6255. | M. May 5/17. |
| | Hunter, A. J. 113. | M. May 7/17. |
| | Johnston, A. 1050. | D/W. Dec. 24/16. Det.D./B. |
| | Keyes, A. 6270. | M. May 7/17. |
| | Park, S. 4566. | W. and M. Feb. 25/17. |
| | Patterson, A. A. 6297. | D/W. Feb. 27/17. Det.D./B. |
| | Spencer, E. H. 2709. | M. May 7/17. |
| | Stevens, G. C. 4580. | M. May 7/17. |
| | *Watts, M. B. 4910. | K. May 7/17. Det.D./B. |

## 10th BATTALION A.I.F.

| Co. | Name | |
|---|---|---|
| | Ash, Sergt. A. A. 387. | M. Feb. 25/17. |
| | Barr, T.-Cpl. D. 2566. | K. May 9/17. Det.D./B. |
| | *Butler, L.-Cpl. A. 1907. | K. April 8/17. Det.D./B. |
| | Campbell, T./Cpl. T. 4449. | M. April 8/17 |
| | Cox, Cpl. A. 303. | M. May 6/17. |
| | Edwards, A. J. 6503. | M. May 6/17. |
| | Moss, W. J. 5799. | M. April 8/17. |
| | *Nation, C. S. 4541. | W. and M. May 6/17. |
| | Nicholls, L.-Cpl. E. J. 1575. | M. May 9/17. |
| | Norris, F. J. 3220A. | M. May 7/17. |
| | Rattigan, P. 1407. | W. and M. Oct. 15/16. |
| D. | Robinson, A. W. 3885. | K. Feb. 17/17. Det.D./B. |

## 11th BATTALION A.I.F.

| Co. | Name | |
|---|---|---|
| | Arthur, T. 6467. | D/W. Feb. 25/17. Det.D./B. |
| | Austin, W. L. 5340. | M. April 16/17. |
| | Barnard, C. G. 3713. | M. April 16/17. |
| | Bath, W. H. 6229. | M. April 16/17. |
| | Batten, E. G. 632. | M. April 16/17. |
| | Bauer, O. 5348. | M. April 16/17. |
| | *Beattie, E. J. 4153. | M. May 16/17. |
| | Bellew, J. H. 5351. | M. April 16/17. |
| | Blackburn, H. 5989. | M. April 16/17. |
| | Boddington, A. R. 2105. | M. April 16/17. |
| | Bowring, L. L. 1307. | M. April 16/17. |
| | Boxall, A. W. 5998. | M. April 16/17. |
| | Brennan, F. 5669. | M. April 16/17. |
| | Bright, W. E. 6237. | M. April 16/17. |
| | Brockwell, L. 5984. | M. April 16/17. |
| | Brown, G. T. 6012. | M. April 16/17. |
| B. | *Brown, H. C. 6726. | W. Unoff. M. May 6/17. |
| | Burfitt, A. 6011. | M. April 16/17. |
| | Burns, J. 6001. | M. April 16/17. |
| | Burns, O. 3740. | M. April 16/17. |

11th Battalion A.I.F.—contd.

| Co. | | |
|---|---|---|
| | Chatterton, E. W. 6250. | M. April 16/17. |
| | Clayton, W. C. 5073. | M. April 16/17. |
| | Collins, W. 5077. | M. April 16/17. |
| | Cusack, T. P. 1926. | M. April 16/17. |
| | Davis, D. W. 5372. | M. April 16/17. |
| | ‡Drew, J. H. H. 5085. | K. May 9/17. Det.D./B. |
| C. | Duncan, L.-Cpl. J. J. 1931. | K. April 16/17. Det.D./B. |
| A. | Durnford, G. 6030. | M. April 16/17. |
| | Durnin, E. V. 5687. | M. April 16/17. |
| | Ellis, A. 3783. | M. April 16/17. |
| | Ellis, L.-Cpl. J. 4188. | M. April 16/17. |
| | Evans, S. C. 1862. | M. April 16/17. |
| | Fallon, L.-Cpl. J. P. 4646. | M. April 16/17. |
| | Farrell, J. A. 5387. | M. April 16/17. |
| | Foley, W. R. 4791. | M. April 16/17. |
| | Gale, L.-Cpl. G. 4202. | M. April 16/17. |
| | Gane, L.-Sergt. G. W. 540. | K. Feb. 20/17. Det.D./B. |
| | Ginbey, H. 5397. | M. April 16/17. |
| | Griffiths, W. P. 4510. | M. April 16/17. |
| A. | Guilmartin, T. E. 5401. | M. April 16/17. |
| | Hanlon, J. H. 6055. | M. April 16/17. |
| | *Harding, T. 2812. | W. Unoff. M. May 6/17. |
| B. | Horner, W. E. 4218. | M. April 16/17. |
| | Huntley, V. D. 6126. | M. April 16/17. |
| | Ingle, L.-Cpl. C. H. 4051. | M. April 16/17. |
| | Jackson, W. H. 4229. | M. April 16/17. |
| | Jarvis, H. T. 1783. | M. April 16/17. |
| | Jarvis, R. 3379. | M. April 16/17. |
| | Jenkins, J. 1877. | M. April 16/17. |
| | Johnson, H. E. 4235. | M. May 6/17. |
| | Jones, E. J. 2910. | M. April 16/17. |
| | Jones, L. A. 4536. | M. April 16/17. |
| | Jones, R. G. 4533. | M. May 6/17. |
| | Keogh, B. 5126. | M. April 16/17. |
| | Key, A. 1379. | M. April 16/17. |
| | Landen, L.-Cpl. D. A. 4244. | M. April 16/17. |
| | Lawrie, J. 6072. | M. April 16/17. |
| | Lavarack, T. 4047. | K. May 6/17. Det.D./B. |
| C. | Leeder, E. A. 5133. | M. April 16/17. |
| | Lewis, J. 3080. | M. April 16/17. |
| | Love, J. 6073. | M. April 16/17. |
| | Lowson, R. J. 70. | M. April 16/17. |
| | Lyons, N. F. 3406. | M. April 16/17. |
| | McCarthy, J. 4560. | M. April 16/17. |
| | McCarthy, T. J. 2894. | M. April 16/17. |
| | McGinn, A. 5145. | M. April 16/17. |
| | McLaughlin, R. 4563. | M. April 16/17. |
| | Martin, W. 6292. | M. April 16/17. |
| | Matthews, M. H. R. 3903. | M. April 16/17. |
| | Milton, G. B. 5154. | M. April 16/17. |
| | Moloney, M. J. 6120. | M. May 6/17. |
| | Monaghan, E. J. 3699. | M. April 16/17. |
| | ‡Moor, C. J. 5157. | M. April 15/17. |
| | Mortimore, J. T. 6299. | M. April 16/17. |
| | Norrie, R. N. 1998. | M. May 6/17. |
| | Oates, C. H. 5169. | M. April 16/17. |
| | O'Brien, J. 2650. | M. April 16/17. |
| | Oddy, W. 6092. | M. April 16/17. |
| | Oden, O. B. 86. | M. April 16/17. |

**11th Battalion A.I.F.—contd.**

| Co. | Name | Casualty |
|---|---|---|
| | Pascall, A. 3442. | M. May 4/17. |
| | Pattison, C. W. E. 3917. | M. April 16/17. |
| | Perrie, V. A. 336A. | M. April 16/17. |
| | Perrin, H. G. 6315. | M. April 16/17. |
| | Petterson, O. H. 2185. | M. April 16/17. |
| | Phillips, L. G. 3923. | M. April 16/17. |
| | Pierce, W. 3444. | M. April 16/17. |
| | Pitchers, S. A. 2440. | M. April 16/17. |
| | Plunkett, J. 4277. | K. April 16/17. Det.D./B. |
| | Plunkett, Sergt. W. 586. | M. April 16/17. |
| | ‡Robertson, S. 6811. | W. Unoff. M. May 6/17. |
| | *Robertson, W. E. 6321. | M. April 16/17. |
| | Robinson, P. 6576. | M. May 6/17. |
| | Sanderson, F. 6581. | M. April 16/17. |
| | ‡Schultz, W. 3458. | K. April 9/17. Det.D./B. |
| | Scott, D. 1826. | M. April 16/17. |
| | ‡Simson, H. M. 6328. | M. April 16/17. |
| | Skelton, E. 5209. | M. April 16/17. |
| | Slavin, J. C. 6335. | M. April 16/17. |
| | Smith, A. 5201. | M. April 16/17. |
| | Smith, W. 6337. | M. April 16/17. |
| | ‡Stagles, W. 1176. | M. April 16/17. |
| | Stevenson, D. C. 6339. | M. April 16/17. |
| | Strang, O. W. 6588. | M. April 16/17. |
| | Sutherland, S. 1412. | M. May 6/17. |
| | Sutton, J. T. 2918. | M. April 16/17. |
| | Synnot, O. B. 6212. | M. April 16/17. |
| | Taylor, J. W. 6342. | M. April 16/17. |
| | Thorpe, C. F. 6591. | M. April 16/17. |
| | Tingey, J. H. 370A. | M. April 16/17. |
| | Townsend, J. D. 3481. | M. April 16/17. |
| | Trigwell, L.-Cpl. 539. | M. April 16/17. |
| | Vincent, L.-Cpl. H. T. 2238. | M. April 16/17. |
| | Waller, G. 1650. | M. April 16/17. |
| | Ward, S. A. 5040. | M. April 16/17. |
| | Warren, W. H. 3138. | M. April 16/17. |
| | Watkins, J. 3505. | M. April 16/17. |
| | ‡Watts, C. T. W. 6349. | M. April 16/17. |
| | White, E. J. 3526. | M. May 6/17. |
| | Wibberley, J. W. 4004. | M. April 16/17. |
| | Willox, W. J. 6844. | M. May 8/17. |
| C. | Wilson, A. 3509. | K. April 11/17. Det.D./B. |
| | Wilson, H. C. 6838. | M. May 6/17. |
| | Wise, T.-Sergt. G. W. 612. | M. April 16/17. |
| | Woodings, J. W. 116. | M. April 16/17. |
| | Worrall, T. E. 5233. | M. April 16/17. |
| | Wragg, A. 2246. | K. April 6/17. Det.D./B. |

**12th BATTALION A.I.F.**

|  |  |
|---|---|
| Alcock, H. 6229. | K. April 6-10/17. Det.D./B. |
| Applely, Capt. A. H. | K. May 6/17. Det.D./B. |
| *Beard, T. J. 5662. | K. April 15/17. Det.D./B. |
| *Birkett, L. J. 376. | K. May 5-8/17. Det.D./B. |
| Bond, F. J. 4763. | K. April 6-10/17. Det.D./B. |
| Bryan, D. 4651. | M. April 10/17. |
| *Buck, C. 6476. | W. and M. April 6-10/17. |

**12th Battalion A.I.F.—contd.**

| Co. | | |
|---|---|---|
| | *Cooke, C. C. 2840A. | W. and M. May 5-8/17. |
| | Davies, Cpl. G. F. 5372. | K. April 15/17. Det.D./B. |
| | Davern, J. T. 2231. | K. April 6-10/17. Det.D./B. |
| | Ellston, H. R. 6270. | K. April 6/17. Det.D./B. |
| | Gittus, C. 6831. | M. May 5-8/17. |
| | *Gordon, J. A. 2852A. | W. and M. April 6-10/17. |
| | ‡Groom, C. J. 4790. | W. and M. May 5-8/17. |
| | ‡Gruby, A. J. 4744. | K. May 5-8/17. Det.D./B. |
| | Gurr, Sergt. M. L. 2602. | M. April 10/17. |
| | Hall, R. 152. | M. April 15/17. |
| | ‡Hardy, Cpl. R. C. 2778. | D/W. May 7/17. Det.D./B. |
| | *Hite, C. E. 2843. | W. and M. April 6-10/17. |
| | Johnson, G. A. 6046. | K. June 18/17. Det.D./B. |
| | Irving, W. 4379. | K. April 10/17. Det.D./B. |
| | Kearney, T. 1616. | K. April 10/17. Det.D./B. |
| | Lee, L. D. 6766. | M. May 5-8/17. |
| | Marriner, L.-Cpl. L. W. 30. | M. May 5-8/17. |
| | Marsh, A. T. 2643. | K. May 5-8/17. Det.D./B. |
| | ‡Melrose, W. 950. | K. April 5/17. Det.D./B. |
| | Mercer, R. C. 1965. | M. May 5-8/17. |
| | Newman, R. T. 6773. | K. April 15/17. Det.D./B. |
| | Olding, R. F. 6586. | M. May 5-8/17. |
| | O'Shaughnessey, P. J. 4235. | K. April 15/17. Det.D./B. |
| | ‡Parker, A.-Cpl. C. T. 6802. | K. May 5-8/17. Det.D./B. |
| | *Pearce, B. 6506. | W. and M. May 5-8/17. |
| A. | *Peck, N. J. 4859. | K. April 6-10/17. Det.D./B. |
| | Pullen, H. W. 2666. | M. May 5-8/17. |
| | ‡Richardson, V. A. 2676. | K. April 6-10/17. Det.D./B. |
| | *Rockliff, V. H. 6079. | W. and M. May 5-8/17. |
| | Rollins, L. O. 4596. | K. April 2/17. Det.D./B. |
| | Rootes, J. H. 2898. | M. April 15/17. |
| | *Ross, F. C. 5761. | K. Feb. 25/17. Det.D./B. |
| | *Stevens, A. H. J. 6524. | W. and M. April 6-10/17. |
| | *Stewart, E. J. 4027. | W. and M. April 6-10/17. |
| | Stone, W. 3069. | M. April 10/17. |
| | ‡Tilley, A. J. 311. | K. April 6-10/17. Det.D./B. |
| | ‡Trueman, C. W. 4030. | K. April 15/17. Det.D./B. |
| | *Whatson, G. 2413. | K. May 7/17. Det.D./B. |
| | *Wickens, R. G. 91. | K. April 6-10/17. Det.D./B. |
| | Williams, A. D. 6366. | M. May 5-8/17. |
| | Wilson, A. 2817. | M. April 15/17. |
| | *Woods, R. T. 6582. | W. and M. May 5-8/17. |
| | *Youl, 2nd Lieut. J. B. | K. May 5/17. Det.D./B. |

**13th BATTALION A.I.F.**

| Co. | | |
|---|---|---|
| | Adams, L.-Cpl. H. L. 465. | M. April 11/17. |
| | Adams, L.-Cpl. W. 3676. | M. April 11/17. |
| B. | Alexander, C. A. 5126. | M. April 11/17. |
| | Anderson, O. 4129. | M. April 11/17. |
| | Artery, W. A. 2121. | M. April 11/17. |
| | Arthur, A. E. 1200. | M. April 11/17. |
| | Arthur, L.-Cpl. V. J. McC. 5646. | M. April 11/17. |
| | Ashdown, E. A. 1819. (M.G.S.) | W. Unoff. M. April 11/17. |
| | Ashton, C. A. 6460. | M. April 11/17. |
| | Baker, R. 2561. | M. April 11/17. |
| | Bales, P. W. 6952. | M. April 11/17. |

**13th Battalion A.I.F.—contd.**

| Co. |  |  |
|---|---|---|
| | Bannatyne, G. T. 5233. | M. April 11/17. |
| | Barber, G. T. 6221. | M. April 11/17. |
| | Bates, J. 5040. | M. April 11/17. |
| | Bates, C. 1065. | M. April 11/17. |
| | Bean, A. H. 5986. | W. and M. April 11/17. |
| | Benson, L.-Cpl. C. C. 2332. | M. April 11/17. |
| | Benson, J. E. 5978. | M. April 11/17. |
| | *Berkeley, R. 4923 | D/W. Feb. 5/17. Det.D./B. |
| | Berman, B. E. 5049. | M. Feb. 4/17. |
| | Blake, D. 6217. | K. Feb. 4/17. Det.D./B. |
| | Bourne, Sergt. F. H. 2336. | M. April 11/17. |
| | Bradley, F. 2142. | M. April 11/17. |
| | Brannigan, L.-Cpl. J. H. 1691. | M. April 11/17. |
| | Brennan, A. P. 6704. | M. April 11/17. |
| | Buchan, Sergt. G. R. 240 | M. April 11/17. |
| | Burns, D. 2573. | M. April 11/17. |
| | Byron, N. P. 1198. | M. April 11/17. |
| | Carle, W. 2806. | K. Feb. 4/17. Det.D./B. |
| | Christie, D. McD. 66. | M. April 11/17. |
| | *Chapman, M. E. 3285. | W. and M. April 11/17. |
| | Cole, G. E. 6979. | M. April 11/17. |
| | Coman, W. F. 6716. | M. April 11/17. |
| | Conlon, T. J. 5789. | M. April 11/17. |
| | Cook, G. J. 3715. | M. April 11/17. |
| | Cooper, O. 5665. | M. April 11/17. |
| C. XII | Cooper, S. C. 5667. | W. and M. April 11/17. |
| | Corish, Cpl. H. 360. | M. April 11/17. |
| | Cormack, S. G. K. 5997. | M. April 11/17. |
| | Coughlan, T. A. 3720. | K. Feb. 4/17. Det.D./B. |
| | Courtney, W. 5061. | M. April 11/17. |
| | Cross, Sergt. G. P. 1504. | M. April 11/17. |
| | Cullen, Cpl. F. 3029. | M. April 11/17. |
| | Cullen, P. G. 6715. | M. April 11/17. |
| | Cullen, T. H. 1700. | M. April 11/17. |
| | Dawson, J. W. 1714A. | M. April 11/17. |
| | Dixon, H. B. 1351. | M. April 11/17. |
| | Dodgshun, L.-Cpl. E. H. 1209. | M. April 11/17. |
| | Dummet, J. H. 6497. | K. April 11/17. Det.D./B. |
| | Dyer, A. 6005. | M. April 11/17. |
| | Edwards, A. L. 5678. | M. April 11/17. |
| | ‡Evans, A. O. 6512. | K. June 10/17. Det.D./B. |
| | Evans, C 6734. | M. April 11/17. |
| | Fairley, J. A. 6735. | M. April 11/17. |
| | Feeney, W. 6118. | M. April 11/17. |
| | Ferrier, T. 1450. | M. April 11/17. |
| | Flaherty, B. 6254. | M. April 11/17. |
| | Forbes, T. J. 4774. | M. April 11/17. |
| | *Forster, L.-Cpl. H. F. 727. | W. and M. April 11/17. |
| | Fowless, L.-Cpl. A. G. S. 2374. | M. April 11/17. |
| | Frost, P. M. 2517. | W. Unoff. M. April 11/17. |
| | Fullager, T. Y. 3763. | M. April 11/17. |
| | Galloway, J. 775. | M. April 11/17. |
| | Giese, H. 3786. | M. April 11/17. |
| | Gill, N. H. 6745. | M. April 11/17. |
| C. | Gove, Sergt. A. C. 2600. | M. April 11/17. |
| | **Gowing, 2nd Lieut. A. L.** | M. April 11/17. |
| | Griffiths, S. A. G. 6740. | M. April 11/17. |
| | Grimby, A. J. 5690. | M. April 11/17. |
| | Hanckel, F. C. A. 7007. | M. April 11/17. |

13th Battalion A.I.F.—contd.

| Co. | | |
|---|---|---|
| | *Hannon, J. 2612. | K. Feb. 4/17. Det.D./B. |
| | Hayes, G. E. 2766. | M. April 11/17. |
| | Hayne, M. D. 5095. | M. April 11/17. |
| | Hill, E. W. 5105. | K. Feb. 4/17. Det.D./B. |
| | Hobbins, C. A. 1685. | M. April 11/17. |
| | Hogan, L.-Cpl. H. 1953. | M. April 11/17. |
| | Hunt, G. H. 3807. | M. April 11/17. |
| | *Hunter. 6047. | K. April 11/17. Det.D./B. |
| | Huskell, J. F. 4213. | M. April 11/17. |
| | Irvine, D. W. 6055. | M. April 11/17. |
| | James, Sergt. E. 1358. | M. April 11/17. |
| | *Johnson, C. A. 1160. | K. Feb. 4/17. Det.D./B. |
| | Johnson, J. O. 7018. | K. April 11/17. Det.D./B. |
| | Jones, L.-Cpl. R. M. 2057. | M. April 11/17. |
| | Jordan, E. M. 2393. | M. April 11/17. |
| | Kay, C. 6067. | M. April 11/17. |
| | Kelly, T. W. 3075. | K. Feb. 4/17. Det.D./B. |
| | Kerr, L.-Cpl. W. 1359. | M. April 11/17. |
| | King, L. 867. | M. April 11/17. |
| | Knox, T. 6548. | M. April 11/17. |
| | Ladner, E. 4464. | M. April 11/17. |
| A. | Laidlow, G. 1173. | M. April 11/17. |
| | Lamb, R. E. H. 6077. | M. April 11/17. |
| | Larkin, T. M. 2672. | M. April 11/17. |
| | McDonald, A. 758. | W. Unoff. M. April 11/17. |
| | McDonald, H. 6294. | M. April 11/17. |
| | *McElroy, Cpl. C. J. 1798. | K. Feb. 14/17. Det.D./B. |
| | McFarlane, D. R. 659. | K. May 3/16. Det.D./B. |
| | McGee, B. J. 6782. | M. April 11/17. |
| | McLennnn, A. 542. | M. April 11/17. |
| | McNellee, S. 2689. | M. April 11/17. |
| | Mackie, T. 3410. | M. April 11/17. |
| | Mahoney, T. B. 5124. | M. April 11/17. |
| | Manny, A. 2209. | W. and M. Feb. 4/17. |
| | Markham, C. 5727. | K. April 11/17. Det.D./B. |
| | Martin, H. A. 3791. | M. April 11/17. |
| | Mason, L.-Cpl. R. B. 5057. | M. April 11/17. |
| | Matheson, Sergt. D. S. 1796. | M. April 11/17. |
| | Melen, J. O. L. 3735. | D/W. Feb. 5/17. Det.D./B. |
| | Mell, H. A. 6770. | M. April 11/17. |
| | Melville, A. S. 6574. | M. April 11/17. |
| | Menzies, J. 5130. | M. April 11/17. |
| | Moore, H. J. 6781. | M. April 11/17. |
| | Moppett, G. S. 6835. | M. April 11/17. |
| | Morel, C. A. 3578. | W. and M. Feb. 4/17. |
| | Mumby, G. 6291. | M. April 11/17. |
| | Murphy, J. D. 5736. | K. Feb. 4/17. Det.D./B. |
| | Murray, A. 2715. | D/W. Feb. 4/17. Det.D./B. |
| | Murray, H. E. 6772. | M. April 11/17. |
| | Noblet, C. E. 5737. | K. April 11/17. Det.D./B. |
| | Niall, A. S. 5740. | K. April 11/17. Det.D./B. |
| | O'Connor, D. J. 6852. | M. April 11/17. |
| | Packnam, C. H. 4870. | M. April 11/17. |
| | Pond, F. 1514. | M. Feb. 4/17. |
| | Raine, M. W. 6361. | M. April 11/17. |
| | ‡Randell, Lieut. E. | K. June 11/17. Det.D./B. |
| B. | ‡Smith, J. J. 4305. | K. Feb. 4/17. Det.D./B. |
| | Richardson, J. H. 6588. | M. April 11/17. |
| | Richardson, R. M. 2226. | M. April 11/17. |

**13th Battalion A.I.F.—contd.**

| Co. | | |
|---|---|---|
| | Riley, E. H. 6591. | M. April 11/17. |
| | *Russell, R. 5796. | K. April 11/17. Det.D./B. |
| | Russell, W. H. 4289. | M. April 11/17. |
| | Samuels, A. B. 468A. | M. April 11/17. |
| | Saunders, W. 6595. | K. April 11/17. Det.D./B. |
| | Sebbens, E. J. 7073. | M. April 11/17. |
| | Scanlon, E. 2904. | K. Feb. 4/17. Det.D./B. |
| | **Shierlaw, Capt. N. C., R.M.O.** | D/W. April 11/17. Det.D./B. |
| | Singleton, A. V. 6839. | M. April 11/17. |
| | Smith, F. N. 6806. | K. April 11/17. Det.D./B. R/Enq. |
| B. | Smith, J. J. | K. Feb. 4/17. Det.D./B. |
| | Smith, S. V. 6325. | M. April 11/17. |
| | Spring, F. W. 5458. | M. Feb. 4/17. |
| | Spring, W. 5175. | W. and M. April 11/17. |
| B. | Stephens, S. E. 6320. | M. April 11/17. |
| | Steward, D. 5173. | M. April 11/17. |
| | Stewart, G. V. 3990. | K. Feb. 4/17. Det.D./B. |
| | Stewart, J. 6317. | M. April 11/17. |
| | Stone, W. D. 5454. | K. Mar. 4/17. Det.D./B. |
| | Stuart, S. 5187. | M. April 11/17. |
| | Sutton, A. M. 3825. | M. April 11/17. |
| | Swasbrick, J. D. 135. | M. April 11/17. |
| A. | Taylor, H. J. 6114. | K. Feb. 4/17. Det.D./B. |
| | Thompson, L.-Cpl. G. F. 2919. | M. April 11/17. |
| | Thornton, Cpl. H. 215. | M. April 11/17. |
| | Tilghman. 6108. | D/W. Feb. 6/17. Det.D./B. |
| | Tilley, E. H. G. 5770. | M. April 11/17. |
| | Totten, A. I. 6332. | M. April 11/17. |
| | Try, L.-Cpl. E. C. 6364. | M. April 11/17. |
| | Walker, G. C. 3977. | M. April 11/17. |
| | Walker, N. A. 6608. | K. Feb. 4/17. Det.D./B. |
| | Warner, F. H. 6609. | M. April 11/17. |
| | Warwick, L.-Cpl. J. H. 6341. | M. April 11/17. |
| | Watson, E. 688. | M. Feb. 2/17. |
| | Welch, W. F. 6827. | M. April 11/17. |
| | *Wilson, R. J. 5205. | W. and M. April 11/17. |
| | White, Sergt. M. J. 3521. | M. April 11/17. |
| | Youdan, T. G. 5788. | M. April 11/17. |

**14th BATTALION A.I.F.**

| | |
|---|---|
| Abbott, G. 6465. | M. April 11/17. |
| ‡Allen. 5326. | K. April 11/17. Det.D./B. |
| Andrews, A. A. 6214. | M. April 11/17. |
| Archer, F. D. 6457. | M. April 11/17. |
| Baillie, R. C. 4431. | M. April 11/17. |
| Barrkman, H. 3231. | M. April 11/17. |
| Beattie, R. 6470. | M. April 11/17. |
| Berg, H. 8027. | M. April 11/17. |
| ‡Berry, Sergt. R. H. 817. | W. and Unoff. M. April 11/17. |
| Bickford, T.-Cpl. W. 815. | M. April 11/17. |
| Bird, P. C. 5337. | M. April 11/17. |
| Black, L.-Cpl. D. C. R. 5328. | M. April 11/17. |
| ‡Blackman, A. J. 6480. | K. April 11/17. Det.D./B. |
| Blamey, Sergt. R. S. 162. | M. April 11/17. |
| Bott, L.-Cpl. A. B. 6225. | M. April 11/17. |
| Bourdon, A. C. 5989. | M. April 11/17. |
| Brodie, G. B. 6481. | M. April 11/17. |

**14th Battalion A.I.F.—contd.**

| Co. | | |
|---|---|---|
| | Burrows, L.-Cpl. A. 3247. | M. April 11/17. |
| | Catterson, O. H. 3294. | W. April 11/17. |
| | Cavanagh, L.-Cpl. D. J. 923. | M. April 11/17. |
| | Challis, S. G. 5996. | M. April 11/17. |
| | Cheeseman, G. H. 3655. | K. Feb. 2/17. Det.D./B. |
| | Cleary, J. B. 5067. | M. April 11/17. |
| | Clifford, C. W. 6003. | M. April 11/17. |
| | Colquhoun, D. 5985. | K. Dec. 4/16. Det.D./B. |
| | Connelly, W. F. 3287. | M. April 11/17. |
| | Conole, L.-Cpl. W. F. 1925. | M. April 11/17. |
| | Craig, D. 4163. | M. April 11/17. |
| | Crammond, D. R. 3263. | M. April 11/17. |
| | Crowley, P. J. 6488. | M. April 11/17. |
| | Cullen, J. A. 5997. | M. April 11/17. |
| | Cutler, L. H. 6239. | M. April 11/17. |
| | *Dadson, Lieut. F. H. | K. April 11/17. Det.D./B. |
| | Dalrymple, W. G. 4470. | M. April 11/17. |
| | Davies, E. C. 6494. | M. April 11/17. |
| C. | *Davis, F. 4954. | M. April 28/17. |
| | Dickenson, J. P. 3482. | M. April 11/17. |
| | Dickinson, J. 1933. | M. April 11/17. |
| | Dudley, A. G. 4178. | M. April 11/17. |
| | Duff, W. G. 1705. | M. April 11/17. |
| | Edwards, T. J. 3357. | M. April 11/17. |
| | Folwell, E. J. 6023. | K. Feb. 5/17. Det.D./B. |
| C. | Garrett, L.-Cpl. R. C. 4812. | K. April 11/17. Det.D./B. |
| | Giffard, P. H. 3494. | M. April 11/17. |
| | Gillies, L.-Cpl. H. J. 2931. | M. April 11/17. |
| | Glen, L.-Sergt. A. S. 590. | M. April 11/17. |
| | Graf, E. W. 6269. | M. April 11/17. |
| | Grant, L.-Cpl. R. T. 4196. | M. April 11/17. |
| | Green, M. N. 5675. | M. April 11/17. |
| | Greene, L.-Cpl. P. E. 5380. | M. April 11/17. |
| | Greer, L.-Cpl. D. L. 3329. | M. April 11/17. |
| | *Hammerburg, R. M. S. 2604. | M. April 11/17. |
| | Hardy, R. E. 2393. | K. April 11/17. Det.D./B. |
| | Harris, F. 4214. | M. April 11/17. |
| | Harvey, C. H. 6649. | M. April 11/17. |
| | Higgs, L. F. 3353. | M. April 11/17. |
| | Hunt, L. S. 3817. | M. April 11/17. |
| | Irvine, J. F. 4223. | M. April 11/17. |
| | ‡Irwin, E. J. 4222. | K. April 11/17. Det.D./B. |
| | *Jago, J. J. 6039. | M. April 11/17. |
| | Kannan, A. J. 4234. | M. April 11/17. |
| | Kennedy, V. J. 5687. | M. April 11/17. |
| | King, P. G. L. 6295. | K. Feb. 5/17. Det.D./B. |
| | Lambert, W. R. 6300. | M. April 11/17. |
| | LeBrun, L.-Cpl. G. L. 1970. | M. April 11/17. |
| | Lee, J. 4534. | M. April 11/17. |
| | Lewis, P. W. 1166. | M. April 11/17. |
| | Lilley, R. 2738. | M. April 11/17. |
| D. | Long, J. 6303. | M. April 11/17. |
| | Lucas, J. W. 5148. | M. April 11/17. |
| | Luke, J. 6048. | M. April 11/17. |
| | McCarty, J. S. 5163. | M. April 11/17. |
| | McDonald, L.-Cpl. J. 2186. | M. April 11/17. |
| | McDonald, Sergt. R. N. S. 3402. | M. April 11/17. |
| | McGowan, W. 5710. | M. April 11/17. |
| | ‡McKinley, Lieut. H. | D/W. April 11/17. Det.D./B. |

**14th Battalion A.I.F.—contd.**

| Co. | | |
|---|---|---|
| | McKissock, A. 3396. | M. April 11/17. |
| | McLachlan, W. J. S. 6059. | M. April 11/17. |
| | McNamee, N. N. 4258. | M. April 11/17. |
| | McPherson, G. 6396. | M. April 11/17. |
| | Mair, J. 1791. | M. April 11/17. |
| | Manson, J. G. 4546. | M. April 11/17. |
| | Markham, A. 1826. | M. April 11/17. |
| | Mayne, W. 1826. | M. April 11/17. |
| | Mehegan, W. D. 6317. | M. April 11/17. |
| | Menzies, D. 3415. | M. April 11/17. |
| | Miller, Cpl. C. F. 4255. | M. April 11/17. |
| | Mills, F. 6068. | M. April 11/17. |
| | Moir, Cpl. J. H. 2181. | M. April 11/17. |
| | **Mullett, 2nd Lieut. L. H.** | M. April 11/17. |
| | Naylor, G. H. 3099. | M. April 11/17. |
| | Needham, G. P. 6072. | M. April 11/17. |
| | *Neighbour, J. 6073. | W. Unoff. M. April 11/17. |
| | Nelson, A. E. 5714. | M. April 11/17. |
| | Neville, L. F. 6074. | M. April 11/17. |
| | **O'Donnell, 2nd Lieut. M.** | M. April 11/17. |
| | Orr, Sergt. W. 2923. | M. April 11/17. |
| | Parker, C. D. 5426. | M. April 11/17. |
| | Parker, W. J. 6566. | M. April 11/17. |
| | Pateman, H. 5724. | M. April 11/17. |
| | Phillips, G. S. 6338. | M. April 11/17. |
| | Postlewaite, Cpl. C. B. 1995. | M. April 11/17. |
| | Quinton, D. A. 5725. | M. April 11/17. |
| | Riley, T. G. J. 6091. | M. April 11/17. |
| | Roach, A. O. 4596. | M. April 11/17. |
| | Robins, L. 3127. | K. Feb. 5/17. Det.D./B. |
| | ‡Rutter, C. 6083. | W. Unoff. M. April 11/17. |
| | Sanders, P. E. C. 4602. | M. April 11/17. |
| | Scott, D. 3633. | W. Unoff. M. April 11/17. |
| | ‡Sheedy, M. J. 6101. | D/W. April 12/17. Det.D./B. |
| | ‡Smith, C. B. 382. | M. April 11/17. |
| | Steele, C. H. 2026. | M. April 11/17. |
| | Stewart, C. N. 6103. | M. April 11/17. |
| | Storer, Cpl. H. 2434. | M. April 11/17. |
| | Thomas, B. P. 6112. | M. April 11/17. |
| | Thomas, H. V. 5229. | K. Feb. 2/17. Det.D./B. |
| | **Thompson, 2nd Lieut. S. H.** | M. April 11/17. |
| | Townsend, H. G. 6138. | M. April 11/17. |
| | Twigg, A. S. 5461. | M. April 11/17. |
| | Wade, E. R. 5476. | M. April 11/17. |
| | Wade, R. J. L. 2275. | M. April 11/17. |
| | Wallace, L. A. 401. | K. Feb. 4/17. Det.D./B. |
| | Watson, A. H. 1194. | K. Feb. 5/17. Det.D./B. |
| | Wearn, G. H. 4328. | M. April 11/17. |
| | Whelan, N. J. 1707. | M. April 11/17. |
| | Williams, E. J. 6113. | M. April 11/17. |
| | Williams, I. A. 648. | K. Jan. 20/17. Det.D./B. |
| | Wilson, R. J. 3537. | M. April 11/17. |
| D. | Wright, Cpl. F. L. 512. | M. April 11/17. |
| | Young, L.-Cpl. W. T. V. 2919. | M. April 11/17. |
| | Yorke, L. J. 5468A. | M. April 11/17. |

## 15th BATTALION A.I.F.

| Co. | Name | Status |
|---|---|---|
| | *Ash, R. J. 2366. | M. April 11/17. |
| | Baker, E. C. 4741. | M. April 11/17. |
| | Baker, L.-Cpl. G. A. 3574. | M. April 11/17. |
| | **Barnes, 2nd Lieut. F. E.** | M. April 11/17. |
| | Battersby, W. J. 6226. | M. April 11/17. |
| | Belcher, W. 4733. | M. April 11/17. |
| | Benson, Cpl. F. M. 1405. | M. April 11/17. |
| | Boden, A. 5984. | M. April 11/17. |
| C. | Bourne, O. G. 4735. (L.M.G.S.) | M. April 11/17. |
| | Boyle, P. 5340. | M. April 11/17. |
| | Bratchford, A. J. 1688. | K. April 11/17. Det.D./B. R/Enq. |
| A. | Bunter, W. F. 5993. | M. April 11/17. |
| | Burne, C. R. 4742. | M. April 11/17. |
| | Castlesmith, R. 118A. | M. April 11/17. |
| | Cave, L.-Cpl. E. 2788. | M. April 11/17. |
| | Chamberlain, F. H. 4762. | M. April 11/17. |
| | Christian, H. 6237. | M. April 11/17. |
| | Clark, W. S. T. 4761. | K. Feb. 1/17. Det.D./B. R./Enq. |
| | Cole, E. H. 2351. | M. April 11/17. |
| | Cottam, E. J. 5665. | M. Feb. 1/17. |
| | Cronk, E. 4471. | M. April 11/17. |
| | David, T. J. 6486. | M. April 11/17. |
| | Donald, H. J. K. 3932. | M. April 11/17. |
| | Dorrough, B. H. 2671. | M. April 11/17. |
| A. | Evans, Sergt. A. R. 1483. | M. April 11/17. |
| | Fahey, J. B. 6500. | M. April 11/17. |
| | Field, W. A. 1865. | M. April 11/17. |
| | Finn, G. F. L. 1151. | M. April 11/17. |
| | Fitzgerald, J. 5582. | M. April 11/17. |
| | Fleming, Sergt. P. J. 2835. | M. April 11/17. |
| | Fogarty, F. T. 6262. | M. April 11/17. |
| | Fraser, W. G. 6017. | M. April 11/17. |
| | Fuhrman, N. 746. | M. April 11/17. |
| | Gallagher, L.-Cpl. H. 2747. | M. April 11/17. |
| | Gilligan, J. 1493. | K. Feb. 1/17. Det.D./B. |
| | Goodfellow, L.-Cpl. G. G. 3304. | K. Feb. 1/17. Det.D./B. |
| | Green, W. 4902. | M. April 11/17. |
| | Hatton, F. 5412. | M. April 11/17. |
| A. | Hawkins, W. D. 5411. | K. Feb. 1/17. Det.D./B. |
| | Holley, B. 3328. | M. April 11/17. |
| | Holmes, H. F. 5684. | K. April 11/17. Det.D./B. |
| | Holper, Cpl. J. W. B. 449. | M. April 11/17. |
| | Howlett, J. 6270. | M. April 11/17. |
| | Hurley, J. P. K. 5696. | M. April 11/17. |
| | Innes, D. M. B. 6286. | W. and M. Feb. 1/17. |
| | Kershaw, F. 6043. | M. April 11/17. |
| A. | Lake, C. N. 6304. | M. Feb. 1/17. |
| | Lake, W. 1388. | M. April 11/17. |
| | Linter, A. B. 6300. | M. April 11/17. |
| | Lydement, H. J. 4830. | K. April 7/17. Det.D./B. |
| | McAteo, J. 3806. | M. Feb. 1/17. |
| | McGinley, W. 3151. | M. April 11/17. |
| | McGregor, H. J. 5478. | M. Feb. 1/17. |
| | McLean, J. D. 2394. | M. Feb. 1/17. |
| | McLennan, E. S. 6055. | M. April 11/17. |
| | McLoughlin, P. 4850. | M. April 11/17. |
| | Manson, Cpl. A. V. 7088. | M. April 11/17. |
| | Mark, Cpl. E. L. 1062. | M. April 11/17. |
| | Mayfield, F. W. 6218. | M. April 11/17. |

**15th Battalion A.I.F.**—contd.

| Co. | Name | Status |
|---|---|---|
| | Moore, A. J. 5718. | M. April 11/17. |
| | Morley, F. J. 1531. | M. April 11/17. |
| | Moroney, Cpl. M. E. 4861. | M. April 11/17. |
| | Morris, E. T. 6310. | M. April 11/17. |
| | Munro, J. T. 757. | M. April 11/17. |
| | Murtagh, M. 5456. | M. April 11/17. |
| | O'Brien, M. J. 473. | M. April 11/17. |
| | Oliver, N. O. 754. | M. April 11/17. |
| | Palfrey, C. W. 6069. | K. April 11/17. Det.D./B. |
| | **Parcell, V. 4886.** | K. Feb. 1/17. Det.D./B. |
| | *Parker, J. A. 4887. | K. April 11/17. Det.D./B. |
| | Penny, L.-Cpl. H. J. 4882. | M. Feb. 1/17. |
| | Peterson, S. 4874. | M. April 11/17. |
| | Ponting, A. W. 6076. | K. Feb. 1/17. Det.D./B. |
| | **Proctor, 2nd Lieut. J. T. C.** | M. April 11/17. |
| | Punzell, J. J. 5571. | M. April 11/17. |
| | Redmond, J. E. 3125. | W. and M. April 11/17. |
| | Richardson, F. 3429. | M. April 11/17. |
| | Rielly, W. H., 6084. | M. April 11/17. |
| | Rossington, G. M. 640. | M. April 11/17. |
| | Russell, J. 116. | M. April 11/17. |
| | Ryan, J. P. 2634. | M. April 11/17. |
| A. | Smith, Cpl. C. B. 1395. | W. and M. Feb. 1/17. |
| | Smith, H. R. 4396. | M. April 11/17. |
| | Smith, R. E. 5833. | K. Feb. 1/17. Det.D./B. |
| | Smith, S. A. 4898. | M. April 11/17. |
| | Sorenson, J. Y. 2198. | M. April 11/17. |
| B. | Stephens, Cpl. R. J. 1362. | M. April 11/17. |
| | Stewart, L.-Cpl. J. T. 2640. | M. April 11/17. |
| | Stewart, W. J. 3444. | M. April 11/17. |
| | Sweeney, G. 6346. | M. April 11/17. |
| | Sweeney, G. J. 1449. | W. and M. April 11/17. |
| | Taylor, L.-Cpl. H. G. 3876. | M. Feb. 1/17. |
| | Thomas, W. H. 6099. | K. Feb. 1/17. Det.D./B. |
| | Tolstoi, A. 5760. | M. April 11/17. |
| | ‡Trebilco, H. J. 6875. | M. July 3/17. |
| | Urquhart, F. 2423. | M. April 11/17. |
| | **Watson, Capt. J. M.** | M. April 11/17. |
| | Willett, W. H. 6367. | W. and M. April 11/17. |
| | Yates, L.-Cpl. J. E. 215. | M. April 11/17. |
| | Yells, C. A. 216. | M. April 11/17. |
| | Young, C. 543. | M. April 11/17. |
| | Young, L.-Cpl. G. C. 6213. | M. Feb. 1/17. |

**16th BATTALION A.I.F.**

| Co. | Name | Status |
|---|---|---|
| B. | Acres, R. 6228. | W. Unoff. M. Feb. 5/17. |
| | Amey, P. H. 1234. | M. April 11/17. |
| | Bentley, E. L. 6478. | M. April 11/17. |
| | ‡Bleakley, J. T. 6234. | M. April 11/17. |
| | Board, A. J. 6476. | M. April 11/17. |
| | Brusnahan, Sergt. P. J. 1124. | W. and M. April 11/17. |
| A. | Burnand, H. 4578. | M. April 11/17. |
| | Campbell, W. F. 6492. | W. and M. April 11/17. |
| | Cassidy, R. J. 3426. | K. Feb. 2/17. Det.D./B. |
| | Chipper, M. 6243. | M. April 11/17. |
| | Cibich, G. H. 265. | M. April 11/17. |

**16th Battalion A.I.F.—contd.**

**Co.**

Corlett, W. B. 6229. M. April 11/17.
Coverley, J. W. 5346. W. and M. April 11/17.
Cowley, H. T. 5799. M. April 11/17.
Cox. 5077. M. April 11/17.
Crellin, W. H. 5702. M. April 11/17.
Denheith, T. 6251. M. April 11/17.
Divall, B. F. 5706. M. April 11/17.
Douglas, Cpl. S. A. 3454. M. April 11/17.
Drew, W. 6624. M. April 11/17.
Duce, E. 3451. W. and M. April 11/17.
Ecclestone, W. B. 3456. W. and M. April 11/17.
Evans, A. C. 4269. M. April 11/17.
Fathers, E. J. 5714. M. April 11/17.
Flannagan, J. 4813. M. April 11/17.
Foster, L.-Cpl. C. E. 2343. W. and M. April 11/17.
Francis, J. 1268. M. April 11/17.
Gent, L. R. 6022. M. April 11/17.
Gilsenan, W. P. 6025. M. April 11/17.
Glasson, T. 5722. M. April 11/17.
Hartnup, B. 6272. M. April 11/17.
Henderson, L.-Cpl. G. 1319. M. April 11/17.
Henderson, W. F. 5810. M. April 15/17.
Hide, C. 3476. M. April 11/17.
Hinds, C. C. 2485. W. April 11/17.
Hodder, J. A. 5365. M. April 11/17.
Ivy, A. G. H. 2348. K. Feb. 6/17. Det.D./B.
Jackman, L. 1622. K. Oct. 4/16. Det.D./B.
Jacobs, V. N. 6046. W. and M. April 11/17.
Jacobson, F. J. 6042. M. April 11/17.
Jenkins, L.-Cpl. H. T. 2488. M. April 11/17.
Kamman, G. 3128. M. April 11/17.
Keirel, C. T. 5736. M. April 11/17.
Kemble, W. R. 6281. M. April 11/17.
Keenan, C. 6048. M. April 11/17.
Lockwood, G. H. 1761. K. April 11/17. Det.D./B.
McCann, J. 5756. M. April 11/17.
McCarthy, H. E. 5379. M. April 11/17.
*McDougall, J. McK. 6548. Unoff. M. April 10-11/17.
McDowell, W. H. 6540. M. April 11/17.
McGrath, P. 5760. M. April 11/17.
†Main, W. E. 6057. M. April 11/17.
Martin, D. 5149. M. April 11/17.
Martin, E. 5741. M. April 11/17.
Martin, T. W. 3946. M. April 11/17.
Mavor, J. 4957. M. April 11/17.
Meginess, M. 5745. M. April 11/17.
Meginnes, W. M. 5746. M. April 11/17.
Mullins, A.-Cpl. J. 1329. W. and M. April 11/17.
Nottage, R. N. 3059. K. April 11/17. Det.D./B.
Paine, S. 5167. M. April 11/17.
Parsons, J. D. 6073. M. April 11/17.
Pettit, S. E. 6078. M. April 11/17.
Pickering, G. 3034. M. April 11/17.
Poole, H. G. 3977. M. April 11/17.
Prior, L.-Cpl. R. J. 427. W. and M. April 11/17.
Radway, J. 2078. M. April 11/17.
Railt, A. 5186. M. April 11/17.
Rouse, A. A. 5415. M. April 11/17.
Samson, D. 3548. M. April 11/17.

**16th Battalion A.I.F.**—contd.

| Co. | | |
|---|---|---|
| | Saunders, J. J. 5784. | M. April 11/17. |
| A. | Sharpe, Sgt. G. 139. | M. April 11/17. |
| | Shorten, A. 6096. | M. April 11/17. |
| | Slade, H. G. 638 | W. Unoff. M. April 11/17. |
| | Sleight, E. A. 5787. | M. April 11/17. |
| | Skipworth, H. H. 6086. | W. and M. April 11/17. |
| | Smith, W. 4383. | M. April 11/17. |
| | Sparks, L.-Sergt. R. 1861. | M. April 11/17. |
| | Spruce, H. F. 5424. | M. April 11/17. |
| | *Stanley, T. 6831. | M. June 12/17. |
| | ‡Stephen. 6090. | K. April 11/17. Det.D./B. |
| | Sutton, A. B. 5428. | M. April 11/17. |
| C. | Stewart, V. J. K. 5974. | M. April 11/17. |
| | *Teague, J. J. 1830. | M. June 11/17. |
| | Thompson, J. 6342. | M. April 11/17. |
| | Thorp, L.-Cpl. H. 1334. | K. April 11/17. Det.D./B. |
| | Todd, E. A. 1833. | M. April 11/17. |
| | Touzel, C. N. 1790A. | M. April 11/17. |
| | Touzel, Sergt. J. C. 1680. | M. April 11/17. |
| | Trenorden, W. E. 1044. | M. April 11/17. |
| | ‡Verdon. 525. | K. Dec. 22/16. Det.D./B. |
| | Wadeson, L.-Cpl. S. J. 2714. | M. April 11/17. |
| | Waller, W. J. 6350. | M. April 11/17. |
| | Walsh, F. W. 4936. | M. April 11/17. |
| | Walters, J. W. E. 1876A. | M. April 11/17. |
| | Warner, G. W. 814. | M. April 11/17. |
| | Weaver, C. J. 1842A. | M. April 11/17. |
| | Wheeler, R. 168. | M. April 11/17. |
| | White, Cpl. G. W. 5455. | M. April 11/17. |
| | Williams, W. W. 3573. | M. April 11/17. |
| A. | *Wise, C. K. 1874. | K. April 11/17. Det.D./B. |

**17th BATTALION A.I.F.**

| | |
|---|---|
| *Attwood, J. N. 4055. | K. May 3/17. Det.D./B. |
| Baggett, A. E. 4659. | W. and M. May 3/17. |
| Bassett, T. 1884. | M. May 3/17. |
| Beaumont, W. H. 3022. | M. May 3/17. |
| Beddows, A. H. 4060. | M. May 3/17. |
| Black, W. 2591. | M. May 3/17. |
| Bourke, F. R. 1665. | M. May 3/17. |
| Boyton, G. S. 2865. | M. May 3/17. |
| Briggs, F. 3762. | W. and M. May 3/17. |
| *Buckeridge, G. W. 3776. | K. April 15/17. Det.D./B. |
| Brown, J. S. D. 2581. | K. Mar. 2/17. Det.D./B. |
| Brown, L.-Sergt. T. H. 3457. | W. and M. May 3/17. |
| Brown, W. S. 6040. | W. and M. May 3/17. |
| Campbell, G. H. 851. | D/W. April 18/17. Det.D./B. |
| Carroll, W. G. 4989. | K. May 3/17. Det.D./B. |
| *Chick, G. J. 1901. | M. May 3/17. |
| Commons, H. 177. | M. May 3/17. |
| Connor, C. 5555. | M. May 3/17. |
| Cox, E. T. 181. | M. May 3/17. |
| Crewe, W. R. 5686. | M. May 3/17. |
| Dean, L. S. 5810. | W. and M. May 3/17. |
| Dearie, F. J. 3810. | W. and M. May 3/17. |
| Dunn, L.-Cpl. W. P. 2359. | M. May 3/17. |

17th Battalion A.I.F.—contd.

| Co. | Name | Casualty |
|---|---|---|
| | Douglas, G. 2879. | K. April 15/17. Det.D./B. |
| | *Dwyer, Cpl. J. V. 1686. | D. April 17/17. Det.D./B. |
| | ‡Foster, H. C. 4414. | D/W. April 16/17. Det.D./B. |
| | Foster, W. 5346. | M. April 15/17. |
| | *Gallogly, G. H. 1800. | K. April 15/17. Det.D./B. |
| | ‡Gillies, J. G. 6166. | K. April 15/17. Det.D./B. |
| | Gooda, A. C. 1220. | M. May 3/17. |
| | Graham, S. J. 2895A. | M. May 3/17. |
| | Grange, S. W. 5826. | M. April 15/17. |
| | Hamilton, T. A. B. 5834. | M. May 3/17. |
| | Hannay. 2240. | K. April 15/17. Det.D./B. |
| | Harding, E. W. 238. | K. May 3/17. Det.D./B. |
| | *Houston, Lieut. C. | K. May 3/17. Det.D./B. |
| | *Huntley, C. E. 5587. | K. May 3/17. Det.D./B. |
| | Hyde, J. 5833. | M. May 3/17. |
| | Jenson, R. W. 4455. | M. May 3/17. |
| | Jesperson, S. W. 5692. | M. April 15/17. |
| | Jolly, T.-Cpl. R. 591. | M. May 3/17. |
| | Jones, W. 5363. | M. May 3/17. |
| | Kelly. 1232. | K. April 16/17. Det.D./B. |
| | Kemp, L.-Cpl. F. H. 2405. | W. and M. May 3/17. |
| | King, T. P. 5842. | M. April 15/17. |
| | McAuliffe, J. 4486. | M. May 3/17. |
| | *McDermid, L.-Cpl. H. D. 2859. | K. May 3/17. Det.D./B. |
| | McLean, R. D. J. 4492. | K. April 15/17. Det.D./B. |
| | Maltby, G. 5382. | M. May 3/17. |
| | Manson, J. 5873. | W. and M. May 3/17. |
| D. | Martin, Cpl. J. H. 4159. | W. and M. May 3/17. |
| | Milner, R. 4780. | W. and M. April 15/17. |
| | ‡Moore, J. T. 5867. | K. April 15/17. Det.D./B. |
| | Moore, T. 5383. | W. and M. May 3/17. |
| | Moran, J. J. 5376. | M. May 3/17. |
| | Nalder, Lieut. G. F. | M. May 3/17. |
| | Oakman, R. M. T. 5391. | M. May 3/17. |
| | Peachman, W. E. 6125. | M. April 15/17. |
| | Penny, C. E. 6119. | K. April 15/17. Det.D./B. |
| C. | Perkins, W. H. 2971. | K. April 15/17. Det.D./B. |
| | Piper, C. E. 5885. | M. May 3/17. |
| | Rumsey, F. T. 5891. | M. May 3/17. |
| | Rees, T. B. 1102. | M. May 3/17. |
| | Reilly, Cpl. F. 1278. | M. May 3/17. |
| | Regan, R. J. 6132. | M. May 3/17. |
| | Robson, G. H. 5889. | M. May 3/17. |
| | *Ruelle, J. 5627. | K. April 15/17. Det.D./B. |
| | Ryan, L.-Cpl. A. E. 409. | M. May 3/17. |
| | Shick, Sergt. G. J. 1901. | M. May 3/17. |
| | Smithers, J. E. 3621. | W. Unoff. M. Mar. 2/17. |
| | Stuntz, J. 5407. | M. May 3/17. |
| | Sullivan, M. 4236. | M. May 3/17. |
| | Symons, L.-Cpl. F. R. 2287. | K. April 15/17. Det.D./B. |
| | Taplin, Lieut. A. S. | M. May 3/17. |
| | Taylor, T. H. 3933. | M. May 3/17. |
| | *Thomas, C. V. 2988. | K. April 15/17. Det.D./B. |
| | Thompson, J. W. 5448. | K. April 15/17. Det.D./B. |
| | Townsend, B. 5096. | M. May 3/17. |
| | *Tranter, H. 5649. | K. May 3/17. Det.D./B. |
| | Ward, H. 2820. | M. Mar. 11/17. |
| | Ward, R. H. 2673. | K. Feb. 3/17. Det.D./B. |
| | Waters, L.-Cpl. H. P. 5667. | M. May 3/17. |

17th Battalion A.I.F.—contd.

| Co. | Name | |
|---|---|---|
| | Watkins, E. S. 1318. | M. April 15/17. |
| | Whisker, A. N. 5439. | W. and M. May 3/17. |
| | Whitaker, J. 5917. | M. May 3/17. |
| | ‡Whitely, R. J. 5928. | W. and M. May 3/17. |
| | Williams, D. 5666. | M. May 3/17. |
| | Windsor, L. J. 5913. | M. May 3/17. |
| | Worth, H. C. 6155. | M. May 3/17. |
| | *Wong, R. W. 5430. | K. Mar. 2/17. Det.D./B. |
| | Woolfe, N. E. 6182. | M. May 3/17. |
| | Wyatt, L.-Cpl. P. 728. | M. May 3/17. |

## 18th BATTALION A.I.F.

| | | |
|---|---|---|
| | *Adams, W. A. 4651. | K. May 3/17. Det.D./B. |
| | Atfield, H. G. 2551. | K. May 3/17. Det.D./B. |
| C. | *Barlow, Cpl. H. 1880B. | W. and M. May 3/17. |
| B. | Barry, J. 482. | M. May 3/17. |
| A. | Bartlett, A. 377. | Unoff. M. May 3-5/17. |
| B. | Berg, Van den. 667. | M. May 3/17. |
| B. | Bird, G. T. 5786. | K. May 3/17. Det.D./B. |
| A. | Bolton, J. C. 4967. | Unoff. M. May 3-5/17. |
| | *Bolton. 4067. | D/W. May 4/17. Det.D./B. |
| | Boyd, E. B. 4987. | K. Feb. 26/17. Det.D./B. |
| A. | Brickley, W. E. 5785. | K. May 3/17. Det.D./B. |
| A. | Brooks, S. 5556. | M. May 3/17. |
| C. | *Brown, H. 5296. | K. Feb. 26/17. Det.D./B. |
| C. | Byron, C. J. 6032. | M. May 3/17. |
| | *Chapman, Cpl. J. N. 3808. | K. May 3/17. Det.D./B. |
| A. | Clifton, W. A. 4391. | K. May 3/17. Det.D./B. |
| | *Cole, A. E. 3821. | W. and M. May 3/17. |
| | *Collis, S. 5307. | W. and M. May 3/17. |
| | *Corbett, D. E. 5005. | D/W. Nov. 16/16. Det.D./B. |
| D. | Coulter, A. 4392. | M. May 3/17. |
| | Dalton, W. E. 5792. | K. May 3/17. Det.D./B. |
| C. | Dare, F. E. 1897A. | M. May 3/17. |
| | ‡Defraine, W. L. 6052. | W. Unoff. M. May 3/17. |
| | ‡Duncan, R. D. 4415. | K. Feb. 25/17. Det.D./B. |
| C. | Duncan, O. H. G. 1677. | Unoff. M. May 3-5/17. |
| | Eckersley, F. E. 2047. | K. May 3/17. Det.D./B. |
| D. | Evans, Sergt. C. S. 3836. | K. May 3/17. Det.D./B. |
| | Evans, Sergt. H. P. 1890. | K. Nov. 14/16. Det.D./B. |
| | *Fenton, R. 5022. | K. May 3/17. Det.D./B. |
| | ‡Ford, C. A. 6072. | D/W. May 4/17. Det.D./B. |
| D. | ‡Foster, L.-Cpl. C. 4632. | K. May 3/17. Det.D./B. |
| | ‡Garrett, C. M. 3567. | W. and M. May 3/17. |
| D. | Gartrell, R. 4430. | M. May 3/17. |
| A. | Green, E. A. 4436. | M. May 3/17. |
| B. | Griffiths, J. 4756. | M. May 3/17. |
| D. | Hamilton, J. L. 6195. | M. May 3/17. |
| D. | Harris, J. 5039. | M. May 3/17. |
| D. | Hayes, Sergt. D. I. 2680. | K. May 3/17. Det.D./B. |
| D. | Hayes, J. J. 4142. | M. May 3/17. |
| | *Healey, L.-Sergt. R. B. 3853. | W. and M. May 3/17. |
| B. | Hedrick, N. R. 5704. | M. May 3/17. |
| | Hind, R. G. 2655. | K. Nov. 15/16. Det.D./B. |
| D. | Hughes, L. 5801. | M. May 3/17. |
| | *Inskip, G. 6130. | K. April 15/17. Det.D./B. |

**18th Battalion A.I.F.—contd.**

| Co. | | |
|---|---|---|
| D. | Jenkins, A. 479A. | M. May 3/17. |
| B. | Jennings, A. W. 4759. | M. May 3/17. |
| C. | Kelly, J. 5359. | Unoff. M. May 3-5/17. |
| C. | Kemp, G. H. 6113. | M. May 3/17. |
| B. | Kinloch, S. Y. 4168. | M. May 3/17. |
| C. | Lassan, R. A. 5818. | M. May 3/17. |
| | Law, E. W. 4170. | K. Nov. 8/16. Det.D./B. |
| A. | Lester, G. 5819. | M. May 3/17. |
| B. | Livermore, A. 2410 | M. May 3/17. |
| | Lord, A. G. 6121. | K. April 15/17. Det.D./B. |
| | McColl, M. G. 5927. | K. May 3/17. Det.D./B. |
| D. | McDonald, H. N. T. 4199. | M. May 3/17. |
| A. | McGoldrick, T. B. 4200. | M. May 3/17. |
| C. | McKenzie, G. J. 3915. | M. May 3/17. |
| | *McLeod, Cpl. M. 2738. | W. and M. May 3/17. |
| C. | McMann, T. J. 4502. | M. May 3/17. |
| B. | McMullen, A. J. 5639. | M. May 3/17. |
| C. | Marzol, L. M. 5626. | M. May 3/17. |
| D. | Maxwell, H. J. 5364. | M. May 3/17. |
| B. | Michael, L.-Cpl. R. 1965. | K. May 3/17. Det.D./B. |
| C. | Miles, P. J. 6214. | M. May 3/17. |
| B. | Mooney, J. 5623. | M. May 3/17. |
| D. | Murray, J. W. 6174. | M. May 3/17. |
| A. | Norton, T. J. 2964. | M. May 3/17. |
| D. | Pratt, E. H. 5389. | M. May 3/17. |
| A. | Quinn, J. 5658. | K. May 3/17. Det.D./B. |
| | *Richards, W. C. 5396. | K. April 20/17. Det.D./B. |
| | *Ricks, D. J. 199[illegible]. | K. May 3/17. Det.D./B. |
| | ‡Roberts, J. 5871. | K. May 3/17. Det.D./B. |
| | ‡Roberts, R. E. 4720. | M. May 3/17. |
| C. | Ross, J. 4284. | M. May 3/17. |
| | *Sandison, J. D. 5665. | W. Unoff. M. May 3/17. |
| S. | Scanlan, H. 1257. | K. May 3/17. Det.D./B. |
| B. | Smith, F. P. 2003A. | M. May 3/17. |
| | Smith, N. J. 5115. | D/W. Feb. 25/17. Det.D./B. |
| D. | Smithers, W. 6151. | M. May 3/17. |
| C. | Stead, B. C. 5469. | M. May 3/17. |
| A. | Street, F. G. 5887. | M. May 3/17. |
| | *Strickland, L. A. A. 3948. | W. and M. May 3/17. |
| | Tate, G. 1292. | M. May 3/17. |
| D. | Walker, W. H. 4538. | Unoff. M. May 3-5/17. |
| | *Wallace, W. 3617. | K. May 3/17. Det.D./B. |
| | ‡Walsh, D. 5419. | K. May 20/17. Det.D./B. |
| | Ward, W. 5898. | K. May 3/17. Det.D./B. |
| B. | Watt, F. J. 3686. | M. May 3/17. |
| D. | Weisener, C. W. 6160. | K. May 3/17. Det.D./B. |

**19th BATTALION A.I.F.**

| | |
|---|---|
| Agland, F. 3454. | M. Nov. 14/16. |
| Apps, D. E. 2658B. | M. May 3/17. |
| Archer, L.-Cpl. J. 740. | M. May 3/17. |
| Arndell, L. R. 1568A. | M. May 3/17. |
| Ashton, J. R. 752. | M. May 3/17. |
| Attwood, A. W. C. 5783. | M. May 3/17. |
| Austin, C. L. 6618. | D/W. Mar. 6/17. Det.D./B. |
| Austin, Cpl. H. R. 2106. | M. May 3/17. |

19th Battalion A.I.F.—contd.

| Co. | | |
|---|---|---|
| | Baldock, H. R. 4975. | M. May 3/17. |
| | Banks, A. W. 5941. | M. May 3/17. |
| | Bax, B. 1505. | M. Nov. 14/16. |
| | Benson, C. R. 4665. | M. Nov. 14/16. |
| | *Bowman, W. T. 2868. | D/W. April 20/17. Det.D./B. |
| | Boyce, A. F. 5790. | M. May 3/17. |
| | Breckell, C. H. 2583. | M. Nov. 14/16. |
| | Breckenridge, 2nd Lieut. H. | M. May 3/17. |
| | Brennan, G. B. 4063. | K. Nov. 14/16. Det.D./B. |
| | Brien, H. J. 2137. | M. April 15/17. |
| | Brooks, R. C. 4367. | M. Nov. 14/16. |
| | Browne, C. A. 2121. | D/W. Feb. 27/17. Det.D./B. |
| B. | Buckland, J. F. 499. | M. Nov. 14/16. |
| | Buckle, A. 4370. | M. May 3/17. |
| | Burns, B. F. 194. | M. May 3/17. |
| | Burns, J. H. 1076. | M. Nov. 14/16. |
| | Burrows, E. J. 6466. | M. May 3/17. |
| | Callaway, N. 5794. | M. May 3/17. |
| | Cant, 2nd Lieut. J. | K. May 3/17. Det.D./B. |
| | Carlson, L.-Cpl. S. M. 4082. | M. May 3/17. |
| | Carlson, V. 1670. | K. Nov. 14/16. Det.D./B. |
| B. | Carraill, S. J. 2374. | M. Nov. 14/16. |
| | Carroll, Cpl. A. E. 383. | M. May 3/17. |
| | Cheriton, J. G. 6047. | M. May 3/17. |
| | Clark, J. C. 4078. | M. May 3/17. |
| | Clarke, H. J. A. 2365. | M. Nov. 14/16. |
| | Coleman, J. 4382. | M. Nov. 14/16. |
| | ‡Condon, F. J. 2881. | K. May 3/17. Det.D./B. |
| B. | Connolly, H. J. 1674. | M. Nov. 14/16. |
| | Cooke, F. G. 5556. | M. May 3/17. |
| | Cooper, F. 3070. | M. Nov. 14/16. |
| | *Corbett, H. W. 6876A. | W. Unoff. M. May 3/17. |
| | Crank, Cpl. N. H. 819. | M. May 3/17. |
| | Crittenden, R. G. 2883B. | M. May 3/17. |
| | Crossland, S. T. 5428. | M. May 3/17. |
| | Crowley, H. 1104A. | M. May 3/17. |
| | Currie, R. J. 2885B. | K. May 3/17. Det.D./B. |
| | Dale, B. 833. | M. May 3/17. |
| | Davis, C. 2387. | M. May 3/17. |
| | Davis, O. R. S. 3790. | W. and M. Nov. 14/16. |
| | Dawson, Sergt. J. 2182. | M. May 3/17. |
| | Denham, H. 1682. | M. Nov. 14/16. |
| | Denmead, A. J. 3017B. | M. May 3/17. |
| | Deverenn, A. W. 1684. | M. May 3/17. |
| | Drummond, C. 537. | M. Nov. 14/16. |
| | Dunleavy, E. J. 4691. | M. Nov. 14/16. |
| | ‡Egan, C. E. 5333. | W. and M. May 3/17. |
| | Ellis, A. V. 4108. | M. May 3/17. |
| D. | Ellis, T. J. 4107. | K. Nov. 14/16. Det.D./B. |
| | Eltham, S. B. 1688. | M. Nov. 14/16. |
| | Farquharson, Sergt. W. 1689. | M. May 3/17. |
| B. | Fergusson, A. B. 3798. | M. Nov. 14/16. |
| | Flett, J. A. 5815. | M. May 3/17. |
| B. | Foster, S. H. 4116. | M. Nov. 14/16. |
| | Gentle, G. E. 1536. | K. Nov. 14/16. Det.D./B. |
| | Giddings, E. A. V. 4415. | K. Nov. 14/16. Det.D./B. |
| | Gilliatt, L.-Cpl. T. 3845A. | M. May 3/17. |
| | Gleaves, J. 2403. | M. May 3/17. |
| | Glover, L.-Cpl. F. E. 2166A. | M. May 3/17. |
| | *Greaves, J. 5138. | D/W. Mar. 3/17. Det.D./B. |

**19th Battalion A.I.F.—contd.**

| Co. | Name | Report |
| --- | --- | --- |
| | Godding, C. S. 5342. | M. May 3/17. |
| | Goodwin, H. 2144. | K. Nov. 14/16. Det.D./B. R/Enq. |
| A. | Goodwin, W. H. 235. | K. April 20/17. Det.D./B. |
| | Gosper, C. R. R. 6025. | M. May 3/17. |
| | Griffin, J. 4422. | M. Nov. 14/16. |
| B. | Hamilton, A. 564. | K. Nov. 14/16. Det.D./B. |
| | Harpur, W. J. 4424. | K. Nov. 11/16. Det.D./B. R/Enq. |
| | Harrison, J. 4720. | M. Nov. 14/16. |
| B. | Haughey, T. H. J. 4283. | M. Nov. 14/16. |
| | Healey, F. B. 2652. | M. Nov. 14/16. |
| | Heavens, G. 4431. | M. Nov. 14/16. |
| C. | Hoare, T. J. 1086. | K. Nov. 14/16. Det.D./B. |
| | Holt, E. W. 5684. | M. May 3/17. |
| | Houston, G. R. 3868. | M. Nov. 14/16. |
| | Howlinson, A. J. 724. | K. Nov. 14/16. Det.D./B. |
| D. | Ingram, R. S. 4726. | W. and M. Nov. 14/16. |
| | Ireland, B. H. 4448. | K. Nov. 14/16. Det.D./B. |
| | Irving, E. A. 5840. | M. May 3/17. |
| | Isley, Sergt. W. A. 31. | K. Nov. 14/16. Det.D./B. |
| | Kellan, A. 1091. | K. Mar. 1/17. Det.D./B. |
| | Kelly, H. P. 767. | K. Nov. 14/16. Det.D./B. |
| B. | Kelly, E. 4811. | M. Nov. 14/16. |
| | Kelsey, J. H. 5589. | M. May 3/17. |
| | Kiddle, Sergt. J. C. 4291. | M. May 3/17. |
| | Knox, L.-Cpl. J. A. 2165. | M. May 3/17. |
| | Kroll, J. 2923A. | M. May 3/17. |
| | Lang, G. B. 2034A. | M. May 3/17. |
| | Leathart, A. J. 2027B. | M. May 3/17. |
| A. | Lee, C.-S.-M. F. J. 565. | K. Nov. 14/16. Det.D./B. |
| B. | Lee, W. 4160. | M. Nov. 14/16. |
| | Leslie, L.-Sergt. C. W. 1226. | M. May 3/17. |
| | Lloyd, A. V. R. 4201. | M. May 3/17. |
| | Lonergan, T. P. 6095. | K. May 3/17. Det.D./B. |
| A. | Lukeman, C. 4164. | M. Nov. 14/16. |
| | Lutwyche, F. A. 4165. | M. Nov. 14/16. |
| | Lynch, P. 6807. | M. May 3/17. |
| | McCabe, W. 6110. | K. April 16/17. Det.D./B. |
| | McCarthy, F. D. 4743. | M. May 3/17. |
| | McCully, W. 4486. | M. May 3/17. |
| | McEwan, D. 4487. | M. May 3/17. |
| | McIlveen, F. J. 5030. | M. May 3/17. |
| | McInnes, Sergt. L. 598. | M. Nov. 14/16. |
| C. | McKay, J. W. 4813. | M. Nov. 14/16. |
| | McNair, A. V. 5474. | M. May 3/17. |
| | Maher, D. C. 5598. | M. May 3/17. |
| | Mahony, H. J. 4169. | M. Nov. 14/16. |
| | Martin, B. 1095. | M. Nov. 14/16. |
| | **Mason, 2nd Lieut. F. W.** | K. May 3/17. Det.D./B. |
| | Millership, J. 5855. | M. May 3/17. |
| | Miskell, L.-Cpl. M. J. 2206. | M. May 3/17. |
| | Mitchell, J. 2207. | M. May 3/17. |
| | Molloy, H. E. J. 2935A. | M. May 3/17. |
| | Moriaty, H. B. 2941. | M. May 3/17. |
| | Naughton, C. W. 5674. | M. May 3/17. |
| | *Neal, W. A. 5801. | K. May 3/17. Det.D./B. |
| | Neaves, H. C. 1578. | M. Nov. 14/16. |
| | *Nesbitt, A. D. 4498. | K. May 2/17. Det.D./B. |
| | Nicholas, S. J. 4188. | K. Nov. 14/16. Det.D./B. |

**19th Battalion A.I.F.—contd.**

| Co. | Name | |
|---|---|---|
| | Nixon, E. M. 6118. | M. May 3/17. |
| | Nolan, C. H. 5066. | M. May 3/17. |
| | Norris, G. 1425A. | M. May 3/17. |
| | O'Grady, J. A. 5611. | M. May 3/17. |
| | O'Kelly, H. 3894 | K. Nov. 14/16. Det.D./B. |
| | O'Neill, W. 2959A. | M. May 3/17. |
| | Osmond, L. J. 5613. | M. May 3/17. |
| | Padroth, R. P. 3587. | K. May 3/17. Det.D./B. |
| | Parker, O. V. 2956A. | M. May 3/17. |
| | Paxton, R. 4202. | K. Nov. 14/16. Det.D./B. |
| | *Perry, F. 6126. | K. April 15/17. Det.D./B. |
| | Prett, H. P. 2963B. | M. May 3/17. |
| | Price, H. W. 6305. | M. May 3/17. |
| | Priest, E. J. 4212. | M. May 3/17. |
| | Pritchard, R. G. 2961B. | M. May 3/17. |
| | Prosser, T. H. 2964. | M. May 3/17. |
| | Raymond, H. A. 5390. | M. May 3/17. |
| | Read, E. P. 6129. | M. May 3/17. |
| | Reid, D. B. 642. | M. May 3/17. |
| | Richardson, G. F. G. 627. | M. Nov. 14/16. |
| | Rider, J. P. 2974. | K. April 20/17. Det.D./B. |
| | Ring, W. E. 632. | M. May 3/17. |
| | Rogers, A. T. 2206. | K. Nov. 14/16. Det.D./B. |
| | Rosenwax, C. H. 2236. | M. May 3/17. |
| | Sewell, Cpl. C. 2790. | M. May 3/17. |
| | Sibley, W. R. 5676. | M. May 3/17. |
| | Sim, J. G. 1274A. | M. May 3/17. |
| | Simpson, S. T. 1656B. | M. May 3/17. |
| | Sinclair, L.-Cpl. A. 1301. | W. and M. Nov. 14/16. |
| | Smith, B. M. 4674. | M. May 3/17. |
| | Smith, E. A. 2215. | M. May 3/17. |
| | Smith, J. S. 6142. | M. May 3/17. |
| | ‡Smith, Sergt. L. G. 1303. | K. May 3/17. Det.D./B. |
| | Spence, J. 5933. | M. May 3/17. |
| | Spowart, A. 5636. | M. May 3/17. |
| | *Stephens, A. G. 5019. | K. May 3/17. Det.D./B. |
| | Sullivan, L.-Cpl. F. 4251. | M. May 3/17. |
| | Swinbourne, A. C. 2826. | K. Nov. 14/16. Det.D./B. |
| | Thompson, Sergt. H. 336. | M. Nov. 14/16. |
| | *Thornton, A. F. 1381. | D/W. Nov. 12/16. Det.D./B. |
| D. | Tidyman, R. R. 4541. | M. Nov. 14/16. |
| | Torpy, T. P. 686. | M. Nov. 14/16. |
| | Turney, S. J. 4258. | K. Nov. 14/16. Det.D./B. |
| | *Tyson, R. H. 5409. | W. and M. May 3/17. |
| | Wann, R. S. 3862. | K. May 3/17. Det.D./B. |
| | Weygang, F. C. 694. | M. Nov. 14/16. |
| | Williams, F. 4272. | M. Nov. 14/16. |
| B. | Williams, M. A. W. 1004. | M. Nov. 14/16. |
| | Wills, L. P. 2996B. | M. May 3/17. |
| | Woodruffe, A. 4560. | K. Nov. 14/16. Det.D./B. |
| | Wright, T. 2725. | K. Nov. 14/16. Det.D./B. |
| | Young, F. R. C. 5043. | M. May 3/17. |

## 20th BATTALION A.I.F.

‡Andrews, L. 353. K. Nov. 15/16. Det.D./B.
Betts, T. 6037. W. and M. May 3/17.
Bond, Cpl. S. R. 2336. K. May 3/17. Det.D./B.
Boyson, C. M. 810. M. May 3/17.
*Britcher, H. E. 5539. M. May 3/17.
Bushby, H. C. 5784. M. May 3/17.
Clark, L.-Cpl. J. 1157. M. May 3/17.
Cozens, O. F. 4089. M. May 3/17.
*Curney, L.-Cpl. A. J. 4675. K. May 3/17. Det.D./B.
Custiss, E. C. 3060. M. May 3/17.
Davis, J. 530. K. Jan. 30/17. Det.D./B.
*Delbringe, H. J. 6074. W. Unoff. M. May 3/17.
Dumbrell, H. C. 415. K. Nov. 15/16. Det.D./B.
‡Evans, J. B. 5332. K. April 15/17. Det.D./B.
Fagan, F. J. 1192. M. Jan. 2/17.
*Gannaway, A. E. 1071. M. May 3/17.
Garnett, H. J. 4429. M. May 3/17.
*Garton, S. 5341. M. May 3/17.
Gibson, D. H. 5586. K. May 3/17. Det.D./B.
Henderson, J. 4692. K. Nov. 12/16. Det.D./B.
Hughes, G. D. 2686. K. Nov. 20/16. Det.D./B.
D. Jones, E. J. 4810. K. Nov. 16/16. Det.D./B.
D. Jones, F. A. 3926. M. Nov. 16/16.
*Kerr, A. G. 2926A. M. May 3/17.
*Knilands, R. L. S. 4175. D/W. Nov. 18/16. Det.D./B.
*McCoy, L. R. 5380. M. May 3/17.
McDonald, Cpl. T. C. 2470. K. Nov. 15/16. Det.D./B.
McGough, J. 5431. M. May 3/17.
B. McMaster, J. 5867. Unoff. M. May 3/17.
Morrison, A. H. 4735. K Nov. 15/16. Det.D./B.
*Pages, G. S. 2970A. M. May 3/17.
Pautlin, W. R. 2967A. M. May 3/17.
Phillips, A. J. 5885. M. May 3/17.
‡Pitts, R. R., D.C.M. 3858. W Unoff. M. June 29/17.
Read, L.-Cpl. D. C. 5093. M. May 3/17.
Robson. 171. K. Mar. 2/17. Det.D./B.
Rutter, T. F. 5396. M. May 3/17.
Seddon, E. 2222. M. May 3/17.
Shaw, Lieut. E. J. M. May 3/17.
*Smith, Cpl. E. 2822. K. May 2/17. Det.D./B.
*Stonestreet, S. J. 5650. K. May 2/17. Det.D./B.
Tonkin, L. G. 1646A. M. Nov. 14/16.
Waight, C. J. 3007A. W. and M. May 3/17.
Wates, C. J. 2994. M. May 3/17.
*Watts, H. C. 3639. K. May 2/17. Det.D./B.
Whitcombe, S. 4537. K. Feb. 25/17. Det.D./B.
Williams, A. 5671. M. May 3/17.
*Williams, J. 5911. W. and M. May 3/17.
B. *Williams, L.-Cpl. H. E. 3973. K. May 3/17. Det.D./B.
*Wilkinson, H. C. 2995B. M. May 3/17.

## 21st BATTALION A.I.F.

Anderson, F. K. 4356 M. May 3/17.
Barrett, W. J. 4665. K. Dec. 24/16. Det.D./B.
Beattie, Sergt. T. M. M. 2129. M. May 3/17.
‡Bellinger, J. T. 4371. K. Feb. 25/17. Det.D./B.
Bennie, W. A. 5558. M. May 3/17.

**21st Battalion A.I.F.—contd.**

| Co. | | |
|---|---|---|
| | ‡Blore, G. T. 5557. | W. and M. May 4/17. |
| | Brent, J. R. 4982. | M. May 3/17. |
| | Cantwell, P. S. 5116. | M. May 3/17. |
| C. | *Channon, P. T. 4176. | W. Unoff. M. April/17. |
| | Charlton, P. 4685. | M. May 3/17. |
| | Condely, J. P. 5803. | M. Mar. 20/17. |
| | Coltish, L. R. 2149. | M. May 3/17. |
| | Corrigan, A. G. 5565. | M. May 3/17. |
| | Dougherty, W. 3802. | M. May 3/17. |
| | *Elliott, J. W. 4412. | K. Mar. 20/17. Det.D./B. |
| | England, W. J. 6043. | M. May 3/17. |
| | ‡Ennis, W. 2352. | W. Unoff. M. May 3/17. |
| | *Ford, L.-Cpl. C. 381. | K. Mar. 20/17. Det.D./B. |
| | Freyne, J. J. 5600. | M. May 3/17. |
| | Goodman, G. E. 4717. | M. May 3/17. |
| | Greenaway, T.-Cpl. A. T. 4429. | M. May 3/17. |
| | Hagan, C. P. 5342. | M. May 3/17. |
| | Harwood, H. J. 1542. | M. May 3/17. |
| | Helme, H. 5358. | M. May 3/17. |
| | *Hewitt, C. R. 5855. | D/W. Mar. 20/17. Det.D./B. |
| | Hooper, F. J. 6051. | M. May 3/17. |
| | Hughes, F. H. 5346. | K. Mar. 13/17. Det.D./B. |
| | ‡Hughes, J. B. 5619. | D/W. Mar. 21/17. Det.D./B. |
| | Istead, S. C. 4709. | M. May 3/17. |
| | Johnson, H. W. 5453. | M. May 3/17. |
| | Jones, A. E. 4147. | M. May 3/17. |
| | Kerr, J. 3849. | K. Mar. 20/17. Det.D./B. |
| | *Lilly, E. H. 901. | W. and M. May 3/17. |
| A. | ‡McGill, Cpl. W. 2219. | M. May 5/17. |
| | McLean. 1556. | K. April 18/17. Det.D./B. |
| | ‡McPherson, L. J. 4495. | K. Mar. 10/17. Det.D./B. |
| | ‡Martin, W. J. 4756. | K. Mar./17. Det.D./B. |
| | Massey, J. S. 2222. | K. April 22/17. Det.D./B. |
| | Milburn, G. W. 4710. | M. Mar. 20/17. |
| | Milligan, J. L. 5376. | K. Feb. 23/17. Det.D./B. |
| | Mitchell, T.-Cpl. J. L. 1967. | M. May 3/17. |
| | Morgan, W. 4478. | K. Mar. 20/17. Det.D./B. |
| | *Nicol, J. 4497. | D/W. Mar. 20/17. Det.D./B. |
| | *Nicholson, A. H. 6069. | K. May 4/17. Det.D./B. |
| C. Sig. | North, T.-Cpl. A. S. 453. | M. May 3/17. |
| | Perry, H. F. 6164. | M. May 5/17. |
| | Palmer, W. H. 5439. | M. May 5/17. |
| | Plant, J. 5069. | M. May 3/17. |
| | Rainer, L. M. 954. | M. Nov. 15/16. |
| | Rankine, Cpl. E. E. 490. | K. Feb. 25/17. Det.D./B. |
| | Raphell, F. J. 1590. | W. and M. Nov. 15/16. |
| | Rawson, Sergt. H. 1178. | M. May 3/17. |
| | Reynolds, G. 6098. | M. May 5/17. |
| | *Rhynehart, 2nd Lieut. H. L. | K. May 3/17. Det.D./B. |
| | *Richardson, H. 4782. | K. Mar. 20/17. Det.D./B. |
| | Rodgers, A. 4582. | D/W. Dec. 30/16. Det.D./B. |
| | ‡Rogasch. 5688. | K. Mar. 20/17. Det.D./B. |
| | Rooney, G. 6107. | M. May 3/17. |
| | Ross, N. A. 5944. | M. May 3/17. |
| | Scales, H. J. M. 5701. | W. and M. Mar. 20/17. |
| | Simons, J. H. 5911. | M. May 3/17. |
| | Sinclair, A. 2380. | M. Nov. 20/16. |
| | Smallmon, D. A. 6132. | M. May 3/17. |
| | Stevens, E. W. 4527. | M. May 3/17. |

**21st Battalion A.I.F.—contd.**

Co.

| | |
|---|---|
| Sturgeon, H. W. 5914. | K. Mar. 20/17. Det.D./B. |
| Taylor, H. C. 519. | M. May 3/17. |
| ‡Taylor, R. J. 3976. | W. and M. April 4/17. |
| *Thomas, B. 4535. | D/W. Nov. 11/16. Det.D./B. |
| Thompson, W. E. 4233. | K. Mar. 20/17. Det.D./B. |
| Trask, J. W. 4537. | M. May 3/17. |
| Tucker, E. G. 5709. | M. May 3/17. |
| Tucker, R. 3927. | M. May 3/17. |
| Watkins, J. W. 2129. | M. May 3/17. |
| Webb, J. W. 4242. | D/W. Nov. 15/16. Det.D./B. |
| Whitchurch, D. J. 4275. | M. May 3/17. |
| *Whitehead, 2nd Lieut. W. M. | W. and M. May 3/17. |
| *Whitelaw, Sergt. R. A. 1003. | W. and M. May 3/17. |
| Whitford, A. H. 5103. | K. Mar. 20/17. Det.D./B. |
| Whitlock, E. L. 6153. | M. May 3/17. |
| Willcox, R. C. 5712. | M. May 3/17. |

**22nd BATTALION A.I.F.**

| | |
|---|---|
| Adamson, A. T. 5307. | W. and M. May 3/17. |
| ‡Alexander, C. H. 4971 | K. Feb. 25/17. Det.D./B. |
| *Anderson, G. T. 6029. | W. and M. May 3/17. |
| *Andrew, Cpl. P. C. 5537. | W. and M. May 3/17. |
| Armstrong, B. 4059. | M. May 3/17. |
| Amery, A. S. 4974. | M. May 3/17. |
| *Bailey, F. E. 5554. | W. and M. May 3/17. |
| Baines, C. D. 4657. | M. Nov. 13/16. |
| Barker, W. H. 4977. | M. May 3/17. |
| *Batt, H. L. 5971. | W. and M. May 3/17. |
| Berlowitz, J. T. 5787. | M. May 3/17. |
| Bloare, A. E. 4369. | M. May 3/17. |
| *Bosustow, 4375. | W. and M. May 3/17. |
| Bowyer, H. 4985. | M. May 3/17. |
| Browning, W. A. 4383. | W. and M. May 3/17. |
| Callander, N. 1889. | M. Feb. 25/17. |
| Campbell, W. C. 130. | M. May 3/17. |
| Caudry, W. D. 5447. | M. May 3/17. |
| Catton, J. T. 5716. | M. May 3/17. |
| Cobden, R. 6062. | M. May 3/17. |
| Christy, J. W. 6065. | M. May 3/17. |
| Collins, D. 4395. | M. May 3/17. |
| Cowell, G. A. N. 5880. | M. May 3/17. |
| *Crane, E. P. W. 5330. | M. May 3/17. |
| Crawford, F. K. 5331. | W. and M. May 3/17. |
| *Crawford, J. 4683. | W. Unoff. M. May 3/17. |
| *Crump, C. T. W. 4404. | W. and M. May 3/17. |
| ‡Davis, O. V. 2177A. | W. and M. May 3/17. |
| Davidson, W. S. 5001. | M. May 3/17. |
| Davies, A. E. 5576. | M. May 3/17. |
| Dennett, C. H. 2033. | M. May 3/17. |
| Dunkley, C. B. 5781. | M. May 3/17. |
| Elliott, P. N. 5580. | M. May 3/17. |
| Fraser, Lieut. H. P. | M. May 3/17. |
| Foley, F. J. 4431. | M. May 3/17. |
| Gascoyne, A. 155. | M. May 3/17. |

**22nd Battalion A.I.F.—contd.**

| Co. | | |
|---|---|---|
| | Griffiths, H. W. 5885. | M. May 3/17. |
| | Harrington, H. C. 5608. | M. May 3/17. |
| | Hassett, J. M. 5886. | M. May 3/17. |
| | Heady, J. 6092. | M. May 3/17. |
| | Hill, G. J. 4120. | M. May 3/17. |
| | **Hogarth, Capt. E. G.** | K. May 3/17. Det.D./B. |
| | Howat, G. A. 4578. | M. May 3/17. |
| | Hughes, Cpl. R. E. 5296. | M. May 3/17. |
| | Hunt, L. C. A. 5597. | M. May 3/17. |
| D. | Hurley, L.-Cpl. J. C. 5931. | M May 3/17. |
| | *Jago, G. E. 5371. | K. Feb. 10/17. Det.D./B. |
| | Johnston, J. W. 5372. | M. May 3/17. |
| | *Johansen, H. P. B. 4728. | W. and M. May 3/17. |
| | Kinsey, H. L. 416. | M. May 3/17. |
| | Kruger, L.-Cpl. J. H. 5173. | D/W. Feb. 22/17. Det.D./B. |
| | Landers, H. D. M. 6116. | M. May 3/17. |
| | *Levell, H. 5049. | W. and M. May 3/17. |
| | Lewis, C. T. 6113. | M. May 3/17. |
| | Lowe, H. 4742. | M. May 3/17. |
| | *McCowan, N. 5301. | W. and M. May 3/17. |
| | McDonald, C. W. 4506. | W. Nov. 17/16. |
| | McPherson, D. 5067. | W. and M. May 3/17. |
| | Madden, L.-Cpl. W. C. 5379. | M. May 3/17. |
| | Martin, L.-Cpl. C. 1109. | M. May 3/17. |
| | Merritt, F. T. 4491. | M. May 3/17. |
| | Miller, C. 4492. | M. May 3/17. |
| | Mitchell, J. L. 5032. | M. May 3/17. |
| | Mooney, J. P. 4496. | M. May 3/17. |
| | Morrison, W. B. 2728. | M. May 3/17. |
| | Morton, J. T. 200. | M. May 3/17. |
| | Murray, T. J. 216. | W. and M. May 3/17. |
| | Nickson, F. 221. | M. Feb. 25/17. |
| | Noake, A. 3893. | M. May 3/17. |
| | Olsen, H. V. 5651. | M. May 3/17. |
| | Owen, T. H. 661. | M. May 3/17. |
| | Parker, J. McD. 5901. | M. May 3/17. |
| | Penn, L. 6132. | W. and M. May 3/17. |
| | Peterson, C. M. H. 5654. | M. May 3/17. |
| | Petersen, Cpl. J. R. 1724. | W. and M. May 3/17. |
| | Phillips, W. M. 2769. | M. May 3/17. |
| | Price, H. 3901. | M. May 3/17. |
| | Pritchard, W. R. 4778. | M. May 3/17. |
| C. | Prior, A. J. 6135. | M. May 3/17. |
| | Rickard, E. M. 5506. | W. and M. May 3/17. |
| | Renshaw, H. 4194. | M. May 3/17. |
| | Robie, A. D. 5406. | W. and M. May 3/17. |
| | Robinson, L.-Cpl. S. 3230. | M. May 3/17. |
| | Schultze, L.-Cpl. H. 3245. | M. May 3/17. |
| | Scott, P. N. 2410. | M. May 3/17. |
| | Shanks, G. C. R. 5091. | M. May 3/17. |
| | Smith, A. 5822. | M. May 3/17. |
| | Smith, R. F. 5684. | M. Feb. 25/17. |
| D. XVI | *Somers, M. D. 5718. (M.G.S.) | W. and M. May 3/17. |
| | Sutton, Sergt. E. 1108. | M. May 3/17. |
| | Swaney, L.-Cpl. V. 3924. | M. May 3/17. |
| | Swift, L.-Cpl. R. 3941. | M. May 3/17. |
| | Taylor, W. C. 3952. | W. and M. May 3/17. |
| | Tregoning, W. J. 5305. | M. May 3/17. |
| | Underwood, F. T. 6164. | M. May 3/17. |

22nd Battalion A.I.F.—contd.

Co.

| | |
|---|---|
| Wallis, B. T. 6170. | M. May 3/17. |
| West, J. 4801. | M. May 3/17. |
| Wiedeman, O. B. 493. | M. May 3/17. |
| Winsor, A. 4569. | M. May 3/17. |
| Woods, A. 5962. | M. May 3/17. |

## 23rd BATTALION A.I.F.

| | |
|---|---|
| Antonia, A. J. 4267. | M. May 3/17. |
| Arnott, Cpl. G. A. 1212. | M. May 3/17. |
| Bailey, W. 3771 | M. May 3/17. |
| ‡Bain, E. H. H. 5544. | K. May 3/17. Det.D./B. |
| ‡Bamkin, B. C. 4975. | M. May 3/17. |
| Barton, W. 6035. | M. May 3/17. |
| Barndon, Cpl. A. E. 5787. | W. and M. May 3/17. |
| ‡Betts, H. 4063. | K. Mar. 17/17. Det.D./B. |
| Bevan, D. 2570. | M. May 3/17. |
| Bray, Cpl. W. F. 88. | M. Mar. 20/17. |
| Brown, J. E. 5557. | M. May 3/17. |
| ‡Cleary. 5320. | K. Mar. 20/17. Det.D./B. |
| Cooke, R. T. 1889. | K. Nov. 9/16. Det.D./B. |
| Cordingly, A. E. 3799. | M. May 3/17. |
| Cotter, Sergt. G. H. 4999. | W. Unoff. M. May 3/17. |
| Crawford, W. W. 5331. | K. Mar. 7/17. Det.D./B. |
| *Cree. 4080. | W. and M. May 3/17. |
| ‡Daws, J. 3809. | M. May 3/17. |
| Dickson, J. 5337. | M. May 3/17. |
| ‡Down, Cpl. D. 5010. | M. June 3/17. |
| Etheridge, R. 4224. | M. May 3/17. |
| Flett, A. E. 4696. | K. Nov. 8/16. Det.D./B. |
| Gammon, Sergt. W. H. 5699. | K. Mar. 11/17. Det.D./B. |
| Grant, J. A. 4703. | M. May 3/17. |
| Harris, G. A. 4408. | M. May 3/17. |
| Hart, J. O'B. 3847. | M. May 3/17. |
| ‡Hensburgh, L. R. 5368. | W. and M. May 3/17. |
| Hilsby, C. E. 5966. | M. May 3/17. |
| Hinchen, R. J. 5029. | K. Nov. 9/16. Det.D./B. |
| ‡Imrie, A. E. 5377. | W. and M. Mar. 20/17. |
| Jackson, W. J. 4420. | M. Mar. 20/17. |
| ‡Kinsman, 2nd Lieut. H. S. | K. May 3/17. Det.D./B. |
| Kirkby, S. 6080. | M. May 3/17. |
| Ladner, C. C. 5131. | W. and M. Mar. 20/17. |
| McAlister, P. W. L. 6095. | M. May 3/17. |
| ‡Macartney, T. 5852. | K. May 3/17. Det.D./B. |
| Mitchell, W. E. 4141. | M. May 3/17. |
| Niven, J. 2075. | M. May 3/17. |
| *O'Connor, W. G. 4158. | K. Mar. 17/17. Det.D./B. |
| Oldfield, T. H. 1245. | M. May 3/17. |
| Orr, V. W. 424. | K. May 3/17. Det.D./B. |
| ‡Pallant, J. A. 2434. | M. May 3/17. |
| ‡Pearce, W. H. 5069. | M. May 3/17. |
| Peters, F. 6101. | M. May 3/17. |
| Piercy, H. W. 5427. | M. May 3/17. |
| Piercy, W. L. 5428. | M. May 3/17. |
| Pridmore, H. W. 5962. | M. May 3/17. |
| *Rankin. 4975. | W. Unoff. M. May 3/17. |
| ‡Riley, Sub.-Cpl. C. 4760. | W. and M. May 3/17. |

**23rd Battalion A.I.F.—contd.**

| Co. | | |
|---|---|---|
| | Ritchie, F. J. 4476. | M. May 3/17. |
| | ‡Roberts, A. O. 5081. | W. and M. May 3/17. |
| | Robinson, J. W. 1269. | M. May 3/17. |
| | Robinson, W. A. 5082. | W. and M. May 3/17. |
| | Russell, Cpl. C. L. 5087. | W. and M. May 3/17. |
| | ‡Ryan, T. J. 5681. | W. and M. May 3/17. |
| | ‡Simmons, J. R. 2455. | M. May 3/17. |
| | ‡Skiller, C. H. 4188. | K. May 3/17. Det.D./B. R/Enq. |
| | Smith, A. J. 3938. | M. May 3/17. |
| | Smith, E. A. 5953. | M. May 3/17. |
| | Smith, M. 6148. | M. May 3/17. |
| | Thompson, M. T. 6191. | M. May 3/17. |
| | ‡Tidd, G. H. 5893. | W. and M. May 3/17. |
| | ‡Tripcony, B. L. 5453. | W. and M. May 3/17. |
| | Ward, W. E. 6133. | M. May 3/17. |
| | Watson, L. J. 5697. | M. May 3/17. |
| | *Wilcox, Sergt. H. L. 1126. | K. Mar. 17/17. Det.D./B. |
| | *Willoughby, L. A. 5458. | K. Mar. 7/17. Det.D./B. |
| | Wyles, J. W. 5905. | M. May 3/17. |

**24th BATTALION A.I.F.**

| | | |
|---|---|---|
| | Arrowsmith, A. 6027. | M. May 3/17. |
| | Blair, R. T. 4981. | M. May 3/17. |
| | *Boak, L.-Cpl. A. J. 2340. | W. and M. May 3/17. |
| | *Brennan, P. 5119. | W. and M. May 3/17. |
| | *Burns, J. A. 6034. | W. and M. May 3/17. |
| | Burns, L.-Cpl. J. R. 2030. | M. May 3/17. |
| D. XVI | *Campbell, J. 5310. | W. and M. May 3/17. |
| | Chamberlain, S. 1325. | M. May 3/17. |
| | *Cohen, L. 3780. | W. and M. May 3/17. |
| | Commins, J. 6043. | M. May 3/17. |
| | Creswick, W. A. 5324. | M. May 3/17. |
| | *Curran, E. L. 6038. | W. and M. May 3/17. |
| | Davidson, Cpl. R. W. 1815. | M. May 3/17. |
| | *Dobinson, A. F. 4686. | W. and M. May 3/17. |
| D. | *Dobson, Sgt. L. F. 769. | M. May 3/17. |
| | Driscoll, J. 1797. | M. May 3/17. |
| | Eckford, A. E. 4407. | M. May 3/17. |
| | *Ewen, E. J. 6052. | K. May 3/17. Det.D./B. |
| | *Flack, J. A. 6165. | M. May 3/17. |
| | Gordon, F. C. 4700. | M. May 3/17. |
| | Haig, R. W. 1806D. | M. May 3/17. |
| | Handford, G. H. 4711. | W. and M. Nov. 14/16. |
| | Haydon, J. S. 5347. | M. May 3/17. |
| | Johnston, H. H. 4448. | M. May 3/17. |
| | King, W. D. 5616. | M. May 3/17. |
| | *Lang, Cpl. H. 903. | W. and M. May 3/17. |
| | Lincoln, J. E. 5153. | M. May 3/17. |
| | Lindsay, L.-Cpl. F. E. 221. | M. May 3/17. |
| | Littlewood, L.-Cpl. E. E. 4139. | M. May 3/17. |
| | Lohman, D. E. 908. | M. May 3/17. |
| | Macbeth, H. R. 4802. | M. May 3/17. |
| | McLesky, R. T. 5879. | M. May 3/17. |
| | *Mallett, A. W. 5050. | W. and M. May 3/17. |
| | Manallack, T. H. H. 5375. | M. May 3/17. |
| | *Manderson, W. 5626. | W. and M. May 5/17. |

**24th Battalion A.I.F.—contd.**

| Co. | Name | Status |
|---|---|---|
| | ‡Murphy, T. M. 5869. | K. Accid. June 1/17. Det.D./B. |
| | Perry, R. 930. | M. May 3/17. |
| | Petch, C.-S.-M. A. W. 584. | M. May 3/17. |
| | Priddle, C. C. 2748. | M. May 3/17. |
| | *Ramage, R. W. 5076. | W. and M. May 2/17. |
| | Rennie, J. 5959. | M. May 3/17. |
| | *Robinson, J. A. 5081. | M. May 3/17. |
| | Rosewarne, W. 4040. | M. May 3/17. |
| | Rolls, J. L. 3625. | M. May 3/17. |
| | Runting, A. 1763. | M. May 3/17. |
| | Rutterford, W. J. 4520. | M. May 5/17. |
| | Smith, F. R. 5423. | M. May 3/17. |
| C. XI | ‡Stanton, W. H. 5428. | K. May 4/17. Det.D./B. |
| | Stewart, A. L. 4204. | M. May 3/17. |
| | *Taylor, E. 5434. | M. May 3/17. |
| D. | Taylor, Sergt. P. H. 1551. | K. May 3/17. Det.D./B. |
| | Tout, L. G. 5677. | M. May 3/17. |
| | *Turnbull, G. A. W. 289. | W. and M. May 4/17. |
| | Swalwell, R. 5901. | M. May 3/17. |
| | Upton, L. J. 5437. | M. May 3/17. |
| | Vallance, E. A. 5904. | M. May 3/17. |
| | Waltho, W. A. 4785. | M. May 3/17. |
| | White, E. C. V. 4792. | M. May 5/17. |
| | *White, R. W. H. 5165. | W. and M. May 3/17. |
| | Young, H. E. 547. | M. May 3/17. |

**25th BATTALION. A.I.F.**

| Co. | Name | Status |
|---|---|---|
| A. | Adams, C. T. 4362. | K. Nov. 14-15/16. Det.D./B. |
| | Anderson, S. A. 4654. | K. Mar. 6/17. Det D./B. |
| | Ballard, H. 3471. | D/W. Nov. 15/16. Det.D./B. |
| D. | Blake, C. F. 3016. | K. Nov. 14/16. Det.D./B. |
| | Carter A B. 1656. | W. and M. Nov. 14/16. |
| | Charles, J. H. 4086. | M. Nov. 14/16. |
| | Chatfield, J. 4989. | D/W. Oct. 28/16. Det.D./B. |
| | Cobb, J. E. 1510. | K. Nov. 14/16. Det.D./B. |
| | *Coghlan, H. H. 2129. | M. Nov. 14/16. |
| | Cross, B. 4687. | W. and M. Nov. 5/16. |
| | Crowley, D. P. 4992. | K. Nov. 14/16. Det.D./B. |
| | *Davies, F. 4796. | K. Nov. 4/16. Det.D./B. |
| C. | Dawe, S. F. 615. | M. Nov. 14/16. |
| | Dwyer, W. 352 | M. Nov. 15/16. |
| | Faull, E. E. 357. | K. Nov. 14/16. Det.D./B. |
| | Ferguson, A. W. 4699. | W. and M. Nov. 14/16. |
| | Ford, T. J. 862. | M. Nov. 14/16. |
| | Francis, A. C. 4435. | K. Nov. 14/16. Det.D./B. |
| | Franklin, D. H. G. 3688. | W. and M. Nov. 14/16. |
| | Fraser, W. 3687. | M. Nov. 5/16. |
| | Gibson, J. 1089 | K. Nov. 14/16. Det.D./B. |
| A. | Goodwin, H. 4708. | K. Nov. 14/16. Det.D./B. |
| | Greenwood, Cpl. S. E. 106. | W. Feb. 16/17. |
| | Grundon, S. 1685. | W. and M. Nov. 14/16. |
| | Hanlon, F. P. 5027. | K. April 23/17. Det.D./B. |
| | Harris, D. R. 4715. | K. Nov. 14/16. Det.D./B. |
| | Healy, 2nd Lieut. | K. Nov. 14/16. Det.D./B. |
| | Hickson, A. S. 5834. | K. May 3-4/17. Det.D./B. |
| | Hill, B. J. 4718. | K. Nov. 14/16. Det.D./B. |

25th Battalion A.I.F.—contd.

| Co. | Name | Status |
|---|---|---|
| | Hughes, H. 4994. | K. Nov. 14/16. Det.D./B. |
| | Hussey, A. D. 1013. | K. April 9/17. Det.D./B. |
| | Jackson, E. J. 3558. | K. Nov. 14/16. Det.D./B. |
| | Lawrence, W. C. 3129. | M. Jan. 16/17. |
| | Lee, B. F. 4163. | M. Nov. 5/16. |
| | Lewis, A. D. 4167. | M. Nov. 14/16. |
| | McIntyre, J. 4739. | M. May 3-4/17. |
| | McLean, J. 459. | K. Nov. 14/16. Det.D./B. |
| | McMunn, J. 4187. | K. Nov. 14/16. Det.D./B. |
| B. | McNeill, W. C. 4741. | K. Nov. 5/16. Det.D./B. |
| | Mewburn, R. 3141. | M. Nov. 5/16. |
| | *Moxham, W. G. 5620. | D/W. May 3-5/17. Det.D./B. |
| | Murphy, C. 690. | M. Nov. 14/16. |
| | Murphy, E. 4178. | K. Nov. 14/16. Det.D./B. |
| | Nicholls, F. W. 4195. | K. Nov. 14/16. Det.D./B. |
| B. | Palmes, Sig. B. 4798. (Sig. S.) | K. May 3/17. Det.D./B. |
| C. | Penn, J. H. 1685. | M. Nov. 14/16. |
| | Pentecost, E. I. 4749 | K. Nov. 14/16. Det.D./B. R./Enq. |
| | Peters, A.-Cpl. A. D. 4065. | M. Nov. 5/16. |
| C. | Piggott, H. L. 4750. | K. Nov. 14/16. Det.D./B. |
| | Pym, Sergt. F. 1082. | K. Nov. 14/16. Det.D./B. |
| | Rash, P. A. R. 4227. | D/W. Oct. 19/16. Det.D./B. |
| | Rockwell, W. P. 4760. | K. Nov. 14/16. Det.D./B. |
| | Salvage, F. T. 2249. | K. April 23/17. Det.D./B. |
| | Sutherland, J. D. G. 4772. | M. Nov. 14/16. |
| | Thompson, C. L. 4773 | M. Nov. 5/16. |
| | Tripcony, A. 5655. | K. May 3/17. Det.D./B. |
| | Tuddenham, W. C. 252. | M. Nov. 14/16. |
| | Turner, Cpl. J. 767. | K. Nov. 14/16. Det.D./B. |
| | Vinnicombe, H. V. 4780. | K. Nov. 5/16. Det.D./B. |
| | Wells, W. G. 4784. | K. Nov. 14/16. Det.D./B. |
| | Williams, R. 5938. | M. May 8/17. |
| | Wilson, A. 4248. | M. Nov. 14/16. |
| | Woock, C. 3302. | M. Nov. 14/16. |

26th BATTALION A.I.F.

| Co. | Name | Status |
|---|---|---|
| | Adey, E. 3753. | K. Feb. 9/17. Det.D./B. |
| | Aitken, M. 3755. | K. Nov. 5/16. Det.D./B. |
| | Archer, V. M. 4800. | M. Nov. 14/16. |
| C. | Attridge, C. 4664. | K. Nov. 16/16. Det.D./B. |
| | Bain, W. T. 4101. | K. Nov. 14/16. Det.D./B. |
| | Bansley, G. A. 3687. | W. and M. Nov. 14/16. |
| | Berg, F. D. E. 4986. | M. Nov. 14/16. |
| | Brennan, F. P. 6007. (Late 5288.) | M. Nov. 14/16. Re-op./enq. |
| | Burge, G. J. 372. | K. Nov. 5/16. Det.D./B. |
| | Cameron, J. 4116. | M. May 3/17. |
| | Cammane, M. H. 3636. | M. Nov. 5/16. |
| | ‡Carey, D. 5556. | W. Unoff. M. April 19/17. |
| | Cogan, G. P. 5562. | K. May 3/17. Det.D./B. R/Enq. |
| | ‡Cole, G. 4568. | W. Unoff. M. May 3/17. |
| | Collie, W. 3475. | K. Nov. 5/16. Det.D./B. |
| | Cottell, C.-S.-M. G. C. 993. | M. Nov. 14/16. |
| | Cox, J. S. 845. | K. Nov. 5/16. Det.D./B. |
| | Craig, Sergt. H. S. 1665. | K. Nov. 14/16. Det.D./B. |
| | Davern, Dvr. L. 1043. | M. Nov. 5/16. |

**26th Battalion A.I.F.—contd.**

| Co. | Name | |
|---|---|---|
| | Davis, F. W. 1070. | W. and M. Nov. 5/16. |
| | Donoghue, J. B. 4259. | K. Nov. 5/16. Det.D./B. |
| | Eeles, A. 4719. | M. Nov. 14/16. |
| | Evans, A. T. 5328. | M. Mar. 26/17. |
| | Fisher, F. 5587. | M. May 3/17. |
| | Gadd, L. V. 3654. | K. Nov. 5/16. Det.D./B. |
| | ‡Garthwaite, H. E. 5838. | D/W. May 11/17. Det.D./B. |
| | Gaynor, G. W. 5596. | M. May 3/17. |
| | Haines, A. S. C. 2490. | K. Mar. 26/17. Det.D./B. |
| | Hall, A. 1103. | M. Nov. 5/16. |
| | Hambrook, A. W. 3557. | M. Nov. 14/16. |
| | Hamlyn, E. A. 4148. | K. Nov. 14/16. Det.D./B. |
| | Harding, W. R. B. 5350. | M. May 3/17. |
| | Harrison, P. H. 2454. | K. Nov. 5/16. Det.D./B. |
| A. | Heckrath, C. A. 1210. | M. Nov. 14/16. |
| | Henderson, J. 4732. | M. Nov. 14/16. |
| | Hill, E. L. 5048. | M. Nov. 14/16. |
| | Hodges, C. F. 520A. | M. Nov. 14/16. |
| | Hunter, W. R. 1645A. | M. May 6/17. |
| | James, W. L. 1029. | K. April 21/17. Det.D./B. |
| | Jones, W. 5416. | M. April 26/17. |
| | Kelly, L. E. 5615. | M. May 3/17. |
| | Kirby, N. J. 4742. | M. Nov. 5/16. |
| | Lawn, J. E. 6000. | M. Nov. 14/16. |
| | Leo, J. F. 912. | D/W. Nov. 11/16. Det.D./B. |
| A. | Leonard, D. 5067. | M. Nov. 5/16. |
| A. | MacFarlane, J. P. 2197. | M. Nov. 14/16. |
| A. | Mackintosh, L.-Cpl. E. D. 4171. | M. Nov. 14/16. |
| B. | McIntyre, W. C. C. 2150. | K. Mar. 26/17. Det.D./B. |
| | Metcalfe, R. 1919. | M. Nov. 14/16. |
| | Mitchell, P. 485. | M. Nov. 14/16. |
| | Murfett, R. D. 3682. | M. Nov. 14/16. |
| | Nolan, P. 1948. | M. Nov. 5/16. |
| | Orr, W. J. 1731. | K. Oct. 16/16. Det.D./B. |
| | ‡Parkinson. 5093. | K. Mar. 26/17. Det.D./B. |
| | *Pearson, J. D. 4243. | K. Nov. 5/16. Det.D./B. |
| | Quick, Sergt. R. R. 4358. | M. Nov. 14/16. |
| | Ronaldson, R. A. 1701. | W. Unoff. M. Mar. 26/17. |
| | Russell, H. 4197. | M. Nov. 14/16. |
| | Samson, A. R. 4203. | K. Nov. 5/16. Det.D./B. |
| | Scott, Sergt. R. S. 405. | K. Nov. 5/16. Det.D./B. |
| | Scott, W. B. 1954. | M. Nov. 5/16. |
| B. | ‡Simpson, A. 5413. | W. Unoff. M. May 3/17. |
| | Simpson, J. 5102. | K. Nov. 5/16. Det.D./B. |
| | Smart, Sergt. R. 415. | K. Nov. 14/16. Det.D./B. |
| | Smith, H. O. 4212. | K. Mar. 26/17. Det.D./B. |
| | Swain. 3709. | K. Mar. 2/17. Det.D./B. |
| | Tindall, C. 4217. | K. Mar. 2/17. Det.D./B. |
| | Von Stieglitz, R. O. 5701. | M. Mar. 26/17. |
| | Wallace, L.-Sergt. L. H. L. 434. | M. Nov. 14/16. |
| | Walthall. 2268. | K. May 3/17. Det.D./B. |
| | Wood, J. 2185. | K. Nov. 14/16. Det.D./B. |
| A. | ‡Wood, J. W. 3156. | K. May 3/17. Det.D./B. |
| | *Woodgate, H. G. S. 5704. | K. May 3/17. Det.D./B. |
| | Wooldridge, Sergt. G. W. 228. | K. Nov. 14/16. Det.D./B. |

**27th BATTALION A.I.F.**

| Co. | | |
|---|---|---|
| | Adam, G. B. 2330. | K. Nov. 5/16. Det.D./B. |
| D. | Aitken, L.-Cpl. R. A. S. 4971. | K. Nov. 5/16. Det.D./B. |
| | Aylet, F. T. L. 5796. | K. Mar. 26/17. Det.D./B. |
| | Axon, H. L. 4374. | K. Nov. 5/16. Det.D./B. |
| B. | Bartlett, G. J. F. 4059. | K. Mar. 3/17. Det.D./B. |
| C. | Bell, C. H. 505. | K. Nov. 5/16. Det.D./B. |
| | Bennie, W. C. 5308. | K. Mar. 3/17. Det.D./B. |
| | Berryman, F. J. 3017. | K. Nov. 5/16. Det.D./B. |
| | Bird, A. W. 508. | K. Nov. 5/16. Det.D./B. |
| | Bootes, C. E. 510. | K. Nov. 5/16. Det.D./B. |
| | Branson, L. J. 4656. | K. Nov. 5/16. Det.D./B. |
| | Brown, C. C. W. 516. | K. Nov. 5/16. Det.D./B. |
| | Brown, W. 2126. | W. and M. Nov. 5/16. |
| | Carman, L.-Cpl. C. C. 521. | M. Nov. 5/16. |
| | Charlton, J. H. 766. | M. Nov. 5/16. |
| | Condon, P. 2457. | M. Nov. 5/16. |
| A. | Davison, E. G. 2027. | K. Mar. 21/17. Det.D./B. |
| | Dawson, T. J. 3081. | K. Nov. 18/16. Det.D./B. |
| | Dutton, H. 546. | K. Nov. 5/16. Det.D./B. |
| | Earls, F. B. 4109. | K. about Nov. 5/16. Det.D./B. |
| A. | Ede, C. F. 2139. | K. Nov. 5/16. Det.D./B. |
| | Edwards, C. C. 4703. | K. Nov. 5/16. Det.D./B. |
| | Fancelli, C. O. 3812. | K. Nov. 5/16. Det.D./B. |
| | Flett, L.-Cpl. J. R. 3111. | K. Nov. 5/16. Det.D./B. |
| | Gleeson, J. 4716. | K. Nov. 5/16. Det.D./B. |
| | Gooding, H. P. 4435. | K. Nov. 5/16. Det.D./B. |
| | Grimes, Q. 3126. | W. and M. Nov. 5/16. |
| | Halliday, A. O. 1717. | M. Nov. 5/16. |
| | Higgs, G. E. 5014. | M. Nov. 5/16. |
| | Highman, H. R. 588. | K. Nov. 5/16. Det.D./B. |
| D. | Hooper, A. 833. | K. Nov. 5/16. Det.D./B. |
| | Hopkins, A. B. 3154. | M. Nov. 5/16. |
| | Horne, B. T. 4798. | W. and M. Nov. 5/16. |
| | Houston, A. 2172. | K. Nov. 5/16. Det.D./B. |
| C. | Hutton, R. 4451. | K. Nov. 5/16. Det.D./B. |
| | Jacobs, A. M. 4453. | K. May 21/17. Det.D./B. |
| | Jackaman, Cpl. W. R. 3163. | M. Nov. 5/16. R/Enq. |
| | Johnson, M. 4146. | M. Nov. 5/16. |
| | Jones, C. W. A. 1656A. | K. Nov. 5/16. Det.D./B. |
| | Knowles, R. H. 617. | K. Nov. 5/16. Det.D./B. |
| | Leane, Cpl. A. H. 1055. | K. Nov. 5/16. Det.D./B. |
| | Leksman, R. 4264. | M. Nov. 5/16. |
| | Lever, H. P. 1774. | K. Nov. 5/16. Det.D./B. |
| | Lucas, 2nd Lieut. A. S. | K. May 2/17. Det.D./B. |
| | Matthews, T. R. 4745. | K. Nov. 5/16. Det.D./B. |
| | Milde, B. J. 5621. | K. Mar. 3/17. Det.D./B. |
| | Moffert, G. 5380. | M. Mar. 26/17. |
| | Moppett, W. A. 4171. | M. Nov. 5/16. |
| | Muller, J. F. W. 6303. | M. Mar. 2/17. |
| | Murray, R. 4800. | K. Nov. 5/16. Det.D./B. |
| | Nelson, L. G. 2403. | K. Nov. 5/16. Det.D./B. |
| | Parnell, J. M. 3881. | K. Nov. 5/16. Det.D./B. |
| | Parsons, L. T. 4189. | M. Nov. 5/16. |
| | Pearce, F. P. 3248. | M. Nov. 5/16. |
| | Perry, Cpl. R. B. 1965. | M. Nov. 5/16. |
| | Polain, H. J. 4190. | W. and M. Nov. 5/16. |
| | Reid, W. R. 4500. | K. Nov. 5/16. Det.D./B. |
| | Roberts, Cpl. F. J. 680. | M. Nov. 5/16. |
| | Roberts, G. 4505. | M. Nov. 5/16. |

**27th Battalion A.I.F.—contd.**

| Co. | Name | Remarks |
|---|---|---|
| C. | Robertson, W. G. 681. | K. Nov. 5/16. Det.D./B. |
| | Rogers, G. E. 4200. | K. Nov. 5/16. Det.D./B. |
| | Ryan, J. A. 4260. | K. Nov. 5/16. Det.D./B |
| | Slater, C. H. 690. | K. Nov. 5/16. Det.D./B. |
| | Smith, Caley-, Sergt. O. E. 760. | M. Nov. 5/16. |
| | Smith, G. 3279. | M. Nov. 5/16. |
| | Smith, J. 4802. | M. Nov. 5/16. |
| | Smith, J. C. 4761. | M. Nov. 5/16. |
| | Smith, N. R. 5070. | K. Nov. 5/16. Det.D./B. |
| | Smith, W. A. 384A. | K. Nov. 5/16. Det.D./B. |
| | Steer, L. 2482B. | D/W. Feb. 27/17. Det.D./B. |
| | Stevens, F. R. 1611. | K. Nov. 5/16. Det.D./B. |
| | Tart, A. E. 4220. | K. Nov. 5/16. Det.D./B. |
| | Tasker, T. A. C. 4221. | K. Mar. 2/17. Det.D./B. |
| | Thaxton, C. E. 4533. | K. Nov. 5/16. Det.D./B. |
| C. | Thomas, A. 2238. | M. Nov. 5/16. |
| | Thompson, A. 3285. | K. Nov. 5/16. Det.D./B. |
| C. | Thorn, Sig. A. 2238. | M. Nov. 5/16. |
| | Toms, W. H. 706. | W. and M. Nov. 5/16. |
| | Tymons, C. J. 947. | K. Nov. 5/16. Det.D./B. |
| | Williams, Sergt. A. 725. | K. Nov. 5/16. Det.D./B. |
| | Wilton, E. 1721A. | M. Nov. 5/16. |
| | Wingrove, R. A. 4781. | K. Nov. 5/16. Det.D./B. |
| | Woolcock, J. W. 4786. | K. Nov. 18/16. Det.D./B. |

**28th BATTALION A.I.F.**

| Co. | Name | Remarks |
|---|---|---|
| | *Ahnall, 2nd Lieut. K. | K. Feb. 28/17. Det.D./B. |
| | Armes, G. A. 569A. | K. Nov. 3-6/16. Det.D./B. |
| | *Bamford, C. H. 5558. | W. and M. May 3/17. |
| D. | Bennett, H. M. 4379. | K. Nov. 3-6/16. Det.D./B |
| | Bennett, R. W. 1622. | K. Nov. 3-6/16. Det.D./B. |
| | Bleakley, H. 4678. | M. Nov. 5/16. |
| | Bleakley, W. N. 4679. | K. Nov. 3-6/16. Det.D./B. |
| | Bock, T. 4682. | M. Nov. 3-6/16. |
| | Bonsey, W. H. 4076. | K. Nov. 3-6/16. Det.D./B. |
| | Booker, W. 3045. | M. Nov. 3-6/16. |
| | Carter, P. H. 341A. | M. Nov. 3-6/16. |
| | Clark, G. A. 5828. | W. and M. May 3/17. |
| D. | Cole, L. 1634. | K. Nov. 3-6/16. Det.D./B. |
| | Cornelius, M. S. 3071. | M. Nov. 16-18/16. |
| | Craig, A. L. 2476. | K. Nov. 5/16. Det.D./B |
| | Cruickshank, T. W. 5570. | W. and M. May 3/17. |
| | Dean, J. A. 63A. | W. and M. Nov. 3-6/16. |
| | Deans, F. R. 5539. | M. May 3/17. |
| | Dedman, F. C. 4719. | M. Nov. 3-6/16. |
| | Dickinson, G. 5843. | M. May 3/17. |
| | Dunstan, S. A. 270. | M. Nov. 3-6/16. |
| | Durrant, G. T. 4728. | M. Nov. 3-6/16. |
| B. | ‡Edington, T. 5848. | D/W. Mar. 25/17. Det.D./B. |
| | Fidler, T. 1645A. | M. Nov. 3-6/16. |
| | ‡Firkin, L.-Cpl. J. | K. Dec. 31/16. Det.D./B |
| | Forrest, R. 4426. | M. Nov. 3-6/16. |
| | Gardiner, T. J. F. 5015. | K. May 3/17. Det.D./B. |
| | Garth, Sergt. T. G. 782. | M. Nov. 3-6/16. |
| A. | Gartung, F. 1718A. | K. Nov. 3-6/16. Det.D./B. |
| | Goodman, H. 3111. | K. Nov. 3/16. Det.D./B. |

28th Battalion A.I.F.—contd.

| Co. | | |
|---|---|---|
| | Groat, D. 1941. | M. Nov. 3-6/16. |
| | Hicks, E. 442. | K. Nov. 16/16. Det.D./B. |
| | *Hind, J. 3143. | W. and M. May 3/17. |
| | Hislop, P. M. 4445. | M. Nov. 3-6/16. |
| | Howard, T. F. 3845. | M. Nov. 3-6/16. |
| | Humphries, W. 4755. | M. Nov. 3-6/16. |
| | *Johnson, W. B. 1957. | W. and M. May 3/17. |
| C. | Joyce, G. 1740. | K. Nov. 3-6/16. Det.D./B. |
| | Kelly, F. M. 3164. | M. Nov. 3-6/16. |
| | Kirwan, E. J. 4768. | M. May 5/17. |
| | Lawrence, J. W. 5626. | D/W. Mar. 26/17. Det.D./B. |
| | Livingstone, G. P. 4775. | M. Nov. 3-6/16. |
| | Longmore, T. 1207. | M. Nov. 16-18/16. |
| | ‡Lucas, F. W. 5629. | K. Mar. 26/17. Det.D./B. |
| | McCormack, J. J. 5896. | M. May 3/17. |
| | McEvoy, A. 742. | W. and M. Nov. 16-18/16. |
| | McGinniss, F. W. 2417. | M. Nov. 3-6/16. |
| | McNeill, W. W. 4365. | M. Nov. 3-6/16. |
| | Martin, S. J. 4185. | K. Nov. 3-6/16. Det.D./B. |
| | *Meadows, H. C. 5639. (M.G.S.) | K. Mar. 26/17. Det.D./B. |
| | Morris, W. G. 1725. | M. Nov. 16-18/16. |
| | Moyle, E. T. 348. | W. and M. Nov. 3-6/16. |
| | Myers, N. O. 4782. | K. Nov. 3-6/16. Det.D./B. |
| | Nalder, F. L. 4497. | K. Nov. 3-6/16. Det.D./B. |
| | Nelson, H. 3217. | K. Feb. 2/17. Det.D./B. |
| | Nicholls, D. A. 6126. | M. May 3/17. |
| | O'Connor, T. P. 4191. | K. Nov. 3-6/16. Det.D./B. |
| | O'Reilly, L.-Cpl. J. T. 5296. | K. May 3/17. Det.D./B. |
| | Parsons, Cpl. C. W. G. 1768. | M. Nov. 3-6/16. |
| | Payne, C. T. 4509. | M. Nov. 3-6/16. |
| | ‡Phillips, B. 2429. | M. May 14-15/17. |
| | Pickthorn, L.-Cpl. A. E. 365. | M. Nov. 3-6/16. |
| | Plummer, J. D. 4789. | M. May 3/17. |
| | Price, C. W. 2200. | K. Oct. 16/16. Det.D./B. |
| | Pritchard, F. 4519. | M. Nov. 3-6/16. |
| | Randall, Cpl. F. C. J. 4530. | K. Nov. 3-6/16. Det.D./B. |
| | Russell, R. A. C. 5916A. | K. May 3/17. Det.D./B. |
| | Rust, J. D. 1097. | M. Nov. 16-18/16. |
| | Scott, F. W. 4535. | M. Nov. 3-6/16. |
| | Seal, T.-Cpl. E. 691. | M. May 3/17. |
| | Smith, Cpl. F. W. 4661. | M. Nov. 3-6/16. |
| | Smith, S. H. 4223. | W. and M. Nov. 16-18/16. |
| | Stewart, J. 518. | M. Nov. 16-18/16. |
| | Stopher, A. H. 951. | K. Feb. 12/17. Det.D./B. |
| | ‡Tanner, A.-Sergt. F. 4311. | K. Nov. 3-6/16. Det.D./B. |
| | Thomson, J. L. 980 | M. Nov. 3-6/16. |
| | Webber, H. P. 3883. | K. Jan. 27/17. Det.D./B. |
| C. | Wilson, L.-Cpl. B. R. 546. | K. Nov. 3-6/16. Det.D./B. |

29th BATTALION A.I.F.

| | |
|---|---|
| Alexander, A. 454. | M. Mar. 23/17. |
| Clark, E. A. 1366. | K. Nov. 24/16. Det.D./B. |
| ‡Lofthouse, L.-Cpl. J. 2945. | K. Mar. 23/17. Det.D./B. R/Enq. |
| McVicars, J. 2719. | K. Nov. 22/16. Det.D./B. |
| Nelson, R. J. 305. | K. Nov. 24/16. Det.D./B. |
| O'Donnell, T. 315. | K. Dec. 4/16. Det.D./B. |

**29th Battalion A.I.F.—contd.**

Co.

Patterson, F. G. 2729. M. Mar. 23/17.
*Schulze, E. A. L. 2991. K. Mar. 23/17. Det.D./B
Shaw, S. 936. K. Feb. 12/17. Det.D./B.
Shimlick, W. 2759. M. Mar. 23/17.
‡Stimpson, C. J. 2758. K. Oct. 27/16. Det.D./B.
Waters, E. 376. K. Mar. 23/17. Det.D./B.
Williams, C. E. 2442. D/W. Oct. 24/16. Det.D./B.
Wood, Lieut. H. V. K. Mar. 3/17. Det.D./B.

**30th BATTALION A.I.F.**

Butcher, A. E. 3195. K. Mar. 12/17. Det.D./B.
Dalton, C. B. 2011. W. and M. Nov. 2/16.
Davey, O. C. T. 4174. K. Nov. 27/16. Det.D./B.
*Dowling, S. J. 3541. K. May 12/17. Det.D./B.
Kean, W. F. 2673. K. Mar. 22/17. Det.D./B.
Knight, W. 2962. K. Mar. 22/17. Det.D./B.
Page, C. R. 3607. K. Mar. 23/17. Det.D./B.
Wright, H. 4302. K. Mar. 23/17. Det.D./B.

**31st BATTALION A.I.F.**

Bruce, L.-Cpl. J. D. 1524. K. Nov. 21/16. Det.D./B.
‡Cumming. 540. K. Oct. 28/16. Det.D./B.
Johnson, H. P. 880A. W. and M. Dec. 9/16.
Shoemark. 2456. D/W. Jan. 25/17. Det.D./B.
Treherne, G. R. 3048. D/W. Nov. 16/16. Det.D./B.
Washington, D. 3059. D/W. Oct. 26/16. Det.D./B.
Westbury, C. A. 792. D/W. Nov. 1/16. Det.D./B.
Wilson, O. W. 2999. K. Oct. 21/16. Det.D./B.

**32nd BATTALION A.I.F.**

‡Anderson, P. M. 1205. M. June 20/17.
Chapman, W. D. 3785. K. Feb. 16/17. Det.D./B.
Dibden, J. A. 2912. K. Nov. 1/16. Det.D./B.
Fiegert, E. A. 2605. K. Dec. 2/16. Det.D./B.
Owler, N. 3354. M. Dec. 9/16.
‡Walker, J. 1186. W. and M. June 20/17.

**33rd BATTALION A.I.F.**

‡Allison, G. H. W. 2273. K. June 9/17. Det.D./B.
Carroll, J. W. 2190. M. May 25/17.
‡Denny, G. 1817. K. June 8/17. Det.D./B.
‡Galvin, S. B. 2561 D. May 25/17. Det.D./B.
‡Gardner. 708. K. June 7/17. Det.D./B.
Kennedy, R. 1481. (L.M.G.S.) K. Mar. 5/17. Det.D./B.
‡Linklater, Capt. C. H. M. June 7-9/17.
‡Montgomery, G. W. 1209. K. June 7/17. Det.D./B.
‡Mulhall. 1969. K. June 7/17. Det.D./B.

**33rd Battalion A.I.F.—contd.**

| Co. | | |
|---|---|---|
| | †Robertson, S. T. 1239. | K. June 7/17. Det.D./B. |
| | †Schofield, W. 1901A. | W. Unoff. M. June 7/17. |
| | †Stanton. 5087. | D/W. June 2/17. Det.D./B. |
| | Stuart, R. 5091A. | M. May 29/17. |
| | †Taylor. 882. | K. June 7/17. Det.D./B. |
| B. | †Taylor Lind-, Sergt. W. 564. | K. June 28/17. Det.D./B. |
| | †Wilson, E. C. 2150. | K. June 7/17. Det.D./B. |
| | *Young, Cpl. R. M. 912. | K. June 6/17. Det.D./B. |

**34th BATTALION A.I.F.**

| | |
|---|---|
| *Corbett, E. B. H. 1087. | K. May 18/17. Det.D./B. |
| †Fidler, W. E. F. 65. | K. June 7/17. Det.D./B. |
| †Gilfillan, G. 2072. | K. May 17/17. Det.D./B. |
| †Joel. 1837. | K. June 7/17. Det.D./B. |
| ***Shannon, Lieut. E.** | K. June 1/17. Det.D./B. |
| †Stibbard, B. 1981. | K. June 7/17. Det.D./B. |
| †Sullivan, J. L. 1924. | K. June 7/17. Det.D./B. |
| ***Warner, Lieut. L.** | D/W. June 8/17. Det.D./B. |

**35th BATTALION A.I.F.**

| Co. | | |
|---|---|---|
| | †Ayre, J. 14. | K. June 1/17. Det.D./B. |
| | *Butler, H. S. 2529. | K. May 25/17. Det.D./B. |
| | †Carter, F. J. 2293. | K. June 11/17. Det.D./B. |
| | **†Clarke, Denton Lieut. T.** | K. June 7/17. Det.D./B. |
| | †Davis. 2304. | K. June 8/17. Det.D./B. |
| | †Ebrill, C. 417. | K. May 29/17. Det.D./B. |
| D. | *Floate, A. 1945. | K. June 7/17. Det.D./B. |
| | †Forster, S. I. 1384. | K. May 25/17. Det.D./B. |
| | †Hush, P. A. 1924. | K. May 29/17. Det.D./B. |
| | *Idstein, V. F. 2173. | K. May 29/17. Det.D./B. |
| | *Johns. 2614. | K. May 3/17. Det.D./B. |
| | *Leeson, N. M. 2347. | K. May 25/17. Det.D./B. |
| | †Moore. 495. | K. June 8/17. Det.D./B. |
| | †Nichol, W. A. 2645. | K. June 23/17. Det.D./B. |
| | †Norris, G. 1910. | K. June 7/17. Det.D./B. |
| | †O'Brien. 2368. | K. June 8/17. Det.D./B. |
| | †Stevenson, G. G. 2403. | K. June 7/17. Det.D./B. |
| | †Worland, R. C. C. 2899. | K. June 10/17. Det.D./B. |

**36th BATTALION A.I.F.**

| | |
|---|---|
| †Bradley, H. 2280. | K. June 8/17. Det.D./B. |
| **†Burns, Lieut. V. A.** | D/W. June 11/17. Det.D./B. |
| †Carroll. 227. | K. June 1/17. Det.D./B. |
| *Cowled, G. H. 1954. | K. April 30/17. Det.D./B. |
| †Diews, C. H. J. 5006. | D/W. June 8/17. |
| †Farmery, G. 4998. | K. June 8/17. Det.D./B. |
| †Grouse. 1827. | K. June 10/17. Det.D./B. |
| *Hicks, F. H. 5031. | K. May 28/17. Det.D./B. |
| †Kirchener, T.-Cpl. G. 110. | K. June 11/17. Det.D./B. |
| **†Piggott, Capt. F.** | K. June 10/17. Det.D./B. |

**36th Battalion A.I.F.—contd**

| Co. | Name | Status |
|---|---|---|
| | *Scott, J. L. 874. | D/W. June 8/17. Det.D./B. |
| | ‡Sieman, P. H. 2130. | K. June 10/17. Det.D./B. |
| | ‡Stead, W. J. 370. | K. June 7/17. Det.D./B. |
| | ‡Tickle. 241. | K. June 10/17. Det.D./B. |
| | ‡Walker. 2682. | K. June 10/17. Det.D./B. |
| | ‡Wilson, S. B. 5041. | M. June 10/17. |
| | ‡Wright. 2407. | K. June 10/17. Det.D./B. |

**37th BATTALION A.I.F.**

| Co. | Name | Status |
|---|---|---|
| | Brown, E. J. 827. | K. Jan. 28/17. Det.D./B. |
| | *Brown, J. H. 830. | M. June 7-9/17. |
| | Connolly, E. 1041. | K June 6-9/17. Det.D./B. |
| | *Cooper, R. J. B. P. 1562. | K. Jan. 28/17. Det.D./B. |
| | Conquest, A. C. 1159. | W. and M. Feb. 27/17. |
| | ‡Creswick, T. S. 2530. | W. Unoff. M. June 7-9/17. |
| | ‡Derrick, H. 1625. | K. June 8/17. Det.D./B. |
| | Gapes, A. W. 275. | K. Feb. 27/17. Det.D./B. |
| | Glynn, M. T. 276. | M. June 7-9/17. |
| | ‡Griffiths, A. I. 2565. | K. June 7/17. Det.D./B. |
| | ‡Hosking, E. E. 1055. | K. April 23/17. Det.D./B. |
| C. | *Jarrett, 2nd W.O. W. T. 912. | K. June 7-9/17. Det.D./B. |
| | *Jorgensen, N. A. 917. | M. June 7-9/17. |
| | ‡Lowrie, C. R. 1222. | W. Unoff. M. April 23/17. |
| | ‡McComb, H. H. 948. | D/W. Feb. 23/17. Det.D./B. |
| | *McGuiness, A. 2616. | M. June 7-9/17. |
| | ‡Nelson, C. A. 2457 | D/W. June 9/17. Det.D./B. |
| | Richardson, H. 1264. | K. Feb. 27/17. Det.D./B. |
| | *Rose, L.-Cpl. A. H. 983. | M. June 7-9/17. |
| B. | *Sanders, R. E. 1909. | K. June 7-9/17. Det.D./B. |
| | ‡Webb, G. F. 2408. | K. June 7-9/17. Det.D./B. |

**38th BATTALION A.I.F.**

|  |  |
|---|---|
| Allen, T. P. 206. | M. May 28/17. |
| *Brown, J. 2527. | M. June 7-9/17. |
| Chapman, C. V. 5981. | M. May 28/17. |
| ‡Donald, H. G. 6001A. | M. June 7-9/17. |
| Fewell, A. 1169. | M. Jan. 1/17. |
| ‡Finlay, H. J. 2562. | K. May 15/17. Det.D./B. |
| *Goulson, R. G. 1036. | M. June 7-9/17. |
| Gunning, Gnr. W. J. 1176. | M. Jan. 1/17. |
| Killingsworth, 2nd Lieut. H. L. | M. May 28/17. |
| *McCormack, A. 1882. | M. June 7-9/17. |
| ‡Nathan, E. W. 1258. | K. April 20/17. Det.D./B. |
| ‡Nelson. 627. | K. Feb. 27/17. Det.D./B. |
| *Nield, W. J. 630. | D/W. Feb. 27/17. Det.D./B. |
| ‡Page, W. R. 2621. | K. June 9/17. Det.D./B. |
| *Ridgway, G. E. 2626. | K. May 29/17. Det.D./B. |

**39th BATTALION A.I.F.**

|  |  |
|---|---|
| ‡Gallagher, N. 885. | K. April 30/17. Det.D./B. |
| ‡Glover. 116. | K. Feb. 6/17. Det.D./B. |

## 40th BATTALION A.I.F.

| Co. | | |
|---|---|---|
| | *Baker, A. W. 1793. | M. June 7/17. |
| | *Huxley, C. H. A. 5723. | K. June 8/17. Det.D./B. |
| | Leitch, R. W. 441. | M. May 31/17. |
| | *McDougall. 682. | K. June 7/17. Det.D./B. |
| | ‡Morey, W. S. 5747. | K. June 7/17. Det.D./B. |
| | Russell, H. McD. 1928. | M. May 31/17. |
| | Smith, C. A. 589. | K. April 9/17. Det.D./B. |

## 41st BATTALION A.I.F.

| | |
|---|---|
| *Crowe, J. J. 404. | K. April 23/17. Det.D./B. |
| *Cummins, W. D. 396 | K. June 1/17. Det.D./B. |
| ‡Harmes, F. L. 440. | K. July 8/17. Det.D./B. |
| *Hamilton. 886. | K. June 14/17. Det.D./B. |
| Hazell, G. P. 442. | M. June 7/17. |
| Kennedy, W. F. E. 101. | M. June 7/17. |
| ‡McFarlane, J. McD. 937. | D/W. June 10/17. Det.D./B. |
| Martin, E. 693. | M. June 7/17. |
| ‡Mills. 2126. | K. June 10/17. Det.D./B. |
| ‡Weatherstone. 1098. | K. June 2/17. |
| Williams, A. E. 305. | M. June 7/17. |

## 42nd BATTALION A.I.F.

| | | |
|---|---|---|
| | ‡Barrett. 516. | K. June 10/17. Det.D./B |
| C. | *Brewster, L.-Cpl. E. V. 529. | K. Feb. 4/17. Det.D./B. |
| | *Hawthorne, W. A. J. 1849. | K. June 9/17. Det.D./B. |
| | *Ibbotson, A. S. 3312. | K. June 10/17. Det.D./B. |
| | *McMurtrie, A. 848. | K. Mar. 7/17. Det.D./B. |
| | ‡Mullen. 1136. | K. June 9/17. Det.D./B. |
| | *Rodger, L.-Cpl. A. 686. | K. June 10/17. Det.D./B. |
| | Shaw, Cpl. A. J. 1772. | K. Feb. 5/17. Det.D./B. |
| | *Tucker. 231. | K. April 5/17. Det.D./B. |
| | ‡Webb, H. 2411. | K. June 9/17. Det.D./B. |

## 43rd BATTALION A.I.F.

| | | |
|---|---|---|
| | ‡Clark, Lieut. E. D. | D/W. June 8/17. |
| | *Colman, Lieut. F. | K. June 4/17. Det.D./B. |
| | *Foster, E. 669. | W. Unoff. M. Mar. 18/17. |
| | *Lands, Sergt. H. C. 1729. | K. Feb. 13/17. Det.D./B. |
| B. | *Shute, A. J. 3983. | K. June 7/17. Det.D./B. |

## 44th BATTALION A.I.F.

| | | |
|---|---|---|
| | Barley, A. R. 1788A. | M. June 4/17. |
| | Clifford, D. M. 523. | M. June 4/17. |
| | *Frearson, T.-Cpl. C. C. J. 865 | M. June 4/17. |
| | ‡Graham, J. F. 2166. | M. June 10/17. |
| | Graham, M. R. 419. | M. June 4/17. |
| A. | *Green, G. 48. | Unoff. M. June 15/17. |

**44th Battalion A.I.F.—contd.**

| Co. | Name | Status |
|---|---|---|
| | *Hardman, J. C. 187. | K. June 8/17. Det.D./B. |
| | McGrath, F. L. 2610. | M. June 4/17. |
| | *Matthews, E. A. 2124. | D/W. June 9/17. Det.D./B. |
| | Palmer, Cpl. C. R. 1937. | M. June 4/17. |
| | Rooke, T. 811. | M. Mar. 14/17. |
| | ‡Short, W. J. 913. | D/W. June 1/17. Det.D./B. |
| | ‡Wood, W. F. 434. | M. June 11/17. |

**45th BATTALION A.I.F.**

| Co. | Name | Status |
|---|---|---|
| | *Allen, Lieut. H. B. | K. June 7/17. Det.D./B. |
| | *Arthur, R. C. 1668A. | M. June 7/17. |
| | ‡Ash, R. J. 2366. | M. April 11/17. |
| | *Austin, H. B. 4726A. | M. June 7/17. |
| | *Barker, E. H. 5044. | M. June 7/17. |
| D. | ‡Blenkinsop, Sergt. J. D. 710. | K. June 9/17. Det.D./B. |
| | *Bourne, M. 2958. | M. June 7/17. |
| | *Boxsell, C. O. 2617. | M. June 7/17. |
| | *Campbell, D. C. 2270. | M. June 7/17. |
| | ‡Cook. 3121. | K. June 7/17. Det.D./B. |
| | ‡Crome, C. 2148. | K. June 9/17. Det.D./B. |
| | *Curson, Sergt. E. E. 1706. | M. June 7/17. |
| | Dawes, H. R. 4499. | K. April 11/17. Det.D./B. |
| | *DeBoynton, A. 3122. | M. June 10/17. |
| | *Douglas, Cpl. A. B. 2765. | M. June 7/17. |
| | *Duncan, A. A. 1731A. | M. June 7/17. |
| | ‡Ede, T. A. J. 3920. | K. June 9/17. Det.D./B. |
| | *Estick, B. H. 1628. | M. June 7/17. |
| | *Fairless, Cpl. C. C. 4183. | M. June 7/17. |
| | *Falconer, R. 2178. | M. June 7/17. |
| | *Findlay, T. 3263. | M. June 7/17. |
| | *Goodwin, V. L. 2907. | M. June 7/17. |
| | ‡Gow, D. 1746. | M. June 6/17. |
| | *Hampton, W. H. 1752. | M. June 7/17. |
| | *Hannam, W. H. 2196. | K. Feb. 21/17. Det.D./B. |
| | *Harris, J. H. 2431A. | M. June 7/17. |
| | *Haynes, F. A. 3163. | M. June 7/17. |
| | *Heard, W. 2654. | M. June 7/17. |
| | *Hemming, L.-Cpl. G. H. 3809. | M. June 9/17. |
| | Hills, B. 2189. | D/W. Jan. 24/17. Det.D./B. |
| | *Jones. 2658. | K. June 12/17. Det.D./B. |
| | *Kennealy, M. 3993. | M. June 7/17. |
| | *Langlands, F. 2449. | M. June 7/17. |
| | *Langridge, T.-Cpl. C. J. 2631. | M. June 7/17. |
| | *Martens, Cpl. W. 1788. | M. June 7/17. |
| | Martin, J. G. 1957 | K. Feb. 21/17. Det.D./B. |
| | *Mason, H. H. 1956. | M. June 7/17. |
| | ‡Mayne, W. H. 1371. | K. June 7/17. Det.D./B. |
| | ‡Miller, L.-Cpl. W. B. R. 2653. | K. June 7/17. Det.D./B. |
| | *Miners, S. H. O. 3199. | M. June 7/17. |
| | *Moore, C. A. 2675. | M. June 7/17. |
| | Morrish. 2212. | K. June 8/17. Det.D./B. |
| | ‡Munger, A. 3207. | K. June 9/17. Det.D./B. |
| | *Murphy, N. A. 3189. | M. June 10/17. |
| | *O'Connor, G. W. 1645. | M. June 7/17. |
| | ‡Owen, J. 2740. | D/W. Nov. 23/16. Det.D./B. |
| | *Perston, J. R. 2698. | K. Feb. 21/17. Det.D./B. |

**45th Battalion A.I.F.—contd.**

| Co. | | |
|---|---|---|
| | *Phillips, G. G. T. R. 2704. | M. **June 7/17.** |
| | *Polmear, R. 1881. | M. **June 7/17.** |
| | ‡Pringle. 3426. | K. **May 7/17.** Det.D./B. |
| | *Ramsay, J. R. 3888. | M. **June 7/17.** |
| | *Reilly, T. 3007. | M. **June 7/17.** |
| | *Robinson, J. 5219. | M. **June 7/17.** |
| | *Rumsey, L.-Cpl. N. E. 2478. | M. **June 7/17.** |
| | Rushton, C. 5450. | K. **April 11/17.** Det.D./B. |
| D. | ‡Ryan, W. W. S. 3443. | K. **June 7/17.** Det.D./B. |
| | *Scott, H. T. 1670. | M. **June 7/17.** |
| | *Smith, F. 3015. | M. **June 7/17.** |
| | *Stuart, F. 3990. | M. **June 7/17.** |
| | Taylor, J. T. 5465. | D/W. **Feb. 25/17.** Det.D./B. |
| | Tilbrook, J. 2488. | M. **April 11/17.** |
| | *Tozer, J. 3286. | M. **June 7/17.** |
| | *Walker, V. K. 2028. | M. **June 7/17.** |
| | *Waring. 3647. | K. **May 29/17.** Det.D./B. |
| | *White, N. N. 2252. | M. **June 7/17.** |
| | *White, R. 3517A. | M. **June 7/17.** |
| | *Wickers, W. T. 2696A. | M. **June 7/17.** |
| | ‡Wootton, S. K. 2025. | K. **June 7/17.** Det.D./B. |

**46th BATTALION A.I.F.**

| | | |
|---|---|---|
| | Abrahams, E. L. 5646. | W. and M. **April 11/17.** |
| | Alexander, G. H. 4728A. | M. **April 11/17.** |
| | ‡Batters, A. 2032. | W. and M. **April 11/17.** |
| C. | Beale, Sergt. H. A. 299. | W. and M. **April 11/17.** |
| | Beggs, F. W. 2817. | M. **April 11/17.** |
| | Belden. C. M. 2033. | M. **April 11/17.** |
| | Bell, L.-Cpl. G. McJ. 4735. | W. and M. **April 11/17.** |
| | Bell, S. 5654. | M. **April 11/17.** |
| | Benham, R. A. 2542. | M. **April 11/17.** |
| C. | *Bennett, J. R. D. 1885. | K. **April 9/17.** Det.D./B. |
| | Berry, J. H. 4736. | W. and M. **April 11/17.** |
| | Booth. 2819. | M. **April 11/17.** |
| | *Bradley, J. 4443. | K. **April 11/17.** Det.D./B. |
| | Brauer, L.-Cpl. W. A. C. 555. | M. **April 11/17.** |
| | Bridge, W. 5053. | M. **April 11/17.** |
| | *Brown, J. 3012. | W. and M. **April 11/17.** |
| | Buchanan, G. C. 2463. | W and M. **April 11/17.** |
| | ‡Buls, H. 2454. | W. and M. **April 11/17.** |
| | ‡Burley, L.-Cpl. T. M. 2034. | W. and M. **April 11/17.** |
| | Burns, M. D. 5659. | M. **April 11/17.** |
| | Burton, T.-Cpl. G. S. 2384B. | W. and M. **April 11/17.** |
| | Caithness, C. P. J. 2385. | M. **April 11/17.** |
| | Campbell, W. G. 2304. | W. and M. **April 11/17.** |
| | Challis, G. E. 2165. | M. **April 11/17.** |
| | Chiswall, F. A. 1821. | M. **April 11/17.** |
| | *Clingan, C. G. 2163. | W. and M. **April 11/17.** |
| | Collins, W. E. 2161. | M. **April 11/17.** |
| | Considine, P. 4475. | M. **April 11/17.** |
| | Cook, Cpl. P. E. 4470. | M. **April 11/17.** |
| | Copeman, A. J. 1680. | M. **April 11/17.** |
| | Cox, C. M. 3713. | M. **April 11/17.** |
| | Crawford, T. 2354. | W. and M. **April 11/17.** |
| | Cremer, Sergt. E. W. 3021. | M. **April 11/17.** |

**46th Battalion A.I.F.—contd.**

Co.

| | |
|---|---|
| Crichton, W. R. 2397. | M. April 11/17. |
| Crouch, C. 2157. | W. and M. April 11/17. |
| ‡Davies, A. H. 4480. | K. April 11/17. Det.D./B. |
| Dawson, C. F. 2176. | W. and M. April 11/17. |
| Dickman, W. H. 2173. | M. April 11/17. |
| ‡Dunn. 1641. | K. Oct. 10/16. Det.D./B. |
| ‡Dusting. H. J. 4486. | W. and M. April 11/17. |
| Fahmel, A. E. 2187. | M. April 11/17. |
| Featherby, A. C. 2409. | M. April 11/17. |
| Firmin, A. 1694. | M. April 11/17. |
| Fletcher, D. J. 3319. | W. and M. April 11/17. |
| Foote, A. 227. | M. April 11/17. |
| ‡Freeman, J. H. 1915A. | K. June 11/17. Det.D./B. |
| Gammon, A. 2655. | M. April 11/17. |
| Gathercole, W. 3750. | M. April 11/17. |
| Goerty, H. W. P. 1917. | M. April 11/17. |
| Graham, G. H. M. 1910 | W. and M. April 11/17. |
| Grainger, O. 2294. | W. and M. April 11/17. |
| Gray, F. W. 2197. | M. April 11/17. |
| Green, A. E. 2192. | W. and M. April 11/17. |
| Green, H. G. 2198. | M. April 11/17. |
| Gronland, H. 14555. | M. April 11/17. |
| Haase, Cpl. R. T. 4955. | M. April 11/17. |
| Hamunn, G. 4825. | M. April 11/17. |
| Harber, A. E. 2210. | M. April 11/17. |
| *Hatt, C. L. 2427. | K. April 11/17. Det.D./B. |
| Hayne, T. A. 949. | M. April 11/17. |
| Hull, W. J. 2479. | M. April 11/17. |
| Jones, J. J. 5132. | W. and M. April 11/17. |
| Joyce, M. J. 3786. | M. April 11/17. |
| Laing, J. O. 2284. | W. and M. April 11/17. |
| Laskie, N. W. 2706. | M. April 11/17. |
| Lawrence, J. H. 3059. | W. and M. April 11/17. |
| Lewis, W. P. 2407. | M. April 11/17. |
| Lewis, Cpl. W. W. 3045. | W. and M. April 11/17. |
| Liddiard, L.-Cpl. A. C. 3825. | M. April 11/17. |
| Lindon, L.-Cpl. W. 4529. | M. April 11/17. |
| ‡Love, P. M. 3327. | K. April 11/17. Det.D./B. |
| Lucas, G. 1728. | M. April 11/17. |
| McDonald, Cpl. R. 3082. | W. and M. April 11/17. |
| McEwan, L.-Cpl. R. A. 4553. | M. April 11/17. |
| McGrath, P. J. 1820. | M. April 11/17. |
| McKellar, D. M. 2800. | M. April 11/17. |
| McMillan, H. C. 4264. | M. April 11/17. |
| **McPherson, Capt. J. J.** | K. June 12/17. Det.D./B. |
| McRae, A. 4560. | M. April 11/17. |
| ‡Manzie, G. S. 2722. | K. April 11/17. Det.D./B. |
| Malhaffy, K. L. 2720. | M. April 11/17. |
| Martin, A. P. 1355. | W. and M. April 11/17. |
| ‡Millett, L. J. 3430. | K. April 11/17. Det.D./B. |
| ‡Mills, H. E. 4539. | K. April 11/17. Det.D./B. |
| *Morehouse, L. B. C. 2466. | M. Apri 11/17. |
| Molyneux, D. P. 4542. | M. April 11/17. |
| Monico, J. B. 1961. | M. April 11/17. |
| Ninnis, F. L. 544. | D/W. Nov 15/16. Det.D./B. |
| Nuttall, A. J. 3854. | M. April 11/17. |
| O'Callaghan, J. E. 1832. | M. April 11/17. |
| O'Connell, H. D. 1971. | K. April 11/17. Det.D./B. |
| Parker, E. L. C. 2479. | M. April 11/17. |

**46th Battalion A.I.F.—contd.**

Co.

| | |
|---|---|
| ‡Parker, F. C. 3110. | K. April 11/17. Det.D./B. |
| Pontin, Sergt. N. M. 3120. | W. and M. April 11/17. |
| Randle, R. 3931. | M. April 11/17. |
| **Roads, L.-Cpl. H. 5753.** | W. and M. April 11/17. |
| Rooney, Sergt. Chas. R. 3896. | W. and M. April 11/17. |
| Ross, N. 2248. | W. and M. April 11/17. |
| Rowley, C. W. 4303. | M. April 11/17. |
| Rutherford, H. 3885. | M. April 11/17. |
| *Rutherford, W. A. 414A. | W. Unoff. M. April 11/17. |
| Slater, H. L. 2755. | M. April 11/17. |
| Sweeney, G. J. 4346. | M. April 11/17. |
| Travis, W. 5221. | M. April 11/17. |
| Tuck, H. T. 3937. | K. April 11/17. Det.D./B. |
| Voumard, H. H. L. 2004. | M. April 11/17. |
| Wade, T. 2466. | M. April 11/17. |
| **Walker, 2nd Lieut. F.** | M. April 11/17. |
| Walker, G. 4322. | M. April 11/17. |
| Williams, F. 2005. | M. April 11/17. |
| Williams, J. H. 5775. | M. April 11/17. |

**47th BATTALION A.I.F.**

| | |
|---|---|
| Alison, J. A. 2125. | M. April 11/17. |
| ‡Andersen, A. C. 2604. | K. June 6/17. Det.D./B. |
| ***Armitage, 2nd Lieut. R. M.** | K. April 11/17. Det.D./B. |
| Bartley, P. 5035. | M. April 11/17. |
| *Beaton, C. 2392. | M. June 7/17. |
| *Beckman, J. 2624A. | M. June 7/17. |
| ‡Benn, W. J. 1971. | K. June 7/17. Det.D./B. |
| Beitzel, L.-Cpl. F. W. 3007. | M. April 11/17. |
| Budgen, W. E. 2391. | M. April 11/17. |
| *Burgess, R. W. 1635. | M. June 7/17. |
| *Cavanagh, C. C. 2748B. | M. June 7/17. |
| ‡Cecini, J. F. 1641. | M. June 7/17. |
| *Clarkson, A. 1887. | M. June 7/17. |
| Collins, R. O. 2400. | M. April 11/17. |
| Cooper, Cpl. A. 3297. | M. April 11/17. |
| Cutler, R. W. 2407A. | M. April 11/17. |
| Doody, W. 2195. | W. and M. Nov. 15/16. |
| *Evans, G. M. 5084. | M. June 7/17. |
| ‡Fallick, P. H. 2425. | K. June 7/17. Det.D./B. |
| ‡Farr, R. 4165. | K. June 7/17. Det.D./B. |
| *Findlay, D. G. 2648. | M. June 7/17. |
| *Flanagan, W. V. 2646. | M. June 7/17. |
| *Grant, D. 2655. | M. June 7/17. |
| ‡Handley. 5106. | K. June 7/17. Det.D./B. |
| *Hill, T. G. 2905. | M. June 7/17. |
| Horton, R. F. 5115. | K. April 11/17. Det.D./B. |
| ‡Hunter, C. 2661. | M. June 7/17. |
| *Jackson, G. 1674. | M. June 7/17. |
| Johnson, W. 2444. | M. April 11/17. |
| *Jorgenson, A. 203; | M. June 7/17. |
| **‡Kelly, 2nd Lieut.** (Late 1666.) | K. April 11/17. Det.D./B. |
| *Leng, T. 248. | M. June 7/17. |
| *Lowry, T. M. 3795. | M. June 7/17. |
| McCormack, T. 1601. | K. April 11/17. Det.D./B. |
| *McKenzie, D. H. 3911. | M. June 7/17. |

**47th Battalion A.I.F.—contd.**

| Co. | | |
|---|---|---|
| | McLeod, Cpl. W. H. B. 2777. | M. April 11/17. |
| | Marshall, G. 1725. | M. April 11/17. |
| | *Martin, A. 2213A. | M. June 7/17. |
| | *Mear, C. 4557. | M. June 7/17. |
| | *Mitchell, H. 3011A. | M. June 7/17. |
| | Murphy, J. 3399. | M. April 11/17. |
| | *Noud, W. J. 4568. | D/W. May 14/17. Det.D./B. |
| | *Pagan, J. 1717. | M. June 7/17. |
| | *Park, H. S. 2485. | M. June 7/17. |
| | *Pettiford, G. L. 2489. | M. June 7/17. |
| | *Pleass, E. L. 1762. | M. June 7/17. |
| | Price, J. G. 4639. | M. April 11/17. |
| | ***Salmon, Lieut. D. F.** | K. June 8/17. Det.D./B. |
| | Spiers, U. A. 1956. | M. April 11/17. |
| | ‡Strang, Cpl. J. T. F. 608. | M. June 7/17. |
| | *Strong, W. 2505. | M. June 7/17. |
| | *Taylor, S. 2309A. | M. June 6/17. |
| | *Viles, K. McL. 3104. | M. June 7/17. |
| | ***Walker, 2nd Lieut. A. R.** | K. June 9/17. Det.D./B. |
| | Weston, R. 1759. | M. April 11/17. |
| | Williams, T. E. 2514 | M. April 11/17. |
| | *Willis, W. W. 3968. | M. June 7/17. |

**48th BATTALION A.I.F.**

| | | |
|---|---|---|
| | Anderson, K. C. 421. | W. and M. April 11/17. |
| | Andrews, A. F. S. 2623A. | M. April 11/17. |
| | *Baldry. 4950. | K. April 11/17. Det.D./B. |
| | Baldwin, A. A. 2296A. | M. April 11/17. |
| | Barber, J. R. 2123A. | W. and M. April 11/17. |
| | Barrett, R. H. E. 2125. | M. April 11/17. |
| | Bates, B. S. 1879. | M. April 11/17. |
| | Bates, G. T. 1880. | M. April 11/17. |
| | Boucher, A. 2633. | M. April 11/17. |
| | Brooks, Cpl. C. 1888. | M. April 11/17. |
| | Bruce, A. E. 2639. | M. April 11/17. |
| | Burlave, C. C. 3016. | M. April 11/17. |
| A. | Burn, L.-Cpl. R. W. 3228. | M. April 11/17. |
| | Buswell, G. E. 4758. | M. April 11/17. |
| | Christian, A. J. 2136. | M. April 11/17. |
| | Clapp, J. 1650. | M. April 11/17. |
| | Cleary, A. H. 2461. | M. April 11/17. |
| | Colebatch, C.-S.-M. H. E. 2332. | M. April 11/17. |
| D. | Collier, G. 5078 | M. April 11/17. |
| | Coombs, J. J. 2142. | M. April 11/17. |
| | Coombs, K. 2314. | M. April 11/17. |
| | Coombs, N. 2399. | W. and M. April 11/17. |
| | Cooper, L.-Sergt. J. C. 3063. | W. and M. April 11/17. |
| | ‡Cooper, S. R. 5679. | W. and M. April 11/17. |
| | Crowe, L.-Cpl. R. C. 1998A. | W. and M. April 11/17. |
| | Cundy, W. D. 5680. | M. April 11/17. |
| | Dalziell, E. R. 2650. | M. April 11/17. |
| | Davies, H. G. 4794. | M. April 11/17. |
| | Deane, L.-Cpl. J. S. 1905. | M. April 11/17. |
| | Dolan, M. 2290. | M. April 11/17. |
| | Douglas, A. L. 3032 | K. April 8/17. Det.D./B. |
| | Douglas. 2720. | Unoff. M. April 11/17. |

**48th Battalion A.I.F.—contd.**

| Co. | | |
|---|---|---|
| | Doyle, W. 2649. | M. April 11/17. |
| C. | Emmins, A. O. 3044. | M. April 11/17. |
| | Evans, C. R. 1911. | M. April 11/17. |
| C. | Evans, R. H. 3041. | M. April 11/17. |
| | Flynn, L.-Cpl. T. J. 4810. | M. April 11/17. |
| | **Forsyth, Codrington-, Lieut. G. P.** | M. April 11/17. |
| | Foster, Sergt. A. B. 16. | W. and M. April 11/17 |
| | Gallagher, A. W. 1919. | M. April 11/17. |
| | Gibson, G. W. 2665. | M. April 11/17. |
| | Glover, H. 4147. | M. April 11/17. |
| | Gregory, A. 2276. | M. April 11/17. |
| | **Hammond, 2nd Lieut. H. J.** | M. April 11/17. |
| | Harris, Sergt. D. 2151A. | M. April 11/17. |
| | Harvey, L.-Cpl. L. W. 1169. | M. April 11/17. |
| | Healy, J. S. 2673. | W. and M. April 11/17. |
| | Hebenton, T 4948. | M. April 11/17. |
| | Hobbs, H. H. 2424. | M. April 11/17. |
| | Holland, H. J. 1934. | M. April 11/17. |
| | Horne, A. V. 5711. | M. April 11/17. |
| | Hutton, E. N. 3012. | M. April 11/17. |
| | Ireland, W. J. 1937. | W. and M. April 11/17. |
| | James, W. 1679. | K. April 11/17. Det.D./B. |
| | Johnston, L.-Cpl. J. F. 5040. | M. April 11/17. |
| | Kelly, L. A. 2057. | W. and M. April 11/17. |
| | Klintworth, H. L. 1946. | M. April 11/17. |
| | Lahey, Cpl. H. J. 3087A. | M. April 11/17. |
| | **Lease, Capt. A. E.** | M. April 11/17. |
| | Le Brun, W. H. 1950. | M. April 11/17. |
| | Leonard, E. H. M. 1690. | M. April 11/17. |
| | Levett, A. R. 2195. | W. and M. April 11/17. |
| | Louden, H. G. A. 2698. | M. April 11/17. |
| | Love, S. E. 4163. | M. April 11/17. |
| | Lowe, R. 5133. | M. April 11/17. |
| | Lyne, D. 2699. | M. April 11/17. |
| | McCabe, J. 2706. | M. April 11/17. |
| | McKinnon, A. 2705. | M. April 11/17. |
| | McLellan, J. H. 1709. | M. April 11/17. |
| | McMahen, M. 1964. | M. April 11/17. |
| | Mahony, C. 935A. | M. April 11/17. |
| | March, D. G. 2720B. | M. April 11/17. |
| | Marshall, W. J. 2714. | M April 11/17. |
| | Masters, R. 3724. | M. April 11/17. |
| | Mayell, E. J. 5728. | M. April 11/17. |
| | Mesney, V. W. 2712. | M. April 11/17. |
| | Miatke, F. A. 3729. | M. April 11/17. |
| | Mounce, C. A. 518. | W. and M. April 11/17. |
| | Myers, J. E. 2459. | M. April 11/17. |
| | Nicholson, Sergt. J. W. 3111. | M. April 11/17. |
| | Noy, E. H. 3740. | M. April 11/17. |
| | Noy, L. C. 588. | M. April 11/17. |
| | O'Brien, L.-Cpl. J. D. 2467A. | M. April 11/17. |
| | O'Dea, J. 1967. | M. April 11/17. |
| | O'Sullivan, G. P. 4681. | M. April 11/17. |
| | Oxman, A. W. 4684. | M. April 11/17. |
| | Page, A. J. 3117. | M. April 11/17. |
| | Parsons, W. G. 5849. | M. April 11/17. |
| | Patterson, O. N. 2470. | M. April 11/17. |
| | Richards, R. M. 3302. | M. April 11/17. |
| | Rigby, J. W. 1724. | M. April 11/17. |

**48th Battalion A.I.F.—contd.**

Co.

| | | |
|---|---|---|
| | Roberts, H. E. 1976. | M. April 11/17. |
| | **Shadwick, Lieut. J. A.** | M. April 11/17. |
| | Shepherd, H. R. 2243. | M. April 11/17. |
| | *Sheridan, E. 4033. | M. June 9/17. |
| | 'Shueard, W. G. 2492. | M. April 11/17. |
| | Sims, F. A. 2984. | M. April 11/17. |
| | Sims, F. G. 2983. | M. April 11/17. |
| | Smith, A. 2489. | M. April 11/17. |
| | Speck, J. C. 1938. | M. April 11/17. |
| | Ticklie, L.-Cpl. A. S. 4347. | M. April 11/17. |
| | Trelour, P. C. 2751. | W. and M. April 11/17. |
| | Turley, G. C. 1997. | K. Mar. 8/17. Det.D./B. |
| | Turner, C. C. 2499. | M. April 11/17. |
| | Tutt, A. 2477. | M., France, April 11/17. |
| | Vawdrey, T. F. 4428. | K. Nov. 26/16. Det.D./B. |
| | Viney, E. G. 2259. | M. April 11/17. |
| | Wachman, Cpl. R. 4451. | M. April 11/17. |
| | Ward, A. 2453A. | M April 11/17. |
| | Warren, Cpl. U. G. 1385. | M. April 11/17. |
| | Watson, J. R. 2002. | M. April 11/17. |
| | Wiese, R. G. W. 2507. | M. April 11/17. |
| | Williams, L.-Cpl. G. S. 2838. | M. April 11/17. |
| | Wooldridge, S. J. C. G. 2012. | M. April 11/17. |
| | Wright, D. L. 2510. | M. April 11/17. |
| | Wright, L.-Cpl. E. J. 2033A. | M. April 11/17. |

**49th BATTALION A.I.F.**

| | | |
|---|---|---|
| | ‡Allen, J. 2614. | M. June 7/17. |
| | ‡Allen, J. E. 2616A. | M. June 7/17. |
| | ‡Anderson. 5207. | K. June 17/17. Det.D./B. |
| | ‡Black, C. M. 5037. | K. Nov. 23/16. Det.D./B. |
| A. | ‡Blake, Sergt. J. T. 2143. | K. June 7/17. Det.D./B. |
| | ‡Carmody. 566. | K. June 7/17. Det.D./B. |
| | ‡Cash, P. 5059. | K. June 7/17. Det.D./B. |
| | Clark, E. W. 233. | D/W. Nov. 15/16. |
| | ‡Cloughley, J. H. 5063. | K. June 7/17. Det.D./B. |
| | ‡Coleman. 3310. | K. June 7/17. Det.D./B. |
| | Craies, C. S. 5064. | W. and M. Oct. 6/16. |
| | ‡Crawford, N. L. 2641. | M. June 7/17. |
| | ‡Dalglish. 1262. | W. Unoff. M. June 7/17. |
| | ‡Dodd, A. S. 3003. | K. June 7/17. Det.D./B. |
| | ‡Druitt. 2472. | K. June 7/17. Det.D./B. |
| | ‡English, S. C. 3804. | K. June 7/17. Det.D./B. |
| | ‡Field, A. S. 3234. | K. June 7/17. Det.D./B. |
| | ‡Frendenberg, B. C. 2896. | M. June 7/17. |
| | ‡Frederick, O. R. 3724. | M. June 7/17. |
| | ‡Grieve, A. M. 2911. | M. June 7/17. |
| | ‡Guerin, J. F. T. 2910. | M. June 7/17. |
| | *Hodges, S. W. 3831. | K. April 5/17. Det.D./B. |
| | ‡Johnson, H. H. 2193A. | M. June 7/17. |
| | ‡McClelland, R. J. 2697A. | M. June 7/17. |
| | ‡McMachon, J. M. 5147. | M. June 7/17. |
| | ‡Moylan. 3844. | K. June 6/17. Det.D./B. |
| | O'Neill, T. G. 5148. | K. April 5/17 Det.D./B. |
| | ‡Palmer. 2789. | K. June 7/17. Det.D./B. |
| | ‡Pedder, F. E. 909. | M. June 7/17. |

**49th Battalion A.I.F.—contd.**

| Co. | | |
|---|---|---|
| | ‡Penrose, R. M. 3559. | K. **June 6/17.** Det.D./B. |
| | ‡Quailey, G. D. 2981. | M. **June 7/17.** |
| | ‡Quinn, M. J. 2486. | M. **June 7/17.** |
| | ‡Spull. 2882. | M. **June 7/17.** |
| | ‡Stewart, R. W. 1070. | K. **April 11/17.** Det.D./B. |
| | ‡Tarling, Cpl. G. H. 2403. | M. **June 7/17.** |
| | ‡Whear, C.-S.-M. H. J. 3527. | M. **June 7/17.** |
| | White. 4528. | K. **April 2/17.** Det.D./B. |
| | ‡Wilkinson, E 3936. | M. **June 7/17.** |
| | ‡Williams. 3694. | K. **May 3/17.** Det.D./B. |

**50th BATTALION A.I.F.**

| | | |
|---|---|---|
| | *Aitken, L.-Cpl. F. H. 4727. | M. **June 9/17.** |
| | ‡Banfoot, J. C. 3544. | M. **June 7/17.** |
| | ***Bidstrup, Lieut. H. L.** | K. **April 3/17.** Det.D./B. |
| | *Coleman. 4995. | K. **May 8/17.** Det.D./B. |
| | *Dougal, H. P. 2907. | K. **April 11/17.** Det.D./B. |
| | Dwiar, J. J. 2908. | K. **April 2/17.** Det.D./B. |
| | Emery, Cpl. H. W. 2611A. | M. **April 2/17.** |
| | Goodes, L.-Cpl. E. A. 1528. | M. **April 2/17.** |
| | *George, E. H. 3321. | W. and M. **April 2/17.** |
| B. | *Harper, A.-Cpl. H. G. 3838. | K. **April 2/17.** Det.D./B. |
| | Harvie, A. G. 4797. | K. **Nov. 19/16.** Det.D./B. |
| | ‡Hayford, H. R. 2774. | M. **June 7/17.** |
| | Hepworth, J. 2680. | K. **April 2/17** R/Enq. Det.D./B. |
| | *Hughes, H. G. 4497. | K. **April 2/17.** Det.D./B. |
| | Joyce, Cpl. H. 3042. | K. **April 2/17.** Det.D./B. |
| | *Kelly, F. 3367. | M. **June 10/17.** |
| | Kernick, H. P. 2940. | K. **April 2/17.** Det.D./B. R/Enq. |
| | *Miller, J. H. T. 4224. | M. **June 10/17.** |
| | Mochrie, J. A. 2224. | K. **April 2/17.** Det.D./B. |
| | Norman, E. L. 1958. | M. **April 2/17.** |
| | O'Reilly, J. F. 2964. | K. **April 2/17.** Det.D./B. |
| | Reid, A. E. 4561. | M. **April 2/17.** |
| | ‡Shea, P. 3202. | K. **April 2/17.** Det.D./B. |
| | ***Sheard, Lieut. E. T.** | K. **Mar. 27/17.** Det.D./B. |
| | Taylor, L.-Cpl. J. 3913. | K. **April 2/17.** Det.D./B. |
| | Tucker, A. N. 1998. | K. **April 2/17.** Det.D./B. |
| | Walsh, W. 2735A. | M. **April 2/17.** |
| | *Washington, O. 3002. | K. **April 2/17.** Det.D./B. |
| | *Watson, Cpl. F. C. 3521. | M. **June 8/17.** |
| | *Wills, L.-Sergt. S. 602. | D/W. **April 3/17.** Det.D./B. |
| | Woodgate, J. J. 4309. | K. **April 2/17.** Det.D./B. |

**51st BATTALION A.I.F.**

| | | |
|---|---|---|
| | Bentley, D. V. 2859. | K. **May 1/17.** Det.D./B. |
| | ‡Burke, W. 1624. | D/W. **April 12/17.** Det.D./B. |
| B. | ‡Dunn, A. J. 2595. | K. **Oct. 3/16.** Det.D./B. |
| A. | ‡Grime, L.-Cpl. E. M. 3346. | K. **April 2/17.** Det.D./B. |
| | Haley, F. L. 3853. | K. **Nov. 3/16.** Det.D./B. |
| | Kerry, T. W. 3559. | M. **April 2/17.** |
| | Morris, Sergt. J. W. 1866. | D/W. **April 4/17.** Det.D./B. |
| | *Perkins, A. E. 2959. | K. **May 12/17.** Det.D./B. |

## 52nd BATTALION A.I.F.

| Co. | Name | Status |
|---|---|---|
| | *Andrews, T. L. 2124. | M. June 7/17. |
| | Barker, O. A. 4447. | M. April 12/17. |
| | ‡Bowles. 2115. | K. June 7/17. Det.D./B. |
| | ‡Burns, J. 2126. | K. June 8/17. Det.D./B. |
| | *Carmichael, G. D. 2634. | M. June 10/17. |
| | Chance, T. W. 1818. | K. Jan. 19/17. Det.D./B. |
| | *Cheeseman, W. J. E. 2147. | M. June 7/17. |
| | ‡Cragg, E. 31. | K. June 7/17. Det.D./B. |
| | ‡Evans, G. 1104. | M. June 11/17. |
| | ‡Fitzgerald. 2653. | D/W. June 10/17. Det.D./B. |
| | *Hanlon, T. 2670. | M. June 7/17. |
| | ‡Kelly, R. M. 2531. | K. June 7/17. Det.D./B. |
| | ‡Laidlow, A. B. 2691. | K. June 9/17. Det.D./B. |
| | *Land, S. J. 1926. | M. June 7/17. |
| | Moore, Cpl. K. C. 2578. | M. April 11/17. |
| | Noonan, J. 2717. | K. April 2/17. Det.D./B. |
| | Pennington. 453. | K. April 2/17. Det.D./B. |
| | ‡Robertson, A. 2240. | K. June 7/17. Det.D./B. |
| D. | ‡Sheppard, R. M. 1734. | K. Feb./17. Det.D./B. |
| | ‡Shipton, A. W. 5183. | K. June 11/17. Det.D./B. |
| | ‡Turner, P. G. 2747. | K. June 9/17. Det.D./B. |

## 53rd BATTALION A.I.F.

| Co. | Name | Status |
|---|---|---|
| | Adams, J. 355. | K. Mar. 20/17. Det.D./B. |
| | Black, N. S. 2375. | K. April 2/17. Det.D./B. |
| | Clark, Cpl. J. 4085. | K. Nov. 4/16. Det.D./B |
| | *Cooper, 2nd Lieut. A. E. | K. Mar. 29/17. Det.D./B. |
| | Cummins, F. W. 2638A. | W. and M. Mar. 31/17. |
| | Dark, A. W. 1157. | D/W. Nov. 5/16. Det.D./B |
| | Earl, G. W. 5359. | W. and M. Nov. 5/16. |
| | Fair, H. S. 1907. | K. April 3/17. Det.D./B. |
| | Hudson, R. 4798. | K. Mar. 16/17. Det.D./B. |
| | ‡Jackson, J. 1562. | K. May 23/17. Det.D./B. |
| | ‡Mitchell. 3563. | K. June 20/17. Det.D./B. |
| | Powter, E. L. 4919. | D/W. Nov. 1/16. Det.D./B. |
| | Ray, S. A. 125A. | M. Oct. 29/16. |
| | *Walker, A. W. 2796. | K. May 11/17. Det D./B. |
| B. | Weston, J. C. 2304. | D/W. Oct. 27/16. Det.D./B. |

## 54th BATTALION A.I.F.

| Co. | Name | Status |
|---|---|---|
| | *Arthurson, D. H. 5032. | K. May 15/17. Det.D./B. |
| | *Butler, C. D. 3479. (L.M.G.S.) | K. May 15/17. Det.D./B. |
| | *Compton, H. G. 1617. | K. May 15/17. Det.D./B. |
| | *Doyle, R. J. 2150. | K. May 15/17. Det.D./B. |
| | *Edwards, T. 3032. | K. May 15/17. Det.D./B. |
| | *Finn, J. 4289. | W. and M. May 15/17. |
| | *Gately, B. 4292. | K. May 15/17. Det.D./B. |
| | *Gospar, H. R. 2906. | K. May 15/17. Det.D./B. |
| | *Gulley, F. 1603. | K. May 15/17. Det.D./B. |
| | *Holmes. 2903. | K. May 16/17. Det.D./B. |
| | *Hurley, S. N. 5367. | K. May 15/17. Det.D./B. |
| | Kerin, W. J. 4249. | D/W. Nov. 2/16. Det.D./B. |
| | Leslie, R. J. 4509. | K. Oct. 27/16. Det.D./B. |

**54th Battalion A.I.F.—contd.**

| Co. | Name | Details |
|---|---|---|
| | ‡McInerney. 2097. | K. May 15/17. Det.D./B. |
| | *McRae, F. A. 3658. | K. May 15/17. Det.D./B. |
| | ‡Mann, C. F. 3223. | K. May 23/17. Det.D./B. |
| | *Marshall, E. 5738. | K. May 15/17. Det.D./B. |
| | *Mealy, P. 4266. | K. May 15/17. Det.D./B. |
| | *Millynn, R. B. 4207. | K. May 15/17. Det.D./B. |
| | ‡Newman, W. H. S. 840. | K. May 15/17. Det.D./B. |
| | Owen, W. T. 5484. | M. Dec. 7/16. |
| | *Poole, B. 873. | K. May 15/17. Det.D./B. |
| | *Richards, T. J. 2959 | K. May 15/17. Det.D./B. |
| | Scrutton, A. E. 2971. | K. Mar. 2/17. Det.D./B. |
| | *Swanson, H. W. 5210. | K. May 15/17. Det.D./B. |
| | ‡Taber. 4614. | K. June 15/17. Det.D./B. |
| | Taylor, C. S. 1882. | D/W. Oct. 30/16. Det.D./B. |
| | Tilling. 4612. | D/W. Oct. 27/16. Det.D..B. |

**55th BATTALION A.I.F.**

| Co. | Name | Details |
|---|---|---|
| | *Amour, P. W. 4728. | K. April 2/17. Det.D./B. |
| | *Akhurst, C. W. 2990. | K. May 10/17. Det.D./B. |
| | *Bradford, A. 2786. | K. April 2/17. Det.D./B. |
| | Bryant, H. W. 2266. | K. May 9/17. Det.D./B. |
| | Caldwell, J. D. 5344. | K. April 2/17. Det.D./B. |
| | Churchill. 3033. | D/W. April 6/17. Det.D./B. |
| | ‡Collier, L. P. 2637. | K. April 2/17. Det.D./B. |
| | Cullen, T. H. 5349. | K. April 2/17. Det.D./B. |
| | Donovan, S. 3827. | M. Oct. 23/16. |
| | Greathead, H. P. 1907. | K. April 2/17. Det.D./B. |
| | *Hollingsworth, C. 2424. | W. Unoff. M. May 11/17. |
| | *Holloway, Cpl. L. T. 2919. | K. May 9/17. Det.D./B. |
| | Ipkendanz, L.-Cpl. E. 2985. | D/W. May 13/17. Det.D./B. |
| | Jones, R. A. 4710. | M. Oct. 23/16. |
| | *Kay. 3154. | K. April 2/17. Det.D./B. |
| | McAllister, H. W. 2462. | K. May 15/17. Det.D./B. |
| | *Meyer, F. H. G. 3138. | D/W. Oct. 14/16. Det.D./B. |
| | Miles. 5406. | Unoff. K. April 2/17. Det.D./B. |
| | Moore, W. M. 1945. | K. April 3/17. Det.D./B. |
| | ‡O'Reilly, G. H. 2482. | D/W. May 14/17. Det.D./B. |
| D. | Reynolds, F. B. 1966. | W. Unoff. M. Mar. 30/16. |
| | Seaman, G. A. 2924. | K. April 2/17. Det.D./B. |
| | *Shepherd, L. 179. | K. May 9/17. Det.D./B. |
| | *Smith, R. C. 5445. | K. May 5/17. Det.D./B. |
| | ‡Westlake, H. B. 2378. | K. May 14/17. Det.D./B. |

**56th BATTALION A.I.F.**

| Co. | Name | Details |
|---|---|---|
| | Bradney, J. 2376. | M. April 2/17. |
| | Brown, R. J. 2566. | K. April 2/17. Det.D./B. |
| | *Carty, W. J. 2384. | K. April 2/17. Det.D./B. |
| | Dilworth, I. D. 3537. | M. April 2/17. |
| | Durkin, A. F. 2643. | M. April 2/17. |
| | *Frew, A. S. 3152. | K. April 2/17. Det.D./B. |
| | Glassington, L. G. 2038. | K. April 2/17. Det.D./B. |
| | Glazebrook, R. 3096. | K. April 2/17. Det.D./B. |
| | *Goldsbrough, H. 4795. | D/W. April 4/17. Det.D./B. |

**56th Battalion A.I.F.—contd.**

| Co. | Name | Casualty |
|---|---|---|
| | ‡Gorman. 5104. | K. Mar. 2/17. Det.D./B. |
| | Helson, A. P. 1673. | M. Oct. 22/16. |
| | ‡Herd, L. G. 2186. | K. May 11/17. Det.D./B. |
| | Johns, W. J. 2195. | K. April 2/17. Det.D./B. |
| | ‡Kelly, G. 1752. | K. May 19/17. Det.D./B. |
| | Kew, W. C. 5408. | K. April 3/17. Det.D./B. |
| | *Lane, A. W. J. 2200. | K. April 2/17. Det.D./B. |
| | ‡Leadnell, W. C. 1684. | K. April 2/17. Det.D./B. |
| | *Lygoe, R. P. 5056. | K. May 16/17. Det.D./B. |
| D. | *McColl, C.-Q.-M.-S. M. P. 2884. | K. May 20/17. Det.D./B. |
| | McConagh, W. 4849. | M. April 2/17. |
| | *McDonald, R. W. 3842. | K. April 3/17. Det.D./B. |
| | McIntosh, A. 1694. | K. April 2/17. Det.D./B. |
| | Mackenzie, L.-Cpl. D. A. 2700. | K. April 3/17. Det.D./B. |
| A. | *McMillan, L.-Cpl. W. S. 2754. | K. April 2/17. Det.D./B. |
| | Matthews, T. W. B. 5421. | K. April 2/17. Det.D./B. |
| | ‡Monkhouse, C. E. 3080. | W. Unoff. M. April 2/17. |
| | Naismith, O. 1703. | K. April 2/17. Det.D./B. |
| | Noble, G. 2233. | M. April 2/17. |
| | O'Connor, Sergt. T. W. 3219. | D/W. Dec. 24/16. Det.D./B. |
| | Preece, E. 2504. | K. April 2/17. Det.D./B. |
| | Richards, J. P. 1719. | D/W. Dec. 6/16. Det.D./B. |
| | *Roberts, H. V. 2468. | K. April 2/17. Det.D./B. |
| | *Stapleton, J. E. 1769. | K. April 2/17. Det.D./B. |
| | *Watts, A. 2753. | D/W. May 19/16. Det.D./B. |
| | Walther, M. H. 3311. | K. April 2/17. Det.D./B. |
| | Warren, H. 3141. | K. April 2/17. Det.D./B. |

**57th BATTALION A.I.F.**

| Co. | Name | Casualty |
|---|---|---|
| | *Bright, S. W. 2619. | K. Mar. 26/17. Det.D./B. |
| | Burton, Cpl. J. A. 2132. | D/W. April 1/17. Det.D./B. |
| A. | *Holmes, T. 2262. | K. Mar. 26/17. Det.D./B. |
| | ‡McGrath, P. 2690. | K. Mar. 15/17. Det.D./B. |
| | O'Connor, T. H. 4878. | M. Feb. 13/17. |
| | *Quigg, W. M. 2719. | K. Feb. 2/17. Det.D./B. |
| | Saltau, L.-Cpl. B. J. 115. | K. Mar. 15/17. Det.D./B. |
| | *Timms, A.-Cpl. A. H. 2034. | D/W. Mar. 25/17. Det.D./B. |
| | Ward, G. R. 2826. | D/W. Mar. 26/17. Det.D./B. |

**58th BATTALION A.I.F.**

|  |  |
|---|---|
| Biggs, Cpl. A. 4443. | M. May 12/17. |
| *Birrell, N. S. 4432. | K. May 12/17. Det.D./B. |
| Bonstead, H. W. 4433. | M. May 13/17. |
| Calder, D. W. 1759. | M. May 11/17. |
| Clarke, J. A. 1242. | M. Oct. 31/16. |
| Clinton, H. J. 2387. | M. May 13/17. |
| ‡Disher, L.-Cpl. P. W. 2642. | W. Unoff. M. May '7/17. |
| ‡Easton, J. N. 2892. | K. May 11/17. Det.D./B. |
| *Field, G. T. 5097. | K. Nov. 22/16. Det.D./B. |
| Flynn, T. 1909. | K. Feb. 4/17. Det.D./B. |
| *Gillies, J. L. 2902. | K. Mar. 23/17. Det.D./B. |
| ‡Gordon, W. J. 4790. | K. May 12/17. Det.D./B. |
| Hindebrand, L.-Cpl. C. 2657. | M. May 12/17. |

58th Battalion A.I.F.—contd.

| Co. | | |
|---|---|---|
| | *Howarth, E. 2433. | K. Mar. 26/17. Det.D./B. |
| | Huntley, J. W. 2435. | M. Mar. 27/17. |
| | King, A. L. 4533. | D/W. Dec. 1/16. Det.D./B |
| | Kirwan, A. 1727. | M. May 12/17. |
| | Liddin, P. T. 2457. | K. Feb. 4/17. Det.D./B. |
| | McGregor, H. K. 2697. | W. and M. Nov. 23/16. |
| C. | Millard, Sig. V. C. 2717. | W. and M. Nov. 22/16. |
| | Morton, F. L. G. 3006. | M. May 12/17. |
| | Murray, W. J G. 5147. | M. Mar. 27/17. |
| | North. 2220. | K. Feb. 27/17. Det.D./B. |
| | Pearson, 2nd Lieut. E. R. | K. Mar. 26/17. Det.D./B. |
| | Peters, J. 2711. | M. May 12/17. |
| D. | Porter, A. W. 2950. | K. May 10/17. Det.D./B. |
| | ‡Rollins. 2012. | K. Mar. 25/17. Det.D./B. |
| | *Thomas E. 1738. | W. Unoff. M. May 12/17. |
| | Weir, W. 2048. | W. and M. Nov. 23/16. |
| | Whatman, W. J. 4617. | W. and M. Nov 23/16. |
| | *White. 2978. | K. May 10/17. Det.D./B. |
| | *Worner, W. A. 2452. | K. Mar. 26/17. Det.D./B. |

59th BATTALION A.I.F.

| | |
|---|---|
| Crombie, P. C. 5357. | K. Mar. 24/17. Det.D./B. |
| Glen, W. G. 2409. | K. Mar. 15/17. Det.D./B. |
| Hade, E. T. 1188. | W. Nov. 30/16. |
| *Hall, H. A. 5087. | K. Dec. 21/16. Det.D./B. |
| Kennedy, L.-Cpl. J. H. W. 2122. | K. Mar. 27/17. Det.D./B. |
| McMillan, M. 2753. (M.G.S.) | K. Oct. 22/16. Det.D./B. |
| *Mitchell, Lieut. T. | K. May 12/17. Det.D./B. |
| *Nugent, J. F. 2446. | D/W. Mar. 25/17. Det.D./B. |
| Richmond, A. C. P. 3012. | K. April 5/17 Det.D./B. |
| Stanford. 5406. | D/W. Mar. 13/17. Det.D./B. |
| Webb, R. J. 5223. | K. Nov. 22/16. Det.D./B. |

60th BATTALION A.I.F.

| | | |
|---|---|---|
| | Bishop, S. G. 1135 | K. Nov. 27/16. Det.D./B. |
| | *Burrgram, A. H. 2858. | D/W. May 10/17. Det.D./B. |
| | Cain, W. J. 3037. | M., 1916. |
| | Challis, F. H. 2644. | M. May 12/17. |
| | Foley, M. L. 1762. | M. May 12/17. |
| | Ferguson, F. E. 2673A. | M. May 12/17. |
| | Harvey, L. A. 5380. | K. April 2/17. Det.D./B. |
| | Irwin, V. T. 3007. | M. May 12/17. |
| | *Kerr, W. W. 1929. | K. May 12/17. Det.D./B. |
| | Milgate, E. A. 2199. | M. May 12/17. |
| | ‡Newman, Sergt. J. 1980. | W. and M. May 12/17. |
| | *Oldfield, G. H. 2221. | K. Mar. 1/17. Det.D./B. |
| A. | Sherrin, H. L., 3630. | K. Nov. 22/16. Det.D./B. |
| | *Ulann, H. T. 2196. | K. May 4/17. Det.D./B. |
| | ‡Wheatley, A. H. 2989. | Gassed May 15/17. |

## 5th DIVISIONAL HEADQUARTERS A.I.F.

Peak, H. E. 425. K. Oct. 28/16. Det.D./B.

## 1st INFANTRY BRIGADE H.Q. A.I.F.

*Pomroy, O. F. 2187. K. May 5/17. Det.D./B.

## PIONEER BATTALIONS A.I.F.

| Batt | Co. |  |  |
|---|---|---|---|
| 1 | | Chapman, H. E. 1969. | K. Mar. 14/17. Det.D./B. |
| 1 | | Ellis, L.-Sergt. T. B. 4182. | D/W. Dec. 20/16. Det.D./B. |
| 2 | | Bake, H. E. L. 1656. | K. May 5/17. Det.D./B. |
| 2 | | Bell, S. 3306. | M. May 5/17. |
| 2 | | Bourke, W. J. 2112. | W. and M. Nov. 14/16. |
| 2 | | Browne, H. 2884. | K. Nov. 14/16. Det.D./B. |
| *2 | A. | Denton, Cpl. A. O. 531. | K. May 5/17. Det.D./B. |
| 2 | | Fogarty, S. J. 2625. | K. Nov. 14/16. Det.D./B. |
| *2 | | Healey, H. 3825. | K. May 3/17. Det.D./B. |
| 2 | | Hegarty, P. H. 2193. | M. May 3/17. |
| ‡2 | | Henry, W. 4216. | K. Nov. 14/16. Det.D./B. |
| 2 | | Manefield, A. 2054A. | K. Nov. 14/16. Det.D./B. |
| 2 | | Nichol, J. C. 2217. | M. May 3/17. |
| *2 | | Renfry, H. A. 1279. | K. May 5/17. Det.D./B. |
| *2 | | Sharp, E. 2511. | K. Mar. 11/17. Det.D./B. |
| 2 | A. | Thomas, E. 3660. | M. Nov. 11/16. |
| 2 | | Trewick, R. 2723. | K. May 3/17. Det.D./B. |
| 2 | | Vigar, Sergt. W. S. 712. | K. May 6/17. Det.D./B. |
| *3 | | Bradford, W. G. 1505. | K. Mar. 20/17. Det.D./B. |
| *3 | | Smeaton, T. V. 909. | K. June 9/17. Det.D./B. |
| 4 | | Hamilton, W. E. 1883. | K. Dec. 3/16. Det.D./B. |
| ‡4 | | Kluck. 3476. | K. June 12/17. Det.D./B. |
| *4 | | McDonnell, E. 2166. | K. April 21/17. Det.D./B. |
| *4 | | Reid, Lieut. J. C. D. | D/W. June 10/17. Det.D./B. |
| ‡5 | | Orgill, A. G. 675. | K. April 11/17. Det.D./B. |
| *5 | | Scown, A. T. 2682. | K. Oct. 30/16. Det.D./B. |

## MACHINE GUN COMPANIES A.I.F.

| Co. |  |  |
|---|---|---|
| ‡1 | Holl, R. 303. | K. Nov. 6/16. Det.D./B. |
| 2 | Thomas, J. R. 5190. | M. April 11/17. |
| *3 | Miller, Sergt. W. R. 1901. | K. May 6/17. Det.D./B. |
| 4 | Brady, G. 277. | M. April 11/17. |
| 4 | Counsel, Sergt. W. J. 1172. | M. April 11/17. |
| 4 | Finlayson, C. 4191. | M. April 11/17. |
| 4 | Graham, G. A. 1728. | M. April 11/17. |
| 4 | Head, J. 242. | M. April 11/17. |
| 4 | Knights, E. 330. | M. April 11/17. |
| 4 | McEntee, T.-Cpl. C. W. 2505. | M. April 11/17. |
| 4 | Moore, G. 1782. | M. April 11/17. |
| 4 | Price, P. P. 1967. | M. April 11/17. |
| 4 | Smith, A. J. 293. | M. April 11/17. |
| 4 | Whitchurch, W. G. 1859. | K. April 11/17. Det.D./B. |
| 5 | Farrell, L.-Cpl. J. V. 1385. | K. Nov. 14/16. Det.D./B. |
| 5 | Lumond, T.-Cpl. G. H. 2703. | M. May 5/17. |

**Machine Gun Companies A.I.F.—contd.**

| Co. | Name | |
|---|---|---|
| 5 | McPhail, D. 286. | M. May 5/17. |
| 5 | Murphy, A. A. 466. | K. May 5/17. Det.D./B. |
| 5 | Pinches, E. 296. | M. May 5/17. |
| 5 | Smith, T. St. P. 4241. | K. May 5/17. Det.D./B. |
| ‡5 | Smith. 5. | K. May 5/17. Det.D./B. |
| ‡5 | Stillman, L.-Cpl. W. E. 91. | K. April 15/17. Det.D./B. |
| 7 | McDonald, A. 697. | D/W. Jan. 10/17. Det.D./B. |
| *9 | Bannister, R. T. A. 2036. | K. June 8/17. Det.D./B. |
| 9 | Taylor, E. J. 126. | K. Feb. 24/17. Det.D./B. |
| 12 | Dahler, W. 280A. | M. April 11/17. |
| 12 | Fraser, Cpl. R. 4274. | M. April 11/17. |
| 12 | **Hartley, Lieut. J. W. M.** | D/W. Jan. 9/17. Det.D./B. |
| 12 | Mitchell, T.-Sergt. J. J. 3633. | M. April 11/17. |
| *12 | Owen, W. 517. | M. June 7/17. |
| *13 | McCarthy, W. 244. | D/W. Mar. 30/17. Det.D./B. |
| 13 | Martin, L.-Cpl. G. 163. | M. Mar. 28/17. |
| ‡13 | Roach, M. J. 2243. | K. June 4/17. Det.D./B. |
| *13 | **Tooth, 2nd Lieut. J. L.** | K. June 8/17. Det.D./B. |
| *14 | Anderson, J. A. 276. | K. April 2/17. Det.D./B. |
| *14 | Howard, Sergt. A. E. 3115. | K. May 11/17. Det.D./B. |
| *14 | West, F. G. 477. | K. May 15/17. Det.D./B. |
| *14 | Wiles, W. J. 334. | K. May 12/17. Det.D./B. |
| ‡22 | [illegible]air, J. 386A. | K. April 21/17. Det.D./B. |

## LIGHT HORSE REGIMENTS A.I.F.

| Squad. | **1st Regiment.** | |
|---|---|---|
| | Adams, F. J. 831. | M. Mar. 26/17. |
| | Alexander, G. 701. | M. Mar. 26/17. |
| | *Haleley, J. D. M. 59. | K. Mar. 21/17. Det.D./B. |
| | Stanton, F. T. 2952. | D/W., Egypt, Jan. 9/17. Det.D./B |
| | Struthers, J. R. 187. | K. Dec. 21/16. Det.D./B. |
| | Taylor, P. E. 465. | M. Mar. 26/17. |
| | **2nd Regiment.** | |
| | Browne, Sgt. T. McD. 299. | D/W. April 20/17. Det.D./B. |
| | ‡Nash, J. 1261. | M. June 7/17. |
| | **3rd Regiment.** | |
| | White, J. V. 1081. | D/W., Egypt, Jan. 12/17. Det D./B. |
| | **4th Regiment.** | |
| | ‡Berryman. 1081. | K. June 25/17. Det.D./B. |
| | Letts, G. 1053. | K. Nov. 13/16. Det.D./B. |
| | **8th Regiment.** | |
| | Denchar. 197. | D/W. May 16/17. Det.D./B. |
| | **Higgins, Capt. M. B.** | K., Egypt, Dec. 23/16. Det D./B |
| B. | Nairn, A. 1355. | K., Egypt, Dec. 2/16. Det.D./B. |
| | **9th Regiment.** | |
| | ‡Johnson, R. J. J. 139. | K. June 27/17. Det.D./B. R/Enq. |
| A. | Pix, L.-Cpl. H. R. A. 179. | K., Egypt, Dec. 23/16. Det.D./B. |
| C. | *Tomkins, Sergt. S. J. 495. | D/W. April 19/17. Det D./B. |

Light Horse Regiments A.I.F.—contd.

| Squad. | 10th Regiment. | |
|---|---|---|
| | Gilbert, W. 35. | K., Egypt, Jan. 9/17. Det.D./B. |
| | Hall, G. F. 2301. | M., Egypt., April 19/17. |
| A. | Knowles, Trooper W. D. 1407. | K., Egypt, Jan. 9/17. Det.D./B. |
| | Throssell, Lieut. E. | K. April 19/17. Det.D./B. |
| | **11th Regiment.** | |
| | Brennan, Lieut. W. | D/W. April 20/17. Det.D./B. |
| | Campbell, Tpr. F. B. 113. | M., Egypt., April 19/17. |
| | ‡Donnelly. 51. | K. April 19/17. Det.D./B. |
| | Rathbone. 1963. | K. April 24/17. Det.D./B. |
| | **12th Regiment.** | |
| | *Fitzgerald, H. 763. | K. April 19/17. Det.D./B. |
| | *McIntosh, Lt.-Col. | D/W., Egypt, April 24/17. Det.D./B. |
| | ‡Ward, W. C. 1587. | D/W. April 19/17. Det.D./B. |
| | **13th Regiment.** | |
| B. Squad. | Williams, Tpr. J. S. 1434. | K. Mar. 23/17. Det.D./B. |

FIELD ARTILLERY A.I.F.

| Bgde. | Batty. | | |
|---|---|---|---|
| *2 | 4 | Cavell, Sgt. L. C. 885. | K. April 9/17. Det.D./B. |
| 2 | 6 | Gardiner, E. R., W. 1280. | M. April 15/17. |
| 2 | | Hudson, B. R. 10344. | D/W. Dec. 22-23/16. Det.D./B. |
| *2 | | McLean, J. J. 11778. | D/W. Mar. 13/17. Det.D./B. |
| 2 | | Miller, G. C. S. | D/W. Mar. 4/17. Det.D./B. |
| *2 | | Nobel, J. A. 5342. | K. April 23/17. Det.D./B. |
| *3 | 9 | Bowen, P. J. 1953. | K. Nov. 14/16. Det.D./B. |
| 3 | | Cavage, C. R. 9613. | K. Dec. 23/16. Det.D./B. |
| *4 | 10 | Donohue, S. 11827. | D/W. April 7/17. Det.D./B. |
| ‡4 | | Lewis, A. E. 10273. | K. May 27/17. Det.D./B. |
| *4 | | Mack, Capt. B. H. R. M. O. | K. April 10/17. Det.D./B. |
| ‡4 | | Olsen. 7796 | K. May 27/17. Det.D./B. |
| *4 | 11 | Pottage, C. A. E. 6563. | K. Mar. 28/17. Det.D./B. |
| 4 | | Proctor, F. 2281. | K. Jan. 4/17. Det.D./B. |
| 4 | | Sheil, F. J. W. 1707. | D/W. April 20/17. Det.D./B. |
| 4 | 10 | Young, G. L. 2707. | K. April 16/17. Det.D./B. |
| ‡5 | | Benjafield, E. W. 29919. | D/W. April 14/17. Det.D./B. |
| 5 | 14 | Coombes, C. A. 10134. | K. April 13/17. Det.D./B. |
| 5 | 13 | Criseford, W. R. 9389. | K. April 23/17. Det.D./B. |
| 5 | 14 | Iredale, J. E. 29295. | K. April 19/17. Det.D./B. |
| *5 | 15 | Rainey, J. R. 1566. | D/W. April 23/17. Det.D./B. |
| ‡5 | 15 | Reynoldson, L. M. 874. | K. April 20/17. Det.D./B. |
| ‡6 | | Jarvis. 15640. | K. June 12/17. Det.D./B. |
| *6 | | Kilmartin, J. D. 8196. | K. June 1/17. Det.D./B. |
| ‡7 | | Mounter. 18505. | K. June 18/17. Det.D./B. |
| ‡8 | 30 | Mathieson, J. 22039. | W. Unoff. M. June 4/17. |
| 10 | | Robertson, Sergt. D. 2442. | M. May 3/17. |
| *10 | | Sumner, T. 11126. | K. April 23/17. Det.D./B. |
| ‡11 | | Agnew. 4726. | K. April 15/17. Det.D./B. |
| 11 | | Connors, E. S. 4474. | K. Dec. 30/16. Det.D./B. |
| 11* | | Follington, A. E. 209. | D/W. Feb. 26/17. Det.D./B. |
| 11 | | King, T. J. 2052. | K. April 15/17. Det.D./B. |
| ‡11 | | Hamilton, T. 3037. | D/W. June 7/17. Det.D./B. |
| 11 | 42 | Hansen. 2041. | D/W. Feb. 26/17. Det.D./B. |

**Field Artillery A.I.F.—contd.**

| Bgde. | Batty. | | |
|---|---|---|---|
| 11 | 61 | Wickham. 94. | K. May 3/17. Det.D./B. |
| ‡12 | 42 | Coghlan, M. G. 20931. | D/W. May 3/17. Det.D./B. |
| 12 | | Daw, A. J. 20933. | K. May 3/17. Det.D./B. |
| *12 | 47 | Mair, H. M. 255A. | K. May 7/17. |
| 13 | 51 | Collings, C. A. 3516. | K. Nov. 19/16. Det.D./B. |
| ‡13 | | Davis. 3117. | K. April 11/17. Det.D./B. |
| 13 | | Kinmance, F. V. 21. | D/W. Jan. 4/17. Det.D./B. |
| ‡14 | | Taylor. 17132. | K. June 21/17. Det.D./B. |
| ‡21 | 24 | Albeitz, F. 9611. | D/W. Nov. 14/17. Det.D./B. |
| 21 | 23 | Jordan, A. W. 4443. | K. Oct. 14/16. Det.D./B. |
| ‡ | 31 | Dyson, Lieut. A. N. | D/W. June 8/17. Det.D./B. |
| 23 | 36 | Cameron, G. G. 22369. | D/W. Jan. 23/17. Det.D./B. |

**SIEGE BRIGADE.**

| | | | |
|---|---|---|---|
| 11 | | Toohey, M. J. 4496. | D/W. Dec. 9/16. Det.D./B. |
| | 36 | Woodland, E. E. 664. | K. April 3/17. Det.D./B. |
| 33 | 36 | Hill, C. W. 228. | D/W. April 27/17. Det.D./B. |
| ? | 36 | Scotcher, Bomb. A. 14 8. | K. April 23/17. Det.D./B. |

**HOWITZER BATTERIES.**

| | | | |
|---|---|---|---|
| ‡ | 101 | Willans, L.-Cpl. L. O. 19158. | K. June 14/17. Det.D./B. |
| * | 105 | Bayliss, A. J. 10121. | K. May 3/17. Det.D./B. |
| * | 108 | Winch, Sergt. F. J. 20175. | D/W. May 23/17. Det.D./B. |
| ‡ | 110 | Gore. 391. | K. June 14/17. Det.D./B. |
| | 112 | Hendry, A. E. 10864. | K. Feb. 27/17. Det.D./B. |
| | 113 | Beilby, Gnr. R. E. 2571. | M. Jan. 12/17. |
| * | 125 | Whitehead, J. H. 25684. | K. May 16/17. Det.D./B. |

**AMMUNITION COLUMN.**

| | | |
|---|---|---|
| 4 Div. | Wood, W. R. 2363. | D/W. Nov. 28/16. Det.D./B. |

**LIGHT TRENCH MORTAR BATTERIES**

| | | |
|---|---|---|
| 3 | Montgomery, H. A. 1062. | M. May 6-10/17. |
| 4 | Coleman, P. 5350. | M. April 11/17. |
| ‡4. | Gunst, F. S. 5106. | K. April 11/17. Det.D./B. |
| 4 | Harrison, V. 3600. | D/W. April 11/17. Det.D./B. |
| 4 | Keeman, T. 3933. | M. April 11/17. |
| 4 | Miller, G. 3412. | M. April 11/17. |
| 4 | Officer, G. T. 2003. | M. April 11/17. |
| 4 | Ryan, P. 2520. | M. April 11/17. |
| 4 | Smith, J. D. 3433. | M. April 11/17. |
| 4 | Webber, W. F. 3978. | M. April 11/17. |
| 4 | Weight, H. S. 2716. | M. April 11/17. |
| 5 | Rundle, F. 2766. | M. May 3/17. |
| 6 | Carter, E. M. 1192. | W. and M. May 5/17. |
| *6 A. | Geyer, H. C. 882. | K. May 4/17. Det.D./B. |
| 8 | Hustler, T. 534A. | M. May 3/17. |
| 8 | Hunter, H. D. 2333. | M. May 3/17. |
| *8 | Marriott, A. R. 2484. | K. May 3/17. Det.D./B. |
| *9 | Alexander, Lieut. C. H. | K. June 8/17. Det.D./B. |

**Light Trench Mortar Batteries—contd.**

| Batty. | | |
|---|---|---|
| 9 | **Brown, Capt. H. P.** | K. May 12/17. Det.D./B. |
| 9 | Williams, G. W. 914. | K. Dec. 20/16. Det.D./B. |
| *10 | Northey, S. H. 1246. | K. June 1/17. Det.D./B. |
| *12 | Henricksen, V. C. 3168A. | M. June 10/17. |
| *12 | Howell, W. H. 1292. | M. June 8/17. |
| *12 | Sutherland, W. F. 4631. | M. June 7/17. |
| 3 Div. | Geraty, P. W. 74. | K. Dec. 23/16. Det.D./B. |

## MEDIUM TRENCH MORTAR BATTERIES.

| | | |
|---|---|---|
| ‡X/2 A. | Haskew, H. S. 28966. | W. and M. July 12/17. |
| *X/4 A. | Langdon, L. G. 2717. | W. Unoff. M. May 3/17. |
| ‡X/4 A. | Smart, T-Bomb. J. C. 4619. | K. Jan. 31/17. Det.D./B. |

## HEAVY TRENCH MORTAR BATTERIES.

| | | |
|---|---|---|
| 3 Div. | **Rutledge, Lieut. N.** | K. June 3/17. Det.D./B. |
| V/4 A. | Denny, W. E. 3512. | K. Dec. 7/16. Det.D./B. |
| V/4 A. | McDonald, W. E. 4858. | M. April 11/17. |
| *V/4 A. | Parkes, J. H. 2348. | M. May 3/17. |

## HEAVY AND MEDIUM TRENCH MORTAR BATTERIES.

| | | |
|---|---|---|
| 4 | Bermingham, F. 3230. | M. May 3/17. |
| 4 | Dwyer, P. B. 1178. | M. May 3/17. |
| 4 | Lodge, A. L. 4532. | M. May 3/17. |
| 4 | Meldrum, W. C. 5476. | M. May 3/17. |
| 4 | Michell, S. J. 2719A. | M. May 3/17. |
| 4 | Mitchell, W. 2222. | M. May 5/17. |
| 4 | Moore, H. 2050. | M. May 3/17. |
| 4 | Mortimer, R. J. 2003. | M. May 3/17. |
| *4 Div. | Moss, J. 814. | K. May 3/17. Det.D./B. |
| 4 | Parsons, A. E. S. 1643. | M. May 3/17. |
| 4 | Pascall, A. 3442. | M. May 3/17. |
| 4 | Powell, F. J. 2011. | M. May 3/17. |
| 4 | Reid, J. 3481. | M. May 3/17. |
| 4 | Reidy, M. S. 1608A. | M. May 3/17. |

## ENGINEERS A.I.F.

| | | |
|---|---|---|
| 1 Field Co. | Donohue, J. T. 6457. | D/W. Feb. 25/17. Det.D./B. |
| 2 | Pearce, E. 6346. | M. Nov. 2/16. |
| 2 | Struckey, V. F. 10944. | K. April 10/17. Det.D./B. |
| 3 | Hair, A. W. 7228. | M. May 3/17. |
| 3 | **McMahon, 2nd Lieut. J. T.** | K. April 9/17. Det.D./B. |
| ‡4 | Coulson, J. C. 1933. | K. April 4/17. Det.D./B. |
| 5 | **Scarr, Lieut. F. S.** | M. May 6-7/17. |
| 6 | **Gilchrist, Capt. W.** | K. May 3/17. Det.D./B. |
| 6 | Greenan, Spr. J. 6592. | D/W. Nov. 20/16, Det.D./B. |
| *6 | Woolley, D. S. 15747. | K. May 8/17. Det.D./B. |
| 7 | Dooley, J. A. 7474. | M. Nov. 14/16. |
| 7 | Morgan, E. G. 6690. | K. Nov. 14/16. Det.D./B. R/Enq. |
| ‡9 | Hayton. 9884. | K. May 31/17. Det.D./B. |
| *11 | Murray. D. A. | K. June 6/17. Det.D./B. |

## MOUNTED DIVISIONAL ENGINEERS.

| | | |
|---|---|---|
| 1 Squad. | Maguire, R. M. 2415. | M. Mar. 26/17. |
| B. Trp. Sig. | Curnou, L.-Cpl. R. M. 6785. | M., Egypt, April 19/17. |

## TUNNELLING COMPANIES.

| | | |
|---|---|---|
| ‡2 | Berry, C. 5281. | Unoff. M. July 10/17. |
| ‡2 | **Mortensen, 2nd Lt. W. M.** | M. July 10/17. |
| *3 | **Coulter, Major L. J.** | K. June 26/17. Det.D./B. |
| ‡3 | Griffen, F. 1283. | M. June 28/17. |

## SIGNALLING COMPANY.

| Div. | Sec. | | |
|---|---|---|---|
| 2 Div. | · | **Rentoul, Lieut. D. N.** | W. and M. May 3/17. |
| 4 | 3 | Nattrass, L.-Cpl. E. A. 1732. | W. Unoff. M. April 11/17. |

## IMPERIAL CAMEL CORPS A.I.F.

| Batt. | | |
|---|---|---|
| ‡1 | Armitage, G. 2633. | W. Unoff. M. April 19/17. |
| 1 | Biggs, L.-Cpl. R. 244. | M. April 19/17. |
| ‡1 | Eaton, F. G. 1384. | W. Unoff. M. April 19/17. |
| 1 | Edwards, H. T. N. 2815. | K. April 19/17. Det.D./B. |
| 1 | **Ellis, 2nd Lieut. W. T.** | M. April 19/17. |
| ‡1 | Falk. 12. | K. April 19/17. Det.D./B. |
| 1 | Finlay, Sergt W. 49. | M. April 19/17. |
| 1 | Gibson, A. 2340. | K. April 19/17. Det.D./B. |
| 1 | Gregory, Spr. V. C. 1181. | M. April 19/17. |
| 1 | Hope, Cpl. W. L. 3013. | M. April 19/17. |
| 1 | Kerr, J. A. B. 2812. | M. April 19/17. |
| 1 | Konsten, W. 1026. | M. April 19/17. |
| 1 | Lawson, J. H. 2630A. | M. April 19/17. |
| 1 | Lovick, Spr. R. L. 2156. | M. April 19/17. |
| 1 | Manley, Spr. G. A. 1056. | M. April 19/17. |
| | **Rae, Capt. W.** | K. Mar. 27/17. Det.D./B. |
| 1 | Reardon, Tpr. W. 2668. | M. April 19/17. |
| *1 | Sleeman, G. 4331. | D/W. April 11/17. Det.D./B. |
| 1 | Smith, L.-Cpl. C. C. 2367. | M. April 19/17. |
| 1 | Ware, L.-Cpl. W. J. 551. | M. April 19/17. |
| 3 Corps | Bailey. 1543. | K. Jan. 9/17. Det.D./B. |
| 13 Corps | Vincent, C. 2174. | D. Egypt. Nov. 21/16 Det.D./B. |
| 12 Co. | Kincaird, Morse-, Cpl. F. H. 1020. | K. Jan. 9/17. Det.D./B. |
| 1 Sec. | Cook, A. W. 1962. | M. April 19/17. |

## CYCLE COMPANY A.I.F.

| | | |
|---|---|---|
| 2 | Gooden, H. K. 3828. | M. Nov. 5/16. |

## FLYING CORPS A.I.F.

| | | |
|---|---|---|
| ‡ | **Norvill, Lieut. V. A.** | M. June 29/17. |
| 1 Squad. | **Steele, Lieut. N. L.** | M. April 20/17. |
| * | **Tonks, Lieut. H. A. C.** | K. June 21/17. Det.D./B. |
| ‡45 | **Hewson, 2nd Lt. T.** (Att. R.F.C.) | M. July 7/17. |
| ‡67 | **Vautin, 2nd Lieut. C. H.** | M. July 8/17, Egypt. |

## ARMY MEDICAL CORPS A.I.F.

| | | |
|---|---|---|
| Med. Ser. | Daly, Col. | M., bel. drowned, April 15/17. |
| 1 Fld. Amb. | Brophy, A. M. 1509. | K. April 18/17. Det.D./B. R/Enq. |
| *1 | Leask, J. 14718. | K. May 4/17. Det.D./B. |
| *3 | Sharp, R. R. 5390. | D/W. May 7/17. Det.D./B. |
| *4 | Aynsley, R. 991. | K. May 6/17. Det.D./B. |
| ‡4 | Cush, H. 4364. | K. June 8/17. Det.D./B. |
| ‡4 | Fuller, R. G. M. 16225. | K. June 8/17. Det.D./B. |
| ‡5 | Davis, C. F. H. 8736. | K. May 1/17. Det.D./B. |
| 5 | Portus. 5622. | K. April 23/17. Det.D./B. |
| *6 | Elms, J. W. 16128. | K. April 21-22/17. Det.D./B. |
| ‡6 | Sales, H. T. 8419. | D/W. Jan. 1/17. Det.D./B. |
| 9 | Dyer, L.-Sergt. A. E. 11956. | K. April 8/17. Det.D./B. |
| 13 | Richards, A. E. 8100. | K. Mar. 27/17. Det.D./B. |

## ARMY SERVICE CORPS A.I.F.

| | | |
|---|---|---|
| 1 Div. | Jeffreys, C. R. (Cleaner). 2492. | K. accid. Jan. 21/17. Det.D./B. |
| 14 | Knapman, A. R. 5657. | D/W. April 7/17. Det.D./B. |
| 16 | Cruickshanks. 397. | W. Unoff. M. June 5/17. |

## FIELD BAKERY A.I.F.

| | | |
|---|---|---|
| 5 | Childs. 1166. | Uoff. K. Feb. 22/17. Det.D./B. |

THIS LIST CANCELS ALL PREVIOUS LISTS.

# CANADIAN BRANCH.

## British Red Cross

AND

## Order of St. John.

AUGUST 1st, 1917.

# ENQUIRY LIST.

# FRANCE AND BELGIUM.

14, COCKSPUR STREET,
LONDON, S.W.

1C

# CANADIAN IMPERIAL FORCES.

**The names with ‡ are New Enquiries; those with * have appeared in the Supplement.**

## CANADIAN LIGHT HORSE.

| | | |
|---|---|---|
| | **Murray, Lieut. J. H.** | W. and M. April 10/17. |
| | Silcox, H. A. 114530. | D/W. 4th Can. Fld Amb. Det.D./B. |

## FORT GARRY HORSE.

| | | |
|---|---|---|
| | Carle, Cpl. R. P. 117178. | M. Mar. 25/17. |
| A. | Landells, C. 225691. | D/W. Mar. 25/17. Det.D./B. |
| A. | Proctor, G. L. 117489. | M. Mar. 25/17. |

## ROYAL CANADIAN DRAGOONS.

| | | |
|---|---|---|
| | Wilson, L.-Cpl. J. 3679. | M. Mar. 25/17. |

## 1st CANADIAN DIV. AMM. COLUMN.

| | | |
|---|---|---|
| | Wright, Dvr. M. G. 348249. | K. April 9/17. Det.D./B. |

## CANADIAN SIEGE ARTILLERY.

| | | |
|---|---|---|
| 5th Batty. | Speck, Gnr. D. R. 346878. | K. April 8/17. Det.D./B. |

## CANADIAN FIELD ARTILLERY.

### 1st Brigade.

| | | |
|---|---|---|
| | MacDonald, D. A. 1260733. | M., bel. W. May 8/17. |
| | Wainwright, John McL. 349196. | D/W. May 8/17. 4th Canadian Fld. Amb. Det.D./B. |

### 2nd Brigade.

| | | |
|---|---|---|
| 7 Batty. | Ripley, R. A. 86000. | K. April 28/17. Det.D./B. |

### 9th Brigade.

| | | |
|---|---|---|
| 33 Batty. | Thomson, Dvr. C. C. E. 310629. | K. April 29/17. Det.D./B. |

## CANADIAN ENGINEERS.

### Tunnelling Company.

| | | |
|---|---|---|
| | Martin, J. 7676 | M. April 24/16. |
| | Murray, John. 10582. | M. Sept. 7/16. |

## CANADIAN DIVISIONAL ENGINEERS.

| | | |
|---|---|---|
| | **McPhee, Capt. M. N.** | M., bel. drowned, April 17/17. |
| ‡2 | Ward, C. W. 405456. | W. and M. May 3/17. |
| 2 Div. 5 Fld. Co. | Rayns, G. 908045. | M. May 28/17. |
| 3 8th Co. | Kirton, Spr. George B. 505006. | K. April 9/17. Det.D./B. |
| 4 11 Co. | Surphlis, A.-2nd Cpl. C. E. 503867. | M. Mar. 1/17. |
| 2 Fld. Co. | Coldrey, Spr. K. A. 2210. | M. May 3/17. |
| 2 Fld. Co. | Bartlett, E. W. 505698. | M. May 3/17. |
| 10 Fld. Co. | Rowland, Spr. C. W. 504368. | M. Feb. 12/17. |
| 12 Fld. Co. | Gillen, Spr. J. 504742. | M., bel. K. Mar. 1/17. |
| 12 Fld. Co. | Millard, Spr. J. T. 504782. | M., bel. K. Mar. 1/17. |

## 3rd CANADIAN RAILWAY TROOPS.

| | | |
|---|---|---|
| | **Hamilton, Capt. H. E. R.** | K. May 19/17. Det.D./B. |

## 5th CANADIAN RAILWAY TROOPS.

| | | |
|---|---|---|
| *C. | Allen, J. 127524. | K. May 14/17. Det.D./B. |

## CANADIAN MACHINE GUN COMPANIES.

### 1st Division.

| | | |
|---|---|---|
| 1 | Raeside, Cpl. R. A4181. | K. April 13/17. Det.D./B. |
| 2 | Hale, G. G. 438937. | D/W. April 28/17. Det.D./B. |
| 2 | Stewart, W. 138697. | K. Sept. 26/16. Det.D./B. |

### 2nd Division.

| | | |
|---|---|---|
| | Donovan, R. 475062. | K. April 9/17. Det.D./B. |
| | Harpell, Michael Andrew. 883767. | K. May 10/17. Det.D./B. |
| | Milroy, L.-Cpl. A. M. 66093. | W. and M. Sept. 17/16. |
| *5 Co. | Graham, D. W. 475267. | K. May 3/17. Det.D./B. |
| ‡14 | Stringer, R. E. 166123. | K. April 28/17. Det.D./B. |

### 4th Division.

| | | |
|---|---|---|
| ‡10 Co. | Ritchie, Jas. Earnest. 488655. | K. June 3/17. Det.D./B. |
| 12 | Latham, C. C. 132432. | W. and M. April 9/17. |

## MACHINE GUN COMPANY.

| | | |
|---|---|---|
| Bordens | Singleton, L. J. 230. | D/W. Sept. 26/16. No. 3 Canadian Fld. Amb. Det.D./B. |

## CANADIAN INFANTRY.

| | | | |
|---|---|---|---|
| *1 | | Althouse, S. 195802. | W. and M. May 3/17. |
| 1 | | Benton, A. 772285. | W. and M. April 9/17. |
| 1 | C. | Camfield, W. 406489. | W. and M. Sept. 2/16. |
| 1 | | Capes, L.-Cpl. A. G. 178237. | M. May 3/17. |
| ‡1 | | Cavill, Sergt. A. H. 814200. | W. and M. May 5/17. |
| 1 | | Cheney, M. O. 177937. | M. May 3/17. |
| 1 | | Chorlton, J. 772258. | M. May 3/17. |
| 1 | | Cooper, J. A. 406701. | M. May 3/17. |
| *1 | | Crawford, R. M. 657646. | W. and M. May 3/17. |
| 1 | | Dawson, W. S. 772105. | M. May 3/17. |
| 1 | | Demorest, H. A. 644763. | M. May 3/17. |
| *1 | | Dowling, T. 195942. | W. and M. May 3/17. |
| 1 | | Dubeau, J. M. 644577. | M. May 3/17. |
| *1 | | Dye, A. 772138. | W. and M. May 3/17. |
| 1 | | Ebel, W. R. 657157. | M. May 3/17. |
| 1 | | Edwards, S. E. A2297. | M., bel. K. Sept. 23/16. |
| *1 | | Edwards, F. C. 402729. | W. and M. May 3/17. |
| 1 | | Eyre, M. 472077. | M. May 3/17. |
| 1 | | Fahey, J. 772286. | M. May 3/17. |
| 1 | | Falcon, A. E. 444110. | K. June 13/16. Det.D./B. |
| 1 | B. | Flowerday, C. A. 642662. | K. April 9/17. Det.D./B. |
| 1 | | Foster, J. A23909. | M. May 3/17. |
| *1 | | Gould, W. 163343. | K. April 9/17. Det.D./B. |
| 1 | | Gullen, W. R. 772521. | M. May 3/17. |
| 1 | A. | Guy, J. 772384. | M. May 3/17. |
| 1 | | Headon, A. G. 727757. | M. May 3/17. |
| 1 | | Heath, F. J. 772960. | M., bel. K. April 9/17. |
| 1 | | Henson, T. 675536. | M. May 3/17. |
| *1 | | Hodgin, W. 177927. | M. Sept. 22/16. |
| *1 | | Jinks, J. 195614. | M. April 9/17. |
| 1 | | Kennedy, F. 177176. | M. April 9/17. |
| *1 | | Kiernan, J. 163382. | W. and M. May 3/17. |
| 1 | | Krueger, J. 201631. | M., bel. K. April 12/17. |
| 1 | | Lee, F. W. A2924. | W. and M. June 13/16. |
| *1 | | Leitch, J. 177281. | W. and M. April 9/17. |
| 1 | A. | Leith, H. J. 189004. | M., bel. K. April 10/17. |
| 1 | | Martin, W. 773035. | M. May 3/17. |
| *1 | | Martin, J. 823709. | W. and M. May 3/17. |
| 1 | | Meyers, T. J. 823015. | M. May 3/17. |
| 1 | | McCaskil, K. J. 658068. | M. May 3/17. |
| 1 | | McConnell, Q. 18413. | D/W. April 11/17. Det.D./B |
| 1 | | MacDonald, H. T. 401308. | M., bel. K. June 14/16. |
| 1 | | MacFie, J. M. 658027. | M. May 3/17. |
| 1 | C. | McMullen, E. A. 159142. | K. April 5/17. Det.D./B. |
| *1 | | Ness, G. W. 772496. | W. and M. May 3/17. |
| 1 | | Newman, Sergt. A. A2585. | D/W. April 23/17. Det.D./B. |
| 1 | B. | O'Grady, David. 195622. | M. May 3/17. |
| *1 | | Pelky, F. 657268. | W. and M. May 3/17. |
| 1 | B. | Pentecost, N. A. 201467. | K. April 9/17. Det.D./B. |
| 1 | C. | Phillips, Geo. L. 657358. | M. May 3/17. |
| *1 | | Porter, F. V. 675072. | W. and M. May 3/17. |
| 1 | B. | Prentice, G. 642738. | M. April 9/17. |
| 1 | | Robson, J. J. 739724. | M. May 4/17. |
| *1 | | Russell, A. 406455. | W. and M. May 3/17. |
| 1 | | Sherrick, P. C. 164186. | K. Sept. 9/16. Det.D./B. |
| ‡1 | | Sluman, S. 675053. | M. May 3/17. |
| 1 | | Stewart, E. W. V659520. | M. May 3/17. |
| *1 | | Tear, D. 195316. | W. and M. May 3/17. |
| 1 | | Turner, F. A. 675855. | M. May 5/17. |
| *1 | | Vallely, Sergt. H. A54. | W. and M. May 3/17. |

**Canadian Infantry—contd**

| | | |
|---|---|---|
| 1 | Warriner, E. N. 643988. | M. May 3/17. |
| 1 | Weakley, N. O. 675575. | M. May 3/17. |
| •1 | Weatherston J. B. 406214. | W. and M. May 3/17. |
| •1 | White, O. 22644. | W. and M. May 3/17. |
| 1 | Willets, J. 772340. | M. May 3/17. |
| 1 | Williams, J. 190266. | M. April 9/17. |
| 1 | Williams, B. C. 305118. | M. May 3/17. |
| •1 | Wood, H. S. 412444. | W. and M. May 3/17. |
| 1 D. | Woods, G. A. 644034. | M. May 3/17. |
| 1 | Woodward, J. R. 7103. | M. May 3/17. |
| 1 C. | Wynne, C. B. 177984. | K. April 9/17. Det.D./B. |
| 2 | **Coombe, Lieut. E. H.** | K. May 3/17. Det.D./B. |
| 2 | Austin, Arthur Ed. 189460. | K. April 25/17. Det.D./B. |
| 2 | Baker, V. A. 455210. | M. May 3-4/17. |
| 2 | Barkley, E. I. 634170. | M. May 3-4/17. |
| 2 B. | Barnett, F. C. 375967. | M. May 3-4/17. |
| 2 B. | Catley, Edward. 454056. | K. May 4/17. Det.D./B. |
| 2 | Crane, Emmett Joseph. 437347. | K. May 4/17. Det.D./B. |
| 2 | Dufor, F. 745361. | M. May 3-4/17. |
| 2 D. | Easey, Arthur. 675697. | Unoff. W. and M. May 3/17. |
| 2 | Essery, T. 603121. | D/W. May 3/17. Det.D./B. |
| 2 | Gittins, J. M. 142615. | M. May 3-4/17. |
| 2 | Haight, C. L. 190177. | M. May 3-4/17. |
| 2 A. | Hefferman, Wm. 647004. | M. May 3-4/17. |
| ‡2 | Hunt, H. 675702. | W. and M. May 3/17. |
| 2 | Insley, E. A. 412123. | D/W. April 9/17. Det.D./B. |
| ‡2 | Jeffries, Albert L. 745023. | K. May 3/17. Det.D./B. |
| 2 | Kuhn, J. 633035. | M. May 3-4/17. |
| ‡2 | Martin, Sergt. 401107. | Unoff. W. and M. May 4/17. |
| ‡2 | Mitchell, C. 634144. | M., bel. K. May 3/17. |
| 2 | Molloy, G. L. 402573. | M. May 3-4/17. |
| 2 | Paterson, A. 746179. | M. May 3-4/17. |
| 2 | Shiniker, F. 630169. | M. May 3-4/17. |
| 2 | Singleton, B. 461308. | K. May 3/17. Det.D./B. |
| 2 | Smith, R. 8378. | M. May 3-4/17. |
| 2 | Soloman, J. 408893. | D/W. April 12/17. Det.D./B. |
| 2 | Treadwell, F. W. 868298. | M. May 3-4/17. |
| 2 | Waltire, H. 436123. | M. May 3-4/17. |
| 2 | Wiles, C. 8159. | M. May 3-4/17. |
| ‡2 D. | Williams, Edward T. 195436. | Unoff. M. May 4/17. |
| 2 | Woodman, C. D. 745503. | M., bel. K. April 5/17. |
| 3 | Basford, W. H. 63117. | M. May 4/17. |
| •3 B. | Buckland, F. G. 788554. | W. and M. May 3/17. |
| 3 | Burke, R. E. 767210. | M. May 3/17. |
| 3 | Burleigh, W. H. 172103. | M. Nov. 8/16. |
| 3 | Caron, F. 63192. | M. May 3/17. |
| •3 | Devereux, P. 404223. | W. and M. May 3/17. |
| 3 | Dingdale, J. 478918. | M. Oct. 2/16. |
| 3 D. (M.G.S.) | Donlevy, M. 788876. | M. May 3/17. |
| •3 | Hackett, T. 172201. | W. and M. May 3/17. |
| 3 D. | Head, Charles R. 138298. | K. Oct. 8/16. Det.D./B. |
| 3 D. | Hyde, D. 171635. | M. May 3/17. |
| •3 | Johnson, D. 183796. | W. and M. May 3/17. |
| 3 | La Rose, Z. 416041. | W. and M. June 13/16. |
| 3 | Letorski, J. 788510. | M. May 3/17. |
| 3 | Luesevage, F. 788916. | M. May 3/17. |
| •3 | Lunn, E. I. 784095. | K. May 3/17. Det.D./B. |
| •3 | Martin, S. 788920. | W. and M. May 3/17. |
| •3 B. | Morrow, M. 427845. | W. and M. May 3/17. |
| 3 | Mount, R. W. 784190. | M. May 3/17. |

**Canadian Infantry—contd.**

| | | |
|---|---|---|
| 3 | McDonald, R. B. 763167. | M. April 24/17. |
| 3 | McGregor, J. A. 603243. | W. and M. Dec. 9/16. |
| *3 | McKinley, C. H. 201439. | W. and M. May 3/17. |
| 3 A. | Pentney, W. M. 785135. | M. May 3/17. |
| *3 | Peters, C. 787331. | W. and M. May 3/17. |
| *3 | Price, L. 426450. | W. and M. May 3/17. |
| *3 | Smith, F. W. 138969. | W. and M. May 3/17. |
| *3 | Spark, R. C. 769550. | W. and M. May 3/17. |
| 3 | Thomas, W. 784511. | M. May 3/17. |
| 3 | Welch, J. 404233. | W. and M., bel. K. May 3/17. |
| 3 B. | Wesley, F. J. 139709. | W. and M. Oct. 8/16. |
| *3 | Wilson, J. 171710. (Bomb. S.). | K. Oct. 8/16. Det.D./B. |
| 3 | Yankel, L.-Cpl. M. 486613. | W. and M. Oct. 8/16. |
| 4 C. | Hastings, L.-Sgt. Chas. 491115. | K. April 11/17. Det.D./B. |
| ‡4 B. | Mews, R. M. 769489. | K. April 9/17. Det.D./B. |
| 4 | McGrath, W. C. 730237. (Att. 1st Entrenching Bn.) | K. April 9/17. Det.D./B. |
| 4 C. | Olde, J. 401015. | K. April 9/17. Det.D./B. |
| 4 | Scott, W. A. A36037. | W. and M. Oct. 8/16. |
| 4 Scout S. | Simmonds, A.-L.-Cpl. P. C. K. 21242. | K. April 24/17. Det.D./B. |
| 4 B. | Turner, W. 201506. | M. Oct. 8/16. |
| 5 | **McLean, Lieut. E. L. B.** | K. April 9/17. Det.D./B. |
| 5 | Archer, J. A40158. | W., bel. K. Sept. 26-27/16. |
| 5 | Bain, T. 1428. | M. April 28/17. |
| *5 | Ballard, A. H. 12825. | W. and M. April 28/17. |
| *5 | Beck, A. G. 925219. | M. April 28/17. |
| 5 | Bowers, A. 467494. | M. April 28/17. |
| 5 A. | Buchanan, David. 925170. | K. April 28/17. Det.D./B. |
| 5 | Burright, M. T. 926037. | K. April 9/17. Det.D./B. |
| 5 | Cuming, W. 466575. | K. Sept. 26-27/16. Det.D./B. |
| 5 C. | Delaney, John J. 198225. | M. April 28/17. |
| 5 | Dorian, J. 95403. | M. April 28/17. |
| ‡5 | Ewart, F. R. 908013. | K. April 28/17. Det.D./B. |
| 5 | Jardine, David. A40512. | W. and M. Sept. 26/16. |
| *5 | Jones, W. 105678. | W. and M. April 28/17. |
| 5 | Kearney, T. J. 460342. | K. April 28/17. Det.D./B. |
| ‡5 D. | King, Alexander. 925483. | D/W. April 10/17. Det.D./B. |
| 5 | Kirk, J. A. 907920. | M. April 28/17. |
| 5 | LeRoy, J. H. 440239. | D/W. April 28/17. Det.D./B. (No. 3 Can. Fld. Amb.) |
| 5 | Long, A. 622083. | W. and M. April 28/17. |
| 5 | Lovatt, S. 423165. | K. April 28/17. Det.D./B. |
| 5 | Marsh, G. H. 926038. | W. and M. April 28/17. |
| 5 | Mason, A. P. 440258. | K. April 28/17. Det.D./B. |
| 5 D. | McGhan, Sergt. Lloyd J. 466061. | K. April 9/17. Det.D./B. |
| 5 C. | Pack, J. H. 907613. | K. April 28/17. Det.D./B. |
| 5 C. | Price, C. O. E. 467245. | K. April 28/17. Det.D./B. |
| 5 A. | Quilty, J. 466625. | K. April 9/17. Det.D./B. |
| 5 | Smith, C. H. 105695. | M. April 28/17. |
| *5 | Smith, G. A24215. | W. and M. April 28/17. |
| *5 | Smith, J. 925070. | W. and M. April 28/17. |
| 5 | Smith, T. L. 925469. | W. and M. April 28/17. |
| 5 | Smith, D. E. 925470. | M. April 28/17. |
| 5 | Solleroz, P. 925690. | M. April 28/17. |
| 5 D. | Street, Albert E. 887303. | M. April 28/17. |
| 5 | Talbot, R. V. 1078065. | M. April 28/17. |
| 5 D. | Wilkinson, W. 908164. | K. April 28/17. Det.D./B. |
| 5 | Zacharko, M. 907637. | M. April 28/17. |
| 7 | Cadwallader, H. T. 183279. | M. April 9/17. |

**Canadian Infantry—contd.**

| | | |
|---|---|---|
| *7 | Dulake, R. L. 701085. | K. April 8-10/17. Det.D./B. |
| 7 A. | Ffoulkes, J. W. McA. 183216. | K. April 8-10/17. Det.D./B. |
| 7 | Locke, S. 446687. | K. April 13/17. Det.D./B. |
| 7 | Munro, C. McL. 790648. | K. April 9/17. Det.D./B. |
| 7 | Robertson, G. W. 760990. | M. April 9-10/17. |
| 7 C. | Smyth, E. S. 467521. | K. April 28/17. Det.D./B. |
| 7 | Walker, A. C. A.28719. | M. April 9-10/17. |
| 7 D. | Walters. 760170. | K. April 14/17. Det.D./B. |
| 7 B. | Youle, Sergt. J. W. 77434. | K. April 13/17. Det.D./B. |
| 7 Gren. S. | Young, J. E. 429568. | M. Feb. 27/17. |
| 8 B. | Bailey, F. A. 460238. | K. April 28/17. Det.D./B. |
| 8 | Barnwell, S. 187221. | M. April 28/17. |
| 8 | Bolton, R. F. 830680. | K. April 2/17. Det.D./B. |
| 8 | Booth, R. C. 552439. | W. and M. April 28/17. |
| 8 | Brown, W. J. 159604. | M., bel. K. April 14/17. |
| 8 | Bytheway, J. 460466. | M. April 28/17. |
| 8 C. | Gibbons, Timothy. A22072. | K. Sept. 26/16. Det.D./B. |
| 8 | Gibbs, T. C. 624832. | K. April 28/17. Det.D./B. |
| 8 | Hampton, W. 424868. | M. April 28/17. |
| 8 | Hancocks, F. 438018. | M., bel. K. April 28/17. |
| 8 | Harding, W. S. 115983. | K. April 28/17. Det.D./B. |
| 8 A. | Hayman, S. 466726. | K. April 28/17. Det.D./B. |
| 8 | Jameson, A. W. 186767. | K. April 28/17. Det.D./B. |
| 8 | Jaques, J. 101315. | M., bel. K. Sept. 26/16. |
| 8 | Kasp, P. 829268. | W. and M. April 28/17. |
| 8 | Lauder, J. 292245. | M. April 28/17. |
| 8 | Mahood, H. J. 442927. | M. April 28/17. |
| 8 | Miller, F. 291337. | M. April 28/17. |
| 8 | Mowat, R. S. 875014. | M. April 14/17. |
| 8 | Musto, A.-Cpl. W. 422289. | M. April 28/17. |
| *8 | McCarthy, C.-S.-M. J. 150154. | W. and M. April 28/17. |
| 8 | McNutt, M. R. 228346. | W. and M. April 28/17. |
| 8 T.M.B. | Pallant, W. B. 425178. | K. April 10/17. Det.D./B. |
| 8 | Parrish, J. R. 830138. | M. April 28/17. |
| 8 | Patterson, N. E. 227111. | M. April 28/17. |
| 8 | Peel, W. N. H. 874140. | W. and M. April 28/17. |
| 8 C. M.G.S. | Pook, E. 186658. | W. and M. April 28/17. |
| 8 C. | Ryons, Alfred. 84764. | K. Sept. 26/16. Det.D./B. |
| 8 | Scott, J. 45292. | M., bel. W. April 28/17. |
| 8 | Smith, G. S. 187704. | W. and M. April 28/17. |
| 8 | Steedman, W. 829454. | W. and M. April 28/17. |
| 8 | Stockdale, F. 622686. | K. Oct. 15/16. Det.D./B. |
| 8 C. | Storey, Harry. A22158. | K. April 14/17. Det.D./B. |
| 8 B. | Swindells, G. A. 460176. | K. Sept. 26/16. Det.D./B. |
| 8 | Tainsh, G. D. 552548. | W. and M. April 28/17. |
| 8 | Thompson, W. R. 187817. | M. April 28/17. |
| 8 D. | Tingley, A. E. 830262. | M. April 28/17. |
| 8 | Wilson, W. 829792. | W. and M. April 28/17. |
| 8 | Youds, W. 829798. | M., bel. K. April 28/17. |
| 10 | **Jackson, Lieut. H. A. L. C.** | K. April 28/17. Det.D./B. |
| *10 | Blake, Harold P. 625074. | K. April 9/17. Det.D./B. |
| 10 D. | Brown, J. 227007. | K. April 28/17. Det.D./B. |
| 10 | Coughlin, A. 434462. | M. April 28/17. |
| 10 D. | Davenport, T. 426041. | K. April 9/17. Det.D./B. |
| 10 C. | Dyson, L. 227015. | K. April 28/17. Det.D./B. |
| 10 | Harkness, J. 20634. | W. and M. Sept. 26/16. |
| 10 | Harris, L.-Cpl. W. A. 466741. | K. April 9/17. Det.D./B. |
| 10 | Johnson, A.-L.-Cpl. E. E. 20637. | M. April 28/17. |
| 10 B. | Mack, C. 20146. | K. Sept. 26/16. Det.D./B. |
| *10 B. | Marshall, W. 253075. | K. April 28/17. Det.D./B. |

**Canadian Infantry—contd.**

| | | |
|---|---|---|
| 10 | McCarthy, F. 467471. | M. April 26/17. |
| 10 B. | McGhee, J. 252757. | M. April 28/17. |
| 10 D. | Parkinson, Oliver J. 467592. | K. Sept. 26/16. Det.D./B. |
| ‡10 D. | Reid, W. H. 808554. | K. April 9/17. Det.D./B. |
| ‡10 | Sentell, Victor. 817342. | K. April 9/17. Det.D./B. |
| 10 A. | Sheppard, E. N. 808427. | K. April 9/17. Det.D./B. |
| 10 | Skinner, E. 466949. | M. Sept. 26/16. |
| 10 | Smith, W. 466224. | M. Sept. 26/16. |
| 10 | Thomson, A. 20671. | M. Sept. 26/16. |
| 10 | Towson, G. A. 160506. | M. April 9/17. |
| 10 | Ushunashi, T. 895063. | M. April 28/17. |
| 10 | Wilkinson, R. 430402. | K. April 28/17. Det.D./B. |
| •10 | Wilson, Percy A. 552918. | K. April 9/17. Det.D./B. |
| 10 L.G.S. | Wyatt, L. 808659. | K. April 28/17. Det.D./B. |
| 10 | Zuidema, S. 808240. | M. April 28/17. |
| •13 | **Smith, Lieut. J. L.** | M. June 29/17. |
| 13 A. | Brearley, Norman O. 602786. | K. April 20/17. Det.D./B. |
| •13 | Gray, William Smith. 193066. | K. April 16/17. Det.D./B. |
| 13 | MacGillivray, G. 199360. | M. April 13/17. |
| •13 | Sheehan, J. P. 841277. | K. April 30/17. Det.D./B. |
| 13 | Sweetman, C. 416104. | K. April 9/17. Det.D./B. |
| 13 | Ward, P. 426974. | Pres. died Sept. 5/16. Det.D./B. |
| 14 | **Beaton, Capt. W. E.** | W. and M. Sept. 26/16. |
| •14 | Belleveaux, T. 416833. | M. June 8/17. |
| 14 | Booth, H. 796174. | K. April 9/17. Det.D./B. |
| 14 | Carson, J. 441840. | K. Sept. 26/16. Det.D./B. |
| 14 | Crerar, J. S. 797213. | K. April 9/17. Det.D./B. |
| 14 | Ford, E. 823375. | M. April 9/17. |
| 14 | Hirshuk, H. 448121. | M. April 9/17. |
| 14 | Judge, R. H. 602835. | M. April 9/17. |
| 14 | Low, W. C. 796609. | M. April 9/17. |
| 14 | Martin, E. 448968. | M. April 9/17. |
| 14 | McRae, O. R. 712829. | W. and M. April 9/17. |
| 14 | Richmond, R. A. A. 841403. | K. Feb. 1/17. Det.D./B. |
| 14 | Staples, E. A. 823760. | M. April 9/17. |
| 14 D. | Turner, W. C. 841644. | K. April 9/17. Det.D./B. |
| 15 | Burford, E. S. 192871. | K. April 9/17. Det.D./B. |
| 15 A. | Chalmer, Edward L. 778397. | K. April 9/17. Det.D./B. |
| 15 | Davie, A. 799830. | K. April 9/17. Det.D./B. |
| 15 | Fodon, H. R. 799778. | M. Mar. 2/17. |
| 15 B. | Greggs, Walter. 46149. | K. April 9/17. Det.D./B. |
| •15 | Hunter, Cpl. W. 77718. | K. April 9/17. Det.D./B. |
| ‡15 C. | Lugger, R. H. 799705. | K. April 9/17. Det.D./B. |
| 15 B. | Manning, G. E. 192865. | K. April 9/17. Det.D./B. |
| ‡15 | Mosley, T.-Cpl. 447705. | K. April 9/17. Det.D./B. |
| 15 A. | McDonald, William. 799594. | K. April 9/17. Det.D./B. |
| 15 D. | McFadyen, G. 02727. | M. April 14/17. |
| 15 B. | McKay, Eric. 799360. | K. April 21/17. Det.D./B. |
| 15 D. | Sullivan, Joseph. 802476. | K. April 9/17. Det.D./B. |
| •15 | Toward, A. C. 437588. | M. June 10/17. |
| 15 | White, N. G. 799771. | K. April 4/17. Det.D./B. |
| 16 | **Irving, Lieut. A. B.** | M. Oct. 9/16. |
| ‡16 A. | Bethell, W. E. 719115. | K. April 9/17. Det.D./B. |
| •16 B. | Broad, Thomas P. 150818. | M. Oct. 8-9/17. |
| 16 D. | Cheeseman, H. 736106. | K. April 9/17. Det.D./B. |
| 16 | Colledge, W. E. 736556. | K. April 9/17. Det.D./B. |
| 16 | Dickson, W. F. 160168. | K. April 9/17. Det.D./B. |
| 16 C. | Dunn, W. 718402. | K. April 18/17. Det.D./B. |
| 16 C. | Harman, R. C. 192519. | K. Oct. 8/16. Det.D./B. |
| •16 D. | MacKinnon, A. C. 181108. | K. April 9/17. Det.D./B. |

**Canadian Infantry—contd.**

| | | |
|---|---|---|
| 16 C. | MacRae, Wm. Murray. 426606. | W. and M. Sept. 4-7/16. |
| 16 | Phillips, F. V. 105741. | Unoff. K. April 9/17. Det.D./B. |
| 16 | Prime, F. 721128. | K. April 28-30/17. Det.D./B. |
| 16 | Ramsay, R. 736849. | W. and M. April 9/17. |
| 16 | Scott, J. A. 421081. | K. Aug. 4/16. Det.D./B. |
| 16 | Tallman, Albert E. 859301. | M. April 9/17. |
| *16 | Wilson, R. 721062. | M. June 6/17. |
| 18 | **Wright, Lieut. William Richard.** | K. May 13/17. Det.D./B. |
| 18 A. | Belcher, Cecil R. 123194. | W. and M. April 9/17. |
| 18 | Devitt, B. 769131. | M. April 9/17. |
| 18 | Fairburn, E. 227098. | M. April 9/17. |
| 18 C. | Hickey, H. C. 160943. | D/W. April 9/17. No. 1 Canadian Field Ambulance. |
| 18 | Jenkins, W. 775949. | M. May 28/17. |
| 18 | Kidney, J. 769565. | M. May 9/17. |
| 18 | LaLonde, W. 63568. | M. May 28/17. |
| 18 | Middleton, W. 823379. | M. May 27/17. |
| ‡18 | Moore, J. E. 769463. | K. May 23/17. Det.D./B. |
| 18 | McKane, C. J. 226610 | M. May 28/17. |
| 18 B. | Ross, A. 803217. | M. May 9/17. |
| 18 D. | Sims, T. B. 770250. | K. May 23/17. Det.D./B. |
| 18 | Skelly, L. R. 803015. | M. Mar. 24/17. |
| 19 | **Laurie, Lieut. J. G.** | K. May 9/17. Det.D./B. |
| 19 | Allard, T. E. 172096. | K. April 9/17. Det.D./B. |
| 19 | Ayles, W. J. 766529. | M., bel. K. May 9/17. |
| *19 | Batterbee, L.-Cpl. A. 56171. | W. and M. May 9/17. |
| 19 B. | Blair, J. 172117. | M. May 9/17. |
| *19 | Blows, Cpl. A. 55371. | W. and M. May 8/17. |
| 19 | Bray, R. 814691. | M. April 13/17. |
| 19 | Britt, F. V. 767212. | M. May 9/17. |
| 19 | Burd, R. J. 210122. | M. May 9/17. |
| 19 | Clarke, H. 757727. | M. May 9/17. |
| 19 | Clark, J. 766157. | M. May 9/17. |
| 19 B. | Colley, Earl Clifford. 190304. | M. May 9/17. |
| 19 | Cook, W. A. W. 766200. | M. May 9/17. |
| 19 | Cooper, G. 862271. | M. May 9/17. |
| 19 | Cosgrove, W. C. 863172 | M. May 9/17. |
| 19 | Cowan, W. 862428. | M. May 9/17. |
| *19 | Crawley, A.-Sergt. H. 55397. | W. and M. May 9/17. |
| *19 | Crowe, J. R. 408756. | W. and M. May 9/17. |
| 19 | Davies, G. 863068. | M. May 9/17. |
| 19 | Edsall, V. L. 739371. | M. May 9/17. |
| 19 A. | Fisher, A. 151664. | W. and M. April 9/17. |
| 19 C. | Ford, John Lane. 201792. | M. May 9/17. |
| 19 C. | Fraser, A.-L.-Cpl. C. H. 183850. | M. May 9/17. |
| 19 | Freeland, G. A., 213516. | M. May 9/17. |
| *19 | Giebner, W. A. 745080. | W. and M. May 9/17. |
| 19 | Gordon, W. G. 766199. | M. May 9/17. |
| 19 C. | Griffin, R. N. 766202. | M. May 9/17. |
| 19 C. | Haines, G. 766206. | M. May 9/17. |
| 19 | Hedges, H. G. 757091, | M. May 9/17. |
| 19 C. | Hill, R. H. 405565. | M. May 9/17. |
| 19 | Houston, J. 56076. | M. May 9/17. |
| 19 C. | Iredale, T. G. 56166. | M. May 9/17. |
| 19 | Melville, H. 766267 | M. May 9/17. |
| 19 | Midgley, W. 745128. | M. May 9/17. |
| *19 | Murdoch, R. 673. | W. and M. May 8/17. |
| 19 | MacFarlane, J. H. 403105. | M. May 9/17. |
| 19 D. | McGuinness, T. J. 214311. | K. May 9/17. Det.D./B. |
| 19 C. | McKellar, Donald B. 766260. | M. May 9/17. |

**Canadian Infantry—contd.**

| | | |
|---|---|---|
| 19 | Neilly, V. E. 643662. | M. May 9/17. |
| 19 | Payne, J. W. 767158. | M., bel. K. May 9/17. |
| 19 B. | Pearce, E. D. 706665. | M. May 9/17. |
| 19 | Prince, A. 643487. | M. May 9/17. |
| 19 C. | Reeve, A.-Sergt. F. 192285. | M. May 9/17. |
| 19 | Reynolds, L. 454903. | M. May 9/17. |
| *19 | Scott, J. 121654. | W. and M. May 9/17. |
| 19 | Sedore, R. 745178. | M. May 9/17. |
| 19 | Sleep, W. W. 408877. | M. May 9/17. |
| 19 B. | Smith, H. W. 797010. | M. May 9/17. |
| 19 | Spicer, L.-Cpl. F. J. 135399. | M. May 9/17. |
| 19 | Tripp, A.-Cpl. G. H. 135315. | M., May 9/17. |
| 19 | Turnbull, E. 657752. | M. May 9/17. |
| '19 | Tweedale, A.-Cpl. G. A. 55729. | M. May 9/17. |
| 19 A. | Vaughan, E. M. B. 180811. | M. May 9/17. |
| 20 | **Little, Lieut. J. H.** | K. April 10/17. Det.D./B. |
| 20 | Batkin, W. H. F. 228529. | M. May 9/17. |
| 20 A. | Bell, Cecil G. 835717. | M. May 9/17. |
| ‡20 | Harper, S. W. 766391. | Unoff. W. and M. May 9/17. |
| 20 | Waiteshuk, F. I. 152728. | M. May 8/17. |
| 21 | Alder, H. 141364. | K. April 9/17. Det.D./B. |
| 21 | Ashman, J. C. 805794. | M. April 9/17. |
| 21 | Blowing, T. 59074. | M. May 9/17. |
| 21 | Boudreau, A. J. 445479. | M. May 10/17. |
| 21 A. | Burton, H. 775991. | K. April 21/17. Det.D./B. |
| 21 | Canniff, E. 220087. | M. May 9/17. |
| 21 | Clue, Charles J. 204407. | K. April 9/17. Det.D./B. |
| 21 | Codd, E. T. 455250. | K. April 9/17. Det.D./B. |
| 21 | Dyer, Cpl. J. 59284. | M. April 9/17. |
| 21 | Endersby, L.-Cpl. A. J. 59300. | M. May 9/17. |
| *21 | Gauthier, Rene. 454423. | D/W. May 8/17. No. 4 Can. Field Amb. Det.D./B. |
| 21 C. | Green, Leo. L. 444831. | K. April 9/17. Det.D./B. |
| 21 | Hobden, J. M. 726080. | M. April 9/17. |
| 21 | Lemmon, M. 636650. | M. May 10/17. |
| 21 | Montonia, E. W. 211113. | M. April 9/17. |
| 21 | Scott, N. J. 141771. | W. and M. Oct. 1/16. |
| 21 | Stinson, C. H. 725549. | M. May 9/17. |
| 21 | Tripp, J. A. 725600. | M. May 9/17. |
| ‡22 | Arsenault, Theo. V. 443300. | K. May 5/17. Det.D./B. |
| 22 | Bacon, O. 417274. | M. Sept. 18/16. |
| 22 | Gagne, P. 454454. | M. Sept. 18/16. |
| 22 | Grivel, J. 61474. | M. Oct. 4/16. |
| 22 | LeMay, L.-Cpl. E. 61595. | M. Sept. 18/16. |
| 22 | Nelson, J. 120844. | M. April 14/17. |
| 22 | Villeneuve, Edouard. 120972. | K. Dec. 25/16. Det.D./B. |
| 24 | Arbing, H. S. 742794. | K. April 9/17. Det.D./B. |
| 24 * | Coughtry, W. H. 841176. | M. April 9/17. |
| 24 D. | Gallagher, E. T. 288956. | K. April 9/17. Det.D./B. |
| 24 | Gilmore, J. A. 742473. | M. April 9/17. |
| 24 | Kimball, Harold C. 749295. | K. April 9/17. Det.D./B. |
| ‡24 | Kuchar, W. 742116. | W. and M. April 9/17. |
| 24 | Leslie, D. Y. 412762. | K. May 18/17. Det.D./B. |
| *24 C. | Maxwell, James G. 742185. | K. April 9/17. Det.D./B. |
| *24 | Moore, John L. 602299. | K. May 5/17. Det.D./B. |
| 24 B. | Mullins, E. J. 65648. | K. April 9/17. Det.D./B. |
| 24 | McElwain, F. W. 742639. | M. April 9/17. |
| 24 | Parton, W. 701258. | M. April 9/17. |
| 24 | Petters, S. W. 842161. | M. April 9/17. |
| 24 | Rabey, W. 889855. | M. April 9/17. |

Canadian Infantry—contd.

24 Robertson, C. W. 700725. M. April 9/17.
24 Rose, H. 65848. K. Mar. 24/17. Det.D./B.
25 Arsenault, B. 712702. M. April 28/17.
25 Addis, J. 161297. M. April 28/17.
25 Bates, G. A. 174229. M. April 28/17.
25 Bentley, A. L. 733069. M. April 9/17.
25 Brewer, V. B. 818230. M. April 9/17.
25 Bryson, L. W. 715094. M. April 9/17.
25 Burgess, A. B. 734229. M. April 9/17.
‡25 A. Clerihew, G. W. 183225. M. April 29/17.
‡25 Feindel, L. C. 733727. K. April 9/17. Det.D./B.
25 Frizell, J. A. 901004. M. April 28/17.
25 Goldstein, J. 715842. M. April 9/17.
25 Goodwin, M. H. 734307. M. April 29/17.
25 Graham, Hugh. 181157. W. and M. April 9/17.
*25 A. Gunn, J. 469294. W. and M. Oct. 1/16.
25 Guy, Jack. 68369. K. Sept. 12/16. Det.D./B.
25 Jefferson, W. 733168. M. April 29/17.
*25 Johnson, E. J. 901037. K. April 9/17. Det.D./B.
25 C. Kennedy, George. 901016. M. May 3/17.
*25 C. Kennedy, J. L. 901058. K. May 20/17. Det.D./B.
25 Lewis, E. M. 469278. M. April 29/17.
*25 Martinson, L. E. 901540. K. May 3/17. Det.D./B.
25 Morash, A. E. 733806. M. April 9/17.
‡25 Mossman, H. M. 733363. M. July 5/17.
25 Muraview, A. 449042. M. April 9/17.
25 Murphy, G. H. 734240. M. May 9/17.
25 Murree, G. S. 67164. M. April 29/17.
25 Miles, C. H. 733051. M. April 29/17.
25 McNeil, J. A. 67870. M. April 28/17.
25 Perry, E. 142127. M. April 29/17.
25 Purdy, C. C. C. 733404. M. April 29/17.
*25 Shkarovsky, P. 417665. M. April 9/17.
25 D. Smith, H. 180848. M. April 28/17.
25 Stevens, G. M. 733352. M. April 28/17.
25 Sumiejski, A. R. 716253. M. April 28/17.
‡25 Towers, A. M. 180325. K. April 28/17. Det.D./B.
*25 D. Veinotte, Baxter Harris. 734518. K. April 9/17. Det.D./B.
25 Williams, W. R. 901361. M. April 28/17.
25 Woodley, S. C. 415785. M. April 29/17.
‡26 C. Ashe J. F. 710173. D/W. April 9/17 Det.D./B. (No. 1 Can. Fld. Amb.)
‡26 Hutchinson, Hector E. 716066. K. Jan. 16/17. Det.D./B.
26 Raymond, Sergt. R. B. 69839. D/W. April 9/17. Det.D./B.
27 Gell, Lieut. E. V. W. and M. May 3/17.
*27 Allan, J. E. 874171. M. May 3/17.
27 Appleton, K. 438957. M. May 3/17.
27 Armstrong, A. 622058. M. April 10/17.
27 D. Binnie, G. 874789. M. May 3/17.
27 Black, A. 874072. M. May 3/17.
*27 Boyle, H. W. 186031. M. May 3/17.
27 B. Bramwell, R. S. 460459. M. May 3/17.
27 D. Cameron, W. R. 69163. M. April 18/17.
27 Chisholm, D. A. 874222. M. May 3/17.
*27 Davis, Cpl. C. 71250. M. May 3/17.
27 Dudgeon, J. 874493. M. May 3/17.
27 Fowler, W. V. 624642. K. April 10/17. Det.D./B.
27 B. Fulford, A. T. 874240. M. May 3/17.
27 Garwell, L.-Cpl. G. E. 424394. M. May 3/17.
*27 Hawkins, C. F. 184079. M. May 3/17.

**Canadian Infantry—contd.**

| | | |
|---|---|---|
| *27 | Hunt, G. 216488. | M. May 3/17. |
| 27 B. | Jeans, G. 552290. | M. May 3/17. |
| 27 | Johnston, W. 234322. | M. May 3/17. |
| 27 E. | Jones, D. E. 187612. | M. May 3/17. |
| 27 | Kidd, A. J. 625534. | M. May 3/17. |
| *27 | Knight, C. 115575. | M. May 3/17. |
| *27 | Lane, F. 875298. | M. May 3/17. |
| 27 | Maher, J. H. 186625. | M. May 3/17. |
| 27 | Matthews, S. 228171. | M. May 3/17. |
| 27 | Messner, G. 874392. | M. May 3/17. |
| 27 | Morrison, F. H. 186196. | K. April 10/17. Det.D./B. |
| *27 | Morison, W. H. 874666. | M. May 3/17. |
| 27 | Muskett, W. 217071. | M. May 3/17. |
| 27 | MacGregor, J. L. 225823. | M. May 3/17. |
| *27 | McPherson, P. 234931. | M. May 3/17. |
| 27 | Riches, J. E. 874263. | M. May 3/17. |
| 27 | Robie, R. R. 875389. | M. May 3/17. |
| 27 D. | Simpson, V. J. 151919. | M. May 3/17. |
| 27 D. | Smith, Paul U. 186706. | M. May 3/17. |
| 27 | Smith, R. G. 622722. | M. May 3/17. |
| 27 B. | Smith, W. F. 874305. | M. May 3/17. |
| 27 | Swanson, J. 875048. | M. May 3/17. |
| 27 | Thorington, S. R. 875148. | M. May 3/17. |
| 27 | Vogel, W. 186271. | M. May 3/17. |
| *27 | Watson. 552812. | M. May 3/17. |
| 27 | Wright, E. L. 460643. | M. April 10/17. |
| 28 C. | Belcher, T. 781632. | M. May 8/17. |
| 28 | Forbes, James. 426004. | Pres. D. Sept. 15/16. Det.D./B. |
| 28 | Hesseltine, J. R. 440923. | K. Sept. 15/16. Det.D./B. |
| 28 | Rees, M. J. 104038. | K. Sept. 15/16. Det.D./B. |
| *28 D. | Robson, L.-Cpl. S. 74073. | W. and M. May 8/17. |
| 28 | Shirriff, F. M. 460627. | K. May 8/17. Det.D./B. |
| 29 | **McIntyre, Lieut. W. G.** | D/W. April 10/17. Det.D./B. |
| 29 | Brewer, H. 463227. | M. May 24/17. |
| 29 | Clark, W. H. 48529. | M. May 24/17. |
| 29 | Cook, S. B. 464197. | W. and M. May 8/17. |
| 29 C. | Donegan, Cpl. G. W. 183555. | Unoff. W. and M. May 3/17. |
| 29 | Harris, F. 116055. | M. May 8/17. |
| 29 C. | Lance, Charles G. 76196. | W. and M. May 8/17. |
| 29 A. | Lewis, A. A. 645011. | M. May 8/17. |
| 29 | Nevard, W. 790295. | K. April 10/17. Det.D./B. |
| 29 B. | Paquette, Hy. 401379. | M. May 8/17. |
| 29 | Wight, Gordon. 628989. | W. and M. Dec. 18/16. |
| 31 | **Cordiner, Lieut. R. C.** | K. April 12/17. Det.D./B. |
| 31 | Baldwin, W. 874283. | M. May 3/17. |
| 31 | Beaton, H. E. 430076. | M. Sept. 27/16. |
| *31 | Berget, O. 696800. | W. and M. May 3/17. |
| 31 | Campbell, S. 424647. | W. and M. Sept. 27/16. |
| 31 C. | Cannon, A. 696796. | W. and M. May 3/17. |
| 31 | Coates, C. R. 696844. | M. May 2/17. |
| 31 C. | Cowie, A. 161092. | M. May 3/17. |
| *31 | Donegan, A.-Cpl. G. W. 183555. | W. and M. May 3/17. |
| 31 | Duhaime, N. 808578. | M. May 3/17. |
| 31 | Elsey, J. T. 696286. | K. May 1/17. Det.D./B. |
| 31 | Erickson, C. G. 696727. | M. May 3/17. |
| *31 | Gilman, C. I. 697019. | W. and M. May 3/17. |
| 31 | Ingram, J. J. 696793. | M. May 3/17. |
| *31 | Jackson, J. H. 696835. | W. and M. May 3/17. |
| 31 | Johnson, P. 101127. | W. and M. Sept. 27/16. |
| 31 | Jones, R. F. 100421. | M. May 3/17. |

**Canadian Infantry—contd.**

| | | |
|---|---|---|
| 31 | Keyes, W. E. G. 79213. | W. and M. May 3/17. |
| 31 | Kimball, J. 696247. | M. May 3/17. |
| *31 D. | King, Henry. 80212. | K. May 3/17. Det.D./B. |
| 31 | Lancaster, C. 79759. | M. May 3/17. |
| 31 | Leif, W. R. 808225. | M. May 3/17. |
| 31 | Maitland, A.-L.-Cpl. G. R. 160726. | M. May 3/17. |
| 31 | Meechan, P. 183666. | W. and M. May 3/17. |
| 31 | Millar, J. 160444. | M. May 3/17. |
| 31 D. | Mould, H. J. 80263. | W. and M. Mar. 29-30/17. |
| 31 B. | MacDonald, Allen. 435718. | M. May 3/17. |
| 31 | O'Keefe, J. 101742. | W. and M. Mar. 29/17. |
| 31 D. | Owen, H. W. 100698. | W. and M. Mar. 29/17. |
| 31 | Peck, A. L. 79431. | W. and M. April 6/16. |
| 31 | Redshaw, J. W. 161034. | M. May 3/17. |
| 31 C. | Richardson, J. M. 100713. | K. Sept. 15/16. Det.D./B. |
| *31 | Ripley, R. J. 696713. | W. and M. May 3/17. |
| 31 | Rumberg, O. A. 696988. | M. May 3/17. |
| 31 | Saunders, W. 183644. | M. May 3/17. |
| 31 | Seward, J. B. 696624. | M. May 3/17. |
| 31 | Shakalevich, K. 697003. | M. May 3/17. |
| 31 | Stratton, A. P. 466320. | M. May 5/17. |
| 31 | Thom, A. W. 696576. | M. May 3/17. |
| 31 C. | Tilson, L.-Cpl. H. 115508. | M. May 3/17. |
| 31 D. | Todd, P. F. 696009. | M. May 3/17. |
| 31 B. | Tole, Pt E. 101238. | M. Sept. 27/16. |
| 31 | Waugh, V. E. 115754. | M. May 3/17. |
| 31 | Wedderburn, L. H. 696110. | M. May 3/17. |
| 31 | Wiseman, Andrew. 811870. | M. May 3/17. |
| 38 | **Hill, Lieut. H. F.** | M. April 9/17. |
| 38 | Clarke, F. W. 775976. | M. April 9/17. |
| 38 | Cosby, W. 725533. | M. April 9/17. |
| 38 | Cox, E. W. 726046. | M. April 9/17. |
| 38 | Fiedler, C. 725240. | M. April 9/17. |
| 38 | Gardiner, L. 410745. | M. April 9/17. |
| *38 D. | Heyd, John G. A. 189977. | K. April 9/17. Det.D./B. |
| *38 | Knight, Charles A., 775985. | D/W. April 10/17. No. 12 Can. Fld. Amb. Det.D./B. |
| 38 A. | Moore, P. 787646. | M. April 9/17. |
| 38 | McCreadie, Robert. 410830. | K. April 9/17. Det.D./B. |
| 38 A. | McDonald, C. 669665. | K. April 9/17. Det.D./B. |
| 38 | Pollitt, G. 725015. | M. April 9/17. |
| 38 | Rainford, Cpl. R. 410863. | K. April 9/17. Det.D./B. |
| 38 | Searle, W. L. 410882. | M. April 9/17. |
| 38 | Siedler, C. 725240. | M. April 9/17. |
| 38 | White, P. V. 220502. | K. Oct. 29/16. Det.D./B. |
| 42 | **Hilton, Lieut. H. B.** | K. April 9-10/17. Det.D./B. |
| ‡42 | Bass, A. E. 794258. | M. April 9/17. |
| 42 | Bradley, H. P. 684402. | K. April 9/17. Det.D./B. |
| 42 B. | Conway, S. M. 283441. | K. April 9/17. Det.D./B. |
| 42 | Eden, E. 418749. | W. and M. April 9/17. |
| 42 | England, A. J. 418301. | M. April 9/17. |
| 42 | Emerson, J. M. 412105. | K. April 9/17. Det.D./B. |
| 42 | Furlotte, J. 793565. | M. April 9-11/17. |
| 42 | Henderson, J. 901266. | K. Jan. 30/17. Det.D./B. |
| 42 | Kenny, R. 793927. | M. April 9-11/17. |
| 42 | LaViolette, A. D. 842319. | M. April 9-11/17. |
| 42 | McDonald, D. A. 901635. | M. April 9-11/17. |
| 42 C. | McMillan, W. H. 414913. | K. Sept. 16/16. Det.D./B. |
| 42 | Pipes, B. 228911 | K. April 9/17. Det.D./B. |

**Canadian Infantry—contd.**

| | | |
|---|---|---|
| 42 | Saunders, W. 701240. | M. April 9-11/17. |
| 42 A. | Walker, Ellis. 441495. | K. April 9/17. Det.D./B. |
| 42 C. | Welsh, C. J. 282661. | W. and M. April 9/17. |
| 43 Gren. S. | Don, A. 153166. | K. Sept. 21/16. Det.D./B. |
| 43 | Morton, James McK. 736659. | K. May 24/17. Det.D./B. |
| 43 | MacDougall, R. W. 155059. | M. April 16/17. |
| •43 | MacTavish, D. T. 736787. | K. April 15/17. Det.D./B. |
| 43 | Peters, D. 736806. | M., bel. P/W. Mar. 15/17. |
| 43 | Simpson, R. 859751. | M. April 16/17. |
| 43 | Stuart, J. 859638. | K. April 5/17. Det.D./B. |
| 43 | Woodworth, W. B. 415632. | K. April 5/17. Det.D./B. |
| 43 B. | Wright, A. C. 700424. | M. May 3/17. |
| 4[illegible] | **Robertson, Lieut. C. G.** | M. April 9-12/17. |
| 44 | **Smith, Lieut. S. S.** | M. June 3/17. |
| 44 | **Stibbard, Capt. S.** | M. June 3/17. |
| •44 | Atkinson, P. S. 460669. | M. June 3/17. |
| •44 | Beatty, M. I. 291949. | M. June 3/17. |
| •44 | Belly, P. 888516. | M. June 3/17. |
| •44 D. | Bennett, A. E. M. 234882. | M. June 3/17. |
| •44 | Bennett, F. V. 830046. | W. and M. May 9/17. |
| •44 | Black, W. E. 859988. | W. and M. May 10/17. |
| •44 A. | Brown, R. 830416. | W. and M. May 10/17. |
| •44 | Connolly, W. 829224. | M. June 3/17. |
| 44 A. | Cullen, E. G. 829710. | K. April 12/17. Det.D./B. |
| •44 | Curran, W. 829608. | M. June 3/17. |
| 44 | Dodwell, R. F. 718571. | K. April 10/17. Det.D./B. |
| 44 | Evans, W. 460716. | W. and M. Nov. 18/16. |
| 44 | Faulder, J. 859111. | M. Feb. 13/17. |
| ‡44 | French, H. 829613. | W. and M. June 3/17. |
| •44 | Fuller, H. J. 234362 | M. June 3/17. |
| •44 | Gamble, A. 234106. | M. June 3/17. |
| •44 | Holland, W. 234056. | M. June 3/17. |
| •44 | Hollett, C. H. 234963. | M. June 3/17. |
| •44 | Howden, J. W. 829253. | M. June 3/17. |
| 44 | Jenson, A. 472716. | M. April 12/17. |
| •44 | Kirkpatrick, J. F. 127573. | M. June 3/17. |
| •44 | Kolomies, A. 886190. | M. June 3/17. |
| •44 | Lane, W. 829773. | M. June 3/17. |
| 44 | Lavallee, C. 220319. | W. and M. April 10/17. |
| •44 | Lawson, W. 829278. | M. June 3/17. |
| 44 | Lien, G. 622561. | M. Feb. 13/17. |
| •44 | Linfoot, J 234935. | M. June 3/17. |
| •44 | Luxton, V. J. 829002. | M. June 3/17. |
| •44 | Maracle, P. 219361. | W. and M. May 10/17. |
| •44 | Marriott, I. 234323. | M. June 3/17. |
| •44 | McDiarmid, C. 725544. | M. June 3/17. |
| 44 | McIntosh, C. J. 830679. | W. and M. April 10/17. |
| ‡44 | McKenzie, A. 693120. | W. and M. June 3/17. |
| •44 | Nicholson, O. McK. 235124. | M. June 3/17. |
| ‡44 | Osmond, F. T. G. 829684. | W. and M. June 3/17. |
| •44 | Paterson, J. 220533. | W. and M. May 7/17. |
| •44 | Pikula, T. 887929. | M. June 3/17. |
| •44 | Portianka, B. 886462. | M. June 3/17. |
| •44 | Priddell, H. S. 135552. | M. June 3/17. |
| •44 | Reed, F. G. 127260. | M. June 3/17. |
| •44 | Rochan, E. F. 622898. | M. June 3/17. |
| ‡44 | Rogers, Cpl. C. E. 474227. | W. and M. June 3/17. |
| •44 C. | Roscoe, T. E. 830208. | M. June 3/17. |
| •44 | Saville, E. J. 871296. | M. June 3/17. |
| ‡44 B. | Scott, Sergt. G. 460415. | W. and M. June 3/17. |

**Canadian Infantry—contd.**

| | | |
|---|---|---|
| *44 | Sced, W. 460616. | M. June 3/17. |
| *44 | Sergechuk, M. 886613. | M. June 3/17. |
| *44 | Sigurdson, S. W. 829335. | M. June 3/17. |
| *44 | Spiess, G. A. 625189. | M. June 3/17. |
| *44 | Squair, F. V. 460628. | M. June 3/17. |
| *44 | Swain, Sergt. J. S. S. 234014. | M. June 3/17. |
| *44 D. | Tarrant, A. H. 234889. | M. June 3/17. |
| *44 | Taylor, W. L. 234622. | M. June 3/17. |
| *44 | Taylor, W. 234774. | M. June 3/17. |
| *44 | Till, G. B. 830227. | M. June 3/17. |
| *44 | Tyreman, T. H. 291849. | M. June 3/17. |
| *44 | Vollett, E. 291897. | M. June 3/17. |
| *44 | Walker, C. H. 292185. | W. and M. May 8/17. |
| *44 | Wihero, B. 199001. | M. June 3/17. |
| *44 | Wood, W. H. 219003. | M. June 3/17. |
| *44 | Yeomans, Cpl. L. 292360. | M. June 3/17. |
| *44 | Younger, M. 830607. | M. June 3/17. |
| 46 | Alberg, W. 624240. | W. and M. April 13/17. |
| 46 | Barlee, Herbert Dalling. 912000. | K. April 12/17. Det.D./B. |
| 46 | Campbell, F. E. 911863. | K. April 12/17. Det.D./B. |
| 46 | Collins, J. P. 472854. | W. and M. Feb. 13/17. |
| *46 D. | Conolly, George. 487487. | K. June 3/17. Det.D./B. |
| 46 | Evans, G. A. 911814. | M. May 6/17. |
| 46 | Hanger, H. 886450. | M. April 13/17. |
| 46 | Lea, R. D. 440461. | M. April 10/17. |
| 46 | Metyl, J. 474268. | M. April 12/17. |
| *46 | Moore, Hugh. 437255. | Pres. died Oct. 25/17. Det.D./B. |
| 46 | Morrison, Cpl. E. J. 472282. | W. and M. April 12/17. |
| 46 D. | McKinven, P. 437403. | W. and M. Feb. 13/17. |
| 46 B. | Storr, F. 474055. | W. and M. Feb. 13/17. |
| 46 | Teale, A. 886426. | M. Mar. 31/17. |
| 46 | Thorne, A. A. 475427. | M. April 10/17. |
| 46 | Traves, E. T. 911810. | M. May 5/17. |
| 47 | Anderson, W. 790663. | W. and M. April 13/17. |
| 47 D. | Bateman, M. G. 790655. | M. Mar. 16/17. |
| 47 | Bond, L. A. 688215. | W. and M. Mar. 31/17. |
| 47 | Bosman, J. 629061. | M. April 13/17. |
| 47 | Bucknam, G. S. 18001. | M. May 5-7/17. |
| 47 | Carlson, S. 227687. | M. May 5-7/17. |
| 47 A. | Connor, Maurice. 181133. | M. May 5-7/17. |
| 47 | Couper, J. 116853. | W. and M. May 6/17. |
| 47 | Coyle, J. J. 628146. | M., bel. K. May 6/17. |
| 47 | Craig, J. 687377. | M. May 5-7/17. |
| 47 C. | Cullington, A. H. 790231. | M. Mar. 16/17. |
| 47 | Daniels, A. E. 628613. | M. Mar. 31/17. |
| 47 | Duncan, D. E. 811812. | M. May 5-7/17. |
| 47 | Englehart, R. H. 645125. | M. Mar. 16/17. |
| 47 | Gibson, A. B. 811500. | W. and M. May 5-7/17. |
| 47 | Hanson, C. 116910. | M. Mar. 31/17. |
| 47 | Kidd, L.-Cpl. Walter. 628098. | K. April 13/17. Det.D./B. |
| 47 | Mallon, Daniel. 464143. | W. and M. April 11/17 |
| 47 | McGill, A. 646185. | M. Mar. 31/17. |
| 47 | Nault, W. 220427. | M. Mar. 16/17. |
| 47 | Newcombe, J. H. 791171. | K. April 13/17. Det.D./B. |
| 47 C. | Pearce, P. C. 687993. | M. April 13/17. |
| 47 C. | Pease, O. A. 687539. | D/W. Mar. 4/17. Det.D./B. (12th Canadian Fld. Amb.) |
| 47 | Phillips, T. W. 629054. | M. Mar. 31/17. |
| 47 | Raine, E. E. 812147. | M. Mar. 31/17. |
| 47 | Ransome, J. M. 812219. | M. Mar. 16/17. |

**Canadian Infantry—contd.**

| | | |
|---|---|---|
| 47 | Roberts, H. W. 687633. | M. Mar. 16/17. |
| 47 | Slavin, J. D. 116504. | W. and M. Mar. 16/17. |
| 47 | Smithrim, C. H. 688295. | M. May 5-7/17. |
| 47 | Thom, R. 736265. | M. Mar. 16/17. |
| 47 | Triggs, H. 790810. | M. Mar. 16/17. |
| 47 | Trueman, J. 688085. | M. April 13/17. |
| 47 M.G.S. | Turner, A.-L.-Cpl. Ernest Muncaster. 269567. | K. Mar. 16/17. Det.D./B. |
| 47 | Wills, W. A. 629582. | M. May 5-7/17. |
| 49 D. | **Downton, Lieut. J. G.** | M., bel. K. June 9/17. |
| 49 | **Pope-Henessy, Lieut. H.** | M., bel. K. April 28/17. |
| *49 | Campbell, H. 904074. | M. June 9/17. |
| *49 | Cottrell, T. E. 160763. | M. June 9/17. |
| *49 | Dunning, Cpl. G. G. 101411. | M. June 9/17. |
| 49 | Foote, R. 100850. | K. Oct. 4/16. Det.D./B. |
| ‡49 | Mealey, W. C. 100576. | M. Oct. 8/16. |
| *49 | Monson, J. 808473. | M. June 9/17. |
| *49 | McDonald, D. 904834. | M. June 9/17. |
| *49 | McDonald, A. R. 904914. | M. June 9/17. |
| *49 | McManus, F. 436216. | M. June 9/17. |
| *49 | Peterson, H. 808723. | M. June 9/17. |
| 49 C. | Riggall, R. 781704. | K. April 30/17. Det.D./B. |
| *49 | Roxburgh, W. 811346. | M. June 9/17. |
| *49 | Sleeman, M. 904315. | M. June 9/17. |
| *49 | Slye, S. J. 808142. | M. June 9/17. |
| *49 | Watson, L.-Cpl. J. F. T. 160187. | M. June 9/17. |
| 50 | **Ambery, Lieut. G. E.** | W. and M. June 3/17. |
| *50 | **Devine, Lieut. H.** | K. June 3/17. Det.D./B. |
| 50 | **Ladler, Lieut. J.** | M. April 25/17. |
| 50 D. | Adams, J. 435118. | M. Feb. 13/17. |
| 50 | Aylwin, G. J. 812232. | K. April 10/17. Det.D./B. |
| 50 | Babb, H. W. 696854. | W. and M. April 10/17. |
| *50 | Bailey, G. J. 781797. | M. June 3/17. |
| *50 | Bell, A. T. 883272. | M. June 3/17. |
| *50 | Bethune, L. 696780. | M. June 3/17. |
| *50 | Bishop, L. C. 832321. | M. June 3/17. |
| *50 | Bowhay, B. A. 88371. | M. June 3/17. |
| *50 | Brown, J. D. 696641. | M. June 3/17. |
| *50 | Buess, E. 808480. | M. June 3/17. |
| *50 C. | Clarke, J. W. 696190. | M. June 3/17. |
| *50 D. | Collett, F. 808414. | M. June 3/17. |
| 50 | Cox, O. 160451. | M., bel. K. Feb. 3/17. |
| *50 | Curry, R. 808885. | M. June 3/17. |
| 50 | Cussack, G. 434256. | M. Feb. 13/17. |
| *50 B. | Dawson, Thos. 696954. | M. June 3/17. |
| ‡50 | Easson, A. 434587. | W. and M. June 3/17. |
| 50 | Ellis, F. 161000. | M. Feb. 13/17. |
| 50 | Evans, J. 434765. | K. Nov. 18/16. Det.D./B. |
| 50 | Everrett, R. 447320. | M. Nov. 19/16. |
| 50 | Francis, D. 781657. | W. and M. April 10/17. |
| *50 | Goodall, D. M. 696250. | M. June 3/17. |
| *50 | Hall, J. 808783. | M. June 3/17. |
| *50 | Hamel, I. 145869. | M. June 3/17. |
| *50 | Harpham, W. 782453. | M. June 3/17. |
| 50 | Howard, C. 220065. | M. April 12/17. |
| *50 | Hutchinson, J. 220160. | M. June 3/17. |
| *50 | Jackson, W. 219273. | W. and M. May 9/17. |
| *50 B. | Johnson, J. A. 696194. | M. June 3/17. |
| 50 | Katayama, K. 697062. | M. May 7/17. |
| 50 C. | Kempton, L.-Cpl. J. 160163. | W. and M. April 10/17. |

Canadian Infantry—contd.

| | | |
|---|---|---|
| ‡50 | Linnen, A. W. 625359. | W. and M. June 3/17. |
| ‡50 | Lobban, J. H. 696903. | W. and M. June 3/17. |
| ‡50 | Malcolm, F. J. 808795. | W. and M. June 3/17. |
| 50 | Maracle, W. 220513. | M., bel. K. Feb. 3/17. |
| *50 | Mazur, S. 808412. | M. June 3/17. |
| *50 | McAlpine, D. 696546. | M. June 3/17. |
| 50 A. | McArthur, Peter. 781202. | K. Mar. 31/17. Det.D./B. |
| 50 | McAskill, A. P. 808957. | K. Mar. 31/17. Det.D./B. |
| 50 | McLean, H. J. 624737. | M. Feb. 13/17. |
| 50 C. | McLennan, W. 809175. | K. April 12/17. Det.D./B. |
| *50 | Narraway, Sergt. T. A. 434567. | W. and M. June 3/17. |
| 50 C. | Neil, A. 435354. | K. April 10/17. Det.D./B. |
| *50 C. | Nelson, J. 808529. | M. June 3/17. |
| *50 | Palmer, H. W. 808015. | M. June 3/17. |
| 50 | Parslow, H. H. 809153. | K. June 3/17. Det.D./B. |
| 50 | Paterson, R. 434526. | K. Feb. 4/17. Det.D./B. |
| ‡50 | Patrick, L. 883670. | W. and M. June 3/17. |
| *50 | Pattison, J. G. 808887. | M. June 3/17. |
| ‡50 | Riddell, R. A. 624623. | W. and M. June 3/17. |
| 50 | St. John, R. R. 812113. | W. and M. April 10/17. |
| 50 | Scott, J. 447414. | M., bel. K. Feb. 3/17. |
| 50 | Shuttleworth, T. 782193. | M. Feb. 13/17. |
| 50 | Sleep, F. L. 435460. | M. Feb. 13/17. |
| 50 | Stafford, J. S. 624567. | W. and M. April 12/17. |
| ‡50 | Stevenson, A. W. 446787. | K. April 25/17. Det.D./B. |
| 50 | Strong, B. 447963. | M. Nov. 19/16. |
| 50 | Takenchi, Y. 696981. | W. and M. April 10/17. |
| ‡50 | Tolman, C. 696959. | W. and M. June 3/17. |
| *50 | Warrington, A. 811754. | M. June 3/17. |
| 50 B. | Westlake, H. C. 219570. | K. Oct. 27/16. Det.D./B. |
| *50 | Zuehlke, F. 625138. | M. June 3/17. |
| ‡52 | Clarke, R. 438701. | M., bel. K. June 29/17. |
| 52 | Howell, Thomas E. 150447. | K. Sept. 16/16. Det.D./B. |
| 52 | McMillan, S. 441884. | K. Sept. 16/16. Det.D./B. |
| 54 | **Dodworth, Lieut. C. G.** | K. Nov. 18/16. Det.D./B. |
| 54 | **Johnson, Lieut. R. L.** | K. April 9/17. Det.D./B. |
| 54 E. | Beck, J. 707122. | K. April 9/17. Det.D./B. |
| 54 D. | Blaine, E. J. 187531. | M. Nov. 18/16. |
| 54 | Brown, W. 760409. | M. April 9/17. |
| 54 | Clayton, T. 102828. | M. Mar. 1/17. |
| 54 C. | Conklin, R. C. 760156. | K. April 9/17. Det.D./B. |
| 54 | Cook, W. H. 464492. | K. April 9/17. Det.D./B. |
| 54 | Craig, J. Duncan B. 707241. | K. April 9/17. Det.D./B. |
| 54 | Harland, W. P. 687769. | K. April 9/17. Det.D./B. |
| 54 | Horton, J. K. 474038. | K. Mar. 1/17. Det.D./B. |
| 54 | Hutton, J. A. 219810 | M. Nov. 18/16. |
| 54 | Hynes, T. J. 645671. | K. April 9/17. Det.D./B. |
| 54 | Ingram, E. M. 443623. | M. April 9/17. |
| 54 | Irvine, R. F. 443486. | K. Mar. 27/17. Det.D./B |
| 54 | Jerram, J. 442409. | M. Nov. 18/16. |
| 54 A. | Kellett, J. W. 442514. | K. Mar. 1/17. Det.D./B. |
| ‡54 | Lake, L.-Cpl. Arthur W. 700439. | K. April 9/17. Det.D./B. |
| 54 | Little, F. 760773. | K. Mar. 1/17. Det.D./B. |
| 54 D. | Littler, H. 931477. | K. April 9/17. Det.D./B. |
| 54 | Marshall, W. 688002. | W. and M. Mar. 1/17. |
| 54 | Martin, F. 645036. | K. Mar. 27/17. Det.D./B. |
| 54 | Moor, F. 688273. | M. Mar. 1/17. |
| 54 | Murrison, W. J. 115836. | K. Nov. 18/16. Det.D./B. |
| 54 S/B. | Myers, J. H. 443956. | K. Nov. 18/16. Det.D./B. |
| 54 | McDowell, J. 411197. | M. April 1/17. |

**Canadian Infantry—contd.**

| | | |
|---|---|---|
| 54 | McIntyre, D. 160462. | M. April 9/17. |
| 54 | McKay, A. 160205. | M. April 9/17. |
| 54 D. | Olliver, J. 931564. | K. April 9/17. Det.D./B. |
| 54 | Prout, G. 160990. | K. Nov. 14/16. Det.D./B. |
| 54 D. | Radford, W. F. 760866. | K. April 9/17. Det.D./B. |
| 54 B. | Rintoul, J. 646178. | K. April 9/17. Det.D./B. |
| 54 | Shaw, L.-Cpl. A. F. 443955. | K. April 18/16. Det.D./B. |
| 54 | Shuttleworth, Allen I. 688155. | K. Mar. 1/17. Det.D./B. |
| 54 C. | Simm, R. G. 760165. | K. April 9/17. Det.D./B. |
| 54 B. | Stenstrom, John B. 403844. | K. April 9/17. Det.D./B. |
| 54 | Walsh, M. 687881. | M. Mar. 1/17. |
| 54 A. | Whetton, T. G. 474076. | K. Mar. 1/17. Det.D./B. |
| 54 | Williams, H. 706243. | M. April 9/17. |
| ‡58 | Collins, F. W. 678292. | M. June 18/17. |
| 58 | Flatt, Sergt. A. 453026. | W. and M. Oct. 8/16. |
| 58 | Grant, W. 654167. | M. April 6/17. |
| 58 | McBride, George. 11654615. | K. April 12/17. Det.D./B. |
| ‡58 | Smith, G. F. A. 426869. | M. July 1/17. |
| ‡58 | Stevens, L. W. 210021. | M. July 1/17. |
| ‡58 | Walker, E. 228480. | M. July 1/17. |
| 67 A. | Glen, J. 102560. | M. Feb. 13/17. |
| 67 | Lindsey, J. 102521. | M. Feb. 13/17. |
| 72 | **Manley, Lieut. J. F.** | K. April 9/17. Det.D./B. |
| 72 | **McLennan, Lieut. J. D.** | K. April 9/17. Det.D./B. |
| 72 | Anderson, S. 472749. | M. Mar. 1/17. |
| 72 | Ansell, A.-Sergt. W. S. 466171. | K. April 4/17. Det.D./B. |
| 72 C. | Cran, R. G. 129441. | M. April 9/17. |
| 72 A. | Curror, Cpl. A. T. J. 474128. | M. Mar. 1/17. |
| 72 D. | Dawson, S. L. 130312. | K. April 9/17. Det.D./B. |
| 72 | Dennis, G. E. 472944. | M. Mar. 1/17. |
| 72 | Donnelly, W. 102026. | M. Mar. 1/17. |
| 72 | Lawson, T. B. 474184. | M. Mar. 1/17. |
| 72 C. | Lloyd, F. H. 130053. | M. Mar. 1/17. |
| 72 D. | Miller, George. 129916. | D/W. April 10/17. No. 12 Canadian Field Ambulance. |
| ‡72 | McMaster, J. 129423. | M. June 28/17. |
| 72 | McPherson, A.-Cpl. G. 466084. | K. April 9/17. Det.D./B. |
| 72 | Oatway, W. H. 130150. | K. April 9/17. Det.D/B. |
| ‡72 | Packer, G. H. 687536. | K. May 28/17. |
| 72 D. | Partridge, H. G. 160210. | M. Mar. 1/17. |
| 72 ‡3 Co. | Pettigrew, I. E. C. 116850. | K. April 9/17. Det.D/B. |
| 72 | Scott, R. 116277. | M. Mar. 1/17. |
| ‡72 | Thomas, L. 129538. | M. June 28/17. |
| 72 | Troughton, T. 474667. | K. April 9/17. Det.D./B. |
| 72 | Twort, P. 129588. | M. Mar. 1/17. |
| 72 A. | Wilkinson, Richard. 160277. | K. April 9/17. Det.D/B. |
| 73 | Allen, G. W. 648021. | M. Mar. 1/17. |
| ‡73 | Baird, H. 144246. | M., bel. K. Feb. 4/17. |
| 73 | Bartlett, W. 754043. | M., bel. K. Feb. 4/17. |
| 73 | Bye, T H. 754108. | M Feb. 4/17. |
| 73 | Dixon, W. 649130. | M. Mar. 1/17. |
| 73 | Ducharne, T. 648266. | M. Mar. 1/17. |
| 73 A. | Dugan, Cpl. James L. 132089. | K. Mar. 1/17. Det.D./B. |
| 73 | Fortner, A. 877752. | M. Mar. 1/17. |
| 73 | Gamache, W. 755197. | M. Mar. 1/17. |
| 73 B. | Geddes, J. 144084. | M. Mar. 1/17. |
| 73 | Harris, G. H. 123570. | M. Mar. 1/17. |
| 73 | Kerr, Richard. 18159. | K. Feb. 23/17. Det.D./B. |
| 73 B. | Kitching, A. 132695. | M. Mar. 1/17. |
| 73 | Misinishkotewe, V. 755136. | D/W. April 9/17. Det.D./B. |

**Canadian Infantry—contd.**

| | | |
|---|---|---|
| 73 | McCallum, W. J. W. 132478. | M. April 9/17. |
| 73 | McKinnon, U. 164154. | M., bel. K. Feb. 4/17. |
| 73 | McShadden, J. 164155. | K. Mar. 1/17. Det.D./B. |
| 73 | Phillips, R. 145204. | M. Mar. 1/17. |
| 73 B. | Prew, L.-Cpl. H. 132173. | M. Mar. 1/17. |
| 73 D. | Roberts, L.-Cpl. J. L. 487263. | K. Mar. 29/17. Det.D./B. |
| 7' C. | Simpson, L.-Cpl. M. 132892. | K. April 9/17. Det.D./B. |
| 73 | Teeples, L. G. 145621. | M. Feb. 4/17. |
| 73 | Upton, W. F. 163714. | M. Mar. 1/17. |
| 73 | White, A. W. 127600. | M. Mar. 1/17. |
| 73 | Whitehead, F. G. 132972. | M. Mar. 1/17. |
| 75 | **Harding, Lieut. W.** | M. April 9-12/17. |
| 75 | **Hewson, Lieut. C. E.** | K. April 9/17. Det.D./B. |
| 75 | **Morrison, Lieut. C. S. M.** | M. April 9-12/17. |
| 75 | **Pratt, Lieut. W. J.** | D/W. June 10/17. Det.D./B. |
| 75 | **Winchester, Lieut. M. M.** | M. April 9-12/17. |
| 75 | **Workman, Lieut. M. J.** | K. April 9/17. Det.D./B. |
| 75 | Abbot, D. 228447. | M. April 9/17. |
| 75 A. | Andrews, L.-Cpl. J. 163278. | M. April 9/17. |
| 75 C. | Appleton, H. E. 681240. | K. Mar. 1/17. Det.D./B. |
| 75 | Axbey, H. W. 681161. | M. Mar. 1/17. |
| 75 B. | Bennett, Walter C. 164620. | K. Mar. 1/17. Det.D./B. |
| 75 A. | Brett, F. S. 163294. | K. Nov. 18/16. Det.D./B. |
| 75 A. | Brown, Fred. 670057. | K. April 9/17. Det.D./B. |
| 75 | Cain, F. J. 805027. | M. April 9/17. |
| 75 | Church, S. G. 163799. | M. April 9/17. |
| *75 | Clark, J. 760081. | M. June 8/17. |
| 75 | Clayton, L. M. 805032. | M. Mar. 1/17. |
| *75 | Collett, L.-Cpl. F. 113143. | K. April 9/17. Det.D./B. |
| *75 | Collie, W. 681712. | M. June 8/17. |
| 75 | Collins, W. R. 159054. | M. April 9/17. |
| 75 A. | Corbett, Cyril. 760810. | K. April 3/17. Det.D./B. |
| 75 C. | Craigie, George. 760079. | K. Mar. 31/17. Det.D./B. |
| 75 A. | Craigie, John. 760080. | K. Mar. 31/17. Det.D./B. |
| *75 | Dunlop, J. S. 678573. | M. June 8/17. |
| 75 | Elson (alias Wallace), R. B. 228024. | M. April 9/17. |
| 75 | Eyles, L. 164442. | M. Mar. 1/17. |
| 75 | Ferguson, C. C. 805557. | M. Mar. 1/17. |
| 75 | Gould, N. 164673. | W. and M. Nov. 18/16. |
| *75 | Grossman, M. 669837. | M. June 8/17. |
| 75 | Hall, T. K. 681154. | M. April 9/17. |
| 75 | Hanna, R. F. 669178. | K. April 9/17. Det.D./B. |
| 75 | Hanson, N. 219646. | M. Mar. 1/17. |
| 75 | Heard, W. Harry. 220514. | K. Mar. 1/17. Det.D./B. |
| 75 | Hilton, J. M. 164105. | M. April 9/17. |
| 75 | Hyatt, J. B. W. 210396. | M. April 9/17. |
| 75 | Irvine, T. J. 219816. | M. April 9/17. |
| *75 | Jackson, R. 760130. | M. June 8/17. |
| 75 C. | Johnson, Andrew. 171257. | K. April 9/17. Det.D./B. |
| *75 | Kaiser, E. L. 669871. | M. June 8/17. |
| *75 | Kemshead, Leslie I. 163851. | K. April 3/17. Det.D./B. |
| 75 | Kettyle, Walter S. 657352. | K. Mar. 1/17. Det.D./B. |
| 75 | Lawrence, T. 730279. | M. Mar. 1/17. |
| *75 | Le Claire, George. 789221. | K. Mar. 1/17. Det.D./B. |
| 75 D. | Lee, Alexander. 164609. | K. Mar. 1/17. Det.D./B. |
| 75 | Marsh, Herbert L. 210586. | K. April 9/17. Det.D./B. |
| 75 | Millard, H. 805225. | M. Mar. 1/17. |
| 75 | Mitchell, W. J. 220210. | M. Mar. 1/17. |
| 75 | Mitcheson, J. P. 228184. | M. Mar. 1/17. |
| *75 | Moffatt, W. H. 228058. | M. June 8/17. |

**Canadian Infantry—contd.**

| | | |
|---|---|---|
| *75 | Munday, A.-L.-Cpl. T. L. 787037. | M. June 8/17. |
| 75 D. | McDiarmid, V. L. 219202. | M. April 9/17. |
| *75 | McEachern, J. 725149. | M. June 8/17. |
| 75 | McIlvride, P. 164507. | K. April 9/17. Det.D./B. |
| 75 | Petroff, L. 164169. | M. Mar. 1/17. |
| 75 C. | Porter, H. 163896. | W. and M. Nov. 18/16. |
| *75 | Scully, L. 163160. | M. June 8/17. |
| *75 | Shaw, P. 788581 | M. June 8/17. |
| 75 M.G.S. | Sime, Walter F. F. 138028. | K. April 9/17. Det.D./B. |
| 75 | Simon, O. J. 730456. | M. Mar. 1/17. |
| 75 C. | Sisson, J. A. 805241. | M. April 9/17. |
| 75 | Smith, Geo. Watt. 237398. | K. June 8/17 Det.D./B. |
| 75 | Staples, J. O. 805361. | M. April 9/17. |
| 75 | Stevens, Arthur. 681122. | K. Mar. 1/17. Det.D./B. |
| 75 | Sutton, J. W. 163080. | W. and M. Nov. 18/16. |
| ‡75 | Thomas, W. 140200. | K. Nov. 18/16. Det.D./B. |
| 75 | Tilton, C. 210905. | M. April 9/17. |
| 75 | Troy, J. W. 210923. | M. April 9/17. |
| 75 | Tufts, Arthur Z. 787678. | K. Mar. 1/17. Det.D./B. |
| *75 | Turner, W. A. 681099. | K. April 9/17. Det.D./B. |
| 75 | Vincent, A. 164518. | M. Mar. 1/17. |
| *75 | Wilson, J. 138996. | M. June 8/17. |
| 78 | **Benson, Lieut. S. P.** | K. April 9/17. Det.D./B. |
| 78 | **Carruthers, Lieut. T. F.** | M. April 9/17. |
| 78 | **Glasgow, Lieut. I. H.** | M. April 9/17. |
| 78 | **McCarthy, Lieut. R. B.** | K. April 9/17. Det.D./B. |
| 78 | Adams, H. O. 624654. | M. April 9/17. |
| 78 A. | Allman, Sergt. E. G. 229288. | D/W. Mar. 31/17. Det.D./B |
| *78 | Armshaw, G. H. 874188. | K. April 9/17. Det.D./B. |
| 78 | Armstrong, W. L. 625098. | K. April 9/17. Det.D./B. |
| 78 | Backlund, G. J. 216110. | M. April 9/17. |
| 78 | Bell, J. B. 875329. | M. April 9/17. |
| 78 | Bolton, Cpl. W. G. 186026. | M. April 9/17. |
| 78 | Booth, W. 808328. | M. April 9/17. |
| 78 D. | Cambin, Charles H. 721007. | K. April 9/17. Det.D./B. |
| 78 | Chisholm, G. R. 148804. | M. April 9/17. |
| 78 | Cools, H. 722063. | M. April 9/17. |
| 78 C. | Copping, A. W. 624686. | K. April 9/17. Det.D./B. |
| 78 | Crozier, D. 875253. | M. April 9/17. |
| 78 | Dickson, Cpl. D. A. F. 874202. | K. April 9/17. Det.D./B. |
| 78 B. | Fleming, W. E. 186115. | M. April 9/17. |
| 78 | Foote, Fred. 148679. | K. April 9/17. Det.D./B. |
| 78 D. | Friend, A. 216124. | M. April 9/17. |
| 78 C. | Graham, L. T. 148743. | K. April 9/17. Det.D./B. |
| 78 A. | Green, Victor George. 234479. | K. April 9/17. Det.D./B. |
| 78 B. | Henry, W. J. 721468. | M. April 9/17. |
| 78 A. | Hinks, Arthur E. J. 234808. | K. April 9/17. Det.D./B. |
| *78 | Hogg, D. 216342. | M. April 9/17. |
| 78 A. | Hooker, Leon A. 721016. | M. April 9/17. |
| 78 B. | Houghton, F. 234629. | M. April 9/17. |
| 78 | Howard, G. R. 147812. | M. April 9/17. |
| 78 B. | Hurd, C. L. 216059. | M. April 9/17. |
| 78 | Kidd, George. 147481. | K. Nov. 3/16. Det.D./B. |
| ‡78 | King, Cpl. W. J. 148647. | D/W. April 14/17. Det.D./B. |
| 78 | Lawledge, W. E. 871668. | M. April 9/17. |
| 78 D. | Magdelin, A. G. 871104. | M. April 9/17. |
| 78 B. | Miller, H. 148490. | K. April 9/17. Det.D./B. |
| 78 C. | Mowat, T. 721037. | M. April 9/17. |
| 78 | O'Neill, J. 220428. | M. April 9/17. |
| 78 C. | Palmer, R. C. 148141. | K. April 9/17. Det.D./B. |

**Canadian Infantry—contd.**

| | | |
|---|---|---|
| 78 | Pickering, L.-Cpl. E. 148442. | K. April 9/17. Det.D./B. |
| 78 | Porter, G. L. 147623. | M. April 9/17. |
| 78 D. | Preston, William Russell. 148769. | K. April 9/17. Det.D./B. |
| 78 | Pritchard, O. W. R. 871585. | M. April 9/17. |
| 78 | Rose, A. 187150. | M. April 9/17. |
| 78 | Roussin, A. 148374. | K. April 9/17. Det.D./B. |
| 78 | Roy, C. E. 624110. | M. April 9/17. |
| 78 D. | Russell, G. E. 148762. | M. April 9/17. |
| 78 | Russell, G. 875413. | M. April 9/17. |
| 78 B. | Setter, A. B. 871237. | M. April 9/17. |
| 78 | Shipley, J. 225688. | M. April 9/17. |
| 78 E. | Sims, F. A. 871068. | M. April 9/17. |
| 78 C. | Skinner, G. 148466. | K. April 9/17. Det.D./B. |
| 78 | Smith, W. F. G. 624392. | M. April 9/17. |
| 78 | Steadman, J. N. 871056. | K. April 9/17. Det.D./B. |
| 78 | Stefanson, J. 722232. | M. April 9/17. |
| 78 | Stewart, W. A. L. 147948. | M. April 9/17. |
| 78 | Taylor, H. A. 874571. | M. April 9/17. |
| *78 | Thompson, Joseph B. 187876. | K. April 9/17. Det.D./B. |
| 78 A. | Thompson, J. H. 216789. | M. April 9/17. |
| 78 A. | Tuck, H. M. 147437. | M. April 9/17. |
| 78 | Turner, J. C. 722311. | M. April 9/17. |
| 78 B. | Ward, C. 625101. | M. April 9/17. |
| 78 C. | Webber, F. 625257. | M. April 9/17. |
| 78 D. | Wilson, G. A. 148739. | M. April 9/17. |
| 78 C. | Young, A.-Sergt. D. 148066. | M. April 9/17. |
| ‡85 | Archibald, W. B. 901757. | M. June 29/17. |
| ‡85 | Baker, R. 223426. | M. June 29/17. |
| *85 | Greens, L.-Cpl. J. 222334. | W. and M. April 9/17. |
| ‡85 | Hopkins, Cpl. R. W. E. 222063. | M. June 29/17. |
| *85 | Kent, R. F. 222068. | M. April 9/17. |
| ‡85 | Wardle, H. S. 736429. | M. June 29/17. |
| 85 | Wheaton, Jack M. 222135. | K. April 9/17. Det.D./B. |
| ‡85 | Woodworth, L. C. 223095. | M. June 29/17. |
| 87 | **Joy, Major E. W.** | K. April 9/17. Det.D./B. |
| 87 D. | Aaron, J. R. 144995. | M. April 9/17. |
| 87 | Beringer, F. 144208. | M. April 9/17. |
| 87 | Blake, T. 805007. | M. April 9/17. |
| 87 A. | Brown, M. 177217. | M. April 9/17. |
| 87 A. | Brush, L. 715174. | M. April 9/17. |
| 87 | Cormack, C. T. L. 177365. | K. Mar. 1/17. Det.D./B. |
| 87 | Cully, W. J. 178324. | K. Mar. 1/17. Det.D./B. |
| 87 | Curtis, H. C. 814042. | K. April 6/17. Det.D./B. |
| 87 | Deuel, R. S. 177873. | M. May 10/17. |
| 87 D. | FitzPatrick, Sergt. Wm. Herbert. 177255. | K. Nov. 18/16. Det.D./B. |
| *87 | Fruish, L.-Cpl. R. 138575. | M. June 9/17. |
| 87 T.M.B. | Henderson, James G. 540342. | K. Nov. 18/16. Det.D./B |
| 87 | Johnston, A./L.-Cpl. W. C. 145491. | M. April 9/17. |
| 87 | Lampman, C. F. 757110. | M. April 9/17. |
| 87 | Leadbetter, F. 715888. | M. April 9/17. |
| 87 A. | Malchelosse, R. 805423. | M. April 9/17. |
| 87 | Malley, A. 793894. | M., bel. K. May 10/17. |
| 87 D. | Moffatt, G. W. 757128. | M. April 9/17. |
| *87 | Murphy, J. A. 177955. | M. June 9/17. |
| 87 | McGregor, D. E. 907531. | K. Jan. 9/17. Det.D./B. |
| *87 | McKenzie, J. 794198. | M. June 9/17. |
| *87 | Organ, J. 793110. | M. June 9/17. |
| 87 C. | Phillips, A.-C.-M.-S. Wm. 177001. | K. April 9/17. Det.D./B. |

**Canadian Infantry—contd.**

| | | |
|---|---|---|
| *87 | Richardson, D. 767195. | M. June 9/17. |
| 87 | Robertson, D. D. 907156. | K. Jan. 9/17. Det.D./B. |
| *87 | Smith, Sergt. F. 457018. | M. June 9/17. |
| 87 | Soucy, M. 117204. | M., bel. K. Nov. 16/16. |
| 87 | Sykes, J. 757805. | M. April 9/17. |
| 87 | Taylor, H. J. 715344. | M. April 9/17. |
| *87 | Thompson, J. 793573. | M. June 9/17. |
| *87 | Ward, J. J. 793168. | M. June 9/17. |
| *87 | Wilson, M. 773025. | M. June 9/17. |
| *87 | Wynn, S. 715106. | K. April 9/17. Det.D./B. |
| *102 D. | Bryson, R. P. 760178. | K. May 11/17. Det.D./B. |
| *102 | Burns, A. E. 760838. | M. June 13/17. |
| 102 | Colman, A. 907161. | M. April 9/17. |
| *102 | Dagg, W. A. R. 788560. | W. and M. June 13/17. |
| 102 | Dickie, Thos. H. 252050. | K. April 9/17. Det.D./B. |
| 102 | Dudley, A. A. 706496. | K. April 9/17. Det.D./B. |
| 102 | Edmond, R. F. 790682. | W. and M. April 9/17. |
| 102 A. | Hunter, David Ainslie. 911777. | K. April 9/17. Det.D./B. |
| 102 D. | Kerr, J. C. 907814. | M. April 9/17. |
| 102 | Maitland-Dougall, H. K. 706658. | W. and M. April 9/17. |
| 102 | Marriette, J. W. 760741. | K. April 9/17. Det.D./B. |
| ‡102 | Moore, J. 706482. | W. and M. June 13/17. |
| *102 | McNally, L.-Cpl. J. E. 703663. | M. June 13/17. |
| 102 | Peters, J. 907532. | W. and M. April 9/17. |
| ‡102 | Porter, H. E. D. 135209. | D/W. April16/17. Det.D./B. |
| 102 E. | Thacker, G. W. 426356. | K. April 9/17. Det.D./B. |
| 102 | Waters, W. S. 707017. | K. April 9/17. Det.D./B. |
| 102 | Wilson, E. E. 161146. | K. Nov. 10/16. Det.D./B. |
| 104 | Boyd, A.-C.-S.-M. T. L. 769068. | D/W. April 26/17. 11th Canadian Fld. Amb. Det.D./B. |
| 116 D. | McInnes, David G. 757870. | K. April 11/17. Det.D./B. |
| 124 | **Pearce, Lieut. G. MacK.** | K. April 26/17. Det.D./B. |
| *124 | Raymer, Sergt. R. G. 769362. | M. June 3/17. |

**P. P. CANADIAN LIGHT INFANTRY.**

| | | |
|---|---|---|
| | Beutlich-Miller, F. 228386. | K. May 9-10/17. Det.D./B. |
| | Blakstad, O. Stanley. 552748. | K. Mar. 28/17. Det.D./B. |
| | Brown, C. E. 487420. | W. and M. April 9-10/17. |
| A. | Davidson, A. P. 51030. | K. April 9-10/17. Det.D./B. |
| | Garrow, W. J. 47855. | K. June 2/16. Det.D./B. |
| C. | Gillen, P. 228343. | W. and M. April 9-10/17. |
| | Holmes, L. 207358. | K. April 9-10/17. Det.D./B. |
| | Rennie, James. 785156. | W. and M. April 9-10/17. |
| | Trow, A. S. 487284. | K. April 9-10/17. Det.D./B. |
| | Williams, T. A. 859512. | K. April 9-10/17. Det.D./B. |

## CANADIAN MOUNTED RIFLES.

| | | |
|---|---|---|
| 1 | **Stuart, Lieut. C. M.** | K. April 9-10/17. Det.D./B. |
| 1 | Appleby, W. 718681. | M. April 7-10/17. |
| 1 M.G.S. | Atkinson, George Nelson. 108068. | K. Sept. 15/16. Det.D./B. |
| 1 | Bairstow, F. 216725. | W. and M. April 7-10/17. |
| ‡1 | Burnett, H. A. 187510. | K. April 7-10/17. Det.D./B. |
| 1 | Dougan, H. 152363. | W. and M. Sept. 15/16. |
| 1 A. | Kesson, John. 105902. | K. April 7-10/17. Det.D./B. |
| 1 | Luprt, W. 186184. | M. April 7-10/17. |
| 1 | Milne, E. J. 216445. | K. April 7-10/17. Det.D./B. |
| ‡1 | Murdock, A. 151827. | W. and M. Sept. 15/16. |
| 1 | Rogers, J. 136183. | M., bel. K. Oct. 2/16. |
| 1 B. | Ross, K. T. 292178. | M. April 7-10/17. |
| 1 | Savard, L. 718925. | M. April 7-10/17. |
| 1 B. | Sproule, Alexander. 117094. | M. June 5/16. |
| 1 B. | Thickett, Albert. 718398. | M. April 7-10/17. |
| 2 D. | Adams, Leonard V. 687245. | K. April 9/17. Det.D./B. |
| *2 A. | Armstrong, Jas. 227669. | W. and M. April 9/17. |
| *2 | Baggs, W. F. 116776. | W. and M. April 9/17. |
| 2 | Doman, R. 180609. | K. Sept. 30/16. Det.D./B. |
| 2 | Gleason, T. S. 160280. | M. April 10/17. |
| 2 | Grendon, W. 781106. | M. April 9/17. |
| 2 | Henderson, G. 687891. | M. April 9/17. |
| 2 | Jackson, S. J. 700068. | M. April 9/17. |
| 2 | Jansen, T. J. 462773. | M. April 10/17. |
| 2 | McKenzie, J. G. 116787. | K. April 9/17. Det.D./B. |
| *2 | Taylor, J. 116744. | W. and M. April 9/17. |
| *2 | Wisson, R. C. A. 687069. | W. and M. April 9/17. |
| *4 | Kelsey, Cpl. L. N. 157100. | W. and M., bel. K. April 9/17. |
| 4 | Lizmore, Cpl Robert. 401122. | K. Oct. 1/16. Det.D./B. |
| 4 | Maracle, A. 225608. | M. April 9/17. |
| 4 A. | Mort, Andrew A. 838543. | M. April 9/17. |
| *4 | McMillan, W. J. 838146. | W. and M., bel. K. April 11/17. |
| ‡4 | Powell, W. E. 835528. | K. April 23/17. Det.D./B. |
| 4 | Smyth, M. 159636. | M., bel. K. April 9/17. |
| 5 | **Bynum, Lieut. W. F.** | M. April 9-10/17. |
| 5 | Colling, L.-Cpl. Clarence A. 406905. | K. June 2-5/16. Det.D./B. |
| 5 | Harding, J. J. 709315. | M., bel. K. April 9/17. |
| 5 | May, G. H. 110368. | M., bel. drowned April 17/17. |
| 5 | Smyth, L. 110524. | K. Sept. 15/16. Det.D./B. |
| ‡5 | Steeves, C. O. 832325. | M. June 26/17. |
| 5 A. Squad. | Stewart, Thomas E. W. | K. Oct. 2/16. Det.D./B. |
| 5 | Veinott, Alec. 415414. | K. Oct. 11/16. Det.D./B. |

## ROYAL CANADIAN REGIMENT.

| | | |
|---|---|---|
| | Briggs, H. C. 552426. | M. Oct. 8/16. |
| | Brunet, L. I. 455788. | M. April 9/17. |
| A. | Bull, C. H. 445113. | K. April 9/17. Det.D./B. |
| | Carbonell, H. J. 477150. | K. April 9/17. Det.D./B. |
| | Chenier, W. 814813. | M. April 9/17. |
| | Currie, H. L. 444449. | K. April 9/17. Det.D./B. |
| A. | De Blaquiere. 160541. | Unoff. M. Oct. 8/16. |
| D. | Douglas, Sergt. F. J. 477258. | W. and M. April 9/17. |

**Royal Canadian Regiment—contd.**

| | | |
|---|---|---|
| | Fielding, C. P. 715061. | K. April 9/17. Det.D./B. |
| | Furlotte, A. G. 445378. | M. April 9/17. |
| ‡ | Lansley, D. 478927. | K. June 8/17. Det.D./B. |
| | Montgomery, N. L. 818211. | M. April 9/17. |
| | MacAskill, Campbell. 477556. | K. April 9/17. Det.D./B. |
| ‡ | McCarthy, J. 460790. | Pres. Died Sept. 16/16. Det.D./B. |
| D. | Pask, C. L. 455259. | K. April 9/17. Det.D./B. |
| | Potter, M. M. 207760. | M. April 9/17. |
| | Rolland, H. 1033143. | M. April 9/17. |
| | Shave, A. 478557. | M. Oct. 8/16. |
| | Young, J. F. 657494. | K. April 9/17. Det.D./B. |

# INDEX.

## FLANDERS, MEDITERRANEAN & PERSIAN GULF ENQUIRIES.

# INDEX—*contd.*

## FLANDERS, MEDITERRANEAN & PERSIAN GULF ENQUIRIES—*contd.*

Printed in the United Kingdom
by Lightning Source UK Ltd.
118458UK00001B/250